$82.95

D1490384

Readings in

PLANNING

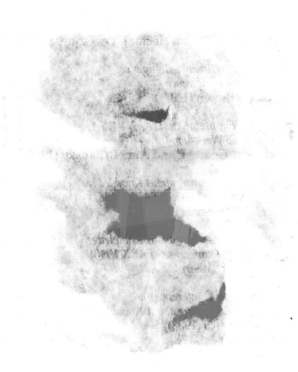

THE MORGAN KAUFMANN SERIES
IN REPRESENTATION AND REASONING

Series editor, Ronald J. Brachman (AT&T Bell Laboratories)

BOOKS

James Allen, James Hendler, and Austin Tate, editors
Readings in Planning (1990)

James Allen, Henry Kautz, Richard Pelavin, and Joshua Tenenberg
Reasoning About Plans (1990)

Ronald J. Brachman and Hector Levesque, editors
Readings in Knowledge Representation (1985)

Ernest Davis
Representations of Commonsense Knowledge (1990)

Matthew L. Ginsberg, editor
Readings in Nonmonotonic Reasoning (1987)

Judea Pearl
Probabilistic Reasoning in Intelligent Systems:
Networks of Plausible Inference (1988)

Glenn Shafer and Judea Pearl, editors
Readings in Uncertain Reasoning (1990)

John Sowa
Principles of Semantic Networks (1990)

Daniel S. Weld and Johan de Kleer, editors
Readings in Qualitative Reasoning about Physical Systems (1990)

David E. Wilkins
Practical Planning:
Extending the Classical AI Planning Paradigm (1988)

PROCEEDINGS

Proceedings of the First International Conference on Principles of
Knowledge Representation and Reasoning (KR 1989)
edited by Ronald J. Brachman, Hector J. Levesque, and Raymond Reiter (1989)

The Frame Problem in Artificial Intelligence:
Proceedings of the 1987 Conference
edited by Frank M. Brown (1987)

Reasoning about Actions and Plans:
Proceedings of the 1986 Workshop
edited by Michael P. Georgeff and Amy L. Lansky (1987)

Theoretical Aspects of Reasoning about Knowledge:
Proceedings of the First Conference (TARK 1986)
edited by Joseph P. Halpern (1986)

Theoretical Aspects of Reasoning about Knowledge:
Proceedings of the Third Conference (TARK 1990)
edited by Rohit Parikh (1990)

Proceedings of the Second Conference on
Theoretical Aspects of Reasoning about Knowledge (TARK 1988)
edited by Moshe Y. Vardi (1988)

Readings in

PLANNING

Edited by

James Allen
University of Rochester

James Hendler
University of Maryland

Austin Tate
University of Edinburgh

Morgan Kaufmann Publishers, Inc.
San Mateo, California

Editor Michael B. Morgan
Production Editor Sharon Montooth
Typesetter Merry Finley, Desktop Productions
Cover Designer Victoria Philp
Copy Editor Robert Klinginsmith

Cover Image: Created by Michael Morse, School of Visual Arts, M.F.A.
Computer Art Department. The image was initially created by a
digitizing camera, then manipulated using an Apple computer
and Adobe Photoshop 1.0 Software.

MORGAN KAUFMANN PUBLISHERS, INC.
Editorial Office:
   2929 Campus Drive, Suite 260
   San Mateo, California 94403
© 1990 by Morgan Kaufmann Publishers, Inc.
All rights reserved
Printed in the United States of America

No part of this publication may be reproduced, stored in a retrieval system,
or transmitted in any form or by any means—electronic, mechanical, photo-
copying, recording, or otherwise—without the prior written permission of
the publisher.

94 93 92 91   5 4 3 2

Library of Congress Cataloging-in-Publication Data

Readings in planning / edited by James Allen, James Hendler, and
   Austin Tate.
      p. cm. -- (The Morgan Kaufmann series in representation and
   reasoning)
      Includes index.
      ISBN 1-55860-130-9
      1. Artificial intelligence. I. Allen, James, 1950-
   II. Hendler, James A. III. Tate, Austin. IV. Series.
   Q335.5R32 1990
      006.3--dc20   90-4624
                                                                      CIP

CONTENTS

Contents   viii

FOREWORD

In the early days of artificial intelligence, the word "planning" meant something different than what it means today. In their summary description of the problem-solving behavior of humans, Feigenbaum and Feldman[1] wrote: "A subject using a *planning* method abstracts or simplifies a complex problem. He then solves the simpler problem and uses the information obtained in the solution of the simpler problem in the solution of the original complex problem. This technique has also been included in GPS..."

Around 1970, my colleagues and I at SRI began using the word "plan" in its more usual sense: *a detailed formulation of a program of action*.[2] This volume contains many of the important papers that propose and explore techniques for automatically formulating and using such programs of action. And, recalling the earlier definition, many of the papers are concerned with *hierarchical planning*, in which the high level actions that achieve a simpler, more abstract goal are used to guide the search for primitive actions to achieve a more detailed one.

Action. How closely associated it is with intelligence! Animals act; plants do not (except in a strained and limited sense). Animals are intelligent; plants are not. And the most intelligent animals (I suppose that's us) are able to think before acting and condition actions on thoughts. Thinking about the consequences of actions before being forced to experience them is the essential part of planning; the result of such thinking is a plan, and the most important part of a plan is the part that specifies what to do next. Since all animals act, *something* tells them what to do next, but we really don't know to what extent animals other than ourselves make and use plans.

We, the planning animals, know that planning is necessary for effective action, and therefore most artificial intelligence researchers want their computer systems to plan. The enterprise of attempting to build such systems has uncovered a multitude of questions about how to represent and reason about the effects of actions. We have the *frame problem*, the *qualification problem*, and the *ramification problem*—to name a few.

Because there are animals that seem too simple to be capable of planning but are nevertheless capable of quite complex behavior (consider the bee, for example), some artificial intelligence researchers[3] have decided to concentrate first on systems that act but that do not plan. It is as if those researchers believed that the ontogeny of artificial intelligence must recapitulate the phylogeny of natural intelligence.

The present volume contains most of the important work of researchers (myself included) who predict that we can bypass those eons of evolutionary history that produced only dull animals which made no plans. We want to build machines straightaway that would rank high

---

[1]Feigenbaum, E. A., and Feldman, J., *Computers and Thought*, McGraw-Hill, New York, 1963, page 278.

[2]*Webster's Ninth New Collegiate Dictionary*, First Digital Edition, NeXT Inc. and Merriam-Webster, Inc., Merriam-Webster, Springfield, MA, 1988.

[3]See, for example, Brooks, Rodney A., "A Robust Layered Control System for a Mobile Robot," *IEEE Journal of Robotics and Automation*, March 1986.

on the evolutionary scale, perhaps machines as good as or better than humans are in terms of thinking about what we are going to do before doing it. It's worth a try! And judging from the results reported here, we are making good progress.

Can we combine our work on planning with the results of the "action-without-planning" school? In Chapter 11, we begin to see a synthesis emerging. Certainly, some systems (even those that ordinarily base their actions on plans) will sometimes have to act quickly when there is no time to make a plan. A frontier problem, only now beginning to receive much attention, is how to build autonomous agents that have the ability to base actions both on complex and deep reasoning, as well as on more "instinctive," built-in patterns—using each method appropriately depending on the situation.

Other frontier problems are suggested by the analogy between planning and learning. Learning occurs when an agent modifies its behavior based on experiences in the world it inhabits. Planning occurs when an agent selects behavior based on "experiences" in an internal model of its world. Some initial attempts to link these two activities are reported in Chapter 9. It is also intriguing to speculate about whether or not recent work in "genetic algorithms" (which model evolutionary processes) might inform both learning and planning research. In a certain sense, learning is simulated evolution, and planning is simulated learning.

Pioneers who want to explore these and other frontiers of artificial intelligence research can do no better than to outfit themselves first with what is already known about planning, and the best of that knowledge is contained in this volume.

NILS J. NILSSON

Preface

Early in the growth of the field of artificial intelligence it was recognized that an important behavior for any intelligent agent was the ability to plan a set of actions to accomplish its goals. The attempt to realize programs with this ability has resulted in one of AI's main subdisciplines—the field of planning.

Since the first published papers on planning in the late 1950s, the field has grown and papers have appeared in virtually all of the major AI conferences and journals. Although numerous review articles on planning have appeared over the years, no systematic attempt to collect the major papers in this field into one volume has been made previously. Courses on planning have been difficult to teach due to the need to gather a large number of papers from disparate sources. In addition, although most AI texts have an introduction to planning, those wishing to begin applying the planning technology have not been able to find a volume pointing out the seminal papers in the field.

The goal of this book is to remedy this situation by bringing together in one place a set of readings that can be used to develop a familiarity with the planning literature, with the major AI theory underlying planning, and with recent papers in the field indicating several directions of current research.

This volume comprises four sections. The first section is a collection of papers introducing the field of planning. These papers are intended for those familiar with AI concepts, but lacking some familiarity with the research in planning. The second section presents work describing important advances in planning systems developed over the past 30 years. The third section concerns AI research in the areas underlying planning: representation of time and coping with the frame problem. This section also includes some papers that formalize planning systems described in the second section. A final section is included that presents some short papers discussing several directions in which current planning research is moving.

In putting together this volume several hard decisions needed to be made. The AI literature in planning is quite diverse and to include all the strands in a single volume would be impossible for the following reasons:

1. Planning systems have traditionally fallen into two major classes: domain-independent planners, which concentrate on the control mechanisms of planning, and domain-dependent planners which concentrate on using domain heuristics to encourage efficient search. The editors decided to concentrate on domain-independent planning in the current volume as it was felt that the more general design principles described herein would be applicable to a wider range of planning work.

2. Planning is related to many other subareas of AI. The underlying theoretical material in this volume is restricted to papers that were deemed to have an explicit relation to an understanding of planning systems. This necessarily meant leaving out much important work in logic and knowledge representation (much of which is available in other issues of the Readings series).

3. Many realistic applications of AI planning methods require extensive reasoning about time, limited resources and other constraints. Although this is an exciting area of current research, space limitations constrain us to including only a few early papers addressing this theme. Pointers to further reading on this subject can be found in the introductory material and in the included papers.

4. The area of plan recognition is a rich literature that is clearly related to the planning area. Unfortunately, to include enough papers on recognition to provide a fair treatment would require significantly more space than was available.

Putting together this volume would have been a far greater undertaking without the efforts of the people who contributed articles, many of whom also provided early feedback on the purpose of the volume or reviewed the proposed set of papers prior to solicitation of the manuscripts. In addition, support from Mike Morgan and Sharon Montooth of Morgan-Kaufmann Publishers was invaluable in bringing this volume to fruition. Finally, on a more personal note, we thank our family and friends who supported us during this effort.

Part I

Introduction to Planning

Chapter 1

Introduction to Planning

Although the field of planning has been an integral part of AI for over 30 years, papers that summarize and introduce this work have been few and far between. This lack has become an especially acute problem in recent years, when a renewed interest in planning has produced a spate of research based on earlier results—researchers have been so busy pursuing this area that few have stopped to look back and synthesize the results to date. In this chapter we present three papers that present overviews of work in planning. These papers assume the reader is familiar with the concepts and techniques of artificial intelligence research but do not assume familiarity with the planning literature. Thus, we include them to help the reader to handle the more technical material appearing later in this collection.

The first paper we present, by Georgeff (1987), appeared in the *Annual Reviews in Computing Science*. Georgeff presents a broad overview of the field of planning, describing both formal work in the foundations of planning systems and some of the past work in developing planning systems. This paper is more general than the two that follow and provides an accessible introduction to the area of planning.

The second paper in this chapter, by Tate, Hendler, and Drummond, is an expansion of an earlier paper written by Tate and Drummond that provided an overview of work in the development of programs for generating plans. In the current paper, the authors provide a more technical introduction to the techniques and terminology in the area of planning. The paper serves as an extended glossary, and we hope it will provide definitions of concepts necessary to the complete understanding of the papers appearing later in this volume. A more introductory version of this article is scheduled to appear in *AI Magazine*, Summer, 1990.

The final paper in this chapter was written by James Allen for this volume. The paper provides a more detailed description of the issues involved in the formal treatment of planning problems. Allen describes the basic problems that must be accounted for in formalizing models of planning and reviews some of the techniques that have been used in the past.

Papers referenced herein but not included in this volume:

Hendler, J., Tate, A., and Drummond, M. (1990). "AI Planning: Systems and Techniques" *AI Magazine*, Summer, 1990.

Ann. Rev. Comput. Sci. 1987. 2: 359–400
Copyright © 1987 by Annual Reviews Inc. All rights reserved

PLANNING

Michael P. Georgeff[1]

Artificial Intelligence Center, SRI International, Menlo Park, California 94025

1. INTRODUCTION

The ability to act appropriately in dynamic environments is critical to the survival of all living creatures. For lower life forms, it seems that sufficient capability is provided by stimulus-response and feedback mechanisms. Higher life forms, however, must be able to anticipate the future and form plans of action to achieve their goals. Reasoning about actions and plans can thus be seen as fundamental to the development of intelligent machines that are capable of dealing effectively with real-world problems.

Researchers in artificial intelligence (AI) have long been concerned with this area of investigation (McCarthy 1968). But, as with most of AI, it is often difficult to relate the different streams of research and to understand how one technique compares with others. Much of this difficulty derives from the varied (and sometimes confused) terminology and the great diversity of problems that arise in real-world planning. Indeed, there are few practical planning systems for which the class of appropriate applications can be clearly delineated.

This article attempts to clarify some of the issues that are important in reasoning about actions and plans. As the field is still young, it would be premature to expect us to have a stable foundation on which to build a discipline of planning. Nevertheless, I hope that the following discussion contributes toward that objective and that it will help the reader to evaluate the pertinent literature.

2. THE REPRESENTATION OF ACTIONS AND EVENTS

Humans spend a great deal of time deciding and reasoning about actions, some with much deliberation and some without any forethought. They may have numerous desires that they wish fulfilled, some more strongly than others. It is often necessary to accommodate conflicting desires, to choose among them, and to reason about how best to accomplish those that are chosen. This choice, and the means chosen to realize these ends, will depend upon currently held beliefs about present and future situations, and upon any commitments or intentions that may have been earlier decided upon. Often it will be necessary to obtain more information about the tasks to be performed, either prior to choosing a plan of action or during its execution. Furthermore, our knowledge of the world itself is frequently incomplete, making it necessary for us to have some means of forming reasonable assumptions about the possible occurrence of other events or the behaviors of other agents.

All this has to be accomplished in a complex and dynamic world populated with many other agents. The agent planning or deciding upon possible courses of action can choose from an enormous repertoire of actions, and these in turn can influence the world in exceedingly complicated ways. Moreover, because of the presence of other agents and processes, the environment is subject to continuous change—even as the planner deliberates on how best to achieve its goals.

2.1 Models of Action

To tackle the kind of problems mentioned above, we first have to understand clearly what entities we are to reason about. The traditional approach has been to consider that, at any given moment, the world is in one of a potentially infinite number of *states* or *situations*. A world state may be viewed as a snapshot of the world at a given instant of time. A sequence of world states is usually called a *behavior*, one that stretches back to the beginning of time or forward to its end is called a *world history* or a *chronicle*. Such a world history, for example, may represent the past history of the actual world, or some potential future behavior.

The world can change its state only by the occurrence of an *event* or *action*. An *event type* is usually modeled as a set of behaviors, representing all possible occurrences of the event in all possible world histories. Thus, the event type "John running around a track three times" corresponds to all possible behaviors in which John does exactly that—namely, runs around *some* track during *some* interval at *some* location exactly three times. An *event instance* is a particular occurrence of an event type in a

---

[1] Also affiliated with the Center for the Study of Language and Information, Stanford University, Stanford, California.

8756–7016/87/1115–0359$02.00

particular world history. However, where there is no ambiguity, we shall call event types simply events.

An *action* is a special kind of event—namely, one that is *performed* by some agent, usually in some intentional way. For example, a tree's shedding of its leaves is an event but not an action; John's running around a track is an action (in which John is the agent). Philosophers make much of this distinction between actions and events, primarily because they are interested in activities that an agent decides upon, rather than those events that are not caused by the agent (such as leaves falling from a tree) or that involve the agent in some unintentional way (such as tripping over a rug) (Davis 1979). For our purposes, however, we can treat these terms synonymously.

We shall begin by restricting our attention to domains in which there is no concurrent activity, as could be used to represent a single agent acting in a static environment. In these domains, it is only necessary to consider the initial and final states of any given event, as nothing can happen during the event to change its outcome. Consequently, an event can be modeled as a set of pairs of initial and final states, rather than as a set of complete behaviors. If, in addition, we limit ourselves to deterministic events, this relation between initial and final states will be functional; that is, the initial state in which an event occurs will uniquely determine the resulting final state. Of course, there may be certain states in which an event cannot be initiated; that set of states in which it *can* is usually called the *domain* of the event.

Events may be composed from other events in a number of ways. As they are just relations (or, in the more general case, sets of behaviors), the two simplest means of composition are set union and intersection. For example, the intersection of the event in which Mary hugs John and the event in which Mary kisses John is the event in which Mary both hugs *and* kisses John. We can also compose events sequentially; for example, to yield the event in which Mary first hugs John and then kisses him.

We also want to be able to say that certain *properties* hold of world states. For example, in some given state, it might be that a specified block is on top of some other block, or that its color is red. But what kind of entities are such properties? For example, consider the property of redness. In a static world, we might model this property as a set of individuals (or objects)—namely, those that are red. However, in dynamic worlds, the individuals that are red can vary from state to state; we therefore cannot model redness in this way.

One approach is to view the properties of the domain as relating to particular states. Thus, instead of representing redness as a set of individuals, it is instead represented by a relation on individuals and states; a

pair $[A, s]$ would be a member of this relation just in case A were red in state s. Such entities are commonly called *situational relations*.

Another, more elegant way to handle this problem is to introduce the notion of a *fluent* (McCarthy & Hayes 1969), which is a function defined on world states. Essentially, a given fluent corresponds to some property of world states, and its value in a given state is the value of that property in that state. For example, the property of redness could be represented by a fluent whose *value* in a given state is the set of individuals that are red in that state.

Fluents come in a variety of types. A fluent whose value in a given state is either *true* or *false* is usually called a *propositional* fluent. For example, the property of it being raining could be represented by a propositional fluent that has the value *true* in those states in which it is raining and the value *false* when it is not raining. An equivalent view of propositional fluents identifies them with the set of states for which the property is true.

Fluents can also represent individuals (such as agents and objects); their value in a given state will be some specific individual that exists in that state. For example, one may have a fluent representing Caesar; the value of this fluent in any state will be whoever happens to be the emperor of Rome at that point in time. Similarly, one can introduce fluents whose value in a given state is a relation over individuals, or fluents whose values are functions from individuals to individuals (Montague 1974). The former are typically called *relational fluents*, the latter *functional fluents*.[2]

2.2   *The Situation Calculus*

Of course, in any interesting domain, it is infeasible to specify explicitly the functions and relations representing events and fluents. We therefore need some formal language for describing and reasoning about them. [Those unfamiliar with logical formalism and its use in AI should refer to the article by Levesque on knowledge representation in Volume 1 of this series (Levesque 1986) and Hayes' beautifully clear exposition of naive physics (Hayes 1985).]

McCarthy (McCarthy & Hayes 1969) proposed a formal calculus of situations (states) which has become the classical approach to this problem. In the variant we describe here, the logical terms of the calculus are used to denote the states, events, and fluents of the problem domain. For example, the event term $puton(A, B)$ could be used to denote the action in

[2] A good introduction to many of these concepts, including some of the logics mentioned in Section 2.2, can be found in the first six chapters of Dowty et al (1981). Note, however, that fluents are therein called *intensions*.

which block A is placed on top of block B. Similarly, the fluent term $on(A,B)$ could designate the fluent representing the proposition that A is on top of B. We could also introduce other event terms to denote composite events and other fluent terms to denote the different kinds of fluents and various individuals (such as A and B) in the domain.

The predicates in this situation calculus are used primarily to make statements about the values of fluents in particular states. For propositional fluents, we shall use the expression $holds(f,s)$ to mean that the fluent f has value *true* in state s. For example, $holds(on(A,B),s)$ will be true if the fluent denoted by $on(A,B)$ has value *true* in state s; that is, if block A is on top of B in s. We can use other predicates and function symbols to describe the properties of other kinds of fluents (Manna & Waldinger 1987; McCarthy & Hayes 1969; Montague 1974).

We must also be able to specify the state transitions associated with any particular event in the problem domain. The usual way to do this is to introduce the term $result(e,s)$ to designate the state resulting from the performance of event e in state s. For example, $result(puton(A,B),s)$ denotes the state that results when the action $puton(A,B)$ is initiated in state s. We can also use the *result* function to characterize those states that are *reachable* by the agent from some given state. That is, for any state s and any performable action e, the state denoted by $result(e,s)$ will be reachable from s and, in turn, from any other state from which s is itself reachable.

The well-formed formulas of this situation calculus may also contain the usual logical connectives and quantifiers. With this machinery, we can now express general assertions about the effects of actions and events when carried out in particular situations. For example, we can express the result of putting block A on top of block B as follows:

$$\forall s \cdot holds(clear(A),s) \land holds(clear(B),s)$$
$$\supset holds(on(A,B),result(puton(A,B),s)).$$

This statement is intended to mean that if blocks A and B are initially clear, then after the action $puton(A,B)$ has been performed, block A will be on top of B.

One problem with the above approach is the apparently large number of axioms needed to describe what properties are *unaffected* by events. For example, if block B were known to be red prior to our placing block A upon it, we would not be able to conclude, on the basis of the previous axiom alone, that block B would still be red afterwards. To do so, we require an additional axiom stating that the movement of block A does not change the color of block B:

$$\forall s \cdot holds(color(B,red),s) \supset holds(color(B,red),result(puton(A,B),s)).$$

In fact, we would have to provide similar axioms for every property of the domain left unaffected by the action. These are called *frame axioms*; being forced to specify them is commonly known as the *frame problem* (Hayes 1973).

Various other logical formalisms have been developed for representing and reasoning about dynamic domains. The most common are the *modal logics*, which avoid the explicit use of terms representing world state. One type of modal logic, called *temporal logic*, introduces various *temporal operators* for describing properties of world histories (Prior 1967). For example, the fact that it will rain sometime in the future can be represented by the formula $\Diamond raining$. Here, the temporal operator $\Diamond$ represents the temporal modality "at some time in the future"; the formula $\Diamond \phi$ means that there exists some future state for which the formula ϕ is true. The use of temporal operators corresponds closely to the way *tense* is used in natural languages; thus, it is claimed, these logics provide a natural and convenient means for describing the temporal properties of given domains.

Process logics are another kind of modal logic in which explicit mention of state is avoided (Nishimura 1980). These logics are based on the same model of the world as described above, but introduce programs (or plans) as additional entities in the domain (see Section 3.1). *Dynamic logics* can be viewed as a special class of process logics that are concerned solely with the input-output behavior of programs (Harel 1979). Hence, these logics are concerned with binary relations on world states rather than with entire behaviors. Harel (1984) provides a good review of dynamic and related logics.

2.3 The STRIPS Representation

The STRIPS representation of actions, originally proposed by Fikes & Nilsson (1971), is one of the most widely used alternatives to the situation calculus. It was introduced to overcome what were seen primarily as computational difficulties in using the situation calculus to construct plans. The major problem was to avoid (*a*) the specification of a potentially large number of frame axioms, and (*b*) the necessity of having the planner consider these axioms in determining the properties that hold at each point in the plan.

In the STRIPS representation, a world state is represented by a set of logical formulas, the conjunction of which is intended to describe the given state. Actions or events are represented by so-called *operators*. An operator consists of a *precondition*, an *add list*, and a *delete list*. Given a description of a world state s, the precondition of an operator is a logical formula that specifies whether or not the corresponding action can be performed in s, and the add and delete lists specify how to obtain a representation of the world state resulting from the performance of the action in s. In particular, the add list specifies the set of formulas that are true in the resulting state and must therefore be added to the set of formulas representing s, while the delete list specifies the set of formulas that may no longer be true and must therefore be deleted from the description of s. This scheme for determining the descriptions of successive states is called the *STRIPS rule*.

For example, the following STRIPS operator can be taken to represent the action that moves block A from location 0 to location 1.

Precondition: $loc(A,0) \land clear(A)$
Add list: $\{loc(A,1)\}$
Delete list: $\{loc(A,0)\}$.

Let's say that some world is described by the formulas $\{loc(A,0), clear(A), red(A)\}$. Given this set of formulas, it is possible (trivially in this case) to prove that the precondition holds, so that the operator is then considered applicable to this world description. The description of the world resulting from application of this operator is $\{loc(A,1), clear(A), red(A)\}$.

It is important to note that the formulas appearing in the delete list of an operator are not necessarily *false* in the resulting state; rather, the truth value of each of these formulas is considered unknown (unless it can be deduced from other information about the resulting state). Operators can also be parameterized and thus can represent a whole class of actions.

Although the operators in STRIPS are intended to describe actions that transform world states into other world states, they actually define *syntactic* transformations on *descriptions* of world states. STRIPS should thus be viewed as a form of logic and the STRIPS rule as a *rule of inference* within this logic. Given this perspective, it is necessary to specify the conditions under which the STRIPS rule is *sound*. That is, for each operator and its associated action, the formulas generated by application of the operator should indeed be true in the state resulting from the performance of the action. Surprisingly, only very recently has anyone attempted to provide such a semantics, though the importance of doing so has long been recognized.

The problem is that soundness is not possible to achieve if the STRIPS rule is allowed to apply to arbitrary formulas. One way around this difficulty is to specify a set of *allowable* formulas and require that only such formulas occur in world descriptions, operator add lists, and operator delete lists (although the preconditions of an operator can involve arbitrary formulas). Lifschitz (1987b) shows that such a system is sound if, for every

operator and its associated action, (a) every allowable formula that appears in the operator's add list is satisfied in the state resulting from the performance of the action, and (b) every allowable formula that is satisfied in the state in which the action is initiated and does not belong to the operator's delete list is satisfied in the resulting state. The latter condition is commonly known as the *STRIPS assumption*.

As described, the STRIPS representation avoids the specification of frame axioms that state what properties are left unchanged by the occurrence of actions. Furthermore, the lack of frame axioms allows a planner to better focus its search effort. On the other hand, STRIPS is not nearly as expressive as the situation calculus (Waldinger 1977). In particular, the STRIPS representation compels us to include in an operator's delete list all allowable formulas that could possibly be affected by the action, even if the truth value of some of these could be deduced from other axioms. For example, even if we were given an axiom stating that when Fred dies he stops breathing, an operator representing the fatal shooting of Fred would nonetheless have to include in its delete list *both* effects of the shooting.

To overcome this difficulty, it is tempting to modify the STRIPS rule so that formulas that can be *proved* false in the resulting state need not be included in an operator's delete list. This leads to the *extended STRIPS assumption*, which states that any formula that is satisfied in the initiating state and does not belong to the delete list will be satisfied in the resulting state, *unless* it is inconsistent to assume so. Unfortunately, no one has yet provided an adequate semantics for such an approach (Reiter 1980).

Another alternative is to allow any kind of formula to appear in state and operator descriptions and to modify the STRIPS rule so that only a certain class of *basic* formulas is passed from state to state. The idea is that the truth value of a nonbasic formula in the state resulting from application of an operator cannot be determined using the STRIPS rule; it must instead be derived from other formulas that are true in that state. In this way, we can often simplify considerably the add lists of operators. [Some early attempts to implement this idea (Fahlman 1974; Fikes 1975) were flawed (Waldinger 1977), and later implementations (Wilkins 1984) appear to work only under certain restrictions.]

Yet another variant representation is described by Pednault (1986). Each action is represented by an operator that describes how performance of the action affects the relations, functions, and constants of the problem domain. As with the STRIPS representation, the state variable is suppressed and frame axioms need not be supplied. For a restricted but commonly occurring class of actions, the representation appears as expressive as the situation calculus.

3. PLAN SYNTHESIS

Plan synthesis concerns the construction of some plan of action for one or more agents to achieve some specified goal or goals, given the constraints of the world in which these agents are operating. In its most general form, it is necessary to take into account the various degrees to which the agents desire that their goals be fulfilled, the various risks involved, and the limitations to further reasoning arising from the real-time constraints of the environment. However, we shall begin with the simpler problem in which an agent's goals are consistent and all of the same utility; we shall disregard reasoning about the consequences of plan failure, and we shall not concern ourselves with real-time issues. [In philosophy, this kind of planning is commonly called *means-ends reasoning*, and is considered to be just one of the many components comprising rational activity (Bratman 1987; Davidson 1980).]

3.1 *Plans*

The essential component of a plan is that, when given to an agent or machine to perform or *execute*, it will produce some behavior. For example, a program for a computer is a particular kind of plan. Exactly what behavior occurs in a given situation will depend on the agent (or machine) that attempts to execute the plan, as well as on the environment in which that agent is embedded. In domains populated by more than one agent, plans may be assigned to a number of agents to execute cooperatively; such plans are often called *multiagent* plans.

The execution of a plan, of course, need not always be successful. Thus, there are at least two types of behavior associated with any plan: those that can be considered successful, in that the agent manages to execute each part of the plan without failure, and those that are generated by the plan but that, for some reason or another, turn out to be unsuccessful. As a rule, an unsuccessful behavior is one in which the agent has executed part of the plan successfully but then failed to execute some subsequent step. In many applications, both kinds of behavior must be taken into consideration — one's choice of plans often depends on the likelihood of plan failure and its consequences (Georgeff & Lansky 1986a).

Plans usually have a definite structure that depends on how the plan has been composed from more primitive components. The standard ways of composing plans include *sequencing* (resulting in sequential plans), *choice* (conditional plans), *iteration* (iterative plans), and *recursion* (recursive plans). One can also define *nondeterministic* operators that allow an arbitrary choice of which component to execute next and *parallel* operators to allow for concurrent activity.

The components of such composite plans are usually called *subplans*; the basic plan elements admitting of no further decomposition are called *atomic* or *primitive* plans (or, somewhat misleadingly, *atomic actions*). Plans can have other properties as well; which ones are considered important will often depend on the domain of application. For example, a plan may be of a certain type, or have an associated risk or likelihood of success.

It is not necessary that a plan be composed solely of atomic elements. For example, a plan for the evening might simply be to get dressed and then go to the theater, without it being specified how either of these activities should be accomplished. Similarly, we may fully detail each of the steps in a plan but leave unspecified the order in which they should be performed. Such plans are often called *partial* plans.

To reason about plans, we have to introduce additional *plan terms* into our formal language of events and actions. A plan term simply denotes a plan, in the same way that state terms, event terms, and fluent terms denote respectively states, events, and fluents. Furthermore, we need to introduce various function symbols and predicates to describe the allowed plan composition operators and any other properties we choose to ascribe to plans.

As mentioned above, one of the most important properties of a plan is the set of successful behaviors it generates. In the case that there is no concurrent activity, this can be reduced to considering simply the transformation from initial to final states. Let's represent the fact that state s_2 results from the execution of plan **p** by agent M when initiated in state s_1 by the expression *generate*$(M, \mathbf{p}, s_1, s_2)$. With this, we can now describe the effects of plan execution and the properties of the various plan composition operators.

For example, for some particular agent M and plan **p**, we might have

$$\forall s_1, s_2 \cdot holds(\phi, s_1) \supset (generate(M, \mathbf{p}, s_1, s_2) \supset holds(\psi, s_2)).$$

That is, if **p** is executed by agent M in a state in which ϕ holds, at the completion of execution ψ will hold. Assuming a fixed agent, we shall write the above formula simply as $exec(\mathbf{p}, \psi)$.

Strictly speaking, plans are not actions. We might have some predicates that apply to plans (such as whether or not they are partial, conditional, or unreliable) but that clearly do not apply to actions. However, predicates such as *generate* (and *exec*) allow us to specify the relation between plans and the actions or behaviors they generate. Process logic and dynamic logic may be viewed as variant notations for describing the same relation. However, some authors (Green 1969; Pelavin & Allen 1986) *equate* plans with the state transformations or events they generate. Used carefully, and in well-circumscribed problem domains, this can be the most frugal way to do things; in more general settings, however, it is restrictive and can lead to unnecessary confusion.

Finally, we need to consider what a *goal* is. Goals are important because they are the things that agents try to accomplish in executing their plans of action. In most of the early AI literature, a goal was considered to be simply some specified set of world states; an agent would be said to accomplish or achieve its goal if it managed to attain one of these states. For this reason, these goals are often called *end goals* or *goals of attainment*. Other researchers take goals to be some desired *transformation* from some set of possible initial states to some set of final states. This is typically the case in the area of automatic programming, in which one attempts to synthesize programs that meet certain input-output requirements.

However, real-world agents have goals that are more complex than these. For example, an agent may have a goal to *maintain* some condition over an interval of time, such as to remain in a position of power. Some goals of maintenance correspond to the *prevention* of some condition. For example, one might have the goal of preventing Congress from discovering how certain illegally obtained funds are distributed. There may also be goals in which the properties of some final state are not particularly important, but where the intervening *sequence of activities* is—for example, where the goal to call in at a Swiss bank prior to returning home. Thus, in general, we can consider a goal to be some set of state sequences or behaviors; an agent succeeds in achieving such a goal if the actual behavior of the world turns out to be an element of this set.

Because in the general case goals are just particular sets of behaviors, they may be composed in the same way that events are. For example, the goal to place the books on the bookshelf and the goal to place the cups on the table can be combined to form the single composite goal to place both the books on the bookshelf *and* the cups on the table. Goals can also be composed sequentially; in this case, the composite goal may be to *first* place the books on the bookshelf and *subsequently* place the cups on the table. The behaviors corresponding to the former composite goal, of course, may be different from those corresponding to the latter one. In the first case, the goal is to achieve a state in which both the books are on the bookshelf *and* the cups are on the table, but there is no requirement regarding the order in which these tasks should be performed. In the second case, the ordering of tasks is specified, but there is no requirement that the books remain on the bookshelf while the cups are placed on the table.

Goal descriptions are often viewed as *specifications* for a plan: They describe the successful behaviors that execution of the plan should produce. Goals of attainment can be specified by stating simply the conditions that should hold after execution of the plan. Thus, they can be adequately described using the language we introduced in Section 2 for describing the properties of world states. Goals of transformation can be similarly specified. For describing more general kinds of goal, however, we must be able to express properties of sequences of states or events. To do this, we need the more expressive formalisms developed for multiagent domains (see Section 4).

3.2   General Deductive Approaches

Given a formulation of actions and world states as described in Section 2, the simplest approach to planning is to prove—by means of some automatic or interactive theorem-proving system—the existence of a sequence of actions that will achieve the goal condition. More precisely, suppose that we have some end goal ψ and that the initial state satisfies some condition ϕ. Then the theorem to be proved is

$$\forall s \cdot holds(\phi, s) \supset \exists z \cdot holds(\psi, z) \wedge reachable(z, s).$$

That is, we are required to prove that there exists a state z, reachable from s, in which the goal ψ holds, given that ϕ holds in the initial state s. For example, a plan to clear a block A, given an initial state in which B is on top of A and C is on B, could be constructed by proving the theorem

$$\forall s \cdot holds(on(C, B), s) \wedge holds(on(B, A), s)$$
$$\supset \exists z \cdot holds(clear(A), z) \wedge reachable(z, s)$$

If done carefully, the proof could lead to a solution of the form

$$\forall s \cdot holds(on(C, B), s) \wedge holds(on(B, A), s) \supset$$
$$holds(clear(A), result(puton(B, table), result(puton(C, table), s))).$$

That is, if C is initially on B, which in turn is on A, then A will be clear in the state resulting from depositing C and then B on the table.

Green (1969) was the first to implement this idea. As he observed, however, it is essential to have the theorem prover provide the right kind of constructive proof. For example, consider being faced with a choice of two doors, behind one of which is a ferocious lion and the other a young maiden. In trying to maximize your lifespan, a theorem prover may well suggest that you simply open the door behind which lies the young maiden. Unfortunately, you may only be able to ascertain the maiden's location after opening the door—too late for you but of little concern to the planning system. This difficulty arises because the sequence of actions constructed by the planner can be conditional on properties of *future* states; that is, on properties that the agent executing the plan is not in a position to determine.

Manna & Waldinger (1987) show how many of these problems can be solved by reasoning about plans rather than actions. The planning technique they develop is based on the following scheme. For a goal condition ϕ and initial state satisfying ψ, we attempt to prove the theorem

$$\exists p \cdot exec(p, \phi, \psi) \wedge executable(p).$$

The aim is to find a plan **p** that satisfies this theorem. For example, a solution to the problem given above would be

$$exec((puton(B, table); (puton(C, table)), on(B, A) \wedge on(C, B), clear(A)),$$

where the symbol ";" represents the sequential composition of plans. The requirement regarding executability is included to prevent the planner from returning trivial or nonexecutable plans; this requirement is usually left implicit.

Conditional plans are not difficult to construct in this framework. For example, consider that we can construct two plans p_1 and p_2 that satisfy respectively $exec(p_1, \gamma \wedge \phi, \psi)$ and $exec(p_2, \neg \gamma \wedge \phi, \psi)$. Then it is straightforward to show that the conditional plan $p = $ **if** γ **then** p_1 **else** p_2 satisfies $exec(p, \phi, \psi)$. However, one must be careful in introducing conditionals, as they can expand the search space of potential solutions considerably.

The construction of plans involving recursion is difficult. To handle recursion, we have to provide the theorem prover with an induction axiom. There are various kinds of induction axioms that one can use. Manna & Waldinger (1987) use the principle of well-founded induction—that is, induction over a well-founded relation. This is a general rule that applies to many subject domains, but there are two difficulties. First, each domain will have its own well-founded relations, which must be specified explicitly. Second, it is often necessary to strengthen the goal constraint so as to have the benefit of a strong enough induction hypothesis to make things work out properly. With human intuition, it may not be difficult to formulate such strengthened goals, but even in simple cases the requisite strengthening seems to be beyond the capability of current theorem provers.

Iteration is often as problematic as recursion. It is not difficult to insert a *fixed* iterative subplan into a plan, provided that we have appropriate axioms describing its behavior. However, it is not a simple matter to *synthesize* an iterative subplan. One approach would be to first form a recursive plan (with all its attendant problems) and then transform this, if possible, into an iterative plan. Strong (1971), for example, shows how to convert certain classes of recursive plans (programs) into iterative ones.

This part is not difficult; the truly hard task is constructing the recursive plan to begin with.

However, in some cases, the synthesis of iterative plans is straightforward. For example, if a certain goal condition has to be satisfied for some arbitrary number of objects, it is often possible to construct a plan that accomplishes the goal for one of the objects and then iterate that plan over all the remaining objects.

Instead of the situation calculus, any of the modal logics discussed in Section 2.2 could alternatively be used to represent knowledge of the problem domain (Lansky 1987a; S. Rosenschein 1981; Stuart 1985). Unfortunately, for most domains of interest it appears that we require the expressive power of first-order modal logics, for which suitable theorem provers are currently unavailable. An exception to this is the work of Stuart (1985). He is concerned with the synchronization properties of plans, which can be adequately described using propositional modal logic.

3.3 Planning as Search

The basis of planning is to find, out of all the possible actions that an agent can perform, which, if any, will result in the world's behaving as specified by the goal conditions, and in what order these actions should occur. It can thus be viewed as a straightforward search problem: Find some or all possible orderings of the agent's actions that would result in achieving the specified goal, given the constraints of the world in which the agent is embedded. The number of possible action orderings is equal to the factorial of the number of actions performable by the agent. This makes the *general* problem computationally intractable (or what is usually called NP-hard).

Thus, a considerable part of the research effort in planning has been directed to finding effective ways of reducing this search, either by formulating the problem in some appropriate way, restricting the class of problems that can be represented, or by careful choice in the manner in which potential plans are examined [see Levesque (1986) for a discussion of similar issues].

There are two common ways of viewing plan search techniques. One is to perceive the process as searching through a space of world states, with the transitions between states corresponding to the actions performable by the agent. Another view is that the search takes place through a space of partial plans, in which each node in the search space corresponds to a partially completed plan. The latter view is the more general, as the first can be seen as a special case in which the partial plan is extended by adding a primitive plan element to either end of the current partial plan.

Thus, we can characterize most approaches to the planning problem as follows. Each node in the search space corresponds to some possibly partial plan of action to achieve the given goal. The search space is expanded by further elaborating some component of plan formed so far. We shall call the ways in which plans can be elaborated *plan specialization operators*.[3] The plan space can be searched with a variety of techniques, both classical and heuristic (Nilsson 1980; Tate 1984).

At each stage, a very general plan (which admits of a potentially large number of behaviors) is increasingly refined until it becomes very specific. As it becomes more specific, the set of behaviors that can potentially satisfy the plan becomes smaller and smaller. The process continues until the plan is specific enough to be considered a solution to the problem; usually this is taken to mean that the plan can be executed by some specified agent. Alternatively, we can view the whole process as continually refining the *specifications* for a plan; that is, by reducing progressively the original goal to some composition of subgoals.

A different approach to planning involves plan *modification* rather than plan specialization. Thus, beginning with a plan that only *approximates* the goal specifications, various *plan modification operators* are applied repeatedly in an attempt to improve the approximation. Unlike plan specialization, the problem with plan modification is that it is often difficult to determine whether or not a particular modification yields a plan that is any closer to a solution. In many cases, a combination of plan specialization and modification can be used effectively. Furthermore, many techniques that are framed in terms of plan modification can be recast as equivalent plan-specialization techniques and vice versa.

In the next few sections, we shall examine the more important of these specialized planning techniques. For many of these, there exists a corresponding deductive method whereby certain constraints are imposed on the order in which inferences are drawn (Genesereth & Nilsson 1987; Kowalski 1979; Manna & Waldinger 1987).

3.4 *Progression and Regression*

Before we consider specific planning techniques, let us introduce some new terminology. Consider a primitive plan **a** that, for some conditions ϕ and ψ, satisfies $exec(\mathbf{a}, \phi, \psi)$. That is, we are guaranteed that, after initiation of **a** in a state in which ϕ holds, ψ will hold at the completion of execution. If ψ is the strongest condition for which we can prove that this holds, we shall call ψ the *strongest provable postcondition* of **a** with respect to ϕ. We

can similarly define the *weakest provable precondition* of **a** with respect to ψ to be the weakest condition ϕ that guarantees that ψ will hold if **a** is initiated in a state in which ϕ holds. Analogously, we can apply these terms to actions as well as plans.

Let's now consider how we could form a plan to achieve a goal ψ, starting from an initial world in which ϕ holds. That is, we are required to find a plan **p** that satisfies $exec(\mathbf{p}, \phi, \psi)$. For any primitive plan element **a**, this condition will be satisfied for **p** if:

1. $\mathbf{p} = \mathbf{NIL}$ and $\forall s \cdot holds(\phi, s) \supset holds(\psi, s)$.
2. $\mathbf{p} = \mathbf{a}; \mathbf{q}$, where **q** satisfies $exec(\mathbf{q}, \gamma, \psi)$ and γ is the strongest provable postcondition of **a**.
3. $\mathbf{p} = \mathbf{q}; \mathbf{a}$, where **q** satisfies $exec(\mathbf{q}, \phi, \gamma)$ and γ is the weakest provable precondition of **a** and ψ.
4. $\mathbf{p} = \mathbf{q}_1; \mathbf{a}; \mathbf{q}_2$, where, for some γ_1 and γ_2, **a** satisfies $exec(\mathbf{a}, \gamma_1, \gamma_2)$, $\mathbf{q}_1$ satisfies $exec(\mathbf{q}_1, \phi, \gamma_1)$, and $\mathbf{q}_2$ satisfies $exec(\mathbf{q}_2, \gamma_2, \psi)$.

Case 1 simply says that if the goal condition is already satisfied, we need not plan anymore—i.e. the empty plan (**NIL**) will do. Now consider case 2. Let's say that we are guaranteed that if we execute some primitive plan **a** in a state in which ϕ holds, γ will be true in the resulting state. Thus, if the plan begins with the element **a**, the rest of the plan must take us from a state in which γ is true to one in which ψ is true. We can take γ to be any condition that is guaranteed to hold after the execution of **a** but, to spare ourselves from planning for situations that cannot possibly occur, it is best to take γ to be the strongest of these conditions. Thus, case 2 amounts simply to forward-chaining from the initial state and is usually called *progression*. Case 3 is similar to case 2, except that we chain backward from the goal. It is usually called *regression*; the condition γ is often called the *regressed goal*. Case 4 is tantamount to choosing a primitive plan element somewhere in the middle of the plan, then trying to patch the plan at either end. In fact, case 4 is a generalization of cases 2 and 3.

It is straightforward to construct a simple planner that uses these rules recursively to build a plan. Initially the planner starts with the fully unelaborated plan **p**, then specializes this plan recursively, applying rules 2, 3, or 4 until, finally, rule 1 can be applied. Clearly, whether or not a solution is obtained will depend on the choice of rules and the choice of primitive plan elements at each step. The algorithm works for any plan or action representation, requiring only that we be able to determine plan (or action) postconditions and preconditions, as described above. For example, GPS (Newell & Simon 1963) and STRIPS (Fikes & Nilsson 1971) use STRIPS-like action representations and rules 1 and 4, whereas S. Rosenschein

[3] Note that plan specialization operators are not the same as plan composition operators, although often there is a correspondence between the two. The former operators map partial plans into more specific plans; the latter map some tuple of plans into a composite plan.

for each goal will be interference free) is known as the *strong linearity* assumption (Sussman 1973).

Unfortunately, in many cases of interest, the plans that are produced for each subgoal turn out not to be interference free. It may nevertheless be possible to construct plans under the strong linearity assumption and, should they interfere with one another, patch them together in some way so that the desired goals are still achieved. Some early planners [notably HACKER (Sussman 1973) and INTERPLAN (Tate 1974)] adopted this approach: They would construct plans that are flawed by interference with one another and then try to fix them by reordering the operations in the plans. These systems backtrack when they find interference; they reorder a couple of subgoals and then start planning to achieve them in the new order. However, this can be inefficient and is somewhat restricted in the class of problems that can be solved (Waldinger 1977).

Waldinger (1977) developed a more general planning method that, in forming a plan for a particular subgoal, took account of the constraints imposed by the subplans for previously solved subgoals. That is, he first constructs a plan to achieve one of the subgoals, without regard to any others. He then tries to achieve the next subgoal while maintaining the constraints imposed by the first plan. In particular, the first subgoal and its regressed conditions, as obtained from the initial plan, become goals of maintenance that must be satisfied by the new plan. These goals of maintenance are usually called *protected* conditions.

Kowalski (1979) and Warren (1974) follow essentially the same approach as Waldinger. Kowalski also examines ways of improving the efficiency of planning by combining regression and progression in various ways. However, none of these methods is complete (that is, none guarantees to find a solution if one exists), primarily because they match the regressed goals with the initial state prematurely. This deficiency was corrected by Pednault, who presents perhaps the most advanced version of this technique (Pednault 1986).

The foregoing approaches can be used with any sufficiently expressive action representation. Warren restricts himself to a simple STRIPS-like representation. An extended form of the STRIPS assumption is embedded in both the Waldinger and Kowalski systems. This, however, is not dealt with adequately by either author, so that the semantics of their action representations is not made clear. For example, Waldinger simply states that he uses "a default rule stating that, if no other regression rule applies, a given relation is assumed to be left unchanged by [the] action." This leads to serious semantic difficulties (Reiter 1980). Kowalski (1979) introduces a predicate *Diff*, the truth value of which is determined according to the *syntactic* structure of the terms that appear as arguments. Again the mean-

(1981) employs dynamic logic to describe the effects of actions and uses rules 1, 2, and 3.

Rather than specify the execution properties of primitive plans alone (using STRIPS or some other variant), it can also be useful to provide information on the execution of partial plans. For example, it may be that going out to dinner and then to the theater results in one being happy, irrespective of the way in which this plan is eventually realized. I have elsewhere (Georgeff & Lansky 1986a) called this *procedural knowledge*, on the grounds that such facts describe properties regarding the execution of certain procedures or plans. Lansky and I show how such procedural knowledge can be used effectively for handling quite complex tasks, such as fault diagnosis on the space shuttle (Georgeff & Lansky 1986b) and the control of autonomous robots (Georgeff et al 1987). The plan operators used in NOAH (Sacerdoti 1977), DEVISER (Vere 1983), and SIPE (Wilkins 1984) (see Section 3.6) also allow the representation of procedural knowledge, although in more restrictive forms.

3.5 *Exploiting Commutativity*

Unfortunately, simple progression and regression techniques are too inefficient to be useful in most interesting planning problems. But is there anything better we can do? In the worst case, the answer is no—we simply have to explore all possible action orderings. However, the real world is not always so unkind.

For example, consider that one has a goal of stacking cups on a table *and* putting books on a bookshelf. It is often possible to construct plans that satisfy each of these component goals without regard to the other, then to combine these plans in some way to achieve the composite goal. (This might not be the case, however, if the cups were initially on the bookshelf or the books strewn randomly atop the table.)

For any two goals, if a plan for achieving one goal does not interfere with a plan to achieve the other goal, we say that the two plans are *interference free* (Georgeff 1984) or *commutative* (Nilsson 1980; Pednault 1986) with respect to these goals.[4] If this condition holds, any interleaving of these two plans will satisfy both goals (Georgeff 1984; Lassez & Maher 1983). Partitioning the problem-solving space in this way can lead to a substantial reduction in the complexity of the problem, as it reduces the number of action orderings that need be considered. The assumption that two given goals can be solved independently (i.e. that the plans constructed

---

[4]In fact, these two notions are not identical. Plans that are interference free with respect to particular goals need not be commutative, and vice versa.

ing of this is unclear. Pednault (1986), on the other hand, uses an extended form of the STRIPS representation that does have a well-defined semantics.

For techniques that aim to exploit commutativity, it is clearly desirable that any composite goals be decomposed into maximally independent subgoals. However, unless one introduces some notion of independence (see Section 4.2), such decompositions are not possible to determine. In fact, all existing planners decompose composite goals on the basis of their *syntactic* structure alone, rather than on any properties of the domain itself. The reason that this often appears to work is probably a result of the way the predicates chosen to represent the world reflect some kind of underlying independence that has not been made explicit. For example, given the composite goal of stacking cups on the table and books on the bookshelf, one possible decomposition is into two subgoals, one of which is to stack half the cups and half the books and the other to stack the remainder of the cups and books. Clearly, in most situations, this turns out to be a poor decomposition of the composite goal; that most planners don't make this decomposition is simply a result of fortuitous choice of domain predicates. However, there are some cases in which this decomposition actually *is* the best one; for example, when half the cups are stored together with half the books in one container and the rest of the cups and books in another container.

3.6   Improving Search

The techniques outlined above provide only a limited number of plan specialization and modification operators and apply only to those cases in which the goal descriptions (plan specifications) consist of a *conjunction* of simpler goal conditions. Furthermore, these operators are such that their application always results in a linear ordering of primitive plan elements. They are thus often called *linear* planners.

However, the search can often be improved by deferring decisions on the ordering of plan elements until such decisions are forced; by that time, we could well have acquired the information we need to make a wise choice. This is the technique adopted by the so-called *nonlinear planners*. These planners allow the partial plans formed during the search to be arbitrary partial orders over plan elements. Thus, instead of arbitrarily choosing an ordering of plan elements, they are left unordered until some conflict is detected among them, at which time some ordering constraint is imposed to remove the conflict. Nonlinear planners therefore do not have to commit themselves prematurely to a specific linear order of actions and can get by with less backtracking than otherwise. Examples of such planners include NOAH (Sacerdoti 1977), NONLIN (Tate 1977), DEVISER (Vere 1983), and SIPE (Wilkins 1984).

Another way in which we can defer making decisions that, at some later stage, may have to be retracted, is to allow the individuals (objects) that appear in a plan to be partially specified. This can be achieved by accumulating *constraints* on the properties that these individuals must satisfy, and by deferring the selection of any particular individual as long as possible (Stefik 1981a; Wilkins 1984). For example, we may know that to perform a certain block-moving action the block being moved must weigh under five pounds. Instead of selecting a particular block that meets this constraint, we instead just post that constraint on the value of the logical variable denoting the block. Later, if we discover that the block should be red as well, we can then attempt to select a block that meets both requirements. This technique can be easily implemented by associating a list of constraints with each such variable and periodically checking these constraints for consistency. Mutual constraints among variables may be similarly handled.

Efficiency can often be further improved by introducing additional plan specialization and plan modification operators. Most nonlinear planners provide a great variety of such operators. For a restricted class of problems, Chapman (1985) and Pednault (1986) furnish a complete set of plan specialization and modification operators, and prove soundness and completeness for their systems. They also provide a good review of the techniques and failings of other nonlinear planners. Chapman also analyzes the complexity of various classes of these planners. Of course, these planners are no more efficient than their linear counterparts in the worst case.

3.7   Hierarchical Planners

The major disadvantage of the planners discussed so far is that they do not distinguish between activities that are critical to the success of the plan and those that are merely details. As a result, these planners can get bogged down in a mass of minutiae. For example, in planning a trip to Europe, it is usually a waste of time to consider, prior to sketching an itinerary, the purchase of tickets or the manner of travelling to the airport.

The method of *hierarchical planning* is first to construct an abstract plan in which the details are left unspecified, and then to refine these components into more detailed subplans until enough of the plan has been elaborated to ensure its success. The advantage of this approach is that the plan is first developed at a level at which the details are not computationally overwhelming.

For an approach to be truly hierarchical, we require that the abstract planning space be a *homomorphic image* of the original (ground) problem. Let us assume we have some function g that maps partial plans in the ground problem space into partial plans in the abstract space. Also, for any plan composition operator C in the ground space, let C' be the corresponding composition operator in the abstract space. Then, if p_1 and p_2 are partial plans in the ground space, we require that

$$g(C(p_1, p_2)) = C'(g(p_1), g(p_2)).$$

This simply captures the fact that the abstraction should preserve the structure of the original problem.

These requirements ensure that if we find a solution at the ground level there will exist a corresponding solution at the abstract level. Furthermore, they ensure that any plan constructed at the abstract level will be composed of plan elements that can be solved *independently* of one another at the lower levels of abstraction. Indeed, it is in this manner that the complexity of the problem is factored. The method can be extended to multiple levels of abstraction in a straightforward way.

There have been a number of attempts to devise hierarchical planning systems. The system ABSTRIPS (Sacerdoti 1973) induced appropriate homomorphisms by neglecting the predicates specifying details of the domain and only retaining the important ones. Thus, for example, in determining how to get from Palo Alto to London, the predicates describing the possession of plane tickets or the relative location of, say, Palo Alto to San Francisco airport may be initially neglected. This simplifies planning the global itinerary, leaving the details of how to collect the plane tickets and how to travel from home to the airport to be determined at lower levels of abstraction. S. Rosenschein (1981) describes another hierarchical planning method in which the homomorphism between levels is given by the relationship between primitive plan elements, at the one level, and elaborated plans at the next lower level—what Rosenschein describes as the relation of being "correctly implemented."

Unfortunately, the notion of hierarchical planning is confused in much of the AI literature. In particular, there is considerable misunderstanding about the requirement that the problems at lower levels of abstraction be independently solvable. This does not mean that the plans formed at the lower levels of abstraction must be independent of the features of other plans formed at these levels. The important point is that any features upon which these plans may mutually depend should be reflected at the higher abstraction levels (i.e. be retained by the homomorphic mapping g). This ensures that any interactions are taken into account in the abstract space and the lower levels can pursue their planning independently of one another. Of course, this approach only works if the number of features that have to be reflected at the higher levels is considerably smaller than the number of features that the lower levels must deal with in their planning. For example, it may be that a certain stove can only accommodate two

saucepans at a time. In planning the overall preparation of a meal, it is important that this information be retained. In this way, the plan formed at the abstract level can account for the potential interference between the cookings of various dishes, and the cookings themselves can then be separately and independently planned. The resource mechanism used in SIPE (Wilkins 1984) serves exactly this purpose.

Most hierarchical planners [e.g. ABSTRIPS (Sacerdoti 1973) and Rosenschein's hierarchical planner (S. Rosenschein 1981)] first form an abstract plan and only then consider construction of the lower-level plans. Stefik (1981), on the other hand, describes an approach in which the planning at the lower levels of abstraction may proceed before the abstract plan is fully elaborated. This is achieved by allowing the abstract plan to be partial with respect to the values of certain critical variables and letting the lower-level plans post global constraints on these values (although he describes this process somewhat differently). In this way, planning need not proceed top-down—from the abstract space to the lower-level spaces—but rather can move back and forth between levels of abstraction.

The plan specialization operators used in some of the nonlinear planners [such as NOAH (Sacerdoti 1977), NONLIN (Tate 1977), SIPE (Wilkins 1984), and DEVISER (Vere 1983)] also allow planning at higher levels of abstraction prior to concentrating on the finer details of a plan. However, these planners are *not* strictly hierarchical. The difficulty is that even if all the subplans produced at lower levels of abstraction are successful (i.e. satisfy the plan constraints imposed by the higher levels of abstraction) it may still not be possible to combine them into a solution of the original problem (S. Rosenschein 1981). Furthermore, the potential for global interactions is dependent on arbitrarily fine details of the lower-level solutions, and the advantages of hierarchy are thus largely lost. There are also difficulties in the way that the STRIPS assumption manifests itself in planning at the higher levels of abstraction; Wilkins (1985a) discusses this problem in more detail and offers a solution.

3.8 Other Planning Techniques

The planning techniques we have discussed so far are all domain independent, in the sense that the representation schemes and reasoning mechanisms are general and can be applied to a variety of problem domains. However, in many cases, techniques specific to the application may be preferable. Many such specialized planning systems have been developed, mostly concerned with robotic control, navigation, and manipulation. For example, Gouzenes (1984) has investigated techniques for solving collision-avoidance problems, Brooks (1983) considers planning collision-free motions for pick-and-place operations, and Myers (1985) describes a collision-avoidance algorithm suited to multiple robot arms operating concurrently. Krogh & Thorpe (1986) have combined algorithms for path planning and dynamic steering control into a scheme for real-time control of autonomous vehicles in uncertain environments, and Kuan (1984) describes a hierarchical method for spatial planning. Lozano-Perez (1980) was one of the first researchers to demonstrate the utility of changes of representation in spatial planning. McDermott & Davis (1984) describe an approach to path planning in uncertain surroundings, and Brooks (1985b) has devised a symbolic map representation whose primitives are suited to the task of navigation and that is explicitly grounded on the assumption that observations of the world are approximate and control is inaccurate.

In many applications, it is necessary to plan not only to achieve certain conditions in the world but also to *acquire* information about the world. Relatively little work has been done in this area. Both Moore (1980) and Morgenstern (1986) propose to treat this problem by explicitly reasoning about the knowledge state of the planning agent. In such a framework, a test is viewed as an action that increases the knowledge of the agent, and can be reasoned about in the same way as other actions. In many cases, however, we can get by with a much simpler notion of a test. For example, Manna & Waldinger (1987) allow a set of primitive tests to be specified directly and utilize these in forming conditional plans. Lansky and I (Georgeff & Lansky 1986a) represent tests simply as plans that are guaranteed to fail if the condition being tested is false at the moment of plan initiation. In this manner, plans involving complex tests can be constructed without having to reason about the knowledge state of the planner.

Sometimes, one must be able to reason explicitly about units of time and the expected duration of events. For example, in planning the purchase of a used car, it may be necessary to know that the bank closes at 3 PM, and that the time taken to travel to the bank is about 15 minutes, depending on traffic density. Furthermore, it is often necessary to reason about the probabilities of event occurrences and the likelihood of future situations. Some initial work in these areas can be found in Bell & Tate (1985), Dean (1984, 1985), Fox (1984), Vere (1983), and Wesley et al (1979).

3.9 Planning and Scheduling

The problem of scheduling can be considered a special case of the planning problem. Essentially, one has a set of activities to carry out while satisfying some set of goal and domain constraints. Unlike the aforementioned planning problems, however, these activities are usually completely detailed, requiring no means-ends analysis. The question is how to put these activities together while maintaining whatever constraints are imposed by the problem domain. These constraints usually concern the availability of resources (such as a certain machine being available to perform one activity at a time) and timing requirements (such that a certain plan must be completed by a specified time). More often than not, the problem involves more than one agent and therefore is really a special case of the multiagent planning problem discussed in Section 4, below.

The class of problems considered by scheduling systems, moreover, often goes beyond those handled by traditional planning systems. For example, the domain constraints are often much richer than those considered by traditional planning systems. In addition, one usually wants an optimal or nearly optimal solution. Furthermore, many of the goals and constraints are *soft*; that is, while it is desirable that they be met, they *can* be relaxed if necessary (at a certain cost). Thus, scheduling requires some kind of cost-benefit analysis to determine the optimal solution.

There are various standard mathematical techniques for solving scheduling problems. However, the combinatorics encountered makes them unsuitable for most real-world applications, especially when rescheduling is involved. On the other hand, there have been few attempts in AI to tackle this challenge. Fox (1984) has developed a number of systems for handling a broad range of scheduling constraints, and has explored the use of special heuristics to constrain the search. As yet, however, the general principles underlying this work remain to be examined (Fox 1986).

3.10 Operator Choice and Metaplanning

As more and more plan specialization operators are introduced, one is faced with the problem of when (i.e. in which order) to apply them. There are various ways of handling this problem. The simplest, and most common, is to specify some particular order and embed this directly in the planning algorithm. Another approach is to specify, for each operator, the conditions under which it should be used. The operators are then invoked (triggered) nondeterministically, depending on the current state of the planner. These techniques are usually called *opportunistic planners* (Hayes-Roth 1985).

Alternatively, one can consider the problem of how to go about constructing a plan (which operators should be expanded next, which goal to work on, how to decompose a goal, when to backtrack, how to make choices of means to a given end, etc) as itself a problem in planning. One would thus provide rules describing possible planning methodologies and let the system determine automatically, for each particular case, the best way to go about constructing a plan. This kind of approach is often referred to as *metaplanning* (Dawson & Siklossy 1977; Genesereth 1983; Georgeff & Lansky 1986a; Stefik 1981b; Wilensky 1981). The obvious problem with metaplanning is to ensure that the time saved in better constraining the search is not lost in reasoning about how to achieve this focus of effort.

Metaplanning can be viewed as describing or axiomatizing the process of planning. In its fullest generality, it could involve the synthesis of metalevel plans based on the properties of basic metalevel actions (Stefik 1981b). However, metaplanning is rarely used in this general way. Rather, the metalevel axiomatization usually serves as a convenient way to describe various planning strategies to some generic planning system, without hardwiring them into the interpreter. Thus, for example, to have the system construct plans in some manner one would simply provide the system with an axiomatization of that particular planning technique. In addition, we can in this way describe plan specialization and modification operators that are intended specifically for certain domains.

4. MULTIAGENT DOMAINS

Most real worlds involve dynamic processes beyond the control of an agent. Furthermore, they may be populated with other agents—some cooperative, some adversarial, and others who are simply disinterested. The single-agent planners we have been considering are not applicable in such domains. These planners cannot reason about actions that the agent has no control over and that, moreover, may or may not occur concurrently with what the agent is doing. There is no way to express nonperformance of an action, let alone to reason about it.

We therefore need to develop models of actions and plans that are different from those we have previously considered. We need theories of what it means for one action to interfere with another. Many interactions are harmful, leading to unforseen consequences or deadlock. Some are beneficial, even essential (such as lifting an object by simultaneously applying pressure from both sides). We should be able to state the result of the concurrence of two events or actions. We need to consider cooperative planning in the presence of adversaries. and how to form contingency plans. In addition, we shall require systems capable of reasoning about the beliefs and intentions of other agents and how to communicate effectively both to exchange information and to coordinate plans of action. Furthermore, these systems will sometimes need to infer the beliefs, goals, and intentions of other agents from observation of their behaviors.

4.1 *Action Representations*

Multiagent domains are those having the potential for concurrent activity among multiple agents or other dynamic processes. The entities introduced in earlier sections—world states, histories, fluents, actions, events, and

plans—can also form the basis for reasoning in these domains. However, most of the simplifying assumptions we made for handling single-agent domains cannot be usefully employed here. In particular, it is not possible to consider every action as a relation on states, as the effects of performing actions concurrently depends on what happens *during* the actions (Georgeff 1983; Pelavin & Allen 1986). For example, in a production line making various industrial components, it is important to know what machines are used during each activity so that potential resource conflicts can be identified.

In addition, we need more powerful and expressive formalisms for representing and reasoning about world histories. For example, we should be able to express environmental conditions such as "The bank will stay open until 3pm" and "If it rains overnight, it will be icy next morning." Similarly, we have to be able to reason about a great variety of goals, including goals of maintenance and goals satisfying various ordering constraints (Pelavin & Allen 1986).

As before, we can take an event type to be a set of state sequences, representing all possible occurrences of the event *in all possible situations* (Allen 1984; Georgeff 1987; McDermott 1982, 1985; Pelavin & Allen 1986). Unlike single-agent domains, however. the set of behaviors associated with a given event must include those in which other events occur *concurrently* or *simultaneously* with the given event. For example, the event type corresponding to "John running around a track three times" must include behaviors in which other events (such as the launch of the space shuttle, it being raining, or John being accompanied by other runners) are occurring concurrently.

One possible approach is to approximate concurrent activity by using an interleaving approximation (Georgeff 1983, 1984; Pednault 1987). This renders the problem amenable to the planning techniques that are used for single-agent domains. However. it is not possible to model simultaneous events using such an approach, which limits its usefulness in some domains.

Another approach to reasoning about multiagent domains is to extend the situation calculus to allow reasoning about world histories and simultaneous events. I show elsewhere (Georgeff 1987) how this can be done by introducing the notion of an atomic event, which can be viewed as an instantaneous transition from one world state to another. Atomic events cannot be modeled as functions on world state, as it would then be impossible for two such events to occur simultaneously (unless they had exactly the same effect on the world). Given this perspective, the transition relation of an atomic event places restrictions on those world relations that are directly affected by the event but leaves most others to vary freely (depending upon what else is happening in the world). This is in contrast to the classical approach, which views an event as changing some world relations but leaving most of them unaltered.

I also introduce a notion of *independence* to describe the region of influence of given events. This turns out to be critical for reasoning about the persistence of world properties and other issues that arise in multiagent domains. Indeed, what makes planning useful for survival is the fact that we can structure the world in a way that keeps most properties and events independent of one another, thus allowing us to reason about the future without complete knowledge of all the events that could possibly be occurring.

McDermott (1982) provides a somewhat different formalism for describing multiagent domains, although the underlying model of actions and events is essentially as described above. Perhaps the most important difference is that world histories are taken to be dense intervals of states, rather than sequences; that is, for any two states in any given world history, there always exists a distinct state that occurs between them. The aim of this extension is to allow reasoning about continuous processes and may also facilitate reasoning about hierarchical systems.

Allen and Pelavin (Allen 1984; Pelavin & Allen 1986) introduce yet another formalism based on a variation of this model of actions and events. The major difference is that fluents are viewed as functions on *intervals* of states, rather than as functions on states. Thus, in this formalism, *holds(raining, i)* would mean that it is raining over the interval of time *i*, which might be, for example, some particular period on some specific day. The aim is that, by using intervals rather than states, we obtain a more natural and possibly more tractable language for describing and reasoning about multiagent domains. A similar approach has been developed by Kowalski & Sergot (1986).

Note that in these interval-based calculi, world states per se need not be included in the underlying model; indeed, intervals become the basic entities that appear in world histories. The ways intervals relate to one another are more complex than for states, however. Whereas in a given world history, states can only either precede or succeed one another. intervals can also meet, contain, and overlap one another in a variety of ways. Some work on formalizing the interval calculus and its underlying models can be found in Allen (1982), Kowalski & Sergot (1986), Ladkin (1987), Ladkin & Maddux (1987), Pelavin & Allen (1986), Sadri (1986), and van Bentham (1984).

Yet another approach is suggested by Lansky (1987a), who considers events as primitive and defines state derivatively in terms of event sequences. Properties that hold of world states are then restricted to being temporal properties of event sequences. For example, one might identify the property "waiting for service" with the condition that an event of type "request" has occurred and has not been followed by an event of type "serve." Lansky uses a temporal logic for expressing general facts about world histories and, in part, for reasoning about them also.

4.2   Causality and Process

One problem I have not yet addressed is the apparent complexity of the axioms that describe the effects of actions. For example, while it might seem reasonable to state that the location of block *B* is independent of the movement of block *A*, this is simply untrue, as everyone knows, in most interesting worlds. Whether or not the location of *B* is independent of the movement of *A* will depend on a host of conditions, such as whether *B* is in front of *A*, on top of *A*, atop *A* but tied to a door, and so on.

One way to solve this problem is by introducing a notion of *causality*.[5] Two kinds of causality suggest themselves: one in which an event causes the simultaneous occurrence of another event; the other in which an event causes the occurrence of a subsequent event. These two kinds of causality suffice to describe the behavior of any procedure, process, or device that is based on discrete (rather than continuous) events.

For example, we might have a causal law to express the fact that, whenever a block is moved, any block atop it and not somehow restrained (e.g. by a string tied to a door) will also move. According to this view, causation is simply a relation between atomic events that is conditional on the state of the world at the time of the events. Causation must also be related to the temporal ordering of events; for example, one would want to assume that an event cannot cause another event that precedes it. Various treatments of causality can be found in several sources (Allen 1984; Lansky 1987a; McDermott 1982; Shoham 1986). Most of these view causality as a simple relation between events; Shoham (1987), however, takes a radical view and defines causality in terms of the *knowledge state* of the agent. Wilkins (1987) indicates how causal laws could be used effectively in traditional planning systems.

It is often convenient to be able to reason about groups of causally interrelated events as single entities. Such groupings of events, together with the causal laws that relate them to one another, are usually called

[5] Although it might appear that the notion of causality also arises in single-agent domains, there seems little point in developing a theory of causality suited to such worlds. The power of causal reasoning lies in describing the properties of dynamic environments in which the actions of an agent may affect or initiate actions by other agents or processes.

processes [although Allen (1984) uses the term quite differently]. For example, we might want to amalgamate the actions and events that constitute the internal workings of a robot, or those that pertain to each component in a complex physical system. A machine (or agent) together with a plan of action may also be viewed as a special kind of process.

Charniak & McDermott (1985) examine how everyday processes may be reasoned about. For example, they consider the problem of reasoning about the filling of a bathtub and how we can infer that it will eventually fill up if the tap is turned on (and the plug not pulled). However, they do not indicate how to provide an adequate formalism for describing such processes, particularly with regard to their interaction with other, possibly concurrent processes.

Indeed, the strength of the concept of process derives from the way the interaction among events in different processes is strictly limited. Surprisingly, there has been little work in AI in this direction, although similar notions have been around for a long time. For example, Hayes (1985) describes the situation in which two people agree to meet in a week. They then part, one going to London and the other remaining in San Francisco. They both lead eventful weeks, each independently of the other, and duly meet as arranged. To describe this using world states, we have to say what each of them is doing just before and just after each noteworthy event involving the other. As Hayes remarks, this is clearly silly.

One approach to this problem is to specify a set of processes and classify various events and fluents as being either internal or external with respect to these processes (Georgeff 1987a; Lansky 1987b). If we then require that there be no *direct* causal relationship between internal and external events, the only way the internal events of a given process can influence external events (or vice versa) is through indirect causation by an event that belongs to neither category. Within the framework of concurrency theory, these intermediary events (more accurately, event types) are often called *ports*. Processes thus impose causal boundaries and independence properties on a problem domain, and can thereby substantially reduce cominatorial complexity (Georgeff 1987a; Lansky 1987b).

The identifiability of processes depends strongly on the problem domain. In standard programming systems (at least those that are well structured), processes can be used to represent scope rules and are fairly easy to specify. In complex physical systems, it is often the case that many of the properties of one subsystem will be independent of the majority of actions performed by other subsystems; thus these subsystems naturally correspond to processes as defined here. Lansky (1987a,b) gives other examples in which processes are readily specified. In other situations, such specification might be more complicated. Moreover, in many real-world situations, depen-

dence will vary as the spheres of influence and the potential for interaction change over time (Hayes 1985).

If we are to exploit the notion of process effectively, it is also important to define various composition operators and to show how properties of the behaviors of the composite processes can be determined from the behaviors of their individual components. For example, we should be able to write down descriptions of the behaviors of individual agents and, from these descriptions, deduce properties of groups of agents acting concurrently. We should *not* have to consider the internal behaviors of each of these agents to determine how the group as a whole behaves. The existing literature on concurrency theory (Hoare 1985; Milner 1980) provides a number of useful composition operators, though this area remains to be explored (Georgeff 1987a).

4.3 *Multiagent Planning*

Despite the variety of formalisms developed for reasoning about multiagent domains, relatively few planning systems have been fully implemented. Allen & Koomen (1983) describe a simple planner, based on a restricted form of interval logic (Allen 1984). While this technique is effective for relatively simple problems, it is not obvious that the approach would be useful in more complex domains. Furthermore, the semantics of their action representation is unclear, particularly with respect to the meaning of concurrent activity. Kowalski & Sergot (1986) also describe systems for reasoning about events based on interval calculi. Again, it appears that the class of problems that can be considered is limited; however, these techniques appear adequate for a large range of dynamic database applications.

Another issue concerns how separate plans can be combined in a way that avoids interference among the agents executing the plans. In such a setting, one could imagine a number of agents each forming their own plans and then, after communicating their intentions (plans) to one another or a centralized scheduler, modifying these to avoid interference. To solve this problem, it is necessary to ascertain, from descriptions of the actions occurring in the individual plans, which actions could interfere with one another and in what manner (Georgeff 1984). After this has been determined, a coordinated plan that precludes such interference must then be constructed. This plan can be formed by inserting appropriate synchronization actions (interagent communications) into the original plans to ensure that only interference-free orderings will be allowed (Georgeff 1983). Stuart (1985) formalized this approach and implemented a synchronizer based on techniques developed by Manna & Wolper (1981).

As the above work shows, the notion of intending or committing to a course of behavior is an important cooperative principal. Some researchers have investigated how multiple agents can cooperate and resolve conflicts by reasoning locally about potential payoffs and risks (J. Rosenschein 1986; J. Rosenschein & Genesereth 1984). Other research has focused on the use of global organizational strategies for coordinating the behavior of agents operating asynchronously (Corkill & Lesser 1983). Another interesting development is the work of Durfee et al (1985) on distributed analysis of sensory information. They show that, by reasoning about the local plans of others, individual tracking agents can form partial global plans that lead to satisfactory performance even in rapidly changing environments. Reasoning about communication is discussed by J. Rosenschein (1982) and Cohen & Levesque (1985).

Lansky (1987b) has developed a multiagent planner that exploits causal independencies. Unlike the approaches described above, constraints between events have to be specified explicitly. However, the system accommodates a wide class of plan-synchronization constraints. Also, the process of plan synchronization is not limited to a strategy of planning to separately achieve each component task and then combining the results. Instead, a more general, adaptable strategy is used that can bounce back and forth between local (i.e. single-agent) and global (multiagent) contexts, adding events where necessary for purposes of synchronization. Planning loci can be composed hierarchically or even overlap.

5.   THE FRAME PROBLEM

Although the so-called frame problem has been regarded as presenting a major difficulty for reasoning about actions and plans, there is still considerable disagreement over what it actually is. Some researchers, for example, see the problem as largely a matter of combinatorics (McCarthy & Hayes 1969; Reiter 1980); others view it as a problem of reasoning with incomplete information (McDermott 1982); and yet others believe it relates to the difficulty of enabling systems to notice salient properties of the world (Haugeland 1985). I shall take the problem to be simply that of constructing a formulation in which it is possible to readily specify and reason about the properties of events and situations. This gives rise to at least five related subproblems, which I discuss below.

The first of these is what I shall call the *combinatorial problem*. While it does not appear too difficult to give axioms that describe the *changes* wrought by some given action, it seems unreasonable to have to write down axioms describing all the properties *unaffected* by the action. Axioms of the latter kind are usually called *frame axioms* (McCarthy & Hayes 1969) and, in general, they need to be given (or, at least, be deducible)

for all property-action pairs. (Note that I use "unaffected" rather than "unchanging." This is an important distinction if we want to allow for concurrent events, as in most real-world domains.) The real problem here is to avoid *explicitly* writing down (or having to reason with) all the frame axioms for every property-action pair. Most solutions to this problem attempt to formalize some closed-world assumption regarding the specification of these dependencies.

As McCarthy was the first to observe (McCarthy 1980), two further problems arise as a result of the fact that specifying the effects of actions is usually subject to qualification. The first sort of qualification has to do with the conditions under which the action effects certain *changes* in the world. This is what I call the *precondition qualification* problem [also variously called the intraframe problem (Shoham 1986) and, simply, the qualification problem (McCarthy 1980)]. The second sort of qualification concerns the extent of influence of the action (or what remains *unaffected* by the action). I call it the *frame qualification* problem [also called the interframe problem (Shoham 1986) and the persistence problem (McDermott 1982)]. Let me give examples of these two kinds of qualification.

First, consider that we are trying to determine what happens if Mary fires a loaded gun (at point-blank range) at Fred (Hanks & McDermott 1986). Given such a scenario, we should be able to derive, without having to state a host of qualifications, that Fred dies as a result of the shooting. However, if we then discover that (or are given an extra axiom to the effect that) the gun was loaded with a blank round, the conclusion (that Fred dies) should be defeasible—i.e. we should be able to accommodate the notion of Fred's possibly being alive after the firing. This is the precondition qualification problem. Most solutions to this problem aim to formalize the rule: "These are the only *preconditions* that matter as far as the performance of the action is concerned, *unless* it can be shown otherwise."

As an example of the frame qualification problem, consider the point at which Mary loads the gun prior to firing it at Fred. All things being equal, it should be possible to derive that Fred's state of being *is* unaffected by loading the gun. However, if we discover that Fred actually died while the gun was being loaded, it should be possible (without changing the theory, except for the additional axiom about the time of Fred's death) to accommodate this without inconsistency and, if desired, to derive other theorems about the resulting situation. Most solutions to this problem attempt to formalize the rule thus: "These are the only *effects* of the action (given the preconditions), *unless* it can be shown otherwise." Solutions to this last problem often provide a solution to the combinatorial problem; the two problems, however, are clearly distinct.

6.1 Execution Monitoring Systems

Most existing architectures for embedded planning systems consist of a plan constructor and a plan executor. As a rule, the plan constructor plans an entire course of action before commencing execution of the plan (Fikes & Nilsson 1971; Vere 1983; Wilkins 1985b). The plan itself is usually composed of primitive actions—that is, actions that are directly performable by the system. The rationale for this approach, of course, is to ensure that the planned sequence of actions will actually achieve the prescribed goal. As the plan is executed, the system performs the primitive actions in the plan by calling various low-level routines. Usually, execution is monitored to ensure that these routines achieve the desired effects; if they do not, the system may return control to the plan constructor so that it can modify the existing plan appropriately.

Various techniques have been developed for monitoring the execution of plans and replanning upon noticing potential plan failure (Fikes & Nilsson 1971; Wilkins 1985b). The basis for most of these approaches is to retain with the plan an explicit description of the conditions that are required to hold for correct plan execution. Throughout execution, these conditions are periodically checked. If any condition turns out to be unexpectedly false, a replanning module is invoked. This module uses various plan-modification operators to change the plan, or returns to some earlier stage in the plan formation process and attempts to reconstruct the plan given the changed conditions.

However, in real-world domains, much of the information about how best to achieve a given goal is acquired during plan execution. For example, in planning to get from home to the airport, the particular sequence of actions performed depends on information acquired on the way—such as which turnoff to take, which lane to get into, when to slow down and speed up, and so on. Traditional planners can only cope with this uncertainty in two ways: (a) by building highly conditional plans, most of whose branches will never be used, or (b) by leaving low-level tasks to be accomplished by fixed primitive operators that are themselves highly conditional [e.g. the intermediate level actions (ILAs) used by SHAKEY (Nilsson 1984)]. The first approach only works in limited domains—the environment is usually too dynamic to anticipate all possible contingencies. The second approach simply relegates the problem to the primitive operators themselves, and does not provide any mechanism by which the higher-level planner can control their behavior.

To overcome this problem, at least in part, there has been some work on developing planning systems that interleave plan formation and execution (Davis & Chien 1977; Durfee & Lesser 1986). Such systems are better-

The fourth problem concerns the ability to write down certain axioms of invariance regarding world states. Following Finger (1986) I shall call this the *ramification problem*. For example, I should be able to formulate an axiom stating that everyone stops breathing when they die. Then I should be able to state that the effect of shooting a loaded gun at Fred results in his death without having to specify that it also results in cessation of his breathing. This latter effect of the shooting action should be inferable from the first axiom describing the consequences of dying. This seems straightforward, but a problem arises from the fact that such axioms can complicate the solution of the previous problems.

The fifth problem, which I call the *independence problem*, arises primarily in multiagent domains. In a dynamic world, or one populated with many agents, we want out solutions to allow for the independent activities of other agents. Most importantly, we do not want to have to specify explicitly all the external events that might occur. But if we leave the occurrence of such events unspecified, we do not want a solution to the previously mentioned problems to overcommit us to a world in which these events are thereby assumed *not* to have occurred.

There are a great variety of approaches to these problems, including the use of default logics (Reiter 1980); nonmonotonic logics (McDermott 1982); consistency arguments (Dean 1984); minimization of the effects of actions (Lifschitz 1987b), abnormalities (McCarthy 1984), event occurrences (Georgeff 1987b), and ignorance (Shoham 1986): and some ad hoc devices (Hayes 1973). All can be viewed as metatheories regarding the making of appropriate *assumptions* about the given problem domain (Poole et al 1986). This kind of reasoning will necessarily be *nonmonotonic*: In the light of additional evidence, some assumptions may need to be withdrawn, together with any conclusions based on those assumptions.

There are, however, serious difficulties in providing an acceptable semantics for many of these approaches (Hayes 1973; Reiter 1980), and many don't yield the intended results (Hanks & McDermott 1986). Furthermore, it is not clear how to implement most of these schemes efficiently. Brown (1987) has collected the most recent papers regarding this issue.

6. EMBEDDED SYSTEMS

Of course, the ability to plan and reason about actions and plans is not much help unless the agent doing the planning can survive in the world in which it is embedded. This brings us to perhaps the most important and also most neglected area of planning research—the design of systems that are actually *situated* in the world and that must operate effectively given the real-time constraints of their environment.

A number of systems developed for the control of robots have a high degree of reactivity (Albus 1981; Albus et al 1981). Even SHAKEY (Nilsson 1984) utilized reactive procedures (ILAs) to realize the primitive actions of the high-level planner (STRIPS), and this idea is pursued further in some recent work by Nilsson (1985). Another approach is advocated by Brooks (1985a), who proposes decomposition of the problem into *task-achieving* units in which distinct behaviors of the robot are realized separately, each making use of the robot's sensors, effectors, and reasoning capabilities as needed. This is in contrast to the traditional approach in which the system is structured according to *functional* capabilities, resulting in separate, self-contained modules for performing such tasks as perception, planning, and task execution. Kaelbling (1987) proposes an interesting hybrid architecture based on similar ideas.

Such architectures could lead to more viable and robust systems than the traditionally structured systems. Yet most of this work has not addressed the issues of general problem-solving and commonsense reasoning; the work is instead almost exclusively devoted to problems of navigation and execution of low-level actions. It remains to extend or integrate these techniques with systems that have the ability to completely change goal priorities, to modify, defer, or abandon current plans, and to reason about what is best to do in light of the current situation.

6.3 Rational Agents

Another promising approach to providing the kind of high-level goal-directed reasoning capabilities, together with the reactivity required for survival in the real world, is to consider planning systems as rational agents that are endowed with the psychological attitudes of belief, desire, and intention. The problem that then arises is specifying the properties we expect of these attitudes, the ways they interrelate, and the ways they determine rational behavior in a situated agent.

The role of beliefs and desires in reasoning about action has a long history in the philosophical literature (Davidson 1980). However, only relatively recently has the role of intentions been carefully examined (Bratman 1987). Moreover, there remain some major difficulties in formalizing these ideas. One serious problem is simply to choose an appropriate semantics for these notions. In particular, it is important to take into account the fact that the beliefs, desires, and intentions of an agent are *intensional* objects rather than *extensional* ones. For example, someone who does not know that the President of the United States is Ronald Reagan may well desire to meet one but not the other. Halpern (1986) provides an excellent collection of papers on reasoning about knowledge and belief. The most serious attempt to formalize some basic principles governing the rational

suited to real worlds than the kind of systems described above, as decisions can be deferred until they *have* to be made. The reason for deferring decisions is that an agent can only acquire *more* information as time passes; thus, the quality of its decisions can only be expected to improve. Of course, there are limitations resulting from the need to coordinate activities in advance and the difficulty of manipulating large amounts of information, but some degree of deferred decision-making is clearly desirable.

6.2 Reactive Systems

Real-time constraints pose yet further problems for traditionally structured systems. First, the planning techniques typically used by these systems are very time-consuming. While this may be acceptable in some situations, it is not suited to domains where replanning is frequently necessary and where system viability depends on readiness to act. In real-world domains, unanticipated events are the norm rather than the exception, necessitating frequent replanning. Furthermore, the real-time constraints of the domain often require almost immediate reaction to changed circumstances, allowing insufficient time for this type of planning.

A second drawback of traditional planning systems is that they usually provide no mechanisms for responding to new situations or goals during plan execution, let alone during plan formation. Indeed, the very survival of an autonomous system may depend on its ability to react quickly to new situations and to modify its goals and intentions accordingly. These systems should be able to reason about their current intentions, changing and modifying these in the light of their possibly changing beliefs and goals. While many existing planners have replanning capabilities, none have yet accommodated modifications to the system's underlying set of goal priorities.

Finally, traditional planners are overcommitted to the planning strategy itself. No matter what the situation, or how urgent the need for action, these systems *always* spend as much time as necessary to plan and reason about achieving a given goal before performing any external actions whatsoever. They do not have the ability to decide when to stop planning, nor to reason about the trade-offs between further planning and longer available execution time. Furthermore, these planners are committed to a single planning technique and cannot opt for different methods in different situations. This clearly mitigates against survival in the real world. Even systems that interleave planning and execution are still strongly committed to achieving the goals that were initially set them. They have no mechanisms for changing focus, adopting different goals, or reacting to sudden and unexpected changes in their environment.

balance among an agent's beliefs, intentions, and consequent actions can be found in the work of Cohen & Levesque (1987).

Lansky and I have been largely concerned with means-ends reasoning in dynamic environments, and with the way partial plans affect practical reasoning and govern future behavior (Georgeff & Lansky 1986b). We have developed a highly reactive system, called PRS, to which is attributed attitudes of belief, desire, and intention. Because these attitudes are explicitly represented, they can be manipulated and reasoned about, result-ing in complex goal-directed and reflective behaviors. The system consists of a *data base* containing current *beliefs* or facts about the world, a set of current *goals* or *desires* to be realized, a set of *procedures* or *plans* describing how certain sequences of actions and tests may be performed to achieve given goals or to react to particular situations, and an *interpreter* or *reasoning mechanism* for manipulating these components. At any moment, the system also has a *process stack*, containing all currently active plans, which can be viewed as the system's current *intentions* for achieving its goals or reacting to some observed situation.

The set of plans includes not only procedural knowledge about a specific domain, but also *metalevel* plans—that is, information about the manipu-lation of the beliefs, desires, and intentions of the system itself. For example, a typical metalevel plan would supply a method for choosing among multiple relevant plans, for achieving a conjunction of goals, or for deciding how much more planning or reasoning can be undertaken, given the real-time constraints of the problem domain.

The system operates by first forming a partial overall plan, then figuring out near-term means, executing any actions that are immediately appli-cable, further expanding the near-term plan, executing further, and so on. At any time, the plans the system intends to execute (i.e. the selected plans) are structurally partial—that is, while certain general goals have been decided upon, specific questions about the means to attain these ends are left open for future reasoning.

Furthermore, not all options that are considered by the system arise as a result of means-end reasoning. Changes in the environment may lead to changes in the system's beliefs, which in turn may result in the con-sideration of new plans that are not means to any already intended end. For example, the system may decide to drop its current goals and intentions completely, adopting new ones in their stead. This ability is vital in worlds in which emergencies of various degrees of severity can occur during the performance of other, less important tasks.

While the above work attempts to show how means-ends reasoning may be accomplished by systems situated in real-world environments, little research has been done in providing theories of *decision-making* that are appropriate to resource-bounded agents. Researchers in philosophy, as well as decision theory, have long been concerned with the question of how a rational agent weighs alternative courses of action (Jeffrey 1983). This work has largely assumed, either explicitly or implicitly, idealized agents with unbounded computational resources. In reality, however, agents do not have arbitrarily long to decide how to act, for the world is changing around them while they deliberate. If deliberation continues for too long, they very beliefs and desires upon which deliberation is based, as well as the real circumstances of the action, may change. These and related issues are explored by Bratman (1987) and Thomason (1987). Dean (1987) discusses some methods whereby a planning system can recognize the difficulty of the problems it is attempting to solve and, depending on the time it has to consider the matter and what it stands to gain or lose, produce solutions that are reasonable given the circumstances.

Systems that are situated in worlds populated with other agents also have to be able to reason about the behaviors and capabilities of these other systems. This requires complex reasoning about interprocess com-munication (Appelt 1985; Cohen & Levesque 1985) and the ability to infer the beliefs, goals, and intentions of agents from observations of their behavior (Pollack 1986, 1987). The challenge remains, however, to design situated planning systems capable of even the simplest kinds of rational behavior.

ACKNOWLEDGMENTS

I wish to thank particularly Amy Lansky, Nils Nilsson, Martha Pollack, and Dave Wilkins for their critical readings of earlier drafts of this paper. I am also indebted to Margaret Olender for her patient preparation of the bibliography and to Savel Kliachko for his erudite editorial advice.

The preparation of this paper has been made possible by a gift from the System Development Foundation, by the Office of Naval Research under Contract No. N00014-85-C-0251, and by the National Aeronautics and Space Administration, Ames Research Center, under Contract No. NAS2-12521.

Literature Cited

Albus, J. S., Anthony, A. J., Nagel, R. N. 1981. Theory and practice of hierarchical control. In *Proc. Twenty-Third IEEE Comput. Soc. Int. Conf.*
Albus, J. S. 1981. *Brains, Behavior, and Robotics.* Peterborough, NH: McGraw-Hill
Allen, J. F. 1982. Maintaining knowledge about temporal intervals. *Commun. ACM* 26: 832-43
Allen, J. F. 1984. Towards a general theory of action and time. *Artif. Intell.* 23: 123-54
Allen, J. F., Koomen, J. A. 1983. Planning using a temporal world model. In *Proc. Eighth Int. Joint Conf. Artif. Intell.*, Karlsruhe, West Germany, pp. 741-47

Appelt, D. E. 1985. Planning English referring expressions. *Artif. Intell.* 26: 1–34

Bell, C. E., Tate, A. 1985. Using temporal constraints to restrict search in a planner. In *Proc. Third Workshop Alvey IKBS Programme Planning Spec. Interest Group,* Sunningdale, Oxfordshire, UK

Bratman, M. 1987. *Intention, Plans, and Practical Reason.* Cambridge, Mass: Harvard Univ. Press. Forthcoming

Brooks, R. A. 1983. Planning collision-free motions for pick-and-place operations. *Int. J. Robot. Res.* 2(4): 19–40

Brooks, R. A. 1985a. *A Robust Layered Control System for a Mobile Robot.* Tech. Rep. 864, Artif. Intell. Lab. Cambridge, Mass: MIT

Brooks, R. A. 1985b. Visual map making for a mobile robot. In *Proc. IEEE Conf. Robot. Automat.* St. Louis, Missouri, pp. 824–29

Brown, F. 1987. *The Frame Problem in Artificial Intelligence: Proceedings of the 1987 Workshop.* Los Altos, Calif: Morgan Kaufmann

Chapman, D. 1985. *Planning for conjunctive goals.* Master's thesis MIT-AI-802, MIT

Charniak, E., McDermott, D. 1985. *Introduction to Artificial Intelligence.* Reading, Mass: Addison-Wesley

Cohen, P. R., Levesque, H. J. 1985. Speech acts and the recognition of shared plans. In *Proc. Twenty-Third Conf. Assoc. Comput. Linguist.,* Stanford, California, pp. 49–59

Cohen, P. R., Levesque, H. J. 1987. Persistence, intention, and commitment. In *Reasoning about Actions and Plans: Proceedings of the 1986 Workshop,* pp. 297–340. Los Altos, Calif: Morgan Kaufmann

Corkill, D. D., Lesser, V. R. 1983. The use of meta-level control for coordination in a distributed problem solving network. In *Proc. Eighth Int. Joint Conf. Artif. Intell.,* pp. 748–56

Davidson, D. 1980. *Actions and Events.* Oxford: Clarendon Press

Davis, L. H. 1979. *Theory and Action, Foundations of Philosophy Series.* Englewood Cliffs, NJ: Prentice-Hall

Davis, P. R., Chien, R. T. 1977. Using and reusing partial plans. In *Proc. Fifth Int. Joint Conf. Artif. Intell.,* Cambridge, Massachusetts, p. 494

Dawson, C., Siklossy, L. 1977. The role of preprocessing in problem solving systems. In *Proc. Fifth Int. Joint Conf. Artif. Intell.,* Cambridge, Massachusetts, pp. 465–71

Dean, T. 1984. Planning and temporal reasoning under uncertainty. In *Proc. IEEE Workshop Knowledge-Based Syst.,* Denver, Colorado

Dean, T. 1985. *An Approach to Reasoning about Time for Planning and Problem Solving.* Tech. Rep. 433. New Haven, Conn: Comput. Sci. Dept., Yale Univ.

Dean, T. 1987. Intractability and time-dependent planning. In *Reasoning about Actions and Plans: Proceedings of the 1986 Workshop,* pp. 245–66. Los Altos, Calif: Morgan Kaufmann

Dowty, D. R., Wall, R. E., Peters, S. 1981. *Introduction to Montague Semantics. Synthese Language Library.* Boston, Mass: Reidel

Durfee, E. H., Lesser, V. R. 1986. Incremental planning to control a blackboard-based problem solver. In *Proc. Fifth Natl. Conf. Artif. Intell.* Philadelphia, Penn., pp. 58–64

Durfee, E. H., Lesser, V. R., Corkill, D. D. 1985. Increasing coherence in a distributed problem solving network. In *Proc. Eighth Int. Joint Conf. Artif. Intell.,* Los Angeles, California, pp. 1025–30

Fahlman, S. E. 1974. A planning system for robot construction tasks. *Artif. Intell.* 5: 1–49

Fikes, R. E. 1975. Deductive retrieval mechanisms for state description models. In *Proc. Fourth Int. Joint Conf. Artif. Intell.* Tbilisi, USSR, pp. 99–106

Fikes, R. E., Nilsson, N. J. 1971. STRIPS: a new approach to the application of theorem proving to problem solving. *Artif. Intell.* 2: 189–208

Finger, J. J. 1986. *Exploiting Constraints in Design Synthesis.* PhD thesis, Stanford Univ., Stanford, California

Fox, M. S. 1984. ISIS—a knowledge-based system for factory scheduling. *Expert Syst.* 1(1): 24–49

Fox, M. S. 1986. Observations on the role of constraints in problem solving. In *Proc. Sixth Can. Conf. Artif. Intell.,* Montreal, pp. 172–87

Genesereth, M. R. 1983. An overview of meta-level architecture. In *Proc. Third Natl. Conf. Artif. Intell.,* pp. 119–24

Genesereth, M. R., Nilsson, N. J. 1987. *Logical Foundations of Artificial Intelligence.* Los Altos, Calif: Morgan Kaufmann

Georgeff, M. P., Lansky, A. L., Schoppers, M. 1987. *Reasoning and Planning in Dynamic Domains: An Experiment with a Mobile Robot.* Tech. Note 380. Menlo Park, Calif: Artif. Intell. Cent., SRI Int.

Georgeff, M. P. 1983. Communication and interaction in multiagent planning. In *Proc. Third Natl. Conf. Artif. Intell.,* Washington, DC, pp. 125–29

Georgeff, M. P. 1984. A theory of action for multiagent planning. In *Proc. Fourth Natl. Conf. Artif. Intell.,* Austin, Texas, pp. 121–25

Georgeff, M. P. 1987a. Actions, processes, and causality. In *Reasoning about Actions and Plans: Proceedings of the 1986 Workshop,* pp. 99–122. Los Altos, Calif: Morgan Kaufmann

Georgeff, M. P. 1987b. Many agents are better than one. In *The Frame Problem in Artificial Intelligence: Proceedings of the 1987 Workshop.* Los Altos, Calif: Morgan Kaufmann

Georgeff, M. P., Lansky, A. L. 1986a. Procedural knowledge. In *Proc. IEEE. Spec. Iss. Knowledge Representation,* 74: 1383–98

Georgeff, M. P., Lansky, A. L. 1986b. *A System for Reasoning in Dynamic Domains: Fault Diagnosis on the Space Shuttle.* Tech. Note 375. Menlo Park, Calif: Artif. Intell. Cent., SRI Int.

Gouzenes, L. 1984. Strategies for solving collision-free trajectories problems for mobile and manipulator robots. *Int. J. Robot. Res.* 3(4): 51–65

Green, C. C. 1969. Application of theorem proving to problem solving. In *Proc. First Int. Joint Conf. Artif. Intell.,* Washington, DC, pp. 219–39

Halpern, J. 1986. *Theoretical Aspects of Reasoning about Knowledge: Proceedings of the 1986 Conference.* Los Altos, Calif: Morgan Kaufmann

Hanks, S., McDermott, D. 1986. Default reasoning, nonmonotonic logics, and the frame problem. In *Proc. Fifth Natl. Conf. Artif. Intell.,* Philadelphia, Pennsylvania, pp. 328–33

Harel, D. 1979. *First Order Dynamic Logic. Springer Lect. Notes in Comput. Sci.* 68

Harel, D. 1984. Dynamic Logic. *Handbook of Philosophical Logic, Vol. II.* NY: Reidel

Haugeland, J. 1985. *Artificial Intelligence: The Very Idea.* Cambridge, Mass: MIT Press

Hayes, P. J. 1973. The frame problem and related problems in artificial intelligence. In *Artificial and Human Thinking,* ed. A. Elithorn, D. Jones, pp. 45–59. San Francisco: Jossey-Bass

Hayes, P. J. 1985. The second naive physics manifesto. In *Readings in Knowledge Representation,* pp. 467–85. Los Altos, Calif: Morgan Kaufmann

Hayes-Roth, B. 1985. A blackboard architecture for control. *Artif. Intell.* 26(3): 251–321

Hoare, C. A. R. 1985. *Communicating Sequential Processes. Series in Computer Science.* Englewood Cliffs, NJ: Prentice Hall

Jeffrey, R. 1983. *The Logic of Decision.* Chicago: Univ. Chicago Press

Kaelbling, L. P. 1987. An architecture for intelligent reactive systems. In *Reasoning about Actions and Plans: Proceedings of the 1986 Workshop,* pp. 395–410. Los Altos, Calif: Morgan Kaufmann

Kowalski, R. 1979. *Logic for Problem Solving.* NY: North Holland

Kowalski, R. A., Sergot, M. J. 1986. A logic-based calculus of events. *New Generation Comput.*

Krogh, B. H., Thorpe, C. E. 1986. Integrated path planning and dynamic steering control for autonomous vehicles. In *Proc. 1986 IEEE Int. Conf. Robot. Automat..* San Francisco, California, pp. 1664–69

Kuan, D. T. 1984. Terrain map knowledge representation for spatial planning. In *Proc. IEEE First Natl. Conf. Artif. Intell. Appl.,* Denver, Colorado, December, pp. 578–84

Ladkin, P. B. 1987. The completeness of a natural system for reasoning with time intervals. In *Proc. Tenth Int. Joint Conf. Artif. Intell.,* Milan, Italy

Ladkin, P. B., Maddux, R. D. 1987. *The algebra of convex time intervals. Kestrel Inst. Tech. Rep. KES.U.87.2*

Lansky, A. L. 1987a. A representation of parallel activity based on events, structure, and causality. In *Reasoning about Actions and Plans: Proceedings of the 1986 Workshop,* pp. 123–59. Los Altos, Calif: Morgan Kaufmann

Lansky, A. L. 1987b. *Localized Representation and Planning Methods for Parallel Domains.* In *Proc. Natl. Conf. Artif. Intell.,* Seattle, Washington

Lassez, J. L., Maher, M. 1983. The denotational semantics of horn clauses as a production system. In *Proc. Natl. Conf. Artif. Intell.,* Washington, DC, pp. 229–31

Levesque, H. J. 1986. Knowledge representation and reasoning. *Ann. Rev. Comput. Sci.* 1: 255–87

Lifschitz, V. 1987a. Formal theories of action. In *The Frame Problem in Artificial Intelligence: Proceedings of the 1987 Workshop.* Los Altos, Calif: Morgan Kaufmann

Lifschitz, V. 1987b. On the semantics of STRIPS. In *Reasoning about Actions and Plans: Proceedings of the 1986 Workshop,* Timberline, Oregon

Lozano-Perez, T. 1980. *Spatial Planning: A Configuration Space Approach. AI Memo 605.* Cambridge, Mass: AI Lab, MIT

Manna, Z., Waldinger, R. J. 1987. A theory of plans. In *Reasoning about Actions and Plans: Proceedings of the 1986 Workshop,* pp. 11–45. Los Altos, Calif: Morgan Kaufmann

Manna, Z., Wolper, P. 1981. *Synthesis of Communicating Processes from Temporal Logic Specifications. Tech. Rep. STAN-CS-81-872.* Stanford, Calif: Comput. Sci. Dept. Stanford Univ.

van Betham, J. 1984. Tense logic and time. *Notre Dame J. Formal Logic* 25(1): 1-16

Vere, S. 1983. Planning in time: windows and durations for activities and goals. *IEEE Trans. Pattern Analysis Mach. Intell.* 5(3): 246-67

Waldinger, R. 1977. Achieving several goals simultaneously. *Mach. Intell.* 8: 94-136

Warren, D. H. D. 1974. *WARPLAN: A system for generating plans.* Tech. Rep. Edinburgh: Univ. Edinburgh

Wesley, L. P., Lowrance, J. D., Garvey, T. D. 1979. *Reasoning about Control: An Evidential Approach.* Tech. Note 324. Menlo Park, Calif: Artif. Intell. Cent., SRI Int.

Wilensky, R. 1981. Meta-planning: representing and using knowledge about planning in problem solving and natural language understanding. *Cognit. Sci.* 5: 197-233

Wilkins, D. E. 1984. Domain independent planning: representation and plan generation. *Artif. Intell.* 22: 269-301

Wilkins, D. E. 1985a. *Hierarchical Planning: Definition and Implementation.* Tech. Note 370. Menlo Park, Calif: Artif. Intell. Cent., SRI Int.

Wilkins, D. E. 1985b. Recovering from execution errors in SIPE. *Comput. Intell.* 1: 33-45

Wilkins, D. E. 1987. *Using causal rules in planning.* Tech. Note 410. Menlo Park, Calif: Artif. Intell. Cent., SRI Int.

Stefik, M. 1981a. Planning with constraints (MOLGEN: Part 1). *Artif. Intell.* 16(2): 111-40

Stefik, M. 1981b. Planning with constraints (MOLGEN: Part 2). *Artif. Intell.* 16(2): 141-70

Strong, H. R. 1971. Translating recursive equations into flowcharts. *J. Comput. Syst. Sci.* 5(3): 254-85

Stuart, C. J. 1985. *Synchronization of Multiagent Plans Using A Temporal Logic Theorem Prover.* Tech. Note 350. Menlo Park, Calif: Artif. Intell. Cent., SRI Int.

Sussman, G. J. 1973. *A Computational Model of Skill Aquisition.* Tech. Rep. AI TR-297. Cambridge, Mass: Artif. Intell. Lab. MIT

Tate, A. 1974. *INTERPLAN: A plan generation system which can deal with interactions between goals.* Memo MIP-R-109. Edinburgh: Mach. Intell. Res. Unit, Univ. Edinburgh

Tate, A. 1977. Generating project networks. In *Proc. Fifth Int. Joint Conf. Artif. Intell.,* Cambridge, Massachusetts, pp. 888-93

Tate, A. 1984. *Hierarchical Planning.* In *Altey IKBS Expert Systems Theme—First Workshop,* Oxford, March. Also *D.A.I. Res. Pap. 221,* Univ. Edinburgh

Thomason, R. H. 1987. The context-sensitivity of belief and desire. In *Reasoning about Actions and Plans: Proceedings of the 1986 Workshop,* pp. 341-60. Los Altos, Calif: Morgan Kaufmann

McCarthy, J. 1968. Programs with common sense. In *Semantic Information Processing,* ed. M. Minsky. Cambridge, Mass: MIT Press

McCarthy, J. 1980. Circumscription—a form of nonmonotonic reasoning. *Artif. Intell.* 13: 27-39

McCarthy, J. 1984. Applications of circumscription to formalizing common sense knowledge. In *Proc. AAAI Nonmonotonic Reasoning Workshop,* pp. 295-324

McCarthy, J., Hayes, P. J. 1969. Some philosophical problems from the standpoint of artificial intelligence. *Mach. Intell.* 4: 463-502

McDermott, D. 1982. A temporal logic for reasoning about processes and plans. *Cognit. Sci.* 6: 101-55

McDermott, D. 1985. Reasoning about plans. In *Formal Theories of the Commonsense World,* ed. J. R. Hobbs, R. C. Moore, pp. 269-317. Norwood. NJ: Ablex

McDermott, D., Davis, E. 1984. Planning routes through uncertain territory. *Artif. Intell.* 22(2): 107-56

Milner, R. 1980. *A Calculus of Communicating Systems. Springer Lect. Notes in Comput. Sci. 92*

Montague, R. 1974. Deterministic theories. In *Formal Philosophy: Selected Papers of Richard Montague,* ed. R. H. Thomason. New Haven: Yale Univ. Press

Moore, R. C. 1980. *Reasoning about Knowledge and Action.* Tech. Note 191. Menlo Park, Calif: Artif. Intell. Cent., SRI Int.

Morgenstern, L. 1986. A first order theory of planning, knowledge, and action. In *Theoretical Aspects of Reasoning about Knowledge: Proceedings of the 1986 Conference,* ed. J. Halpern, pp. 99-114. Los Altos, Calif: Morgan Kaufmann

Myers, J. K. 1985. Multiarm collision avoidance using the potential-field approach. *Soc. Photo-Optic. Instru. Eng.* 580: 78-87

Newell, A., Simon, H. A. 1963. GPS, a program that simulates human thought. In *Computers and Thought,* ed. E. A. Feigenbaum, J. Feldman, pp. 279-93. NY: McGraw-Hill

Nilsson, N. J. 1980. *Principles of Artificial Intelligence.* Palo Alto. Calif: Tioga Publ.

Nilsson, N. J. 1984. *Shakey the Robot.* Tech. Note 323. Menlo Park, Calif: Artif. Intell. Cent., SRI Int.

Nilsson, N. J. 1985. *Triangle Tables: A Proposal for a Robot Programming Language.* Tech. Note 347. Menlo Park, Calif: Artif. Intell. Cent., SRI Int.

Nishimura, H. 1980. Descriptively complete process logic. *Acta Inform.* 14: 359-69

Pednault, E. P. D. 1986. Toward a mathematical theory of plan synthesis. PhD thesis. Stanford Univ.. Stanford, Calif.

Pednault, E. P. D. 1987. Solving multiagent dynamic world problems in the classical planning framework. In *Reasoning about Actions and Plans: Proceedings of the 1986 Workshop,* pp. 42-82. Los Altos, Calif: Morgan Kaufmann

Pelavin, R., Allen, J. F. 1986. A formal logic of plans in a temporally rich domain. In *Proc. IEEE, Spec. Iss. Knowledge Representation,* 74: 1364-82

Pollack, M. E. 1986. Inferring domain plans in question answering. PhD thesis. Univ. Pennsylvania

Pollack, M. E. 1987. A model of plan inference that distinguishes between the beliefs of actors and observers. In *Reasoning about Actions and Plans: Proceedings of the 1986 Workshop,* pp. 279-95. Los Altos, Calif: Morgan Kaufmann

Poole, D. L., Goebel, R. G., Aleliunas, R. 1986. *Theorist: a Logical Reasoning System for Defaults and Diagnosis.* NY: Springer-Verlag

Prior, A. N. 1967. *Past, Present and Future.* Oxford: Clarendon Press

Reiter, R. 1980. A logic for default reasoning. *Artif. Intell.* 13: 81-132

Rosenschein, J. S. 1982. Synchronization of multiagent plans. In *Proc. Conf. Artif. Intell.,* Stanford, California, pp. 115-19

Rosenschein, J. S., Genesereth, M. R. 1984. *Communication and Cooperation.* Tech. Rep. 84-5, Heur. Program. Proj. Stanford. Calif: Comput. Sci. Dept., Stanford Univ.

Rosenschein, J. S. 1986. Rational interaction: cooperation among intelligent agents. PhD thesis. Stanford Univ.

Rosenschein, S. J. 1981. Plan synthesis: a logical perspective. In *Proc. Seventh Int. Joint Conf. Artif. Intell.,* pp. 331-37. Vancouver, British Columbia

Sacerdoti, E. D. 1973. Planning in a hierarchy of abstraction spaces. In *Proc. Third Int. Joint Conf. Artif. Intell.,* Stanford. California, pp. 412-30

Sacerdoti, E. D. 1977. *A Structure for Plans and Behavior.* NY: Elsevier, North Holland

Sadri, F. 1986. Representing and reasoning about time and events: three recent approaches. Department of Computing. Imperial College, London

Shoham, Y. 1986. Chronological ignorance: time, nonmonotonicity, necessity and causal theories. In *Proc. Fifth Natl. Conf. Artif. Intell.,* Philadelphia, Pennsylvania. pp. 389-93

Shoham, Y. 1987. What is the frame problem. In *Reasoning about Actions and Plans: Proceedings of the 1986 Workshop,* pp. 83-98. Los Altos, Calif: Morgan Kaufmann

A Review of AI Planning Techniques

Austin Tate

Artificial Intelligence Applications Institute
University of Edinburgh

James Hendler

Computer Science Department
University of Maryland

Mark Drummond

Sterling Software
AI Research Branch
NASA Ames Research Center

1. Introduction

A long standing problem in the field of automated reasoning is that of designing systems which can describe a set of actions (or plan) which can be expected to allow the system to reach a desired goal. Ideally, the set of actions so produced is then passed on to a robot, a manufacturing system, or some other form of effector, which can follow the plan and produce the desired result. The design of such "planners" has been with AI since its earliest days, and a large number of techniques have been introduced in progressively more ambitious systems over a long period. In addition, planning research has introduced many problems to the field of AI. Some examples include:

- Representing and reasoning about time, causality and intentions
- Physical or other constraints on suitable solutions
- Uncertainty in the execution of plans
- Sensation and perception of the "real world" and holding beliefs about it
- Multiple agents who may cooperate or interfere

Planning problems, like most AI topics, have been attacked in two major ways: approaches which try to understand and solve the general problem without use of domain specific knowledge, and approaches which use domain heuristics directly. In planning, these are often referred to as *domain-dependent* approaches (which use domain-specific heuristics to control the planner's operation), and *domain-independent* approaches (in which the planning knowledge representation and algorithms are expected to work for a reasonably large variety of application domains). The issues involved in the design of domain-dependent planners are those generally found in applied approaches to AI — the need to justify solutions, the difficulty of knowledge acquisition, and the fact that the design principles may not map well from one application domain to another.

Work in domain-independent planning has formed the bulk of the AI research in the area of planning. The long history of these efforts (see figure 1) has led to the discovery of many

An early version of this article appeared in the *Knowledge Engineering Review* Volume 1 Number 2 pages 4–17, June 1985. Part of that review along with a tutorial introduction to the field appeared in the planning chapter of *Knowledge Engineering* Volume 1 published by McGraw–Hill (editor H.Adeli) in 1990. A more intoductory version of this paper is scheduled to appear in AI Magazine (Summer, 1990).

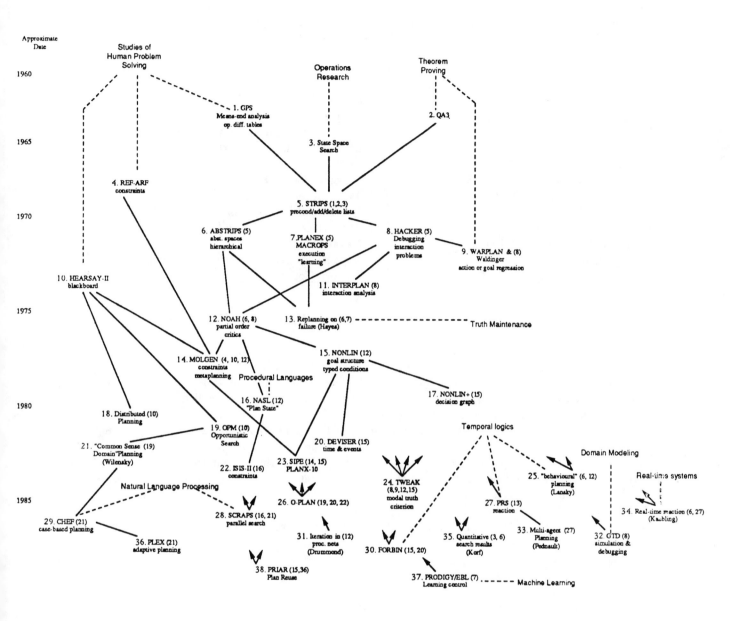

Figure 1: A brief chronology of some well–known planning systems.

Numbers in parentheses represent systems on which each planner has built directly (also shown as solid lines where possible). Dotted lines represent some of the important outside areas influencing the development of planning systems.

recurring problems, as well as to certain standard solutions. In addition, there have been a number of attempts to combine the planning techniques available at a given time into prototypes able to cope with increasingly more realistic application domains. (Table 1 shows an example of some of these efforts and the domains to which they were applied.)

Planner	Domain
STRIPS (Fikes & Nilsson, 1972a)	Simple Robot Control
HACKER (Sussman, 1973)	Simple Program Generation
NOAH (Sacerdoti, 1977)	Mechanical Engineers apprentice supervision
NONLIN (Tate, 1977)	Electricity Turbine Overhaul
NASL (McDermott, 1978)	Electronic Circuit Design
OPM (Hayes–Roth & Hayes–Roth, 1979)	Journey Planning
ISIS–II (Fox et. al., 1981)	Job Shop Scheduling (Turbine Production)
MOLGEN (Stefik, 1981a)	Experiment Planning in Molecular Genetics
SIPE (Wilkins, 1983)	Aircraft Carrier Mission Planning
NONLIN+ (Tate & Whiter, 1984)	Naval Logistics
DEVISER (Vere, 1983)	Voyager Spacecraft Mission Sequencing
FORBIN (Miller et. al., 1985)	Factory Control

Table 1: Numerous planning systems have attempted to integrate available planning techniques and apply them to application domains.

The goal of this article is to familiarize the reader with some of the important problems which have arisen in the design of planning systems, and some of the many solutions which have been developed in the over thirty years of planning research. In this paper we will try to provide a broad coverage of the major ideas in the field of AI planning and attempt to show the direction in which current research is going. We will define some of the terms commonly used in the planning literature, describe some of the basic issues arising out of the design of planning systems, and survey results in the area. (Due to the recurrence of many themes throughout the planning literature, we will survey the field on the basis of areas of interest rather than in terms of its chronological development.) Such a task is virtually never–ending, and any finite document must per force be incomplete. Thus, in addition to our discussion of the issues we have provided references to connect each idea to the appropriate literature and to allow readers access to the papers most relevant to their own research or applications work.

2. Planning Terminology

An AI planning system is charged with generating a *plan* which is one possible *solution* to a specified *problem*. The plan generated will be composed out of *operator schemata*, provided to the system for each domain of application. This section briefly considers the meaning of each of these terms and how they relate to one another.

A problem is characterized by an initial state and goal state description. The initial state description tells the planning system the way the world is "right now". The goal state description tells the planning system the way we want the world to look when the plan has been executed. The world in which planning takes place is often called the *application domain*. We will sometimes refer to the goal state description as simply "the goal." In many systems, a goal may be transformed into a set of other, usually simpler, goals called "sub–goals."

Operator schemata characterize *actions*. (The terms *action* and *event* are often used interchangeably in the AI planning literature, and certainly will be here.) *Schemata* primarily describe actions in terms of their preconditions and effects. Plans are built out of these operator schemata. Each operator schemata characterizes a *class* of possible actions, by containing a set of variables which can be replaced by constants to derive operator *instances* that describe specific, individual, actions. When the distinction doesn't matter, we'll use the term *operator* to stand for both operator schemata and operator instances. An action which the planner considers to be directly executable is referred to as a *primitive action*, or simply as a *primitive*.

Pickup(x)

Precondition:	ONTABLE(x) ^ HANDEMPTY ^ CLEAR(x)
Delete List:	ONTABLE(x) HANDEMPTY CLEAR(x)
Add List:	HOLDING(x)

Figure 2: A typical STRIPS operator.

The operator *Pick-up* contains a precondition formula, add and delete lists. Thus, pick-up can be used to lift an object which must be on the table, the hand must be empty, and the object must be clear (from the preconditions). After pickup, the object is not on the table and is not clear, and the hand is no longer empty (from the delete-list), also the hand is known to be holding the object (from the add-list).

A commonly used terminology throughout the AI planning literature is that of *STRIPS operators* (Fikes, et.al., 1972a; 1972b). These operators, first used in the early planning program STRIPS, describe an action by means of three parts: a *precondition* formula, an *add-list* and a *delete-list* (see Figure 2). An operator's precondition formula (or simply, the operator's preconditions) give facts that must hold before the operator can be applied. The add-list and delete-list are used in concert to simulate action occurrence. If an operator's preconditions hold in a state then the operator can be applied. Applying an operator means acting on its add-list and delete-list to produce a new state. The new state is produced by first deleting all formulas given in the delete-list and then adding all formulas in the add-list. Although newer planning systems (discussed later) do depart from this approach, the terminology of STRIPS operators is fairly standard and we will use it often in this article.

A plan is an organized collection of operators. A plan is said to be a *solution* to a given problem if the plan is applicable in the problem's initial state, and if after plan execution, the goal is true. What does it mean for a plan to be "applicable"? Assume that there is some operator in the plan that must be executed first. Then the plan is *applicable* if all the preconditions for the execution of this first operator hold in the initial state. Repeated analysis can determine whether or not all operators can be applied in the order specified by the plan. This analysis is referred to as *temporal projection*. The first state considered in the projection is the problem's initial state. Repeated operator applications produce intermediate state descriptions. If the goal is true at the end of this projection then the plan is a solution to the specified problem.

So, the inputs to a typical AI planning system are a set of operator schemata and a problem that is characterized by an initial state description and goal. The output from the planner is a plan which under projection satisfies the goal. The process connecting the input and output is known by various names. Common names are plan *generation*, plan *synthesis* and plan *construction*. A planner is called *domain independent* in the sense that the plan representation language and plan generation (or synthesis, or construction) algorithms are expected to work for a reasonably large

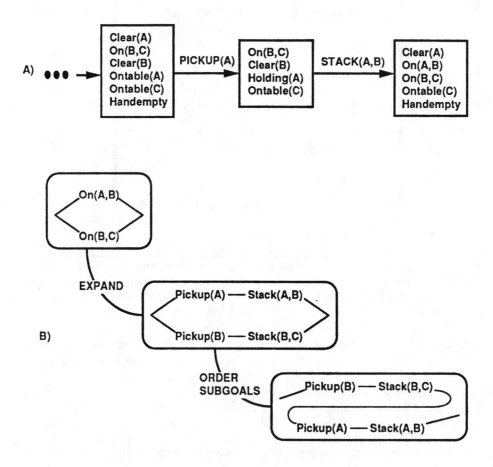

Figure 3: Partial solutions to the problem "(On A B)&(On B C)"

Figure 3a (based on STRIPS) shows a typical state-space and a sequence of operators, representing a partial solution. Figure 3b (based on NOAH) shows the plan as a partial ordering of actions representing a partial solution.

variety of application domains. While this view of planning is slightly restrictive, it will suffice for the purposes of this overview.

A planner is organized so that it defines a search space and then seeks a point in that search space which is defined as a solution. Planners differ as to how they define their search space. Some (most of the pre–1975 planners) define points in the search space as "states" of the application's world at various times. This "world state" can be traversed by applying any applicable operator to some chosen state leading to a different point in the search space. A problem solution can be defined as a sequence of operators that can traverse the search space from some initial state to some state defined as satisfying the goal. Thus, a state–space plan contains descriptions of states of the world the plan is to be executed in, and move operators which correspond to the actions to be carried out to execute the plan. A state–space solution is trivial to recognize: it is quite simply a path from some initial state to a state satisfying the goal specification (see Figure 3a).

Other (most of the post–1975) planners define points in the search space as partially elaborated plans. One point in this space is changed into another using any applicable planning transformation such as the expansion of an action to a greater level of detail, the inclusion of an additional ordering constraint between actions to resolve some interaction between effects of unordered actions, etc.. Given some initial (skeleton) plan defining a point in this "partial plan search space", a sequence of plan transformations must be applied which lead to a fully detailed plan that satisfies the goal (see Figure 3b). A plan is considered to be complete when all of the goals can be realized as a set of primitive actions (totally– or partially–ordered depending on the planner).

Systems which search through the space of partial plans have typically represented plans as an "action–ordering" in which the actions, described by operators, are strung together with temporal ordering relations. The most famous example of such plans are Sacerdoti's (1975) *Procedural Nets* (see section 3). Action–ordering plans describe the relationships among actions directly, rather than through states and predicates contained within states.

In an action–ordering representation a plan need not completely specify the conditions that each action affects. The plan can simply order two actions without specifying intermediate states. In contrast, state–based plan structures typically require complete specification of these intermediate states. This is particularly difficult for use in describing complicated causal and temporal relationships *between* actions. Thus, many complex domains are quite difficult to encode using a state–based approach (cf. Lansky, 1987), and action–ordering approaches have become the more generally used technique.

3. Planning as Search

As described above, the essence of planning is a search problem. The program must traverse a potentially large search space and find a plan which satisfies the goal and is applicable starting in the initial state. This search can be quite difficult as the search space may contain many interactions between different states or partial plans. As such, it is not surprising that even simple planning problems can be shown to be exponential (Chapman, 1987). The problems of organizing the heuristic search, choosing what to do in cases of failure, and generally finding ways of making more informed choices have therefore been among the most discussed in the planning literature. A good quantitative discussion of planning viewed as heuristic search can be found in Korf (1987).

State Space Search

Early approaches to planning sought to apply legal "moves" to some initial state to search for a state that satisfied the given goals. There was a great deal of overlap with game playing work. Heuristic evaluation functions were employed to rate the various intermediate states produced to estimate their "closeness" to a goal state (e.g., in A* (Hart et al, 1968) and the Graph Traverser (Doran & Michie, 1966). Later techniques have used many other search strategies.

Means–ends Analysis

To reduce the number of intermediate states considered, only those operators or activities that can satisfy some outstanding goal may be considered. These in turn can introduce new (hopefully simpler) sub–goals. This was introduced in GPS (Newell & Simon, 1963) and used in many later systems.

Search Reduction through Least Commitment[†]

Least commitment plan representations[†] may be used to allow a wider set of possible distinct plans to be represented in a single search space state when a partial–plan search–based planner is used. Examples of such representations include the use of a parallel plan to represent a number of possible action orderings prior to a commitment becoming necessary (e.g. in NOAH (Sacerdoti, 1975)), or the posting of constraints on objects referred to in the plan rather than making an arbitrary selection (e.g. in MOLGEN (Stefik,1981a)).

Select and Commit

Some systems, especially ones which introduced important new techniques, did not search through the possible alternatives at all. Selections were made on the basis of the information available locally and then a commitment to that solution path was made. Of course, this meant that some problems could not be solved. However, since these systems were typically demonstrated on particular applications for which one technique was most appropriate, the approach was often successful at arriving at a solution directly. Very often, techniques demonstrated in isolation in this way were incorporated in later planners that could search for alternatives and use the method alongside others depending on their relevance.

Depth–first Backtracking

A simple method of considering alternative solution paths (especially when there are only a few to choose from due to the use of means–ends analysis, etc.) is to save the state of the solution at each point at which there are alternative ways to proceed and to keep a record of the alternative choices. The first is chosen and search continues. If there is any failure, the saved state at the last choice point is restored and the next alternative taken (if there are none, "backtracking" continues over previous decisions). Simple stack based implementation techniques can be used for this process (for example, as done in Prolog).

Beam Search

This is a search method which considers all possible solutions within a pre–constrained area so that they can be compared. Such a method is normally used when tight search space constraints are known and hence the solution space considered by the beam search is expected to be small. It is also normally employed along with other heuristic search methods so that a choice can be made of the "best" solutions found amongst the solutions to some sub–problem which have been proposed by a beam search (e.g., ISIS–II (Fox, Allen, & Strohm, 1981)).

One–then–Best Backtracking

Since there is often good local information available to indicate the preferred solution path, it is often appropriate to try the best choice indicated by local heuristic information before considering the many alternatives that may be available should the local choice prove faulty. Taken to the extreme, depth–first search gives something of the flavor of such a search strategy. However, gradual wandering from a valid solution path could entail backtracking through many levels when a failure is detected. An alternative is to focus on the

----

† Some people use the term "least commitment" to refer only to the ordering of plan steps in a partial–order planner. We use the term in the broader sense, referring to any aspect of a planner which only commits to a particular choice when forced by some constraints.

choice currently being made and try to select one of the local choices which seems most promising. This continues while all is going well (perhaps with some cut–off points to take a long, hard look at how well things are going). However, if a failure occurs, the *entire* set of alternatives which have been generated (and ranked by a heuristic evaluator) are re–considered to select the re–focusing point for the search (e.g., in NONLIN (Tate, 1977)).

Dependency–Directed Search

It is well known that any backtracking system based on saved states and resumption points (whether depth–first or heuristically controlled) can waste much valuable search effort. There may be several unrelated parts to a solution. If it so happens that backtracking on one part has to go back beyond points at which work was done on an unrelated part, all effort on the unrelated part will be lost. Examples of work that have explored this include Hayes (1975), Stallman and Sussman (1977), NONLIN+Decision Graph (Daniel, 1983) and MOLGEN (Stefik, 1981a,b) to some extent. Such systems do not keep saved states of the solution at choice points. Instead they record the dependencies between decisions, the assumptions on which they are based and the alternatives from which a selection can be made. They then use methods for undoing a failure by propagating and undoing all of the dependent parts of the solution. This leaves unrelated parts intact irrespective of whether they were worked on after some undone part of the solution. Truth maintenance systems (particularly ATMS') have been proposed as one way of implementing such systems efficiently.

Opportunistic Search

Some systems do not take a fixed (goal–driven or data–driven) directional approach to solving a problem. Instead, a current "focus" for the search is identified on the basis of the most constrained operation that can be performed. This may be suggested by comparison of the current goals with the initial world model state, by consideration of the number of likely outcomes of making a selection, by the degree to which goals are instantiated, etc. Any problem solving component may summarize its requirements for the solution as constraints on possible solutions or restrictions of the values of variables representing objects being manipulated. They can then suspend their operation until further information becomes available on which a more definite choice can be made (for example, MOLGEN (Stefik, 1981a)). Many such systems operate using a blackboard architecture through which the various components can communicate via constraint information (e.g., Hearsay–II (Erman et al, 1980), and OPM (Hayes–Roth & Hayes–Roth, 1979)). The scheduling of the various tasks associated with arriving at a solution may also be dealt with through the blackboard.

Meta–level Planning

There are a number of planning systems which have an operator–like representation of the different types of plan transformations available to the planner. A separate search is made to decide which of these is best applied at any point; this happens before decisions are taken about the details of the particular application plan being produced (e.g., MOLGEN (Stefik, 1981a,b), and Wilensky (1981a)). This technique is often used in opportunistic planners.

Distributed Planning

Some systems have gone further in distributing the sources of problem solving expertise or knowledge. They allow fully distributed planning with the sub–problems being passed between specialized planning experts. The use of the experts or the types of things they can do may be controlled through a centralized blackboard and executive (with a system rather like priority scheduling of parallel processes) or may be controlled in a more distributed fashion via pairwise negotiation. Examples of relevant work include Smith's (1977) Contract Net, Corkill (1979), Kornfeld (1979), Konolige and Nilsson (1980) Georgeff (1982), and Corkill and Lesser (1983).

General Pruning of the Search Space

Besides the basic methods of reducing the search space by selection of relevant operators in means–ends analysis, many other methods of reducing the search space size have been employed in planners. Some are identified here.

- By considering "higher priority" goals first in hierarchical planners (e.g., ABSTRIPS (Sacerdoti, 1973), and LAWALY (Siklossy & Dreussi, 1975)).

- By detecting and correcting for interactions in an intelligent fashion; for example, Waldinger's (1975) Goal Regression, INTERPLAN's "approach" and "Ticklist" (Tate, 1975), NOAH (Sacerdoti, 1975) and NONLIN (Tate, 1977).

- By rejection of states or plans that are known to be impossible or in violation of some rule about the state or plan (e.g., Warplan's (Warren, 1974) *imposs* statements, Allen and Koomen's (1983) *domain constraints*, and Drummond and Currie's (1989a, 1989b) technique of *temporal coherence*). A variant on this approach, using a domain model to simulate the results of planning operators was used in Simmons & Davis' (1987) Generate–Test–Debug planner.

- By checks on resource usage levels, time constraints on actions, etc. (e.g.,DEVISER (Vere, 1983), SIPE (Wilkins, 1983), NONLIN+ (Tate & Whiter, 1984)).

- by providing heuristics which utilize the naturally occurring structures within a domain. Lansky's (1988) GEMPLAN, a multiagent planner uses "locality" or domain structure to partition domain information as well as the planning space and provides a way of partitioning the planning search space into smaller, localized search spaces.

- By using parallelism to briefly examine many potential choices. The program SCRAPS (Hendler, 1986) used a parallel, breadth first, marker–passing search algorithm, coupled with heuristics concerning potential effects of various interactions to suggest possible choices or to rule out potential paths (thus reducing the search space).

4. Hierarchy/Abstraction Levels

The order in which several simultaneous goals are tackled can have a marked effect on the efficiency of the search process for a solution. In some early planners, it can make the difference between finding a solution and looping round on the same goals repeatedly or getting solutions with redundant steps. Some approaches to ordering the various goals involve separating the goals into levels of importance or priority (the more abstract and general goals being worked on first and the more concrete or detailed levels being filled in later).

Strict Search by Levels

The early hierarchical systems (e.g., ABSTRIPS (Sacerdoti, 1973); LAWALY (Siklossy & Dreussi, 1975); NOAH (Sacerdoti, 1977)) formed a solution at the most abstract level and then made a commitment to this solution. The lower levels were then planned using the pre–set skeleton plan formed at the upper levels. No backtracking to the higher levels was possible.

Non–strict by Levels

Later systems (e.g., NONLIN (Tate, 1977)) treat the abstraction levels as a guide to a skeleton solution, but are able to re–plan or consider alternatives at any level if a solution cannot be found, or if problems with part of a solution indicate that a higher level choice was faulty.

Opportunistic by Levels

Other hierarchical systems use the abstraction levels as one guide to the ordering of goals, but have other mechanisms that can be considered alongside this. Some systems are able to determine when a particular choice (at whatever level) is sufficiently constrained to be a preferable goal to work on at any time (e.g., MOLGEN (Stefik, 1981a,b)).

Concurrent Processing of Levels

A relatively recent approach has included attempting to build models which can plan at different levels of the hierarchy concurrently. A mathematical analysis of some properties which allow systems to assume independence of level effects in some cases has been performed (Yang, 1989). Attempts to use this approach in the building of systems are currently underway (Nau et. al., 1989). GEMPLAN (Lansky, 1988) also allows for simultaneous use of events at varying levels. Thus, the planning operators may use events at whatever level is appropriate to a stated goal or constraint. A formal theory of abstraction of abstraction, allowing for concurrent processing of levels and for the control of information flow between levels is also being explored currently (Hendler & Subrahmanian, 1990).

5. Goal Ordering and Interaction Detection and Correction

A common way of categorizing planning systems is according to the way in which they manage interactions between goals and the way in which they structure operators in a plan. In terms of goal interactions, there are planners which make the so-called "linearity assumption", that is, that solving one goal and then following this with the solution to other goals will be successful. This assumption is valid in some domains since the solutions to different goals may often be decoupled. Some planners do not make the linearity assumption, and are prepared to consider arbitrary interleavings of all goals and subgoals.

In terms of plan structure, there are "total order" planners and "partial order" planners. A total order planner uses a sequence of operators to represent the plans in its search space. A partial order planner represents a plan as a partially ordered network of operators and performs least–commitment in the sense that it only introduces ordering links between operators when problems in the developing plan demand it.

In this section we review the progress from total order planners to partial order planners, and discuss some of the mechanisms that have been used for managing goal interactions.

Total Order – Interactions Ignored
> If the separate sub–goals are solved sequentially and then a simple check made to see if the conjunction of goals then holds (e.g., in STRIPS (Fikes & Nilsson, 1971)), this can lead to mutual goal or subgoal interference which at best can lead to redundant actions in the plan and at worst may get the planner into an endless cycle of re-introducing and trying to satisfy the same goal over and over again.

Total Order – Interactions Detected
> In early systems that recognised the importance of detecting "bugs" with the "linearity assumption" (e.g., HACKER (Sussman, 1973)), corrections were attempted by backtracking to points where alternative goal orderings could be tried (as part of the overall search space). This could solve some types of problems.

Total Order – Interactions Detected – Corrected by Action Regression
> One method of correcting for detected interactions is to allow the interfering action (just being introduced to satisfy some goal) to be placed at different (earlier) points in the partial linear plan until a position is found where there is no interaction (e.g., WARPLAN (Warren, 1974)). Unfortunately this can lead to the inclusion of redundant actions since the action may not be necessary (or may not be the best choice) when moved earlier in the plan.

Total Order – Interactions Detected – Corrected by Goal Regression
> The problem of regressing the action chosen to satisfy a goal back through the plan to correct for an interaction can be solved by regressing the goal itself when an interaction with some particular solution fails (e.g., Waldinger, 1975). This has the advantage that redundant actions are not included if the goal is already solved at some earlier point in the plan.

Total Order – Interactions Detected – Corrected by Analysis
> A representation called "Goal Structure" was introduced in INTERPLAN (Tate, 1975) to record the link between an effect of one action that was a precondition (subgoal) of a later one. This representation is additional to the ordering links

between the actions themselves (as some actions have effects that are used much later in the plan). Sussman (1973) referred to this as the "teleology" of the plan. Interactions are detected as an interference between some new action or goal being introduced and one or more previous goal structures. This mehtod could consider fewer re–orderings of the given goals and subgoals than the regression methods.

Partial Order – Interactions Detected – Limited Correction

NOAH (Sacerdoti, 1975), the first partial–order planner[†], incorporated code called "critics" which were used to search for interactions between parts of the plan. It used a Table of Multiple Effects (TOME) to aid in discovering the interactions. The TOME was modelled on the concept of Goal Structure as it appeared in INTER-PLAN. Once detected, NOAH could correct for interactions in a limited way suited to the applications it was employed on. This was primarily due to the limitation in NOAH that no alternatives could be considered – the best choice was committed to at each stage.

Partial Order – Interactions Detected – Corrected by Analysis

The detection of interactions by analysis of the underlying "Goal Structure" was added to NONLIN (Tate, 1977) a partial order planner modelled on NOAH. In NON-LIN, the minimum set of orderings necessary to resolve any interaction could be suggested by the introduction of ordering links into a partial order plan only when this became essential. The NONLIN system could consider alternatives if failures on any chosen search branch occurred. Techniques to analyze the condition structure of a plan and to detect and correct for interactions have also been proposed in PLANX–10 (Sridharan & Bresina, 1985), SIPE's "Plan Rationale" (Wilkins, 1983) and Dean's (1985) work.

Partial Order – Interactions Detected and Corrected – Time Limits Handled

When individual goals or actions in a plan have time constraints on when they can be satisfied or performed, the detection and correction of interactions must be sensitive to the temporal displacement introduced . This normally further limits the number of legal solutions that can be proposed. These capabilities were realized in the DEVISER system (Vere, 1983), a NONLIN–like system which allowed for planning in the presence of deadlines and external events.

Partial Order – Interactions Detected and Corrected – Resources Handled

The use of objects being manipulated as scarce resources on which usage conflicts occur and need to be avoided was incorporated in the MOLGEN (Stefik, 1981a) and SIPE (Wilkins, 1983) planners. Viewing time as such a resource is an active topic being considered in current research (Dean & Boddy, 1987).

6. Planning with Conditionals and Iterators

Most of the search space control techniques, goal ordering and interaction correction mechanisms developed in AI planners to date have been oriented towards the generation of plans which are fully or partially ordered sequences of primitive actions. However, there has been some effort on the generation of plans which contain conditionals ("if ... then ... else ...") and iterators ("repeat ... until ...").

Black Box Approach to Conditionals and Iterators

A conditional or iterator which can be modelled as a single entity and for which the differences between the multiple paths or the individual loops are not important can be handled by many of the planning systems and techniques already described.

[†] NOAH is often referred to as the first "non–linear" planner —— the term being used in this context to refer to the partially ordered plan structures employed by the system. NOAH was the first planner that did not require the operators in a plan to be totally ordered with respect to time. This was a great insight and aspects of this representation are still under formal analysis today. But we feel that the term "non–linear" is too easily confused with issues surrounding the "linearity assumption". To help avoid this confusion we will not refer to planners which use partially ordered plans as non–linear, but rather, will say that such planners *use* partially ordered plans; thus, they are "partial order planners".

NOAH (Sacerdoti, 1975) explicitly dealt with such packaged conditionals and iterators. SIPE (Wilkins, 1983) was able to deal with iteration which repeated a planned action sequence on each member of a set of parameters (which could be objects or points on an aircraft flight trajectory).

Conditionals: Branch and Case Analysis

Conditionals were handled in WARPLAN–C (Warren, 1976) by branching the plan at the conditional and performing separate planning on the two branches using the assumption that the statement in the conditional was true in one branch and false in the other. This lead to a case analysis of the separate branches to produce a plan that was tree–structured (see also, Schoppers (1987)). In addition, Drummond (1985) has designed a mechanism for representing disjunction and iteration and for predicting the behavior of the system where these were present.

Conditionals: Branch and Re–Join

There has been relatively little work in the mainstream AI planning literature which has attempted a full treatment of conditionals which can branch and rejoin later in the plan and for which the black box approach was not sufficient. However, work on automatic programming and theorem proving has considered this area. See, for example, Luckham and Buchanan (1974) and Dershowitz (1985). The latter reference has an extensive bibliography of papers on automatic programming and shows how AI planning research overlaps with this work.

7. Domain Representation

Many AI systems have introduced formalisms or constructs for capturing the information about the application domain and for making that knowledge available to a planning system[†]. Once again, later systems have often built on the best aspects of earlier efforts.

Differences

The early means–ends analysis systems selected appropriate operators to apply to a problem by considering the differences between the goal state and the initial state. The General Problem Solver, GPS (Newell & Simon, 1963), associated the operators for the problem with the changes they could make in the world (i.e. the state in which they were applied).

Add/Delete/Precondition Lists

Based on the situation calculus (McCarthy & Hayes 1969), Green's (1969) QA3, and the notion of differences from GPS (Newell & Simon, 1963), STRIPS (Fikes & Nilsson, 1971) makes the assumption that the initial world model is only changed by a set of additions to and deletions from the statements modelling the world state, everything else remaining unchanged. (This is sometimes called the "STRIPS assumption".) STRIPS then defined an operator as having an add–list, a delete–list and a preconditions–formula (to define the applicability or sub–goaling conditions). Operators could be selected on the basis of goals which occur on their add–lists (statements added to the world model).

Abstraction Levels on Goals

The hierarchical systems introduced the ability to specify the abstraction or criticality levels of the various statements that could be made about a world state (e.g., ABSTRIPS (Sacerdoti, 1973); LAWALY (Siklossy & Dreussi, 1975)).

Partial–orders on plan segments in hierarchical planners

NOAH (Sacerdoti, 1975), allowed plan steps to be left unordered until some need was found to linearize them. NOAH had procedurally specified "SOUP" (Semantics Of User's Problem) code to introduce appropriate methods of achieving goals or orderings to correct for interactions into the network of actions.

_____

[†] As mentioned in the introduction, in this article we are concentrating on work in the area of domain-independent planning systems. A large amount of work in representing specific domain information for planning systems has also been done. Some good examples can be found in the Proceedings of the DARPA workshop on Knowledge–based planning, Austin Texas, Dec. 1987.

Declarative Partial–order representation

Later planners introduced declarative representations for operators in extensions of the STRIPS operator type of formalism (e.g., NONLIN'S Task Formalism (Tate, 1977) and SIPE Notation (Wilkins, 1983)). As well as add, delete and precondition lists, an "expansion" of the operator to a lower level of detail could be specified as a partial order on suitable sub–actions and sub–goals.

Intent of plan steps

Some systems distinguish between ordering relationships on actions and the purposes of the actions with respect to where in the plan their effects are required. Such information was first made available through the STRIPS "triangle tables" (Fikes et. al., 1972a) to aid in re–use of parts of plans in new situations. In HACKER (Sussman, 1973), the information is kept as protection intervals (Sussman used the term "teleology") and was used to detect "protection violations" which led HACKER to consider alternative ways to perform a task being tried. In Tate's INTERPLAN (1975) and NONLIN (1977; 1984b) systems, such information (called "Goal Structure") was used to be more precise about interaction detection and aided in suggesting appropriate corrections. PLANX–10 (Sridharan & Bresina, 1985) and SIPE (Wilkins, 1983) have internal structures similar to Goal Structure.

Time Windows and Events

DEVISER (Vere, 1983) has provided a method for specifying a time window on goals and activities. External events and their time of occurrence can also be given. Delayed events caused some time after a planned action can be specified.

Action Logics and Formal Models

Formal models of actions, processes and states have been a recurring theme of AI work and this has impacted on AI planning work. Some of the work has its roots in Process models and Finite State Automata. The majority of the AI planning techniques reviewed in this paper are most suited to planning for discrete activities. Some of the work on formal models and action logics admit reasoning about continuous processes. Such topics require a survey in their own right and are only briefly touched upon here. Example references include (Moore, 1980; McDermott, 1978). Recent research in AI planning is taking more account of such work. In addition, an effort is being made to extend temporal representations to handle simultaneously occuring events and event interactions. The use of these extended representations for planning is discussed by Pednault (1987) and Lansky (1987).

8. Time and Resource Handling

It is becoming increasingly important in planning systems to perform on realistic applications where resources of various types are limited. Also, planners are being used in domains where time considerations must be accounted for. Several systems have explored this area.

Compute Time and Resource Usage

In a project planning domain, NONLIN maintained information about the durations of the various activities and used this to compute earliest and latest start times for each action. A critical path of actions could be found. A "cost" measure could also be kept with each activity. This information was used in an extension to the NONLIN planner that could selectively remove costly activities or lengthy activities from a plan and replace them with others that either reduced the cost or the duration depending on the limitation that was exceeded (see Daniel, 1983). More recent work on NONLIN+ (Tate & Whiter, 1984) has added the capability of representing multiple limited resources and making selection from appropriate activities on the basis of reducing some overall computed "preference" between them. The definition of shared objects as resources and the declaration of the use of such resources in operators was provided in SIPE (Wilkins, 1983). DEVISER (Vere, 1983) could also handle consumable resources (such as fuel).

Preference Constraints

ISIS–II (Fox et al, 1981) allows a wide variety of constraints on the problem to be specified. Some of these can be in the form of preferences, or "soft" constraints, which are used to guide the search for acceptable solutions.

Event and Time Specifications for Actions

Deviser (Vere, 1983) allowed a "time window" to be specified for any goal or action. External events could be described as having some effect at a particular time. The planner propagated the temporal links between these time windows, progressively narrowing them as they became constrained by other actions. It could detect when some plan step prevented a goal from being achieved or an activity from being executed at the required time. In such a case, backtracking was used to consider alternative solutions. Airplan (Masui et al, 1983) was able to reason about time intervals and about how concurrent actions in these intervals could interact. EXCALIBUR (Drabble, 1988) allowed for planning in the face of external continuous processes which were modelled qualitatively. A model for flexibly reasoning about time in the context of planning, called a time map manager, was developed by Dean and McDermott (1987).

O–Plan (Bell & Tate, 1985) uniformly represents time constraints (and resource usage) by a numeric *(min, max)* pair which bound the actual values for activity duration, activity start and finish times, and delays between activities. The actual values may be uncertain for various reasons, such as the plan being at a high abstraction level, not having chosen values for objects referred to in the plan, or uncertainty in modeling the domain. Constraints can be stated on the time and resource values which may lead to the planner finding that some plans in its search space are invalid.

Flexible Time Handling

Much more flexible handling of the propagation of temporal constraints between the steps of a plan is being considered in the widespread research effort on temporal logic. A discussion of this work is presented in Allen (1990).

9. Planning and Execution

Most of the systems described so far have assumed that the planner is possessed of complete knowledge of the current state of the world and the cause–and–effect relationships that govern changes in that world. Clearly this approach is in need of revision in situations where separate execution cannot be guaranteed to succeed. This can occur when agents outside of the control of the planner may cause changes in the environment or where the planner may be uncertain of information that can only be ascertained while the plan is being run. Planning in such environments cannot be guaranteed to succeed even in cases where plans could be efficiently computed otherwise (Sanborn & Hendler, 1987). A number of alternatives and refinements to the generate and execute approach have now been suggested.

Interleaved Planning and Execution

McDermott's (1978) NASL system differed from the classical approach by generating plans a step at a time and executing each step as it was generated. This made the planner more susceptible to errors caused by interactions, but made it less susceptible to errors caused by change in the environment. SIPE (Wilkins, 1983) allowed a user to provide a measure of separate execution and generation by allowing the user to guide the planning process and to request changes to the plan during execution. PRS (Georgeff & Lansky, 1987) uses "metareasoning" during execution to recognize problems which may cause additional planning.

Replanning

Execution time failures can either be planned for (see next section) or dealt with upon occurence. This latter approach, known as replanning, typically is assumed to occur when a planner recognizes a mismatch between the expected and actual state of the world. Hayes (1975) proposed that the subgoal trees and decision graphs used in the formation of the plan could be used to guide replanning. Daniel (1983) explored the use of a similar mechanism in a partial order planner. SIPE (Wilkins, 1983) also used such an approach. Kambhampati (1989; Kambhampati & Hendler, 1989) has shown that a subset of this information, known as the validation structure, can provide the same guidance. A formal treatment of replanning can be found in Morgenstern, (1987).

Planning for Failure

An alternative to replanning is to actually expect potential failures and to plan for them. This can involve planning for expected possibilities, such as waiting for a light to turn green before crossing a street (Drummond, 1986), or it can involve scheduling monitoring tasks — tests to be run at execution time, associated with fixes to be used in the case of failed tests (cf. Doyle, et. al, 1986). An example of this (Kaelbling, 1987) would be having a robot check to see if two walls were equidistant at some point during the traversal of a hallway. If not, the robot achieves this equidistance, and then continues. Schoppers (1987) has proposed taking disjunctive planning to an extreme by generating execution time "universal" plans which can deal with all possible contigencies.

Dealing with Environmental Change

The STRIPS/PLANEX (Fikes et. al., 1972a) system was used to plan the motion of a robot called *Shakey* and to control it as it pushed a set of boxes through a number of interconnecting rooms. A well known SRI film shows *Shakey* following a STRIPS generated plan using the PLANEX execution monitor. Charley Rosen, the SRI AI Lab founder, dressed in a sinister cloak, appears and disrupts the position of the boxes during execution. PLANEX makes use of the triangle table (described previously, section 7) to recover. This technique, however, proves to be inefficient in dealing with a rapidly changing world. Much recent work has dealt with designing mechanisms which can react to significant change in the environment. This work achieves responsiveness by giving up complex planning for shallow planning or planning using tightly coupled sensing and action (Rosenschein, 1982; Chapman & Agre, 1987; Hendler & Sanborn, 1987). Some of this work, however, has dealt directly with the issues of how to map from planning to reaction. Firby (1989) proposes "reactive action packages" which essentially replace the operators in the system with procedures that include a reactive component. Kaelbling's and Rosenschein's (1988) GAPPS system is a compiler that translates constraint expressions into directly executable circuits for use in robotic control systems. Georgeff and Lansky (1987) describe the use of a meta-reasoning system which can choose actions based on the goals being pursued by the system. Ambros–Ingerson and Steel (1987) propose an approach to integrating planning and execution for changing domains using an agenda–driven control structure in which action which are serially initiated can run concurrently, with information acquiring actions (for monitoring the environment) included.

Uncertainty in Planning

Another source of execution time problems may arise when uncertainty exists during plan generation. If the planner cannot model the real world with complete information, but instead uses some sort of probability–based model, it must deal with low probability events that may occur during execution. (This problem arises in a very significant way for systems which use real sensors to perceive the world). Work using probability estimates during plan generation includes Dean et. al (1989) and Dean & Kanazawa (1989). Segre (1988) examines the issue of execution time failures of plans based on uncertain information.

Planning for Planning

An important part of planning in dynamic domains involves making tradeoffs— specifically trading precision in decision making for time in responding to events. In the last few years, a number of researchers have attempted to improve the responsiveness of planning systems operating in dynamic domains by directly reasoning about the utility of planning (Dean, 1987; Horvitz, 1988; Russell & Wefald, 1989). This work has involved an examination both of reasoning about these trade–offs during plan generation (Kanazawa and Dean, 1989; Heckerman et al, 1989) or during execution (Boddy and Dean, 1989; Horvitz et al, 1989).

10. Learning and Memory

The concentration in planning has been on generating plans from scratch, not learning from experience. Thus, much of the classical work in planning has been "ahistoric"— that is, asked to solve the same problem again the planner performs no better than it did the first time. Recently, due both to the gains being made in machine learning and the new work on case–based reasoning, designing planning systems which learn from experience has emerged as an important new research direction.

Operator Learning

> The earliest approach to learning in plans was the MACROPs (for macro–operators) work of (Fikes et al 1982) which extended STRIPS to do some limited learning from its failures. When a portion of a plan was found to have succeeded, the entire set of operators could be turned into a single operator whose preconditions and effects were identical with the preconditions and effects of the operator sequence. The operators were generalized by using variables to replace the constants found in the specific solution from which the new operator had been derived. Minton's (1985) Prodigy/EBL system used a similar approach, but applied an explanation–based learning algorithm to provide more accurate generalizations.

Memory–based planning

> Case–based reasoning approaches to planning have also been attempted. In these situations a problem solver finds an old plan that may be applicable in the new situation and modifies it accordingly. Many of these systems have concentrated on guiding the search for the old plan (e.g. JULIA (Kolodner, 1987); CHEF (Hammond, 1986)) and then use a fairly simple mapping to produce the new plan. PLEXUS (Alterman, 1988) used information about the new context to guide the reuse of an existing plan. The PRIAR reuse framework (Kambhampati, 1989) applies a case–based approach in the classical planning framework. PRIAR is an extension to NONLIN (Tate, 1977) which allows the planner to annotate plans being created with information about the dependency structure between operators in the completed plan. This information is then used to guide retrieval, reuse, and replanning.

11. Summary

Planning systems have been an active research topic within Artificial Intelligence for nearly thirty years. There have been a number of techniques developed during that period which still form an essential part of many of today's AI planning systems. In this paper we have tried to provide a broad coverage of the major ideas in the field of AI planning, and have attempted to show the direction in which current research is going. Such a task is never–ending, and any finite document must per force be incomplete. We have provided references to connect each idea to the appropriate literature and to allow readers immediate access to the papers most relevant to their research or applications work.

12. Recommended Reading

A good and reasonably up–to–date account of AI planning techniques and systems is given in Charniak and McDermott's (1985) *Introduction to Artificial Intelligence* textbook. In particular, chapter 9 and sections of chapters 5 and 7 are relevant. Somewhat earlier material is provided in Elaine Rich's (1983) *Artificial Intelligence* textbook. Nilsson's (1980) book on the *Principles of Artificial Intelligence* provides a uniform treatment of planning techniques available up to the time it was published. There are several useful summaries of early AI planning work in the *Handbook of Artificial Intelligence* (Barr & Feigenbuam, 1981) volume I section II.D and volume III sections XI.B, XI.C and XV. A collection of recent papers concerning planning can be found in Georgeff and Lansky's (1987) *Reasoning about Actions and Plans*.

Barr, A. and Feigenbaum, E.A. (1981) "The Handbook of Artificial Intelligence" William

Kaufmann, Los Angeles, Ca.

Charniak, E. and McDermott, D.V. (1985) "Introduction to Artificial Intelligence", Addison–Wesley.

Georgeff, M. and Lansky, A. (eds.) (1987) "Reasoning about actions and plans," Morgan–Kaufman, Los Altos, Ca.

Nilsson, N.J. (1980) "Principles of Artificial Intelligence", Tioga Press, Palo Alto, Calif.

Rich, E. (1983) "Artificial Intelligence", McGraw–Hill, New York.

Acknowledgements

The work of the Planning Group at AIAI is supported by the UK Science and Engineering Research Council (under IED grant 1320, GR/F 36545) and the United States Air Force (under contract EOARD–88–0044). J. Hendler is also affiliated with the Systems Research Center and the UM Institute for Advanced Computer Studies. His work is funded in part by the US Office of Naval Research grant N00014–88–K–0560 and NSF grant IRI–8907890. A portion of Mark Drummond's work at the NASA Ames Research Center is funded by the Air Force Office of Scientific Research, Artificial Intelligence Research Program.

We are grateful for input from research colleagues active in AI planning who have helped us structure this review. We hope that we have not misrepresented anyone in showing how the research themes, techniques and planning systems relate to one another.

13. References

Allen, J. "Formal models of planning" in Allen, Hendler, and Tate (eds.) Readings in Planning.

Allen, J.F. and Koomen, J.A. (1983) "Planning Using a Temporal World Model", IJCAI–83, Karlsruhe, West Germany. pp 741–747 [TIMELOGIC]

Altermann, R. (1988) "Adaptive Planning," Cognitive Science, 12. [PLEXUS]

Ambros–Ingerson, J. & Steel, S., "Integrating planning, execution, and monitoring", AAAI–88, St. Paul, Minn., pp 83–88.

Appelt, D.E. (1985) "Planning English Referring Expressions", Artificial Intelligence, 26, pp 1–33. [KAMP]

Bell, C.E. and Tate, A. (1985) "Using Temporal Constraints to Restrict Search in a Planner", Proceedings of the Third Workshop of the Alvey IKBS Programme Planning Special Interest Group, Sunningdale, Oxfordshire, UK, April 1985. Available through the Institute of Electrical Engineers, London, UK [O–PLAN]

Boddy, M. and Dean, T. (1989) "Solving Time–Dependent Planning Problems" Proceedings IJCAI–89, Detroit, Michigan pp 979–984.

Bresina, J.L. (1981) "An Interactive Planner that Creates a Structured Annotated Trace of its Operation", Rutgers University, Computer Science Research Laboratory, Report CBM–TR–123. [PLANX–10]

Chapman, D. (1985) Nonlinear planning: a rigorous reconstruction. In proc. of IJCAI–85. pp. 1022–1024. [TWEAK]

Chapman, D. (1987) "Planning for Conjunctive Goals," Artificial Intelligence (32), 1987, pp.

333–377. [TWEAK]

Chapman, D. and Agre, P. (1987) "Abstract Reasoning as Emergent from Concrete Activity" in Georgeff, M. and Lansky, A. (eds.) Reasoning about Actions and Plans, Morgan–Kaufmann, Los Altos, Ca.

Corkill, D.D. (1979) "Hierarchical Planning in a Distributed Environment", IJCAI–79, Tokyo, Japan pp 168–175.

Corkill, D.D. and Lesser, V.R. (1983) "The Use of Meta–level Control for Coordination in a Distributed Problem Solving Network", IJCAI–83, Karlsruhe, West Germany. pp 748–756

Currie, K. and Tate, A. (1985) "O–Plan – Control in the Open Planner Architecture" BCS Expert Systems Conference, Cambridge University Press, UK. [O–PLAN]

Daniel, L. (1983). "Planning and Operations Research", in "Artificial Intelligence: Tools, Techniques and Applications", Harper and Row, New York. [NONLIN]

Davis, R. and Smith, R. (1983) "Negotiation as a Metaphor for Distributed Problem Solving", Artificial Intelligence, 20, pp 63–109.

Davis, P.R. and Chien, R.T. (1977) "Using and Re–using Partial Plans", IJCAI–77, Cambridge, Mass., USA.

Dean, T. (1985) "Temporal Reasoning Involving Counterfactuals and Disjunctions", IJCAI–85, Los Angeles, Calif. [TNMS]

Dean, T. "Intractability and time–dependent planning" in Georgeff, M. & Lanksy, A. (eds) Reasoning about Actions and Plans, Morgan–Kaufmann, Los Altos, CA..

Dean, T. and Boddy, M. (1987) "Reasoning about Partially Ordered Events," Artificial Intelligence 36, pp 375–399

Dean, T., Firby, J., and Miller, D., (1989) Hierarchical Planning Involving Deadlines, Travel Time and Resources Computational Intelligence (3). [FORBIN]

Dean, T. & McDermott, D. (1987) "Temporal data base management," Artificial Intelligence, 32.   Dershowitz, N. (1985) "Synthetic programming", Artificial Intelligence, 25, pp 323–373.

Doran, J.E. and Michie, D. (1966) "Experiments with the Graph Traverser Program" Proceedings of the Royal Society, A, pp 235–259. [GRAPH TRAVERSER]

Doran, J.E. and Trayner, C. (1985) "Distributed Planning and Execution – Teamwork 1", Computer Science Technical Report, University of Essex, UK [TEAMWORK]

Doyle, J. (1979) "A Truth Maintenance System", Artificial Intelligence, 12, pp 231–272.

Doyle, R.J., Atkinson, D.J., and Doshi, R.S. (1986) "Generating perception requests and expectations to verify the execution of plans" Proc. of AAAI–86, Philadelphia, PA.

Drabble, B. (1988) "Planning and Reasoning with Processes" The Eighth Workshop of the Alvey Planning Special Interest Group, Institute of Electrical Engineers, Nottingham, UK, pp 25–40. [EXCALIBUR]

Drummond, M. (1985). Refining and extending the procedural net. Proc. of IJCAI–85, pp. 1010–1012.

Drummond, M., and K.W. Currie (1989a) Exploiting Temporal Coherence in Non–linear Plan Construction. Computational Intelligence, March, 1989.

Drummond, M., and K.W. Currie (1989b) Goal Ordering in Partially Ordered Plans. Proceedings of IJCAI–89 , Detroit, Michigan.

Duffay, P. and Latombe, J–C (1983) "An Approach to Automatic Robot Programming Based on Inductive Learning", IMAG, Grenbole, France. [TROPIC]

Erman, L.D., Hayes–Roth, F., Lesser, V.R. and Reddy, D.R. (1980) "The HEARSAY–II Speech–understanding System: Integrating Knowledge to Resolve Uncertainty", ACM Computing Surveys, 12, No.2.

Fahlman, S.E. (1974) "A Planning System for Robot Construction Tasks" Artificial Intelligence, 5, pp 1–49.

Faletti, J. (1982) "PANDORA – A Program for Doing Commonsense Reasoning Planning in Complex Situations", AAAI–82, Pittsburgh, Pa., USA, Aug, 1982. [PANDORA]

Fikes, R.E. (1970) "REF–ARF: A System for Solving Problems stated as Procedures", Artificial Intelligence", 1, pp 27–120. [REF–ARF]

Fikes, R.E. (1982) "A Commitment–based Framework for Describing Informal Cooperative Work", Cognitive Science, 6, pp 331–347.

Fikes, R.E. and Nilsson, N.J. (1971) "STRIPS: a New Approach to the Application of Theorem Proving to Problem Solving", Artificial Intelligence, 2, pp 189–208. [STRIPS]

Fikes, R.E., Hart, P.E. and Nilsson, N.J. (1972a) "Learning and Executing Generalised Robot Plans", Artificial Intelligence, 3. [STRIPS/PLANEX]

Fikes, R.E., Hart, P.E. and Nilsson, N.J. (1972b) "Some New Directions in Robot Problem Solving", in "Machine Intelligence 7", Meltzer, B. and Michie, D., eds., Edinburgh University Press. [STRIPS]

Firby, J. (1989) "Adaptive Execution in Complex Dynamic Worlds," Doctoral Dissertation, Department of Computer Science, Yale University. [RAPS]

Fox, M.S., Allen, B. and Strohm, G. (1981) "Job Shop Scheduling: an Investigation in Constraint–based Reasoning", IJCAI–81, Vancouver, British Columbia, Canada, August 1981. [ISIS–II]

Georgeff, M. (1982) "Communication and Interaction in Multi–agent Planning Systems", AAAI–3.

Georgeff, M. and Lansky, A. (1985) "A Procedural Logic", IJCAI–85, Los Angeles, Calif., Aug 1985.

Georgeff, M, and Lansky, A. (1987) "Reactive Reasoning and Planning" Proceedings of AAAI–87. [PRS]

Green, C.C. (1969) "Theorem Proving by Resolution as a basis for Question Answering" in Machine Intelligence 4, eds. Meltzer, B. and Michie, D., Edinburgh University Press.

Hammond, K. (1986) "Chef: A model of case–based planning" Proceedings of AAAI–86. [CHEF]

Hart, P., Nilsson, N., and Raphael, B. (1968) "A formal basis for the heuristic determination of minimum cost paths", IEEE Transactions System Science and Cybernetics, SSC–4(2), pp. 100–107. [A*]

Hayes, P.J. (1975) "A Representation for Robot Plans", Advance papers of IJCAI–75, Tbilisi, USSR.

Hayes–Roth, B. and Hayes–Roth, F. (1979) "A Cognitive Model of Planning", Cognitive Science, pp 275–310. [OPM]

Hayes–Roth, B. (1983a) "The Blackboard Architecture: A General Framework for Problem Solving?", Heuristic Programming Project Report No. HPP–83–30. Stanford University. May 1983.

Hayes–Roth, B. (1983b) "A Blackboard Model of Control", Heuristic Programming Project Report No. HPP–83–38. Stanford University. June 1983. [OPM]

Heckerman, D., Breese, J. and Horvitz, E. (1989) "The Compilation of Decision Models" Proceedings of the 1989 Workshop on Uncertainty in Artificial Intelligence, Windsor, Ontario pp 162–173

Hendler, J.A. (1986) Integrating Marker–passing and Problem Solving: A spreading activation approach to improved choice in planning i. Doctoral Thesis, Dept. of Computer Science, Brown University, 1986 ii. (1987) Lawrence Erlbaum Associates, Norwood, N.J. [SCRAPS]

Hendler, J. and Sanborn, J. (1987) "Planning and reaction in dynamic domains" Proceedings DARPA Workshop on Planning, Austin, Tx. [DR/CROS]

Hendrix, G. (1973) "Modelling Simultaneous Actions and Continuous Processes", Artificial Intelligence, 4, pp 145–180.

Horvitz, E. (1988) "Reasoning Under Varying and Uncertain Resource Constraints," Proceedings AAAI–88, St. Paul, Minnesota. pp 111–116.

Horvitz, E. and Cooper, G. and Heckerman, D. (1989) "Reflection and Action Under Scarce Resources: Theoretical Principles and Empirical Study" Proceedings IJCAI–89, Detroit, Michigan. pp 1121–1127

Kaelbling, L. (1987) "An Architecture for Intelligent Reactive Systems" in Georgeff, M. & Lanksy, A. (eds) Reasoning about Actions and Plans, Morgan–Kaufmann, Los Altos, CA.. [REXX]

Kaelbling, L.P. (1988) Goals as Parallel Program Specifications. Proceedings of AAAI–88. St. Paul, Minnesota. pp. 60–65. [GAPPS]

Kahn, K. and Gorry, G.A. (1977) "Mechanizing Temporal Knowledge" Artificial Intelligence, 9, pp 87–108.

Kambhampati, S. (1989) Flexible Reuse and Modification in Hierarchical planning: a Validation Structure Based Approach, Doctoral dissertation, Dept. of Computer Science, University of Maryland. [PRIAR]

Kambhampati, S. and Hendler, J. (1989), "Flexible Reuse of Plans via Annotation and Verification", Proceedings of Fifth IEEE Conference on Applications of Artificial Intelligence, Miami, Florida. [PRIAR]

Kanazawa, K. and Dean, T., (1989) "A Model for Projection and Action" Proceedings IJCAI–89, Detroit, Michigan pp 985–99

Kolodner, J. (1987) "Case–based Problem Solving," Proceedings of the 4th International Workshop on Machine Learning, UC Irvine. [JULIA]

Konolige, K. (1983) "A Deductive Model of Belief", IJCAI–83, Karlsruhe, West Germany, pp 377–381.

Konolige, K. and Nilsson, N.J. (1980) "Multi–agent Planning Systems", AAAI–1, Stanford, Ca., USA. pp 138–142.

Korf, R.E., (1987) "Planning as Search: A Quantitative Approach," Artificial Intelligence, (33), 1987, pp. 65–88.

Kornfeld, W.A. (1979) "ETHER: a Parallel Problem Solving System" IJCAI–79, Tokyo, Japan. pp 490–492

Lansky, A. (1985) Behavioral specification and planning for multiagent domains. Tech. note 360, SRI International, Menlo Park, CA. [GEMPLAN]

Lansky, A.L. (1988). Localized Event–Based Reasoning for Multiagent Domains. Computational Intelligence Journal. [GEMPLAN]

Latombe, J–C. (1976) "Artificial Intelligence in Computer–aided Design – The TROPIC System", Stanford Research Institute AI Center Technical Note 125, Menlo Park, Ca., USA. [TROPIC]

Lenat, D.B. (1975) "BEINGS: Knowledge as Interacting Experts", IJCAI–75, Tbilisi, USSR. pp 126–133 [PUP]

London, P. (1977) "A Dependency–based Modelling Mechanism for Problem Solving", Dept of Computer Science, University of Maryland, Memo. TR–589.

Luckham, D.C. and Buchanan, J.R. (1974) "Automatic Generation of Programs Containing Conditional Statements", AISB Summer Conference, University of Sussex, UK, pp 102–126.

Masui,S., McDermott, J. and Sobel, A. (1983) "Decision–Making in Time Critical Situations", IJCAI–83, Karlsruhe, West Germany. pp 233–235 [AIRPLAN]

McCarthy, J. and Hayes, P.J. (1969) "Some Philosophical Problems from the Standpoint of Artificial Intelligence", in Machine Intelligence 4, ed. Meltzer, B. and Michie, D., Edinburgh University Press.

McDermott, D.V. (1978) "Planning and Acting" Cognitive Science, Vol. 2. [NASL]

McDermott, D.V. (1982) "A Temporal Logic for Reasoning about Processes and Plans", Cognitive Science, 6, pp 101–155.

McDermott, D.V. and Doyle, J. (1979) "An Introduction to Non–monotonic Logic", IJCAI–79, Tokyo, Japan. pp 562–567.

Mellish, C.S. (1984) "Towards Top–down Generation of Multi–paragraph Text", Proceedings of the Sixth European Conference on Artificial Intelligence, Pisa, Italy. pp 229.

Miller, D., Firby, J, and Dean, T. (1985) "Deadlines, travel time, and robot problem solving." Proc. of IJCAI–85. pp. 1052–1054. [FORBIN]

Minton, S. (1985) "Selectively Generalizing Plans for Problem–Solving" IJCAI–85, pp 596–599 [Prodigy/EBL]

Moore, R. (1980) "Reasoning about Knowledge and Action", SRI AI Center Report No. 191.

Morgenstern, L. (1987) "Replanning" Proceedings DARPA Knowledge–Based Planning Workshop, Austin, Tx.

Mostow, D.J. (1983) "A Problem Solver for Making Advice Operational", Proc. AAAI 3, pp 179–283.

Nau, D., Yang, Q., and Hendler, J. (1989), "Planning for Multiple Goals with Limited Interactions," Proceedings of Fifth IEEE Conference on Applications of Artificial Intelligence, Miami, Florida. [SIPS]

Newell, A. and Simon, H.A. (1963) "GPS: a Program that Simulates Human Thought", in Feigenbaum, E.A. and Feldman, J. eds Computers and Thought (McGraw–Hill, New York, 1963). [GPS]

Nilsson, N.J. (1971) Problem Solving Methods in Artificial Intelligence McGraw–Hill. [STRIPS/ABSTRIPS/RSTRIPS]

Pednault, E. (1987) Solving Multi–agent dynamic world problems in the classical planning framework, in Georgeff, M. & Lanksy, A. (eds) Reasoning about Actions and Plans, Morgan–Kaufmann, Los Altos, CA..

Reiger, C. and London, P. (1977) "Subgoal Protection and Unravelling During Plan Synthesis", IJCAI–77, Cambridge, Mass., USA.

Rich, C. (1981) "A Formal Representation for Plans in the Programmer's Apprentice", IJCAI–81, Vancouver, British Columbia, Canada. pp 1044–1052.

Rich, C., Shrobe, H.E. and Waters, R.C. (1979) "Overview of the Programmer's Apprentice", IJCAI–79, Tokyo, Japan. pp 827–828.

Rosenschein, S.J. (1981) "Plan Synthesis: A Logical Perspective", IJCAI–81, Vancouver, British Columbia, Canada.

Rosenschein, S. (1982) "Synchronization of Multi–agent Plans", Proceedings AAAI–82.

Russell, S.. and Wefald, E. (1989) "Principles of Metareasoning" Proceedings of the First International Conference on Principles of Knowledge Representation and Reasoning, Morgan–Kaufman Los Altos, California.

Sacerdoti, E.D. (1973) "Planning in a Hierarchy of Abstraction Spaces", Advance papers of IJCAI–73, Palo Alto, Ca., USA. [ABSTRIPS]

Sacerdoti, E.D. (1975) "The Non–linear Nature of Plans", Advance papers of IJCAI–75, Tbilisi, USSR. [NOAH]

Sacerdoti, E.D. (1977) "A Structure for Plans and Behaviour", Elsevier–North Holland. [NOAH]

Sacerdoti, E.D. (1979) "Problem Solving Tactics", IJCAI–79, Tokyo, Japan. [NOAH]

Sanborn, J. and Hendler, J. (1988) Monitoring and Reacting: Planning in dynamic domains, International Journal of AI and Engineering, 3(2), April, 1988. [DR/CROS]

Sathi, A., Fox, M.S. and Greenberg, M. (1985) "Representation of Activity Knowledge for Project Management", IEEE Special Issue of Transactions on Pattern Analysis and Machine Intelligence, July, 1985. [CALLISTO]

Schank, R.C. and Abelson, R.P. (1977) "Scripts, Plans, Goals and Understanding", Lawrence Erlbaum Press, Hillsdale, New Jersey, USA.

Schoppers, M. (1987) "Universal plans for reactive robots in unpredictable domains," Proceedings IJCAI–87.

Segre, A. (1988) Machine Learning od Robot Assembly Plans, Kluwer Academic Publishers, Norwell, MA.

Siklossy, L. and Roach, J. (1973) "Proving the Impossible is Impossible is Possible: Disproofs based on Hereditary Partitions", IJCAI–73, Palo Alto, Calif. [DISPROVER/LAWALY]

Siklossy, L. and Dreussi, J. (1975) "An Efficient Robot Planner that Generates its own Procedures", IJCAI–73 Palo Alto, Ca., USA. [LAWALY]

Simmons, R. and Davis, R. (1987) "Generate, Test and Debug: Combining Associational Rules and Causal Models," Proceedings IJCAI–87, pp. 1071–1078. [G–T–D]

Smith, R.G. (1977) "The Contract Net: a Formalism for the Control of Distributed Problem Solving", IJCAI–77, Cambridge, Mass, USA. pp 472.

Smith, R.G. (1979) "A Framework for Distributed Problem Solving", IJCAI–79, Tokyo, Japan.

Sridharan, A. and Bresina, J.L. (1985) "Knowledge structures for planning in realistic domains." *Computers and Mathematics with Applications (Special Issue on Knowledge Representation)*. Vol. 11(5), pp. 457–480. [PLANX–10]

Stallman, R.M. and Sussman, G.J. (1977) "Forward Reasoning and Dependency Directed Backtracking", Artificial Intelligence, 9, pp 135–196.

Steele, G.L. and Sussman, G.J. (1978) "Constraints", MIT AI Lab Memo 502.

Stefik, M.J. (1981a) "Planning with Constraints", Artificial Intelligence, 16, pp 111–140. [MOLGEN]

Stefik, M.J. (1981b) "Planning and Meta–planning", Artificial Intelligence, 16, pp 141–169. [MOLGEN]

Sussman, G.A. (1973) "A Computational Model of Skill Acquisition", M.I.T. AI Lab. Memo no. AI–TR–297. [HACKER]

Sussman, G.A. and McDermott, D.V. (1972) "Why Conniving is Better than Planning", MIT AI Lab. Memo 255A. [CONNIVER]

Tate, A. (1975) "Interacting Goals and Their Use", IJCAI–75, Tbilisi, USSR. pp 215–218 [INTERPLAN]

Tate, A. (1977) "Project Planning Using a Hierarchical Non–linear Planner", Dept. of Artificial Intelligence Report 25, Edinburgh University. [NONLIN]

Tate, A. (1977) "Generating Project Networks", IJCAI–77, Boston, Ma., USA. [NONLIN]

Tate, A. (1984a) "Planning and Condition Monitoring in a FMS", International Conference on Flexible Automation Systems", Institute of Electrical Engineers, London, UK July 1984. [NONLIN]

Tate, A. (1984b) "Goal Structure: Capturing the Intent of Plans", European Conference on Artificial Intelligence, Pisa, Italy, September 1984. [NONLIN]

Tate, A. and Whiter, A.M. (1984) "Planning with Multiple Resource Constraints and an Application to a Naval Planning Problem", First Conference on the Applications of Artificial Intelligence, Denver, Colorado, USA. December 1984. [NONLIN+]

Vere, S. (1983) "Planning in Time: Windows and Durations for Activities and Goals", IEEE Trans. on Pattern Analysis and Machine Intelligence, PAMI-5, No. 3, pp. 246–267. [DEVISER]

Vilain, M.B. (1980) "A System for Reasoning about Time", AAAI-2.

Waldinger, R. (1975) "Achieving Several Goals Simultaneously", SRI AI Center Technical Note 107, SRI, Menlo Park, Ca., USA.

Warren, D.H.D. (1974) "WARPLAN: a System for Generating Plans", Dept. of Computational Logic Memo 76. Artificial Intelligence, Edinburgh University. [WARPLAN]

Warren, D.H.D. (1976) "Generating Conditional Plans and programs", Proceedings of the AISB Summer Conference, University of Edinburgh, UK, pp 344–354 [WARPLAN-C]

Wilensky, R. (1978) "Understanding Goal-based Stories", Dept. of Computer Science, Yale University, Research Report No. 140. [PAM]

Wilensky, R. (1981a) "Meta-planning: Representing and Using Knowledge about Planning in Problem Solving and Natural Language Understanding", Cognitive Science, 5, pp 197–233.

Wilensky, R. (1981b) "A Model for Planning in Complex Situations", Electronics Research Lab. Memo. No. UCB/ERL M81/49, University of California, Berkeley, Ca., USA.

Wilensky, R. (1983) "Planning and Understanding", Addison-Wesley, Reading, Mass.

Wilkins, D.E. and Robinson, A.E. (1981) "An Interactive Planning System", SRI Technical Note 245. [SIPE]

Wilkins, D.E. (1983) "Representation in a Domain-Independent Planner", IJCAI-83, Karlsruhe, West Germany.pp 733–740 [SIPE]

Wilkins, D.E. (1988) Practical Planning – Extending the classical AI planning paradigm, Morgan-Kaufmann. [SIPE/SIPE-II]

Yang, Q. (1989) Improving the Efficiency of Planning, Doctoral dissertation, Dept. of Computer Science, University of Maryland. [SIPS]

Formal Models of Planning

James Allen
Department of Computer Science
University of Rochester
Rochester, New York

The area of planning includes a large number of complex problems, requiring a wide range of techniques in order to achieve a reasonable solutions. The purpose of specifying formal models of planning is to better define the capabilities and limitations of various approaches. This work is particularly important at the present time, as researchers are attempting to extend existing planning methods developed for simple domains to real problems. Formal models are important because they allow researchers to focus on the ultimate capabilities and limitations of an approach. In particular, a formal model allows one to examine problems independently of the procedural problem of finding a plan. This is not to suggest that research on building actual planning systems is not worthwhile, but only to point out that if the representation used by the system is not powerful enough to be able to state the problem and the solution, then there is no point trying to build a system for the problem using that representation. While this might seem uncontroversial, it is important for, without a formal description, it is often extremely difficult to characterize what problems a given system could ultimately solve.

Research in formal models view planning as a reasoning process within some mathematical language, typically a logic of some sort. These models allow one to consider how planning systems may be extended or integrated into more general reasoning systems. To deal with non–toy worlds, a planning system may need to support common–sense reasoning about the world, reasoning about natural processes, causal effects, other agent's actions and motivations, and many other issues. Such abilities cannot simply be grafted on as another module that interfaces with a traditional planning system. Rather, there is a continuum from reasoning purely about one's actions (i.e. planning) to common–sense reasoning about the world. In order to recognize and prevent a glass ball from rolling off a table, for instance, the agent must use common–sense knowledge to predict that the rolling ball will continue to roll until it reaches the table edge, and then will fall and most likely shatter. With this knowledge, the agent may then plan to block the ball before it reaches the edge. This problem cannot be solved without a planner that can predict the behavior of the world using common–sense knowledge. The language of logic provides a common framework for investigating the representation of plans, common–sense knowledge, and other presentation problems within a single framework.

While the glass–ball scenario is a simple everyday problem, problems of this class are beyond the capabilities of any planning system built to date. The question is, however, whether it is the case that such situations are inherently beyond the general approach used (and hence new models must be developed), or it is simply the case that the existing approaches have not been developed sufficiently yet. Having formal models of plan representations allows us to give a reasonably concise answer to this question. It is impossible, for instance, for a state–based representation using the STRIPS assumption to represent this situation, so planners built on this model will not be extendable to such problems. In other cases, say the situation calculus, the framework may not handle such situations as currently defined, but the approach may be extendable, preserving the essential characteristics of the initial formulation, to a representation that can describe such situations. As we shall see, a considerable amount of the recent work in planning has focused on exploring representations that support temporally–explicit representations that can describe common–sense knowledge, actions and plans within a uniform framework.

There are many different aspects of planning that one could attempt to formalize. The issues discussed above, namely the representation of the world, and the representation of actions, have received the most attention. Another central area of planning in need of formal analysis concerns the issues of search. With a formal representation, it is possible to determine inherent complexity bounds on any algorithm that can guarantee finding a solution if one exists. Chapman (1987, Chapter 7) gives a good example of this, producing complexity results for the class of planning algorithms based on non–linear planning. Georgeff's (1987, Chapter 1) review article gives an excellent overview of the different representations used in planning systems. Here I will explore a few of the key representations in more detail, focusing on their advantages and disadvantages. Rather than develop this chronologically, I'll move from the most constrained representations to the most expressive.

A basic representation technique, which has been most influential in the systems built to date, is the STRIPS state–based representation. These systems maintain a database of atomic propositions that represent a state of the world at a particular instant of time. As such, the propositions are atemporal and represent static properties of the world. For example, we can simply assert that a certain object is red in a state, but we cannot easily assert that a certain object is currently falling to the ground, or that a certain other object will explode in a few minutes. Actions are not explicitly represented in the world representation – i.e. as part of the state. Rather actions are state–transformation operators, which map a state capturing the world before the action to a state immediately following the action using syntactic transformations. These transformations are defined by specifying the explicit manipulation of the assertions in the database: an action's effects specify what formulas to delete from the initial database and which formulas to add. Such operations cannot directly be modelled as logical inference, and such systems could only be specified procedurally until recently. Lifschitz (1987, Chapter 7) identified constraints on the updates that an action can make that allow one to define notions of soundness and consistency, but the representation defining the actions remains external to the representation of the world. As a result, successful use of this representation depends on making several very restrictive assumptions about the domains, namely

> Only one action can occur at any time;
> Nothing changes except as the result of the planned actions; and
> Actions are effectively instantaneous (since nothing may happen or change while they are being performed).

Because the action representation is not part of the world representation, it is not clear how these restrictions could be relaxed in any general way. Complex interactions between the actions and the world are simply not expressible. As one example, actions that have different effects in different situations cannot be described directly.

It is important to realize that most non–linear planners make the same assumptions about the world representation as described above. Actions are still distinct from the world representation, and the world is updated using the same add/delete operations defined with the actions. The planning algorithms, of course, are different with these systems, but the range of situations that such planners can represent and potentially solve are exactly the same as the STRIPS–style planners. This is not so obvious since most of the descriptions of such planners concentrate on the techniques for maintaining the partial action ordering during the search, and examine the techniques for possible interactions between the actions. There is little discussion of what the state of the world is at any point in the plan. Tate (1977, Chapter 5) discussed this in the light of answering questions about the plan, and Chapman (1987, Chapter 7) explicitly examined this issue in his formal construction of non–linear planners. It is exactly the necessity to reduce the non–linear plans to the set of possible linear plans, and hence world state sequences, that leads to the complexity results that Chapman found.

While much can be done to extend this formalism in ways that are useful for particular applications, these extensions generally remain ad–hoc, and depend on the programmer's ingenuity to guarantee that the planner will be able to find a solution. For example, Vere (1983, Chapter 5) added temporal indices and durations to each state and coupled his planner with a PERT–style scheduling algorithm to generate schedules. The basic limitations of the state– based approach, however, such as the inability to reason about actions with conditional effects, or simultaneous interacting actions, restrict the applicability of these extensions. For instance, Vere could represent external events, but only if it is known precisely when they occur, and they cannot be affected by any planned action. Overlapping actions can be scheduled, but only because the set of actions in his domain are independent of each other – i.e. their effects are the same no matter what else is going on simultaneously. While these extensions are useful in some domains, they remain inherently limited because of the expressive weakness of the underlying representation.

The situation calculus (McCarthy & Hayes, 1969, Chapter 6) is a considerably more powerful representation that explicitly includes actions in the representation. A situation is a complete snapshot of the world at some instant in time, essentially an abstraction of the STRIPS state. Since situations are infinite, they are not explicitly describable by listing all the propositions as in the state–based approach. Instead, the situation calculus provides a language for partially specifying knowledge about a situation. Situations are objects in the domain and described by terms in the logic. They define a notion of fluents, which are functions operating on situations. For example, on(A,B) is a fluent that takes a situation and produces true if A is on B in that situation. Alternatively, we can view On as a three place predicate, the third argument being a situation. Thus On(A,B,s) asserts that A is on B in situation s. The crucial fluent for defining actions is Result(p,a,s), which is a function that produces the situation that results from person p performing action a in situation s. The paper by Green in this volume describes a planner built fairly directly on this formalism.

The situation calculus is defined within a variant of the predicate calculus, so much richer interactions between the world and actions are expressible. For instance, an action Toggle, which turns a light on if it is off, and turns it off if it is on, can be defined directly by the axioms:

$$\forall(p,s)\ NearSwitch(p,s)\ \&\ LightOn(s) \rightarrow LightOff(l,\ result(p,Toggle,s))$$
$$\forall(p,s)\ NearSwitch(p,s)\ \&\ LightOff(s) \rightarrow LightOn(l,\ result(p,Toggle,s))$$

In other words, if person p is near the switch and the light is on, then the light will be off in the situation that results for performing the Toggle action. If the light is initially off, on the other hand, the light will be on in the resulting situation. Similarly, the situation calculus can describe actions that have disjunctive preconditions, or even disjunctive effects. The principal reason the situation calculus is more powerful, however, is that the STRIPS assumption is not an inherent part of the formalism. In particular, there is no assumption that nothing changes except for the effects explicitly indicated in the action definition. While this allows richer problems and plans to be described, it opens the door to a wide range of new problems often commonly referred to as the "frame problem". The more complex the interactions allowed between actions, the more difficult it is to precisely state the necessary prerequisites of an action or predict the effects of an action. But these problems are not a result of the formalism itself, they are an inherent part of reasoning about more complex, and realistic, domains. Thus the same issues will arise in any formalism where the effects of actions may be conditional on the state of the world, where external events may occur, and where more than one action may occur at the same time.

Something close to the STRIPS assumption can be incorporated into a variant of the situation calculus by using the techniques in non–monotonic logic. In its most radical form, we could formalize the notion that nothing changes in the world except that which logically follows from the effects of the action. Or we can formalize the notion that as little changes in the world as possible. While there are problems with these simple approaches, it is important to remember that these questions cannot even be asked within the simple STRIPS–based representation. The richer representation brings us closer to an adequate representation of the world, and hence introduces new problems that need solutions. Dealing with variants of the frame problem is an extremely active area of work at present. Hanks & McDermott (1987, Chapter 8) give a good survey of the major approaches.

The situation calculus, however, does not provide a convenient representation for reasoning about simultaneous action or external events because of the functional nature of the Result function (i.e. an action uniquely defines a resulting situation, so the result cannot change based on what other actions or events are occurring at the same time). There is some work directly generalizing the formalism, but most of the work addressing these issues has involved the development of explicit temporal logics for the world representation. In particular, rather than associating assertions with instantaneous situations, assertions are associated with the interval of time over which they are true. McDermott (1982, Chapter 6) builds such a logic out of time instants, maintaining a close correspondence to the situations in the situation calculus. Allen (1984, Chapter 6) rejects situations as the basic building blocks altogether, and develops a representation directly in terms of temporal intervals. The problems that originally arose as the frame problem do not disappear with these new representations, however. Rather than having to determine what is true in a particular situation, McDermott and Allen now have to deal with the problem of persistence – given a fact is true now, how long into the future will it stay true? This problem appears no easier than the original frame problem, and progress on either problem will probably transfer to the other. Shoham & McDermott (1988, Chapter 8) discuss this issue in depth.

Explicit temporal models have no problem representing simultaneous actions, or any complex overlapping of actions, and can represent external events as well. To handle complex interactions between overlapping actions, however, the representation must also explicitly handle notions of future possibility. McDermott used a branching time model for this approach, and a similar technique was developed by Pelavin and Allen (1987) for

Allen's interval logic. These are the most expressive formal representations of actions and plans developed in AI to date.

As to be expected, the development of more powerful representations precedes the development of practical planning systems that can use these representations. In addition, the representations are sufficiently expressive that we can prove that optimal search methods are not realizable. But this is also the case with planners based on the STRIPS representation. Brute–force construction of plans from first principles is not generally feasible. The majority of papers in this volume attest to this fact and explore methods of avoiding such brute–force search. Whichever techniques are ultimately used, however, real–world planners will need to be able to represent complex real–world situations and hence eventually need to use expressive representations such as those developed in the formal work.

References to papers not appearing in this volume:

Pelavin, R. & Allen, J. (1987) A model for concurrent actions having temporal extent, Proc. AAAI–87.

Part II

Planning Systems

Chapter 2

Beginnings

Three areas of scientific study were combined early in the development of AI planning systems: human cognition, operations research, and theorem proving. This section begins with two early papers that represent attempts to apply the lessons learned in those fields to the problem of generating plans of action. The first paper we present describes the early work by Newell, Shaw, and Simon (1963) on the General Problem Solver (GPS), a system that led to a number of insights that have continued to influence the systems being built today—the main one being the use of Means-ends Analysis as a technique to direct search. The second paper in this chapter, Green (1969), describes work on the QA3 problem solver, which followed this development and which provided a computational base for building planning systems at SRI in the late 1960s.

Perhaps the single most influential planning system to date is the STRIPS planner. Methods of representing actions were introduced in STRIPS that are still employed in many current systems and that still are the subject of active theoretical study. The STRIPS system is perhaps the earliest example of an engineering approach to building a planning system intended to actually operate in its chosen domain—in this case in the generation of control plans for the SRI Shakey robot. Theoretical advances and formal representations were used, but a pragmatic approach to constructing an operational planner was also taken.

A sample of the many influential STRIPS papers by Fikes and Nilsson (1971) is included in this section. Chapter 4, "Planning and Acting," includes another paper that describes some of the software and techniques associated with the STRIPS system which allowed plans to be generalized and reused and parts to be repaired or reexecuted on failure. All these topics are still very much on the research agenda for AI planning.

This chapter finishes with a representative paper on the early work on introducing abstraction level reasoning into AI planners. The work by Sacerdoti (1973) on the system ABSTRIPS is represented here. Siklossy and Dreussi (1975) also worked on the LAWALY hierarchical planner, which had similar objectives, around the same period. These early systems were mainly concerned with different levels of abstraction for the description of the effects and preconditions of actions. Later hierarchical planners, such as NOAH (Sacerdoti, 1975, Chapter 3), also used task breakdowns of the actions themselves into subactions.

Papers referenced herein but not included in this volume:

Siklossy, L., and Dreussi, J. (1975). "An Efficient Robot Planner That Generates Its Own Procedures," *IJCAI-75*.

GPS, A PROGRAM THAT SIMULATES HUMAN THOUGHT

by Allen Newell & H. A. Simon

This article is concerned with the psychology of human thinking. It sets forth a theory to explain how some humans try to solve some simple formal problems. The research from which the theory emerged is intimately related to the field of information processing and the construction of intelligent automata, and the theory is expressed in the form of a computer program. The rapid technical advances in the art of programming digital computers to do sophisticated tasks have made such a theory feasible.

It is often argued that a careful line must be drawn between the attempt to *accomplish* with machines the same tasks that humans perform, and the attempt to *simulate* the processes humans actually use to accomplish these tasks. The program discussed in the report, GPS (General Problem Solver), maximally confuses the two approaches—with mutual benefit. GPS has previously been described as an attempt to build a problem-solving program (Newell, Shaw, and Simon, 1959a, 1960a), and in our own research it remains a major vehicle for exploring the area of artificial intelligence. Simultaneously, variants of GPS provide simulations of human behavior (Newell and Simon, 1961a). It is this latter aspect—the use of GPS as a theory of human problem-solving—that we want to focus on exclusively here, with special attention to the relation between the theory and the data.

As a context for the discussion that is to follow, let us make some brief comments on some history of psychology. At the beginning of this century the prevailing thesis in psychology was Associationism. It was an atomistic doctrine, which postulated a theory of hard little elements, either sensations or ideas, that became hooked or associated together without modifica-

tion. It was a mechanistic doctrine, with simple fixed laws of contiguity in time and space to account for the formation of new associations. Those were its assumptions. Behavior proceeded by the stream of associations: Each association produced its successors, and acquired new attachments with the sensations arriving from the environment.

In the first decade of the century a reaction developed to this doctrine through the work of the Wurzburg school. Rejecting the notion of a completely self-determining stream of associations, it introduced the task (*Aufgabe*) as a necessary factor in describing the process of thinking. The task gave direction to thought. A noteworthy innovation of the Wurzburg school was the use of systematic introspection to shed light on the thinking process and the contents of consciousness. The result was a blend of mechanics and phenomenalism, which gave rise in turn to two divergent antitheses, Behaviorism and the Gestalt movement.

The behavioristic reaction insisted that introspection was a highly unstable, subjective procedure, whose futility was amply demonstrated in the controversy on imageless thought. Behaviorism reformulated the task of psychology as one of explaining the response of organisms as a function of the stimuli impinging upon them and measuring both objectively. However, Behaviorism accepted, and indeed reinforced, the mechanistic assumption that the connections between stimulus and response were formed and maintained as simple, determinate functions of the environment.

The Gestalt reaction took an opposite turn. It rejected the mechanistic nature of the associationist doctrine but maintained the value of phenomenal observation. In many ways it continued the Wurzburg school's insistence that thinking was more than association—thinking has direction given to it by the task or by the set of the subject. Gestalt psychology elaborated this doctrine in genuinely new ways in terms of holistic principles of organization.

Today psychology lives in a state of relatively stable tension between the poles of Behaviorism and Gestalt psychology. All of us have internalized the major lessons of both: We treat skeptically the subjective elements in our experiments and agree that all notions must eventually be made operational by means of behavioral measures. We also recognize that a human being is a tremendously complex, organized system, and that the simple schemes of modern behavioristic psychology seem hardly to reflect this at all.

An Experimental Situation

In this context, then, consider the following situation. A human subject, a student in engineering in an American college, sits in front of a blackboard on which are written the following expressions:

Newell, A., & H. A. Simon, "GPS: A Program that Simulates Human Thought", in E. A. Feigenbaum & J. Feldman (eds.), *Computers and Thought*, 279-293, R. Oldenbourg KG., 1963. ©1963 by R. Oldenbourg KG. and the author.

$$(R \supset \sim P) \cdot (\sim R \supset Q) \mid \sim (\sim Q \cdot P)$$

This is a problem in elementary symbolic logic, but the student does not know it. He does know that he has twelve rules for manipulating expressions containing letters connected by "dots" (·), "wedges" (∨), "horseshoes" (⊃), and "tildes" (∼), which stand respectively for "and," "or," "implies," and "not." These rules, given in Fig. 1, show that expressions of certain forms (at the tails of the arrows) can be transformed into expressions of somewhat different form (at the heads of the arrows). (Double arrows indicate transformations can take place in either direction).

Objects are formed by building up expressions from letters (P, Q, R, ...) and connectives · (dot), ∨ (wedge), ⊃ (horseshoe), and ∼ (tilde). Examples are P, ∼Q, P∨Q, ∼(R⊃S)· ∼P; ∼∼P is equivalent to P throughout. Twelve rules exist for transforming expressions (where A, B, and C may be any expressions or subexpressions):

R1.	A · B → B · A ; A ∨ B → B ∨ A	Applies to main expression only.
R2.	A ⊃ B → ∼ B ⊃ ∼ A	Applies to main expression only.
R3.	A · A → A ; A ∨ A → A	
R4.	A · (B · C) ↔ (A · B) · C ; A ∨ (B ∨ C) ↔ (A ∨ B) ∨ C	
R5.	A ∨ B ↔ ∼(∼A · ∼B)	
R6.	A ⊃ B ↔ ∼ A ∨ B	
R7.	A · (B ∨ C) ↔ (A · B) ∨ (A · C) ; A ∨ (B · C) ↔ (A ∨ B) · (A ∨ C)	
R8.	A · B → A ; A · B → B	A and B are two main expressions.
R9.	A → A ∨ X	
R10.	A ; B → A · B	A and B are two main expressions.
R11.	A ; A ⊃ B → B	A and A ⊃ B are two main expressions.
R12.	A ⊃ B ; B ⊃ C → A ⊃ C	A ⊃ B and B ⊃ C are two main expressions.

Example, showing subject's entire course of solution on problem:

1.	(R ⊃ ∼ P) · (∼ R ⊃ Q)	∼ (∼ Q · P)
2.	(∼ R ∨ ∼ P) · (R ∨ Q)	Rule 6 applied to left and right of 1.
3.	(∼ R ∨ ∼ P) · (∼ R ⊃ Q)	Rule 6 applied to left of 1.
4.	R ⊃ ∼ P	Rule 8 applied to 1.
5.	∼ R ∨ ∼ P	Rule 6 applied to 4.
6.	∼ R ⊃ Q	Rule 8 applied to 1.
7.	R ∨ Q	Rule 6 applied to 6.
8.	(∼ R ∨ ∼ P) · (R ∨ Q)	Rule 10 applied to 5. and 7.
9.	P ⊃ ∼ R	Rule 2 applied to 4.
10.	∼ Q ⊃ R	Rule 2 applied to 6.
11.	∼ P ∨ Q	Rule 12 applied to 6. and 9.
12.	∼ (P · ∼ Q)	Rule 6 applied to 11.
13.	∼ (∼ Q · P)	Rule 5 applied to 12.
14.	∼ (∼ Q · P)	Rule 1 applied to 13. QED.

Figure 1. The task of symbolic logic.

Well, looking at the left hand side of the equation, first we want to eliminate one of the sides by using rule 8. It appears too complicated to work with first. Now – no, – no, I can't do that because I will be eliminating either the Q or the P in that total expression. I won't do that at first. Now I'm looking for a way to get rid of the horseshoe inside the two brackets that appear on the left and right sides of the equation. And I don't see it. Yeh, if you apply rule 6 to both sides of the equation, from there I'm going to see if I can apply rule 7.

Experimenter writes: 2.   (∼ R ∨ ∼ P) · (R ∨ Q)

I can almost apply rule 7, but one R needs a tilde. So I'll have to look for another rule. I'm going to see if I can change that R to a tilde R. As a matter of fact, I should have used rule 6 on only the left hand side of the equation. So use rule 6, but only on the left hand side.

Experimenter writes: 3.   (∼ R ∨ ∼ P) · (∼ R ⊃ Q)

Now I'll apply rule 7 as it is expressed. Both – excuse me, excuse me, it can't be done because of the horseshoe. So – now I'm looking – scanning the rules here for a second, and seeing if I can change the R to a ∼R in the second equation, but I don't see any way of doing it. (Sigh.) I'm just sort of lost for a second.

Figure 2. Subject's protocol on first part of problem.

tion.) The subject has practiced applying the rules, but he has previously done only one other problem like this. The experimenter has instructed him that his problem is to obtain the expression in the upper right corner from the expression in the upper left corner using the twelve rules. At any time the subject can request the experimenter to apply one of the rules to an expression that is already on the blackboard. If the transformation is legal, the experimenter writes down the new expression in the left-hand column, with the name of the rule in the right-hand column beside it. The subject's actual course of solution is shown beneath the rules in Fig. 1.

The subject was also asked to talk aloud as he worked; his comments were recorded and then transcribed into a "protocol," —*i.e.*, a verbatim record of all that he or the experimenter said during the experiment. The initial section of this subject's protocol is reproduced in Fig. 2.

The Problem of Explanation

It is now proposed that the protocol of Fig. 2 constitutes data about human behavior that are to be explained by a psychological theory. But what are we to make of this? Are we back to the introspections of the Wurzburgers? And how are we to extract information from the behavior of a single subject when we have not defined the operational measures we wish to consider?

There is little difficulty in viewing this situation through behavioristic eyes. The verbal utterances of the subject are as much behavior as would be his arm movements or galvanic skin responses. The subject was not introspecting; he was simply emitting a continuous stream of verbal behavior while solving the problem. Our task is to find a model of the human problem-solver that explains the salient features of this stream of behavior. This stream contains not only the subject's extemporaneous comments, but also his commands to the experimenter, which determine whether he solves the problem or not.

Although this way of viewing the behavior answers the questions stated above, it raises some of its own. How is one to deal with such variable behavior? Isn't language behavior considered among the most complex human behavior? How does one make reliable inferences from a single sample of data on a single subject?

The answers to these questions rest upon the recent, striking advances that have been made in computers, computer programming and artificial intelligence. We have learned that a computer is a general manipulator of symbols—not just a manipulator of numbers. Basically, a computer is a transformer of patterns. By suitable devices, most notably its addressing logic, these patterns can be given all the essential characteristics of linguistic symbols. They can be copied and formed into expressions. We have known this abstractly since Turing's work in the midthirties, but it is only recently that computers have become powerful enough to let us actually explore the capabilities of complex symbol manipulating systems.

For our purpose here, the most important branch of these explorations is the attempt to construct programs that solve tasks requiring intelligence. Considerable success has already been attained (Gelernter, 1959b; Kilburn et al, 1959; Minsky, 1961a; Newell, Shaw, and Simon, 1957a, 1958b; Samuel, 1959a; Tonge, 1960). These accomplishments form a body of ideas and techniques that allow a new approach to the building of psychological theories. (Much of the work on artificial intelligence, especially our own, has been partly motivated by concern for psychology; hence, the resulting rapprochement is not entirely coincidental.)

We may then conceive of an intelligent program that manipulates symbols in the same way that our subject does—by taking as inputs the symbolic logic expressions, and producing as ouputs a sequence of rule applications that coincides with the subject's. If we observed this program in operation, it would be considering various rules and evaluating various expressions, the same sorts of things we see expressed in the protocol of the subject. If the fit of such a program were close enough to the overt behavior of our human subject—*i.e.*, to the protocol—then it would constitute a good theory of the subject's problem-solving.

Conceptually the matter is perfectly straightforward. A program prescribes in abstract terms (expressed in some programming language) how a set of symbols in a memory is to be transformed through time. It is completely analogous to a set of difference equations that prescribes the transformation of a set of numbers through time. Given enough information about an individual, a program could be written that would describe the symbolic behavior of that individual. Each individual would be described by a different program, and those aspects of human problem-solving that are not idiosyncratic would emerge as the common structure and content of the programs of many individuals.

But is it possible to write programs that do the kinds of manipulation that humans do? Given a specific protocol, such as the one of Fig. 2, is it possible to induct the program of the subject? How well does a program fit the data? The remainder of the report will be devoted to answering some of these questions by means of the single example already presented. We will consider only how GPS behaves on the first part of the problem, and we will compare it in detail with the subject's behavior as revealed in the protocol. This will shed considerable light on how far we can consider programs as theories of human problem-solving.

The GPS Program

We will only briefly recapitulate the GPS program, since our description will add little to what has already been published (Newell, Shaw, and Simon, 1959a, 1960a). GPS deals with a task environment consisting of *objects* which can be transformed by various *operators*; it detects *differences* between objects; and it organizes the information about the task environment into *goals*. Each goal is a collection of information that defines what constitutes goal attainment, makes available the various kinds of information relevant to attaining the goal, and relates the information to other goals. There are three types of goals:

Transform object A into object B,
Reduce difference D between object A and object B,
Apply operator Q to object A.

For the task of symbolic logic, the objects are logic expressions; the operators are the twelve rules (actually the specific variants of them); and the differences are expressions like "change connective" or "add a term." Thus the objects and operators are given by the task; whereas the differences are something GPS brings to the problem. They represent the ways of relating operators to their respective effects upon objects.

Basically, the GPS program is a way of achieving a goal by setting up subgoals whose attainment leads to the attainment of the initial goal. GPS has various schemes, called methods, for doing this. Three crucial methods are presented in Fig. 3, one method associated with each goal type.

means that the operator affects objects with respect to the difference. Operationally, relevance can be determined by applying the matching process already used to the input and output forms of the operators, due account being taken of variables. The results can be summarized in a table of connections, as shown in Fig. 3, which lists for each difference the operators that are relevant to it. This table also lists the differences that GPS recognizes. [This set is somewhat different from the one given in Newell, Shaw, and Simon (1959a); it corresponds to the program we will deal with in this report.] If a relevant operator, Q, is found, it is subjected to a preliminary test of feasibility, one version of which is given in Fig. 3. If the operator passes this test, a subgoal is set up to apply the operator to the object. If the operator is successfully applied, a new object, A', is produced which is a modification of the original one in the direction of reducing the difference. (Of course, other modifications may also have occurred which nullify the usefulness of the new object.)

If the goal is to apply an operator, the first step is to see if the conditions of the operator are satisfied. The preliminary test above by no means guarantees this. If the conditions are satisfied, then the output, A, can be generated. If the conditions are not satisfied, then some difference, D, has been detected and a subgoal is created to reduce this difference, just as with the transform goal. Similarly, if a modified object, A', is obtained, a new subgoal is formed to try to apply the operator to this new object.

These methods form a recursive system that generates a tree of subgoals in attempting to attain a given goal. For every new difficulty that is encountered a new subgoal is created to overcome this difficulty. GPS has a number of tests it applies to keep the expansion of this goal tree from proceeding in unprofitable directions. The most important of these is a test which is applied to new subgoals for reducing differences. GPS contains an ordering of the differences, so that some differences are considered easier than others. This ordering is given by the table of connections in Fig. 3, which lists the most difficult differences first. GPS will not try a subgoal if it is harder than one of its supergoals. It will also not try a goal if it follows an easier goal. That is, GPS insists on working on the hard differences first and expects to find easier ones as it goes along. The other tests that GPS applies involve external limits (*e.g.*, a limit on the total depth of a goal tree it will tolerate) and whether new objects or goals are identical to ones already generated.

GPS *on the Problem*

The description we have just given is adequate to verify the reasonableness, although not the detail, of a trace of GPS's behavior on a specific problem. (In particular we have not described how the two-line rule, R10

Thus, to transform an object A into an object B, the objects are first matched—put into correspondence and compared element by element. If the match reveals a difference, D, between the two objects, then a subgoal is set up to reduce this difference. If this subgoal is attained, a new object, A', is produced which (hopefully) no longer has the difference D when compared with object B. Then a new subgoal is created to transform A' into B. If the transformation succeeds, the entire goal has been attained in two steps: from A to A' and from A' to B.

If the goal is to reduce the difference between two objects, the first step is to find an operator that is relevant to this difference. Relevance here

Goal: Transform object A into object B

Goal: Reduce difference D between object A and object B

Goal: Apply operator Q to object A

For the logic task of the text:

Feasibility test (preliminary):
Is the mean connective the same? (e.g., A·B → B fails against PvQ)
Is the operator too big? (e.g., (AvB)·(AvC) → Av(B·C) fails against P·Q)
Is the operator too easy? (e.g., A → A·A applies to anything)
Are the side conditions satisfied? (e.g., R8 applies only to main expressions)

Table of connections

	R1	R2	R3	R4	R5	R6	R7	R8	R9	R10	R11	R12
Add terms									x		x	x
Delete terms								x	x		x	x
Change connective					x	x	x	x			x	x
Change sign				x		x						
Change lower sign			x		x							
Change grouping			x				x					
Change position	x											

× means some variant of the rule is relevant. GPS will pick the appropriate variant.

Figure 3. Methods for GPS.

through R12, are handled, since they do not enter into the protocol we are examining.) In Fig. 4, we give the trace on the initial part of problem D1. Indentation is used to indicate the relation of a subgoal to a goal. Although the methods are not shown, they can clearly be inferred from the goals that occur.

The initial problem is to transform L1 into L0. Matching L1 into L0 reveals that there are R's in L1 and no R's in L0. This difference leads to the formulation of a reduce goal, which for readability has been given its functional name, *Delete*. The attempt to reach this goal leads to a search for rules which finds rule 8. Since there are two forms of rule 8, both of which are admissible, GPS chooses the first. (Variants of rules are not indicated, but can be inferred easily from the trace.) Since rule 8 is

applicable, a new object, L2, is produced. Following the method for transform goals, at the next step a new goal has been generated: to transform L2 into L0. This in turn leads to another reduce goal: to restore a Q to L2. But this goal is rejected by the evaluation, since adding a term is more difficult than deleting a term. GPS then returns to goal 2 and seeks another rule which will delete terms. This time it finds the other form of rule 8 and goes through a similar excursion, ending with the rejection of goal 8.

Returning again to goal 2 to find another rule for deleting terms, GPS obtains rule 7. It selects the variant $(A \vee B) \cdot (A \vee C) \rightarrow A \vee (B \cdot C)$, since only this one both decreases terms and has a dot as its main connective. Rule 7 is not immediately applicable; GPS first discovers that there is a difference of connective in the left subexpression, and then that there is one in the right subexpression. In both cases it finds and applies rule 6 to change the connective from horseshoe to wedge, obtaining successively L4 and L5. But the new expression reveals a difference in sign, which leads again to rule 6—that is, to the same rule as before, but perceived as accomplishing a different function. Rule 6 produces L6, which happens to be identical with L4 although GPS does not notice the identity here. This leads, in goal 19, to the difference in connective being redetected; whereupon the goal is finally rejected as representing no progress over goal 13. Further attempts to find alternative ways to change signs or connectives fail to yield anything. This ends the episode.

Comparison of the GPS Trace with the Protocol

We now have a highly detailed trace of what GPS did. What can we find in the subject's protocol that either confirms or refutes the assertion that this program is a detailed model of the symbol manipulations the subject is carrying out? What sort of correspondence can we expect? The program does not provide us with an English language output that can be put into one-one correspondence with the words of the subject. We have not even given GPS a goal to "do the task and talk at the same time," which would be a necessary reformulation if we were to attempt a correspondence in such detail. On the other hand, the trace, backed up by our knowledge of how it was generated, does provide a complete record of all the task content that was considered by GPS, and the order in which it was taken up. Hence, we should expect to find every feature of the protocol that concerns the task mirrored in an essential way in the program trace. The converse is not true, since many things concerning the task surely occurred without the subject's commenting on them (or even being aware of them). Thus, our test of correspondence is one-sided but exacting.

```
L0    ~(~Q·P)
L1    (R⊃~P)·(~R⊃Q)

GOAL 1  TRANSFORM L1 INTO L0
GOAL 2  DELETE R FROM L1
  GOAL 3  APPLY R8 TO L1
    PRODUCES L2  R⊃~P

GOAL 4  TRANSFORM L2 INTO L0
  GOAL 5  ADD Q TO L2
    REJECT

GOAL 2
  GOAL 6  APPLY R8 TO L1
    PRODUCES L3  ~R⊃Q

GOAL 7  TRANSFORM L3 INTO L0
  GOAL 8  ADD P TO L3
    REJECT

GOAL 2
  GOAL 9  APPLY R7 TO L1
    GOAL 10  CHANGE CONNECTIVE TO V IN LEFT L1
      GOAL 11  APPLY R6 TO LEFT L1
        PRODUCES L4  (~R∨~P)·(~R⊃Q)

  GOAL 12  APPLY R7 TO L4
    GOAL 13  CHANGE CONNECTIVE TO V IN RIGHT L4
      GOAL 14  APPLY R6 TO RIGHT L4
        PRODUCES L5  (~R∨~P)·(R∨Q)

    GOAL 15  APPLY R7 TO L5
      GOAL 16  CHANGE SIGN OF LEFT RIGHT L5
        GOAL 17  APPLY R6 TO RIGHT L5
          PRODUCES L6  (~R∨~P)·(~R⊃Q)

      GOAL 18  APPLY R7 TO L6
        GOAL 19  CHANGE CONNECTIVE TO V
                 IN RIGHT L6
          REJECT

      GOAL 16
        NOTHING MORE

    GOAL 13
      NOTHING MORE

  GOAL 10
    NOTHING MORE
```

Figure 4. Trace of GPS on first part of problem.

Let us start with the first sentence of the subject's protocol (Fig. 2):

Well, looking at the left-hand side of the equation, first we want to eliminate one of the sides by using rule 8.

We see here a desire to decrease L1 or eliminate something from it, and the selection of rule 8 as the means to do this. This stands in direct correspondence with goals 1, 2, and 3 of the trace.
Let us skip to the third and fourth sentences:

Now,—no,—no, I can't do that because I will be eliminating either the Q or the P in that total expression. I won't do that at first.

We see here a direct expression of the covert application of rule 8, the subsequent comparison of the resulting expression with LO, and the rejection of this course of action because it deletes a letter that is required in the final expression. It would be hard to find a set of words that expressed these ideas more clearly. Conversely, if the mechanism of the program (or something essentially similar to it) were not operating, it would be hard to explain why the subject uttered the remarks that he did.

One discrepancy is quite clear. The subject handled both forms of rule 8 together, at least as far as his comment is concerned. GPS, on the other hand, took a separate cycle of consideration for each form. Possibly the subject followed the program covertly and simply reported the two results together. However, we would feel that the fit was better if GPS had proceeded something as follows:

```
GOAL 2 DELETE R FROM L1
    GOAL 3 APPLY R8 TO L1
        PRODUCES L2 R⊃~P OR ~R⊃Q

GOAL 4 TRANSFORM L2 INTO LO
    GOAL 5 ADD Q TO R⊃~P OR ADD P TO ~R⊃Q
        REJECT
```

We will consider further evidence on this point later.
Let us return to the second sentence, which we skipped over:

It appears too complicated to work with first.

Nothing in the program is in simple correspondence with this statement, though it is easy to imagine some possible explanations. For example, this could merely be an expression of the matching—of the fact that L1 is such a big expression that the subject cannot absorb all its detail. There is not enough data locally to determine what part of the trace should correspond to this statement, so the sentence must stand as an unexplained element of the subject's behavior.

Now let us consider the next few sentences of the protocol:

Now I'm looking for a way to get rid of the horseshoe inside the two brackets that appear on the left and right side of the equation. And I don't see it. Yeh, if you apply rule 6 to both sides of the equation, from there I'm going to see if I can apply rule 7.

This is in direct correspondence with goals 9 through 14 of the trace. The comment at the end makes it clear that applying rule 7 is the main concern and that changing connectives is required in order to accomplish this. Further, the protocol shows clearly that rule 6 was selected as the means. All three rule selections provide some confirmation that a preliminary test for feasibility was made by the subject—as by GPS—in the reduce goal method. If there was not selection on the main connective, why wasn't rule 5 selected instead of rule 6? Or why wasn't the $(A \cdot B) \lor (A \cdot C) \rightarrow A \cdot (B \lor C)$ form of rule 7 selected?

However, there is a discrepancy between trace and protocol, for the subject handles both applications of rule 6 simultaneously, (and apparently was also handling the two differences simultaneously); whereas GPS handles them sequentially. This is similar to the discrepancy noted earlier in handling rule 8. Since we now have two examples of parallel processing, it is likely that there is a real difference on this score. Again, we would feel better if GPS proceeded somewhat as follows:

```
GOAL 9 APPLY R7 TO L1
    GOAL 10 CHANGE CONNECTIVE TO ∨ IN LEFT L1 AND RIGHT L1
        GOAL 11 APPLY R6 TO LEFT L1 AND RIGHT L1
            PRODUCES L5 (~R∨~P)·(R∨Q)
```

A common feature of both these discrepancies is that forming the compound expressions does not complicate the methods in any essential way. Thus, in the case involving rule 8, the two results stem from the same input form, and require only the single match. In the case involving rule 7, a single search was made for a rule and the rule applied to both parts simultaneously, just as if only a single unit was involved.

There are two aspects in which the protocol provides information that the program is not equipped to explain. First, the subject handled the application of rule 6 covertly but commanded the experimenter to make the applications of rule 6 on the board. The version of GPS used here did not make any distinction between internal and external actions. To this extent it fails to be an adequate model. The overt-covert distinction has consequences that run throughout a problem, since expressions on the blackboard have very different memory characteristics from expressions generated only in the head. Second, this version of GPS does not simulate the search process sufficiently well to provide a correspondent to "And I don't see it. Yeh, . . .". This requires providing a facsimile of the rule sheet, and distinguishing search on the sheet from searches in the memory.

The next few sentences read:

I can almost apply rule 7, but one R needs a tilde. So I'll have to look for another rule. I'm going to see if I can change that R to a tilde R.

Again the trace and the protocol agree on the difference that is seen. They also agree that this difference was not attended to earlier, even though it was present. Some fine structure of the data also agrees with the trace. The right-hand R is taken as having the difference (R to ~R) rather than the left-hand one, although either is possible. This preference arises in the program (and presumably in the subject) from the language habit of working from left to right. It is not without consequences, however, since it determines whether the subject goes to work on the left side or the right side of the expression; hence, it can affect the entire course of events for quite a while. Similarly, in the rule 8 episode the subject apparently worked from left to right and from top to bottom in order to arrive at "Q or P" rather than "P or Q." This may seem like concern with excessively detailed features of the protocol, yet those details support the contention that what is going on inside the human system is quite akin to the symbol manipulations going on inside GPS.

The next portion of the protocol is:

As a matter of fact, I should have used rule 6 on only the left-hand side of the equation. So use 6, but only on the left-hand side.

Here we have a strong departure from the GPS trace, although, curiously enough, the trace and the protocol end up at the same spot, $(\sim R \vee \sim P) \cdot (\sim R \supset Q)$. Both the subject and GPS found rule 6 as the appropriate one to change signs. At this point GPS simply applied the rule to the current expression; whereas the subject went back and corrected the previous application. Nothing exists in the program that corresponds to this. The most direct explanation is that the application of rule 6 in the inverse direction is perceived by the subject as undoing the previous application of rule 6. After following out this line of reasoning, he then takes the simpler (and less foolish-appearing) alternative, which is to correct the original action.

The final segment of the protocol reads:

Now I'll apply rule 7 as it is expressed. Both—excuse me, excuse me, it can't be done because of the horseshoe. So—now I'm looking— scanning the rules here for a second, and seeing if I can change the R to ~R in the second equation, but I don't see any way of doing it. (Sigh). I'm just sort of lost for a second.

The trace and the protocol are again in good agreement. This is one of the few self-correcting errors we have encountered. The protocol records the futile search for additional operators to affect the differences of sign and connective, always with negative results. The final comment of mild despair can be interpreted as reflecting the impact of several successive failures.

Summary of the Fit of the Trace to the Protocol

Let us take stock of the agreements and disagreements between the trace and the protocol. The program provides a complete explanation of the subject's task behavior with five exceptions of varying degrees of seriousness.

There are two aspects in which GPS is unprepared to simulate the subject's behavior: in distinguishing between the internal and external worlds, and in an adequate representation of the spaces in which the search for rules takes place. Both of these are generalized deficiencies that can be remedied. It will remain to be seen how well GPS can then explain data about these aspects of behavior.

The subject handles certain sets of items in parallel by using compound expressions; whereas GPS handles all items one at a time. In the example examined here, no striking differences in problem solving occur as a result, but larger discrepancies could arise under other conditions. It is fairly clear how GPS could be extended to incorporate this feature.

There are two cases in which nothing corresponds in the program to some clear task-oriented behavior in the protocol. One of these, the early comment about "complication," seems to be mostly a case of insufficient information. The program is making numerous comparisons and evaluations which could give rise to comments of the type in question. Thus this error does not seem too serious. The other case, involving the "should have . . ." passage, does seem serious. It clearly implies a mechanism (maybe a whole set of them) that is not in GPS. Adding the mechanism required to handle this one passage could significantly increase the total capabilities of the program. For example, there might be no reasonable way to accomplish this except to provide GPS with a little continuous hindsight about its past actions.

An additional general caution must be suggested. The quantity of data is not large considering the size and complexity of the program. This implies that there are many degrees of freedom available to fit the program to the data. More important, we have no good way to assess how many relevant degrees of freedom a program possesses, and thus to know how easy it is to fit alternative programs. All we do know is that numerous minor modifications could certainly be made, but that no one has proposed any major alternative theories that provide anything like a comparably detailed explanation of human problem-solving data.

It would help if we knew something of how idiosyncratic the program was. We have discussed it here only in relation to one sample of data for one subject. We know enough about subjects on logic problems to assert that the same mechanisms show up repeatedly, but we cannot discuss these data here in detail. In addition, several recent investigations more generally support the concept of information processing theories of human thinking (Bruner et al., 1956; Feigenbaum, 1961a; Feldman, 1961a; Hovland and Hunt, 1960; Miller et al., 1960).

Conclusion

We have been concerned in this report with showing that the techniques that have emerged for constructing sophisticated problem-solving programs also provide us with new, strong tools for constructing theories of human thinking. They allow us to merge the rigor and objectivity associated with Behaviorism with the wealth of data and complex behavior associated with the Gestalt movement. To this end their key feature is not that they provide a general framework for understanding problem-solving behavior (although they do that, too), but that they finally reveal with great clarity that the free behavior of a reasonably intelligent human can be understood as the product of a complex but finite and determinate set of laws. Although we know this only for small fragments of behavior, the depth of the explanation is striking.

APPLICATION OF THEOREM PROVING TO PROBLEM SOLVING[*†]

Cordell Green
Stanford Research Institute
Menlo Park, California

Abstract

This paper shows how an extension of the resolution proof procedure can be used to construct problem solutions. The extended proof procedure can solve problems involving state transformations. The paper explores several alternate problem representations and provides a discussion of solutions to sample problems including the "Monkey and Bananas" puzzle and the "Tower of Hanoi" puzzle. The paper exhibits solutions to these problems obtained by QA3, a computer program based on these theorem-proving methods. In addition, the paper shows how QA3 can write simple computer programs and can solve practical problems for a simple robot.

Key Words: Theorem proving, resolution, problem solving, automatic programming, program writing, robots, state transformations, question answering.

Automatic theorem proving by the resolution proof procedure[1]§ represents perhaps the most powerful known method for automatically determining the validity of a statement of first-order logic. In an earlier paper Green and Raphael[2] illustrated how an extended resolution procedure can be used as a question answerer--e.g., if the statement $(\exists x)P(x)$ can be shown to follow from a set of axioms by the resolution proof procedure, then the extended proof procedure will find or construct an x that satisfies P(x). This earlier paper (1) showed how one can axiomatize simple question-answering subjects, (2) described a question-answering program called QA2 based on this procedure, and (3) presented examples of simple question-answering dialogues with QA2. In a more recent paper[3] the author (1) presents the answer construction method in detail and proves its correctness, (2) describes the latest version of the program, QA3, and (3) introduces state-transformation methods into the constructive proof formalism. In addition to the question-answering applications illustrated in these earlier papers, QA3 has been used as an SRI robot[4] problem solver and as an automatic program writer. The purpose of this paper is

twofold: (1) to explore the question of predicate calculus representation for state-transformation problems in general, and (2) to elaborate upon robot and program-writing applications of this approach and the mechanisms underlying them.

Exactly how one can use logic and theorem proving for problem solving requires careful thought on the part of the user. Judging from my experience, and that of others using QA2 and QA3, one of the first difficulties encountered is the representation of problems, especially state-transformation problems, by statements in formal logic. Interest has been shown in seeing several detailed examples that illustrate alternate methods of axiomatizing such problems--i.e., techniques for "programming" in first-order logic. This paper provides detailed examples of various methods of representation. After presenting methods in Secs. I and II, a solution to the classic "Monkey and Bananas" problem is provided in Sec. III. Next, Sec. IV compares several alternate representations for the "Tower of Hanoi" puzzle. Two applications, robot problem solving and automatic programming, are discussed in Secs. V and VI, respectively.

I. An Introduction to State-Transformation Methods

The concepts of states and state transformations have of course been in existence for a long time, and the usefulness of these concepts for problem solving is well known. The purpose of this paper is not to discuss states and state transformations as such, but instead to show how these concepts can be used by an automatic resolution theorem prover. In practice, the employment of these methods has greatly extended the problem-solving capacity of QA2 and QA3. McCarthy and Hayes[5] present a relevant discussion of philosophical problems involved in attempting such formalizations.

First we will present a simple example. We begin by considering how a particular universe of discourse might be described in logic.

Facts describing the universe of discourse are expressed in the form of statements of mathematical logic. Questions or problems are stated as conjectures to be proved. If a theorem is proved, then the nature of our extended theorem prover is such that the proof is "constructive"-- i.e., if the theorem asserts the existence of an object then the proof finds or constructs such an object.

At any given moment the universe under consideration may be said to be in a given state.

---

* This research is a part of Project Defender and was supported by the Advanced Research Projects Agency of the Department of Defense and was monitored by Rome Air Development Center under Contracts AF 30(602)-4147 and F30602-69-C-0056.

† This preprint is a preliminary version and is subject to modification prior to publication.

§ References are listed at the end of this paper.

Used by permission of the International Joint Conferences on Artificial Intelligence, Inc.

We will represent a particular state by a subscripted s--e.g., s_{17}. The letter s, with no subscript, will be a variable, ranging over states. A state is described by means of predicates. For example, if the predicate $AT(object_1,b,s_1)$ is true, then in state s_1 the object, $object_1$, is at position b. Let this predicate be axiom A1:

A1. $AT(object_1,b,s_1)$.

The question "Where is $object_1$ in state s_1?" can be expressed in logic as the theorem $(\exists x)AT(object_1,x,s_1)$. The answer found by using system QA3 to prove this theorem is "yes, x = b."

Changes in states are brought about by performing actions and sequences of actions. An action can be represented by an action function that maps states into new states (achieved by executing the action). An axiom describing the effect of an action is typically of the form

$$(\forall s)[P(s) \supset Q(f(s))]$$

where s is a state variable
  P is a predicate describing a state
  f is an action function (corresponding to some action) that maps a state into a new state (achieved by executing the action)
  Q is a predicate describing the new state.

(Entities such as P and f are termed "situational fluents" by McCarthy.)

As an example, consider an axiom describing the fact that $object_1$ can be pushed from point b to point c. The axiom is

A2. $(\forall s)[AT(object_1,b,s) \supset$

  $AT(object_1,c,push(object_1,b,c,s))]$.

The function $push(object_1,b,c,s)$ corresponds to the action of pushing $object_1$ from b to c. (Assume, for example, that a robot is the executor of these actions.)

Now consider the question, "Does there exist a sequence of actions such that $object_1$ is at point c?" Equivalently, one may ask, "Does there exist a state, possibly resulting from applying action functions to an initial state s_1, such that $object_1$ is at point c?" This question, in logic, is $(\exists s)AT(object_1,c,s)$, and the answer, provided by the theorem-proving program applied to axioms A1 and A2, is "yes, $s = push(object_1,b,c,s_1)$."

Suppose a third axiom indicates that $object_1$ can be pushed from c to d:

A3. $(\forall s)[AT(object_1,c,s) \supset$

  $AT(object_1,d,push(object_1,c,d,s))]$.

Together, these three axioms imply that starting in state s_1, $object_1$ can be pushed from b to c and then from c to d. This sequence of actions (a program for our robot) can be expressed by the composition of the two push functions, $push(object_1,c,d,push(object_1,b,c,s_1))$. The normal order of function evaluation, from the innermost function to the outermost, gives the correct sequence in which to perform the actions.

To find this solution to the problem of getting $object_1$ to position d, the following conjecture is posed to the theorem prover: "Does there exist a state such that $object_1$ is at position d?" or, stated in logic, $(\exists s)AT(object_1,d,s)$. The answer returned is "yes, $s = push(object_1,c,d,push(object_1,b,c,s_1))$."

The proof by resolution, given below, demonstrates how the desired answer is formed as a composition of action functions, thus describing a sequence of necessary actions. The mechanism for finding this answer is a special literal,* the "answer literal." This method of finding an answer is explained in detail in Ref. 3. For our purposes here, we will just show how it works by example. In the proof below, each answer literal is displayed beneath the clause containing it. At each step in the proof the answer literal will contain the current value of the object being constructed by the theorem prover. In this example the object being constructed is the sequence of actions s. So initially the answer literal ANSWER(s) is added to the clause representing the negation of the question. (One can interpret this clause, Clause 1, as "either $object_1$ is not at d in state s, or s is an answer.") The state variable s, inside the answer literal, is the "place holder" where the solution sequence is constructed. The construction process in this proof consists of successive instantiations of s. An instantiation of s can occur whenever a literal containing s is instantiated in the creation of a resolvent. Each instantiation* of s fills in a new action or an argument of an action function. In general, a particular inference step in the proof (either by factoring* or resolving*) need not necessarily further instantiate s. For example, the step might be an inference that verifies that some particular property holds for the current answer at that step in the proof. The final step in the proof yields Clause 7, "an answer is $push(object_1,c,d,push(object_1,b,c,s_1))$," which terminates the proof.

---

* We assume the reader is familiar with the vocabulary of the field of theorem proving by resolution as described in Refs. 1, 7, and 8.

Proof

1. $\sim$AT(object$_1$,d,s)   Negation of theorem

    ANSWER(s)

2. $\sim$AT(object$_1$,c,s) $\lor$ Axiom A3

    AT(object$_1$,d,push(object$_1$,c,d,s))

3. $\sim$AT(object$_1$,c,s)   Resolve 1,2

    ANSWER(push(object$_1$,c,d,s))

4. $\sim$AT(object$_1$,b,s) $\lor$ Axiom A2

    AT(object$_1$,c,push(object$_1$,b,c,s))

5. $\sim$AT(object$_1$,b,s)   Resolve 3,4

    ANSWER(push(object$_1$,c,d,

        push(object$_1$,b,c,s)))

6. AT(object$_1$,b,s$_1$)   Axiom A1

7. Contradiction   Resolve 5,6

    ANSWER(push(object$_1$,c,d,

        push(object$_1$,b,c,s$_1$)))

For the particular proof exhibited here, the order of generating the solution sequence during the search for the proof happens to be the same order in which the printout of the proof indicates s is instantiated. This order consists of working backward from the goal by filling in the last action, then the next-to-last action, etc. In general, the order in which the solution sequence is generated depends upon the proof strategy, since the proof strategy determines the order in which clauses are resolved or factored. The proof that this method always produces correct answers, given in Ref. 4, shows that the answers are correct regardless of the proof strategy used.

II. Refinements of the Method

The purpose of this section is to discuss variations of the formulation presented in the previous section and to show how other considerations such as time and conditional operations can be brought into the formalism. The reader who is interested in applications rather than additional material on representation may omit Secs. II, III, and IV, and read Secs. V and VI.

A. An Alternate Formulation

The first subject we shall discuss is an alternate to the previously given formulation. We shall refer to the original, presented in Sec. I, as formulation I, and this alternate as formulation II. Formulation II corresponds to a system-theoretic notion of state transformations. The _state transformation function_ for a system gives the mapping of an action and a state into a new state. Let f represent the state transformation function, whose arguments are an action

and a state and whose value is the new state obtained by applying the action to the state. Let $\{a_i\}$ be the actions, and _nil_ be the null action. Let g be a function that maps two actions into a single composite action whose effect is the same as that of the argument actions applied sequentially. For example, axioms of the following form would partially define the state transformation function f:

B1. $(\forall s)[P(s) \supset Q(f(a_1,s))]$

B2. $(\forall s)[f(nil,s) = s]$

B3. $(\forall s,a_i,a_j)[f(a_j,f(a_i,s)) = f(g(a_i,a_j),s)]$.

The predicates P and Q represent descriptors of states. Axiom B1 describes the result of an action a_1 applied to the class of states that are equivalent in that they all have the property $P(s)$. The resulting states are thus equivalent in that they have property $Q(s)$. Axiom B2 indicates that the null action has no effect. The equation in B3 says that the effect of the composite action sequence $g(a_i,a_j)$ is the same as that of actions a_i and a_j applied sequentially. The question posed in this formulation can include an initial state--e.g., a question might be $(\exists x)Q(f(x,s_0))$, meaning "Does there exist a sequence of actions x that maps state s_0 into a state satisfying the predicate Q?" Observe that we are not insisting on finding a particular sequence of actions, but any sequence that leads us to a satisfactory state within the target class of states.

This representation is more complex, but has the advantage over the previous representation that both the starting state of a transformation and the sequence of actions are explicitly given as the arguments of the state-transformation function. Thus, one can quantify over, or specify in particular, either the starting state or the sequence, or both.

Next we shall show how other considerations can be brought into a state-transformation formalism. Both the original formulation (I) and the alternate (II) will be used as needed.

B. No Change of State

This kind of statement represents an implication that holds for a fixed state. An axiom typical of this class might describe the relationship between movable objects; e.g., if x is to the left of y and y is to the left of z, then x is to the left of z.

$$(\forall x,y,z,s)[LEFT(x,y,s) \land LEFT(y,z,s) \supset LEFT(x,z,s)]$$

C. Time

Time can be a function of a state, to express the timing of actions and states. For example, if the function time(s) gives the time of an instantaneous state, in the axiom

$$(\forall s)\big[P(s) \supset \big[Q(f(s)) \wedge$$

$$EQUAL(difference(time(f(s)),time(s)),\tau)\big]\big],$$

where $P(s)$ describes the initial state and $Q(s)$ describes the final state, the state transformation takes τ seconds to complete.

D.   State-Independent Truths

An example is

$$(\forall x,y,z)\big[EQUAL(plus(x,17),z) \supset$$

$$EQUAL(difference(z,x),17)\big]$$

illustrating how functions and predicates are explicitly made state independent by not taking states as arguments.

E.   Descriptors of Transformations

A descriptor or modifier of an action may be added in the form of a predicate that takes as an argument the state transformation that is to be described. For example,

WISHED-FOR(f(action,state),person)

might indicate a wished-for occurrence of an action;

LOCATION(f(action,state),place)

indicates that an action occurred at a certain place.

F.   Disjunctive Answers

Consider a case in which an action results in one of two possibilities. As an example, consider an automaton that is to move from a to d.

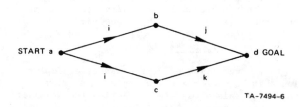

TA-7494-6

The above figure shows that action i leads to either b or c from a. The function f is single-valued but we don't know its value. The goal d can be reached from b by action j, or from c by action k. In the formalization given below it is possible to prove that the goal is reachable although a correct sequence of actions necessary

to reach the goal is not generated. Instead, the answer produced is a disjunction of two sequences-- $j(i(s_0))$ or $k(i(s_0))$.

We use formulation I. Axiom M1 specifies the starting state s_0 and starting position a. Axioms M2, M3, and M4 specify positions resulting from the allowed moves.

M1. $AT(a,s_0)$

M2. $(\forall s)\big[AT(a,s) \supset AT(b,i(s)) \vee AT(c,i(s))\big]$

M3. $(\forall s)\big[AT(b,s) \supset AT(d,j(s))\big]$

M4. $(\forall s)\big[AT(c,s) \supset AT(d,k(s))\big]$

To find if the goal d is reachable, we ask the following question:

Question: $(\exists s)AT(d,s)$

to which an answer is:

Answer: Yes, $s = j(i(s_0))$ or $s = k(i(s_0))$.

The proof is:

Proof

1.	$\sim AT(d,s)$	Negation of theorem
	$\underline{ANSWER}(s)$	
2.	$\sim AT(b,s) \vee AT(d,j(s))$	Axiom M3
3.	$\sim AT(b,s)$	From 1,2
	$\underline{ANSWER}(j(s))$	
4.	$\sim AT(c,s) \vee AT(d,k(s))$	Axiom M4
5.	$\sim AT(c,s)$	From 1,4
	$\underline{ANSWER}(k(s))$	
6.	$\sim AT(a,s) \vee$ $AT(b,i(s)) \vee AT(c,i(s))$	Axiom M2
7.	$\sim AT(a,s) \vee AT(b,i(s))$	From 5,6
	$\underline{ANSWER}(k(i(s)))$	
8.	$\sim AT(a,s)$	From 3,7
	$\underline{ANSWER}(j(i(s))) \vee \underline{ANSWER}(k(i(s)))$	
9.	$AT(a,s_0)$	Axiom M1
10.	Contradiction	From 8,9
	$\underline{ANSWER}(j(i(s_0))) \vee \underline{ANSWER}(k(i(s_0)))$	

Observe that clause 8 has two answers, one coming from clause 3 corresponding to the action k and one from clause 7 corresponding to the action j. This shows how an "or" answer can arise.

G.   Answers with Conditionals

A conditional operation such as "if p then q else r" allows a program to branch to either operation q or r depending upon the outcome of the test condition p. By allowing a conditional operation, a better solution to the above problem is made possible, namely, "beginning in state s_o take action i; if at b take action j, otherwise take action k."

Consider the problem above that yields disjunctive answers. The information in the above problem formulation, axioms M1 through M4, plus additional information allows the creation of a program with a conditional and a test operation. The following additional information is needed, which we shall furnish in the form of axioms.

The first addition needed is a conditional operation, along with a description of what the operation does. Since our programs are in the form of functions, a conditional function is needed. One such possible function is the LISP conditional function "cond" which will be discussed in Sec. VI. However, another function, a simple "select" function is slightly easier to describe and will be used here. The function select(x,y,z,w) is defined to have the value z if x equals y and w otherwise.

M5. $(\forall x,y,z,w)[x = y \supset select(x,y,z,w) = z]$

M6. $(\forall x,y,z,w)[x \neq y \supset select(x,y,z,w) = w]$

The second addition needed is a test operation, along with a description of what it does. Since our programs are in the form of functions, a test function is needed. We shall use "atf", meaning "at-function." The function "atf" applied to a state yields the location in that state, e.g., $atf(s_o) = a$. The atf function is described by

M7. $(\forall x,s)[AT(x,s) \equiv (atf(s) = x)]$.

These axioms lead to the solution

$$s = select(atf(i(s_o)),b,j(i(s_o)),k(i(s_o))),$$

meaning "if at b after applying i to s_o, take action j otherwise action k."

Although the new axioms allow the conditional solution, just the addition of these axioms does not guarantee that disjunctive answers will not occur. To prevent the possibility of disjunctive answers, we simply tell the theorem prover not to accept any clauses having two answers that don't unify.

What may be a preferable problem formulation and solution can result from the use of the alternative state formulation, II, exemplified in axioms B1, B2, and B3 above. Recall that f(i,s) is the state transformation function that maps action i and state s into a new state, the function g(i,j) maps the action i and the action j into the

sequence of the two actions--i then j. The interrelation of f and g is described by

B3. $(\forall i,j,s)[f(j,f(i,s)) = f(g(i,j),s)]$

Axioms M1 through M4 remain the same but axioms M5, M6, and M7 are replaced. The new select function is described by the two axioms:

M5'. $(\forall i,j,s,p,b)[test(p,s) = b \supset$
$$f(select(p,b,i,j),s) = f(i,s)]$$

M6'. $(\forall i,j,s,p,b)[test(p,s) \neq b \supset$
$$f(select(p,b,i,j),s) = f(j,s)],$$

where the function test applies the test condition p (which will correspond to atf for this problem) to state s. The test condition atf is defined by

M7'. $(\forall x,s)[AT(x,s) \equiv test(atf,s) = x]$.

The new solution is

$$s = f(g(i,select(atf,b,j,k)),s_o).$$

Further discussion of program writing, including recursion, is given in Sec. VI.

Another method of forming conditional answers is possible. This involves inspecting an existence proof such as the one given in Sec. II-F above. First, such a proof is generated in which clauses having multiple answers are allowed. The conditional operation is constructed by observing the two literals which are resolved upon to generate the two-answer clause. For example, in the above proof clauses 3 and 7 resolve to yield 8. This step is repeated below, using the variable s' in 3 to emphasize that s' is different from s in 7.

Clause 3. $\sim AT(b,s')$

ANSWER(j(s'))

Clause 7. $\sim AT(a,s) \lor AT(b,(i(s)))$

ANSWER(k(i(s)))

Clause 8. $\sim AT(a,s)$

ANSWER(j(s)) $\lor$ ANSWER(k(i(s)))

Clause 3 may be read as "if at b in state s', the answer is to take action j when in state s'." Clause 7 may be read as "if not at b in state i(s) and if at a in state s, the answer is to take action k when in state i(s)." Observing that the resolution binds s' to i(s) in Clause 8, one knows from Clauses 3 and 7 the test condition by which one decides which answer to choose in Clause 8, "if at a in state s the answer depends on i(s); if at b in i(s) take action j; otherwise take action k."

This discussion illustrates that the creation of a clause with two answer literals indicates that a conditional operation is needed to create a single conditional answer. This information provides a useful heuristic for the program-writing applications of QA3: When a clause having two answer literals is about to be generated, let the proof strategy call for the axioms that describe the conditional operation (such as M5 and M6). These axioms are then applied to create a single conditional answer.

Waldinger and Lee[5] have implemented a program-writing program PROW that also uses a resolution theorem prover to create constructive proofs, but by a different method than that of QA3. (The second method for creating conditionals by combining two answers is closely related to a technique used in PROW.) Information about (1) the target program operations, (2) the general relationship of the problem statement and axioms to the allowed target program operations including the test conditions, and (3) the syntax of the target language, is embedded in the PROW program. In QA3 this information is all in the axioms--such as axioms M5, M6, and M7.

H. Acquisition of Information

Another situation that arises in problem solving is one in which at the time the problem is stated and a solution is to be produced, there is insufficient information to completely specify a solution. More precisely, the solution cannot name every action and test condition in advance. As an example, consider a robot that is to move from a to c. The action i leads from a to b but no path to c is known, as illustrated below.

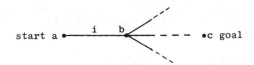

However, once point b is reached, more information can be acquired--for example, a guide to the area lives at b and will provide a path to point c if asked. Or perhaps once point b is reached, the robot might use its sensors to observe or discover paths to c.

To formalize this, assume that the action ask-path(b,c) will result in a proper path to c, when taken at b. For simplicity, assume that the name of the path is equal to the state resulting from asking the question. Using formulation II, one suitable set of axioms is:

N1. $AT(a, s_0) \land PATH(a,b,i)$

N2. $(\forall s,x,y,j)[AT(x,s) \land PATH(x,y,j) \supset$
        $AT(y, f(j,s))]$

N3. $(\forall s)[AT(b,s) \supset PATH(b,c,f(ask\text{-}path(b,c),s)) \land$
        $AT(b, f(ask\text{-}path(b,c),s))]$

where PATH(a,b,i) means that i is a path from a to b. The question $(\exists s)AT(c,s)$ results in the solution,

"yes, s = f(f(ask-path(b,c),f(i,s)),f(i,s))".

Axiom N3 illustrates an important aspect of this formalism for problem solving: If a condition (such as the robot's) is made state dependent, then we must specify how this condition changes when the state is changed. Thus in axiom N3 we must indicate that the robot's location is not changed by asking for a path. In a pure theorem-proving formalism, this means that if we want to know any condition in a given state, we must prove what that condition is. If a large number of state-dependent conditions need to be known at each state in a solution, then the theorem prover must prove what each condition is at each state in a conjectured solution. In such a case the theorem prover will take a long time to find the solution. McCarthy[5] refers to this problem as the <u>frame problem</u>, where the word "frame" refers to the frame of reference or the set of relevant conditions. Discussion of a method for easing this problem is presented in Sec. V.

I. Assignment Operations

An assignment operation is one that assigns a value to a variable. An example of an assignment is the statement a ← h(a), meaning that the value of a is to be changed to the value of the function h(a). In our representation, we shall use an assignment function--i.e., assign(a,h(a)). Using Formulation II this function is described by the axiom

$$(\forall a, a_0, s)[VALUE(a, a_0, s) \supset$$
$$VALUE(a, h(a_0), f(assign(a,h(a)),s))]$$

where the predicate VALUE(a, a_0, s) means that variable a has value a_0 in state s.

III. An Example:
The Monkey and The Bananas

To illustrate the methods described earlier, we present an axiomatization of McCarthy's "Monkey and Bananas" problem.

The monkey is faced with the problem of getting a bunch of bananas hanging from the ceiling just beyond his reach. To solve the problem, the monkey must push a box to an empty place under the bananas, climb on top of the box, and then reach them.

The constants are monkey, box, bananas, and under-bananas. The functions are reach, climb, and move, meaning the following:

reach(m,z,s)   The state resulting from the action of m reaching z, starting from state s

climb(m,b,s)   The state resulting from the action of m climbing b, starting from state s

move(m,b,u,s) The state resulting from the action of m moving b to place u, starting from state s.

The predicates are:

MOVABLE(b)   b is movable

AT(m,u,s)   m is at place u in state s

ON(m,b,s)   m is on b in state s

HAS(m,z,s)   m has z in state s

CLIMBABLE(m,b,s) m can climb b in state s

REACHABLE(m,b,s) m can reach b in state s.

The axioms* are:

MB1. MOVABLE(box)

MB2. AT(box, $place_b$, s_0)

MB3. $(\forall x) \sim$ AT(x, under-bananas, s_0)

MB4. $(\forall b, p_1, p_2, s)[[$ AT(b, p_1, s) $\land$ MOVABLE(b) $\land$

$(\forall x) \sim$ AT(x, p_2, s) $] \supset$

[AT(b, p_2, move(monkey, b, p_2, s)) $\land$

AT(monkey, p_2, move(monkey, b, p_2, s))]]

MB5. $(\forall s)$ CLIMBABLE(monkey, box, s)

MB6. $(\forall m, p, b, s)[[$ AT(b, p, s) $\land$ CLIMBABLE(m, b, s) $] \supset$

[AT(b, p, climb(m, b, s)) $\land$

ON(m, b, climb(m, b, s))]]

MB7. $(\forall s)[[$ AT(box, under-bananas, s) $\land$

ON(monkey, box, s) $] \supset$

REACHABLE(monkey, bananas, s)]

---

* The astute reader will notice that the axioms leave much to be desired. In keeping with the "toy problem" tradition we present an unrealistic axiomatization of this unrealistic problem. The problem's value lies in the fact that it is a reasonably interesting problem that may be familiar to the reader.

MB8. $(\forall m, z, s)[$ REACHABLE(m, z, s) $\supset$

HAS(m, z, reach(m, z, s))].

The question is "Does there exist a state s (sequence of actions) in which the monkey has the bananas?"

QUESTION: $(\exists s)$ HAS(monkey, bananas, s).

The answer is yes,

s = reach(monkey, bananas, climb(monkey,

box, move(monkey, box, under-bananas, s_0))).

By executing this function, the monkey gets the bananas. The monkey must, of course, execute the functions in the usual order, starting with the innermost and working outward. Thus he first moves the box under the bananas, then climbs on the box, and then reaches the bananas.

The printout of the proof is given in the appendix.

IV. Formalizations for the Tower of Hanoi Puzzle

The first applications of our question-answering programs were to "question-answering" examples. Commonly used question-answering examples have short proofs, and usually there are a few obvious formulations for a given subject area. (The major difficulty in question-answering problems usually is searching a large data base, rather than finding a long and difficult proof.) Typically any reasonable formulation works well. As one goes on to problems like the Tower of Hanoi puzzle, more effort is required to find a representation that is suitable for efficient problem solving.

This puzzle has proved to be an interesting study of representation. Several people using QA3 have set up axiom systems for the puzzle. Apparently, a "good" axiomatization--one leading to quick solutions--is not entirely obvious, since many axiomatizations did not result in solutions. In this section we will present and compare several alternate representations, including ones that lead to a solution.

There are three pegs--peg_1, peg_2, and peg_3. There are a number of discs each of whose diameter is different from that of all the other discs. Initially all discs are stacked on peg_1, in order of descending size. The three-disc version is illustrated below.

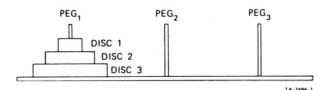

TA-7494-7

The object of the puzzle is to find a sequence of moves that will transfer all the discs from peg_1 to peg_3. The allowed moves consist of taking the top disc from any peg and placing it on another peg, but a disc can never be placed on top of a smaller disc.

In order to correctly specify the problem, any formalization must: (1) specify the positions of the discs for each state; (2) specify how actions change the position of the discs; and (3) specify the rules of the game, i.e., what is legal.

Let the predicate ON specify disc positions. In the simplest representation the predicate ON specifies the position of one disc--e.g., $ON(disc_1, peg_1, s)$ says that in state s $disc_1$ is on peg_1. This representation requires one predicate to specify the position of each disc. The relative position of each disc either must be specified by another statement, or else if two discs are on the same peg it must be implicitly understood that they are in the proper order. Perhaps the simplest extension is to allow the predicate another argument that specifies the position of the disc--i.e., $ON(disc_1, peg_1, position_2, s)$. Again, this requires many statements to specify a complete configuration.

Since various moves are constructing stacks of discs, and since stacks can be represented as lists, consider as an alternative representation a list to represent a stack of discs. Let the function $\ell(x, y)$ represent the list that has x as its first element (representing the top disc in the stack) and y as the rest of the list (representing the rest of the discs in the stack). This function ℓ corresponds to the "cons" function in LISP. Let nil be the empty list. The statement $ON(\ell(disc_1, \ell(disc_2, nil)), peg_1, s)$ asserts that the stack having top disc, $disc_1$, and second disc, $disc_2$, is on peg_1. This representation illustrates a useful technique in logic--namely, the use of functions as the construction (and selection) operators. This notion is consistent with the use of action functions as constructors of sequences.

Next, consider how to express possible changes in states. Perhaps the simplest idea is to say that a given state implies that certain moves are legal. One must then have other statements indicating the result of each move. This method is a bit lengthy. It is easier to express in one statement the fact that given some state, a new state is the result of a move. Thus one such move to a new state is described by $(\forall s)[ON(\ell(disc_1, nil), peg_1, s) \land ON(nil, peg_2, s) \land ON(\ell(disc_2, \ell(disc_3, nil)), peg_3, s) \supset ON(nil, peg_1, move(disc_1, peg_1, peg_2, s)) \land ON(\ell(disc_1, nil), peg_2, move(disc_1, peg_1, peg_2, s)) \land ON(\ell(disc_2, \ell(disc_3, nil)), peg_3, move(disc_1, peg_1, peg_2, s))]$.

With this method it is possible to enumerate all possible moves and configuration combinations. However, it is still easier to use variables to represent whole classes of states and moves. Thus

$(\forall s, x, y, z, p_i, p_j, p_k, d)[ON(\ell(d, x), p_i, s) \land ON(y, p_j, s) \land ON(z, p_k, s) \supset ON(x, p_i, move(d, p_i, p_j, s)) \land ON(\ell(d, y), p_j, move(d, p_i, p_j, s)) \land ON(z, p_k, move(d, p_i, p_j, s))]$ specifies a whole class of moves. The problem here is that additional restrictions must be added so that illegal states cannot be part of a solution. In the previous formalism, one could let the axioms enumerate just the legal moves and states, thus preventing incorrect solutions.

The first method for adding restrictions is to have a predicate that restricts moves to just the legitimate states. Since the starting state is legal, one might think that only legal states can be reached. However, the resolution process (set-of-support strategy[7]) typically works backward from the goal state toward states that can reach the goal state--such states are sometimes called "forcing states." Thus illegal but forcing states can be reached by working backward from the goal state. This does not allow for incorrect solutions, since the only forcing states that can appear in the solution must be those reached from the starting state (which is a legal state). The restriction of moving only to new legal states thus prevents an error. But the search is unnecessarily large, since the theorem prover is considering illegal states that cannot lead to a solution. So a better solution is to eliminate these illegal forcing states by allowing moves only from legal states to legal states. This is perhaps the best specification, in a sense. Such an axiom is $(\forall s, x, y, z, p_i, p_j, p_k, d)[ON(\ell(d, x), p_i, s) \land ON(y, p_j, s) \land ON(z, p_k, s) \land LEGAL(\ell(d, x)) \land LEGAL(\ell(d, y)) \land DISTINCT(p_i, p_j, p_k) \supset ON(x, p_i, move(d, p_i, p_j, s)) \land ON(\ell(d, y), p_j, move(d, p_i, p_j, s)) \land ON(z, p_k, move(d, p_i, p_j, s))]$. The predicate $LEGAL(x)$ is true if and only if the discs are listed in order of increasing size. (One can "cheat" and have a simpler axiom by omitting the predicate that requires that the state resulting from a move have a legal stack of discs. Since the set-of-support strategy forces the theorem prover to work backward starting from a legal final state, it will only consider legal states. However, one is then using an axiomatization that, by itself, is incorrect.) The additional LEGAL predicate is a typical example of how additional information in the axioms results in a quicker solution. The predicate $DISTINCT(p_i, p_j, p_k)$ means no two pegs are equal.

The clauses generated during the search that are concerned with illegal states are subsumed[8] by ~LEGAL predicates such as $(\forall s)\sim LEGAL(\ell(disc_2, \ell(disc_1, x)))$. The stacks are formed by placing one new disc on top of a legal stack. If the new top disc is smaller than the old top disc then it is of course smaller than all the others on the stack. Thus the legal stack axioms need only to specify that the top disc is smaller than the second disc for a stack to be legal. This blocks the construction of incorrect stacks.

One complete axiomatization is as follows:

AX1. $(\forall x,y,z,m,n,p_i,p_j,p_k)[ON(\ell(d(m),x),p_i,s) \wedge$

$ON(y,p_j,s) \wedge ON(z,p_k,s) \wedge$

$DISTINCT(p_i,p_j,p_k) \wedge LEGAL(\ell(d(m),x)) \wedge$

$LEGAL(\ell(d(n),y)) \supset$

$ON(x,p_i,move(d(m),p_i,p_j,s)) \wedge$

$ON(\ell(d(m),y),p_j,move(d(m),p_i,p_j,s)) \wedge$

$ON(z,p_k,move(d(m),p_i,p_j,s))]$

AX2. $(\forall m,n,x)[LEGAL(\ell(d(m),\ell(d(n),x))) \equiv$

$LESS(m,n)] \wedge (\forall n)LEGAL(\ell(d(n),nil)) \wedge$

$LEGAL(nil)$

Instead of naming each disc, the disc number n is an argument of the function d(n) that represents the <u>n</u>th disc. This representation illustrates how the proof procedure can be shortened by solving frequent decidable subproblems with special available tools--namely, the LISP programming language. The theorem prover uses LISP (the "lessp" function) to evaluate the LESS(n,m) predicate--a very quick step. This mechanism has the effect of generating, wherever needed, such axioms as ~LESS(3,2) or LESS(2,3) to resolve against or subsume literals in generated clauses. Similarly, LISP evaluates the DISTINCT predicate.

Note that the move axiom, AX1, breaks up into three clauses, each clause specifying the change in the task for one particular peg. The process of making one move requires nine binary resolutions, and two binary factorings of clauses.

Still other solutions are possible by using special term-matching capabilities in QA3 that extend the unification and subsumption algorithms to include list terms, set terms, and certain types of symmetries.

In another axiomatization, the complete configuration of the puzzle in a given state is specified by the predicate ON. ON(x,y,z,s) means that in state s, stack x in on peg_1, stack y is on peg_2, and stack z is on peg_3. Thus if the predicate $ON(\ell(d_1,\ell(d_2,nil))),nil,\ell(d_3,nil),s_k)$ holds, the stack $d_1 - d_2$ is on peg_1 and d_3 is on peg_3. The predicate LEGAL again indicates that a given stack of discs is allowed.

Two kinds of axioms are required--move axioms and legal stack axioms. One legal stack axiom is $LEGAL(\ell(d_1,\ell(d_2,nil)))$. One move axiom is $(\forall d,x,y,z,s)[ON(\ell(d,x),y,z,s) \wedge LEGAL(\ell(d,x)) \wedge$ $LEGAL(\ell(d,y)) \supset ON(x,\ell(d,y),z,move(d,p_1,p_2,s))]$. This axiom states that disc d can be moved from peg_1 to peg_2 if the initial stack on peg_1 is legal and the resultant stack on peg_2 is legal.

In this last-mentioned formalization, using 13 axioms to specify the problem, QA3 easily solved this problem for the three-disc puzzle. During the search for a proof, 98 clauses were generated buy only 25 of the clauses were accepted. Of the

25, 12 were not in the proof. The solution entails seven moves, thus passing through eight states (counting the initial and final states). The 12 clauses not in the proof correspond to searching through 5 states that are not used in the solution. Thus the solution is found rather easily. Of course, if a sufficiently poor axiomatization is chosen--one requiring an enumeration of enough correct and incorrect disc positions--the system becomes saturated and fails to obtain a solution within time and space constraints. An important factor in the proof search is the elimination of extra clauses corresponding to alternate paths that reach a given state. In the above problem it happens that the subsumption heuristic[8] eliminates 73 of these redundant clauses. However, this particular use of subsumption is problem dependent, thus one must examine any given problem formulation to determine whether or not subsumption will eliminate alternate paths to equivalent states.

The four-disc version of the puzzle can be much more difficult than the three-disc puzzle in terms of search. At about this level of difficulty one must be somewhat more careful to obtain a low-cost solution.

Ernst[9] formalizes the notion of "difference" used by GPS and shows what properties these differences must possess for GPS to succeed on a problem. He then presents a "good" set of differences for the Tower of Hanoi problem. Utilizing this information, GPS solves the problem for four discs, considering no incorrect states in its search. Thus Ernst has chosen a set of differences that guide GPS directly to the solution.

Another method of solution is possible. First, solve the three-disc puzzle. Save the solution to the three-disc puzzle (using the answer statement[4]). Then ask for a solution to the four-disc puzzle. The solution then is: Move the top three discs from peg_1 to peg_2; move $disc_4$ from peg_1 to peg_3; move the three discs on peg_2 to peg_3. This method produces a much easier solution. But this can be considered as cheating, since the machine is "guided" to a solution by being told which subproblem to first solve and store away. The use of the differences by GPS similarly lets the problem solver be "guided" toward a solution.

There is another possibly more desirable solution. The four-disc puzzle can be posed as the problem, with no three-disc solution. If the solution of the three-disc puzzle occurs during the search for a solution to the four-disc puzzle, and if it is automatically recognized and saved as a lemma, then the four-disc solution should follow easily.

Finally, if an induction axiom is provided, the axioms imply a solution in the form of a recursive program that solves the puzzle for an arbitrary number of discs. Aiko Hormann[10] discusses the related solutions of the four-disc problem by the program GAKU (not an automatic theorem-proving program). The solutions by lemma finding, induction, and search guided by differences have not been run on QA3.

V.   Applications to the Robot Project

A.   Introduction to Robot Problem Solving

In this section we discuss how theorem-proving methods are being tested for several applications in the Stanford Research Institute Artificial Intelligence Group's Automaton (robot). We emphasize that this section describes work that is now in progress, rather than work that is completed. These methods represent explorations in problem solving, rather than final decisions about how the robot is to do problem solving. An overview of the current status of the entire SRI robot project is provided by Nilsson[4]. Coles[11] has developed an English-to-logic translator that is part of the robot.

We use theorem-proving methods for three purposes, the simplest being the use of QA3 as a central information storage and retrieval system that is accessible to various parts of the system as well as the human users. The data base of QA3 is thus one of the robot's models of its world, including itself.

A second use is as an experimental tool to test out a particular problem formulation. When a suitable formulation is found, it may then be desirable to write a faster or more efficient specific program that implements this formulation, perhaps involving little or no search. If the special program is not as general as the axiom system is, so that the special program fails in certain cases, the axioms can be retained to be used in the troublesome cases. Both solutions can be made available by storing, as the first axiom to be tried, a special axiom that describes the special solution. The predicate-evaluation mechanism can then call LISP to run the special solution. If it fails, the other axioms will then be used.

The third use is as a real-time problem solver. In the implementation we are now using, statements of logic--clauses--are the basic units of information. Statements are derived from several sources: teletype entries, axioms stored in memory, clauses or statements generated by the theorem prover, and statements evaluated by programs--subroutines in LISP, FORTRAN, or machine language. These programs can use robot sensors and sensory data to verify, disprove, or generate statements of logic.

The SRI robot is a cart on wheels, having a TV camera and a range-finder mounted on the cart. There are bumpers on the cart, but no arms or grasping agents, so the only way the robot can manipulate its environment is by simple pushing actions. Given this rather severe restriction of no grasping, the robot must be clever to effectively solve problems involving modifying its world. We present below some axioms for robot problem solving.

The first axiom describes the move routines of the robot:

R1. $(\forall s, p_1, p_2, path_{12})[AT(robot, p_1, s) \land$

$PATH(p_1, p_2, path_{12}, s) \supset$

$AT(robot, p_2, move(robot, path_{12}, s))]$.

This axiom says that if the robot is at p_1 and there is a path to p_2, the robot will be at p_2 after moving along the path. The predicate PATH indicates there exists a robot-path, $path_{12}$, from place p_1 to place p_2. A robot-path is a path adequate for the robot's movement. The terms p_1 and p_2 describe the position of the robot.

In general, it may be very inefficient to use the theorem prover to find the $path_{12}$ such that $PATH(p_1, p_2, path_{12})$ is true. Several existing FORTRAN subroutines, having sophisticated problem-solving capabilities of their own, may be used to determine a good path through obstacles on level ground. We will show later a case where the theorem prover may be used to find a more obscure kind of path. For the less obscure paths, the axiom R1 is merely a description of the semantics of these FORTRAN programs, so that new and meaningful programs can be generated by QA3 by using the efficient path-generating programs as subprograms. The "predicate-evaluation" mechanism is used to call the FORTRAN path-finding routines. The effect of this evaluation mechanism is the same as if the family of axioms of the form $PATH(p_1, p_2, path_{12})$ for all p_1 and p_2 such that $path_{12}$ exists, were all stored in memory and available to the theorem prover.

The second axiom is a push axiom that describes the effect of pushing an object. The robot has no arm or graspers, just a bumper. Its world consists of large objects such as boxes, wedges, cubes, etc. These objects are roughly the same size as the robot itself.

The basic predicate that specifies the position of an object is ATO, meaning at-object. The predicate

$ATO(object_1, description_1, position_1, s_1)$

indicates that $object_1$, having structural description "$description_1$", is in position "$position_1$", in state "s_1". At the time of this writing, a particular set of "standard" structure descriptions has not yet been selected. So far several have been used. The simplest description is a point whose position is at the estimated center of gravity of the object. This description is used for the FORTRAN "push in a straight line" routine. Since all the objects in the robot's world are polyhedrons, reasonably simple complete structural descriptions are possible. For example, one structural description consists of the set of polygons that form the surface of the polyhedron. In turn, the structure of the polygons is given by the set of vertices in its boundary. Connectivity of structures can be stated explicitly or else implied by common boundaries. The position of an object is given by a mapping of the topologically-described structure into the robot's coordinate system. Such structural descriptions may be given as axioms or supplied by the scene-analysis programs used by the robot.

A basic axiom describing the robot's manipulation of an object is

R2.

$$(\forall s, obj_1, desc_1, pos_1, pos_2)[ATO(obj_1, desc_1, pos_1, s) \land$$
$$MOVABLE(obj_1) \land ROTATE\text{-}TRANSLATE\text{-}ABLE(desc_1,$$
$$pos_1, pos_2) \land OBJECT\text{-}PATH(desc_1, pos_1, pos_2,$$
$$path_{12}, s) \supset ATO(obj_1, desc_1, pos_2, push(obj_1,$$
$$path_{12}, s))]$$

This axiom says that if object 1, described by description 1, is at position 1, and object 1 is movable, and object 1 can be theoretically rotated and translated to the new position 2, and there is an object-path from 1 to 2, then object 1 will be at position 2 as a result of pushing it along the path. The predicate ROTATE-TRANSLATABLE($desc_1, pos_1, pos_2$) checks the necessary condition that the object can be theoretically rotated and translated into the new position. The predicate OBJECT-PATH($desc_1, pos_1, pos_2, path_{12}$) means that pos_2 is the estimated new position resulting from pushing along push-path, $path_{12}$.

Let us now return to the frame problem. More specifically, in a state resulting from pushing an object, how can we indicate the location of objects which were not pushed? One such axiom is

R3. $(\forall obj_1, obj_2, desc_1, pos_1, path_{12}, s)[ATO(obj_1,$
$desc_1, pos_1, s) \land \sim SAME(obj_1, obj_2) \supset$
$ATO(obj_1, desc_1, pos_1, push(obj_2, path_{12}, s))].$

This axiom says that all objects that are not the same as the pushed object are unmoved. The predicate evaluation mechanism is used to evaluate SAME and speed up the proof. One can use this predicate evaluation mechanism, and perhaps other fast methods for handling classes of deductions (such as special representations of state-dependent information and special programs for updating this information--which is done in the robot), but another problem remains. Observe that axiom R3 assumes that only the objects directly pushed by the robot move. This is not always the case, since an object being pushed might accidentally strike another object and move it. This leads to the question of dealing with the real world and using axioms to approximate the real world.

B. Real-World Problem Solving: Feedback

Our descriptions of the real world, axiomatic or otherwise, are at best only approximations. For example, the new position of an object moved by the robot will not necessarily be accurately predicted, even if one goes to great extremes to calculate a predicted new position. The robot does not have a grasp on the object so that some slippage may occur. The floor surface is not uniform and smooth. The weight distribution of objects is not known. There is only rudimentary kinesthetic sensing feedback--namely, whether or not the bumper is still in contact with the object. Thus it appears that a large feedback loop iterating toward a solution, is necessary: Form a plan for pushing the object (possibly using the push axiom), push according to the plan, back up, take a look, see where the object is, compare the position to the desired position, start over again. The new position (to some level of accuracy) is provided by the sensors of the robot. This new position is compared to the position predicted by the axiom. If the move is not successful, the predicate (provided by sensors in the new state) that reasonably accurately gives the object's position in the new state must be used as the description of the initial state for the next attempt.

This feedback method can be extended to sequences of actions. Consider the problem: Find s_f such that $P_3(s_f)$ is true. Suppose the starting state is s_0, with property $P_0(s_0)$. Suppose the axioms are as follows:

$$P_0(s_0)$$
$$(\forall s)[P_0(s) \supset P_1(f_1(s))]$$
$$(\forall s)[P_1(s) \supset P_2(f_2(s))]$$
$$(\forall s)[P_2(s) \supset P_3(f_3(s))].$$

The sequence of actions $f_3(f_2(f_1(s_0)))$ transforms state s_0 with property $P_0(s_0)$ into state s_f having property $P_3(s_f)$.

The solution is thus $s_f = f_3(f_2(f_1(s_0)))$.

Corresponding to each "theoretical" predicate $P_i(s)$ is a corresponding "real-word" predicate $P_i'(s)$. The truth value of $P_i'(s)$ is determined by sensors and the robot's internal model of the world. It has built-in bounds on how close its measurements must be to the correct values in order to assert that it is true.* The proof implies the following description of the result after each step of execution of $f_3(f_2(f_1(s_0)))$:

---

* At this time, a many-valued logic having degrees of truth is not used, although this is an interesting possibility.

Actions and Successive States	Predicted Theoretical Results	Predicted Real-World Results
s_0	$P_0(s_0)$	$P'_0(s_0)$
$s_1 = f_1(s_0)$	$P_1(s_1)$	$P'_1(s_1)$
$s_2 = f_2(s_1)$	$P_2(s_2)$	$P'_2(s_2)$
$s_f = f_3(s_2)$	$P_3(s_3)$	$P'_3(s_f)$

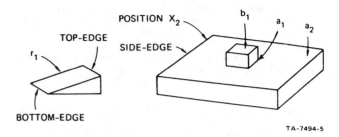

TA-7494-5

To measure progress after, say, the ith step, one checks that $P'_i(s_i)$ is true. If not, then some other condition $P''_i(s_i)$ holds and a new problem is generated, given $P''_i(s_i)$ as the starting point. If new information is present, such as is the case when the robot hits an obstacle that is not in its model, the model is updated before a new solution is attempted. The position of this new object of course invalidates the previous plan--i.e., had the new object's position been known, the previous plan would not have been generated.

The new solution may still be able to use that part of the old solution that is not invalidated by any new information. For example, if $P'_i(s_i)$ holds, it may still be possible to reach the jth intermediate state and then continue the planned sequence of actions from the jth state. However, the object-pushing axiom is an example of an axiom that probably will incorrectly predict results and yet no further information, except for the new position, will be available. For this case, the best approach is probably to iterate toward the target state by repeated use of the push axiom to generate a new plan. Hopefully, the process converges.

For a given axiomatization feedback does not necessarily make it any easier to find a proof. However, knowing that the system uses feedback allows us to choose a simpler and less accurate axiom system. Simple axiom systems can then lead to shorter proofs.

One can envision formalizing this entire problem-solving process, including the notion of feedback, verifying whether or not a given condition is met, updating the model, recursively calling the theorem prover, etc. The author has not attempted such a formalization, although he has written a first-order formalization of the theorem prover's own problem-solving strategy. This raises the very interesting possibility of self-modification of strategy; however, in practice such problems lie well beyond the current theorem-proving capacity of the program.

C. A Simple Robot Problem

Now let us consider a problem requiring the use of a ramp to roll onto a platform, as illustrated below.

The goal is to push the box b_1 from position x_1 to x_2. To get onto the platform, the robot must push the ramp r_1 to the platform, and then roll up the ramp onto the platform.

A simple problem formulation can use a special ramp-using axiom such as

R4. $(\forall x_1, x_2, s, \text{top-edge}, \text{bottom-edge}, \text{ramp}_1)$
$[\text{AT-RAMP}(\text{ramp}_1, \text{top-edge}, x_2, \text{bottom-edge},$
$x_1, s) \wedge \text{AT-PLATFORM}(\text{side-edge}, x_2, s) \supset$
$\text{AT}(\text{robot}, x_2, \text{climb}(\text{ramp}_1, x_1, s))]$

with the obvious meaning. Such a solution is quick but leaves much to be desired in terms of generality.

A more general problem statement is one in which the robot has a description of its own capabilities, and a translation of this statement of its abilities into the basic terms that describe its sensory and human-given model of the world. It then learns from a fundamental level to deal with the world. Such a knowledge doesn't make for the quickest solution to a frequently-encountered problem, but certainly does lend itself to learning, greater degrees of problem-solving, and self-reliance in a new problem situation.

Closer to this extreme of greatest generality is the following axiomatization.

R5. $(\forall x_1, x_2, r)[\text{RECTANGLE}(r, x_1, x_2) \wedge$
$\text{LESSP}(\text{maxslope}(r), k_0) \wedge \text{LESSP}(r_0, \text{width}(r))$
$\text{CLEAR}(\text{space}(r, h_0), s) \wedge \text{SOLID}(r) \supset$
$\text{PATH}(x_1, x_2, r)].$

This axiom says that r describes a rectangle having ends x_1 and x_2. The maximum slope is less than a constant k_0, the width of r is greater than the robot's width w_0, the space above r to the robot's height h_0 is clear, and the rectangle r has a solid surface.

Two paths can be joined as follows:

R6. $(\forall x_1, x_2, x_3, r_1, r_2)[PATH(x_1, x_2, r_1) \wedge$
         $PATH(x_2, x_3, r_2) \supset PATH(x_1, x_3, join(r_1, r_2))]$.

From these two axioms (R5 and R6), the push axiom (R2), and a recognition of a solid object that can be used as a ramp, a solution can be obtained in terms of climb, push, join, etc. This more general method of solution would of course be slower than using the special ramp axiom. On the other hand, the more general method will probably be more useful if the robot will be required to construct a ramp, or recognize and push over a potential ramp that is standing on its wide end.

The danger in trying the more general methods is that one may be asking the theorem prover to re-derive some significant portion of math or physics, in order to solve some simple problem.

VI.   Automatic Programming

A.   Introduction

The automatic writing, checking, and debugging of computer programs are problems of great interest both for their independent importance and as useful tools for intelligent machines. This section shows how a theorem prover can be used to solve certain automatic programming problems. The formalization given here will be used to precisely state and solve the problem of automatic generation of programs, including recursive programs, along with concurrent generation of proofs of the correctness of these programs. Thus any programs automatically written by this method have no errors.

We shall take LISP[12],[13] as our example of a programming language. In the LISP language, a function is described by two entities: (1) its value, and (2) its side effect. Side effects can be described in terms of their effect upon the state of the program. Methods for describing state-transformation operations, as well as methods for the automatic writing of programs in a state-transformation language, were presented in Secs. I and II. For simplicity, in this section we shall discuss "pure" LISP, in which a LISP function corresponds to the standard notion of a function--i.e., it has a value but no side effect.

Thus we shall use pure LISP 1.5 without the program feature, which is essentially the lambda calculus. In this restricted system, a LISP program is merely a function. For example, the LISP function car applied to a list returns the first element of the list. Thus if the variable x has as value the list (a b c), then car(x) = a. The LISP function cdr yields the remainder of the list, thus CDR(x) = (b c), and car(cdr(x)) = b. There are several approaches one may take in formalizing LISP; the one given here is a simple mapping from LISP's lambda calculus to the predicate calculus. LISP programs are represented by functions. The syntax of pure LISP 1.5, is normal function composition, and the corresponding syntax for the formalization is also function composition. LISP "predicates" are represented in LISP--and in this

formalization--as functions having either the value NIL (false) or else a value not equal to NIL (true). The semantics are given by axioms relating LISP functions to list structures, e.g., $(\forall x,y) car(cons(x,y)) = x$, where cons(x,y) is the list whose first element is x and whose remainder is y.

In our formulation of programming problems, we emphasize the distinction between the program (represented as a function in LISP), that solves a problem and a test for the validity of a solution to a problem (represented as a predicate in logic). It is often much easier to construct the predicate than it is to construct the function. Indeed, one may say that a problem is not well defined until an effective test for its solution is provided.

For example, suppose we wish to write a program that sorts a list. This problem is not fully specified until the meaning of "sort" is explained; and the method of explanation we choose is to provide a predicate R(x,y) that is true if list y is a sorted version of list x and false otherwise. (The precise method of defining this relation R will be given later.)

In general, our approach to using a theorem prover to solve programming problems in LISP requires that we give the theorem prover two sets of initial axioms:

(1)   Axioms defining the functions and constructs of the subset of LISP to be used

(2)   Axioms defining an input-output relation such as the relation R(x,y), which is to be true if and only if x is any input of the appropriate form for some LISP program and y is the corresponding output to be produced by such a program.

Given this relation R, and the LISP axioms, by having the theorem prover prove (or disprove) the appropriate question we can formulate the following four kinds of programming problems: checking, simulation, verifying (debugging), and program writing. These problems may be explained using the sort program as an example as follows:

(1) Checking: The form of the question is R(a,b) where a and b are two given lists. By proving R(a,b) true or false, b is checked to be either a sorted version of a or not. The desired answer is accordingly either yes or no.

(2) Simulation: The form of the question is $(\exists x)R(a,x)$, where a is a given input list. If the question $(\exists x)R(a,x)$ is answered yes, then a sorted version of x exists and a sorted version is constructed by the theorem prover. Thus the theorem prover acts as a sort program. If the answer is no, then it has proved that a sorted version of x does not exist (an impossible answer if a is a proper list).

(3) Verifying: The form of the question is $(\forall x)R(x,g(x))$, where g(x) is a program written

by the user. This mode is known as verifying, debugging, proving a program correct, or proving a program incorrect. If the answer to $(\forall x)R(x,g(x))$ is yes, then $g(x)$ sorts every proper input list and the program is correct. If the answer is no, a counterexample list c, that the program will not sort, must be constructed by the theorem prover. This mode requires induction axioms to prove that looping or recursive programs converge.

(4) Program Writing: The form of the question is $(\forall x)(\exists y)R(x,y)$. In this synthesis mode the program is to be constructed or else proved impossible to construct. If the answer is yes, then a program, say $f(x)$, must be constructed that will sort all proper input lists. If the answer is no, an unsortable list (impossible, in this case) must be produced. This mode also requires induction axioms. The form of the problem statement shown here is oversimplified for the sake of clarity. The exact form will be shown later.

In addition to the possibility of "yes" answer and the "no" answer, there is always the possibility of a "no proof found" answer if the search is halted by some time or space bound. The elimination of disjunctive answers, which is assumed in this section, was explained in Sec. B.

These methods are summarized in the following table. The reader may view $R(x,y)$ as representing some general desired input-output relationship.

Programming Problem	Form of Question	Desired Answer
(1) Checking	$R(a,b)$	yes or no
(2) Simulation	$(\exists x)R(a,x)$	yes, x = b or no
(3) Verifying	$(\forall x)R(x,g(x))$	yes or no, x = c
(4) Program Writing	$(\forall x)(\exists y)R(x,y)$	yes, y = f(x) or no, x = c

We now present an axiomatization of LISP followed by two axiomatizations of the sort relation R (one for a special case and one more general).

B. Axiomatization of a Subset of LISP

All LISP functions and predicates will be written in small letters. The functions "equal(x,y)," "at(x)," and "null(x)" evaluate to "nil" if false and something not equal to "nil," say "T," if true. The predicates of first-order logic that are used to describe LISP are written in capital letters. These, of course, have truth values.

The version of LISP described here does not distinguish between an S-expression and a copy of that S-expression. There is some redundancy in the following formulation, in that certain functions and predicates could have been defined in terms of others; however, the redundancy allows us to state the problem more concisely. Also, some axioms could have been eliminated since they are

derivable from others, but are included for clarity. The variables x, y, and z are bound by universal quantifiers, but the quantifiers are omitted for the sake of readability wherever possible. The formulation is given below:

Predicates	Meaning
NULL(x)	x = nil
LIST(x)	x is a list
ATOM(x)	x is an atom
x = y	x is equal to y

Functions	Meaning
car(x)	The first element of the list x.
cdr(x)	The rest of the list x.
cons(x,y)	If y is a list then the value of cons(x,y) is a new list that has x as its first element and y as the rest of the list, e.g., cons(1,(2 3)) = (1 2 3). If y is an atom instead of a list, cons(x,y) has as value a "dotted pair," e.g., cons(1,2) = (1·2).
cond(x,y,z)	The conditional statement, if x = nil then y else z. Note that the syntax of this function is slightly different than the usual LISP syntax.
nil	The null (empty) list containing no elements.
equal(x,y)	Equality test, whose value is "nil" if x does not equal y.
atom(x)	Atom test, whose value is "nil" if x is not an atom.
null(x)	Null test, whose value is "nil" if x is not equal to nil.

Axioms

L1: $x = car(cons(x,y))$

L2: $y = cdr(cons(x,y))$

L3: $\sim ATOM(x) \supset x = cons(car(x),cdr(x))$

L4: $\sim ATOM(cons(x,y))$

L5: $ATOM(nil)$

L6: $x = nil \supset cond(x,y,z) = z$

L7: $x \neq nil \supset cond(x,y,z) = y$

L8: $x = y \equiv equal(x,y) \neq nil$

L9: $ATOM(x) \equiv atom(x) \neq nil$

L10: $NULL(x) \equiv null(x) \neq nil$

C. A Simplified Sort Problem

Before examining a more general sort problem, consider the following very simple special case.

Instead of a list-sorting program, consider a program that "sorts" a dotted pair of two distinct numbers; i.e., given an input pair the program returns as an output pair the same two numbers, but the first number of the output pair must be smaller than the second. To specify such a program, we must define the simple version of R, $R_0(x,y)$. Let us say that a dotted pair of numbers is "sorted" if the first number is less than the second. Thus $R_0(x,y)$ is true if and only if y equals x when x is sorted and y is the reverse of x when x is not sorted. Stated more precisely, we have

R1.　$(\forall x,y)\{R_0(x,y) \equiv [[car(x) < cdr(x) \supset y = x]$

$\wedge [car(x) \nless cdr(x) \supset car(y) = cdr(x) \wedge$

$cdr(y) = car(x)]]\}$.

The correspondence of the LISP "lessp" function to the "less-than" relation is provided in the following axiom:

R2.　$(\forall x,y)[lessp(x,y) \neq nil \equiv x < y]$.

Using the predicate R_0 we will give examples of four programming problems and their solutions:

(1) Checking:

　　Q:　$R_0(cons(2,1),cons(1,2))$

　　A:　yes

(2) Simulation:

　　Q:　$(\exists x)R_0(cons(2,1),x)$

　　A:　yes, x = cons(1,2)

(3) Verifying:

　　Q:　$(\forall x)R_0(x,cond(lessp(car(x),cdr(x)),x,$

　　　　$cons(cdr(x),car(x)))$

　　A:　yes

Thus the program supplied by the user is correct.

(4) Program writing:

　　Q:　$(\forall x)(\exists x)R_0(x,y)$

　　A:　yes, y = cond(lessp(car(x),cdr(x)),

　　　　x,cons(cdr(x),car(x)))

Translated into a more readable form, the program is:

　　if car(x) < cdr(x) **then** x **else**

　　　　cons(cdr(x),car(x)).

Given only the necessary axioms--L1, L2, L6, L7, R1, and R2--QA3 found a proof that constructed the sort program shown above. The paramodulation[14],[15] rule of inference was used to handle equality.

We now turn to a more difficult problem.

D.　The Sort Axioms

The definition of the predicate R is in terms of the predicates ON and SD. The meaning of these predicates is given below:

　　R(x,y)　A predicate stating that if x is a list of numbers with no number occurring more than once in the list, then y is a list containing the same elements as x, and y is sorted, i.e., the numbers are arranged in order of increasing size.

　　ON(x,y)　A predicate stating that x is an element on the list y.

　　SD(x)　A predicate stating that the list x is sorted.

First we define R(x,y), that y is a sorted version of x, as follows:

S1.　$(\forall x,y)\{R(x,y) \equiv [(\forall z)[ON(z,x) \equiv ON(z,y)] \wedge$

$SD(y)]$

Thus a sorted version y of list x contains the same elements as x and is sorted.

Next we define, recursively, the predicate ON(x,y):

S2.　$(\forall x,y)\{ON(x,y) \equiv [\sim ATOM(y) \wedge [x = car(y) \vee$

$ON(x,cdr(y))]]\}$

This axiom states that x is on y if and only if x is the first element of y or if x is on the rest of y.

Next we define the meaning of a sorted list:

S3.　$(\forall x)\{SD(x) \equiv [NULL(x) \vee [\sim ATOM(x) \wedge$

$NULL(cdr(x))] \vee [\sim ATOM(x) \wedge \sim NULL(cdr(x)) \wedge$

$car(x) \leq car(cdr(x)) \wedge SD(cdr(x))]]\}$.

This axiom states that x is sorted if and only if x is empty, or x contains only one element, or the first element of x is less than the second element and the rest of x is sorted.

To simplify the problem statement we assume that the arguments of the predicates and functions range only over the proper type of objects--i.e., either numbers or lists. In effect, we are assuming that the input list will indeed be a properly formed list of numbers. (The problem statement could be modified to specify correct types by using predicates such as NUMBERP(x)--true only if x is, say, a real number).

The problem is made simpler by using a "merge" function. This function, and a predicate P describing the merge function are named and described as follows:

sort(x)   A LISP sort function (to be constructed) giving as its value a sorted version of x.

merge(x,u)   A LISP merge function merging x into the sorted list u, such that the list returned contains the elements of u, and also contains x, and this list is sorted.

P(x,u,y)   A predicate stating that y is the result of merging x into the sorted list u.

We define P(x,u,y), that y is u with x merged into it:

S4. $(\forall x,u,y)\{P(x,u,y) \equiv [SD(u) \supset [SD(y) \wedge$

$(\forall z)(ON(z,y) \equiv (ON(z,u) \vee z = x))]]\}.$

Thus P(x,u,y) holds if and only if the fact that u is sorted implies that y contains x in addition to the elements of u, and y is sorted. One such merge function is merge(x,u) = cond(null(u),cons(x,u), cond(lessp(x,car(u)),cons(x,u),cons(car(u),merge(x, cdr(u))))).

The axiom required to describe the merge function is:

S5. $(\forall x,u)P(x,u,merge(x,u)).$

This completes a description of the predicates ON, SD, R, and P. Together, these specify the input-output relation for a sort function and a merge function. Before posing the problems to the theorem prover, we need to introduce axioms that describe the convergence of recursive functions.

E.   Induction Axioms

In order to prove that a recursive function converges to the proper value, the theorem prover requires an induction axiom. An example of an induction principle is that if one keeps taking "cdr" of a finite list, one will reach the end of the list in a finite number of steps. This is analogous to an induction principle on the nonnegative integers, i.e., let "P" be a predicate, and "h" a function. Then for finite lists,

$[P(h(nil)) \wedge (\forall x) [\sim ATOM(x) \wedge P(h(cdr(x))) \supset$

$P(h(x))]] \supset (\forall z)P(h(z))$

is analogous to

$[P(h(0)) \wedge (\forall n)[n \neq 0 \wedge P(h(n-1)) \supset$

$P(h(n))]] \supset (\forall m)P(h(m))$

for nonnegative integers.

There are other kinds of induction criteria besides the one given above. Unfortunately, for each recursive function that is to be shown to converge, the appropriate induction axiom must be carefully formulated by the user. The induction axiom also serves the purpose of introducing the

name of the function to be written. We will now give the problem statement for the sort program, introducing appropriate induction information where necessary.

F.   The Sort Problem

Examples illustrating the four kinds of problems are shown below.

(1) Checking:

   Q: R(cons(2,cons(1,nil)),cons(1,cons(2,nil)))

   A: yes

(2) Simulation:

   Q: $(\exists x)R(cons(2,cons(1,nil)),x)$

   A: yes, x = cons(1,cons(2,nil))

(3) Verifying: Now consider the verifying or debugging problem. Suppose we are given a proposed definition of a sort function and we want to know if it is correct. Suppose the proposed definition is

S6. $(\forall x)[sort(x) \equiv cond(null(x),nil,merge(car(x),$

$sort(cdr(x))))].$

Thus sort is defined in terms of car, cdr, cond, null, merge, and sort. Each of these functions except sort is already described by previously given axioms. We also need the appropriate induction axiom in terms of sort. Of course, the particular induction axiom needed depends on the definition of the particular sort function given. For this sort function the particular induction axiom needed is

S7. $[R(nil,sort(nil)) \wedge (\forall x)[\sim ATOM(x) \wedge$

$R(cdr(x),sort(cdr(x))) \supset R(x,sort(x))]] \supset$

$(\forall y)R(y,sort(y)).$

The following conjecture can then be posed to the theorem prover:

   Q: $(\forall x)R(x,sort(x))$

   A: yes

(4) Program writing: The next problem is that of synthesizing or writing a sort function. We assume, of course, that no definition such as S6 is provided. Certain information needed for this particular problem might be considered to be a part of this particular problem statement rather than a part of the data base. We shall phrase the question so that in addition to its primary purpose of asking for a solution, the question provides three more pieces of information: (a) The question assigns a name to the function that is to be constructed. A recursive function is defined in terms of itself, so to construct this definition the name of the function must be known (or else created internally). (b) The question specifies the number of arguments of the function that is to be considered.

(c) The question (rather than an induction axiom) gives the particular inductive hypothesis to be used in constructing the function.

In this form, the question and answer are

$$Q: \quad (\forall x)(\exists y)\{R(nil,y) \wedge [[\sim ATOM(x) \wedge$$
$$R(cdr(x),sort(cdr(x)))] \supset R(x,y)]\}$$

$$A: \quad yes, \ y = cond(equal(x,nil),nil,merge$$
$$(car(x),sort(cdr(x)))).$$

Thus the question names the function to be "sort" and specifies that it is a function of one argument. The question gives the inductive hypothesis-- that the function sorts cdr(x)--and then asks for a function that sorts x. When the answer y is found, y is labeled to be the function sort(x).

Using this formulation QA3 was unable to write the sort program in a reasonable amount of time, although the author did find a correct proof within the resolution formalism*. The creation of the merge function can also be posed to the theorem prover by the same methods.

G.   Discussion of Automatic Programming Problems

The axioms and conjectures given here illus- trate the fundamental ideas of automatic program- ming. However, this work as well as earlier work by Simon,[16] Slagle,[17] Floyd,[18] Manna,[19] and others pro- vides merely a small part of what needs to be done. Below we present discussion of issues that might profit from fruther investigation.

Loops. One obvious extension of this method is to create programs that have loops rather than recursion. A simple technique exists for carrying out this operation. First, one writes just recurs- ive functions. Many recursive functions can then be converted into iteration--i.e., faster-running loops that do not use a stack. McCarthy[20] gives criteria that determine how to convert recursion to iteration. An algorithm for determining cases in which recursion can be converted to iteration, and then performing the conversion process is embedded in modern LISP compilers. This algorithm could be applied to recursive functions written by the theorem-proving program.

Separation of Aspects of Problem Solving. Let us divide information into three types: (1) Infor- mation concerning the problem description and semantics. An example of such information is given in the axiom $AT(a,s_0)$, or axiom S1 that defines a sorted list. (2) Information concerning the target programming language, such as the axiom $[x = nil \supset cond(x,y,z) = z]$. (3) Information concerning the interrelation of the problem and the target lan- guage, such as $[LESS(x,y) \equiv lessp(x,y) \neq nil]$.

These kinds of information are not, of course, mutually exclusive.

In the axiom systems presented, no distinction is made between such classes of information. Con- sequently, during the search for a proof the theorem prover might attempt to use axioms of type 1 for pur- poses where it needs information of type 2. Such attempts lead nowhere and generate useless clauses. However, as discussed in Sec. II-G, we can place in the proof strategy our knowledge of when such infor- mation is to be used, thus leading to more efficient proofs. One such method--calling for the conditional axioms at the right time, as discussed in Sec. II-G-- has been implemented in QA3.

The PROW program of Waldinger and Lee[6] provides a very promising method of separating the problem of proof construction from the problem of program construction. In their system, the only axioms used are those that describe the subject--i.e., state the problem. Their proof that a solution exists does not directly construct the program. Instead, information about the target programming language, as well as information about the relation- ship of the target-programming language to the problem-statement language, is in another part of the PROW program--the "post-processor." The post- processor then uses this information to convert the completed proof into a program. The post- processor also converts recursion into loops and allows several target programming languages.

If our goal is to do automatic programming involving complex programs, we will probably wish to do some optimization or problem solving on the target language itself. For this reason we might want to have axioms that give the semantics of the target language, and also allow the intercommunica- tion of information in the problem-statement lan- guage with information in the target language. Two possibilities for how to do this efficiently suggest themselves: (a) Use the methods presented here in which all information is in first-order logic. To gain efficiency, use special problem- solving strategies that minimize unnecessary inter- action; (b) Use a higher-order logic system, in which the program construction is separated from the proof construction, possibly by being at another level. The program construction process might then be described in terms of the first- order existence proof.

Problem Formulation. The axiomatization given here has considerable room for improvement: Missing portions of LISP include the program features and the use of lambda to bind variables. The functions to be written must be named by the user, and the number of arguments must also be specified by the user.

Heuristics for Program-Writing Problems. Two heuristics have been considered so far. The first consists of examining the program as it is con- structed (by looking inside the answer literal). Even though the syntax is guaranteed correct, the answer literal may contain various nonsense or undefined constructions (such as car(nil)). Any

---

* After this paper was written the problem was re- formulated using a different set of axioms. In the new formulation QA3 created the sort program "sort(x) = cond(x,merge(car(x),sort(cdr(x))),nil).

clause containing such constructed answers should be eliminated. Another heuristic is to actually run the partial program by a pseudo-LISP interpreter on a sample problem. The theorem prover knows the correct performance on these sample problems because they have either been solutions or else counterexamples to program-simulation questions that were stored in memory, or else they have been provided by the user. If the pseudo-LISP interpreter can produce a partial output that is incorrect, the partial program can be eliminated. If done properly, such a method might be valuable, but in our limited experience, its usefulness is not yet clear.

Higher-Level Programming Concepts. A necessary requirement for practical program writing is the development of higher-level concepts (such as the LISP "map" function) that describe the use of frequently employed constructs (functions) or partial constructs.

Induction. The various methods of proof by induction should be studied further and related to the kinds of problems in which they are useful. The automatic selection or generation of appropriate induction axioms would be most helpful.

Program Segmentation. Another interesting problem is that of automatically generating the specifications for the subfunctions to be called before writing these functions. For example, in our system, the sort problem was divided into two problems: First, specify and create a merge function, next specify a sort function and then construct this function in terms of the merge function. The segmentation into two problems and the specification of each problem was provided by the user.

VII. Discussion

The theorem prover may be considered an "interpreter" for a high-level assertional or declarative language--logic. As in the case with most high-level programming languages the user may be somewhat distant from the efficiency of "logic" programs unless he knows something about the strategies of the system.

The first applications of QA2 and QA3 were to "question answering." Typical question-answering applications are usually easy for a resolution-type theorem prover. Examples of such easy problem sets given QA3 include the questions done by Raphael's SIR,[21] Slagle's DEDUCOM,[17] and Cooper's chemistry question-answering program.[22] Usually there are a few obvious formulations for some subject area, and any reasonable formulation works well. As one goes to harder problems like the Tower of Hanoi puzzle, and program-writing problems, good and reasonably well-thought-out representations are necessary for efficient problem solving.

Some representations are better than others only because of the particular strategy used to search for a proof. It would be desirable if the theorem prover could adopt the best strategy for a given problem and representation, or even change the representation. I don't believe these goals are impossible, but at present it is not done. However, a library of strategy programs and a strategy language is slowly evolving in QA3. To change strategies in the present version the user must know about set-of-support and other program parameters such as level bound[1] and term-depth bound. To radically change the strategy, the user presently has to know the LISP language and must be able to modify certain strategy sections of the program. In practice, several individuals who have used the system have modified the search strategies to suit their needs. To add and debug a new heuristic or to modify a search strategy where reprogramming is required seems to take from a few minutes to several days, perhaps averaging one day. Ultimately it is intended that the system will be able to write simple strategy programs itself, and "understand" the semantics of its strategies.

Experience with the robot applications and the automatic programming applications emphasize the need for a very versatile logical system. A suitable higher-order logic system seems to be one of the best candidates. Several recent papers are relevant to this topic. A promising higher order system has been proposed by Robinson.[23] Banerji[24] discusses a higher order language. One crucial factor in an inference system is a suitable method for the treatment of the equality relation. Discussion of methods for the treatment of equality is provided by Wos and Robinson,[14] and Robinson and Wos,[15] and Kowalski.[25] McCarthy and Hayes[5] include a discussion of modal logics.

The theorem-proving program can be used as an experimental tool in the testing of problem formulations. In exploring difficult problems it can be useful to write a computer program to test a problem formulation and solution technique, since the machine tends to sharpen one's understanding of the problem. I believe that in some problem-solving applications the "high-level language" of logic along with a theorem-proving program can be a quick programming method for testing ideas. One reason is that a representation in the form of an axiom system can correspond quite closely to one's conceptualization of a problem. Another reason is that it is sometimes easier to reformulate an axiom system rather than to rewrite a problem-solving program, and this ease of reformulation facilitates exploration.

Resolution theorem-proving methods are shown in this paper to have the potential to serve as a general problem-solving system. A modified theorem-proving program can write simple robot problems, and solve simple puzzles. Much work remains to be done before such a system is capable of solving problems that are difficult by human standards.

Acknowledgment

I would like to acknowledge valuable discussions with Dr. Bertram Raphael and Mr. Robert Yates.

REFERENCES

1. J. A. Robinson, "The Present State of Mechanical Theorem Proving," a paper presented at the Fourth Systems Symposium, Cleveland, Ohio, November 19-20, 1968 (proceedings to be published).

2. C. Green and B. Raphael, "The Use of Theorem-Proving Techniques in Question-Answering Systems," Proc. 23rd Nat'l. Conf. ACM, (Thompson Book Company, Washington, D.C., 1968).

3. C. Green, "Theorem Proving by Resolution as a Basis for Question-Answering Systems," Machine Intelligence 4, D. Michie and B. Meltzer, Eds. (Edinburgh University Press, Edinburgh, Scotland, 1969).

4. N. J. Nilsson, "A Mobile Automaton: An Application of Artificial Intelligence Techniques," a paper presented at the International Joint Conference on Artificial Intelligence, Washington, D.C., May 7-9, 1969 (proceedings to be published).

5. J. McCarthy and P. Hayes, "Some Philosophical Problems from the Standpoint of Artificial Intelligence," Machine Intelligence 4, D. Michie and B. Meltzer, Eds. (Edinburgh University Press, Edinburgh, Scotland, 1969).

6. R. J. Waldinger and R. C. T. Lee, "PROW: A Step Toward Automatic Program Writing," a paper presented at the International Joint Conference on Artificial Intelligence, Washington, D.C., May 7-9, 1969 (proceedings to be published).

7. L. Wos, G. A. Robinson, and D. F. Carson, "Efficiency and Completeness of the Set of Support Strategy in Theorem Proving," J.ACM, Vol. 12, No. 4, pp. 536-541 (October 1965).

8. J. A. Robinson, "A Machine-Oriented Logic Based on the Resolution Principle," J.ACM, Vol. 12, No. 1, pp. 23-41 (January 1965).

9. George Ernst, "Sufficient Conditions for the Success of GPS," Report No. SRC-68-17, Systems Research Center, Case Western Reserve University, Celveland, Ohio (July 1968).

10. A. Hormann, "How a Computer System Can Learn," IEEE Spectrum (July 1964).

11. L. S. Coles, "Talking With a Robot in English," paper submitted at the International Joint Conference on Artificial Intelligence, Washington, D.C., May 7-9, 1969 (proceedings to be published).

12. John McCarthy, Paul W. Abrahams, Daniel J. Edwards, Timothy P. Hart, and Michael I. Levin, LISP 1.5 Programmer's Manual (The MIT Press, Cambridge, Mass., 1962).

13. C. Weissman, LISP 1.5 Primer (Dickenson Publishing Company, Inc., Belmont, Calif., 1967).

14. Lawrence Wos and George Robinson, "Paramodulation and Set of Support," summary of paper presented at the IRIA Symposium on Automatic Demonstration at Versailles, France, December 16-21, 1968 (proceedings to be published).

15. G. Robinson and L. Wos, "Paramodulation and Theorem-Proving in First-Order Theories with Equality," Machine Intelligence 4, B. Meltzer and D. Michie, Eds. (Edinburgh University Press, Edinburgh, Scotland, 1969).

16. H. Simon, "Experiments with a Heuristic Compiler," J.ACM, Vol. 10, pp. 493-506 (October 1963).

17. J. R. Slagle, "Experiments with a Deductive, Question-Answering Program," Comm. ACM, Vol. 8, pp. 792-798 (December 1965).

18. R. W. Floyd, "The Verifying Compiler," Computer Science Research Review, Carnegie Mellon University (December 1967).

19. Z. Manna, "The Correctness of Programs," J. Computer and Systems Sciences, Vol. 3 (1969).

20. J. McCarthy, "Towards a Mathematical Science of Computation," Proceedings ICIP (North Holland Publishing Company, Amsterdam, 1962).

21. B. Raphael, "A Computer Program Which 'Understands'," Proc. FJCC, pp. 577-589 (1964).

22. W. S. Cooper, "Fact Retrieval and Deductive Question Answering Information Retrieval Systems," J.ACM, Vol. 11, pp. 117-137 (April 1964).

23. J. A. Robinson, "Mechanizing Higher Order Logic," Machine Intelligence 4, D. Michie and B. Meltzer, Eds. (Edinburgh University Press, Edinburgh, Scotland, 1969).

24. R. B. Banerji, "A Language for Pattern Recognition," Pattern Recognition, Vol. 1, No. 1, pp. 63-74 (1968).

25. R. Kowalski, "The Case for Using Equality Axioms in Automatic Demonstration," paper presented at the IRIA Symposium on Automatic Demonstration at Versailles, France, December 16-21, 1968 (proceedings to be published).

APPENDIX

The axioms for the Monkey and Bananas problem are listed below, followed by the proof. The term SK24(S,P2,P1,B) that first appears in clause 16 of the proof is a Skolem function generated by the elimination of (∀x) in the conversion of axiom MB4 to quantifier-free clause form. (One may think of it as the object that is not at place P2 in state S.)

LIST MONKEY

MB1   (MOVABLE BOX)

MB2   (FA(X)(NOT(AT X UNDER-BANANAS SØ)))

MB3   (AT BOX PLACEB SØ)

MB4   (FA(B P1 P2 S)(IF(AND(AT B P1 S)(MOVABLE B)(FA(X)(NOT(AT X P2 S))))(AND(AT MONKEY P2 (MOVE(MONKEY B P2 S))(AT B P2(MOVE MONKEY B P2 S)))))

MB5   (FA(S)(CLIMBABLE MONKEY BOX S))

MB6   (FA(M P B S)(IF(AND(AT B P S)(CLIMBABLE M B S))(AND(AT B P(CLIMB M B S))(ON M B (CLIMB M B S)))))

MB7   (FA(S)(IF(AND(AT BOX UNDER-BANANAS S)(ON MONKEY BOX S))(REACHABLE MONKEY BANANAS S)))

MB8   (FA(M B S)(IF(REACHABLE M B S)(HAS M B(REACH M B S))))

DONE

Q   (EX(S)(HAS MONKEY BANANAS S))

A   YES, S = REACH(MONKEY,BANANAS,CLIMB(MONKEY,BOX,MOVE(MONKEY,BOX,UNDER-BANANAS,SØ)))

PROOF

1	-AT(X,UNDER-BANANAS,SØ)	AXIOM
2	AT(BOX,PLACEB,SØ)	AXIOM
3	CLIMBABLE(MONKEY,BOX,S)	AXIOM
4	-HAS(MONKEY,BANANAS,S)	NEG OF THM
	ANSWER(S)	
5	HAS(M,B,REACH(M,B,S)) -REACHABLE(M,B,S)	AXIOM
6	-REACHABLE(MONKEY,BANANAS,S)	FROM 4,5
	ANSWER(REACH(MONKEY,BANANAS,S))	
7	REACHABLE(MONKEY,BANANAS,S) -AT(BOX,UNDER-BANANAS,S) -ON(MONKEY,BOX,S)	AXIOM
8	-AT(BOX,UNDER-BANANAS,S) -ON(MONKEY,BOX,S)	FROM 6,7
	ANSWER(REACH(MONKEY,BANANAS,S))	
9	ON(M,B,CLIMB(M,B,S)) -AT(B,P,S) -CLIMBABLE(M,B,S)	AXIOM
10	-AT(BOX,UNDER-BANANAS,CLIMB(MONKEY,BOX,S)) -AT(BOX,P,S) -CLIMBABLE(MONKEY,BOX,S)	FROM 8,9
	ANSWER(REACH(MONKEY,BANANAS,CLIMB(MONKEY,BOX,S)))	
11	-AT(BOX,UNDER-BANANAS,CLIMB(MONKEY,BOX,S)) -AT(BOX,P,S)	FROM 3,10
	ANSWER(REACH(MONKEY,BANANAS,CLIMB(MONKEY,BOX,S)))	
12	AT(B,P,CLIMB(M,B,S)) -AT(B,P,S) -CLIMBABLE(M,B,S)	AXIOM
13	-AT(BOX,XX1,S) -AT(BOX,UNDER-BANANAS,S) -CLIMBABLE(MONKEY,BOX,S)	FROM 11,12
	ANSWER(REACH(MONKEY,BANANAS,CLIMB(MONKEY,BOX,S)))	
14	-AT(BOX,XX1,S) -AT(BOX,UNDER-BANANAS,S)	FROM 3,13
	ANSWER(REACH(MONKEY,BANANAS,CLIMB(MONKEY,BOX,S)))	
15	-AT(BOX,UNDER-BANANAS,X)	FACTOR 14
	ANSWER(REACH(MONKEY,BANANAS,CLIMB(MONKEY,BOX,S)))	
16	AT(B,P2,MOVE(MONKEY,B,P2,S)) -MOVABLE(B) -AT(B,P1,S) AT(SK24(S,P2,P1,B),P2,S)	AXIOM

```
17   -MOVABLE(BOX)   -AT(BOX,P1,S)   AT(SK24(S,UNDER-BANANAS,P1,BOX),UNDER-BANANAS,S)       FROM 15,16
         ANSWER(REACH(MONKEY,BANANAS,CLIMB(MONKEY,BOX,MOVE(MONKEY,BOX,UNDER-BANANAS,S))))
18   -MOVABLE(BOX)   AT(SK24(SØ,UNDER-BANANAS,PLACEB,BOX),UNDER-BANANAS,SØ)                  FROM 2,17
         ANSWER(REACH(MONKEY,BANANAS,CLIMB(MONKEY,BOX,MOVE(MONKEY,BOX,UNDER-BANANAS,SØ))))
19   -MOVABLE(BOX)                                                                          FROM 1,18
         ANSWER(REACH(MONKEY,BANANAS,CLIMB(MONKEY,BOX,MOVE(MONKEY,BOX,UNDER-BANANAS,SØ))))
20   MOVABLE(BOX)                                                                           AXIOM
21   CONTRADICTION                                                                          FROM 19,20
         ANSWER(REACH(MONKEY,BANANAS,CLIMB(MONKEY,BOX,MOVE(MONKEY,BOX,UNDER-BANANAS,SØ))))

11 CLAUSES LEFT
28 CLAUSES GENERATED
22 CLAUSES ENTERED
```

STRIPS: A New Approach to the Application of Theorem Proving to Problem Solving[1]

Richard E. Fikes
Nils J. Nilsson

Stanford Research Institute. Menlo Park. California

Recommended by B. Raphael

Presented at the 2nd IJCAI. Imperial College. London, England. September 1–3, 1971.

ABSTRACT

We describe a new problem solver called STRIPS that attempts to find a sequence of operators in a space of world models to transform a given initial world model into a model in which a given goal formula can be proven to be true. STRIPS represents a world model as an arbitrary collection of first-order predicate calculus formulas and is designed to work with models consisting of large numbers of formulas. It employs a resolution theorem prover to answer questions of particular models and uses means-ends analysis to guide it to the desired goal-satisfying model.

DESCRIPTIVE TERMS
Problem solving, theorem proving. robot planning, heuristic search.

1. Introduction

This paper describes a new problem-solving program called STRIPS (*ST*anford *R*esearch *I*nstitute *P*roblem *S*olver). An initial version of the program has been implemented in LISP on a PDP-10 and is being used in conjunction with robot research at SRI. STRIPS is a member of the class of problem solvers that search a space of "world models" to find one in which a given goal is achieved. For any world model, we assume that there exists a set

[1] The research reported herein was sponsored by the Advanced Research Projects Agency and the National Aeronautics and Space Administration under Contract NAS12-2221.

of applicable operators, each of which transforms the world model to some other world model. The task of the problem solver is to find some composition of operators that transforms a given initial world model into one that satisfies some stated goal condition.

This framework for problem solving has been central to much of the research in artificial intelligence [1]. Our primary interest here is in the class of problems faced by a robot in re-arranging objects and in navigating, i.e., problems that require quite complex and general world models compared to those needed in the solution of puzzles and games. In puzzles and games, a simple matrix or list structure is usually adequate to represent a state of the problem. The world model for a robot problem solver, however, must include a large number of facts and relations dealing with the position of the robot and the positions and attributes of various objects, open spaces, and boundaries. In STRIPS, a world model is represented by a set of well-formed formulas (wffs) of the first-order predicate calculus.

Operators are the basic elements from which a solution is built. For robot problems, each operator corresponds to an *action routine*[2] whose execution causes a robot to take certain actions. For example, we might have a routine that causes it to go through a doorway, a routine that causes it to push a box, and perhaps dozens of others.

Green [4] implemented a problem-solving system that depended exclusively on formal theorem-proving methods to search for the appropriate sequence of operators. While Green's formulation represented a significant step in the development of problem-solvers, it suffered some serious disadvantages connected with the "frame problem"[3] that prevented it from solving nontrivial problems.

In STRIPS, we surmount these difficulties by separating entirely the processes of theorem proving from those of searching through a space of world models. This separation allows us to employ separate strategies for these two activities and thereby improve the overall performance of the system. Theorem-proving methods are used only *within* a given world model to answer questions about it concerning which operators are applicable and whether or not goals have been satisfied. For searching through the space of world models, STRIPS uses a GPS-like means-end analysis strategy [6]. This com-

[2] The reader should keep in mind the distinction between an *operator* and its associated *action routine*. Execution of action routines actually causes the robot to take actions. Application of operators to world models occurs during the planning (i.e., problem solving) phase when an attempt is being made to find a sequence of operators whose associated action routines will produce a desired state of the world. (See the papers by Munson [2] and Fikes [3] for discussions of the relationships between STRIPS and the robot executive and monitoring functions.)

[3] Space does not allow a full discussion of the frame problem; for a thorough treatment, see [5].

bination of means-ends analysis and formal theorem-proving methods allows objects (world models) much more complex and general than any of those used in GPS and provides more powerful search heuristics than those found in theorem-proving programs.

We proceed by describing the operation of STRIPS in terms of the conventions used to represent the search space for a problem and the search methods used to find a solution. We then discuss the details of implementation and present some examples.

2. The Operation of STRIPS

2.1. The Problem Space

The problem space for STRIPS is defined by the initial world model, the set of available operators and their effects on world models, and the goal statement.

As already mentioned, STRIPS represents a world model by a set of well-formed formulas (wffs). For example, to describe a world model in which the robot is at location a and boxes B and C are at locations b and c we would include the following wffs:

$$ATR(a)$$
$$AT(B, b)$$
$$AT(C, c).$$

We might also include the wff

$$(\forall u\, \forall x\, \forall y)\{[AT(u, x) \land (x \neq y)] \Rightarrow\, \sim AT(u, y)\}$$

to state the general rule that an object in one place is not in a different place. Using first-order predicate calculus wffs, we can represent quite complex world models and can use existing theorem-proving programs to answer questions about a model.

The available operators are grouped into families called schemata. Consider for example the operator *goto* for moving the robot from one point on the floor to another. Here there is really a distinct operator for each different pair of points, but it is convenient to group all of these into a family goto (m, n) parameterized by the initial position[4] m and the final position n. We say that goto (m, n) is an operator *schema* whose members are obtained by substituting specific constants for the *parameters* m and n. In STRIPS, when an operator is applied to a world model, specific constants will already have been chosen for the operator parameters.

Each operator is defined by an operator description consisting of two main

[4] The parameters m and n are each really vector-valued, but we avoid vector notation here for simplicity. In general, we denote constants by letters near the beginning of the alphabet $(a, b, c, \ldots)$, parameters by letters in the middle of the alphabet $(m, n, \ldots)$, and quantified variables by letters near the end of the alphabet (x, y, z).

parts: a description of the effects of the operator, and the conditions under which the operator is applicable. The effects of an operator are simply defined by a list of wffs that must be added to the model and a list of wffs that are no longer true and therefore must be deleted. We shall discuss the process of calculating these effects in more detail later. It is convenient to state the applicability condition, or *precondition*, for an operator schema as a *wff schema*. To determine whether or not there is an instance of an operator schema applicable to a world model, we must be able to prove that there is an instance of the corresponding wff schema that logically follows from the model.

For example, consider the question of applying instances of the operator subschema goto (m, b) to a world model containing the wff ATR(a), where a and b are constants. If the precondition wff schema of goto (m, n) is ATR(m), then we find that the instance ATR(a) can be proved from the world model. Thus, an applicable instance of goto(m, b) is goto(a, b).

It is important to distinguish between the parameters appearing in wff schemata and ordinary existentially and universally quantified variables that may also appear. Certain modifications must be made to theorem-proving programs to enable them to handle wff schemata; these are discussed later.

Goal statements are also represented by wffs. For example, the task "Get Boxes B and C to Location a" might be stated as the wff:

$$AT(B, a) \land AT(C, a).$$

To summarize, the problem space for STRIPS is defined by three entities:

(1) An initial world model, which is a set of wffs describing the present state of the world.
(2) A set of operators, including a description of their effects and their precondition wff schemata.
(3) A goal condition stated as a wff.

The problem is solved when STRIPS produces a world model that satisfies the goal wff.

2.2. The Search Strategy

In a very simple problem-solving system, we might first apply all of the applicable operators to the initial world model to create a set of successor models. We would continue to apply all applicable operators to these successors and to their descendants (say in breadth-first fashion) until a model was produced in which the goal formula was a theorem. However, since we envision uses in which the number of operators applicable to any given world model might be quite large, such a simple system would generate an undesirably large tree of world models and would thus be impractical.

Instead, we have adopted the GPS strategy of extracting "differences" between the present world model and the goal and of identifying operators that are "relevant" to reducing these differences [6]. Once a relevant operator has been determined, we attempt to solve the subproblem of producing a world model to which it is applicable. If such a model is found, then we apply the relevant operator and reconsider the original goal in the resulting model. In this section, we review this basic GPS search strategy as employed by STRIPS.

STRIPS begins by employing a theorem prover to attempt to prove that the goal wff G_0 follows from the set M_0 of wffs describing the initial world model. If G_0 does follow from M_0, the task is trivially solved in the initial model. Otherwise, the theorem prover will fail to find a proof. In this case, the uncompleted proof is taken to be the "difference" between M_0 and G_0. Next, operators that might be relevant to "reducing" this difference are sought. These are the operators whose effects on world models would enable the proof to be continued. In determining relevance, the parameters of the operators may be partially or fully instantiated. The corresponding instantiated precondition wff schemata (of the relevant operators) are then taken to be new subgoals.

Consider the trivially simple example in which the task is for the robot to go to location b. The goal wff is thus ATR(b), and unless the robot is already at location b, the initial proof attempt will be unsuccessful. Now, certainly the instance goto(m, b) of the operator goto(m, n) is relevant to reducing the difference because its effect would allow the proof to be continued (in this case, completed). Accordingly, the corresponding precondition wff schema, say ATR(m), is used as a subgoal.

STRIPS works on a subgoal using the same technique. Suppose the precondition wff schema G is selected as the first subgoal to be worked on. STRIPS again uses a theorem prover in an attempt to find instances of G that follow from the initial world model M_0. Here again, there are two possibilities. If no proof can be found, STRIPS uses the incomplete proof as a difference, and sets up (sub) subgoals corresponding to their precondition wffs. If STRIPS does find an instance of G that follows from M_0, then the corresponding operator instance is used to transform M_0 into a new world model M_1. In our previous simple example, the subgoal wff schema G was ATR(m). If the initial model contains the wff ATR(a), then an instance of G— namely ATR(a)—can be proved from M_0. In this case, the corresponding operator instance goto(a, b) is applied to M_0 to produce the new model, M_1. STRIPS then continues by attempting to prove G_0 from M_1. In our example, G_0 trivially follows from M_1 and we are through. However, if no proof could be found, subgoals for this problem would be set up and the process would continue.

The hierarchy of goal, subgoals, and models generated by the search process is represented by a *search tree*. Each node of the search tree has the form (⟨world model⟩, ⟨goal list⟩), and represents the problem of trying to achieve the sub-goals on the goal list (in order) from the indicated world model.

An example of such a search tree is shown in Fig. 1. The top node (M_0, (G_0)) represents the main task of achieving goal G_0 from world model M_0.

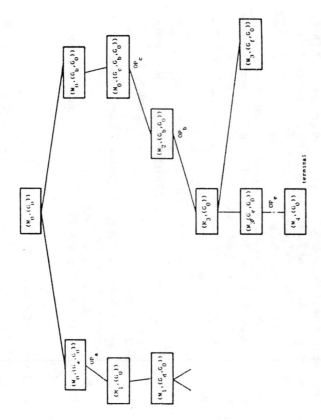

FIG. 1. A typical STRIPS search tree.

In this case, two alternative subgoals G_a and G_b are set up. These are added to the front of the goal lists in the two successor nodes. Pursuing one of these subgoals, suppose that in the node (M_0, (G_a, G_0)), goal G_a is satisfied in M_0; the corresponding operator, say OP_a. is then applied to M_0 to yield M_1. Thus, along this branch, the problem is now to satisfy goal G_0 from M_1, and this problem is represented by the node (M_1, (G_0)). Along the other path, suppose G_c is set up as a subgoal for achieving G_b and thus the node (M_0, (G_c, G_b, G_0)) is created. Suppose G_c is satisfied in M_0 and thus OP_c is applied to M_0 yielding M_2. Now STRIPS must still solve the subproblem G_b before attempting the main goal G_0. Thus, the result of applying OP_c is to replace M_0 by M_2 and to remove G_c from the goal list to produce the node (M_2, (G_b, G_0)).

This process continues until STRIPS produces the node $(M_4, (G_0))$. Here suppose G_0 can be proved directly from M_4 so that this node is terminal. The solution sequence of operators is thus (OP_c, OP_b, OP_e).

This example search tree indicates clearly that when an operator is found to be relevant, it is not known where it will occur in the completed plan; that is, it may be applicable to the initial model and therefore be the first operator applied, its effects may imply the goal so that it is the last operator applied, or it may be some intermediate step toward the goal. This flexible search strategy embodied in STRIPS combines many of the advantages of both forward search (from the initial model toward the goal) and backward search (from the goal toward the initial model).

the difference (i.e., the uncompleted proof) is stored with the node. Except for those successor nodes generated as a result of applying operators, the process of successor generation is as follows: STRIPS selects a node and uses the difference stored with this node to select a relevant operator. It uses the precondition of this operator to generate a new successor. (If all of the node's successors have already been generated, STRIPS selects some other node still having uncompleted successors.) A flowchart summarizing the STRIPS search process is shown in Fig. 2.

STRIPS has a heuristic mechanism to select nodes with uncompleted successors to work on next. For this purpose we use an evaluation function that takes into account such factors as the number of remaining goals on the goal list, the number and types of predicates in the remaining goal formulas, and the complexity of the difference attached to the node.

3. Implementation

3.1. Theorem-Proving with Parameters

In this section, we discuss the more important details of our implementation of STRIPS; we begin by describing the automatic theorem-proving component.

STRIPS uses the resolution theorem-prover QA3.5 [7] when attempting to prove goal and sub-goal wffs. We assume that the reader is familiar with resolution proof techniques for the predicate calculus [1]. These techniques must be extended to handle the parameters occurring in wff schemas; we discuss these extensions next.

The general situation is that we have some goal wff schema $G(\bar{p})$, say, that is to be proved from a set M of clauses where $\bar{p}$ is a set of schema parameters. Following the general strategy of resolution theorem provers, we attempt to prove the inconsistency of the set $\{M \cup \sim G(\bar{p})\}$. That is, we attempt to find an instance $\bar{p}'$ of $\bar{p}$ for which $\{M \cup \sim G(\bar{p}')\}$ is inconsistent.

We have been able to use the standard unification algorithm of the resolution method to compute the appropriate instances of schema variables during the search for a proof. This algorithm has the advantage that it finds the most general instances of parameters needed to effect unification. To use the unification algorithm we must specify how it is to treat parameters. The following substitution types are allowable components of the output of the modified unification algorithm:

- *Terms that can be substituted for a variable*: variables, constants, parameters, and functional terms not containing the variable.
- *Terms that can be substituted for a parameter*: constants, parameters, and functional terms not containing Skolem functions, variables, or the parameter.

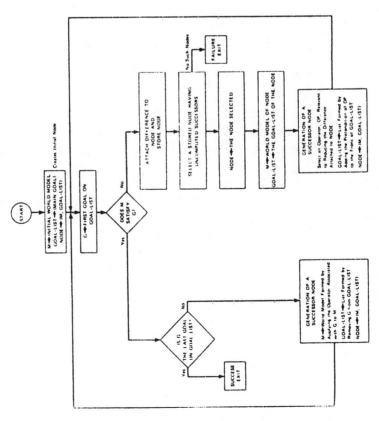

Fig. 2. Flow chart for STRIPS.

Whenever STRIPS generates a successor node, it immediately tests to see if the first goal on the goal list is satisfied in the new node's model. If so, the corresponding operator is applied, generating a new successor node; if not,

The fact that the same parameter may have multiple occurrences in a set of clauses demands another modification to the theorem prover. Suppose two clauses C_1 and C_2 resolve to form clause C and that in the process some term t is substituted for parameter p. Then we must make sure that p is replaced by t in all of the clauses that are descendants of C.

3.2. Operator Descriptions and Applications

We have already mentioned that to define an operator, we must state the preconditions under which it is applicable and its effects on a world model schema. Preconditions are stated as wff schemata. For example, suppose $G(\bar{p})$ is the operator precondition schema of an operator $O(\bar{p})$. $\bar{p}$ is a set of parameters, and M is a world model. Then if $\bar{p}'$ is a constant instance of $\bar{p}$ for which $\{M \cup \sim G(\bar{p}')\}$ is contradictory, then STRIPS can apply operator $O(\bar{p}')$ to world model M.

We next need a way to state the effects of operator application on world models. These effects are simply described by two lists. On the *delete list* we specify those clauses in the original model that might no longer be true in the new model. On the *add list* are those clauses that might not have been true in the original model but are true in the new model.

For example, consider an operator push(k, m, n) for pushing object k from m to n. Such an operator might be described as follows:

push(k, m, n)

Precondition:	ATR(m)
	∧ AT(k, m)
delete list	ATR(m);
	AT(k, m)
add list	ATR(n);
	AT(k, n)

The parameters of an operator schema are instantiated by constants at the time of operator application. Some instantiations are made while deciding what instances of an operator schema are relevant to reducing a difference, and the rest are made while deciding what instances of an operator are applicable in a given world model. Thus, when the add and delete lists are used to create new world models, all parameters occurring in them will have been replaced by constants.

(We can make certain modifications to STRIPS to allow it to apply operators with uninstantiated parameters. These applications will produce world model schemata. This generalization complicates somewhat the simple add and delete-list rules for computing new world models and needs further study.)

For certain operators it is convenient to be able merely to specify the *form* of clauses to be deleted. For example, one of the effects of a robot *goto* operator must be to delete information about the direction that the robot was originally facing even though such information might not have been represented by one of the parameters of the operator. In this case we would include the atom FACING($) on the delete list of *goto* with the convention that any atom of the form FACING($), regardless of the value of $, would be deleted.

When an operator description is written, it may not be possible to name explicitly all the atoms that should appear on the delete list. For example, it may be the case that a world model contains clauses that are derived from other clauses in the model. Thus, from AT(B1, a) and from AT(B2, $a+\Delta$), we might derive NEXTTO(B1, B2) and insert it into the model. Now, if one of the clauses on which the derived clause depends is deleted, then the derived clause must also be deleted.

We deal with this problem by defining a set of primitive predicates (e.g., AT, ATR) and relating all other predicates to this primitive set. In particular, we require the delete list of an operator description to indicate all the atoms containing primitive predicates that should be deleted when the operator is applied. Also, we require that any nonprimitive clause in the world model have associated with it those primitive clauses on which its validity depends. (A primitive clause is one which contains only primitive predicates.) For example, the clause NEXTTO(B1, B2) would have associated with it the clauses AT(B1, a) and AT(B2, $a+\Delta$).

By using these conventions, we can be assured that primitive clauses will be correctly deleted during operator applications, and that the validity of nonprimitive clauses can be determined whenever they are used in a deduction by checking to see if all of the primitive clauses on which the nonprimitive clause depends are still in the world model.

3.3. Computing Differences and Relevant Operators

STRIPS uses the GPS strategy of attempting to apply those operators that are relevant to reducing a difference between a world model and a goal or subgoal. We use the theorem prover as a key part of this mechanism.

Suppose we have just created a new node in the search tree represented by $(M, (G_i, G_{i-1}, \ldots, G_0))$. The theorem prover is called to attempt to find a contradiction for the set $\{M \cup \sim G_i\}$. If one can be found, the operator whose precondition was G_i is applied to M and the process continues.

Here, though, we are interested in the case in which no contradiction is obtained after investing some prespecified amount of theorem-proving effort. The uncompleted proof P is represented by the set of clauses that form the negation of the goal wff plus all of their descendants (if any), less any clauses eliminated by editing strategies (such as subsumption and predicate evaluation). We take P to be the difference between M and G_i and attach P to the node.[5]

Later, in attempting to compute a successor to this node with incomplete proof P attached, we first must select a relevant operator. The quest for relevant operators proceeds in two steps. In the first step an ordered list of candidate operators is created. The selection of candidate operators is based on a simple comparison of the predicates in the difference clauses with those on the add lists of the operator descriptions. For example, if the difference contained a clause having in it the negation of a position predicate AT, then the operator *push* would be considered as a candidate for this difference.

The second step in finding an operator relevant to a given difference involves employing the theorem prover to determine if clauses on the add list of a candidate operator can be used to "resolve away" clauses in the difference (i.e., to see if the proof can be continued based on the effects of the operator). If the theorem prover can in fact produce new resolvents that are descendants of the add list clauses, then the candidate operator (properly instantiated) is considered to be a relevant operator for the difference set.

Note that the consideration of one candidate operator schema may produce several relevant operator instances. For example, if the difference set contains the unit clauses $\sim$ ATR(a) and $\sim$ ATR(b), then there are two relevant instances of goto(m, n), namely goto(m, a) and goto(m, b). Each new resolvent that is a descendant of the operator's add list clauses is used to form a relevant instance of the operator by applying to the operator's parameters the same substitutions that were made during the production of the resolvent.

3.4. Efficient Representation of World Models

A primary design issue in the implementation of a system such as STRIPS is how to satisfy the storage requirements of a search tree in which each node may contain a different world model. We would like to use STRIPS in a robot or question-answering environment where the initial world model may consist of hundreds of wffs. For such applications it is infeasible to recopy completely a world model each time a new model is produced by application of an operator.

We have dealt with this problem in STRIPS by first assuming that most of the wffs in a problem's initial world model will not be changed by the application of operators. This is certainly true for the class of robot problems with which we are currently concerned. For these problems most of the wffs in a model describe rooms, walls, doors, and objects, or specify general properties of the world, which are true in all models. The only wffs that might be changed in all models are the ones that describe the status of the robot and any objects which it manipulates.

Given this assumption, we have implemented the following scheme for handling multiple world models. All the wffs for all world models are stored in a common memory structure. Associated with each wff (i.e., clause) is a visibility flag, and QA3.5 has been modified to consider only clauses from the memory structure that are marked as visible. Hence, we can "define" a particular world model for QA3.5 by marking that model's clauses visible and all other clauses invisible. When clauses are entered into the initial world model, they are all marked as visible. Clauses that are not changed remain visible throughout STRIPS' search for a solution.

Each world model produced by STRIPS is defined by two clause lists. The first list, DELETIONS, names all those clauses from the initial world model that are no longer present in the model being defined. The second list, ADDITIONS, names all those clauses in the model being defined that are not also in the initial model. These lists represent the changes in the initial model needed to form the model being defined, and our assumption implies they will contain only a small number of clauses.

To specify a given world model to QA3.5, STRIPS marks visible the clauses on the model's ADDITIONS list and marks invisible the clauses on the model's DELETIONS list. When the call to QA3.5 is completed, the visibility markings of these clauses are returned to their previous settings.

When an operator is applied to a world model, the DELETIONS list of the new world model is a copy of the DELETIONS list of the old model plus any clauses from the initial model that are deleted by the operator. The ADDITIONS list of the new model consists of the clauses from the old model's ADDITIONS list, as transformed by the operator, plus the clauses from the operator's add list.

3.5. An Example

Tracing through the main points of a simple example helps to illustrate the various mechanisms in STRIPS. Suppose we want a robot to gather together three objects and that the initial world model is given by:

$$M_0: \left\{ \begin{array}{l} ATR(a) \\ AT(BOX1, b) \\ AT(BOX2, c) \\ AT(BOX3, d) \end{array} \right\}$$

The goal wff describing this task is

$$G_0: (\exists x)[AT(BOX1, x) \wedge AT(BOX2, x) \wedge AT(BOX3, x)].$$

If P is very large we can heuristically select some part of P as the difference.

Its negated form is

$$\sim G_0: \sim \text{AT}(\text{BOX1}, x) \lor \sim \text{AT}(\text{BOX2}, x) \lor \sim \text{AT}(\text{BOX3}, x).$$

(In $\sim G_0$, the term x is a universally quantified variable.)
We admit the following operators:

(1) *push* (k, m, n): Robot pushes object k from place m to place n.

Precondition: $\text{AT}(k, m) \land \text{ATR}(m)$
Negated precondition: $\sim \text{AT}(k, m) \lor \sim \text{ATR}(m)$
Delete list: ATR(m)
              AT(k, m)
Add list: AT(k, n)
           ATR(n)

(2) *goto*(m, n): Robot goes from place m to place n.

Precondition: ATR(m)
Negated precondition: $\sim$ ATR(m)
Delete list: ATR(m)
Add list: ATR(n)

Following the flow chart of Fig. 2, STRIPS first creates the initial node $(M_0, (G_0))$ and attempts to find a contradiction to $\{M_0 \cup \sim G_0\}$. This attempt is unsuccessful; suppose the incomplete proof is:

$$\sim \text{AT}(\text{BOX1}, x) \lor \sim \text{AT}(\text{BOX2}, x) \lor \sim \text{AT}(\text{BOX3}, x)$$

$$\text{AT}(\text{BOX1}, b) \quad \text{AT}(\text{BOX2}, c) \quad \text{AT}(\text{BOX3}, d)$$

$$\sim \text{AT}(\text{BOX1}, c) \lor \sim \text{AT}(\text{BOX3}, c)$$

$$\sim \text{AT}(\text{BOX2}, b) \lor \sim \text{AT}(\text{BOX3}, b)$$

$$\sim \text{AT}(\text{BOX1}, d) \lor \sim \text{AT}(\text{BOX2}, d)$$

We attach this incomplete proof to the node and then select the node to have a successor computed.

The only candidate operator is push(k, m, n). Using the add list clause AT(k, n), we can continue the uncompleted proof in one of several ways depending on the substitutions made for k and n. Each of these substitutions produces a relevant instance of push. One of these is:

$$OP_1: \text{push}(\text{BOX2}, m, b)$$

given by the substitutions BOX2 for k and b for n. Its associated precondition (in negated form) is:

$$\sim G_1: \sim \text{AT}(\text{BOX2}, m) \lor \sim \text{ATR}(m).$$

Suppose OP_1 is selected and used to create a successor node. (Later in the search process another successor using one of the other relevant instances of push might be computed if our original selection did not lead to a solution.) Selecting OP_1 leads to the computation of the successor node $(M_0, (G_1, G_0))$. STRIPS next attempts to find a contradiction for $\{M_0 \cup \sim G_1\}$. The uncompleted proof (difference) attached to the node contains:

$$\sim \text{AT}(\text{BOX2}, m) \lor \sim \text{ATR}(m)$$

$$\text{AT}(\text{BOX2}, c)$$

$$\sim \text{ATR}(c) \qquad \sim \text{AT}(\text{BOX2}, a)$$

$$\text{ATR}(a)$$

When this node is later selected to have a successor computed, one of the candidate operators is goto(m, n). The relevant instance is determined to be

$$OP_2: \text{goto}(m, c)$$

with (negated) precondition

$$\sim G_2: \text{ATR}(m).$$

This relevant operator results in the successor node $(M_0, (G_2, G_1, G_0))$. Nest STRIPS determines that $(M_0 \cup \sim G_2)$ is contradictory with $m = a$. Thus, STRIPS applies the operator goto(a, c) to M_0 to yield

$$M_1: \begin{cases} \text{ATR}(c) \\ \text{AT}(\text{BOX1}, b) \\ \text{AT}(\text{BOX2}, c) \\ \text{AT}(\text{BOX3}, d) \end{cases}.$$

The successor node is $(M_1, (G_1, G_0))$. Immediately, STRIPS determines that $(M_1 \cup \sim G_0)$ is contradictory with $m = c$. Thus, STRIPS applies the operator push(BOX2, c, b) to yield

$$M_2: \begin{cases} \text{ATR}(b) \\ \text{AT}(\text{BOX1}, b) \\ \text{AT}(\text{BOX2}, b) \\ \text{AT}(\text{BOX3}, d) \end{cases}.$$

The resulting successor node is $(M_2, (G_0))$, and thus STRIPS reconsiders the original problem but now beginning with world model M_2. The rest of the solution proceeds in similar fashion.

Our implementation of STRIPS easily produces the solution {goto(a, c), push(BOX2, c, b), goto(b, d), push(BOX3, d, b)}. (Incidentally, Green's theorem-proving problem-solver [4] has not been able to obtain a solution to this version of the 3-Boxes problem. It did solve a simpler version of the problem designed to require only two operator applications.)

4. Example Problems Solved by STRIPS

STRIPS has been designed to be a general-purpose problem solver for robot tasks, and thus must be able to work with a variety of operators and with a world model containing a large number of facts and relations. This section describes its performance on three different tasks. The initial world model for all three tasks consists of a corridor with four rooms and doorways (see Fig. 3) and is described by the list of axioms in Table 1. Initially, the robot

TABLE 1. Formulation for STRIPS Tasks.

Initial World Model

$(\forall x \forall y \forall z)[\text{CONNECTS}(x,y,z) \Rightarrow \text{CONNECTS}(x,z,y)]$	INROOM(BOX1,ROOM1)
CONNECTS(DOOR1,ROOM1,ROOM5)	INROOM(BOX2,ROOM1)
CONNECTS(DOOR2,ROOM2,ROOM5)	INROOM(BOX3,ROOM1)
CONNECTS(DOOR3,ROOM3,ROOM5)	INROOM(ROBOT,ROOM1)
CONNECTS(DOOR4,ROOM4,ROOM5)	INROOM(LIGHTSWITCH1,ROOM1)
LOCINROOM(f,ROOM4)	PUSHABLE(BOX1)
AT(BOX1,a)	PUSHABLE(BOX2)
AT(BOX2,b)	PUSHABLE(BOX3)
AT(BOX3,c)	ONFLOOR
AT(LIGHTSWITCH1,d)	STATUS(LIGHTSWITCH1,OFF)
ATROBOT(e)	TYPE(LIGHTSWITCH1,LIGHTSWITCH)
TYPE(BOX1,BOX)	
TYPE(BOX2,BOX)	
TYPE(BOX3,BOX)	
TYPE(D4,DOOR)	
TYPE(D3,DOOR)	
TYPE(D2,DOOR)	
TYPE(D1,DOOR)	

Operators

goto1(m): Robot goes to coordinate location m.
 Preconditions:
  $(\text{ONFLOOR}) \wedge (\exists x)[\text{INROOM}(\text{ROBOT},x) \wedge \text{LOCINROOM}(m,x)]$
 Delete list: ATROBOT($\hat{s}$),NEXTTO(ROBOT,$\hat{s}$)
 Add list: ATROBOT(m)

goto2(m): Robot goes next to item m.
 Preconditions:
  $(\text{ONFLOOR}) \wedge \{(\exists x)[\text{INROOM}(\text{ROBOT},x) \wedge \text{INROOM}(m,x)] \vee (\exists x)(\exists y)$
   $[\text{INROOM}(\text{ROBOT},x) \wedge \text{CONNECTS}(m,x,y)]\}$
 Delete list: ATROBOT($\hat{s}$),NEXTTO(ROBOT,$\hat{s}$)
 Add list: NEXTTO(ROBOT,m)

pushto(m,n): robot pushes object m next to item n
 Precondition:
  $\text{PUSHABLE}(m) \wedge \text{ONFLOOR} \wedge \text{NEXTTO}(\text{ROBOT},m) \wedge \{(\exists x)[\text{INROOM}(m,x)$
   $\wedge \text{INROOM}(n,x)] \vee (\exists x:\exists y)[\text{INROOM}(m,x) \wedge \text{CONNECTS}(n,x,y)]\}$
 Delete list: AT ROBOT ($\hat{s}$) NEXTTO (ROBOT $\hat{s}$) NEXTTO ($\hat{s}$,m)
      AT (m$\hat{s}$)   NEXTTO (m$\hat{s}$)
 Add list: NEXTTO(n,m)
     NEXTTO(n,m)
     NEXTTO(ROBOT,m)

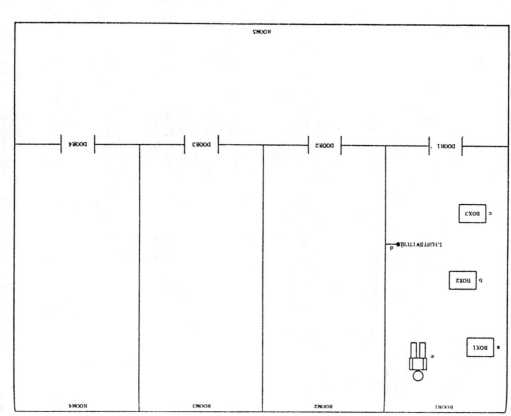

FIG. 3. Room plan for the robot tasks.

is in ROOM1 at location e. Also in ROOM1 are three boxes and a lightswitch: BOX1 at location a, BOX2 at location b, and BOX3 at location c; and a lightswitch. LIGHTSWITCH1 at location d. The lightswitch is high on a wall out of normal reach of the robot.

The first task is to turn on the lightswitch. The robot can solve this problem by going to one of the three boxes, pushing it to the lightswitch, climbing on the box[6] and turning on the lightswitch. The second task is to push the three boxes in ROOM1 together. (This task is a more realistic elaboration of the three-box problem used as an example in the last section.) The third task is for the robot to go to a designated location. f, in ROOM4.

The operators that are given to STRIPS to solve these problems are described in Table 1. For convenience we define two "goto" operators, goto1 and goto2. The operator goto1(m) takes the robot to any *coordinate* location m in the same room as the robot. The operator goto2(m) takes the robot next to any *item* m (e.g., lightswitch, door, or box) in the same room as the robot. The operator pushto(m, n) pushes any pushable object m next to any *item* n (e.g., lightswitch, door or box) in the same room as the robot. Additionally, we have operators for turning on lightswitches, going through doorways, and climbing on and off boxes. The precise formulation of the preconditions and the effects of these operators is contained in Table 1.

turnonlight(m): robot turns on lightswitch m.
Precondition: $\{(\exists n)[\text{TYPE}(n,\text{BOX}) \wedge \text{ON}(\text{ROBOT},n) \wedge \text{NEXTO}(n,m)]\}$
 $\wedge \text{TYPE}(m,\text{LIGHTSWITCH})$
Delete list: STATUS(m,OFF)
 Add list: STATUS(m,ON)

climbonbox(m): Robot climbs up on box m.
Preconditions:
 ONFLOOR $\wedge$ TYPE(m,BOX) $\wedge$ NEXTTO(ROBOT,m)
Delete list: ATROBOT($\$$),ONFLOOR
 Add list: ON(ROBOT,m)

climboffbox(m): Robot climbs off box m.
Preconditions:
 TYPE(m,BOX) $\wedge$ ON(ROBOT,m)
Delete list: ON(ROBOT,m)
 Add list: ONFLOOR

gothrudoor (k,l,m): Robot goes through door k from room l into room m.
Preconditions:
 NEXTTO(ROBOT,k) $\wedge$ CONNECTS(k,l,m) $\wedge$ INROOM(ROBOT,l) $\wedge$ ONFLOOR
Delete list: ATROBOT($\$$),NEXTTO(ROBOT,$\$$),INROOM(ROBOT,$\$$)
 Add list: INROOM(ROBOT,m)

Tasks

1. *Turn on the lightswitch*
 Goal wff: STATUS(LIGHTSWITCH1,ON)
 STRIPS solution: {goto2(BOX1),climbonbox(BOX1),climboffbox(BOX1),
  pushto(BOX1,LIGHTSWITCH1),climbonbox(BOX1),
  turnonlight(LIGHTSWITCH1)}

2. *Push three boxes together*
 Goal wff: NEXTTO(BOX1,BOX2) $\wedge$ NEXTTO(BOX2,BOX3)
 STRIPS solution: {goto2(BOX2),pushto(BOX2,BOX1),goto2(BOX3),pushto
  (BOX3,BOX2)}

3. *Go to a location in another room*
 Goal wff: ATROBOT(f)
 STRIPS solution: {goto2(DOOR1), gothrudoor(DOOR1,ROOM1,ROOM5),
  goto2(DOOR4),gothrudoor(DOOR4,ROOM5,ROOM4),
  goto1(f)}

TABLE 2. Performance of STRIPS on Three Tasks.

	Time taken (in seconds)		Number of nodes		Number of operator applications	
	Total	Theorem-proving	On solution path	In search tree	On solution path	In search tree
Turn on the lightswitch	113.1	83.0	13	21	6	6
Push three boxes together	66.0	49.6	9	9	4	4
Go to a location in another room	123.0	104.9	11	12	5	5

We also list in Table 1 the goal wffs for the three tasks and the solutions obtained by STRIPS. Some performance figures for these solutions are shown in Table 2. In Table 2, the figures in the "Time Taken" column represent the CPU time (excluding garbage collection) used by STRIPS in finding a solution. Although some parts of our program are compiled, most of the time is spent running interpretive code; hence, we do not attach much importance to these times. We note that in all cases most of the time is spent doing theorem proving (in QA3.5).

The next columns of Table 2 indicate the number of nodes generated and the number of operator applications both in the search tree and along the solution path. (Recall from Fig. 2 that some successor nodes do not correspond to operator applications.) We see from these figures that the general search heuristics built into STRIPS provide a highly directed search toward the goal. These heuristics presently give the search a large "depth-first" component, and for this reason STRIPS obtains an interesting but non-optimal solution to the "turn on the light-switch" problem.

[6] This task is a robot version of the so-called "Monkey and Bananas" problem. STRIPS can solve the problem even though the current SRI robot is incapable of climbing boxes and turning on lightswitches.

5. Future Plans and Problems

The current implementation of STRIPS can be extended in several directions. These extensions will be the subject of much of our problem-solving research activities in the immediate future. We mention some of these briefly.

We have seen that STRIPS constructs a problem-solving tree whose nodes represent subproblems. In a problem-solving process of this sort, there must be a mechanism to decide which node to work on next. Currently, we use an evaluation function that incorporates such factors as the number and the estimated difficulty of the remaining subgoals, the cost of the operators applied so far, and the complexity of the current difference. We expect to devote a good deal of effort to devising and experimenting with various evaluation functions and other ordering techniques.

Another area for future research concerns the synthesis of more complex procedures than those consisting of simple linear sequences of operators. Specifically, we want to be able to generate procedures involving iteration (or recursion) and conditional branching. In short, we would like STRIPS to be able to generate computer programs. Several researchers [4, 8, 9] have already considered the problem of automatic program synthesis and we expect to be able to use some of their ideas in STRIPS.

We are also interested in getting STRIPS to "learn" by having it define new operators for itself on the basis of previous problem solutions. These new operators could then be used to solve even more difficult problems. It would be important to be able to generalize to parameters any constants appearing in a new operator; otherwise, the new operator would not be general enough to warrant saving. One approach [10] that appears promising is to modify STRIPS so that it solves every problem presented to it in terms of generalized parameters rather than in terms of constants appearing in the specific problem statements. Hewitt [11] discusses a related process that he calls "procedural abstraction". He suggests that, from a few instances of a procedure, a general version can sometimes be synthesized.

This type of learning provides part of our rationale for working on automatic problem solvers such as STRIPS. Some researchers have questioned the value of systems for automatically chaining together operators into higher-level procedures that themselves could have been "hand coded" quite easily in the first place. Their viewpoint seems to be that a robot system should be provided a priori with a repertoire of all of the operators and procedures that it will ever need.

We agree that it is desirable to provide a priori a large number of specialized operators, but such a repertoire will nevertheless be finite. To accomplish tasks just outside the boundary of a priori abilities requires a process for chaining together existing operators into more complex ones. We are interested in a system whose operator repertoire can "grow" in this fashion.

Clearly one must not give such a system a problem too far away from the boundary of known abilities, because the combinatorics of search will then make a solution unlikely. However, a truly "intelligent" system ought always to be able to solve slightly more difficult problems than any it has solved before.

ACKNOWLEDGEMENT

The development of the ideas embodied in STRIPS has been the result of the combined efforts of the present authors, Bertram Raphael, Thomas Garvey, John Munson, and Richard Waldinger, all members of the Artificial Intelligence Group at SRI.

The research reported herein was sponsored by the Advanced Research Projects Agency and the National Aeronautics and Space Administration under Contract NAS12–2221.

REFERENCES

1. Nilsson, N. J. *Problem-Solving Methods in Artificial Intelligence*. McGraw-Hill Book Company, New York, New York, 1971.
2. Munson, J. H. Robot planning, execution, and monitoring in an uncertain environment. *Proc. 2nd Int'l. Joint Conf. Artificial Intelligence*, London, England (September 13, 1971).
3. Fikes, R. E. Monitored execution of robot plans produced by STRIPS. *Proc. IFIP 71*, Ljubljana, Yugoslavia (August 1971).
4. Green, C. Application of theorem proving to problem solving. *Proc. Int'l. Joint Conf. Artificial Intelligence*, Washington, D.C. (May 1969).
5. Raphael, B. The frame problem in problem-solving systems. *Proc. Adv. Study Inst. on Artificial Intelligence and Heuristic Programming*, Menaggio, Italy (August 1970).
6. Ernst, G. and Newell, A. *GPS: A Case Study in Generality and Problem Solving*. ACM Monograph Series. Academic Press, New York, New York, 1969.
7. Garvey, T. and Kling, R. User's guide to QA3.5 Question-Answering System. Stanford Research Institute Artificial Intelligence Group Technical Note 15, Menlo Park, California (December 1969).
8. Waldinger, R. and Lee, R. PROW: A step toward automatic program writing. *Proc. Int'l. Conf. Artificial Intelligence*, Washington, D.C. (May 1969).
9. Manna, Z. and Waldinger, R. Towards automatic program synthesis. *Comm. ACM.* 14, No. 3 (March 1971).
10. Hart, P. E. and Nilsson, N. J. The construction of generalized plans as an approach toward learning. Stanford Research Institute Artificial Intelligence Group Memo, Menlo Park, California (5 April 1971).
11. Hewitt, C. PLANNER: A language for Manipulating models and proving theorems in a robot. Artificial Intelligence Memo No. 168 (Revised), Project MAC, Massachusetts Institute of Technology, Cambridge, Massachusetts (August 1970).

Planning in a Hierarchy of Abstraction Spaces*

Earl D. Sacerdoti

Stanford Research Institute, Artificial Intelligence Center, Menlo Park, Calif. 94025, U.S.A.

Recommended by P. Winston

ABSTRACT

A problem domain can be represented as a hierarchy of abstraction spaces in which successively finer levels of detail are introduced. The problem solver ABSTRIPS, a modification of STRIPS, can define an abstraction space hierarchy from the STRIPS representation of a problem domain, and it can utilize the hierarchy in solving problems. Examples of the system's performance are presented that demonstrate the significant increases in problem-solving power that this approach provides. Then some further implications of the hierarchical planning approach are explored.

1. Introduction

General purpose problem solvers, such as STRIPS [3, 4] or GPS [2], must do their work using general purpose search heuristics. Unfortunately, by using such heuristics, it is not possible to solve any reasonably complex set of problems in a reasonably complex domain. Regardless of how good such heuristics are at directing search, attempts to traverse a complex problem space can be caught in a combinatorial quagmire.

This paper presents an approach to augmenting the power of the heuristic search process. The essence of this approach is to utilize a means for discriminating between important information and details in the problem space. By planning in a hierarchy of abstraction spaces in which successive levels of detail are introduced, significant increases in problem-solving power have been achieved.

* The work reported herein was sponsored by the Advanced Research Projects Agency of the Department of Defense under Contract DAHC04-72-C-0008 with the U.S. Army Research Office.

Artificial Intelligence **5** (1974), 115–135

Copyright © 1974 by North-Holland Publishing Company

Section 2 sketches the hierarchical planning approach and gives motivation for its use. Sections 3 and 4 describe the definition and use of abstraction spaces by ABSTRIPS (Abstraction-Based STRIPS), a modification of the STRIPS problem-solving system that incorporates this approach. Section 5 describes the performance of the system. Section 6 discusses the implications of this approach for problem solving and for robotics.

2. The Motivation for Using Abstraction Spaces in Problem Solving

It was not quite fair to assert in the previous section that a complex problem domain is beyond the combinatorial capability of general purpose problem solvers. A problem solver deals not with the problem domain itself, but with some representation of that domain. So it would be more correct to state that a complex representation exceeds the scope of general purpose problem solvers.

Unfortunately, a straightforward transcription of a complex problem domain will yield a complex representation. However, a well-chosen transcription can lead to a simpler representation. By choosing such a simplifying representation, one can have the problem solver do its work in a context that is simple enough for some useful problem solving to take place.

In other words, the heuristic search through the simplifying representation will be of sufficiently short duration that a goal state in the problem space can be reached. Such a representation displays what McCarthy and Hayes [7] term "heuristic adequacy".

Attempts to achieve simplifying representations, such as the "macro operator", or MACROP, of the STRIPS problem solver [3], have heretofore tried to preserve, in McCarthy and Hayes' terminology, "epistemological adequacy"; that is, the simplifying representations had to preserve all the detail that was needed to solve the problem at hand. A MACROP simplifies the representation of a problem domain by providing a means of selecting at one time an entire sequence of primitive operators, linked in a semantically sensible manner. But it preserves every detail of the preconditions and effects of its constituent operators.

Such simplifying representations can provide only limited enhancement to the power of a problem-solving system because of a somewhat dismaying fact: For a sufficiently complex problem domain, no epistemologically adequate representation can be heuristically adequate.

Epistemological adequacy implies that every relevant detail is properly dealt with. But attention to detail is precisely what defeats heuristic adequacy. A good heuristic evaluation function will enable a problem solver to reject most of the possible paths in a situation space. But if all the details are

Artificial Intelligence **5** (1974), 115–135

attended to, the evaluation function must be applied at all the nodes at which the details are affected. The combinatorics of the expanding search space will enable the problem solver to solve only rather simple problems.

A superior approach to problem solving would be to search first through an *abstraction space*, a simplifying representation of the problem space in which unimportant details are ignored. When a solution to the problem in the abstraction space is discovered, all that remains is to account for the details of the linkup between the steps of the solution. This can be regarded as a sequence of subproblems in the original problem space. If they can be solved, a solution to the overall problem will have been achieved. If they cannot be solved, more planning in the abstraction space is required to discover an alternative solution.

Pólya [9] cites the importance of this approach for human problem solving. It has been used by computer programs to find proofs in symbolic logic [8] (ignoring the nature of the connectives and the ordering of symbols as details) and to detect edges in scenes [6] (using a shrunken picture with less detail).

The concept can readily be extended to a hierarchy of spaces, each dealing with fewer details than the ground space below it and with more details than the abstraction space above it. By considering details only when a successful plan in a higher level space gives strong evidence of their importance, a heuristic search process will investigate a greatly reduced portion of the search space.

The process of abstraction defined in Section 3 is general in that it is not domain-dependent. But it is highly structured and very dependent on the syntax of the problem domain. It is a first step, providing no capability for a "representational shift" that would restate a difficult problem in terms that render its solution markedly easier. Rather, it employs a series of representational nudges that increase the power of the heuristic search process over a problem space.

3. Automated Definition of Abstraction Spaces

The following sections describe the ABSTRIPS system, a modification of the STRIPS problem solver [3, 4]. A brief description of the aspects of STRIPS that are relevant to the discussion to follow is presented below.[1] The reader is encouraged to see [3, Section 2] for a brief but thorough summary of the operation of STRIPS or [4] for a full description.

[1] In the interests of brevity and clarity, no further mention will be made of the MACROPs in the STRIPS system. A MACROP is the result of generalizing a previously completed plan. Most of its valid subsequences of operators can be extracted for use in further planning. Each such subsequence could be treated by ABSTRIPS like a primitive operator.

Artificial Intelligence **5** (1974), 115–135

Briefly, the representation of a problem domain with which STRIPS deals consists of:

(1) *A world model.* The world model is a set of wffs in the predicate calculus, describing facts (e.g., CONNECTS(DOOR1, ROOM1, ROOM2)) or laws (e.g., $(\forall Rx, Ry, Dx)$ CONNECTS(Dx, Rx, Ry) $\Leftrightarrow$ CONNECTS(Dx, Ry, Rx)) of the problem domain.

(2) *A set of operator descriptions.* Each action in the problem domain is represented by an "operator" for changing one model into another. An operator is defined by a precondition wff, an add list, and a delete list. For an operator to be applicable in a given model, its precondition wff must be satisfied. The add and delete lists describe which wffs are changed when an application of the operator transforms the world model.

A problem is stated to STRIPS as a goal wff. STRIPS must develop a sequence of operator applications that will lead to a world model in which the goal wff is true. A GPS-like means-ends analysis strategy [2] is employed to generate the operator sequence.

A "difference" between the initial model and the goal model is extracted. STRIPS determines which instances of which operators would reduce the difference; the instance that most reduces the difference is selected. If it is applicable in the initial state (i.e., its precondition wff is true in the initial world model), the operator is applied, and a new world model created. If the goal wff is true in the new model, STRIPS is done. If not, the difference between the new state and the goal state is extracted. and the process continues.

If the operator instance that most reduced the difference is not applicable in the initial state (i.e., its precondition wff is not provable in the world model), the precondition is set up as a subgoal wff. STRIPS will then try to develop a sequence of operator applications that will lead to a world model in which the subgoal wff is true. If the subgoal is achieved, the operator instance can be applied as before. If not, another operator instance is selected, and the process continues as before.

3.1. Abstraction spaces in the STRIPS context

For a practical problem-solving system, one would like to have an abstraction space differ from its ground space enough to achieve a significant improvement in problem-solving efficiency, but yet not so much as to make the mapping from abstraction space to ground space complex and time-consuming.

For the STRIPS system, this criterion is met by having the abstraction spaces differ from their ground spaces only in the level of detail used to specify the preconditions of operators. Although the change in representation provided by this choice may seem intuitively insufficient. it satisfies the

Artificial Intelligence **5** (1974), 115–135

criterion well. The world model can remain unchanged; there is no need to delete unimportant details from it because they can simply be ignored. No operators need be deleted in their entirety; if all they do is achieve details, they will never be selected as relevant. Any change to the add or delete lists of the operators would cause the operators' effects to be very different in different spaces. Since the applicability of a particular operator at some intermediate state might depend on any effects of any previously applied operators, the mapping of plans among spaces would be rendered too complex.

Thus, an abstraction space in the STRIPS context differs from its ground space only in the preconditions of its operators. The precondition wffs in an abstraction space will have fewer literals than those in its ground space. The literals omitted will be those that are "details" in the sense that a simple plan can be found to achieve them once the more "critical" literals have been achieved. For instance, consider a PUSHTHRUDR operator, which describes the effects of a robot pushing a particular object through a doorway into an adjacent room. In a high level abstraction space, the operator would be applicable whenever the object was pushable and a doorway into the desired room existed. In a lower level space, it would also be required that the robot and the object be in the room connected by the doorway with the target room. In a still lower abstraction space, the door would also have to be open. Finally, in the original representation of the problem space, the robot would also have to be next to the box, and the box would have to be next to the door.

For ABSTRIPS to be able to discriminate among various levels of detail, each literal within the preconditions of each operator in a problem domain is assigned a "criticality" value at the time the domain is first defined. Only the most critical literals will be in the highest abstraction space, whereas in lower spaces less critical ones will also appear.

3.2. Assigning criticality to the literals of a precondition

There are many possible approaches to the assignment of criticality values to the literals of an operator's precondition wff. They span a range from a manual assignment as part of the specification of the problem domain to a completely automatic assignment of criticalities.

At one extreme, the definition of a problem domain could include an explicit specification of criticalities, reflecting the definer's intuition about the domain. For example, if one were to define a "Turn on the lamp(ℓ)" operator, he might say it was essential that ℓ be a lamp. He might say it was very important to be in the room with the lamp, less important that the lamp's cord be plugged in, and still less important to be next to the lamp. Specifying

the criticality value of a literal by a number preceding it in braces, one might define the precondition wff of the "Turn on the lamp" operator as

$$\{4\}\text{TYPE}(\ell,\text{lamp}) \land (\exists rx)\{3\}\text{INROOM}(\text{Me},rx) \land \{3\}\text{INROOM}(\ell,rx) \land \{2\}\text{PLUGGED-IN}(\ell) \land \{1\}\text{NEXTTO}(\text{Me},\ell).$$

At the other extreme, a scheme can be developed to perform an exhaustive analysis of the $n!$ possible orderings of the n literals in a precondition in order to determine which literals can be achieved once other literals are assumed to be true. The results of this analysis can be used to specify the criticality values for literals of the precondition.

For ABSTRIPS, an intermediate approach to criticality assignment was adopted. A predetermined (partial) ordering of all the predicates used in describing the problem domain was used to specify an order for examining the literals of the precondition wffs of all the operators in the domain. First, all literals whose truth value could not be changed by any operator in the domain were assigned a maximum criticality value. Then, each remaining literal was examined in an order determined by the partial ordering. If a short plan could be found to achieve a literal from a state in which all previously processed literals were assumed to be true, then the literal in question was said to be a detail and was assigned a criticality equal to its rank in the partial ordering. If no such plan could be found, the literal was assigned a criticality greater than the highest rank in the partial order. For the domain including the "Turn on the lamp(ℓ)" operator, the partial ordering might look like the following:

TYPE( ) COLOR( )		(Rank 4)
INROOM( )		(Rank 3)
PLUGGED-IN( ) UNPLUGGED( )		(Rank 2)
NEXTTO( )		(Rank 1)

The TYPE(ℓ,lamp) literal could not be changed by any operator in the domain, and so it would be assigned a maximum criticality (6, in this case). The two INROOM literals would be examined next (an arbitrary order can be chosen for literals whose predicates have equal rank in the partial ordering). They cannot be achieved from a state in which TYPE(ℓ,lamp) is asserted, and so they would be assigned a criticality greater than the highest rank in the partial order, in this case 5. PLUGGED-IN(ℓ) can be achieved from a state in which the INROOM literals and the TYPE literal are true. It can be achieved by a plan to go to the lamp cord, pick it up, bring it to a socket, and plug it in. So it would be assigned a criticality equal to its rank in the partial ordering, namely, 2. Similarly, a plan can be found to achieve

NEXTTO(Me,ℓ) from a state in which the previously processed literals are true, and so it would be assigned a criticality of 1.

Regardless of the method used to determine the criticality values, they define a hierarchy of abstraction spaces. The next section shows how such a hierarchy can be used to aid the planning process.

4. Utilization of Abstraction Spaces in Planning

To take advantage of the hierarchical planning approach offered by the use of abstraction spaces, the ABSTRIPS system—whose flow of control is shown in Fig. 1—has a recursive executive program. This program accepts two parameters. The first is a criticality value indicating the abstraction space in which planning is to occur. The second is a list of nodes from the search tree in the higher space, representing a skeleton plan. When a new problem is posed to ABSTRIPS, the external interface program sets the preconditions of a dummy operator to the goal wff. The domain's maximum criticality, which was determined when criticalities were assigned, is retrieved. The executive is called with the criticality set to the maximum and the skeleton consisting of the dummy operator.

Within the highest abstraction space, the executive plans to achieve the preconditions of the dummy step in the skeleton plan, i.e., the main goal. When a plan is found, the executive computes the criticality of the next lowest space in which planning is needed, and it builds a skeleton of nodes along the path of the successful plan. The executive then invokes itself recursively. The new invocation solves in turn the subproblems of bridging the gaps between steps in the skeleton plan and of ensuring that the steps in the skeleton plan are still applicable at the appropriate points in the new plan. The final step in the skeleton is always the dummy operator, and so the final applicability check ensures that the original goal has been reached. When all subproblems have been solved, the executive invokes itself for planning in a still lower space. This recursion continues until a complete plan is built up in the problem space itself.

This search strategy might be termed a "length-first" search. It pushes the planning process in each abstraction space all the way to the original goal state before beginning to plan in a lower space. This enables the system to recognize as early as possible the steps that would lead to dead ends or very inefficient plans.

If any subproblem in a particular space cannot be solved, control is returned to the process in its abstraction space. The search tree is restored to its state prior to the selection of the node that led to failure in the ground space. That node is eliminated from consideration, and the search for a successful plan at the higher level continues.

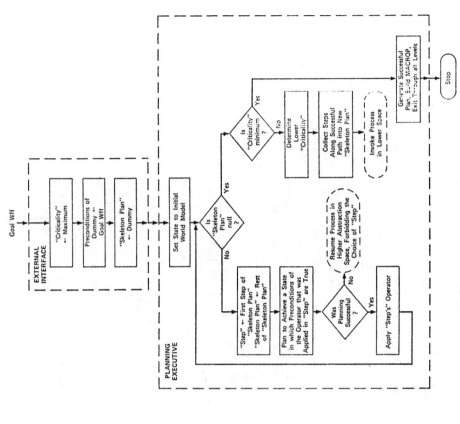

Fig. 1. Flow of control of ABSTRIPS.

This failure mechanism is analogous to the automatic backtracking feature of the PLANNER language [5]. It has the major defect that when a failure of a lower level process is reported, the process and the context in which the failure occurred are no longer around for analysis. So ABSTRIPS relies heavily on being able to produce good plans at the highest level.

This requirement has led to two modifications to the search algorithm originally employed by STRIPS. The first is an alteration of the evaluation function used to select which node in the search tree to expand next. STRIPS emphasizes the estimated cost of achieving the goal from the given node and de-emphasizes the cost of arriving at the node from the initial state. Thus, it has a tendency to find a slightly longer plan quickly, rather than the cheapest plan more slowly. But each extra step in a high abstraction space is likely to lead to many extra steps in the corresponding plan in the problem space. Thus, for ABSTRIPS, the evaluation function has itself been made a function of the level of abstraction. At the highest level, ABSTRIPS gives equal weight to the cost of reaching a given node and to the estimated cost of reaching the goal from that node. This evaluation function changes incrementally as the level of abstraction decreases, until it reaches the old STRIPS function at the level of the problem space.

The second modification involves postponing the selection of one among several equivalent instances of a relevant operator. During the process of selecting relevant operators to reduce a particular difference, a partial instantiation of the operators' parameters may occur. For example, if the difference were that the robot was not in Room 3, then the operator "Go through a door into a room" might be selected and instantiated to "Go through a door into Room 3". The preconditions of this operator would then be analyzed by the theorem prover to determine which door to choose. If several choices seem equally good to STRIPS (i.e., the states in which the various choices can be applied are equally difficult to reach), then it would arbitrarily pick a door.

For ABSTRIPS, alternative instantiations in an abstraction space might appear equivalent, and yet one choice might be substantially superior when further details are considered. So ABSTRIPS defers its decision when more than one equivalent "best choice" of a relevant operator is found. The partially instantiated relevant operator (e.g., "Go through a door into Room 3") is used in planning. When subsequent analysis in a lower abstraction space reveals a preferred instantiation, that instantiation is then chosen. If this selection should eventually lead to failure, the other instantiations can still be chosen through the backtracking mechanism.

In summary, hierarchical planning using abstraction spaces in a "length-first" search technique postpones extending the search tree through the levels concerned with the detailed preconditions of an operator until it knows that doing so will be highly effectual in reaching the goal (because the operator lies along an almost certainly successful path). By avoiding work on fruitless branches of the search tree, the technique achieves significant efficiencies in the formulation of complex plans.

5.　Examples of ABSTRIPS' Performance

To clarify the issues raised and the way in which the ABSTRIPS system works, the system's performance is traced through some examples below. The

ABSTRIPS system consists of some 370 INTERLISP functions, which run as compiled code on a PDP-10 computer. All the examples presented were drawn from the environment of the Stanford Research Institute mobile robot. The domain consists of seven rooms interconnected by doorways. Operators have been defined that model the robot's ability to navigate to any object or location within a room, to push boxes within a room or through a doorway, to navigate through a doorway, to block a doorway using a box, and to unblock a doorway. In addition, fictitious operators have been defined to model the opening and closing of doors; these actions are beyond the robot's capabilities. In all, 167 predicate calculus wffs have been defined as axioms to model the robot domain.

The definition of the domain is essentially identical to the one used for the examples in the latest report on the STRIPS system [3].

5.1.　Definition of abstraction spaces

To enable the system to assign criticality values properly to the literals of the preconditions of the operators, two additional axioms, representing laws about the world, were included in the world model:

$$(\forall x)\text{PUSHABLE}(x) \supset \text{TYPE}(x,\text{OBJECT})$$

and

$$(\forall x)\text{STATUS}(x,\text{CLOSED}) \equiv \neg\text{STATUS}(x,\text{OPEN}).$$

The criticality determination algorithm required approximately five minutes of running time. The resulting operator descriptions are listed below. The number in braces preceding each literal in the precondition wffs represents the criticality of the literal. The literal will appear in the precondition in abstraction spaces of criticality less than or equal to the number in braces.

GOTOB(bx)　*Go to object bx.*
Preconditions: {6}TYPE(bx,OBJECT),(∃rx)[{5}INROOM(bx,rx) ∧ {5}INROOM(ROBOT,rx)]
Deletions: AT(ROBOT,$1,$2),NEXTTO(ROBOT,$1)
Additions: *NEXTTO(ROBOT,bx)

GOTO(dx)　*Go to door dx.*
Preconditions: {6}TYPE(dx,DOOR),(∃rx)(∃ry) [{5}INROOM(ROBOT,rx) ∧ {6}CONNECTS(dx,rx,ry)]
Deletions: AT(ROBOT,$1,$2),NEXTTO(ROBOT,$1)
Additions: *NEXTTO(ROBOT,dx)

GOTOL(x,y)　*Go to coordinate location (x,y).*
Preconditions: (∃rx)[{5}INROOM(ROBOT,rx) ∧ {6}LOCINROOM(x,y,rx)]

Deletions: AT(ROBOT,$1,$2),NEXTTO(ROBOT,$1),
Additions: *AT(ROBOT,x,y)

PUSHB(bx,by) *Push bx to object by.*
Preconditions: {6}TYPE(by,OBJECT),{6}PUSHABLE(bx),
{1}NEXTTO(ROBOT,bx),(∃rx)[{5}INROOM(bx,rx) ∧
{5}INROOM(ROBOT,rx)]
Deletions: AT(ROBOT,$1,$2),NEXTTO(ROBOT,$1),
AT(bx,$1,$2),NEXTTO(bx,$1),NEXTTO($1,bx)
Additions: *NEXTTO(by,bx),*NEXTTO(bx,by),NEXTTO(ROBOT,bx)

PUSHD(bx,dx) *Push bx to door dx.*
Preconditions: {6}PUSHABLE(bx),{6}TYPE(dx,DOOR),
{1}NEXTTO(ROBOT,bx),
(∃rx)(∃ry)[{5}INROOM(ROBOT,rx) ∧
{5}INROOM(bx,rx) ∧ {6}CONNECTS(dx,rx,ry)]
Deletions: AT(ROBOT,$1,$2),NEXTTO(ROBOT,$1),
AT(bx,$1,$2),NEXTTO(bx,$1),NEXTTO($1,bx)
Additions: *NEXTTO(bx,dx),NEXTTO(ROBOT,bx)

PUSHL(bx,x,y) *Push bx to coordinate location (x,y).*
Preconditions: {6}PUSHABLE(bx),{1}NEXTTO(ROBOT,bx),
(∃rx)[{5}INROOM(ROBOT,rx) ∧
{5}INROOM(bx,rx) ∧ {6}LOCINROOM(x,y,rx)]
Deletions: AT(ROBOT,$1,$2),NEXTTO(ROBOT,$1),
AT(bx,$1,$2),NEXTTO(bx,$1),NEXTTO(ROBOT,bx)
Additions: *AT(bx,x,y),NEXTTO(ROBOT,bx)

GOTHRUDR(dx,rx) *Go through door dx into room rx.*
Preconditions: {6}TYPE(dx,DOOR),{6}TYPE(rx,ROOM),
{2}STATUS(dx,OPEN),(∃ry)[{5}INROOM(ROBOT,ry) ∧
{6}CONNECTS(dx,ry,rx)]
Deletions: AT(ROBOT,$1,$2),NEXTTO(ROBOT,$1),
INROOM(ROBOT,$1)
Additions: *INROOM(ROBOT,rx)

PUSHTHRUDR(bx,dx,rx) *Push bx through door dx into room rx.*
Preconditions: {6}PUSHABLE(bx),{6}TYPE(dx,DOOR),
{6}TYPE(rx,ROOM),{2}STATUS(dx,OPEN),
{1}NEXTTO(bx,dx),{1}NEXTTO(ROBOT,bx),
(∃ry)[{5}INROOM(bx,ry) ∧ {5}INROOM(ROBOT,ry) ∧
{6}CONNECTS(dx,ry,rx)]
Deletions: AT(ROBOT,$1,$2),NEXTTO(ROBOT,$1),
AT(bx,$1,$2),NEXTTO(bx,$1),NEXTTO($1,bx),
INROOM(ROBOT,$1),INROOM(bx,$1)

Additions: *INROOM(bx,rx),INROOM(ROBOT,rx),
NEXTTO(ROBOT,bx)

OPEN(dx) *Open door dx.*
Preconditions: {6}TYPE(dx,DOOR),{5}STATUS(dx,CLOSED),
{5}NEXTTO(ROBOT,dx)
Deletions: STATUS(dx,CLOSED)
Additions: *STATUS(dx,OPEN)

CLOSE(dx) *Close door dx.*
Preconditions: {6}TYPE(dx,DOOR),{5}STATUS(dx,OPEN),
{5}NEXTTO(ROBOT,dx)
Deletions: STATUS(dx,OPEN)
Additions: *STATUS(dx,CLOSED)

Note: The addition clauses preceded by an asterisk are the *primary additions* of the operator. When STRIPS or ABSTRIPS searches for a relevant operator, it considers only primary addition clauses.

5.2. A detailed sample problem

Fig. 2 depicts the initial model that was defined for this problem. The robot is in Room RRIL. The door between RRIL and RCLK is closed. BOX1

FIG. 2. Initial state for the sample problem.

FIG. 3. A state in which the goal of the sample problem is satisfied.

and BOX2 are both in RPDP. The problem is for the system to plan to achieve a state in which the two boxes are next to one another and the robot is in Room RUNI, as in Fig. 3. The goal wff for this problem is:

NEXTTO(BOX1,BOX2) ∧ INROOM(ROBOT,RUNI).

STRIPS was able to solve this problem without using abstraction spaces. However, its solution required the exploration of 119 nodes in the search tree, only 23 of which were on the successful path. This exploration took over 30 minutes of computer time. Fig. 4(a) depicts the search tree.

was satisfied when Par12 was instantiated to DUNIMYS. So

GOTHRUDR(DUNIMYS,RUN1)

was applied, and this generated a state in which the goal wff was true. Fig. 4(b) depicts the search tree in the highest abstraction space. The positioning of the nodes suggests the correspondence to the nodes in the STRIPS search tree.

A skeleton plan was built consisting of the nodes at which the two operators were applied. The plan was:

PUSHB(BOX2,BOX1).   GOTHRUDR(DUNIMYS,RUN1).

Planning then began in the space of criticality 5.

The first subgoal was the precondition wff in this abstraction space of the first operator, PUSHB(BOX1,BOX2). The difference between the initial state and the one in which the wff was true was INROOM(ROBOT,RPDP). Operator instances relevant to reducing this difference were

GOTHRUDR(Par17,RPDP) and PUSHTHRUDR(ROBOT,Par20,RPDP).

The precondition wff of the first was tested, but it was not completely satisfied. There were still differences INROOM(ROBOT,RMYS) or INROOM (ROBOT,RCLK) before GOTHRUDR(Par17,RPDP) could be applied (i.e., the robot was not yet in a room adjoining RPDP). The PUSHTHRUDR operator was completely inapplicable because the robot is not a pushable object.

Then ABSTRIPS tried to reduce the differences that would render GOTHRUDR(Par17,RPDP) applicable. Four relevant operators were found. The first was GOTHRUDR(Par22,RMYS), and its precondition wff was not satisfied either (the robot was not in a room adjoining RMYS). The second relevant operator was GOTHRUDR(Par22,RCLK), and its precondition wff was satisfied when Par22 was instantiated to DCLKRIL. So GOTHRUDR(DCLKRIL,RCLK) was applied, producing a state in which GOTHRUDR(DPDPCLK,RPDP) was applicable. That operator was applied, producing a state in which the initial subgoal, the precondition wff of PUSHB(BOX2,BOX1), was true. The PUSHB operator was then applied.

Then a new subgoal was set up, in which the preconditions of GOTHRUDR(DUNIMYS,RUN1) in this space were true. The difference between the current state and the subgoal state was INROOM(ROBOT, RMYS). GOTHRUDR(Par27,RMYS) was selected as a relevant operator, and its preconditions were satisfied when Par27 was bound to DMYSPDP. So GOTHRUDR(DMYSPDP,RMYS) was applied, producing a state in which the subgoal was satified. The operator associated with this subgoal, GOTHRUDR(DUNIMYS,RUN1), was applied, and the goal state was again reached. Fig. 4(c) shows the search trees in this space.

Artificial Intelligence **5** (1974), 115–135

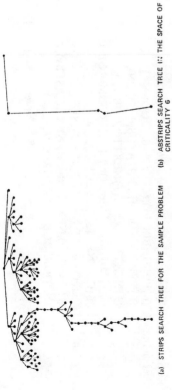

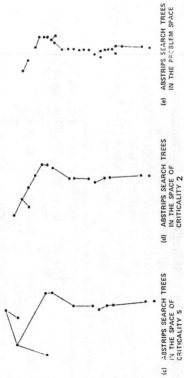

(a) STRIPS SEARCH TREE FOR THE SAMPLE PROBLEM

(b) ABSTRIPS SEARCH TREE IN THE SPACE OF CRITICALITY 6

(c) ABSTRIPS SEARCH TREES IN THE SPACE OF CRITICALITY 5

(d) ABSTRIPS SEARCH TREES IN THE SPACE OF CRITICALITY 2

(e) ABSTRIPS SEARCH TREES IN THE PROBLEM SPACE

FIG. 4. Search trees for the sample problem.

ABSTRIPS first examined the problem in an abstraction space in which the only precondition clauses considered were those whose truth value could never be altered by the robot. The difference between the initial state and the goal state was computed. The difference was the goal wff itself. Five relevant operator instances were computed. The first of these, PUSHB(BOX2, BOX1), was examined. Its precondition wff in this abstraction space was true in the initial state; so the operator was applied. This resulted in a new state in which the robot, BOX1, and BOX2 were next to each other. The difference between this state and the goal state was computed and found to be INROOM(ROBOT,RUN1). Two relevant operator instances were found, and the first, GOTHRUDR(Par12,RUN1), was examined. (Par12 is an uninstantiated parameter.) Its precondition wff in this abstraction space,

TYPE(RUN1,ROOM) ∧ TYPE(Par12,DOOR)
∧ (∃ry)CONNECTS(Par12,ry,RUN1),

Artificial Intelligence **5** (1974), 115–135

The following new skeleton plan was built up:

GOTHRUDR(DCLKRIL,RCLK); GOTHRUDR(DPDPCLK.RPDP);
PUSHB(BOX2,BOX1); GOTHRUDR(DMYSPDP,RMYS);
GOTHRUDR(DUNIMYS,RUNI).

The planning process was then reinvoked in an abstraction space of criticality 2.

The first subgoal, the precondition wff of the first step in the skeleton plan, GOTHRUDR(DCLKRIL,RCLK), was not satisfied in the initial model. The difference was STATUS(DCLKRIL,OPEN). An analysis showed that it could be eliminated by applying GOTOD(DCLKRIL) and then OPEN (DCLKRIL). This resulted in a state that satisfied the first subgoal. So GOTHRUDR(DCLKRIL,RCLK) was applied.

Each of the remaining subgoals of the process in this abstraction space were immediately satisfiable, and so each step of the skeleton plan was applied in turn, resulting in a state in which the original goal was satisfied. The skeleton plan produced was GOTOD(DCLKRIL); OPEN(DCLKRIL), followed by all the steps of the previous skeleton plan. Fig. 4(d) shows the search trees in this space.

Finally, planning took place in the ground space, the space including literals of criticality 1. The first three steps of the skeleton plan were applied in turn. But the preconditions of GOTHRUDR(DPDPCLK,RPDP) were not satisfiable in a state in which the robot had just come through DCLKRIL. The difference was NEXTTO(ROBOT,DPDPCLK), and analysis indicated that it could be eliminated by applying GOTOD(DPDPCLK), enabling GOTHRUDR(DPDPCLK,RPDP) to be applied.

The next subgoal, the preconditions of PUSHB(BOX2,BOX1), was not satisfied at this point. The difference was NEXTTO(ROBOT,BOX2), which could be eliminated by an application of the first relevant operator selected, GOTOB(BOX2). After PUSHB(BOX2,BOX1) was applied, the next two subgoals failed because the robot was not next to the appropriate door. An analysis similar to the one that occurred with DPDPCLK was performed, enabling ABSTRIPS to finish the plan with an operator to go to and an operator to go through DMYSPDP and DUNIMYS.

Note that the planning in this space is just as if STRIPS were given seven small problems to solve consecutively, without the benefit of MACROPS. The search trees for the ground space are shown in Fig. 4(e). The entire planning process for ABSTRIPS produced 60 nodes, 54 of which were on the successful path in one space or another. This process required 5:28 of computer time. This is less than one-fifth of the time required by the non-hierarchical STRIPS.

TABLE 1
Comparison of planning times and search trees

	PROBLEM 1	PROBLEM 2	PROBLEM 3	PROBLEM 4	PROBLEM 5
ABSTRIPS					
Time to find plan (minutes)	1:54	2:55	2:24	2:30	6:41
Total nodes in search trees	25	34	30	33	63
—by spaces[a]	5, 5, 5, 10	5, 7, 15	3, 4, 11, 12	5, 7, 14	5, 17, 16, 25
Nodes on solution path	24	32	28	32	54
—by spaces[a]	5, 5, 9	5, 7, 13	3, 4, 10, 11	5, 7, 13	5, 11, 15, 23
Operators in plan	4	6	5	6	11
STRIPS					
Time to find plan (minutes)	1:40	5:44	4:34	9:47	>20:00[b]
Total nodes in search tree	10	33	22	51	—
Nodes on solution path	9	13	11	15	—
Operators in plan	4	6	5	7	—
STRIPS with MACROPS					
Time to find plan (minutes)	1:40	2:06	5:18	3:00	5:49
Total nodes in search tree	10	6	14	6	14
Nodes on solution path	6	6	6	6	14
Operators in plan	4	6	5	9	11

[a] The number of nodes from the search tree in each space, from the one of highest criticality to the problem space itself.
[b] STRIPS had not solved Problem 5 after 20 minutes.

Unfortunately, while these special purpose programs display intelligent behavior within their limited domain, they are worth little in any other domain. Can a more generally intelligent system be constructed that, when presented with task-specific knowledge (basic to which is the description of the problem domain), can incorporate that knowledge into its search heuristics?

The process of automated definition of abstraction space offers a possible approach. By applying a general purpose problem solver to a particular domain in the most general manner described in Section 3, a task-specific detail hierarchy can be built up. The ability of a system to discriminate important considerations from mere details is an important aspect of task-specific knowledge.

A further aspect of task-specific knowledge is the facility for negotiating those areas of the search space that are easily traversable. In the hierarchical representation framework, easily traversable areas correspond to sub-problems of achieving details, once the more critical aspects of a problem have been solved.

The ABSTRIPS system determines that a given literal is a detail when it has built a small plan to achieve a state in which it is true. That small plan can be saved as a MACROP, to be used as the first-choice relevant operator whenever the detail needs to be achieved. The relatively small number of MACROPs formed in this way, when added to the set of basic operators, constitute a basic body of knowledge about how to solve problems in a particular task domain.

6.2 Planning with multiple outcome operators

The use of a hierarchical representation can greatly simplify the process of creating conditional plans, plans with information gathering operators, and plans with loops. This is because the outcomes of these operators are un-certain only to a particular level of detail. Thus, in a higher abstraction space a simple specification can adequately model the preconditions and effects of the operators, although some of the effects may have to be described in terms of uninstantiated parameters. A drawback to this approach is that, as noted in Section 3, the mapping of plans among spaces becomes difficult when the effects of operators are abstracted. Nevertheless, the simplicity of representation of these rather complex operators renders this scheme attractive.

As an example, in planning to drive to the airport to catch a plane, one would use a "Park the car" operator. Such an operator might have the effect of "If Lot A is not full, park inside Lot A. Else if Lot B is not full, park inside Lot B. Else drive around, and then park the car." If one plans at a high level of abstraction to drive to the airport, he does not consider the

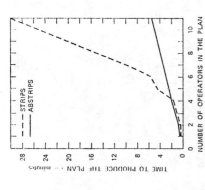

Fig. 5. Planning time as a function of plan length.

5.3. Other examples

The set of tasks from the most recent report on STRIPS [3] was run on ABSTRIPS. The running times and the search trees are compared with those from the STRIPS system in Table 1. Fig. 5 plots the planning time as a function of plan length for STRIPS and ABSTRIPS on an extended set of problems from the robot domain.

6. Further Implications of the Use of Abstraction Spaces in Planning

This paper has shown how the representation of a problem domain as a hierarchy of abstraction spaces dramatically improved the performance of a problem solver. This section briefly considers the implications of such a hierarchical representation for some other problem areas in robotics and problem solving.

6.1. Learning task-specific knowledge

General-purpose problem solvers have tended to be weak problem solvers. Because the heuristics they use to guide the search through the problem space must be generally applicable, they are not especially powerful in any particular task domain. On the other hand, special purpose programs to solve problems in a particular domain have been notably successful. The HEURISTIC DENDRAL program [1] and the game playing programs display far more problem-solving power in their particular domains of competence than a general purpose problem solver could muster. This competence is derived to a large degree from the great amount of task-specific knowledge that has been incorporated into their search heuristics.

"Park the car" operator in its full complexity. Rather, he considers an image of the operator in an abstraction space in which no uncertainties exist. It might have the simple precondition AT(CAR,AIRPORT) and might cause the clause PARKED-IN-LOT(CAR,Parameter 37) to be added to the model. Further planning could continue without considering as separate cases states in which PARKED-IN-LOT(CAR,LOT A) or PARKED-IN-LOT(CAR,LOT B) were true.

6.3. An integrated robot system

A primary motivation for building the STRIPS system, and its offspring ABSTRIPS, was to build plans for a mobile robot. In the Stanford Research Institute robot system, the operator descriptions are models for actions that the robot can actually take. The actions modeled are termed "intermediate level actions" (ILAs). When they are executed, they invoke "low level actions" (LLAs), which are concerned with initiating and monitoring motion of the robot. These routines in turn pass commands to, and receive information from, a program in a PDP-15 computer, which communicates with the robot itself via a radio link.

The ground space as viewed by ABSTRIPS is in fact just another abstraction space from the point of view of plans built up from basic operations at lower levels. The problem solver can be extended to handle successively finer levels of detail until a ground space is reached in which the only remaining details are to roll the robot around. This offers the enticing possibility of a fully integrated planning and execution system. But the interaction of planning and execution would require that the plans that such a system built be different from the traditional form of plan built by problem solvers.

For a system that deals with complex problems in a real world, as opposed to a simulated one, it is undesirable to solve an entire problem with an epistemologically adequate plan. There are too many reasonably likely outcomes for each real-world operation. The number of hypothetically possible states of the world attainable by a particular plan will grow exponentially with the length of the plan. Most of the effort of such a system would be spent reasoning about world states that would never be achieved, and very little of it would be spent moving the robot toward its goals.

It is desired that the system's planning efforts focus on reasoning about states of the world that are likely to be traversed in the course of robot execution. Thus, the overall planning should be roughed out in an abstraction space that ignores enough levels of detail so that the rough plan is fairly certain to succeed.

A few steps of the plan can be used as a skeleton, to which more detailed steps are added in a manner similar to ABSTRIPS. These new steps are fairly certain to succeed at the level of detail to which they are specified. Even more

detailed steps can be filled in for the beginning portion of this subplan, and the process can continue until a short subplan of low-level robot commands is built. These can be executed in sequence. Any deviations between the actual state of the world and the hypothesized results of the subplan will hopefully be mere details to the space that is an abstraction of the robot commands. Thus, the remaining steps of the plan in this space, as well as all higher spaces, are still on the solution path.

Further building and extending of the various subplans can then take place, including a new bottom-level subplan to move the robot. This subplan will accurately reflect the precise results of previous execution, and so it will be fully appropriate for achieving the ultimate goal. The process of alternatively adding detailed steps to the plan and then actually executing some steps can continue until the goal is achieved.

If a grievous failure occurs at some point in execution and nondetails in higher models no longer reflect the actual state of the world, subplans at affected levels of detail can propagate the failure up to an abstraction space in which the deviation from the predicted world model was a detail. Replanning can be initiated from this level of abstraction, thus reusing the results of as much as possible of the previous planning.

Therefore, by using a hierarchy of abstraction spaces to mask uncertainties in the real world effects of planned operations, an effectively integrated robot planning and executing system can be created. By dealing with a hierarchy of short, simple plans, such a system will be able to cope effectively with truly complex problems.

ACKNOWLEDGMENTS

The author is indebted to Richard Fikes, Peter Hart, and Nils Nilsson for their enthusiastic encouragement and intellectual support. The research reported in this paper was supported by the Advanced Research Projects Agency of the Department of Defense under Contract DAHC04-72-C-0008 with the U.S. Army Research Office.

REFERENCES

1. Buchanan, B. Sutherland, G., and Feigenbaum, E. HEURISTIC DENDRAL: A program for generating explanatory hypotheses in organic chemistry. *Machine Intelligence* 4, B. Meltzer and D. Michie (eds.), American Elsevier, New York (1969), 209–254.
2. Ernst, G., and Newell, A. *GPS: A Case Study in Generality and Problem Solving.* ACM Monograph Series, Academic Press, New York (1969).
3. Fikes, R. E., Hart, P. E., and Nilsson, N. J. Learning and executing generalized robot plans. *Artificial Intelligence* 3 (1972), 251–288.
4. Fikes, R. E., and Nilsson, N. J. STRIPS: A new approach to the application of theorem proving to problem solving. *Artificial Intelligence* 2 (3/4) (1971), 189–208.
5. Hewitt, C. Description and theoretical analysis (using schemata) of PLANNER: A language for proving theorems and manipulating models in a robot. Ph.D. Thesis Dept. of Mathematics, Massachusetts Inst. of Technol., Cambridge, Mass. (1972).

6. Kelly. M. D. Edge detection in pictures by computer using planning. *Machine Intelligence 6*, B. Meltzer and D. Michie (eds.), American Elsevier, New York (1971), 397–409.

7. McCarthy, J., and Hayes, P. Some philosophical problems from the standpoint of artificial intelligence. *Machine Intelligence 4*, B. Meltzer and D. Michie (eds.), American Elsevier, New York (1969), 463–502.

8. Newell, A., Shaw, J. C., and Simon, H. A. Report on a general problem solving program. *Proc. Intern. Conf. on Information Processing*, UNESCO, Paris (1960), 256–264.

9. Pólya, G. *How to Solve It*. Princeton Univ. Press, Princeton, N.J. (1945). §.

Received January 1974

Chapter 3

Interactions and Dependencies

The methods and planning systems described in Chapter 2 are often called linear planners because they produced plans in which the actions were fully ordered. During the early to mid 1970s, considerable effort was spent on finding methods to exploit the simple and efficient linear stepwise approach to producing plans, whereby one goal was tackled and then the resulting plan was used as a basis for tackling a second goal. It was recognized that interaction problems resulted from a poor choice of the order in which goals were tackled. The research led to solutions for problems arising when a second goal interfered with the successful achievement of the first goal.

The first paper we present, describing Sussman's (1974) HACKER system, looks at the underlying teleology (conditions and effects, goal structure or intentions) of plan steps and at debugging a simple linear approach when interactions were detected. HACKER was not flexible in ensuring that all ways were proposed to correct the interactions. However, Sussman's work did lay the foundation for later work on "protection" of teleologically important effects of plan steps over the interval where they were required to satisfy a condition of a later step.

A simple block-stacking problem that became known as the Sussman Anomaly (see figure) was also popularized by this work as an example of the type of interacting goal problem that could not be solved by any top-level reordering of the goals tackled. It was a problem that could not be solved by STRIPS and HACKER, for example. It is difficult to believe now that a whole generation of AI planning researchers spent years of their lives trying to understand why this was so difficult!

Waldinger's (1975) paper, the next one we present, describes a now classic method for dealing with a conjunction of goals where the individual solutions could interact. His method allows for a solution to be built incrementally as each goal is tackled, but whenever the solution to a later goal interferes with an existing plan for the goals already solved, the goal is "regressed" through the plan, i.e., the position of the goal is moved to an earlier point where there may be no interaction. The goal can be tried at any position right back to the start of the plan that already exists.

Warren's (1975) approach to solving the interaction problem was similar, but in the case of his WARPLAN system, the specific actions chosen to achieve a goal were regressed to earlier positions in the plan. In some cases, this process did lead to longer plans than were needed. We present a paper on WARPLAN (Warren, 1975) because of interest in the system as the first planner written in PROLOG. It was small and compact and used PROLOG backtracking for searches. It has been used by a number of people as a teaching aid. The paper included in this volume contains the complete planner.

A number of other approaches to handling interaction problems were published in the mid-1970's. One method, in Tate's INTERPLAN planner (Tate, 1975), used a variant of the HACKER concept of the use of the teleological structure of the plan to debug an

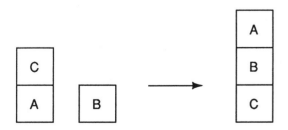

Figure: Sussman Anomaly—The three block problem

initial linear approach to tracking conjunctive goals. A paper is not included in this chapter, because the same idea was generalized for use in later planners (see Currie and Tate, 1985, Chapter 5).

Concern with avoidance of repetitive generation of valid parts of plans that had interacting sections led to methods of recording which parts of plans depended on which other parts. This dependency information could then be used to selectively undo faulty sections, leaving the valid parts intact. An early paper by Hayes (1975) describing such methods is included in this chapter. Hayes built a journey planner that used a dependency graph to record dependencies on components of plans for travel within Europe on trains, planes, and ships. The dependency graph could be used to selectively undo parts of the plan when failures occurred at plan or execution time. Much work has been done since this time on dependency directed backtracking, truth maintenance, reason maintenance, etc.

The papers included up to this point have described planners in which the plans generated were fully ordered sequences of actions. The systems commit to some ordering of goals or actions and then fix, or debug, problems that emerge with such an approach. The last two papers in this chapter describe planners that avoided making commitments until reasons for making a choice were evident.

Sacerdoti's (1975) NOAH planner allowed goals and actions to remain unordered with respect to one another until some interaction was detected between them. His planner allowed a plan to be represented as a partial order on the goals and actions. A least-commitment approach was taken to correct any interactions that the system did find (putting just enough ordering constraints in to resolve the problems detected). NOAH also represented its actions in a hierarchical way.

The last paper in this chapter describes the MOLGEN system (Stefik, 1981), which is interesting because of its ability to post constraints on objects referred to in the plan. A commitment to some specific instance of an object could be avoided until further evidence became available as to the best choice to make.

The collection of planning methods described in this chapter put in place the building bricks used to construct a number of integrated planning systems. A collection of papers concerning these systems are presented in Chapter 5.

Paper referenced herein but not included in this volume:

Tate, A. (1975). "Interacting Goals and Their Use," *IJCAI-75*, Tbilisi, USSR.

The Virtuous Nature of Bugs

by Gerald Jay Sussman

How much time has each of us spent tracking down some bug in a computer program, an electronic device, or a mathematical proof? At such times it may seem that a bug is at best a nuisance, at worst a disaster. Has it ever occurred to you that bugs are manifestations of powerful strategies of creative thinking? That, perhaps, creating and removing bugs are _necessary_ steps in the normal process of solving a problem? Recent research at the MIT AI Laboratory [Sussman 1973] [Goldstein 1973] [Fahlman 1973] indicates that this is precisely the case.

While "bug" is hard to define, I do not mean those trivial failures of oversight, of manipulation, or typing, that plague us continually. I mean real, conceptual errors.

Recently, I have completed the design of HACKER, a computational model of skill acquisition. HACKER is a problem-solving system whose performance improves with practice. This investigation has elucidated several important aspects of problem solving, including: the relationship of problem-solving to learning; the relationship between imperative and declarative aspects of knowledge; the nature of plans and their teleological structure; and the role of bugs and debugging in the refinement of plans.

A theory of problem solving:

A human problem-solver first tries to classify his problem into a subclass for which he knows a solution method. If he can, he applies that method. If he cannot, he must construct a new method by applying some more general problem-solving strategies to his knowledge of the domain. In constructing the new method, he is careful to avoid certain pitfalls he has previously encountered and he may use methods he has previously constructed to solve subproblems of the given problem. The new method is committed to memory for future use. If any method, new or old, fails on a problem for which it is expected to work, the failure is examined and analyzed. As a result the method may be modified to accommodate the new problem. Often the analysis of the failure can also be classified and abstracted to be remembered as a pitfall to avoid in the future when constructing new methods.

How HACKER embodies this theory:

Please examine figure 1. HACKER, when attacking a problem (in the Blocks World [Winograd 1971]), first checks to see if he has a program in his Answer Library whose pattern of applicability matches the problem statement. If so, he runs that program. If not, he must write a new program, using some general knowledge of programming techniques applied to his knowledge of the Blocks World. Any proposed program is criticized to avoid certain bugs he has previously encountered. He may use subroutines (in the Answer Library) he has previously constructed to solve subproblems of the given problem. After criticism, the proposed solution program is tried out. The new program is stored in the Answer Library, indexed by an applicability pattern derived from the statement of the problem for which it was written, so that it can be used to solve similar problems in the future. If any program, new or old, manifests a bug when it is applied to a problem which matches its pattern of applicability, general debugging knowledge is used to classify the mode of failure. Often, the nature of the bug can be summarized and remembered as a critic. The program is patched to fix the bug and tried again.

The origins of bugs:

HACKER has ways of repairing bugs when they come up, but how do bugs come up? There are several important sources of bugs. Sometimes, because of generalizations made when a new program is inserted in the Answer Library, a program is applied to a kind of situation which was not anticipated when the program was written. Other bugs result from unanticipated interactions between the steps of a proposed solution. Let us examine the genesis and repair of a bug of this latter kind.

Suppose that one is confronted with a composite goal, in which the problem is to achieve the conjunction of two conditions. In the absence of any further knowledge about the structure of the problem, what is a rational strategy to follow in attempting to solve the problem? The simplest approach, which has had great success in the history of science, is to begin with a "linear theory" -- to assume that the two subgoals can be achieved by independent processes. Thus, the <u>linear theory plan</u> is to break up the conjunction into its components, and then achieve each component independently, with the hope that there will be no interference between the subproblem solutions. Of course, this assumption is often false, and leads to a bug, but it is a place to start. Understanding the nature of the resulting bug will often point out the correct patch to make and may lead to a more fundamental understanding of the problem domain.

Consider, for example, HACKER's behavior on the following problem: Suppose that there are 3 blocks on the table, A,B and C, and we ask HACKER to build a 3-high tower:

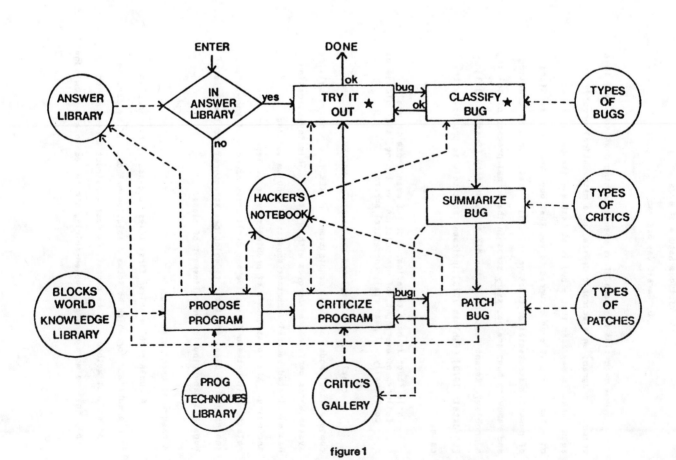

figure 1

(ACHIEVE (AND (ON A B) (ON B C)))

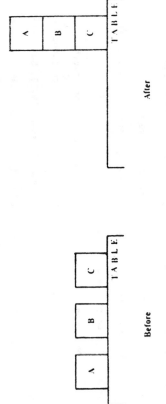

Before

After

(Please assume that HACKER has already written a program to (ACHIEVE (ON x y)) for any bricks x,y.) HACKER cannot find any program in his Answer Library which matches the given conjunction problem. HACKER then goes into program proposal mode. He fishes about for a strategy which matches the problem posed. The linear theory for achieving conjunctions is retrieved. It suggests the plan:

(TO AND2 (ACHIEVE (AND (ON A B) (ON B C)))
L3: (ACHIEVE (ON A B))
L4: (ACHIEVE (ON B C)))

That is, in simplified HACKER syntax: first try to get A on B, then try to get B on C. If the subgoals are independent, their order doesn't matter, so the arbitrary order from the problem statement is used. The proposal is then passed by the criticizer (which doesn't know anything about this kind of problem -- yet) and tried out.

Of course, it has a bug. The program, AND2, first puts A on B. Next it tries to put B on C, but that means it must grasp B. It cannot move B with A on it (a physical restriction of the robot's hand), so it removes A from B and puts it on the table. (This is part of that Answer Library subroutine which HACKER has constructed to solve some earlier problem of the form (ACHIEVE (ON x y)) and which is being used here.) Next, it puts B on C and is done. But it failed to achieve its overall purpose -- A is no longer on B!

Actually, in HACKER, the program would never get this far.

Besides proposing the plan, the linear theory also placed the following teleological commentary for that plan into HACKER's Notebook (Figure 1):

(PURPOSE L3 (TRUE (ON A B)) AND2)
(PURPOSE L4 (TRUE (ON B C)) AND2)

These state that the author of the plan expected that A would be on B starting after line L3 and remain there at least until the program AND2 was done (the fourth position could have contained a line number in a more complex plan where L3 was a *prerequisite* step rather than a *main step*) and B would be on C starting after line L4 and remain there until AND2 was done. When a program is executed for the first time, it is executed in CAREFUL mode. In CAREFUL mode these comments are interpreted along with the lines to which they are attached. A daemon was set after L3 to *protect* the truth of (ON A B) until AND2 is done.

This daemon interrupted the execution of L4 at the moment A was lifted off of B. The bug is thus manifest as a PROTECTION-VIOLATION and caught *in flagrante delicto*. Control now passes from the interrupted process to the bug classifier.

Types of Bugs:

We have seen how a bug can be constructed when a powerful but imperfect method of *plausible* inference is invoked. What do we do when such a bug comes up? Until recently, it was thought that a very good idea would have been to include a combinatorial search mechanism (e.g. backtracking) to unwind the problem solver back to some earlier point where the next most plausible proposal could be selected and tried out. The hitch with this idea is that this kind of search rapidly leads to a combinatorial explosion -- just what is this "next most plausible" proposal? It might be that the next most plausible proposal will fail in precisely the way that the current one does and that only the one-hundredth most plausible will succeed. Perhaps the program should re-evaluate its plausibilities on the basis of this failure. That is, the program should be able to learn from its mistakes, not only so as not to make the same error again, but to be positively guided by analysis of the structure of the mistake. (See [Sussman 1972] for a more complete argument)

If this conclusion is to be taken seriously it becomes important to better understand the nature of bugs; to classify and name the bugs and repair strategies. The idea of thinking of bugs as important concepts and BUG as a "powerful idea" may seem surprising; but we suspect that isolating and systematizing them may become as important in the study of intelligence as classifying interactions has become in physics!

Now let's see how HACKER understands the above mentioned bug, which has manifested itself as a protection violation. What is its underlying cause? The basic strategy of HACKER in debugging a bug manifestation is to compare (a model of) the behavior of the misbehaving program with various prototypical bug patterns. If a match is found, the program is said to be suffering from a bug which is an instance of the prototype.

What constitutes a model of the behavior of the misbehaving program, and how is it constructed? The details of the construction of a process model are described elsewhere [Sussman 1973], but here is one scheme. At the time of the PROTECTION-VIOLATION interrupt, the bug classifier has access to an essentially complete chronological history of the problem-solving process which was interrupted. (A human debugger often uses a "tracer" to help him construct such a history, but special features of CONNIVER [McDermott 1972] provide this and more in CAREFUL mode.; HACKER also has access to a complete teleological commentary of his proposed solution and access to variable bindings and other relevant data.

The bug classifier begins by noting two pointers, the current control point, and the origin of the protection comment whose scope was violated. These pointers are then traced with the help of the relevant teleological commentary and history as follows:

```
Where was I?      In 1: (PUTON A TABLE)

Why?              Main Step in 2: (ACHIEVE (ON A TABLE))

Why?              Main Step in 3: (ACHIEVE (NOT (ON A B)))

Why?              Main Step Generic in 4: (ACHIEVE (CLEARTOP B))

Why?              Prerequisite Step for 5: (PUTON B C)

Why?              Main Step in 6: (ACHIEVE (ON B C))

Why?              Main Step in 7: (ACHIEVE (AND (ON A B) (ON B C))):

                  8: COMMAND

Who complained?   9: Protect (TRUE (ON A B))

Why?              Result of 10: (ACHIEVE (ON A B))

Why?              Main Step in 7: (ACHIEVE (AND (ON A B) (ON B C)))
```

A Main Step is a step in a program whose purpose is to achieve a result which contributes to the overall goal of the program. Its purpose comment states that the result achieved by that step is needed until the program returns to its caller. A Prerequisite Step is one whose purpose is to set up for the execution of some other step. The result of this trace can be summarized in the following schematic

This structure matches a particular prototype bug called

PREREQUISITE-CLOBBERS-BROTHER-GOAL (PCBG):

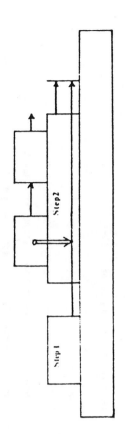

By this I mean a bug which is due to an interaction between two program steps whose purpose scopes terminate at the same time. A prerequisite step (or any number of main steps for a prerequisite step -- the matcher can compress main step scopes but prerequisite step scopes must be explicitly represented -- [Sussman 1973]) for a main stop in the code for step 2 clobbered the result of step 1. In this case, the process of achieving (CLEARTOP B), a prerequisite of (PUTON B C), which is a main step in L4:(ACHIEVE (ON B C)), destroys the truth of (ON A B), the result of L3:(ACHIEVE (ON A B)). Since both L3 and L4 are main steps in AND2 their purpose scopes terminate when AND2 returns.

Just how much generality is there in the concept PCBG? Perhaps it is just peculiar to the Blocks World? In fact, PCBG is a very common form of non-linearity.

If, for example, one wants to paint the ceiling, it is simultaneously necessary that the paint be on the platform and that the painter be on the platform. The linear strategy is to achieve each subgoal independently. The painter can either first lift the can to the ladder platform, and then climb the ladder, which works; or he can

diagram of the buggy process:

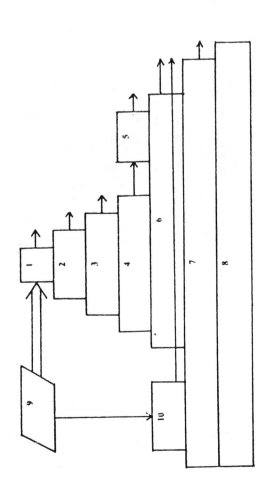

Each box in this diagram is a stack frame of the process. The horizontal dimension is its extent in time; the vertical dimension is the depth of functional application. Thus, the blocks labeled 7 and 8 (the AND2 frame and command level frame respectively) exist from the time the command is typed until it returns. Frame number 10 is the frame of line L3:(ACHIEVE (ON A B)) and frame number 6 is the frame of line L4:(ACHIEVE (ON B C)). Frame number 9 is special -- it is the protection daemon on the result of L3. It points at the accused violator. The horizontal arrows indicate the scopes of the purposes of the steps. Arrows which terminate on boxes are prerequisite step scopes. (In this trace there is only one prerequisite scope, from 4 to 5.) Other arrows are main step scopes.

first climb the ladder and then lift the can, which doesn't work.

Once he is on the ladder, he has no access to the can on the ground.

He must first come down to get the paint (clobbering the previously achieved subgoal of being on the ladder). Climbing down -- to achieve the prerequisite to lifting the paint can -- has clobbered the brother goal of being on the ladder.

In programming, too, one often runs into PCBG's. Consider the problem of compiling the LISP expression (F 3 (G 4)). If the argument passing convention is to load the arguments into successive argument registers and then call the function, we see that the call to function F requires that 3 be in register 1 and the result of (G 4) be in register 2. If we try the obvious order -- first put 3 in register 1, then calculate (G 4) and put it in register 2 -- we find that we must load 1 with 4 to call G, thus clobbering the brother goal of having 3 in register 1.

Fixing the Bug:

Now that the bug is classified, can we come up with a modification to the plan (program) which eliminates the bug? The offending prerequisite must, in any case, be accomplished before its target step. Its scope must extend until that step. But since the first and second conjuncts are brothers (they are both for the same target), their scopes must overlap. Thus, since the scope of the first conjunct and the scope of the prerequisite of a main step for the second step are incompatible, the only way to prevent the overlap is to move the step for the second conjunct ahead of the step for the first. We must assign an order to the plan. Thus, the patcher changes the plan as follows:

```
(TO AND2 (ACHIEVE (AND (ON A B) (ON B C)))
   L4:  (ACHIEVE (ON B C))
   L3:  (ACHIEVE (ON A B)))
```

A new comment is added to HACKER's notebook summarizing this ordering constraint (BEFORE L4 L3). The program is patched and the result works. In this case a critic is compiled which summarizes what has been learned (How this happens is beyond the scope of this paper -- see [Sussman 1973]): If for any blocks a, b, and c we are proposing program which has lines with the purposes of getting a on b and b on c, we must compile the line which puts b on c before the one which puts a on b. Applied recursively, this advice is sufficient to ensur that any program which piles up bricks will do it in the correct orde -- from the bottom-up.

Other bugs:

Of course, not every bug is a PCBG -- not even every bug whic manifests as a protection violation. If, for example, we try to bui an arch -- (ACHIEVE (AND (ON A B) (ON A C))) -- with a linear theory plan, the bug will manifest as a protection violation but no interchange or other simple modification of the linear theory plan c succeed. This kind of bug is a DIRECT-CONFLICT-BROTHERS (DCB) whic can only be resolved using more Blocks World knowledge. In [Sussman 1973] I classify three other types of bugs (but not DCB).

Conclusions:

We can draw the conclusion that to be effective, a problem-solver need not know the precise way to solve each kind of problem. Perhaps a better strategy is to attempt to break a hard problem up into subproblems. Sometimes these subproblems can be solved independently, in which case the linear theory plan will work

Bibliography

[Fahlman 1973]
Fahlman, Scott
A Planning System For Robot Construction Tasks
AI TR-283 (May 1973) MIT-AI-Laboratory

[Goldstein 1973]
Goldstein, Ira
Understanding Fixed Instruction Turtle Programs
PhD Thesis (September 1973) MIT-AI-Laboratory

[Hewitt 1971]
Hewitt, Carl
"Procedural Semantics: Models of Procedures and the Teaching of Procedures"
Courant Computer Science Symposium 8 (1971)

[McDermott 1972]
McDermott, D.V. and Sussman, G.J
The CONNIVER Reference Manual
AI Memo 259 MIT-AI-Laboratory (May 1972) (Revised July 1973)

[Sacerdoti 1973]
Sacerdoti, Earl
"Planning in a Hierarchy of Abstraction Spaces"
IJCAI-73 (1973)

[Sussman 1973]
Sussman, G.J.
A Computational Model of Skill Acquisition
AI TR-297 MIT-AI-Laboratory (August 1973)

[Sussman 1972]
Sussman, G.J. and McDermott, D.V.
"From PLANNER to CONNIVER - A Genetic Approach"
FJCC (1972)

[Winograd 1970]
Winograd, T.
Procedures as a Representation for Data in a Computer Program for Understanding Natural Language
AI TR-17 (MAC TR-84) MIT-AI-Laboratory (February 1971)

Sometimes the steps of the plan will interact and debugging will be necessary. And sometimes, because of prior experience, we may know that a particular kind of problem may require a particular kind of nonlinear plan, such as the ordered plan required for the problem discussed here.

The appearance of a few bugs need not be seen as evidence of a limitation of problem solving ability, but rather as a step in the effective use of a powerful problem solving strategy -- approximation of the solution of a problem with an almost-right plan. This strategy becomes powerful if the bug manifestation that results from the failure of such an almost-right plan can be used to focus the problem-solver on the source of the difficulty. A problem-solver based on debugging need not thrash blindly for an alternate plan but can be led by the analysis of the failure -- provided that adequate bug classifying and repairing knowledge is available.

Thus, I believe that effective problem solving depends as much on how well one understands one's errors as on how carefully and knowledgably one makes one's initial choices at decision points. The key to understanding one's errors is in understanding how one's intentions and purposes relate to his plans and actions. This indicates that an important part of the knowledge of a problem-solver is in teleological commentary about how the subparts of the performance knowledge relate to each other so as to achieve the overall goals of the system. It also indicates the need for knowledge about how to trace out bugs and about the kinds of bugs that might be met in applying a given kind of plausible plan.

Achieving Several Goals Simultaneously*

Richard Waldinger

Artificial Intelligence Center
Stanford Research Institute

In the synthesis of a plan or computer program, the problem of achieving several goals simultaneously presents special difficulties, since a plan to achieve one goal may interfere with attaining the others. This paper develops the following strategy: to achieve two goals simultaneously, develop a plan to achieve one of them and then modify that plan to achieve the second as well. A systematic program modification technique is presented to support this strategy. The technique requires the introduction of a special "skeleton model" to represent a changing world that can accommodate modifications in the plan. This skeleton model also provides a novel approach to the "frame problem."

The strategy is illustrated by its application to three examples. Two examples involve synthesizing the following programs: interchanging the values of two variables and sorting three variables. The third entails formulating tricky blocks-world plans. The strategy has been implemented in a simple QLISP program.

It is argued that skeleton modelling is valuable as a planning technique apart from its use in plan modification, particularly because it facilitates the representation of "influential actions" whose effects may be far reaching.

The second part of the paper is a critical survey of contemporary planning literature, which compares our approach with other techniques for facing the same problems. The following is the outline of contents.

CONTENTS

INTRODUCTION

> My feet want to dance in the sun
> My head wants to rest in the shade
> The Lord says "Go out and have fun!"
> But the landlord says "Your rent ain't paid!"
>
> E.Y. Harburg, *Finian's Rainbow*

It is often easier to achieve either of two goals than to achieve both at the same time. In the course of achieving the second goal we may undo the effects of achieving the first. Terry Winograd points out in a *Psychology Today* article (Winograd, 1974) that his blocks program

cannot carry out the command, "Build a stack without touching any pyramids," because it has no way to work on one goal (building a stack) while keeping track of another one (avoiding contact with pyramids).

The reasoning subprograms of his natural language processor "have a sort of one-track mind unsuited to complicated tasks."

In program synthesis, such "simultaneous goal" problems are rampant. A

*The research reported herein was sponsored by the National Science Foundation under Grant GJ-36146.

Reproduced with permission from Machine Intelligence 8, by Richard Waldinger, Published in 1977 by Ellis Norwood Limited, Chichester.

typical example: the goal of a sort program is to rearrange an array in ascending order while ensuring at the same time that the resulting array is a permutation of the original. Simultaneous goal problems occur in mathematical equation solving, in robot tasks, and in real life as well.

An earlier paper (Manna and Waldinger, 1974) proposes a method for dealing with simultaneous goal problems in program synthesis. The present paper elaborates on the description of the method, reports on its implementation, discusses its application to general planning and robot problem solving, and points out some of its shortcomings and some projected improvements.

The general strategy proposed in (Manna and Waldinger, 1974) is: in order to construct a plan to achieve P and Q, construct a plan to achieve P, and then modify that plan to achieve Q as well. In the course of the modification, the relation P is "protected": no modifications that might make P false are permitted. If no satisfactory modification is found, the same strategy is attempted with the roles of P and Q reversed.

The earlier paper considers the construction of programs with branches and recursive loops; here, the discussion is strictly limited to the construction of straight-line programs. The simultaneous goal strategy can be integrated with the branch and loop formation techniques discussed in our earlier paper; however, this integration has not yet been implemented. Furthermore, the straight-line case is rich enough to be interesting in its own right.

The paper is divided into two main parts. Part 1 describes the simultaneous goal strategy in full detail, the program modification technique, and the modelling structure that the strategy requires. The strategy is illustrated by several examples, including the development of programs to interchange the values of two variables and to sort three variables, and the solution of the "anomaly" blocks-world problem from Sussman's (Sussman, 1973) thesis. These examples are not chosen to be impressive; they have been refined to present no difficulties other than the simultaneous goal problem itself.

Part 2 tries to relate this work to some other problem-solving efforts, and provides a critical survey of the way these systems represent a changing world in terms of the framework developed in Part 1. A summary of Part 2 appears in Section 2.9.

PART 1

SIMULTANEOUS GOALS, PROGRAM MODIFICATION, AND THE REPRESENTATION OF ACTIONS

1.1 A description of our approach

1.1.1 Achieving primitive goals

Below, the boarhound and the boar
Pursue their pattern as before
But reconciled among the stars.

T.S. Eliot, *Four Quartets*

Before we are ready to face multiple simultaneous goals, it may be helpful to say a few words about our approach to simple goals. Our system has a number of built-in techniques and knowledge of the kinds of goal to which each technique applies. When faced with a new goal, the system tries to determine if that goal is already true in its model of the world—if the goal is true it is already achieved. Otherwise, the system retrieves those techniques that seem applicable. Each of these techniques is attempted in turn until one of them is successful.

An important clue to the choice of technique is the form of the given goal. For instance, suppose we are working on blocks-world problems, and we are faced with the goal that block A be directly on top of block B. Assume that we have an arm that can move only one block at a time. Then we may build in the following strategy applicable to all goals of form, "Achieve: x is on y": clear the top of x and the top of y, and then put x on y. That x be clear is a new goal, which may already be true in the model, or which may need to be achieved itself (by moving some other block from the top of x to the table, say). "Put x on y" is a step in the plan we are developing. If we can successfully apply this technique, we have developed a plan to put A directly on top of B. However, for a variety of reasons this technique may fail, and then we will have to try another technique.

An example from the program synthesis domain: suppose our goal is to achieve that a variable X have some value b. One approach to goals of this form is to achieve that some other variable v has some value b, and then execute the assignment statement $X \leftarrow v$.* Here again, the relation "v has value b" is a subgoal, which may already be true or which may need to be achieved by inserting some other instructions into the plan. The assignment statement $X \leftarrow v$ is an operation that this technique itself inserts into the plan. (Note that if we are not careful, this technique will be applicable to its own subgoal, perhaps resulting in an infinite computation.) Of course, there may be other techniques to achieve goals of form "X has value b"; if the original technique fails, the others are applied.

The practice of retrieving techniques according to the form of the goal and then trying them each in turn until one is successful is called "pattern-directed function invocation," after Hewitt, 1972). A problem solver organized around the single-mindedness that Winograd complains of. When given multiple simultaneous goals, we would like to be able to apply the techniques applicable to each goal and somehow combine the results into a single coherent plan that achieves all of them at once.

1.1.2 Goal regression

Change lays not her hand upon truth.

A.C. Swinburne, *Poems: Dedication*

---

*We use a lower case "v" but an upper case "X" because here, X is the name of a specific variable while v is a symbol that can be instantiated to represent any variable.

Our approach to simultaneous goals depends heavily on having an effective program modification technique. Our program modification technique in turn depends on knowing how our program instructions interact with the relations we use to specify the program's goals.

Suppose P is a relation and F is an action of program instruction; if P is true, and we execute F, then of course we have no guarantee that P will still be true. However, given P, it is always possible to find a relation P' such that achieving P' and then executing F guarantees that P will be true afterwards. For example, in a simple blocks world if P is "block C is clear" (meaning C has no blocks on top of it) and F is "Put block A on block B," then P' is the relation "C is clear or A is on C": for if C is clear before putting A on B, then C will still be clear afterwards, while if A is on C before being put on B, then the action itself will clear the top of C.*

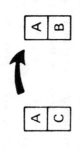

FIGURE 1

We will demand that P' be the weakest relation that ensures the subsequent truth of P; in other words, if P' is not true before executing F, P may not be true afterwards. Otherwise, we could always take P' to be the relation that is always false. We will call P' the result of passing P back over F, and we will call the operation of passing P back "regression."

Another example: suppose F is an assignment statement "$X \leftarrow t$" where X is a variable and t an expression, and let P be any relation between the values of the variables of our program, written P(X). Then P' is P(t), the relation obtained by replacing X by t in P(X). For if P(t) is true before executing $X \leftarrow t$, then P(X) will certainly be true afterwards. For instance, if P(X) is "$X=A*B$," and F is "$X \leftarrow U*V$," then $P'=P(U*V)$ is "$U*V=A*B$," for if $U*V=A*B$ before executing $X \leftarrow U*V$, then $X=A*B$ afterwards. Furthermore, if $U*V=A*B$ is false before the assignment, then $X=A*B$ will be false afterwards.

Note that if X does not occur in P(X), then P(t) is the same as P(X); the instruction has no effect on the truth of the relation.

Regression will play an important part in our program modification technique and also in the way we construct our models. The use of a static relational description to describe a dynamic program has been variously attributed to (Floyd, 1967), (Naur, 1966), (Turing, 1950), and (Goldstine and von Neumann, 1947), but the observation that it is technically simpler to look at the "weakest preconditions" of a relation (passing it back), as we do, instead of the "strongest

*We assume that the blocks are all the same size, so that only one block can fit immediately on top of another.

postconditions" (passing it forward), appears to be due to (Manna, 1968), (Hoare, 1969), and (King, 1969). The term "weakest precondition" is Dijkstra's (1975); we will not use it because the word "precondition" has a different meaning in the artificial intelligence literature. All these authors apply the idea to proving the correctness of programs; (Manna, 1974) contains a survey of this application. We now go on to show how the idea applies to program modification as well.

1.1.3 Plan modification

It is a bad plan that admits of no modification.

Publilius Syrus, *Sententiae*

In order to achieve a goal of form P and Q, we construct a plan F that achieves P, and then modify F so that it achieves Q while still achieving P. The simplest way to modify F is to add new instructions to the end so as to achieve Q. This method is called a "linear theory plan" by Sussman (Sussman, 1973). However, this linear strategy may be flatly inadequate; for instance, executing the plan F may destroy objects or information necessary to achieve Q. Furthermore, even if Q can be achieved by some composite plan ⟨F:G⟩ (execute F, then execute G), how can we be sure that plan G will not cause P to be made false?

However, we may also modify F by adding new instructions to the beginning or middle, or by changing instructions that are already there. Let us assume that F is a linear sequence of instructions $\langle F_1,...,F_n \rangle$. As we have seen, in order to achieve Q after executing F, it suffices to achieve Q' immediately before executing F_n, where Q' is the result of passing Q back over F_n. Similarly, it suffices to achieve Q'' immediately before executing F_{n-1}, where Q'' is the result of passing Q' back over F_{n-1}.

How can we benefit by passing a goal back over steps in the plan? A goal that is difficult or impossible to achieve after F has been executed may be easier to achieve at some earlier point in the plan. Furthermore, if achieving Q after executing F destroys the truth of P, it is possible that planning to achieve Q' or Q'' earlier will not disturb P at all; a planner should be free to achieve Q in any of these ways.

How is the planner supposed to know how to pass a relation back over a given plan step? First of all, the information can be given explicitly, as one of a set of rules. These "regression rules," which can themselves be expressed as programs, are regarded as part of the definition of the plan step. Alternatively, if a relation is defined in terms of other relations, it may be possible to pass back those defining relations. Furthermore, if the plan step is defined in terms of simpler component plan steps, then knowing how to pass relations back over the components allows one to pass the relation back over the original plan step. Finally, if no information at all exists as to how to pass a relation back over a plan step, it is assumed that the plan step has absolutely no effect on the relation. This assumption makes it unnecessary to state a large number of rules, each saying that a certain action has no effect at all on a certain relation. Thus we avoid the so-called "frame problem" (cf. [McCarthy and Hayes, 1969]).

In modifying a program it is necessary to ensure that it still achieves the purpose for which it was originally intended. This task is performed by the protection mechanism we will now describe.

1.1.4 Protection

> Protection is not a principle, but an expedient.
>
> *Disraeli, Speech*

Our strategy for achieving two goals P and Q simultaneously requires that after developing a plan F that achieves P we modify F so that it still achieves Q while still achieving P. This strategy requires that in the course of modifying F the system should remember that F was originally intended to achieve P and check that it still does. It does this by means of a device called the protection point: we attach P to the end of F as a comment. This comment has imperative force: no modifications are permitted in F that do not preserve the truth of P at the end of the modified plan. We will say that we are protecting P at the end of F. Any action that destroys the truth of P will be said to violate P. Relations may be protected at any point in a plan; if a relation is protected at a certain point, that relation must be true when control passes through that point.*

Protection has purposes other than ensuring that simultaneous goals do not interfere with each other: for instance, if an action requires that a certain condition be true before it can be applied, we must protect that condition at the point before the action is taken to see that no modification in the plan can violate it.

In order to ensure that a modification cannot violate any of the protected relations, we check each of these relations to see that it is still true after the proposed modification has been made: otherwise, the modification must be retracted.

In the next section we will examine a very simple example involving two simultaneous goals in order to demonstrate the techniques we have described.

1.1.5 A very simple example

Suppose we have three blocks, A, B, and C, sitting on a table.

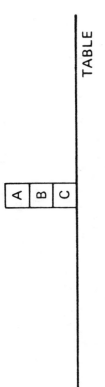

TABLE

FIGURE 2

*(Sussman, 1973) was the first to use protection in program synthesis, and to apply it to the simultaneous goal problem.

Our goal is to make a tower of the three blocks, with A on top and C on the bottom.

TABLE

FIGURE 3

We express this goal as a conjunction of two goals. "A is on B" and "B is on C." (We'll forget about saying that C is on the table.) Of course, if we approach these goals in the reverse order we have no problem: we simply put B on top of C and then put A on top of B; no destructive interactions arise. However, if we approach them in the given order we run into a blind alley.

We first attempt to achieve that A is on top of B. In order to do this, we see if A and B are clear (they are), and then we plan to put A on top of B. We have thus planned to achieve our first goal. Because we will now work on another goal to be achieved simultaneously we protect the relation that A is on top of B. We will adopt a notation for representing plans under development in which the left-most column will represent the steps of the plan, the second column will represent the anticipated model or state of the world between the respective plan steps, and the third column will represent any goals that we have yet to achieve, and relations that have already been achieved but must be protected at that point. In this notation our plan so far is as follows:

Plan	Model	Comments
		Protect: A is clear
		Protect: B is clear
Put A on B		Achieve: B is on C
		Protect: A is on B

FIGURE 4

In order to put A on top of B we must be sure that A and B are both clear: therefore we have protected these two relations at the point before the action is applied. (Of course, the action itself violates one of the conditions afterwards: we merely want to ensure that the conditions will be true immediately before the action is applied, regardless of what modifications are made to the plan.) We put the goal "Achieve: B is on C" after the plan step and not before because we are initially attempting to achieve the goal by adding steps to the end of the plan and not the beginning.

Now, since our arm can lift only one block at a time, we will be forced to put A back on the table again in order to get B on top of C. This will violate our protected relation (A is on B) so we cannot hope to achieve our second goal by adding instructions to the end of the plan. But we can still try to pass the goal back over the plan. The goal "B is on C" passed back over the plan "Put A on B" is simply "B is on C" itself, because putting A on B will not alter whether or not B is on C. The plan state so far is as follows:

Plan	Model	Comments
Put A on B	A B C / A on B, C	Achieve: B is on C Protect: A is clear Protect: B is clear Protect: A is on B

FIGURE 5

The goal "B is on C" now occurs before the plan step.

Our goal "B in on C" can now be achieved by simply putting B on C; the appropriate plan step will be added to the beginning of the plan instead of to the end. The resulting plan state is illustrated in Figure 6.

avoid backing up and reversing the order in which the goals are approached. This technique will not always prevent such goal reordering; however, we will see that it will allow us to solve some problems that cannot readily be solved, regardless of the order in which the goals are attempted.

The reader may note that the model following the plan step "Put A on B" changes between Figure 5 and Figure 6, because of the insertion of the earlier plan step "Put B on C." It we maintained a model corresponding to each plan step, we would be faced with the task of updating the entire sequence of models following every insertion to reflect the action of the new plan step. This can be an arduous chore if the model is at all large. Instead we maintain only a scanty "skeleton" model that is not affected by an alteration, and generate or "flesh out" other portions of the model as needed, using the same regression method that we introduced earlier as a program modification technique.

1.1.6 Skeleton models

Following each step in the developing plan we have a model, which for our purposes may be regarded as a list of relations that are certain to be true following the execution of that plan step. For instance, following the step "Put A on B" we include in the model the relation "A is on B" and perhaps the relation "A is clear," meaning that no block is on top of A. However, we do not usually include any information about the location of B, for example, because, unless protected, the location of B can be changed by inserting new steps earlier in the plan.

Similarly, after an assignment statement $X \leftarrow t$ we do no generally include the fact that X has value 2 even if we believe that t has value 2 before the statement is executed, because subsequent modifications to the beginning of the program could change the value of t, unless that value is protected. In fact, the model following an assignment statement may be absolutely empty.

In addition to the models that follow each statement in the plan, we have an initial model that describes that situation at the beginning (as given by the problem statement), and we have a global model of the "eternal verities," relations such as x=x, that are unchanged by any action or the passage of time. Information in the global model is implicitly present in all the other models.

The models that follow each action in the plan are incomplete: much knowledge about the situation is not included explicitly. How are we to compensate for this deficiency?

Suppose that we are given a plan $F_1,...,F_n$, and we need to know whether some relation Q is true after execution of step F_i. We first see if Q is explicitly in the model following F_i; in other words, we see if Q is an immediate consequence of the execution of F_1. If not, we simply pass Q back over the plan step F_i, yielding a perhaps altered relation Q'. We then check if Q' is in the preceding model. The justification for this measure is clear: Q' has been defined as the relation that must be true before the execution of F_i in order that Q will be true afterwards.

If we fail to determine if Q' is true, we pass Q' back over F_{i-1} and repeat the

Plan	Model	Comments
Put B on C	A B C / B on C	Protect: B is clear Protect: C is clear
Put A on B	A on B, C	Protect: A is clear Protect: B is clear
	A on B on C	Protect: B is on C Protect: A is on B

FIGURE 6

Note that the new plan step did not interfere with any of the protected relations; otherwise we would have had to retract the step and find some other solution. As it is, the two-step plan "Put B on C; Put A on B" achieves the desired goal. The method of passing goals back over plan steps has enabled us to

process until we have passed Q all the way back to the initial model. If we are still unable to determine whether Q is true we must give up. Even if we determine that Q is true, we must generally resist the temptation to add it to the model that follows F_i; unless Q is protected, later plan alterations could make Q false, and then the model would be inaccurate.

An example: suppose we are given a model in which block A is on C, but blocks A and B both have a clear top.

FIGURE 7

We somehow develop the plan step "Put A on B," and we are led to inquire if C is clear. We cannot determine this from the model that follows "Put A on B," because that model only contains the relations "A is on B" and "A is clear." However, we can pass that relation back over the plan step using a regression rule (as described in Section 1.1.2), leading us to ask if "C is clear or A is on C." Since we know "A is on C" initially, we can conclude "C is clear" in the model following the plan step.

The skeleton model is a technique in which the partial plan that has been constructed is regarded as a central part of the model. Important relationships and the plan itself are in the model explicitly; other relationships may be inferred using the regression rules.

It is traditional in problem solving to distinguish between rules that work backwards from the goal and rules that work forwards from the present state of the world. In Hewitt's (Hewitt, 1972) terminology, these rules are called "consequent theorems" and "antecedent theorems" respectively. Regression rules are a special kind of consequent theorem that can refer explicitly to steps in the plan as well as relations in the model. (Kowalski, 1974) and (Warren, 1974) also discuss the application of regression rules as a modelling technique.

The use of skeleton models means that if a relation P is protected at the end of a plan, no modification can be made at any point in the plan that will not leave P true at the end, because, in checking the truth of P after the modification has been made, we will percolate P back up through the plan, and the unfortunate interaction between P and the new plan step will be discovered.

For instance, suppose a plan step X ← Y achieves a protected relation P(X), and a new instruction Y ← Z is inserted at the beginning of the plan, where P(Z) is false. We will try to check that the protected relation P(X) is still true at the end of the modified program. Using regression, we will therefore check if P(Y) is true in the middle of the program, and thus that P(Z) is true at the beginning. Since P(Z) is false, we will detect a protection violation and reject the proposed modification.

This mechanism means that it is necessary to protect a relation only at the point at which we need it to be true. In the previous example, we must protect P(X) after the assignment statement X ← Y, but we need not protect P(Y) before the statement; the latter protection is implicit in the former.

A description of how skeleton models can be implemented using the "context" mechanism of the new artificial intelligence programming languages occurs in Section 2.7.

We have concluded the general description of our approach to simultaneous goals. The balance of Part 1 concerns how this technique has been applied to specific subject domains in order to solve the sample problems.

1.2 Interchanging the values of two variables

1.2.1 Relations that refer to variables

So first, your memory I'll jog,
And say: A CAT IS NOT A DOG.
T.S. Eliot, *Old Possum's Book
of Practical Cats*

In the next section we will show the synthesis of a more complex program whose specification is represented as a set of simultaneous goals. The subject domain of this program will be variables and their values. However, we must first examine a certain kind of relation more closely: the relation that refers directly to the variable itself, as opposed to its value. For instance, the relation "variable X has value a," written "X:a," refers both to the variable X and its value a. The relations "variable X is identical to variable Y," written "X≈Y," and its negation "variable X is distinct from variable Y," written "X≠Y," refer to variables X and Y, but do not refer at all to their values. X≠Y means "X and Y are not identical," and is true regardless of whether X and Y have the same value. Relations such as ≈, which do not refer to values at all, are not affected by assignment statements or any program instructions we are going to consider. Relations such as ":" are more complicated. For instance, the relation X:a passed back over the assignment statement X ← Y yields Y:a, where X and Y are both variables. (A more general rule covers the case in which an arbitrary term plays the role of the variable Y, but we will have no need to consider this case in the following examples.) A more complex situation arises if the variable in the relation is existentially quantified. Such a situation arises if the relation is a goal to find a variable with a certain value. For instance, how do we pass back a goal such as "Find a variable v such that v:a" over the instruction X ← Y? If there is a variable v such that v:a before the assignment statement is executed, and if that variable is distinct from X, then certainly v:a after the execution of X ← Y. Furthermore, if Y:a before the execution, then v can be identical to X as well. Therefore, passing the goal "Find a variable v such that v:a" back over the assignment statement X ← Y yields

We will assume the system knows verities such as x≈x, X≠Y, or X≠Z. In the example of the next section we will use one additional fact about the relation ≠: the fact that we can always invent a new variable. In particular, we will assume we can find a variable v such that v≠X by taking v to be the value of a program GENSYM that invents a new symbol every time it is called.

There is, of course, much more to be said about these peculiar relations that refer to variables themselves. They do not follow the usual Floyd-Naur-Manna-King-Hoare rule for the assignment statement. However, the discussion in this section will be enough to carry us through our next example.

1.2.2 The solution to the two variable problem*

  But above and beyond there's still one name left over,
  And that is the name that you never will guess
  The name that no human research can discover—
  But THE CAT HIMSELF KNOWS, and will never confess.
          T.S. Eliot, *Old Possum's Book of Practical Cats*

The problem of exchanging the values of two variables is a common beginner's programming example. It is difficult because it requires the use of a "temporary" variable for storage. Part of the interest of this synthesis involves the system itself originating the idea of using a generated variable for temporary storage.

We are given two variables X and Y, whose initial values are a and b; in other words, X:a and Y:b. Our goal is to produce a program that achieves X:b and Y:a simultaneously.

Recall that our strategy when faced with a goal P and Q is to try to form a plan to achieve P, and then to modify that plan to achieve Q as well. Thus our first step is to form a plan to achieve X:b.

For a goal of form X:b we have a technique (Section 1.1.1) that tells us to find a variable v such that v:b and then execute the assignment statement X ← v. We have such a v, namely Y. Therefore, we develop a plan, X ← Y, that achieves X:b. We must now modify this plan to achieve Y:a while protecting the relation X:b that the plan was developed to achieve. In our tabular notation:

Plan	Model		Comments	
	X:a	Y:b	Achieve:	Y:a
				X:b
X ← Y	X:b	Y:b	Protect:	X:b

FIGURE 8

"Find a variable v such that
    v≠X and v:a
  or v≈X and Y:a."

(In our table we record the full model at each stage even though the implementation does not store this model explicitly.

In trying to achieve Y:a we attempt to find a variable v such that v:a. Once we have executed X ← Y, no such variable exists. However, we pass the goal "Find v such that v:a" back over the plan step X ← Y, yielding

    Find v such that
        v≠X and v:a
      or v≈X and Y:a,

as explained in the preceding section. We now attempt to achieve this goal at the beginning of the plan. In tabular form

Plan	Model		Comments	
	X:a	Y:b	Achieve:	Find v such that
				v≠X and v:a
				or v≈X and Y:a
X ← Y	X:b	Y:b	Protect:	X:b

FIGURE 9

Once the outstanding goal is achieved, we will add an assignment statement Y ← v to the end of the program, where v is the variable that achieves the goal.

If we work on the goals in the given order, we try to find a v such that v≠X. Here we know that GENSYM will give us a new variable name, say G₁, guaranteed to be distinct from X. Our problem is now to achieve the first conjunct, namely G₁:a. But this can easily be achieved by inserting the assignment statement G₁ ← X at the beginning of the plan, since X:a initially. Inserting this instruction does not disturb our protected relation.

We have been trying to find a v satisfying the disjunction

    v≠X and v:a
  or v≈X and Y:a

We have satisfied the first disjunct, and therefore we can ignore the second. (We

---

*Another way of approaching this problem is discussed in (Green *et al.*, 1974). Green's system has the concept of temporary variable built in. He uses a convention of inserting a comment whenever information is destroyed, so that a patch can be inserted later in case the destroyed information turns out to be important.

will consider later what happens if we reverse the order in which we approach some of the subgoals.)

We have thus managed to find a v such that v:a at the end of the program, namely $v \approx G_1$. Since our ultimate purpose in finding such a v was to achieve Y:a, we append to our program the assignment statement $Y \leftarrow G_1$. This addition violates no protected relations, and achieves the last of the extant goals. The final program is thus

Plan	Model			Comments	
	X:a	Y:b			
$G_1 \leftarrow X$	X:a	Y:b	G_1:a		
$X \leftarrow Y$	X:b	Y:b	G_1:a		
$Y \leftarrow G_1$	X:b	Y:a	G_1:a	Protect:	Y:a
	X:b	Y:a	G_1:a	Protect:	X:b

FIGURE 10

The program has "invented" the concept of "temporary variable" by combining two pieces of already existing knowledge: the fact that GENSYM produces a variable distinct from any given variable, and the rule for passing a goal "Find a v such that v:a" back over an assignment statement. Of course, we could have built in the temporary variable concept itself, and then the solution would have been found more easily. But in this case the invention process is of more interest than the task itself.

Notice that at no point in the construction did we violate a protected relation. This is because of the fortunate order in which we have approached our subgoals. For example, if we had chosen to work on the disjunct

$$v \approx X \text{ and } Y:a$$

instead of

$$v \not\approx X \text{ and } v:a,$$

we would have inserted the assignment statement $Y \leftarrow X$ at the beginning of the program in order to achieve Y:a, and we would have proposed the program

$$Y \leftarrow X$$
$$X \leftarrow Y$$
$$Y \leftarrow X$$

which violates the protected relation X:b. Other alternative choices in this synthesis are either successful or terminated with equal dispatch.

1.3 Sorting three variables*

1.3.1 Sorting two variables

In our next example we will see how to construct a program to sort the values of three variables. This program will use as a primitive the instruction sort2, which sorts the values of two variables. Before we can proceed with the example, therefore, we must consider how to pass a relation back over the instruction sort2.

Executing sort2(X Y) will leave X and Y unchanged if X is less than or equal to Y $(X \leq Y)$, but will interchange the values of X and Y otherwise. Let P(X Y) be any relation between the values of X and Y. We must construct a relation P'(X Y) such that if P'(X Y) is true before sorting X and Y, P(X Y) will be true afterwards. Clearly, if $X \leq Y$, it suffices to know that P(X Y) itself is true before sorting, because the sorting operation will not change the values. On the other hand, if $Y < X$ it suffices to know P(Y X), the expression derived from P(X Y) by exchanging X and Y, because the values of X and Y will be interchanged by the sorting. Therefore, the relation P'(X Y) is the conjunction

$$\text{if } X \leq Y \text{ then P(X Y)}$$
$$\text{and if } Y < X \text{ then P(Y X)}$$

A similar argument shows that the above P' is as weak as possible. The same line of reasoning applies even if X or Y does not actually occur in P. For instance, if X does not occur, P(Y X) is simply P(X Y) with Y replaced by X.

Given the appropriate definition of sort2, it is straightforward to derive the above relation mechanically (e.g., see [Manna, 1974]). However, that would require the system to know about conditional expressions, and we do not wish to discuss those statements here. For our purposes, it suffices to assume that the system knows explicitly how to pass a relation back over a sort2 instruction.

1.3.2 Achieving an implication

We have excluded the use of conditionals in the programs we construct. However, we cannot afford to exclude the goals of form "if P then Q" from the specifications for the program being constructed. For instance, such specifications can be introduced by passing any relation back over a sort2 instruction.

*This problem is also discussed in (Green, *et al.*, 1974). Green allows the use of program branches and the program he derives has the form of a nested conditional statement. Green's use of the case analysis avoids any protection violations in his solution: the interaction between the subgoals plays a much lesser role in Green's formulation of the problem. Some other work in the synthesis of sort programs (see [Green and Barstow, 1975], [Darlington, 1975]) does not consider "in-place" sorts at all; goal interactions are still important, but protection issues of the type we are considering do not arise. However, Darlington's concept of "pushing in" a function is the analogue of regression for programs in which nested functional terms play the role of sequential program instructions.

The form of these specifications suggests that the forbidden conditional expression be used in achieving them. Therefore, for purposes of this example we will introduce a particularly simple-minded strategy: to achieve a goal of form "if P then Q," first test if P is known to be false: if so, the goal is already achieved. Otherwise, assume P is true and attempt to achieve Q.

The strategy is simple-minded because it does not allow the program being constructed to itself test whether P is true; a more sophisticated strategy would produce a conditional expression, and the resulting program would be more efficient. However, the simple strategy will carry us through our next example.

1.3.3 The solution to the three-sort problem

Given three variables, X, Y, and Z, we want to rearrange their values so that X≤Y and Y≤Z. Either of these goals can be achieved independently, by executing sort2(X Y) or sort2(Y Z) respectively. However, the simple linear strategy of concatenating these two instructions does not work; the program

```
sort2(X Y)
sort2(Y Z)
```

will not sort X, Y, and Z if Z is initially the smallest of the three. On the other hand, the simultaneous goal strategy we have introduced does work in a straightforward way.

In order to apply our strategy, we first achieve one of our goals, say X≤Y, using the primitive instruction sort2(X Y). We then try to modify our program to achieve Y≤Z as well. In modifying the program we protect the relation X≤Y. In tabular form, the situation is as follows:

Plan	Model	Comments
sort2(X Y)	X≤Y	Achieve: Y≤Z Protect: X≤Y

FIGURE 11

As we have pointed out, simply appending a plan step sort2(Y Z) will violate the protected relation X≤Y. Therefore we pass the goal back to see if we can achieve it at an earlier stage. The regressed relation, as explained in the previous section, is

if X≤Y then Y≤Z
and if Y≤X then X≤Z.

(This relation effectively states that Z is the largest of the three numbers.) Our situation therefore is as follows:

Plan	Model	Comments
sort2(X Y)	X≤Y	Achieve: if X≤Y then Y≤Z and if Y≤X then X≤Z Protect: X≤Y

FIGURE 12

We must now try to achieve the remaining goal. This goal is itself a conjunction and is handled by the simultaneous goal strategy. The first conjunct, "if X≤Y then Y≤Z," is an implication. Therefore we first test to see if X≤Y might be known to be false, in which case the implication would be true. However, nothing is known about whether X≤Y, so we assume it to be true and resign ourselves to achieving the consequent Y≤Z: this can easily be done using the primitive instruction sort2(Y Z). Inserting this instruction at the beginning of the plan does not interfere with the protected relation X≤Y: the protection point is immediately preceded by the instruction sort2(X Y). Our situation is therefore as follows:

Plan	Model	Comments
sort2(Y Z)	Y≤Z	Achieve: if Y<X then X≤Z Protect: if X≤Y then Y≤Z
sort2(X Y)	X≤Y	Protect: X≤Y

FIGURE 13

(Notice that we do not reproduce the complete model for this example, but only include the skeleton model.)

We have achieved the goal "if X≤Y then Y≤Z," which is one of two simultaneous goals. We therefore protect the relation we have just achieved and attempt to modify the program to achieve the remaining goal, "if Y≤X then X≤Z." Again, we cannot disprove Y≤X and therefore we attempt to achieve the consequent, X≤Z. This goal can be achieved immediately by executing sort2(X Z), but we must check that none of the protected relations is disturbed. Our situation is

Plan	Model	Comments
sort2(Y Z)	Y≤Z	
sort2(X Z)	X≤Z	Protect: if X≤Y then Y≤Z
sort2(X Y)	X≤Y	Protect: X≤Y

FIGURE 14

The second protected relation $X \leq Y$ is still preserved: the first presents us with a bit more difficulty, but is in fact true: a human might notice that Z is the largest of the three numbers at this point. Perhaps it is worth explaining how the system verifies this protected relation, thereby illustrating the use of the skeleton model.

After executing the second instruction sort2(X Z), the only information in skeleton model is that $X \leq Z$. This is not enough to establish that the protected relation is undisturbed. The system therefore passes the relation back to an earlier model and tries to prove it there. The regressed relation is

$$\text{if } X \leq Z \text{ then (if } X \leq Y \text{ then } Y \leq Z)$$
$$\text{and if } Z \leqslant X \text{ then (if } Z \leqslant Y \text{ then } Y \leqslant X).$$

The earlier model tells us that $Y \leq Z$ [because we have just executed sort2(Y Z)]. The first conjunct is thus easy to prove: the conclusion $Y \leq Z$ is known explicitly by the model. The second conjunct follows from transitivity: since we know $Y \leq Z$ from the model and $Z \leqslant X$ from the hypothesis we can conclude that $Y \leqslant X$. (This sort of reasoning is performed by a mechansim described in [Waldinger and Levitt, 1974]). The program in Figure 14 is therefore correct as it stands (although additional relationships should be protected if the plan is to undergo further modification).

It is pleasing that this last bit of deduction was not noticed by Manna and Waldinger in preparing the 1974 paper, but was an original discovery of the program, which was implemented afterwards. Manna and Waldinger assumed the protected relation would be violated and went through a somewhat longer process to arrive at an equivalent program. This is one of those not-so-rare cases in which a program debugs its programmer.

In order to show how these ideas apply to robot-type problems we discuss one further example, Sussman's "anomaly," in the next section.

1.4 The Sussman "anomaly"

We include this problem because it has received a good deal of attention in the robot planning literature (e.g., [Sussman, 1973; Warren, 1974; Tate, 1974; Hewitt, 1975; Sacerdoti, 1975]). However, for reasons that we will explore in Part 2, the solution does not exercise the capabilities of the system as fully as the previous two examples. We are given three blocks in the following configuration:

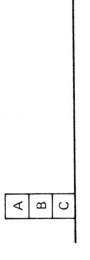

FIGURE 15

We are asked to rearrange them into this configuration:*

FIGURE 16

The goal is thus a simple conjunction "A is on B and B is on C." (We will forget about the table.)

The anomaly is one of the simplest blocks-world problems for which the linear strategy does not work regardless of the order in which we approach the subgoals: if we clear A and put A on B we cannot put B on C without removing A:

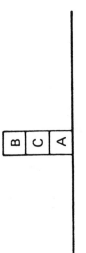

FIGURE 17

(Remember the arm can lift only one block at a time.)

On the other hand, if we put B on C first, we have buried A and cannot put it on top of B without disturbing the other blocks:

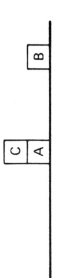

FIGURE 18

Our technique can solve this problem regardless of the order in which it attacks the goals. We will consider just one of these orderings: Assume we attempt to achieve "A is on B." The system will generate subgoals to clear A and B. B is already clear, and A will be cleared by putting C on the table. Then A will be put on B. This much can be done by the elementary strategy for achieving the "on" relationship (Section 1.1.1). Our situation is as follows:

---

*This problem was proposed by Allan Brown. Perhaps many children thought of it earlier but did not recognize that it was hard.

Plan	Model	Comments
Put C on TABLE		Protect: C is clear
Put A on B		Protect: A is clear / Protect: B is clear
		Achieve: B is on C / Protect: A is on B

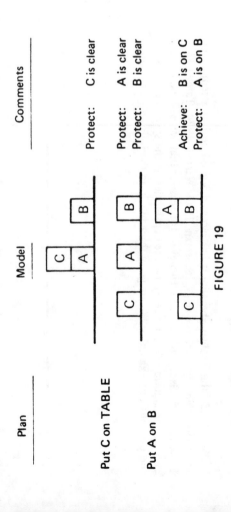

FIGURE 19

We protect "A is on B" because we want to modify the plan to achieve "B is on C" while still achieving "A is on B." We protect "A is clear" and "B is clear" earlier in order to make sure that the operation "Put A on B" will still be legal after the modifications are made.

Now, we have seen that we cannot achieve "B is on C" by adding new steps to the end of the plan without disturbing the protected relation "A is on B." Therefore we again pass the goal back to an earlier stage in the plan, hoping to achieve it before the protected relationship is established.

Passing "B is on C" back over the plan step "Put A on B" yields "B is on C" itself: whether B is on C or not is unaffected by putting A on B. The situation is thus:

Plan	Model	Comments
Put C on TABLE		Protect: C is clear
		Achieve: B is on C / Protect: A is clear / Protect: B is clear
Put A on B		Protect: A is on B

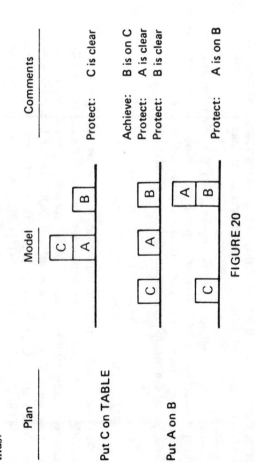

FIGURE 20

The goal "B is on C" can be easily achieved at the earlier stage: B and C are both clear, so we can simply put B on C. Furthermore this operation does not violate any of the protected relations. Since all goals have been achieved, our final plan is as follows:

Plan	Model	Comments
Put C on TABLE		Protect: C is clear
Put B on C		Protect: B is clear / Protect: C is clear
Put A on B		Protect: A is clear / Protect: B is clear
		Protect: A is on B / Protect: B is on C

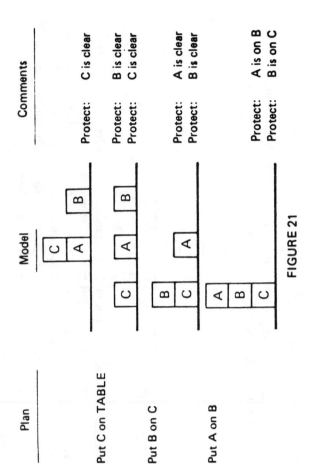

FIGURE 21

The solution is similar if the order in which the goals are attempted is reversed. This completes the last of our examples. In the next section we discuss some of the limitations of this approach, and consider how they might be transcended.

1.5 Limitations and next steps

> Odin. . .of all powers mightiest far art thou
> Lord over men of Earth, and Gods in heaven,
> Yet even from thee thyself hath been withheld.
> One thing: to undo what thou thyself hast ruled.
>
> Matthew Arnold, *Balder Dead*

The policy maintained by our implementation is to allow no protection violations at all: if a proposed modification causes a violation, that modification is rejected. This policy is a bit rigid and can sometimes inhibit the search for a solution.

For instance, consider the blocks problem in which initially the blocks are as follows:

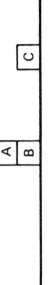

FIGURE 22

and in which the goal is to construct the following stack:

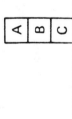

FIGURE 23

The goal may be considered to be the conjunction of two goals, "A is on B" and "B is on C." If these goals are approached in the reverse order, the system has no problem: it clears B by putting A on the table, puts B on C and then puts A on B. However, if the system approaches the goals in the given order, it will attempt to achieve "A is on B" first. This relation is already true, so the system protects it while trying to achieve the goal "B is on C." Here the system is baffled: it cannot put B on C without clearing B, thereby violating the protected relation. Passing the goal backwards into the plan is of no use: there are no plan steps to back it over. Clearly we would like to relax the restriction against protection violation until B is safely on C, and then reachieve the relation "A is on B," but our policy does not permit such a maneuver. The system is forced to reorder the goals in order to find a solution.

The restriction against violating protected relations also lengthens the search in generating the program to sort three variables. If these violations were permitted, a correct program

sort2(X Y)
sort2(Y Z)
sort2(X Y)

could be constructed without the use of regression at all. Why not permit violations, under the condition that a "contract" is maintained to reachieve protected relations that have been violated?

Indeed, such a strategy is quite natural, but we have two objections to it. First, suppose in the course of reachieving one protected relation we violate another. Are we to reachieve that relation later as well, and so on, perhaps ad infinitum? For example, in searching for a plan to reverse the contents of two variables it is possible to generate the infinite sequence of plans

X ← Y,
Y ← X,
X ← Y,

X ← Y
Y ← X
X ← Y,
Y ← X
X ← Y
Y ← X
X ← Y, ...

Each plan corrects a protection violation perpetrated by the previous plan—but commits an equally heinous violation itself. (This objection is a bit naive: one could invent safeguards against such aberrations, as has been done by Sussman (Sussman, 1973) and Green et al. (Green et al., 1974).

The second objection: allowing temporary protection violations can result in inefficient plans. For example, we could generate the following plan for solving the Sussman anomaly:

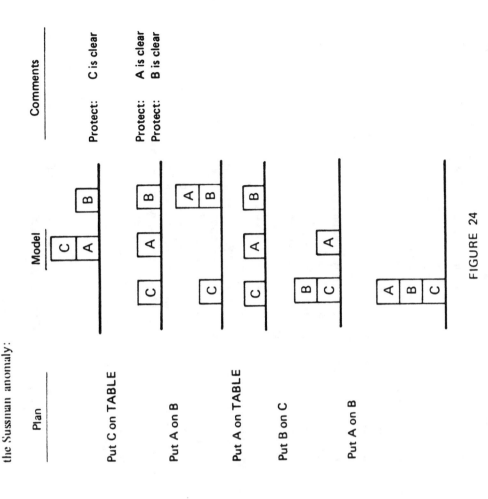

Plan	Model	Comments
Put C on TABLE		Protect: C is clear
Put A on B		Protect: A is clear Protect: B is clear
Put A on TABLE		
Put B on C		
Put A on B		

FIGURE 24

This plan is correct but inefficient: We have put A on B only to put A back on the table again because a protection violation was temporarily admitted. In a similar way, Sussman's HACKER produces an equally inefficient plan, approaching the goals in the opposite order. Of course, the plans could later be optimized, but allowing protection violations seems to encourage inefficiency in the plan produced.

Nevertheless, we feel that permitting temporary protection violations in a controlled way is a natural strategy that may be admitted in future versions of the program.

A more serious limitation of our implementation is that the only way it can modify plans is by adding new instructions, never by changing instructions that are already there. For example, suppose we have the initial configuration

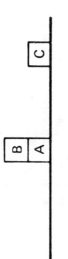

FIGURE 25

and our goal is to construct the stack

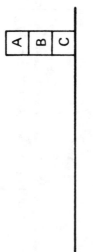

FIGURE 26

Assuming we approach the goal "A is on B" first, we are quite likely to put B on the table and then put A on B. In modifying the plan to achieve "B is on C," it would be clever to plan to put B on C instead of the table, but this sort of modification is beyong the system's capabilities. The "formal object" approach of Sussman (Sussman, 1973) would handle this properly: there, the decision about where to put B (in clearing A) would be deferred until we attempted the second goal "B is on C." However, other sorts of modifications require achieving the same goals in entirely different ways in order to accomodate the demands of the additional specification. Certain protected relations might never be achieved at all in the modified program if the higher level goal that constituted the "purpose" of the protected subgoal could be achieved in some other way. To effect such modifications will require that in the course of modifying a program we retain some of the goal-subgoal hierarchy that caused the original program to be constructed. Such modifications are in the spirit of our approach, but beyond the capabilities of our simple implementation.

The plans we have constructed in our paper are "straight-line" programs; they involve no loops or branches. The system as it exists contains a subsystem for constructing programs with branches and recursive loops (cf. [Manna and Waldinger, 1974]); however, these programs are free of side effects. Since the mechanisms for loop branch construction have not been integrated with the system that constructs structure-altering programs of the sort we have discussed in this paper. Nevertheless, these mechanisms are entirely consistent, and we

intend to unite them. Our hand simulations indicate that the system will then be able to construct a variety of array-sorting routines.

The use of goal regression for these more complex programs has been studied by many as a way of proving programs correct. Passing relations back into branches is straightforward (Floyd, 1967, Hoare 1969); passing a relation back into a loop, on the other hand, may require ingenuity to generalize the relation. This problem is discussed by (Katz and Manna, 1973; Wegbreit, 1974; Boyer and Moore, 1973; Moore, 1975) and others, but it is by no means "solved."

All the loops constructed by our synthesizer will initially be recursive: we intend to introduce iteration only during a subsequent optimization phase, following (Darlington and Burstall, 1973).

The way we have implemented skeleton modelling may be remarkably inefficient, particularly if the plan being constructed is to have many steps. It may take a long time to pass a relation back so far, and the transformed relation may grow alarmingly. There are many ways one might consider to make skeleton modelling more efficient. We prefer not to speculate on which of these ways will actually help until we have tried to implement some of them.

We regard program modification as a valuable synthesis technique apart from its role in achieving goals simultaneously. Often we can construct a program by modifying another program that achieves a goal that is somehow similar or analogous. For instance, in (Manna and Waldinger, 1974) we show how a unification algorithm could be constructed by modifying a pattern matcher. Another sort of program modification is optimization: here we try to modify the program to achieve the same goal more efficiently. It is our hope that systems with the ability to modify their own programs will be able to adapt to new situations without needing to be "general." Before that can happen, however, program modification techniques must be developed beyond what has been done here.

This concludes our discussion of the simultaneous goal strategy. In the next part of this paper we discuss how some other problem solvers have approached some of the same problems.

PART 2

THE REPRESENTATION OF ACTIONS AND SITUATIONS IN CONTEMPORARY PROBLEM SOLVING

> Time present and time past
> Are both perhaps present in time future,
> And time future contained in time past.
> If all time is eternally present
> All time is unredeemable.
>
> T.S. Eliot, *Four Quartets*

In the rest of this paper we will examine a number of problem-solving systems, asking the same question of each system: how are actions and their effects on the world represented? Thus we will not emphasize simultaneous goals in this section, and in discussing a system we will often ignore the very facets that make it unusual. Many of these systems approach problems of far greater complexity than those we have addressed in Part 2, problems involved in manipulating many more objects, and more complex structures. When we compare our approach to theirs, please bear in mind that our implementation has not been extended to handle the problems that our hand simulation dispatches with such ease.

2.1 The classical problem solvers

In the General Problem Solver (GPS) (see [Newell, Shaw, and Simon, 1960]), the various states of the world were completely independent. For each state, GPS had to construct a new model: no information from one state was assumed to carry through to the next automatically, and it was the responsibility of each "operator" (the description of an action) to tell how to construct a new model. The form of the states themselves was not dictated by GPS and varied from one domain to another.

The resolution-based problem solvers (e.g., [Green, 1969; Waldinger and Lee, 1969]) maintained the GPS convention that *every* action was assumed capable of destroying any relation: in other words it was necessary to state explicitly such observations as that turning on a light switch does not alter the location of any of the objects in a room. To supply a large number of these facts (often called "frame axioms") was tedious, and they tended to distract the problem solver as well. Since most actions leave most of the world unchanged, we want our representation of the world to be biased to expect actions not to affect most existing relations. For a number of reasons we demand that these "obvious" facts be submerged in the representation, so that we (and our system) can focus our attention on the important things, the things that change.

The STRIPS problem solver (Fikes and Nilsson, 1971) was introduced to overcome these obstacles. In order to eliminate the frame axioms, STRIPS adopted the assumption that a given relation is left unchanged by an action unless it is explicitly mentioned in the "addlist" or the "deletelist" of the action: relations in the addlist are always true after the action is performed, while relations in the deletelist are not assumed to be true afterwards even if they were true before. Thus the frame axioms are assumed implicitly for every action and relation unless the relation is included in the addlist or deletelist of the action. For instance, a (robot) action "go from A to B" might have "the robot is at B" in its addlist and "the robot is at A" in its deletelist. A relation such as "box C is in room 1" would be assumed to be unaffected by the action because it is not mentioned in either the addlist or the deletelist of the operator.

Henceforth, we shall refer to the belief that an action leaves all the relations in the model unchanged, unless specified otherwise, as the "STRIPS assumption."

A STRIPS model of a world situation, like a STRIPS operator, consists of an addlist and a deletelist. The addlist contains those relations that are true in the corresponding situation but that may not have been true in the initial situation, and the deletelist contains those relations that may not be true in the corresponding situation even though they were true initially. Thus one can determine which relations are true, given the current model and the initial list of relations. Also, given a model and an operator, it is easy to apply the operator to the model and derive a new model. The STRIPS scheme keeps a complete record of all the past states of the system, while allowing the various models to share quite a bit of structure.

STRIPS operators are appealingly simple. In the next section we will examine how the sorts of techniques we have discussed apply if the actions are all STRIPS operators.

2.2 Regression and STRIPS operators

Suppose an action is represented as a STRIPS operator, and that the members of the addlist and the deletelist are all atomic—that is, they contain no logical connectives or quantifiers. It is singularly simple to pass a relation back over such an operator, because the interaction between the operator and the relation are completely specified by the addlist and the deletelist. In order for a relation to be true after the application of such an operator, it must (1) belong to the addlist of the operator, or else (2) be true before application of the operator and not belong to the deletelist of the operator. Thus the rule for passing any relation back over such a STRIPS operator is implicit in the operator description itself.

For instance, an operator such as "move A from B to C" might have addlist "A is on C" and "B is clear" and deletelist "A is on B" and "C is clear." Thus, when passed back over this operator, the relation "A is on C" becomes true, "A is on B" becomes false, and "C is on D" remains the same. The simplicity of regression in this case indicates that we should express our actions in this form whenever possible.

The problem-solver WARPLAN (Warren, 1974) uses precisely the same sort of skeleton model as we do, and uses an identical strategy for handling simultaneous goals, but restricts itself to an atomic add-deletelist representation for operators, thus achieving a marvelous simplicity. Although we imagine that WARPLAN would require extension before it could handle the sort problem or the interchanging of variable values, the principles involved in the WARPLAN design are a special case of those given here.

Thus the clarity of actions expressed in this form makes reasoning about them exceedingly easy. However, many have found the add-deletelist format for representing actions too restrictive. With the advent of the "artificial intelligence programming languages," it became more fashionable to represent actions "procedurally," so that the system designer could describe the effects of the action using the full power of a programming language. We shall examine the impact of the STRIPS assumption on some of these systems in the next section.

2.3 The use of contexts to represent a changing world

What is past, even the fool knows.

Homer, *Iliad*

The new AI languages include PLANNER (Hewitt, 1972), QA4 (Rulifson, *et al.*, 1972). CONNIVER (McDermott and Sussman, 1972) and QLISP (Wilber, 1976), a variant of QA4. A comparative survey of these languages is provided in (Bobrow and Raphael, 1974). Implementers of problem solvers in these languages are fond of saying their systems represent actions "procedurally," as computer programs, rather than "declaratively," as axioms or add-delete lists. Yet in each of these systems the STRIPS assumption is firmly embedded, and the procedures attempt to maintain an updated model by deleting some relations and adding others; which relations an action adds or deletes depends on a computation instead of being explicitly listed beforehand. The STRIPS assumption is expressed not procedurally or declaratively but structurally: it is built into the choice of representation. The more primitive systems (e.g., [Winograd, 1971; Buchanan and Luckham, 1974]), implemented in an early version of PLANNER, maintained a single model which they updated by adding and deleting relations.* This scheme made it impossible for the system to recall any but the most recent world situation without "backtracking," passing control back to an earlier state and effectively undoing any intermediate side effects. The more recent trend† has been to incorporate the newer assumption by a particular use of the "context" mechanism and its use in building what we will call an "archeological model."

The context mechanism in QA4, CONNIVER, QLISP, AP/1, and HBASE operates roughly as follows: Each of these systems has a data base; assertions can be made and subsequently retrieved. Assertions and queries in these systems are always made with respect to an implicit or explicit context. If T_1 is a context, and we assert that B is on C with respect to T_1, the system will store that fact and answer accordingly to queries made with respect to T_1. There is an operation known as "pushing" a context that produces a new context, an immediate "descendant" of the original "parent" context. We may push T_1 any number of times, each time getting a new immediate descendant of T_1. If T_2 is a descendant of T_1, any assertion made with respect to T_1 will be available to queries made with respect to T_2.

---

*We do not mean to imply that all these systems were copying STRIPS; Winograd's work was done at the same time.

†See, for example, (Derksen, *et al.*, 1972; Sussman, 1973; Fahlman, 1974; McDermott, 1974; Fikes, 1975). (Balzer, *et al.*, 1974 and Tate, 1974) use the context mechanism of the AP/1 programming system and the HBASE data base system (Barrow, 1974), respectively, in exactly the same way.

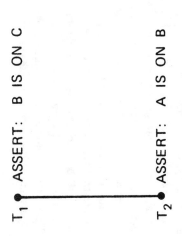

T_1 ASSERT: B IS ON C

T_2 ASSERT: A IS ON B

FIGURE 27

Thus if we ask whether B is on C with respect to T_2, we will be told "Yes" (in some fashion). However, assertions made with respect to that descendant are "invisible" to queries made with respect to its parent or any other context aside from its own descendants. For instance, if A is asserted to be on B with respect to T_2, that information will not be available to queries made with respect to T_1 (see Figure 27).

It is also possible to "delete" a relation with respect to a given context. If I delete the fact that B is on C with respect to T_2, the system will be unable to determine whether B is on C with respect to T_2 (on any of its descendants), but it will still know that B is on C with respect to T_1:

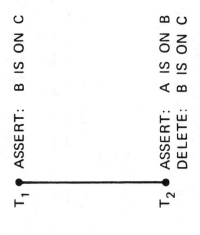

T_1 ASSERT: B IS ON C

T_2 ASSERT: A IS ON B
         DELETE: B IS ON C

FIGURE 28

The convention taken in planning systems implemented in languages with such a "context-structured data base" has been to equate each situation with a context. Furthermore, if some action occurs in a given situation T_1, resulting in a new situation, the usual practice has been to equate the new situation with an immediate descendant T_2 of the given context T_1. Any relations that are produced by the action are asserted with respect to T_2; any relations that may be disturbed by the action are deleted with respect to T_2. Other relations are still accessible in the new context. Thus if we are in situation T_1 and move block A onto block B from on top of block C, we construct a descendant T_2, asserting that A is on B and deleting that A is on C with respect to T_2. If B was known to be on block D in situation T_1, that information will still be available in situation T_2.

If T_2 is succeeded by another situation T_3, T_3 will be represented by a descendant of T_2, and so on. The structure of the sequence of contexts is represented as

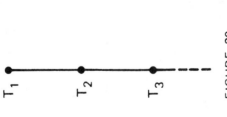

FIGURE 29

Each context is a descendant of the preceding context.

We will call this representation of the world an "archeological" model because it allows us to dig into successive layers of context in order to uncover the past.

In the balance of this paper we will propose that the archeological model is not always ideal. Because any assertion true in a context is automatically true in its descendants (unless specifically deleted), the use of archaeological models implicitly incorporates the STRIPS assumption, and accepts the STRIPS solution to the frame problem. Therefore, most of the planning systems implemented in the new AI languages use representations like that of STRIPS. We have been paying so much attention to the STRIPS assumption for the following reason: we are about to argue that in the future we may not want this assumption so firmly implanted in the structure of our problem solvers; indeed, some researchers have already begun to feel its constriction.

2.4 Influential actions

> For want of a nail the shoe was lost,
> For want of a shoe the horse was lost,
> For want of a horse the rider was lost,
> For want of a rider the battle was lost,
> For want of a battle the kingdom was lost,
> And all for the want of a horseshoe nail.
>
> Nursery Rhyme

The STRIPS assumption, embedded in the archeological model, has been so universally adopted because it banishes the frame axiom nightmare: it is no longer necessary to mention when an action leaves a relation unaffected because every action is assumed to leave every relation unaffected unless explicitly stated otherwise. The assumption reflects our intuition about the world, and the archeological model represents the assumption in an efficient way. Having found a mechanism that rids us of the headaches of previous generations of artificial intelligence researchers, shouldn't we swear to honor and cherish it forever?

Indeed, so much can be done within the STRIPS-archeological model framework, and so great are the advantages of staying within its boundaries, that we only abandon it with the greatest reluctance. If we were only modelling robot acts we might still be content to update our models by deleting some relations and adding others. The death blow to this approach is dealt by programming language instructions such as the assignment statement.

Suppose we attempt to express an assignment statement $X \leftarrow Y$ by updating an archeological model. We must delete any relation of form $P(X)$; furthermore, for every relation of form $P(Y)$ in the model we must add a relation of form $P(X)$. In addition, we may need to delete a relation of form "there is a z such that z has value b" even though it does not mention X explicitly. We may need to examine each relation in the model in order to determine whether it depends on X maintaining its old value. The consequences of this instruction on a model are so drastic and far reaching that we cannot afford to delete all the relations that the statement has made false.

How are we to represent the effects of an instruction such as sort2(X Y) on a model? If P(X Y) is the conjunction of everything that is known about X or Y, we might delete P(X Y) and assert $X \leq Y$ and (P(X Y) or P(Y X)). This is a massive and unworkable formula if P(X Y) is at all complex; furthermore, it does not express our intuition about the sort, that whether P(X Y) or P(Y X) holds depends on whether or not X was less than or equal to Y before the sort took place. Knowledge of the previous relation between X and Y has been lost.*

Even in the robot domain, for which the STRIPS formalism was orginated, the archeological representation becomes awkward when considering actions with indirect side effects. For example, if a robot is permitted to push more than once box at a time, an operation such as "move box A to point x" can influence the locations of boxes B, C, and D.

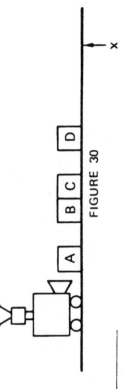

FIGURE 30

---

*A reply to some of this criticism appears in (Warren, 1976).

This situation becomes worse as the number of elements in the world increases: in moving a complex subassembly of a piece of equipment, we must change the location of every component of the subassembly. If we turn a subassembly upside down, we must replace every relation of form "x is on y" by the relation "y is on x," if x and y are components of the inverted assembly.

These actions are clumsy to model archeologically because so many relations need to be added and deleted from the model, and these relations may involve objects that are not explicitly mentioned by the operator. Furthermore, the operators are insensitive to whether or not these relations are relevant to the problem being solved.

Many of the more recent planning and modelling systems have been attempting to represent these "influential" actions, and we will soon examine how they have overcome the above obstacles. First let us point out that regression provides one technique for modelling these actions; for instance, we need not determine the location of any component indirectly affected by an action until a query concerning that component arises: thus, though many components may be moved, the system need only be concerned with a few of them. When a query about the location does arise, the regression technique will allow the new location to be determined from the original location and from the sequence of actions that has been performed on the subassembly. In particular, if the robot in the previous example (Figure 30) has moved the stack 10 feet to the right in moving box A to point x, the new location of box C will also be several feet to the right of the old location: of course, there is no need to compute the new location of C unless that information is requested.

We have seen that archeological models embed the **STRIPS** assumption; however, many of the more recent planning systems, while retaining the archeological structure, have been attempting to model actions that must be classified as influential. We will see in the next section how they have resolved the discrepancy.

2.5   Escaping from the STRIPS assumption

Once the archeological model was adopted, the designers of problem solvers devised mechanisms to loosen the STRIPS assumption embedded in their choice of representation.

Fahlman (Fahlman, 1974), using **CONNIVER**, wanted to simulate a robot that could lift and transport an entire stack or assembly of blocks in one step by carefully raising and moving the bottom block. We characterize this action as "influential" because many blocks will have their location changed when the bottom block is moved. Aware of the difficulty of maintaining a completely updated model, Fahlman distinguishes between "primary" and "secondary" relations. Primary relationships, such as the locations of the blocks, are fundamental to the description of the scene: an updated model is kept of all primary relationships. Secondary relationships, such as whether or not two blocks are touching, are defined in terms of the primary relationships and therefore can be deduced from the model, and added to it, only as needed. The system has

thereby avoided deducing large quantities of irrelevant, redundant secondary relationships.

Notice, however, that keeping an updated model of just the primary relationships may still be a sizable chore: for instance, at any moment the system must know the location of every block in the model, even though these locations are often themselves redundant; when a large subassembly is moved, the locations of each of the blocks in the subassembly can be computed from the location of the subassembly itself.

Furthermore, in Fahlman's system if a primary relationship is changed, all the secondary relationships that have been derived from that primary relationship and added to the model must be deleted at once to avoid potential inconsistency.

The modelling system of the SRI Computer Based Consultant (Fikes, 1975), implemented in QLISP, distinguishes between derived and explicitly asserted relations for the same reason that Fahlman distinguishes between primary and secondary data. However, in the SRI system the same relation might be derived in one instance and explicitly asserted in another. Thus the location of a component could very well be derived from the location of a subassembly.

Like the Fahlman system, the SRI system deletes all the information derived from an assertion when it deletes the assertion itself.

Note that the SRI system does not behave at all well if the user tries to assert a complex relationship explicitly, say, in a problem description. For instance, suppose the user says that block B is between blocks A and C. If the system then moves block A, it will still report that B is between A and C, because that relationship was explicitly asserted and not derived: the system has no way of knowing that it depends on the location of A.

The Fahlman system avoids this difficulty only by forbidding the user to assert any secondary relationships.

Both the Fikes and the Fahlman systems have the following scheme: define actions in terms of the important relationships that they modify, and then define the lesser relationships in terms of the important relationships. This simplifies the description of actions, makes model updating more efficient, and allows the system designer to introduce new relationships without needing to modify the actions' descriptions.

However, it may be impossible to define some lesser relationships in terms of the important ones; we may need to know directly how the lesser relationships are affected by actions. The moving of subassemblies provides a convenient example of this phenomenon.

Consider a row of blocks on a table.

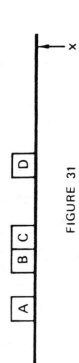

FIGURE 31

If skeleton models are adopted, the context mechanism need not be dropped altogether as a way of representing distinct world situations; however, descendent contexts cannot be used to represent successive world states. Our implementation of skeleton models uses contexts in a different way, which we will outline in the next section.

2.6 The use of contexts to implement skeleton models

Recall that we can "push" a given context any number of times, creating a new immediate descendant with every push. These new contexts are independent from each other–none of them is descended from any of the others, and an assertion made with respect to one of them will be invisible to the rest.

In our implementation of skeleton models we represent each situation by a context, but successive situations are all immediate descendents of a single global context T. Thus if situation T_2 results from situation T_1 by performing some act, T_1 and T_2 will both be immediate descendents of T, created by pushing T; T_2 will not be a descendant of T_1. We can represent the skeleton model context structure as follows:

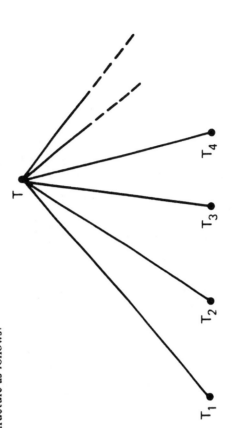

FIGURE 32

Asserting a relation with respect to T_1 does not automatically make it true with respect to T_2, and so on. The only relations asserted in the global context T are the eternal verities.

Since the structure of the skeleton model does not imply any relationship at all between successive states, we represent such knowledge procedurally, by the regression rules for passing a relation back from one state to the preceding one. We suffer a possible loss of efficiency in abandoning the archeological model, but we gain in flexibility and in our ability to represent influential operators efficiently. We do not need to struggle against the assumption incorporated into our representation.

We want to move A several feet to the right, to point x. We can either slide A or lift it. If we lift it, blocks B, C, and D will stay where they are, whereas if we slide it, we will inadvertently carry the others along. It is expensive to expect the slide operator to update the model to include the new locations of all the blocks it affects: there may be many of these intermediate blocks and they may not be important to the problem being solved. On the other hand, we cannot expect an archeological system to deduce the new location of B from the new model in case that information turns out to be needed: in order to compute the location of B, the system needs to know whether A has been lifted or slid, and that information is not part of a conventional model. Thus, in an archeological model, locations of intermediate blocks must always be computed at the time the slide is added to the plan.

If skeleton models are adopted, on the other hand, the actions in the plan form an integral part of the model. If A is slid to x, only the new location of A would be explicitly included in the new model. If subsequently we need to determine the location of B, a regression rule sees that A has been slid and asks whether B is in the path of the slide; if not, the location of B after the slide is the same as before; otherwise, the new location of B is somewhere to the right of A.

In both the archeological and the skeletal representations, knowledge about the side effects of sliding must be explicitly expressed. In the skeleton model, the new locations of the intermediate blocks need not be computed until they are needed.

In archeological modelling, the description of an action must be expressed completely in a single operator. For an action with many side effects, the operator is likely to be a rather large and opaque program. Skeleton modelling does not eliminate the need to describe the effects of an action explicitly; however, it does allow the description to be spread over many smaller, and usually clearer programs. Furthermore, one can alter a system to handle new relations merely by adding new regression rules, without changing any previously defined operators. In short, skeleton modelling can sometimes make a system more transparent and modular, as well as more efficient.

Skeleton models do not discard the STRIPS assumption. If this assumption were abandoned, the frame problem would be back upon us at once: for every relation and action it would be necessary to state or deduce a regression rule whether or not the action had any effect at all on the relation. Instead, skeleton models contain a default rule stating that if no other regression rule applies, a given relation is assumed to be left unchanged by a given action. This rule states the STRIPS assumption precisely but does not freeze it into a structure. We have lost in efficiency if actions really do have few side effects, because the archeological model does embed the STRIPS assumption in a structural way and requires no computation if it applies, whereas a skeleton model can only apply the assumption after all the regression rules have failed. The extent to which this modelling technique will be economic depends entirely on the "influence" of actions of the plan—the degree to which they affect the relations in the model.

Of course, it is possible to implement skeleton models without using a context mechanism. Problem solvers of the sort advocated by Kowalski (Kowalski, 1974) or implemented by Warren (Warren, 1974) embed a skeleton model representation in a predicate logic formalism in which states of the world are represented by explicit state variables, just as in the early theorem-proving approach. These systems are especially elegant in that the regression rules are indistinguishable from the operator descriptions. They both accept the STRIPS add-deletelist operator representation, but we can envision their incorporating the sort of regression we have employed without requiring any fundamental changes in structure. Hewitt (Hewitt, 1975) has indicated that a version of what we have called skeleton modelling has also been developed independently in the actor formalism, and Sacerdoti (Sacerdoti, 1975) uses another version in conjunction with the procedural net approach.

2.7 Hypothetical worlds

What might have been is an abstraction
Remaining a perpetual possibility
Only in a world of speculation.
What might have been and what has been
Point to one end, which is always present.
Footfalls echo in the memory
Down the passage which we did not take
Towards the door we never opened
Into the rose-garden.

                                 T.S. Eliot, *Four Quartets*

Although so far we have avoided discussing the formation of conditional plans in this paper, it may now be useful to note that using descendent contexts to split into alternate hypothetical worlds (cf. [Rulifson, *et al.*, 1972; McDermott, 1974; Manna and Waldinger, 1974]) is entirely consistent with using independent contexts in skeleton models, but presents something of a problem to archeological models.

In both archeological and skeletal models it is common to represent hypothetical worlds by descendent contexts. For instance, to prepare alternate plans depending on whether or not it is raining in a situation represented by context T_1, two new contexts T_1' and T_1'' are formed, corresponding to the cases in which it is raining and it is not raining, respectively. T_1' and T_1'' are both descendents of T_1, so that any relations known in T_1 will automatically be assumed about T_1' and T_1'' also, as one would have hoped. Furthermore, in T_1' it is asserted to be raining, while in T_1'' it is asserted not to be raining.

The plan for the rainy case would be represented as a sequence of contexts that follows T_1'. In an archeological model these would be successive descendants of T_1' (Figure 33), while in a skeleton model these would be independent contexts linked by regression rules. A similar sequence of contexts beginning with T_1'' would correspond to the plan for the case in which it is not rainy.

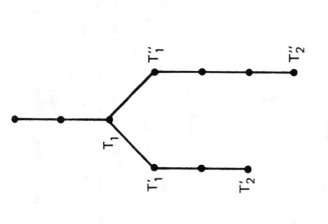

FIGURE 33

Eventually we may reach a situation T_2' and T_2'' in each plan, respectively, after which it becomes irrelevant whether or not it was raining in T_1. In other words our ultimate goal may now be achieved by a single plan that will work in either T_2' or T_2''. Therefore we would like to join our two plans back together into a single plan; we want to form a new context T_2 such that P is true in T_2 if and only if it is true in both T_2' and T_2''. This can be done in a skeleton model by creating an independent context T_2 linked to the previous contexts by the following regression rule: to establish R in T_2, establish R in both T_2' and T_2''.

The situation becomes more difficult if one attempts to maintain an updated archeological model. One could take the following approach: if P and Q are the conjunction of all that is known in T_2' and T_2'', respectively, then assert (P or Q) with respect to T_2. However, (P or Q) is likely to be an unwieldy formula, and we may have lost the information that P corresponds to the rainy situation and Q to the nonrainy one.

We regret that our treatment of hypothetical situations is so terse. A discussion of our own approach, with examples, is given in (Manna and Waldinger, 1974).

2.8 Complexity

Home is where one starts from. As we grow older
The world becomes stranger, the pattern more complicated
Of dead and living.

                                 T.S. Eliot, *Four Quartets*

Perhaps we should say a few words contrasting the work reported here with recent work of Sussman (Sussman, 1973) and Sacerdoti (Sacerdoti, 1975). Although both of these works deal in some of their aspects with simultaneous goals, the principal thrust of their interests is different from ours, and so comparisons are likely to be shallow.

Sussman's main interest is the acquisition of knowledge. Thus he wants his system to learn how to handle simultaneous goals, and is more concerned with learning than with simultaneous goals themselves. We, on the other hand, want our system to know how to handle simultaneous goals from the start, and are not (at present) concerned with learning at all.

The sort of program modification we do is distinct from debugging: the program we are modifying correctly achieves one goal, and we want it to achieve another. We also refrain from actually executing our programs, and ultimately produce programs that are guaranteed correct, whereas Sussman produces programs that may have undiscovered bugs. It is plausible that in tackling more complex problems we will want to introduce bugs and later correct them. We imagine this happening in problems involving several levels of detail: a program may work correctly in a crude way, but still contain many minor errors. The problems we have been considering are simple enough so that we have not been forced into using these techniques.

Similarly we view Sacerdoti's procedural nets, like his earlier abstraction hierarchies (Sacerdoti, 1974) as a way of dealing with complexity by submerging detail until a grossly correct plan has been developed. Then the plan is examined in greater depth, and difficulties are ironed out as they emerge. The Sacerdoti formalism can easily represent actions with many subsidiary side effects: these effects are considered only after the initial (approximate) plan has been formulated.

In approaching several simultaneous goals, Sacerdoti develops plans to achieve each of the goals separately; as interactions between the plans are observed, the system will impose orderings on the steps ("Step F_i from plan F must be executed before step G_j from plan G") and even alter the plans themselves to make them impervious to the effects of the other plans. Actions are represented essentially by addlists and deletelists, and the "critics" (cf. [Sussman, 1973]) that recognize the interactions between plans rely strongly on this representation, although the critic principle is more general.

Sacerdoti's approach to simultaneous goals is partially dictated by his application: a consultant system advising a human amateur in a repair task. The user may choose to order the plan steps in any of a number of valid ways; the system cannot force an order except where that order is necessary to avoid harmful interactions; therefore it maintains a highly parallel plan whenever possible until the user himself has selected the order. In a sense, Sacerdoti's system must anticipate all possible plans to achieve a task.

Sacerdoti's idea, deciding what order in which to approach goals only after having done some planning for each of them, is intriguing and avoids a certain

amount of goal reordering. However, we believe we will not make best use of hierarchical planning until we are ready to wade into deeper waters of complexity.

2.9 Recapitulation

You say I am repeating
Something I have said before. I shall say it again.
T.S. Eliot, *Four Quartets*

In this section we will briefly repeat the main points of the argument in Part 2.

The earliest problem solvers maintained entirely separate models corresponding to each state of the world. In GPS, each operator had the responsibility of constructing a completely new model, whereas in the resolution-based systems the description of the new model created by an action was distributed between several axioms, some describing how relationships were changed by the action, and others (the frame axioms) telling which relationships remained the same.

In an effort to do away with troublesome and obvious frame axioms, later problem solvers adopted what we have called the "STRIPS assumption," that any action will not change most relations, and therefore they described an action by telling which relations it adds and which relations it deletes from the model. The "addlists" and "deletelists" were either given explicitly or computed. Any relation not explicitly added or deleted by an action was assumed to be unaffected.

Systems implemented in artificial intelligence programming languages having a "context" feature tended to incorporate the STRIPS assumption by equating states of the world with contexts, and representing states that occur after a given state by successive descendants of the given context; since any relation asserted with respect to the given context is considered to be true with respect to any of its descendents unless explicitly deleted, the STRIPS assumption is expressed structurally in this "archeological" representation.

Meanwhile, the designers of problem-solving systems entered domains in which the STRIPS assumption began to break down: areas in which the world was modelled in such detail, or in which objects were so highly interrelated, that actions might have many consequences, most of which were irrelevant to the problem at hand. The STRIPS assumption and the archeological structure that expresses it become an obstacle here: it would be cumbersome and inefficient for the description of the action to have to make all these changes in the model. Recent problem solvers have attempted to escape from the STRIPS assumption by distinguishing between the important relations, which are always updated in the model, and the lesser relations, which are defined in terms of the important relations and which are only updated as necessary. These measures are inadequate largely because the designer of the system is prevented from stating explicitly how the lesser relationships are affected by the various actions.

The regression technique advocated here and elsewhere provides a method whereby the actions in the plan become an important part of the model, from which a relational description of the world can be "fleshed out" as necessary. The context mechanism can be used to represent this type of "skeleton model," but successive states are represented as parallel contexts instead of descendants. This latter representation has the additional advantage of being consistent with the use of descendent contexts to represent hypothetical worlds, and with the program modification technique introduced in Part 1.

In my end is my beginning.
T.S. Eliot, *Four Quartets*

ACKNOWLEDGMENTS

This work has been developed through discussions with Zohar Manna and Earl Sacerdoti. The manuscript has benefited from the comments of Rich Fikes, Earl Sacerdoti, and Bert Raphael. The ideas presented here have also been influenced by conversations with Mike Wilber, Bob Boyer, Nachum Dershowitz, Rod Burstall, John Darlington, Gordon Plotkin, Bob Kowalski, Alan Bundy, Bernie Elspas, Nils Nilsson, Peter Hart, Ben Wegbreit, Carl Hewitt, Harry Barrow, Cordell Green, Avra Cohn, Dave Barstow, Doug Lenat, and Lou Steinberg. Mike Wilber has been of special assistance in the use of the QLISP system, which is based on INTERLISP. Our efforts have been encouraged by the environments provided by the Artificial Intelligence Center at SRI, the Department of Artificial Intelligence at the University of Edinburgh, and the Applied Mathematics Department at Weizmann Institute. Linda Katuna and Lorraine Staight prepared many versions of the manuscript.

The National Science Foundation Office of Computing Activities supported this work through Grant GJ.36146.

REFERENCES

Balzer, R.M., N.R. Greenfeld, M.J. Kay, W.C. Mann, W.R. Ryder, D. Wilczynski, and A.L. Zobrist (1974) Domain-independent automatic programming. *Information Processing 74: Proc IFIP 74*, 2, 326-330.

Barrow, H.G. (1974) HBASE. *POP-2 Library Documentation*, Department of Artificial Intelligence, University of Edinburgh, Edinburgh.

Bobrow, D.G. and B. Raphael (1974) New programming languages for artificial intelligence research. *ACM Computer Surveys*, 6, 3, 155-174.

Boyer, R.S. and JS Moore (1973) Proving theorems about LISP functions. *Proc IJCAI3*, 486-493, Stanford, CA, also in *JACM*, 22, 1, 129-144.

Buchanan, J.R. and D.C. Luckham (1974) On automating the construction of programs. *Informal Memo*, Artificial Intelligence Laboratory, Stanford University, Stanford, CA.

Darlington, J. (1975) Application of Program Transformation to Program Synthesis. *Proc Colloques IRIA: Proving and improving programs*, 133-144, Arc et Senans, France.

Darlington, J. and R.M. Burstall (1973) A system which automatically improves programs. *Proc IJCAI3*, 479-485, Stanford, CA.

Derksen, J., J.F. Rulifson and R.J. Waldinger (1972) The QA4 language applied to robot planning. *AFIPS 41*, Part II, 1181-1187.

Dijkstra, E.W. (1975) Guarded commands, non-determinacy and a calculus for the derivation of programs. *Proceedings, International Conference on Reliable Software* 2-2.13, Los Angeles, CA.

Fahlman, S. (1974) A planning system for robot construction tasks. *Artificial Intelligence*, 5, 1, 1-49.

Fikes, R.E. (1975) Deductive retrieval mechanisms for state description models. *Technical Note 106*, Artificial Intelligence Center, Stanford Research Institute, Menlo Park, CA.

Fikes, R.E and N.J. Nilsson (1971) STRIPS: A new approach to the application of theorem proving in problem solving, *Artificial Intelligence*, 2, 3/4, 189-208.

Floyd, R.W. (1967) Assigning meanings to programs. *Mathematical Aspects of Computer Science*, Proceedings of a Symposium on Applied Mathematics Vol. 19, American Mathematical Society, 19-32.

Goldstine, H.H. and J. von Neumann (1947) Planning and Coding Problems for an Electronic Computer Instrument. *Collected Works of John von Neumann* 5, 80-235 (Pergamon Press, New York, 1963).

Green, C.C. (1969) Application of theorem proving to problem solving. *Proc IJCAI* 219-239, Washington, DC.

Green, C.C., R.J. Waldinger, D.R. Barstow, R. Elschlager, D.B. Lenat, B.P. McCune, D.E. Shaw and L.I. Steinberg (1974) Progress report on program-understanding systems. *Memo AIM-240*, Stanford Artificial Intelligence Laboratory, Stanford University, Stanford, CA.

Green, C.C. and D. Barstow (1976) A hypothetical dialogue exhibiting a knowledge base for a program-understanding system. *Machine Intelligence 8*, (eds. Elcock, E.W. and Michie, D.), Ellis Horwood Ltd. and John Wiley.

Hewitt, C. (1972) Description and Theoretical Analysis (using Schemata) of PLANNER: A Language for Proving Theorems and Manipulating Models in a Robot. *Ph.D. Thesis* Massachusetts Institute of Technology, Cambridge, Mass.

Hewitt, C. (1975) How to use what you know. *Proc IJCAI4*, 189-198, Tbilisi, Georgia, USSR.

Hoare, C.A.R. (1969) An axiomatic basis for computer programming. *CACM*, 12, 10, 576-580, 583.

Katz, S.M. and Z. Manna (1976) Logical analysis of programs, *CACM* 19, 4, 188-206.

King, J.C. (1969) A Program Verifier. *Ph.D. Thesis*, Department of Computer Science, Carnegie-Mellon University, Pittsburgh, PA.

Kowalski, R. (1974) Logic for Problem Solving. *Memo No. 75*, Department of Computational Logic, University of Edinburgh, Edinburgh.

Manna, Z. (1968) Termination of Algorithms, *Ph.D. Thesis* Department of Computer Science, Carnegie-Mellon University, Pittsburgh, PA.

Manna, Z. (1974) *Mathematical Theory of Computation* McGraw Hill, New York.

Manna, Z. and R.J. Waldinger (1974) Knowledge and reasoning in program synthesis. *Artificial Intelligence* 6 2, 175-208.

McCarthy, J. and P. Hayes (1969) Some philosophical problems from the standpoint of artificial intelligence, *Machine Intelligence 4*, (eds. Meltzer, B. and Michie, D.), American Elsevier, New York.

McDermott, D.V. (1974) Assimilation of new information by a natural language-understanding system, *AI Memo 291*, Artificial Intelligence Laboratory, Massachusetts Institute of Technology, Cambridge, MA.

McDermott, D.V. and G.J. Sussman (1972) The Conniver Reference Manual. *AI Memo 259* (revised 1973), Artificial Intelligence Laboratory, Massachusetts Institute of Technology, Cambridge, MA.

Moore, JS (1975) Introducing iteration into the pure LISP theorem prover. *IEEE Transactions on Software Engineering*, SE-1, 3, 328-338.

Naur, P. (1966) Proof of algorithms by general snapshots. *BIT* 6, 4, 310-316.

Newell, A., J.C. Shaw, and H.A. Simon (1960) Report of a General Problem-Solving Program for a Computer. *Information Processing, Proceedings of an International Con-*

ference on Information Processing, 256-264. UNESCO, Paris, France.

Rulifson, J.F., J.A.C. Derksen, and R.J. Waldinger (1972) QA4: A procedural calculus for intuitive reasoning. *Technical Note 73*, Artificial Intelligence Center, Stanford Research Institute, Menlo Park, CA.

Sacerdoti, E.D. (1974) Planning in a Hierarchy of Abstraction Spaces *Artificial Intelligence*, 5, 2, 115-135.

Sacerdoti, E.D. (1975) The non-linear nature of plans. *Proc IJCAI4*, 206-214, Tbilisi, Georgia, USSR.

Sussman, G.J. (1973) A Computational Model of Skill Acquisition. *Ph.D. Thesis*, Massachusetts Institute of Technology, Cambridge, MA.

Tate, A. (1974) INTERPLAN: A plan generation system that can deal with interactions between goals. *Memorandum MIP-R-109*, Machine Intelligence Research Unit, University of Edinburgh, Edinburgh.

Turing, A.M. (1950) Checking a large routine. *Report of a Conference on High Speed Automatic Calculating Machines*, 66-69. University of Toronto, Toronto.

Waldinger, R.J. and R.C.T. Lee (1969) PROW: A step toward automatic program writing. *Proc IJCAI*, 241-252, Washington, D.C.

Waldinger, R.J. and K.N. Levitt (1974) Reasoning about programs. *Artificial Intelligence*, 5, 3, 235-316.

Warren, D.H.D. (1976) Generating Conditional Plans and Programs. *Proc AISB Summer Conference*, 344-354, Edinburgh.

Wegbreit, B. (1974) The synthesis of loop predicates, *CACM 17*, 2, 102-112.

Wilber, M. A QLISP Reference Manual. *Technical Note 118*, Artificial Intelligence Center, Stanford Research Institute, Menlo Park, CA.

Winograd, T. (1971) Procedures as a Representation for Data in a Computer Program for Understanding Natural Language. *Ph.D. Thesis*, Massachusetts Institute of Technology, Cambridge, MA. also appears as *Understanding Natural Language* Academic Press, New York, NY.

Winograd, T., (1974) Artificial Intelligence—when will computers understand people? *Psychology Today*, 7, 12, 73-79.

Extract from Prolog for Programmers
By F. Kluźniak and S. Szpakowicz

---

8   TWO CASE STUDIES

8.1. PLANNING

We shall consider planning with respect to a finite, usually small, set of **objects** to which simple **actions** from a finite, and also small, set are applicable. Objects constitute a closed "**world**". The **state** of the "world" is, by definition, the set of all **relationships** that hold between its objects; we also call these relationships **facts** about objects. As a result of an action, some relationships cease or begin to hold; we say that an action **deletes** or **adds** facts. A fact established by an action is also called a **goal achieved** by this action. Every action transforms one state into another. **Planning** consists in finding a sequence of actions that lead from a given **initial state** to a given **final state**.

As an example, we shall describe one of the so-called cube worlds. There are three cubes, *a, b, c,* and *floor*. All we can do with them is stack cubes on cubes or on the floor. There are two types of facts concerning a cube U and an object W: U is sitting on W, and U is clear (this means that nothing is sitting on U). The set of possible states is determined by naming all meaningless (i.e. impossible or forbidden) combinations of facts:

—A cube X sitting on a *clear* cube Y;
—A cube sitting on two different objects;
—Two different cubes sitting on the same cube;
—An object sitting on itself.

There is one kind of action: move a single clear block, either from another block onto the floor, or from an object onto another clear block (the object must differ from both blocks). As a result of moving X from Y onto Z, X is sitting on Z instead of Y, Y is clear (unless it is the floor), Z is not clear (unless it is the floor).

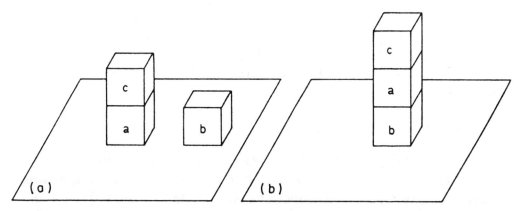

FIG. 8.1   (a) An initial state of the cubes world. (b) A final state of the cubes world.

Even in this microscopic world, planning may require some sophistication. It is reasonable to postulate that a desirable fact, once added, will never be deleted (otherwise we risk an infinite loop). However, let the initial state be that of Fig. 8.1a, described by a conjunction of five facts:

a on floor, b on floor, c on a, clear(b), clear(c).

Let the final state be that of Fig. 8.1b, described by a conjunction of two goals: c on a, a on b. The first goal is trivially achieved. To put a on b, though, we must remove c from a, i.e. destroy an already achieved goal. The simple strategy of achieving goals one by one (and freezing all relevant facts) would not work in this case.

In a more crowded "world", a state might comprise so many facts that its direct representation (as a list, say) would be impractical. Moreover, even a small change might require copying large data structures. Clausal representation is free from this disadvantage but it is unwieldy when a change must be undone, and of course planning is a trial–and–error process. What we need is a method of incrementally describing incremental changes, and making them easily undoable.

A state and an action determine the next state, if we assume that the action does not affect facts not mentioned explicitly in the description of the action's effects as added or deleted. Given an initial state and a plan, i.e. a sequence of actions, we can check whether a fact holds in the resulting final state. To undo an action, we remove it from the plan (in practice, this may be slightly more complicated).

For any particular planning problem, the initial state can be considered fixed. The final state should be given implicitly, as a conjunction of facts to be established by a plan we are going to find. This approach was taken by D. H. D. Warren in his remarkable planning program, WARPLAN.

In WARPLAN, world description is separated from the planning procedure (see Listing 8.1, pp. 221–223, lines 1–26, for the description of our cube world). Objects are given implicitly, in descriptions of actions and facts. Actions are defined by three procedures. The two-parameter procedure

can(Action, Precondition)

serves as a catalogue—one clause per action; Precondition is a conjunction of facts that must hold for Action to be applicable. A conjunction is either a fact, or a pair of conjunctions constructed by the infix functor &, e.g. c on a & a on b.

Two other procedures,

add(Fact, Action)
del(Fact, Action)

give facts added and deleted by available actions (and, conversely, actions which can add or delete a fact). Impossible combinations of facts are listed in the procedure

imposs(Conjunction)

In these four procedures, we can use variables instead of world objects to express general laws, e.g. "a clear cube U is sitting on a cube V":

U on V & notequal(V, floor) & clear(U)

For efficiency, facts that hold in the initial state, and are unaffected by any action, are listed in the procedure

always(Fact)

Other facts that hold in the initial state are supplied by the procedure

given(InitialStateName, Fact)

The initial state is denoted by its name, e.g. *start*. A state derived from it by actions A1, ..., An is denoted by the term

InitialStateName : A1 : ⋯ : An,

e.g.

start : move(c,a, floor) : move(a, floor, b) : move(c, floor, a)

The planning program (Listing 8.2, pp. 224–226) operates independently of specific world descriptions. It assumes the presence of an appropriate data base whose coherence is the responsibility of the user.

The program begins with a conjunction of facts (i.e. the description of a desired final state) and the empty plan. In each step, the conjunction shrinks and/or the plan grows: successive intermediate states approximate the final state. Roughly speaking, the plan is constructed backwards: we look for preconditions of actions that achieve the final state, then for preconditions of actions that achieve those preconditions, etc. Unless a fact holds in an intermediate state, the program chooses an action that adds this fact, inserts the action into the current partial plan, removes the fact from the current conjunction and adds to it the action's preconditions.

A partial plan usually contains variables. For example, to achieve a on b, we use the action move(a, V, b), whose precondition includes the fact a on V (for an unknown V). Such variables require some care: the fact U on c may, in general, differ from a on V, even though the two terms are unifiable. We can either use the built-in procedure == to compare facts, or temporarily instantiate their variables (by the built-in procedure *numbervars*) prior to the comparison.

In addition to the current conjunction and plan, the program maintains a conjunction of desirable facts already planned for. No newly inserted action can destroy any of these *preserved* facts.

The program is amazingly concise. In Warren's original paper it was accompanied by many pages of detailed considerations. Hence, the absence of proper comments in the program text. Below we shall present, in our own words, some indispensable technical explanations.

The main planning routine, *plan*, is called only if the final state description is not inconsistent (lines 10–13), i.e. if it does not imply one of the impossible combinations of facts. *plan* has three input parameters—facts to be achieved, facts already achieved (initially *true*; see line 13) and the current plan—and one output parameter, the final plan. The procedure *solve* is called for each fact of the initial goal list (see lines 30–32). It has five parameters: a fact to be established, preserved facts, the current plan, preserved facts after *solve* has succeeded and the new plan.

Every clause of *solve* accounts for a different status of the fact (lines 35–39). It may be always true; it may be true by virtue of general laws external to "worlds" (e.g. equality or inequality of objects will be checked by this clause); it may hold in the state described by the current plan (to preserve it, we add it to the facts planned for; see lines 83–84); otherwise (the last clause) we choose an action and call *achieve*.

The procedure *achieve* (lines 41–49) tries to apply a given action, i.e. to insert it into the current plan (as the last action, or as the last but one, etc.). The action U is applicable if it deletes none of the preserved facts, and if its precondition is consistent with these facts and if a plan for achieving this precondition can be constructed. Notice that possible additions to P (preserved facts) made by the recursive call on *plan* are invisible to *achieve*: they are only needed "locally" during the construction of the intermediate plan T1. The additional call on *preserves* (line 45) is necessary because of variables in the plan. For example, the action move(b, a, W) need not delete the fact clear(c), so *preserves* lets it through; however, *plan* may instantiate W as c, and this ought to cause a failure.

If, for any of these reasons, the action U cannot be added at the end of the plan, *achieve* will try to undo the last action V and insert U earlier into the plan. This is only possible if V does not delete the fact to be added by U. The procedure *retrace* (lines 65–73) removes from the set of preserved facts all facts that may be established by V but are different from V's preconditions. Specifically, it removes the facts added by V (lines 68–69) and the facts that constitute the precondition of V (lines 70–71)—the latter facts will be re-inserted by *append* (see lines 66, 86–87)[1].

A few comments on the remaining procedures. A fact holds after executing a given plan (lines 52–55), if it is *given* or added by one of the actions, and preserved by all subsequent actions (if any). Two conjunctions, C and P, are inconsistent (lines 76–78, 93–97) if C&P contains all facts of an impossible combination S, except those which—like *not-equal*—are tested "metaphysically" (see line 95). For disjoint C, S this cannot be the case—hence the call on *intersect* which is relatively cheap. Two object descriptions X and Y, with variables instantiated by *number-vars* in *mkground* (line 101), may refer to the same object if X = Y or X = 'V'(_) or Y = 'V'(_)—see line 99. The procedure *elem* (lines 89–91) extracts single facts from a nested conjunction; it can be used both to test membership, and to generate facts.

Now that you have acquainted yourself with the planning program, try it on a richer world. Here is the world of a robot that walks around several rooms, moves some boxes, etc. (see Listing 8.1, lines 33–101). Figure 8.2 depicts an initial state of this world. There are six points, five rooms, four doors, three boxes, a light switch, and the robot. Nine types of facts are considered: at(Object, Point), on(Object, Box), nextto(Object1, Object2), pushable(Object), inroom(Object, Room), locinroom(Point, Room), connects(Door, Room1, Room2), status(Lightswitch, OnOff), onfloor—the latter characterizes the robot. Only the robot performs actions—there are seven of them (see lines 64–77).

---

[1] The special treatment of V's preconditions is necessary for actions which add facts listed among their own preconditions. If *retrace* simply deleted V's effects, such preconditions could be lost from the list of facts which must be preserved by U, and those parts of the plan which achieve "locally desirable" goals could inadvertently be destroyed in the insertion process.

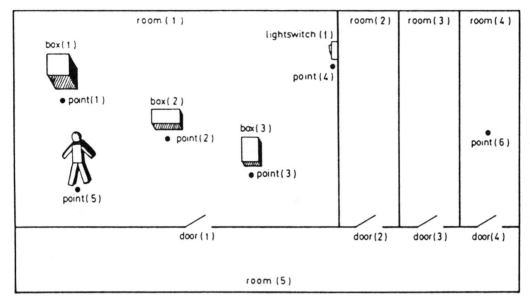

FIG. 8.2 "STRIPS" world.

The procedure *del* merits a comment. It is supposed to delete more than it should—we count on *add* to straighten the situation out. For example, the action turnon(S) removes whatever status of S may be recorded (line 54); "a moment later" it adds the appropriate fact (line 39). The clauses in lines 49–50 say that a moved object X is no longer "next to" anything. However, this does not apply to the robot manipulating a box (lines 46–48)—*del* fails, i.e. the fact is *not* deleted.

For sample results, see Listing 8.3, p. 227.

Although WARPLAN is a feat of ingenuity, there is much more to planning than it does account for. For one thing, the plans it generates need not be optimal, i.e. contain the least possible number of actions. For example, action U in *achieve* (lines 47–49) is executed when it preserves V's precondition P; if we checked that U establishes P, we might delete actions which had been planned to establish it. A much more profound problem: in general, it is likely that conditional or iterative plans will be required, rather than sequential (the robot explores the world).

Even with these (and other) limitations, and despite exponential time complexity, WARPLAN is an excellent tool for experiments with rigorous world descriptions. One example is the world of a robot that assembles cars. Warren has also demonstrated how his program can be used to compile arithmetic expressions into machine code (the code is treated as a plan for placing some values in some registers).

```
1   % % % % WARPLAN - cube worlds
2
3   :- op( 50, xfx, on ).
4
5   add( U on W, move( U, V, W ) ).
6   add( clear( V ), move( U, V, W ) ).
7
8   del( U on Z, move( U, V, W ) ).
9   del( clear( W ), move( U, V, W ) ).
10
11  can( move( U, V, floor ),
12      U on V & notequal( V, floor ) & clear( U ) ).
13  can( move( U, V, W ),
14      clear( W ) & U on V & notequal( U, W ) & clear( U ) ).
15
16  imposs( X on Y & clear( Y ) ).
17  imposs( X on Y & X on Z & notequal( Y, Z ) ).
18  imposs( X on Z & Y on Z & notequal( Z, floor ) & notequal( X, Y ) ).
19  imposs( X on X ).
20
21  % The three blocks problem.
22  given( start, a on floor ).
23  given( start, b on floor ).
24  given( start, c on a ).
25  given( start, clear( b ) ).
26  given( start, clear( c ) ).
27
28  :- plans( c on a & a on b, start ).
29  :- plans( a on b & b on c, start ).
30  :- delop( 'on' ), redefine.
31  % ----------------------------------------
32
33  % % % % WARPLAN -- the STRIPS problem
34
35  add( at( robot, P ), goto1( P, R ) ).
36  add( nextto( robot, X ), goto2( X, R ) ).
37  add( nextto( X, Y ), pushto( X, Y, R ) ).
38  add( nextto( Y, X ), pushto( X, Y, R ) ).
```

LISTING 8.1 WARPLAN—Examples of worlds. (*continued*)

```
39   add( status( S, on ), turnon( S ) ).
40   add( on( robot, B ), climbon( B ) ).
41   add( onfloor, climboff( B ) ).
42   add( inroom( robot, R2 ), gothrough( D, R1, R2 ) ).
43
44   del( at( X, Z ), U ) :- moved( X, U ).
45   del( nextto( Z, robot ), U ) :- del( nextto( robot, Z ), U ).
46   del( nextto( robot, X ), pushto( X, Y, R ) ) :- !.
47   del( nextto( robot, B ), climbon( B ) ) :- !, fail.
48   del( nextto( robot, B ), climboff( B ) ) :- !, fail.
49   del( nextto( X, Z ), U ) :- moved( X, U ).
50   del( nextto( Z, X ), U ) :- moved( X, U ).
51   del( on( X, Z ), U ) :- moved( X, U ).
52   del( onfloor, climbon( B ) ).
53   del( inroom( robot, Z ), gothrough( D, R1, R2 ) ).
54   del( status( S, Z ), turnon( S ) ).
55
56   moved( robot, goto1( P, R ) ).
57   moved( robot, goto2( X, R ) ).
58   moved( X, pushto( X, Y, R ) ).
59   moved( robot, climbon( B ) ).
60   moved( robot, climboff( B ) ).
61   moved( robot, gothrough( D, R1, R2 ) ).
62
63   can( goto1( P, R ),
64        locinroom( P, R ) & inroom( robot, R ) & onfloor ).
65   can( goto2( X, R ),
66        inroom( X, R ) & inroom( robot, R ) & onfloor ).
67   can( turnon( lightswitch(S) ),
68        on( robot, box(1) ) & nextto( box(1), lightswitch(S) ) ).
69   can( pushto( X, Y, R ),
70        pushable( X ) & inroom( Y, R ) & inroom( robot, R ) &
71        nextto( robot, X ) & onfloor ).
72   can( gothrough( D, R1, R2 ),
73        connects( D, R1, R2 ) & inroom( robot, R1 ) &
74        nextto( robot, D ) & onfloor ).
75   can( climboff( box(B) ), on( robot, box(B) ) ).
```

```
77   can( climbon( box(B) ), nextto( robot, box(B) ) & onfloor ).
78
79   always( inroom( D, R1 ) ) :- always( connects( D, R2, R1 ) ).
80   always( connects( D, R2, R1 ) ) :- connects1( D, R1, R2 ).
81   always( connects( D, R1, R2 ) ) :- connects1( D, R1, R2 ).
82   always( pushable( box(N) ) ).
83   always( locinroom( point(N), room(1) ) ) :- range( N, 1, 5 ).
84   always( locinroom( point(6), room(4) ) ).
85   always( inroom( lightswitch(1), room(1) ) ).
86   always( at( lightswitch(1), point(4) ) ).
87
88   connects1( door(N), room(N), room(5) ) :- range( N, 1, 4 ).
89
90   range( M, M, _ ).
91   range( M, L, N ) :-
92      L < N, L1 is L + 1, range( M, L1, N ).
93
94   imposs( at( X, Y ) & at( X, Z ) & notequal( Y, Z ) ).
95
96   given( strips1, at( box(N), point(N) ) ) :- range( N, 1, 3 ).
97   given( strips1, at( robot, point(5) ) ).
98   given( strips1, inroom( box(N), room(1) ) ) :- range( N, 1, 3 ).
99   given( strips1, onfloor ).
100  given( strips1, status( lightswitch(1), off ) ).
101  given( strips1, inroom( robot, room(1) ) ).
102
103  % a few tests.
104  :- plans( at( robot, point(5) ), strips1 ).
105  :- plans( at( robot, point(1) ) & at( robot, point(2) ), strips1 ).
106  :- plans( at( robot, point(4) ), strips1 ).
107  :- plans( status( lightswitch(1), on ), strips1 ).
108  :- plans( at( robot, point(6) ), strips1 ).
109  :- plans( nextto( box(1), box(2) ) & nextto( box(3), box(2) ), strips1 ).
```

LISTING 8.1   *(Continued)*

```prolog
1   % X X X X X X          WARPLAN - A System for Generating Plans
2   % X X X X X X
3   % X X X X X X
4
5   % X X X  The general planner.
6   % X      -------------------
7   :- op( 200, xfx, & ), op( 100, xfx, : ).
8
9   % Generate and output a plan.
10  plans( C, _ ) :-
11     inconsistent( C, true ), !, write( 'Impossible.' ), nl.
12  plans( C, T ) :-
13     plan( C, true, T, T1 ), output( T1 ), !.
14  plans( _, _ ) :-
15     write( 'Can''t do this.' ), nl.
16
17  output( Xs:X ) :-
18     numbervars( Xs:X, 1, _ ), output1( Xs ), output2( X, '.' ).
19  output( _ ) :- write( 'Nothing need be done.' ), nl.
20
21  output1( Xs:X ) :-  !, output1( Xs ), output2( X, ':' ).
22  output1( X ) :- output2( X, ':' ).
23
24  output2( Item, Funct ) :-  write( Item ), write( Funct ), nl.
25
26  % Main planning routine.
27  %  Definitions of 'always', 'imposs', 'given', 'can', 'add', 'del' -
28  %  see specific world descriptions.
29
30  plan( X&C, P, T, T2 ) :-
31     !, solve( X, P, T, P1, T1 ), plan( C, P1, T1, T2 ).
32  plan( X, P, T, T1 ) :- solve( X, P, T, _, T1 ).
33
34  % Ways of solving a goal.
35  solve( X, P, T, T ) :-  always( X ).
36  solve( X, P, T, T ) :-  X.
```

```prolog
37  solve( X, F, T, F1, T ) :- holds( X, T ), and( X, F, F1 ).
38  solve( X, F, T, X&F, T1 ) :- achieve( X, U, F, T, T1 ).
39
40
41  % Methods of achieving a goal -
42  % by extension:
43  achieve( -, U, F, T, T1=U ) :-
44      preserves( U, F ), can( U, C ), not inconsistent( C, F ),
45      plan( C, F, T, T1 ), preserves( U, F ).
46  % by insertion:
47  achieve( X, U, F, T=V, T1=V ) :-
48      preserved( X, V ), retrace( F, V, F1 ),
49      achieve( X, U, F1, T, T1 ), preserved( X, V ).
50
51  % Check if a fact holds in a given state.
52  holds( X, -:=V ) :- add( X, V ).
53  holds( X, T:V ) :-
54      !, preserved( X, V ), holds( X, T ), preserved( X, V ).
55  holds( X, T ) :- given( T, X ).
56
57  % Prove that an action preserves a fact.
58  preserves( U, X&C ) :- preserved( X, U ), preserves( U, C ).
59  preserves( -, true ).
60
61  preserved( X, V ) :- check( pres( X, V ) ).
62  pres( X, V ) :- mkground( X&V ), not del( X, V ).
63
64  % Retracing a goal already achieved.
65  retrace( X&F, V, C, F1 ) :-
66      add( Y, V ), X == Y, !, retrace( F, V, C, F1 ).
67
68  retrace( X&F, V, C, F1 ) :-
69      can( V, C ), retrace( F, V, C, F1 ), append( C, F1, F2 ).
70  retrace( X&F, V, C, F1 ) :-
71      elem( Y, C ), X == Y, !, retrace( F, V, C, F1 ).
```

LISTING 8.2   WARPLAN—The general planner. (*continued*)

```
72   retrace( X&F, V, C, X&F1 )   :-   retrace( F, V, C, F1 ).
73   retrace( true, _, _, true ).
74
75   % Inconsistency with a goal already achieved.
76   inconsistent( C, F )   :-
77       mkground( C&F ),  imposs( S ),
78       check( intersect( C, S ) ), implied( S, C&F ),  !.
79
80   % % % Utilities.
81   % -----------------
82
83   and( X, F, F )   :-   elem( Y, F ),   X == Y,   !.
84   and( X, F, X&F ).
85
86   append( X&C, F, X&F1 )   :-   !,   append( C, F, F1 ).
87   append( X, F, X&F ).
88
89   elem( X, Y&_ )   :-   elem( X, Y ).
90   elem( X, _&C )   :-   !,   elem( X, C ).
91   elem( X, X ).
92
93   implied( S1&S2, C )   :-   !,   implied( S1, C ),   implied( S2, C ).
94   implied( X, C )   :-   elem( X, C ).
95   implied( X, _ )   :-   X.
96
97   intersect( S1, S2 )   :-   elem( X, S1 ),   elem( X, S2 ).
98
99   notequal( X, Y )   :-   not X==Y ,   not X='V'(_) ,   not Y='V'(_).
100
101  mkground( X )   :-   numbervars(X, 0, _ ).
```

LISTING 8.2 *(Continued)*

```
1
2      c on a  &  a on b
3
4      start :
5      move( c, a, floor ) :
6      move( a, floor, b ) :
7      move( c, floor, a ).
8
9      a on b  &  b on c
10
11     start :
12     move( c, a, floor ) :
13     move( b, floor, c ) :
14     move( a, floor, b ).
15
16     at( robot, point(5) )
17
18     Nothing need be done.
19
20     at( robot, point(1) )  &  at( robot, point(2) )
21
22     Impossible.
23
24     at( robot, point(4) )
25
26     strips1 :
27     goto1( point( 4 ), room( 1 ) ).
28
29     status( lightswitch(1), on )
30
31     strips1 :
32     goto2( box( 1 ), room( 1 ) ) :
33     pushto( box( 1 ), lightswitch( 1 ), room( 1 ) ) :
34     climbon( box( 1 ) ) :
35     turnon( lightswitch( 1 ) ).
36
37     at( robot, point(6) )
38
39     strips1 :
40     goto2( door( 1 ), room( 1 ) ) :
41     gothrough( door( 1 ), room( 1 ), room( 5 ) ) :
42     goto2( door( 4 ), room( 5 ) ) :
43     gothrough( door( 4 ), room( 5 ), room( 4 ) ) :
44     goto1( point( 6 ), room( 4 ) ).
45
46     nextto( box(1), box(2) )  &  nextto( box(3), box(2) )
47
48     strips1 :
49     goto2( box( 1 ), room( 1 ) ) :
50     pushto( box( 1 ), box( 2 ), room( 1 ) ) :
51     goto2( box( 3 ), room( 1 ) ) :
52     pushto( box( 3 ), box( 2 ), room( 1 ) ).
```

LISTING 8.3   WARPLAN—Sample results.

BIBLIOGRAPHIC NOTES

WARPLAN is described in Warren (1974). Our presentation has been greatly influenced by this excellent paper. The program we publish here is a slightly cleaned-up version of the text given in Coelho *et al.* (1980), where all the mentioned examples of worlds can also be found. The robot's world was introduced by Fikes and Nilsson (1971) as a test case for their system STRIPS; Warren (1974) used it to compare the performance of the two systems. An extension of WARPLAN, intended for generating conditional plans, was described in Warren (1976).

REFERENCES

Coelho H., Cotta J.C., and Pereira L.M. (1980) "How to Solve It in Prolog" Laboratorio Nacional de Enginharia Civil, Lisboa.

Fikes, R.E., and Nilsson, N.J. (1971) "STRIPS: A New Approach to the Application of Theorem Proving to Problem Solving," *Artificial Intelligence*, 2, pp. 189–208.

Warren, D.H.D. (1974) "WARPLAN: A System for Generating Plans," Dept. of Computational Logic Memo 76. Artificial Intelligence, Edinburgh University.

Warren, D.H.D. (1976) "Generating Conditional Plans and Programs," Proceedings of the AISB Summer Conference, University of Edinburgh, UK, pp. 344–354.

A REPRESENTATION FOR ROBOT PLANS

Philip J. Hayes
Institute for the Study of Semantics and Cognition
6976 Castagnola, Switzerland

Abstract

A representation for robot plans is proposed. The representation of a given plan reflects the structure of the process which produced the plan. This information is useful in both the original construction of the plan and its subsequent modification if unforeseen events cause execution failures. A programmed system that constructs and executes (in simulation) plans for journeys using a large system of public transport is described to illustrate the advantages of the representation. It is also shown how the representation could be used for more typical robot-planning worlds.

1. Introduction

Since most robots must function in a world whose behaviour they cannot hope to predict exactly, they must be prepared for plans they make to fail during execution. (As usual, a plan is a linear sequence of actions or operations intended to transform some initial state of the robot's world into some goal state.) Such failures may occur because some action in the plan fails to have its expected effect or because of some unpredictable event outside the control of the robot. In any case, after such a failure the robot must be able to modify its plan to cope with the unexpected turn of events.

Rather than throw away the original plan and start again from scratch, it is clearly desirable that as much as possible of the work that went into constructing the old plan should be reused in producing a modified version. One previous system, STRIPS[1,2], that dealt with replanning after execution failures, tried to save work by making arbitrary subsequences of operations from the original plan available to the replanning process as primitive operations. No attention, however, was paid to the way in which such subsequences were originally intended to contribute to the fulfillment of the goal of the plan, thus, at times, leading to rather arbitrary uses of them. Such a scheme does not try and use any of the problem analysis that went into constructing the original plan but only its results.

More hierarchically structured systems[3,4] have proposed that plans should be sketched out at some level of detail abstracted from that of the robot's primitive actions, and each step fully detailed only as it is executed. Such an approach, while giving an inbuilt flexibility with regard to details, runs the risk of disaster if some of the unelaborated steps turn out to be impossible because of some complication at the more detailed levels.

The scheme of plan representation presented in this paper is primarily designed to facilitate the reconstruction of detailed plans after failure in execution. It does this by explicitly recording in the representation of a particular plan the structure of the process which produced that plan. The information thus recorded includes the choices made during the construction of a plan, how they advanced the construction of the plan in terms of sub-goaling and refinement of details, and how they are logically related to each other. After failure this information enables that part of the development of a plan due to decisions invalidated by the circumstances of failure to be precisely identified and discarded. The resulting data structure represents that part of the original problem analysis which is still applicable after the failure*. Use of this structure by the replanning mechanism will avoid the corresponding part of the original planning effort being duplicated during replanning.

While the representation makes as few assumptions as possible about planning processes, it is basically oriented to processes based on hierarchical levels of detail[3,4,5]. By making information about all steps of a plan constantly available, the representation facilitates plan making for worlds in which the effects of operators tend to interfere with each other to a significant extent. It also permits different parts of the execution sequence to be developed in an order and to relative levels of depth, dependent only on the constraints of the problem domain. Such an ability is useful when there are different certainties as to whether the different steps of an undetailed skeleton plan can be successfully developed to a detailed level.

Use of the representation forms the basis of a working robot planning and (simulated) execution system described in section 3. Some aspects of the system implemented are atypical of robot planning domains in general, and so a discussion of how the representation would be used with a more usual robot world follows in section 4.

2. The Representation

A plan in the proposed representation consists of two interlinked data structures: a tree which represents the subgoal structure of the plan and a graph which represents the logical relationships of the decisions taken in constructing the plan. This representation and its uses are described below in general terms; for detailed examples see section 3.

---

*In fact it does not always represent all of it, since there can be decisions that are still appropriate after failure, but are discarded because they were originally based on one of the decisions invalidated by the failure.

IJCAI 1975 pp. 181-188
Used by permission of the International Joint Conferences on Artificial Intelligence, Inc.

Each node of the subgoal tree of a plan (subsequently jnode) corresponds to a goal and the action necessary to achieve it.   (These two concepts are sufficiently close that it is often useful to blur any distinction between them.)   Subgoaling is represented by the branching of the tree (with a left to right time ordering).   Thus

$$X \atop {Y \quad Z}$$

would indicate that goal X has been split into subgoal Y and subgoal Z (or equivalently that the action required to achieve X can be split into an action that will achieve Y followed by an action that will achieve Z).   The root of the tree corresponds to the top-level goal of the plan, while in a complete plan the tips of the tree correspond to primitive actions.   For a system using a hierarchy of levels of detail, progress along a branch from root to tip would thus be naturally accompanied by an increasing amount of detail.

Besides just representing a goal or action, each jnode can contain any other information about that goal or action that is helpful to the plan construction process.   In particular, information about the expected state of the world before or after the action could be thus represented.   Communication and co-operation between processes constructing different steps in the same plan can be greatly facilitated by having such information for every step in the plan constantly available.

The nodes of the decision graph of a plan (subsequently dnodes) are in one-one correspondence with the decisions made during the construction of that plan.   The parent-child relation of the graph indicates logical dependence of the child on the parent.   Logical dependence of one decision on another here means that the process which made the second decision was influenced by some direct consequence of the first.   A graph structure is necessary to represent such logical dependencies, because the effects of two quite independent decisions can influence the making of a third.

Each dnode has two-way pointers from it to those jnodes created as a direct consequence of its decision.   These pointers can be used in conjunction with a graph structure to precisely identify all the effects both direct and indirect of a decision on the development of a plan.   The process of removing the effects (thus identified) of a decision from a plan is known as UNDOING the decision and consists of:

a)   removing the decision from the graph and all the jnodes pointed to by the decision from the tree;

b)   UNDOING the children of the decision in the graph.

This UNDO mechanism forms the basis of the method for reconstructing plans after failure in execution.   The basic idea is to identify the most logically senior decisions inappropriate to the unexpected situation, UNDO them, and then use what is left of the original plan representation as a basis for plan reconstruction.   To this end, each decision must have a resumption point of the plan construction process associated with it.   Use of this resumption point should result in the plan construction process being reentered to remake the decision in the light of all currently available information.

In more detail the replanning mechanism works as follows.   When an execution failure occurs, the execution monitoring system is assumed to designate a set of jnodes as unexecutable, these jnodes being the most senior that could be so designated.   Then:

1.   all portions of the subgoal tree successfully executed are discarded, together with any dnodes directly responsible only for discarded jnodes,

2.   all information in the tree, made inaccurate as a result of the circumstances of failure, is updated,

3.   for each jnode, A, of the unexecutable set

a)   if A has already been removed from the tree nothing more is done, otherwise

b)   the dnode, D, directly responsible for A is UNDONE,

c)   the plan construction process is reentered through the resumption point of D,

d)   if the reentered plan construction process terminates successfully nothing more is done, otherwise

e)   if A is not the root of the tree, it is replaced by its parent and step b) is looped to, otherwise

f)   replanning is assumed to be impossible.

If this mechanism is always to produce a complete plan, the resumption point associated with a decision must not only remake its own decision, but also any other dependent decisions needed to produce a complete plan.   Such an arrangement may not always be feasible.   In such cases those jnodes on the frontier of the subgoal tree that were not primitive at the end of the above process would have to be found and developed until they were.   This problem does not, however, arise with the system to be described in the next section.

3.   A Working System Based on Use of the Representation

The representation described above forms the basis of a working system for the construction and (simulated) execution of plans.   The plans concern the journeys of a (robot) traveller through a network of rail, sea and air public transport services.   The system contains a considerable amount of knowledge in procedural form about how to make plans in such a domain.   It is not, however, tied to a particular network, but accepts the definition of such a network in tabular form as initial data.   This definition comprises lists of connections, timetables for those connections and some geographical data (concerning the positions of towns and the relative positions of countries and seas).

The network used for example purposes is extensive. It connects 84 European centres using 43 rail services, 7 sea services and 55 air services giving in excess of 500 town to town connections and more than 2000 primitive journeys (journeys between two centres using one service at a particular time). The services used are all taken from real world timetables. The geographical area covered by the network is shown in figure 1. For the sake of readability, only a small subset of the network is shown, but this subset includes all the routes used in the examples.

FIGURE 1

- - - - air services

───── sea services

............rail services

Some of the Routes in the

Example Transport Network

The system can construct plans subject to certain constraints of time and cost. These constraints can be both global (e.g. on the overall cost of a journey) and local (e.g. on the time of arrival at a particular place). The system can also cope with the occurrence of "unexpected" events during the simulated execution of a journey. It checks their relevance to the journey and if necessary modifies the plan using the replanning mechanism described in the previous section.

The system uses its domain dependent knowledge to good effect and a planning time of around 20 seconds is typical for a journey involving six primitive journeys. The plan produced is "reasonable" though not necessarily optimal. The system was coded in POP-2 on an ICL 4130 computer.

Figure 2 shows the subgoal tree and decision graph of a plan produced by the system for going from Manchester to Nice by train and boat. (This plan is, in fact, optimal with respect to both time and cost for a journey in the example network from Manchester to Nice using surface transport.)

Because of the nature of the domain, all jnodes correspond to journeys of varying degrees of specification. The correspondence between increase in detail and increase in depth of the tree will be clear. Times are represented by a 24-hour clock time plus a day, thus 17:30 2 means 5:30 p.m. on day 2 of the journey. The list of numbers in brackets associated with each dnode indicates which jnodes were created as a direct result of each dnode.

The function of each decision shown in figure 2 (b) is as follows:

Decision 0 is a dummy decision which is notionally responsible for all the unchangeable features of the world.

Decision 1 chooses surface transport as the mode of travel. Because a sea, the English Channel, lies between Manchester and Nice, it results in subgoaling the original goal into three subgoals: to get to the Channel, to cross it, and to get to Nice.

Decision 2 chooses the route for the Channel crossing and thus refines jnodes 2, 3 and 4 into the more detailed jnodes 6, 5 and 7 respectively.

Decision 3 fixes a time for the sea crossing, refining jnode 5 still further. Since the sea crossings are rarer than the rail connections, unnecessary waiting is minimized if rail times are fitted to sea times rather than the other way round. The situation after this decision is an example of the concurrent use of differing levels of detail for different steps of the plan.

Decision 4 fixes the route for the train journey as far as the Channel crossing, but is independent of decision 3 even though made after it. Decision 7 is similar.

Decision 5 fixes a time for the train journey immediately before the Channel crossing. It depends on a routing decision (4) and a timing decision (3) which are independent, but an alteration in either would require the reconsideration of decision 5. Decision 8 is similar.

Decisions 6, 9 and 10 are other timing decisions which depend on a routing decision and its dependent timing decision.

The domain dependent expertise of the planning system is encoded in a number of special functions called dfunctions. Each dfunction has its own special area of knowledge and is associated with the making of a particular sort of decision. Dfunctions are parameterless and are expected to extract all the knowledge they require from the decision graph and subgoal tree representing the existing state of the plan.

There are seven main dfunctions:

TRYSORP which chooses between air and surface transport,

TRAINS, BOATS, and PLANES which choose routes for rail, sea and air journeys respectively,

TRAINTIME, SEATIME and PLANETIME which choose times for journeys by rail, sea and air respectively.

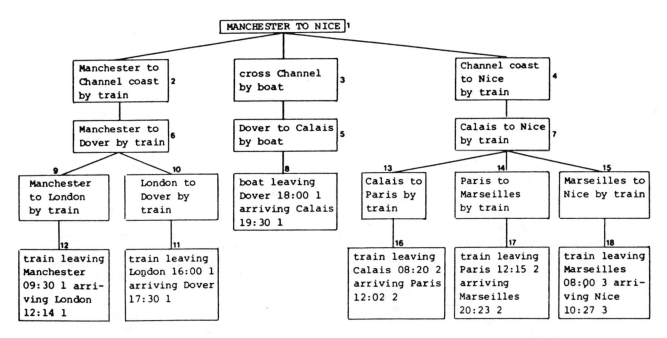

FIGURE 2 (a)   Subgoal tree of plan for journey from Manchester to Nice

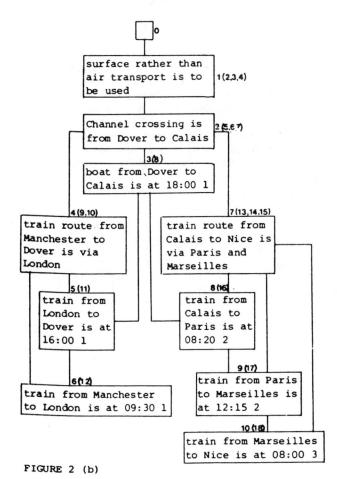

FIGURE 2 (b)

Decision Graph of plan for
journey from Manchester to Nice

Since dfunctions take all their information from the plan representation existing at the time they are called, they make ideal resumption points for use with the replanning mechanism described in the previous section.   Indeed, this is the reason they were so designed.

The entire planning system runs under a simple backtracking regime.   The problems with automatic backtracking are well known[6], and this feature of the system is undesirable.   However, since emphasis is placed on trying to make good decisions at the first attempt, the bad points of backtracking do not have as much impact as they might.   See reference 8 for a discussion of how the representation can be used to ameliorate backtracking for those plan construction processes using it.   The unimplemented scheme proposed there is based on the fact that the representation enables a decision to be remade without remaking chronologically subsequent but logically independent decisions.

Use of the representation can also help the plan construction process in handling the global constraints of time and cost that can be imposed on a journey.   The system deals with these constraints by associating with each jnode an estimate of the time and cost of the journey it represents. The more specified the journey, naturally the more accurate the estimate.   At any time the most up-to-date estimate for the whole journey can be obtained by summing the individual estimates of the jnodes on the current frontier of the tree, making allowance for waiting times and overnight stops. If this estimate is much outside the prescribed limit, then the development of the plan along the current lines can be discontinued immediately, thus wasting as little effort as possible.   Such an approach leads to little time being spent on journeys for which the allowance is grossly inadequate, but more on journeys for which the allowance falls just short.

The computer output produced by a simulated execution of the example plan described above is:

AT MANCHESTER WAITING FOR A TRAIN TO
LONDON

09:30 1 LEAVING MANCHESTER ON WAY TO LONDON BY
TRAIN

12:14 1 ARRIVING IN LONDON WAITING FOR A TRAIN
TO DOVER

14:00 1 TRAIN FROM MARSEILLES TO NICE AT 08:00
CANCELLED

REPLANNING

AT LONDON WAITING FOR A TRAIN TO DOVER

16:00 1 LEAVING LONDON ON WAY TO DOVER BY TRAIN

16:30 1 BOAT ACROSS THE CHANNEL FROM DOVER TO
CALAIS AT 18:00 CANCELLED

17:30 1 ARRIVING IN DOVER

REPLANNING

AT DOVER WAITING FOR A BOAT TO CALAIS

22:00 1 LEAVING DOVER ON WAY TO CALAIS BY BOAT

23:30 1 ARRIVING IN CALAIS STAYING IN CALAIS
FOR THE NIGHT

23:45 1 STORMS IN THE CHANNEL

08:20 2 LEAVING CALAIS ON WAY TO PARIS BY TRAIN

10:00 2 ALL TRAINS BETWEEN PARIS AND MARSEILLES
CANCELLED

12:02 2 ARRIVING IN PARIS

REPLANNING

AT PARIS WAITING FOR A TRAIN TO NIMES

09:03 3 LEAVING PARIS ON WAY TO NIMES BY TRAIN

20:25 3 ARRIVING IN NIMES WAITING FOR A TRAIN
TO MARSEILLES

21:53 3 LEAVING NIMES ON WAY TO MARSEILLES BY
TRAIN

23:15 3 ARRIVING IN MARSEILLES STAYING IN MAR-
SEILLES FOR THE NIGHT

13:00 4 LEAVING MARSEILLES ON WAY TO NICE BY TRAIN

15:20 4 ARRIVING IN NICE JOURNEY FINISHED

During this execution, four unexpected events occur and replanning is necessary for three of them. Following the execution in detail will make clear the workings of the replanning mechanism (step numbers refer to the description in section 2).

Execution proceeds normally until 14:00 1 when the train from Marseilles to Nice at 08:00 is with-. drawn. This means that the final step in the plan, jnode 18, is unexecutable and so replanning commences. The successfully executed part of the plan i.e. the journey from Manchester to London (jnodes 9, 12 and dnode 6) is discarded (step 1). The starting points of jnodes 1, 2, 6 are changed to London and the time and cost limits for the journey decremented by the amount already used (step 2). The decision, dnode 10, responsible for the unexecutable step in the plan is UNDONE resulting in the removal of jnode 18 and dnode 10 (step 3b). The plan construction process is then reentered through the dfunction, TRAINTIME, associated with dnode 10 (step 3c). TRAINTIME chooses another time for the Marseilles-Nice journey and a complete revised plan results. This new plan uses all the original plan (minus the Manchester-London journey) except that jnode 18 is replaced by jnode 19, a journey from Marseilles to Nice at 13:00 3, and decision 10 is

replaced by decision 11, the choice of that service.

Execution of the revised plan is then resumed, but has not continued for long when the boat service that was to be used is cancelled. The decision responsible for the choice of that service is decision 3. After removing the successfully completed part of the plan, i.e. everything involved in getting as far as Dover, dnode 3 is therefore UNDONE. Its UNDOING leads also to the UNDOING of dnodes 8, 9 and 11, i.e. all the remaining timing decisions (for they were chosen to fit in with it) and consequently to the removing of all the timed jnodes (8, 16, 17, 19). Note that decision 7, the rail routing decision, though made chronologically after decision 3 is logically independent of it and therefore unaffected. The planning process is then reentered through the resumption point of decision 3, the dfunction SEATIME, and produces the retimed plan shown in figure 3.

Execution of this newly revised plan then continues with the retimed Channel crossing. The next event, even though it causes all boat services across the Channel to be cancelled, does not affect execution of the plan since, by the time it occurs, the Channel has been successfully crossed.

The final event of the journey (which refers to the direct line from Paris to Marseilles via Lyons) is handled similarly to the first two. This time very little of the original plan can be saved because the routing decision for France, dnode 7, is rendered invalid, and all of the journey that is left is the trip through France. Invocation of TRAINS, the dfunction of dnode 7, produces the plan which finally leads without further interruption from Paris to Nice.

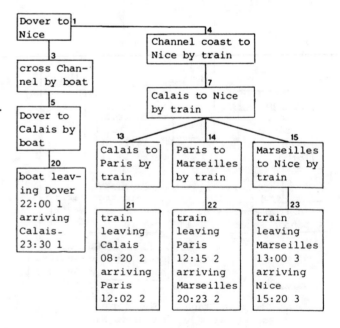

Figure 3 (a)   Subgoal tree of a plan reconstructed after an execution failure

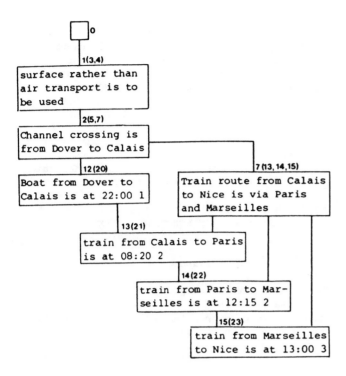

Figure 3 (b) Decision graph of a plan reconstructed after an execution failure

4. Representing Plans for More Typical Robot Worlds

The system described above is atypical of
robot planning systems. Most other systems are
concerned with worlds in which e.g. a mobile robot
pushes blocks around through a network of rooms[1,3,5],
or a one-handed robot moves blocks about on a table
top[7]. The essential difference between these
worlds and the transport world lies in the number
of features of the world that change or can be
changed in a predictable way. For the transport
world such features are few and fixed (only the
robot's position and consequently the amounts of
time and money available to it), while for the
other worlds they are numerous and variable (e.g.
the position of every block).

The systems mentioned above that deal with
such domains all use some sort of data base to
model the changing features of their worlds. This
data base contains a record of all changeable features of the world and is typically updated in a
simulation of execution as plan construction proceeds. If the representation is to make explicitly
available at all times information about every step
in a plan, one data base is insufficient for use
with it. There must be several, one for each jnode
in the plan. To provide for each jnode a separate
data base containing mention of all changeable features of the world is, however, unnecessarily wasteful. It is possible and even advantageous to use
one global data base plus a linked incremental
system of alterations to it.

In this scheme, each jnode has attached to it
an <u>alteration</u>, i.e. a record of the changes expected to be brought about by the action associated

with it. The presence or absence of any piece of
information in the data base representing the expected state of the world after the execution of
some jnode can then be found by looking back along
the frontier of the tree, starting with that jnode,
for the first mention of that item in an alteration.
An item can be mentioned as being either present or
absent, but the first mention of it discovered determines its status. If the item is not mentioned
in any of the alterations, its status is the same
as its status in the global data base describing
the initial state of the world. An example will
make this clearer.

Consider the simple world shown in figure 4
with a robot, two boxes, four rooms and four connecting doors. Figure 5 shows the tree and graph
of a plan to transform it from the configuration
shown in figure 4 to one in which the two boxes are
next to each other. The primitive actions shown
in the plan are similar to those used by STRIPS[1]
for a similar world. No assumptions are made, however, about the type of process which produced the
plan or about the order in which its several steps
were elaborated.

The global data base representing the initial
state of the world might contain the following
items:

(IN ROBOT ROOM1) (IN BOX1 ROOM2) (IN BOX2 ROOM3)

(CLOSED DOOR1) (OPEN DOOR2) (OPEN DOOR3)
                            (OPEN DOOR4)

plus other information describing static features
of the world such as DOOR1 connects ROOM1 and
ROOM2 or that the two boxes are pushable.

The alterations associated with each jnode
might be as follows:

1. (NEXTO BOX1 BOX2)
2. (IN ROBOT ROOM2) (NEXTO ROBOT BOX1)
    -(IN ROBOT $) -(NEXTO ROBOT $)
3. as 2, but without (NEXTO ROBOT BOX1)
4. (NEXTO ROBOT DOOR1) -(NEXTO ROBOT $)
5.& 7. same as 3.
6. -(CLOSED DOOR1) (OPEN DOOR1)
8. (NEXTO ROBOT BOX1) -(NEXTO ROBOT $)
9. (IN ROBOT ROOM3) (IN BOX1 ROOM3)
                (NEXTO BOX1 BOX2)
    -(IN ROBOT $) -(IN BOX1 $) plus A
10. as 9, without (NEXTO BOX1 BOX2)
11. (NEXTO BOX2 DOOR2) plus A
12.& 13. same as 10.
14. (NEXTO BOX1 BOX2) plus A

where A is (NEXTO ROBOT BOX1) -(NEXTO ROBOT $)
        -(NEXTO BOX1 $) -(NEXTO $ BOX1)
    - denotes the absence of that item
    $ is a free variable that stands for anything

Thus -(IN ROBOT $) denotes the absence of all
items of that form, i.e. it cancels any specification of which room the robot is in. The positive
items of an alteration take precedence over its
negative items when conflicts arise.

In this complete plan, the room the robot is
expected to be in after the execution of jnode 13
is found directly from the alteration of jnode 13,

since it contains (IN ROBOT ROOM3). For jnode 11, however, it is necessary to follow the frontier back until jnode 7, to find this information, since the alterations of neither jnode 11 nor jnode 8 contain an item of the form (IN ROBOT room). Similarly the expected position of BOX2 after the execution of every jnode will always be found from the global data base since no mention of it is made in any alteration either positively or negatively.

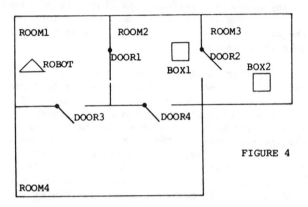

FIGURE 4

Initial world in more typical
robot planning domain

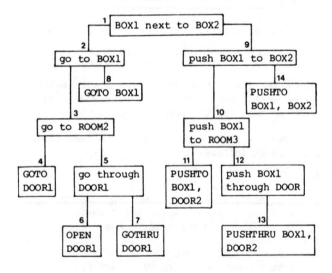

FIGURE 5 (a) Subgoal tree of plan for pushing
the two boxes in figure 4 together

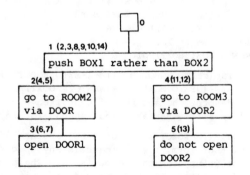

FIGURE 5 (b) Decision graph of plan for pushing
the two boxes in figure 4 together

Using such a scheme with predicates which give essentially the same information at differing levels of detail can lead to difficulties when different steps of a plan are at different levels of detail. Suppose, for example, that jnode 8 was further developed to specify (AT ROBOT X), X being the position the robot must be in to push BOX1 in the proper direction. Then the data bases of all subsequent jnodes in the execution sequence would contain this (for them) erroneous information. One solution is to ensure that whenever a new peice of information is established, all other information both at the same and lower levels of detail that could conflict should be erased. Thus including (IN ROBOT room) in an alteration would also entail the inclusion of -(IN ROBOT $), -(NEXTO ROBOT $) and -(AT ROBOT $) in the same alteration.

An important advantage of the incremental scheme is related to this problem. Any details filled in about one step of a plan become immediately available in the data bases of all subsequent steps of the plan, providing, of course, no intervening alteration contradicts the detail. Thus the data base of one jnode can be updated by development of a completely different step of the plan. For example, in the above plan, jnode 14 is already in existence immediately after decision 1 is made. (CLOSED DOOR1) is present in its data base, since the item is present in the original data base and no intervening alteration existing at that time mentions it. However, after decision 3 has been made, jnode 6 is present on the frontier of the tree and its alteration removes (CLOSED DOOR1) from the data base of jnode 14 and inserts (OPEN DOOR1) in its place.

This data base scheme makes the construction of the decision graph straightforward. A decision directly depends exactly on those other decisions which first established the information influencing its formation. Thus if information from the alteration of a jnode influences a decision, that decision depends on the decision responsible for the creation of the eldest ancestor of that jnode whose alteration contains the same information.

The advantages of having information about the entire plan constantly available are more apparent in a world where different steps of the same plan are more likely to interfere with each other. An example of such a world is the well known BLOCKS world of Winograd[7]. The robot in this world cannot lift up a block which has other blocks on top of it. To manipulate such a block, it must first clear off its top by putting the supported blocks somewhere else, usually on the table. Such tactics can lead to problems when one block occupies the space needed for another. Such problems are resolved rather inefficiently by backtracking in Winograd's system. If the above representation were used, a plan could be developed as far as possible down each branch of its tree until it was necessary to choose definite places on the table in which to put the blocks. A place for each block could then be chosen using the information in the tree about all the other objects which had to be fitted in, thus eliminating the need for trial and error backtracking search.

The method of plan reconstruction after execution failure, based on use of the representation and described in section 2, works in exactly the same manner as illustrated in section 3. For example, suppose in the execution of the present plan, the robot discovered when it got to DOOR1 that it was not only CLOSED but LOCKED. It would apply the replanning procedure to jnode 5, as the most senior unexecutable ancestor of jnode 6, the unexecutable primitive action of opening DOOR1. Firstly, jnode 4 would be discarded since it had already been successfully executed. Then the global data base would be updated with the current position of the robot and the fact that DOOR1 is LOCKED. Dnode 2, the choice of the robot's route from ROOM1 to ROOM2, is the decision directly responsible for jnode 5, so it would be UNDONE, removing jnodes 5, 6 and 7 from the tree and dnodes 2 and 3 from the graph. Since the knowledge that DOOR1 is locked is available, reentering the planning process should then result in the route from ROOM1 to ROOM2 via ROOM4 being chosen. In the new plan, thus produced, the tree representing the robot's going from ROOM1 to ROOM2 would grow from the original jnode 3. All the rest of the plan about pushing BOX1 through DOOR2 would, of course, remain intact throughout this process.

5. Conclusion

A representation for robot plans has been presented which can assist in both the construction and execution of such plans. Use of the representation was illustrated by a description of a working planning and execution system concerned with the journeyings of a robot traveller in a network of public transport services. The problem domain of this system is atypical of robot planning systems in general, but it was also shown how the representation could be used for more typical worlds. The examples of the use of the representation indicated a number of features of it:

When a failure occurs during execution, the representation enables the discarding of those parts of the plan invalidated by the failure and thus reconstruction of the plan based on the selective reuse of the analysis made by the original planning process.

The structure of the representation is oriented towards planning systems using hierarchical levels of detail, and enables details to be filled in in an order unrelated to execution order. It also facilitates the use of information about one part of a plan in constructing other parts of the same plan.

The representation makes these contributions to plan construction and execution, because, for a particular plan, it reflects the structure of the process which produced the plan. The present representation is able to reflect the structures of currently typical planning processes. For more advanced processes with more structure a representation capable of reflecting the extra structure would probably give further benefits similar to the ones mentioned above.

Acknowledgements

This paper is based on a University of Edinburgh Master of Philosophy thesis[8]. As in that, I would like to thank my supervisors Harry Barrow and Donald Michie for their guidance and encouragement. My financial support at Edinburgh was provided by the Science Research Council.

References

1. Fikes, R. E. and Nilsson, N. J. "STRIPS: A New Approach to the Application of Theorem Proving to Problem Solving", Artificial Intelligence, vol. 2, 1971, pp. 189-208.

2. Fikes, R. E., Hart, P. E. and Nilsson, N. J., "Learning and Executing Generalized Robot Plans" Artificial Intelligence, vol. 3, 1972, pp. 251-288.

3. Sacerdoti, E., "Planning in a Hierarchy of Abstraction Spaces", Proceedings of the Third International Joint Conference on Artificial Intelligence, Stanford, California, 1973., pp. 412-422.

4. Nilsson, N. J., "A Hierarchical Robot Planning and Execution System", AIC Technical Note 76, SRI Project 1187, Stanford Research Institute, California, 1973.

5. Siklossy, L. and Dreussi, J. "An efficient Robot Planner which Generates its own Procedures", Proceedings of the Third International Joint Conference on Artificial Intelligence, Stanford, California, 1973, pp. 423-430.

6. Sussman, G. J. and McDermott, D. V., "Why Conniving is Better than Planning", AI Memo 255A, Massachusetts Institute of Technology, Cambridge, Mass. 1972.

7. Winograd, T., "Procedures as a Representation for Data in a Computer Program for Understanding Natural Language", Project MAC TR-84, Massachusetts Institute of Technology, Cambridge, Mass., 1971.

8. Hayes, P. J., "Structuring of Robot Plans by Successive Refinement and Decision Dependency", M. Phil. Thesis, School of Artificial Intelligence, University of Edinburgh, Edinburgh, 1973.

THE NONLINEAR NATURE OF PLANS

Earl D. Sacerdoti
Artificial Intelligence Center
Stanford Research Institute
Menlo Park, California U.S.A.

ABSTRACT

We usually think of plans as linear sequences of actions. This is because plans are usually executed one step at a time. But plans themselves are not constrained by limitations of linearity. This paper describes a new information structure, called the procedural net, that represents a plan as a partial ordering of actions with respect to time. By avoiding premature commitments to a particular order for achieving subgoals, a problem-solving system using this representation can deal easily and directly with problems that are otherwise very difficult to solve.

I   INTRODUCTION

When we think of plans in our everyday lives, or conceive of plans for a computer to carry out, we usually think of them as linear sequences of actions. The sequence may include conditional tests or loops, but the basic idea is still to do one step after another.

Although the execution of a plan is essentially linear, a plan itself may be thought of as a partial ordering of actions with respect to time.

This paper will show how, for certain classes of problems, the representation of plans as nonlinear sequences of actions enables a problem solving system to deal easily and directly with problems that are otherwise very difficult to solve.

II   AN EXAMPLE

To motivate the use of a nonlinear representation, let us develop an elementary example in a simple environment that consists of three blocks and a table. In the initial state, Block C is on Block A, and Block B is by itself. The goal is to achieve a new configuration of blocks, as shown in Figure 1. It is expressed as a conjunction: Block A is on Block B, and Block B is on Block C.

There is only one action that can be applied to the blocks. PUTON (X,Y) will put Block X on Y. PUTON (X,Y) is not applicable unless X has a clear top, and unless Y is the table or it has a clear top. The problem is to develop a sequence of actions that will achieve the goal state.

This example is presented by Sussman (1) as an "anomalous situation" for which his HACKER program could not produce an optimal solution. Other planning programs using means-ends analysis, for example STRIPS (2) and ABSTRIPS (3), also produce non-optimal solutions. Optimal solutions to the problem are produced by programs of Tate (4) and Warren (5), whose approaches will be discussed in Section VII below.

Let us see what a planning system using means-ends analysis would do under the assumption that plans must be linear. It will try to achieve in turn each of the conjuncts describing the goal state. Suppose it tried to put A on B first. After clearing A by doing PUTON (C,TABLE), the first subgoal can be achieved by doing PUTON (A,B). But now, in order to put B on C, B will have to be re-cleared, thus undoing the subgoal it achieved first.

On the other hand, the system might decide to put B on C first. This can be done immediately in the initial state. But now when the system tries to put A on B, it finds it is even further from its goal than it was in the initial state.

So the planner is in trouble. It must perform a more sophisticated analysis to put the subgoals in the proper order.

But the problem is easy to solve if plans are represented as partial orderings. A planner can begin with an oversimplified plan that considers the subgoals of putting A on B and putting B on C as parallel, independent operations. When it looks at the subplans in more detail, a simple analysis will determine the interactions between them. Potential conflicts can be resolved by imposing linear constraints on some of the detailed actions.

In subsequent sections we will show how a planner that is freed from the assumption of linearity is able to solve problems of this type directly, constructively, and without backtracking.

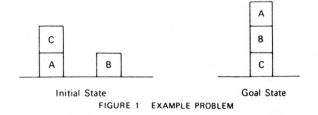

Initial State   Goal State
FIGURE 1   EXAMPLE PROBLEM

Used by permission of the International Joint Conferences on Artificial Intelligence, Inc.

III NOAH

NOAH (Nets of Action Hierarchies) is a problem solving and execution monitoring system that uses a nonlinear representation of plans. The system is being used for SRI's computer based consultant project (6), and has many aspects that are not directly relevant to the point of this paper. We will present a simplified explanation of the procedural net (NOAH's representation for actions and plans) of SOUP (the language for giving the system task-specific knowledge) and of the planning algorithm. A complete discussion of the system will appear elsewhere (7).

NOAH is implemented in QLISP (8), and runs as compiled code on a PDP-10 computer under the TENEX time-sharing system.

A.   The Procedural Net

The system's plans are built up in a data structure called the procedural net, which has characteristics of both procedural and declarative representations.

Basically, the procedural net is a network of nodes, each of which contains procedural information, declarative information, and pointers to other nodes. Each node represents a particular action at some level of detail. The nodes are linked to form hierarchical descriptions of operations, and to form plans of action.

Nodes at each level of the hierarchy are linked in a partially ordered time sequence by predecessor and successor links. Each such sequence represents a plan at a particular level of detail.

The nodes discussed in this paper are of four types: GOAL nodes represent a goal to be achieved; PHANTOM nodes represent goals that should already be true at the time they are encountered; SPLIT nodes have a single predecessor and multiple successors, and represent a forking of the partial ordering; JOIN nodes have multiple predecessors and a single successor, and represent a rejoining of subplans within the partial ordering.

Each node points to a body of code. The action that the node represents can be simulated by evaluating the body. The evaluation will cause new nodes, representing more detailed actions, to be added to the net. It will also update a hypothesized world model to reflect the effects of the more detailed actions.

Associated with each node is an add list and a delete list. These lists are computed when the node is created. They contain symbolic expressions representing the changes to the world model caused by the action that the node represents.

Node types are designated as follows:

Description of action	Description of action	S	J
GOAL	**PHANTOM**	**SPLIT**	**JOIN**

FIGURE 2   GRAPHIC REPRESENTATION OF A NODE

Figure 2 shows the graphic notation used in this paper to display a node of a procedural net.

As an example, let us examine a procedural net representing a hierarchy of plans to paint a ceiling and paint a stepladder. The plan can be represented, in an abstract way, as a single node as shown in Figure 3a. In more detail, the plan is a conjunction, and might be represented as in Figure 3b. The more detailed subplans to achieve these two goals might be "Get paint, get ladder, then apply paint to ceiling," and "Get paint, then apply paint to ladder," as depicted in Figure 3c. The plan depicted in Figure 3d will be explained below.

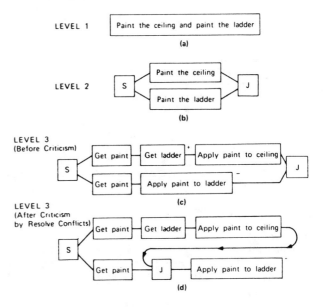

FIGURE 3   PROCEDURAL NET FOR PAINTING

The pictorial representation used here suppresses much of the information associated with each node. The add and delete lists, for instance, are not indicated in the diagrams. They are not hard to infer, however. For example, "Get ladder" will cause "Has ladder" to be added to the world model, and "Apply paint to ceiling" might delete "Has paint."

Precondition-subgoal relationships are inferred by the system from pointers that indicate which nodes represent expansions in greater detail of other nodes. These pointers are also omitted in the pictorial representation. The system assumes that every action but the last in such an expansion is a precondition for the last action.

B. Task-specific Knowledge

Knowledge about the task domain is given to the system in procedural form, written in the SOUP (Semantics of User's Problem) language. SOUP is an extension of QLISP (8) that is interpreted in an unusual fashion, as described in the next section.

As an example, let us examine the SOUP code for blocks problems such as that presented in Section II above. The complete semantics of the actions of this domain are expressed by two functions, which are shown in Figure 4. The code for the function CLEAR says, "If the variable X is TABLE, then it is already "clear." Otherwise, see if some block Y is on X. If so, clear Y and then remove Y by putting it somewhere else."

The code for the function PUTON says, "To put X on Y, first clear X and Y. Then place X on Y (and thus Y is no longer clear)."

Figure 4

SOUP Code for the Blocks Problems

```
(CLEAR
  (QLAMBDA (CLEARTOP ←X)
     (OR (EQ $X (QUOTE TABLE))
         (QPROG (←Y)
            (ATTEMPT (PIS (ON ←Y $X))
               THEN (PGOAL (Clear $Y)
                           (CLEARTOP $Y)
                           APPLY
                           (CLEAR))
                    (PDENY (ON $Y $X))
                    (PGOAL (Put $Y on top of ←Z)
                           (ON $Y ←Z)
                           APPLY NIL))
            (RETURN))))))

(PUTON
  (QLAMBDA (ON ←X ←Y)
     (PAND (PGOAL (Clear $X)
                  (CLEARTOP $X)
                  APPLY
                  (CLEAR))
           (PGOAL (Clear $Y)
                  (CLEARTOP $Y)
                  APPLY
                  (CLEAR)))
     (PGOAL (Put $X on top of $Y)
            (ON $X $Y)
            APPLY NIL)
     (PDENY (CLEARTOP $Y))))
```

C. The Planning Algorithm

Initially, NOAH is given a goal to achieve. NOAH first builds a procedural net that consists of a single goal node to achieve the given goal. This node has a list of all relevant SOUP functions as its body, and represents the plan to achieve the goal at a very high level of abstraction. This one-step plan may then be expanded.

The planning algorithm of the NOAH system is simple. It expands the most detailed plan in a procedural net by expanding each node of the plan. The nodes are expanded in the order of their position in the time sequence. The expansion of each node produces child nodes. Each child node contains a more detailed model of the action it represents. The detailed models are queried during the creation of subsequent nodes in the time sequence. (Note that they are not queried during the expansion of parallel nodes in parallel branches of the plan.) Thus by creating subplans for each node in the plan, a new, more detailed plan will be created.

The individual subplan for each node will be correct, but there is as yet no guarantee that the new plan, taken as a whole, will be correct. There may be interactions between the new, detailed steps that render the overall plan invalid. For example, the individual expansions involved in generating the plan in Figure 3c from that in Figure 3b are correct, yet the overall plan is invalid, since it allows for painting the ladder before painting the ceiling.

Before the new detailed plan is presumed to work, the planning system must take an overall look at it to ensure that the local expansions make global sense together. This global examination is provided by a set of critics. The critics serve a purpose somewhat similar to that of the critics of Sussman's HACKER (1), except that for NOAH they are constructive critics, designed to add constraints to as yet unconstrained plans, whereas for HACKER they were destructive critics whose purpose was to reject incorrect assumptions reflected in the plans.

The algorithm for the planning process, then, is as follows:
   (1) Simulate the most detailed plan in the procedural net. This will have the effect of producing a new, more detailed plan.
   (2) Criticize the new plan, performing any necessary reordering or elimination of redundant operations.
   (3) Go to Step 1.

Clearly, this algorithm is an oversimplification, but for the purposes of this paper we may imagine that the planning process continues until no new details are uncovered. (In fact, for the complete problem solving and execution monitoring system, a local decision must be made at every node about whether it should be expanded.)

IV CRITICS

The critics described here are general-purpose critics, appropriate to any problem solving task. In addition to these, other task-specific critics may be specified for any particular domain.

A.   The "Resolve Conflicts" Critic

The Resolve Conflicts critic examines those portions of a plan that represent conjuncts to be achieved in parallel. In particular, it looks at the add and delete lists of each node in each conjunctive subplan. If an action in one conjunct deletes an expression that is a precondition for a subgoal in another conjunct, then a conflict has occurred. The subgoal is endangered because, during execution, its precondition might be negated by the action in the parallel branch of the plan. (An implicit assumption being made here is that all of a subgoal's preconditions must remain true until the subgoal is executed.) The conflict may be resolved by requiring the endangered subgoal to be achieved before the action that would delete the precondition.

For example, the painting plan depicted in Figure 3c contains a conflict. "Apply paint to ladder" will effectively delete "Has ladder," which is on the add list of "Get ladder." In such a situation, a conflict would occur, since "Has ladder" is a precondition of "Apply paint to ceiling." The conflict is denoted in the pictorial representation by a plus sign (+) over the precondition and a minus sign (−) over the step that violated it. The conflict can be resolved by requiring that the endangered subgoal ("Apply paint to ceiling") be done before the violating step ("Apply paint to ladder").

If the conflict were resolved in this manner, the resulting plan would appear as in Figure 3d.

A similar conflict occurs if an action in one conjunct deletes an expression that is a precondition for a following subgoal. In this case, the precondition must be re-achieved after the deleting action.

Conflicts of this type are very easy to spot. The critic simply builds a table of multiple effects. This table contains an entry for each expression that was asserted or denied by more than one node in the current plan. A conflict is recognized when an expression that is asserted at some node is denied at a node that is not the asserting node's subgoal.

Note that a precondition may legally be denied by its own subgoal. For example, to put Block A on Block B, B must have a clear top. This precondition will be denied by the action of putting A on B.

B.   The "Use Existing Objects" Critic

In addition to specifying the right actions in the right order, a complete plan must specify the objects that the actions are to manipulate. For NOAH, this specification is accomplished by binding the unbound variables (those prefixed by a left arrow) in the PGOAL statements of the SOUP code.

During the course of planning, NOAH will avoid binding a variable to a specific object unless a clear best choice for the binding is available. When no specific object is clearly best, the planner will generate a formal object to bind to the variable. The formal object is essentially a place holder for an entity that is as yet unspecified. The formal objects described here are similar in spirit to those used by Sussman in his HACKER program (1), and to the uninstantiated parameters in relevant operators as used by ABSTRIPS (3).

The strategy of allowing actions with unbound arguments to be inserted into a plan has several advantages. First, it enables the system to avoid making arbitrary, and therefore possibly wrong, choices on the basis of insufficient information. Furthermore, it allows the system to deal with world models that are only partially specified by producing plans that are only partially specified.

However, after a plan has been completed at some level of detail, it may be clear that a formal object can be replaced by some object that was mentioned elsewhere in the plan. The Use Existing Objects critic will replace formal objects by real ones whenever possible. This may involve merging nodes from different portions of the plan, resulting in reordering or partial linearization.

For example, a more detailed expansion of the painting plan might specify putting the ladder at Place ^{001} to paint it, and at Under-Ceiling for painting the ceiling. The Use Existing Objects critic would optimize the plan by replacing Place001 with Under-Ceiling.

C.   The "Eliminate Redundant Preconditions" Critic

During the simulation phase of the planning process, every precondition that is encountered is explicitly stored in the procedural net. This is so that the critics will be able to analyze the complete precondition-subgoal structure of each new subplan. But after the other critics have done their work, and the plan has been altered to reflect the interactions of all the steps, the altered plan may well specify redundant preconditions.

For instance, in our painting example, "Get paint" appears twice in the plan. This critic recognizes the redundancy by examining the same table of multiple effects that was used by Resolve Conflicts. The extra preconditions are eliminated to conserve storage and avoid redundant planning at more detailed levels for achieving them.

V THE EXAMPLE, AGAIN

We are now ready to see how NOAH solves the problem posed in Section II. The initial state is expressed to the system as a set of QLISP assertions:

        (ON C A)
        (CLEARTOP B)
        (CLEARTOP C)

NOAH is invoked with the goal: (AND (ON A B) (ON B C)).

The system builds an initial procedural net that consists of a single GOAL node. The node is to achieve the given goal; its body is a list of the task-specific SOUP functions, in this case CLEAR and PUTON. It then applies the planning algorithm to this one-step plan, which is depicted in Figure 5a.

The conjunction is split up, so that each of its conjuncts is achieved independently. PUTON is the relevant function for achieving both conjuncts, but the system does not immediately invoke PUTON. Rather, the system builds a new GOAL node in the procedural net to represent each invocation. The nodes are to achieve (ON A B) or (ON B C), and have PUTON as their body. The original plan has now been completely simulated to a greater level of detail, and so the critics are applied. At this level, they find no problems with the plan that was generated. The new plan is shown in Figure 5b.

The new plan is now expanded. When the GOAL nodes for achieving (ON A B) and (ON B C) are simulated, PUTON is applied to each goal expression. PUTON causes the generation of a new level of GOAL nodes. When the entire plan has been simulated, the resulting new plan appears as in Figure 5c. The nodes of the plan are numbered to aid in explaining the actions of the critics.

The critics are now applied to the new plan. Resolve Conflicts generates a table of all the expressions that were asserted or denied more than once during the simulation. The table is shown in Figure 6a. This table is then reduced by eliminating from consideration those preconditions that are denied by their own subgoals. For example, (CLEARTOP C) is a precondition for the subgoal (ON B C), so it is not a conflict that achieving (ON B C) at Node 6 makes (CLEARTOP C) false. Now, any expression for which there is only a single remaining effect is removed from the table. The resulting table, shown in Figure 6b, displays all the conflicts created by the assumption of nonlinearity.

Resolve Conflicts now reorders the plan by placing the endangered subgoal (Node 6, achieving (ON B C)) before the violating step (Node 3, a-

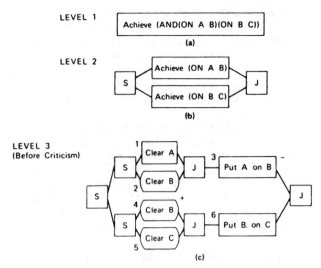

LEVEL 1   (a)

LEVEL 2   (b)

LEVEL 3 (Before Criticism)   (c)

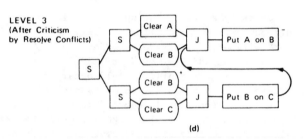

LEVEL 3 (After Criticism by Resolve Conflicts)   (d)

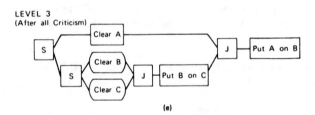

LEVEL 3 (After all Criticism)   (e)

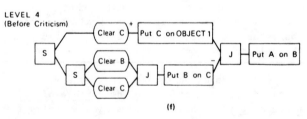

LEVEL 4 (Before Criticism)   (f)

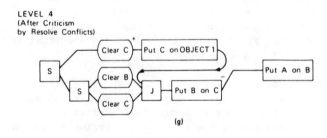

LEVEL 4 (After Criticism by Resolve Conflicts)   (g)

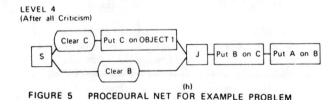

LEVEL 4 (After all Criticism)   (h)

FIGURE 5   PROCEDURAL NET FOR EXAMPLE PROBLEM

Figure 6

TABLE OF MULTIPLE EFFECTS FOR
EXAMPLE PROBLEMS
(Node numbers refer to Figure 5c.)

6a - Original Table

CLEARTOP B: Asserted - Node 2 ("Clear B")
             Denied - Node 3 ("Put A on B")
             Asserted - Node 4 ("Clear B")
CLEARTOP C: Asserted - Node 5 ("Clear C")
             Denied - Node 6 ("Put B on C")

6b - Refined Table

CLEARTOP B: Denied - Node 3 ("Put A on B")
             Asserted - Node 4 ("Clear B")

chieving (ON A B)). The transformed plan is shown
in Figure 5d.

   Since no formal objects were generated at
this level of detail, Use Existing Objects does
not transform the plan further. Eliminate Redundant Preconditions is now applied, and the resulting plan is shown in Figure 5e. Note that the
major restriction in the solution to the problem,
that B must be placed on C before A is placed on
B, has been incorporated into the plan. This has
been accomplished directly, constructively, and
without backtracking.

   The critics having been applied, the system
simulates the new plan. This results in the
generation of a new, yet more detailed plan, shown
in Figure 5f. The critics are then applied. An
analysis similar to that described above enables
Resolve Conflicts to discover that (CLEARTOP C)
might be violated when achieving (ON B C). Thus,
the plan is rearranged, as shown in Figure 5g, so
that (ON C Object1), the endangered subgoal, is
achieved before (ON B C).

   Use Existing Objects again finds no formal
objects that can be unified with existing ones.
After Eliminate Redundant Preconditions cleans
up the plan, it appears as in Figure 5h. The
final plan is: Put C on Object 1; Put B on C; Put
A on B. Essentially, the plan is now completely
linearized. The planning system has chosen the
correct ordering for the subgoals, without backtracking or wasted computation. By avoiding a
premature commitment to a linear plan, the system never had to undo a random choice made on the
basis of insufficient information.

VI OTHER EXAMPLES

   In this section a number of other
blocks world examples will be presented. The
problems and their solutions will be displayed
graphically, and only points of special interest
will be discussed in the text.

A. Four Blocks

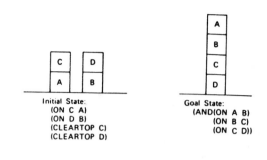

Initial State:
(ON C A)
(ON D B)
(CLEARTOP C)
(CLEARTOP D)

Goal State:
(AND(ON A B)
(ON B C)
(ON C D))

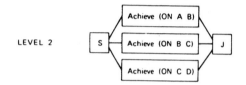

LEVEL 1   Achieve (AND(ON A B)(ON B C)(ON C D))

The conjunctive goal is split into parallel goals.

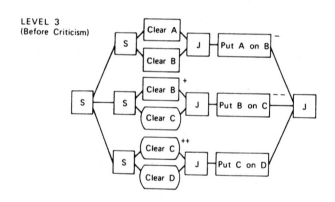

LEVEL 2

LEVEL 3
(Before Criticism)

Resolve Conflicts notices two cases of a
precondition (+) negated by a parallel operation
(-).

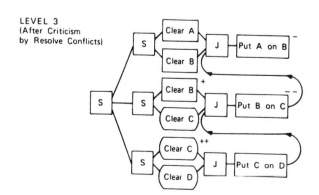

LEVEL 3
(After Criticism
by Resolve Conflicts)

Eliminate Redundant Preconditions cleans up the plan.

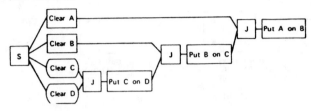

LEVEL 3
(After all Criticism)

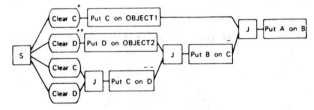

LEVEL 4
(Before Criticism)

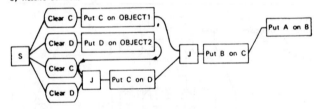

LEVEL 4
(After Criticism
by Resolve Conflicts)

Use Existing Objects notices that the plan can be simplified by unifying the formal object, Object1, with Block D. The nodes that refer to putting C on D and on Object1 are merged.

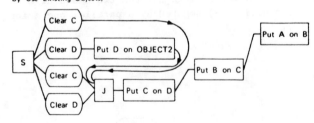

LEVEL 4
(After Criticism
by Use Existing Objects)

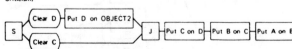

LEVEL 4
(After all
Criticism)

The final plan is: Put D on Object2, Put C on D, Put B on C, Put A on B.

B.   Creative Destruction

This problem can only be solved by undoing a subgoal that is already achieved.

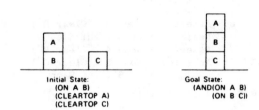

Initial State:
(ON A B)
(CLEARTOP A)
(CLEARTOP C)

Goal State:
(AND(ON A B)
(ON B C))

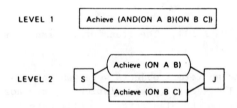

LEVEL 1   Achieve (AND(ON A B)(ON B C))

LEVEL 2

The first conjunct is a PHANTOM goal, since it is already true in the initial world model.

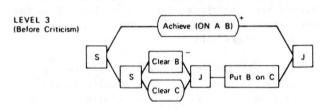

LEVEL 3
(Before Criticism)

Resolve Conflicts notices that one node (−) deletes a precondition for a subsequent subgoal. The precondition in this case is (ON A B), and the subgoal is the initial conjunctive goal. The system therefore alters the PHANTOM goal (+) to become a genuine goal, to be achieved in time for the subsequent subgoal.

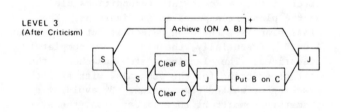

LEVEL 3
(After Criticism)

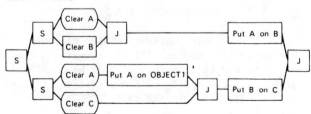

LEVEL 4
(Before Criticism)

Resolve Conflicts notices that (CLEARTOP B) is asserted by one node (+) and deleted by another (-). It therefore reorders the plan.

LEVEL 4
(After Criticism
by Resolve Conflicts)

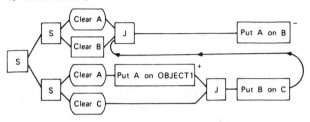

Eliminate Redundant Preconditions cleans up the plan.

LEVEL 4
(After Criticism)

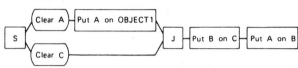

The final plan is: Put A on Object1, Put B on C, Put A on B.

VII DISCUSSION

We have seen how a variety of problems which can be represented as conjunctive goals have simple, straightforward solutions in NOAH. There are a number of other problem solving systems that use alternative approaches to solve similar problems. Among these are Sussman's use of debugging (1,9), Tate's search in a space of "tick lists" (4), and the approach of passing actions backward over a partial plan, which is used by Manna and Waldinger (10) and Warren (5).

The approach presented in this paper is in many ways antithetical to that of Sussman's HACKER. HACKER attacks conjunctive goals by making a "linear" assumption. That is, conjunctive goals are assumed to be independent and additive, and so to achieve the overall goal each conjunct may be achieved in sequence. The system is explicitly aware of this assumption. If the developing plan fails, it can be debugged by comparing the problem that occurred with the known types of problems generated by the assumption of linearity. As bugs are encountered and solved, a collection of critics is developed, each of which notices that a certain type of bug has occurred in a plan.

HACKER does a lot of wasted work. While the problem solver will eventually produce a correct plan, it does so in many cases by iterating through a cycle of building a wrong plan, then applying all known critics to suggest revisions of the plan, then building a new (still potentially wrong) plan.

NOAH makes no rash assumptions, but preserves all the freedom of ordering that is implicit in the statement of a conjunctive goal. It assumes the conjuncts are independent, but the nonlinear representation frees it from worrying about additivity. It applies its critics constructively, to linearize the plan only when necessary. By waiting until it knows the nature of the conjuncts' interactions, NOAH is sure to place actions in the correct order, and thus needs never undo the effects of a false assumption.

Tate's INTERPLAN performs a search for a correct linear ordering by using both debugging and backtracking. INTERPLAN does this not by creating alternative sequences of actions, but rather by examining a tabular representation of the interactions between conjunctive goals. Tate demonstrated that a planner can perform reasoning about plans by dealing with information that is much simpler than the plan itself. This concept has been used extensively by the critics in NOAH, which do much of their analysis on the tables of multiple effects rather than on the plans themselves.

Manna and Waldinger and Warren build linear plans in non-sequential order. They require that the partial plan at every stage be a linear one. However, they allow additions to the plan by insertion of new actions into the body of the plan, rather than restricting new actions to appear at the end. This approach has the advantage of being constructive, in the sense that when the planner adds each step to the plan, it takes into account all the interactions between conjuncts that it knows about. But by forcing the plan to be linear at all intermediate stages, these planners must do unnecessary search with backtracking, or sophisticated plan optimization to find the correct order in which to attack the conjuncts.

VII FURTHER WORK

This paper deals with a deceptively simple idea: a plan may have the structure of a partial ordering. The planning system described here is primitive and incomplete, and a more complete one will be required to fully explore the implications of this representation of plans. The system does not now deal with disjunctive subgoals (for example, to paint the ceiling, get paint and either a ladder or a table).

The current system also fails to deal with what might be termed "non-linearizable interactions." These are interactions between subgoals where no simple ordering of the actions that achieve each subgoal independently will achieve the overall goal. An example of this arises in the problem of exchanging the contents of two registers.

The most serious deficiency in the current system is its lack of awareness about the auxiliary computations specified in the procedural semantics (the SOUP code) of a task domain. The procedural net representation lets the system be aware of the goals and subgoals that the planner has decided to tackle, but it does not preserve any information about the computation that resulted in those decisions. In some cases, a reordering of subgoals might alter the state in which one of these computations would be carried out. Then the computation might produce different results.

Space does not permit adequate discussion of these issues here. The interested reader will find it elsewhere (7). It is worth noting, however, that the system as it now stands has been used successfully for SRI's Computer Based Consultant, where it creates for the casual observer a surprising sense of richness. This suggests not that NOAH is very sophisticated, but that the mechanisms of intelligence may not be as complex as we think.

ACKNOWLEDGMENTS

The ideas presented in this paper have been stimulated and sharpened by discussions with Richard Waldinger, Richard Fikes, Nils Nilsson, and Austin Tate. The research reported in this paper was sponsored by the Advanced Research Projects Agency of the Department of Defense under Contract DAHC04-72-C-008 with the U.S. Army Research Office.

REFERENCES

1. Sussman, G. J., "A Computational Model of Skill Acquisition," Tech, Note AI TR-297, Artificial Intelligence Laboratory, MIT, Cambridge, Ma., August 1973

2. Fikes, R. E., and Nilsson, N. J., "STRIPS: A New Approach to the Application of Theorem Proving to Problem Solving," Artificial Intelligence, Vol. 2, pp. 189-208, 1971

3. Sacerdoti, E. D., "Planning in a Hierarchy of Abstraction Spaces," Artificial Intelligence, Vol. 5, No. 2, pp. 115-135, 1974

4. Tate, A., "INTERPLAN: A Plan Generation System which can deal with Interactions between Goals," Memorandum MIP-R-109, Machine Intelligence Research Unit, University of Edinburgh, December 1974

5. Warren, D.H.D., "WARPLAN: A System for Generating Plans," Memo No. 76, Department of Computational Logic, University of Edinburgh, June 1974

6. Hart, P. E., "Progress on a Computer-Based Consultant," Tech. Note 99, Artificial Intelligence Center, SRI, Menlo Park, CA., January 1975

7. Sacerdoti, E. D., "A Structure for Plans and Behavior," forthcoming Ph.D. thesis, Stanford University

8. Reboh, R., and Sacerdoti, E. D., "A Preliminary QLISP Manual," Tech. Note 81, Artificial Intelligence Center, SRI, Menlo Park, Ca., August 1973

9. Sussman, G. J., "The Virtuous Nature of Bugs," Proc. AISB Summer Conference, July 1974

10. Manna, Z. and Waldinger, R., "Knowledge and Reasoning In Program Synthesis," Tech. Note 98, Artificial Intelligence Center, SRI, Menlo Park, Ca., November 1974

Planning with Constraints (MOLGEN: Part 1)

Mark Stefik*

Computer Science Department, Stanford University, Stanford, CA 94305, U.S.A.

Recommended by Daniel G. Bobrow

ABSTRACT

Hierarchical planners distinguish between important considerations and details. A hierarchical planner creates descriptions of abstract states and divides its planning task into subproblems for refining the abstract states. The abstract states enable it to focus on important considerations, thereby avoiding the burden of trying to deal with everything at once. In most practical planning problems, however, the subproblems interact. Without the ability to handle these interactions, hierarchical planners can deal effectively only with idealized cases where subproblems are independent and can be solved separately.

This paper presents an approach to hierarchical planning, termed constraint posting, that uses constraints to represent the interactions between subproblems. Constraints are dynamically formulated and propagated during hierarchical planning, and used to coordinate the solutions of nearly independent subproblems. This is illustrated with a computer program, called MOLGEN, that plans gene-cloning experiments in molecular genetics.

1. Introduction

Divide each problem that you examine into as many parts as you can and as you need to solve them more easily. Descartes, *OEuvres*, vol. VI, p. 18; "Discours de la Methods"

This rule of Descartes is of little use as long as the art of dividing ... remains unexplained. ... By dividing his problem into unsuitable parts, the inexperienced problem-solver may increase his difficulty. Leibniz, *Philosophische Schriften*, edited by Gerhart, vol. IV, p. 331 from Polya [12]

Subproblems interact. This observation is central to problem solving, particularly planning and design. When interactions can be anticipated, they can guide the division of labor. When they are discovered late, the required changes can be difficult and expensive to incorporate. The difficulty of managing interactions is compounded by problem size and complexity. In large design projects, unforeseen interactions often consume a substantial share of the work of project managers [2].

This paper is concerned with ways to cope with and exploit interactions in design. Section 2 presents the *constraint posting* approach for managing interactions in design. Constraint posting has been implemented in a computer program (named MOLGEN) that has planned a few experiments in molecular genetics. In Section 3, the design of an experiment is used to illustrate the constraint posting ideas. In Section 4, the effectiveness of constraint posting on the sample problem is examined. The remaining sections trace the intellectual connections to other work on problem solving and propose suggestions for further research.

This is the first of two papers about my thesis research on MOLGEN. Both papers are concerned with the use and organization of knowledge to make planning effective. This paper discusses the use of constraints to organize knowledge about subproblems in hierarchical planning. A companion paper [21] discusses the use of levels to organize control knowledge. It also develops a rationale for deciding when a planner should use heuristic reasoning.

The research was carried out as part of the MOLGEN project at Stanford. A long term goal of this project is to build a knowledge-based program to assist geneticists in planning laboratory experiments. Towards that goal, two prototype planning systems have been constructed and used as vehicles for testing ideas about planning [7, 20].

2. The Constraint Posting Approach to Design

The constraint posting approach depends on the view of systems as aggregates of *loosely coupled* subsystems. It models the design of such systems in terms of operations on constraints.

2.1. Nearly independent subproblems

In *Sciences of the Artificial* [18], Simon discussed the study and design of complex systems. He observed that when we study a complex system, whether it is natural or man-made, we often divide it into subsystems that can be studied separately without constant attention to their interactions. For example, in studying an automobile, we delineate subsystems such as the electrical system, fuel system, engine, and the brake system; in an animal, we delineate the nervous system, circulatory system, and the digestive system.

Similarly, when we design complex systems, we tend to first map out the design in terms of subsystems. Designers have advocated this top-down ap-

* Current address: Xerox Palo Alto Research Center. 3333 Coyote Hill Road, Palo Alto. CA 94304, U.S.A.

Artificial Intelligence 16 (1981) 111-140

0004-3702/81/0000–0000/$02.50 ©North-Holland Publishing Company

proach for the design of such diverse things as computer programs, machines, and buildings. This approach is so familiar and universally practiced that we seldom consider the motivations for it. Some of these motivations are: (1) the apparent complexity of the design problem is often reduced by partitioning it into subproblems, and (2) the partitioning can be done before the specifications of the subsystems are worked out because most of the details are irrelevant to the global design, and (3) the labor and expertise of designing the detailed subsystems can often be divided among several specialists.

A key step in design is to minimize the interactions between separate subsystems. Simon coined the phrase *nearly decomposable system* to characterize the way that a complex system can be built from loosely coupled subsystems. Winograd [26] addressed the same point in representational terms:

"... we must worry about finding the right decomposition to reduce the apparent complexity, but we must also remember that interactions among subsystems are weak but *not negligible*. In representational terms, this forces us to have representations which facilitate the weak interactions."

The view of a system in terms of *nearly decomposable* subsystems corresponds to the view of the design process in terms of *nearly independent* subproblems. In hierarchical planning a solution is first sketched out in terms of abstract steps, which are refined into specific plan steps during the planning process as shown in Fig. 1. The abstract steps and their subsequent refinements

correspond to *nearly decomposable* subsystems; they are connected together in a plan and the output of each plan step must match the required input of the following plan step. These input/output relationships make a plan work as a whole. The design subproblems, that is, the refinements of the abstract plan steps into specific steps, are only nearly independent. They are not completely independent because their solutions must interface correctly. When the abstractions partition the plan into nearly independent subproblems, interactions do not dominate the planning process. However, efficient planning usually requires that the weak interactions be taken into account during the planning process. The key idea in constraint posting is to use constraints to represent the interactions between subproblems.

2.2. The meanings of constraints

For the purposes of planning, constraints can have several different interpretations. A constraint expresses a relationship among plan variables. Constraints are represented as predicates. For example, consider the following:

(Lambda (Gene DNA-structure) (Contains Gene DNA-Structure)).

If the **Lambda** variables (*Gene* and *DNA-Structure*) are bound to the constants *Tc⁻-gene* and *DNA-13*, then the predicate Contains may be evaluated to determine whether the *Tc⁻-gene* is contained in *DNA-13*. The full representation of constraints implemented in MOLGEN allows the plan variables to have different names than the **Lambda** variables and contains other information related to the constraint. Constraints may involve more than two variables; they may also apply over sets of variables.

The first interpretation of constraints is as *elimination rules* from the perspective of object selection. A constraint in MOLGEN is associated with a set of plan variables that usually refer to laboratory objects. When the variables are not yet bound, the constraint may be interpreted as a condition to be satisfied. It *constrains* the set of allowable bindings; potential selections are eliminated if they do not satisfy the constraint.

A second interpretation of constraints is as partial descriptions and *commitments* from the perspective of plan refinement. During the process of planning, there are many opportunities for deciding which part of a plan to make more specific. A least-commitment approach is to defer decisions as long as possible. A constraint is essentially a partial description of an object; a selection is a full description. By formulating constraints about objects, MOLGEN is able to make commitments about partial descriptions of the objects without making specific selections.

A third interpretation of constraints is as a **communication medium** for expressing interactions between subproblems. A constraint represents an in-

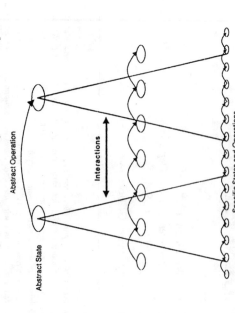

FIG. 1. Nearly independent subproblems. The upper level represents an abstract (or less detailed) plan. The arcs represent abstract operations and the circles represent abstract states. In hierarchical planning, such abstract plans are *refined* into more specific plans, as suggested by the *refinement-cones*. Each cone can be viewed as a refinement-subproblem. Interactions between the refinement subproblems need to be managed during planning.

tended relationship between (possibly uninstantiated) plan variables. In MOLGEN, these variables are often shared among various steps in the plan; they represent objects having a rich set of relationships. For example, they may represent laboratory objects which are to be constructed out of other laboratory objects. If a problem solver has a calculus of expressions, it can take constraints relating to variables in one part of the plan and infer new constraints relating to variables in another part of the plan, even though the variables themselves are still unbound. This amounts to the propagation of constraints in a plan, and we will see that this enables a problem solver to coordinate the solution of subproblems.

2.3. Operations on constraints

The constraint posting approach is essentially a marriage of ideas from hierarchical planning and constraint satisfaction. It distinguishes three operations on constraints:

(1) constraint formulation,
(2) constraint propagation,
(3) constraint satisfaction.

All of these operations could be broadly characterized as inferences in problem solving. A major point of this paper is that it is useful to consider these operations in terms of the substantially different roles they play in the problem solving process.

Constraint formulation is the adding of new constraints as commitments in the design process. A planner can proceed hierarchically by formulating constraints of increasing detail as planning progresses. Thus, a problem solver that can introduce new constraints need not work with all of the details at once. This idea is consistent with the common experience of working on problems that are imprecisely formulated, but which become more tightly specified during the solution process. In contrast, the traditional constraint satisfaction approach works with a fixed number of constraints that are all known at the beginning.

Constraint propagation is the creation of new constraints from old constraints in a plan. In MOLGEN, this operation performs communication between refinement subproblems during planning. Refinement subproblems are usually under-constrained when viewed in isolation because there are many choices for refining abstractions in genetics plans. When constraints are propagated, they bring together the requirements from separate parts of the problem. Constraint propagation makes possible a *least-commitment* strategy of deferring decisions for as long as possible. The problem solver works to keep its options open, and reasons by elimination when constraints from other subproblems become known.

Constraint satisfaction is the operation of finding values for variables so that a set of constraints on the variables is satisfied. Constraint satisfaction can take different forms. For example, linear programming is a constraint satisfaction method that assigns numeric values of variables satisfying linear inequalities. Constraints in MOLGEN describe requirements about laboratory objects needed in the plans; constraint satisfaction implements a 'buy or build' decision process. MOLGEN first tries to satisfy the constraints by selecting an available object 'off the shelf'. Computationally, this involves searching MOLGEN's knowledge base for a record of an object that is marked as available and which satisfies the constraints. For example, MOLGEN might search for an organism carrying a particular gene on its chromosome. If the search process fails, MOLGEN marks the constraint as unsatisfied and may later propose building an object to satisfy the constraint. In such a case, the construction of the object becomes a subgoal in the plan. When the constraints and variables come from different subproblems, constraint satisfaction plays a coordinating role by pooling the constraints and intersecting their solutions.

3. An Example of Planning with Constraints

This section illustrates the constraint posting idea with an experiment that was planned by MOLGEN. MOLGEN has been used to plan experiments in a class of synthesis problems known as gene cloning experiments.[1] The goal in gene cloning experiments is to use bacteria as a biological system for synthesizing a desired protein product. The experiments involve splicing a gene coding for the protein into bacteria, so that the bacteria will manufacture it. The laboratory plan illustrated in this example is a solution to a gene cloning problem called the *rat-insulin problem* which was reported by Ullrich et al. in 1977 [24].

Before starting the example, it should be mentioned that the main use of MOLGEN is as a vehicle for testing approaches to reasoning about design. It would be misleading to suggest that MOLGEN is currently a useful computational aid for geneticists. MOLGEN's knowledge base is too narrow and there are serious difficulties in upgrading MOLGEN to a routinely useful system (see Section 6.2). The rat-insulin experiment is one of a few gene cloning experiments that have been planned by MOLGEN. Even in this narrow class of experiments, there are laboratory techniques (e.g., involving protein transcription) that are currently beyond MOLGEN's ken, and experiments which MOLGEN fails to solve satisfactorily. The trace of MOLGEN's reasoning in this experiment took over 30 pages of computer print out (without annotations). The interested reader is referred to Stefik [20] for a complete trace of the planning of this experiment.

[1] A very readable review of these experiments is available in Gilbert and Villa-Komaroff [8].

3.1. First steps

The first part of MOLGEN's trace is similar to the behavior of previous problem-solving programs like GPS (Newell [11]). MOLGEN compares goals, finds *differences*, and chooses operators to reduce the differences. Like several recent planning programs (see Section 5.1), MOLGEN plans hierarchically. It uses a simplified model of genetics to set up an abstract plan, and then refines that to a plan of specific laboratory steps. This section shows how MOLGEN sets up an abstract plan for achieving a synthesis goal. The constraint posting ideas do not appear until Section 3.2.

3.1.1. Abstract objects and operators

MOLGEN views synthesis experiments as compositions of four abstract operators called the 'MARS' operators. (The word 'MARS' is an acronym formed from the first letters of their names.)

(1) **Merge**[2] – to put separate parts together to make a whole. *Examples*: connecting DNA structures together (**Ligate**), adding an extrachromosomal vector to an organism (**Transform**).

(2) **Amplify** – to increase the amount of something. *Examples*: incubating bacteria in ideal growth conditions (**Incubate**), introducing something from stock (**Get-Off-Shelf**).

(3) **React** – altering the properties of something. *Examples*: cleaving DNA with a restriction enzyme (**Cleave**), using alkaline phosphatase to change terminal phosphates to hydroxyl groups in DNA molecules (**Add-Hydroxyl**).[3]

(4) **Sort** – to separate a whole into parts according to their properties. *Examples*: separating polynucleotides according to mass and topology (**Electrophoresis**), killing organisms not resistant to a given antibiotic (**Screen**).

MOLGEN's knowledge is represented in a hierarchical knowledge base[4] divided into objects and operators. The knowledge base describes the laboratory entities at various levels of abstraction. The most abstract laboratory operator is called **Lab-Operator**; the next level contains the four **MARS** operators, and the next level contains thirteen specific laboratory operators. The most abstract laboratory object is **Lab-Object**; the next level contains *Antibiotic, Culture, DNA-Struc, Enzyme, Organism,* and *Sample*. This hierarchy is six levels deep and contains descriptions of 74 kinds of objects.

[2] This paper uses the convention that operators are indicated by underlining; objects and steps are indicated by italics. References to units are indicated by capitalizing their first letter: references to slots are indicated by italics with the first letter not capitalized.

[3] This is the usual meaning of *sort* and not the computer science meaning, which requires a linear ordering. Some of the laboratory operators classified as **Sort** operators do provide a linear ordering (such as *Electrophoresis*); others do not (such as *Screen*). An alternative name for this category of operators would be *separative techniques*.

[4] See Stefik [19] for a discussion of the representation language.

3.1.2. Finding a difference

The synthetic goal for the rat-insulin problem is shown in Fig. 2. This goal is a *partial* description of the desired state that leaves some of the details to be filled in by the planner. It describes a culture of an unspecified bacterium, having an unspecified vector that carries gene for rat-insulin. A *vector* is a self-replicating DNA molecule that can be used to transmit genes into bacteria. Bacteriophages and plasmids are typically used as vectors. Determining what bacterium and vector to use is part of the problem. MOLGEN interprets this goal as a request to design a laboratory plan to get the described bacterium.

An important part of creating a laboratory plan is the selection of (possibly abstract) operators. Like several earlier problem solvers, MOLGEN keys its selection of operators by *differences*. MOLGEN's first steps in doing this are shown in Fig. 3. The key item in the figure is the data structure *Difference-1*.

Prototype is SYNTHESIS-PROBLEM

```
GOAL: [CULTURE-1 with
       ORGANISMS: [BACTERIUM-1 with
                   EXOSOMES: [VECTOR-1 with
                              GENES: [RAT-INSULIN]]]]

TO-PLAN:        META-PLAN-INTERPRETER

PLAN-NUMBER:  1

DESCR:    This synthesis problem is to clone the
          gene for rat-insulin. This problem was
          discussed by Ullrich et al. in Science,
          Vol. 196, pp. 1313-1319.
```

Fig. 2. Goal of the rat-insulin problem. *Bacterium-1* and *Vector-1* are variables, which will become instantiated during planning. The goal slot contains a symbolic description of the synthetic goal.

```
>STRATEGY-STEP-1 (FOCUS)
>PLAN-STEP-1 (FIND-UNUSUAL-FEATURES) Input: ($LAB-GOAL-1)
<PLAN-STEP-1 DONE SUCCESS Output: (DIFFERENCE-1)

·····  DIFFERENCE-1 ·····

MISMATCH:        EXOSOMES
OBJECT:          BACTERIUM-1
COMPARED-TO:     BACTERIUM
LEVEL:           2
DEFN-ROLE:       MORE-SPECIFIC
TYPE:            PART-OF
EXCEPTIONS:      (VECTOR-1 (*P VECTOR))
REPRESENTATION:  LIST
MAKER:           PLAN-STEP-1
DESCR:           Created by FIND-UNUSUAL-FEATURES
```

Fig. 3. Finding unusual features. The *Find-Unusual-Features* design operator compares the objects in *Lab-Goal-1* against their prototypes, and outputs a description of their unique features as *Difference-1*. (It quits after finding the highest level difference.)

Difference-1 summarizes the unusual features of the bacterium described in the goal (*Bacterium-1*) that were found when it was compared to the prototypical bacterium in the genetics knowledge base. The interpretation of *Difference-1* is that *Bacterium-1* was unusual in that it had a specific vector (*Vector-1*) as an exosome.

The rest of Fig. 3 exposes some aspects of MOLGEN's planning machinery that are the topic of the companion paper. For now it is enough to know that in addition to laboratory operators which operate on laboratory objects, MOLGEN has operators which operate on *plans*. These operators are further classified as *planning* (or design) operators, which operate on plans, and *meta-planning* (or strategy) operators, which control the design steps. These operators are described in detail in the companion paper. The design operators represent the constraint posting approach in terms of operators for refining objects and operators, creating and propagating constraints, simulating laboratory steps, and finding differences. The design operator in Fig. 3 is *Find-Unusual-Features*.

MOLGEN's progress in planning takes place in a series of *steps*, which are executed. In Fig. 3, the start of execution of a step is indicated in the trace by a line beginning with the symbols '→'. The name of the operator follows in parentheses (e.g., *Focus* in the first line). The names of the objects input to the operator in the step, if any, follow. The termination of a step is indicated by a line beginning with the symbols '←' and followed by the step name, an indication of the status of the step at termination, an indication of the reason for the status, and the names of the objects output from the step. Finally, a representation of each of the objects output from the step is printed.

3.1.3. Making an abstract plan

Starting with *Difference-1*, MOLGEN goes on to develop an abstract plan. It

```
-----LAB-STEP-1-----
-> PLAN-STEP-2 (PROPOSE-OPERATORS) Input: (DIFFERENCE-1)
<- PLAN-STEP-2 DONE SUCCESS Output: (LAB-STEP-1)

OPERATOR:     MERGE
INPUT:
OUTPUT:
FWD-GOAL:     $LAB-GOAL-1
STATUS:       PROPOSED
REASON:       APPLICABLE
NEXTSTEPS:
PREVSTEPS:
DESCR:        Created to reduce: (DIFFERENCE-1)
MAKER:        PLAN-STEP-2
```

FIG. 4. Proposing the first laboratory step. *Lab-Step-1* is a partially instantiated laboratory step in the abstract plan. It specifies that the operator is *Merge*. No previous or following steps in the plan are known yet. The *input* and *output* slots will be filled with descriptions of the objects that are input and output to the laboratory step. The *fwd-goal* slot refers to a description of the intended output of the step.

begins by partially instantiating a laboratory step (*Lab-Step-1*) as shown in Fig. 4. This step is created by the design operator, **Propose-Operators**. It specifies the abstract operator, **Merge**, but not what objects will be merged or any previous or next steps in the plan. The next few design operations fill in the backwards goals in *Lab-Step-1*, and propose additional steps. They are omitted here for brevity. When they have been executed, MOLGEN has the two-step abstract laboratory plan in Fig. 5. The planning in this part of the trace has been quite straightforward; it is about to get more interesting.

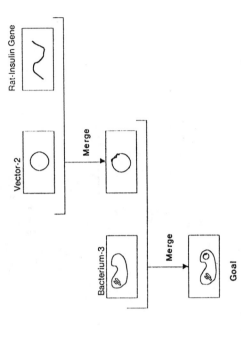

FIG. 5. MOLGEN's abstract plan. This figure characterizes the experiment in terms of two abstract *Merge* operations.

3.2. Introducing a constraint

In the next part of the trace, MOLGEN refines its abstract plan. Fig. 6 shows the important developments:

(1) The specific laboratory operator, **Transform**, has replaced the abstract operator, **Merge**.

(2) The *input* slot of *Lab-Step-1* has been filled with a description of the objects being combined.

(3) *Constraint-1* has been introduced to the plan.

The formulation of *Constraint-1* illustrates an important aspect of MOLGEN's decision-making. When MOLGEN decided to refine **Merge** to the **Transform** operator, the bacterium and vector in *Lab-Step-1* were still unspecified. For **Transform** to work properly, it is necessary that the bacterium and vector be biologically compatible. One approach would be for MOLGEN to immediately select a bacterium and vector for compatibility, and to bind the

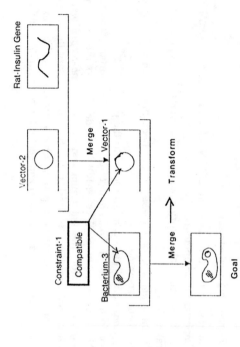

FIG. 7. The plan after introducing the compatibility constraint.

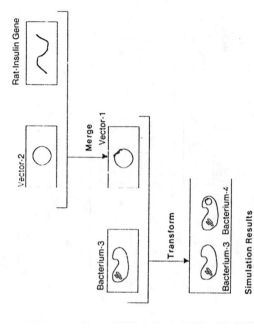

FIG. 8. Simulation of the *Transform* step predicts that some of the bacteria will not get the vector.

```
>PLAN-STEP-6 (REFINE-OPERATOR) Input: (LAB-STEP-1)
<--PLAN-STEP-6 DONE SUCCESS
  Output: (LAB-STEP-1 REFINEMENT-1 CONSTRAINT-1)

-----LAB-STEP-1-----

OPERATOR:    TRANSFORM
INPUT:       [SAMPLE-1 with
              STRUCS: [VECTOR-1 with
              GENES: [RAT-INSULIN]].
              CULTURE-1 with
              ORGANISMS: [BACTERIUM-3]]
OUTPUT:      $LAB-GOAL-1
FWD-GOAL:    REFINED
STATUS:      NEW-OPERATOR
REASON:
NEXTSTEPS:   [LAB-STEP-2]
PREVSTEPS:   Created to reduce: (DIFFERENCE-1)
DESCR:       PLAN-STEP-2
MAKER:

-----REFINEMENT-1-----

ABSTRACT:    MERGE
SPECIFIC:    TRANSFORM
CONSTRAINTS: [CONSTRAINT-1]
GOODLIST:
LAB-STEP:    LAB-STEP-1
MAKER:       PLAN-STEP-6
DESCR:

-----CONSTRAINT-1-----

TYPE:        MANDATORY
ARGS:        [BACTERIUM-3,
              VECTOR-1]
PREDICATE:   (LAMBDA (BACTERIUM VECTOR)
              COMPATIBLE BACTERIUM VECTOR))
STATUS:      PROPOSED
REASON:      FORMULATED
MAKER:       PLAN-STEP-6
LAB-STEP:    LAB-STEP-1
DESCR:       From refinement of MERGE to TRANSFORM in LAB-
              STEP-1
```

FIG. 6. Refinement of *Lab-Step-1* introduces the constraint that the bacterium (*Bacterium-3* from *Culture-1*) and the vector (*Vector-1* from Sample-1) must be compatible. (The syntax of *Constraint-1* has been simplified slightly by eliminating the expression which tests whether enough information is available to evaluate the constraint.)

plan variables (*Bacterium-3* and *Vector-1*) accordingly. The trouble with this approach is that it would preclude the consideration of other constraints that might be uncovered later in the planning process. Since many combinations of values are possible for these variables, MOLGEN decides to keep its options open. Instead of choosing values for the variables, it formulates a constraint on their values that can be taken into account in a later constraint satisfaction step. *Constraint-1* states that the bacterium and vector input to the *Transform* step must be compatible. By posting the constraint, MOLGEN makes the requirement explicit so that it can be combined with other constraints. This deferring of decisions until necessary is part of a *least-commitment* approach to problem solving. Fig. 7 illustrates the plan at this stage pictorially.

3.3. Predicting results of a lab step

One of the important ideas for using symbolic representations is symbolic execution. For each of its laboratory operators, MOLGEN has a simulation model which it can use to predict the results of a laboratory step. The simulation of *Transform* in *Lab-Step-1* is illustrated in Fig. 8. The simulation takes account of the fact that transformation in the laboratory never works to completion. Transformation is essentially the absorption of vectors across cell membranes. In practice, some of the bacteria inevitably end up without vectors. Thus, the output of *Lab-Step-1* includes *Bacterium-4*, which has the vector, and *Bacterium-3*, which does not.

3.4. Introducing a variable

When MOLGEN compares the simulation output of *Lab-Step-1* with the goals, it discovers the extra bacteria resulting from the incompleteness of the *Transform* step. The comparison process yields a difference, which is used to key the selection of an abstract laboratory operator (**Sort**) to remove the bacterium. After several planning steps similar to what we have already seen, MOLGEN refines the **Sort** operator to the **Screen** operator, which kills bacteria with an antibiotic as shown in Fig. 9. This particular refinement introduces some of the most interesting constraints in the plan. When **Refine-operator** looks for a specialized kind of **Sort** to remove unwanted bacteria, it finds only the **Screen** laboratory operator, which kills the bacteria with an antibiotic. This means that an antibiotic must be introduced into the plan. The antibiotic should kill the extra bacteria, those without the vector (*Bacterium-3*) but not harm the others (*Bacterium-4*). Although MOLGEN could arbitrarily choose an antibiotic at this point, it prudently decides to defer the decision in case other factors are found that bear on the selection. In order to refer to an antibiotic without selecting a particular one from the knowledge base, MOLGEN introduces the variable, *Antibiotic-1*, and posts a pair of constraints to indicate which of the bacteria are supposed to be resistant to it.

3.5. Propagating constraints

Subproblems in plans interact. A simple form of interaction occurs when variables are shared between subproblems. In this case, constraints from the subproblems are combined when a value for the variable is determined. A more complicated way to account for interactions is to propagate symbolic constraints between subproblems. In such cases, new constraint expressions are inferred from other constraint expressions on possibly distinct variables.

The virtue of constraint propagation can be seen by viewing planning as a *generate-and-test* process. Constraints are the rules for pruning in the *test* part of the process. The key to efficiency in finding solutions is to apply constraints as early as possible, so that branches corresponding to possible plans can be eliminated before much computational effort is expended. When constraints can be propagated across partial solutions to subproblems, they enable a planner to anticipate interactions and effectively prune some possible choices without generating them.

An example of constraint propagation is shown in Fig. 10. The figure shows the plan at a much later point than where we left off in the previous section. In this propagation, the constraints on which bacteria resist the antibiotic are converted, through a series of transformations, into a constraint on the selection of the vector at the top of the figure. The propagation process approximates the following genetics argument:

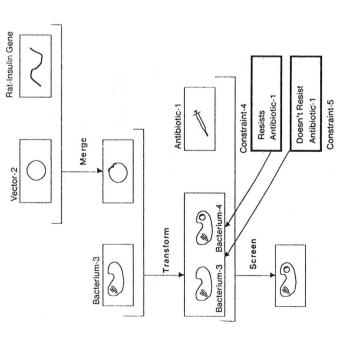

FIG. 9. Introducing an antibiotic. To get rid of the unwanted bacteria, a **Screen** step is proposed, which utilizes an antibiotic. At this point in the plan, MOLGEN has not yet determined the type of bacteria. It introduces some new constraints that tie the selection of the bacteria to the selection of the antibiotic.

3.6. Satisfying constraints

The third operation on constraints is constraint satisfaction. Constraints in MOLGEN describe restrictions on laboratory object in plans; satisfaction is simply a search of the knowledge base for records of available objects that satisfy the constraints on the plan variables. Fig. 11 illustrates an example of constraint satisfaction. *Constraint-1* is the constraint we saw earlier requiring compatibility for values for the variables *Bacterium-3* and *Vector-1*. **Refine-Object** is the name of the design operator for constraint satisfaction on laboratory objects. It searches the knowledge base for possible bindings and records them in the data structure *Tuple-1*. (These should properly be termed 'tuple-sets', since they represent sets of solutions expressed as *n*-tuples.) 'Tuple' data structures list the possible solutions to constraints. The interpretation of *Tuple-1* is that *Bacterium-3* can be bound only to *E. coli*, and that *Vector-1* can be bound to any of four plasmids (e.g., *Col. E1*) listed in the figure.

As discussed further in Section 6.3, MOLGEN uses distinct variable names to refer to objects at different times in the plan, that is, in distinct states. Such variables are linked by a *same-type* relationship in the representation language; solutions for one variable imply solutions for others. For example, *Bacterium-3* is known to be the same type of bacterium as *Bacterium-4*. When MOLGEN anchored *Bacterium-3*, it propagated the information to *Bacterium-1* and *Bacterium-4* as well.

As MOLGEN picks constraints to satisfy, it sometimes discovers that the objects are mentioned in several constraints. In such cases, the tuples are combined and the solutions are intersected. This is shown in Fig. 12 where the constraint satisfaction step integrates the results of satisfying *Constraint-7* with

```
-> PLAN-STEP-15 (REFINE-OBJECT) Input: (CONSTRAINT-1)
     (Anchoring BACTERIUM-3 to ECOLI)
     (Updating slots: GRAMSTAIN MORPHOLOGY in BACTERIUM-1)
     (Updating slots: GRAMSTAIN MORPHOLOGY in BACTERIUM-4)
<- PLAN-STEP-15 DONE SUCCESS Output: (TUPLE-1)

-----TUPLE-1-----

     CONSTRAINTS:     [CONSTRAINT-1]
     VARIABLES:       [BACTERIUM-3,
                       VECTOR-1]
     PRIMARIES:       [BACTERIUM-3,
                       VECTOR-1]
     COMPATIBLES:     (((BACTERIUM-3   ECOLI)
                       VECTOR-1 COLEI
                       PSC101 PBR322 PMB9)))
     MAKER:           PLAN-STEP-15
     DESCR:
```

FIG. 11. Satisfying a constraint. Constraint satisfaction involves a 'buy or build' decision. Here MOLGEN searches the knowledge base for combinations of bacteria and vectors that satisfy the compatibility constraint.

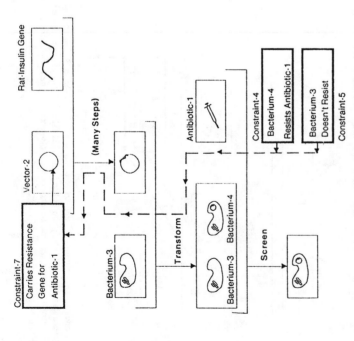

FIG. 10. Propagating Constraints. The constraint propagation process creates new constraints in the plan from existing constraints. This process regresses constraints through the plan in time. one step at a time.

By *Constraint-4*, *Bacterium-4* is resistant to *Antibiotic-1*. By *Constraint-5*, *Bacterium-3* is not resistant. Resistance to an antibiotic is conferred by a resistance gene, which can be either on the bacterial chromosome, or on some extrachromosomal element. The two bacteria are of the same type, that is, they have the same chromosome. This means that the resistance can not be conferred by a resistance gene on the bacterial chromosome. Therefore the resistance gene must be conferred by an extra-chromosomal element. *Vector-1* is the only exosome in *Bacterium-4* that is not in *Bacterium-3*. Therefore, *Vector-1* must carry a resistance gene for *Antibiotic-1*. *Vector-1* was constructed from *Vector-2* and the rat-insulin gene. Since the rat-insulin gene carries no resistance genes for any antibiotic. a resistance gene must be carried by *Vector-2*. (This is the predicate of *Constraint-7*.)

TABLE 1. Final solutions to the constraints

Solution	Bacterium	Vector	Antibiotic	Enzyme	Linker
1	E. coli	pBR322	Tetracycline	HIND3	HIND3DECAMER
2	E. coli	pBR322	Ampicillin	HIND3	HIND3DECAMER
3	E. coli	pSC101	Tetracycline	HIND3	HIND3DECAMER
4	E. coli	pMB9	Tetracycline	HIND3	HIND3DECAMER

reported by Ullrich et al. [24]. A picture of MOLGEN's plan for the experiment is shown in Fig. 13.

In reporting their experiments, geneticists customarily report only the details of their final experiments. Infrequently they report some of their thoughts in planning an experiment and even less frequently are any of the constraints reported. In review articles (such as Boyer [1]) one can sometimes find a discussion of the constraints or experimental considerations once the technique has worked its way into the methodology of the field. The constraints that MOLGEN formulated in the rat-insulin problem are listed below together with a description of their introduction to the plan:

(1) *The bacterium should be biologically compatible with the vector.*
(Formulated as a commitment when **Merge** was refined to **Transform** in *Lab-Step-1*.)

(2) *The vector should have sticky ends prior to ligation in Lab-Step-2 for some restriction enzyme (Restriction-Enzyme-1).*
(Formulated as a commitment when **Merge** was refined to **Ligate** in *Lab-Step-2*.)

(3) *The DNA carrying the Rat-insulin gene should have sticky ends for Restriction-Enzyme-1 prior to ligation in Lab-Step-2.*
(Formulated as a commitment when **Merge** was refined to **Ligate** in *Lab-Step-2*.)

(4) *The bacterium carrying the plasmid (Bacterium-4) should be resistant to some antibiotic (Antibiotic-1).*
(Formulated as a commitment when **Sort** was refined to **Screen** in *Lab-Step-4*.)

(5) *The bacterium without the plasmid (Bacterium-3) should not be resistant to Antibiotic-1.*
(Formulated as a commitment when **Sort** was refined to **Screen** in *Lab-Step-4*.)

(6) *The vector input to the transformation step (Vector-1) should carry a resistance gene for Antibiotic-1.*
(Result of propagating *Constraint-4* and *Constraint-5* through the **Transform** operator in *Lab-Step-1*.)

```
>PLAN-STEP-33 (REFINE-OBJECT) Input: (CONSTRAINT-6)
<-PLAN-STEP-33 CANCELLED REPLACED Output: (NONE)
>PLAN-STEP-35 (REFINE-OBJECT) Input: (CONSTRAINT-7)
<-PLAN-STEP-35 DONE SUCCESS Output: (TUPLE-2)

        -----TUPLE-2-----

CONSTRAINTS:   [CONSTRAINT-3, CONSTRAINT-2, CONSTRAINT-1,
               CONSTRAINT-7]
VARIABLES:     [RESTRICTION-ENZYME-1,
               VECTOR-2,
               BACTERIUM-3,
               VECTOR-1,
               ANTIBIOTIC-1]
PRIMARIES:     [RESTRICTION-ENZYME-1,
               VECTOR-2,
               BACTERIUM-3,
               ANTIBIOTIC-1]
COMPATIBLES:   (((RESTRICTION-ENZYME-1 RESTRICTION-
               ENZYME)
               (BACTERIUM-3 E.COLI)
               (ANTIBIOTIC-1 COLICIN-E1)
               (VECTOR-2 COL.E1))
               ((RESTRICTION-ENZYME-1 RESTRICTION
               ENZYME)
               (BACTERIUM-3 E.COLI)
               (ANTIBIOTIC-1 TETRACYCLINE AMPICILLIN)
               (VECTOR-2 PBR322))
               ((RESTRICTION-ENZYME-1 RESTRICTION-
               ENZYME)
               (BACTERIUM-3 E.COLI)
               (ANTIBIOTIC-1 TETRACYCLINE)
               (VECTOR-2 PMB9 PSC101)))
MAKER:         PLAN-STEP-21
```

FIG. 12. Integrating constraints. MOLGEN uses a *tuple* notation to keep track of possible values for variables. When constraints are introduced, constraints are considered which tie together variables from different tuples, the requirements are combined.

the other constraints in *Tuple-2*. *Constraint-7* is a constraint requiring that *Vector-2* carry a resistance gene for *Antibiotic-1*.

3.7. Finishing the plan

The rest of the trace of MOLGEN's performance on this experiment uses the same kinds of problem solving techniques that we have seen already. New constraints are introduced about restriction enzymes and resistance genes and more variables are introduced and anchored as the constraints on the plan accumulate. In *Lab-Step-7*, MOLGEN introduced a 'molecular adapter' (*Linker-1*) so that the rat-insulin gene can be readily attached to the vector. At this point, the solution was somewhat predetermined in that MOLGEN's knowledge base only had one available linker (called *Hind3decamer*) that could be used. This narrowed the number of possible solutions to the accumulated constraints more than would have been possible if a full complement of linkers had been available. Even so, MOLGEN had four solutions after satisfying all of the constraints as shown in Table 1. The fourth solution was the one

(8) *Restriction-Enzyme-1 should not cut the resistance gene for Antibiotic-1.*
(Result of propagating *Constraint-7* through the *Cleave* operator in *Lab-Step-5*.)

(9) *Restriction-Enzyme-1 should not cut the rat-insulin gene.*
(Result of propagating *Constraint-2* through the *Cleave* operator in *Lab-Step-5*.)

(10) *The vector should have a site for Restriction-Enzyme-1.*
(Formulated as a commitment when *React* was refined to *Cleave* in *Lab-Step-5*.)

(11) *The DNA carrying the rat-insulin gene should have a site for Restriction-Enzyme-1.*
(Result of propagating *Constraint-3* through the *Cleave* operator in *Lab-Step-6*.)

(12) *The linker should have a site for Restriction-Enzyme-1.*
(Formulated as a commitment when *React* was refined to *Cleave* in *Lab-Step-7*.)

If MOLGEN had a more detailed model of genetics (i.e., including the logic of gene promoters) even more constraints would have been formulated.

4. The Effectiveness of Constraint Posting

The power of constraint posting comes largely from two abilities: (1) the ability to plan hierarchically by introducing new constraints and variables, and (2) the ability to anticipate interference between subproblems (using constraint propagation) and to eliminate the interfering solutions. The effectiveness of this during the planning of the rat-insulin problem is illustrated in Table 2.

Each row in the table corresponds to the introduction of a constraint in the plan; the first row shows the situation before any constraints have been introduced. The shaded squares in each row indicate which variables are involved in the constraint. For example, the *compatibility* constraint in the second row involves the variables *Bacterium* and *Vector*. The power of constraint formulation is illustrated by the column labeled 'Total Combinations', which shows how the number of solutions decreases from 3456 to 4 as constraints are added. This column shows the number of acceptable combinations of values for all of the variables. These numbers understate the combinations seen by MOLGEN because they reflect the use of genetics knowledge to reduce the combinatorics. For example, a plan actually contains many variables representing bacteria at different stages of planning. MOLGEN knows that these bacteria represent an *equivalence class* for the purposes of constraint satisfaction, because no laboratory operator will change a bacterium from one type to another. If the variables were counted independently, the columns would be *powers* of the numbers shown. In the first row, no com-

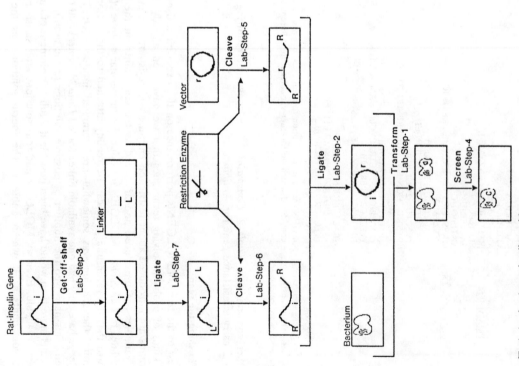

Fig. 13. Final plan for the rat-insulin problem.

(7) *The vector out of which Vector-1 is made should carry a resistance gene for Antibiotic-1.*
(Result of propagating *Constraint-6* through the *Ligate* operator in *Lab-Step-2*.)

chart, the number of solutions for the *Vector* variable decreases from 4 to 3, even though it is not involved directly in the new constraint. This is because constraint satisfaction implicitly includes all of the previous constraints. All of the solutions involving the eliminated vector (a subset of the 10 solutions satisfying the previous constraints) also involved a particular solution for the *Enzyme* variable. When the last constraint reduced the number of possible enzymes from 6 to 1, it eliminated all of the solutions that permitted the deleted value for the *Vector* variable. This shows how the bookkeeping of constraint satisfaction automatically coordinates requirements from different parts of the problem.

5. Relationships to Other Work

The constraint posting approach builds on previous research in hierarchical planning, subgoal interactions, and constraint satisfaction. Several recent and detailed reviews of this research are available with extensive bibliographies [13, 15, 20]. In the interest of brevity, the following discussion will be limited to the main ideas.

5.1. Hierarchical planning

Many AI programs have had the ability to break a problem into subproblems, that is, to find a solution by a *divide and conquer* strategy. However, a program uses a *hierarchical* approach only if it has the additional capability to defer consideration of the details of a problem. *Non-hierarchical* programs suffer from the tyranny of detail. If in the course of solving a problem there is something they need to know, they must determine it immediately. This fault is expressed in the common wisdom as 'not being able to see the forest for the trees'. Abstraction, as the basis for hierarchical planning, is a way of suppressing detail. It was used in the General Problem Solver (GPS) reported by Newell, Shaw, and Simon, for finding proofs in propositional logic. Hierarchical approaches have been integral to most recent planning programs.

When hierarchical and non-hierarchical approaches have been systematically compared the former have usually dominated. For example, the ABSTRIPS program (Sacerdoti [17]) was a version of the non-hierarchical STRIPS planning program, retro-fitted with a scheme for abstract reasoning. In this comparative study of the two programs on a sequence of blocks world problems, Sacerdoti reported that ABSTRIPS was substantially more efficient than STRIPS, and that the effect increased dramatically as longer plans were tried. Hierarchical and non-hierarchical methods have also been compared in special purpose applications, such as Paxton's study [14] of approaches to speech recognition. Paxton's measurements indicated that a hierarchical 'island-driving' approach does not necessarily dominate a simpler left-to-right processing approach. When planning islands are formed by an abstraction process, the

TABLE 2. Elimination of Solutions

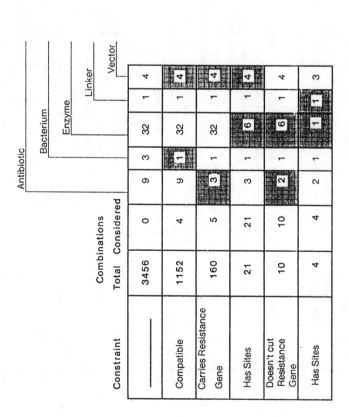

Constraint	Combinations		Antibiotic	Bacterium	Enzyme	Linker	Vector
	Total	Considered	9	3	32	1	4
——	3456	0	9	3	32	1	4
Compatible	1152	4	9	1	32	1	4
Carries Resistance Gene	160	5	3	1	32	1	4
Has Sites	21	21	3	1	6	1	4
Doesn't cut Resistance Gene	10	10	2	1	6	1	4
Has Sites	4	4	2	1	1	1	3

binations are ruled out and 3456 is the product of the number of solutions for each variable. As planning continues, the possible solutions are only a subset of this because some of the combinations are ruled out.

Because MOLGEN does not consider solutions for variables until they are introduced, it works with a substantially reduced number of combinations as shown in the column labeled 'Considered Combinations'. MOLGEN introduces new variables as it plans hierarchically. For example, the variable *Enzyme* is not really considered in the problem until it first appears in a constraint for sites on a vector. Thus, hierarchical planning greatly reduces MOLGEN's bookkeeping requirements during constraint satisfaction. The largest number of combinations that MOLGEN needed to simultaneously record during planning was 21, when the *Enzyme* variable was introduced.

The global control of interactions is illustrated in the declining numbers of solutions for each variable. A decrease in the number of solutions for a variable usually happens only when an additional constraint involving that variable is introduced. For example, the number of solutions for the *Bacterium* variable is reduced from 3 to 1 by the first constraint. In the last row of the

abstraction process must be appropriate. In the terminology of this article, the abstraction process must divide the planning decisions into nearly independent (or loosely-coupled) subproblems. As a practical matter, the more loosely the subproblems are coupled, the better the hierarchical approaches have performed because the methods for handling interactions between subproblems have been weak.

MOLGEN differs from these earlier hierarchical planning programs in its ability to add details to a plan by adding constraints. This approach to hierarchical planning avoids the issue of trying to assign global criticality levels to the domain vocabulary (as in ABSTRIPS), and reflects the perspective that commitments in planning can be characterized as new constraints. This facilitates knowledge-based approaches to backtracking that examine the reasons for making commitments in planning.

5.2. Interactions between subproblems

When subproblems in a problem do not interact, they can be solved independently. However, the experience with problem-solving programs in the past few years has shown that this ideal situation is unusual in real world problems. Interactions appear even in highly simplified AI domains such as the blocks world. Recognition of this has led researchers to focus on the nature of interactions to determine how they should be taken into account during planning.

The first of the recent programs to focus on the interactions between steps was the HACKER program reported by Sussman [22]. HACKER solved problems in the blocks world by making some simplifying assumptions to create an initial plan, and then *debugging* the plan. HACKER's main assumption (termed the *linearity assumption*) was that to solve a conjunction of goals, each one may be solved in sequence. In many simple blocks world problems, the effects of satisfying one goal interfere with solving another one. Sussman created procedures called *critics* that could recognize such interference. HACKER was often able to repair the plan by rearranging the steps in the plan.

Other approaches to satisfying conjunctive goals have been explored by Tate and Waldinger. In his INTERPLAN program. Tate's approach was to abstract the original goals and to determine holding periods over which they could be assumed to be true. INTERPLAN analyzed these periods with a view toward moving goals around to ease conflict situations. Waldinger [25] developed an approach called *goal regression* for problems from program synthesis and blocks world. It involved creating a plan to solve one of several goals followed by constructive modifications to achieve the other goals. It differed from HACKER in that it used notation about protection of goals to guide the linear placement of actions in the plan. Thus, rather than building incorrect plans and

then debugging them, it built partial linear plans in non-sequential order. The term *goal regression* is suggestive of the way the program worked, moving goals backwards through the planned actions to where they did not interfere.

A novel approach to planning with interfering conjunctive goals was reported by Sacerdoti [16] for his NOAH program. NOAH avoided HACKER's linearity assumption by considering the plan steps as parallel (that is, partially ordered) as long as possible. NOAH had *constructive* critics which sequenced the steps according to the interactions that were uncovered. If an action for one goal deleted an expression that was a precondition of a conjunctive goal, then the action with the endangered precondition was moved first so that it would be performed first. In 1977 Tate [23] extended these techniques somewhat in his planning program, NONLIN, which he applied to blocks world problems and to generator maintenance in power stations.

MOLGEN is like NOAH in its use of a least commitment strategy for handling interactions. NOAH used this idea for resolving the order of operators; MOLGEN used it mostly for object selection. (See Stefik [21] for a discussion of MOLGEN's recourse to heuristic reasoning when least commitment fails.) Constraint propagation in MOLGEN is like Waldinger's goal regression, except that MOLGEN is a hierarchical planner. Section 6 discusses some weaknesses in MOLGEN's representation of time which bear on the use of constraint propagation across planning situations.

5.3. Reasoning with constraints

This section discusses several AI programs that use constraints. It begins with search, a model for problem solving in AI in which solutions are found by traversing a space of possibilities for candidates that satisfy some constraints.

DENDRAL and its descendant CONGEN (Buchanan and Feigenbaum [3]) are examples of programs that use constraint-satisfaction. CONGEN accepts as input a set of constraints about chemical structures – an atomic formula, lists of required and disallowed substructures, and partial specifications of inter-atomic connections. It searches for solutions using a hierarchical *generate-and-test* approach. An exhaustive depth-first generator of chemical structures delivers partial solutions for testing against the constraints. CONGEN's applicability to practical problems depends on (1) the availability and use of powerful problem-specific constraints for limiting the generation of candidates, and on (2) the application of these constraints early in the generation process.

When constraints can be applied early in the solution process on partial solutions, the time to solution can usually be reduced. This leads to the idea of processing the constraints in ways that facilitate their early application. In 1970, Fikes [5] reported a problem-specification language and problem solver, REF-ARF, that was able to represent and solve a number of discrete numeric and symbolic constraint satisfaction problems. REF-ARF combined backtracking with constraint manipulation routines. Given a partial instantiation of the variables, these routines attempted to simplify the remaining constraints by reducing choices for the other variables or by deriving a contradiction. For example, an unbound variable could be expressed as a function of bound variables to yield an immediate solution. By alternating constraint manipulation and variable instantiation, REF-ARF demonstrated an impressive performance that was much superior to backtracking methods, which require complete variable instantiation before acceptance tests can be applied. Mackworth [9] and Freuder [6] have recently reviewed some sources of redundancy in backtracking and have suggested ways to improve efficiency.

For several years, several researchers as MIT have been working on programs for electronic circuit analysis and design. In 1977, McDermott [10] reported an ambitiously conceived program (NASL) for designing electrical circuits. NASL designed circuits hierarchically by combining and instantiating schemata representing functional subcircuits; it was capable of propagating and manipulating various kinds of algebraic constraints about circuits. Although NASL was never fully implemented and relied on human intervention for the more difficult aspects of constraint manipulation, this research established some of the ideas for later design programs. In 1978, Sussman and de Kleer [4] reported the SYN program for the *synthesis* phase of circuit design, that is, for determining the parameters of a circuit given desiderata for its behavior. Solution of the parameters by algebraic means (i.e., solving equations) is infeasible. SYN introduces constraints by making engineering assumptions about the operation of various components (e.g., by assuming that a transistor is in its linear operating region) and then propagates them through the circuit using electrical laws. The constraints are composed of algebraic expressions with variables. In some cases, SYN introduces variables for unknowns. It combines and reduces the resulting algebraic expressions using an adaptation of a rational simplifier from MACSYMA.

MOLGEN differs from constraint satisfaction programs like DENDRAL and REF-ARF in that it is not limited to the initial set of constraints. MOLGEN formulates constraints dynamically as it runs. NASL and SYN both augmented the constraint satisfaction idea with the use of constraint propagation between subproblems. Many of the ideas that were important for MOLGEN were anticipated in NASL, although they were not implemented.

6. Limitations and Further Research

Research often raises more questions than it answers. While this paper offers some suggestions for understanding the process of design in terms of constraint posting, it leaves open several fundamental questions about the constraints themselves. The following sections raise some issues about constraints and the representation of time, the generality of MOLGEN's ability to use constraints, and some practical limitations of MOLGEN.

6.1. Constraints and meta-constraints

The generality of MOLGEN's ability to reason with constraints stems from the simple requirements of constraint satisfaction. Constraint satisfaction requires only the ability to *evaluate* constraints. As long as MOLGEN can *generate* potential solutions, it can easily test whether arbitrary constraints are satisfied. This use of constraints for testing ignores the more powerful idea of using them to guide generation, by applying them early to partial solutions.

MOLGEN's ability to apply constraints early depends on its implementation of constraint propagation, which has some serious weaknesses. MOLGEN's constraint propagation operators are based strictly on *syntactic matches* of the constraints. Unfortunately, MOLGEN has no capability for recognizing the equivalence of logical predicates in constraints. Although MOLGEN is able to propagate constraints that it was generated, it has no ability to propagate logically equivalent variations of these constraints or arbitrary constraints outside of its limited vocabulary. This results in a practical limitation on MOLGEN's ability to use constraints; while it may eventually generate a plan that satisfies a new constraint, it may practically take too long for MOLGEN to propose a satisfactory plan if it can only apply the constraint late in the planning process.

A second limitation is that MOLGEN's does not use constraints to describe processes; all of the examples in this paper deal only with object specification. The simplest example of this would be to constrain the selection of laboratory operators. The difficulty is that MOLGEN lacks powerful ways to describe processes. No constraints on *partial process descriptions* have been developed within the representational framework used in MOLGEN.

A third limitation is that MOLGEN's does not use *meta*-constraints. First-order constraints are about the objects in the plans; *meta*-constraints would be about the plan or the planning process. For example, there could be a constraint that the plan have no more than twelve steps, or constraints on its overall yield or time of execution. In the companion paper, we will see that MOLGEN's interpreter is organized in layers. Within this layered structure, the knowledge about manipulating constraints simply appears at too low a level to support constraint reasoning about the design process.

6.2. The knowledge acquisition bottleneck

Although ideas like *meta*-constraints have some exotic appeal, it is difficult to assess their impact on making a practical system. To keep things in perspective, it is worth remarking on a serious practical limitation to the use of computers in problem solving: the difficulty of getting the relevant knowledge into the computer. This difficulty is compounded in a rapidly expanding field like molecular genetics because the knowledge can quickly become out of date. Most knowledge-based systems (including MOLGEN) fail to use what they know to make the transfer of expertise less painful. They don't take an active part in trying to understand what they are told and don't improve their ability to acquire new knowledge.

Constraint posting is a knowledge intensive style of problem solving; it requires substantial knowledge about when to formulate constraints and how to propagate them. Missing knowledge about constraint formulation has a more serious effect than missing knowledge about constraint propagation. When MOLGEN fails to formulate some necessary constraint in planning, it fails to model the genetics accurately and may propose experiments that will not work in the laboratory. When MOLGEN fails to propagate constraints, interference between planning decisions will not be discovered until much extra work is done. This results in only a *soft failure* in planning; MOLGEN may still plan successfully, but only after much extra backtracking. In practical terms, the amount of extra computation can sometimes mean that MOLGEN will never finish. The difficulty of incorporating such knowledge easily into a knowledge base illustrates the need for more research in knowledge acquisition.

6.3. Representing time

MOLGEN uses an inadequate representation of time. To deal with the changes in objects over time, MOLGEN changes the names of the objects. At different points in a plan, a bacterium may be known as *Bacterium-1*, or *Bacterium-3*, or some other name. These different names refer to the same bacterium in different 'states'. The determination of the times during which various constraints are satisfied is indicated indirectly by the names of the objects that are referenced. While this approach is good enough to indicate when constraints are satisfied (in terms of states), it does not provide a satisfactory representation of time for further planning work. For example, it does not facilitate (1) reasoning explicitly about the periods of satisfaction of constraints or (2) maintaining records of distinct possible worlds.

Reasoning about possible futures is tricky because what will happen depends on what we do and on things that we do not know about. For example, we want to reason as far into the future as knowledge and commitments permit. I know of no planning programs which can realistically reason about the future or construct useful scenarios. To do this, they would need to understand the limits of their knowledge and the sources of uncertainty about the future.

7. Summary

This paper presents an approach to hierarchical planning which focusses on the use and interpretation of constraints. Constraints are viewed (1) as elimination rules for ruling out solutions, (2) as commitments made by the planner to partially describe solutions, and (3) as a communication medium for expressing interactions between subproblems. Constraint posting is an approach to hierarchical planning which exploits the different interpretations of constraints to plan effectively. It formulates constraints during hierarchical planning to add new commitments and propagates them so that they can be utilized early in the design process to eliminate interfering solutions.

A computer program has been implemented with a genetics knowledge base to test the idea of constraint posting. It models the experiment design process in terms of operations on constraints: formulation, propagation, and satisfaction. Constraint formulation adds details to parts of the plan. Constraint propagation spreads information between the nearly independent subproblems. Constraint satisfaction finds values for the variables subject to constraints from the subproblems.

Constraint posting is a knowledge intensive approach to problem solving. An impediment to the routine application of such approaches is the lack of effective means for transferring such information into a computer. This work does not address the knowledge acquisition issue but has identified several kinds of inferential knowledge for handling constraints.

ACKNOWLEDGMENT

The research reported here was drawn from my thesis [20]. Special thanks to my advisor, Bruce Buchanan, and the other members of my reading committee: Edward Feigenbaum, Joshua Lederberg, Earl Sacerdoti, and Randall Davis. Thanks also to the members of the MOLGEN project—Douglas Brutlag, Jerry Feitelson, Peter Friedland, and Lawrence Kedes for their help. Thanks to Daniel Bobrow, Lewis Creary, and Austin Henderson for helpful comments on earlier drafts of this paper. Research on MOLGEN was funded by the National Science Foundation grant NSF MCS 78-02777. General support for the planning research was provided by DARPA Contract MDA 903-77-C-0322. Computing support was provided by the SUMEX facility under Biotechnology Resource Grant RR-00785.

REFERENCES

1. Boyer, H.W., Betlach, M., Bolivar, F., Rodriguez, F., Shine, J. and Goodman, H.M. The construction of molecular cloning vehicles, in: Beers, R.F. and Bassett, E.G. Eds., *Recombinant Molecules: Impact on Science and Society* (Raven Press, New York, 1977).
2. Brooks, F.P., *The Mythical Man-month: Essays on Software Engineering* (Addison-Wesley Publishing Company, Reading, MA, 1975).
3. Buchanan, B.G. and Feigenbaum, E.A.. DENDRAL and Meta-DENDRAL: Their applications dimension. *Artificial Intelligence* 11 (1978) 5-24.
4. de Kleer, J. and Sussman, G.J., Propagation of constraints applied to circuit synthesis. MIT AI Memo 485 (September 1978).
5. Fikes, R.E., REF-ARF: A system for solving problems stated as procedures. *Artificial Intelligence* 1 (1970) 27-120.
6. Freuder, E.C. Synthesizing constraint expressions, *Communications of the ACM* 21(11) (1978) 958-966.
7. Friedland, P.. Knowledge-based hierarchical planning in molecular genetics. Doctoral Dis-

sertation, Computer Science Department, Stanford University. (Also Computer Science Department Report STAN-CS-79-771.)

8. Gilbert, W. and Villa-Komaroff, L., Useful proteins from recombinant bacteria, *Sci. Am.* (April 1980) 74–94.

9. Mackworth, A.K., Consistency in networks of relations, *Artificial Intelligence* **8** (1977) 99–118.

10. McDermott, D.V., Flexibility and efficiency in a computer program for designing circuits, Doctoral Dissertation, Massachusetts Institute of Technology, Report AI-TR-402 (June 1977).

11. Newell, A. and Simon, H.A., GPS, A program that simulates human thought, in: Feigenbaum, E.A. and Feldman, J., Eds., *Computers and Thought* (McGraw-Hill, New York, 1963).

12. Polya, G., *Mathematical Discovery*. 2 (John Wiley and Sons, New York, 1965).

13. Nilsson, N.J., *Principles of Artificial Intelligence* (Tioga Publishing Co., Palo Alto, 1980).

14. Paxton, W.H., A framework for speech understanding, Doctoral Dissertation, Computer Science Department, Stanford University (1977). (Also SRI Artificial Intelligence Center Technical Note 142).

15. Sacerdoti, E.D., Problem solving tactics. *Proceedings of the Sixth International Joint Conference on Artificial Intelligence* (August 1979) 1077–1085.

16. Sacerdoti, E.D., *A Structure for Plans and Behavior*. (American Elsevier Publishing Company, New York, 1977 (originally published, 1975)).

17. Sacerdoti, E.D., Planning in a hierarchy of abstraction spaces, *Artificial Intelligence* **5**(2) (1974) 115–135.

18. Simon, H.A., The science of design and the architecture of complexity, in: *Sciences of the Artificial* (MIT press, Cambridge, 1969).

19. Stefik, M.J., An examination of a frame-structured representation system, *Proceedings of the Sixth International Joint Conference on Artificial Intelligence* (1979) 845–852.

20. Stefik, M.J., *Planning with constraints*, Doctoral Dissertation, Computer Science Department, Stanford University (January 1980). (Also Stanford Computer Science Department Report No. STAN-CS-80-784.)

21. Stefik, M.J., Planning and meta-planning, *Artificial Intelligence* **16**(2) (1981) 141–170 [this issue].

22. Sussman, G.J., *A Computer Model of Skill Acquisition* (American Elsevier, New York, 1975).

23. Tate, A., Generating project networks. *Proceedings of the Fifth International Joint Conference on Artificial Intelligence* (1977) 888–900.

24. Ullrich, A., Shine, J., Chirgwin, J., Pictet, R., Tischer, E., Rutter, W.J. and Goodman, H.M., Rat insulin genes: construction of plasmids containing the coding sequences, *Science* **196** (June 1977) 1313–1319.

25. Waldinger, R., *Achieving several goals simultaneously*, SRI Artificial Intelligence Center Technical Note 107 (July 1975).

26. Winograd, T., Frame representations and the procedural/declarative controversy, in: Bobrow, D.G. and Collins, A., Eds., *Representation and Understanding: Studies in Cognitive Science* (Academic Press, New York, 1975).

Received June 1980; revised version received September 1980

Chapter 4

Planning and Acting

The papers in Chapters 2 and 3 define what has come to be known as the "classical planning framework." In such systems, the planner returns an ordered set of operators which, if applied in the initial state, using the given ordering (partial or total, depending on the planner), will result in the goal state being reached. To guarantee that interactions between the actions chosen by the planner do not cause unexpected results, the system "debugs" the plan during its generation. In a sense, these systems can be viewed as plan "compilers" (a term introduced in McDermott [1977]) which generate a plan and then use various techniques (for example, NOAH's critics) to perform "optimizations" that can create a more efficient final plan (for example, realizing that one block could be moved directly to another without first being placed on the table). The ability to do this, however, is based on a strong assumption: All change in the environment must be knowable to the planner (so that the final state after planning can be demonstrated to hold true). As planning domains get more complex, allowing other agents or outside forces to introduce change (violating the above assumption), the notion of separate generation and execution of plans cannot be guaranteed to work.

The first paper in this chapter discusses this problem in the context of the STRIPS system. In a now-famous movie, STRIPS was used to plan the motion of a robot called Shakey and to control it as it pushed a set of boxes through a number of interconnecting rooms. At one point in the film, Shakey is following a STRIPS-generated plan. Charley Rosen, the SRI AI Lab founder, dressed in a sinister looking cloak, appears and disrupts the position of the boxes. STRIPS, using information stored in "macro-operators," is able to recover. The use of information learned during planning to help replan after an exe-

cution-time failure is described in this paper. A recent abridged collection of papers describing aspects of the Shakey system can be found in Nilsson, 1984.

Feldman and Sproull (1977), the second paper presented here, examines another aspect of planning and acting. They argue that a planner may not have the necessary time to completely plan all the aspects of every possible action. If the planner is time limited (like a monkey that is getting hungrier and hungrier and must get bananas before it starves), then it must be able to use nonoptimal (and possibly risky) plans to achieve its goals. This paper is one of the first to discuss the use of decision theoretical measures (utility functions and probability estimates) in planning, an area currently regaining interest in the planning community.

McDermott (1978) describes a planning system, called NASL, which did not make the assumption that all of the effects of actions could be summarized as state changes or that they could be fully explicated and stored in effect tables. Instead, it assumed that planning steps were achieved on the fly—it expanded and executed pieces of the plan as it went along. Thus, it could not use syntactic means of checking for the interactions between subplans, as was done in NOAH, etc. However, NASL could use logical inference to conditionally retrieve the add and delete statements used by its operators. Thus, NASL's behavior could be changed by conditions of the environment—for example, it might have a different "to-add" rule for a "going" action depending on whether the action resulted in reaching a final destination. This use of deductive retrieval allowed NASL to provide a uniform treatment of its planning operators, regardless of whether they succeeded or failed during execution (an ability not available in the classical framework).

The next paper we present, Hayes-Roth and Hayes-Roth (1977), brings up another aspect of plan generation. Their efforts centered on a cognitive model of planning in the everyday world, rather than on a simplified block's world. They point out that in such cases, it is very important to take into account that many choices may be made at various points during planning. Further, rather than one of these being "correct," there might be many appropriate actions. Thus, the issue of choosing one from a large number of options was an area they focused on. This paper introduced two important new ideas: meta-planning, the use of planning strategies to guide operator choice, and opportunistic planning, the ability to recognize when execution-time events can provide for the satisfaction of the system's goals. (In addition, this work was one of the first to use a blackboard architecture for planning and also to use the propagation of constraints to help eliminate possible plan choices.)

Wilensky (1981) uses ideas arising from both natural-language processing and planning research to devise a model for planning in everyday situations. This system, an elaboration and expansion of many of the ideas presented in the Hayes-Roth and Hayes-Roth paper, also provides for the use of meta-planning and opportunistic planning. The system was based on a set of principles that included associating plans with goals in the system's memory, projecting future worlds based on a world model and a set of plans, detecting interactions between several plans and goals, using these interactions to influence other plans, and evaluating alternative scenarios of plans. A more comprehensive description of Wilensky's work can be found in Wilensky, 1983.

The final paper included in this chapter, Hendler (1985), describes one aspect of the SCRAPS planning system, which extended McDermott's NASL planner to handle problems of the type discussed in Wilensky's work. The primary innovation of the SCRAPS system was the addition of a marker-passing search mechanism to be used to improve the choices made by the planner. Because NASL was unable to project future actions, it might miss choices that could lead to optimal plans or make choices that lead to disastrous results. A combination of the massively parallel marker-passing mechanism and an efficient heuristic path checker enabled SCRAPS to project actions and improve the choices made. In addition, opportunistic situations could be detected early without the need for a special meta-planning mechanism. A more comprehensive description of the SCRAPS system can be found in Hendler, 1988.

Papers referenced herein but not included in this volume:

Hendler, J. (1988). *Integrating Marker-Passing and Problem-Solving: A Spreading Activation Approach to Improved Choice in Planning*, Lawrence Erlbaum Associates, Hillsdale, NJ.

McDermott, D. (1977). "Flexibility and Efficiency in a Computer Program for Designing Circuits," Technical Report AI-TR-402, MIT AI Lab., Cambridge, MA.

Nilsson, N. (1984). "Shakey the Robot," Technical Note 323, SRI International, Menlo Park, CA.

Wilensky, R. (1983). "Planning and Understanding," Addison-Wesley, Reading, MA.

Learning and Executing Generalized Robot Plans[1]

Richard E. Fikes, Peter E. Hart and Nils J. Nilsson

Stanford Research Institute, Menlo Park, California 94025

Recommended by D. Michie

ABSTRACT

In this paper we describe some major new additions to the STRIPS robot problem-solving system. The first addition is a process for generalizing a plan produced by STRIPS so that problem-specific constants appearing in the plan are replaced by problem-independent parameters.

The generalized plan, stored in a convenient format called a triangle table, has two important functions. The more obvious function is as a single macro action that can be used by STRIPS—either in whole or in part—during the solution of a subsequent problem. Perhaps less obviously, the generalized plan also plays a central part in the process that monitors the real-world execution of a plan, and allows the robot to react "intelligently" to unexpected consequences of actions.

We conclude with a discussion of experiments with the system on several example problems.

1. Introduction

In this paper we describe a system of computer programs for controlling a mobile robot. This system can conceive and execute plans enabling the robot to accomplish certain tasks such as pushing boxes from one room to another in a simple but real environment. Although these sorts of tasks are commonly thought to demand little skill or intelligence, they pose important conceptual problems and can require quite complex planning and execution strategies.

In previous papers, we described two important components of our robot system, namely, STRIPS [1] and PLANEX [2]. When a task statement is given to the robot, STRIPS produces a plan consisting of a sequence of pre-programmed actions, and PLANEX supervises the execution of this sequence to accomplish the task. In this paper we present a major new addition to the original capabilities of STRIPS and PLANEX that enables the system to generalize and then save a solution to a particular problem. This generalization capability is used in two ways. The more obvious use of a generalized plan is as a "macro action" that can be used as a single component of a new plan to solve a new problem. When used in this fashion, generalization becomes a powerful form of learning that can reduce the planning time for similar tasks as well as allow the formation of much longer plans, previously beyond the combinatoric capabilities of STRIPS.

The second use of generalized plans involves the supervision or monitoring of plan execution. Often, a real-world robot must reexecute a portion of its plan because of some failure that occurred during the first attempt at execution. At such a time, the system has more flexibility if it is not restricted to repeating identically the unsuccessful portion of the plan, but instead can reexecute the offending actions with different arguments.

Before getting into details (and defining just what we mean by *generalize*), we present in outline form a scenario that illustrates some of the capabilities of the system. Suppose we give a robot the task "Close window WIND1 and turn off light LITE1."[2] To accomplish this, let us say that the robot decides to push box BOX1 to window WIND1, climb BOX1 in order to close the window, and then proceed to turn off light LITE1. First, the system generalizes this specific plan to produce a plan that can, under certain specified conditions, close an arbitrary window (not just WIND1) and turn off an arbitrary light. Next, the system applies the appropriate version of this generalized plan to the specific problem at hand, namely, "close WIND1 and turn off LITE1." While executing the appropriate version, let us suppose that the robot fails to push BOX1 to the window because, say, it discovers another box is already under the window. The PLANEX supervisor will recognize that this new box will serve the purpose that BOX1 was to serve, and the plan execution will proceed.

Now let us suppose that, after finishing the first task, the robot is given a new problem, "Close window WIND5 and lock door DOOR1." The system is capable of recognizing that a portion of the old generalized plan can help solve the new task. Thus, the sequence of several component actions needed to close the window can be readily obtained as a single macro action, and the planning time required to solve the new problem thereby reduced.

We shall begin with a brief review of the problem-solving program STRIPS. Then we shall review a novel format for storing plans that conveniently

[1] The research reported herein was supported at SRI by the Advance Research Projects Agency of the Department of Defense, monitored by the U.S. Army Research Office-Durham under Contract DAHC04 72 C 0008.

[2] The scenario is imaginary; our robot cannot actually turn off light switches or close windows.

allows most of the legitimate $2^n - 1$ subsequences of an n-step plan to be extracted as a unit in a subsequent planning activity. We then describe a process by which constants appearing in the plan can be converted to parameters so that each plan can handle a family of different tasks. Thus generalized, the plan can be stored (i.e., learned) for future use. Next, we review the operation of PLANEX and discuss how generalized plans are used during execution to increase the system's capabilities for responding to unplanned-for situations. Finally, we discuss how STRIPS uses stored plans to compose more complex ones and describe some experiments with a sequence of learning tasks.

2. Summary of Strips

2.1. Description

Because STRIPS is basic to our discussion, let us briefly outline its operation. (For a complete discussion and additional examples, see [1].) The primitive actions available to the robot vehicle are precoded in a set of action routines. For example, execution of the routine GOTHRU(D1,R1,R2) causes the robot vehicle actually to go through the doorway D1 from room R1 to room R2. The robot system keeps track of where the robot vehicle is and stores its other knowledge of the world in a model [3] composed of well-formed formulas (wffs) in the predicate calculus. Thus, the system knows that there is a doorway D1 between rooms R1 and R2 by the presence of the wff CONNECTS-ROOMS(D1,R1,R2) in the model.

Tasks are given to the system in the form of predicate calculus wffs. To direct the robot to go to room R2, we pose for it the goal wff INROOM(ROBOT,R2). The planning system, STRIPS, then attempts to find a sequence of primitive actions that would change the world in such a way that the goal wff is true in the correspondingly changed model. In order to generate a plan of actions, STRIPS needs to know about the effects of these actions; that is, STRIPS must have a model of each action. The model actions are called *operators* and, just as the actions change the world, the operators transform one model into another. By applying a sequence of operators to the initial world model, STRIPS can produce a sequence of models (representing hypothetical worlds) ultimately ending in a model in which the goal wff is true. Presumably then, execution of the sequence of actions corresponding to these operators would change the world to accomplish the task.

Each STRIPS operator must be described in some convenient way. We characterize each operator in the repertoire by three entities: an *add list*, a *delete list*, and a *precondition wff*. The meanings of these entities are straightforward. An operator is applicable to a given model only if its precondition is true in that model.

---

[3] Our use of the word "model" is consistent with customary terminology in Artificial Intelligence. We hope there will be no confusion between our use of the word and its technical definition in logic, namely an interpretation for a set of formulas.

. wff is satisfied in that model. The effect of applying an (assumed applicable) operator to a given model is to delete from the model all those clauses specified by the delete list and to add to the model all those clauses specified by the add list. Hence, the add and delete lists prescribe how an operator transforms one state into another.

Within this basic framework STRIPS operates in a GPS-like manner [6]. First, it tries to establish that a goal wff is satisfied by a model. (STRIPS uses the QA3 resolution-based theorem prover [3] in its attempts to prove goal wffs.) If the goal wff cannot be proved, STRIPS selects a "relevant" operator that is likely to produce a model in which the goal wff is "more nearly" satisfied. In order to apply a selected operator the precondition wff of that operator must of course be satisfied; this precondition becomes a new subgoal and the process is repeated. At some point we expect to find that the precondition of a relevant operator is already satisfied in the current model. When this happens the operator is *applied*; the initial model is transformed on the basis of the add and delete lists of the operator, and the model thus created is treated in effect as a new initial model of the world.

To complete our review of STRIPS we must indicate how relevant operators are selected. An operator is needed only if a subgoal cannot be proved from the wffs defining a model. In this case the operators are scanned to find one whose add and delete list specifies clauses that would allow the proof to continue. Specifically, STRIPS searches for an operator whose add list specifies clauses that would allow the proof to be successfully continued (if not completed). When an add list is found whose clauses do in fact permit an adequate continuation of the proof, then the associated operator is declared relevant; moreover, the substitutions used in the proof continuation serve to instantiate at least partially the arguments of the operator. Typically, more than one relevant operator instance will be found. Thus, the entire STRIPS planning process takes the form of a tree search so that the consequences of considering different relevant operators can be explored. In summary, then, the "inner loop" of STRIPS works as follows:

(1) Select a subgoal and try to establish that it is true in the appropriate model. If it is, go to Step 4. Otherwise:

(2) Choose as a relevant operator one whose add list specifies clauses that allow the incomplete proof of Step 1 to be continued.

(3) The appropriately instantiated precondition wff of the selected operator constitutes a new subgoal. Go to Step 1.

(4) If the subgoal is the main goal, terminate. Otherwise, create a new model by applying the operator whose precondition is the subgoal just established. Go to Step 1.

The final output of STRIPS, then, is a list of instantiated operators whose corresponding actions will achieve the goal.

2.2. An Example

An understanding of STRIPS is greatly aided by an elementary example. The following example considers the simple task of fetching a box from an adjacent room. Let us suppose that the initial state of the world is as shown below:

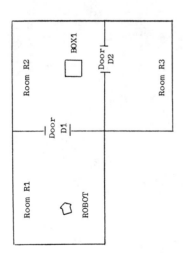

Initial Model

M₀: INROOM(ROBOT,R1)
CONNECTS(D1,R1,R2)
CONNECTS(D2,R2,R3)
BOX(BOX1)
INROOM(BOX1,R2)

$(\forall x \, \forall y \, \forall z)[\text{CONNECTS}(x,y,z) \Rightarrow \text{CONNECTS}(x,z,y)]$

Goal wff

G₀: $(\exists x)[\text{BOX}(x) \wedge \text{INROOM}(x,\text{R1})]$

We assume for this example that models can be transformed by two operators GOTHRU and PUSHTHRU, having the descriptions given below. Each description specifies an *operator schema* indexed by schema variables. We will call schema variables *parameters*, and denote them by strings beginning with lower-case letters. A particular member of an operator schema is obtained by instantiating all the parameters in its description to constants. It is a straightforward matter to modify a resolution theorem prover to handle wffs containing parameters [1], but for present purposes we need only know that the modification ensures that each parameter can be bound only to one constant; hence, the operator arguments (which may be parameters) can assume unique values. (In all of the following we denote constants by strings beginning with capital letters and quantified variables by x, y or z):

GOTHRU(d,r1,r2)
(Robot goes through Door d from Room r1 into Room r2.)
Precondition wff
INROOM(ROBOT,r1) ∧ CONNECTS(d,r1,r2)
Delete List
INROOM(ROBOT,$)
(Our convention here is to delete any clause containing a predicate of the form INROOM(ROBOT,$) for any value of $.)
Add List
INROOM(ROBOT,r2)

PUSHTHRU(b,d,r1,r2)
(Robot pushes Object b through Door d from Room r1 into Room r2.)
Precondition wff
INROOM(b,r1) ∧ INROOM(ROBOT,r1) ∧ CONNECTS(d,r1,r2)
Delete List
INROOM(ROBOT,$)
INROOM(b,$)
Add List
INROOM(ROBOT,r2)
INROOM(b,r2).

When STRIPS is given the problem it first attempts to prove the goal G_0 from the initial model M_0. This proof cannot be completed; however, were the model to contain other clauses, such as INROOM(BOX1,R1), the proof attempt could continue. STRIPS determines that the operator PUSHTHRU can provide the desired clause; in particular, the partial instance PUSHTHRU(BOX1,d,r1,R1) provides the wff INROOM(BOX1,R1). The precondition G_1 for this instance of PUSHTHRU is

G_1: INROOM(BOX1,r1)
∧ INROOM(ROBOT,r1)
∧ CONNECTS(d,r1,R1).

This precondition is set up as a subgoal and STRIPS tries to prove it from M_0. Although no proof for G_1 can be found, STRIPS determines that if r1 = R2 and d = D1, then the proof of G_1 could continue were the model to contain INROOM(ROBOT,R2). Again STRIPS checks operators for one whose effects could continue the proof and settles on the instance GOTHRU(d,r1,R2). Its precondition is the next subgoal, namely:

G_2: INROOM(ROBOT,r1)
∧ CONNECTS(d,r1,R2).

STRIPS is able to prove G_2 from M_0, using the substitutions r1 = R1 and d = D1. It therefore applies GOTHRU(D1,R1,R2) to M_0 to yield:

M_1: INROOM(ROBOT,R2)
 CONNECTS(D1,R1,R2)
 CONNECTS(D2,R2,R3)
 BOX(BOX1)
 INROOM(BOX1,R2)

$(\forall x \forall y \forall z)[\text{CONNECTS}(x,y,z) \Rightarrow \text{CONNECTS}(x,z,y)]$.

Now STRIPS attempts to prove the subgoal G_1 from the new model M_1. The proof is successful with the instantiations r1 = R2, d = D1. These substitutions yield the operator instance PUSHTHRU(BOX1,D1,R2,R1), which applied to M_1 yields

M_2: INROOM(ROBOT,R1)
 CONNECTS(D1,R1,R2)
 CONNECTS(D1,R2,R3)
 BOX(BOX1)
 INROOM(BOX1,R1)

$(\forall x \forall y \forall z)[\text{CONNECTS}(x,y,z) \Rightarrow \text{CONNECTS}(x,z,y)]$.

Next, STRIPS attempts to prove the original goal, G_0, from M_2. This attempt is successful and the final operator sequence is

GOTHRU(D1,R1,R2)
PUSHTHRU(BOX1,D1,R2,R1).

We have just seen how STRIPS computes a specific plan to solve a particular problem. The next step is to generalize the specific plan by replacing constants by new parameters. In other words, we wish to elevate our particular plan to the status of a plan schema, or macro operator, analogous to the primitive operators we were given initially. Moreover, we would like to store a macro operator in such a way as to make any of its legitimate subsequences also available to STRIPS. In the next section we describe a storage format, called a *triangle table*, that has this property. Our procedure for plan generalization will be explained after we have discussed triangle tables and their properties.

3. Triangle Tables

Suppose STRIPS has just computed a plan consisting of the sequence of n operators $OP_1, OP_2, \ldots, OP_n$. In what form should this plan be presented to

PLANEX, the system responsible for monitoring the execution of plans? In what form should it be saved? For purposes of monitoring execution, PLANEX needs at every step to be able to answer such questions as

(a) Has the portion of the plan executed so far produced the expected results?

(b) What portion of the plan needs to be executed next so that after its execution the task will be accomplished?

(c) Can this portion be executed in the current state of the world?

Also, for purposes of saving plans so that portions of them can be used in a later planning process, we need to know the preconditions and effects of any portion of the plan.

If we are to have efficient methods for answering Questions (a)–(c), we must store a plan in a way that plainly reveals its internal structure. In particular, we must be able to identify the role of each operator in the overall plan: what its important effects are (as opposed to side effects) and why these effects are needed in the plan. To accomplish this, we decided to store plans in a tabular form called a *triangle table*.[4]

A triangle table is a lower triangular array where rows and columns correspond to the operators of the plan.

An example of a triangle table is shown in Fig. 1. (The reader may temporarily ignore the heavily outlined rectangle.) The columns of the table, with the exception of Column zero, are labelled with the names of the operators of the plan, in this example $OP_1, \ldots, OP_4$. For each Column i, $i = 1, \ldots, 4$, we place in the top cell the add list A_i of operator OP_i. Going down the ith column, we place in consecutive cells the portion of A_i that survives the application of subsequent operators. Thus, $A_{1/2}$ denotes those clauses in A_1 not deleted by OP_2; $A_{1/2,3}$ denotes those clauses in $A_{1/2}$ not deleted by OP_3, and so forth. Thus, the ijth cell of the matrix contains those wffs added by the jth operator that are still true at the time of application of the ith operator.

We can now interpret the contents of the ith row of the table, excluding the left-most column. Since each cell in the ith row (excluding the left-most) contains statements added by one of the first $(i-1)$ operators but not deleted by any of those operators, we see that the union of the cells in the ith row (excluding the left-most) specifies the add list obtained by applying the $(i-1)$st *head* of the plain; i.e., by applying in sequence $OP_1, \ldots, OP_{i-1}$. We denote by $A_{1,\ldots,j}$ the add list achieved by the first j operators applied in sequence. The union of the cells in the bottom row of a triangle table evidently specifies the add list of the complete sequence.

The left-most column of the triangle table, which we have thus far ignored, is involved with the preconditions for the stored plan. During the formation

[4] We are indebted to John Munson who prompted us to try a tabular format.

of the plan, STRIPS produced a proof of each operator's preconditions from the model to which the operator was applied. We will define the set of clauses used to prove a formula as the *support* of that formula. We wish to ensure that the *i*th row of a triangle table contains all the wffs in the support of those preconditions for Operator *i*. In general, some clauses in the support for Operator *i* will have been added by the first *i* − 1 operators in the plan and will therefore be included in Row *i*, as described in the previous paragraphs.

	0	1	2	3	4
1	PC_1	OP_1			
2	PC_2	A_1	OP_2		
3	PC_3	$A_{1/2}$	A_2	OP_3	
4	PC_4	$A_{1/2,3}$	$A_{2/3}$	A_3	OP_4
5		$A_{1/2,3,4}$	$A_{2/3,4}$	$A_{3/4}$	A_4

FIG. 1. A triangle table.

The remainder of the support clauses appeared in the initial model and were not deleted by any of the first *i* − 1 operators. These clauses, which we denote by PC_i, are precisely the clauses that are entered into the left-most (Column 0) cell of Row *i*. Hence, we see that Column 0 of a triangle table contains those clauses from the initial model that were used in the precondition proofs for the plan. It is convenient to flag the clauses in each Row *i* that are in the support for Operator *i* and hereafter speak of them as *marked* clauses; by construction, all clauses in Column 0 are marked. Note that in proving the preconditions of operators, STRIPS must save the support clauses so that the triangle table can be constructed.

As an example, we show in Fig. 2 the triangle table for the plan discussed in the previous section. The clauses that are marked by an asterisk "*" were all used in the proofs of preconditions.

We have seen how the marked clauses on Row *i* constitute the support of

the preconditions for the *i*th operator. Let us now investigate the preconditions for the *i*th *tail* of the plan—that is, the preconditions for applying the operator sequence $OP_i, OP_{i+1}, \ldots, OP_n$. The key observation here is that the *i*th tail is applicable to a model if the model already contains that portion of the support of each operator in the tail that is not supplied within the tail itself. This observation may be formulated more precisely by introducing the notion of a *kernel* of a triangle table. We define the *i*th kernel of a table to be the unique rectangular subarray containing the lower left-most cell and Row *i*. We assert now that the *i*th tail of a plan is applicable to a model if all the marked clauses in the *i*th kernel are true in that model. Let us see by example why this is so.

1	*INROOM(ROBOT,R1) *CONNECTS(D1,R1,R2)	GOTHRU(D1,R1,R2)	
2	*INROOM(BOX1,R2) *CONNECTS(D1,R1,R2) *CONNECTS(x,y,z) ⊃ CONNECTS(x,z,y)	*INROOM(ROBOT,R2)	PUSHTHRU(BOX1,D1,R2,R1)
3			INROOM(ROBOT,R1) INROOM(BOX1,R1)

FIG. 2. Triangle table for example plan. (A "*" preceding a clause indicates a "marked" clause.)

Consider again Fig. 1, in which we have heavily outlined Kernel 3. Let us assume that all marked clauses in this kernel are true in the current model. (When all the marked clauses in a kernel are true, we shall say that the kernel is true.) Certainly, OP_3 is applicable; the marked clauses in Row 3 are true, and these marked clauses support the proof of the preconditions of OP_3. Suppose now that OP_3 is applied to the current model to produce a new model in which A_3, the set of clauses added by OP_3, is true. Evidently, OP_4 is now applicable, since all the marked clauses in Row 4 are true; those clauses within the outlined kernel were true before applying OP_3 (and by construction of the triangle table are still true), and those outside the kernel (that is, A_3)

are true because they were added by OP_3. Thus, the truth of the marked clauses in Kernel 3 is a sufficient condition for the applicability of the tail of the plan beginning with OP_3.

We have some additional observations to make about triangle tables before moving on to the matter of plan generalization. First, notice that Kernel 1—that is, the left-most column of a triangle table—constitutes a set of sufficient conditions for the applicability of the entire plan. Thus, we can take the conjunction of the clauses in Column 0 to be a precondition formula for the whole plan.

A second observation may help the reader gain a little more insight into the structure of triangle tables. Consider again the table of Fig. 1, and let us suppose this time that Kernel 2 is true. Since Kernel 2 is true, the sequence OP_2, OP_3, OP_4 is applicable. Upon applying OP_2, which is immediately applicable because the marked clauses in Row 2 are true, we effectively add Column 2 to the table. Moreover, we lose interest in Row 2 because OP_2 has already been applied. Thus the application of OP_2 transforms a true Kernel 2 into a true Kernel 3, and the application of the operators in the tail of the plan can continue.

4. Generalizing Plans

4.1. Motivation

The need for plan generalization in a learning system is readily apparent. Consider the specific plan produced in the example of Section 2:

GOTHRU(D1,R1,R2)
PUSHTHRU(BOX1,D1,R2,R1).

While this sequence solves the original task, it probably doesn't warrant being saved for the future unless, of course, we expect that the robot would often need to go from Room R1 through Door D1 to Room R2 to push back the specific box, BOX1, through Door D1 into Room R1. We would like to generalize the plan so that it could be free from the specific constants, D1, R1, R2, and BOX1 and could be used in situations involving arbitrary doors, rooms, and boxes.

In considering possible procedures for generalizing plans we must first reject the naive suggestion of merely replacing each constant in the plan by a parameter. Some of the constants may really need to have specific values in order for the plan to work at all. For example, consider a modification of our box-fetching plan in which the second step of the plan is an operator that *only* pushes objects from room R2 into room R1. The specific plan might then be

GOTHRU(D1,R1,R2)
SPECIALPUSH(BOX1).

When we generalize this plan we cannot replace all constants by parameters, since the plan only works when the third argument of GOTHRU is R2. We would want our procedure to recognize this fact and produce the plan

GOTHRU(d1,r1,R2)
SPECIALPUSH(b1).

Another reason for rejecting the simple replacement of constants by parameters is that there is often more generality readily available in many plans than this simple procedure will extract. For example, the form of our box-pushing plan, GOTHRU followed by PUSHTHRU, does not require that the room in which the robot begins be the same room into which the box is pushed. Hence the plan could be generalized as follows:

GOTHRU(d1,r1,r2)
PUSHTHRU(b,d2,r2,r3)

and be used to go from one room to an adjacent second room and push a box to an adjacent third room.

Our plan-generalization procedure overcomes these difficulties by taking into account the internal structure of the plan and the preconditions of each operator. The remainder of this section is a description of this generalization procedure.

4.2. The Generalization Procedure

The first step in our generalization procedure is to "lift" the triangle table to its most general form as follows: We first replace every occurrence of a constant in the clauses of the left-most column by a new parameter. (Multiple occurrences of the same constant are replaced by distinct parameters.) Then the remainder of the table is filled in with appropriate add clauses assuming completely uninstantiated operators (i.e., as these add clauses appear in the operator descriptions), and assuming the same deletions as occurred in the original table. As an example, Fig. 3 shows the table from Fig. 2 in its most general form.

The lifted table thus obtained is too general; we wish to constrain it so that the marked clauses in each row support the preconditions of the operator on that row, while retaining the property that the lifted table has the original table as an instance. To determine the constraints we redo each operator's precondition proof using the support clauses in the lifted table as axioms and the precondition formulas from the operator descriptions as the theorems to be proved. Each new proof is constructed by performing at each step resolutions on the same clauses and unifications on the same literals as in the original proof. This proof process ensures that each original proof is an instance of the new

The substitutions from the proof are made in the table and then the following precondition proof for PUSHTHRU(p14,p15,p16,p17) is performed:

Negation of Theorem: ~INROOM(ROBOT,p16) ∨ ~INROOM(p14,p16) ∨ ~CONNECTS(p15,p16,p17)

Axiom: INROOM(p6,p7)

~INROOM(ROBOT,p7) ∨ ~CONNECTS(p15,p7,p17)

Axiom: INROOM(ROBOT,p5)

~CONNECTS(p15,p5,p17)

Axiom: ~CONNECTS(x,y,z) ∨ CONNECTS(x,z,y)

~CONNECTS(p15,p17,p5)

Axiom: CONNECTS(p8,p9,p10)

nil

Substitutions

p6→p14
p7→p16

p5→p7

p8→p15
p9→p17
p5→p10

The substitutions from this proof are then used to produce the triangle table shown in Fig. 4.

The two proofs have constrained the plan so that the room into which the first operator takes the robot is the same room that contains the object to be pushed by the second operator. The robot's initial room and the target room for the push, however, remain distinct parameters constrained only by the precondition requirements that they each be adjacent to the object's initial room.

4.3. Two Refinements

Before a generalized plan is stored, two additional processing steps are carried out—one to improve efficiency and the other to remove possible inconsistencies. The first step eliminates some cases of overgeneralization produced during the lifting process and therefore makes more efficient the use of the plan by STRIPS and PLANEX. Often a clause in a plan's initial model will be in the support set of more than one operator, and therefore will appear more than once in Column 0 of the triangle table. When the table is lifted, each occurrence of the clause will generate new parameters. For example, in Fig. 3, CONNECTS(D1,R1,R2) was lifted to CONNECTS(p3,p4,p5) and to CONNECTS(p8,p9,p10). In many cases this lifting pro-

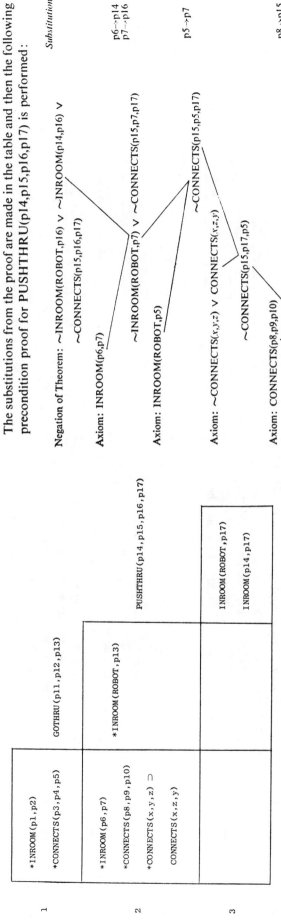

Fig. 3. Triangle table after initial lifting process.

generalized proof and therefore provides the basis for ensuring that the original table is an instance of the lifted table. Any substitutions of parameters for constants or for other parameters in the new proofs act as constraints on the generality of the plan and must be reflected in the lifted table. Hence these parameter substitutions are made throughout the lifted table and the generalized plan. The table resulting from the substitutions determined by the new proofs is constrained in the desired way.

Consider the effects of the new precondition proofs on the example table shown in Fig. 3. The precondition proof for GOTHRU(p11,p12,p13) proceeds as follows:

Negation of Theorem: ~INROOM(ROBOT,p12) ∨ ~CONNECTS(p11,p12,p13).

Axiom: INROOM(p1,p2)

~CONNECTS(p11,p2,p13)

Axiom: CONNECTS(p3,p4,p5)

nil

Substitutions

ROBOT→p1
p2→p12

p3→p11
p2→p4
p5→p13

INROOM example above, thereby making the two occurrences of the clause identical, but would not generate any constraining substitutions for the CONNECTS clause in the box-fetching example.

The second processing step that is performed before the plan is stored is needed to avoid inconsistencies that can occur in the lifted tables. The difficulty can be illustrated with the following example.

Consider a simple plan, PUSH(BOX1,LOC1), PUSH(BOX2,LOC2), for pushing two boxes to two locations. The unlifted triangle table for this plan might be as shown in Fig. 5a, where for simplicity we have not shown all clauses. When this table is lifted and the precondition proofs redone, no constraints are placed on the lifted table and it has the form shown in Fig. 5b. Suppose now that STRIPS were to use this plan with box1 and box2 instantiated to the same object and loc1 and loc2 instantiated to distinct locations. In that case STRIPS would evidently have a plan for achieving a state in which the same object is simultaneously at two different places!

	0	1	2
1	---	PUSH(BOX1,LOC1)	
2	---	AT(BOX1,LOC1)	PUSH(BOX2,LOC2)
3	---	AT(BOX1,LOC1)	AT(BOX2,LOC2)

(a) Unlifted Table

	0	1	2
1	---	PUSH(box1,loc1)	
2	---	AT(box1,loc1)	PUSH(box2,loc2)
3	---	AT(box1,loc1)	AT(box2,loc2)

(b) Inconsistent Lifted Table

	0	1	2
1	---	PUSH(box1,loc1)	
2	---	AT(box1,loc1)	PUSH(box2,loc2)
3	---	$box1 \neq box2 \supset$ AT(box1,loc1)	AT(box2,loc2)

(c) Correct Lifted Table

FIG. 5. Triangle table for box-pushing plan.

	0	1	2
1	*INROOM(ROBOT,p2) *CONNECTS(p3,p2,p5)	GOTHRU(p3,p2,p5)	
2	*INROOM(p6,p5) *CONNECTS(p8,p9,p5) *CONNECTS(x,y,z) ⊃	*INROOM(ROBOT,p5)	PUSHTHRU(p6,p8,p5,p9)
3	CONNECTS(x,z,y)		INROOM(ROBOT,p9) INROOM(p6,p9)

FIG. 4. Final form of triangle table for generalized plan.

cedure enhances the generality of the plan (as it did for the box-fetching plan by allowing the first and third rooms to be distinct), but it also produces cases of over-generalization that, while not incorrect, can lead to inefficiencies. For example, consider a case in which INROOM(BOX1,R1) appears twice in Column 0 of a triangle table. When the table is lifted, the occurrences of the clause in Column 0 might become INROOM(p1,p2) and INROOM(p3,p4). If the precondition proofs cause p1 to be substituted for p3, but do not constrain p2 and p4, then we have a plan whose preconditions include the clauses

INROOM(p1,p2) and
INROOM(p1,p4).

Therefore we have a plan whose preconditions allow Object p1 to be in two distinct rooms at the same time, even though we know that in any semantically correct model Object p1 will be in only one room.

We eliminate most cases of this overgeneralization by recognizing those cases where two parameters are produced from a single occurrence of a constant in a single clause; if both such parameters do not appear as arguments of operators in the plan, then they can be bound together and one substituted for the other throughout the table without effectively inhibiting the generality of the plan. This procedure would substitute p2 for p4 in the

The source of this embarrassment lies in the assumption made above that the deletions in the lifted table can be the same as in the unlifted table. In our example, the clause AT(box1,loc1) should be deleted by the PUSH(box2, loc2) operator in the case where box1 and box2 are bound to the same object, but not deleted otherwise. Using the deletion algorithm described below, we represent this situation in the lifted table by replacing the clause AT(box1, loc1) in Row 3 by the clause form of

box1 ≠ box2 ⊃ AT(box1,loc1)

as shown in Fig. 5(c). This implication serves us well since the theorem prover can deduce AT(box1,loc1) as being part of the plan's additions list for exactly those cases in which box1 and box2 are distinct.

We now consider in general how deletions are correctly accounted for in the lifted triangle tables. After all the precondition proofs are redone for the lifted table, the delete list of each operator is considered beginning with the first operator and continuing in sequence through the plan. The delete list of the *i*th operator is applied to the clauses in Row *i* of the table to determine which clauses should appear in Row *i* + 1 of the table.[5] Recall that an operator's delete list is specified to STRIPS as a list of literals, and any clause that unifies with one of these literals is deleted. Application of the delete list will cause the lifted table to be modified only when a unification with a delete literal requires that a parameter p1 be replaced by another parameter p2 or by a constant C1. In that case the clause will unify with the delete literal only when p1 and p2 are instantiated to the same constant or when p1 is instantiated to C1. Hence the clause is replaced in the next row of the table by an implication as follows:

p1 ≠ p2 ⊃ clause   or
p1 ≠ C1 ⊃ clause.

This implication allows the theorem prover to deduce the clause in only those cases where the operator's delete list would not have deleted it from the model.

If the clause that is replaced by the implication in a conditional deletion is part of the support of an operator in the plan (i.e., the clause is marked), then the implication must be accompanied by another addition to the table. In particular, if a clause CL1 is part of the support for the *j*th operator of the plan and CL1 is replaced in Row *j* of the table by the implication p1 ≠ p2 ⊃ CL1, then p1 ≠ p2 must be added as a marked clause to Cell (*j*,0) of the table. This addition to the table ensures that the *j*th operator's preconditions can be proved from the marked clauses in Row *j* of the table. The preconditions proof previously obtained will remain valid with the addition of a

[5] This characterization of the deletion applications requires that we include in Cell (1, 0) of the table all the clauses that appear anywhere in Column 0. The resulting redundant occurrences of Column 0 clauses can be edited out before the table is stored.

preliminary proof step in which clause CL1 is derived from p1 ≠ p2 and p1 ≠ p2 ⊃ CL1.

After these two processing steps are completed, the generalized plan is ready to be stored away as a macro operator, or *MACROP*, for later use by STRIPS and PLANEX.

5. Execution Strategies

5.1. Requirements for the Plan Executor

In this section we shall describe how a program called PLANEX uses triangle tables to monitor the execution of plans. An early version of PLANEX was described by Fikes [2]. It is now being used in conjunction with STRIPS and the MACROP generation procedures to control the SRI robot [4].

One of the novel elements introduced into artificial intelligence research by work on robots is the study of execution strategies and how they interact with planning activities. Since robot plans must ultimately be executed in the real world by a mechanical device, as opposed to being carried out in a mathematical space or by a simulator, consideration must be given by the executor to the possibility that operations in the plan may not accomplish what they were intended to, that data obtained from sensory devices may be inaccurate, and that mechanical tolerances may introduce errors as the plan is executed. Many of these problems of plan execution would disappear if our system generated a whole new plan after each execution step. Obviously, such a strategy would be too costly, so we instead seek a plan execution scheme with the following properties:

(1) When new information obtained during plan execution implies that some remaining portion of the plan need not be executed, the executor should recognize such information and omit the unneeded plan steps.

(2) When execution of some portion of the plan fails to achieve the intended results, the executor should recognize the failure and either direct reexecution of some portion of the plan or, as a default, call for a replanning activity.

5.2. Preparation of the MACROP for Execution

Rather than working with the specific version of the plan originally produced by STRIPS, PLANEX uses the generalized MACROP to guide execution. The generalized plan allows a modest amount of replanning by the executor should parts of the plan fail in certain ways.

Before a MACROP can be used by PLANEX, its parameters must be partially instantiated using the specific constants of the goal wff. This specializes the MACROP to the specific task at hand while it leaves as general as possible the conditions under which it can be executed. This partial instantiation process is quite simple: We put in the lower left-most cell of the triangle table those clauses from the original model that were used by STRIPS in proving the goal wff. Then we use all of the clauses in the entire last row of the MACROP to prove the goal wff. Those substitutions made during this proof are then made on the entire MACROP. In addition we mark those clauses in the last row of the MACROP that were used to support the goal wff proof. This version of the MACROP is the one used to control execution.[6]

Let us illustrate what we have said about preparing a MACROP for execution by considering our example of fetching a box. In Fig. 4, we have the MACROP for this task. In Section 2, the goal wff for this task was given as

$$(\exists x)[\text{BOX}(x) \wedge \text{INROOM}(x, \text{R1})].$$

In the proof of this goal wff we used the clause BOX(BOX1) from the original model, M_0. Therefore, we insert this clause in Cell (3,0) of the triangle table. We now use the clauses in Row 3 of the MACROP in Fig. 4 (together with BOX(BOX1), just inserted) to prove the goal wff. That is, we use BOX(BOX1), INROOM(ROBOT,p9) and INROOM(p6,p9) to prove $(\exists x)[\text{BOX}(x) \wedge \text{INROOM}(x, \text{R1})]$. The substitutions made in obtaining the proof are BOX1 for p6 and R1 for p9. When these substitutions are applied to the MACROP of Fig. 4 and the support clauses for the new proof are marked, we obtain the execution MACROP shown in Fig. 6.

5.3. The PLANEX Execution Strategy

Our strategy for monitoring the execution of plans makes use of the kernels of the execution MACROP. Recall that the ith kernel of a triangle table for an n-step plan is the unique rectangular subarray containing Row i and Cell $(n + 1, 0)$. The importance of the ith kernel stems from the fact that it contains (as marked clauses) the support of the operator sequence $\{OP_i, \ldots, OP_n\}$. Thus if at some stage of plan execution the marked clauses in the ith kernel are provable, then we know that the ith tail is an appropriate operator sequence for achieving the goal. At each state of execution we must have at least one true kernel if we are to continue execution of the plan.

At the beginning of execution we know that the first kernel is true, since the initial model was used by STRIPS when the plan was created. But at later stages, unplanned outcomes might place us either unexpectedly close to the goal or throw us off the track completely. Our present implementation adopts a rather optimistic bias. We check each kernel in turn starting with the highest numbered one (which is the last row of the MACROP) and work backwards from the goal until we find a kernel that is true. If the goal kernel (the last row) is true, execution halts; otherwise we determine if the next-to-last kernel is true, and so on, until we find a true kernel k_i and a corresponding tail of the plan $\{OP_i, \ldots, OP_n\}$. The execution strategy then executes the action corresponding to OP_i and checks the outcome, as before, by searching for the highest-numbered true kernel. In an "ideal" world this procedure merely executes in order each operator in the plan. On the other hand, the procedure has the freedom to omit execution of unnecessary operators and to overcome failures by repeating the execution of operators. Replanning by STRIPS is initiated when no kernels are true.[7]

When checking to see if a kernel is true, we check to see if some instance of the conjunction of marked clauses in the kernel can be proved from the present model. Once such an instance is found, we determine the corresponding instance of the first operator in the tail of the plan and execute the action corresponding to that instance. Thus the generality of representation of the execution MACROP allows a great deal of flexibility in plan execution. For example, consider a case where PLANEX is executing a plan that takes the robot from one room through a second room into a third room. If, when the robot attempts to go through the door connecting the second and third rooms, the door is found to be locked, then PLANEX may be able to

[7] Typically, when replanning is necessary it is sufficient to produce a short sequence of operators to "get back onto the track" of the original plan. Since STRIPS has the MACROP for the original plan in its repertoire of operators, the new plan can often be formed by composing a sequence of operators and appending it to an appropriate tail of the MACROP.

1	*INROOM(ROBOT,p2)	*CONNECTS(p3,p2,p10)	GOTHRU(p3,p2,p10)		
2	*INROOM(BOX1,p10)	*CONNECTS(p8,R1,p10) *CONNECTS(x,y,z) ⊃ CONNECTS(x,z,y)	*INROOM(ROBOT,p10)	PUSHTHRU(BOX1,p8,p10,R1)	
3	*BOX(BOX1)			INROOM(ROBOT,R1) *INROOM(BOX1,R1)	

FIG. 6. Execution MACROP for the fetch a box task.

[6] Some increase in generality can be obtained by putting in the lower leftmost cell of the triangle table *generalized* versions of the original model clauses. Some of the parameters in these generalized clauses might remain unbound in the proof of the goal wff, thereby making the table more general. In our implementation we shunned this additional complication.

reinstantiate parameters so that the first part of the plan can be reexecuted to take the robot from the second room through some new fourth room and then into the target third room.

An interesting by-product of our optimistic strategy of examining kernels in backwards order is that PLANEX sometimes remedies certain blunders made by STRIPS. Occasionally, STRIPS produces a plan containing an entirely superfluous subsequence—for example, a subsequence of the form OP, OP^{-1}, where OP^{-1} precisely negates the effects of OP. (Such a "detour" in a plan would reflect inadequacies in the search heuristics used by STRIPS.) During plan execution, however, PLANEX would effectively recognize that the state following OP^{-1} is the same as the state preceding OP, and would therefore not execute the superfluous subsequence.

5.4. The PLANEX Scanning Algorithm

The triangle table is a compact way of representing the kernels of a MACROP; most cells of the table occur in more than one kernel. We have exploited this economy of representation by designing an efficient algorithm for finding the highest-numbered true kernel. This algorithm, called the *PLANEX scan*, involves a cell-by-cell scan of the triangle table. We give a brief description of it here and refer the reader to Fikes [2] for more details. Each cell examined is evaluated as either *True* (i.e., all the marked clauses are provable from the current model) or *False*. The interest of the algorithm stems from the order in which cells are examined. Let us call a kernel "potentially true" at some stage in the scan if all evaluated cells of the kernel are true. The scan algorithm can then be succinctly stated as: *Among all unevaluated cells in the highest-indexed potentially true kernel, evaluate the left-most. Break "left-most ties" arbitrarily.* The reader can verify that, roughly speaking, this table-scanning rule results in a left-to-right, bottom-to-top scan of the table. However, the table is never scanned to the right of any cell already evaluated as false. An equivalent statement of the algorithm is "Among all unevaluated cells, evaluate the cell common to the largest number of potentially true kernels. Break ties arbitrarily." We conjecture that this scanning algorithm is optimal in the sense that it evaluates, on the average, fewer cells than any other scan guaranteed always to find the highest true kernel. A proof of this conjecture has not been found.

As the cells in the table are scanned we will be making substitutions for the MACROP parameters as dictated by the proofs of the cells' clauses. It is important to note that a substitution made to establish the truth of clauses in a particular cell must be applied to the entire table. When there are alternative choices about which substitutions to make, we keep a tree of possibilities so that backtracking can occur if needed.

6. Planning with MACROPS

In the preceding sections, we described the construction of MACROPS and how they are used to control execution. Now let us consider how a MACROP can be used by STRIPS during a subsequent planning process.

6.1. Extracting a Relevant Operator Sequence from a MACROP

Recall that the $(i + 1)$st row of a triangle table (excluding the first cell) represents the add list, $A_{1, \ldots, i}$, of the ith head of the plan, i.e. of the sequence $OP_1, \ldots, OP_i$. An n-step plan presents STRIPS with n alternative add lists, any one of which can be used to reduce a difference encountered during the normal planning process. STRIPS tests the relevance of each of a MACROP's add lists in the usual fashion, and the add lists that provide the greatest reduction in the difference are selected. Often a given set of relevant clauses will appear in more than one row of the table. In that case only the lowest-numbered row is selected, since this choice results in the shortest operator sequence capable of producing the desired clauses.

Suppose that STRIPS selects the ith add list $A_{1, \ldots, i}$; $i < n$. Since this add list is achieved by applying in sequence $OP_1, \ldots, OP_i$, we will obviously not be interested in the application of $OP_{i+1}, \ldots, OP_m$, and will therefore not be interested in establishing any of the preconditions for these operators. Now in general, some steps of a plan are needed only to establish preconditions for subsequent steps. If we lose interest in a tail of a plan, then the relevant instance of the MACROP need not contain those operators whose sole purpose is to establish preconditions for the tail. Also, STRIPS will, in general, have used only some subset of $A_{1, \ldots, i}$ in establishing the relevance of the ith head of the plan. Any of the first i operators that does not add some clause in this subset or help establish the preconditions for some operator that adds a clause in the subset is not needed in the relevant instance of the MACROP.

Conceptually, then, we can think of a single triangle table as representing a family of generalized operators. Upon the selection by STRIPS of a relevant add list, we must extract from this family an economical parameterized operator achieving the add list. In the following paragraphs, we will explain by means of an example an editing algorithm for accomplishing this task of operator extraction.

6.2. The Editing Algorithm

Consider the illustrative triangle table shown in Fig. 7. Each of the numbers within cells represents a single clause. The circled clauses are "marked" in the sense described earlier; that is, they are used to prove the precondition of the operator whose name appears on the same row. A summary of the structure

These clauses have been indicated on the table by an asterisk (*). The editing algorithm proceeds by examining the table to determine what effects of individual operators are not needed; we can therefore remove all circle marks from Row 7, since those marks indicate the support of the preconditions of OP_7. We now inspect the columns, beginning with Column 6 and going from right to left, to find the first column with no marks of either kind (circles or asterisks). Column 4 is the first such column. The absence of marked clauses in Column 4 means that the clauses added by OP_4 are not needed to reduce the difference and are not required to prove the pre-condition of any subsequent operator; hence OP_4 will not be in the edited operator sequence and we can unmark all clauses in Row 4. Continuing our right-to-left scan of the columns, we note that Column 3 contains no marked clauses. (Recall that we have already unmarked Clause 18.) We therefore delete OP_3 from the plan and unmark all clauses in Row 3. Continuing the scan, we note that Column 1 contains no marked entries (we have already unmarked Clause 11), and therefore we can delete OP_1 and the marked entries in Row 1.

The result of this editing process is to reduce the original seven-step plan to the compact three-step plan, $\{OP_2, OP_5, OP_6\}$, whose add list specifically includes the relevant clauses. The structure of this plan is shown below.

OPERATOR	PRECONDITION SUPPORT SUPPLIED BY	PRECONDITION SUPPORT SUPPLIED TO
OP_2	I	OP_5, F
OP_5	I, OP_2	OP_6, F
OP_6	I, OP_5	F

6.3. Use of Edited MACROPS as Relevant Operators

Once an edited MACROP has been constructed, we would like STRIPS to use it in the same manner as any other operator. We have some latitude though, in specifying the preconditions of the MACROP. An obvious choice would be to use the conjunction of the clauses in the left-most column, but there is a difficulty with this straightforward choice that can be made clear with the aid of a simple example. Suppose we are currently in a state in which the first kernel of an edited MACROP—that is, its left-most column—is false, but suppose further that, say, the third kernel is true. Since the third kernel is true, the tail of the MACROP beginning with OP_3 is immediately applicable and would produce the desired relevant additions to the model. If STRIPS were to ignore this opportunity and set up the left-most column of the MACROP as a subgoal, it would thereby take the proverbial one step backward to go two steps forward.

This example suggests that we employ a PLANEX scan on the edited table

of this plan is shown below, where "I" refers to the initial state and "F" to the final state:

	OP_1	OP_2	OP_3	OP_4	OP_5	OP_6	OP_7	
1	⊙(1,2)							
2	⊙(3)	11,12 / 13						
3	(4,5)	11,12	14,15 / 16					
4	(6)	⊙(11),12	15,16	17,18 / 19,20				
5	(7)	12	⊙(16)	17,18 / 19,20	21,22 / 23			
6	⊙(8,9)	12	16	17,18	21,22	⊙(24)		
7	⊙(10)	16	17,⊙(18)	21,22	24	⊙(25)		
8		16	17	21	24		26	
	0	1	2	3	4	5	6	7

TA-8973-13

Fig. 7. MACROP with marked clauses.

OPERATOR	PRECONDITION SUPPORT SUPPLIED BY	PRECONDITION SUPPORT SUPPLIED TO
OP_1	I	OP_4
OP_2	I	OP_5
OP_3	I	OP_7, F
OP_4	I, OP_1	F
OP_5	I, OP_2	OP_6, F
OP_6	I, OP_5	OP_7
OP_7	I, OP_3, OP_6	F

Suppose now that STRIPS selects $A_1, ..., _6$ as the desired add list and, in particular, selects Clause 16 and Clause 25 as the particular members of the add list that are relevant to reducing the difference of immediate interest.

so that all tails of the relevant MACROP will be tested for applicability. If an applicable tail is found, STRIPS applies, in sequence, each operator in this tail to produce a new planning model. Each operator application is performed in the usual manner using the add and delete lists of the individual operators. If the PLANEX scan fails to find a true kernel, then no tail is set up as a subgoal to be achieved by STRIPS. Actually, any kernel would constitute a perfectly good subgoal and, in principle, the disjunction of all the kernels would be better still. Unfortunately, this disjunction places excessive demands on both the theorem prover and the STRIPS executive, so we restrict ourselves to consideration of the first kernel.

We have seen that STRIPS uses a MACROP during planning by extracting a relevant subsequence of the MACROP's operators, and then including that subsequence in the new plan being constructed. When the new plan is made into a MACROP it is often the case that it will contain add lists that are subsets of add lists in already existing tables. For example, if an entire existing MACROP is used in the construction of a new plan, and the parameter substitutions in the new MACROP correspond to those in the old MACROP, then each add list in the old MACROP will be a subset of an add list in the new MACROP. To assist STRIPS in its use of MACROPS, we have designed a procedure that will remove redundant add lists from consideration during planning, and in cases where an entire MACROP is contained within another, will delete the contained MACROP from the system.

Our procedure takes the following action: If every instance of the operator sequence that is the ith head of some MACROP is also an instance of a sequence occurring anywhere else in the same or some other MACROP, then all the add lists in that head (i.e. Rows 2 through $i + 1$) are disallowed for consideration by STRIPS.[8] For example, consider the following two generalized plans:

Plan A: OPA(p1),OPB(p1,p2),OPC(p3),OPD(p3,C1),OPA(p3,C1),OPB(p4,p5)

Plan B: OPC(p6),OPD(p6,C1),OPA(p7),OPF(p6,p7).

Rows 2 and 3 of Plan A are disallowed for consideration as add lists since every instance of the sequence, OPA(p1),OPB(p1,p2), is also an instance of the sequence, OPA(p3),OPB(p4,p5), that occurs at the end of Plan A. Rows 2 and 3 of Plan B are disallowed because of the sequence, OPC(p3),OPD-(p3,C1), that occurs in Plan A. Note that Row 4 of Plan B could not be disallowed for consideration by Plan A since there are instances of the sequence, OPC(p6),OPD(p6,C1),OPA(p7), that are not instances of OPC(p3),OPD(p3,C1),OPA(p3).

This procedure is applied whenever a new MACROP is added to the system. It has proved to be quite effective at minimizing the number of

[8] Note that the first row of a MACROP contains no add clauses.

MACROP add lists that STRIPS must consider during planning. (See Section 7, for examples.) A difficulty arises in the use of this procedure when the same operator appears in two MACROPs and the support sets for the precondition proofs of that operator differ markedly in the two triangle tables. This can occur, for example, when the precondition is a disjunction of two wffs and in one case the first disjunct was proven to be true and in the other case the second disjunct was proven to be true. In those situations the two occurrences of the operator should not be considered as instances of the same operator since each occurrence effectively had different preconditions. A refinement of our procedure that would include an appropriate comparison of the support sets could be employed to overcome this difficulty.

7. Experimental Results

The mechanisms we have described for generating and using MACROPS have been implemented as additions and modifications to the existing STRIPS and PLANEX systems. In this section we will describe the results of some of the experiments we have run with the new system. Problems were posed to the system in the SRI robot's current experimental environment of seven rooms, eight doors, and several boxes about two feet high. The robot is a mobile vehicle equipped with touch sensors, a television camera, and a push bar that allows the robot to push the boxes [4]. A typical state of this experimental environment is modeled by STRIPS using about 160 axioms.

7.1. Operator Descriptions

The operator descriptions given to STRIPS for these experiments model the robot's preprogrammed action routines for moving the robot next to a door in a room, next to a box in a room, to a location in a room, or through a door. There are also operators that model action routines for pushing a box next to another box in a room, to a location in a room, or through a door. In addition, we have included operator descriptions that model fictitious action routines for opening and closing doors. These descriptions are as follows:

GOTOB(bx) Go to object bx.
Preconditions: TYPE(bx,OBJECT),(∃rx)[INROOM(bx,rx) ∧ INROOM(ROBOT,rx)]
Deletions: AT(ROBOT,$1,$2),NEXTTO(ROBOT,$1)
Additions: *NEXTTO(ROBOT,bx)

GOTOD(dx) Go to door dx.
Preconditions: TYPE(dx,DOOR),(∃rx)(∃ry)[INROOM(ROBOT,rx) ∧ CONNECTS(dx,rx,ry)]
Deletions: AT(ROBOT,$1,$2),NEXTTO(ROBOT,$1)
Additions: *NEXTTO(ROBOT,dx)

GOTOL(x,y) Go to coordinate location (x,y).
Preconditions: (∃rx)[INROOM(ROBOT,rx) ∧ LOCINROOM(x,y,rx)]
Deletions: AT(ROBOT,$1,$2),NEXTTO(ROBOT,$1)
Additions: *AT(ROBOT,x,y)

operator applications actually occurring in the STRIPS solution. STRIPS' attention was directed to the rooms shown in the diagrams by closing the doors connecting all other rooms.

The plan for the first problem in the sequence pushes two boxes together and then takes the robot into an adjacent room. The second problem is similar to the first except that different rooms and different boxes are involved, and the robot begins in a room adjacent to the room containing the boxes. STRIPS uses a tail of MACROP1 to get the robot into the room with the boxes and then uses the entire MACROP1 to complete the plan.

The third problem involves taking the robot from one room through a second room and into a third room, with the added complication that the door connecting the second and third rooms is closed. STRIPS first decides to use MACROP2 with the box-pushing sequence edited out and then finds that the door must be opened; to get the robot next to the closed door, a head of MACROP2 is selected with the box-pushing sequence again edited out. After formation of the plan to go to the door and open it, the PLANEX scan observes that only the final operator of the first relevant instance of MAC-ROP2 is needed to complete the plan.

The fourth problem requires that three boxes be pushed together, with the robot beginning in a room adjacent to the room containing the boxes. A head of MACROP2 is used to get the robot into the room with the boxes and to push two of them together; the box-pushing sequence of MACROP2 is used to complete the plan, again with the assistance of the PLANEX scan.

The fifth problem requires the robot to go from one room into a second room, open a door that leads into a third room, go through the third room into a fourth room, and then push together two pairs of boxes. The plan, which is formed by combining all of MACROP4 with all of MACROP3, is well beyond the range of plans producible by STRIPS without the use of MACROPs. Note that although MACROP4 was created by lifting a plan that pushed three boxes together, it has enough generality to handle this form of a four-box problem. Note also that MACROP1, MACROP3, and MACROP4 have been recognized as redundant and deleted, so that the net result of this learning sequence is to add only MACROP2 and MACROP5 to the system.

In Table I we present a table showing the search tree sizes and running times for the five problems. The problems were run both with and without the use of MACROPs for comparison. Even when MACROPs were not being used for planning we include the MACROP production time since PLANEX needs the MACROP to monitor plan execution. Note that the times and the search tree sizes are all smaller when MACROPS are used and that the MACROPs allow longer plans to be formed without necessarily incurring an exponential increase in planning time.

PUSHB(bx,by) *Push bx to object by.*
Preconditions: TYPE(by,OBJECT),PUSHABLE(bx),NEXTTO(ROBOT,bx),
($\exists rx$)[INROOM(bx,rx) $\wedge$ INROOM(by,rx)]
Deletions: AT(ROBOT,$1,$2),NEXTTO(ROBOT,$1),AT($bx$,$1,$2),NEXTTO($bx$,$1),
NEXTTO($1,$bx$)
Additions: *NEXTTO(bx,dx),NEXTTO(ROBOT,bx)

PUSHD(bx,dx) *Push bx to door dx.*
Preconditions: PUSHABLE(bx),TYPE(dx,DOOR),NEXTTO(ROBOT,bx)
($\exists rx$)($\exists ry$)[INROOM(bx,rx) $\wedge$ CONNECTS(dx,rx,ry)]
Deletions: AT(ROBOT,$1,$2),NEXTTO(ROBOT,$1),AT($bx$,$1,$2),NEXTTO($bx$,$1),
NEXTTO($1,$bx$)
Additions: *NEXTTO(bx,dx),NEXTTO(ROBOT,bx)

PUSHL(bx,x,y) *Push bx to coordinate location (x,y).*
Preconditions: PUSHABLE(bx),NEXTTO(ROBOT,bx),($\exists rx$)[INROOM(ROBOT,rx) $\wedge$
LOCINROOM(x,y,rx)]
Deletions: AT(ROBOT,$1,$2),NEXTTO(ROBOT,$1),AT($bx$,$1,$2),NEXTTO($bx$,$1),
NEXTTO($1,$bx$)
Additions: *AT(bx,x,y),NEXTTO(ROBOT,bx)

GOTHRUDR(dx,rx) *Go through door dx into room rx.*
Preconditions: TYPE(dx,DOOR),STATUS(dx,OPEN),TYPE(rx,ROOM),
NEXTTO(ROBOT,dx) ($\exists ry$)[INROOM(ROBOT,ry) $\wedge$ CONNECTS(dx,ry,rx)]
Deletions: AT(ROBOT,$1,$2),NEXTTO(ROBOT,$1),INROOM(ROBOT,$1)
Additions: *INROOM(ROBOT,rx)

PUSHTHRUDR(bx,dx,rx) *Push bx through door dx into room rx.*
Preconditions: PUSHABLE(bx),TYPE(dx,DOOR),STATUS(dx,OPEN),TYPE(rx,
ROOM),NEXTTO(bx,dx),NEXTTO(ROBOT,bx),($\exists ry$)[INROOM(bx,ry) $\wedge$
CONNECTS(dx,ry,rx)]
Deletions: AT(ROBOT,$1,$2),NEXTTO(ROBOT,$1),AT($bx$,$1,$2),NEXTTO($bx$,$1),
NEXTTO($1,$bx$),INROOM(ROBOT,$1),INROOM(bx,$1)
Additions: *INROOM(bx,rx),INROOM(ROBOT,rx),NEXTTO(ROBOT,bx)

OPEN(dx) *Open door dx.*
Preconditions: NEXTTO(ROBOT,dx),TYPE(dx,DOOR),STATUS(dx,CLOSED)
Deletions: STATUS(dx,CLOSED)
Additions: *STATUS(dx,OPEN)

CLOSE(dx) *Close door dx.*
Preconditions: NEXTTO(ROBOT,dx),TYPE(dx,DOOR),STATUS(dx,OPEN)
Deletions: STATUS(dx,OPEN)
Additions: *STATUS(dx,CLOSED)

Note. The addition clauses preceded by an asterisk are the *primary additions* of the operator. When STRIPS searches for a relevant operator is considers only these primary addition clauses.

7.2. Example Problems

7.2.1. SUMMARY. A sequence of five problems was designed to illustrate the various ways in which MACROPs are used during planning. We show in the next subsection an annotated trace of the system's behaviour for each problem in the sequence. Each trace is preceded by a diagram of the problem's initial and final states, and includes the sequence of subgoal generations and

TABLE I
Statistics for STRIPS behavior

	PROBLEM 1	PROBLEM 2	PROBLEM 3	PROBLEM 4	PROBLEM 5
Without MACROPS					
Total time (minutes)	3 : 05	9 : 42	7 : 03	14 : 09	–
Time to produce MACROP	1 : 00	1 : 28	1 : 11	1 : 43	–
Time to find unlifted plan	2 : 05	8 : 14	5 : 52	12 : 26	–
Total nodes in search tree	10	33	22	51	–
Nodes on solution path	9	13	11	15	–
Operators in plan	4	6	5	7	–
With MACROPS					
Total time (minutes)	3 : 05	3 : 54	6 : 34	4 : 37	9 : 13
Time to produce MACROP	1 : 00	1 : 32	1 : 16	1 : 37	3 : 24
Time to find unlifted plan	2 : 05	2 : 22	5 : 18	3 : 00	5 : 49
Total nodes in search tree	10	9	14	9	14
Nodes on solution path	9	9	9	9	14
Operators in plan	4	6	5	6	11

STRIPS is written in BBN-LISP and runs as compiled code on a PDP-10 computer under the TENEX time-sharing system.
STRIPS could not solve Problem 5 without using MACROPs.

7.2.2. ANNOTATED TRACE OF SYSTEM BEHAVIOR FOR EACH EXAMPLE PROBLEM.

Problem 1

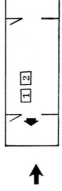

G1: INROOM(ROBOT,RRAM) ∧ NEXTTO(BOX1,BOX2)
*****
    G1 is the task statement.
*****
G2: Preconditions for PUSHB(BOX2,BOX1)
G3: Preconditions for GOTOB(BOX2)
Apply GOTOB(BOX2)
Apply PUSHB(BOX2,BOX1)
G4: Preconditions for GOTHRUDR(par18,RRAM)
Apply GOTHRUDR(par18,RRAM)
G6: Preconditions for GOTOD(DRAMCLK)
*****
    G5 was the precondition for an operator that did not appear in the completed plan.
*****

Apply GOTOD(DRAMCLK)
Apply GOTHRUDR(DRAMCLK,RRAM)
Solution

Form MACROP1(par29,par37,par45,par54,par33)
*****
    The parameter list for a MACROP contains all the parameters that occur in the triangle table.
*****

GOTOB(par29)
PUSHB(par29,par37)
GOTOD(par45)
GOTHRUDR(par45,par54)
*****
    The generalized plan pushes two boxes together and takes the robot into an adjacent room, given that the robot and the boxes are initially all in the same room.
*****

Set first additions row of MACROP1 to 3.
*****
    STRIPS will consider only rows numbered 3 and higher as add lists during planning. Rows 1 and 2 of a triangle table are never considered as add lists since there are no add clauses in Row 1, and the add clauses in Row 2 are redundant with respect to the operator description of the first operator in the MACROP.
*****

Problem 2

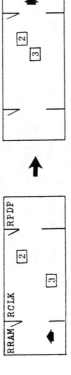

G1: INROOM(ROBOT,RPDP) ∧ NEXTTO(BOX2,BOX3)
*****
    G1 is the task statement.
*****
G2: Preconditions for MACROP1:5(BOX3,BOX2,par3,RPDP,par5)
*****
    The notation MACROP1:5 means that Row 5 of MACROP1 is selected as a relevant add list. MACROP1 is instantiated so that Row 5 contains the relevant clauses INROOM(ROBOT,RPDP) added by GOTHRUDR(par3,RPDP) and NEXTTO(BOX2,BOX3) added by PUSHB(BOX3,BOX2). All four operators in MACROP1 are needed to produce these relevant clauses. No kernels in the triangle table are satisfied. A difference consisting of the single clause INROOM (ROBOT,RCLK) is extracted from the first kernel.
*****

G3:   Preconditions for MACROP1:5(par17,par18,par19,RCLK,par21)
*****
Row 5 of MACROP1 is again selected as a relevant add list. MACROP1 is instantiated so that Row 5 contains the relevant clause INROOM-(ROBOT,RCLK) added by GOTHRUDR(par19,RCLK). Only the last two operators in MACROP1 are needed to produce the relevant clause.
*****
Kernel 3 satisfied
*****
Kernel 3 is the precondition for the last two operators in MACROP1.
*****
Apply GOTOD(DRAMCLK)
Apply GOTHRUDR(DRAMCLK,RCLK)
Kernel 1 satisfied
Apply GOTOB(BOX3)
Apply PUSHB(BOX3,BOX2)
Apply GOTOD(DPDPCLK)
Apply GOTHRUDR(DPDPCLK,RPDP)
Solution

Form MACROP2(par27,par52,par72,par91,par111,par38,par40)
GOTOD(par27)
GOTHRUDR(par27,par40)
GOTOB(par52)
PUSHB(par52,par72)
GOTOD(par91)
GOTHRUDR(par91,par111)
*****
The generalized plan takes the robot from one room into an adjacent room, pushes two boxes together in the second room, and then takes the robot into a third room adjacent to the second.
*****
Erase MACROP1.
*****
MACROP1 is completely contained in MACROP2.
*****
The first two operators of MACROP2 match the last two operators of MACROP2.
*****
Set first additions row of MACROP2 to 4.
*****
The first two operators of MACROP2 match the last two operators of MACROP2.
*****

G1:   INROOM(ROBOT,RPDP)
*****
G1 is the task statement.
*****
G2:   Preconditions for MACROP2:7(par1,par2,par3,par4,RPDP,par6,par7)
*****
Row 7 of MACROP2 is selected as a relevant add list. MACROP2 is instantiated so that Row 7 contains the relevant clause INROOM-(ROBOT,RPDP) added by GOTHRUDR(par4,RPDP). Only the first, second, fifth, and sixth operators are needed to produce this relevant clause. No kernels in the triangle table are satisfied. A difference consisting of the single clause STATUS(DPDPCLK,OPEN) is extracted from the first kernel.
*****
G5:   Preconditions for OPEN(DPDPCLK)
*****
After considering two other relevant operators for achieving G1, STRIPS returns to the solution path. OPEN(DPDPCLK) is found to be a relevant operator and a difference consisting of the single clause NEXTTO(ROBOT,DPDPCLK) is extracted from the preconditions.
*****
G9:   Preconditions for MACROP2:6(par15,par16,par17,DPDPCLK,par19, par20,par21)
*****
After considering three other relevant operators for achieving G5, STRIPS selects Row 6 of MACROP2 as a relevant add list. MACROP2 is instantiated so that Row 6 contains the relevant clause NEXTTO-(ROBOT,DPDPCLK) added by GOTOD(DPDPCLK). Only the first, second, and fifth operators are needed to produce this relevant clause.
*****
Kernel 1 satisfied.
Apply GOTOD(DRAMCLK)
Apply GOTHRUDR(DRAMCLK,RCLK)
Apply GOTOD(DPDPCLK)
Apply OPEN(DPDPCLK)
Kernel 6 satisfied
*****
A PLANEX scan is used so that all kernels are checked. Kernel 6 is the precondition for the final operator in the relevant instance of MACROP2.
*****
Apply GOTHRUDR(DPDPCLK,RPDP)
Solution

Form MACROP3(par24,par59,par82,par32,par42)
GOTOD(par24)
GOTHRUDR(par24,par42)
GOTOD(par59)
OPEN(par59)
GOTHRUDR(par59,par82)

Problem 3

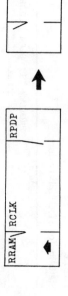

*****
The generalized plan takes the robot from one room into an adjacent room, then to a closed door in the second room, opens the closed door, and then takes the robot through the opened door into a third room.
*****
The first two operators of MACROP3 match the first two operators of MACROP2.
*****
Set first additions row of MACROP3 to 4.
*****

Problem 4

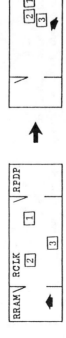

G1: NEXTTO(BOX1,BOX2) ∧ NEXTTO(BOX2,BOX3)

    G1 is the task statement.
*****
G2: Preconditions for MACROP2:5(par1,BOX2,BOX1,par4,par5,par6,par7)
*****
Row 5 of MACROP2 is selected as a relevant add list. MACROP2 is instantiated so that Row 5 contains the relevant clause NEXTTO-(BOX1,BOX2) added by PUSHB(BOX2,BOX1). All of the first four operators in MACROP2 are needed to produce this relevant clause.
*****
Kernel 1 satisfied
Apply GOTOD(DRAMCLK)
Apply GOTHRUDR(DRAMCLK,RCLK)
Apply GOTOB(BOX2)
Apply PUSHB(BOX2,BOX1)
G3: Preconditions for MACROP2:5(par19,BOX3,BOX2,par22,par23,par24,par25)
*****
Row 5 of MACROP2 is selected as before. The instantiation is so that Row 5 contains the relevant clause NEXTTO(BOX2,BOX3) added by PUSHB(BOX3,BOX2). Again all of the first four operators are included in the relevant instance of MACROP2.
*****
Kernel 3 satisfied
*****
A PLANEX scan is used so that all kernels are checked. Kernel 3 is the precondition for the third and fourth operators.
*****
Apply GOTOB(BOX3)
Apply PUSHB(BOX3,BOX2)
Solution

Form MACROP4(par37,par80,par102,par123,par134,par57,par59)
    GOTOD(par37)
    GOTHRUDR(par37,par59)
    GOTOB(par80)
    PUSHB(par80,par102)
    GOTOB(par123)
    PUSHB(par123,par134)
*****
The generalized plan takes the robot from one room into an adjacent room, pushes one box to a second box, and then pushes a third box to a fourth box.
*****
Set first additions row of MACROP2 to 6.
*****
The first 4 operators of MACROP2 match the first 4 operators of MACROP4.
*****
Set first additions row of MACROP4 to 4.
*****
The first 2 operators of MACROP4 match the last 2 operators of MACROP2.
*****

Problem 5

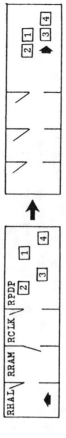

G1: NEXTTO(BOX1,BOX2) ∧ NEXTTO(BOX3,BOX4)

    G1 is the task statement.
*****
G2: Preconditions for MACROP4:7(par13,BOX2,BOX1,BOX3,BOX4,par18,par19)
*****
Row 7 of MACROP4 is selected as a relevant add list. MACROP4 is instantiated so that Row 7 contains the relevant clauses NEXTTO(BOX1,BOX2) added by PUSHB(BOX2,BOX1) and NEXTTO(BOX3,BOX4) added by PUSHB(BOX3,BOX4). All six operators in MACROP4 are needed to produce these relevant clauses. No kernels in the triangle table are satisfied. A difference consisting of the single clause INROOM(ROBOT,RCLK) is extracted from the first kernel.
*****
G3: Preconditions for MACROP3:6(par27,par28,RCLK,par30,par31)
*****
Row 6 of MACROP3 is selected as a relevant add list. MACROP3 is instantiated so that Row 6 contains the relevant clause INROOM-(ROBOT,RCLK) added by GOTHRUDR(par28,RCLK). All five

robot environment that culminated in the production of a 19-operator plan for fetching three boxes from three different rooms and then pushing the three boxes together. This final MACROP subsumed the seven earlier ones so that only one MACROP was retained by the system. Subsequences of the 19-step MACROP could be used to fetch boxes, push boxes together, move the robot from room to room, etc.

The experiments we have been discussing show the use of MACROPs during planning. We have also run experiments with PLANEX to illustrate the use of MACROPs during plan execution. One such experiment is documented in a report [4] and film [5] that illustrate how PLANEX monitors robot task execution in the seven-room experimental environment. One interesting sequence in this experiment involves the robot attempting to go from one room through a second room into a third room. After entering the second room, the robot discovers that a box is blocking the door that leads into the third room. Since PLANEX is working with a generalized plan, the difficulty can be overcome by finding a different instance of the plan's first kernel that is satisfied. This new instantiation of the plan's parameters causes the robot to be sent from the second room into a fourth room and then into the target third room.

8. Conclusions

We have presented in considerable detail methods by which a problem-solving program can "learn" old solutions and use them both to monitor real-world execution and to aid in the solution of new problems. We view these methods as representing only a preliminary excursion into an area that, in the long run, may hold high potential for the design of "intelligent" robots. Before such potential is realized, however, there are a number of substantial technical problems to be solved; in this final section we briefly point out a few of these.

8.1. Abstracting Preconditions

It is a commonplace observation that successful problem solvers (human or machine) must plan at a level of detail appropriate to the problem at hand. In typical problem-solving programs, the level of detail is set a priori by the experimenter when he carefully selects the representations employed. This situation changes when the problem solver can create its own MAC-ROPS. Now we have the possibility of creating powerful macro operators whose specification is at the same level of detail as each component operator. In terms of our system, we may create a large triangle table whose preconditions (its first kernel) is the conjunction of so many literals that the theorem prover has little hope of success. What we need is a way of appropriately

operators in MACROP3 are needed to produce this relevant clause.
*****
Kernel 1 satisfied
 Apply GOTOD(DRAMHAL)
 Apply GOTHRUDR(DRAMHAL,RRAM)
 Apply GOTOD(DRAMCLK)
 Apply OPEN(DRAMCLK)
 Apply GOTHRUDR(DRAMCLK,RCLK)
Kernel 1 satisfied
 Apply GOTOD(DPDPCLK)
 Apply GOTHRUDR(DPDPCLK,RPDP)
 Apply GOTOB(BOX2)
 Apply PUSHB(BOX2,BOX1)
 Apply GOTOB(BOX3)
 Apply PUSHB(BOX3,BOX4)
Solution
Form MACROP5(par44,par87,par151,par208,par237,par265,par294,par180,par130, par64,par66)
 GOTOD(par44)
 GOTHRUDR(par44,par66)
 GOTOD(par87)
 OPEN(par87)
 GOTHRUDR(par87,par130)
 GOTOD(par151)
 GOTHRUDR(par151,par180)
 GOTOB(par208)
 PUSHB(par208,par237)
 GOTOB(par265)
 PUSHB(par265,par294)
*****
The generalized plan takes the robot from one room into a second room, opens a door leading to a third room, takes the robot through the third room into a fourth room, and then pushes together two pairs of boxes.
*****
Erase MACROP3.
Erase MACROP4.
*****
MACROP3 and MACROP4 are completely contained in MACROP5.
*****
Set first additions row of MACROP5 to 4.
*****
The first two operators of MACROP5 match the sixth and seventh operators of MACROP5.
*****

7.3. Further Experiments

In another set of experiments that were run with the new system, the primary goal was to produce long plans. We ran a sequence of eight problems in our

(Please see p. 288 for conclusion to this paper.)

Decision Theory and Artificial Intelligence II: The Hungry Monkey*

Jerome A. Feldman

University of Rochester

Robert F. Sproull

Xerox Palo Alto Research Center

This paper describes a problem-solving framework in which aspects of mathematical decision theory are incorporated into symbolic problem-solving techniques currently predominant in artificial intelligence. The utility function of decision theory is used to reveal tradeoffs among competing strategies for achieving various goals, taking into account such factors as reliability, the complexity of steps in the strategy, and the value of the goal. The utility function on strategies can therefore be used as a guide when searching for good strategies. It is also used to formulate solutions to the problems of how to acquire a world model, how much planning effort is worthwhile, and whether verification tests should be performed. These techniques are illustrated by application to the classic monkey and bananas problem.

1. INTRODUCTION

Mathematical decision theory is concerned with decision making under conditions of uncertainty. Because this is also a major concern of artificial intelligence, one would expect considerable interaction between the disciplines. Although there has been some (primarily in the study of search algorithms, see Hart, Nilsson, & Raphael, 1968), the two fields have presented basically competing paradigms. It is the purpose of this and related papers (Yakimovsky & Feldman, 1974) to show how artificial intelligence problems can be attacked by methods derived from decision theory. More generally, we are concerned with how to combine numeric and symbolic reasoning.

The central idea of mathematical decision theory is that a numerical utility function can be used to evaluate decisions (see Chernoff & Moses, 1959, or Raiffa, 1970, for introductions to decision theory). A single numerical value is used to summarize the advantages of a set of actions. A typical utility function would be the profits realized from a particular investment outcome. Although it

might seem that the use of a single number could preclude the choice of an optimal strategy in some cases, the central theorem of decision theory shows essentially that this cannot happen. The presentation of this theorem is beyond the scope of this paper (see deGroot, 1970), for an elementary presentation), but the result can be stated simply: if various outcomes have known utilities and known probabilities of occurrence, then any acceptable (admissible) strategy is equivalent to one which maximizes expected utility. Different strategies arise from different assumptions about probability and utility functions. Both kinds of functions are subjective models of the behavior of the problem domain and may be quite complex.

The first, and perhaps the best, argument for a numerical utility function is that the choice between alternative courses of action is often intrinsically numerical. One chooses the cheapest, or fastest, or strongest alternative. We have found that many problems in robot problem solving are virtually inexpressible in nonnumerical terms.

Another main use of a numerical utility function is in "comparing the incomparable." If flying is faster and safer than driving, but more expensive and subject to delay, how can we choose which to do? What change in price would cause us to choose otherwise? The expected utilities of the alternative decisions answer these questions. By contrast, a heuristic program capable of comparing differing strategies must have rules covering all possible combinations of goals and circumstances, and the addition of new alternatives may require significant reprogramming. In a decision-theory formulation, much of the complexity in the tradeoff comparisons is embodied in the structure of the utility function. A vast controversy-filled literature testifies to the intricacies of utility and probability assessments that attempt to model tradeoffs made by humans (Tversky & Kahneman, 1974). Our objective is considerably simpler: the design of the utility function need not address values only within a particular problem.

Our first major application of decision-theoretic methods in robotics attacked the problem of image segmentation (Yakimovsky & Feldman, 1974). The problem of segmentation, breaking a complex image into sections, is a central one in machine perception; the analogous problem arises in the analysis of speech (Woods, 1974) and in other complex problems. The approach applies Bayesian decision theory and problem-dependent information (semantics) to determine an acceptable segmentation of the image. This program was quite successful and the general ideas are being widely adopted (Garvey Tenenbaum, 1974; Tenenbaum, 1973).

However, the image segmentation effort did not explore all advantages of decision-theoretic formulations. Image analysis has been a peripheral problem in AI and has often been attacked by partially numerical techniques. We believe that many problems in AI can be clarified by abandoning a strictly "symbolic data processing" viewpoint and by employing decision-theoretic techniques.

The central problem addressed in this paper is that of planning and acting. This is a core issue in AI and becomes increasingly important as we begin to

*This research was supported in part by the Advanced Research Projects Agency of the Department of Defense under contract DAHC 15-73-C-0435, ARPA order 2494, and in part by the Xerox Corporation. Reprints may be obtained from Jerome A. Feldman, Computer Science Department, University of Rochester, Rochester, N.Y.

Cognitive Science 1, 1977, pp. 158-192

tion about the position of objects with an "AT" assertion that associates an object and its Cartesian coordinate position. Additional assertions declare boxes to be climbable and pushable and bananas to be edible. An initial set of assertions might be:

```
(AT MONKEY 9 9 0)
(AT BANANAS 0 0 5)
(AT BOX 2 2 0)
(HEIGHT BOX 5)
(CLIMBABLE BOX)
(PUSHABLE BOX)
(EDIBLE BANANAS)
```

The operators are specified below. If all assertions in the list of preconditions are in the assertion data base, then the operator can be applied. Application of an operator causes assertions in the delete list to be deleted from the data base, and those in the add list to be added. (The functions X, Y, and Z refer to the coordinate entries in the AT predicate. The symbol $ will match any value in the corresponding position in the assertion.)

```
WALKTO(α)
  Preconditions:  (AT MONKEY $ $ 0)
  Delete list:    (AT MONKEY $ $ 0)
  Add list:       (AT MONKEY X(α) Y(α) 0)

PUSHTO(α,β)
  Preconditions:  (AT MONKEY X(α) Y(α) 0)
                  (PUSHABLE α)
                  (AT α $ $ 0)
  Delete list:    (AT MONKEY $ $ 0)
                  (AT α $ $ 0)
  Add list:       (AT MONKEY X(β) Y(β) 0)
                  (AT α X(β) Y(β) 0)

CLIMB(α)
  Preconditions:  (CLIMBABLE α)
                  (AT MONKEY X(α) Y(α) 0)
  Delete list:    (AT MONKEY $ $ 0)
  Add list:       (AT MONKEY X(α) Y(α) HEIGHT(α))

CONSUME(α)
  Preconditions:  (EDIBLE α)
                  (AT MONKEY X(α) Y(α) Z(α))
  Delete list:    (EDIBLE α)
  Add list:       (FED)
```

The problem solver, given the goal (FED), would generate the plan:

```
WALKTO(BOX)
PUSHTO(BOX,BANANAS)
CLIMB(BOX)
CONSUME(BANANAS)
```

apply AI techniques to real problems. The vehicle used for discussion in this paper is the classic "Monkey and Bananas" problem. It is a simple, well-known problem which can be extended naturally to include many of the basic issues we wish to address. These issues include planning under uncertainty, assessing costs and risks, error recovery, the value of information, and the cost of planning.

Because the monkey's world may seem rather artificial, the reader may prefer a more practical example. The issues of uncertainty, cost, risk, and information gathering seem easy to appreciate in the case of the "wheelless student," the real-life problem of buying a used automobile. A typical procedure is first to read newspaper advertisements and bulletin boards to assess the situation generally. Then, at relatively low cost, one can telephone various purveyors of cars and inquire about them. At some point, one must actually go to the effort of seeing and driving certain of these. There are professional diagnostic services which can be employed at considerable cost to further test the car. In each of these steps, one must decide when to stop that stage and go on to the next one. One does not, of course, proceed in strict order; there will normally be alternatives at several different levels of investigation.

Notice that the "plan" itself is trivial: read, telephone, look, drive, professionally test, and buy. It is the application of this plan to the world situation which is difficult. We believe that much intelligent activity is characterized by complex applications of simple plans, and this belief has led us to concentrate on the closely related questions of plan elaboration and execution.

The following four sections illustrate the applications of decision theory to AI with the monkey and bananas example. The first section describes the use of simple decision-theoretic techniques applied to symbolic problem solving. The subsequent sections illustrate a broader application of techniques, particularly for allocation of resources to planning and acting. The indented paragraphs describe generalizations of ideas in the example which may be ignored on first reading.

2. DECISION THEORY IN SYMBOLIC PROBLEM SOLVING

Decision theory helps a symbolic problem-solver search for the best plan that achieves a given goal. A utility function on plans can govern a search strategy that explores plans of high utility; the search terminates by announcing the plan of highest utility.

We shall illustrate how symbolic problem solving and decision analysis can be combined with the classical example: *A hungry monkey is in a room in which a bunch of bananas hangs from the ceiling. The monkey cannot reach the bananas. There is, however, a movable box in the room; if the box is under the bananas and the monkey stands on the box he can reach the bananas and eat.* The goal for a symbolic problem solver is to find a plan that will feed the monkey.

A typical problem solver is given a symbolic model of the problem and searches for a combination of "operators" that achieves a given goal. A possible symbolic model, specified in the style of a modern AI language, records informa-

In a robotics experiment, the original assertions and this sequence of operators can be used as a set of commands to software and hardware subsystems that would cause a robot to simulate the actions of the monkey.

If the problem statement and the corresponding symbolic information given to the problem solver were expanded to include multiple tools, multiple sources of food, or multiple goals, the problem solver could generate other plans as well. If the initial assertions model several boxes, a plan for each box can be generated. However, if the symbolic model becomes at all large and intricate, the combinatorial explosion would overwhelm any present problem solver.

Computing the Utility of a Plan

The utility of any one of the WALKTO, PUSHTO, CLIMB, CONSUME plans is derived from a *utility model* that accompanies the symbolic model. It is a measure of the value of executing each of the steps in the plan and thus achieving the goal. We shall assume for now that this utility can be expressed as a sum of contributions from individual steps and a contribution representing the value of achieving the goal (*Note:* This eludes several important considerations such as risk which will be treated later.)

For each goal, we assign a function that evaluates the utility of achieving the goal. In our example, we shall assign $U_e = 200$ to the goal of eating, that is, to state in which the monkey is fed. Goals of less value to the monkey are assigned correspondingly smaller utilities. For later reference, we shall assume that the next most desirable goal is ''don't bother trying to eat,'' which has utility U_{db}.

The utility associated with executing each step of the plan is often called the ''cost'' of the step. A robotics experiment that simulates each operator with a collection of processes, including computation and control of a robot vehicle or manipulator, might use cost assignments that express the consumption of resources required to accomplish each step. Table 1 specifies an assignment of negative-valued cost functions C that reflect the expenditure of resources required for each step.

WALKTO(α). The monkey walks from its present location (x_m, y_m) to $(X(\alpha), Y(\alpha))$. The cost is $C_w = -1 *$ distance$((x_m, y_m),(X(\alpha), Y(\alpha)))$.

PUSHTO(α, β). The monkey pushes the object α to the location $X(\beta), Y(\beta)$. $C_p = -10 *$ distance$((X(\alpha), Y(\alpha)),(X(\beta), Y(\beta)))$.

CLIMB(α). The monkey climbs the object α. $C_b = -20$.

CONSUME(α). The monkey consumes the food α. $C_e = -5$.

Using this model, the total utility of the symbolic plan WALKTO, PUSHTO, CLIMB, CONSUME is: $U_{total} = C_w + C_p + C_b + C_e + U_e$. The utility of the next best plan is U_{db}.

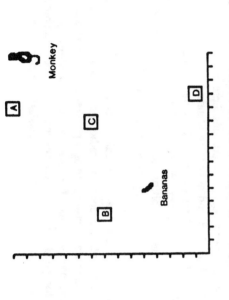

FIG. 1 Map showing the location of the monkey, the bananas and four boxes. The axes indicate an (x, y) coordinate system.

Comparing Alternative Plans

The plan with greatest utility can be selected for execution: it is the ''best'' of the plans generated by the symbolic problem solver, as evaluated by the utility model. To illustrate the power of comparing plans, consider generating plans using each of the four boxes shown in the ''map'' of Fig. 1. Table 1 shows the total utilities of the WALKTO, PUSHTO, CLIMB, CONSUME plans using the different boxes. The plan to use box B has the greatest utility and is therefore selected as the best plan. This simple utility model adds considerable capability to the problem solver. The location of the boxes and the cost functions determine which box is selected as the best one to use. For example, if $C_p = C_w$, box C will be preferred rather than B. If the initial position of the monkey changes, different boxes may be preferred. (Figure 2a shows a map of regions in which the monkey might start out, together with the preferred box in each region (the map is made assuming $C_p = -2*$distance).)

TABLE 1

	C_w	C_p	C_b	C_c	U_e	U_{total}
Box A	-3	-117	-20	-5	200	55
Box B	-13	-36	-20	-5	200	126
Box C	-6	-64	-20	-5	200	105
Box D	-13	-81	-20	-5	200	81

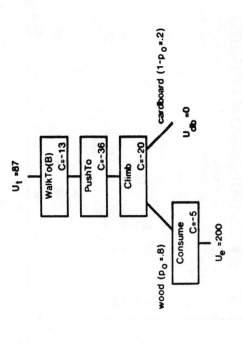

FIG. 3   A decision tree for a plan in which CLIMB may fail.

failure-recovery plans of higher utility may exist: a plan to clear away the destroyed cardboard box and to try using another box may have a higher utility than U_t. Techniques for devising failure recoveries will be more fully developed below; we shall temporarily assume the utility of the failure outcome to be U_{cb}.

The utility of the plan is calculated as the mathematical *expectation* of the utilities of the individual outcomes, that is:

$$U_{total} = \Sigma \, p_i U_i$$

where U_i is the total utility of a particular path in the "decision tree," and p_i is the probability of taking the path ($\Sigma p_i = 1$). For Fig. 3, the total utility U_{total} is $p_0(C_w + C_p + C_c + U_e) + (1 - p_0)(C_w + C_p + C_b + U_{cb})$.

This technique allows the planner to trade off cost and reliability; classical AI problem solvers have no means of expressing these tradeoffs. For example, if we use the costs of Table 1 and assume an identical p_0 for all boxes, no change occurs in the selection of the best plan. However, if the probabilities differ for various boxes, a reliable plan may be preferred to a less reliable one. For example, if p_{0c} is the probability that box C is wood, p_{0b} that of box B, and $p_{0c} > p_{0b} + .11$, the expected utility of using box C will be greater than that of using box B.

The expected utility is a numerical measure of the merits of the *strategy* expressed by the plan. It does not predict that executing the plan will have an outcome of comparable utility, but only predicts the *average* utility of outcomes of many executions. Thus, if we use the *expected utility* as a measure when searching for good plans, we do not guarantee good outcomes; only good strategies. (This notion is central to classical decision theory; see deGroot, 1970.)

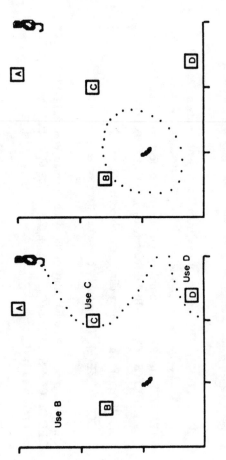

FIG. 2   (a) Regions of box preference by initial monkey position. (b) Region in which a box preferred to B must lie.

The cost functions also provide answers to a number of questions that an intelligent strategist must pose. For example, when should one try to find a box of higher utility than any presently located, and where should one search? (Figure 2b shows the region in which a box preferred to B would have to lie.)

Another important class of strategic questions concerns what decision theorists call "sensitivity analysis": how much confidence can be placed in the identification of the best plan? Is it substantially better than the next best, or do the utilities show that the planner is nearly indifferent to the choice? Do slight inaccuracies in the map or model cause a substantial change in the choice of best strategy? We shall later return to these important questions.

Coping with Uncertainty

Execution of a plan can go awry and produce outcomes considerably different from the desired goal. Clearly the reliability of a plan must be incorporated into the calculation of its utility. Decision theory shows how to weight the utility of an outcome with its probability of occurrence and thus to calculate a total utility that expresses the consequences of possible failures.

Let us augment the monkey-and-bananas problem by introducing a simple kind of failure: *There are two kinds of boxes in the room: wooden and cardboard. Cardboard boxes will not support the monkey; wooden ones will.*

When the plan outline is applied to a box of unknown type, either the box is wood and the monkey succeeds in eating, or it is cardboard and he fails (see Fig. 3). In the absence of more precise information about the box to which the plan is applied, we shall use a single probability p_0 to express the likelihood that the box is wooden. In addition, we shall assign a utility to the failure outcome. A simple assignment is U_{cb}, corresponding to abandoning the quest for food. However,

Finding Good Plans

Because the utility of a plan can be used to compare the merits of competing plans, it can be used to guide a search for good plans. The basic idea is to search by expanding paths of greatest expected utility. A number of algorithms have been devised that can use numerical measures to guide such a search (see surveys in Lawler & Wood, 1966, and Nilsson, 1971). Thus, augmenting the symbolic model with a numerical utility model widens the range of applicable search techniques.

Using numerical measures to guide search is not new to AI. Many game-playing programs employ a numerical score to represent the desirability of a board position and to guide a search. In fact, a game-playing program that uses a plausible move generator and a numerical evaluation of progress toward a win is a simple example of a combination of symbolic and (ad hoc) utility models in problem solving. Robotics problem-solving programs (e.g., STRIPS, see Fikes & Nilsson, 1971)[1] have also used simple numerical measures, such as the number of operators in a plan, as a search guide.

Searching can be guided in several ways; we shall illustrate "progressive deepening" and "pruning" as examples. The A* algorithm (Nilsson, 1971; Pohl, 1973) is typical of a progressive-deepening approach: a nonterminal node, N, of a search tree is expanded if it lies on the most promising path. The measure of promise is an estimate of the utility of the complete plan, computed as the sum of two terms: g, a measure of the "costs" ascribed to the nodes already included in the path (i.e., the total cost of the steps from the root node to N), and h, an upper bound estimate of the utility of a path from N to the goal. (Note: All "costs" are negative. Thus an upper bound on a set of costs is one for which resource expenditure is least.) These terms for the monkey and bananas example might be:

g(node) = ΣC_i from root to node
h(node) = (upper-bound estimate of costs from node to the goal) + U_e

The calculation of g requires calculating the contribution to the utility of the steps of the partially complete plan. It is for this reason that we have formulated our utility model as a sum of terms attributable to individual steps of the plan. The estimate used for h can be based on a simple "state-difference" approach, for example, if, at node N, the monkey is not located at the bananas, then an upper bound on h is the cost of moving the monkey to the bananas.

Progressive deepening uses a running estimate of the path utility to guide application of further planning effort. One advantage of this technique is that it will automatically attenuate the processing of plans that loop: such plans are abandoned because, as steps are added to the plan, g decreases continually without an offsetting increase in h.

"Pruning" is characteristic of several kinds of search algorithms that avoid exploring portions of the tree because the optimal plan can be shown to lie elsewhere. Many algorithms in use in operations research, known generically as "branch and bound" algorithms, have this property. The basic idea is to ignore paths that have an upper bound on their utility that is less than the utility achievable by some other path. A similar technique, for minimax trees, is called "alpha–beta," which has been extended for use with decision trees (Nilsson, 1971; Pauker & Kassirer, 1975).

The key information that guides pruning is the *bounds* information: the tighter the bounds, the more pruning necessary. Bounding the utility of a plan such as that of Fig. 3 requires bounding the utility of the part of the plan that is incomplete, the failure path. Bounding the failure path is equivalent to bounding the utility of the possible recovery strategies. One way to do this is as follows:

Lower bound: Don't bother with the current goal, and assign utility U_{db} to the failure. Thus the lower bound is $U_l = C_w + C_p + C_b + p_0(C_c + U_e) + (1-p_0)U_{db}$.

Upper bound: Assume that the failure caused no damage, and that there is an alternative plan as good as the present one. (Note: Given that a good plan fails, we do not have to assume that there exists a *better* one, because that will be covered by cases involving other boxes.)

$$U_u = C_w + C_p + C_b + p_0(C_c + U_e) + (1-p_0)U_u$$
$$U_u = (C_w + C_p - C_b)/p_0 + C_c + U_e$$

If we perform these calculations for all boxes, as in Table 1, we obtain Table 2. This bounding scheme shows clearly that utilities of plans involving boxes A, C, or D cannot exceed even the lower bound on using box B. Thus portions of the tree that call for boxes A, C, and D to be used to reach the bananas are pruned.

The numerical utility model thus furnishes information that is useful in guiding search. This information, whether encoded in cost functions or in bounding schemes, can easily involve "domain-dependent" information, as exemplified by our assignment of a function of distance to the cost of walking. The symbolic model also constrains search: the symbolic preconditions are used to avoid searching foolish plans, for example, ones that reach for the bananas when the monkey is not nearby. This technique can be implemented in the new AI lan-

TABLE 2

Box	U_l	U_u
A	16	20
B	87	109
C	66	82
D	42	52

[1] Use of A* was revealed in a private communication.

guages (see survey in Bobrow & Raphael, 1974) by instantiating each subgoal pursuit as a separate process and including bounds estimates and costs when proposing new subgoals. A branch-and-bound algorithm, such as A^*, can then schedule the processes (subgoals), always executing the most promising subgoal. Such dynamic allocation of effort to problem-solving processes motivated the design of the SAIL multiple process structure (Feldman, 1972).

3. IMPROVING THE PLAN

In this section, we will focus on improvements that can be made to a plan prior to its execution. A plan outline can often be altered to yield a greater expected utility by making detailed, often local, improvements to the plan. The measure of improvement in this *plan elaboration* process is the increase in expected utility resulting from filling in details.

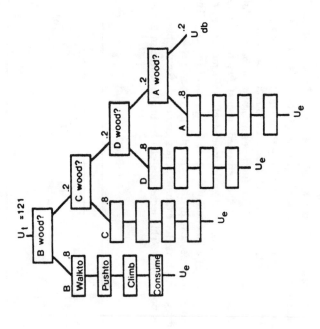

FIG. 5   Inserting costless tests for wooden boxes.

A plan can be improved by developing plans to recover from failures in the original outline. The failure in Fig. 3 can be elaborated with steps to clear away the mess, choose an alternative box, and try to use it to reach the bananas. Such an elaboration is shown in Fig. 4; the expected utility of the plan has risen from 87 to 96 as a result of the elaboration. The increase occurs because the plan to deal with the failure of box B (i.e., to try again with box C) has a higher utility than that of giving up (45 vs. 0). This process can be carried on indefinitely, but if the probability of failure is fairly low, the cost of additional planning may exceed the slight improvement in expected utility. (Generating plans for recovering from failures is similar to the generation of the original plan: a symbolic problem solver can provide plan outlines; the alternative recovery strategies are compared with utility measurements.)

Elaborating failures tightens the bounds on a plan. Figure 4 has a set of bounds shown in brackets as a triple: lower bound, expected value, and upper bound. Bounds are assessed from bottom to top; the triple with a prime symbol is calculated using the U_u formula, then the effects are propagated up through the tree. This process yields a rather tight bound on the utility of using box B (cf. Table 2).

Another kind of plan improvement can be achieved by introducing steps in the plan to gather information, and thereby reduce the uncertainty in the outcome. A simple example is shown in Fig. 5: a perfect and costless test determines whether each box is wooden. If the test announces that a box is wooden, which happens

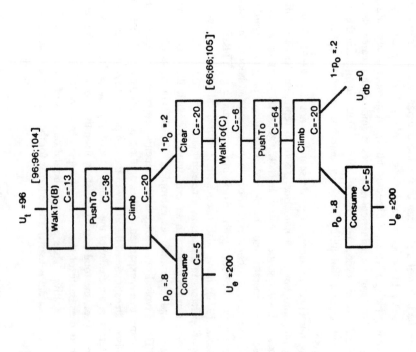

FIG. 4   Elaboration to increase the utility of failure in CLIMB. The numbers in brackets are explained in the text.

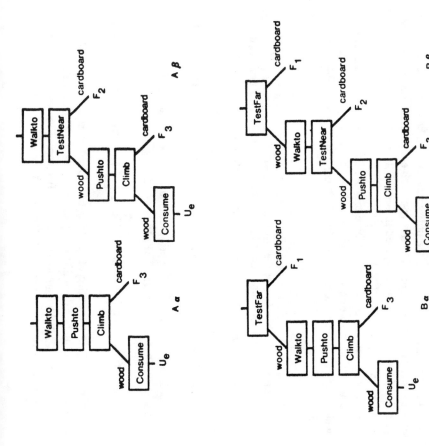

with probability p_0, then the plan to use that box is guaranteed to be successful. If the test announces that a box is cardboard, the next best plan is tried, and so forth. Adding these tests causes U_{total} to rise to 121.

A more realistic model of such information gathering incorporates the expenditure of resources required to perform the test and for the possibility that the test gives an incorrect answer. We shall define two such tests that can be used to elaborate the monkey-and-bananas plan:

TEST-FAR: A visual test measures whether a box is wooden. It does not require that the monkey be located near the box. It has a cost C_{tf}. The answer is characterized by two conditional probabilities p_{tw} and p_{tc}.

$p_{tw} = \Pr\{\text{test announces "wood"} \mid \text{box is wooden}\}$
$(1 - p_{tw}) = \Pr\{\text{test announces "cardboard"} \mid \text{box is wooden}\}\ )$

$p_{tc} = \Pr\{\text{test announces "wood"} \mid \text{box is cardboard}\}$
$(1 - p_{tc}) = \Pr\{\text{test announces "cardboard"} \mid \text{box is cardboard}\}\ )$

If the test always yields correct answers, $p_{tw} = 1$ and $p_{tc} = 0$.

TEST-NEAR: This test is analogous to TEST-FAR, but the monkey must be at the same location as the box being tested. This test might involve "thumping" the box. Cost C_{tn}. The behavior is characterized by:

$p_{nw} = \Pr\{\text{test announces "wood"} \mid \text{box is wooden}\}$
$p_{nc} = \Pr\{\text{test announces "wood"} \mid \text{box is cardboard}\}$
If the test always yields correct answers $p_{nw} = 1$ and $p_{nc} = 0$.

Adding these tests to the plan outline produces the four strategies shown in Fig. 6. In order to calculate the expected utilities of these plans, and thereby choose the best one, we must describe the consequences of performing a test. We shall use a simple Bayesian model: a test causes a change in the probability that the tested box is wooden, according to Bayes rule:

$\Pr\{\text{box is wood} \mid \text{TEST-FAR announces "wood"}\}$
$$= \frac{p_{tw}\Pr\{\text{box is wood}\}}{p_{tw}\Pr\{\text{box is wood}\} + p_{tc}(1 - \Pr\{\text{box is wood}\})}$$

$\Pr\{\text{box is wood} \mid \text{TEST-FAR announces "cardboard"}\}$
$$= \frac{(1 - p_{tw})\Pr\{\text{box is wood}\}}{(1 - p_{tw})\Pr\{\text{box is wood}\} + (1 - p_{tc})(1 - \Pr\{\text{box is wood}\})}$$

In these equations, $\Pr\{\text{box is wood}\}$ is the *prior probability* that the box is wood, and $\Pr\{\text{box is wood} \mid \text{TEST-FAR}\}$ is the *posterior probability* that it is wood. Analogous relations hold for TEST-NEAR.

FIG. 6 Four strategies using TEST-NEAR and TEST-FAR.

We also need to calculate the probabilities of taking each of the two paths that emanate from the TEST operation:

$\Pr\{\text{test announces "wood"}\} = p_{tw}\Pr\{\text{box is wood}\} + p_{tc}(1 - \Pr\{\text{box is wood}\})$
$\Pr\{\text{test announces "cardboard"}\} = 1 - \Pr\{\text{test announces "wood"}\}$

As an example of these calculations, we shall evaluate the expected utility of the $B\alpha$ strategy of Fig. 6 applied to box B, with the prior probability of finding a wooden box, p_0, set to 0.8, the performance of TEST-FAR characterized by $C_{tf} = -20$, $p_{tw} = 0.9$, and $p_{tc} = 0.1$, and the failure utilities U_{F1} and U_{F2} set to 0.

account. Although we may in principle reduce these errors by refining the model, we shall always be faced with insignificantly small differences.

Elaborations cause the search space to grow quite large because of the various choices of inclusion and exclusion of tests, the increased number of failures that require recovery strategies, etc. The search would be wholly impractical without a guide such as the branch-and-bound algorithm. We shall address below other methods of combating the "combinatorial explosion" during elaboration.

For each of the three paths through the tree, we must calculate the probability the path is taken and the utility of the path:

Path	U_i	Path probability
TEST-FAR, F_1	-20	$\Pr\{\text{test announces "cardboard"}\}$ $= 1 - (p_{tw}p_o + p_{tc}(1-p_o)) = .26$
TEST-FAR, WALKTO, PUSHTO, CLIMB, F_3	-89	$\Pr\{\text{box is cardboard}\,|\,\text{test announces "wood"}\}*$ $\Pr\{\text{test announces "wood"}\}$ $= [1 - (p_{tw}p_o)/(p_{tw}p_o + p_{tc}(1-p_o))]* .74 = .02$
TEST-FAR, WALKTO, PUSHTO, CLIMB, CONSUME, U_e	106	$\Pr\{\text{box is wood}\,|\,\text{test announces "wood"}\}\,*$ $\Pr\{\text{test announces "wood"}\}$ $= [(p_{tw}p_o)/(p_{tw}p_o + p_{tc}(1-p_o))] * .74 = .72$

The expected utility is $EU = \Sigma p_i U_i = 69$. Similar calculations for all four strategies, applied to box B, are recorded in Table 3. For the given set of costs, utilities, and probabilities, strategy $A\beta$ is selected. The strategy can be improved still further by elaboration to cope with the failures F_2 and F_3, as described above. Using both methods, a strategy with expected utility 105 turns out to be optimal.

The model of testing reveals tradeoffs among various information-gathering strategies as differences in utility. If the insertion of tests in a plan causes the expected utility of a plan to rise, the test is providing information that helps reduce the uncertainty of the outcome. Decision theory calls the increase in utility the "value of information."

If different strategies have nearly identical utilities, as do $A\alpha$ and $A\beta$ in Table 3, the planner might announce indifference between the strategies, and perhaps use other methods to decide which one to pursue. Such small differences may be insignificant when uncertainties in the probability or utility models are taken into

4. WORLD MODEL ACQUISITION

The planning activities described in previous sections have assumed that the planner has a complete model of the world. Because acquiring such a "world model" and locating all the boxes is a sizable task, an efficient strategy for feeding the monkey must make efficient allocation of resources to build the model.

A decision-theoretic model of the acquisition process can express the cost and reliability of an acquisition operator and the utility and probability of locating an object in the world. Once again, the utility measure can be used to search for an efficient strategy. A key concept in this approach is that the expected utility of a plan that uses an object, as computed in Section 2, can be used to estimate the value of locating the object.

The vision strategy must decide where to look. For our example, we shall use a grid to divide the world into regions and use a utility calculation to decide which region should be scrutinized. We shall use a simple acquisition operator LOOKAT:

LOOKAT(x,y). Examine the unit square at (x,y) with a vision system to determine if a box lies in the square. The cost of the operator is $C_{x,y}$. The outcome of the operator could be characterized by the two probabilities:

$$p_{tb} = \Pr\{\text{LOOKAT}(x,y) \text{ announces "box"}\,|\,\text{box at } (x,y)\}$$
$$p_{ln} = \Pr\{\text{LOOKAT}(x,y) \text{ announces "box"}\,|\,\text{no box at } (x,y)\}$$

In the remainder of the example, we shall assume $p_{tb} = 1$ and $p_{ln} = 0$.

In addition, we shall require a priori estimates of the probability that a box lies in a square, $\Pr\{\text{box at } (x,y)\}$. The utility of looking at a square is thus:

$$U_{look\text{-}x,y} = C_{x,y} + \Pr\{\text{box at } (x,y)\}\, U_{box\text{-}x,y} + (1 - \Pr\{\text{box at } (x,y)\})\, U_{fail}$$

where $U_{box\text{-}x,y}$ is the utility of using a box found at square (x,y), which is estimated by evaluating the utility of a plan outline (e.g., Fig. 3) without elaboration. The $U_{look\text{-}x,y}$ values are calculated for all squares, and the square with the largest value is chosen as the best place to look for a box.

TABLE 3

Strategy	E U
$A\alpha$	87 (cf. Fig. 3)
$A\beta$	88
$B\alpha$	69
$B\beta$	63

$C_w = -1 * \text{distance}$	$C_{tf} = -20$
$C_p = -10 * \text{distance}$	$C_{tn} = -10$
$C_b = -20$	$p_{tw} = .9$
$C_c = -5$	$p_{tc} = .1$
$U_c = 200$	$p_{wc} = 0$
$U_{f_t} = 0$	$p_o = .8$

The vision plan can also be elaborated. If the LOOKAT operator fails to locate a box, we might apply the LOOKAT operator to another square, and so forth (Fig. 7). This is just like coping with failure in CLIMB—we chose an alternative. Calculating the order in which to look at squares in this case is straightforward: the square with the largest value of $U_{box,x,y} + C_{x,y} / \Pr\{\text{box at } (x,y)\}$ is examined first, that with second largest next, etc.

Analogous to adding TEST-NEAR and TEST-FAR operators might be adding CHANGE-LENS or TURN-ON-MORE-LIGHTS operations to improve the probability of success of the vision operator. A more subtle elaboration might include WALKTO operators to position the monkey for better viewing of a particular region; this would of course influence the values of $U_{box,x,y}$ by changing the initial position of the monkey.

The utility of an acquisition plan is an attempt to measure the benefit of augmenting the information in the world model. Finding objects may permit using plans of higher utility; or it may show that a navigational path is blocked. Absence of objects may be useful when planning a collision-free route. Hence the utility that is assigned to a particular outcome of a vision operator is the utility of the information for the current set of plans. The utility of acquisition is further increased because new world-model information may give rise to alternative plans not previously considered.

The results of the LOOKAT operation change information in the world model. If a box is located, it is recorded in the model. In all cases, the subjective probability that a box is located in the scrutinized square, $\Pr\{\text{box at } (x,y)\}$, is modified. This is analogous to the treatment of TEST-NEAR and TEST-FAR: Bayes' rule is used to update $\Pr\{\text{box at } (x,y)\}$ just as it is used to update $\Pr\{\text{box is wood}\}$ as a result of the TESTs. This means that once a square is looked at and found not to contain a box, it will probably not be tested again.

The a priori values for the $\Pr\{\text{box at } (x,y)\}$ are supplied by a function that can contain considerable information about the world. If boxes are more common in the garage than in the house, this can be expressed in the probability assessments.

The results of looking at a square may have implications other than the success or failure in locating a box. An object needed to execute a competing plan may be located, thereby causing the utility of such a plan to rise. Or the information detected by LOOKAT may alter probabilities that boxes exist in surrounding squares (e.g., finding a fireplace may cause one to suspect that no boxes lie nearby; if piles of boxes are common, finding a box may increase chances of finding others nearby).

The previous discussion suggests that we look for only one box, and then use it. However, once a single box has been located, we can consider alternatives: use the one that is found or look for another one. If a second box is located, it may have higher utility than the first, or may improve the plan to use the first box because the second is available as backup.

Because acquisition operators change the world model, the results can cause widespread changes to the utilities of current plans. We could, in principle, model an acquisition operator with a large number of outcomes and generate plans for each contingency although a large number of eventually useless plans would result. A mechanism to control the amount of planning ahead and to permit periodic reevaluation of plans is clearly needed. The next section addresses this topic.

5. THE TRINITY: LOOK, THINK, ACT

At some point, the planning operations sketched in the previous sections must be halted and the best plan actually executed. In fact, planning must be severely limited, lest planning resources be wasted in any of numerous ways, such as generating detailed plans for paths that are never encountered or planning without adequate world model information or pursuing complicated elaborations that increase plan utilities only slightly. However, if planning is curtailed, we must be able to resume planning later on.

What is needed is an efficient scheduling of planning, looking, and acting. The scheduler decides in some way which activity is most beneficial at the moment, grants it a resource quantum, and then repeats. A natural quantum for looking and acting is execution of one of the "operators," such as LOOKAT or WALKTO. A natural quantum for planning might be one iteration of a branch-and-bound algorithm, or the addition of one elaboration to a plan.

The decision to plan or to execute can be made with a utility measure. We compare the utility of looking (i.e., executing a step in the best acquisition plan), acting (i.e., executing a step in the best action plan), or additional planning (i.e.,

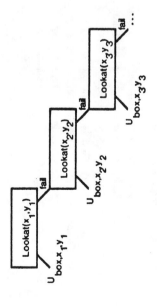

FIG. 7   Correcting failures in LOOKAT by examining more squares.

adjustments in the utilities of various available plans. This mixing of planning and acting is a uniform framework for providing ''monitoring'' and ''verification'' functions in robotics systems (Grape, 1973; Munson, 1971).

6. BEYOND THE EXAMPLE

The monkey-and-bananas example used in the preceding four sections fails to bring out some of the potential uses of decision theory. This section expands on the techniques illustrated in the example.

The Model

The design of the abstracted model of the world, comprising the symbolic operators, the outcomes of operators, and the probability and utility assessments, is a key to the performance of the system. On the one hand, we contend that a repertoire of symbolic operators alone, as used in many robotics systems, generates plans that are blatantly wasteful of resources. The augmented operators described in the monkey-and-bananas example, which include cost and reliability measures, still fall far short of a complete model of ''reality.'' Yet if the model gets too complicated, with many possible elaborations, outcomes, and failures, the search may grow unmanageably large.

Modeling the Operators. The cost/outcome model of system operators strives to summarize, in a few functions, the behavior of large, complicated subsystems for vision or action. Surely the complexity cannot be captured in a few simple functions. On the other hand, an excessively precise model of the operation of the subsystems would paralyze planning, turning it into a huge simulation. A numerical summary form for expressing performance of subsystems for vision or action which permits computation on the bounds and estimates (expectations) of performance is quite powerful.

Symbolic Models. The symbolic model gives rise to plan outlines that constrain the remaining search to *reasonable* plans. In our example, the symbolic model will not generate a plan to fly to the box; flying is not reasonable. Thus, utility analysis is not applied to arbitrary sequences of operators which violate logical conditions (i.e., sequences in which the preconditions for each step are not met) or which are not reasonably likely to achieve the given goal.

Utility Functions. The utility function must capture the tradeoffs the planning system is expected to make among reasonable plans. In the monkey-and-bananas example, we assign simple cost functions to each operator and a fixed utility to being fed. This permits tradeoffs among boxes at different locations to be expressed. However, the linear additive property of our utility function (the

---

elaborating existing plans with branch-and-bound as a guide, or developing more symbolic plans). Unfortunately, specifying a utility function that reflects the benefits of future planning is quite difficult.

Decision theorists have addressed a problem called ''cost of analysis,'' which is loosely related to the notion of planning cost used here (Matheson, 1968). In a practical analysis, the cost of building a model and assessing probability and utility values is often large enough to try to estimate the value of various alternative analyses. This calculation is often modeled as a set of initial tests of varying cost that give different sorts of information about prevailing probability distributions. The tests and their costs correspond to the various analysis choices (Matheson, 1968).

In our case, planning is the application of the model to a particular situation, which may involve substantial symbolic reasoning, tree expansion, etc. We desire simply to discount the value of a partial plan by the cost of the processing required to generate the details needed for execution.

A simple ad hoc approach can be used to *limit* planning activities, that is, to specify a stopping criterion. The difference between the upper bound and expected utilities of a plan for vision or action is a limit on the improvement in the plan that infinite planning would achieve. We have the choice between executing the plan as it stands, and receiving (on the average) the expected utility, and spending some effort planning (say, the cost is C_{plan}) and receiving, *at most*, the upper bound on the plan. Comparing the utilities of these two alternatives, we have:

Execute: ($U_{execute}$) $U_{execute} = U_{plan\ expectation}$
Plan with cost C_{plan}: (U_{plan}) $U_{plan} \leq C_{plan} + U_{upper\ bound}$

If $U_{plan} > U_{execute}$, we choose to plan. This constrains the planning effort: $C_{plan} \geq U_{plan\ expectation} - U_{upper\ bound}$. Thus the additional planning effort is limited by the difference between the upper bound and the expected utility. Obviously this is a crude approximation and could be refined.

This approach essentially compares the risk of the current plan (as estimated by the difference between the upper bound and the expectation) with the cost of further planning. It does not attempt to predict the actual value of planning, but rather measures the cost and maximum value of planning steps. It would certainly be better to use the expected value of the benefits of planning if this quantity could be computed.

The main loop of the system plans until such a stopping criterion is reached, and then either looks or acts, whichever has the greater utility. Then the process repeats. The outcomes of looking or acting are, of course, recorded and cause

1. How to decide what to look for. The utilities of competing plans provide a measure of which objects are important to the system. These measures can propagate to the lowest level of a vision subsystem, appearing as preferences of, for example, operators to locate corners or operators to measure texture. The task of assimilating low-level vision information and "recognizing" objects may also make efficient use of such information.

2. How to decide when to look. When should vision operators be invoked to locate objects needed in a particular plan? The elaboration process can apply vision operators both earlier and later, using the expected utility to decide whether improvements result. Two simple examples illustrate the need for careful consideration of when to look:

A block-stacking task requires two blocks; both are located with vision before the manipulator is used. Because one block hides another from the camera's viewpoint, locating the second block is extremely costly. If the arm had moved the first block away to a stack, the second would *then* be found easily.

A block-stacking task requires two blocks; one is located, and moved to the stack. The attempt to locate a second block fails completely—there is not one available. The goal is unsatisfiable, and could have been abandoned before manipulation effort was expended.

These simple scenarios suggest that it may be advantageous to acquire a complete world model before planning. First, as illustrated in the second example, failure to find enough parts to satisfy a goal causes failure early, which is more efficient than detecting the failure later. Second, more information often permits cleverer plans: if many blocks have been located, an optimal assignment of blocks to locations in the stack can be made (Fahlman, 1974). Third, there are often economies in making measurements in parallel. In robotics domains, this may mean that the TV camera need be read only once; or it permits planning aperture, orientation, and other parameter settings that can apply to groups of visual inquiries. (If the strategy is laid out as in Fig. 7, we can compute the expected number of LOOKAT operations required, and set the camera viewing parameters to look at the spots specified in the first LOOKATs.) In medical diagnosis, making parallel measurements may shorten hospital stays or reduce the number of costly preparations for tests (Ginsberg, 1969).

There are also advantages in delaying vision. First, better observation conditions may exist after several execution steps have been performed, as illustrated above. Second, the omnipresent opportunity to destroy information argues for delaying its gathering: if the arm drops a block on a collection of carefully located objects, the location effort is largely wasted. Third, late vision may benefit from additional world-model information which may help decide where to look.

The utility measure can express the tradeoffs between these two extremes. If, for example, toothpicks occur rarely in the world, a plan requiring a toothpick

total utility is a simple sum of independent contributions of the operators) cannot express certain preferences, especially aversion to risk.

The utility calculation can be modified to be more comprehensive. A trivial extension will express risk aversion: Let the utility of a plan be $U = f(\Sigma C_i + U_o)$, where the C_i are the costs of the steps in the plan, U_o is the contribution of the outcome, and f is a convex monotonically increasing function (see, for example, Raiffa, 1970, for an explanation of how this construction models risk). Further extension permits the costs to be interdependent; the utility is then a function of all steps in the plan.

Because the utility function will be evaluated frequently during the search and elaboration processes, the expense of its computation is important. An additive property permits the calculation of the utility of a partial path to be local and incremental, rather than global. Even if the utility of a traveler, for example, is a nonlinear function of total transit time and total fares, running totals of elapsed time and spent money can be kept with each node, and the nonlinear utility function f can be computed locally. In this case, each operator is characterized by a cost vector C_i which expresses the resources required to accomplish the step (e.g., time, energy, money, etc.). Then the total utility of a path can be written as $g(\Sigma C_i + U_o)$.

The information that must be associated with each node of the decision tree is often local and compact, as this example indicates. A few numbers for utility calculations, probability of reaching the node, and a small amount of information about state changes caused by the operator at the node suffice. If the state information needed by the symbolic problem solver can also be represented compactly, a system will be able to explore many alternatives without excessive space requirements.

Vision and Other Acquisition Operators. Historically, the vision portions of a robotics experiment have been the most complex, the most consuming of resources, and the most failure-prone of the entire system. Similarly, in a medical domain, the cost and risk of gathering information can be quite high. Consequently, we desire that a planner generate reasonable strategies for acquisition. For the purposes of planning a good overall strategy, we must strike a balance between a "black box" model of vision subsystems and a detailed model of their performance.

The important point is that a utility function is a natural way to compare differing information-gathering strategies, to measure the benefits of improving them, and so forth. We do not attempt here to expand the repertoire of basic vision techniques, but rather to provide a framework in which good vision strategies can be planned. Within the vision subsystems, additional planning will certainly occur, perhaps generating symbolic plans (e.g., acquire the chair by first scanning vertically for the chair back, then look for the seat, Garvey & Tenenbaum, 1974), or perhaps using theories of optimal testing (e.g., sequential decision theory, see deGroot, 1970; Bolles, 1976).

tem's activity is not known precisely. For example, if the subsystem is to turn on lights, we may not know whether the lights work. Elaboration can decide between two approaches by computing their utilities: either continuing obliviously, hoping that the operator worked correctly, or applying some test that is capable of determining the state of nature. If an operator were inserted by elaboration to turn on lights, the utility of the original plan without lights is known, and can be used to decide whether a test that verifies the strength of illumination increases the expected utility.

The Role of the Symbolic Problem Solver

The chief function of the symbolic problem solver is to provide plan outlines for elaboration and execution. Ideally, planning occurs at various levels of detail: the initial planning is done in a highly abstracted model of the world, with an associated abstracted utility model so that estimates of the utility of the plan can be made, thus permitting comparison of competing goals. Further planning is accomplished using more detailed models. (This technique is drawn from current symbolic problem solvers, see Sacerdoti, 1974, 1975; Sproull, 1977.)

Generating the initial plan outlines may require no search at all: a system may use so few outlines or the outlines may be so simple that they are stored as "constants" and simply retrieved for purposes of elaboration and execution. This technique is more attractive if plan outlines may contain variables (for example, the object BOX in our initial plan outline could be a variable); the symbolic problem solver instantiates an outline for each possible application. The outlines for the monkey-and-bananas problem, the wheelless student, and even for block-stacking tasks (see Fig. 8) are of this simple nature.

may be improved by locating the toothpick early. Similarly, if a particularly error-prone step may destroy information, late information gathering might be preferred. The elaboration process considers moving these vision operations to early positions in the plan; it uses the utility measure to decide whether the change is advantageous.

3. *How to decide where to look.* The main techniques used to decide where to look were discussed in the example: a probability density function and utility function on objects in the world together specify where to look. A great deal of information, both a priori information about the world and the results of previous tests and actions, can be expressed in the probabilities. The particular formulation given in the example has the virtue that the choice of squares and examination sequence has a very simple solution that requires no search. The operations research literature contains analyses of methods for searching for objects that also yield such closed-form solutions (Cozzolino, 1972).

Bayesian Models. In the monkey-and-bananas example, results of tests are modeled with Bayes' rule: a posterior probability is computed as a function of the prior probability and some properties of the test.

One problem with this technique is that it makes the often unwarranted assumption that the tests are independent. Strategy Bβ of Fig. 6 has a path that applies both TEST-FAR and TEST-NEAR. In this case, the independence assumption may be violated: if both tests are visual, they may be prone to similar errors in, say, dimly lit scenes, and hence have correlated results. In principle, this problem can be resolved by using different values for the performance of TEST-NEAR (i.e. p_{nc} and p_{nc}) if the test follows a TEST-FAR on the same box, although quantifying the dependencies may be difficult.

If the probability and utility models are extended to their most general form, in which all quantities are modeled as distributions rather than as discrete values, the expressive power of the model is enhanced. For example, Bayes' rule for the LOOKAT operator, which modifies a distribution function on the position of a box, can record the uncertainty in the location of the box. This information may be useful to calculate probabilities of success of subsequent operators. For example, the success of a GRASP operator in picking up a box with a mechanical arm depends on the precision with which the location of the box is known; the stability of a stack of boxes depends on the precision with which they are located, picked up, and stacked (Taylor, 1976). If the success of the plan is sufficiently impaired by imprecise location information, elaboration may find it beneficial to insert more precise tests that reduce the uncertainty. A simple representation of a distribution function (e.g., mean and standard deviation) may suffice for these calculations (Sproull, 1977).

Modeling Execution Operators. The planning system views "execution" as calling upon a vision or action subsystem to perform a particular task, and then recording the results. However, it may happen that the outcome of the subsys-

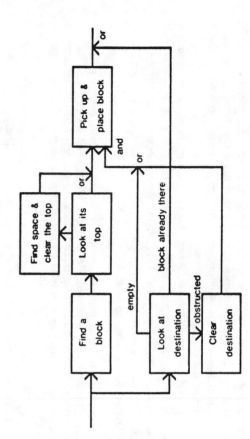

FIG. 8   A plan outline for block stacking.

inserting tests that will affect the outcome of subsequent steps, that is, tests that modify a parameter used to calculate the cost or outcome probabilities of a subsequent step. Determining how to insert tests that change the basic plan outline by changing the state of the world (e.g., tests that require the monkey to make additional moves for a better view) is very difficult.

3. Changing operators. The model may provide several operators that accomplish the same operation (from the standpoint of the symbolic model) but with different costs, or different reliabilities, etc. Thus we might have two operators: WALKTO and WALKTO-AVOIDING-OBSTACLES. The choice of operator (or subgraph of the plan outline) is controlled by utility appraisals.

4. Moving operators. If a plan outline is a sequential union of several outlines (e.g., stacking two blocks, the QA4 "buy groceries and mail a letter" problem (Rulifson, Derksen, & Waldinger, 1972), or certain assembly problems (Taylor, 1976)) it may be advantageous to reorder some of the steps. A simple case, the grouping of vision operations, was discussed above. In general, however, this is a very hard problem. The decision-theory techniques provide a useful way to decide if progress is being made, but they do not obviate the recalculation of the utility of symbolic reasoning to decide whether the plan outline remains legal.

The elaboration process has a strong parallel with trial evaluation: a plan modification is tentatively made, the utility of the new plan is computed, and the modification is saved if the utility rises. Thus a test will be inserted if its "value of information" is greater than its cost because the recalculation of the utility automatically incorporates both of these influences.

The elaboration process needs heuristics in order to keep the search reasonably efficient. The monkey-and-bananas example shows such an effect: the vision planning uses an estimate of the utility of actually using a box; the execution planning uses an estimate of the utility of locating and using a box that is currently unavailable. Figure 10 shows such a situation schematically: the utility

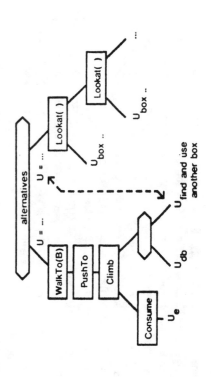

FIG. 10   Estimating a recovery utility.

The plan outlines delivered to the elaboration process require additional symbolic information. Some is "state" information that is used to match preconditions of various elaborations (e.g., TEST-NEAR information can be inserted only when the monkey and box are at the same location). Some is "recovery" information, specifying how a recovery from a particular error may be accomplished. We have already demonstrated the simplest form of this: on failure, choose another top-level alternative. More complicated error recoveries try to make a fix-up and then join the original plan again. This procedure changes the decision tree into a *graph*, and permits a somewhat more efficient search; joining an existing plan saves having to generate a fresh one. The problem solver can generate, for each outcome of an operator, one or more reasonable failure-recovery approaches. Then the elaboration process will calculate which of the approaches is best (see Fig. 9).

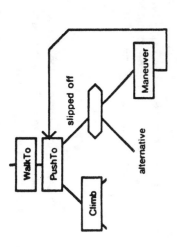

FIG. 9   A recovery strategy.

Elaborating

The elaboration process, which explores improvements to plan outlines using the utility function as a measure of progress, includes the following operations:

1. Fixing failures. Paths in the plan outline that end in failure are expanded to recover. Often, this involves pursuing another top-level alternative plan. In this case, an estimate of the utility of fixing up the failure is the current utility assessment of the top-level alternative. This is, of course, not completely correct, because the state of the world used to compute the top-level utility is not the same as that after a failure. For example, in the monkey-and-bananas problem, failure F_3 (Fig. 6) leaves the monkey under the bananas, and the ruins of a cardboard box under the monkey. Later, if the search for good strategies indicates effort should be devoted to this plan, the failure elaboration may be improved from an estimate to an explicit plan.

2. Inserting steps. The insertion of tests has already been demonstrated; the location of such insertions is governed by preconditions on the test and state information provided in the plan outline. The elaboration process only considers

of the best vision plan is used as an estimate of the utility of a recovery strategy that uses an as yet to be located alternative box; the vision calculation uses an unelaborated utility of using a box (in conjunction with any that already exist) should it be found. Thus both the vision and action planning activities each make use of the other's approximate utilities.

Looking, Thinking, Acting

The allocation of effort among the various activities of the system, looking, planning, and acting, can be thought of as a scheduler, allocating resources to the task of highest priority. Priority is, of course, determined by a utility measure. This approach has several implications for the design of the system.

First, planning is incremental. After a vision or action step, the results are recorded, perhaps causing changes in the utility or probability assignments of some pending plans, and planning is continued. Since *every* alternative plan is in some sense "active" (i.e., the planning is complete to some level of detail, at least enough to estimate a utility to compare with other plans), each outcome can cause the planner to "reexamine the alternatives," and perhaps adopt an entirely different strategy. The vision routines may also take advantage of the incremental organization, using latest utility estimates of objects needed to plan a vision strategy.

Second, the formulation helps prevent needless detailed advance planning. Some elaborations consume planning effort, although their contribution to increasing plan utility is slight; the effort is weighted by the probability of reaching a particular part of the tree. As execution progresses, however, some of these alternatives will vanish (paths not taken) and some utilities will increase, thus making detailed planning more attractive. The planning horizon at any level of abstraction thus precedes the execution in a controlled fashion. This property can be exploited to delay certain specific planning activities. An example from robot block stacking is the freespace problem: if a free spot is needed in which to place an object temporarily, it is advantageous to delay assigning the location until absolutely necessary; it may be easy to examine available alternatives at the time the space is needed.

Our simple formulation of the utility of planning can undoubtedly be considerably improved. Ideally, various intuitive measures of planning progress, such as the number of alternative branches remaining to be explored, or estimates of what clever but costly planning tricks may accomplish, could be included in the utility measure. This measure should provide ample rewards for carefully assessing the economics of planning.

7. THE PARADIGM

This paper advances the view that a combination of decision-theoretic and symbolic artificial intelligence paradigms offers advantages not available to either individually. This section explores this claim.

The Two Fields

Some readers will have already objected that our suggestions do not increase the range of problems solvable by decision theory or symbolic processing, that each is a powerful and complete paradigm, and that our remarks bear on efficiency considerations alone. The pure symbolic processor claims that he can achieve the effects we describe by dividing numeric ranges into a small number of "symbolic values" (e.g., temperature into COLD, COOL, WARM and HOT) that suffice for a given problem. Information about tradeoffs can be encoded as a set of symbolic preferences: (FED and WALKED-A-LONG-DISTANCE) is preferred to ((not FED) and WALKED-A-SHORT-DISTANCE). Or he will assess tradeoffs numerically by instantiating theorems of number theory, analysis, and algebra. This gives rise to crude and awkward models in cases where a small amount of numerical processing is more natural and accurate.

The pure mathematical programmer, on the other hand, will mathematize all constraints or move complexity into value or reward functions. He will formulate any search as a shortest path problem with appropriate arc weights and propose dynamic programming to calculate a solution. The result is often a huge state space for very simple problems, making numerical solution simply infeasible.

Practitioners of either field adopt more moderate approaches: the AI designer finds many problems suited to partially numerical approaches. Similarly, the decision theorist engages in a substantial amount of symbolic reasoning to formulate his model and to apply it intelligently to the situation; he may also use "heuristic" solution techniques on large problems. A human analyst will perform the reasoning required to build a decision tree intelligently, one that represents sensible plans. From the point of view of AI, this construction process is itself an endeavor of interest.

From the point of view of decision theory, our formulation aims to permit a computer program to emulate a good decision analyst. Such an analyst combines formulating plans and searching decision trees to arrive at a solution. A good analyst will monitor the implementation of the decisions, keeping abreast of exogenous changes in the utilities on which his solution was based, formulating additional plans, etc. Our technique attempts to emulate this activity. This is in contrast to conventional computer programs used to search one static tree exhaustively.

From the point of view of AI, the advantage of decision theory is the ability to find solutions that are "optimal" in some model. Although the approach requires a certain amount of search to find solutions, several powerful methods are available to limit the search.

1. The symbolic problem solver constrains the search later undertaken to perfect a strategy. The elaboration search does not try strategies involving many combinations of many operators, but is limited to those strategies that include certain key steps specified by the problem solver. The basic recovery strategies,

that is, the instructions for plan elaboration in case of failure, are also provided by the symbolic problem solver. Information attached to the plan outline is used to guide plan elaboration. For example, tests which have certain preconditions (e.g., that the monkey is "at" a box) are considered only at points in the plan outline that meet the conditions. A rough plan generated in simplified, abstract space, can be used to constrain the more careful planning (Sacerdoti, 1974, 1975). These are examples of basic search-limiting methods of AI not practiced in decision analysis programs.

2. A number of decision-theoretic techniques limit search. Branch-and-bound methods limit search based on bounds derived from the utility models. In addition, one can *prove* that the failure F_1 in Fig. 6 should not include paths that persist in using the same box (i.e., paths that disregard the outcome of the test): every such strategy is dominated by one that simply does not perform the test at all. Such "utility theorems" limit search.

Another example of search limiting occurs when the plan outline specifies a loop. Any paths that involve loops continue to incur increased costs as they are expanded, but the ultimate utility is fixed. The loop thus expends effort without approaching the goal; such paths will be cut off by the branch-and-bound algorithm.

3. Domain-independent heuristics can be applied to limit search. One such heuristic is to explore paths of high probability first, and perhaps be willing to bound pessimistically those paths of low probability. Although pure decision theory looks dimly on this technique because even paths of low probability may have unbounded utilities, in many cases we can meaningfully assign bounds to the utilities.

4. Domain-dependent heuristics can limit search. Although these techniques may require a certain amount of reprogramming for each new domain, they are probably far more powerful than domain-independent methods. The current AI trend toward knowledge-based systems (Bobrow & Collins, 1975; Fikes, 1976; Nilsson, 1974) is due in part to benefits of distributing domain knowledge throughout systems. Such techniques are equally applicable in our framework.

Certain of the recovery mechanisms, for example, using another top-level alternative, are domain independent, as is the method of approximating the utility of such an alternative plan.

Search-limiting heuristics are not without drawback—the resulting search may not guarantee finding the optimal solution, that is, it is not admissible. However, the utility measure still allows us to extract the best plan among those developed in the search.

The Combination

What the two fields of decision theory and artificial intelligence offer is a collection of techniques that can be applied judiciously to solve problems. There are cases when applying decision theory is difficult or adds little to AI techniques:

Insignificant costs. The benefit of optimal planning may simply be too low if the costs of the planning and execution are themselves insignificant or if the planning costs greatly exceed the execution costs.

Identical values. A problem may give rise to solutions of identical preference. A theorem-proving program may not be at all concerned with finding the shortest proof or with the expense of the search. A program that attempts to "understand" a paragraph of natural language in order to answer questions about it is likewise not concerned with optimization but with capturing a conceptual structure. In these cases, the utility function on outcomes is nearly constant, and gives no information to the search.

Both of these examples are characterized by the intuition that the domain is inherently symbolic: the understanding problem is to build a conceptual structure that is communicated as a string of words; the theorem-proving task, even as practiced by humans, is primarily symbolic manipulation. There are notions of "best" solutions in both cases, but they are second-order considerations.

Partial plans. Classical decision theory deals only with complete plans, and cannot cope with extremely large search problems in which it is impractical to enumerate all plans (e.g., chess, with 10^{160} nodes). Some AI programs deal with this problem by using a heuristic estimate of the value of a partial plan to approximate the value of a complete plan (Newell, Shaw, & Simon, 1958).

The heuristic estimate is often "backed up" through several steps of the partial plan in order to calculate the utility of the entire plan. This technique reduces somewhat the sensitivity of the overall utility calculation to errors in the heuristic estimate. In spite of this reduction, errors in the utility are a major concern (Pohl 1973). It is sometimes possible for a program to "learn" which estimates give rise to the smallest errors (Samuel, 1967).

Modeling difficulties. It may be very difficult to construct a utility and probability model that applies to the problem. Although the central theorem of decision theory shows that any choice of a "best" plan is an implied assessment of utilities and probabilities, it still may be difficult to cast the model in numerical terms.

A particularly painful aspect of this problem is presented by Bayes' rule: if we use the rule to calculate the probability distribution resulting from a sequence of tests, a potentially huge number of conditional probabilities (or probability distributions) is required. This difficulty, coupled with that of extracting probability information from humans, has led to several alternative "rules of inference" for computing likelihood information based on test outcomes (e.g., Shortliffe, 1974). This is an important current research topic.

But there are also ways in which decision theory adds considerable power.

Convenient representation. Utility and probability models are often convenient ways of representing parameters of a problem; they thereby ease parameter modification by a designer or by a user with a slightly different problem. For

the lowest planning cost. Thus although the space of outcome utilities is constant, the utilities of various alternative planning approaches are not. This second space has been important to the development of search programs; it corresponds, for example, to the evaluation functions in game-playing programs.

When the costs, uncertainties, and outcomes of the planning process itself are considered in controlling a planning and execution system, the system does "optimal planning." Although the plans generated may not be optimal, the entire process, including planning, is optimal. This suggests an extended notion of admissibility that includes consideration of planning costs.

Detection problems. AI has embraced a number of problems that have significant *detection* components: speech understanding and machine vision are the most obvious examples. The problems of efficient detection, and especially of uncertainty in the results, are at the heart of decision theory. In an AI setting, the knowledge gained from detection operations must be incorporated into higher-level reasoning that has significant symbolic components. It is perhaps in these problems that the approach we propose is most advantageous, for it unifies inherently numerical computation (detection) with symbolic reasoning (understanding). Indeed, it is these areas that gave rise to the approach and saw early applications (Bolles, 1976; Garvey & Tenenbaum, 1974; Tenenbaum, 1973; Yakimovsky & Feldman, 1974).

The fields of AI and decision theory clearly have much to offer each other; each provides insights and techniques for solutions to information-processing problems. Researchers in each discipline should learn from the other.

ACKNOWLEDGMENTS

The authors are grateful to many people, especially Dan Bobrow, whose suggestions greatly improved this paper.

APPENDIX: CLOSED FORMS, LEARNING, AND SENSITIVITY ANALYSIS

If a planner is repeatedly given similar problems to solve, much of the searching and elaboration performed each time is wasteful. Ideally, a strategy could be labeled with a set of conditions under which it is optimal; the optimal strategy can be later retrieved by examining the necessary conditions. Such conditions might take the form of rules. For example, a decision rule for the monkey-and-bananas problem with one box is:

$$\text{if } d_m < 50 \text{ then} \quad (\text{if } d_b < 3 \text{ then } A\alpha \text{ else } A\beta)$$
$$\text{else} \quad (\text{if } d_b < 8 - d_m/10 \text{ then } A\alpha \text{ else } B\alpha)$$

The variables in the rule are d_m, the distance from the monkey to the box, and d_b, the distance from the box to the bananas; all other parameters of the problem are assumed fixed to values of Table 3. The rule does not attempt to compare the

example, if a vision operator is modified to use a faster algorithm and therefore less computer time, a small modification to the utility model will suffice to alter the performance of an entire vision system correctly. It would be less obvious how to modify a set of symbolic heuristics that governs the application of the operator.

A simple utility function may express the tradeoffs among the various resources the system consumes (money, elapsed time, etc.). The information that governs the tradeoffs the system actually makes is thus localized and easily modifiable. Some such modifications can be made by the system itself in reaction to complaints about its behavior, the changes could require only simple numerical calculations to compute new parameters for the utility model. It is less obvious how a program should itself "learn" heuristics.

Finally, because decision theory is continually being applied to real-world problems, new models are built, refined, and used. For example, efforts are underway to provide doctors with decision-theory models to help plan the diagnosis and treatment of various diseases (Ginsberg, 1969; Pauker & Kassirer, 1975). Computer aids to such decision making can take advantage of the models.

Ubiquity of planning. Such models are not limited to application in traditional "AI" domains. For example, an optimizing compiler embarks upon substantial symbolic reasoning to plan efficient object code for a program; sophisticated optimizers measure or estimate how often a section of code is executed and use this as an estimate of the utility of an optimization. An extended utility structure would permit trading off different forms of optimization and including the user's utility function. Automatic programming, and in particular automatic coding (Low, 1974), seem to involve the same kinds of planning and elaboration mechanisms presented here.

Optimal planning. A decision-theoretic model of a planning process itself can be used to make planning decisions and thus to control allocation of effort to planning tasks. Many AI programs such as planners, problem solvers, parsers, and "understanders" require such guidance in the application of available methods: Is it more important to plan further ahead or to investigate detail of the current plan (Sacerdoti, 1974)? How far should consequences of a situation be investigated (Rieger, 1975)? Increasingly, this problem becomes one of controlling a number of processes which are "triggered" by various changes in the world model, and which are responsible for exploring consequences of the change (Bobrow & Winograd, 1976). If two alternative parsings of a sentence appear similar in a crude analysis, should one be examined in detail, or should both be explored uniformly (Paxton & Robinson, 1973)? How are alternative hypotheses pursued (Woods, 1974)?

Even if the plans themselves have constant utility, optimal planning is useful. For example, in a theorem prover, we are given a set of clauses and must decide which of several resolutions to make; if we can calculate the cost of planning a solution from a given set of clauses, we choose the resolution which gives rise to

eating strategies to plans for pursuing other goals. Rather, it is a convenient way to retrieve a good strategy based on a small number of symbolic requirements (existence of bananas and box) and some parameters (C_s, p_s, and d_s). After retrieving the best eating strategy, its utility can be compared with that of other plans.

Unfortunately, generating concise rules to cover a wide variety of situations is not a trivial task. We can, of course, always resort to planning and searching decision trees if a precomputed strategy is lacking. Furthermore, the results of each search could be stored for ready reference in the future. But a deeper problem makes this difficult: if small changes to any parameter result in different strategies, the number of rules could grow unreasonably large.

We could try to partition the space of parameter values, associating a rule with each cell of the partition. The problem then is to find an appropriate partition. One technique for developing a partition might be called "learning." Initially, a coarse partition is chosen, and strategies or rules are associated with each cell as needed. In addition, a number is kept with each cell that records the average utility actually achieved by the strategy in the past. If this number falls substantially below the expected utility of the strategy, we suspect that the strategy is not valid throughout the cell, and refine the partition. Such a scheme is used in Yakimovsky and Feldman (1974) under manual control.

Alternatively, sensitivity analysis can help devise a partition. Such analysis, if it can be carried out, can answer questions such as "Over what range of parameter values is a strategy rule such as the example valid?" Insignificant changes in the utility, to which the planner is indifferent, need not cause repartitioning. In simple cases when the symbolic expressions for utility calculations are available, partial differentiation can help determine the effect of parameter changes on the utility.

Sensitivity analysis is useful to the planner even if we are not computing a partition. During elaboration, the usefulness of a test that measures a particular parameter is gauged by the change in utility as a result of a change in parameter value. Also, since many of the parameter values may be only approximate, or even subject to gross errors because of unreliable measurements of the state of nature, the sensitivity analysis can warn of gross changes in strategy within the range of parameter variation.

REFERENCES

Bobrow, D. G., & Collins, A. (Eds.) *Representation and understanding*. New York: Academic Press, 1975.

Bobrow, D. G., & Raphael, B. New programming languages for AI research. *Computing Surveys*, 1974, **6**, No. 3.

Bobrow, D. G., & Winograd, T. An overview of KRL, a knowledge representation language. Computer Sciences Laboratory, Xerox Palo Alto Research Center, 1976. Published in *Cognitive Science* 1, 1977, 3–46.

Bolles, R. Vision for automated assembly. PhD thesis, Computer Science Dept., Stanford University, 1976.

Chernoff, H., & Moses, L. *Elementary decision theory*. New York: Wiley, 1959.

Cozzolino, J. M. Search for an unknown number of objects of nonuniform size. *Operations Research*, 1972, **20**, 293.

deGroot, M. H. *Optimal statistical decisions*. New York: McGraw-Hill, 1970.

Fahlman, S. A planning system for robot construction tasks. *Artificial Intelligence*, 1974, **5**, No. 1.

Feldman, J. A., Low, J. R., Taylor, R., and Swinehart, B. Recent developments in SAIL—An ALGOL-based language for artificial intelligence. *Proceedings of the Fall Joint Computer Conference*, 1972.

Fikes, R. E. Knowledge representation in automatic planning systems. Tech. Note 119, Artificial Intelligence Center, Stanford Research Institute, Menlo Park, California, 1976.

Fikes, R. E., & Nilsson, N. J. STRIPS: A new approach to the application of theorem proving in problem solving. *Artificial Intelligence*. 1971, **2**, 189.

Garvey, T., & Tenenbaum, J. M. On the automatic generation of programs for locating objects in office scenes. *Proceedings of the Second International Joint Conference on Pattern Recognition*, IEEE 74-CH0885-4C, August 1974, p. 162.

Ginsberg, A. S. Decision analysis in clinical patient management with an application to the pleural effusion problem. PhD thesis, Stanford University, 1969.

Grape, G. Model based (intermediate level) computer vision. PhD thesis, Computer Science Dept., Stanford University, Stanford, California, 1973.

Hart, P., Nilsson, N. J., & Raphael, B. A formal basis for the heuristic determination of minimum cost paths. *IEEE Transactions on Systems Science and Cybernetics*, 1968, **SSC-4**, 100.

Lawler, E. and Wood, D. Branch and bound methods: a survey. *Operations Research*, 1966, **14**, 699.

Low, J. R. Automatic coding: choice of data structures. Stanford Artificial Intelligence Project AIM 242, Stanford, Calif., August 1974.

Matheson, J. E. The economic value of analysis and computation. *IEEE Transactions on Systems Science and Cybernetics*, 1968, **SSC-4**, 325.

Munson, J. H. Robot planning, execution and monitoring in an uncertain environment. *Proceedings of the Second International Joint Conference on AI*. September, 1971, p. 338.

Newell, A., Shaw, J., & Simon, H. Chess playing programs and the problem of complexity. *IBM Journal of Research and Development*. 1958, **2**, 320. Reprinted in E. Feigenbaum & J. Feldman (Eds.), *Computers and thought*. New York: McGraw-Hill, 1963.

Nilsson, N. J. Artificial intelligence. *Proc. IFIP Congress*, 1974, p. 778.

Nilsson, N. J. *Problem-solving methods in artificial intelligence*. New York: McGraw-Hill, 1971.

Pauker, S. G., & Kassirer, J. P. Therapeutic decision making: A cost-benefit analysis. *New England Journal of Medicine*. 1975, **239**, 229–234.

Paxton, W. H., & Robinson, A. E. A parser for a speech understanding system. *Proceedings of the Third International Joint Conference on AI*. August, 1973, p. 216.

Pohl, I. The avoidance of (relative) catastrophe, heuristic competence, genuine dynamic weighting and computational issues in heuristic problem solving. *Proceedings of the Third International Joint Conference on AI*. August 1973, p. 12.

Raiffa, H. *Decision analysis: introductory lectures on choices under uncertainty*. Reading, Mass.: Addison Wesley, 1970.

Rieger, C. J. Conceptual memory. In R. Schank (Ed.), *Conceptual information processing*. Amsterdam: North-Holland, 1975.

Rulifson, J. F., Derksen, J. A., & Waldinger, R. J. QA4: A procedural calculus for intuitive reasoning. Tech. Note 73, Artificial Intelligence Center, Stanford Research Institute, Menlo Park, California, 1972.

Sacerdoti, E. Planning in a hierarchy of abstraction spaces. *Artificial Intelligence*, 1974, **5**, 115–135.

Sacerdoti, E. A structure for plans and behavior. Tech. Note 109, Artificial Intelligence Center, Stanford Research Institute, Menlo Park, California, 1975.

Samuel, A. L. Some studies in machine learning using the game of checkers, II. Recent progress. *IBM Journal of Research and Development*, 1967, **11**, No. 6.

Shortliffe, E. H. MYCIN: A rule-based computer program for advising physicians regarding antimicrobial therapy selection. AI Memo 251, Stanford Artificial Intelligence Project, Stanford, Calif., October, 1974.

Slagle, J. R., & Lee. R. C. T. Application of game tree searching techniques to sequential pattern recognition. *Communications of the ACM*, 1971, **14**, 103.

Sproull, R. F. Strategy construction using a synthesis of heuristic and decision-theoretic methods. PhD thesis, Computer Science Dept., Stanford University, 1977.

Taylor, R. H. Assembly Robot Program Automation. PhD thesis, Computer Science Dept., Stanford University, 1976.

Tenenbaum, J. M. On locating objects by their distinguishing features in multisensory images. *Computer graphics and image processing*, 1973, **2**, No. 3/4.

Tversky, A., & Kahneman, D. Judgement under uncertainty: heuristics and biases. *Science*, 1974, **185**, No. 4157, 1124.

Woods, W. A. Motivation and overview of BBN Speechlis: An experimental prototype for speech understanding research. *IEEE Symposium on Speech Recognition*, IEEE 74-CH0878-9 AE, April 1974.

Yakimovsky, Y., & Feldman, J. Decision theory and artificial intelligence: I. A semantics-based region analyzer. *Artificial Intelligence*, 1974, **5**, 349–371.

Planning and Acting*

DREW MCDERMOTT

Yale University

A new theory of problem solving is presented, which embeds problem solving in the theory of action; in this theory, a problem is just a difficult action. Making this work requires a sophisticated language for talking about plans and their execution. This language allows a broad range of types of action, and can also be used to express rules for choosing and scheduling plans. To ensure flexibility, the problem solver consists of an interpreter driven by a theorem prover which actually manipulates formulas of the language. Many examples of the use of the system are given, including an extended treatment of the world of blocks. Limitations and extensions of the system are discussed at length. It is concluded that a rule-based problem solver is necessary and feasible, but that much more work remains to be done on the underlying theory of planning and acting.

1. INTRODUCTION

The following are all examples of *problems:*

Move these disks from this peg to that one, one at a time, moving only the top disk from one peg to another, and avoiding ever having a larger disk resting on a smaller disk.

Design a stereo system that has a linear frequency response over the range of human hearing, and that sells for less than $500.

Keep our political enemies from finding out who authorized the break-in at opposition headquarters and the payment of hush money to the burglars.

Win this chess game.

Live on a professional salary.

Don't overcook the beans.

Find a way for John to keep his mistress without Mary getting angry.

The theory of problem solving is the study of problems and their solutions. The literature in this theory (Ernst & Newell, 1969; Nilsson, 1971; Newell & Simon, 1972; Rieger & London, 1977; Sacerdoti, 1975; Schank & Abelson, 1977; Siklossy & Dreussi, 1973; Sussman, 1975) shows that the theory is still in its infancy. No two authors agree on what a problem or a solution is. There is no universally agreed-upon set of methods for obtaining solutions.

The purpose of this paper is to present yet another theory of problem solving. In some ways it is general enough to encompass more types of problem than previous theories, but generality in some areas has constrained the theory too much in others. Fortunately, experience with it, and a computer program, the NASL interpreter, based on it, points the way toward improvements. I will deal with the theory, the implementation, and the improvements, in that order.

A brief precis of that theory: problem solving is part of the study of *action*. A problem is a difficult action. Solving a problem is the construction and successful execution of a plan to carry it out. Doing this efficiently depends on shallow deduction about evolving plans and the effects of actions.

Before I begin, let me sketch what I think the goals of a theory of problem solving are (cf. Newell & Simon, 1972). There are several goals such a theory might have:

Power. A theory will include a set of solution techniques. The more types of problem these techniques solve, the more successful the theory.

Analytical adequacy. A theory must contain notations for problems, plans, events, causes and effects, and more. The more these notations allow us to say, the better this goal will be met. (McCarthy has called this "epistemological" adequacy; see McCarthy & Hayes, 1969.)

Heuristic adequacy. Some of the notations I just described will be available to the problem solver the theory discusses. We would like for rules and facts expressed in these notations to be accessible at the appropriate times. (This concept is also due to McCarthy.) We can distinguish two subgoals here: *weak heuristic adequacy* for a given set of facts is met by producing any program at all that can be shown to embody all those facts; *strong heuristic adequacy* for a notation is met by a program which can accept any set of facts in the notation and make use of them. The highest level in this sequence in *additivity,* achieved by a strongly heuristically adequate program which can accept one new fact at a time and reconfigure itself incrementally to make use of it.

Application independence. A theory of problem solving may support implementation of a problem solver, but there are other possible applications. For example, the theory is involved in understanding the actions of other planners (Schank & Abelson, 1977; Wilensky, 1977).

Empirical veracity. If the theory is intended to be a theory of *human* plan formation and understanding, it must explain what humans can and cannot do as much as possible.

There is no theory today which even attempts to meet all of these goals. Mine is no exception. In fact, the only goals I have kept in mind are analytical

*Much of the work reported herein was conducted at the Artificial Intelligence Laboratory, a Massachusetts Institute of Technology research program supported in part by the Advanced Research Projects Agency of the Department of Defense, and monitored by the Office of Naval Research under contract number N00014-75-C-0643. The rest was supported by a Josiah Willard Gibbs Instructorship at Yale University.

Request for reprints should be sent to the author at Department of Computer Science, Yale University, 10 Hillhouse Avenue, New Haven, Conn. 06520.

adequacy and additivity. Whatever power a problem solver based on my theory has will be due to its ability to retrieve knowledge about plans. Application independence is met only to the degree that it is encouraged by the flexibility required for additivity. Empirical veracity has not played a part except as a loose guide.

2. A THEORY OF PLANNING AND ACTING

A *problem solver* operates by *reducing problems* to simpler subproblems repeatedly until immediately solvable (*primitive*) problems are reached. The result is a *plan* which must be *executed* in order to realize a solution to the problem. (These definitions are to some extent arbitrary. All of these terms have been used in other ways.)

This is an abstract description of a problem solver (cf. Nilsson, 1971). To get a useful theory, we must be more precise about the details. Here are some design decisions that must be made:

1. What is a problem? What does it mean for one to be reduced?
2. Is the choice of reduction deterministic?
3. How are simultaneous subproblems handled?
4. Is execution necessary? (Sometimes a plan is all we care about.)
5. How are planning and execution interleaved?
6. How are errors at planning and execution time handled?

To begin, let us construe the notion of problem very broadly. In previous theories, a problem has often been characterized as a state of affairs to be brought about or an object to be generated (Newell & Simon, 1972). For example, a problem solver like NOAH (Sacerdoti, 1975) or GPS (Ernst & Newell, 1969) can have the goal, "Get block A on block B and block B on block C." This is certainly an important class of problems. However, there are many problems which do not fit into this mold, such as

"Prevent Little Nell from being mashed by the train."
"Wait here for five minutes."
"Promise me you will pay me five dollars."
"Think of a fallible Irishman."
"Avoid firing the budget director while retaining credibility."
"Keep track of the number of sheep on this birch bark."
"Design a circuit which converts a square wave into a sine wave."

One could think of artificial ways of forcing these to be state changes. (E.g., "Think of an x" could be "Get the name of an x into your STM.") But about all they really have in common is that they can be described as "actions" of various degrees of abstractness. Some actions bring states about, some alter the course of events, some are purely mental, and some can be described only as influencing the execution of other actions.

So I introduce the notion of *task*—any describable action to which the interpreter is committed. A *problem* is then any task whose action cannot be immediately carried out. Reducing such a task amounts to finding a collection of *subtasks* such that the problem task may be carried out by doing all the subtasks. The collection of subtasks is called a *plan*.

Before I proceed with a description of how problems are solved, I should add a little structure to the apparently amorphous notion of "task." Tasks can be classified along three dimensions (Fig. 1). (This list is not necessarily exhaustive.)

PROBLEMATICITY
  Primitive
  Problematic
MONASTICISM
  Inferential
  Worldly
PARASITISM
  Primary
  Secondary

FIG. 1 Taxonomies of actions.

The first I have already described. A task is either primitive (in various ways to be described later), or it is problematic, and requires a plan of execution. The second classification is on the basis of whether the action has any effects in the "real world." If not, it is said to be *inferential*. Otherwise, it is *worldly*. "Think of a fallible Irishman" is inferential. The classification by parasitism is to distinguish *primary* actions, whose intent may be specified in isolation, from *secondary* actions, which are executed successfully by executing some other task in a particular way. For example, the task, "Win the war without alienating the middle class," may be reduced to two tasks, "Win the war," and "Avoid alienating the middle class." The first of these is primary, the second is parasitic upon it. A secondary task is also called a *policy*. Such a task may be primitive or problematic, just like a primary task.

When a problematic task is to be reduced, a problem solver needs to construct a collection of subtasks that together suffice to carry it out. Several mechanisms for doing this have been tried (Ernst & Newell, 1969; Hewitt, 1972; McDermott, 1977a; Rieger, 1976). All use some variant of the procedure, "Extract 'features' of the problem statement, and use them to retrieve subproblem schemata (via an 'index' of some kind) which can be instantiated to give a plan." An indexed collection of subproblem schemata is called a *plan schema*. In the index, each plan schema has some kind of description of when it is appropriate; the description must "match" the extracted features in some way. (I am being vague here in order to be general. For concreteness, let me mention that this retrieval job is carried out in NASL by a theorem prover operating on a PLANNER-type data base. This is to increase the chances of achieving strong heuristic adequacy. See Section 3.)

No matter how the retrieval is accomplished, we must deal with the issue of what to do if more than one reduction of a problem presents itself. One thing a problem solver can do is explore all possibilities, by backtracking or more sophisticated control regimes. This choice leads to the classic AND/OR graph-search idea (Nilsson, 1971).

Unfortunately, this approach is unsuitable if we want to deal with both planning and execution. If execution is included in the problem-solving process, then at some point one plan must be selected to guide action in the "real world." If it fails, the state of the world will in general have been changed enough by the attempt so that the alternative plans are out of date.

Here is a situation in which human performance is a guide. Humans rely on a rather different approach from AND/OR graph search: they try something, wait until an error has been made, and then correct it. The difference between the two approaches is simple. If the "state of the world" is thought of as an internal data structure, completely under control, it is just as easy or easier to return to an earlier state and try something else as it is to generate a new one. But if states of the world are really states of the whole wide world, over which one's information is limited and one's control slight, quite the opposite is the case.

In many applications, the choice is clear. If you are building a robot, you must treat the real world with respect. In other cases, it is fairly clear that the problem solver is the master of the situation. A plan for doing an indefinite integration is, in a sense, already executed as soon as it is found.

For many interesting problem domains, however, we can choose to distinguish between planning and execution, even if all the action ultimately takes place only in the problem solver's head. For example, in the domain of electronic circuit design (McDermott, 1977b), taking this attitude amounts to treating the current circuit model as though it were a diagram on a piece of paper. Altering such a diagram requires actually erasing lines or starting with a fresh sheet of paper, and is not a matter of simply "popping things off a stack." This attitude is appropriate any time a problem model is so complex that the system cannot assign responsibility for every feature of it. (Otherwise, bookkeeping techniques exist for undoing exactly the right things in case of error. These techniques are called "dependency-directed backtracking"; see Stallman & Sussman, 1977.)

In most problem areas, we do not know how to assign responsibility in all cases. Besides, we want a theory that is general enough to apply to real-world problem solution. Therefore, I have made the following design decision: every task has just one reduction. The plan representation is a pure "AND" graph.

One way to achieve this is to insist that plan schemata be indexed in such a way that only one schema is retrieved in reducing a task. If two schemata perform similar actions, they must be differentiated by adding enough clauses to their descriptions to ensure that the circumstances under which they would be retrieved are disjoint. However, this approach tends to defeat additivity. A new schema could not be judged in isolation; it would be erroneous if its description overlapped that of another schema. At best, this approach leads to large, unreadable schema descriptions, reversing the recent trend in "knowledge engineering" (Feigenbaum, 1977) toward representing information as sets of small rules, the ideal being for each fact about a problem domain to correspond to one rule. These rules may be used in explaining things to a user (cf. Davis, 1976), so the rules themselves must not require explanation. Besides, the same rules may be involved in different competitions later, and will need further revision. The more unreadable they become, the harder this will be for the user. (By "user" I usually mean the domain expert whose knowledge is being translated into plan schemata.)

Consider an example from the domain of electronic circuit design (McDermott, 1977b). If acquiring a common-collector amplifier is known to be a good way of achieving high input impedance, this fact may be represented by describing "Make a common-collector" as a good way to carry out, "Make an amplifier," in the presence of a high-impedance requirement. Now, say that the system is to be told about field-effect transistors (FETs). Since they have a high input impedance, a very similar fact will be added regarding the FET "common-source" amplifier. A request to make an amplifier will cause both of these schemata to be retrieved. We could force the user to revise one or both of the schema descriptions until only one is appropriate in this situation. But this will make revision harder if FETs later compete with vacuum tubes.

To add to all the trouble, sometimes the user will want to be able to express rules for synthesizing a brand new alternative task reduction "on the fly" when two task reductions have been suggested in response to different aspects of a situation.

The solution is to face up to the necessity for treating "choice between alternatives" as a basic situation of problem solving. When two or more task reductions present themselves, the problem solver must *choose* among them. Since there is no general criterion for such a choice, the choice process must be able to retrieve *choice rules* by methods similar in principle to those used for retrieving plans (in my theory, using the same theorem prover). These rules can select among alternatives, or replace them with new ones.

One reason choice rules must be ad hoc is that the choice of a task reduction can depend on what other tasks are simultaneously active. This raises the issue of coordination of simultaneous subproblem solutions. In a sense, this is the main issue in problem solving. There are many ways in which tasks can interfere with each other. Executing one task the wrong way can make other tasks impossible (Ernst & Newell, 1969). For example, if you cool your coffee by mixing it with antifreeze, it is no longer possible to drink it. Scheduling tasks in the right order can be important (Sacerdoti, 1975). Painting yourself into a corner may be thought of as a scheduling error. There may be resources like money to be allocated to several tasks (Freeman & Newell, 1971). Spending too much on one solution can block solving other tasks.

There are so many kinds of task conflict that there are probably no general ways to handle all of them. Instead, I have opted for provision of formal mechanisms by which user rules can guide task coordination. User rules can, in particular, guide choosing and scheduling of plans. In extreme cases, plan schemata can be tailor-made for reducing *sets* of tasks. For example, in engineering design an engineer will know several standard mechanisms which have more than one purpose. A good chess move often has more than one purpose. Such plans are sometimes necessary for efficiency, sometimes essential for there to be any solution at all to a set of problems.

With these design decisions made, we can turn to a very difficult matter: the relation between planning and execution. To what degree are planning and execution interleaved? Is all execution postponed until completion of planning? Or should a problem solver be able to execute incomplete plans?

Previous systems, such as STRIPS (Fikes & Nilsson, 1971) and NOAH (Sacerdoti, 1975), have usually developed a complete plan (at some level of abstraction) before trying to execute it. The problem with doing things this way is that the proper plan for a task usually depends upon the state of the world when the task is to be executed, and this state is difficult to compute in advance. (It would be easier if all actions could be defined as state changes.)

Therefore, I have made practically the opposite decision. In my theory, tasks may be executed as soon as scheduling rules permit. Executing a "problematic" task means reducing it and executing the resulting subtasks. Executing a primitive task means calling a piece of LISP code. (Actually, many primitives are defined as a list of changes to the world model, which are just carried out. See below.)

This control regime causes planning and execution to be tightly interleaved. In fact, the problem solver does not distinguish two different "phases." It picks a task to work on, executing it if it is primitive, reducing it otherwise. This arrangement prevents the system from trying to reduce a task unless it can be executed. This bars it from employing an algorithm like Sacerdoti's (1975) "reduce-criticize" loop. This is the price it pays for being able to execute very general actions.

Let me summarize the system so far. A problem is a nonprimitive task. A task is an arbitrary, nameable activity, which may be defined in terms quite remote from simple state changes. A plan for a problem is a network of subtasks to carry it out. (The network links are subtask and scheduling relationships.) Tasks are reduced by retrieving and instantiating plan schemata. If more than one is found, choice rules are retrieved and used to choose among them. Primitive tasks are executed as soon as scheduling rules allow.

This theory is rather different from the usual AND/OR graph-search theory. It raises some new issues: What happens if no task reduction can be retrieved? What if executing a task fails? How does one tell when a task is successful? How does one reedit the task network? All of these questions fall within the area of *error correction.* The first concerns planning errors; the rest, execution errors. A planning error occurs when no plan can be found to reduce a task. In the

AND/OR tradition, this is a sign that a wrong choice was made sometime in the past, so the current branch of the AND/OR tree should be pruned. In my theory, choices are made under the guidance of choice rules, so they are assumed to be correct; besides, the alternatives have not been retained. The only thing left to do is "try harder." A problem which cannot be solved as stated must be *restated.* For example, a problem in electronics that is intractable in the time domain may be easy to solve in the frequency domain. I do not have a "general theory of restatement" (but see McDermott, 1977b, and cf. Mark, 1977, and Moore & Newell, 1974). The theory merely specifies that transforming a task into a solvable set of tasks may itself become a task of the system. This is called *rephrasing.*

My theory of execution errors is still fairly primitive. The basic notion of this theory is that correcting an error is to be treated as a task like any other. There is no outside monitor like a backtracker (Ernst & Newell, 1969; Stallman & Sussman, 1977) or triangle-table searcher (Fikes, 1971) to put the problem solver back on the track. Instead, I distinguish a set of error-correcting actions. Any task with an error-correcting subtask that has not been finished yet is said to be *failing.* For example, remembering something you forgot to pick up at the supermarket is to be modeled as creating an error-correcting task to go and get it. Until this task is finished, the task, "Go shopping," is failing. The way in which this is done will be described in the next section. The main weakness of the theory is that it does not allow a failing task to be abandoned. I will describe in Section 5 alterations to the error-correction machinery to make it more flexible.

3. IMPLEMENTATION

My intent so far has been to provide a set of concepts broad enough to be useful in talking of problem solving. This has been in pursuit of analytical adequacy. Before proceeding, I would like to sketch my approach to strong heuristic adequacy. It is important not just that *we* have a theory of action, that is, a notation for talking about problems and solutions, but that the problem solver itself have access to the same notations. The way I have arranged this has been described in earlier papers (McDermott, 1977a,b,c). The problem solver maintains a data base of predicate-calculus statements, some of which describe the state of the world, and some of which describe the state of the problem solver. The data base is managed by a theorem prover which does forward deductions from formulas as they are added to the data base, and backward deductions to retrieve plan schemata and choice rules. The notation for tasks and plans must be rich enough to ensure that these deductions are short and fast. That is, most of what the system wants to know about the current solution attempt must already be in the plan representation. The operation of the theorem prover STP is beyond the scope of this paper (see McDermott, 1977d). In the course of explaining the task network interpreter, I will describe relevant aspects of the deductive language and inferer.

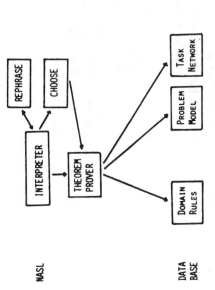

FIG. 2 The NASL problem solver.

The deductive language has the following syntax: Formulas consist of functions or predicates and their arguments, enclosed in parentheses. "Block A is on block B" might be presented (ON A B). (This syntax is slightly simplified from that used in McDermott, 1977b.) Formulas are used to describe the state of the problem, and the rules governing them. LISP data structures are used to represent only transient state information. The state of the problem solver is defined by formulas which specify the current tasks and the relationships between them.

A word of warning: The description of the implementation gets a little messy in places. The vocabularies for describing the problem solver's state are rather large—for good reasons, I believe (McDermott, 1977c). It would be nice if the meanings of all of these formulas could be given independently of how the problem solver uses them. Then, after you understood their intended meanings, I could tell you how the problem solver worked. The only remaining task would be to convince you that the solver was faithful to the semantics (cf. Hayes, 1977). Unfortunately, I am very far from being able to do this; the way the problem solver handles the formulas *is* what they mean. I will discuss ways in which this situation could be improved in Section 5. For now, try not to get too bogged down, but appreciate the many places where the problem-solving interpreter does clever things.

To begin, tasks are defined by formulas of this form:

```
(TASK name ⟨ -input-pvars- ⟩
    (LAMBDA ( -vars- ) action)
    ⟨ -output-pvars- ⟩)
```

The tuples of "input pvars" and "output pvars" are used for passing information from one task to another. ("Pvar" abbreviates "plan variable.") Unlike the notations of most problem solvers, this one allows information to be computed by one step and passed to the next. This would be necessary for execution of the plan, "Think of someone who would be willing to lend you $100, and ask him for it," as a way of getting $100. Here is how these tasks might be described:

```
(TASK GET-MONEY ⟨⟩
    (LAMBDA ( ) (ACHIEVE '(I have $100))) ⟨⟩)

(TASK FIND-SUCKER ⟨⟩
    (LAMBDA ( ) (FIND (LAMBDA (X)
                (?X would be willing to give me $100))))
    ⟨'(SUCKER-1)⟩)

(TASK SQUEEZE ⟨'(SUCKER-1)⟩
    (LAMBDA (X) (ask ?X for $100)) ⟨⟩)

(SUBTASK FIND-SUCKER GET-MONEY)
(SUBTASK SQUEEZE GET-MONEY)
(SUCCESSOR FIND-SUCKER SQUEEZE)
```

The lower-case parts of these formulas are those I do not care to try to formalize. The rest is authentic NASL notation. ("?" prefixes bound and free variables. The single quotes marking certain subformulas are intended to indicate that the "meaning" rather than the "value" of an expression is referred to. All this means for our purposes is that substitution of equals into a quoted context is not allowed.) The task SQUEEZE takes as input the person thought of by the task FIND-SUCKER. The last three formulas indicate relationships holding between tasks. The first task is a supertask of the other two, which together make up the plan for carrying it out. In addition, the "find" task is a predecessor of the "ask" task. The execution of a successor is supposed to be postponed until execution of its predecessors has been taken care of. (I will be more precise about this below.)

Pvar values are kept in the data base in formulas of the form

$$(\Rightarrow \text{'pvar value})$$

This is not the only use of this notation. In general, $(\Rightarrow \text{'x y})$ is a version of equality which prescribes replacing a formula subsumed by x with the appropriate instance of y whenever the theorem prover generates one (cf. Bledsoe & Tyson, 1975). The single quote is necessary to keep the system from rewriting $(\Rightarrow x\ y)$ as $(\Rightarrow y\ y)$. The main loop of the interpreter is:

Pick a task to work on

If it is primitive,

Then Execute it
Else Reduce it
Repeat until there are no more tasks

The first step of the interpreter cycle, picking a task, is done in cooperation with a system of forward deduction of SUCCESSOR relations. The axioms that support these deductions are the user's responsibility. (The system will insert a SUCCESSOR link between a task that sets a pvar and one that uses it. So the link between FIND-SUCKER and SQUEEZE above would be inserted by the system.)

The system chooses at random from the tasks it is permitted to do next by existing SUCCESSOR relationships. This may sound computationally expensive, but it is not. When a task is created, it is given two "statuses," which go through various transitions. Its *task status* is an indication of whether work has begun on it, and whether it is finished. Its *enablement status* expresses its relation to other tasks.

TASK-STATUS:	PENDING		ACTIVE	FINISHED
ENAB-STATUS:	BLOCKED	ENABLED	SUBS-ENABLED	SUCCS-ENABLED

FIG. 3 Life history of a task.

These stages in the life of a task are represented by formulas of the form:

(⇒ '(TASK-STATUS task) pending-active-finished)
(⇒ '(ENAB-STATUS task) blocked-enabled-etc)

It should be clear what the three task statuses mean. The task-status is used mainly by user rules. The interpreter is interested in the enab-status. The scheduling I mentioned before is accomplished by picking an enabled task at random.

A task is enabled when all of its predecessors have entered the state "succs-enabled," and all of its supertasks have entered the state "subs-enabled." Whenever a task enters either of these two states, the interpreter recomputes the enab-status of all its successors or subtasks.

Notice that a task can have its successors enabled before it is finished. This is to allow a task to be reduced to main steps plus cleanup steps that do not have to be done before one can go on. For example, if pounding a nail into the wall is a predecessor to some other task, like hanging a picture on it, the hammer does not have to be put away before the picture is hung, even though putting away the hammer is a subtask of pounding a nail into something (cf. Charniak, 1976). If a subtask does have to be done before its supertask's successors can be begun, we write (MAIN subtask supertask).

Another feature to notice is that the interpreter will choke if there is a loop of SUCCESSOR links among a group of tasks; that is, if a task is related to itself by a chain of such links. Such a task will never become enabled. In the current implementation, it is the user's responsibility to prevent this from happening.

Once a task is picked, the interpreter goes to work on it. (Before doing so, it changes its status from PENDING to ACTIVE.) First the interpreter finds all the input pvars' values, and applies the action slot of the task definition to them to get a *task action*. In the example I gave before, if FIND-SUCKER sets (SUCKER-1) to JOE, the task action of SQUEEZE will be "ask JOE for $100."

What the interpreter does now depends upon whether the task action is primitive or problematic. An action can be primitive in two ways. There is a set of primitives built in to NASL, which are defined by LISP functions. In addition, the user can supply an open-ended set of primitives defined by "model-manipulation axioms." These are deductive rules used to conclude formulas of the form

(MOD-MANIP task-name action deletelist addlist)

where the deletelist and addlist are tuples of propositions. For example, we might define MOVE with

(→ (AND (AT ?X ?PLACE1) (NOT (= ?PLACE1 ?PLACE2))
    (MOD-MANIP ?TASK (MOVE ?X ?PLACE2)
      ⟨'(AT ?X ?PLACE1)⟩
      ⟨'(AT ?X ?PLACE2)⟩))

meaning, "If something is at one place, moving it to a different place leaves it there." ("P implies Q" is written (→ P Q). In the actual system, you have to tell the system the direction in which to use the implication (Hewitt, 1972; McDermott, 1977b).) This is all very traditional; see Fikes and Nilsson (1971). Executing this action involves updating the current "data pool" representing what the theorem prover believes (McDermott, 1977b).

A few primitives are defined by LISP functions, which are just executed to carry out the primitive. Sometimes the function does something or returns a value. A very common "primitive" is DO-SUBNET, which is used to annex an entire subnet, and actually does nothing itself. The action

(DO-SUBNET plan-schema pvars-map)

instantiates a plan schema. This is the way canned plans are referenced for use in reducing tasks. The schema instance is created by making up a name for it and recording

(PLAN-INSTANCE name plan-schema super-task)

It is up to the user to supply forward deduction rules to cause the appropriate subtasks to be inferred.

enters its special "choice" or "rephrasing" protocol, which I will describe in a moment.

There is a circumstance under which all of this machinery will be bypassed. If NASL finds a problematic task for which the formula

```
(REDUCED task-name)
```

is already in the data base, it does nothing but enable its subtasks. This is to handle tasks which are reduced entirely by forward deduction. For example, a plan schema may have subtasks which carry out more than the task the schema is indexed under. These side benefits are indicated by formulas of the form

```
(→ (PLAN-INSTANCE ?PI schema ?SUP)
   (REDUCED some-other-task))
```

So far I have described what happens when the theorem prover retrieves exactly one way to carry out a problematic task. I discussed in Section 2 the need for a choice mechanism when more than one is retrieved. This is box labeled CHOOSE in Fig. 2.

The first thing the chooser does is to create a new "choice situation," defined by a formula of the form

```
(CHOICE name context goal-formula)
```

The system makes up a name. The context depends upon whether the system is making the choice of a task reduction, in which case it will be the symbol EXEC, or whether it is making the choice of an object to carry out an inferential task (usually with action (FIND pred)), in which case the context will be the name of the inferential task. Finally, the "goal-formula" is a representation of the theorem-prover goal that is giving trouble. This cannot be a proposition, since we want to be able to ask questions like, "Is this piece of the goal formula a variable?" (NASL is in principle very Tarskian!) It is in fact a data structure representing a proposition. I indicate this by surrounding such an object with [brackets].

I will use an example from the domain of electronic circuit design (McDermott, 1977b). The choice of a way to make an amplifier would be begun by recording

```
(CHOICE C53 EXEC
        [TO-DO TSK437 (MAKE AMPLIFIER) (⟨STAGE1⟩)]
        ?WAY])
```

Next, the chooser records, for each of the answers the theorem prover found, a formula of the form

```
(OPTION choice-name option-name answer-formula)
```

Here is how one would create the plan for getting money that I showed earlier. We define the plan-schema BORROW-SCHEMA thus:

```
(→ (PLAN-INSTANCE ?PI (BORROW-SCHEMA ?AMOUNT) ?SUP)
   (AND (TASK (FIND-SUCKER ?PI) ⟨⟩
         (LAMBDA ()
           (FIND (LAMBDA (X)
             (?X would be willing
               to lend me ?AMOUNT))))
           ⟨⟨SUCKER-1 ?PI⟩⟩)
        (TASK (SQUEEZE ?PI) ⟨⟨SUCKER-1 ?PI⟩⟩
          (LAMBDA (X) (ask ?X for ?AMOUNT))  ⟨⟩)
        (SUBTASK (FIND-SUCKER ?PI) ?SUP)
        (SUBTASK (SQUEEZE ?PI) ?SUP) )
        (MAIN (SQUEEZE ?PI) ?SUP) ))
```

and index it thus (see below):

```
(TO-DO ?TASK (ACHIEVE '(I have ?AMOUNT)) ⟨⟩
       (DO-SUBNET (BORROW-SCHEMA ?AMOUNT) ⟨⟩))
```

The vars-map slot of DO-SUBNET is used when the supertask has output pvars, which must be identified with output pvars from the schema's steps. (The attentive reader will have noticed that instantiating this schema will not produce exactly the tasks of the previous example. The tasks and pvars will all have names of the form "(symbol plan-instance-name)." The reason is to avoid collision with other tasks derived from other instances of the same schema.)

A task elaborated in this way will be labeled FINISHED when all its subtasks are finished. It will have enablement status SUCCS-ENABLED when all of its MAIN subtasks have that status. The formula (MAIN (SQUEEZE ?PI) ?SUP) indicates, as I mentioned before, that (SQUEEZE i) is a "main step" of the plan instance "i."

"Macro actions" like DO-SUBNET are on the border between real primitives and problematic tasks. They never actually appear in the task network, but are found in TO-DO formulas like the one I used to index the BORROW-SCHEMA. (ACHIEVE...) is a true problematic action. When the NASL interpreter finds one of these enabled, it tries to reduce it by asking the theorem prover to prove constructively the existence theorem

```
(TO-DO task-name problem-action output-pvars ?WAY)
```

That is, find an action ?WAY such that executing ?WAY carries out problem-action. If the theorem prover returns exactly one way, a new task with this action is created, enabled, and made the MAIN subtask of the current task (unless it is a macro, in which case it is just executed, attaching a plan instance. This is what would happen in reducing the task GET-MONEY.). If the theorem prover does not return exactly one value, a "planning error" has taken place, and NASL

with a different (newly created) name for each option. Here again I make use of the device of using data structures to talk about formulas. A typical option might look like:

```
(OPTION C53 A54
    [TO-DO TSK437 (MAKE AMPLIFIER) '(STAGE1)]
    (MAKE COMMON-COLLECTOR)])
```

The expectation is that the appearance of these various formulas in the data base will cause forward deduction of formulas expressing ''advice'' appropriate to the situation. This advice will be found in the next phase of the choice protocol. In this phase, the system tries to prove theorems of the following sorts:

```
(RULE-OUT option-name)
(RULE-IN option-name)
(RULE-TOGETHER ( -option-names- ) new-answer-formula)
```

It will be able to to if it has rules like this:

```
(→ (AND (CHOICE ?C EXEC
    [TO-DO _?TNAME (MAKE AMPLIFIER)
        ⟨_?AMPNAME⟩
        _?WAYVAR])
    (OPTION ?C ?A
    [TO-DO _?TNAME (MAKE AMPLIFIER)
        ⟨_?AMPNAME⟩
        (MAKE FET)])
    (desired operating current of circuit is very low))
    ; For ways of expressing and accessing
    ; desired circuit characteristics,
    ; see McDermott, 1977b.
    (RULE-IN ?A))
```

which says, ''If making a FET is an option, and the desired operating current of the circuit is very low, RULE-IN the FET option.'' (In a formula like this, the ''_'' construction is used for doing pattern matching against data structures. If [P _?X] is matched against [P A], the result has ?X bound to [A], not A. Note that [P ?X] does not match [P A] at all.) Deduction of a RULE-OUT causes an option to be thrown away. A RULE-IN causes all but RULEd-IN options to be discarded. A RULE-TOGETHER is more complex (and more ad hoc). It causes the named options to be thrown away, but a new option to be constructed, which is intended to be a synthesis of the old ones. This is important in electronic design, but I will have nothing more to say about it here (see McDermott, 1977b, 1978).

The system searches through rules of this kind cyclically. On each loop, it looks for RULE-OUTs, RULE-INs, and RULE-TOGETHERs, in that order. If at any time only one option is left, it becomes the choice. Otherwise, the cycle continues. If no changes occur in the set of options on a given iteration, a formula of the form

```
(QUIESCENCE choice-name)
```

is added to the data base, in an effort to trigger more forward deductions. The intent of this device is to enable the user to express backup rules of the form, ''If all other things are equal,....'' as implications of the form (→ (QUIES-CENCE...)...).

Finally, I should mention what happens when the theorem prover is unable to retrieve any ways of carrying out a task. As I said before, this is a signal to ''try harder.'' All this means in the current implementation is that a new ''rephrasing'' task is created, with action

```
(REPHRASE losing-task action-formula output-pvars)
```

whose job it is to reduce the losing task. It is up to user-supplied rules to suggest ways of doing this. I will not discuss this further, because I consider it an unsuccessful part of the NASL theory. The rephraser (like the choice protocol) is allowed to manipulate a formula as an arbitrary data structure, and not just do unifications against it. This division of formula manipulations may appear arbitrary to users, and thus defeat additivity, since a new task reduction fact may be expressed in two different ways. At the same time, there is little discipline in how formula manipulation is done. This makes it hard for a system to explain its actions. The root problem here is that rephrasing as implemented embodies no *theory* of what rephrasing a problem really is. (For attempts at such a theory, see Mark, 1977, the design rephrasing plan of McDermott, 1977b, and, with a grain of salt, Moore & Newell, 1974.)

Before I give an extended example of the use of the system, I should say something about the execution of secondary tasks, or ''policies.'' Recall that a secondary task is one whose execution amounts to an alteration in the execution of some primary task. This definition seems a little mysterious by itself, since it does not actually suggest what the interpreter does when it is confronted with a secondary action.

There are two principal ways a policy influences execution of other tasks. The most common way by far is a simple consequence of the way NASL is organized. This is for the (TASK...) formula and other formulas defining a secondary task to take part in deductions that influence the way other tasks are carried out. There are two obvious ways this can happen: in rules of the form, ''policy so-and-so implies (TO-DO...),'' and in rules of the form, ''policy such-and-such implies (RULE-IN...) or (RULE-OUT...).'' Whenever a policy definition takes part in a task reduction, the steps of the selected plan are made subtasks of the policy as well as the primary task of which they are the reduction. For example, clauses such as ''low operating current is desired'' in the choice-protocol illustration above are most naturally expressed as checks of active policies. (See McDermott, 1977b.) When things are done this way, the task with action (MAKE FET) will have two supertasks: ''MAKE AMPLIFIER'' and ''keep current low.'' This is just what we require.

The second way is to have primitive policies. These must be fairly rare, since implementing a new one may require potential changes to the way NASL handles almost any action. The only substantive primitive policy action is

(MONITOR formula (LAMBDA (var) action))

which does nothing unless some task removes the formula (as a model effect). Then a new subtask will be created with the given action, with var bound to the name of the task that did the removal. (In a sense, using MONITOR is not really different from the more common use of policies I described in the last paragraph; the other, one depends upon triggering action from deduction of a new formula; the other, from erasure of an old one. In a well-disciplined deductive system, where we are not allowed ''ERASING'' theorems à la Hewitt (1972), we must make one alternative a primitive action.)

Of course, we need a formal primitive policy for policies to reduce to in the case where we just want them to sit there and take part in deductions. For this purpose I supply the action PRIM. If a policy is reduced to (PRIM *SETUP), it is made ACTIVE and its successors are enabled. If it is reduced to (PRIM *BE-GUN), it is made ACTIVE, but its successors are not enabled until it is FINISHED. (See below.)

Keep in mind that policies are, in principle, executed like other tasks. They go through the same status transitions (Fig. 3), and a problematic policy must be reduced. I hope it is clear that there is nothing new about policies. All problem solvers (indeed, all computer programs) maintain constraints on action. The novelty in NASL is that the policies are made explicit and of the same form as other tasks, so they may easily take part in deductions.

There are some differences in the way policy states are represented. A secondary task has, in addition to its usual defining formulas, two formulas

(POLICY task-name action)
(SCOPE secondary-task-name primary-task-name)

The second of these defines the *scope* of the policy, the primary task which the policy is supposed to influence. User rules are usually responsible for adding this formula. (A policy may have more than one scope. A scopeless policy is possible. ''Avoid death'' is an example from real life.)

Another difference is that, since a policy does not have a tidy list of subtasks defining it, special provision must be made for executing its ''steps'' and finishing it. There is no contradiction in a policy having steps; a secondary task may

have primary as well as secondary subtasks. For instance, the policy, ''Keep track of the number of sheep on this birch bark,'' involves actually making a mark occasionally. This is accomplished by generating pseudo-tasks with action

(CONTINUE policy-task action)

In the sheep-counting example, this might mean having a rule of the form, ''If you observe a sheep leaving the pen, then there is a task with action (CONTINUE (SHEEP-COUNT) (count number of sheep)).'' These pseudo-actions are reduced by calling the theorem prover with a pattern of the form (TO-CONTINUE policy-task action ?WAY); this is a lot like reducing the policy all over again. To count sheep, we might have the rule, ''(TO-CONTINUE ?POL (count number of sheep) (make mark on birch bark).'' The subtasks generated by rules like this are attached to the original policy task as well as the pseudo-task. (This is easier to use than to grasp!)

Finally, some special action must sometimes be taken to finish a secondary task. When all the primary subtasks of a task are FINISHED, the secondary subtasks are finished by creating subtasks with action (FINISH policy-task action). For example, we must have a sheep-counting rule of the form, ''(TO-DO ?FTASK (FINISH ?POL (count sheep)) ⟨⟩ (total up the marks on the birch bark)).''

4. AN EXTENDED EXAMPLE

In this section I will show the application of the NASL technique to the ''blocks world'' (Sacerdoti, 1975; Sussman, 1975). I have several purposes in doing so. I want to illustrate the mechanisms I discussed in the last section. Putting the discussion in the context of the blocks world (the ''E. Coli.'' of AI as Winston, 1977, puts it) will enable you to compare NASL to previous problem solvers. The discussion will be in the form of an annotated listing, in ''genetic'' order. That is, I will start with a primitive problem solver, and add rules to it to make it more sophisticated. This will allow you to judge the degree to which additivity is encouraged by NASL's structure. (Of course, without a natural-language interface and rule debugger like Davis's (1976) TEIRESIAS, ''encouraged'' is the most I can claim.)

The blocks world was not chosen because it is particularly easy to express its rules in NASL. The NASL notation was developed for electronic design and common-sense reasoning. In some places it is awkward to express certain blocks-world constructs. (Indeed, if our goal were to duplicate a previous system exactly, we would have some trouble. See the discussion of an attempt to duplicate NOAH (Sacerdoti, 1975) in McDermott (1977b), which was not so successful.) On the other hand, the way NASL encourages talk about some things is, I believe, superior to previous methods.

Circumstances have prevented me from actually running the problem solver I

234 Chapter 4 *Planning and Acting*

am about to discuss, so I cannot guarantee that the rules have no bugs. However, I have had enough experience with NASL in similar situations in the past to be able to point out where the current theorem prover would have problems and the system would run slowly. Aside from this fixable problem, the structure of NASL will guarantee strong heuristic adequacy with the rule set I will give.

In this section, I will use lower case letters for rules set off from the text.

Many of the problems in the blocks world are of the form: "Bring about condition x," written (ACHIEVE 'x). (The quote is needed because the condition's current status is not at issue.) One rule that we need is this:

```
(defmla to-do-achieve
  (→ c ?p
    (to-do ?task (achieve '?p) ⟨⟩ (output ⟨⟩)))))
```

A few new notational frills: I give names to each rule with the construction (DEFMLA name rule). I have added after the implication arrow a letter indicating how the implication is to be used. The possible combinations are:

```
(→ C p q) — To prove q, prove p
(→ A p q) — If p is recorded, record q
(→ G p q) — Prove p, and, for each instance generated,
            record an instance of q
```

(cf. Hewitt, 1972). I recommend ignoring these "use" letters when first trying to understand each rule. First understand what conclusions the rule allows you to draw, then note how it is necessary to "cheat" to get the system to draw the right conclusions.

In the rule TO-DO-ACHIEVE, the action (OUTPUT ⟨⟩) is a no-op primitive. It can return a tuple of terms to be assigned to pvars, but we do not need this feature here. So the rule says, "If ?P is already true, (ACHIEVE '?P) is done by a no-op."

If ?P is not true, more powerful methods will have to be found. For example, to achieve a conjunction, we have the following schema

```
(defmla conj-plan
  (→ a (plan-instance ?plan (conj-schema ?c1 ?c2) ?sup)
    (and (task (conj-1 ?plan) ⟨⟩
               (lambda () (achieve ?c1)  )
            ⟨⟩)
         (task (conj-2 ?plan)  ⟨⟩
               (lambda ( ) (achieve ?c2)  )
            ⟨⟩)
         (subtask (conj-1 ?plan) ?sup)
         (subtask (conj-2 ?plan) ?sup)
         (main (conj-1 ?plan) ?sup)
         (main (conj-2 ?plan) ?sup))))
```

```
(defmla to-do-ach-and
  (to-do ?task (achieve '(and ?c1 ?c2)) ⟨⟩
    (do-subnet (conj-schema '?c1 ?c2) ⟨⟩))))
```

These rules are independent of the blocks world, and merely suggest achieving a conjunction by achieving, in no particular order, each of its conjuncts (cf. Sacerdoti, 1975).

The rules are technically correct always, but can be inefficient if the conjunction is already true. We could revise the formula TO-DO-ACH-AND, but, in pursuit of additivity, let us instead add a new choice rule:

```
(defmla choose-easy-way-out
  (→ a (option ?choice ?a [to-do —?tsk —?act —?outs
                          (output —?x)])
    (rule-in ?a)))
```

("If a no-op suffices to do a task, don't consider anything else.")

Other schemata will depend on the domain conditions we are interested in achieving. The main such condition in the blocks world is (ON a b), which is true if a is directly above (supported by) b. We can define

```
(defmla clear-defn-1
  (→ c (forall (y) (not (on ?y ?x)))
    (clear ?x)))
```

```
(defmla clear-defn-2
  (→ a (clear ?x) (forall (y) (not (on ?y ?x)))))
```

Further, our knowledge of ON is complete:

```
(defmla pres-not-on
  (forall (x y) (presumably '(not (on ?x ?y)))))
```

That is, if the system does not know about an ON relationship, it is assumed not to exist. (PRESUMABLY p) is defined by the built-in rule ((PRESUMABLY '?X) ↔ (→ C (CONSISTENTLY '?X) ?X)). CONSISTENTLY is defined procedurally, by a call to the theorem prover. If (NOT p) cannot be proved, (CONSISTENTLY p) is proved (McCarthy & Hayes, 1969; McDermott, 1977b).)

There is room for one object on top of another if the supporting object is clear or is the table:

```
(defmla space-for-defn-1
  (→ c (clear ?y) (space-for ?x ?y)))
```

```
(defmla space-for-defn-2
  (space-for ?x table))
```

Here is the basic plan schema for achieving ON-ness:

The intended meaning of (PREREQ supertask preparatory-subtask main-subtask ⟨ -propositions- ⟩) is that the propositions are to be kept true from the end of the preparatory subtask to the beginning of the main subtask.

We must do something similar for the conjunction-achiever, since the intent there is to have all the conjuncts true when the plan is completed. In this case, there is no "main" subtask, so we invent one:

```
(defmla and-plan-prereqs
 (→ a (plan-instance ?plan (conj-schema ?c1 ?c2) ?sup)
  (and (task (synchronizer ?plan)⟨⟩
      (lambda ( ) (output ⟨⟩)) ⟨⟩)
   (prereq ?sup
    (conj-1 ?plan) (synchronizer ?plan)
    ⟨?c1⟩)
   (prereq ?sup
    (conj-2 ?plan) (synchronizer ?plan)
    ⟨?c2⟩))))
```

PREREQ is defined thus:

```
(defmla prereq-defn
 (→ a (prereq ?sup ?prep ?main ?props)
  (and
   (successor ?prep ?main)
   (subtask ?prep ?sup)
   (subtask ?main ?sup)
   (→ g (elt ?p ?props)        ;For each ?p in ?props,
    (exists (pol)              ;there is a policy ...
     (and (task ?pol ⟨⟩
       (lambda ()
        (protect ?p  ;... to "protect" ?p
          ?prep ?main ))
       ⟨⟩)
      (scope ?pol ?sup)
      (subtask ?pol ?sup)
      (successor ?pol ?prep))))))))
```

I have implemented "keep p true" by setting up a policy of protecting p during the critical period between the preparatory step and the main step. (The formula (SUCCESSOR ?POL ?T1) expresses the fact that the policy task must be reduced, i.e., set up, before the preparatory subtask.)

PROTECT is not a NASL primitive. (Perhaps it should be; on the other hand, perhaps it is not as ubiquitous or simple as has been thought.) Here is how it is done:

```
(defmla on-plan
 (→ a (plan-instance ?plan (ach-on-schema ?x ?y) ?sup)
  (and
   (task (clear-step ?plan) ⟨⟩
    (lambda ( ) (achieve '(clear ?x))) ⟨⟩)
   (task (find-space-step ?plan) ⟨⟩
    (lambda ( ) (achieve '(space-for ?x ?y))) ⟨⟩)
   (task (move-step ?plan) ⟨⟩
    (lambda ( ) (puton ?x ?y)) ⟨⟩)
   (subtask (move-step ?plan) ?sup)
   (subtask (clear-step ?plan) ?sup)
   (subtask (find-space ?plan) ?sup)
   (successor (clear-step ?plan) (move-step ?plan))
   (successor (find-space-step ?plan) (move-step ?plan))
   (main (move-step ?plan) ?sup))))
```

Of course, we need

```
(defmla puton-defn-1
 (→ c (on ?a ?x)
  (mod-manip ?task (puton ?a ?b) ⟨'(on ?a ?x)⟩ ⟨⟩)))

(defmla puton-defn-2
 (mod-manip ?task (puton ?a ?b) ⟨⟩ ⟨'(on ?a ?b)⟩))
```

The schema is made available by this rule:

```
(defmla to-do-ach-on
 (to-do ?task (achieve '(on ?x ?y)) ⟨⟩
  (do-subnet (ach-on-schema ?x ?y) ⟨⟩)))
```

The schema for achieving ON-ness is incomplete, because the successor relation is not strong enough. There will often be other tasks around which are unordered with respect to MOVE-STEP and its predecessors. These tasks may interfere with the conditions ACHIEVEd by CLEAR-STEP and FIND-SPACE-STEP. These conditions are achieved in preparation for the main task MOVE-STEP. So we must in addition specify

```
(defmla on-plan-prereqs
 (→ a (plan-instance ?plan (ach-on-schema ?x ?y) ?sup)
  (and
   (prereq ?sup (clear-step ?plan) (move-step ?plan)
     ⟨'(clear ?x)⟩)
   (prereq ?sup (find-space-step ?plan) (move-step ?plan)
     ⟨'(space-for ?x ?y)⟩))))
```

```
(defmla to-do-protect
  (→ c (→ '(den ?fmla) ?prop)
    (to-do ?pol (protect '?prop ?prep ?main) ⟨⟩
      (monitor ?fmla
        (lambda (interloper)
          (protect-check ?pol ?interloper
            '?prop ?prep ?main))))))
```

The protected fact is monitored. (The left-hand side of the implication calculates ?FMLA, a data structure representing the formula to be monitored, from ?PROP, the proposition being protected. It does this by deducing a data structure whose denotation (DEN) is ?PROP. See Section 3.) If the fact is ever erased, a task with action (PROTECT-CHECK ... fact...) is created. This task will register a "protection-violation" complaint (cf. Sussman, 1975):

```
(defmla to-do-protect-check-1
  (→ c (and (= (enab-status ?prep) succs-enabled)
            (= (task-status ?main) pending))
    (tc-do ?task
      (protect-check ?pol ?interloper ?prop
        ?prep ?main)
      ⟨⟩
      (get-rid-of
        (protection-violation ?prop ?interloper
          ?pol ?prep ?main)))))
```

but only if the problem solver is between the preparatory task and its main step. Otherwise, the protection policy is simply CONTINUEd:

```
(defmla to-do-protect-check-2
  (→ c (and (= (enab-status ?prep) succs-enabled)
            (= (task-status ?main) pending))
    (to-do ?task
      (protect-check ?pol ?interloper ?prop
        ?prep ?main)
      ⟨⟩
      (continue ?pol (protect ?prop ?prep ?main)))))
```

In the false-alarm case, there must be rules for how to CONTINUE and FINISH protecting:

```
(defmla to-continue-protect
  (→ c (to-do ?task (protect ?p ?prep main) ⟨⟩ ?x)
    (to-continue ?task (protect ?p ?prep ?main) ?x)))
```

("Any way to do protection is a way to continue protection.")

```
(defmla to-finish-protect
  (to-do ?task (finish ?pol (protect ?p ?prep ?main)) ⟨⟩
    (output ⟨⟩)))
```

("To finish protecting, just cease.")

Before pursuing the handling of protection violation, I must backpedal a bit. The plans I just gave, while simple and clear, will not handle the original protections I wanted! The problem is that (CLEAR...) and (SPACE-FOR...) are complex predicates deduced from simpler formulas. This by itself is not enough to cause problems, since the NASL data base is smart enough to erase consequences of erased formulas, but some of the supporters of the formulas to be protected are of the form (CONSISTENTLY...), and what is consistent one moment may be inconsistent the next. (This could all be handled nicely by Doyle's (1977) "truth maintenance.") So we must add a couple of rules to make sure the interpreter notices the erasures. (This is definitely an ugly part of the blocks world problem solver.)

```
(defmla ugly-rule-1
  (→ a (task ?pol ⟨⟩
    (lambda () (protect '(clear ?x) ?prep ?main)) ⟨⟩)
    (→ a (→ '(task-status ?pol) active)
      (→ a (→ '(task-status ?prep) finished)
        (→ a (on ?y ?x)
          (exists (ugly-task)
            (s ' (and
              (task ?ugly-task ⟨⟩
                (lambda ()
                  (erase '(clear ?x))))
                ⟨⟩
              (successor ?ugly-task
                ?main))))))))))
```

(S 'p) means p starts to be true. If (on ?y ?x) is erased, the tasks derived from it will remain. (NASL is doing real deduction, not disguised demon firing. That is, the consequent of an implication is a proposition which is true only as long as the antecedent remains true. Ideally, what we would like is to have the truth of the task formula depend upon (ON ?Y ?X) having been true, but the language is not powerful enough to say this, so I resort to the "S" device.)

```
(defmla ugly-rule-2
  (→ a (task ?pol ⟨⟩
    (lambda () (protect '(space-for ?x ?y)
      ?prep ?main))
    ⟨⟩
    (→ g (not (= ?y table))
```

```
      (lambda (z)
         (achieve '(on ?y ?z))) ⟨⟩
   (subtask (find-place-step ?y ?plan)
            ?sup)
   (subtask (move-step ?y ?plan) ?sup)
   (main (move-step ?y ?plan) ?sup))))))
```

(defmla is-place-table (is place table))

(defmla are-places-blocks
  (→ c (is block ?x) (is place ?x)))

(defmla to-do-ach-clear
  (to-do ?task (achieve ;(clear ?x)) ⟨⟩
  (do-subnet (ach-clear-schema ?x) ⟨⟩)))

(defmla to-do-ach-space-for
  (to-do ?task (achieve '(space-for ?x ?y)) ⟨⟩
  (achieve '(clear ?y))))

I note with some satisfaction that we have had to introduce no new notation. CLEAR-PLAN defines ACH-CLEAR-SCHEMA, which suggests clearing a block by creating a task for each block on it to put that block elsewhere. The rule as written is underspecified, since it does not say where to put a displaced block. This is a matter of some complexity (cf. Sacerdoti, 1975), but at least we have the following choice principle:

(defmla choose-table-ceteris-paribus
  (→ a (choice ?c (find-place-step ?block ?plan) ?fmla)
     (→ a (quiescence ?c)
        (→ a (option ?c ?a
             [and (is place table)
                  (not (= table -- ?x))])
           (rule-in ?a)))))

That is, if other rules say nothing, and the table is an option, choose the table. Now, how are protection violations to be handled? I mentioned error correction very briefly in Section 2, but said nothing about it in Section 3, because almost no error correction is currently implemented. The only error-correction action is (GET-RID-OF mistake-description), and that only by convention. (For example, if a FIND can think of no objects satisfying its argument, the LISP function implementing it signals failure, and the interpreter places a (GET-RID-OF (PRIM-FAILURE (FIND . . .))) in the task network.)

```
(→ a (→ '(task-status ?pol) active)
   (→ a (→ '(task-status ?prep? finished)
      (→ a (on ?z ?y)
         (exists (ugly-task)
            (s ' (and
               (task ?ugly-task ⟨⟩
                  (lambda ()
                     (erase
                        '(space-for
                          ?x ?y)))
                  ⟨⟩))
               (successor
                  ?ugly-task
                  ?main)))))))))
```

(defmla ugliest-rule-of-all
  (mod-manip ?task (erase '?p) ⟨'?p⟩ ⟨⟩))

This last rule is really ugly, since it allows an action, ERASE, which does not really correspond to any well-defined action in the world. (How would you carry out, "Erase 'The Empire State Building is in New York'"?) I freely admit that NASL as it stands is prone to all this ugliness; perhaps it will convince future generations of the necessity of having this data base maintenance done automatically, and not by explicit erasure. It is a blow to additivity to have to duplicate here the same information that we had in SPACE-FOR-DEFN-1,2 and CLEAR-DEFN-1,2. This is the last ugliness we shall encounter.

Before we look at the handling of protection violation, let me give another plan schema:

(defmla clear-plan
  (→ a (plan-instance ?plan (ach-clear-schema ?x) ?sup)
     (→ a (→ '(task-status ?sup) active)
        (→ g (on ?y ?x)
           (S ' (and
              (task (find-place-step ?y ?plan)
                 ⟨⟩
                 (lambda ()
                    (find
                       (lambda (z)
                          (and (is place ?z)
                               (not (= ?z
                                       ?x))))))
                 ⟨'(place ?y ?plan)⟩)
              (task (move-step ?y ?plan)
                 ⟨'(place ?y ?plan)⟩
```
```

Even with this crude machinery, we can write some interesting rules.

```
(defmla gro-pv-plan
 (→ a (plan-instance ?plan
       (gro-pv-schema ?prop ?loser ?pol
                      ?prep ?main)
       ?sup)
 (and
  (task (continue-step ?plan) ⟨⟩
   (lambda ()
    (continue ?pol
     (protect ?prop ?prep ?main)))
   ⟨⟩)
  (task (redo-step ?plan) ⟨⟩
   (lambda ( ) (achieve ?prop)) ⟨⟩)
  (subtask (redo-step ?plan) ?sup)
  (subtask (continue-step ?plan) ?sup)
  (successor (continue-step ?plan) (redo-step ?plan))
  (successor (redo-step ?plan) ?main)
 (→ g
  (and (consistently
   '(not (exists (purpose)
    (and (purpose ?loser ?purpose)
     (succ* ?main ?purpose)))))
   (purpose ?loser ?purpose))
  (successor ?purpose (redo-step ?plan)))  )))

(defmla purpose-defn ;PURPOSE is a generalization of PREREQ
 (→ c (and (main* ?task ?superprep)
       (prereq ?x ?superprep ?supermain ?props))
  (purpose ?task ?supermain)) )

(defmla succ*-defn-1 ;SUCC* is the transitive...
 (→ c (or (successor ?t1 ?t2)
       (and (successor ?t1 ?t3) (succ* ?t3 ?t2)))
  (succ* ?t1 ?t2)))

(defmla succ*-defn-2 ;... and reflexive closure of SUCCESSOR
 (succ* ?t1 ?t1) )

(defmla succ*-defn-3 ;... plus successors of supertasks
 (→ (and (main ?t1 ?t3) (successor ?t3 ?t4) (succ* ?t4 ?t2))
  (succ* ?t1 t2))  )
```

```
(defmla main*-defn-1 ;MAIN* is the transitive...
 (→ c (or (main ?t1 ?t2)
       (and (main ?t1 ?t3) (main* ?t3 ?t2)))
  (main* ?t1 ?t2)))

(defmla main*-defn-2 ;... and reflexive closure of MAIN
 (main* ?t ?t))
```

In other words, if a protected proposition is removed, it should be reachieved, but only after the interfering process is completed. This is accomplished, naturally, by the deduction of new successor links. Unfortunately, since it is the user's responsibility to avoid loops of successor links, we have to do a slightly awkward test to make sure the rule does not introduce loops. A loop here would mean that the violated proposition is itself a prerequisite (of a prerequisite of . . .) some purpose of the violator. So we have no choice but to continue carrying out the two competing task networks in parallel. Unfortunately, this raises the possibility of infinite loops. For example, the silly action (ACHIEVE '(AND (ON A B) (ON A TABLE))) would result in a deadly embrace of repeated violations. So we must qualify the use of the schema thus:

```
(defmla to-do-gro-pv
 (→ c (consistently '(not (purpose ?loser ?main)))
   (to-do ?task
   (get-rid-of (protection-violation
                ?prop ?loser ?pol ?prep ?main))
   ⟨⟩
   (do-subnet (gro-pv-schema ?prop ?loser) ⟨⟩)))))
```

That is, if the protection violator and violatee are both in service of exactly the same main step, this schema will not solve the problem, and we will need other,

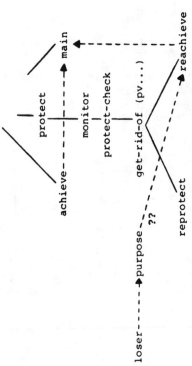

FIG. 4 Task network for protection violation.

```
(→ g (removes ?x ?p)
    (→ g (consistently '(not (succ* ?x ?purp)))
       (successor ?purp ?x)))))
```

REMOVES does the same thing as Sacerdoti's table of multiple effects (with the same efficiency, assuming an efficient data base).

```
(defmla removes-defn-1
  (→ a (⇒ '(task-status ?task) pending)
     (s '(→ a (task-action ?task ?a)
            (→ g (and (mod-manip ?task ?a
                                 ?erasures ?additions)
                      (elt ?p ?erasures))
               (removes ?task ?p))))))
```

(The formula (TASK-ACTION task action) is provided by the system as soon as all the input pvars of a task have been found.) However, we cannot do lookahead as easily as Sacerdoti. We may miss some conflicts involving un-PENDING actions, because we need to know the model manipulations that will be done before we know the contents of the model at execution time. The best we can do is:

```
(defmla removes-defn-2
  (→ a (task-action ?task ?a)
     (→ g (and (forall (r)
                  (T ?r (mod-manip ?task ?a
                                   ?erasures ?additions))
                  (elt ?p ?erasures))
               (removes ?task ?p)))))
```

The use of (T ?R . . .) in this formula is my first mention of the modal operator "T." T takes two arguments, a "possible world," or "reference point," and a proposition, and asserts that the proposition is true at the reference point. This is not really a very well thought out feature of NASL. The only purpose of using it here is to capture the idea that one can be sure a task will remove a proposition if it removes it no matter what the state of the world is. This is far weaker than the tests made by NOAH in similar circumstances. However, for NOAH to do this correctly requires a careful sequence of interleaved task reductions and world-model recomputations. (This was pointed out by Rod McGuire, personal communication.) This is impossible in the more realistic task notation used by NASL.

We can also use a few more statements about REMOVES:

```
(defmla removes-defn-3
  (→ a (task-action ?task (achieve '?p))
     (→ c (forall (r) (T ?r (→ ?p (not ?q)))
        (removes ?task ?q))))
```

more specific rules. (These will be execution-time analogues of Sacerdoti's (1975) "Resolve Double Cross" critic.)

(The reason for the use of CONSISTENTLY in testing the problem-solver state is that the system has perfect knowledge of its own state. Compare the rule PRES-NOT-ON above. By the way, the processing of transitivity axioms like MAIN*-DEFN and SUCC*-DEFN is a typical place where the current theorem prover can run very slowly. This could be rectified by having a special-purpose transitivity handler (McDermott, 1977d).)

A diagram will make this whole set of rules easier to visualize. Figure 4 shows the state of the task network after a protection violation has been handled. If main = purpose, the plan schema does not apply. If main is not a predecessor of purpose, the plan says to make purpose a predecessor of "reachieve." Otherwise, continue execution and correct later errors as you find them. (You may find it amusing to try all possible execution orders of the action (ACHIEVE '(AND (ON A B) (ON B C))) in the initial state with (ON C A).)

I invite you to compare this approach to those of Sussman (1975), Rieger and London (1977), and Sacerdoti (1975). I find mine more appealing, not because it is more sophisticated and general (it isn't), but because it treats protection violation as an execution-time phenomenon. In the majority of everyday protection violations, it is too late to plan around the problem when it is detected, and there is no point in trying to learn something very general from a circumstance that will never be duplicated again. For example, say you are peeling potatoes. You open the kitchen garbage-can lid as a preparation for throwing away the peelings. Then you open a drawer to get the peeler. It happens that you opened the lid so that it rested against the drawer, so it flops back shut. At this point, it is pointless to compile a critic (Sussman, 1975) about opening garbage-can lids in the presence of drawers. (It could be one of millions of critics you would need.) But the rules I just gave capture what you should do exactly. They suggest checking why the drawer had to be opened; this task, "get the peeler," will be a ?PURPOSE in GRO-PV-PLAN. A new task, "open the lid again," will be created, but this time placed after "get the peeler."

Is our problem solver complete? No. There are several gaps in what I have given so far. We could remedy these defects, and I will discuss some remedies in a moment, but there will always be more rules we could add to a problem solver, especially if we try to add new problems and plans, and have to deal with their interactions. The important requirement is that new rules be addable as they come up.

For example, let us say we wished to add a few critics of Sacerdoti's sort. After all, if it is possible to catch a bug before it happens, we might as well. Here is a version of the "Resolve Conflicts" critic:

```
(defmla resolve-conflicts
  (→ a (prereq ?sup ?prep ?purp ?props)
     (→ g (elt ?p ?props)
```

(I would not really want to guarantee that NASL's theorem prover would be able to handle this.)

```
(defmla removes-special-1
  (→ a (task-action ?task (achieve '(clear ?x)))
     (removes ?task '(on ?y ?x))))

(defmla removes-special-2
  (→ a (task-action ?task (achieve '(space-for ?y ?x)))
     (→ g (not (= ?x table))
        (removes ?task '(on ?z ?x)))))
```

These last two rules are special-purpose aids to the problem solver, and do nothing but add entries to the "table of multiple effects."

I should point out that NASL will not guarantee that these rules apply when they are appropriate. Whether an interference is caught in advance depends upon the other hand, it would be nice if you could write rules to force reductions tages and disadvantages. It seems more realistic than NOAH's rigid sequence of "reduce—criticize" loops, which can force "overplanning," the production of plans which are rendered invalid by execution errors before they are reached. On the other hand, it would be nice if you could write rules to force reductions independent of execution order when it seemed appropriate. NASL never allows you to do this, and this is a failure in my attempt at heuristic adequacy. In the next section, I will discuss this and other weaknesses at greater length.

5. TRANSCENDING NASL'S LIMITS

The two goals I had in developing NASL were analytical and heuristic adequacy. Obviously, neither has been achieved, although some progress has been made. Design decisions made in pursuit of analytical flexibility have made the task of actual analysis more difficult. Some interpreter features have defeated additivity. In this section, I will discuss problems of both these kinds. In the next, I will make a more upbeat summary of NASL's strengths.

The major analytical inadequacies of NASL are:

Lack of an inferential theory of time and events.
No notion of "success conditions" for a task.
No theory of error correction.
Absence of a class of actions which are neither inferential nor worldly, but just edit the task network.
No theory of rephrasing.

The major heuristic inadequacies of NASL are:

Dissimilarity between the choice mechanism and the task mechanism.
Rigidity in reasoning about loops of SUCCESSOR relationships and other scheduling structures.
Inefficiencies of the theorem prover.

On balance, the system comes closer to achieving heuristic than analytical adequacy.

The most glaring problem in the first list is the lack of a real theory of time, actions, and events. The interpreter apparently causes statements like (POLICY name action) to come true by the way it behaves, but it cannot, and we cannot, say much about what these statements mean. This makes some reasoning processes impossible. In Section 4, we were forced to state some fairly weak rules for detecting in advance certain task interferences. We were kept from saying very much about the effects of a task that was not enabled. In this case, it was not terribly important, and, in general, it is not worth a special effort to make sure that every foreseeable interaction is foreseen, since there will always be some unforeseeable ones that will have to be dealt with. But what is troublesome is our inability to write any rules at all which refer to future courses of events, or which recommend reducing a task in advance. For example, in planning a trip to town, we might want a rule that says, "If any task, even a BLOCKED one, may involve going to town, reduce it now to make sure we do not have to make two trips." Reducing a task while its predecessors are still PENDING involves calculating what the world will look like when its predecessors have run. This requires a theory of time.

If the purpose of every task were to effect a state change, we could adopt a standard temporal logic (McCarthy & Hayes, 1969; Rescher & Urquhart, 1971). This logic is well enough understood to permit very efficient algorithms for detecting task interferences (Sacerdoti, 1975) and for more specialized duties.

Unfortunately, as I stressed at the outset, the effects of tasks, and events in general, are not usually specifiable as states of the world that are brought about. Take the example of the action, "Prevent Little Nell from being mashed by the train" (Nell being tied to the tracks and the train coming). What is true before the execution of this action that is not true afterward? It cannot be, "Nell will be mashed," since, after the action, we can see that Nell was not going to be mashed. We could take some axiomatization of the temporal operator Fp ("p is going to be true in some future state") in which multiple possible futures are allowed (Rescher & Urquhart, 1971). Before the rescue, we have (F (Little Nell mashed)); after, (NOT (F (Little Nell mashed))) (Doyle, personal communication). However, this is too weak a sense of "prevent." It is in this sense that I prevent tigers from entering my office by locking the door. How can we capture the idea that an event was not just possible, but was *going to occur* "unless something happened"?

This is a very difficult problem. It seems to me that the language for talking about such things will have to include at least the following elements. There must be very abstract entities called "events" and "processes." An event is associated with a proposition being true at some approximate time. However, to say that an event "exists" is not to commit ourselves to its happening. We would like to talk about events like the South's winning the Civil War. For each event, there must be a way of talking about the entire course of history that must occur for that event to have happened. The statement "event so-and-so occurred" must be true only in such a history. Within such a history, we may if we wish refer to the state of affairs just after the event occurred, and in this way get back to simple state changes when appropriate.

A process is an entity associated with a possible sequence of events. If the process is happening, then its events are going to happen unless other factors make it provable that they will not happen, but even then the process still exists. For example, a causal description of an electronic circuit with feedback must refer to two causal processes which fight it out over a voltage value (de Kleer, 1976 "personal communication). Unless the radio malfunctions, neither process will ever succeed in realizing its events, but the two processes nonetheless exist. Is there a calculus for talking about such things? (Some of the concepts of Rieger's (1976) "common-sense algorithms" look promising. One would have to combine his notion of "tendency" with explicit notations for time and truth.)

If we had a calculus of this kind, we would be able to specify *success conditions* for tasks. The success conditions for a task are propositions supposed to hold true if and only if the task is successful. They provide a characterization of the immediate end of a task which is independent of, and more general than, how it is reduced. I succeeded in convincing myself that such conditions were unnecessary, because either a task is primitive (and will tell us when it fails), or it is reduced to a set of tasks (and succeeds if all its subtasks do), or it cannot be reduced (in which case it has failed). This argument is fallacious on several grounds. (1) Tasks can have effects via inference, as I said most policies did (Section 3). Tasks derived because of the presence of an active policy will be made subtasks of it, but the success of the subtasks derived this way is not sufficient for the success of the policy. If a policy like, "Keep costs low," never gets a chance to influence a choice, it will fail with no indication. (2) Some plans are just not foolproof. All of their steps can execute successfully without thereby executing their supertasks. For example, one way to start a car is to insert the key in the ignition and turn it a certain angle. You can do the insertion and the turning perfectly and still have the car not start. We could put an explicit test for success into the plan, but then we would have to do this for almost all plans. (3) It smacks of hubris to assume that all plan schemata we give the problem solver are correct. If a plan is wrong, there is no way to know it without some independent success criterion.

If we had success criteria, how would we use them? In some circumstances (a version of "careful mode," à la Sussman, 1975), we might want to test the criteria of all tasks or some selected tasks to make sure they worked. Notice that it is not sufficient to wait until the task is finished to check it. A protection policy, for instance, must be noted as failing as soon as its protectee is erased. For a more complete answer, we must turn to the topic of error correction,

obviously crucial in my cosmology, and obviously neglected hitherto. There are a couple of issues here: detecting errors and doing something about them.

Error detection can, I think, be modeled as a data-base maintenance process. When a task is being worked on, the statement, "Task so-and-so is succeeding," is added to the data base as an assumption, and supports the statement of its success conditions. If nothing untoward happens, these conditions will just be believed. In particular, if asked, the system will explain itself based on the assumption that its actions will be successful. (This is ordinary "careless mode.") When some part of a success condition is violated, this will cause a contradiction to appear in the data base. Handling this contradiction (McDermott, 1974; Stallman & Sussman, 1977) requires finding its immediate antecedents and their supporters, and considering which to reject; if "Task so-and-so is succeeding" appears to be the culprit, a failing task has been detected. (In a "truth maintenance" system of this kind (see Doyle, 1977), there would probably be no need for MONITOR to be a primitive, since the system would always be looking for contradictions. We could just list "p" among the success conditions of "(PROTECT p).")

Once an error has been detected, it must be corrected. If this merely involves taking extra corrective actions, as in the GRO-PV-PLAN of Section 4, no extensions to the current scheme are required. Unfortunately, there are plenty of cases where more must be done. For example, if you are dialing a phone number, and your hand slips, an error is detected (presumably, in this case, by a clash between kinesthetic "success conditions" and reports from the hand). At this point, there are seven subtasks of the main task, "Dial number n," one subtask for each digit. If your hand slips on digit four, there are three FINISHED tasks behind you and three PENDING tasks ahead of you. Clearly, it is pointless to try redialing the digit just dialed. Instead, you retrieve a (very) standard plan to correct the problem. In NASL terms, you add to the task network a task with action (GET-RID-OF (TASK-FAILURE "hand slipped")), and retrieve the plan for such a task which says, "Throw away the upcoming tasks, enqueue a task to push down the buttons until a dial tone is reattained, and enqueue seven successor tasks to dial each digit again."

The only part of this which is new is the action, "Re-reduce a task, throwing away its old plan." There is no room for this action in the life history of a task (Fig. 3). To make it possible, we must allow tasks to become derailed into a new category, "abandoned." There is probably a primitive, "Re-reduce task ...," which causes the plan beneath a task to be abandoned, and calls the retrieval machinery all over again to find a new plan.

This is only one of a class of actions which are neither worldly nor inferential, but just edit the task network. Such actions would allow generalization of the existing scheduling machinery. For example, we would like to have an action, "Reduce task," which caused a task to be reduced, whether it was executable or not. This would require being able to calculate the state of the world when the

Finally, in the long run there must be a theory of rephrasing, "thinking harder." I mention this only for completeness. I am disappointed in NASL's performance in this area, but have no good suggestions for improvement. The applications of rephrasing in McDermott (1977b) are worthwhile, but cannot really be shown all to be examples of the same phenomenon. In particular, the rephrasing device has been used for three rather different purposes: as a way of "cheating" on Tarskianism, by allowing manipulation of formulas as arbitrary data structures; as a way of allowing backup plan schemata which will not even be thought of unless the first wave can be shown to be inapplicable; and as a way of capturing the idea of "cookbook" problem transformations such as the move to the frequency domain in signal-processing applications. In addition, there is the process modeled by Sussman (1975) of using rule-generating rules when existing plan schemata ("Answer Libary entries") do not apply. If this last process is rephrasing, then rephrasing is strongly involved with learning.

In the remainder of this section, I will say a little about failures to achieve heuristic adequacy in NASL. Many of these seem simple to correct compared to analytical inadequacies. For example, there is a problem with the additivity of the choice protocol. If two persons write two different packages of choice rules for a situation, chances are they will interact in unpredicted and unfortunate ways. For example, one may RULE-OUT what the other RULEd-IN. They may both rule things in, and be left with too many things, or rule everything out between them. They may impose different conventions about the meaning of QUIESCENCE.

The solution to all these problems is simple. Get rid of the choice protocol, and replace it with a task of the form (CHOOSE . . .), with built-in success conditions, and no built-in plans. The success conditions are clear: that only one option remain. It is up to the user to supply plans. If two users supply plans, the system will make an intelligible request for rules to choose between *them.*

A similar "taskification" could be helpful in handling the problem of loops of SUCCESSOR relationships. Currently tasks involved in such loops just never become ENABLED. To get rid of this bug, such a situation must be noticed, and give rise to a task of the form, "Choose which order to do these in." There are plenty of scheduling rules one can think of which are awkward to express as simple implications for reasons exactly analogous to those I gave in Section 2 to justify the choice protocol: if you are forced to qualify every rule concluding a SUCCESSOR relationship to avoid collision with other such rules, additivity is **defeated. The rule GRO-PV-PLAN is a good example. Choosing order of execution of tasks should be invokable explicitly even when a successor loop has not been detected.** For example, here is a chain of reasoning I went through recently. Given an unwashed apple and an orange, which do you eat first? Well, you must **wash the apple before you eat it, and you must wash your hands after you eat the orange. If you are planning to do some washing, do it all at once if possible. If**

task was executable, so, like everything else I have mentioned, it depends on a better logic of time. If this action were available, more NOAH-like rules could be given to NASL.

At this point, while I am visualizing what an error-correcting NASL would look like, I should compare this approach to error correction with previous approaches. There are three. The most sophisticated by far is Sacerdoti's (1975) approach, from which there is much to learn. He provided a model of execution monitoring, from which there is much to learn. He provided a model of execution (the instruction of an apprentice) and of errors (the apprentice making a mistake) which allowed his program to perform insightful error recovery. The main defect in this work is the assumption that the plan is correct, and that all errors are due to faulty "effectors." Another approach is Fikes's (1971) robot execution monitor. In my opinion, this made too many assumptions about the basic soundness and comprehensiveness of the plan.

The earliest approach was GPS (Ernst & Newell, 1969). GPS is not often thought of as an execution monitor, its nondeterministic executive ensures that it really is not. But a deterministic GPS that was not allowed to take moves back would be a very nice model of execution. All plan execution must be of the form, *"Try something, see if it works, then try something else."* This is essentially GPS's brand of means–ends analysis.

To make this point clear, let me say a few words about the very first problem I gave as an example in this paper: the Tower of Hanoi problem. This kind of problem was important in the early days of problem solving, but appears exceedingly awkward to handle from the point of view of the more recent PLANNER-NOAH family of which NASL is a member. This is because the "modern" approach is oriented around retrieval and coordination of complex partial plans rather than construction of operator sequences from operators. It strains credulity to assume the existence of such a plan in the case of an artificial puzzle. So, in a sense, the later tradition has abandoned hope of solving puzzles in a general way.

However, I believe there is a niche for puzzles in the "knowledge-based problem reduction" tradition. They are problems which require a large amount of error handling. That is, a good problem solver of this type will attack a puzzle of this kind by trying something. It will almost certainly fail, and have to move pieces back. Whether this is done with a mechanical arm or merely simulated is unimportant. Such a problem solver will flounder a lot on such a problem, and in general behave a lot like people do. For example, it will not be able to detect repeated states automatically, as GPS would. The reason is clear: in realistic problem solving, a state will *never* be repeated. (At least the statement, "I've been here before," will be true the second time and not the first.) Ad hoc and buggy rules for detecting loops in a particular solution attempt will have to be supplied or devised. Frustration mechanisms will have to be supplied to provide a conservative escape hatch. A problem solver that can solve problems as complex as Sacerdoti's will, I suggest, necessarily have to act out a clumsy caricature of GPS's elegance on simple problems.

you eat the orange first, you can do the hand washing and apple washing simultaneously, so eat the orange first. I leave it as an exercise for the reader to see what rules must apply to have this chain of reasoning noticed. (I believe NOAH could do this nicely, but only by enforcing a rigid order of reduction and criticism.)

Finally, the theorem prover used by NASL is too clumsy and slow. A theorem prover used for retrieving plan schemata should be simple-minded and efficient, tailored for this one application. In McDermott (1977b) I pointed out that there was some question as to the division of labor between the theorem prover and inferential tasks. I now think the theorem prover should be forbidden to do any complex reasoning. See McDermott (1977d) for discussion.

6. CONCLUSIONS

I have described a notation for talking about problems and plans, and a problem solver which operates by manipulating a data base containing formulas in that notation. The goals of this effort were an analytically adequate notation and a heuristically adequate program. The second goal was met to a greater degree than the first.

The problem solver is unique in that it welcomes rules which talk of a very broad class of actions, problems, and plans. The vocabularies and syntax of these rules encourage access to important properties of the current solution attempt by way of shallow deductions. It is easy, once the notation is learned, to think of a fact the problem solver ought to know, and express it as a rule.

The control structure of the problem solver is completely deterministic. Non-determinism is confined to a simple theorem prover which retrieves plan schemata for use in attacking a problem. If the theorem prover returns more than one possible plan, choice rules are retrieved to help choose among them. If a choice later leads to trouble, error-correction plans must be found to eliminate it. There is no backup.

I hope I have shown convincingly that problem solving is not itself a solved problem. In a sense, we have only begun to understand it. The major requirement for future progress in this domain is a flexible logic of time and action.

ACKNOWLEDGMENTS

I wish to express my thanks for ideas and criticism to Eugene Charniak, Jon Doyle, Johan de Kleer, Chuck Rieger, Gerald Sussman, Robert Wilensky, and others too numerous to mention.

REFERENCES

Bledsoe. W. W., & Tyson. M. The UT interactive prover. The University of Texas at Austin. Departments of Mathematics and Computer Sciences Automatic Theorem Proving Project Memo ATP 17. 1975.

Charniak. E. A framed PAINTING: The representation of a common sense knowledge fragment. Geneva: Institut pour les Etudes Semantiques et Cognitives Working Paper 28, 1976. Published in *Cognitive Science.* 1977, 4, 355–394.

Davis, R. Applications of meta level knowledge to the construction, maintenance, and use of large knowledge bases. Palo Alto: Stanford AI Laboratory Memo, 283, 1976.

Doyle. J. Truth maintenance systems for problem solving. Cambridge. Mass.: MIT AI Laboratory Technical Report 419, 1977.

Ernst. G., & Newell, A. *GPS: A case study in generality and problem-solving.* New York: Academic Press, 1969.

Feigenbaum. E. The art of artificial intelligence: themes and case studies of knowledge engineering. *Proceedings of the Fifth International Joint Conference on Artificial Intelligence.* 1977. pp. 1014–1029.

Fikes, R. E. Monitored execution of robot plans produced by STRIPS. *Proc. IFIP Congress,* Ljubljana, Yugoslavia. pp. 189–194.

Fikes, R. E., & Nilsson, N. J. 1971. STRIPS: a new approach to the application of theorem proving to problem solving. *Artificial Intelligence.* 1971, 2, 189–208.

Freeman, P., & Newell, A. A model for functional reasoning in design. *Proceedings of the Second International Joint Conference on Artificial Intelligence,* 1971. pp. 621–640.

Hayes, P. J. In defense of logic. *Proceedings of the Second International Joint Conference on Artificial Intelligence,* 1977. pp. 559–565.

Hewitt, C. Description and theoretical analysis (using schemata) of PLANNER: a language for proving theorems and manipulating models in a robot. Cambridge: MIT AI Laboratory Technical Report 258, 1972.

De Kleer, J., Doyle, J., Steele, G. L., & Sussman, G. J. Explicit control of reasoning. Cambridge: MIT AI laboratory Memo 427. 1977. Also in *Proceedings of the conference on AI and programming languages.* Rochester. New York. Pp. 116–125.

Mark, W. S. The reformulation approach to building expert systems. *Proceedings of the Fifth International Joint Conference on Artificial Intelligence,* 1977. pp. 329–335.

McCarthy, J., & Hayes, P. J. Some philosophical problems from the standpoint of artificial intelligence. In Meltzer & D. Michie (Eds.), *Machine intelligence,* Vol. 4. New York: American Elsevier. 1969. Pp. 463–502.

McDermott, D. Assimilation of new information by a natural language-understanding system. Cambridge. Mass.: MIT AI Laboratory Technical Report 291, 1974.

McDermott, D. A deductive model of control of a problem solver. *Proceedings of the workshop on pattern-directed inference systems* (SIGART Newsletter no. 63). 1977. Pp. 2–7. (a)

McDermott, D. Flexibility and efficiency in a computer program for designing circuits. Cambridge: MIT AI Laboratory Technical Report 402, 1977. (b)

McDermott, D. Vocabularies for problem solver state descriptions. *Proceedings of the Fifth International Joint Conference on Artificial Intelligence.* 1977. pp. 229–234. (c)

McDermott, D. Deduction in the pejorative sense. Presented at Workshop on Automatic Deduction, MIT. 1977. (d)

McDermott, D. Circuit design as problem solving. *Proceedings of the IFIP workshop on artificial intelligence and pattern recognition in computer-aided design.* New York: Springer Verlag. 1978.

Moore. J., & Newell. A. How can Merlin understand? In L. Gregg (Ed.). *Knowledge and cognition.* Hillsdale. N.J.: Lawrence Erlbaum Associates, 1974. Pp. 201–252.

Newell. A.. & Simon. H. A. *Human problem solving.* Englewood Cliffs. N.J.: Prentice-Hall, 1972.

Nilsson. N. J. *Problem-solving methods in artificial intelligence.* New York: McGraw-Hill, 1971.

Rescher. N., & Urquhart. A. *Temporal logic.* New York: Springer-Verlag. 1971.

Rieger. C. An organization of knowledge for problem solving and language comprehension. *Artificial Intelligence.* 1976. 7, 89–127.

Rieger, C., & London, P. Subgoal protection and unravelling during plan synthesis. *Proceedings of the Fifth International Joint Conference on Artificial Intelligence.* 1977. pp. 487–493.

Sacerdoti, E. D. A structure for plans and behavior. Menlo Park: SRI AI Center Technical Note 109. 1975.

Schank, R., & Abelson, R. *Scripts, plans, goals, and understanding.* Hillsdale, N.J.: Lawrence Erlbaum Associates, 1977.

Siklossy, L., & Dreussi, J. An efficient robot planner which generates its own procedures. *Proceedings of the Third International Joint Conference on Artificial Intelligence.* 1973. pp. 423–430.

Stallman, R., & Sussman, G. J. Forward reasoning and dependency-directed backtracking in a system for computer-aided circuit analysis. *Artificial Intelligence,* 1977, **9**, 135–196.

Sussman, G. J. *A computer model of skill acquisition.* New York: American Elsevier, 1975.

Wilensky, R. PAM, a program that infers intentions. *Proceedings of the Fifth International Joint Conference on Artificial Intelligence.* 1977. p. 15.

Winston, P. *Artificial intelligence.* Reading, Mass.: Addison-Wesley, 1977.

Cognitive Science 3(4) 1979 pp. 275-310

A Cognitive Model of Planning*

BARBARA HAYES-ROTH

AND

FREDERICK HAYES-ROTH

The Rand Corporation, Santa Monica, California

This paper presents a cognitive model of the planning process. The model generalizes the theoretical architecture of the Hearsay-II system. Thus, it assumes that planning comprises the activities of a variety of cognitive "specialists." Each specialist can suggest certain kinds of decisions for incorporation into the plan in progress. These include decisions about: (a) how to approach the planning problem; (b) what knowledge bears on the problem; (c) what kinds of actions to try to plan; (d) what specific actions to plan; and (e) how to allocate cognitive resources during planning. Within each of these categories, different specialists suggest decisions at different levels of abstraction. The activities of the various specialists are not coordinated in any systematic way. Instead, the specialists operate opportunistically, suggesting decisions whenever promising opportunities arise. The paper presents a detailed account of the model and illustrates its performance with a "thinking aloud" protocol. The paper contrasts the proposed model of a computer simulation of the model. It also describes the performance with successive refinement models and attempts to resolve apparent differences between the two points of view.

1. INTRODUCTION

Planning is a familiar cognitive activity. We all have many opportunities to decide how we will behave in future situations. For example, we plan how to get to work in the morning, where and with whom to eat lunch, and how to spend our evenings. We also make longer-term plans, such as what to do on our vacations, how to celebrate Christmas, and what career path to follow. Thus, planning influences many activities, from the most mundane to the most consequential, in everyday life.

We define planning as the predetermination of a course of action aimed at achieving some goal. It is the first stage of a two-stage problem-solving process. The second stage entails monitoring and guiding the execution of the plan to a successful conclusion. We refer to these two stages as *planning and control*. This paper focuses on the planning stage of planning and control. We have two main objectives: to characterize the planning process and to propose a theoretical account of it.

Sacerdoti's (1975) work is probably the best-known previous research on planning. His computer program, NOAH, implements a successive refinement approach to planning. NOAH formulates problems in terms of high-level goals that specify sequences of actions (for example, the monkey should get the bananas and then eat them). NOAH expands each constituent subgoal into additional subgoals, maintaining any indeterminate sequential orderings as long as possible. In this manner, NOAH eventually generates correct plans specifying sequences of elementary actions. When executed, these actions transform initial conditions into a series of intermediate conditions, culminating in the goal state. (See also: Ernst & Newell, 1969; Fahlman, 1974; Fikes, 1977; Fikes & Nilsson, 1971; Sacerdoti, 1974; Sussman, 1973).

While not incompatible with successive-refinement models, our view of planning is somewhat different. We share the assumption that planning processes operate in a two-dimensional planning space defined on time and abstraction dimensions. However, we assume that people's planning activity is largely *opportunistic*. That is, at each point in the process, the planner's current decisions and observations suggest various opportunities for plan development. The planner's subsequent decisions follow up on selected opportunities. Sometimes, these decision-sequences follow an orderly path and produce a neat top-down expansion as described above. However, some decisions and observations might also suggest less orderly opportunities for plan development. For example, a decision about how to conduct initial planned activities might illuminate certain constraints on the planning of later activities and cause the planner to refocus attention on that phase of the plan. Similarly, certain low-level refinements of a previous, abstract plan might suggest an alternative abstract plan to replace the original one.

In general, the assumption that people plan opportunistically implies that interim decisions can lead to subsequent decisions at arbitrary points in the planning space. Thus, a decision at a given level of abstraction, specifying an action to be taken at a particular point in time, may influence subsequent decisions at higher or lower levels of abstraction, specifying actions to be taken at earlier or later points in time.

This view of the planning process suggests that planners will produce many coherent decision sequences, but some less coherent sequences as well. In extreme cases, the overall process might appear chaotic. The relative orderliness of particular planning processes presumably reflects individual differences among planners as well as different task demands.

We have tried to develop a theoretical framework that can accommodate both systematic approaches to planning, like successive refinement, and the more

*ONR Contract N00014-78-C-0039, NR 157-411 supported this research. We thank Bob Anderson, Ed Feigenbaum, Penny Nii, Perry Thorndyke and members of the Rand Cognitive Sciences Brownbag for many valuable discussions of this research. Bob Anderson, Bill Faught, Phil Klahr, Stan Rosenschein, and Bob Wesson provided useful comments on an earlier version of this manuscript. We thank Allan Collins for outstanding editorial assistance. Send reprint requests to: Barbara Hayes-Roth, The Rand Corporation, 1700 Main Street, Santa Monica, California, 90406.

1. Let's go back down the errand list. Pick up medicine for the dog at veterinary supplies. That's definitely a primary, anything taking care of health. Fan belt for refrigerator. Definitely a primary because you need to keep the refrigerator. Checking out two out of three luxury apartments. It's got to be a secondary, another browse. Meet the friend at one of the restaurants for lunch. All right. Now, that's going to be able to be varied I hope. That's a primary though because it's an appointment, something you have to do. Buy a toy for the dog at the pet store. If you pass it, sure. If not, the dog can play with something else. Movie in one of the movie theaters. Better write that down, those movie times, 1, 3, or 5. Write that down on my sheet just to remember. And that's a primary because it's something I have to do. Pick up the watch at the watch repair. That's one of those borderline ones. Do you need your watch or not? Give it a primary. Special order a book at the bookstore.

2. We're having an awful lot of primaries in this one. It's going to be a busy day.

3. Fresh vegetables at the grocery. That's another primary. You need the food. Gardening magazine at the newsstand. Definitely secondary. All the many obligations of life.

4. Geez, can you believe all these primaries?

5. All right. We are now at the health club.

6. What is going to be the closest one?

7. The appliance store is a few blocks away. The medicine for the dog at the vet's office isn't too far away. Movie theaters—let's hold off on that for a little while. Pick up the watch. That's all the way across town. Special order a book at the bookstore.

8. Probably it would be best if we headed in a southeasterly direction. Start heading this way. I can see later on there are a million things I want to do in that part of town.

9. No we're not. We could end up with a movie just before we get the car. I had thought at first that I might head in a southeasterly direction because there's a grocery store, a watch repair, a movie theater all in that general area. Also a luxury apartment. However, near my parking lot also is a movie, which would make it convenient to get out of the movie and go to the car. But I think we can still end up that way.

10. All right. Apparently the closest one to the health club is going to be the vet's shop. So I might as well get that out of the way. It's a primary and it's the closest. We'll start . . .

    [The experimenter mentions that he has overlooked the nearby restaurant and flower shop.]

11. Oh, how foolish of me. You're right. I can still do that and still head in the general direction.

12. But, then again, that puts a whole new light on things. We do have a bookstore. We do have . . . OK. Break up town into sections. We'll call them northwest and southeast. See how many primaries are in that section. Down here in the southeast section, we have the grocery store, the watch repair and the movie theater. In the northwest section we have the grocery store, the flower shop, the vet's shop, and the restaurant.

13. And since we are leaving at 11:00, we might be able to get those chores done so that some time when I'm in the area, hit that restaurant. Let's try for that. Get as many of those out of the way as possible. We really could have a nice day here.

14. OK. First choice number one. At 11:00 we leave the health club. Easily, no doubt about it, we can be right across the street in 5 minutes to the flower shop. Here we go. Flower shop at 11:05. Let's give ourselves 10 minutes to browse through some bouquets and different floral arrangements.

Figure 1. Thinking aloud protocol from the errand-planning task.

generally opportunistic process described above. The next section of the paper presents a "thinking-aloud" protocol that illustrates the kind of behavior the model must explain. Section 3 describes the proposed planning model. Section 4 shows how the model could produce the thinking-aloud protocol. Section 5 describes a computer implementation of the model and compares its performance to the performance of the human subject. Section 6 addresses questions of theoretical complexity. Section 7 attempts to resolve apparent differences between the proposed model and successive refinement models. Section 8 summarizes our conclusions.

2. PLANNING A DAY'S ERRANDS

The thinking aloud protocol in Figure 1 illustrates the kind of behavior a comprehensive planning model must explain. A college graduate produced it while planning a hypothetical day's errands. We have collected a total of thirty protocols from five different subjects performing six different versions of such errand-planning tasks. The protocol shown in Figure 1 is representative of this set.

The subject began with the following problem description:

You have just finished working out at the health club. It is 11:00 and you can plan the rest of your day as you like. However, you must pick up your car from the Maple Street parking garage by 5:30 and then head home. You'd also like to see a movie today, if possible. Show times at both movie theaters are 1:00, 3:00, and 5:00. Both movies are on your "must see" list, but go to whichever one most conveniently fits into your plan. Your other errands are as follows:

> pick up medicine for your dog at the vet;
> buy a fan belt for your refrigerator at the appliance store;
> check out two of the three luxury apartments;
> meet a friend for lunch at one of the restaurants;
> buy a toy for your dog at the pet store;
> pick up your watch at the watch repair;
> special order a book at the bookstore;
> buy fresh vegetables at the grocery;
> buy a gardening magazine at the newsstand;
> go to the florist to send flowers to a friend in the hospital

Note that the problem description specifies more errands than the subject could reasonably expect to accomplish in the time available. The subject's task was to formulate a realistic plan indicating which errands he would do, when he would do them, and how he would travel among them.

Figure 2 shows the hypothetical town in which the subject planned his errands. Each of the pictures on the map symbolizes a particular store or other destination. The subject was quite familiar with both the symbology and the layout of the town. In addition, the map was available during planning.

We have numbered small sections of the protocol in Figure 1 to facilitate the discussion. Also, for convenience, we refer to specific errands by the names of the associated stores or other destinations.

15. You know, you want to take care in sending the right type of flowers. That's something to deal with personal relationships.

16. At 11:10 we go north on Belmont Avenue to the Chestnut Street intersection with Belmont and on the northwest corner is a grocery.

17. Oh, real bad. Don't want to buy the groceries now because groceries rot. You're going to be taking them with you all day long. Going to have to put the groceries way towards the end.

18. And that could change it again. This is not one of my days. I have those every now and again. Let's go with our original plan. Head to the southeast corner.

19. Still leaving the flower shop at 11:10. And we are going to go to the vet's shop next for medicine for the dog. We'll be there at 11:15, be out by 11:20. The vet's shop.

20. Proceeding down Oak Street. I think it would be, let's give ourselves a little short-cut.

21. Maybe we'll knock off a secondary task too.

22. Proceed down Oak Street to Belmont. Belmont south to the card and gift shop, or rather, to the department store. Cut through the department store to Johnson Street to the newsstand. Pick up our gardening magazine at the newsstand.

23. We're heading this way. We're going to make a definite southeast arrow.

24. Third item will be the newsstand since we are heading in that direction. Often I like to do that. I know buying a gardening magazine is hardly a primary thing to do, but since I'm heading that way, it's only going to take a second. Let's do it. Get it out of the way. Sometimes you'll find at the end of the day you've done all your primary stuff, but you still have all those little nuisance secondary items that you wish you would have gotten done. So, 11:20 we left the vet's office. We should arrive 11:25 at the newsstand. 11:30 we've left the newsstand.

25. Now let's start over here. We're going to be in trouble a little bit because of that appliance store hanging way up north. So we could: appliance store is a primary. It's got to be done.

26. All right, let's do this. This could work out. Market Square, we leave the Market Square exit of the newsstand up to Washington, arrive at the pet store, buy a toy for the dog at the pet store. We're there at 11:35, out at 11:40. Pretty good. 11:40. Proceeding east just slightly, up north Dunbar Street to the appliance store, we arrive there at 11:45, and we leave there, fan belt, leave at 11:50.

27. We're looking good. We've knocked off a couple of secondaries that really we hadn't planned on, but because of the locations of some stores that are in the way that could be convenient.

28. Now it's 11:50, right near noontime.

29. And I think one of the next things to do, checking our primaries, what we have left to do, would be to go to the restaurant. And we can be at the restaurant at 5 minutes to noon. We're going to go down Dunbar Street, south on Dunbar Street to Washington, to the restaurant which is located on the very eastern edge of the map. Meeting our friend there for lunch at 11:55, allowing a nice leisurely lunch. No, oh yeah. An hour. 12:55.

30. Now we've got to start being concerned about a few other things. We can pick up the car from the Maple Street garage by 5:30.

31. It's 12:55, done with lunch. Primary left to do, see a movie, pick up a watch, special order a book, and get fresh vegetables.

32. So then with what we have left now to do is special order a book at a bookstore and pick up the watch at the watch repair.

33. So, I think we can make this a very nice trip. We're at the restaurant on Washington Avenue. Let's proceed west one block to Madison, south to Cedar Street. Cedar Street west right there at the intersection of Cedar and Madison is the watch repair. Pick up the watch at the watch repair. We should be at the watch repair by 1:05. Give us a good 10 minutes. 1:05 at the watch repair. Pick up a watch. We're out of there by 1:10.

34. Now I'm going to go just a slight back down Madison to one of the luxury apartments. I arrive at one of the luxury apartments at 1:15. I allow myself 15 minutes to browse. Two bathroom apartment. 1:30. Now I'm leaving that.

35. Next, I'm going to go west on Lakeshore, north on Dunbar, west on Cedar to the bookstore. And I will arrive at the bookstore at 1:35. Special order my book, 1:40.

36. From the bookstore I can go west on Cedar Street just a hair, down Kingsway, to a second luxury apartment. Find out what's happening at that luxury apartment. And I'm there at 1:45, allowing myself another 15 minutes there, 2:00 we're out.

37. We're taken care of checking out 2 out of 3 luxury apartments. We ordered our book.

38. Now we do have a problem. It's 2:00 and all we have left to do is see a movie and get the vegetables. And that's where I think I've blown this plan. I've got an hour left there before the movie.

39. So the best way to eliminate as much time as possible since we are now located at the Cedar Lakeshore apartments. That's not going to be . . .

40. If I go get the groceries now, it's not really going to be consistent with the plans throughout the day because I've been holding off on the groceries for rotting. If I take them to a movie. . . Vegetables don't really perish like ice cream.

41. We leave the luxury apartment on Lakeshore, proceed due east to Dunbar, and we're at the grocery store at 2:05. 2:05 at the grocery store. Hunt around for fresh vegetables, and we can give ourselves 20 minutes there. So we leave there at 2:25.

42. We leave there and we proceed up Dunbar, north to Cedar, Cedar west to the movie theater.

43. We probably arrive at the movie theater at 2:35. 2:35 we arrive at the movie theater which still gives us 25 minutes to kill before the next showing. But that's that. We're going to have to simply do it. I'm going to have to go with it for right now.

44. The plan seems to have worked well enough up until then. We made better time than we had thought. That happens in life sometimes. How did I get here so fast?

45. 2:25. We catch the 3:00 showing. We leave there at 5:00. Proceed immediately down Johnson, up Belmont to the parking structure, and we're there at 5:05 at the parking structure. We had to pick it up by 5:30.

46. Got everything done, the only problem being having a little bit of time to kill in that one period.

47. You could have stretched out, to make things fair, you could have said, well, okay, I'll give myself an hour and 15 minutes at lunch, but as I did plan it, I did come up 30 minutes over. 25 minutes there. And that's a little bit of, when that happens you feel bad. You remember the old Ben Franklin saying about don't kill time because it's time that kills us. And I hate to have time to waste. I've got to have things work very nicely.

In sections 1–4, the subject defines his goal and characterizes his task. Thus, in 1 and 3, he uses world knowledge to categorize the errands on his list as either primary errands, which he feels he must do, or secondary errands. In 2 and 4, he infers that, given the time constraints, his goal will be difficult to achieve.

In sections 5–7, the subject begins planning how to go about doing his errands. Notice that he begins planning at a fairly detailed level of abstraction. He has made only one kind of prior high-level decision—defining his goal. He has not considered what might be an efficient way to organize his plan. He has not made any effort to group his errands. He does not take his final location into consideration. Instead he immediately begins sequencing individual errands, working forward in time from his initial location. Thus, he ascertains his initial location, the health club, indicates that he wants to sequence the closest errand next, and begins locating the primary errands on his list, looking for the closest one.

In section 8, the subject changes his level of abstraction. In the course of looking for the closest errand to his current location, he apparently discovers a cluster of errands in the southeast corner of town. This observation leads him to make a decision at a "higher" or more abstract level than he had previously. Thus, he decides to treat the errands in the southeast corner as a cluster. He plans to go to the southeast corner and do those errands at about the same time.

In section 9, the subject modifies his high-level cluster. He discovers that one of the errands in the cluster, the movie, can also be done on the west side of town, near his final destination, the Maple Street parking structure. He changes back to the more detailed level of abstraction. Planning backward in time from his final location, he decides to end his day by going to the movie and then picking up his car. In so doing, he removes the movie from the high-level cluster.

In section 10, the subject begins to instantiate his high-level plan to go to the southeast corner at the lower, errand-sequencing level. Again, he is looking for the closest errand on his way, and he chooses the vet.

At that point, the experimenter interrupts to point out to the subject that he has overlooked several closer errands.

In sections 11 and 12, the subject incorporates the new information into his planning. His first reaction, in 11, is to continue working at the errand-sequencing level, simply considering the newly identified errands among those he might do next. However, additional observation at this level leads him to make a decision at the more abstract level. Again, he decides to treat a group of errands, those in the northwest corner of town, as a cluster. This leads him to revise his high-level plan to include two clusters of errands, the northwest cluster and the southeast cluster.

In section 13, the subject begins instantiating his new high-level plan. He notes the initial time, 11:00, and the presence of a restaurant, another errand in the northwest cluster. These observations lead him to formulate an intermediate level plan regarding how to sequence errands within the northwest cluster. He

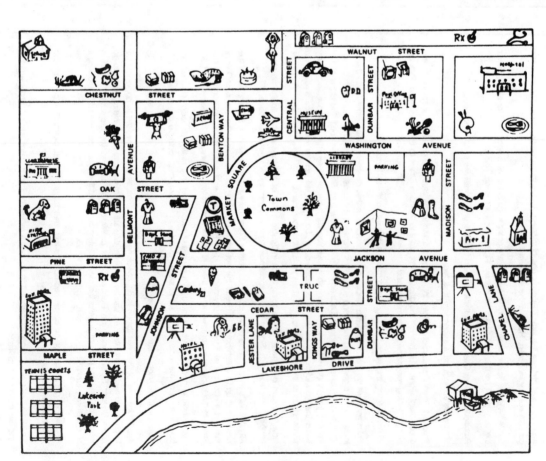

Figure 2. Town map for the errand-planning task.

decides to sequence the errands in that cluster to permit him to arrive at the restaurant in time for lunch.

In sections 14–15, the subject works on instantiating his revised high-level plan at a very detailed level of abstraction. Here, he not only sequences individual errands (the florist and the grocery), he specifies the exact routes he will take among them. In addition, the subject mentally simulates execution of his plan in progress, estimating how long each errand should take and computing the "current" time at each stage of the plan.

In section 16, the subject's mental simulation suggests the inference that his groceries will perish if he picks them up early in the day. This leads him to revise his low-level plan, assigning the grocery a sequential position at the end of the plan.

In section 17, the subject decides to abandon his two cluster high-level plan in favor of his original high-level plan including only the southeast cluster. Presumably he decided that, without the grocery, there were not enough errands in the northwest cluster to occupy him until lunch.

In section 18, the subject begins instantiating his original high-level plan at a more detailed level. Again, he sequences individual errands (the florist and the civet) and specifies exact routes among them, mentally simulating execution of his plan as he formulates it.

In sections 19–23, the subject continues working at the lowest level of abstraction. He works on planning his route from the sequenced errands to the southeast corner, mentally simulating execution of his plan in the process. In so doing, he notices a "short-cut" through the card and gift shop and incorporates it into his plan, later replacing it with one through the department store. He then notices that taking the short-cut will put him very near the newsstand. Although the newsstand is a secondary errand, he decides to incorporate it in his plan because it is so convenient. Thus, a decision at the lowest level of abstraction leads him to make a decision at the next higher level. Note also that this decision implies addition of the newsstand to the subject's definition of the goal.

In sections 24–26, the subject continues working at a low level of abstraction. He notes that his high-level plan does not include any provision for the appliance store, a primary errand. He plans to go there directly, temporarily ignoring his high-level plan to go to the southeast corner. He also notices that another secondary errand, the pet store, is on the way to the appliance store and, because it is so convenient, incorporates that errand into his plan. Again, he plans at the level of sequencing errands and specifying routes and simulates execution of the plan as he goes along. Note that these decisions imply addition of the pet store to the subject's definition of the goal. (Note also that, while the short-cut planned in 19–23 was a short-cut to the southeast corner, it is a detour in the planned route to the appliance store.)

The remainder of the protocol (sections 27–45) documents the completion of the subject's plan. In the interests of brevity, we simply summarize this part of

the protocol. Basically, the subject decides to incorporate the appliance store and the restaurant before finally arriving at the southeast corner. Then he plans all of the remaining errands, including all remaining secondary errands. Figure 9 below shows the subject's final plan.

This protocol illustrates a number of the points made above. First, the subject's plan develops incrementally at various points in the planning space we described. He plans actions at various points in the plan's temporal sequence, and he also plans at different levels of abstraction. Second, the subject appears to plan opportunistically, "jumping about" in the planning space to develop promising aspects of the plan in progress. For example, the planner does not plan strictly forward in time. Instead, he plans temporally-anchored sub-plans at arbitrary points on the time dimension and eventually concatenates the sub-plans. Similarly, the planner does not plan in a systematic top-down fashion across the different levels of abstraction. He frequently plans low-level sequences of errands or routes in the absence, and sometimes in violation, of a prescriptive high-level plan. Finally, decisions at a given point in the planning space appear to influence subsequent decisions at both later and earlier points in the temporal sequence and at both higher and lower levels of abstraction. The protocol contains examples of each of these kinds of influence.

The protocol illustrates another important component of the planning process—the ability to simulate execution of a plan mentally and to use the results of the simulation to guide subsequent planning. Mental simulation can answer a variety of questions for the subject: At what time will I arrive at (or leave) a particular destination? How long will I take to perform a certain action? What sequence of operations will I perform to satisfy a particular sub-goal? How long will it take to execute a plan or partial plan? What effects will my actions produce? What have I accomplished so far? The subject can use this information to evaluate and revise prior planning and to constrain subsequent planning.

The subject performs two kinds of mental simulation corresponding to *time-driven* and *event-driven* processes. Sometimes he simulates his plan by mentally stepping through a sequence of time units for each planned action (e.g., walking, carrying a package, performing an errand). With each successive step, he extrapolates the results of each planned action, updating his understanding of the "current state" accordingly. At other times, the subject performs "event-driven" simulation. In this case, he mentally moves directly from one planned situation to another, ignoring any actions in the intervening temporal interval. He then computes certain consequences arising from the transition.

More importantly, in the present context, the subject simulates execution of plans at different levels of abstraction. Thus, in sections 14–15, he simulates execution of a detailed plan. By stepping through his plan, the subject computes expected times for performing individual errands and traveling specific routes. In sections 24–26, the subject simulates execution of his high-level plan for performing errands in the northwest and then those in the southeast. Here, he performs event-driven simulation, inferring that if he executes his high-level plan, proceeding directly to the southeast corner of town, he will neglect a primary errand.

In the next section, we describe the proposed planning model in detail. The model postulates specific levels of abstraction and a structural organization for the planning space. In addition, it postulates decision-making mechanisms that permit theoretical interpretation of subjects' apparently chaotic progress through the planning space.

3. AN OPPORTUNISTIC MODEL OF PLANNING

Overview

The proposed model assumes that the planning process comprises the independent actions of many distinct cognitive *specialists* (akin to demons in Selfridge's (1959) Pandemonium model). Each specialist makes tentative *decisions* for incorporation into a tentative *plan*. Further, different specialists influence different aspects of the plan. For example, some specialists suggest high-level, abstract additions to the plan, while others suggest detailed sequences of specific actions.

All specialists record their decisions in a common data structure, called the *blackboard*. The blackboard enables the specialists to interact and communicate. Each specialist can retrieve prior *decisions* of interest from the blackboard, regardless of which specialists recorded them. The specialist combines these earlier decisions with its own decision-making heuristics to generate new decisions.

The model partitions the blackboard into several *planes* containing conceptually different categories of decisions. For example, one plane contains decisions about explicitly planned activities, while another contains decisions about data that might be useful in generating planned activities. The model further partitions each plane into several *levels* of abstraction. These partitionings serve two functions. First, they provide a conceptual taxonomy of the decisions made during planning. Second, they restrict the number of prior decisions each individual specialist must consider in generating its own decisions (see also Englemore & Nii, 1977). Thus, most specialists deal with information that occurs at only a few levels of particular planes of the blackboard.

The proposed model generalizes the theoretical architecture developed by Reddy and his associates (Cf. CMU Computer Science Research Group, 1977; Lesser, Fennell, Erman, & Reddy, 1975; Erman & Lesser, 1975; Lesser & Erman, 1977; Hayes–Roth & Lesser, 1977) for the Hearsay-II speech-understanding system. Others have since applied it to image understanding (Prager, Nagin, Kohler, Hanson, & Riseman, 1977), reading comprehension (Rumelhart, 1976), protein-crystallographic analysis (Nii & Feigenbaum, 1977),

and inductive inference (Soloway & Riseman, 1977). The proposed model is, to our knowledge, the first attempt to adapt the Hearsay-II architecture to a "generation" problem. We describe it in detail below.

Specialists

As mentioned above, independent cognitive specialists generate decisions during the planning process. The model operationalizes specialists as condition-action rules.

The condition component describes circumstances under which the specialist can contribute to the plan. Ordinarily, the condition requires the planner to have made certain prior decisions. However, it may also require satisfaction of other, arbitrarily complex criteria. For example, one specialist's condition might require a prior decision to organize the plan by spatial clusters of errands and prior identification of useful clusters.

The action component defines the specialist's behavior. The action may include an arbitrary amount of computation, but always results in the generation of a new decision or modification of a prior decision. For example, one specialist might detect and identify spatial clusters of errands on the map. Another might generate an abstract organizational design for the plan as a whole.

Thus, specialists generalize the symbol-manipulation capabilities of production rules (Newell & Simon, 1972) to more complex, pattern-directed activity (see also: CMU Computer Science Research Group, 1977; Hayes-Roth, Waterman, & Lenat, 1978; Lenat, 1975).

The Blackboard

As discussed above, specialists record their decisions in a common data structure called the blackboard. The blackboard contains five conceptual planes: *plan, plan-abstractions, knowledge-base, executive* and *meta-plan*. We characterize each of these below.

We have already characterized the plan plane in our discussion of the thinking-aloud protocol. Decisions on this plane represent actions the planner intends to take in the world. For example, the planner might decide to travel in a circle around town, performing errands along the way, or to travel from the florist to the vet along Belmont Avenue and Oak Street. Both of these decisions describe explicit actions the planner intends to carry out.

Decisions on the plan-abstractions plane characterize desired attributes of potential plan decisions. Thus, these decisions indicate the kinds of actions the planner would like to take without specifying the actions themselves. For example, the planner might decide to go to the closest errand next. This decision characterizes a desired sequence of errands, but does not identify a particular

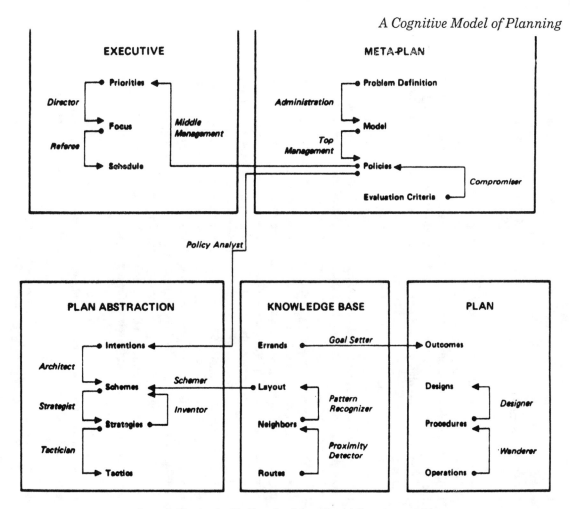

Figure 3. The planning blackboard and the actions of illustrative specialists.

sequence. Similarly, the planner might decide to organize the plan around spatial clusters of errands. Again, this decision characterizes a desired abstract plan, but does not instantiate it (i.e. does not specify particular spatial clusters).

The knowledge-base contains observations and computations regarding relationships in the world that might bear on the planning process. These computations are useful in suggesting plan-abstractions and instantiating them in the plan. For example, the planner might ascertain that the florist is the closest errand to the health club. That information would permit instantiation of a prior plan-abstraction decision to go to the closest errand next. As a second example, the planner might observe that several errand-sites cluster in close proximity on the map. That observation might suggest a subsequent plan-abstraction decision to organize the plan around several such spatially arrayed clusters.

Plan, plan-abstractions, and knowledge-base decisions determine features of the developing plan. Executive decisions, by contrast, determine features of the planning process. Thus, the executive plane contains decisions about the allocation of cognitive resources during the planning process. These decisions determine which aspect of the plan the planner will develop and which specialist the planner will bring to bear at each point in the process. For example, the planner might decide to determine which errands to include in the plan before working out the details of the plan. As a second example, the planner might decide to focus on working out routes among previously sequenced errands.

The meta-plan plane contains decisions about how to approach the planning problem. These decisions reflect the planner's understanding of the problem, the methods she or he intends to apply to it, and the criteria she or he will use to evaluate prospective solutions.

As mentioned above, the model further partitions each plane of the blackboard into several levels of abstraction. In the following sections, we describe the postulated levels of abstraction for each of the five planes (see Figure 3 on p. 288).

Levels of the Plan Plane. The plan plane has four levels of abstraction. Decisions at the four levels form a potential hierarchy, with decisions at each level specifying a more refined plan than those at the next higher level. Beginning at the most abstract level, *outcomes* indicate what the planner intends to accomplish by executing the finished plan. For the errand-planning task, outcomes indicate what errands the planner intends to accomplish by executing the plan. For example, the planner might decide to accomplish the desired errands at the florist, the vet, and the grocery store. At the next lower level, *designs* characterize the general behavioral approach by which the planner intends to achieve the outcomes. For the errand-planning task, designs characterize the general order in which the planner intends to perform errands. For example, the planner might decide to head toward the southeast cluster. Next, *procedures* specify specific sequences of gross actions. For the errand-planning task, procedures specify sequences of errands. For example, the planner might decide to go to the vet after the florist. Finally, *operations* specify sequences of more minute actions. For the errand-planning task, operations specify the details of performing individual errands and the routes by which the planner will proceed from each errand to the next. For example, the planner might decide to travel from the vet to the florist via Belmont Avenue and Oak Street.[1]

Levels of the Plan-Abstractions Plane. The plan-abstractions plane contains four levels. Each level characterizes types of decisions suggested for incorporation into the corresponding level of the plan plane. For example, the planner might indicate an *intention* to establish all of the "critical" errands as the outcome of the plan. At the next lower level, the planner might generate a *scheme* that suggests generating a design featuring spatial clusters of errands. At the next level, the planner might develop a *strategy* to go to the closest errand next, characterizing a desirable procedure level decision. Finally, the planner might adopt a *tactic* to search for a short-cut between one errand and the next, characterizing a desirable operation level decision.

Levels of the Knowledge Base Plane. The knowledge base also has four levels of abstraction. Each level contains observations and computations useful in suggesting decisions at the corresponding level of the plan-abstractions plane or instantiating them at the corresponding level of the plan plane. Because the levels of the knowledge base contain problem-specific information, we have given them problem-specific names. At the *errand* level, for example, the planner might determine the relative importance of each desired errand. At the *layout* level, the planner might observe that several errands form a convenient spatial cluster. At the *neighbor* level, the planner might observe that two planned errands are near one another. At the *route* level, the planner might detect a short-cut.

Levels of the Executive Plane. The executive plane has three levels of abstraction. Decisions made at the three levels on this plane form a hierarchy, with decisions at each level potentially refining ones at the level above. Beginning at the top, *priority* decisions establish principles for allocating cognitive resources during the entire planning process. These decisions generally indicate preferences for allocating processing activity to certain areas of the planning blackboard before others. For example, the planner, by approaching the errand-planning task as a resource-limited scheduling problem, might decide to determine which errands to do before working out the details of the plan. At the next lower level, *focus* decisions indicate what kind of decision to make at a specific point in time. For example, the planner might decide to focus attention on generating an operation-level refinement of a previously generated procedure. Finally, *schedule* decisions resolve any remaining conflicts among competing specialists. If, given current priorities and focus decisions, more than one specialist can make a contribution to the plan, the planner must make schedule decisions to decide among them. Schedule decisions select specialists on the basis of relative efficiency, reliability, etc. (Hayes-Roth & Lesser, 1977).

Levels of the Meta-Plan Plane. The meta-plan plane has four levels: *problem definition, problem-solving model, policies,* and *evaluation criteria.* Unlike the levels on the other four planes, these levels do not produce a neat hierarchy of decisions. However, they emphasize different aspects of the subject's approach to the planning problem and relate in systematic ways to the other planes of the blackboard.

Beginning at the top, problem definition decisions characterize the planner's own formulation of the task. These include descriptions of goals, available resources, possible actions, and constraints. For the errand-planning task, the problem definition would reflect the subject's understanding of the list of errands, contextual information, and associated instructions.

The chosen problem-solving model indicates how the planner intends to represent the problem and generate potential solutions. For example, the planner might view the errand-planning task as an instance of the familiar "traveling salesman" problem (Christophides, 1975) and approach the problem accordingly. Problem-solving models can also consist of general problem-solving strategies, such as "divide and conquer," "define and successively refine" (Aho, Hopcroft, & Ullman, 1974), etc. The planner presumably chooses a particular problem-solving model from known alternatives in response to specific problem characteristics. The problem-solving model, in turn, bears directly on subsequent executive decisions. For example, adoption of the traveling salesman model should lead to basically "bottom-up" executive decisions. That is, the planner should focus attention on the procedures and operations levels of the plan plane and on corresponding levels of the plan-abstractions and knowledge-base planes.

The planner's policies specify global constraints and desirable features for the developing plan. For example, the planner might decide that the plan must be efficient or that it should minimize certain risks. Some policy decisions derive implicitly from particular problem-solving models. For example, the traveling salesman model naturally implies a route-efficiency policy. Other policies are model-independent. In either case, policy decisions bear directly on subsequent plan-abstractions decisions. Particular policy decisions make particular plan-abstractions more or less desirable. For example, the route efficiency policy favors a strategy to go to the closest errand next. By contrast, it inhibits an intention to achieve only the most important errands.

[1]Obviously, partitioning plan decisions into four discrete categories is arbitrary and probably over-simplified. However, we find these categories intuitively appealing and they provide a convenient terminology for discussion. In addition, Hayes-Roth and Thorndyke (1979) have shown that theoretically naive subjects group statements drawn from planning protocols in exactly these four categories.

Finally, solution-evaluation criteria specify how the planner intends to evaluate prospective plans. For example, the planner might decide to speculate on what could go wrong during execution and insure that the plan is robust over those contingencies. Again, some of these decisions derive implicitly from particular problem-solving models, while others are independent. Obviously, the planner brings these criteria to bear on the developing plan and uses them to determine which plan decisions to preserve and which to change.

Control of the Planning Process

Under the control of the executive, the planning process proceeds through a series of "cycles" during which various specialists execute their actions. At the beginning of each cycle, some number of specialists have been invoked—that is, their conditions have been satisfied. The executive selects one of the invoked specialists to execute its action—that is, to generate a new decision and record it on the blackboard. The new decision invokes additional specialists and the next cycle begins. This process ordinarily continues until: (a) the planner has integrated mutually consistent decisions into a complete plan; and (b) the planner has decided that the existing plan satisfies important evaluation criteria. Under certain circumstances, the process might also terminate in failure.

schedule decisions. As discussed above, at each point in the sequence of recorded decisions, a schedule decision selects one of the currently invoked specialists to execute its action. We have omitted these decisions from Figures 4–8 for simplicity. However, it is appropriate to assume that a schedule decision selected each of the indicated specialist actions (noted by arrows).

Figure 4 shows the blackboard representation of sections 1–4 of the protocol. In sections 1 and 3, the subject works through the list of errands, assigning binary importance values (primary versus secondary) to each one. In sections 2 and 4, the subject remarks that the large number of primary errands implies that he will have a busy day. According to our assumptions, a specialist calculates importance values for individual errands and records these at the errands level of the knowledge base. However, we assume that a considerable amount of activity, unstated in the protocol, preceded and motivated this action. Figure 4 shows the blackboard representation of this implicit activity.

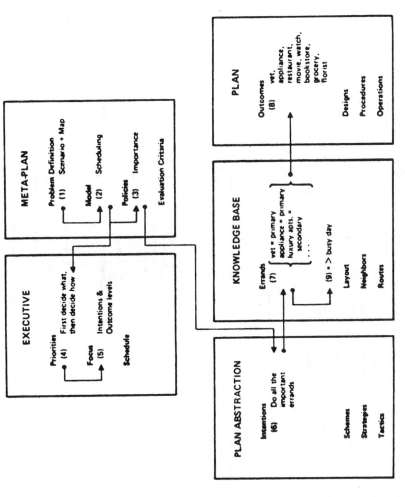

Figure 4. Blackboard representation of sections 1–4 of the protocol.

4. ANALYSIS OF THE PLANNING PROTOCOL UNDER THE OPPORTUNISTIC MODEL

In this section, we use the proposed model to "parse" sections 1–10 of the protocol. We intend this exercise to demonstrate the descriptive power of the model. Of course, the psychological validity of the model rests on more than this informal sufficiency test. In subsequent sections of the paper, we discuss a more formal sufficiency test based on a computer simulation and summarize several empirical tests of the model's assumptions.

Figures 4–8 show blackboard representations of sections 1–10 of the protocol as individual decisions. They also show how individual specialists respond to the presence of particular decisions on the blackboard by generating other decisions and recording them at appropriate locations on the blackboard. Each arrow represents the invocation and execution of a specialist. Thus, an arrow from one decision to another indicates that the former decision invoked a specialist that recorded the latter decision. In order to clarify the flow of activity, we have numbered decisions in Figures 4–8 according to their presumed order of occurrence. Note, however, that arrows need not connect consecutively numbered decisions. Occasionally, an early decision invokes a specialist that is not scheduled until after one or more other specialists have been scheduled and added their decisions to the blackboard.

We have omitted only one kind of decision from these illustrations—

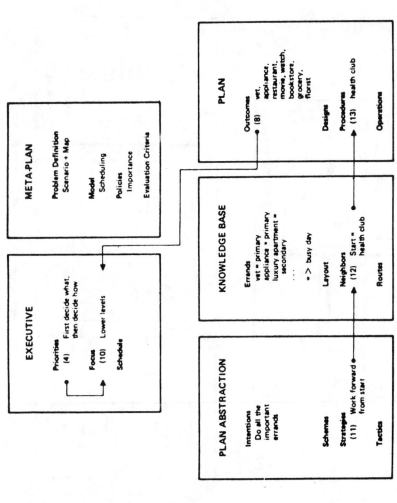

Figure 5. Blackboard representation of section 5 of the protocol.

The subject begins the task with a problem definition (1), including the scenario and map provided by the experimenter. The protocol suggests that the subject categorizes the problem as a resource-limited scheduling problem (2). In other words, the subject apparently views the task as one in which he cannot do all of the things he wants to do and, therefore, must decide which things to do and then how to do them. The appearance of this problem-solving model on the blackboard presumably invokes two other specialists, One generates and records a useful policy (3), emphasizing the importance of individual errands. The other generates and records an appropriate set of priorities (4). The priorities, in turn, motivate a decision to focus on the intentions and outcomes levels of the plan-abstraction and plan planes (5). Given this focus and the errand-importance policy, a specialist records an intention to do all the important errands (6). This intention presumably invokes the specialist described above that calculates the errand-importance values actually stated in the protocol (7). This activity implies another unstated decision, that the intended outcomes should include the designated primary errands (8). Finally, the statements in sections 2 and 4 of the protocol imply that the errand-importance calculations invoke another specialist that infers: "It's going to be a busy day." (9).

Figure 5 shows the blackboard representation of section 5 of the protocol. In section 5, the subject states: "All right. We are now at the health club." This statement conveys a procedure-level specification of the initial location (13). Figure 5 shows the implicit sequence of activity that produced this statement, given the prior state of the blackboard shown in Figure 4. First, having decided what to do (8), the subject proceeds to his second priority, deciding how to do it. Accordingly, he changes focus to the lower levels of the blackboard (10). Given this focus, a strategy-generating specialist records its decision to plan forward from the initial location (11). This decision motivates another specialist to identify the initial location at the procedure level of the blackboard (13).

Figure 6 shows the blackboard representation of sections 6–8 of the protocol. In section 6, the subject asks, "What is going to be the closest one?" This question indicates a strategic decision to plan to perform the closest errand next in the procedure sequence (14). The appearance of this strategy on the blackboard invokes a specialist that evaluates the relative proximities of other primary errands to the initial location, the health club (15). Section 7 of the protocol describes these evaluations.

Section 8 of the protocol reflects a discontinuity in the planning process. The preceding statements aim toward recording the second errand in the procedural sequence. Instead, however, the subject states in section 8: "Probably it would be best if we headed in a southeasterly direction. Start heading this way. I can see later on there are a million things I want to do in that part of town." This statement expresses a higher-level design, recorded on the blackboard as a decision to perform the errands in the southeast cluster, performing whatever other

errands occur along the route from the initial location to the southeast cluster (18).

Let us consider how the subject might have arrived at this design. The subject's immediately-preceding overt activity, evaluation of proximities, requires him to locate each errand in the list. In doing so, the subject locates (at least) three consecutive errands, the movie, the watch repair, and the bookstore, in the southeast corner of town. Apparently, this sequence of visual observations invokes a specialist that identifies clusters of errands and records the identity of the detected cluster at the layout level of the knowledge base (16). The appearance of the cluster on the blackboard invokes another specialist that generates schemes. It suggests exploiting the spatial cluster of errands by organizing a design around it (17). Another specialist responds to the new scheme and the identified cluster by recording the appropriate design on the blackboard (18).

Figure 7 shows the blackboard representation of section 9 of the protocol. In section 9, the subject indicates a procedure decision to sequence the movie

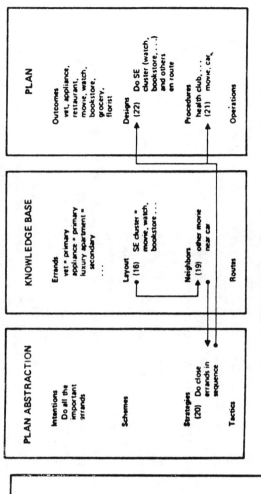

Figure 7. Blackboard representation of section 9 of the protocol.

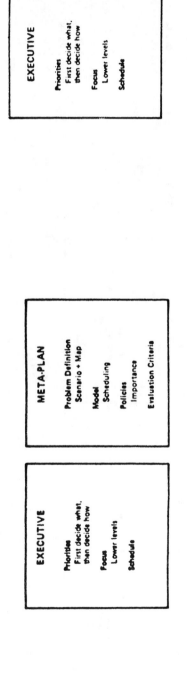

Figure 6. Blackboard representation of sections 6—8 of the protocol.

right before picking up his car at the end of the day (21). He tells us explicitly that, in so doing, he is removing the movie from the previously-defined southeast cluster (22). He also tells us why he has made this decision: because it would be "convenient to get out of the movie and go to the car" (20).

Figure 7 models these decisions, beginning with the subject's prior definition of the southeast cluster (16). Presumably, attention to one of the errands in the cluster, the movie, invokes a specialist that notices another movie on the west

side of town close to the parking structure (19). The proximity of these two errands invokes a specialist that suggests a more general strategy to perform two proximate errands in sequence (20). This new strategy invokes another specialist that records the suggested sequence, movie-car, at the procedure level of the plan plane (21) and amends the prior design accordingly (22).

Figure 8 shows the blackboard representation of section 10 of the protocol. In section 10, the subject decides to go to the vet after the health club because it is the closest primary errand. Thus, section 10 conveys a procedure-level decision (26) and the strategy that motivated it (24). We assume that the presence of a modified design on the blackboard motivates a narrowing of the focus to aim at instantiating the design at the procedure level (23). In accordance with this focus, the design also invokes a specialist that generates a strategy to do the closest the postulated levels on all five planes of the blackboard. Further, the subject makes decisions opportunistically. Rather than working systematically through the levels along either of the two dimensions, he enters the planning space at various points and moves about freely within it. The subject's observations and computations on the available data (the map and the scenario) exert a powerful influence on the point in the planning space at which he makes each successive decision. This produces a strong ''bottom-up'' component to the planning process. However, prior decisions at both higher and lower levels influence the subject's decisions, as assumed by the model.

5. COMPUTER SIMULATION

We have implemented a computer simulation of the planning model described above. The simulation is written in INTERLISP. It contains an internal representation of the map shown in Figure 1, a blackboard structure to organize planning decisions, and about forty specialists. (See Hayes-Roth, Hayes-Roth, Rosenschein, & Cammarata (1979) for a detailed description of the simulation.)

We designed the specialists to model some of the knowledge in our subject's protocol. Following the reasoning used in section 4, we postulated condition-action rules for producing many of the decisions in the protocol, as well as rules for producing the necessary intermediate decisions. The specialists generalize these rules. For example. in section 8 of the protocol, the subject notices that certain errands appear in close proximity in the southeast part of town. Based on this section of the protocol, we designed a specialist whose condition requires that at least three errands have been located on the map and that they appear in the same region (northwest, northeast, southwest, or southeast). Its action is to identify as a cluster any set of errands that satisfies its condition. Thus, this specialist can identify not only the particular clusters the subject noticed, but other clusters as well.

The simulation includes specialists for most of the condition-action rules inferred from the protocol. However, we did not attempt to capture all of the subject's idiosyncracies. For example, although the subject used several slightly different navigation rules, the simulation has only one. Thus, the simulation represents an approximate model of the subject's knowledge.

We can evaluate two aspects of the simulation's performance: the plans it produces and the process by which it produces them. We discuss each of these below.

Figure 9 shows the plan the subject produced for the problem discussed above. Figure 10 shows the plan produced by the simulation. The two plans are quite similar. Both plans include all primary errands and at least some of the secondary errands. While the subject included all secondary errands, the simulation included only one very convenient secondary errand. While the simulation and the subject planned different routes, both routes are fairly efficient, though clearly sub-optimal. Both the simulation and the subject planned to arrive at

errand in the right direction (24). This strategy invokes a specialist that evaluates the proximities of individual errands at the neighbors level of the knowledge base (25). Finally, the observation that the vet is the closest errand to the initial location, the health club, invokes a specialist that records the vet as the next errand in the procedural sequence (26).

We can analyze the remainder of the protocol in much the same fashion. However, we conclude the analysis at this stage for brevity.

The analysis reinforces the main points made in section 2. The subject plans at different points in the planning space along both temporal and abstractness dimensions. In particular, the subject appears to make decisions at each of

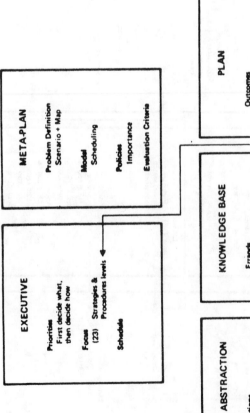
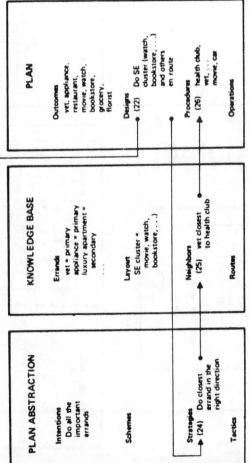

Figure 8. Blackboard representation of section 10 of the protocol.

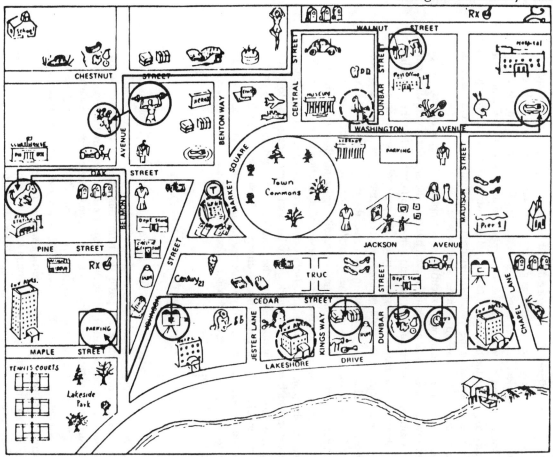

Figure 10. Plan produced by the computer simulation.

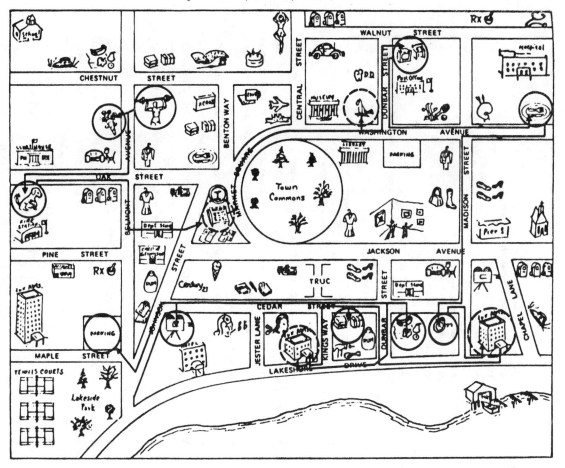

Figure 9. Plan produced by the human subject.

subject's protocol. Common decisions are preceded by "*" in Fig. 11. Of course, the remainder of the simulation's protocol does not always mirror the subject's protocol as closely as the section in Figure 11. Two factors produce the divergences.

First, as mentioned above, the simulation does not contain the entire set of specialists used by the subject. Thus, the simulation occasionally uses a specialist that is slightly different from the one the subject uses. This produces differences in both the protocols and the resulting plans. For example, in section 18 of the protocol, the subject decides to go from the health club to the vet on the way to the southeast part of town. At the same point in its protocol, the simulation decided to go from the health club to the appliance store. Both were trying to find the closest errand along the way, but they used slightly different specialists, and, as a consequence, chose different errands.

Second, the simulation's executive is incomplete. On some cycles, two or more invoked specialists are equally attractive and the simulation chooses randomly among them. Frequently, this random choice fails to select the specialist the subject used at that point. In such cases, the protocols also diverge.

In our opinion, it would be unproductive to model the subject's performance at a level of detail sufficient to counteract the effects of these two factors. Therefore, we look for the same general features in the two protocols, rather than exact replication. Such commonalities are readily apparent. Both the simulation and the subject made decisions at various levels of abstraction on each of the five planes of the planning blackboard. Both exhibited many coherent decision sequences in which each decision appeared to build on its predecessors. However, both also frequently "jumped about" the planning blackboard, rather than working systematically along any particular dimension. In particular, both the simulation and the subject occasionally redirected or dramatically changed their own activity in response to fortuitous observations or computations on the available data (e.g., the map).

6. THEORETICAL COMPLEXITY

The opportunistic model seems, at first glance, fairly complex. It postulates five different conceptual "planes" of decisions and several levels of abstraction within each of those planes. It postulates numerous planning specialists whose simultaneous efforts to participate in the planning process require the supervision of a fairly sophisticated executive. Although a number of complex models have proved fruitful in the last few years (Cf., Anderson, 1976; Anderson & Bower, 1973; Rumelhart, Lindsay, & Norman, 1972; Winograd, 1972), most of us still adhere to the law of parsimony, preferring simpler models to complex models.

In fact, the proposed model is computationally quite simple. It postulates a uniform decision mechanism, the specialist, to perform all of the varied decision-making functions planners perform. By modeling executive decisions

---

time-constrained destinations (e.g. the restaurant and the movie) at reasonable times. The major difference between the two plans lies in their relative "realism." The subject's plan is quite unrealistic—one could not execute the complete plan in the time available for doing so. The simulation's plan is somewhat more realistic, primarily because it omits many of the secondary errands.

1–9	[Omitted]
10	Work forward for the starting location.
*11	The starting location is the Health Club which is on Belmont Avenue.
12	Begin at the Health Club.
*13	Go to the closest errand next.
*14	The vet is on Oak Street.
*15	The appliance store is on Walnut Street.
16	The restaurant is on Washington Avenue.
*17	The watch repair is on Cedar Street.
*18	The bookstore is on Cedar Street.
19	The grocery is on Cedar Street.
*20	The watch repair, the bookstore, and the grocery are all in a cluster in the southeast part of town.
21	Organize the plan around spatial clusters.
*22	Proceed from the Health Club toward the southeast cluster.

Figure 11. Excerpt from the simulation's protocol.

Like the subject, the simulation produced a planning protocol—the series of decisions underlying the final plan. Figure 11 shows an excerpt from this protocol—decisions 10–22. (The protocol actually produced by the simulation is a series of decision "nodes" in list notation. Figure 11 translates the protocol into standard English for clarity.)

Decisions 10–22 of the simulation's protocol correspond quite closely to sections 5–8 of the subject's protocol. Recall that, in those sections, the subject identified the health club as the starting location, decided to schedule the closest errand to the health club next, located several errands on the map in his search for the closest errand, detected a cluster of errands in the southeast part of town and, accordingly, decided to head in that general direction.

Now consider the simulation's protocol. Decision 10 establishes a strategy to work forward from the starting location. Decisions 11 and 12 identify the starting location as the health club and establish it as the first errand in the procedure. Decision 13 establishes a strategy to go to the closest errand next. Decisions 14–19 locate individual errands on the map in a search for the closest errand to the health club. Decision 20 detects the cluster of errands in the southeast part of town. Decision 21 suggests organizing an overall design for the plan around the spatial cluster and decision 22 does so.

In addition to performing essentially the same functions the subject performed, the simulation made many of the decisions explicitly declared in the

with the same mechanism, it can account for a wide range of distinct planning styles without additional assumptions. (See Hayes-Roth (1979) for a discussion of executive "flexibility.")

Most of the apparent complexity in the model derives from the details of the blackboard structure. However, the blackboard partitions provide another important computational efficiency. Each specialist gets invoked whenever a new decision on the blackboard satisfies its condition. If the blackboard were simply an unstructured collection of decisions, each specialist would have to examine every new decision to determine whether the decision satisfied its condition. This would require an enormous amount of computation, much of it unnecessary. The blackboard partitions reduce the amount of computation required by permitting each specialist to restrict its "attention" to only those new decisions that occur at particular levels.

The blackboard structure also permits the model to capture an important psychological feature—interruptability. People have the power to interrupt their own cognitive processing at arbitary points. After performing some more or less related processing, they may or may not continue the interrupted task. This interruptability appears throughout our protocols and we believe it is a salient feature of cognitive processing in general. In the proposed model, interruption can occur only between individual decisions. Thus, the blackboard structure embodies our view of possible loci for interruption.

7. COMPARISON WITH SUCCESSIVE REFINEMENT MODELS

As discussed in the introduction to this paper, our view of planning differs somewhat from earlier views of planning as a process of successive refinement. This section explores several differences between the two views and attempts to resolve the differences.

Top-Down versus Multi-Directional Processing

While earlier work has assumed that planning is a top-down process, the proposed model treats planning as a multi-directional process. The diverse observations people make while planning often guide subsequent planning. Some of these observations arise from planning at an abstract level and guide subsequent planning at a more detailed level. The errand-planning protocol illustrates this kind of top-down processing in section 10, where the subject begins to instantiate a previously planned design at the lower procedure level. However, observations also arise from planning at a low level and guide subsequent planning at a more abstract level. The protocol illustrates this kind of bottom-up processing in section 8 where the subject formulates a design based on observations related to previous decisions at the lower procedure level. Many other examples of both

top-down and bottom-up processing appear throughout this protocol and the others we have collected.

The sample protocol confirms the more general assumption of multi-directionality in another way. If the subject were operating in a top-down fashion, he would begin planning at the highest (most abstract) level of the planning space. He could plan at a lower level only if he had already planned that particular subtask at all higher levels. The errand-planning protocol disconfirms this presumption repeatedly. The subject begins forming his actual plan at a relatively low level, the procedure level. Thus, he plans at this level in the absence of any corresponding high-level plans. Similar instances of planning a subtask at a low level without having previously planned it at higher levels appear throughout this protocol and our others. These findings follow directly from the multi-directional assumption. (See Hayes-Roth and Thorndyke, 1979, for additional evidence on this point.)

Complete versus Incremental Planning

A second difference between the earlier view of planning and the proposed model concerns the relative completeness attributed to abstract plans. The earlier work assumes that, while initial plans may be abstract, they will be complete and fully integrated. Under a breadth-first processing assumption, this requires that complete plans at each level must precede any planning at the next lower level. Under a depth-first processing assumption, it requires only that the highest-level plan must be complete before planning activity can proceed at lower levels. Under either assumption, the earlier view presupposes that complete plans will eventually exist at all levels of abstraction.

By contrast, we assume that planning is incremental and, therefore, will rarely produce complete plans in the systematic fashion described above. We assume that people make tentative decisions without the requirement that each one fit into a current, completely integrated plan. As the planner relates each new decision to some subset of his previous decisions, the plan grows by incremental accretion. Further, the developing plan need not grow as a coherent integrated plan. Alternative subplans can develop independently either within or between levels of abstraction. The planner can incorporate these sub-plans into the final plan as she or he wishes.

The sample protocol provides evidence for these assumptions. For example, in section 9, having established only his initial location at the procedure level, the subject plans a sequence of two errands with which to conclude. In the following several sections of the protocol, he intermittently plans alternative designs (none of which covers the planned concluding sequence) and initial sequences of errands (none of which he concatenates with the planned concluding sequence). Similar partial plans appear throughout the protocol as well as in the other protocols we collected. These findings confirm our assumption that specialists record tentative decisions in various locations on the blackboard in response to relevant prior decisions.

Hierarchical versus Heterarchical Plan Structures

Earlier conceptions of plans as hierarchical structures responded to the appealing simplicity of hierarchically structured programs and the successive refinement method. None of our observations denies the putative merits of these hierarchical approaches. Of course, one can always interpret a sequence of actions as a hierarchy with some number of levels. Therefore, one must perform some more informative analysis to contrast hypothesized hierarchical plans with more complex plan structures. More importantly, a satisfactory theory of planning must describe all decisions made during the planning process as well as those that appear in completed plans.

Our efforts to model the planning process suggest that people make many decisions that do not fit a simple hierarchical structure. Under the proposed model, one might attempt to construe the final set of decisions on the plan plane as a hierarchical structure, but our protocols do not provide strong evidence for such a structure. For example, the design maintained throughout most of the sample protocol dictates that errands on the way to the southeast cluster should be performed first followed by those errands within the cluster itself. However, much of the subject's planning at lower levels concerns errands not covered by this design (e.g., the newsstand, the pet store, the appliance store, and the restaurant).

The assumption of hierarchical plan structure becomes more tenuous if we consider the many other kinds of decisions our subject made while planning. We have observed four categories of decisions that do not describe what the subject actually plans to do at all. These correspond to the four remaining planes of the planning blackboard. Thus, the subject makes decisions about data—how long errands should take, how important individual errands are, what the consequences of a particular action might be, etc. He makes decisions about abstract features of plans—what *kinds* of plan decisions might be useful. He makes meta-planning decisions—how to approach the problem and how to constrain and evaluate his plan. Finally, the subject makes executive decisions about how to allocate his cognitive resources during planning. While all of these decisions contribute to the planning process, they do not exhibit a single hierarchical planning structure. For these reasons, we prefer to think in terms of heterarchical plan structures.

Relative Advantages of Hierarchical versus Opportunistic Planning

We might also speculate on the relative merits of hierarchical versus opportunistic planning. The orderly, systematic nature of the top-down process and the simplicity of its hierarchical structure argue in its favor. The recent emphasis on structured programming, a top-down approach to software engineering, reflects these merits (Cf., Dahl, Dykstra, & Hoare, 1972). One might also argue that top-down processes would minimize memory load (Cf., Thorndyke, 1978). The planner could restrict attention to a single area of the hierarchy, rather than attending intermittently to several different areas of the planning space.

On the other hand, planning in tasks fraught with complexity and uncertainty might benefit from less of the discipline imposed by a top-down process. In such complex tasks, general, a priori solutions or problem-solving methods may not exist or may be computationally intractable. Even if some general approach were available, opportunistic planning would free the planner of the burden of maintaining a structurally integrated plan at each decision point. Instead, the planner could formulate and pursue promising partial plans as opportunity suggested.

More importantly, a multi-directional process might produce better plans. It certainly permits more varied plans than a strictly top-down process does. If the planner always began with a fixed high-level plan, she or he could refine it in only a limited number ways. The bottom-up component in multi-directional processing provides a potentially important source of innovation in planning. Low-level decisions and related observations can inspire novel higher-level plans. We observed this in the errand-planning protocol, for example, when the subject generated a high-level design based on observations and decisions made at the lower procedure level. Similarly, Feitelson and Stefik (1977) observed that their expert geneticist deliberately exploited the potential for innovation in bottom-up processing:

> Thus, not only is the planning process largely event driven but sometimes steps are taken somewhat outside the plan of the experiment to make a possibly interesting observation. This kind of behavior reflects the convenience of making certain interesting observations while the equipment is set up. Often this is done to verify the successful completion of an experimental step, but sometimes the observations seem to correspond more to fishing for interesting possibilities. (p. 31)

Resolving the Two Points of View

Although the preceding discussion argues for the proposed opportunistic model in favor of successive refinement models, we would not "reject" either model in favor of the other. Obviously, both models have merit and can best explain different situations. We can suggest three variables which might influence a planner's approach to a particular problem: problem characteristics, individual differences, and expertise.

Problem characteristics could have a major impact on the approach a planner takes. For example, planners might usefully exploit a top-down approach to planning whenever the problem at hand exhibited an inherent hierarchical structure. A study by Byrne (1977) supports this conjecture. His subjects planned

subsequent executive decisions and, consequently, on the planner's progress through the remaining levels of the blackboard. For example, a planner might adopt a "define and successively refine" problem-solving method. Given strict adherence to this method, the planner's formulation of decisions on the plan plane would indeed proceed in a systematic top-down fashion. These are exactly the decisions modeled in the earlier work on top-down planning.

Note that "define and refine" is only one of many problem-solving methods adoptable in the framework of the opportunistic model. Thus, the question is no longer which model is correct, but rather, under what circumstances do planners bring alternative problem-solving methods to bear? We have suggested problem characteristics, individual differences, and expertise as important factors. We should also ask which problem-solving methods work best for different kinds of problems.

8. CONCLUSIONS

The opportunistic model draws on earlier theoretical work in cognitive psychology and artificial intelligence. It incorporates the strongest points of these models with its own assumptions regarding multi-directionality, opportunism, and incrementation in a heterarchical plan structure. We believe that the model is flexible enough to handle the complexity and variability of people's planning behavior. Yet, it is vulnerable to data. We hope the opportunistic model will provide a useful framework for future investigations of the planning process.

REFERENCES

Aho, A. V., Hopcroft, J. E., & Ullman, J. D. *The design and analysis of computer algorithms*. Reading, Mass.: Addison-Wesley, 1974.

Anderson, J. R. *Language, memory, and thought*. Hillsdale, N.J.: Lawrence Erlbaum Associates, 1976.

Anderson, J. R., & Bower, G. H. *Human associative memory*. Washington, D.C.: V. H. Winston, 1973.

Byrne, R. Planning meals: Problem-solving on a real data-base. *Cognition*, 1977, 5, 287–332.

CMU Computer Science Research Group. Summary of the CMU five-year ARPA effort in speech understanding research. Technical Report, Carnegie-Mellon University, 1977.

Christophides, N. *Graph theory: An algorithmic approach*. New York: Academic Press, 1975.

Dahl, O. J., Dykstra, E. W., & Hoare, C. A. R. *Structured programming*. New York: Academic Press, 1972.

Engelmore, R. S., & Nii, H. P. A knowledge-based system for the interpretation of protein x-ray crystallographic data. Report No. STAN-CS-77-589, Stanford University, 1977.

Erman, L. D., & Lesser, V. R. A multi-level organization for problem solving using many diverse cooperating sources of knowledge. *Proceedings of the Fourth International Joint Conference on Artificial Intelligence*. Tbilisi, USSR, 1975, 483–490.

dinner menus. As one might expect, subjects appeared to plan menus by deciding on type of dinner (e.g., Chinese dinner, Christmas dinner), main course (e.g., roast beef, turkey), and accompaniments (e.g., cranberry sauce, mashed potatoes). This is a nice example of a hierarchical planning structure. In addition, Byrne's subjects appeared to make decisions within this structure in a top-down fashion.

By contrast, the errand-planning problems discussed in this paper did not exhibit any obvious hierarchical structure. In such circumstances, planners might reasonably resort to more opportunistic methods. Apparently, this is what our subjects did.

A study by Hayes-Roth (1979) provides more direct evidence for the influence of problem characteristics. She successfully induced alternative planning approaches by manipulating the amount of time available for plan execution. For problems that imposed severe time constraints, most subjects adopted a top-down approach. For problems that imposed minimal time constraints, most subjects adopted a bottom-up approach.

The Hayes-Roth (1979) study also provides evidence for the impact of individual differences on planning methods. Many of her subjects exhibited a strong proclivity to adopt a bottom-up approach regardless of problem characteristics. Even with explicit instruction, some subjects persisted in using the bottom-up approach. Other subjects were more flexible, adopting an appropriate approach in response to problem characteristics or instruction.

Finally, planning expertise might influence which planning model a planner brings to bear on particular problems. A practiced planner working on a familiar, constrained problem may possess well-learned, reliable abstract plans for dealing with the problem. This extensive experience may support the application of standard methods for systematically refining abstract plans. On the other hand, a practiced planner working on an unconstrained problem can also exploit opportunistic methods to advantage. Feitelson's and Stefik's (1977) study of the experiment-planning of an expert molecular geneticist provides a nice illustration:

The experiments described here reflect a combination of goal driven behavior and event driven behavior... If there were no goals, behavior might seem very erratic and follow no general course. If there is no event driven component to the planning process, then the experimental procedure must admit no feedback or changes of plans as a result of observations. Thus, no advantage will be made of fortunate observations. What is being suggested here is that the planning in this experiment involved far more exploitation of events and changes of plan according to the events than the authors had anticipated. (p. 30)

One resolution of the apparent conflict between the two models would simply incorporate the top-down model as a special case of the opportunistic model. We have discussed the importance of the problem-solving method a planner brings to bear on a task. This decision can have a major impact on

Ernst, G. W., & Newell, A. *GPS: A case study in generality and problem solving.* New York: Academic Press, 1969.

Fahlman, S. E. A planning system for robot construction tasks. *Artificial Intelligence,* 1974, *5,* 1–49.

Feitelson, J., & Stefik, M. A case study of the reasoning in a genetics experiment. Heuristic Programming Project, Working Paper 77–18. Department of Computer Science, Stanford University, April 1977.

Fikes, R. E. Knowledge representation in automatic planning systems. In A. K. Jones (ed.), *Perspectives on computer science.* New York: Academic Press, 1977.

Fikes, R. E., & Nilsson, N. J. STRIPS: A new approach to the application of theorem proving to problem solving. *Artificial Intelligence,* 1971, *2,* 189—203.

Hayes-Roth, B. Flexibility in executive strategies. N:1170, The Rand Corporation, Santa Monica, California, 1979.

Hayes-Roth, B., Hayes-Roth, F., Rosenschein, S., & Cammarata, S. Modeling planning as an incremental, opportunistic process. *Proceedings of the Sixth International Joint Conference on Artificial Intelligence.* Tokyo, Japan, 1979.

Hayes-Roth, B., and Thorndyke, P. Decision-making during the planning process. N:1213, The Rand Corporation, Santa Monica, California, 1979.

Hayes-Roth, F., & Lesser, V. R. Focus of attention in the Hearsay-II speech understanding system. *Proceedings of the Fifth International Joint Conference on Artificial Intelligence,* Boston, Mass., 1977, 27–35.

Hayes-Roth, F., Waterman, D. A., & Lenat, D. E. Principles of pattern-directed inference systems. In Waterman D. A. & Hayes-Roth F. (eds.), *Pattern-directed inference systems.* New York: Academic Press, 1978.

Lesser, V. R., Fennell, R. D., Erman, L. D., & Reddy, D. R. Organization of the Hearsay-II speech understanding system. *IEEE Transactions on Acoustics, Speech and Signal Processing,* ASSP-23, 1975, 11–23.

Lesser, V. R., & Erman, L. D. A retrospective view of the Hearsay-II architecture. *Proceedings of the Fifth International Joint Conference on Artificial Intelligence.* Boston, Mass., 1977, 790–800.

Newell, A., & Simon, H. A. *Human problem solving.* Englewood Cliffs, N.J.: Prentice-Hall, 1972.

Nii, H. P., & Feigenbaum, E. A. Rule-based understanding of signals. In D. A. Waterman & F. Hayes-Roth (eds.), *Pattern-directed inference systems.* New York: Academic Press, 1978.

Prager, J., Nagin, P., Kohler, R., Hanson, A., & Riseman, E. Segmentation processes in the VISIONS system. *Proceedings of the Fifth International Joint Conference on Artificial Intelligence,* Boston, Mass., 1977.

Rumelhart, D. E. Toward an interactive model of reading. Technical Report 56, Center for Human Information Processing, University of California at San Diego, La Jolla, Ca., 1976.

Rumelhart, D., Lindsay, P. H., & Norman, D. A. A process model for long-term memory. In E. Tulving & W. Donaldson (eds.), *Organization of memory.* New York: Academic Press, 1972.

Sacerdoti, E. D. Planning in a hierarchy of abstraction spaces. *Artificial Intelligence,* 1974, *5,* 115–135.

Sacerdoti, E. D. A structure for plans and behavior. Technical Note 109, Standford Research Institute, Menlo Park, California, August, 1975.

Selfridge, O. Pandemonium: A paradigm for learning. *Symposium on the mechanization of thought.* London: HM Stationery Office, 1959.

Soloway, E. M., & Riseman, E. M. Knowledge-directed learning. *Proceedings of the Workshop on Pattern-Directed Inference Systems,* special edition of the *SIGART Newsletter.* New York: Association for Computing Machinery, June, 1977.

Sussman, G. J. A computational model of skill acquisition. AI TR-297, Artificial Intelligence Laboratory, Massachusetts Institute of Technology, Cambridge, Mass., 1973.

Thorndyke, P. W. Pattern-directed processing of knowledge from text. In D. A. Waterman & F. Hayes-Roth (eds.), *Pattern-directed inference systems.* New York: Academic Press, 1978.

Winograd, T. A program for understanding natural language *Cognitive Psychology,* 1972, *3.*

A Model for Planning in Complex Situations

ROBERT WILENSKY

Computer Science Division
Department of EECS
University of California, Berkeley

ABSTRACT

A model of planning applicable to complex, commonplace activities is being developed. This model differs from previous approaches in that it is based on the following assumptions: (1) A planning agent must be able to infer its own goals in addition to being able to generate plans for these goals; (2) everyday planning is primarily concerned with reasoning about the interactions between plans and goals; (3) *meta-planning* (formulating knowledge about how to plan in abstract plans and goals, and having the planner use this knowledge to solve its own planning problems) is used as a driving principle; (4) *projection* (simulating hypothetical futures based on current plans and world knowledge) is used to infer goals and debug plans; and (5) planning knowledge should be equally available for understanding as well as for planning.

Coupled together, the mechanisms for implementing these features give rise to a system of considerable power. For example, the ability to infer one's own goals is needed in an autonomous planning agent since it must deal with unexpected situations. However, together with meta-planning knowledge and the ability to project hypothetical futures, this feature enables the planner to detect and reason about complicated goal interactions, anticipate problems with proposed plans, and make choices in the face of competing alternatives.

This model has been developed in detail for the detection and resolution of goal conflicts. In doing so, we postulate several goal conflict resolution strategies, or meta-plans, called RE-PLAN, CHANGE-CIRCUMSTANCE, and SIMULATE-AND-SELECT. The structure and application of these meta-plans is explored in the context of both decision making and understanding the actions of other planners.

INTRODUCTION—SOME TENETS FOR A THEORY OF PLANNING

Much previous work on planning and problem solving has been concerned with either very specialized systems or with highly artificial domains (e.g., consider Fikes & Nilsson 1971; Newell & Simon, 1972; Sussman, 1975; Shortliffe, 1976). More recently, there has been an increase in attention given to planning in commonplace situations. For example, Rieger (1975b) has proposed a set of "common sense algorithms" for reasoning about everyday physical situations; Hayes-Roth and Hayes-Roth (1979) are concerned with how a person might schedule a day's activities; and Carbonell's (1978) POLITICS program reasons dogmatically about political decisions. On another front, Sacerdoti (1977) and McDermott (1978), while operating perhaps in the more traditional problem solving context, have proposed some powerful approaches to problem solving in general.

Everyday Planning is Reasoning about Interactions Between Goals

We have been developing a theory of planning that is concerned with reasoning about commonplace situations. A central tenet of this theory is that most of the planning involved in everyday situations is primarily concerned with the interactions between goals. That is, planning for individual goals is assumed to be a fairly simple matter, consisting primarily of the straightforward application of rather large quantities of world knowledge. The complexity of planning is attributed to the fact that most situations involve numerous goals that interact in complicated ways.

Thus while traditional problem solving research has been concerned with finding the solution to a single, difficult problem (e.g., finding the winning chess move), most everyday problem solving consists of synthesizing solutions to fairly simple, interacting problems. For example, a typical everyday situation that involves the sort of planning we are interested in might be to obtain some nails, and also buy a hammer. The plan for each goal is straightforward: One simply goes to the hardware store, buys the desired item, and returns. The problem lies in recognizing that it is a terrible idea to execute these plans independently. Rather, the seemingly simple common sense plan is to combine the two individual plans, resulting in the plan of going to the hardware store, buying both items, and then returning.

Simple as this situation may be, most conventional planners are ill-equipped to handle it. Although some planning programs have mechanisms for removing redundancies from a plan, they generally lack a mechanism for even noticing this sort of interaction if these plans are derived from heretofore unrelated goals. Perhaps more importantly, the interaction between plans may have more complex ramifications. For example, if enough items are to be purchased at the hardware store, then a better plan might be to take one's car, whereas walking may do otherwise. Thus a good part of planning involves detecting the interactions between goals, figuring out their implications, and then deciding what to do about them.

Request for reprints should be sent to Robert Wilensky, Dept. of EECS, University of California, Berkeley, California, 94720.

Cognition and Brain Theory
Vol. IV, No. 4, Fall 1981

plan will be the solution to the original planning problem.

A typical example of a meta-goal is the goal RESOLVE-GOAL-CONFLICT. A planner would presumably have an instance of this goal whenever it detects that some of its "ordinary" goals are in conflict with one another. The meta-plans for this goal are the various goal conflict resolution strategies available to the planner.

Meta-planning is described in more detail in Wilensky (1980). Here, we give only a brief characterization of its main features and advantages.

Meta-goals are organized by *meta-themes*. These are very general principles of planning that describe situations in which meta-goals come into being. We summarize these briefly:

Meta-themes

1. DON'T WASTE RESOURCES
2. ACHIEVE AS MANY GOALS AS POSSIBLE
3. MAXIMIZE THE VALUE OF THE GOALS ACHIEVED
4. AVOID IMPOSSIBLE GOALS

As an example of how these function, the meta-theme "ACHIEVE AS MANY GOALS AS POSSIBLE" is responsible for detecting goal conflicts. That is, if the planner intends to perform a set of actions that will negatively interact with one another, this meta-theme causes the planner to have the goal of resolving the conflict. If this meta-goal fails, i. e., the planner could not find a way to resolve the conflict, then the meta-theme "MAXIMIZE THE VALUE OF THE GOALS ACHIEVED" springs into action. This meta-theme sets up the goal of arriving at a scenario in which the less valuable goals are abandoned in order to fulfill the more valuable ones. The details of the meta-plans involved in these processes are described at length in the last two sections of this paper.

Meta-planning has a number of advantages over other approaches to planning; these advantages are summarized below.

Meta-planning Knowledge Can be Used for Both Planning and Understanding. As meta-goals and meta-plans are declarative structures in the same sense as are ordinary goals and plans, they may be used to understand situations as well as to plan in them. Thus an understander with access to this knowledge would be able to interpret someone's action as an attempt to resolve a goal conflict, for example. In contrast, planning programs that have the equivalent knowledge embedded procedurally would not be able to conveniently use it to explain someone else's actions.

The Same Planning Mechanism Can Apply to More Difficult Tasks. Meta-planning knowledge generally embodies a set of strategies for com-

Planners Must Infer Goals As Well As Act Upon Them

Before a planner can determine that there is an interaction between its goals, it must of course know what goals it possesses. In most planning systems, high-level goals are simply handed to the planner, often in the form of a problem to be solved. However, an autonomous planner must be able to infer its own goals based upon its overall mission together with the situation in which it finds itself.

For example, a planner may be given the job of maintaining a nuclear reactor. In addition to sustaining the generation of power, the robot may also be in charge of keeping the floors clean, preventing meltdowns, cleaning up dangerous spills, and maintaining itself. However, much of the time, most of these functions are inoperative, e.g., the robot need not be concerned with cleaning up a spill until one occurs. It is desirable to build a planner that can recognize one of these situations when it occurs, and infer the goal it should have at that time. Thus the robot should infer that it has the goal of cleaning up a spill when one occurs, of defending itself and the plant if they are attacked by terrorists, and of replenishing its resources if its power supply is low.

Moreover, goal inference interacts in important ways with other planning capabilities. For example, consider the situation earlier in which a planner is trying to get a hammer and nails from the hardware store. In accomplishing this task, the planner may end up at the hardware store with the hammer and nails. However, it now needs to realize that it should go home with these items. That is, if having the hammer and nails were instrumental to some other task, for example, fixing one's roof, the planner now needs to realize that its plan for obtaining these items has caused it to have the new goal of going home. While the plan for this goal is likely to be trivial, it is crucial that the goal be inferred in order for the entire plan to be effective.

The mechanism that infers goals is used in a similar fashion together with the next two features of this model to provide a facility for detecting and reasoning about the interactions between goals, for anticipating problems with proposed plans, and for making choices in the face of competing alternatives.

Meta-Planning is Used as the Driving Principle

The third salient feature of our theory is that it is based on *meta-planning*. By this I mean that the problems a planner encounters in producing a plan for a given situation may themselves be formulated as goals. These "meta-goals" can then be submitted to the planning mechanism, which treats them just like any other goals. That is, the planner attempts to find a "meta-plan" for this meta-goal; the result of successful application of this

hypothetical world. Since such interactions generally indicate that some important planning principle is not being adhered to, the occurrence of this hypothetical negative interaction is usually a signal to the planner to achieve some particular meta-goal.

Working with projected universes entails some liabilities as well, as does the notion of meta-planning and of using highly declarative representations. However, our claim is that the prices associated with these ideas are prices that must be paid anyway. By putting them together in the manner described here, a good deal of power is obtained for no additional cost.

Planning Knowledge Should be
Equally Available for Understanding

The last tenet of our theory of planning is that it should be equally usable by both a planner and an understander. This is essentially an extension of the point made by Rieger (1975a). That is, while a planner uses its planning knowledge to bring about a desired state of affairs, an understander may need to use this same knowledge to comprehend the actions of a person it is watching or of a character about whom it is reading. For example, a planner with the goal of keeping fit might take up jogging; an understander might use the same knowledge to infer that someone who has taken up jogging may have done so because he had the goal of staying in shape. Planning and understanding are rather different processes, and this will of course be reflected in our planning and understanding mechanisms. However, our theory of planning specifies that knowledge should be represented in a fashion so that it is usable by either mechanism. In particular, we have formulated meta-planning knowledge in terms of explicit goals and plans so that it might be used to understand a situation as well as to act in one.

In the next section, I discuss the general structure of a planning mechanism based on these assumptions. This is the structure used in PANDORA (Plan ANalysis with Dynamic Organization, Revision, and Application), a planning system now under construction at Berkeley. The sections following show how these mechanisms function together in reasoning about *goal conflict situations*. As we have noted, we intend these ideas to be applicable to understanding as well as planning, and in fact, they are being used in a new implementation of PAM, a plan-based, story-understanding system. While we do not discuss the structure of PAM here, the analysis of goal conflicts is presented in a form in which its use in understanding as well as planning may be seen.

THE DESIGN OF A PLANNER BASED ON META-PLANNING

This section describes the overall architecture of a planner based on the

plicated plan interactions. By formulating this knowledge in terms of goals and plans, the same planning architecture that already exists for simpler planning can be used to implement more complicated planning involving multiple goals, etc.

More General Resolution of Traditional Planning Problems. Traditional planners usually treat problems such as goal conflicts by special purpose means — by the introduction of critics, for example (Sussman 1975, Sacerdoti 1977). This is equivalent to having the general problem solver consult an expert when it gets in trouble. The meta-planning allows the general problem solver to call a general problem solver (itself) instead. Thus all the power of such a system can be focused on planning problems, rather than just relying on a few expert tactics. Of course, all the specific knowledge usually embodied in critics would still be available to the general problem solver. But the meta-planning model allows this knowledge to interact with all other knowledge as it now takes part in general reasoning processes.

Representational Advantages. The meta-planning model also provides more flexibility when no solution can be found. Since a meta-goal represents the formulation of a problem, the existence of the problem may be dealt with without being fully resolved. For example, the problem solver may simply decide to accept a flawed plan if the violation is viewed as not being too important, or decide to abandon one of the goals that it can't satisfy. By separating solving the problem from formulating the problem, the problem may be accessed as opposed to treated, an option that most other problem solving models do not allow.

Projection is Used to Infer Goals and Debug Plans

The fourth significant feature of our planning model is that it is based on *projection*. That is, as the planner formulates a plan for a goal, the execution of this plan is simulated in a hypothetical world model. Problems with proposed plans may be detected by examining these hypothetical worlds.

Projection not only enables the planner to find problems with its own plans, but it also enables it to determine that a situation merits having a new goal. For example, sensing an impending danger requires the planner to project from the current state of affairs into a hypothetical world which it finds less desirable. Having done this projection, the planner can infer that it should have the goal of preventing the undesirable state of affairs from coming into being.

Projecting hypothetical realities also allows a general "goal detection" mechanism to work for meta-goals as well as for "ordinary" goals. When proposed plans for goals are projected, interactions will appear in the

tenets just considered. The planner is composed of the following major components:

1. *The Goal Detector.* This mechanism is responsible for determining that the planner has a goal. The goal detector has access to the planner's likes and dislikes, to the state of the world and any changes that may befall it, and to the planner's own internal planning structures and hypothetical world models. The goal detector can therefore establish a new goal because of some change in the environment, because such a goal is instrumental to another goal, or in order to resolve a problem in a planning structure that arises in a hypothetical world model.

2. *The Plan Generator.* The plan generator proposes plans for the goals already detected. It may dredge up stereotyped solutions, it may edit previously known plans to fit the current situation, or it may create fairly novel solutions. The plan generator is also responsible for expanding high-level plans into their primitive components to allow execution.

3. *The Executor.* The executor simply carries out the plan steps as proposed by the plan generator. It is responsible for the detection of errors, although not with their correction.

The importance of the goal detector should be emphasized. As was previously mentioned, most planners merely have their goals stated to them, but a planning system needs to infer its own goals for a number of reasons: An autonomous planner needs to know when it should go into action; it should be able to take advantage of opportunities that present themselves, even if it doesn't have a particular goal in mind at the time; and it should be able to protect itself from dangers from its environment, from other planners, or from consequences of its own plans.

The goal detector operates through the use of a mechanism called the *Noticer.* The Noticer is a general facility in charge of recognizing that something has occurred that is of interest to some part of the system. The Noticer monitors changes in the external environment and in the internal states of the system. When it detects the presence of something that it was previously instructed to monitor, it reports this occurrence to the source that originally told it to look for that thing. The Noticer can be thought of as a collection of IF-ADDED demons whose only action is to report some occurrence to some other mechanism.

Goals are detected by having themes and meta-themes asserted into the Noticer with orders to report to the goal detector. *Theme* is a term used by Schank and Abelson (1977) to mean something that gives rise to a goal; a meta-theme, similarly, is responsible for generating meta-goals. For example, we can assert to the Noticer that when it gets hungry (i. e., when the value of some internal state reaches a certain point), the planner should have the goal of being not hungry (i. e., of changing this value), or that if

someone is threatening to kill the planner, the planner should have the goal of protecting its life. On the meta-level, we might assert that if a goal conflict comes into existence, then the planner should have the meta-goal of resolving this conflict.

Using the Goal Detector to Spot Goal Interactions

The presumption of a goal detector coupled with meta-planning creates a system of considerable power. For example, no separate mechanism is required for detecting goal conflicts or for noticing that a set of proposed plans will squander a resource. The need to resolve conflicts or conserve resources is expressed by formulating descriptions of the various situations in which this may occur, and the appropriate meta-goal to have when it does. By inserting these descriptions into the Noticer to detect meta-goals, goal conflicts and other important goal interactions are handled automatically.

The planner component of our model itself consists of three components:

1. *The Proposer* which suggests plausible plans to try;
2. *The Projector* which tests plans by building hypothetical world models of what it would be like to execute these plans;
3. *The Revisor* which can edit and remove parts of a proposed planning structure.

The Proposer begins by suggesting the most specific plan it knows of that is applicable to the goal. If this plan is rejected or fails, the Proposer will propose successively more general and "creative" solutions. Once the Proposer has suggested a plan, the Projector starts computing what will happen to the world as the plan is executed. The difficult problems in conducting a simulation involve reasoning about "possible world" type situations which are not amenable to standard temporal logic (McCarthy & Hayes, 1969). However, we finesse this issue by defining hypothetical states in terms of what the planner thinks of in the course of plan construction. In other words, our solution is to let the system assert the changes that would be made into a hypothetical data base, in the meantime letting the goal detector have access to these states. Thus if the plan being simulated would result in the planner dying, say, this would constitute a hypothetical undesirable state, which might trigger further goals, etc.

As the Projector hypothetically carries out the plan, and other goals and meta-goals are detected by the goal detector, the original plan may have to be modified. This is done by explicit calls to the Revisor, which knows the plan structure and can make edits or deletions upon request. The modified plan structure is simulated again until it is either found satisfactory or the entire plan is given up and a new one suggested by the Proposer.

Actually, the function of the Projector is somewhat more pervasive than has so far been described. The Projector must be capable of projecting current events into future possibilities based both on the intentions of the planner and on its analysis of those events themselves. For example, if the planner sees a boulder rolling down the mountain, it is the job of the Projector to project the future path that the boulder will traverse. If the projected path crosses that of the planner, for example, a preservation goal should be detected. Thus the Projector is quite powerful and general device that is capable of predicting plausible futures.

REASONING ABOUT GOAL CONFLICTS

In the next two sections we give a more detailed analysis of one particular part of our planning model, namely, the resolution of goal conflicts. The problem is important in its own right; however, the presentation that follows is aimed at demonstrating the kind of "strategy architecture" to which the model is conducive. In particular, the section illustrates a number of important meta-goals and the meta-plans for them, and describes how they would be invoked and utilized by the model. The section also emphasizes the utility of meta-planning for the application of planning knowledge to understanding goal conflicts as well as to planning for them.

Since it is desirable to achieve all of one's goals, a planner faced with a goal conflict ought to attempt to resolve that conflict. We express this by saying that the state of having a goal conflict is a situation that causes the meta-theme "ACHIEVE AS MANY GOALS AS POSSIBLE" to become active. In such a situation, this meta-theme creates the meta-goal RESOLVE-GOAL-CONFLICT. This is a meta-goal because resolving the conflict can be viewed as a planning problem that needs to be solved by the creation of a better plan. In this formulation, the resolution of the goal conflict is performed by the execution of a meta-plan, the result of which will be a set of altered plans whose execution will not interfere with one another.

The knowledge needed to replan around a goal conflict is quite diverse, and may depend upon the particular goals in question and on the nature of the conflict. However, the meta-plans with which this knowledge is applied are rather general. To see why, it is necessary to ask how it is possible for goal conflicts to be resolved at all. There appear to be two ways in which goal conflicts can come about that determine how they may be resolved:

1. The conflict detected is based on the plans for one's goals, rather than on the goals themselves. In this case, it may be possible to achieve the goals by other, non-conflicting plans.

2. The conflict depends upon some additional circumstance or condition

beyond the stated goals or plans. The conflict might therefore be resolved if this circumstance is changed.

We therefore define two very general meta-plans, RE-PLAN and CHANGE-CIRCUMSTANCE. Of course, to be effective, we need to supply these meta-plans with more information; if we use RE-PLAN blindly, for example, we might end up enumerating all possible plans for each conflicting goal, although many of these plan combinations will present the same problem that caused the original goal conflict.

RE-PLAN

There are a number of different re-planning strategies applicable to goal conflict situations. They are given here in order of decreasing specificity. This is in accordance with our belief about the order in which such plans would actually be used, i. e., the most specific one first, then progressively more general ones, until a satisfactory set of plans is found. In this respect, meta-plans are entirely analogous to ordinary plans insofar as the planning process is concerned.

The order of plan application is just a corollary of the First Law of Knowledge Application — "Always use the most specific piece of knowledge applicable."

USE-NORMAL-PLAN Applied to Resolving Goal Conflicts. The most specific re-planning strategy is likewise analogous to the planning strategy for ordinary goals, namely, find a normal plan. A normal plan in the case of goal conflict is to find a stored plan specifically designed for use in a goal conflict between the kinds of goals found in the current situation. For example, consider the following situation:

(1) Mary was very hungry, but she was trying to lose some weight. She decided to take a diet pill.

In (1), there is a conflict between the goal of losing weight and satisfying hunger, as the normal plan for the latter goal involves eating. The RE-PLAN meta-plan is used, and the USE-NORMAL-PLAN strategy applied. The normal plan found that is applicable to both goals is to take a diet pill.

Just as many objects are functionally defined by the role they play in ordinary plans, so some objects are functionally defined by the role they play in plans aimed at resolving specific goal conflicts. Thus a diet pill is an object functionally defined by its ability to resolve the conflict between hunger and weight loss; a raincoat is defined by the role it plays in preventing wetness when one must go outside. In fact, a great deal of mundane planning knowledge appears to consist of plans for resolving specific types of goal conflicts.

Intelligent Use of TRY-ALTERNATE-PLAN to Find Non-Conflicting Set. A general planning strategy that is applicable when a plan cannot be made to work is to try another plan for that goal. In the case of resolving goal conflicts, this means that alternative plans for each conflicting goal can be proposed until a set is found that are not in conflict. As noted earlier, this may be costly, but it will be tried only when no canned conflict resolution plan has been found. Moreover, the plan can provide some intelligent ways of proposing new alternatives that may help keep costs down.

For example, consider the following situation:

(2) John was going outside to pick up the paper when he noticed it was raining. He looked for his raincoat, but he couldn't find it. He decided to get Fido to fetch the paper for him.

Here, John first thought to walk outside, but then found that this would cause a conflict. As his normal plan for resolving this conflict failed, John tried proposing other plans, looking for ones that wouldn't entail his getting wet. Since getting the dog to fetch the paper is such a plan, and since John presumably doesn't care if Fido gets wet, this plan is adopted.

The meta-planning strategy used here is called TRY-ALTERNATIVE-PLAN. The difference between using this meta-plan and blind generate-and-test stragies is that some control can be exerted here over exactly what is undone and what is looked for as a replacement. For example, the backtracking here need not be chronological or dependency-directed, but can be *knowledge-directed.* That is, rather than undo the last planning decision, a planning decision related to either goal can be undone, possibly based on an informed guess.

In addition, when fetching a new plan, it may be possible to specify in the fetch some conditions that the fetched plan may have to meet without actually testing that plan for a conflict. For example, in the case of getting the newspaper when it is raining, we can ask for a plan for getting something that doesn't involve going outside. That is, we can look for a plan for one goal that does not contain an action that leads to the original conflict. If our memory mechanism can handle such requests, then we can retrieve only those plans that do not conflict in the same way that the original plan does.

In order for this to work, TRY-ALTERNATIVE-PLAN needs to know what part of a plan contributed to the goal conflict so it can look for a plan without this action. This generally depends upon the kind of conflict. We can formulate this within the meta-planning framework by defining a meta-plan called MAKE-ATTRIBUTION. Here, MAKE-ATTRIBUTION is used as a subplan of the TRY-ALTERNATIVE-PLAN meta-plan, although we shall make other uses of it below. TRY-ALTERNATIVE-PLAN first asks MAKE-ATTRIBUTION to specify a cause of the problem, and then fetches a new plan without the objectionable element in it.

TRY-ALTERNATIVE-PLAN can also control how far up the proposed goal-subgoal structure it should go to undo a decision. Thus, if no alternative plan for a goal can be found, the goal itself can be questioned if it is a subgoal of some other plan. For example, consider the following scenario:

(3) John was going to get the newspaper when he noticed it was raining. He decided to listen to the radio instead.

Here the entire subgoal of getting the newspaper was eliminated. Since this was apparently a subgoal of finding out the news, the alternative plan of listening to the radio can be substituted. Once again, MAKE-ATTRIBUTION is used to propose a plan that doesn't involve an unwanted step. The difference between this and the last case is that here a plan lying above the conflicting goal is re-planned.

Change-Circumstance

In addition to the RE-PLAN meta-plan, the other general goal conflict resolution strategy is to change the circumstance that contributes to the conflict. This is actually more general than RE-PLAN, because it may be applicable to conflicts where the goals themselves exclude one another, whereas RE-PLAN requires the conflict to be plan-based.

CHANGE-CIRCUMSTANCE can resolve a goal conflict by altering a state of the world that is responsible for the goals conflicting with one another. Once this has been achieved, the original set of plans may be used without encountering the original problem.

For example, consider the following situations:

(4) John had a meeting with his boss in the morning, but he was feeling ill and wanted to stay in bed. He decided to call his boss and try to postpone the meeting until he felt better.

(5) John wanted to live in San Francisco, but he also wanted to live near Mary, and she lived in New York. John tried to persuade Mary to move to San Francisco with him.

In (4), John's conflict is caused by his plan to attend the meeting and his plan to stay home and rest. These plans conflict because of the time constraints on John's meeting, which force the plans to overlap; the plans require John to be in two places at once, so they cannot be executed simultaneously. If the time constraint on attending the meeting were relaxed, however, then the conflict would cease to exist. Thus rather than alter his plans, John can seek to change the circumstances that cause his plans to conflict by attempting to remove the time constraint that is a cause of the difficulty.

In (5), the conflict is between living in San Franciso and being near Mary, who is in New York. The basis for this exclusion involves the location of San Francisco and of Mary. However, if one of these locations were changed so that the distance between them were reduced, then the states would no longer exclude one another. Thus John can attempt to change Mary's location, while still maintaining his original goals.

To decide what circumstance to change, a planner once again needs to analyze the cause of the conflict. Thus CHANGE-CIRCUMSTANCE first requires the use of MAKE-ATTRIBUTION to propose a candidate for alteration. As was the case for RE-PLAN, MAKE-ATTRIBUTION requires access to detailed knowledge about the nature of negative goal interactions in order to find a particular circumstance with which to meddle. An analysis of such interactions appears in Wilensky (1978).

GOAL ABANDONMENT

When attempts to resolve a goal conflict are unsuccessful, a planner must make a decision about what should be salvaged from this situation. The choices here involve abandoning some of the goals completely while pursuing some select subset, or modifying some of the goals so as to avoid the conflict. As was previously mentioned, we consider the latter alternative, goal modification, to be a form of goal abandonment rather than conflict resolution because the strategy does not result in the fulfillment of the original set of goals.

In terms of meta-planning, we can describe goal abandonment situations as follows. The ability to achieve a RESOLVE-GOAL-CONFLICT meta-goal results in the planner having this failed meta-goal on his hands (or more precisely, in his representational space). Having a failed RESOLVE-GOAL-CONFLICT meta-goal is a condition that triggers the meta-theme MAXIMIZE-THE-VALUE-OF-THE-GOALS-ACHIEVED. This triggering condition causes this meta-theme to invoke a new meta-goal, called CHOOSE-MOST-VALUABLE-SCENARIO. This goal is satisfied when the relative worth of various achievable subsets of the conflicting goals is assessed, and the subset offering the greatest potential yield determined.

To achieve this meta-goal, we postulate a SIMULATE-AND-SELECT meta-plan. This plan proposes various combinations of goals to try, and computes the worth of each combination. The most valuable set of goals is returned as the scenario most worth pursuing.

The SIMULATE-AND-SELECT meta-plan

The SIMULATE-AND-SELECT meta-plan has a rich structure. To begin with, it makes a number of presumptions about evaluating the cost and worth of goals and of comparing them to one another. For the purposes at hand, we shall not dwell on exactly how the evaluation is done. Partly this is because the details of how to do this are not completely clear; moreover, they are not crucial for the upcoming discussion. We presume that values can be attributed to individual states in isolation *ceteris paribus*, and that the value of a set can be computed from its parts. This does not presume that the computation is simple; indeed, it may involve the consultation of large amounts of world knowledge. However, we do assume that all values can be made commensurable.

This being said, the SIMULATE-AND-SELECT meta-plan has in effect two distinct options. The first is quite straightforward. It simply involves construction of maximal achievable (i. e., non-conflicting) subsets from among the conflicting goals, and evaluating the net worth of each one. Since we are generally dealing with two goals in a conflict, this means just evaluating the worth of one goal and comparing it to the value of the other. Thus if having the newspaper is deemed more valuable than getting wet, then the planner walks outside to get the newspaper and allows himself to get soaked. Alternatively, a reader trying to understand someone else's behavior would use knowledge about this meta-plan to make inferences about their value system. If we observe John risking getting wet in order to get his morning paper, then we conclude that having his paper is worth more to him than staying dry.

Goal Abandonment versus Goal Substitution. Sometimes, goal abandonment is operating in a sort of disguise. For example, consider the following stories:

(6) John wanted to see the football game, but his wife said she would divorce him if he watched one more game. John settled for watching the tennis match together with his wife.

(7) John wanted to live in San Francisco, but he also wanted to live near Mary, and she lived in New York. John decided he could probably find another girlfriend in San Francisco.

In (6), John must resolve a conflict between his goal of watching the football game and preserving his marriage. On the surface, it appears as if John modifies the goal of watching the football game to watching tennis instead, an activity that John's wife apparently does not object to. Similarly, in (7), John abandons his goal of maintaining his relationship with Mary, and appears to substitute it with the goal of having a similar relationship with somebody else.

Schank and Abelson (1977) describe such situations as instances of *goal substitution*. According to them, goal substitution is a strategy applicable whenever a goal is blocked. They state the rule that "following blockage, the maximum feasible number of valued characteristics of the goal object should be preserved. (p. 109)" As they point out, goals can be "stacked" within a hierarchy of many levels, so for example, wanting to watch the Giants can be an instance of wanting to watch a football game, which in turn is an instance of wanting to watch a sporting event, and so on. Thus if a goal is to be substituted, it is desirable to replace it with a goal occupying as similar a place in the hierarchy as the goal it is replacing. So watching the Jets is likely to be a better substitution for watching the Giants than is watching tennis, which is in turn a better substitute than operating a hydraulic ram.

However, we offer an analysis that is somewhat at odds with theirs. The main problem with Schank and Abelson's formulation is based on a subtle, but important distinction. To understand this problem, consider the question of *why* one goal may be substituted for another. That is, how is it possible that a "similar" goal can be substituted for the original goal? If a goal is truly something that a planner wants to achieve, then why should some other, different state do as well? The answer that Schank and Abelson provide is that the original goal is really just an instantiation of a more general goal; therefore another instantiation will do.

The problem here is that we are forced to conclude that the original goal was not a goal at all, but merely a plan for achieving some real goal. This is clearly the case some of the time, as the following example illustrates:

(8) John needed a pen to sign a letter. When he couldn't find his own, he asked Bill if he could borrow his.

In this example, John at one point seems to have the goal of possessing his pen. When this goal fails, he replaces it with the goal of possessing Bill's pen. On the surface, one goal appears to be substituted by another, similar goal. However, strictly speaking, it is unlikely that John really had the goal of possessing his pen; most likely, his goal *was* "possess some pen" or possibly, "possess a writing implement." But such a goal is too abstract to be achieved directly. While this goal is not specific to the particular writing implement selected, the real world has only individual objects. At some point, one such object must be designated in order for a plan to be executed. That is, in order to have any pen, a planner eventually plans to obtain one particular object.

Because this sort of narrowing down is really part of the planning process rather than part of a planner's goal structure, we refer to it as *plan specification*. Specifically, we postulate a PLAN-SPECIFICATION meta-plan that makes a plan work by supplanting generic descriptions with descriptions of more specific entities (This is in contrast to *goal specification*, a term used by Schank and Abelson to make the conditions of a goal more elaborate. The effects of these two processes are quite different. Plan specification enables the fulfillment of a goal by producing a plan more capable of execution. Goal specification makes fulfillment of a goal more difficult by posing additional constraints that a state must meet to achieve the desired goal).

We can see at once that John wanting his pen in story (8) is almost certainly an instance of plan specification. His goal is to have a writing implement and, as a way of achieving this goal, he used the PLAN-SPECIFICATION meta-plan to produce the plan of obtaining his particular pen. As he failed to execute this plan, he re-specifies by selecting another instance of the generic class of object which he is seeking.

Thus the situation in story (8) obeys Schank and Abelson's hierarchy rules, but it is unrelated to goal substitution; it merely supplants one plan to another and it is therefore simply an instance of re-planning for a goal. In a real goal substitution situation, an actual goal rather than a plan-specified instance of a goal must be substituted. Otherwise this situation is no different than substituting the plan of asking with the plan of begging when the attempt to successfully execute the plan fails.

Most of Schank and Abelson's candidates for goal substitution are actually simple re-planning instances. For example, consider the goal of "enjoy eating at a Chinese restaurant." Schank and Abelson would suggest that this is "dominated" by the goal "enjoy eating good food," and therefore if it fails, then eating at a French restaurant may be substituted as it preserves these salient features. But in fact, these features are not a property of this goal at all. To see this, note that the goal dominating this one may just as easily have been "partake in the Chinese New Year celebration." Now if eating at a Chinese restaurant were blocked, then a reasonable substitute might be "watch the Chinese New Year parade." However, "enjoy eating at a French restaurant" would fail utterly. The explanation for this difference is of course that in both cases, eating at a Chinese restaurant is not a goal, but rather a plan for another goal.

Of course, "enjoy eating at a Chinese restaurant" may very well be a goal, but in that case, it would be unsubstitutable. Since this being a real goal would be most unusual, this may be difficult to see. However, in general such goals are not uncommon. For example, the goal "treat my wife to dinner for her birthday" will hardly be amenable to substitution by replacing my wife with my son, or with her twin sister. And if I really wanted to take her out to dinner, buying her a ring will just not do.

burger,'' we interpret this as "John wanted some generic hamburger," as individual hamburgers are rarely distinguished by one's goals.

This tendency toward normality is why example (7) seems somewhat unusual — one is supposed to value highly the particular individual involved in a relationship, thus realizing that the goal here is actually more abstract comes as somewhat of a surprise.

According to this analysis, goal substitution is just not possible. The semantics of what it means to be a goal are such that if it were substitutable, then our original specification must have been incorrect in the first place. If I said my goal was "treat my wife to dinner for her birthday," but treating her to a fancy lunch was an acceptable substitute, then I must have meant that my original goal was really "treat wife to fancy meal," and the "treat her to dinner," merely a plan.

However, there is still a problem. For if I really desired to treat my wife to dinner, how can it be that if this goal fails, then buying her a ring still seems more appropriate than going to a football game with my best friend? The answer is that when a planner truly has a goal such as taking one's spouse to dinner, he often has other related goals as well. For example, he is likely to have the goal "enjoy a good meal" and "buy wife a present" in addition to the particular desire to take her to dinner. While these goals are in principle unrelated, it happens to be the case that the plan for the latter one is in fact equivalent to the achievement of the other two. That is, in addition to being a goal in its own right, taking one's spouse to dinner is a plan for enjoying a good meal and for buying her a present. Rather than an instance of goal substitution, replacing "take wife to dinner" with "buy her a ring," is actually an abandonment of this goal and of "enjoy good meal," and a respecification of the "buy wife a present" goal with the plan "buy wife a ring" instead of "take wife to dinner."

In sum, goal substitution does not exist. Either we have a case of respecification, in which case the original "goal" was actually a plan, or we have an instance of goal abandonment in which one of the goals abandoned also happened to be equivalent to a plan for another goal, which was subsequently respecified into some new plan.

As an example, suppose we assume John's goal in story (6) above, was really to watch the football game. In this case, he actually abandons this goal completely. However, he might have another goal, "enjoy leisure activity" for which watching the football game is a plan. Thus watching tennis is a new plan specification for this goal, and the original goal that conflicted with preserving his marriage is given up entirely.

This notion of goal abandonment is sufficient to handle situations like (6) and (7), once we realize that there are likely to be a number of goals active here at once. Of course, making such a realization requires knowledge about the normal goal structures people are likely to have. In the case of story understanding, for example, if we are told that a planner desires such and such a state, we use our knowledge of normalcy to infer what the goal really is. Unusually specific or general goals must be described as such explicitly to overcome this default inference. Thus "John wanted to go to New York" is interpreted as the goal "John wanted to *be* in New York," as going in itself is not normally desirable; if we hear "John wanted a ham-

Partial Goal Fulfillment. Goal abandonment can therefore account for a diverse number of complicated situations. However, there is another set of situations that we cannot yet cope with. Consider once again the example of fetching the newspaper in from the rain, in which the original goals are to get the newspaper in from the rain, and to remain dry. Rather than abandon either goal completely, a reasonable alternative is to try to reduce the degree to which one gets wet as much as possible. A plan for remaining as dry as possible while moving through the rain is to run as fast as one can. This plan satisfies one goal entirely, and another to a degree. The total value of this scenario is likely to be greater than the value of staying dry but not getting the paper, and since the other abandonment possibility (getting the paper but getting less soaked) is clearly worse than this (i. e., getting the paper but getting less soaked), the scenario involving partial fulfillment is likely to be adopted.

Partial goal fulfillment is a general principle that is applicable to all goals that involve scalar values. If one wants not to be hungry, being less hungry is not as good as not being hungry at all, but it is better than not being less hungry. That is, it is implicit in what it means to *be* a goal that states closer to the goal have a value less than the goal but greater than those further from the goal.

In the cases where this does not appear to hold, it is usually because the actual goal structure has been incorrectly identified. For example, if it were raining acid rain whose very touch were deadly, getting just a little wet would not be better than getting very wet. But this is because the real goal in this situation is not "don't get wet," but "don't get killed." Not getting wet is simply a plan for this goal when it is raining acid rain. Achieving the plan to a degree does not fulfill the goal at all, and is thus not a very good plan. In the previous case, the goal was not such a binary one, so partial fulfillment is possible. In other words, the goal must refer to a degree-like scale. As the story goes, a father will not be comforted to learn that his unmarried daughter is just a little pregnant.

Partial goal fulfillment provides the SIMULATE-AND-SELECT metaplan with a complicated option. In addition to strict abandonment scenarios, it now also has the possibility of proposing options in which the partial fulfillment of one goal enables the (possibly partial) fulfillment of the other. The process that proposes this partial fulfillment scenario is as follows: MAKE-ATTRIBUTION determines that the problem with the "stay dry" goal is that it requires not going outside. Thus a partial version of this goal is sought that doesn't involve this condition. In the case of not getting wet, the "stay as dry as possible" alternative is postulated because this doesn't require not going outside. This scenario is therefore hypothesized and evaluated along with the strict abandonment options, and the one with the highest value is chosen.

Plausibility Evaluation. So far, we have been assuming that the planner has absolute certainty about each scenario that is envisioned. However, the success of a plan is more apt to be a probabilistic quantity. That is, a planner may believe that an envisioned scenario will fulfill his various goals with different degrees of certainty. Since the degree of expectation of success will affect the overall value of the scenario, the planner must take these factors into account in selecting an option.

For example, if the planner believes that some scenario offers a very small chance of fulfilling a very important goal, but a competing scenario offers a larger chance of fulfilling a less important goal, then these likelihoods must be considered to determine which scenario is to be preferred. Thus crossing the street may be in conflict with not getting hit by a car, and the value of preserving one's life is apt to be greater than the ultimate value of the goal underlying crossing the street. However, the perceived likelihood of such an occurrence is usually so small that it undermines the superior value of that goal from influencing one's plan.

Once the probability of success enters into consideration, we realize that situations we have been calling goal conflicts are actually often only plausible conflicts. That is, all the goal conflict detection and reasoning apparatus that has been discussed so far may be called into play when the planner expects that pursuing one goal may impede the fulfillment of another, but in which the interference may itself only be probabilistic.

Fortunately, these considerations can be accommodated without serious alterations to the planning structures I have proposed if we assume that the planner can attach plausibility judgments to anticipated events and propagate these judgments to the derived scenarios. Then the descriptions of situations used by the goal detector to spot goal conflicts can contain the degree of plausibility of the goal as well. For example, the planner might have a description denoting that walking down a dark alley along at night conflicts to some particular degree with preserving one's money; upon considering such an action, this conflict will be spotted as would an "absolute" conflict. Then the relative values and likelihoods of fulfillments of the goals could be considered to determine the appropriate course of action.

To propagate along plausibility judgments, the planner needs to be able to assess the probability that a plan will succeed if all its preconditions are fulfilled; the interaction with the other plans amounts to assessing the probability that those preconditions will be met. A goal conflict then is a situation in which pursuing one plan lowers the probability of the preconditions for some other plan being met.

In situations in which the likelihood and values of the goals involved are in concord, selecting the most productive scenario is unproblematic. However, in those situations in which the values and expected achievement of goals are inversely related, a way of comparing these quantities is needed. However, the computation of the expected value of plan of action does not appear to be something that people carry out in a principled way. That is, these situations are those in which it is notoriously difficult for people to come to a decision. Possibly, rather than a principled means of computing expected value, a set of heuristics is used. Our theory may be agnostic on this point, however. We need only assume that the value of a scenario computed by SIMULATE-AND-SELECT takes into account the relative likelihood of success in addition to the value of one's goal. In those cases where it cannot, the SIMULATE-AND-SELECT plan may simply fail, leaving the planner in a quandary as to which action to take.

An Example. As many of the situations just described are complicated by the presence of a number of goals all involving the same plan, it is instructive to look at one such situation in some detail. One plan I might have for eating lunch is to go to the Three C's with John and order a crepe. The goal structure behind this plan is actually quite rich. First, there are several goals that this plan is seeking to satisfy. They include:

1. satisfying my hunger, as it is lunch-time and eating most anything will fulfill this goal;
2. enjoying the experience of eating, as I like good food and the crepes at this restaurant are tasty;
3. getting back to the office quickly, as I need to return to my office soon, and this restaurant is nearby;
4. enjoying company, as I prefer not to eat alone, and enjoy John's company;
5. not spending more than four dollars for lunch.

If in fact these are precisely my goals, then the plan I chose is only one of a number of alternatives that might work just as well. For example, I could conceivably go to another restaurant that is equidistant and which serves just as good food, or I might try another companion if the one specified in this plan were not available. These variations would fulfill the actual goals just as well, and thus constitute instances of re-specification rather than goal substitution.

On the other hand, if no restaurant near my office were open, then I might have to settle for the partial fulfillment of a goal, namely, I would attempt to get back as quickly as possible. Or if the only good restaurant nearby served very small portions, I have a goal conflict between "satisfy-hunger" and "enjoy good food." This conflict might be resolved once again by settling for partial fulfillment, achieving "satisfy-hunger as much as possible" rather than "satisfy-hunger."

Alternatively, my original goal structure could have been somewhat different. For example, I might have had an urge for a Three C's crepe, in which case going to another good restaurant would have to be viewed as goal abandonment. Or I might have had some particular reason to talk with John so choosing another co-diner would not be acceptable. It is unlikely, however, that I would have had only very general original goals like "enjoy any activity" and "satisfy some urge," so that when I could find no restaurant opened nearby, I would be just as happy to go to a movie with a friend. Of course, I might actually end up doing so in this situation. But it must be interpreted as abandoning a number of my original goals rather than as finding a different way of achieving them.

SUMMARY AND PROJECTIONS

We have proposed a theory of planning based on the following tenets: (1) Common-sense planning is essentially the consideration of interactions of otherwise simple plans; (2) a planner must be able to deduce its goals as well as produce plans for them; (3) planning problems should be formulated as meta-goals, and solved by the same planning mechanism responsible for the fulfillment of ordinary goals; (4) to accomplish much of its mandate, the planner makes projections of the future based on its current knowledge of the world and its own tentative plans; and (5) knowledge about planning should be usable both by a planner and an understander.

These tenets form the basis for a model of planning whose most salient features are a goal detector and a projector. The goal detector is used to infer goals, including meta-goals, based on the situations in which the planner finds itself; the projector is used to guess what the future will bring based on the planner's current beliefs and plans. As the goal detector has access to the hypothetical situations simulated by the projector, it can detect problems with currently intended plans by noticing their consequences in hypothetical realities. These problems are dealt with by setting up meta-goals to try to assure a more desirable future state of affairs.

We examined this model of planning in the particular domain of goal conflict resolution. Here we found use for the meta-plans RE-PLAN (consisting of USE-NORMAL-PLAN and USE-ALTERNATE-PLAN) and CHANGE-CIRCUMSTANCE for the meta-goal RESOLVE-GOAL-CONFLICT. Both meta-plans make use of the powerful sub-plan MAKE-ATTRIBUTION. For the related goal of CHOOSE-MOST-VALUABLE-SCENARIO, the SIMULATE-AND-SELECT meta-plan is used to create alternatives involving goal abandonment and partial goal fulfillment. MAKE-ATTRIBUTION was found to be useful here as well.

We are currently attempting to test these ideas in two programs. PAM, a story-understanding system, uses knowledge about goal interactions to understand stories involving multiple goals. That is, PAM can detect situations like goal conflict and goal competition and, realizing that these threaten certain meta-goals, PAM will interpret a character's subsequent behavior as a meta-plan to address the negative consequences of these interactions. Thus PAM makes use of the knowledge structures described above, but of course, it does not test the model of planning per se.

Both the model of planning knowledge and of planning is being used in the development of PANDORA (Plan ANalyzer with Dynamic Organization, Revision and Application). PANDORA is given a description of a situation and determines if it has any goals it should act upon. It then creates plans for these goals, using projection to test them. New goals, including meta-goals, may be inferred in the process, possibly causing PANDORA to revise its previous plans.

The following is an example of the kind of planning situation that PANDORA can handle. PANDORA is presented with a task that requires it to get some nails and to get a hammer. PANDORA proposes the normal plans for these goals, which requires it to go to the store, buy the desired item, and return. As the plans involve some common preconditions, the meta-theme "DON'T WASTE RESOURCES" causes PANDORA to have the meta-goal COMBINE-PLANS. A meta-plan associated with this goal synthesizes a new plan that involves going to the store, buying both objects, and returning.

PANDORA can also detect and resolve a number of goal conflict situations. In addition, PANDORA is being used to model the planning processes of a human who needs to cook dinner during a power failure, in which most of the normal plans for one's goals will not be effective.

ACKNOWLEDGEMENTS

Research sponsored by the National Science Foundation under grant MCS79-06543 and by the Office of Naval Research under contract N00014-80-C-0732.

REFERENCES

Carbonell, J. (1978). POLITICS: Automated ideological reasoning, *Cognitive Science*, 2:27-51.

Fikes, R. & Nilsson, N. J. (1971). STRIPS: A new approach to the application of theorem proving to problem solving. *Artifical Intelligence*, 2, 189-208.

Hayes-Roth, B., & Hayes-Roth, F. (1979). A Cognitive Model of Planning, *Cognitive Science*, 3:275-310.

McDermott, D. (1978). Planning and Acting. *Cognitive Science*, 2:

McCarthy, J., & Hayes, P. J. (1969). Some philosophical problems from the standpoint of artificial intelligence. In B. Meltzer & D. Michie (Eds.) *Machine intelligence*, vol. 4. New York: American Elsevier, pp. 463-502.

Newell, A., & Simon, H. A. (1972). *Human problem solving.* Englewood Cliffs, N. J.: Prentice Hall.

Rieger, C. (1975a). *One System for Two Tasks: A Common-sense Algorithm Memory that Solves Problems and Comprehends Language.* MIT AI Lab working paper 114.

Rieger, C. (1975b). The common-sense algorithm as a basis for computer models of human memory, inference, belief, and contextual language comprehension. In *Theoretical issues in natural language processing.* R. Schank & B. L. Nash-Webber (Eds.), Association for Computational Linguistics, Cambridge, Mass.

Sacerdoti, E.D. (1977). *A structure for plans and behavior.* North-Holland, Amsterdam: Elsevier.

Schank, R. C. & Abelson, R. P. (1977). *Scripts, plans, goals, and understanding.* Hillsdale, N. J.: Lawrence Erlbaum Associates.

Shortliffe, E. H. (1976). *MYCIN: Computer-based medical consultations.* New York: American Elsevier.

Stefik, M. J. (1980). Planning and Meta-Planning - MOLGEN: Part 2. Stanford Heuristic Programming Project HPP-80-13 (working paper), Computer Science Department, Stanford University.

Sussman, G. J. (1975). *A computer model of skill acquisition.* New York: American Elsevier.

Wilensky, R. (1978). *Understanding goal-based stories.* Yale University Research Report No. 140.

Wilensky, R. (1980). *Meta-planning: Representing and Using Knowledge about Planning in Problem Solving and Natural Language Understanding.* Berkeley Electronic Research Laboratory Memorandum No. UCB/ERL/M80/33.

Integrating Marker–Passing and Problem Solving

James A. Hendler
Department of Computer Science
Brown University[†]

In this paper we describe how an efficient underlying mechanism, a parallel, spreading activation algorithm, can be used during problem solving. We present this mechanism, chosen due to its demonstrated usefulness for several other cognitive tasks, and show how it can be used to guide the problem solver in choosing correct plans, rejecting plans that violate constraints, or modifying plans as they are generated. Examples of how this technique is used are given, and an implementation of such a system, integrating a marker–passer with a problem solver, is described. The paper discusses some of the desiderata in designing such systems and some of the issues that arise. Some future directions for the work are also described.

1. Introduction

A major problem faced by problem-solving systems today is that of making a choice in the presence of multiple alternatives. It is often the case that the system has access to knowledge that would lead to the optimal solution, or that could avoid a conflict, but this knowledge is not used. Consider the case of a system trying to solve a goal such as *Satisfy hunger*. It must make a choice between alternatives such as *Go to restaurant* and *Eat at home*. In the absence of other knowledge it may not matter which path is chosen, but what if we had already asserted *You have no money* to this system? At this point there is a conflict down the *restaurant* path, but none down the *eat at home* path. Thus the system should choose the latter. Unfortunately, most present day systems are unable to take advantage of this sort of information, and would make the choice at random. At a later point in the problem solving it would encounter the error (assuming it took the *restaurant* path) and be forced to backtrack. Avoiding backtracking has been a primary goal of problem-solving researchers.

In this paper we present a new approach to the issue of choosing paths during problem solving. We propose that a suitably structured "marker-passer", a parallel, spreading activation mechanism, can be used to aid the choice mechanism used by a problem-solver. In this paper we will describe an implementation of such a mechanism, as well as discussing why such a mechanism is desirable.

2. Integrating Marker–Passing and Problem Solving

Present day problem solvers work by using information found in Memory to generate plans. These plans are then subjected to some form of plan Evaluation, either in the form of demons (cf Sussman, 1975; Sacerdoti, 1977) or meta–rules (cf Wilensky, 1983) which critique the plans and if necessary, return them to the problem-solver for

---

[†] This research was supported by Office of Naval Research under contract N00014-79-C-0592.

Copyright, Cognitive Science Society Incorporated, used by permission.

reworking.

Most problem solvers work by making step–wise refinements on subplans until primitive actions are reached. Thus *Restaurant* would be broken down into *enter, order, eat, pay,* and *leave*. *Order* could be broken down into *read menu, decide,* and *tell waitress,* etc. Steps such as *read menu* would be primitive and thus the final plan would be comprised of such steps.

It is this step–wise refinement that causes the problem described in the introduction. At the time we decide which plan to use we do not yet know what steps it will eventually decompose into. However, it is when we try to perform these primitives that the conflicts will most often manifest themselves.

It is clear that if a mechanism could be developed that would examine all these primitive actions looking for possible conflicts and identifying them prior to the making of a choice then the problem solver would benefit. This mechanism would need to find all possible bindings for the variables being passed through the various levels of substeps checking for conflicts.

Unfortunately, such a mechanism does not presently exist. To be computationally viable this mechanism would need to perform deduction extremely quickly. Further, since all possible bindings of any variables need to be examined, large numbers (susceptible to combinatorial explosion) of low–level deductions[†] would need to be done. Parallelism would improve the situation, but not solve it, due to inherent limitations on the efficiency of such deductions and the combinatorics of multiple possibilities of variable bindings.

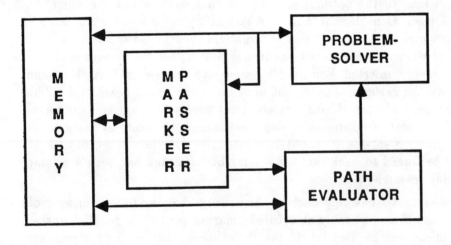

Figure 1: Flow of control

[†] Depending on the type of problem–solver being used these computations could involve unification, pattern–matching, script instantiation, etc. In this paper all of these types of tasks will be referred to as "low–level deductions" for want of a better term.

It is possible, however, to approximate this mechanism with a system that can examine the primitive actions quickly while looking for special features. A Marker-passing system is one such mechanism. It is our contention that by merging a marker-passer with a problem solver we can provide substantial improvement. Our system (Figure 1) has the marker-passer integrated with the problem–solver and plan evaluator. At this point we will discuss exactly what we mean by marker-passing and why we prefer this type of system. Following that we will show some examples of how the marker-passer is integrated into the problem solver.

2.1. What is Marker–Passing?

Marker-passing (cf Quillian, 1966; Fahlman, 1979; Charniak, 1983), a computational model of spreading activation, can be thought of as the marking of nodes adjacent to some node in memory, and then marking all nodes adjacent to those, etc. Thus, for example, in a traditional semantic net system if we marked *CAR* we would then mark *WHEELS, VEHICLE*, and all those concepts directly related to *CAR*. Following this we would then mark *RUBBER, ROUND* and all those concepts relating to *WHEEL*, as well as *TRANSPORTATION* and those concepts relating to *VEHICLE*. This process would proceed until either nothing was left to mark or the process was called to a halt.

By marking first one node and then another we can see how they are related by examining those concepts marked by both. Thus, in this example from Charniak (1983):

John wanted to commit suicide. He got a rope.

We would start passing markers at *suicide* and then pass markers starting at *rope*. This would find an intersection at the node *noose* which would be found both from *suicide* (the instrument of a *hang*) and from *rope* (as a material relation).

The primary difference between the marker-passer defined by Charniak (1983; based on Quillian, 1966) and the parallel model proposed by Fahlman (1979) is that the former will return the path found, rather than reporting the node of intersection (as would the latter). Thus in the example above the marker-passer would return:

SUICIDE –> to do suicide KILL self –> KILL –> HANG is a type of KILL –> HANG –> instrument of HANG is NOOSE –> NOOSE –> NOOSE is made of ROPE –> ROPE

Notice that the marker-passer does not perform any deductions during its run. If we had asserted that the agent and patient of a *hang* had to be different this path would still be found. This would not be a valid path since the definition of *suicide* requires that the agent and patient must be the same. It is this "blind" behaviour that enables us to implement marker-passing efficiently, at the expense of finding some false paths. The issues of evaluating false paths and avoiding their generation are discussed later in this paper (section 4.2).

2.2. Why Marker–Passing?

In considering an underlying mechanism to use for problem-solving it was our desire to find a system with several properties: it must be able to examine many possibilities efficiently, it must return information that the problem-solver can use for making choices, and it would be desirable to start from an existing system, being used for other cognitive problems. Marker-passing fits all three of these criteria.

Earlier, we discussed how the choice mechanism needs to be able to access the primitive actions of our problem-solver. As the marker-passer proceeds from a plan it marks the substeps, the substeps of these, etc. until it reaches the primitives. Since it does not do deduction as it marks it is able to reach these nodes efficiently. Further, existing implementations of marker-passing (Fahlman, 1979; Charniak, Gavin, Hendler, 1983) are formulated so as to be computed in parallel[†] thus gaining efficiency. In section 3 we will show examples of how the problem-solver can take advantage of the marker-passer. Thus, we satisfy our first two criteria.

Our system is not, by any means, the first to propose the use of marker-passing as an underlying mechanism. Quillian (1966) described a system, TLC, in which spreading activation was used to analyze sentence fragments such as "lawyer's client." As these phrases were analyzed the system would "learn" their meaning and thus be able to build to an understanding of more complex sentences. Collins and Loftus (1975) expanded some of Quillian's ideas, and described the psychological relevance of the spreading activation idea.

Fahlman (1979) described a system in which a marker-passing like scheme was used as the basis for a deductive system. In his system, NETL, links between nodes had properties that determine how marks pass over these links. By allowing this feature, many paths that a blind marker-passer would find are avoided. For example, if we wanted to encode the information that "Clyde was a *pink* elephant" we would have a regular link from *Clyde* to *elephant* and another link, called a cancellation link, from *Clyde* to the area where we record that *the color of an elephant is grey*. Fahlman described an implementation scheme for doing many standard deductive inferences using these sorts of links.

Charniak (1983) described the use of the marker-passer as a device for aiding in the process of story comprehension. The marker-passer is used to find possible paths through the frame knowledge database that relate two frames together. These paths enable the system to build up a model of the frames being instantiated. Thus, in the example of section 2.1, the path from *suicide* to *rope* is found by the marker-passer. It returns this information to a higher level mechanism which uses the information for instantiating the *hang* frame and for building a representation of the events in the story.

Hirst (1983) used Charniak's model of marker-passing for word sense disambiguation. Part of his "Polaroid words" system would pass markers between the senses of words being examined. Thus, in the case of the sentence:

The farmer bought the straw.

the marker-passer would find the path between *farmer* and the *hay* meaning of *straw* thus preferring this meaning over the *drinking straw* meaning for which no significant connection would be found. Further, his system explains the difficulties that would be found in disambiguating a sentence such as:

The astronomer married the star.

Granger, Eiselt, and Holbrook (1984) developed a model of parsing based on the spreading activation model. Their program, ATLAST, models the integration of lexical,

---

[†]Due to hardware limitations these systems have been implemented as "psuedo-parallel." That is, although running on serial machines they violate no constraints of locality or temporality that a massively parallel system would need.

syntactic, and pragmatic processes during natural language comprehension. A spreading activation model of memory is used to propose paths that are then evaluated by a filtering mechanism. Those paths found to be significant are pursued by the parser.

3. Examples

The flow of control when we integrate the marker-passer with the problem-solver was shown in figure 1. In general the following occurs: To start, the problem-solver is invoked. In attempting to solve problems it passes markers throughout the knowledge base. When these markers encounter other markers an intersection is found. The paths meeting at this intersection are then returned to the plan evaluation mechanism. This mechanism checks this path for information which can be used to help guide the problem-solver. If no such information is found, the path is ignored.

The system checks to see if this path proposes a solution to an existing problem (see section 3.1 below), causes a conflict (sections 3.2 and 3.3), or suggests a modification to an existing plan (section 3.4). If one of these is identified the system takes appropriate action choosing, rejecting, or modifying the plan as necessary. In this section we will show examples of these situations and informally describe how the system would work. In later sections we will discuss the specifics of this implementation in more detail.

3.1. Example 1

The first example we will examine is one in which the marker-passer can help us identify a correct solution to a problem with many alternatives. In this example we consider the case of

Trying to commit suicide while holding a gun.

Figure 2 shows a simplified view of the knowledge base used in this example.

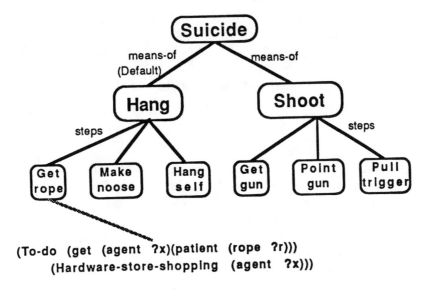

Figure 2: Suicide Information

The system needs to choose between each of the possible ways of commiting suicide shown. It starts by passing markers to each of the alternatives, these in turn mark their subplans, etc. While this goes on we are also passing markers starting with the frame[†] *gun*. Since this marks *gun*, and since *shoot* has as a precondition the possession of a *gun*, we find an intersection. The path

SUICIDE –> to do SUICIDE(x) KILL (x,x) –> KILL –> method of KILL(y,x) is
SHOOT(y,x) –> SHOOT –> precondition of SHOOT(y,x) is possess (y,GUN) –> GUN

is reported to the plan evaluator. Since this path presents a potential solution to the task which has been posed, committing suicide, the plan evaluator can cause the problem solver to prefer the *shoot* plan for achieving the *suicide* goal.

3.2. Example 2

We can also use the marker–passer to reject plans that violate externally generated constraints. Consider, for example, the following situation:

> You are told at some time that the Air Traffic Controllers are on strike. At some later time you are told to plan a trip to California.

Figure 3 shows a simplified view of the knowledge we have in the database.

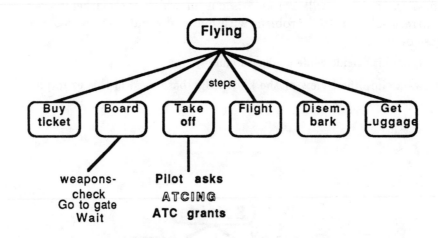

Figure 3: Air Traffic Control

It is important for our problem–solver to realize that the first statement (the ATC strike) is in conflict with our primary choice for the method of getting to California. When the system is given the first sentence it wishes to add it to the database. The system enters this information. It also notices a forward inference rule of the form *IF someone is on strike AND that person has some function THEN that function might not be*

[†]We will use frames here as a generic word for a planning structure. The user may replace it with "script", "schema", "plan" or other such term.

able to happen. Since the Air Traffic Controllers have as their function *ATCing* this would be marked.

We would now ask the system to plan a trip to California. Among the options to choose from will be the *FLY* frame. We will now pass markers on our alternatives. This will mark the *Ticket, Board, Clearance,* and *Take-off* frames, followed by each of the substeps of each of these frames. Since *ATCing* is one of the substeps of *clearance* it will be marked. At this point the marker-passer would recognise that an intersection has been found, and will return the path

> TRIP -> method trip FLY -> FLY -> step of FLY: CLEARANCE -> CLEARANCE -> step of CLEARANCE: ATCING -> ATCING -> ATCING (marked as unachievable by FACT of strike)

This information is passed to the plan evaluator which examines the path. Since ATC-ING has been marked as unachievable the system asserts that it cannot be done. The system now invokes a rule of the form *IF I cannot achieve a step in some plan, THEN I cannot achieve that plan.* Since ATCING is a step in the plan for FLY we can rule out the choice of flying as a method of transport for the problem solver.

3.3. Example 3

Another use of this mechanism is to identify conflicts between parts of plans. As an example consider the case of

Buying a cleaver while on a business trip.

Figure 4 shows a simplified view of the information we use to process this example.

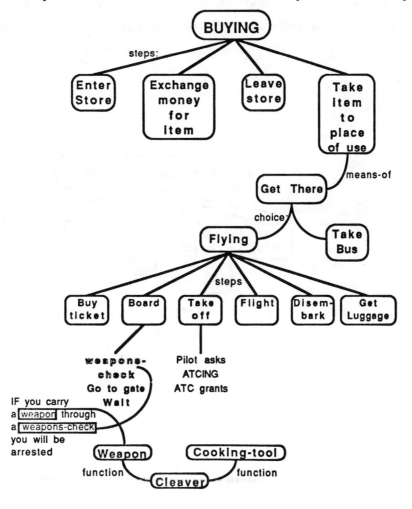

Figure 4: Buying the cleaver

The system starts by attempting to plan the buying of the cleaver. As such it passes markers down the paths for *Cleaver* and for *Buying*. From *cleaver* it use the knowledge that cleavers are used as *kitchen tools* and as *weapons* so it marks these nodes.

The system also marks the information about *buying* which includes the step of taking home that which is bought. Via the substeps of substeps the marker–passer eventually notices that one way to go home is to *fly* and that within *flying* one must pass through a *weapons check*. However, *weapons check* marks *weapon* and finds that it is already marked. Thus, an intersection has been reached and the information is passed to the plan evaluator.

The plan evaluator examines this path and discovers that the intersection involves carrying a weapon through a weapons check, which leads to being arrested, an undesirable state.

The plan evaluator can now use a heuristic which states that *IF a path causes one to reach an undesirable state THEN rule out the plan during which this state is enocuntered.* Since *Flying* is the plan which dominates the *weapons check* we can rule it out as the method of getting the cleaver home. It can then do replanning and either reject the purchase or amend the plan so as to avoid the illegality (and thus check the cleaver in as luggage).

3.4. Example 4

In the final example the marker–passer is used to find an inference rule that causes a modification of an existing plan. Take for example the following (from Wilensky, 1983):

The planner is given the task of fetching a newspaper from outside during a rainstorm.

Figure 5 shows the necessary information, simplified as usual.

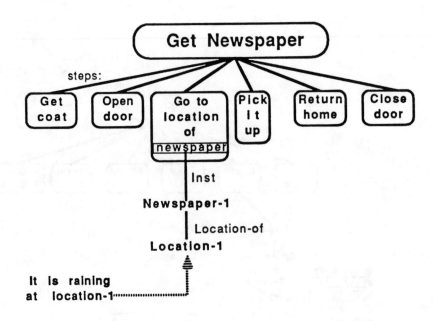

Figure 5: Getting a Newspaper

As before we pass markers from both parts of this problem. We thus mark the elements of the *get newspaper* plan and the *raining* statement. In this case we find the intersection not at one of the nodes of the plan, but at an inference rule in the system. This rule, *If it's raining AND if someone is outside THEN an umbrella should be used by that person*, is now examined by the plan evaluator. Since the person in question will can be bound with the agent of *get newspaper*, the plan will be modified so that that agent takes an umbrella.

4. SCRAPS: An Implementation

We have implemented a system, called SCRAPS, that combines a marker–passer and a problem–solver as described so far. In this section we will describe this implementation and discuss how we avoid some of the potential problems inherent in the design of such a system.

4.1. Implementation Details

SCRAPS is implemented using the problem solver NASL (McDermott, 1978; Charniak, 1982) on a logic–based semantics system, FRAIL (Charniak, Gavin, Hendler, 1983). Built into FRAIL is an implementation of a marker–passer. FRAIL and NASL are both implemented in the NISP dialect of Lisp (McDermott, 1983) and run on several different types of machines.

One important aspect of a marker-passing system has to do with the overall organization of the frame knowledge database being searched. For the purposes of performing marker passing, this database should be viewable as a large network of independent processors, each representing a frame, that are interrelated via links along which markers may be passed. Each frame must be capable of both receiving and passing markers to neighboring frames through these links, which correspond to directed arcs relating frames to each other.

The FRAIL language provides such a system. Frames are translated into logical predicates which are stored in a LISP database as properties on atoms. These atoms serve as frames and the logical predicates serve as links. Thus, FRAIL provides both a logical language for deduction and a semantic–net representation useful for marker-passing.

The NASL problem solver uses FRAIL to retrieve the possible plans usable for satisfying a goal. When more than one plan can be applicable FRAIL uses a simple choice mechanism that checks for plans which are ruled out or ruled in. SCRAPS uses this mechanism as the primary communication between the plan evaluator and the problem-solver. When the marker–passer finds a path that the plan evaluator recognizes as a potential solution, that path is ruled in and all other paths are ruled out. Similarly, when the plan evaluator recognizes a problem it simply rules out that plan which would cause the contradiction. Synchronization is provided by having the problem–solver's choice mechanism wait until a message is received from the plan evaluator allowing it to proceed. Modifications to plans are done by having the plan evaluator make assertions directly into the FRAIL database.

As an example, consider once again the restaurant example of section 1. The system is started with the assertion that no money is available, and thus the *paying* frame is marked as unachievable via a forward chaining rule. We then ask the problem solver to solve the task of *eating* with some specific agent, *agent1*. NASL calls upon FRAIL to retrieve the potential plans and finds both *restaurant* and *eat at home*. As FRAIL retrieves these plans markers are passed. The path from *restaurant* to *money* is found and reported to the Plan Evaluator. The Plan Evaluator recognizes the conflict in the restaurant plan and therefore generates a *rule out* statement. [†] It then signals NASL to continue. NASL now uses its choice mechanism to examine the possibilities. Since the restaurant frame has been ruled out it uses the only other possibility, eat at home, and continues on.

4.2. Implementation Issues

For our system to be efficient it must be the case that the added efficiency of avoiding backtracking outweighs the overhead time spent in evaluating the returns from the marker–passer. If the plan evaluator takes longer to reject false paths than it would take the problem solver to find the correct path then the addition of a marker–passer loses its value. The plan evaluator must be designed so that it can quickly reject those paths with nothing to offer.

In the SCRAPS system the plan evaluator is composed of a set of *ad hoc* heuristics that can examine a path and see if any useful information can be gleaned. These rules serve two purposes: first, we wish to quickly reject paths which are not going to yield useful information, and second, we wish to be able to extract information from those paths which are useful. This is done by passing the path through a series of rules in a cascaded manner. The early rules are designed to reject paths known not to be useful, the later rules are designed to quickly check for a certain feature and pass the rule on to the next heuristic if it is not found.

The early rules work by first checking the node of intersection of a path. If the node of intersection is found to be a "promiscuous" node, one with a very high out–branching factor, the path is probably not useful and can therefore be rejected. If the node of intersection is not of this form, the path is checked to see if certain features can be detected that will cause the rule to be rejected. For example, a rule checks to see if a path is an *ISA Plateau*. This would be the situation if we passed markers from, for example, *dog* and *cat* and found an intersection at *animal*. These sorts of paths are useful for the word sense disambiguation use of marker-passing, but not for problem solving. Eugene Charniak (fortcoming) has been examining the paths returned by the marker–passer and trying to formalize path checking as a resolution proof procedure. As this work becomes practical our system will be changed to use this method for the rejecting of false paths.

Once the obviously useless paths have been rejected the Plan Evaluator then uses the second type of heuristic to see if the path yields valuable data. This is done by having each heuristic designed to quickly examine the path for some feature. If that feature is not found the path evaluator immediately passes this path on to the next heuristic. If none of these heuristics find such a feature then the path is considered uninteresting and rejected. If, however, such a feature is found the path is subjected to closer inspection to see if useful information is yielded. Due to the underlying   logical formalism of FRAIL unification is used as a first test in these situations. If items in the path do not unify it can be rejected.

[†] Readers wanting more details about the format of the rules used by the choice mechanism in FRAIL and NASL are directed to Charniak, Gavin, and Hendler (1983),

As an example of these heuristics consider what the Plan Evaluator would do with the *restaurant* example. With variables included, the path found is of the form:

GOAL EAT (*me*) -> EAT -> To–do EAT(x) use RESTAURANT(x) -> RESTAURANT -> step–of RESTAURANT(x) is PAYING (x y) -> **PAYING** -> PAYING(*me*) is Marked as unachievable

We are also informed that the place where the marks intersect is on the node *Paying*. First we examine the node *Paying* to see if it is inherently uninteresting or "promiscuous." Since it isn't we go on to check the form of the path to see if we have found an ISA plateau (a very efficient heuristic). Again, this test fails, so we do not reject this path. We now move on to the second type of heuristic, those designed to extract information. The first heuristic to fire might be the heuristic checking for meta–rules of the type found in example 3.4. This rule would check the path to see if any of the links was of the form *Meta–rule*. Since none of the links in the path above have this form it is passed on to the next heuristic. This rule checks to see if either of the end–points of the path is marked as unachievable. Since this is the case, the rule is now subjected to closer scrutiny. The unification algorithm is used to see if variables in the path match up. Since, in this case, the person with the *Eat* goal is the same as the person trying to do the *Paying* the unifier reports the match. We now can use this rule to rule out using the restaurant plan as described in section 4.1.

Although, the key factor in designing these heuristics is to make the tests for path rejection as efficient as possible, it is still essential that the number of false paths generated can be held down. If too many paths are found by the marker–passer we lose efficiency since the evaluator must examine all those paths which are reported. If too few paths are reported the correct information can be missed. The marker–passer must be designed so as to constrain the number of paths reported.

We are presently exploring some of the issues involved in the design of such constraints. The marker–passer in FRAIL uses a propagation limitation on markers to help keep down the number of false paths found. Marker–passing is invoked with a certain strength at a starting node. That node divides the strength by the number of nodes it has as neighbors, and passes a marker to each of them with this new strength. Each of these nodes proceeds in turn marking its neighbors with ever decreasing strength. Once strength falls below a certain limit marker–passing stops along that path. Thus, long thin trails are preferred to short multiply branching ones.

Another means of limiting the number of false paths is the removal of marks during processing. At present we have developed a model which degrades marker strength over time, depending on the original strength of the marking. When the strength is sufficiently decremented the mark is removed. Recent work (Granger, Holbrook, 1983), however, has suggested that the removal of marks is a more complex process than the one we have implemented. We are presently examining this issue.

5. Research Directions

Recent work (Wilensky, 1983) has been examining the issues involved when a single agent has multiple goals, or when multiple agents, each with their own goals, are involved in a situation. This work has concentrated on recognizing, and resolving, conflicts between these goals. In section 3.3 we showed an example of how a system like SCRAPS could be used to detect problems caused by a conflict between subgoals during a problem–solving task. Our recent research has been directed at exploring the relationship between these sorts of subgoal conflicts and the multiple agent goal conflicts being examined by Wilensky. It is our belief that SCRAPS can be extended to allow the plan evaluator to work on such tasks.

Take the following example (based on an example from Wilensky, 1978):

Bill wants to get the treasure, but the hoard was guarded by a dragon.

SCRAPS would be invoked to solve two tasks one in which Bill attempts to obtain a treasure, and one in which a dragon attempts to guard a hoard. The marker-passer finds the path from Bill to the dragon via the path relating the treasure to the hoard. The plan evaluator can now examine this path. Since, in this simple case, the variables can be bound consistently the plan evaluator can recognize a potential planning conflict. If it had been the case that Bill had decided that the treasure he wanted was not the hoard but the giant pearl being guarded by the huge octopus, the plan evaluator would fail to match the dragon's treasure and the goal of Bill's quest, and thus the path would be regarded as false and therefore rejected.

The primary problem with extending SCRAPS to handle multiple agent planning is the growth in the number of false paths reported when common objects are used in many of the plans. Consider the following situation:

John wishes to buy a farm. Mary, no relation to John, wants to get a job so she can earn more money. Bill, no relation to either of the others, wishes to go to a restaurant.

Our marker-passer will return paths connecting all of these as potential planning conflicts dealing with *money*. Similar growth in paths are caused by items like *cars*, *clothes*, and any other item common to many plans.

The single-agent version of SCRAPS is able to use a heuristic which rejects paths which meet at common objects. Thus, in the cleaver example of section 3.3 a false path such as:

Cleaver -> ... -> weapons-check -> AGENT of Weapons-check is PERSON ->
-> PERSON -> AGENT of buying is PERSON -> BUYING

can be rejected since the node of intersection, *person*, is involved in so many frames. In the multi-agent cases, however, these false paths cannot be rejected as simply. It now requires using our knowledge base to recognize that, for example, Bill's money, Mary's money, and John's money are all different.[†] We are presently working on redesigning the plan evaluator to handle such cases.

6. Conclusions

Integrating marker-passing with problem solving enables us to avoid backtracking in many problem solving tasks. An efficient underlying mechanism, the marker-passer, is used to choose correct plans, reject plans violating constraints, or to modify existing plans. The marker-passing mechanism is chosen due to its demonstrated usefulness during cognitive tasks.

We have shown that careful attention must be paid to the design of the marker-passer and the plan evaluator for the problem solving process to gain efficiency. At present SCRAPS is able to provide this efficiency boost in several situations. We are

---

[†] To convince oneself that this is true, consider the case where John and Mary are married and share a common bank account.

presently examining other problem solving areas to see if other classes of problem solving behaviours can benefit from this technique.

7. Acknowledgements

The author wishes to acknowledge Eugene Charniak for much aid in the design and critiquing of the work described in this report. Several of the examples used in this paper are based on his work. We also wish to acknowledge Doug Wong's aid in helping to formalize some of the pitfalls inherent in the design of a marker–passer.

8. References

Charniak, E. *Micro–Nasl Reference Manual* Dept. of Computer Science, Brown University, 1982.

Charniak, E. "Passing markers: A theory of contextual influence in language comprehension." *Cognitive Science* 7(*3*), July – Sept. 1983.

Charniak, E. *A Neat Theory of Marker–Passing* Dept. of Computer Science, Brown University, forthcoming.

Charniak, E., Gavin, M.K. and Hendler, J.A. *The FRAIL/NASL Reference Manual.* Brown University Dept. of Computer Science Technical Report No. CS–83–06, Feb. 1983.

Collins, A.M. and Loftus, E.F. "A Spreading–activation theory of semantic processing" *Psychological Review* 82(*6*) pp. 407–428, 1975.

Fahlman, S.E. *NETL: A system for representing and using real–world knowledge* MIT Press, 1979.

Granger, R.H., Eiselt, K.P., and Holbrook, J.K. *Parsing with Parallelism: A Spreading Activation Model of Inference Processing During Text Understanding* University of California at Irvine Artificial Intelligence Project Technical Report #228, Sept. 1984.

Granger, R.H. and Holbrook, J.K. *Perseverers, Recencies, and Deferrers: New experimental Evidence for Multiple Inference Strategies in Understanding.* University of California at Irvine Artificial Intelligence Project Technical Report #195, May 1983.

Hirst. G.J. *Semantic Interpretation Against Ambiguity* Brown University Computer Science Technical Report CS–83–25, Dec. 1983.

McDermott, D.V. "Planning and acting" *Cognitive Science* **2** pp. 71–109, April 1978.

McDermott, D.V. *The NISP Manual* Yale University Computer Science Tech Report U/DCS/RR No. 274, June 1983.

Quillian, M.R. *Semantic Memory* (Scientific Report No. 2) Bolt, Beranek, and Newman, 1966.

Sacerdoti, E.C. *A Structure for Plans and Behavior* Elsevier, 1977.

Sussman, G.J. *A Computer Model of Skill Acquisition* Elsevier, 1975.

Wilensky, R. *Understanding Goal-Based Stories* Yale University Computer Science Research Report No. 140, Sept. 1978

Wilensky, R. *Planning and Understanding* Addison–Wesley, 1983.

2. Fikes, R. E. Monitored execution of robot plans produced by STRIPS. *Proc. IFIP Congress 71*, Ljubljana, Yugoslavia (August 23–28, 1971).
3. Garvey, T. D. and Kling, R. E. User's Guide to QA3.5 Question-Answering System. Technical Note 15, Artificial Intelligence Group, Stanford Research Institute, Menlo Park, California (December 1969).
4. Raphael, B. et al. Research and Applications—Artificial Intelligence. Final Report. Contract NASW-2164, Stanford Research Institute, Menlo Park, California (December 1971).
5. Hart, P. E. and Nilsson, N. J. Shakey: Experiments in Robot Planning and Learning. Film produced at Stanford Research Institute, Menlo Park, California (1972).
6. Ernst, G. and Newell, A. *GPS: A Case Study in Generality and Problem Solving.* ACM Monograph Series. Academic Press, New York, New York, 1969.

Received July 1972; revised version received September 1972.

abstracting the preconditions of a MACROP so that only its "main" preconditions remain. A plan would first be attempted using these abstract preconditions; if successful, a subsequent planning process would fill in the details (and perhaps suggest changes to the abstract plan) as needed. As a rough example of the sort of process we have in mind, suppose we have a MACROP that requires the robot to travel through several doors. An abstract precondition for the MACROP might not contain the requirement that the doors be open on the supposition that, should they be closed, the robot could easily open them at the appropriate time. In whatever manner such a scheme is ultimately implemented, it seems clear that a problem solver will be able to increase its power with experience only if it can use this experience at an appropriate level of abstraction.

8.2. Saving MACROPS

We discussed previously a method for discarding a MACROP when it is subsumed by another, more powerful MACROP. In general, any system that learns plans must also either incorporate a mechanism for forgetting old plans or else face the danger of being swamped by an ever-increasing repertoire of stored plans. One straightforward approach to this problem would be to keep some statistics on the frequencies with which the various MACROPS are used, and discard those that fall below some threshold. We have not, however, experimented with any such mechanisms.

8.3. Other Forms of Learning

The generalization scheme discussed in this paper is but one of many possible forms of machine learning. Another form of learning that would be interesting to investigate involves reconciling predicted and observed behavior. Suppose, by way of example, that an operator OP is originally thought to add Clause C whenever it is applied, but suppose we notice that the action corresponding to OP consistently fails to add C. We would like the system to remedy this situation by taking one of three steps: drop C from the add list of OP, restrict the preconditions of OP to those (if any) that guarantee that C is added by the action, or change the actual action routine so that it does in fact behave as originally advertised. While we offer no algorithms for accomplishing these forms of learning, it is interesting to note that the problem itself arises only when we deal with real, as opposed to simulated, robot systems. It is the occurrence of problems of this sort that persuades us of the continuing interest and importance of robot problem solving.

REFERENCES

1. Fikes, R. E. and Nilsson, N. J. STRIPS: A new approach to the application of theorem proving to problem solving. *Artificial Intelligence* **2** (1971), 189–208.

Chapter 5

Integrated Planning Systems

The engineering approach to building complete AI planners intended to perform in one or more domains is the focus of this chapter. STRIPS (Fikes and Nilsson, 1972, Chapter 2) has already been mentioned as an early example of this approach.

Many of the systems included in this chapter have been published in a variety of papers or books. We have had to select a single paper from amongst many that often deal with some specific aspect of AI planning system work. All of these planners are implemented systems coping with problems of scale and multiple application areas. The techniques embedded in the later planners of this kind draw heavily on the range of papers we have included in this volume. The papers are intended as a lead into the literature on the techniques employed or the applications tackled.

The first paper we present describes Tate's (1977) NONLIN planner, which was based on NOAH, but represented and could cover the full search space (whereas NOAH could not undo any choice already made). NONLIN had at its heart a QA (question-answering) routine which established the necessary plan changes to ensure that some required condition was satisfied at some point in the plan. NONLIN QA produced a full, but minimum, set of alternative plan changes, thus ensuring coverage of the parts of the search space that could contain solutions. (The central component of this style of AI planning system was formalized by Chapman in a paper included in Chapter 7.) NONLIN introduced a number of search restriction techniques to increase the scale of problem that could be tackled. A means to describe the application domain and domain knowledge to reduce the search was introduced (task formalism). A mixture of AI and operations research methods (such as the use of critical path data on durations of activities) also

was employed in the NONLIN planner to prune searches. A later version of NONLIN (Daniel, 1983) had dependency recording, like that in the Hayes paper in Chapter 3, to allow for retention of valid parts of the plans after some failure.

The second paper we present describes Vere's (1983) DEVISER planner, built at the Jet Propulsion Laboratory. DEVISER was based on NONLIN and introduced facilities to reason about actions and goals where time constraints were involved. An ability to interface with externally generated events was also included. The original DEVISER planner was used to generate control sequences for the *Voyager* spacecraft—though none was actually used in real spacecraft. DEVISER continues to be developed; for example, in 1989, DEVISER V was in use at Lockheed's AI Center for planning the activities of a marine vehicle.

The next paper in this chapter presents Wilkins's (1984) SIPE planner. SIPE, developed at SRI International's AI Center, is a comprehensive planning system that reasons about objects in a plan and treats them as resources on which interactions can be monitored and corrected. SIPE has an improved domain description language, including the ability to raise the expressiveness of the domain language over that of earlier integrated planners. Wilkins (1988) gives a full account of the SIPE system. SIPE-2 (Wilkins, 1989) explores its search space more comprehensively than versions described in earlier papers.

Fox's ISIS scheduling system is rather different from the other integrated planners discussed in this chapter. ISIS deals with the representation and manipulation of constraints on the scheduling of resources in a factory. It represents a stream of work that parallels the activity planning work that is the main theme of the papers in this volume. In any realistic planning system, the need to select resources to carry out planned actions and the need to schedule the time periods over which those resources must be reserved is vital. The Fox and Smith (1984) paper included in this chapter serves as a pointer to work that addresses such issues.

O-Plan is a system that builds on the earlier Edinburgh work on planners such as NONLIN. It provides a simplified and extensible architecture for building planners that search a space of partial plans, i.e., that progressively refine a given plan to one that meets the given requirement. The Currie and Tate (1985) paper included herein describes the control aspects of the architecture. A soon-to-be-published paper by Currie and Tate (1990) gives a more comprehensive description of O-Plan.

The final paper in this chapter (Dean et al., 1988) describes the FORBIN planner, developed at Yale University, as an attempt to bring together recent work on temporal reasoning, planning as simulation, and reaction in planning and to use these ideas in the domain of factory scheduling. FORBIN uses a tempo-ral reasoning system to directly model the effects of the passage of time and the interactions between various operations. A time-optimizing scheduler that takes production requirements and constraints into account is also used in the system, thus allowing interaction between planning and scheduling techniques. Recent versions of the system also include a reactive component used to handle unexpected events, such as machine breakdowns and scheduling slippage.

Papers referenced herein but not included in this volume:

Currie, K.W., and Tate, A. (1990). "O-Plan: The Open Planning Architecture," to appear in *AI Journal*.

Daniel, L. (1983). "Planning and Operations Research," in *Artificial Intelligence: Tools, Techniques and Applications*, Harper and Row, New York.

Wilkins, D. E. (1988). Practical Planning: Extending the Classical AI Planning Paradigm, Morgan Kaufman, San Mateo, CA.

Wilkins, D. E. (1989). "Can AI Planners Solve Practical Problems?," SRI AI Center Technical Note 468R.

GENERATING PROJECT NETWORKS

Austin Tate
Department of Artificial Intelligence
University of Edinburgh
Edinburgh Scotland

Abstract

Procedures for optimization and resource allocation in Operations Research first require a project network for the task to be specified. The specification of a project network is at present done in an intuitive way. AI work in plan formation has developed formalisms for specifying primitive activities, and recent work by Sacerdoti (1975a) has developed a planner able to generate a plan as a partially ordered network of actions. The "planning: a joint AI/OR approach" project at Edinburgh has extended such work and provided a hierarchic planner which can aid in the generation of project networks. This paper describes the planner (NONLIN) and the Task Formalism (TF) used to hierarchically specify a domain.

1. AI and OR approaches to planning

The general problem of planning a task is one of very broad scope. Current work in Operations Research (OR) and Artificial Intelligence (AI) has concentrated on different aspects of the problem. We have taken an interdisciplinary approach in the hope that this will lead to a development of both these aspects.

In the OR approach, the planning process falls into two stages.
1. The constituent "jobs" of a plan are specified together with their precedence relationships (i.e. requirements of the form that one job precede another). This information defines a graph, termed a project network.
2. Various operations are performed on the project network to establish schedules and allocate resources (e.g. using critical path analysis).

OR work has been concerned with the second stage of computational operations on a given project network. The preliminary stage is performed in an intuitive, not well understood, and probably haphazard way.

It can be argued that the generation of a project network is important because of the structure it imposes on the task in hand. It forces component jobs to be isolated and necessary orderings between them considered. The project network can be used not only for predictions of how the project will be done, but also as a tool to aid in monitoring its progress and allowing bottlenecks to be identified. However, a considerable amount of effort is expended in the

---

The author's present address is: Edinburgh Regional Computing Centre, Alison House, Nicolson Square, Edinburgh, EH8 9BH, U.K.

manual construction of project networks.

Steps towards automating the process of specifying constituent jobs for some task and for giving the precedence relationships between jobs, have been developed for representing the data to the planning process, i.e. a description of the goals of the plan and the operations (jobs) of which it might consist (notably the representation of operator schemas to STRIPS - Fikes & Nilsson, 1971). The applicability of the AI work on plan formation to the generation of project networks has been restricted because most of the work has concentrated on the production of plans with totally ordered sequences of primitive jobs rather than the networks needed for OR analysis. Avoiding as much unnecessary sequencing of primitive jobs as possible is important to permit effective scheduling by OR techniques. Recently, Sacerdoti (1975a) has explored the use of a planner able to generate a plan as a partially ordered network of actions. This work forms the basis of our approach to aiding a user to generate a project network for some task. Sacerdoti's approach cannot be described here, so a reader unfamiliar with the work should see the reference cited above.

2. An overview of the project

The "planning: a joint AI/OR approach" project has been concerned with aiding a user in the process of constructing a project network. To do this, as in the work of Sacerdoti, we have been investigating the use of a partially ordered network of actions to represent a plan (or project) at any stage of development. Any ordering in the network results from the fact that either
i)   an action achieves a condition for a subsequent action, or
ii)   an action interferes with an important effect of another action and must be removed outside the effects' "range".
Range here is used to mean the time between when a goal is achieved and the point at which it was required to satisfy a condition on a later node.

2.1 Task Formalism (TF)
A formalism (TF) has been specified to enable actions in a domain to be described in a hierarchic fashion. Sub-task descriptions can be written independently of their use at higher levels. The Task Formalism is intended to encourage the writing of modular job descriptions at various levels of detail. Within the specification of each task will be information about
a)   When to introduce an action in the plan
b)   The effects of an action
c)   What conditions must hold before an action can be performed
d)   How to expand an action to lower level actions.

IJCAI 1977 pp. 888-893
Used by permission of the International Joint Conferences on Artificial Intelligence, Inc.

We illustrate the form of TF by an "ACTSCHEMA" from a simple house building task (the complete listing is given in Tate, 1976).

```
ACTSCHEMA DECOR
  PATTERN <<DECORATE>>
  EXPANSION
  1 ACTION <<FASTEN PLASTER AND PLASTER BOARD>>
  2 ACTION <<POUR BASEMENT FLOOR>>
  3 ACTION <<LAY FINISHED FLOORING>>
  4 ACTION <<FINISH CARPENTRY>>
  5 ACTION <<SAND AND VARNISH FLOORS>>
  6 ACTION <<PAINT>>
  ORDERINGS 1 --->3  6 --->5 SEQUENCE 2 TO 5
  CONDITIONS
  UNSUPERVISED <<ROUGH PLUMBING INSTALLED>> AT 1
  UNSUPERVISED <<ROUGH WIRING INSTALLED>> AT 1
  UNSUPERVISED <<AIR CONDITIONING INSTALLED>> AT 1
  UNSUPERVISED <<DRAINS INSTALLED>> AT 2
  UNSUPERVISED <<PLUMBING FINISHED>> AT 6
  SUPERVISED <<PLASTERING FINISHED>> AT 3 FROM 1
  SUPERVISED <<BASEMENT FLOOR LAYED>> AT 3 FROM 2
  SUPERVISED <<FLOORING FINISHED>> AT 4 FROM 3
  SUPERVISED <<CARPENTRY FINISHED>> AT 5 FROM 4
  SUPERVISED <<PAINTED>> AT 5 FROM 6.
END;
```

This schema says that an ACTION node with pattern <<DECORATE>> can be expanded into 6 lower level actions with the following partial ordering:

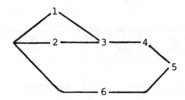

Conditions on nodes in the expansion are given types. SUPERVISED conditions are made true within the expansion of the task (e.g. the ACTION <<PAINT>> (6), achieves the SUPERVISED condition <<PAINTED>> on ACTION 5). UNSUPERVISED conditions are made true by other experts (mainly here by an "INSTALL SERVICES" expert). Another condition type, "USEWHEN", would say that an ACTSCHEMA containing it should not be used unless the condition was already true. It is also possible to specify the EFFECTS on a node of the expansion. In the case of the DECOR schema these would be defined by lower level actions.

2.2 The non-linear planner (NONLIN)

A planner, NONLIN, has been implemented which can generate plans from task descriptions given in the Task Formalism. It generates a plan at progressively greater levels of detail and can handle interactions between sub-plans to produce a plan as a partially-ordered network of actions. The algorithms employed in the planner have been designed so that ordering choices are avoided where possible. However, where a choice does become necessary all choice points are kept for later analysis or re-planning. A simple clear representation of the goal structure (GOST) of a plan is kept (the conditions on nodes of the network together with the points where the conditions are achieved). An example of a GOST entry during a

house building task might be

    <<SUPERVISED <<SCAFFOLDING ERECTED>> TRUE 6>>
    with value [4].

This would mean that <<SCAFFOLDING ERECTED>> had to be true at node 6 and was made true at node 4 (nodes in a network are numbered). Node 4 here will be referred to as a "contributor" to satisfying the condition. It is possible to have several potential contributors. The GOST thus specifies a set of "ranges" for which patterns have a certain value. Goal structure provides information about a plan which would be difficult to extract from the detail of the plan itself. The use of goal structure to direct search in a problem solver was first investigated in Tate (1975). The goal structure of a plan not only provides information to aid the search of the planner, it contains valuable information for monitoring the execution of a plan.

2.3 Comparison with NOAH

NONLIN, as mentioned previously, is based upon the work of Sacerdoti (1975a) on the NOAH planner. We accept the concept of Sacerdoti's work: that ordering constraints should only be imposed between the actions comprising a plan if these are necessary for the achievement of the overall purpose of the plan. However, the NOAH program still had to make choices as to the order that actions were to be placed in a plan to correct for interactions. NOAH made this choice in one particular way. It did not keep any backtrack choice points, so this decision, once made, was irreversible. This leads to an incompleteness of the search space which can render some simple block pushing tasks unachieveable by NOAH (see section 10 of Tate, 1975 for a full account). NONLIN is capable of correcting for an interaction by suggesting two orderings (which are sufficient to ensure the incompleteness of NOAH mentioned above is avoided — see section 4.4). Other operations performed by NOAH deterministically (i.e. without generating alternative courses of action) should also be considered as choice points. Two examples of this are

a)   the choice of which method to use to expand a node where alternatives exist, and

b)   the decision to merge two nodes in a network. If such decisions cannot be undone some problems are unsolvable. NONLIN keeps such choice points. We found it impractical to store all alternatives in a single AND/OR network. Instead, we make choices as they become necessary but keep alternatives for later re-use. As in NOAH, we expect that the first choice taken should lead to a solution since many of the choices made by linear planners have been avoided. Indeed, if failure occurs with the first plan being considered, our experience is that backtracking can lead to long searches since many consequent ordering choices may have been made because of an inappropriate choice early in the generation of the plan. We are tackling this problem by the use of a "Decision Graph" (see Daniel, 1977).

NOAH had no way to distinguish between important effects at nodes which achieved a condition on some later node and unimportant side-effects. If a node was introduced to achieve some goal for a later node, NOAH ensured that any effect at the introduced node was kept true up to the goal node. This can mean that no plan ordering may be found for problems to which solutions exist. NONLIN distinguishes between an effect at a node which satisfies some condition at a later node and other unimportant effects. The goals structure information which NONLIN keeps is used to enable NONLIN to suggest the minimum of two alternative orderings to correct for interactions and to distinguish important effects.

We have given careful attention to the design of a question answering program which behaves correctly for queries in a partially ordered network of nodes. This algorithm is fully described later in this paper. The algorithms used in NOAH failed to take into account interference on the truth of some statements by the effects of actions in parallel with any path from a query node to the initial situation in a plan network.

3. Task Formalism for domain specifications

At the outset of this work the problem of straightforwardly specifying a domain to a problem solver in a hierarchic fashion was recognized as being of primary importance. We wish to allow high level definitions of a task to be given, each part of which can be expanded into lower level descriptions and so on down to some arbitrary level which the user of the program requires as output, or for which "libraries" of lower level plans are available. It should be possible for each component at lower levels to be specified in a modular way — not requiring knowledge of the exact form of other components. Given any particular task, the planner must choose appropriate lower level actions so that each part of a plan can be performed successfully and so that the overall purpose of the plan is achieved.

Sub-task description — the use of condition types

When sub-tasks are being provided, the experts who produce them may know that the constituent jobs ought to be done in a particular order, or know that several jobs can be done together (in parallel). They know that certain conditions ought to hold before some jobs can proceed. For example, a carpet layer knows that before he does his job the floor boards ought to be layed, even though that isn't part of his job. These conditions are not under the supervision of this expert and are the responsibility of others. They will be termed UNSUPERVISED CONDITIONS.

Experts also know that certain conditions must be made to hold under their supervision before their task can be completed. Again, the carpet fitter knows it is his responsibility to get the carpet to the site, but the details of that task may be sub-contracted. Such conditions will be termed SUPERVISED CONDITION. N.B. as we will see these correspond to normal preconditions in means-end analysis driven systems such as

STRIPS (Fikes and Nilsson, 1971).

There is a third type of condition which an expert may impose. Conditions may be stated which must hold before this expert can be called into use at all. For example, consider a block stacking expert which knows how to clear blocks by moving a block on top of the block to be cleared to some other place. If a block cannot be found to be on top of the one to be cleared it is no use calling this expert at all. If the conditions were merely stated as a goal to be achieved before the movement of the upper block to somewhere else was done, we could get into a situation where we actually move some block onto the one to be cleared and then move it off again. Such static conditions on the use of a particular expert will be called USEWHEN CONDITIONS. Usewhen conditions can be considered to be an extension to the check of relevancy of some schema which imposes them.

So, we can distinguish three different types of conditions:
  (a) Unsupervised conditions
  (b) Supervised conditions
  (c) Usewhen conditions

Making a distinction between them can be of great benefit in controlling the number of choice points generated during a search and in choosing an alternative after a failure. Only conditions of type (b) are allowed to cause further expansions to be made to the plan being generated, i.e., allow further experts to be called in to plan to achieve the conditions. This is why they correspond to normal preconditions as specified in STRIPS. If expansions were allowed to achieve the unsupervised and usewhen conditions, we could find that the net contained much redundancy which could be difficult to resolve. It seems better to allocate jobs to appropriate experts.

Example of TF

TF is completely declarative and is based upon the operator schemas provided in STRIPS (Fikes and Nilsson, 1971). A full BNF description of the Task Formalism and further examples of its use are given in Tate (1976). However, some idea of its form can be got from the listing of one "ACTSCHEMA" from a small house building domain in section 2. Below we give a complete listing of the block stacking domain translated from Sacerdoti's (1975a) SOUP code for comparison (ℊ* is a variable prefix).

```
ACTSCHEMA PUTON
    PATTERN <<PUT ℊ*X ON TOP OF ℊ*Y>>
    CONDITIONS USEWHEN <<CLEARTOP ℊ*X>> AT SELF
               USEWHEN <<CLEARTOP ℊ*Y>> AT SELF
               USEWHEN <<ON ℊ*X ℊ*Z>> AT SELF
    EFFECTS + <<ON ℊ*X ℊ*Y>>
            - <<CLEARTOP ℊ*Y>>
            - <<ON ℊ*X ℊ*Z>>
            + <<CLEARTOP ℊ*Z>>
    VARS X UNDEF Y UNDEF Z UNDEF;
END;
```

```
OPSCHEMA MAKEON
    PATTERN <<ON ∮*X ∮*Y>>
    EXPANSION 1 GOAL <<CLEARTOP ∮*X>>
             2 GOAL <<CLEARTOP ∮*Y>>
             3 ACTION <<PUT ∮*X ON TOP OF ∮*Y>>
    ORDERINGS 1 --->3  2 --->3
    VARS X UNDEF Y UNDEF;
END;

OPSCHEMA MAKECLEAR
    PATTERN <<CLEARTOP ∮*X>>
    EXPANSION 1 GOAL <<CLEARTOP ∮*Y>>
             2 <<PUT ∮*Y ON TOP OF ∮*Z>>
    ORDERINGS 1 --->2
    CONDITIONS USEWHEN <<ON ∮*Y ∮*X>> AT 2
               USEWHEN <<CLEARTOP ∮*Z>> AT 2
    VARS X <:NOT TABLE:> Y UNDEF
         Z ◀:AND <:NOT ∮*X:> <:NOT ∮*Y:> :>;
END;

ALWAYS <<CLEARTOP TABLE>>;
```

In the block stacking description, SUPERVISED conditions are omitted. TF fills these in automatically for any GOAL nodes to the following node in an expansion. The PUTON schema does not specify an expansion and only gives further effects and conditions on the action. The ALWAYS statement asserts that <<CLEARTOP TABLE>> is true in any situation. Several schemas can be given which have the same PATTERN. These then being alternative methods of expanding a node with the pattern. Choices between alternatives are handled explicitly by the planner.

4. NONLIN: The Planner

NONLIN starts with a single node representing the task to be planned. The simplified control cycle is similar to that used in NOAH.
1. Expand a node in the network using the expansion from an appropriate schema.
2. Correct for any interactions introduced.
3. Repeat from 1 until there are no further nodes to expand.

The system is run mostly "stand-alone" at present. However, it does support a simple interactive 'top-down' planning process, asking a user for information as it is found to be lacking.

4.1 Representation of the Network

The network is represented as a collection of nodes which are referred to via a subscript, e.g. NODE(4). Each node has associated with it various components:

nodenum	its NODE subscript
nodetype	GOAL, ACTION or PHANTOM*
pattern	used to seek an expansion schema
prenodes	a list of nodes linked immediately before this one
succnodes	a list of nodes linked immediately after this one
nodectxt	a context containing the effects of this node. The partially ordered network of contexts is defined by the

---

*A PHANTOM node is a GOAL node whose pattern was already true in the network at the point where it is placed.

nodectxts and the prenodes and succnodes links.

parentnode	the node was inserted as a result of the expansion of its parentnode
nodemark	a temporary marker used to record the relation of this node to some other node in the network ("BEFORE", "NODE", "AFTER" or "IN PARALLEL"). This is used during question answering.

Other components can be ignored for the purposes of this paper. The network thus described gives the ordering constraints between the nodes in the network. 2 other structures are used to represent a plan, a TOME and a GOST.

Table of Multiple Effects (TOME)

As in Sacerdoti (1975a) we keep a record of what values are given to patterns at each node. The TOME is used during question answering and to detect interactions.

Goal Structure (GOST)

A condition of any type on any node in a plan is stored in GOST together with a list of "contributors". Contributors are nodes, any one of which could make this condition hold. See section 4.3 for the method used to find the contributors for any pattern.

The Goal Structure allows the purposes of any particular effect at any node to be determined (if it has any). This allows interactions to be detected and allows corrections (suggested linearizations) to be sensitive to the important effects of nodes (those which satisfy some condition). Unimportant effects are therefore ignored. Once the interacting effects of nodes are determined and the goal structure is available, simple linearizations can be suggested to remove the interactions (as in INTERPLAN — Tate 1975).

4.2 Expanding a Node

A node is expanded to get more detail of how a task can be performed or a goal achieved.
1) GOAL nodes A goal node is present to state that the pattern of the node should be true at the node. There are three ways this could be achieved.
   a) If the pattern was already true at that point.
   b) If we could introduce links into the network to make the pattern true at that point.
   c) If we could make an expansion of the node which would make the pattern be true.

In cases (a) and (b), the goal node is returned with a new type "PHANTOM". A GOST entry with a special condition type "PHANTOM" is made to show the contributors which make the pattern true at the node. Links will have been put in the network as a result of (b).

In case (c), it is necessary to find an expansion for the pattern and replace the goal node in the network by the expansion. One member of the list of schemas which can be used to expand any pattern is chosen and alternative ways to expand the pattern are kept as choice points.

2) ACTION nodes An action node is present as a command to do something. No attempt is therefore made to see if its pattern is true or can be made true (by linking) as cases (a) and (b) for goal nodes. However, case (c) is performed exactly as for goal nodes. An expansion of the pattern is sought and used to replace the action node in the network. An action node is allowed to have a null expansion. This indicates to the system that the action can be considered primitive and it should not be replaced in the network or expanded further. A shorthand TF form PRIMITIVE ... ; can be used to declare primitives.

4.3 Question answering in a partially ordered network of contexts

Current data base systems which provide a context mechanism, e.g. CONNIVER (McDermott and Sussman, 1972), provide efficient facilities for storing a changing data base by remembering the alterations made to an initial situation. However, they only provide facilities for the determination of the value of a pattern with respect to a given context in a fully ordered tree of contexts. In a tree of contexts there is a strict time sequence along a single context path so answers are fully determinate. In the partially-ordered network, answers will depend on the nodes in parallel with a particular node as well as the answer got by retracing back through a network. This answer, got by retracing through the network, will itself vary as nodes are linked earlier in the network. A full world model kept at each context would have to be continuously updated. So, as for a tree of contexts, it is best to store only the changes to an initial world model at each node.

We have provided a QA system for such a world model which can respond to two kinds of query:
(a) Does statement P have value V at node N in the current network? It could have value definitely V, definitely not V, or be undecidable.
(b) What links would have to be added to the network to make P have a certain value at N if it did not have this value in the given network?
The system finds lists of "critical" nodes in the network and uses these to give a truth result for requests of type (a). The lists contain the information needed to suggest links if a request of type (b) is given.
defns - P-node is a node which gives statement P a value.
  PV-node is a node which gives statement P a value V.
  PV̄-node is a node which gives statement P a value other than V.

a critical node for (P,N) is a node which, in a possible linearization, gives a value to statement P which could be maintained up to node N.
N.B. The critical nodes for (P,N) are
i) the last P-node on each incoming branch to N (ignore P-nodes which are also predecessors of any other critical nodes since there may be redundant links in the network).

ii) all P-nodes which are in parallel with N.

QA (P,V,N) finds the lists of critical P-nodes by marking the other nodes of the network with their position with respect to N and looking for TOME entries for the statement P.
P definitely has value V at node N if there is at least one critical PV-node before node N, and there are no critical PV̄-nodes.* P definitely does not have value V at node N if there is at least one critical PV̄-node and there are no critical PV-nodes.

If neither of these 2 definite cases arises then it may be possible to make P have value V at node N by making suitable links in the network if this is required. We must have at least one critical PV-node linked in before node N and link out all critical PV̄-nodes (both parallel to and before N), so that at least one path from a critical PV-node to N has no PV̄-node in parallel with it. Since both the PV-nodes and PV̄-nodes involved may be contributors to conditions on later nodes, the suggestion of links must be sensitive to the goal structure. The process used to suggest compatible links for this scheme is very similar to the process which corrects for interactions in a network. The common procedure used is described next. It is provided with the lists of critical nodes found during question answering.

4.4 Linking process for the network

There are 2 occasions on which it is necessary to suggest links in the network.
a) to detect and remove interactions
b) to make a statement have a particular value at some node.
We use a common procedure for both these tasks. The overall idea is very simple. It relies on having the goal structure of a network available. Goal structure gives a set of "ranges" for which a statement must have a particular value. A statement is given a value at a particular node and must retain this value up to a node which requires the statement as a condition. Our process simply ensures that there is no overlap between any ranges for which a statement P must have value V and any ranges for which a statement P must have a value other than V (i.e. V̄ in our previous notation). We take into account 2 facts
i) where there are multiple contributors to a condition on any node, we are only constrained to maintain one of them as contributor.
ii) If the condition is only present to make a GOAL node a PHANTOM node we can remove all its contributors if necessary and this will merely force us to consider ways to achieve the GOAL.
The detail of the operation is described in Tate (1976). It emerges that once a pair of conflicting ranges are identified it is necessary to suggest both putting a link from the end of one range to the beginning of the other and vice versa (if this is compatible with the existing links in the network). This is needed to avoid the incompleteness mentioned in section 2.3. This process is a generalization of the interaction correction procedure first suggested for linear problem solvers in Tate (1975).
*The PV-nodes before node N are the "contributors".

It is vital that comparisons of all ranges specified in the goal structure are not being made continuously to check for interactions. Our method ensures that only those ranges jeopardized by any operation on the network need to be checked. We outline below how this is done for the two different uses to which the linking procedure is put.

a) To detect and remove interactions

As effects are added to nodes in the network, they are also recorded in the Table of Multiple Effects (TOME). As they are added we can find if an interaction resulted by performing two checks.

i) see if any parallel node has an opposite value for the statement (a check on the TOME). The network will already have been marked with respect to the node at which the effect was added, as a result of question answering.

ii) see if the node given the effect is in parallel with any range for which the statement must have a different value (a check on the GOST).

The linking procedure is only entered with any conflicting nodes or ranges, thus limiting the computation needed.

b) To make a statement P have a particular value V at some node N

We mentioned in section 4.3 that the QA routine can provide lists of "critical" nodes which can be used to suggest links to make a statement have a particular value at some node. Given these lists, the operation can be performed by ensuring that there is at least one critical PV-node "linked-in" before node N. This may already be the case, but if not, a choice point is made and one of the critical PV-nodes is linked before node N. The linking procedure is then used to "link-out" all critical PV-nodes from the PV-range which establishes the condition on node N. So here again we drastically reduce the potential range conflicts which need to be compared by using the lists of "critical" nodes provided by the question answering routine.

5. Summary

We have used recent work in AI aimed at generating plans as partially ordered networks of actions to aid in project network construction. Such networks are in a suitable form for the use of Operations Research optimization techniques. The present NONLIN system is a development of NOAH (Sacerdoti, 1975a). However, we have sought to improve over NOAH in several important ways.

a) Interactions are corrected for in all legal ways to avoid an incompleteness present in NOAH. In fact only 2 alternative orderings need be considered in order that this is achieved.

b) Interactions are corrected for only on the "important" effects of nodes (those which are required as the contributor to a condition on a later node).

c) We use a question answering procedure which behaves correctly for queries in a partially ordered network of nodes.

d) All alternatives generated at choice points in the planner's search space are kept for backtracking. NOAH did not keep alternatives where it made arbitrary choices.

The provision of an explicit record of the conditions on any node together with the nodes which achieve those conditions (the goal structure of the network) has provided a simplified representation of the plan which is of benefit in directing the planner's search (e.g. for (a) or (b) above). More detail of the NONLIN program and the procedures used can be found in Tate (1976). This paper also gives examples of the use of the program.

We have developed a Task Formalism (TF) to enable a group of people to co-operatively describe a task to the system with the planner's aid. TF is completely declarative and this has aided us in providing the Table of Multiple Effects (TOME) and Goal Structure (GOST). The declarative form of TF descriptions is also proving of use in the design of a "Decision Graph" to localize the alterations which need to be made to a network to recover from a search failure (see Daniel, 1977).

We are currently engaged on an investigation of project planning in the scheduling of generator maintenance in power stations. We hope to gain a better understanding of the formal channels of communication used between the planner in an organization, management who gives directives to the planner and people from whom the planner gets information to enable him to plan a project. We hope to test our present ideas of how this process is performed (as modelled in NONLIN and TF) on a realistic application in this domain.

Acknowledgements

This research work was performed on a Science Research Council Grant held by Professor B. Meltzer (Grant No. B/RG/94455). The work has benefited from discussions with Gottfried Eder and my co-worker on the project, Lesley Daniel.

References

Daniel, L. (1977). Project planning: modifying non-linear plans. Forthcoming DAI Memo.

Fikes, R.E., and Nilsson, N.J. (1971). STRIPS: a new approach to the application of theorem proving to problem solving. *Artificial Intelligence*, 2, pp. 189-208.

McDermott, D.V. & Sussman, G.J. (1972). The CONNIVER Reference Manual, MIT AI Lab., Memo No. 259.

Sacerdoti, E.D., (1975a). The non-linear nature of plans. Advance papers of 4th International Joint Conference on Artificial Intelligence (IJCAI4), Tbilisi, USSR, pp. 206-214.

Sacerdoti, E.D. (1975b). A structure for plans and behaviour, SRI AI Center, Technical Note 109.

Tate, A. (1975). Using goal structure to direct search in a problem solver. Ph.D. thesis, Machine Intelligence Research Unit, University of Edinburgh.

Tate, A. (1976). Project planning using a hierarchic non-linear planner. Research Report No. 25, Department of Artificial Intelligence, University of Edinburgh.

Planning in Time: Windows and Durations for Activities and Goals

STEVEN A. VERE, MEMBER, IEEE

Abstract –A general purpose automated planner/scheduler is described which generates parallel plans to achieve goals with imposed time constraints. Both durations and start time windows may be specified for sets of goal conditions. The parallel plans consist of not just actions but also of events (triggered by circumstances), inferences, and scheduled events (completely beyond the actor's control). Deterministic durations of all such activities are explicitly modeled, and may be any computable function of the activity variables. A start time window for each activity in the plan is updated dynamically during plan generation, in order to maintain consistency with the windows and durations of adjacent activities and goals. The plans are tailored around scheduled events. The final plan network resembles a PERT chart. From this a schedule of nominal start times for each activity is generated. Examples are drawn from the traditional blocksworld and also from a realistic "Spaceworld," in which an autonomous spacecraft photographs objects in deep space and transmits the information to Earth.

Manuscript received November 23, 1981; revised July 29, 1982. This work was supported by the National Aeronautics and Space Administration under Contract NAS 7-100 and presents the results of one phase of research carried out at the Jet Propulsion Laboratory, California Institute of Technology.

The author is with the Information Systems Research Section, Jet Propulsion Laboratory, Pasadena, CA 91109.

Index Terms –Duration, goal directed simulation, planning, problem solving, relational production, scheduled event, scheduling, start time window, temporal planning, time, time constraint.

I. INTRODUCTION

IN PLANNING a course of action to achieve a set of goals, time is often a key parameter. The need to account for time explicitly in artificial intelligence planners has been recognized for a long time [5], [8]. This paper describes features and mechanisms of a general purpose automated planner/scheduler called DEVISER. The program synthesizes plans to achieve goals which may have time restrictions on *when* sets of goals should be achieved and on *how long* the goal conditions should be preserved. Actions and events may have computable, deterministic durations. Scheduled events may occur over which the actor has no control. The principal output of DEVISER is a partially ordered network of activities. For each activity, a duration and a start time "window" are presented. This provides all the information of an activity-on-

0162-8828/83/0500-0246$01.00 © 1983 IEEE

node PERT chart, the starting point for an extensive theory of scheduling in operations research. (See [4], for example.) This concern with time is motivated by the intended application at JPL: the planning and scheduling of actions for autonomous unmanned spacecraft, such as Voyager.

A system in which activities have start times and durations begins to resemble a deterministic simulation. DEVISER adopts the style of discrete event simulation systems, such as SIMSCRIPT [9], in which all changes can be assumed to occur at specific points in time, rather than continuously as in continuous time simulations. However, the program is markedly different from discrete event simulation systems in that it is goal directed and generates its activities in reverse time order.

The capabilities for planning in time have been implemented on top of a parallel planner similar to Tate's NONLIN [16], [17], which in turn is a descendant of Sacerdoti's NOAH [13], the first parallel planner. NONLIN and NOAH generate plans in which the actions are maximally concurrent. The original intent was simply to generate serial plans efficiently. However, parallel plans are also important for systems which can actually execute actions in parallel. By performing actions simultaneously, the total duration of a plan can of course often be reduced, and deadlines can be met which a serial plan would overrun.

The treatment of time in AI planning is uncommon. The air traffic control planner of Wesson [20] is the earliest instance of which I am aware. Wesson's planner, while quite impressive in its application, was a special purpose program. One peculiarity of the air traffic control world is that the goals are negative, avoidance conditions rather than positive attainment conditions. The goal of the controller is to avoid the situation where two or more aircraft approach too closely, either horizontally or vertically. Negative goals are a neglected topic and very interesting. However, it is not clear how Wesson's methods can be adapted to general positive goals. More recently, the AUTOPILOT system [18] has been described. This is a special purpose, distributed planning program for controlling multiple aircraft which seems philosophically descended from Wesson's planner. There is also a report by McDermott [10] on the modeling of time for planning.

The work of Hendrix [8] was an early investigation of actions and events in which time was treated explicitly. However, Hendrix' system would best be described as a deterministic simulation. It did not plan actions to achieve goals. Since then there have been other AI simulation systems which modeled events in time for various purposes, e.g., to solve physics problems or answer questions [2], [3], [7], [12].

Automated planning and problem solving is a vast subfield of artificial intelligence. I have confined my attention here to those works which treat time or parallelism. A paper by Sacerdoti [14] may serve as an entry into the literature for those interested in other facets of planning.

II. Background

A. Preliminary Concepts

An *activity* is by definition an action, event, or inference. An *action* is a change in the world which the actor in a plan may decide to perform. An *event* is a change which is triggered spontaneously by the state of the world. For example, an actor may decide to open a valve on a tank. Given that the valve is open, that there is water in the tank, and that the water is acted on by gravity, an event occurs: the draining of water from the tank. Both actions and events may add and delete facts from a world model. An *inference* is a special kind of activity in which facts are added whose validity depends on the continuing truth of the preconditions of the inference. For example, if (ON x y) (ON y z) → (ABOVE x z) is an inference, then the validity of (ABOVE x z) depends on (ON x y) and (ON y z) continuing to be true. Inferences require special treatment in planning to ensure that inferred assertions are not invalidated by subsequent actions. In timeless planning, activities are either sequential or parallel. With the introduction of time an important special case of sequential activities emerges. Two sequential activities will be called *consecutive* if the second must begin immediately on termination of the first. We will see later that consecutive activities arise in the treatment of spontaneous events.

B. Representation of Activities

In DEVISER all activities are represented by relational productions [19], which are related to STRIPS rules [6]. Relational productions have three components (context, antecedent, and consequent) consisting of unordered sets of literals. The *context* consists of literals which are preconditions for the activity, and whose truth is not affected by the activity. The *antecedent* consists of preconditions which are deleted from the world model when the activity occurs. The *consequent* consists of literals which are added to the world model when the activity occurs.

In this paper relational productions will be presented with the following syntax:

$$(\langle \text{activity-name} \rangle \, \langle \text{activity-type} \rangle$$
$$(\text{CONTEXT} \, \langle \text{list-of-context-literals} \rangle)$$
$$(\langle \text{list-of-antecedent-literals} \rangle) \rightarrow$$
$$(\langle \text{list-of-consequent-literals} \rangle))$$

The activity type is either ACTION, EVENT, or INFERENCE. For example, an unstacking action in a blocksworld might be described by

$$(\text{UNSTACK ACTION}$$
$$(\text{CONTEXT}) \, ((\text{CLEAR } x) \, (\text{ON } x \, y)) \rightarrow$$
$$((\text{HOLDING } x) \, (\text{CLEAR } y)))$$

Here the context component happens to be empty. Throughout this paper, variables in relational productions will be presented in lowercase and constants will be presented in small capitals.

For the moment it will be assumed that all activities occur instantaneously. Section III will describe how the relational production model is extended to describe durations.

C. The Three Operations of the Core Planner

This subsection briefly reviews the three major plan generation operations of the core planner on top of which the various time capabilities have been implemented. The terminology is that of Tate [16], with which the serious reader is assumed to be familiar.

The core planner generates plans by backward chaining from unordered subgoals. There are three basic operations in plan generation: linking, node expansion, and conflict detection and resolution. For each operation there may be several choices. One alternative is selected and the others are saved. If the planner reaches an impasse, it backtracks to the last choice point and tries another alternative. The notion of subgoal hierarchies [15] has been adopted, and there is also a limited advice capability.

The three plan generation operations are as follows.

• *Linking:* If the assertion of a goal node G is achieved by an existing node E in the plan (including the start node), then the planner creates an arc from E to G in the plan network. Of course, E must not be downstream from G in the plan network, since this would create a loop. G becomes a "phantom" node.

• *Node Expansion:* If a subgoal cannot be satisfied by linking, the node is expanded into an activity which achieves the subgoal. Usually the action has preconditions which become new subgoals, and the side effects of the activity must be added to the assertions of the expanded node. Antecedent literals of the activity production are negated and, together with the consequent literals, become the assertions of the node.

• *Conflict Detection, and Resolution by Ordering Parallel Activities:* A conflict exists in a plan network when two parallel nodes assert contradictory literals. Each time a goal node is expanded, new conflicts may be introduced into the plan network. A conflict may also result from the instantiation of an existing literal. Conflicts are resolved by ordering nodes which formerly were unordered.

By resolving all conflicts after each node expansion, we avoid the problem of "regression through a partial ordering" [11, Section 8.3]. In a plan network without conflicts, the truth of any assertion at any point in the network is determinable even when, as is usually the case, the nodes are only partially ordered. Thus, the linking procedure always sees a conflict-free plan network, and is able to judge with certainty whether a goal node assertion has already been achieved.

D. Scheduled Events

A *scheduled event* is an event which is guaranteed to occur at a known time; its occurrence is not under the control of the actor in the plan. Familiar examples are the opening and closing of a bank at known hours or the departures and arrivals of airline flights. In the Spaceworld discussed in Section VII, important scheduled events are the beginning and end of an occultation.

In DEVISER, scheduled events are described just like other events, except that they are specified to occur at a constant time and do not have any preconditions. For example, the opening of a bank at 10 A.M. might be described by

(BANK.OPENS EVENT
        (CONTEXT) NIL → ((BANK OPEN))
        (WINDOW AT 10:00:00)).

(Windows will be discussed in detail in Section IV.) Since scheduled events are guaranteed to occur, they are simply ordered with respect to time of occurrence and inserted into the plan network before plan generation begins. During plan generation other activities are ordered with respect to these scheduled events to satisfy goal nodes or to resolve conflicts. In the process, the start time windows of other activities in the plan are compressed, as will be described in Section V. In this way the three basic operations of plan generation build a plan network around these events without having to extend them any special treatment. Once plan generation begins, there is no distinction between scheduled event nodes and other nodes in the plan network. At present, any event with a fixed time of occurrence is treated as a scheduled event. The more difficult problem of conditional scheduled events, which would occur at known times if certain preconditions are met, has not been studied, solved, or implemented.

E. Procedurally Defined Literals

A *procedurally defined literal* is a literal whose truth is determined by calling a procedure. For example, (LEQ x y) is procedurally defined, since there is a Lisp function which can be called once the values of x and y are known. In contrast, the truth of "ordinary" literals can be determined only by looking in a distributed database (whose contents are modified by actions and events). For example, (ON x y) is an ordinary literal in the blocksworld. Accordingly, a procedurally defined literal may not be added or deleted in an activity description. Such literals may only appear in the context component of a relational production defining an activity. In NOAH and NONLIN, procedurally defined literals were not provided for. Procedurally defined literals provide a link between conventional computation and production rule computation.

F. Function Literals

For reasons of efficiency and convenience, function literals are given special treatment in DEVISER. A *function literal* is a literal whose rightmost term is a function of all the other terms. For example, (FILTER color.1) is a function literal in the Spaceworld. There is only one filter wheel on the TV camera, and it can have only one setting at any instant. Thus, the database cannot contain two literals (FILTER x) and (FILTER y) unless x = y. Similarly, (MOTHER.OF x y) in a geneology world is a function literal. A great many of the literals describing a "world" will typically be functions. Advantage may be made of such function literals: if x ≠ y, then we can be sure that (FILTER x) contradicts (FILTER y). Thus deleted function literals need not be stored explicitly as side effects of an action. For example, if an action x is described by the production

(X ACTION
        (CONTEXT) ((LIGHT RED)) → ((LIGHT GREEN)))

we would normally need to store ~(LIGHT RED) as one of the assertions of the node representing this action. If LIGHT is declared to be a function, this becomes unnecessary. In the conflict detection operation, completely instantiated function literals of n terms are then recognized as contradictory if their first n - 1 terms are identical and their nth terms are distinct. This special treatment of function literals in DEVISER was suggested by a paper by Bundy [1].

G. The VALUE.OF Mechanism

There are circumstances where we desire a term in one literal to be a function of terms in other literals. In DEVISER this is accomplished by the VALUE.OF mechanism. Literals appearing in the context of a production and whose first term is "VALUE.OF" are given special treatment. These literals must have the form (VALUE.OF variable ⟨EVALuable expression⟩). As soon as all variables in the expression have been instantiated, it is EVALuated and that value is substituted for all occurrences of "variable."

To illustrate, suppose we are modeling a RECORD.PICTURE event in a Spaceworld. A digital image is to be recorded on a magnetic tape. Each image occupies a segment 336 mm long on the tape. We want to update the position of the tape under the read/write head. The desired relation is: final.position = initial.position + 336. This would be accomplished with the VALUE.OF mechanism as shown below:

```
(RECORD.PICTURE EVENT
    (CONTEXT
        (IN.CAMERA (PICTURE azimuth color.
            t1 t2 t3))
        (TAPE.RECORDER RECORDING)
        (TAPE.AT initial.position)
        (VALUE.OF final.position
            (initial.position + 336)))
    NIL → ((RECORDED (PICTURE azimuth color.
        t1 t2 t3)) (TAPE.AT final.position))
    (DURATION 48 SECONDS)
    (WINDOW AFTER t1))
```

H. The Implementation of DEVISER

DEVISER is written entirely in INTERLISP. It consists of 185 functions totaling about 4000 lines. The program runs on a DEC KL-10 computer under the TOPS-20 operating system. Once plan generation begins, the only human interaction comes after a solution plan has been obtained and the user is asked if he wants additional alternative solutions to be attempted. The run times reported later in the paper are for a compiled version of the program. All program features described in this paper are implemented, debugged, and working.

III. DURATIONS FOR ACTIVITIES

If time is to be accounted for in planning, the durations of activities must be represented. In DEVISER, durations may be constant or any EVALuable function of the activity variables.

A. Specification of Activity Durations

To specify the duration of an activity, a duration s-expression is attached to the relational production describing the activity, as shown in the following examples. The units are assumed to be second unless stated otherwise.

Example 3.1: A blocksworld action with constant duration of 3 s:

```
(STACK ACTION
    (CONTEXT)
    ((HOLDING x) (CLEAR y)) → ((CLEAR x)
        (ON x y))
    (DURATION 3))
```

Example 3.2: A spaceworld action in which the duration is an arithmetic function of the action variables:

```
(POSITION.TAPE ACTION
    (CONTEXT)
    ((TAPE.AT x)) → ((TAPE.AT y))
    (DURATION (ABS (x - y)) / 7.3))
```

Here the TAPE.AT predicate specifies the position of the read/write head of a tape recorder along a magnetic tape.

Example 3.3: A Spaceworld action in which the duration involves a call to a domain-specific function:

```
(ROLL ACTION
    (CONTEXT
        (NEQ refstar.1 refstar.2)
        (AZIMUTH refstar.1 star1.azimuth)
        (AZIMUTH refstar.2 star2.azimuth))
    ((SC.AZIMUTH star1.azimuth)
        (LOCKED.ONTO refstar.1)) →
    ((SC.AZIMUTH star2.azimuth)
        (LOCKED.ONTO refstar.2))
    (DURATION (84 + 5 * (SCOPE.0.TO.180
        (star2.azimuth - star1.azimuth)))))
```

Here SCOPE.0.TO.180 is a domain-specific function, specially written in Lisp, which converts an angle, possibly negative or larger than 180, into a positive number from 0 to 180 indicating the minimum angle through which the spacecraft must roll.

When a duration expression contains variables, such as star2.azimuth, that expression is not and cannot be EVALuated until all the variables have been instantiated for a particular occurrence of the activity in a plan. Consequently, the duration of an activity in a plan may remain undetermined for some time after a goal node has been expanded. When the duration is finally known, its effect may ripple through the plan both forwards and backwards in time as the windows of adjacent activities are narrowed. This will be amplified in the discussion of window compression in Section V.

B. When Does an Action Produce Its Changes?

In DEVISER all changes in the world model, both additions and deletions, occur at the end of the activity. The conflict resolution mechanisms of the core planner ensure that all preconditions are sustained throughout the duration of an activity. But what of activities with "trigger" preconditions, where the precondition need only be true momentarily rather than throughout the duration of the activity? What about activities where some change takes place immediately. Surprisingly, the "change-on-termination" assumption does not cost any generality. These circumstances can accurately be modeled by two consecutive change-on-termination activities, as will now be explained.

C. Achieving "Trigger" Preconditions

Suppose in the production

```
(X ACTION
    (CONTEXT (A) (B) (C)) NIL → ((D))
    (DURATION 10))
```

we want (B) to be a trigger precondition, i.e., once the action is initiated, it will continue even if (B) becomes false. This may be achieved by decomposing action X into an action consecutive with an event:

```
(x' ACTION
    (CONTEXT (A) (B) (C)) NIL → ((INITIATE.x"))
    (DURATION 0))

(x" EVENT
    (CONTEXT (A) (*CONSECUTIVE (INITIATE.x"))
        (C)) NIL → ((D))
    (DURATION 10))
```

The enclosure of the (INITIATE.x") condition in a special *CONSECUTIVE literal signals the program that the x" event must be consecutive with the activity which achieves (INITIATE.x"). A record is maintained of all nodes which are consecutive. This information is accessed by the procedures which adjust windows during plan generation and select start times in determining a final schedule of actions.

D. Achieving Immediately Deleted Preconditions

Suppose in the following action we want (C) to be deleted immediately when the action begins:

```
(Y ACTION
    (CONTEXT (A) (B)) ((C)) → ((D))
    (DURATION 5))
```

This too can be achieved by decomposing the action into an action consecutive with an event:

```
(Y' ACTION
    (CONTEXT (A) (B)) ((C)) → ((INITIATE.Y"))
    (DURATION 0))

(Y" EVENT
    (CONTEXT (A) (B)) ((*CONSECUTIVE
        (INITIATE.Y"))) → ((D))
    (DURATION 5))
```

Similar decompositions can also be employed to achieve the effect of an action where certain facts become true immediately after the action is initiated or midway through an action, rather than at the end.

These decompositions could easily be performed automatically if syntactic conventions were assumed, as in

```
(z ACTION
    (CONTEXT (A) (*TRIGGER (B)) (C)) NIL → ((D))).
```

However, in my experience these special conditions have occurred so rarely that it has not seemed worth the trouble to provide an automatic decomposition capability.

IV. Windows for Activities and Goals

In the following discussions the standard PERT acronyms will be used:

$$\begin{Bmatrix} E \\ L \end{Bmatrix} \begin{Bmatrix} S \\ F \end{Bmatrix} T \text{ stands for } \begin{Bmatrix} \text{EARLIEST} \\ \text{LATEST} \end{Bmatrix} \begin{Bmatrix} \text{START} \\ \text{FINISH} \end{Bmatrix} \text{TIME.}$$

TABLE I
Translation of Goal Window Options into Triples

WINDOW OPTION	TRANSLATION INTO TRIPLE FORM
(WINDOW AT t)	(t t t)
(WINDOW BEFORE t)	(TIME0 NIL t)
(WINDOW AFTER t)	(t NIL INFINITY)
(WINDOW BETWEEN t1 t2)	(t1 NIL t2)
(WINDOW EARLIEST. IDEAL. LATEST t1 t2 t3)	(t1 t2 t3)

For example, EFT = earliest finish time. The finish time of an activity is its start time plus its duration.

A "window" is typically an upper and lower bound on the time when an activity may occur. In DEVISER, windows may also have an optional ideal time, indicating an ideal or preferred time of occurrence. (The idea of an ideal start time was suggested by K. Blom.) A window is then defined to be a triple (EARLIEST.START.TIME IDEAL LATEST.START.TIME) where EARLIEST.START.TIME and LATEST.START.TIME are real numbers ranging from 0 to infinity, EST ⩽ LST, and IDEAL is either NIL (if no preference exists) or a real number such that EST ⩽ IDEAL ⩽ LST.

In DEVISER, windows may be specified explicitly for goals. Windows for activities are computed dynamically during plan generation, and are derived from goal windows by consideration of the durations of intervening activities and the times of occurrence of scheduled events.

A. Syntactic Options for Goal Windows

All windows are represented internally as triples. As a convenience for the user, a number of syntactic options are provided for specifying goal windows to the program: AT, BEFORE, AFTER, BETWEEN, and EARLIEST.IDEAL.LATEST. Table I shows how these various forms are translated by the program into the triple form for internal use. TIME0 in the second row of the table is an optional input to the program which specifies the time when the plan may begin. Its default value is zero. All time components of a goal window must be numeric constants, expressed either in seconds or in standard "hours: minutes:seconds" form, e.g., 8:23:01.

B. Specification of Windows and Durations for Goals

Once time is introduced into a planner, it becomes possible and desirable to specify goals as more than just a set of conditions to be achieved. We would like to be able to specify when a set of conditions should be achieved and how long the conditions should be maintained. In DEVISER, goal conditions may be partitioned into "packages," and each package may be assigned a window and/or a duration. The default window is "anytime," i.e., (TIME0 NIL INFINITY), and the default duration is 0, i.e., the goal conditions need only hold for an instant.

Following are some examples of such goal specifications.
Example 4.1:

```
(GOALS ((WINDOW BEFORE 15) (ON A B)
    (ON B C)))
```

The meaning of this specification is that for some time t ⩽ 15, both literals must be true at least momentarily.

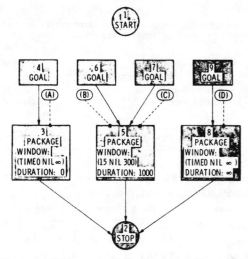

Fig. 1. Initial plan network for the goals in Example 4.3.

Example 4.2:

(GOALS ((WINDOW BEFORE 15) (ON A B))
   ((WINDOW BEFORE 15) (ON B C)))

The meaning of this specification is not identical to the previous one. Here, for some $t_1 \leq 15$, (ON A B) is momentarily achieved, and, for some $t_2 \leq 15$, (ON B C) is momentarily achieved, but the two goal literals need not be true simultaneously.

Example 4.3:

(GOALS ((A))
   ((WINDOW BETWEEN 15 300) (DURATION 1000)
    (B) (C))
   ((DURATION INFINITY) (D)))

Here there are three packages. The first package says (A) must be achieved at least momentarily sometime. The second package says that (B) and (C) must hold simultaneously beginning sometime between 15 and 300, and must continue to hold thereafter for at least 1000 s. The third package says that (D) must be achieved sometime and then must hold forever after.

C. Implementation of Goal Windows and Durations

In timeless planning, as in NONLIN, each goal condition becomes the assertion of a goal node which is sequential to the stop node. This is not satisfactory for achieving groups of goal conditions packaged together with common windows and durations. In DEVISER, there is a distinct *package node* for each package of goal conditions. The package node carries the window and duration associated with the goal conditions, and is sequential to the stop node. Each goal condition is the assertion of a separate goal node, which is sequential to its respective package node. Fig. 1 illustrates this for the goals of Example 4.3. The dashed lines signify that each goal node assertion participates in a "goal structure" relationship (to adopt Tate's terminology) with the respective package node. The conflict detection and resolution mechanisms of the core planner then ensure that the conditions of each goal package

are preserved for the specified duration. For example, conflict resolution will force any activity contradicting (A) to be ordered either after node 3 or before node 4.

D. Activity Windows

Each activity in the plan network also has a window. The default window is (TIME0 NIL INFINITY). As previously mentioned, TIME0 is when planning time begins. A goal node takes its window from the goal specifications, as described in Section IV-B. As planning progresses, the EST and LST bounds on an activity may be revised so as to compress the window. (As a general rule, a window is never widened except when backtracking to an earlier state in plan generation.) The IDEAL component of a window is never modified, and figures only in the selection of start times for actions after generation of the plan network is complete.

The windows of nodes which are sequential in the plan network are dependent. Suppose nodes N1 and N2 are sequential, and D1 is the duration of N1. Then the following inequalities must be satisfied:

$$EST1 + D1 \leq EST2$$
$$LST1 + D1 \leq LST2.$$

Since the window of an activity can not be widened, if the first inequality is not satisfied, we can only increase EST2. If the second inequality is not satisfied, we can only decrease LST1. In both cases it is, of course, necessary to preserve the inequality $ESTi \leq LSTi$ for $i = 1, 2$. If two nodes are consecutive, their windows must satisfy two additional conditions: $EST1 + D1 = EST2$, and $LST1 + D1 = LST2$. These observations on start times form the basis for the window compression procedures presented in Section V. Whenever nodes are linked, expanded, or ordered to resolve conflicts, the windows of those nodes must be reexamined and compressed as necessary to preserve these conditions.

Events are often consecutive after other activities. In most cases, an event occurs as soon as the latest of its preconditions becomes true. Suppose event E is of this type and has preconditions (A) and (B). The event would be described to DEVISER as follows:

(E EVENT
  (CONTEXT (*CONSECUTIVE (A))
   (*CONSECUTIVE (B))) NIL → ((D)))

This serves as a signal to the program that the goal nodes for (A) and (B) must be consecutive to the node for event E.

There are certain cases where an event precondition is not consecutive to the event. For example, in a world of alarm clocks there could be an event:

(ALARM.SOUNDS EVENT
  (CONTEXT (ALARM SET t)) NIL →
   ((ALARM SOUNDING))
  (WINDOW AT t))

Here the precondition (ALARM SET 6AM) will nearly always be achieved many hours before the event occurs. This example also shows that the window for an activity may be derived

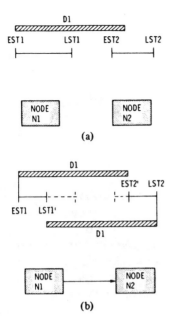

Fig. 2. (a) Windows for nonsequential nodes N1 and N2. (b) The narrowed
windows after ordering N1, N2.

from the variables of that activity. Here the start time for the
event comes from the variable t in the precondition.

V. Window Processing Procedures

As explained in Section IV, the windows of sequential or
consecutive nodes are dependent. Linking and conflict resolution operations in plan generation may cause nodes to become
sequential which formerly were in parallel. Expansion of a
node leads to the evaluation of its duration. Thus all three
operations in plan generation may cause a ripple of window
compressions in the plan network propagating away from the
point where the network is modified. These window compressions will be analyzed in detail in Section V-A. The actual
window compression procedure will be presented in Section
V-B. When a goal node is expanded, it is also necessary to
reconcile its window with the window associated with the
activity into which it is expanded. This process is described
in Section V-E.

A. A Closer Look at Dynamic Window Compression

Fig. 2(a) shows the windows for two nodes N1 and N2 in
time-line style. As before, D1 is the duration of node N1. If
N1 and N2 are made sequential during plan generation, it may
be necessary to modify LST1 and EST2 to maintain the inequalities EST1 + D1 ≤ EST2 and LST1 + D1 ≤ LST2. This is
illustrated in Fig. 2(b). It may be helpful to imagine that the
two bars of length D1 are attached to EST1 and LST2. The
upper bar is connected to EST1 and pushes EST2 right to
EST2′, compressing the window for N2. The lower bar is connected to LST2 and pushes LST1 left to LST1′, compressing the
window for N1. Moving EST2 right may in turn require that
the EST's of nodes downstream from N2 also be moved to the
right. Similarly, nodes upstream from N1 may require their
LST's to be moved left.

If N1 or N2 are consecutive with other plan nodes to the left
or right there are further implications. If there is a node N3

which is consecutive to N2, then EST3 must move right also.
This is because of the additional constraint for consecutive
nodes that their upper and lower bounds must remain separated
by exactly the duration of the earlier node. However, if
several nodes are consecutive to a given (event) node, the LST
of that node is governed by the maximum of the LFT's of
those other nodes. An event cannot begin before the latest
of its consecutive preconditions becomes true.

All these considerations, both for consecutive and nonconsecutive nodes, require that the appropriate window boundaries
be real numbers. If the window boundaries are variables, it is
necessary to wait until they have been instantiated.

In the discussion above, the compression of the windows
occurred when two formerly parallel nodes were ordered. The
same effect occurs if the nodes are already sequential, but the
duration of N1 has not yet been determined. (The duration
may be a function of variables which have not yet been instantiated.) An unknown duration is taken to be 0 when testing the consistency of sequential node windows. When the
duration of N1 at last is known, and if it is nonzero, it may
push EST2 right and LST1 left just as in Fig. 2(b).

From this analysis we see that the revision or instantiation of
an activity's window boundary, or the evaluation of an activity's
duration all may cause ripples both upstream and downstream
in the plan network. As each window boundary is revised, it is
necessary to check that the condition EST ≤ LST is maintained.
If not, the action which triggered the window revision is
aborted and DEVISER must backtrack. All these considerations are embodied in the procedure MODIFY.START.TIMES,
which revises window boundaries as required and returns T
or NIL depending on whether these changes are permissible. Several subordinate subroutines are also presented.
REVISE.CONSECUTIVE.EST and REVISE.CONSECUTIVE.LST
manage the respective window boundaries when consecutive
nodes are involved.

B. The Window Compression Procedure and Subroutines

```
(MODIFY.START.TIMES (NODE1 NODE2)
   (PROG (D1 EST1 LST1 EST2 LST2 EFT1 LFT1 OK
          CONSECUTIVE DURATION.ESTIMATE)

    (CONSECUTIVE = (CONSECUTIVE? NODE1 NODE2))
    (D1 = (CONVERT.DURATION NODE1))
    (* CONVERT.DURATION SETS DURATION.ESTIMATE *)
    (EST1 = (EARLIEST.START.TIME NODE1))
    (EST2 = (EARLIEST.START.TIME NODE2))
    (OK = T)
    (IF (NUMBERP EST1) AND (NUMBERP EST2) THEN
    |  (EFT1 = EST1 + D1)
    |  (IF (EFT1 GT EST2) THEN
    |  |  (SET.EARLIEST.START.TIME NODE2 EFT1)
    |  |  (IF ~(GOAL.NODE? NODE2) THEN
    |  |  |  (ORDER.EST.AGAINST.SCHEDULED.EVENTS
    |  |  |     NODE2)
    |  |  )
    |  |  (IF ~(PROPAGATE.WINDOW.COMPRESSIONS NODE2
    |  |     NODE1) THEN (OK = NIL))
    |  )
```

```
| (IF OK AND CONSECUTIVE AND
| | ~DURATION.ESTIMATE AND
| | ~(GOAL.NODE? NODE1) AND
| | ~(REVISE.CONSECUTIVE.EST NODE1 D1) THEN
| | (OK = NIL)
) )
(LST1 = (LATEST.START.TIME NODE1))
(LST2 = (LATEST.START.TIME NODE2))
(IF OK AND (NUMBERP LST2) AND (NUMBERP LST1)
   THEN
| (LFT1 = LST1 + D1)
| (IF (LFT1 GT LST2) AND ~(EQUAL LST2 INFINITY)
| | AND
| | ~(EQUAL D1 INFINITY) THEN
| | (LST1 = LST2 - D1)
| | (SET.LATEST.START.TIME NODE1 LST1)
| | (IF ~(GOAL.NODE? NODE1) THEN
| | | (ORDER.LST.AGAINST.SCHEDULED.EVENTS
| | |    NODE1)
| | )
| | (IF ~(PROPAGATE.WINDOW.COMPRESSIONS NODE1
| |     NODE2) THEN (OK = NIL))
| )
| (IF OK AND CONSECUTIVE AND
| | ~DURATION.ESTIMATE AND
| | ~(GOAL.NODE? NODE1) AND
| | ~(REVISE.CONSECUTIVE.LST NODE2) THEN
| | (OK = NIL)
) )
(RETURN OK)
(* ------------------------------------------ *)))
(REVISE.CONSECUTIVE.EST (NODE1 D1)
   (* CONSIDER REVISING THE EST OF NODE1, WHICH IS
      CONSECUTIVE TO OTHER NODES. *)
   (PROG (EST3 EST1 EST1' OK)

   (EST1 = (EARLIEST.START.TIME NODE1))
   (OK = T)
   (FOR NODE3 IN (CONSECUTIVE.FROM NODE1) WHILE
   | OK DO
   | (EST3 = (EARLIEST.START.TIME NODE3))
   | (IF ~(VARIABLE? EST3) THEN
   | | (EST1' = (EARLIEST.START.TIME NODE3) - D1)
   | | (IF ~(EQUAL EST1 EST1') THEN
   | | | (IF (LESSP EST1' EST1) THEN
   | | | | (OK = NIL)
   | | | ELSE
   | | | | (SET.EARLIEST.START.TIME NODE1 EST1')
   | | | | (EST1 = EST1')
   | | | | (IF (PROPAGATE.WINDOW.COMPRESSIONS
   | | | | | NODE1 NODE3) THEN
   | | | | | (ORDER.EST.AGAINST.SCHEDULED.EVENTS
   | | | | |    NODE1)
   | | | | ELSE
   | | | | | (OK = NIL)
   ) ) ) ) )
   (RETURN OK)
(* ------------------------------------------ *)))
```

```
(REVISE.CONSECUTIVE.LST (NODE 2)
   (* SEE IF ANY NODES CONSECUTIVE TO NODE2
      SHOULD REDUCE ITS LST. IF ANY EST'S OR
      DURATIONS ARE VARIABLES, DON'T CHANGE THE
      WINDOW. *)
   (PROG (MAXIMUM.LFT THIS.LFT LST3
      MAXIMUM.POSSIBLE? GOVERNING.NODE D3 OK)


   (OK = T)
   (MAXIMUM.POSSIBLE? = T)
   (MAXIMUM.LFT = -INFINITY)
   (FOR NODE3 IN (CONSECUTIVE.TO NODE2) WHILE
   | MAXIMUM.POSSIBLE? DO
   | (LST3 = (LATEST.START.TIME NODE3))
   | (D3 = (GET.DURATION NODE3))
   | (IF (VARIABLE? LST3) OR (VARIABLE? D3) THEN
   | | (MAXIMUM.POSSIBLE? = NIL)
   | ELSE
   | | (THIS.LFT = LST3 + D3)
   | | (IF (GREATERP THIS.LFT MAXIMUM.LFT) THEN
   | | | (MAXIMUM.LFT = THIS.LFT)
   | | | (GOVERNING.NODE = NODE3)
   ) ) )
   (IF MAXIMUM.POSSIBLE? AND
   | (LESSP MAXIMUM.LFT (LATEST.START.TIME NODE2))
   |    THEN
   | (SET.LATEST.START.TIME NODE2 MAXIMUM.LFT)
   | (IF (PROPAGATE.WINDOW.COMPRESSIONS
   | | GOVERNING.NODE) THEN
   | | (ORDER.LST.AGAINST.SCHEDULED.EVENTS NODE2)
   | ELSE
   | | (OK = NIL)
   ) )
   (RETURN OK)
(* ------------------------------------------ *)))
(PROPAGATE.WINDOW.COMPRESSIONS (NODE CALLER)
   (* CALLER WAS RESPONSIBLE FOR COMPRESSING THE
      WINDOW OF NODE. CHECK ALL NEIGHBORS OF
      NODE EXCEPT CALLER TO SEE IF THE CHANGE
      MUST PROPAGATE. *)
   (PROG (EST LST OK UPPER.NEIGHBORS
      LOWER.NEIGHBORS)


   (EST = (EARLIEST.START.TIME NODE))
   (LST = (LATEST.START.TIME NODE))
   (IF (NUMBERP EST) AND (NUMBERP LST) AND
   | (GREATERP EST LST) THEN
   | (RETURN NIL)
   ELSE
   | (OK = T)
   | (UPPER.NEIGHBORS = (REMOVE CALLER (FETCH
   |     PREDECESSORS OF NODE)))
   | (FOR UPPER.NEIGHBOR IN UPPER.NEIGHBORS WHILE
   | | OK DO
   | | (IF ~(MODIFY.START.TIMES UPPER.NEIGHBOR
   | |    NODE) THEN (OK = NIL))
   | )
```

```
|  (IF OK THEN
|  |  (LOWER.NEIGHBORS = (REMOVE CALLER
|  |     (FETCH SUCCESSORS OF NODE)))
|  |  (FOR LOWER.NEIGHBOR IN LOWER.NEIGHBORS
|  |  |  WHILE OK DO
|  |  |  (IF ~(MODIFY.START.TIMES NODE
|  |  |     LOWER.NEIGHBOR) THEN (OK = NIL))
|  )  )
|  (RETURN OK)
)
(* - - - - - - - - - - - - - - - - - - - - - - - - - - - - - - - *)))
(ORDER.EST.AGAINST.SCHEDULED.EVENTS (NODE)
   (* SEE IF NODE SHOULD BE ORDERED WITH RESPECT
      TO ANY OF THE SCHEDULED EVENTS, BASED ON
      ITS EARLIEST START TIME. *)
(* - - - - - - - - - - - - - - - - - - - - - - - - - - - - *))
(ORDER.LST.AGAINST.SCHEDULED.EVENTS (NODE)
   (* SEE IF NODE SHOULD BE ORDERED WITH RESPECT
      TO ANY OF THE SCHEDULED EVENTS, BASED ON
      ITS LATEST START TIME. *)
(* - - - - - - - - - - - - - - - - - - - - - - - - - - - *))
```

C. When MODIFY.START.TIMES is Called

MODIFY.START.TIMES is called just after linking a goal node to another activity node and after ordering two nodes to resolve a conflict. PROPAGATE.WINDOW.COMPRESSIONS is also called just after a node is expanded, so that the node's window becomes consistent with its neighbors. For this call, the "CALLER" argument is NIL. In cases where the duration is a function of variables in the precondition literals, evaluation of the duration may be delayed until these variables have all been instantiated by succeeding plan generation operations. The subroutine which performs instantiations looks at duration expressions and evaluates them as soon as all their variables have been replaced by constants. The instantiation subroutine then calls PROPAGATE.WINDOW.COMPRESSIONS for the node in question, just as after node expansion.

D. Final Determination of Start Times

When the last goal node in the plan network has been eliminated by linking or expansion and all conflicts have been resolved, it is likely that many of the activities will have windows with EST < LST, i.e., the start time of the activity is still not uniquely determined. The IDEAL components of the windows now play their role. It will have been noted that the IDEAL values were never modified during window compression. The result may be that some IDEALS may no longer lie within the EST, LST bounds. In this case we want to select a start time as close to the IDEAL as possible. This will be either the EST or the LST, depending on whether IDEAL < EST or IDEAL > LST. The procedure DETERMINE.START.TIMES, which actually selects start times for each activity based on these considerations, is presented below:

```
(DETERMINE.START.TIMES NIL
   (PROG (EST IDEAL LST)

   (FOR NODE IN NODES.LIST DO
   |  (IDEAL = (IDEAL NODE))
```

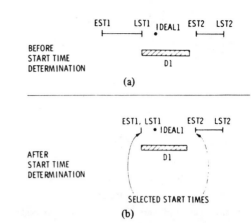

NOT CONSECUTIVE NODES

Fig. 3. Selection of start times for sequential nodes.

```
|  (IF IDEAL THEN
|  |  (EST = (EARLIEST.START.TIME NODE))
|  |  (IF (LESSP IDEAL EST) THEN
|  |  |  (IDEAL = EST)
|  |  ELSE
|  |  |  (LST = (LATEST.START.TIME NODE))
|  |  |  (IF (GREATERP IDEAL LST) THEN
|  |  |  |  (IDEAL = LST)
|  |  ) )
|  |  (SET.EARLIEST.START.TIME NODE IDEAL)
|  |  (SET.LATEST.START.TIME NODE IDEAL)
|  |  (PROPAGATE.WINDOW.COMPRESSIONS NODE NIL)
|  ) )
(RETURN)
))
```

The procedure operates by setting each node's EST and LST to the desired start time. The call to PROPAGATE.WINDOW.COMPRESSIONS is necessary to ensure that the windows of sequential and consecutive nodes remain consistent. PROPAGATE.WINDOW.COMPRESSIONS is guaranteed to succeed here because we are now merely selecting times within previously existing windows. On termination of DETERMINE.START.TIMES, the EST of each node is the desired start time and as close as possible to the specified IDEAL, if any.

As an illustration, Figs. 3 and 4 show the windows of two nodes in timeline form. In Fig. 3 the nodes are assumed not consecutive. The duration D1 is one of many which would be consistent with the windows shown. In Fig. 4, the two nodes are consecutive. This has forced the "width" of the windows to be identical. The duration shown here is the only one consistent with the nodes being consecutive. In both figures, node 1 has an IDEAL while node 2 does not. DETERMINE.START.TIMES sets EST1 to LST1, since this is the closest point to IDEAL1 that lies within the window. For the nonconsecutive case, the window of node 2 is not affected. However, if D1 had been longer, EST2 might have been pushed to the right. For the consecutive case, the closing of window1 to a point has the identical result on window2, because start times for consecutive activities must be exactly D1 apart.

It should be pointed out that this procedure does not guarantee that, say, the sum of all displacements of start times from their IDEALS is minimized. Examples can be

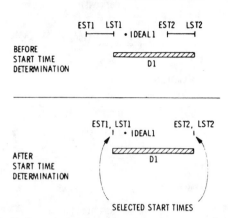

Fig. 4. Selection of start times for consecutive nodes.

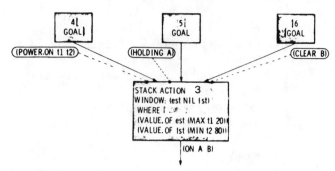

Fig. 5. A node expansion with an uninstantiated window.

constructed involving consecutive nodes where the first node treated by DETERMINE.START.TIMES gets its IDEAL start time, while all the remaining nodes are severely displaced from their IDEALS. The subject of an optimal algorithm for start time selection merits further investigation.

E. Reconciling Production and Goal Node Windows During Node Expansion

Even before expansion, a goal node may already have a window narrower than (TIME0 NIL INFINITY). Conflict resolution may call for ordering existing nodes above a goal node, increasing its EST. The LST of the goal node may have been decreased from infinity to consist with the activity node below. In addition, DEVISER also permits a window to be attached to the activity description productions, as seen earlier in the ALARM.SOUNDS example. When the goal node is expanded into an activity which has its own window, the two windows must be reconciled, if possible, else the expansion must be aborted.

To illustrate, suppose a goal node with assertion (ON A B) and window (20 NIL 80) is expanded into the stack activity described by the following production:

```
(STACK ACTION
    (CONTEXT) ((HOLDING x) (CLEAR y)) →
        ((ON x y) (CLEAR x))
    (WINDOW BEFORE 50)
    (DURATION 5))
```

(The window on this action might result from the fact that the power source will be turned off at time = 55.) In expanding the goal node with this activity, it is necessary to try to reconcile the time constraints from the two sources: the goal node window and the production window. The bounds of the goal node window will always be numeric. If the upper and lower bounds of the production window are also numeric (as in this example), we simply take the maximum of the two lower bounds and the minimum of the two upper bounds. The window for the expanded node in this example then becomes (20 NIL 50).

However, the production window may contain uninstantiated variables. This is the case if the stack action is instead described as follows:

```
(STACK ACTION
    (CONTEXT (POWER.ON t1 t2))
    ((HOLDING x) (CLEAR y)) → ((ON x y) (CLEAR x))
    (WINDOW BETWEEN t1 t2)
    (DURATION 5))
```

Here it is assumed that a POWER.ON literal in the initial state specifies when the power is turned on and off. At the time the node is expanded, t1 and t2 are still variables. It is necessary to set up two VALUE.OF constraints (as described in Section II-G). The result of the expansion is shown in Fig. 5. When goal node 4 is linked to the start node, t1 and t2 are instantiated. The expressions of the two VALUE.OF literals are then completely instantiated. This is detected, the MAX and MIN functions are EVALuated, and the variables est and lst in the window of node 3 are instantiated. This in turn automatically triggers a call to PROPAGATE.WINDOW.COMPRESSIONS to check the windows of adjacent nodes both above and below node 3, possibly propagating changes outward from node 3 in the plan network. In the Spaceworld model of Section VII there are several instances of activities which require variables in their windows. This capability is definitely a practical necessity and not a theoretical frill.

VI. A BLOCKSWORLD MICROEXAMPLE

This section presents a trace of the actions of DEVISER on a complete microexample in the blocksworld. On problems of interesting size it is not feasible to show all the individual steps. For example, the Spaceworld example in Section VII requires hundreds of plan generation operations. There it is only possible to present inputs and outputs

The initial state for this problem is a single block A on a table. A second block B will be "delivered" onto the table at t = 8. This delivery of B exemplifies the treatment of scheduled events. The goal is to achieve (ON A B) before t = 12. Plan time begins at t = 5. The initial situation and goals are input in the following form:

```
(INITIAL.SITUATION (ONTABLE A) (CLEAR A)
    (TIME0 5))
(GOALS ((WINDOW BEFORE 12) (ONTABLE B)
    (ON A B)))
```

The blocksworld actions are as follows:

```
(PICKUP ACTION
    (CONTEXT) ((CLEAR x) (ONTABLE x)) →
        ((HOLDING x))
(DURATION 1))
```

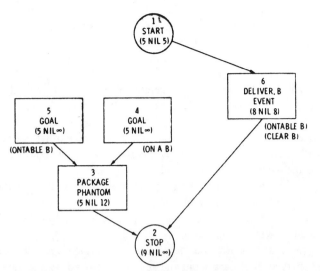

Fig. 6. The initial plan network for the Blocksworld microexample.

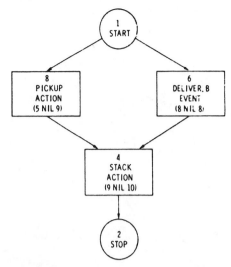

Fig. 7. The final plan network for the Blocksworld microexample.

(PUTDOWN ACTION
    (CONTEXT) ((HOLDING x)) → ((CLEAR x)
        (ONTABLE x))
(DURATION 1))

(STACK ACTION
    (CONTEXT) ((HOLDING x) (CLEAR y)) →
        ((CLEAR x) (ON x y))
(DURATION 2))

(UNSTACK ACTION
    (CONTEXT) ((CLEAR x) (ON x y)) →
        ((HOLDING x) (CLEAR y))
(DURATION 2))

The delivery event is specified by

(DELIVER. B EVENT
    (CONTEXT) NIL → ((ONTABLE B)
        (CLEAR B))
    (DURATION 1)
    (WINDOW AT 8))

The program constructs the initial plan network shown in Fig. 6. The final plan network, without phantom nodes, is shown in Fig. 7. To obtain it, the program performs the 14 plan generation operations listed below. A few adjustments of phantom node windows have been omitted. I recommend the serious reader to take up pencil and paper, draw Fig. 6, and then draw in the effect of each plan generation step.

Plan Generation Steps:

1) Link node 5 to (ONTABLE B) in node 6.

2) Change the EST of node 5 to 9, since the EST of node 6 is 8 and the duration is 1.

3) Change the EST of node 3 to 9, since the EST of node 5 is 9 and the duration is 0.

4) Expand node 4 into a STACK action with assertions (ON A B) (CLEAR A) ~(CLEAR B) ~(HOLDING A) and goal nodes 7 (CLEAR B) and 8 (HOLDING A).

5) Change the LST of node 4 to 10, since the LST of node 3 is 12 and the duration is 2.

6) Detect a conflict over (CLEAR B) involving nodes 4 and 6; order 6, 4.

7) Change the EST of node 4 to 9, since the EST of node 6 is 8 and the duration is 1.

8) Change the EST of node 3 to 11, since the EST of node 4 is 9 and the duration is 2.

9) Change the EST of node 2 to 11, since the EST of node 3 is 11 and the duration is 0.

10) Link node 7 to (CLEAR B) in node 6.

11) Expand node 8 into a PICKUP action, with assertions (HOLDING A) ~(ONTABLE A) ~(CLEAR A) and goal nodes 9 (ONTABLE A) and 10 (CLEAR A).

12) Change the LST of node 8 to 9, since the LST of node 4 is 10 and the duration is 1.

13) Link node 9 to (ONTABLE A) in node 1.

14) Link node 10 to (CLEAR A) in node 1.

The start time for the PICKUP action can be anywhere in the interval (5, 9) and for the STACK action anywhere in the interval (9, 10). Of course, since the two actions are sequential, these start times are dependent. The program simply selects the earliest start time as the planned start time. The result is the following schedule of activities:

START TIME (HH:MM:SS.S)	ID	ACTIVITY	SUBSTITUTION
00:00:05.0	8	PICKUP	A/x
00:00:08.0	6	DELIVER. B	
00:00:09.0	4	STACK	B/y
			A/x

The computation time for this example was 11 s.

As an option, the program will attempt to reduce the duration of the entire plan by starting the "top" actions (those preceded only by the start node or scheduled event nodes) at their LST's and all other actions at their EST's (consistent with the constraints imposed by sequential and consecutive nodes). In this little example, it would start the PICKUP action at t = 9 and the STACK action at t = 10. This would give a shorter plan duration than starting PICKUP at 5 and STACK at 9.

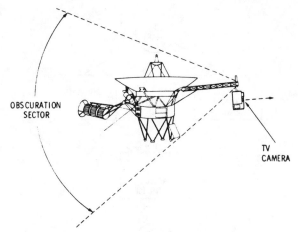

OBSCURATION SECTOR

TV CAMERA

Fig. 8. The Voyager spacecraft and its obscuration sector.

VII. A Spaceworld Example

A. An Overview of the Spaceworld

The "Spaceworld" is a simplified model of the world of JPL's two Voyager spacecraft, which photographed Jupiter, Saturn, and their satellites in 1979, 1980, and 1981. In this model, the goals are the receipt on Earth of pictures of objects in deep space. Not all the numbers in the model hold for the real Voyager; some are entirely fictitious. However, the model is qualitatively accurate. For simplicity, a two-dimensional world is assumed. A TV camera takes still, black-and-white pictures through colored filters at a maximum rate of about one picture per minute. This camera is mounted at the side of the spacecraft on a scan platform, which can be rotated so as to look along any azimuth. However, the sector between 135° and 225° is obscured by the body of the spacecraft, as shown in Fig. 8. A digital image from the camera can reach Earth either by being transmitted immediately or by being recorded on an on-board tape recorder and played back for transmission at a later time. During an occultation, i.e., when a planet or satellite blocks radio signals between the spacecraft and Earth, the only option is to record pictures for later transmission.

A complete set of all the Spaceworld activities in relational production form is presented in Appendix I. Following is a summary in English of the more important ones:

CHANGE.DATA.MODE ACTION—Change the datamode from one setting to another. The datamode controls the routing of data within the spacecraft between the camera, the tape recorder, and the radio transmitter.

DATAMODE.OK INFERENCES—For picture-taking, the datamode must be set to reflect the bit rate at which information can be transmitted to Earth. This datamode in turn influences the time to transmit a single picture frame from the camera.

HIGH.SPEED.SLEW ACTION—Rotate the scan platform at 1°/s.

MEDIUM.SPEED.SLEW ACTION—Rotate the scan platform at 0.1°/s. Slewing the scan platform at either speed induces vibrations which must be allowed to subside before snapping a picture.

PLAYBACK ACTION—Play back data from the tape recorder and transmit it to Earth.

RECORD.PICTURE EVENT—If the datamode is properly set, as soon as a picture is snapped, the image data from the camera is sent to the tape recorder and recorded.

ROLL ACTION—The entire spacecraft is rotated from one angle to another (by firing thrusters). Before the roll, the spacecraft is locked onto one reference star; after the roll, it is locked onto a new reference star. A roll must be performed if an object to be photographed lies in the sector of obscuration between 135° and 225°. The roll, like several other Spaceworld actions, may best be regarded as a call to an action subroutine whose internal details do not concern us.

SET.FILTER ACTION—Change the color filter on the camera lens by rotating the filter wheel.

SHUTTER.CAMERA ACTION—Snap a picture with the TV camera.

START.RECORDING ACTION—Cause the tape recorder to begin recording data from the source controlled by the datamode. In addition to image data from the camera, engineering data may be recorded during a roll.

TRANSMIT.PICTURE EVENT—If the datamode is properly set, as soon as a picture is snapped, it is automatically transmitted to Earth.

VIEWING INFERENCE—Determine from the absolute azimuth of the spacecraft and the spacecraft-relative azimuth of the scan platform the absolute azimuth in which the camera is pointed. This inference also includes a check that this view does not lie within the obscuration sector.

Scheduled Events: The two classes of scheduled events affecting a Spaceworld plan are Earth occultations and deocculations, and datarate changes. The rate at which digital information can be transmitted to Earth varies as tracking stations on Earth "rise" and "set" (from the spacecraft's viewpoint) with the Earth's rotation. For planning purposes, this data rate may be viewed as a step function whose value changes at known times. Each step of the function can be described by a scheduled event which changes the rate to a new value. For example, a change in the data rate to 67.2 kbits/s at time 8000 is represented by the following production:

```
(DATARATE.CHANGE EVENT
    (CONTEXT) NIL → ((DATARATE 67.2))
    (DURATION 5 MINUTES)
    (WINDOW AT 8000))
```

B. A Example Spaceworld Problem

A scene for an example Spaceworld problem is shown in Fig. 9. The spacecraft is passing by the fictional planet Clarion and its two satellites Clotho and Atropos. We want a picture of Clotho at time 2500, looking at an azimuth of 80°. The window for this observation is from 2400 to 2550. We also want a picture of Atropos at time 9000, looking at an azimuth of 170°. The window for the second observation is from 8800 to 9200. This second observation takes place within an occultation. There are three data rate changes within the span of this problem, occuring at the indicated times. The planner's task is to devise a schedule of on-board actions which will accomplish the stated goals. By stating the goals in terms of time and azimuth, we avoid the problem of requiring the

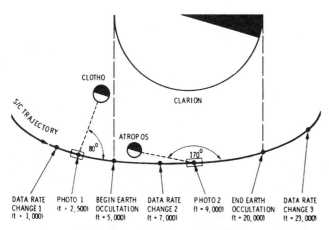

Fig. 9. Scene for a Spaceworld problem.

spacecraft to understand celestial mechanics, which is an un-solved research problem. The major questions to be resolved by the plan of action are as follows. Should high or medium speed slews be performed? To what relative azimuth should the scan platform be slewed? Will it be necessary to perform a roll? What should the datamode settings be? When should the tape recorder be used? Will the tape have to be positioned? Is there sufficient time between the observations to perform all the necessary preparations? When should each action be initiated? A solution for this problem will require the scheduling of 21 actions at 14 different times.

The initial state description and goals specification for this problem are given below:

```
(INITIAL.STATE
    (AZIMUTH ARCTURUS 189)
    (AZIMUTH CANOPUS 0)
    (CAMERA OFF)
    (DATAMODE IM2)
    (DATARATE 35)
    (EARTH IN.VIEW)
    (FILTER CLEAR)
    (GYROS CALIBRATED)
    (GYROS OFF)
    (HEATERS ON)
    (LOCKED.ONTO CANOPUS)
    (PLATFORM STILL)
    (PLATFORM.AZIMUTH 72)
    (SC.AZIMUTH 0)
    (SHUTTER.SPEED 5.76)
    (TAPE.RECORDER OFF)
    (TAPE.AT 50)
    (TAPE.EMPTY 0 2000)
    (TRANSMITTER OFF)
)

(GOALS
    ((RECEIVED.ON.EARTH (PICTURE 80 BLUE 2400
        2500 2550)) (RECEIVED.ON.EARTH (PICTURE
        170 ULTRAVIOLET 8800 9000 9200)))
    ((WINDOW AFTER 25000)
        (ALL.RECORDED.DATA.TRANSMITTED))
```

Note that the windows for the pictures are installed in the PICTURE literals, rather than presented in a meta-level WINDOW literal. This is necessary because these windows apply to the snapping of the picture rather than to goal of receiving the information on Earth, which may occur much later if the picture is recorded on tape and played black. The SHUTTER.-CAMERA action derives its window from components of the PICTURE literal, as seen from the action definition:

```
(SHUTTER.CAMERA ACTION
    (CONTEXT
        (VIEWING azimuth)
        (SHUTTER.SPEED speed)
        (CAMMERA ON)
        (FILTER color.)
        (PLATFORM STILL))
    NIL → ((IN.CAMERA (PICTURE azimuth color.
        t1 t2 t3)))
    (DURATION speed SECONDS)
    (WINDOW EARLIEST.IDEAL.LATEST t1 t2 t3))
```

C. The Machine Generated Parallel Plan

The machine generated parallel plan is presented in Fig. 10 (the figure itself was also machine generated by a separate plotting package programmed by E. Cohen). The plan con-sists of 36 activities, of which 21 are actions. Advantage is taken of the parallelism of which the spacecraft is capable. For example, transmission of the first picture takes place in parallel with the actions of setting the filter wheel and slewing for the second picture. The first picture is transmitted directly. The second picture is recorded on the tape recorder and trans-mitted immediately after the end of occultation. A roll to the star Arcturus must be performed because the second picture would otherwise be obscured by the body of the spacecraft. After playing back the second picture, engineering data re-corded during the roll is played back for transmission to Earth.

From this plan network, a scheduling subroutine determines a start time for each activity, as described in Section V-D. The result is the schedule of activities shown in Appendix II. Execution of this problem took 5 min of CPU time.

VIII. SUMMARY

Mechanisms have been described for extending a parallel planner to treat goals with time constraints and durations. These goals are to be achieved in a world where activities have deterministic durations and scheduled events may occur. A start time window is maintained for each activity in the plan network. Special package nodes hold the window and dura-tion requirements for goal conditions. Constraints on the window boundaries must be satisfied when two nodes are sequential or consecutive. As activities are ordered and dura-tions are evaluated in the course of plan generation, these windows are compressed as necessary. If the boundaries of a window cross, this indicates a time constraint has been violated and the program must backtrack. The final plan is then a partially ordered network in which each activity has a start time window guaranteed to be consistent with that of neighboring activities. From this plan network, a schedule of

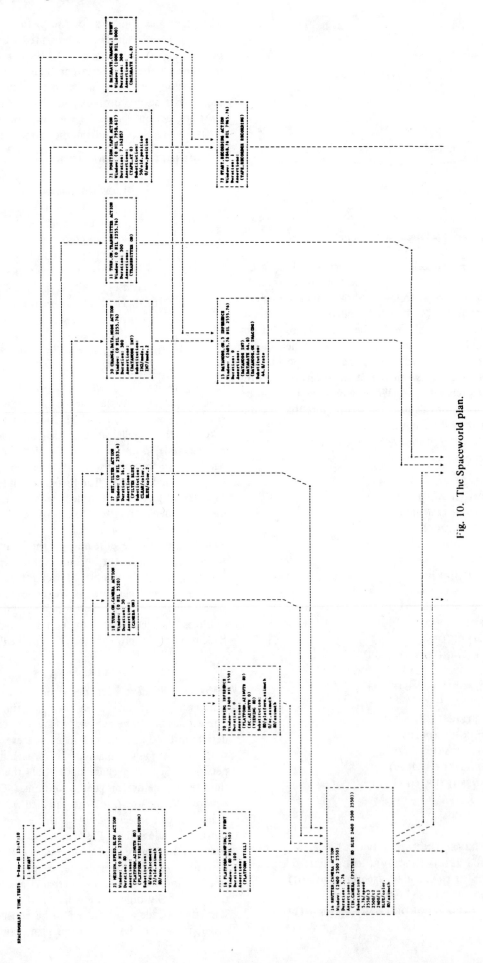

Fig. 10. The Spaceworld plan.

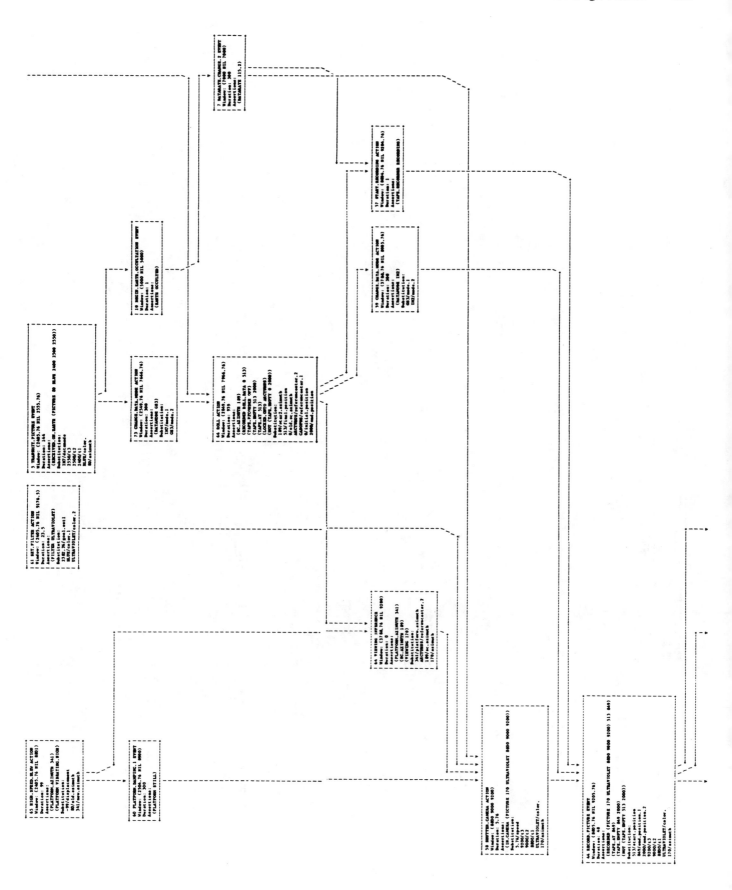

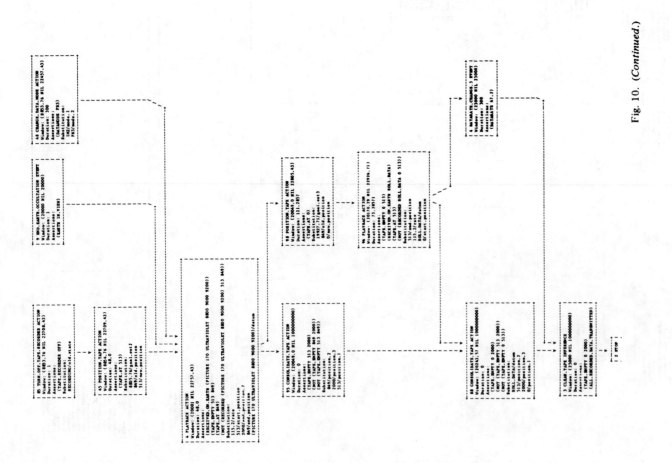

Fig. 10. (*Continued.*)

start times for each activity is computed, while attempting to satisfy requested ideal start times. From one perspective, this system merges planning and deterministic simulation into what might be called goal-directed simulation.

APPENDIX I
THE SPACEWORLD PRODUCTIONS

Following is a list of all productions for the Spaceworld model, preceded by additional miscellaneous program input. The PRIORITIES input specifies the order in which subgoals should be solved for, with the highest priority at the beginning of the list. The FUNCTIONS input lists predicates which form function literals, with the parameter telling the number of arguments of the function. The TYPES are restrictions on substitutions for variables. For example, any variable which begins with "color," must be instantiated with a constant from the specified list: CLEAR, VIOLET, etc. The DOMAIN.FUNCTIONS are short INTERLISP subroutines which are called from within the activity productions. There are times when a conventional subroutine is the most convenient mechanism for achieving a computation. For example, the function SET.FILTER.DURATION computes the time to rotate the color filter wheel from one position to another. This function is called in the duration expression of the SET.FILTER action.

```
(PRIORITIES EARTH IN.CAMERA SHUTTER.SPEED VIEWING
    TAPE.EMPTY RECORDED TAPE.AT LOCKED.ONTO
    AZIMUTH SC.AZIMUTH)


(FUNCTIONS
    (AZIMUTH 1) (CAMERA 0) (DATAMODE 0) (DATARATE 0)
    (EARTH 0) (FILTER 0) (HEATERS 0) (IN.CAMERA 0)
    (PLATFORM 0) (PLATFORM.AZIMUTH 0) (SC.AZIMUTH 0)
    (TAPE.AT 0) (TAPE.RECORDER 0) (TRANSMITTER 0))


(TYPES (COLOR CLEAR VIOLET BLUE ORANGE GREEN
    UNTRAVIOLET CH4 NAD) (MODE IM1 IM2 IM3 IM4 IM5
    IM7 IM9 IM11 IM12 PB1 PB2 PB3 GS1 GS2 GS3)
    (REFERENCESTAR CANOPUS ARCTURUS))


(DOMAIN.FUNCTIONS
(IMAGE.READOUT.DURATION (NLAMBDA (DATAMODE)
    (* CALLED BY THE TRANSMIT.PICTURE EVENT. *)
    (PROG (DURATION)

    (SELECTQ DATAMODE
    |  (IM3 (DURATION = 48))
    |  (IM5 (DURATION = 96))
    |  (IM7 (DURATION = 144))
    |  (IM9 (DURATION = 144))
    |  (IM11 (DURATION = 240))
    |  (IM13 (DURATION = 480))
    |  (HELP "CALL TO IMAGE.READOUT.DURATION WITH
    |      UNKNOWN DATAMODE")
    )
    (RETURN DURATION)
(* - - - - - - - - - - - - - - - - - - - - - - - - - - - - - *))))
```

```
(SCOPE.0.TO.180 (N)
    (* USED BY THE DURATION FUNCTIONS OF ROLL AND
        SLEW TO FIND AN ANGULAR DISPLACEMENT. *)
    (PROG NIL

    (N = (SCOPE.0.TO.360 N))
    (IF (N GT 180) THEN (N = 360 - N))
    (RETURN N)
(* - - - - - - - - - - - - - - - - - - - - - - - - - - - - *)))
(SCOPE.0.TO.360 (N)
    (* TURN N INTO A POSITIVE ANGLE FROM 0 TO 360. *)
    (PROG NIL

    (N = (IREMAINDER N 360))
    (IF (N LT 0) THEN (N = N + 360))
    (RETURN N)
(* - - - - - - - - - - - - - - - - - - - - - - - - - - - *)))
(SET.FILTER.DURATION (NLAMBDA (OLD.COLOR
    NEW.COLOR)
    (PROG (CLEAR VIOLET BLUE ORANGE CH4 GREEN NAD
        ULTRAVIOLET DISTANCE)

    (PUTPROP 'CLEAR 'NUMBER 0)
    (PUTPROP 'VIOLET 'NUMBER 1)
    (PUTPROP 'BLUE 'NUMBER 2)
    (PUTPROP 'ORANGE 'NUMBER 3)
    (PUTPROP 'CH4 'NUMBER 4)
    (PUTPROP 'GREEN 'NUMBER 5)
    (PUTPROP 'NAD 'NUMBER 6)
    (PUTPROP 'ULTRAVIOLET 'NUMBER 7)
    (DISTANCE = (GETPROP NEW.COLOR 'NUMBER) -
        (GETPROP OLD.COLOR 'NUMBER))
    (IF (DISTANCE LT 0) THEN (DISTANCE =
        DISTANCE + 8))
    (RETURN (2.3 * DISTANCE + 12))
(* - - - - - - - - - - - - - - - - - - - - - - - - - - - *))))
(SLEWING.DISPLACEMENT (OLD.AZIMUTH NEW.AZIMUTH)
    (PROG (COUNTERCLOCKWISE.DISPLACEMENT
        CLOCKWISE.DISPLACEMENT)

    (IF (LESSP OLD.AZIMUTH 240) AND (GREATERP
    |  NEW.AZIMUTH 250) THEN
    |  (COUNTERCLOCKWISE.DISPLACEMENT = 1000000)
    ELSE
    |  (COUNTERCLOCKWISE.DISPLACEMENT =
    |      (NEW.AZIMUTH - OLD.AZIMUTH))
    |  (IF (LESSP COUNTERCLOCKWISE.DISPLACEMENT 0)
    |  |  THEN
    |  |  (COUNTERCLOCKWISE.DISPLACEMENT =
    |  |      COUNTERCLOCKWISE.DISPLACEMENT + 360)
    )  )
    (IF (GREATERP OLD.AZIMUTH 250) AND (LESSP
    |  NEW.AZIMUTH 240) THEN
    |  (CLOCKWISE.DISPLACEMENT = 1000000)
    ELSE
    |  (CLOCKWISE.DISPLACEMENT = NEW.AZIMITH -
    |      OLD.AZIMUTH)
```

```
|  (IF (GREATERP CLOCKWISE.DISPLACEMENT 0) THEN
|  |   (CLOCKWISE.DISPLACEMENT =
|  |       CLOCKWISE.DISPLACEMENT - 360)
)  )
(IF (LESSP (ABS CLOCKWISE.DISPLACEMENT)
|        (ABS COUNTERCLOCKWISE.DISPLACEMENT))
|           THEN
|  (RETURN CLOCKWISE.DISPLACEMENT)
ELSE
|  (RETURN COUNTERCLOCKWISE.DISPLACEMENT)
)
(* - - - - - - - - - - - - - - - - - - - - - - - - - - - - - - - *)))
)
```

PRODUCTIONS:

```
(CALIBRATE.GYROS ACTION
    (CONTEXT (GRYOS UP.TO.SPEED)) NIL →
       ((GYROS CALIBRATED))
    (DURATION 4 HOURS))

(CHANGE.DATA.MODE ACTION
    (CONTEXT
       (NEQ mode.1 mode.2)
       (DATAMODE mode.1))
    NIL → ((DATAMODE mode.2))
    (DURATION 5 MINUTES))

(CLEAR.TAPE INFERENCE
    (CONTEXT (TAPE.EMPTY 0 2000)) NIL →
       ((ALL.RECORDED.DATA.TRANSMITTED)))

(CONSOLIDATE.TAPE ACTION
    (CONTEXT)
    ((TAPE.EMPTY position.1 position.2)
       (TAPE.EMPTY position.2 position.3))
    → ((TAPE.EMPTY position.1 position.3))
    (DURATION 0))

(DATAMODE.OK.1 INFERENCE
    (CONTEXT
       (LEQ 115.2 rate)
       (DATARATE rate)
       (DATAMODE IM3)) NIL → ((DATAMODE.OK IMAGING)))

(DATAMODE.OK.2 INFERENCE
    (CONTEXT
       (LEQ 67.2 rate)
       (GREATERP 89.6 rate)
       (DATARATE rate)
       (DATAMODE IM5)) NIL → ((DATAMODE.OK IMAGING)))

(DATAMODE.OK.3 INFERENCE
    (CONTEXT
       (LEQ 44.8 rate)
       (GREATERP 67.2 rate)
       (DATARATE rate)
       (DATAMODE IM7)) NIL → ((DATAMODE.OK IMAGING)))

(DATAMODE.OK.4 INFERENCE
    (CONTEXT
       (LEQ 29.9 rate)
       (GREATERP 44.8 rate)
       (DATARATE rate)
       (DATAMODE IM11)) NIL → ((DATAMODE.OK
          IMAGING)))

(DATAMODE.OK.5 INFERENCE
    (CONTEXT
       (LEQ 19.2 rate)
       (GREATERP 29.9 rate)
       (DATARATE rate)
       (DATAMODE IM13)) NIL → ((DATAMODE.OK
          IMAGING)))

(GYROS.REV.UP EVENT
    (CONTEXT (*CONSECUTIVE (GYROS ON))) NIL →
       ((GRYOS UP.TO.SPEED))
    (DURATION 2 HOURS))

(HIGH.SPEED.SLEW ACTION
    (CONTEXT
       (NEQ old.azimuth new.azimuth)
       (OR (LESSP new.azimuth 240)
          (GREATERP new.azimuth 250))
       (PLATFORM.AZIMUTH old.azimuth)
       (VALUE.OF displacement (SLEWING.DISPLACEMENT
          old.azimuth new.azimuth))
       (GREATERP (ABS displacement) 18))
    NIL → ((PLATFORM.AZIMUTH new.azimuth)
       (PLATFORM VIBRATING.HIGH))
    (DURATION (ABS displacement) SECONDS))

(MEDIUM.SPEED.SLEW ACTION
    (CONTEXT
       (NEQ old.azimuth new.azimuth)
       (OR (LESSP new.azimuth 240)
          (GREATERP new.azimuth 250))
       (PLATFORM.AZIMUTH old.azimuth)
       (VALUE.OF displacement (SLEWING.DISPLACEMENT
          old.azimuth new.azimuth))
       (LEQ (ABS displacement) 18))
    NIL → ((PLATFORM.AZIMUTH new.azimuth)
       (PLATFORM VIBRATING.MEDIUM))
    (DURATION (ABS (displacement * 10)) SECONDS))

(PLATFORM.DAMPING.1 EVENT
    (CONTEXT (*CONSECUTIVE (PLATFORM
       VIBRATING.HIGH)))
    NIL → ((PLATFORM STILL))
    (DURATION 5 MINUTES))

(PLATFORM.DAMPING.2 EVENT
    (CONTEXT (*CONSECUTIVE (PLATFORM
       VIBRATING.MEDIUM)))
    NIL → ((PLATFORM STILL))
    (DURATION 100 SECONDS))
```

(PLAYBACK ACTION
  (CONTEXT
    (TAPE.RECORDER OFF)
    (DATAMODE PB3)
    (DATARATE rate)
    (GREATERP rate 19.2)
    (EARTH IN.VIEW)
    (TAPE.AT start.position))
  ((RECORDED datum start.position end.position))
  → ((TAPE.AT end.position)
    (RECEIVED.ON.EARTH datum)
    (TAPE.EMPTY start.position end.position))
  (DURATION ((ABS (end.position - start.position)) / 7.0)
    SECONDS)
  (PREFERRED.FOR (TAPE.EMPTY start.position
    end.position)))

(POSITION.TAPE ACTION
  (CONTEXT
    (TAPE.RECORDER OFF)
    (NEQ old.position new.position)
    (TAPE.AT old.position))
  NIL → ((TAPE.AT new.position))
  (DURATION ((ABS (new.position - old.position)) / 7.0)
    SECONDS))

(RECORD.PICTURE EVENT
  (CONTEXT
    (GOAL (RECORDED (PICTURE azimuth color. t1 t2 t3)
      start.position end.position.1))
    (DATAMODE IM2)
    (*CONSECUTIVE (IN.CAMERA (PICTURE azimuth color.
      t1 t2 t3)))
    (*CONSECUTIVE (TAPE.RECORDER RECORDING))
    (TAPE.AT start.position)
    (LEQ end.position.1 end.position.2)
    (VALUE.OF end.position.1 (start.position + 336)))
  ((TAPE.EMPTY start.position end.position.2))
  → ((RECORDED (PICTURE azimuth color. t1 t2 t3)
      start.position end.position.1)
    (TAPE.EMPTY end.position.1 end.position.2)
    (TAPE.AT end.position.1))
  (DURATION 48 SECONDS)
  (WINDOW AFTER t1))

(ROLL ACTION
  (CONTEXT
    (GOAL (SC.AZIMUTH star2.azimuth))
    (GYROS CALIBRATED)
    (DATAMODE GS3)
    (*CONSECUTIVE (TAPE.RECORDER RECORDING))
    (TAPE.AT initial.position)
    (VALUE.OF final.position (initial.position + 3 *
      (SCOPE.0.TO.180 (old.sc.azimuth -
      star2.azimuth))))
    (LOCKED.ONTO referencestar.1)
    (SC.AZIMUTH old.sc.azimuth)

(AZIMUTH referencestar.2 star2.azimuth)
    (LEQ final.position end.position)
    (NEQ referencestar.1 referencestar.2))
  ((TAPE.EMPTY initial.position end.position))
  → ((SC.AZIMUTH star2.azimuth)
    (LOCKED.ONTO referencestar.2)
    (TAPE.AT final.position)
    (TAPE.EMPTY final.position end.position)
    (TAPE.RECORDER OFF)
    (RECORDED ROLL.DATA initial.position final.position))
  (DURATION
    (84 + 5 * (SCOPE.0.TO.180 (old.sc.azimuth -
      star2.azimuth))) SECONDS))

(SET.FILTER ACTION
  (CONTEXT
    (NEQ color.1 color.2)
    (FILTER color.1))
  NIL → ((FILTER color.2))
  (DURATION (SET.FILTER.DURATION color.1 color.2)
    SECONDS))

(SHUTTER.CAMERA ACTION
  (CONTEXT
    (VIEWING azimuth)
    (SHUTTER.SPEED speed)
    (CAMERA ON)
    (FILTER color.)
    (PLATFORM STILL))
  NIL → ((IN.CAMERA (PICTURE azimuth color. t1 t2 t3)))
  (DURATION speed SECONDS)
  (WINDOW EARLIEST.IDEAL.LATEST t1 t2 t3))

(START.RECORDING ACTION
  (CONTEXT (TAPE.RECORDER OFF)) NIL →
    ((TAPE.RECORDER RECORDING))
  (DURATION 1 SECOND))

(TRANSMIT.PICTURE EVENT
  (CONTEXT
    (EARTH IN.VIEW)
    (*CONSECUTIVE (IN.CAMERA (PICTURE azimuth color.
      t1 t2 t3)))
    (DATAMODE.OK IMAGING)
    (DATAMODE datamode)
    (TRANSMITTER ON))
  NIL → ((RECEIVED.ON.EARTH (PICTURE azimuth color.
    t1 t2 t3)))
  (DURATION (IMAGE.READOUT.DURATION datamode))
  (WINDOW AFTER t1)
  (PREFERRED.FOR (RECEIVED.ON.EARTH (PICTURE
    azimuth color. t1 t2 t3))))

(TURN.OFF.CAMERA ACTION
  (CONTEXT (CAMERA ON)) NIL → ((CAMERA OFF))
  (DURATION 30 SECONDS))

(TURN.OFF.GYROS ACTION
   (CONTEXT (HEATERS ON) (GYROS ON)) NIL →
      ((GYROS OFF))
   (DURATION 5 MINUTES))

(TURN.OFF.HEATERS ACTION
   (CONTEXT (HEATERS ON)) NIL →((HEATERS OFF))
   (DURATION 3 MINUTES))

(TURN.OFF.TAPE.RECORDER ACTION
   (CONTEXT
      (TAPE.RECORDER old.state)
      (NEQ old.state OFF))
   NIL →((TAPE.RECORDER OFF))
   (DURATION 1 SECOND))

(TURN.ON.CAMERA ACTION
   (CONTEXT (CAMERA OFF)) NIL →((CAMERA ON))
   (DURATION 30 SECONDS))

(TURN.ON.GYROS ACTION
   (CONTEXT (HEATERS OFF) (GYROS OFF)) NIL →
      ((GYROS ON))
   (DURATION 1 SECOND))

(TURN.ON.HEATERS ACTION
   (CONTEXT (HEATERS OFF)) NIL →((HEATERS ON))
   (DURATION 3 MINUTES))

(TURN.ON.TRANSMITTER ACTION
   (CONTEXT (TRANSMITTER OFF)) NIL →
      ((TRANSMITTER ON))
   (DURATION 5 MINUTES))

(VIEWING INFERENCE
   (CONTEXT
      (SC.AZIMUTH sc.azimuth)
      (OR (LESSP platform.azimuth 135)
         (GREATERP platform.azimuth 225))
      (PLATFORM.AZIMUTH platform.azimuth)
      (VALUE.OF platform.azimuth (SCOPE.0.TO.360
         (azimuth - sc.azimuth))))
   NIL →((VIEWING azimuth)))

(BEGIN.EARTH.OCCULTATION EVENT
   (CONTEXT (EARTH IN.VIEW)) NIL →
      ((EARTH OCCULTED))
   (WINDOW AT 5000))

(END.EARTH.OCCULTATION EVENT
   (CONTEXT (EARTH OCCULTED)) NIL →
      ((EARTH IN.VIEW))
   (WINDOW AT 20000))

(DATARATE.CHANGE.1 EVENT
   (CONTEXT) NIL →((DATARATE 44.8))
   (DURATION 5 MINUTES)
   (WINDOW AT 1000))

(DATARATE.CHANGE.2 EVENT
   (CONTEXT) NIL →((DATARATE 115.2))
   (DURATION 5 MINUTES)
   (WINDOW AT 7000))

(DATARATE.CHANGE.3 EVENT
   (CONTEXT) NIL →((DATARATE 67.2))
   (DURATION 5 MINUTES)
   (WINDOW AT 23000))

END

APPENDIX II
SCHEDULE OF ACTIVITIES DERIVED FROM THE SPACEWORLD PLAN

START TIME (HH:MM:SS.S)	ID	ACTIVITY	SUBSTITUTION
00:00:00.0	71	POSITION.TAPE	50/old.position 0/new.position
00:00:00.0	30	CHANGE.DATA.MODE	IM2/mode.1 IM7/mode.2
00:00:00.0	21	MEDIUM.SPEED.SLEW	8/displacement 72/old.azimuth 80/new.azimuth
00:00:00.0	17	SET.FILTER	CLEAR/color.1 BLUE/color.2
00:00:00.0	18	TURN.ON.CAMERA	
00:00:00.0	11	TURN.ON.TRANSMITTER	
00:01:20.0	16	PLATFORM.DAMPING.2	
00:16:40.0	8	DATARATE.CHANGE.1	
00:41:40.0	14	SHUTTER.CAMERA	5.76/speed 2550/t3 2500/t2 2400/t1 BLUE/color. 80/azimuth
00:41:45.7	65	HIGH.SPEED.SLEW	-99/displacement 80/old.azimuth 341/new.azimuth
00:41:45.7	61	SET.FILTER	2382.26/goal.est1 BLUE/color.1 ULTRAVIOLET/color.2

START TIME (HH:MM:SS.S)	ID	ACTIVITY	SUBSTITUTION	START TIME (HH:MM:SS.S)	ID	ACTIVITY	SUBSTITUTION
00:41:45.7	5	TRANSMIT.PICTURE	IM7/datamode 2550/t3 2500/t2 2400/t1 BLUE/color. 80/azimuth	02:30:53.7	85	TURN.OFF.TAPE.-RECORDER	RECORDING/old.-state
				02:30:53.7	48	CHANGE.DATA.MODE	IM2/mode.1 PB3/mode.2
00:43:24.7	60	PLATFORM.DAMPING.1		02:30:54.7	45	POSITION.TAPE	8805.76/goal.est2 849/old.position 513/new.position
00:44:09.7	73	CHANGE.DATA.MODE	IM7/mode.1 GS3/mode.2	05:33:20.0	9	END.EARTH.OCCULTA-TION	
00:49:08.7	72	START.RECORDING					
00:49:09.7	66	ROLL	189/star2.-azimuth 513/final.position 0/old.sc.azimuth ARCTURUS/refer-encestar.2 CANOPUS/refer-encestar.1 0/initial.position 2000/end.position	05:33:21.0	4	PLAYBACK	115.2/rate 513/start.position 2000/end.posi-tion.2 849/end.position (PICTURE 170 ULTRAVIOLET 8800 9000 9200)/datum
				05:34:09.0	98	POSITION.TAPE	19927.71/goal.-est3 849/old.position 0/new.position
01:04:48.7	59	CHANGE.DATA.MODE	GS3/mode.1 IM2/mode.2				
01:23:20.0	10	BEGIN.EARTH.-OCCULTATION		05:34:09.0	95	CONSOLIDATE.TAPE	849/position.2 2000/position.3 513/position.1
01:56:40.0	7	DATARATE.CHANGE.2		05:36:10.2	96	PLAYBACK	513/end.position 115.2/rate ROLL.DATA/ datum 0/start.position
02:30:00.0	58	SHUTTER.CAMERA	5.76/speed 9200/t3 9000/t2 8800/t1 ULTRAVIOLET/ color. 170/azimuth				
				05:37:23.5	88	CONSOLIDATE.TAPE	ROLL.DATA/ datum 513/position.2 2000/position.3 0/position.1
02:30:04.7	57	START.RECORDING					
02:30:05.7	44	RECORD.PICTURE	513/start.posi-tion 849/end.posi-tion.1 2000/end.posi-tion.2 9200/t3 9000/t2 8800/t1 ULTRAVIOLET/ color. 170/azimuth	06:23:20.0	6	DATARATE.CHANGE.3	

REFERENCES

[1] A. Bundy, "Exploiting the properties of functions to control search," Dep. Artificial Intell., Univ. Edinburgh, Res. Rep. 45, Oct. 1977.

[2] J. de Kleer, "Qualitative and quantitative knowledge in classical mechanics," Artificial Intell. Lab., Massachusetts Inst. Technol., Tech. Rep. AI-TR-352, Dec. 1975.

[3] A. Bundy, "Will it reach the top? Predictions in the mechanics world," *Artificial Intell.*, vol. 10, pp. 129–146, Apr. 1978.

[4] S. E. Elmaghraby, *Activity Networks: Project Planning and Control by Network Models.* New York: Wiley, 1977.

[5] R. E. Fikes *et al.*, "Some new directions in robot problem solving," in *Machine Intelligence*, vol. 7, B. Meltzer and D. Michie, Eds. New York: Wiley, 1972.

[6] R. E. Fikes and N. J. Nilsson, "STRIPS: A new approach to the application of theorem proving to problem solving," *Artificial Intell.*, vol. 2, pp. 189–208, 1971.

[7] B. V. Funt, "Problem-solving with diagrammatic representations," *Artificial Intell.*, vol. 13, pp. 201–230, May 1980.

[8] G. G. Hendrix, "Modeling simultaneous actions and continuous processes," *Artificial Intell.*, vol. 4, pp. 145–180, Winter 1973.

[9] P. J. Kiviat *et al.*, *The SIMSCRIPT II Programming Language*. Englewood Cliffs, NJ: Prentice-Hall, 1968.

[10] D. McDermott, "A temporal logic for reasoning about processes and plans," Dep. Comput. Sci., Yale Univ., Res. Rep. 196, 1981.

[11] N. J. Nilsson, *Principles of Artificial Intelligence*. Palo Alto, CA: Tioga, 1980.

[12] C. Rieger and M. Grinberg, "The causal representation and simulation of physical mechanisms," Dep. Comput. Sci., Univ. Maryland, Rep. TR-495, Nov. 1976.

[13] E. D. Sacerdoti, *A Structure for Plans and Behavior*. New York: Elsevier, North-Holland, 1977.

[14] —, "Problem solving tactics," in *Proc. IJCAI*, 1979, pp. 1077–1085.

[15] L. Siklossy and J. Dreussi, "An efficient robot planner which generates its own procedures," in *Proc. IJCAI*, 1973, pp. 423–430.

[16] A. Tate, "Project planning using a hierarchic non-linear planner," Dep. Artificial Intell., Univ. Edinburgh, Rep. 25, Aug. 1976.

[17] —, "Generating project networks," in *Proc. IJCAI*, 1977, pp. 888–893.

[18] P. W. Thorndyke *et al.*, "AUTOPILOT: A distributed planner for air fleet control," in *Proc. IJCAI*, 1981, pp. 171–177.

[19] S. A. Vere, "Relational production systems," *Artificial Intell.*, vol. 8, pp. 47–68, 1977.

[20] R. B. Wesson, "Planning in the world of the air traffic controller," in *Proc. IJCAI*, 1977, pp. 473–479.

Steven A. Vere (M'74) was born in Whittier, CA, in 1945. He received the B.S., M.S., and Ph.D. degrees in engineering from the University of California, Los Angeles, in 1966, 1967, and 1970, respectively.

Between 1970 and 1974 he held staff positions successively at Logicon and Hughes Ground Systems Group, where he did applied research in program verification, higher level language computer architecture, and digital hardware design languages. From 1974 to 1980 he was an Assistant Professor in the Department of Information Engineering at the University of Illinois, Chicago, where he taught computer science and conducted basic research in inductive learning and production systems. Since 1980 he has been with the Information Systems Research Section at the Jet Propulsion Laboratory, Pasadena, CA. His present research interests are intelligent planning, reasoning, and learning systems in the context of space exploration and national defense.

Domain-independent Planning: Representation and Plan Generation

David E. Wilkins

Artificial Intelligence Center, SRI International, Menlo Park, CA 94025, U.S.A.

Recommended by Drew McDermott

ABSTRACT

A domain-independent planning program that supports both automatic and interactive generation of hierarchical, partially ordered plans is described. An improved formalism makes extensive use of constraints and resources to represent domains and actions more powerfully. The formalism also offers efficient methods for representing properties of objects that do not change over time, allows specification of the plan rationale (which includes scoping of conditions and appropriately relating different levels in the hierarchy), and provides the ability to express deductive rules for deducing the effects of actions. The implications of allowing parallel actions in a plan or problem solution are discussed, and new techniques for efficiently detecting and remedying harmful parallel interactions are presented. The most important of these techniques, reasoning about resources, is emphasized and explained. The system supports concurrent exploration of different branches in the search, making best-first search easy to implement.

1. The Planning Problem

The problem of generating a sequence of actions to accomplish a goal is referred to as *planning*. The automation of planning in a computer program involves representing the world, representing actions and their effects on the world, reasoning about the effects of sequences of such actions, reasoning about the interaction of actions that are taking place concurrently, and controlling the search so that plans can be found with reasonable efficiency.

The ability to reason about actions is a core problem for artificial intelligence. It is part of the common-sense reasoning people do all the time. By reasoning about actions, a program could plan your travel for you, control a robot arm in a changing environment, get a computer system or network to accomplish your computing goals, or do any number of other things that are beyond the scope of current systems. This problem is even central to convers-

ing in natural language. First, because many utterances are deliberately *planned* to achieve specific goals, and also because it is often necessary to create your own model of other people's plans in order to understand their utterances. Despite the importance of the planning problem, relatively little has been accomplished in recent years. This paper describes progress on this problem that has resulted from development of a planning program at SRI International.[1]

Planners designed to work efficiently in a single problem domain, though desirable, often depend on the structure of that domain to such an extent that the underlying ideas cannot be readily used in other domains. Usually a new program (often requiring its own unique representation and heuristics) must be developed for each new domain to get reasonable performance. On the other-hand, domain-independent planners yield reasonable planning techniques that are applicable in many domains and provide a general planning capability. Such a common-sense planning capability is likely to require different techniques from those used by an expert planning in his particular domain of expertise, but it is nonetheless essential for people in their daily lives and for intelligent programs. Of course, a general planner should provide representations and methods for including domain-specific knowledge and heuristics.

There is no guarantee, except for human performance, that a large central core of domain-independent planning techniques exists. It is important to enlarge this core as much as possible so we do not have to write a new planner for each new domain. Such motivation lies behind other AI research; for example EMYCIN [14] is an attempt to clarify the domain-independent core of expert systems such as MYCIN, and TEAM [2] provides natural-language access to data bases independent of the domain or structure of the data base. This paper describes an implemented planning program that expands the core of domain-independent planning techniques as it builds on and extends such previous domain-independent planning systems as Sacerdoti's NOAH [9], Tate's NONLIN [13], Sridharan's PLANX10 [10], Vere's DEVISER [15], and SRI's STRIPS [1].

Two features found in many planning systems are also central in this work: hierarchical planning and parallel actions. Hierarchical planning is often necessary for real-world domains, since it helps avoid the tyranny of detail that would result from planning at the most primitive level. The planner can significantly reduce the search space by first planning at abstract levels and then expanding these abstract plans into more detailed plans. Parallel actions are also useful for real-world domains. Such domains are often multieffector or multiagent (e.g., having two robot arms to construct an object, or two editors to work on your report), and the best plans should use these agents in parallel

[1] The research reported here is supported by Air Force Office of Scientific Research Contract F-49620-79-C-0188.

0004-3702/84/$3.00 © 1984, Elsevier Science Publishers B.V. (North-Holland)

whenever possible. This distinguishes planning from much of the work in program synthesis, since the goal there is often a strictly sequential program. A planning system that allows parallel actions must be able to reason about how parallel actions interact with one another, since interference between parallel actions may prevent the plan from accomplishing its goal. This is a major problem for planning systems and a primary focus of this paper.

2. Overview of SIPE

We have designed and implemented (in INTERLISP) a system, SIPE (System for Interactive Planning and Execution Monitoring), that supports domain-independent planning. The program has produced correct parallel plans for problems in four different domains (an extended blocks world, cooking, aircraft operations, and travel planning). The system allows for hierarchical planning and parallel actions. Development of the basic planning system has led to several extensions of previous systems. These include the development of a perspicuous formalism for encoding descriptions of actions, the use of constraints to partially describe objects, the concurrent exploration of alternative plans, the incorporation of heuristics for reasoning about resources. mechanisms that make it possible to perform simple deductions, and advanced abilities to reason about the interaction among parallel actions.

SIPE can generate plans automatically, but, unlike its predecessors, SIPE is designed to also allow interaction with users throughout the planning and plan execution processes. The user is able to watch and, when he wishes, guide and/or control the planning process. Our concern with interaction means that perspicuous representations have been favored and that some search control issues have not been addressed as yet. As the system evolves, more methods for controlling the search will be developed and more problems will be solved automatically. This evolutionary approach has several advantages. From the planning point of view it allows us to address larger, 'real-world' problems that may initially be beyond the capabilities of fully automatic planning techniques, but which could provide interesting research problems. Development of an interactive planner also encourages us to deal with the issue of representing the planning problem in terms that can be easily communicated to a user. This is also important for an automatic planner, because the machine must still be able to communicate about the planning it has performed. Our system raises issues in human–machine interaction, but this paper addresses only the planning aspects of our work.

In SIPE a plan is a set of partially ordered goals and actions. which is composed by the system from operators (the system's description of actions that it may perform). By simply applying operators, plans that do not achieve the desired goal may sometimes be generated, so the system has *critics* that find

potential problems and attempt to avert them. In particular, most of the reasoning about interactions between parallel actions is done by the critics. The plans are represented in procedural nets [9]. primarily for graceful interaction between man and machine. Invariant properties of objects in the domain are represented in a sort hierarchy, which allows inheritance of properties and the posting of constraints on the values of attributes of these objects. The relationships that change over time—and therefore all goals—are represented in a restricted version of first-order predicate calculus that interacts with the knowledge in the sort hierarchy. Operators are represented in an easily understood formalism [6] in which the ability to post constraints on variables is a primary feature. Each of these parts of the system will be described in more detail later.

It should be noted that, like most domain-independent planning systems (DEVISER being an exception), ours assumes discrete time, discrete states, and discrete operators. Time need not be represented explicitly for many tasks, since the ordering links in the procedural network provide the necessary ordering information. It is assumed that each world state that can be reached is discrete and can be represented explicitly. The operators are also discrete, with the effects of an action occurring instantaneously as far as the system is concerned. This applies to a given abstraction level; using hierarchical planning, the system can order the effects that occur at a lower level of detail. These assumptions are acceptable in many real-world domains and have been made by most previous planners. They are however restrictive and prevent many real-world phenomena from being adequately represented. For example, sophisticated reasoning about time and modeling of dynamic processes are not possible within our present framework. Few artificial intelligence programs have addressed these problems (McDermott's recent work being a notable exception [5]).

This paper describes SIPE in more detail by discussing its solutions to four major problems a planner must address. These problems are representation (of the domain, goals, and operators), recognizing and dealing with parallel interactions, controlling the search, and monitoring execution. The next four sections describe these problems and stress new developments in SIPE by comparing it to previous systems.

Most of the new developments are in the areas of representation and parallel interactions. The primary contributions of SIPE are a general constraint language and the ability to reason about resources. The use of constraints makes SIPE more powerful than previous domain-independent planners because it can use constraints both to represent a wider range of domains and to find solutions more efficiently. Resources are a powerful mechanism for reasoning about parallel actions. SIPE allows actions to use objects as resources, then reasons about these resources to find parallel actions that must be linearized. While the concept of resources in SIPE is limited, it is nevertheless quite useful both in the representation of domains and in finding solutions efficiently.

Other important representational contributions of SIPE include deductive operators, efficient methods for representing invariant properties of objects, and mechanisms for representing plan rationale. Many effects of actions are deduced (and thus do not need to be represented explicitly), but the deduction is kept under tight control—thus avoiding the search explosion encountered by more deduction-oriented planners. For greater efficiency, SIPE provides different representations (both a frame-based hierarchy and predicate calculus) for different parts of the domain. (Most domain-independent planners have used a single representation.) In addition, SIPE enables a rich description of plan rationale, thus providing important information for execution monitoring, plan explanation, and critics. These features are described in more detail below.

3. Representation

A central concern in designing a representation for a planning system is how to represent the effects an action has on the state of the world. This means that the frame problem [9] must be solved in an efficient manner. Since we intend that many domains will be encoded in the planning system, it is also necessary that the solution to the frame problem not be too cumbersome. For example, one does not want to have to write a large number of frame axioms for each new action that is defined.

The planning-representation problem involves representing the domain. goals, and operators. Operators are the system's representation of actions that may be performed in the domain or, in the hierarchical case, abstractions of actions that can be performed in the domain. An operator includes a description of how each action changes the state of the world. In a logical formalism such as Rosenschein's adaptation of dynamic logic to planning [8], the same representational formalism may be used for representing the domain, goals. and operators. However, in many planners more concerned with efficiency, including SIPE, there is a different representation for each. The goal is to have a rich enough representation so that many interesting domains can be represented (an advantage of logical formalisms), but this must be measured against the ability of the system to deal with its representations efficiently during the planning process.

3.1. Representation of domain objects and goals

The system provides for representation of domain objects and their invariant properties by nodes linked in a hierarchy. This permits SIPE to incorporate the advantages of frame-based systems (primarily, efficiency), while retaining the power of the predicate calculus for repesenting properties that do vary. Most previous domain-independent planners have used a single representation. Invariant properties do not change as actions planned by the system are performed (e.g., the size of a frying pan does not change when something is cooked in it). Each node can have attributes associated with it and can inherit properties from other nodes in the hierarchy. The values of attributes may be numbers, pointers to other nodes, key words the system recognizes, or any arbitrary string (which can be used only by checking whether it is equal to another such string). The attributes are an integral part of the system, since planning variables contain constraints on the values of attributes of possible instantiations. Constraints are an important part of the system and are discussed in considerable detail later. There are different node types for representing variables, objects, and classes, but these will not be discussed in detail here, since they are similar to those occurring in many representation formalisms—for example, semantic networks and UNITS [11].

All parts of the system are actually nodes in this hierarchy; for example, procedural net nodes, operators, and goals are represented as nodes in the hierarchy. However, unlike variables and domain objects, these latter nodes are near the top of the hierarchy and make use of neither the inheritance of properties nor the constraints on attribute values. The use of a uniform formalism for all parts of the system has been helpful both in implementation and in interaction with users.

A restricted form of first-order predicate calculus is used to represent properties of domain objects and the relationships among them that may change with the performance of actions; it is also therefore used to describe goals as well as the preconditions and effects of operators. Quantifiers are allowed whenever they can be handled efficiently. Universal quantifiers are always permitted in effects, and over negated predicates in preconditions. Existential quantifiers can occur in the preconditions of operators, but not in the effects. Disjunction is also not allowed in effects. These restrictions result from using 'addlists' to solve the frame problem. (Why this is so is described in the next section.) By representing the invariant properties of the domain separately, SIPE reduces the number of formulas in the system and makes deductions more efficient. There is currently no provision for creating or destroying objects as actions are executed, although in some domains this would be useful (e.g., after an omelet has been made, do the original three eggs still exist as objects?).

3.2. Representation of operators

Operators representing actions the system may perform contain information about the objects that participate in the actions (represented as resources and arguments of the actions), what the actions are attempting to achieve (their goals), the effects of the actions when they are performed, and the conditions necessary before the actions can be performed (their preconditions). Before SIPE's representation is described in detail, some basic assumptions made by SIPE about the effects of actions need to be presented.

Determining the state of the world after actions have been performed is

the planner must ascertain whether the intended goals have been achieved), involves solving the frame problem. Here we make what Waldinger [16] has called the STRIPS assumption, which is that all relations mentioned in the world remain unchanged unless an action in the plan specifies that some relation has changed. In STRIPS, an action specifies that a relation has changed by mentioning it on an 'addlist' or 'deletelist'. SIPE is actually an extension of this idea, since it allows some of the changed relations to be deduced instead of being mentioned explicitly in the operators. However, all deduced effects are mentioned explicitly in the final plan, so the basic approach to the frame problem is the same. An alternative to making the STRIPS assumption would be to deduce all changes from general frame axioms. That approach was not taken in SIPE because the deduction problem is large and must be tightly controlled.

Making this assumption imposes requirements on the formalism used for representing the domain, since it must support the STRIPS assumption. While the STRIPS assumption may be very limiting in the representation of rich domains, such as automatic programming, there are many domains of interest for which it causes no problems. For example, the fairly simple environments in which robot arms often operate appear adequately representable in a system embodying the STRIPS assumption. SIPE currently makes the closed-world assumption: any negated predicate is true unless the unnegated form of the predicate is explicitly given in the model or in the effects of an action that has been performed. This is not critical; the system could be changed to assume that a predicate's truth-value is unknown unless an explicit mention of the predicate is found in either negated or unnegated form. (Although in large domains, there may be an enormous number of predicates that are not true.) Deduction in SIPE does not violate the closed-world assumption; it is used only to deduce effects of an action when the action is added to a plan (thus sparing the operator that represents the action from having to specify these effects).

Many features combine to make SIPE's operator description language an improvement over operator descriptions in previous systems. These features will be presented by discussing the sample operator given in Fig. 1, with subsections devoted to the more important features. SIPE has produced correct parallel plans for problems in four different domains, one of which is the blocks world (described in [9]) for which many domain-independent planning systems (e.g., NONLIN and NOAH) have presented solutions. To facilitate comparison with these systems, a PUTON operator for the blocks world in the SIPE formalism is shown in Fig. 1.

3.2.1. *Interfacing different levels of description*

The operator's effects, preconditions, purpose, and goal are all encoded as first-order predicates on variables and objects in the domain. (In this case,

```
OPERATOR: PUTON
ARGUMENTS: BLOCK1, OBJECT1; OBJECT1 IS NOT BLOCK1;
PURPOSE: (ON BLOCK1 OBJECT1);
PLOT:

    PARALLEL
        BRANCH 1:
            GOALS: (CLEARTOP OBJECT1);
            ARGUMENTS: OBJECT1;
        BRANCH 2:
            GOALS: (CLEARTOP BLOCK1);
            ARGUMENTS: BLOCK1;
    END PARALLEL

    PROCESS
        ACTION: PUTON.DETAILED;
        ARGUMENTS: OBJECT1;
        RESOURCES: BLOCK1;
        EFFECTS: (ON BLOCK1 OBJECT1);
    END
```

FIG. 1. A PUTON operator in SIPE.

BLOCK1 and OBJECT1 are variables.) Negated predicates that occur in the effects of an operator essentially remove from the model a fact that was true before, but is no longer true. Although the operator in Fig. 1 has no precondition, operators may specify preconditions that must obtain in the world state before the operator can be applied. The concept of precondition here differs from its counterpart in some planners, since the system will make no effort to make the precondition true. A false precondition simply means that the operator is not appropriate. Conditions that the planner should make true (which may be referred to as preconditions in other planners) are expressed as goals (e.g., the CLEARTOP goals in Fig. 1, which are described below).

Separating this idea of precondition from the goals gives SIPE greater flexibility for two reasons. First, it is plausible that some domains may have actions that will work in certain (possibly undesirable) situations, but that one would not want to work to achieve such a situation for the sake of performing that action. SIPE can easily represent this, whereas a planner that tried to achieve all preconditions might try to make the situation worse in order to apply its 'emergency' operators. Essentially, SIPE is representing knowledge on *how* to achieve goals (i.e., do not try to achieve preconditions). In the general case, there might be still more types of 'precondition', each providing different instructions for how to achieve the goals in the precondition. Second, SIPE's preconditions are useful for connecting different levels of detail in the hierarchy. The precondition of an operator might specify that certain higher-level conditions must be true, while the operator itself specifies goals at a more detailed level. This provides an interface between two different levels of description that was not present in NOAH. In addition, SIPE's preconditions are important for representing deductive operators as described in Section 3.6.

For example, consider the PUTON.DETAILED operator in Fig. 1. The reason for planning at this most abstract level with PUTON: (and a CLEAR operator that is not shown) is to produce a series of PUTON.DETAILED operators that will move the blocks in the correct order. The PUTON.DETAILED operator would then plan the next level of detail, perhaps planning approach vectors to the blocks and finger-moving actions so that commands for a robot arm could be generated. The precondition for PUTON.DETAILED could specify (CLEARTOP BLOCK1) and (CLEARTOP OBJECT1). These goals should have been achieved at a higher level; if they have not, one would not want to plan them at this level of detail. Rather one should go up the hierarchy and plan them at the proper level. With proper operators in a perfect world where planning always begins at the highest level, this would be a redundant check (though still useful for explanatory purposes). In an imperfect world, this technique can be useful for replanning during execution monitoring and for detecting inappropriate commands given by the user interactively (e.g., to plan an action down to a lower level before the proper higher-level goals have been achieved).

The ability to interface between levels is further enhanced by allowing operators to specify the 'purpose' they are trying to achieve at both levels of detail. The PURPOSE attribute of the operator specifies what it is trying to achieve at the lower level of detail and is used to determine plan rationale as described in Section 3.5. The GOAL attribute of an operator specifies what the operator is trying to achieve at the higher level of detail. This is used to determine when to apply the operator (i.e., what goals it will solve). For example, the PUTON.DETAILED operator might have (ON BLOCK1 OBJECT1) as its GOAL, but might also have a PURPOSE that mentions actual coordinates planned about at the lower level of detail. The operator in Fig. 1 does not have a GOAL attribute (in which case SIPE's default is to use the PURPOSE attribute to serve the function of both the PURPOSE and GOAL attributes). A GOAL attribute is not needed here, since both levels of description are the same (i.e., blocks with ON and CLEARTOP predicates). The ability of the formalism to interface two levels of description is important because the real advantage of hierarchical planning stems from the ability to employ different levels of abstraction.

3.2.2. Plots

Operators contain a plot that specifies how the action is to be performed in terms of actions and goals. Like plans, plots are represented as procedural networks. When used by the planning system, the plot can be viewed as instructions for expanding a node in the procedural network to the next level. The plot may specify the next level in the plan at the current one (e.g., in NOAH's blocks world the level of description never changes), or at a more detailed level of description. The plot of an operator can be described either in terms of goals to be achieved (i.e., a predicate to make true), or in terms of processes to be invoked (i.e., an action to be performed). (NOAH represented a process as a goal with only a single choice of action.) Encoding a step as a process implies that only the action it defines can be taken at that point, while encoding a step as a goal implies that any action can be taken that will achieve the goal. Another less explicit difference between encoding a step as a goal or as a process is whether the emphasis is on the situation to be achieved or the actual action being performed.

During planning, an operator is used to expand an already existing GOAL or PROCESS node in the procedural network to produce additional procedural network structure at the next level. For example, the PUTON operator might be applied to a GOAL node in a plan whose goal predicate is (ON A B). Operators contain lists of resources and arguments to be matched with the resources and arguments of the node being expanded. In our example, A and B in the GOAL node are matched with BLOCK1 and OBJECT1 in the PUTON operator when the operator is used to expand the node. The plot of the operator is used as a template for generating two GOAL nodes and one PROCESS node in the plan.

Operators in SIPE provide for posting of constraints on variables, specification of resources, explicit representation of the rationale behind each action, and the use of deduction to determine the effects of actions. Each feature is described below in some detail. SIPE also provides the ability to apply the plots of operators to lists of objects. Variables in an operator can be instantiated to a list of objects by calling a generator function given in the GENERATOR attribute of the CLASS node of the variable. For example, suppose BLOCKS1 is a variable in an operator and the CLASS node for BLOCKS in the sort hierarchy has a function as the value of its GENERATOR attribute. In this case, application of that operator will result in the function being called to instantiate BLOCKS1 (e.g., to a list of blocks). The plot of the operator may then contain an ITERATE-BEGIN and an ITERATE-END, and the plot within these tokens will be reproduced in the resultant procedural net—once for each block in the list BLOCKS1. For example, a CLEARTOP goal could be generated for each block in the list. This is useful for generating paths to move along in the aircraft operations domain, as described in the section on performance.

3.3. Constraints

One of SIPE's most important advances over previous domain-independent planning systems is its ability to construct partial descriptions of unspecified objects. This ability is important both for domain representation (e.g., objects with varying degrees of abstractness can be represented in the same formalism) and for finding solutions efficiently (since decisions can be delayed until partial descriptions provide more information). The subsections below describe the constraint language, explain how it is incorporated into the system, and compare it with other systems. Since almost no previous domain-independent planning systems have used this approach (e.g., NOAH cannot partially describe objects), the constraints in SIPE will be documented in some detail.

3.3.1. SIPE's constraint language

Planning variables that do not yet have an instantiation (these are INDEFINITE nodes in the sort hierarchy) can be partially described by setting constraints on the possible values an instantiation might take. This allows instantiation of the variable to be delayed until it is forced or until as much information as possible has been accumulated, thus preventing incorrect choices from being made. Constraints may place restrictions on the properties of an object (e.g., requiring certain attribute values for it in the sort hierarchy), and may also require that certain relationships exist between an object and other objects (e.g., predicates that must be satisfied in a certain world state). SIPE provides a general language for expressing these constraints on variable bindings so they can be encoded as part of the operator. During planning, the system also generates constraints that are based on interactions within a plan, propagates them to variables in related parts of the network, and finds variable bindings that satisfy all constraints.

The allowable constraints in SIPE on a variable V are listed below:

—CLASS. This constrains V to be in a specific class in the sort hierarchy. In SIPE's operator description language there is implicit typing based on the variable name; therefore, in the PUTON operator in Fig. 1, the variable created for BLOCK1 has a CLASS constraint that requires the instantiation for the variable to be a member of the class BLOCKS. Similarly, the OBJECT1 variable has a CLASS constraint for class OBJECTS.

—NOT-CLASS. V must be instantiated so that it is not a member of a given class.

—PRED. V must be instantiated so that a given predicate (in which V is an argument of the predicate), is true. This results in an explicit number of choices for V's instantiation, since all true facts are known (by the closed-world assumption).

—NOT-PRED. V must be instantiated so that a given predicate (in which V is an argument of the predicate) is not true.

—SAME. V must be instantiated to the same object to which some other given variable is instantiated.

—NOT-SAME. V must not be instantiated to the same object to which some other given variable is instantiated. In the PUTON operator in Fig. 1, the phrase "IS NOT BLOCK1" results in a NOT-SAME constraint being posted on both BLOCK1 and OBJECT1 that requires they not be instantiated to the same thing. Thus, if SIPE is looking for a place to put block A, it will not choose A as the place to put it.

—INSTAN. V must be instantiated to a given object. This could be represented by using SAME applied to objects as well as variables (or using PRED with an EQ predicate), but instantiation is a basic function of the system and warrants its own constraint for a slight gain in efficiency.

—NOT-INSTAN. V must not be instantiated to a given object.

—OPTIONAL-SAME. This is similar to SAME, but merely specifies a preference and is not binding. For example, one would prefer to conserve resources by making two variables be the same object, but, if this is not possible, then different objects are acceptable.

—OPTIONAL-NOT-SAME. This is similar to NOT-SAME, but is not binding. If SIPE notices that a conflict will occur between two parallel actions if two variables are instantiated to the same object, then it will post an OPTIONAL-NOT-SAME constraint on both variables. If it is possible to instantiate them differently, a conflict is avoided. If it is not, they may be made the same—but the system will have to resolve the ensuing conflict (perhaps by not doing things in parallel).

—Any attribute name. This requires a specific value for a specific attribute of an object. For example, the PUTON operator could have specified "BLOCK1 WITH COLOR RED". This would have created a constraint on BLOCK1 requiring the COLOR attribute (in the sort hierarchy) of any possible instantiation to have the value RED. For attributes with numerical values, 'greater than' and 'less than' can also be used. In planning an airline schedule, for example, the operator used for cross-country flights might contain the following variable declaration: "PLANE1 WITH RANGE GREATER THAN 3000".

3.3.2. Using constraints

Constraints add considerably to the complexity of the planner because they interact with all parts of the system. For example, to determine if a goal predicate is true, SIPE must verify whether it matches predicates that are effects earlier in the plan. This may require matching the variables that are arguments to the two predicates, which in turn involves determining whether the constraints on the variables are compatible. In a similar way, constraints also interact with the deductive capability of the system (to be described later). Constraints also affect critics, since determining if two concurrent actions interact may depend on whether their constraints are compatible. SIPE must also solve a general constraint satisfaction problem with reasonable efficiency, although how to control the amount of processing spent on constraint satisfaction is an open and important question. SIPE currently uses a simple and straightforward constraint satisfaction algorithm, though it is modular and replaceable.

During planning, SIPE assumes that it is possible to satisfy any constraint that it cannot prove unsatisfiable. Actual checking by running the constraint satisfaction routine is done only once per level in the hierarchy by the automatic search (as currently implemented). It can also be invoked by a user interactively. This is a good strategy because SIPE discovers most unsatisfiable constraints quickly by using the PRED constraint, which is quite powerful, and by immediately propagating many consequences as soon as constraints are posted.

When SAME and NOT-SAME constraints are added to a variable, similar constraints are immediately propagated to all other variables involved. (This may result in forced instantiations.) Whenever a constraint other than these two is added to a variable, the system verifies that at least one object satisfies all the constraints on this variable. This is fast because of efficient retrieval from the sort hierarchy and because PRED constraints store explicit disjunctive lists of possible instantiations. If only one possible instantiation remains for a variable, that instantiation is made immediately; if no instantiations remain, the current search branch fails immediately.

By accumulating PRED constraints on a variable, the system is assured that any object satisfying all the constraints on a variable will have all the properties required by the plan. A failure in constraint satisfaction can occur only when chains of SAME or NOT-SAME constraints prevent compatible assignments to different variables (each of which has an acceptable instantiation modulo those constraints). For these reasons, most problems are discovered quickly; thus, only occasional checking of the entire constraint satisfaction problem yields acceptable performance.

3.3.3. *Comparison with other systems*

The use of constraints is a major advance over previous domain-independent planning systems. NOAH, for example, would have to represent every property of an object as a predicate and then, to get variables properly instantiated, would have each such predicate as a precondition of an operator or a goal in the plan. In SIPE an operator might declare a variable as "CARGOPLANE1 WITH RANGE 3000" and the plan using this variable can assume it has the proper type of aircraft. In NOAH goals similar to (CARGOPLANE X) and (RANGE X 3000) would have to be included in the operator and achieved as part of the plan. This makes both the operators and plans much longer and harder to use and understand.

In addition to syntactic sugar, constraints in SIPE improve efficiency and expressibility. The constraint satisfaction algorithm used in SIPE takes advantage of the fact that invariant properties of objects are stored directly in the sort hierarchy. The lookup of such properties is much more efficient than the process of looking through the plan to determine which predicates are currently true, as would have to be done in systems like NOAH and NONLIN. In SIPE, finding a cargoplane with the proper range is accomplished with a single efficient lookup in the sort hierarchy. In NOAH, a cargoplane would be chosen without regard to its range, and the range goal may later fail. If NOAH were to backtrack (in actuality it would fail), it would still have to search the whole space in the worst case, going through the overhead of frame reasoning on each lookup. The OPTIONAL-SAME and OPTIONAL-NOT-SAME constraints used in resource reasoning increase expressibility as they cannot be expressed as goals or preconditions in a system like NOAH.

Some domain-dependent systems make use of constraints. Stefik's system [11], one of the few existing planning systems with the ability to construct partial descriptions of an object without identifying it, operates in the domain of molecular genetics. Our system extends Stefik's approach in three ways.

(1) We provide an explicit, general set of constraints that can be used in many domains. Stefik does not present a list of allowable constraints in his system; moreover, some of them that are mentioned seem specifically related to the genetics domain.

(2) Constraints on variables can be evaluated before the variables are fully instantiated. For example, a set can be created that is constrainable to be only bolts, then to be longer than one inch and shorter than two inches, then to have hex heads. This set can be used in planning before its members are identified in the domain.

(3) Partial descriptions can vary with the context, thus permitting simultaneous consideration of alternative plans involving the same unidentified objects. This is described in more detail in the section on search control.

3.4. Resources

One of the major contributions of SIPE is the ability to reason about resources. The formalism for representing operators includes a means of specifying that some of the variables associated with an action or goal will actually serve as resources for the action or goal (e.g., BLOCK1 is declared as a resource in the PUTON.PRIMITIVE action of the PUTON operator in Fig. 1). Resources are to be employed during a particular action and then released, just as a frying pan is used while vegetables are being sauteed in it. Reasoning about resources is a common phenomenon. It is a useful way of representing many domains (e.g., planning an airline flight schedule or planning the cooking of a meal), a natural way for humans to think about problems, and, consequently, an important aid to interaction with the system.

SIPE has specialized knowledge for handling resources: declaration of a resource associated with an action is a way of saying that one precondition of the action is that the resource be available. Mechanisms in the planning system, as they allocate and deallocate resources, automatically check for resource conflicts and ensure that these availability preconditions will be satisfied. One advantage of resources, therefore, is that they help in the axiomatization and representation of domains. The user of the planning system does not have to axiomatize the availability of resources in the domain operators as a precondition. (Such an axiomatization may be difficult, since the critics must use the representation correctly to recognize problems caused by the unavailability of resources.)

Resources enable SIPE's operators and plans to be more succinct and easier to understand than similar operators and plans in domain-independent parallel

to this node, and the rationale for that node being in the plan is that it achieves the higher-level goal. If the operator does not have a PURPOSE attribute, the default is to copy the effects down to the last node of the expansion. In NOAH the assumption was that the last node of an expansion achieved the main purpose, so the effects were always copied down to that node. SIPE therefore provides additional flexibility—for example, operators that include some 'clean-up' or normalization after accomplishing their goal can be represented correctly.

SIPE also keeps track of the rationale for each node that is not there to achieve some higher-level goal. Such a node is put in a plan for the purpose of preparing some later action at that level, and this fact must be recorded so the planner will be able to determine how long a goal condition must be maintained. Nodes within the plot of a SIPE operator may specify later nodes in the plot as the action they are preparing, thus explicitly stating the scope of the node. If no such scope is specified, the default (which takes advantage of the above flexibility) is that the scope of all nodes in the expansion before the node that achieves the purpose of the operator runs to that 'main-purpose' node.

For example, if an expansion consists of three nodes, it may be the case that the first prepares the second, which in turn prepares the third, or it may be that the first two both prepare the third (which we'll consider to be the 'main purpose' of the expansion). NOAH always assumes the latter case is true, which is the default in SIPE if no scoping information is present in the operator. However, SIPE also provides the ability to represent the first case, since the first node could explicitly state that its scope was to last only until the second node. This is important for correcting problematic parallel interactions within a plan and for execution monitoring. If the goal achieved by the first node suddenly became unexpectedly false after the second node was executed (but before execution of the third node), SIPE could perceive that there is no problem, since the first node had to be maintained only until the second node. Such an ability seems desirable. For example, one might wish to represent the operator for seasoning stew as 'open the cupboard', then 'pick up a bay leaf', then 'put bay leaf in stew'. If the cupboard closes after the bay leaf is in hand but before it is put into the stew, the planner should realize that there is no problem.

An alternative approach would be to always have the scope last only until the next node. However, one might want to represent the same operator as 'take the lid off the stew pot', then 'pick up the bay leaf', then 'put bay leaf in the stew'. In this case, it is a problem if the lid is put back prematurely. Whether or not it is possible to solve these problems by using only the default method for scoping (by forcing the user to write possibly contorted operators), the freedom to write operators naturally in unforeseen domains seems to be an advantage. SIPE's ability to represent scoping explicitly provides this added flexibility, and represents an advance over NOAH. HACKER [12] and many

planning systems, such as NOAH and NONLIN. In the latter systems, resource availability would have to be correctly axiomatized, checked, and updated in the preconditions and effects of the operators. It is not clear that it would be possible to do this so that the critics would recognize only the intended conflicts. If it were indeed possible, the resource reasoning in SIPE would be much more efficient than such an axiomatization in the other systems. For example, in NOAH the resolve-conflicts critic would eventually have to notice that posted 'available-resource' effects are in conflict. This could be done only after the entire plan had been expanded and the critics applied. Even then, conflicts between uninstantiated variables might not be detected, since only in an attempt to instantiate them would an actual conflict arise. In SIPE it is known which resources an operator needs before it is expanded. This can result in choosing operators that do not produce conflicts, thereby pruning the search space. SIPE avoids not only the immediate incorrect operator expansion, but also both the entire expansion to the next level and the application of the critics after that. The savings can be considerable in domains that use resources heavily. SIPE can also detect conflicts between uninstantiated variables; if a plan requires two arms as resources and only one arm exists in the world, SIPE can detect this conflict even though the two arm variables have not been instantiated.

The concept of resource implemented in SIPE is fairly limited. More details on how resources are used are given in Section 4.

3.5. Plan rationale

SIPE provides more flexibility in specifying the rationale behind a plan than many domain-independent planners. (The rationale for an action in a plan is 'why' the action is in the plan.) This is needed for determining how long a condition must be maintained, what changes in the world cause problems in the plan, and what the relationship is among different levels in the hierarchy. SIPE constructs links, both between the levels of a plan and within a level, that help express the rationale behind the actions. Both of these are discussed below.

In the procedural networks that represent plans, PROCESS and GOAL nodes represent an action to be performed or a goal to be achieved. When a node is planned to a greater level of detail by applying an operator, the expansion may consist of many nodes. To ascertain when the effects of the higher-level node become true in the more detailed expansion, it must first be established which node in the expansion achieves the higher-level goals. Each operator in SIPE has a PURPOSE attribute that specifies a conjunction of predicates, which is the main purpose of any expansion produced with this operator. When the operator is used to produce an expansion, this PURPOSE attribute is used to determine the node in the piece of procedural net produced by the expansion that achieves the operator's purpose. The higher-level effects are then copied down

systems based on logic are flexible in this manner and NONLIN uses its 'goal structure' to provide most of the benefits described above.

3.6. Deductive operators

In addition to operators describing actions. SIPE allows specification of deductive operators that deduce facts from the current world state. As more complex domains are represented, it becomes increasingly important to deduce the effects of actions from axioms about the world, rather than explicitly representing these effects in operators. Deduction is also necessary for execution monitoring. For example, a sensor might tell the planner that the finger separation of the robot arm has suddenly become zero. The planner must then deduce that the arm is no longer holding block *A* and that the location of block *A* is no longer known.

Domain-independent planners that have used a NOAH-like approach (as opposed to a theorem-proving approach) have not had a deductive capability. Although the addition of some deductive capability is straightforward, it is more difficult to find a good balance between expressibility and efficiency. SIPE provides a deductive capability that is useful, but nevertheless keeps deduction under control by severely restricting the deductions that can be made. The importance of this ability will become more significant as execution monitoring capabilities are expanded.

The deductions that are permitted by SIPE have proved to be useful. For example, the PUTON operator in Fig. 1 lists only (ON BLOCK1 OBJECT1) as an effect. It does not mention which objects are or are not now CLEARTOP, since that is deduced by deductive operators. Because deductive operators in SIPE may include both existential and universal quantifiers, they provide a rich formalism for deducing (possibly conditional) effects of an action. Effects that are deduced in SIPE are considered to be side effects. (Operators can also specify effects as either main or side effects.) Knowing which ones are side effects is important in handling parallel interactions (see next section).

Fig. 2 shows one of the deductive operators in the SIPE blocks world for deducing CLEARTOP relationships. Deductive operators are written in the same formalism as other operators in SIPE, thus permitting the system to control deduction with the same mechanisms it uses to control the application of operators. This also allows constraints to be used and, as this example shows, they play a major role in SIPE's deductive capability.

All deductions that can be made are performed at the time an operator is expanded. The deduced effects are recorded in the procedural net, and the system can proceed just as if all the effects had been listed in the operator. Deductions are not attempted at other points in the planning process. Deductive operators have triggers to control their application. The DCLEAR operator in Fig. 2 is applied whenever an expansion is produced that has an effect which

```
DEDUCTIVE.OPERATOR: DCLEAR
  ARGUMENTS: OBJECT1,OBJECT2,BLOCK3 IS NOT OBJECT2,
             OBJECT4 CLASS EXISTENTIAL IS NOT OBJECT1;
  TRIGGER: (ON OBJECT1 OBJECT2);
  PRECONDITION: (ON OBJECT1 BLOCK3), (NOT (ON OBJECT4 OBJECT3));
  EFFECTS: (CLEARTOP BLOCK3);
```

FIG. 2. A deductive operator in SIPE.

matches (ON OBJECT1 OBJECT2). Deductive operators have no instructions for expanding a node to a greater level of detail. Instead, if the precondition of a deductive operator holds, its effects can be added to the world model (in the same context in which the precondition matched) without changing the existing plan. This may 'achieve' some goal in the plan (by deducing that it has already been achieved), thereby making it unnecessary to plan actions to achieve it. In Fig. 2, matching the precondition will bind BLOCK3 to the block that OBJECT1 was on before it moved to OBJECT2. Since OBJECT4 is constrained to be in the EXISTENTIAL class (see below) and is constrained to not be OBJECT1, the precondition will match (and CLEARTOP of BLOCK3 deduced) only if OBJECT1 is the only object on BLOCK3 (just before moving OBJECT1 to OBJECT2).

The method used for specifying variables as existentially quantified (i.e., constraining them to be in the EXISTENTIAL class) does not provide scoping information. Since only certain types of quantifiers are permitted for efficiency reasons, SIPE interprets preconditions according to defaults that are somewhat non-standard. The scope of each EXISTENTIAL variable appearing as an argument in a predicate is local to that predicate. Each predicate effectively gets a different existential variable. In addition, negated predicates are interpreted as having the quantifier within the scope of the negation. Thus, the variable is effectively universally quantified for negated predicates. As an example, with x declared EXISTENTIAL, the precondition $P(x) \land \neg Q(x)$ is interpreted as $\exists x.P(x) \land \neg\exists x.Q(x)$ (or equivalently, $\exists x.P(x) \land \forall x.\neg Q(x)$). These restrictions make use of SIPE's representation (e.g., the fact that negated predicates are treated differently) to permit handling quantifiers efficiently.

Besides simplifying operators, deductive operators are important in many domains for their ability to represent conditional effects. In NOAH's blocks world, only one block may be on top of another. Consequently, whenever a block is moved, the operator for the move action can be written to state explicitly the effect that the block underneath will be clear. In the more general case in which one large block might have many smaller blocks on top of it, there may or may not be another block on the block underneath, so the effects of the action must be conditional upon this. Since systems like NOAH and NONLIN must mention effects explicitly (universally or existentially quantified variables are not allowed in the description of effects), they cannot represent this more general case with a single move operator. These systems would need two move operators—one for the one-block-on-top case, another for the many-blocks-on-top case. Furthermore, the preconditions for separation of the cases would add an undesirable complication to the representation of the operators.

As the above example shows, SIPE's deductive operators allow certain quantifiers and are powerful enough to handle the general case mentioned. Since SIPE can deduce all the clearing and unclearing effects that occur in the blocks world, the operators themselves do not need to represent them. As domains grow to include many operators, this becomes very convenient. Deductive operators provide a way to distinguish side effects, which can be important. By the use of deduction, more complicated blocks worlds can be represented more elegantly in SIPE than in previous domain-independent planners.

4. Parallel Interactions

As noted before, parallelism is considered beneficial, since optimal plans in many domains require it. (Two segments of a plan are in parallel if the partial ordering of the plan does not specify that one segment must be done before the other.) The approach used in SIPE, therefore, is to keep as much parallelism as possible and then to detect and respond to interactions between parallel branches of a plan. There are three aspects to this situation: recognizing interactions between branches; correcting harmful interactions that keep the plan from accomplishing its overall goal; taking advantage of helpful interactions on parallel branches so as not to produce inefficient plans.

This section first defines helpful and harmful interactions, then describes new features and heuristics in SIPE that aid in handling them. These fall into four areas:

(1) reasoning about resources, which is the major contribution of SIPE;
(2) using constraints to generate correct parallel plans;
(3) explicitly representing the rationale behind each action and goal to help solve harmful interactions correctly;
(4) taking advantage of helpful interactions.

SIPE's abilities to handle parallel actions are best described in the context of a sample problem. The canonical simple problem for thinking about parallel interactions is the three-blocks problem. Blocks A, B, and C are on a table or on one another. The goal is to achieve (ON A B) in conjunction with (ON B C), thus constructing a three-block tower. (Initially the two goals are represented as being in parallel.) To move the blocks, there is a PUTON operator (see Fig. 1, for example) that puts OBJECT1 on OBJECT2. It specifies the goals of making both OBJECT1 and OBJECT2 clear before performing a primitive move action. (The table is assumed to be always clear and a block is clear only when no block is on top of it.) This problem will be utilized below to provide examples of interactions.

4.1. Defining helpful and harmful interactions

If two branches of a plan are in parallel, an interaction is defined to occur when a goal that is trying to be achieved in one branch (at any level in the hierarchy) is made either true or false by an action in the other branch. Since the actions in a plan explicitly list their effects (a feature shared by many planners, such as NOAH and NONLIN), it is always possible to recognize such interactions. (In a hierarchical planner, however, they may not appear until lower levels of the hierarchy of both branches have been planned.) By requiring that a goal be involved in the interaction, we attempt to eliminate interactions that do not affect the outcome of the plan. For this to succeed, the domain must be encoded so that all important relationships are represented as goals at some level. As we shall see later, this is reasonable in SIPE.

The planner can possibly take advantage of a situation in which a goal in one branch is made true in another branch (a helpful interaction). Suppose we solve the three-blocks problem, starting with A and C on the table with B on A. In solving the (ON B C) parallel branch, the planner will plan to move B onto C, thus making A clear and C not clear. Now, while an attempt is made to move A onto B in the (ON A B) branch, the goal of making A clear becomes part of the plan. Since A is not clear in the initial state, the planner may decide to make it true by moving B from A to the table (after which it will move A onto B). In this case it would be better to recognize the helpful effect of making A clear, which happens in the parallel branch. Then the planner could decide to do (ON B C) first, after which both A and B are clear and the (ON A B) goal is easily accomplished.

The planner must decide whether or not to add more ordering constraints to the plan to take advantage of such helpful interactions. Ordering the parallel branches sequentially is the best solution to this problem because (ON B C) must be done first in any case, but in other problems an ordering suggested to take advantage of helpful effects may be the wrong thing to do from the standpoint of eventually achieving the overall goal. In general, the planner cannot make such an ordering decision without error unless it completely investigates all the consequences of such a decision. Since this is not always practical or desirable, planning systems use heuristics to make such decisions. If an interaction is detected that makes a goal false in a parallel branch, there is a problematic (i.e., possibly harmful) interaction, which may mean that the plan is not a valid solution. For example, suppose the planner does not recognize the helpful interaction in our problem and proceeds to plan to put B on the table and A on B in the (ON A B) branch. The plan is no longer a valid solution (if it is assumed that one of the two parallel branches will be executed

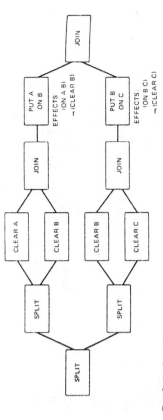

Fig. 3. A plan without resources.

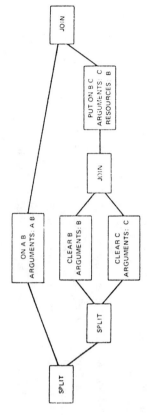

Fig. 4. A plan with resources.

before the other). The planner must recognize this by detecting the problematic interaction. Namely, the goal of having B clear in the (ON $B\ C$) branch is made false in the (ON $A\ B$) branch when A is put onto B. The planner must then decide how to rectify this situation.

As with helpful interactions, there is no easy way to solve harmful interactions. Here too a correct solution may require that all future consequences of an ordering decision be explored. Stratagems other than ordering may be necessary to solve the problem. For example, a new operator may perhaps need to be applied at a higher level. Consider the problem of switching the values of the two registers in a two-register machine. Applying the register-to-register move operator creates a harmful interaction that no ordering can solve, since a value is destroyed. The solution to this interaction involves applying a register-to-memory move operator at a high level in order to store one of the values temporarily. Correcting many types of harmful interactions efficiently seems very difficult in a domain-independent planner—domain specific heuristics may be required. SIPE simplifies the problem by not shuffling actions between two parallel branches (i.e. the problem must be solvable by leaving things in parallel or placing some number of entire parallel branches sequentially before the others.) Although this does prevent some elegant solutions from being found, it retains efficiency while not being overly restrictive.

4.2. Reasoning about resources

The formalism for representing operators in SIPE includes a means of specifying that some of the variables associated with an action or goal actually serve as resources for that action or goal. As we have seen, one advantage of resources is that they help in the axiomatization and representation of domains. Another important advantage of resources is that they facilitate early detection of problematic interactions on parallel branches. The system does not allow one branch to use an object that is also a resource in a parallel branch.

The above example of achieving (ON $A\ B$) and (ON $B\ C$) as a conjunction shows how SIPE uses resource reasoning to help with parallel interactions. Fig. 3 depicts a plan that might be produced by NOAH or NONLIN (or by SIPE without making use of resource reasoning) for this problem. Fig. 4 shows a plan from SIPE using resources in the operators.

In NOAH and NONLIN, both original GOAL nodes are expanded with the PUTON operator or its equivalent. This produces a plan similar to the one shown in Fig. 3. The central problem is to be aware that B must be put on C before A is put on B (otherwise B will not be clear when it is to be moved onto C). NOAH and NONLIN both build up a table of multiple effects (TOME) that tabulates every predicate instance listed as an effect in the parallel expansions of the two GOAL nodes. Using this table, the programs detect that B is made clear in the expansion of (ON $B\ C$), but is made not clear in the (ON $A\ B$)

expansion. Both programs then solve this problem by doing (ON $B\ C$) first.

SIPE uses its resource heuristic to detect this problem and propose the solution without having to generate a TOME. (SIPE does do a TOME-like analysis to detect interactions that do not fit into the resource reasoning paradigm.) When some object is listed in an action as a resource, the system then prevents that particular object from being mentioned as either a resource or an argument in any action or goal that is in parallel. In the PUTON operator, the block being moved is listed as a resource in the primitive PUTON action. Thus, as soon as the expansion of (ON $B\ C$) with the PUTON operator is accomplished and the plan in Fig. 4 produced, SIPE recognizes that the plan is invalid because B is a resource in the expansion of (ON $B\ C$) and an argument in (ON $A\ B$). This can be detected without expanding the (ON $A\ B$) goal at all and without generating a TOME.

This efficient generation of the correct plan depends on listing the block being moved as a resource. This choice is based on domain-dependent heuristic knowledge, and seems reasonable. The robot arm that was moving the block would also be a resource if it were to be represented in the operator. The action of moving an object with an arm causes both the object and the arm to

allows the exact details of SIPE's resource reasoning to be explicated. Domains like cooking make more natural and advantageous use of resources to represent problems such as cooking four dishes in three pans on two burners. It should be noted that the concept of resource as implemented is quite limited. For example, we often think of money or computational power as resources, but these could not be represented in our current implementation. We do plan to implement conditions on *shared resources* in the future, which should express a wider range of resource concepts.

4.3. Constraints and resources assignment

SIPE can accumulate various constraints on unbound variables in a plan, which is useful for taking full advantage of resources to avoid harmful interactions. When variables that are not fully instantiated are listed as resources, the system posts constraints on the variables that point to other variables that are potential resource conflicts. When allocating resources, the system then attempts to instantiate variables so that no resource conflicts will occur. (See the OPTIONAL-NOT-SAME constraint in Section 3.) For example, if a robot arm is used as a resource in the block-moving operators, the system will try to use different robot arms (if they are available) on parallel branches, thus avoiding resource conflicts. If only one arm is available, it will be assigned to both parallel branches in the hope that the plan can later be ordered to resolve the conflict. In this way many harmful interactions are averted by intelligent assignment of resources.

4.4. Solving harmful interactions

The difficulty entailed in eliminating harmful interactions has already been discussed. However, if the system knows why each part of the plan is present, it can use this information to come up with reasonable solutions to some harmful interactions. Suppose a particular predicate is made false at some node on one parallel branch and true at another node on another parallel branch. Depending on the rationale for including these nodes in the plan, it may be the case that the predicate is not relevant to the plan (an extraneous side effect), or must be kept permanently true (the purpose of the plan), or must be kept only temporarily true (a precondition for later achievement of a purpose). SIPE's ability to specify a plan rationale flexibly and to separate side effects from main effects enables it to distinguish these 3 cases accurately, and therefore to represent more problems of this type accurately than could NOAH.

Solutions to a harmful interaction may depend on which of these cases holds. Let us call the three cases side effect, purpose, and precondition, respectively, and analyze the consequent possibilities. If the predicate in conflict on one branch is a precondition, one possible solution is to further order the plan, first doing the segment of the plan that extends from the precondition on through

be physically moved; therefore, they are considered to be resources of the action, since nothing in a parallel branch should try to use the arm, move the object, or even be dependent on their respective current locations. The other blocks are not considered resources because they are not used *during* the moving action (though they could also be specified as resources if desired). Resources can be viewed as a powerful tool that can be utilized by the writer of the operators to represent important domain specific knowledge concerning the behavior of actions.

Not allowing a resource to be mentioned as either a resource or an argument in any action or goal that is in parallel is a strong restriction (though useful in practice). Because this is sometimes too strong a restriction, so SIPE also permits the specification of *shared resources*, whereby a resource in one branch can be an argument in a parallel branch, but not a resource. In the future we would like to have predicates that specify sharing conditions, but this has not yet been implemented.

Resources help in solving harmful interactions, as well as in detecting them. In resource conflicts, no goal is made false on a parallel branch; however, if the resource availability requirements were axiomatized as precondition or goal predicates, an availability goal would be made false on a parallel branch. Thus, resource conflicts are considered to be harmful interactions. SIPE uses a heuristic for solving resource-argument conflicts. Such an interaction occurs when a resource in one parallel branch is used as an argument in another parallel branch (as distinguished from a resource-resource conflict, in which the same object is used as a resource in two parallel branches). This is the type of conflict that occurs in the plan in Fig. 4, since B is a resource in the primitive PUTON action and an argument in (ON A B).

SIPE's heuristic for solving a resource-argument conflict is to put the branch using the object as a resource before the parallel branch using the same object as an argument. In this way SIPE decides that (ON B C) must come before (ON A B) in Fig. 4. This is done without generating a TOME, without expanding the original (ON A B) node, and without analyzing the interaction. The assumption is that an object used as a resource will have its state or location changed by such use; consequently, the associated action must be done first to ensure that it will be 'in place' when later actions occur that employ it as an argument. The above argument may not be convincing, and certainly this heuristic is not guaranteed to be correct, but it is another tool provided by the system that has been proved useful in the four domains encoded in SIPE. By simply setting a flag, the user can prevent the employment of this heuristic if it is inappropriate for a particular domain.

Many interactions that would be harmful in the other systems are dealt with efficiently in SIPE by the resource-reasoning mechanisms. To take full advantage of resources, the system posts constraints. This capability is discussed briefly below. The blocks world example is used above because its simplicity

its corresponding purpose. Once this purpose has been accomplished, there will be no problem in negating the precondition later. This solution applies no matter which of the three cases applies to the predicate in the other conflicting branch.

In case both conflicting predicates are side effects, it is immaterial to us if the truth-value of the predicate changes and thus no real conflict exists. In the case of a side effect that conflicts with a purpose, one solution is to order the plan so that the side effect occurs before the purpose; thus, once the purpose has been accomplished it will remain true. When both conflicting predicates are purposes, there is no possible ordering that will achieve both purposes at the end of the plan. The planner must use a different operator at a higher level or plan to reachieve one of the purposes later. However, none of the above suggestions for dealing with interactions can be guaranteed to produce the best (according to some metric, e.g., shortest) solution.

This has been a brief summary of SIPE's algorithm for dealing with harmful interactions. Systems like NOAH and NONLIN do similar things. However, SIPE provides methods for more precise and efficient detection. It should be emphasized that many interactions that would be problematical in the other systems are dealt with in SIPE by the resource-reasoning mechanisms and therefore do not need to be analyzed. When interactions are being analyzed, SIPE requires that one of the conflicting predicates be a goal (not just a side effect) at some level in the hierarchy. In this way, interactions among side effects that pose no problems are not even detected. This requires that all important predicates be recognized as goals at some level, which is easily done in SIPE's hierarchical planning scheme. SIPE provides for exact expression of the purpose of any goal in its operators, which again leads to better analysis of interactions. The system also distinguishes between main and side effects at each node in the plan. This makes it easy to tell which predicates are of interest to us at any level of the plan without looking up the hierarchy (since higher-level goals will become main effects at lower-level actions).

4.5. Achieving goals through linearization

SIPE recognizes helpful interactions and will try to further order the plan to take advantage of them, although the user can control this interactively if he wishes. If a goal that must be made true on one parallel branch is actually made true on another parallel branch, the system will under certain conditions order the plan so that the other branch occurs first (if this causes no other conflicts).

NOAH was not able to take advantage of such helpful effects. (It did have an 'eliminate redundant preconditions' critic that eliminated preconditions that occurred twice in the plan, but this could not recognize and react appropriately to a single precondition that was an integral part of the plan being achieved unexpectedly during execution.) NONLIN, on the other hand, did have an ability to order the plan in this way. This is an important ability in many real-world domains, since helpful side effects occur frequently. For example, if parallel actions in a robot world both require the same tool, only one branch need plan to get the tool out of the tool box; the other branch should be able to recognize that the tool is already on the table.

5. Search Control

The automatic search in SIPE is a simple depth-first search to a given depth limit without using knowledge for making choices or backtracking. Although SIPE manipulates its representations efficiently, such a search will obviously not perform well on large, complex problems. The problems involved in planning at the metalevel to control the search are discussed below. The poor performance of automatic search is not debilitating in SIPE, since it has been designed and built to support interactive planning. The user can easily invoke planning operations at any level without being required to make tedious choices that could be performed automatically. In SIPE the user can direct low-level and specific planning operations (e.g., 'instantiate PLANE1 to N2636G', 'expand NODE 32 with the PUTON operator'), high-level operations that combine these lower-level ones (e.g., 'expand the whole plan one more level and correct any problems'), or operations at any level between the two (e.g., 'assign resources', 'expand NODE 32 with any operator', 'find and correct harmful interactions'). This interactive ability is quite useful, since the system can be guided through problems that would not be solved in a reasonable amount of time with the automatic search.

An interface to SIPE allows the above examples to be given graphically. This interface has been implemented on a high-resolution black-and-white bitmap display and a color-graphics terminal [7].[2] The planning choices available to the user appear in a menu from which one can be selected by pointing with a mouse or joystick. Similarly, steps in a plan (nodes in the network) can be referred to either by name or by pointing to them.

The procedural networks (plans) produced are presented graphically. The user can choose to view different portions of the plan, do so at different levels of detail, or can look at any alternative plans. The system also provides the information needed by a domain-specific package for displaying the domain configuration. Such a display package has been implemented for the aircraft domain. In this implementation, the user can see a graphic representation of either the actual domain configuration (principally the location of objects) or the one that will exist after some sequence of planned steps. The configuration,

[2] The Office of Naval Research Contract N00014-80-C-0300 supported the application of SIPE to the problem of aircraft spotting, during which the implementation of the interactive component was accomplished.

that planning about the planning process itself can be done in the same way as planning about the domain, enabling use of a single system architecture for both the planning system and its control structure. As Hayes says in [3]: "We need to be able to describe processing strategies in a language at least as rich as that in which we describe the external domains, and for good engineering, it should be the same language." This section makes two points: (1) metaplanning is a vague concept, and (2) interesting metaplanning appears very difficult in a system that makes the STRIPS assumption.

The idea of metaplanning must be clarified because the term is used in a vague way by many people. A major problem in being more precise about metaplanning is that there is often no clear dividing line between the external domain and the planning process (contrary to Wilensky's argument in [17]). Given any particular system, it will likely be obvious what is at a metalevel in that system. But any particular piece of knowledge might be encoded at either the metalevel or the domain level; furthermore, it is not always clear which is best. It is trivial to convert any domain operator into a metaoperator, and many metaoperators can probably be wired into the domain during design of the domain representation. Wilensky claims that metaplanning can be distinguished by the fact that "meta-goals are declarative structures": but certainly all goals in a planner can be declarative. He claims that another distinguishing characteristic is "meta-goals are domain-independent, encoding only knowledge about planning in general". Metagoals actually contain varying amounts of domain-dependent knowledge. Furthermore, this is necessary, since good planning strategies may differ for differing domains.

For example, consider the advice 'use existing objects'. This is a fairly domain-independent concept that is used by Sacerdoti in NOAH [9], and mentioned by Wilensky as a metagoal for metaplanning. However, this idea still involves domain knowledge. In the house-building domain, it is desirable to use the same piece of lumber to support both the roof and the sheetrock on the walls. But in another domain, this may not be a good strategy. On the space shuttle, one may want different functions to be performed by different objects so the plan will be more robust and less vulnerable to the failure of any one object. So the 'use existing objects' idea makes assumptions about the domain that need to be stated. (Perhaps one wants to apply this idea only to certain portions of the domain.) It would be reasonable to design a system in which such an idea was implemented at the lowest planning level and referred to domain objects (e.g., by automatically adding OPTIONAL-SAME constraints to variables). It would also be reasonable to use this idea in the metaplanner as advice to the 'instantiate-variable' planning operator. Thus, the idea contains some domain knowledge and could reasonably be implemented either as part of the domain or at a metalevel.

There are several domain-independent planners in the literature, but none of them does interesting metaplanning. Systems such as SIPE that do hierarchical

generally shown together with a plan or partial plan, corresponds to the expected state following execution of that plan.

One feature of SIPE not found in previous domain-independent planners is the ability to explore alternatives in parallel. This is advantageous in an interactive environment because it allows the user to conduct a best-first search easily. In addition to supporting breadth-first and depth-first planning, the interactive planning operations allow *islands* to be constructed in a plan (to arbitrary levels of detail), and then linked together later. The following sections describe the implementation of parallel alternatives and the use of metaplanning as a means of controlling the search.

5.1. Exploring alternatives in parallel

A context mechanism has been developed to allow constraints on a variable's value to be established relative to specific plan steps. Constraints on a variable's value, as well as its instantiation (possibly determined during the solution of a general constraint-satisfaction problem), can be retrieved only relative to a particular context. This permits the user to shift focus back and forth easily between alternatives.

SIPE accomplishes this in a hierarchical procedural-network paradigm by introducing CHOICE nodes in the procedural networks at each place an alternative can occur. Constraints are stored relative to choice points. Thus, the constraints on a variable at a given point in a plan can be accessed by specifying the path of choices in the plan that is to be followed to reach that point. Different constraints can be retrieved by specifying a different plan (path of choices). This shifting of focus among alternatives cannot be done in systems that use a backtracking algorithm, in which descriptions built up during expansion of one alternative are removed during the backtracking process before another alternative is investigated. Most other planning systems either do not allow alternatives (e.g., NOAH) or use a backtracking algorithm (e.g., Stefik's MOLGEN, NONLIN). An exception is the system described by Hayes-Roth et al. [4], in which a blackboard model is used to allow the shifting of focus among alternatives.

5.2. Metaplanning

The term *metaplanning* is widely used for referring to reasoning about the planning process itself. The control structure of a planning program (which is continually making choices in an attempt to find a plan) is doing metaplanning, though in SIPE only in an uninteresting way since the control structure is simple and contains little knowledge. (Of course, in SIPE the most abstract operators could be written to make use of metaplanning knowledge in a particular domain.) Many researchers have realized that metaplanning is an important element in being able to control the search efficiently, pointing out planning can use abstract operators to encode some metaplanning knowledge, but, as the next paragraph argues, the most interesting metaplanning ideas cannot be encoded in this manner. The only other metaplanning done in such systems is obscure search-control code; no metaknowledge is expressed in the domain-independent formalisms used in these systems for planning in the external domain. There is good reason for this, as these domain-independent formalisms are not adequate for expressing interesting metaknowledge.

These formalisms generally use a *model approach* to representation. (The STRIPS assumption implies a model approach.) Its essential characteristic is that all relationships that hold in the domain are expressed directly (e.g., disjunctions are now allowed), in the sense that the model can be queried in a lookup manner to return an answer quickly about the truth-value of a relationship. This efficient querying ability is, of course, the motivation for the model approach. This approach also means that add and delete lists can be used to solve the frame problem. The disadvantage of the model approach is that many things cannot be represented, since they do not admit to such direct representation. In particular, what we need to say about plans at a metalevel cannot fit easily into the model approach, as it will be hard to represent explicitly (for example) every property of a plan, a failed search branch, an operator, or a constraint that we might want to reason about at the metalevel. The point is that the domain language in these systems is not rich (since it must satisfy this model approach). In particular, it may not be rich enough to do interesting metaplanning, though some metalevel concepts are representable.

6. Execution Monitoring

In real-world domains, things do not always proceed as planned. Therefore, it is desirable to develop better execution-monitoring techniques and better capabilities to replan when things do not go as expected. This may involve planning for tests to verify that things are indeed going as expected. Such tests may be expensive (e.g., taking a picture with a computer vision system) so care must be taken in deciding when to use them. The problem of replanning is also critical. In complex domains it becomes increasingly important to use as much as possible of the old plan, rather than to start all over when things go wrong. SIPE has addressed only some of the problems of execution monitoring; research is continuing in this area. During execution of a plan in SIPE, some person or computer system monitoring the execution can specify what actions have been performed and what changes have occurred in the domain being modeled. In accordance with this, the plan can be updated interactively to cope with unanticipated occurrences. Planning and plan execution can be intermixed by producing a plan for part of an activity and then executing some or all of that plan before elaborating the remaining portion.

At any point in the plan, the user can inform the system of a predicate that is now true (though SIPE may have thought it was false). The program will look through the plan and find all the goals that are affected by this new predicate. Since SIPE understands the rationale of nodes in the plan, it can determine how changes affect the plan. For example, if a later purpose is suddenly and unexpectedly accomplished, SIPE can notice the helpful effect and eliminate a whole section of the plan because it knows the preparatory steps are only there to accomplish the purpose. If an unexpected occurrence causes a problem, the system will suggest all the solutions it can find. Problems can be identified because the rationale for goal nodes is given—SIPE can tell which goals must still be maintained and which have already served their purpose. SIPE's repertoire of techniques for finding such solutions is not very sophisticated, however. It includes:

(1) instantiating a variable differently (e.g., using a different resource if something has gone wrong with the one originally employed in the plan);

(2) finding relevant operators to accomplish a goal that is no longer true (and inserting the new subplan correctly into the original plan);

(3) finding a higher level from which to replan if the problems are widespread.

These few techniques are not trivial. Changing an instantiation involves checking the whole plan to see if any parts might be affected by the new instantiation. Inserting a new subplan in the original plan requires a similar check. SIPE's execution-monitoring capabilities are an extension of those in previous domain-independent planners primarily because the explicit representation of plan rationale allows more sophisticated replanning. The deductive capability is also useful for deducing the effects of unexpected occurrences.

Research is continuing in an effort to expand SIPE's execution-monitoring capabilities. After the deductive capabilities of the system have been improved, it will be able to deduce that something in unknown (as will often be the case during execution monitoring). Having unknown quantities will constitute a fundamental modification of SIPE—even the method of determining whether a predicate is true must be changed. SIPE will also be extended to produce conditional plans and to plan for the use of information-gathering actions. Thus, an unknown quantity might produce a plan with an action to perceive the unknown value, followed by a conditional plan that specifies the correct course of action for each possible outcome of the perception action. We also plan to extend the operator description language so that instructions for handling foreseeable errors can be included in operators. Initial investigations show that this ability will include the incorporation of metalevel predicates that are maintained by the system, for subsequent access by the error-handling instructions.

getting an agent who was currently at SRI to MIT, SIPE would effectively backward chain from the destination to produce solutions with several dozen nodes. The representation was effective and natural for this problem.

8. Conclusion

SIPE's operator description language was designed to be easy to understand (to enable graceful interaction) while being more powerful than those found in previous domain-independent planners. Constraints, resources, and deductive operators all contribute to the power of the representation. Deductive operators allow quantified variables and can therefore be used to make fairly sophisticated deductions, thus eliminating the need to express effects in operators when they can be deduced. They are also useful in distinguishing main effects from side effects.

One of the most important features of SIPE is its ability to constrain the possible values of variables. It is well known that this enables more efficient planning, since choices can be delayed until information has been accumulated. Other advantages of constraints, however, are also critical. A key consideration is that constraints allow convenient expression of a much wider range of problems. Constraint satisfaction finds variable instantiations efficiently by taking advantage of the fact that invariant properties of objects are encoded in the sort hierarchy. Constraints also help prevent harmful parallel interactions.

SIPE incorporates several new mechanisms that make it easier to deal with the parallel-interaction problem. The most significant of these mechanisms is the ability to reason about resources. It has been beneficial in user interaction to have reasoning about resources as a central part of the system, because resources seem to be a natural and intuitive way to think about objects in many domains. Combined with the system's ability to post constraints, resource reasoning helps the system to avoid many harmful interactions, to recognize sooner those interactions that do occur, and to solve some of these interactions more quickly. SIPE's handling of interactions is also improved by its ability to differentiate side effects and to determine correctly the rationale behind actions.

SIPE provides flexibility in specifying the rationale behind a plan. It is able to specify explicitly the scope of a condition and the node that accomplishes higher-level goals. This is useful for determining how long a condition must be maintained and what changes in the world cause problems in the plan, for finding solutions to such problems, and for determining the relationship among different levels in the hierarchy. SIPE also provides new mechanisms for interfacing between two different levels of hierarchical descriptions.

A major difference between SIPE and previous planners is that SIPE is interactive. Its interactive capabilities help the user guide and direct the planning process, thereby allowing alternative plans to be explored concur-

7. Performance of SIPE

SIPE has been tested in four different domains: an extended blocks world, cooking, aircraft operations, and a travel planning task. As these domains do not have large branching factors or search spaces, the automatic search can find solutions. The cooking domain was encoded to demonstrate resource reasoning. SIPE operators naturally represented requirements for frying pans and burners during the cooking of a dish. Problems such as cooking four dishes with three pans on two burners were handled efficiently by the resource reasoning mechanisms in SIPE. Handling a problem means producing plans for cooking as many dishes as possible in parallel, with enough serialization to get the task accomplished with the available resources. Such plans consisted of dozens of nodes in our simple cooking world.

The standard blocks world was encoded in SIPE, with some enrichments (e.g., more than one block could be on top of another). Use of deductive operators made the PUTON operator more readable. Resource reasoning enabled SIPE to find and correct parallel interaction problems quickly. All problems of building three- and five-block towers can be solved efficiently as long as they do not involve shuffling of actions between two parallel branches. A number of other problems involving properties of the blocks and quantifiers were also handled elegantly (making use of the constraints in SIPE). For example, the problem of getting *some* red block on top of *some* blue block is easily represented and solved. (SIPE will choose a red block and a blue block that are already clear, if such exist.) The blocks-world was also extended to include planning the utilization of the robot arm and the mating of two parts. (This means the system must deduce that, when an object moves, all things mated with it move conjointly.) SIPE was adequate for representing this problem.

The aircraft operations problem involved planning the launch of a number of airplanes, given their initial locations. This may involve checking for airworthiness, finding paths from a parking space to a runway. finding paths from a parking space to a fuel station to a runway, and clearing a path if no clear one exists. Problems in this domain included numerous aircraft and long paths, so the plans generated contained hundreds of nodes. Using the automatic search to find paths on the grid would have led to a combinatorial explosion, so path variables were instantiated to a list of locations by a special-purpose generator. SIPE's ability to allow operators to loop over a list enabled the system to generate easily the goals of clearing the locations specified in the list produced by the generator. Using these abilities, SIPE was able to generate large plans automatically for correctly launching many planes from parallel runways.

The travel-planning domain involved agents who could perform actions such as walking, taking a bus. taking a plane. taking a taxi, etc. Given the goal of

rently by means of the context mechanism. Thus, the user can shift focus as he pleases without being required to understand the program's search strategy or backtracking algorithm.

SIPE is not yet robust enough to operate in complex real-world situations. Its execution-monitoring capabilities are currently being expanded. Future research needs to investigate iterative plans, conditional plans, and uncertainty, since these cannot currently be represented.

ACKNOWLEDGMENT

Many people influenced the ideas expressed in this paper. Special thanks go to Ann Robinson who helped design and implement SIPE, and to Nils Nilsson, Stan Rosenschein, and Michael Georgeff for many enlightening discussions.

REFERENCES

1. Fikes, R., Hart, P. and Nilsson, N., Learning and executing generalized robot plans, in: N. Nilsson and B. Webber (Eds.), *Readings in Artificial Intelligence* (Tioga, Palo Alto, CA, 1981) 231–249.
2. Grosz, B. et al., TEAM: A transportable natural-language system, Tech. Note 263, SRI International Artificial Intelligence Center, Menlo Park, CA, 1981.
3. Hayes, P.J., In defense of logic, *Proceedings IJCAI-77*, Cambridge, MA (1977) 559–565.
4. Hayes-Roth, B., Hayes-Roth, F., Rosenschein, S. and Cammarata, S., Modeling planning as an incremental, opportunistic process, *Proceedings IJCAI-79*, Tokyo, Japan (1979) 375–383.
5. McDermott, D., A temporal logic for reasoning about processes and plans, *Cognitive Sci.* 6(2) (1982) 101–155.
6. Robinson, A.E. and Wilkins D.E.. Representing knowledge in an interactive planner, *Proceedings of the First Annual Conference of the AAAI*, Stanford, CA (1980) 148–150.
7. Robinson, A.E., and Wilkins D.E., Man–machine cooperation for action planning, Final Rep., SRI International Artificial Intelligence Center, Menlo Park, CA, 1982.
8. Rosenschein, S., Plan synthesis: A logical perspective, *Proceedings IJCAI-81*, Vancouver, BC (1981) 331–337.
9. Sacerdoti, E., *A Structure for Plans and Behavior* (North-Holland, New York, 1977).
10. Sridharan, N. and Bresina, J., Plan formation in large, realistic domains, *Proceedings CSCSI Conference*, Saskatoon, Saskatchewan (1982) 12–18.
11. Stefik, M., Planning with constraints, *Artificial Intelligence* 16(2) (1981) 111–140.
12. Sussman, G.J., *A Computer Model of Skill Acquisition* (North-Holland, New York, 1975).
13. Tate, A., Generating project networks, *Proceedings IJCAI-77*, Cambridge, MA (1977) 888–893.
14. van Melle, W., A domain-independent production-rule system for consultation programs, *Proceedings IJCAI-79*, Tokyo, Japan (1979) 923–925.
15. Vere, S., Planning in time: Windows and durations for activities and goals, Jet Propulsion Lab., Pasadena, CA, 1981.
16. Waldinger, R., Achieving several goals simultaneously, in: N. Nilsson and B. Webber (Eds.), *Readings in Artificial Intelligence* (Tioga, Palo Alto, CA, 1981) 250–271.
17. Wilensky, R.. Meta-planning, *Proceedings AAAI-80*, Stanford, CA (1980) 334–336.

Received February 1983; revised version received October 1983

ISIS — a knowledge-based system for factory scheduling

Mark S. Fox and Stephen F. Smith
The Robotics Institute, Carnegie-Mellon University,
Pittsburgh, Pennsylvania 15213, USA

Abstract: Analysis of the job shop scheduling domain has indicated that the crux of the scheduling problem is the determination and satisfaction of a large variety of constraints. Schedules are influenced by such diverse and conflicting factors as due date requirements, cost restrictions, production levels, machine capabilities and substitutability, alternative production processes, order characteristics, resource requirements, and resource availability. This paper describes ISIS, a scheduling system capable of incorporating all relevant constraints in the construction of job shop schedules. We examine both the representation of constraints within ISIS, and the manner in which these constraints are used in conducting a constraint-directed search for an acceptable schedule. The important issues relating to the relaxation of constraints are addressed. Finally, the interactive scheduling facilities provided by ISIS are considered.

1. Introduction

The construction of schedules to govern the production of orders in a job shop is a complex problem that is influenced by knowledge accumulated from many different sources in the shop. The acceptability of a particular schedule depends on such diverse and conflicting factors as due date requirements, cost restrictions, production levels, machine capabilities and substitutability, alternative production processes, order characteristics, resource requirements, and resource availability. The problem is a prime candidate for application of artificial intelligence (AI) technology, as human schedulers are overburdened by its complexity and existing computer-based approaches to automatic scheduling incorporate only a fraction of the relevant scheduling knowledge. They use a purely *predictive* approach to scheduling; based on a restricted model of the environment, predictions are made as to when operations are to be performed. The resulting schedules often bear little resemblance to the actual state of the factory, leaving detailed scheduling to the shop-floor supervisor. Automatic scheduling is thus reduced to weekly or monthly runs whose outputs provide guidance in determining future loadings. By viewing the scheduling problem from an AI perspective, it is possible to provide a better solution. Schedule construction can be cast as a constraint-directed activity that is influenced by *all* relevant scheduling knowledge. The

This research was supported, in part, by the Air Force Office of Scientific Research under contract F49620-82-K0017, Westinghouse Electric Corporation, and the Robotics Institute.

Appeared in Expert Systems, July 1984, Vol. 1, No. 1

result is a scheduling system that possesses an additional *reactive* capability; accurate and timely schedules can be constructed in response to the actual current state of the factor. This latter approach is the basis of ISIS, a knowledge-based decision support system for job shop scheduling [1, 2, 3].

Formulating the job shop scheduling problem as a constraint-directed activity raises some interesting research issues. Given the conflicting nature of the domain's constraints, the problem differs from typical constraint satisfaction problems and one cannot rely solely on propagation techniques (e.g. [4, 5, 6, 7]) to arrive at an acceptable solution. Rather, constraints must be selectively *relaxed* and the problem-solving strategy must be one of finding a solution that best satisfies the constraints. This implies that constraints must serve to discriminate among alternative hypotheses as well as to restrict the number of hypotheses generated. Thus, the design of ISIS has focused on

- constructing a knowledge representation that captures the requisite knowledge of the job shop environment and its constraints to support constraint-directed search, and
- developing a search architecture capable of exploiting this constraint knowledge to effectively control the combinatorics of the underlying search space.

The remainder of this paper focuses on the issues surrounding the constraint-directed reasoning approach to job shop schedule construction taken in the design of ISIS. In Section 2 we examine the nature and complexity of the job shop scheduling problem within an actual manufacturing facility. The wide variety of constraints that influence job shop schedules are identified and categorized. This is followed in Section 3 by a description of the constraint representation used to characterize this knowledge within ISIS. In Section 4, the issues surrounding the

use of constraint knowledge are addressed. The constraint-directed search conducted by ISIS to automatically construct job shop schedules is discussed, and some performance results are presented and discussed in Section 5. We turn our attention to the practical capabilities provided by the ISIS interactive scheduling subsystem in Section 6. The additional features of ISIS are summarized in Section 7. Finally, in Section 8, we draw some conclusions based on our experience with the system.

2. The scheduling problem

The job shop scheduling problem can be defined as selecting a sequence of operations (i.e., a process routing) whose execution results in the completion of an order, and assigning times (i.e., start and end times) and resources to each operation. Historically, the scheduling problem has been divided into two separate steps. Process routing selection is typically the product of a planning process, while the assignment of times and resources is typically the purpose of scheduling. Actually, the distinction between planning and scheduling is somewhat fuzzier, as the selection of a routing cannot be made conclusively without generating the accompanying schedule. The admissibility of a process routing depends on the feasibility of each selected operation, and a given operation is feasible only if its resource requirements are satisfied during the time that the operation is to be performed. Thus, the determination of an admissible process routing implies a prior assignment of resources and times to each operation in the routing.

The job shop scheduling problem has been described as NP-hard. Consider the sequencing of just ten orders through five operations. Associating a single machine with each operation (i.e. no alternative routings) and assuming no time gaps in the schedule to be generated, there are $(10!)^5$ or about 10^{32} possible schedules. The situation within an actual manufacturing facility is much more complex. The number of orders, operations, and resources are substantially greater, and the dynamic nature of the shop (e.g. machine breakdowns, order changes, etc.) further complicates the selection process. To illustrate the full complexity of the problem, let us examine a specific job shop scheduling environment.

2.1 The WTCP job shop environment

The Westinghouse Turbine Component Plant (WTCP) in Winston-Salem N.C. was selected as a test domain for investigating the job shop scheduling problem. The primary product of the plant is steam turbine blades. A turbine blade is a complex three-dimensional object produced by a sequence of forging, milling and grinding operations to tolerances of a thousandth of an inch. Thousands of different blade styles are produced in the plant, many of them to be used as replacements in turbines currently in service.

The plant continuously receives orders for one to a thousand blades at a time. Orders fall into at least six categories:

- Forced outages (FO): Orders to replace blades which malfunctioned during operation. It is important to ship these orders as soon as possible.
- Critical replacement (CR) and Ship Direct (SD): Orders to replace blades during scheduled maintenance. Advance warning is provided, but the blades must arrive on time.
- Service and shop orders (SO,SH): Orders for new turbines. Lead times of up to three years may occur.
- Stock orders (ST): Orders for blades to be placed in stock for future needs.

The area of the plant considered by ISIS has 100 to 200 orders in process at any time.

Turbine blades are produced according to a process routing or lineup. A routing specifies a sequence of operations that leads to the finished product. An operation is an activity which defines the resources required (e.g. machines, tools, materials and fixtures), machine set up and run times, and labor requirements. Each type of turbine blade produced in the plant has one or more process routings, each containing ten or more operations. Distinctions between process routings may be as simple as substituting a different machine, or as complex as changing the manufacturing process. The resources needed for an operation are typically shared with other operations in the shop.

During our discussions with WTCP, we found that orders are not scheduled in a uniform manner. Each scheduling decision to be made entails side effects whose importance varies by order, and the generation of a schedule is an iterative process. What quickly became evident was the scheduler's reliance on information other than due dates, process routings, and machine availability. A proposed schedule is distributed to persons in every department in the plant, and each person on the distribution list can provide information which may result in schedule alterations. We found that the scheduler spends only 10%–20% of his time actually scheduling, and 80%–90% of his time communicating with other employees to determine what additional 'constraints' should influence an order's schedule.

From this analysis, we may conclude that the objective of scheduling is not only meeting due dates, but satisfying the many constraints that originate from various parts of the plant. Scheduling is not a distinct function, separate from activities in the rest of the plant, but is highly dependent upon decisions being made elsewhere in the plant. The added complexity imposed by these constraints leads schedulers to produce schedules that are characterized by high work-in-process times, order tardiness, and low machine use. What is needed is a general methodology for using such diverse sources of information in the generation of job shop schedules.

2.2 Constraint categories

Any attempt to provide a general solution to the job shop scheduling problem must begin with an identification of both the set of scheduling constraints to be considered and their effect on the scheduling process. Our analysis of the constraints present in the WTCP plant has yielded five broad categories of constraints. These categories are examined below.

The first category of constraint encountered in the factory is what we call an *organizational goal*. Part of the organization planning process is the generation of measures of how the organization is to perform. These measures act as constraints on one or more organization variables. An organizational goal constraint can be viewed as an expected value of some organization variable. For example:

- *Due dates*: A major concern of a factory is meeting due dates. The lateness of an order affects customer satisfaction.
- *Work-in-progress*: Work-in-progress (WIP) inventory levels are another concern. WIP inventory represents a substantial investment in raw materials and added value. These costs are not recoverable until delivery. Hence, reducing WIP time is desirable.
- *Resource levels*: Another concern is maintaining adequate levels of resources necessary to sustain operations. Resources include personnel, raw materials, tools, etc. Each resource will have associated constraints. For example, labor size must be smoothed over a month's interval, or raw materials inventory may have to be limited to a two day supply.
- *Costs*: Cost reduction can be another important goal. Costs may include material costs, wages, and lost opportunity. Reducing costs may help achieve other goals such as stabiliza-

tion of the workforce.

- *Production levels*: Advance planning also sets production goals for each cost center in the plant. This serves two functions: it designates the primary facilities of the plant by specifying higher production goals, and also specifies a preliminary budget by predicting how much the plant will produce. One outcome of this activity is a forecast of the work shifts that will be run in various areas of the plant.
- *Shop stability*: Shop stability is a function of the number of revisions to a schedule and the amount of disturbance in preparation caused by these revisions. It is an artifact of the time taken to communicate change in the plant and the preparation time.

One can view all organizational goal constraints as being approximations of a simple profit constraint. The goal of an organization is to maximize profits. Scheduling decisions are then made on the basis of current and future costs incurred. For example, not meeting a due date may result in the loss of a customer and, in turn, erosion of profits. The longer the work in process time is, the greater the carrying charge will be for raw materials and value-added operations. Maintaining a designated production level may distribute the cost of the capital equipment in a uniform manner. In practice, most of these costs cannot be accurately determined, and must therefore be estimated.

Physical constraints determine a second category of constraint. Physical constraints specify characteristics which limit functionality. For example, the length of a milling machine's workbed may limit the types of turbine blades that it can be used for. Similarly, there are specific machine set-up and processing times associated with different manufacturing operations.

Causal restrictions constitute a third category of constraint. They define what conditions must be satisfied before initiating an operation. Examples of causal constraints include:

- *Precedence*: A process routing is a sequence of operations. A predence constraint on an operation states that another operation must take place before (or after) it. There may be further modifiers on the constraint in terms of minimum or maximum time between operations, product temperature to be maintained, etc.
- *Resource requirements*: Another causal constraint is the specification of resources that must be present before or during the execution of a process. For example, a milling operation re

quires the presence of certain tools, an operator, fixtures, etc.

A fourth category of constraint is concerned with the *availability* of resources. As resources are assigned to specific operations during production of a schedule, constraints declaring the resources unavailable for other uses during the relevant time periods must be generated and associated with these resources. Resource availability is also constrained by the work shifts designated in the plant, machine maintenance schedules, and other machine down times (e.g. breakdowns).

A fifth category of constraint is *prefer-*

Organizational goals	Due date
	Work-in-process
	Shop stability
	Shifts
	Cost
	Productivity goals
	Quality
Physical constraints	Machine physical constraints
	Set-up times
	Processing time
	Quality
Causal restrictions	Operation alternatives
	Machine alternatives
	Tool requirements
	Material requirements
	Personnel requirements
	Inter-operation transfer times
Availability constraints	Resource reservations
	Machine down time
	Shifts
Preference constraints	Operation preferences
	Machine preferences
	Sequencing preferences

Figure 2.1: Scheduling constraints

ence. A preference constraint can also be viewed as an abstraction of other types of constraints. Consider a preference for a machine. It expresses a floor supervisor's desire that one machine be used instead of another. The reason for the preference may be due to cost or quality, but sufficient information does not exist to derive actual costs. In addition to machine preferences, operation preferences, and order sequencing preferences exemplify this type of constraint.

Figure 2-1 lists the variety of constraints we have identified as well as the categories we have used to classify them.

In a review of commercial scheduling systems we found that most of them provide only simple capacity analysis with an emphasis on meeting due dates. Little or no consideration is given to providing general facilities for representing and using any additional constraints. Moreover, these systems are batch oriented, and meant to be run weekly or monthly; they do not provide real-time control. This was found to be unacceptable by WTCP. On the other hand, management science research has focused on optimal results for artificial problems, or dispatch rules for meeting due dates or maximizing facility use. These solutions are also found to be unsatisfactory for the real-life scheduling problem.

3. Modeling the domain and its constraints

The wide variety of constraints identified above indicate the need for a rich underlying model of the job shop scheduling domain. Detailed knowledge of all facets of the domain, including operations, process routings, machines, work areas, tools, materials, personnel, orders, etc. must be accessible to the scheduling system if it is to intelligently construct job shop schedules. The characterization of this knowledge within ISIS is considered in the following subsections. The ISIS modeling system and its constraint representation are described in turn.

3.1. The ISIS modeling system

The ISIS modeling system contains all the knowledge necessary to plan and schedule production in a job shop environment. The system is built using SRL [8, 9], a flexible knowledge representation system which allows the user to mould the language to his needs. SRL is a frame-based language which encodes concepts as schemata. A schema is a collection of slots and values. Each schema, slot, and/or value may have meta-information attached to it. In addition to attribute knowledge, slots define inter-schema relations, along which slots and values may be inherited. The inheritance semantics of

```
{{ operation
    { IS-A act
       NEXT-OPERATION: "operations which follow this"
       PREVIOUS-OPERATION: "operations which directly precede this"
       ENABLED-BY: "state which enables this action"
       CAUSES: "states caused by this action"
       DURATION: "time of this action"    }    }}
```

Figure 3.1: Operation schema

a relation are user-definable. Figure 3.1 illustrates the basic SRL construct in defining an operation schema.

In this case, the description states that an *operation* IS-A type of act. This view of an operation is further refined to include the attributes (slots) NEXT-OPERATION, PREVIOUS-OPERATION, etc. SRL has been used to support a number of different Intelligent Management System functions [10] including simulation, diagnosis, graphics, project management, and long range planning.

SRL provides ISIS with the capability of modeling a plant at all levels of detail; from physical machine descriptions, to process descriptions, to organizational structures and relations. Some of the uses made of SRL within the ISIS modeling system include:

- *Order definition* — any type of order, e.g. live, forecast, customer, manufacturing, etc., can be created, and updated interactively. New types of orders can be created as needed.
- *Lot definition* — orders may be grouped into lots, which may then be run as a unit through the plant.
- *Resource definition* — resources such as machines, tools, fixtures, materials, and personnel can be defined and used by an extensible set of functions. Resource definitions include substitutability in operations, and their current operation assignments in the plant.
- *Lineup (operation) definition* — the process(es) by which a product is produced may be described as an operations graph. The operations graph describes all alternative operations, processing information, and resource requirements. Operations can be described hierarchically, enabling the description of operations at varying levels of detail.
- *Work area definition* — cost centers, work areas, and any other plant floor

organizations may be defined and resources, sub work areas, etc. can be assigned to them. Possible uses besides scheduling include accounting, personnel, and other functions.
- *Department definition* — departments, personnel, and any other organization structures may be defined, and linked with other parts of the model.
- *Reservation definition* — any resource may be reserved for an activity (operation). ISIS provides full reservation creation and alteration facilities with respect to both interactive and automatic scheduling.
- *Plant organization* — the plant may be described hierarchically both from an organization structure perspective, and a physical layout perspective. This is used to support functions such as color graphics displays of the plant layout.

These descriptive capabilities are provided within the ISIS modeling system through the definition of a variety of primitives for modeling manufacturing organizations. The lowest level provides the basic concepts of states, objects, and acts, related to one another by a set of temporal and causal relations. These primitives provide a general foundation upon which more domain-specific concepts such as those identified above are defined and related. In specifying a process routing, for example, manufacturing operations are defined as acts, and relations such as NEXT-OPERATION are composed from basic temporal and causal relations. Resources required by the operations are expressed as objects, with their allocation represented as states of possession by particular operations. Constraints are represented as meta-information, and can be attached to any schema, slot, or value in the model.

Figure 3.2 gives a flavor of the ISIS job shop scheduling model, schematically depicting a portion of a process routing representing the two sequential oper-

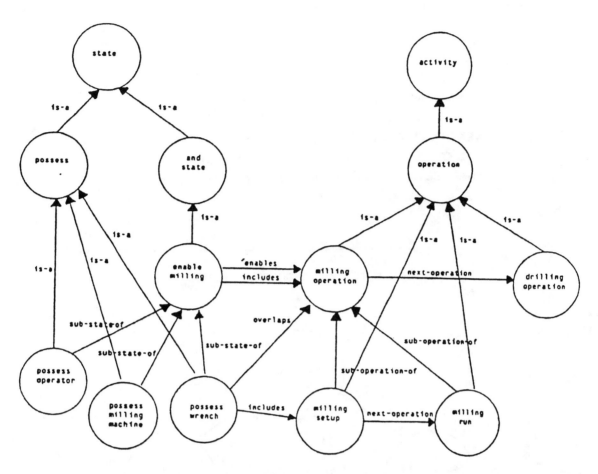

Figure 3.2: Activity model

ations of *milling* and *drilling*. The *milling* operation is defined as the composition of the sub-operations *milling-setup* and *milling-run*, with the NEXT-OPERATION relation specifying precendece between the two. Likewise, NEXT-OPERATION is used to designate *drilling* as the operation immediately following *milling*. The *milling* operation is further defined as being enabled by the *enable-milling* state. This indicates that the *enable-milling* state must exist before the *milling-operation* may be performed. The *enable-milling* state is the conjunction of sub states *possess-operator*, *possess-milling-machine* and *possess-wrench*, each of which is also linked to the *milling* operation via causal (e.g. ENABLES) and temporal

(e.g. OVERLAPS, INCLUDES) relations.

Within the schema representation of such a model, relations appear as slots in the schemata that they relate. The *milling-operation* schema, shown in Figure 3.3, illustrates this point.

Additional schemata are present in the representation to describe the properties of the relations themselves. In the activity model of Figure 3.2, for example, the domain specific relations NEXT-OPER-ATION, SUB-OPERATION-OF, and SUB-STATE-OF are defined in terms of more primitive domain independent relations, forming the relation hierarchy shown in Figure 3.4

```
{{ milling-operation
    { IS·A operation
        WORK·CENTER: milling·center
        DURATION: {{ INSTANCE time·interval
                        DURATION: 5 }}
        NEXT·OPERATION: drilling·operation
        SUB·OPERATION: milling·setup milling·run
        ENABLED·BY: enable·milling  }     }}
```

Figure 3.3: Milling-operation schema

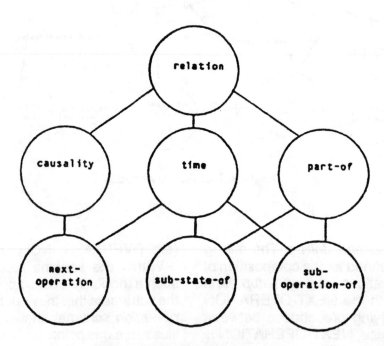

Figure 3.4: Relation hierarchy

3.2. Constraint representation

Given the role of constraints in determining a job shop schedule, a major thrust of our research has centered on identifying and characterizing the constraint knowledge required to support an effective constraint-directed search. Consider the imposition of a due date. In its simplest form, this constraint would be represented by a date alone, the implication being that the job be shipped on that date. In actuality, however, due dates may not always be met, and such a representation provides no information as to how to proceed in these situations. An appropriate representation must include the additional information about the due date that may be necessary in constructing a satisfactory schedule. For example:

- what alternative dates are satisfactory if the original cannot be met?
- what preferences exist for these alternative dates?
- who specified the due date? when? and why?
- how is the satisfaction of the due date related to other constraints such as costs?
- does the satisfaction of the due date constraint positively or negatively affect the satisfaction of other constraints?
- under what circumstances should the due date constraint be considered?
- if there are two or more due date constraints specified for an order, which should be used?

Let us examine the representational issues raised by these examples, and, correspondingly, the salient features of the ISIS constraint representation (additional details may be found in [1, 2, 11]).

One of the central issues that must be addressed by the constraint representation is that of *conflict*. Consider cost and due date constraints. The former may require reduction of costs while the latter may require shipping the order in a short period of time. To accomplish the latter may require using faster, more expensive machines, thereby causing a conflict with the former. In short, it may not be possible to satisfy both constraints, in which case one or both must be *relaxed*. This is implicitly accomplished in mathematical programming and decision theory by means of utility functions and the specifications of relaxation through bounds on a variable's value. In AI, bounds on a variable are usually specified by predicates [5, 12] or choice sets [6, 7].

Given the diversity in the types of constraints present in the job shop scheduling domain, it is necessary to provide a variety of forms for specifying *relaxations* (i.e. alternative values) of constraints. Accordingly, relaxations may be defined within the ISIS constraint representation as either predicates or choice sets, which, in the latter case, are further distinguished as discrete or continuous. However, the simple specification of bounds on a variable provides no means of differentiating between the values falling within these bounds, a capability that is required by ISIS both for generating plausible alternative schedules for consideration and for effectively discriminating among alternative schedules that have been generated to resolve a given conflict. The necessary knowledge is provided by associating a utility with each relaxation specified in a constraint, indicative of its *preference* among the alternatives available.

The relative influence to be exerted by a given constraint, i.e. its *importance*, is a second aspect of the constraint representation. Not all constraints are of equal importance. The due date constraint associated with high priority orders, for example, is likely to be more important than an operation preference constraint. Moreover, the relative importance of different types of constraints may vary from order to order. In one order, the due date may be important, and in another, cost may be important. Both of these forms of differentiation are expressible within the ISIS constraint representation; the former through the association of an absolute measure of importance with each constraint, and the latter by the use of *scheduling goals* which partition the constraints into importance classes and assign weights to be distributed amongst each partition's members. This knowledge enables ISIS to base its choices of which constraints to relax on the relative influence exerted by various constraints.

A third form of constraint knowledge explicitly represented is constraint *relevance*, which defines the conditions under which a constraint should be applied. Given that constraints are attached directly to the schemata, slots, and/or values they constrain, constraint relevance can be determined to a large degree by the proximity of constraints to the portion of the model currently under consideration. A finer level of discrimination is provided by associating a specific procedural test, termed the *context*, with each constraint. However, there are situations in which problems arise if the applicability of constraints is based solely on their context sensitivity to the current situation. First, many constraints tend to vary over time. The number of shifts, for example, fluctuates according to production levels set in the plant. Consequently, different variants of the same constraint type may be applicable during different periods of time. Within the ISIS constraint representation these situations are handled by associating a temporal scope with each variant, organizing the collection of variants according to the temporal relationships among them, and providing a resolution mechanism that exploits the organization. A second problem involves inconsistencies that might arise with respect to a given constraint type. Since ISIS is intended as a multiple user system, different variants of the same constraint type could quite possibly be created and attached to the same object in the model. For example, both the material and marketing departments may place different and conflicting due date constraints on the same order. In this case, a first step has been taken in exploiting an authority model of the organization to resolve such inconsistencies.

A fourth aspect of the constraint representation concerns the *interactions* amongst constraints. Constraints do not exist independently of one another, but rather the satisfaction of a given constraint will typically have a positive or negative effect on the ability to satisfy other constraints. For example, removing a machine's second shift may decrease costs but may also cause an order to miss its due date. These interdependencies are expressed as relations within the ISIS constraint representation, with an associated *sensitivity* measure indicating the extent and direction of the interaction. Knowledge of these interactions is used to diagnose the causes of unsatisfactory final solutions proposed by the system and to suggest relaxations to related constraints which may yield better results.

A final concern is that of constraint *generation*. Many constraints are introduced dynamically as production of the schedule proceeds. For example, a decision to schedule a particular operation during a particular interval of time imposes bounds on the scheduling decisions that must be made for other operations in the production process. The dynamic creation and propagation of constraints is accomplished by attaching constraint generators to appropriate relations in the model.

Figure 3.5 summarizes the knowledge about constraints that is captured within the ISIS constraint representation.

An example of a constraint within the ISIS model is a *due–date–constraint* [Figure 3.6]. It constrains the range (i.e. value) that a slot may have. In particular, it constrains the DUE-DATE slot (relation) associated with an order schema. The specific set of alternative values (or relaxations) designated by this constraint is described by the *due–date–relaxation–spec* schema [Figure 3.7], which is defined as a type of *continuous–relaxation–spec*. A continuous choice relaxation spec restricts the value of a slot to a particular domain, in this case the domain of dates, and specifies a piece-wise linear utility function over this domain. This function provides the basis for determining the

relaxation	specification of allowable alternatives and the preferences amongst them.
importance	the relative influence to be exerted by the constraint.
relevance	the conditions under which the constraint should apply.
interaction	the constraint's interdependencies with other constraints.
generation	a mechanism for creating and propagating constraints.

Figure 3.5: Aspects of constraint knowledge

```
{{ due-date-constraint
    { IS-A range-constraint
        IMPORTANCE:
        CONTEXT: t
        DOMAIN:
            range: (type IS-A order)
        RELATION: due-date
        CONSTRAINED-BY:
            range: (type IS-A due-date-relaxation-spec) }
    PRIORITY-CLASS:    }}
```

Figure 3.6: due-date-constraint schema

```
{{ due-date-relaxation-spec
    { IS-A continuous-relaxation-spec
        DOMAIN: dates
        PIECE-WISE-LINEAR-UTILITY:
        EVALUATOR: interpolate }  }}
```

Figure 3.7: due-date-relaxation-spec schema

utility of any particular value chosen (via interpolation).

4. Constraint-directed search

ISIS has been designed to perform constraint-directed scheduling of job shops, and, as such, provides a framework for incorporating the wide range of constraints that typically influence scheduling decisions. It is able to identify which constraints to satisfy, on an order-by-order basis, and may selectively relax any constraints found to be unsatisfactory. Among the principle characteristics of the automatic scheduling system are:

- *Constraint utilisation* — the general framework enables ISIS to use almost any constraint the user deems appropriate.
- *Multi-level scheduling* — ISIS allows scheduling to be performed at differing levels of detail and perspectives. Included in the current version is a bottleneck analysis whose output is a set of constraints to guide the detailed scheduling of required resources.
- *Bottleneck analysis* — the capacity analysis level of scheduling determines the availability of machines to produce an order. It outputs a set of constraints on when each operation for an order should be performed so as to avoid unnecessary waiting, and tardiness.
- *Detailed scheduling* — the detailed level of scheduling provides complete scheduling of all resources required to

produce an order. It takes into account all relevant constraints, both model and user-defined. As it constructs a schedule, it tests to see how well the schedule satisfies the known constraints. If important constraints cannot be satisfied, they will be relaxed. This level searches for a constraint-satisfying schedule.

The remainder of this section presents an overview of the ISIS approach to automatic job shop scheduling.

In constructing a job shop schedule, ISIS conducts a hierarchical, constraint-directed search in the space of all possible schedules. The different levels of the search provide multiple abstractions of the scheduling problem, each a function of the specific types of constraints that are considered at that level. Control generally flows in a top down fashion, and communication between levels is accomplished via the exchange of constraints. Processing at any given level proceeds in three phases: pre-analysis, search, and post-analysis [Figure 4.1]. The pre-analysis phase determines the bounds of the level's search space, the search phase performs the actual problem solving in this space, and the post-analysis phase assesses the quality of the results produced by the search. If deemed acceptable during post-analysis, the search results are codified as constraints for use at the next lower level of the search. Alternatively, the rejection of search results during post-analysis may lead to an alteration of the search space at

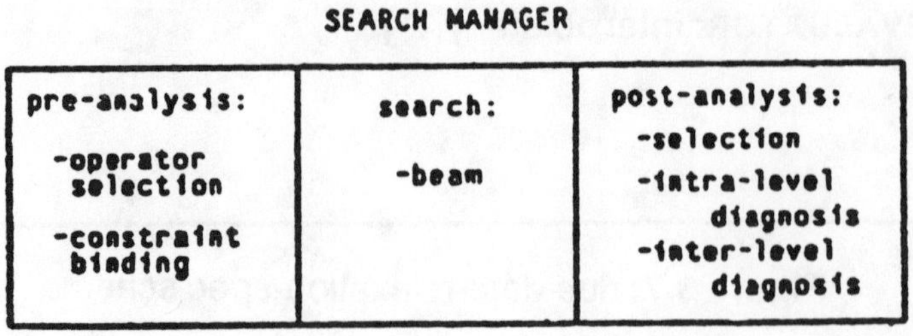

SEARCH MANAGER

pre-analysis:	search:	post-analysis:
-operator selection	-beam	-selection
-constraint binding		-intra-level diagnosis
		-inter-level diagnosis

Figure 4.1: Three phases of a level's processing

the current or a higher level (through the relaxation of one or more constraints), and the subsequent transfer of control back to the affected level.

Four search levels are organized within this framework to construct a job shop schedule. Level one selects an order to be scheduled according to a prioritization algorithm based on the category of the order, and its due date. Level two then performs a capacity analysis of the plant to determine the availability of the machines required by the selected order. Level three performs a detailed scheduling of all resources necessary to produce the order. Finally, level four selects and assigns reservations for resources required in the schedule. The following subsections consider this search architecture in more detail.

decisions imposed by the user. Level one determines the current set of orders to be scheduled and prioritizes them. The scheduling priority assigned to a given order in the set is determined by its priority class (e.g. forced outage), and the closeness of its due date. Orders are then scheduled one at a time in priority order.

4.2. Level two: capacity-based scheduling

Once an order is selected, ISIS analyzes the machine capacity of the plant available to produce the order. The purpose of the capacity analysis is to detect bottlenecks in the plant so that scheduling decisions at level three may be modified (i.e., operations scheduled early enough) to satisfy time constraints such as due date, start date, and work-in-process.

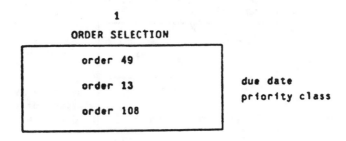

Figure 4.2: Order selection

4.1. Level one: order selection

Order selection [Figure 4.2] establishes the system's global strategy for integrating unscheduled orders into the existing job shop schedule (or loading the shop if no orders have yet been scheduled). The orders of interest at this level fall into two categories: orders that have been newly received at the plant and previously scheduled orders whose schedules have been subsequently invalidated. The invalidation of an order's schedule may occur in response to changes in the status of the plant (e.g. machine breakdowns), changes to the order's description, or

Capacity based scheduling of an order selected by level one proceeds by applying a critical path method (CPM) analysis to the operations involved in the production of the order [Figure 4.3]. By considering estimates of the durations of these operations, the resource reservations previously generated by the detailed scheduling of other orders, and the order's start and due date, this analysis determines the earliest start time and latest finish time for each operation of the selected order. The times generated are then codified as operation time bound constraints and passed to level three. These constraints restrict the start and end times of operations that are subsequently generated during detailed scheduling[1].

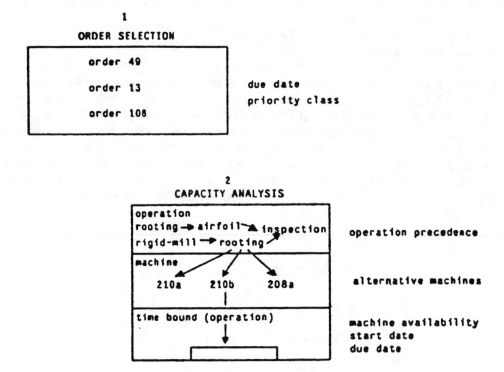

Figure 4.3: Capacity analysis level

4.3. Level three: resource scheduling

Level three [Figure 4.4] extends the scheduling of level two by considering more detailed information about operation resource requirements in addition to machines, and additional constraints such as preferences, physical constraints, etc. Pre-search analysis begins with an examination of the order's constraints, resulting in the determination of the scheduling direction (either forward from the start date or backward from the due date), the creation of any missing constraints (e.g. due dates, work-in-process), and the selection of the set of search operators which will generate the search space. A beam search [13] is then performed using the selected set of search operators. The search space to be explored is composed of states which represent partial schedules. The application of operators to states results in the creation of new states which further specify the partial schedules under development.

---

[1] *The net effect of the interpretation of these constraints is to modify the evaluation function for the search algorithm used at level three.*

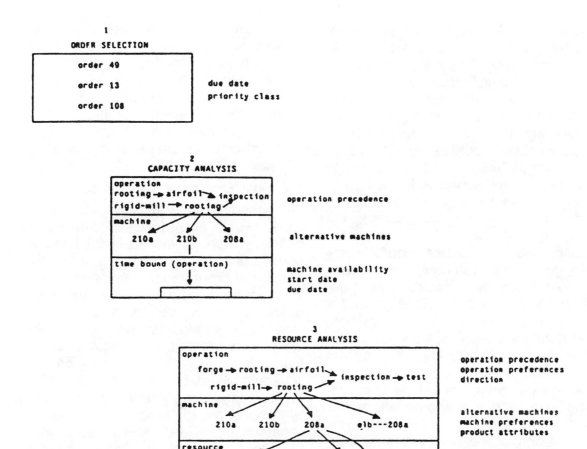

Figure 4.4: Resource scheduling level

Depending on the results of pre-search analysis, the search proceeds either forward or backward through the set of allowable routings for the order. An operator that generates states representing alternative operations initiates the search, in this case generating alternative initial (or final) operations.

Once a state specifying an operation has been generated, other operators extend the search by creating new states which bind particular resources and/or an execution time to the operation.[2] After any given operator is applied, each newly generated state is *rated* by the set of constraints found to be relevant to the state and its ancestors. This set is determined by a resolution process that extracts the constraints attached to each object specified in the state (e.g. machine, tool, order, etc.), and filters them according to the *relevance* criteria described in Section

---

[2] *A variety of alternatives exist for each type of operator. For example, two operators have been tested for choosing the execution time of an operation [see Section 5]. The 'eager reserver' operator chooses the earliest possible reservation for the operation's required resources, and the 'wait and see' operator tentatively reserves as much time as available, leaving the final decision to level four.*

3.2. Each constraint in the resolved set assigns a utility between 0 and 2 to the state, where 0 signifies that the state is not admissible, 1 signifies indifference, and 2 signifies maximum support. These utilities are then weighted by the importance of the assigning constraints and averaged to produce the overall rating of the state. This rating, which reflects the degree to which the partial schedule including this state satisfies the relevant constraints, serves to focus the search on subsequent iterations.

Once a set of candidate schedules has been generated, a rule-based post search analysis examines the candidates to determine if one is acceptable (a function of the ratings assigned to the schedules during the search). If no acceptable schedules are found, then diagnosis is performed. First, the schedules are examined to determine a type of scheduling error and the appropriate repair. Inter-level repair may result in the re-instantiation of the level's search. Pre-analysis is performed again to alter the set of operators and constraints for re-scheduling the order. Inter-level repair is initiated if diagnosis determines that the poor solutions were caused by constraint satisfaction decisions made at another level. Inter-level diagnosis can be performed by analyzing the interaction relations linking constraints. A poor constraint decision at a higher level can be determined by the utilities of constraints affected by it at a lower level, and an alternative value can be chosen.

In attempting to find a solution at this level that best satisfies the constraints, ISIS provides two approaches to the constraint relaxation:

- *Generative relaxation.* Constraints are relaxed in a generative fashion during the heuristic search. The search operators generate states where each state represents an alternative relaxation of one or more constraints.
- *Analytic relaxation.* A rule-based

system analyzes an order during pre-analysis to determine the relative importance of constraints, and, in turn, which should be relaxed. Another set of rules perform a post-search analysis to determine whether the schedule is reasonable, and if not, what other constraints should be strengthened or relaxed.

4.4. Level four: reservation selection

The schedule generated by the detailed scheduling level, and passed to level four of the search, is in near final form. A specific process routing has been selected for the order under consideration, resources have been selected for each operation in the routing, and resource time bound constraints have been associated with each selected resource. Level four [Figure 4.5] finalizes the order's schedule by establishing reservations for each required resource in the schedule. Working within the resource time bound constraints provided by detailed scheduling, local optimizations are performed to minimize the order's work in process time. The resulting resource reservations are added to the existing shop schedule and act as additional constraints for use in the scheduling of subsequent orders.

5. Experimental results

Experiments have been conducted with several versions of the ISIS scheduling system, all based on a portion of the turbine component plant defined by the human plant scheduler. In each experiment, an empty job shop was loaded with a representative set of eighty-five blade orders spanning a period of two years. The various types of constraint knowledge influencing the development of schedules in these experiments included:

- alternative operations,
- alternative machines,
- due dates,
- start dates,
- operation time bounds,
- order priority classification (with orders

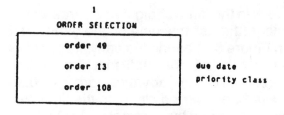

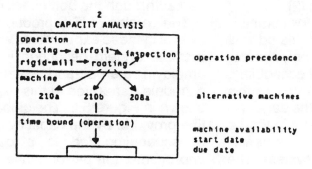

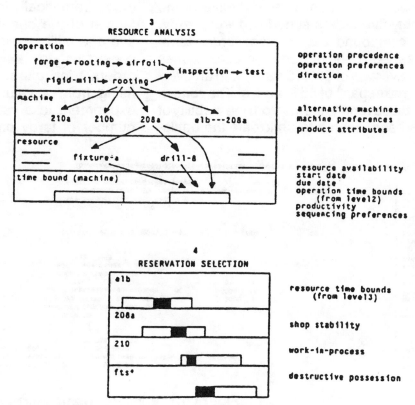

Figure 4.5: Reservation selection level

falling into four priority classes),

- work-in-process restrictions,
- sequencing constraints to reduce set-up time,
- machine constraints on product form and length,
- resource availability, and
- shop stability (minimizing pre-emption).

To date, thirteen experiments have been performed. These experiments have explored the effects of alternative constraints, alternative search operators, and the utility of the hierarchical search architecture. In this section we will examine the results obtained in two selected experiments, which serve to underscore the advantages of the hierarchical search architecture. A detailed discussion of all experiments may be found in [2].

To provide a benchmark for comparison, the initial version of ISIS tested was non-hierarchical, employing only the detailed (beam search) level of scheduling. Assignment of reservation times in this experiment was handled by the eager reserver. The gantt chart[3] shown in Figure 5.1 depicts the schedule that was generated by this version of the system. The schedule is a poor one; sixty-five of the eighty-five orders scheduled were tardy. To compound the problem, order tardiness led to high work-in-process times (an average of 305.15 days) with an overall makespan[4] of 857.4 days. The reason for these results stems from the inability of the beam search to anticipate the bottle-

neck in the 'final straightening area' of the plant (the fts* machine on the gantt chart in Figure 5.1) during the early stages of its search. Had the bottleneck operation been known in advance, orders could have been started closer to the time they were received by the plant and scheduled earlier through the bottleneck operation.

The version of ISIS producing the best results in these experiments was the hierarchical system described in Section 4 employing the wait-and-see reserver. The schedule generated in this experiment is shown in Figure 5.2. The global perspective provided by the capacity based level of scheduling led to a considerable improvement in performance, evidenced most dramatically in the increased satisfaction of the due date constraints. The average utility assigned by the due date constraint to lower priority 'service orders', for example, almost doubled, rising from a value of 0.46 in the first experiment to a value of 0.80. The total number of tardy orders was reduced to

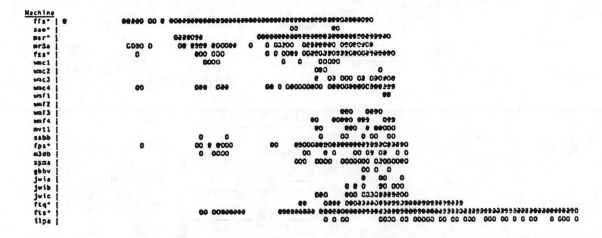

Figure 5.1: Version 1 gantt chart

---

[3]   *Each row represents a machine, and each column a week. If a position in the gantt chart is empty, then the machine is idle for that week. If a position contains an 'o', then it is used for less than 50% of its capacity. If the position contains a '@', then over 50% of its capacity is used. Machines that are encountered earlier in the process routings appear closer to the top of the chart.*

---

[4]   *Makespan is the time taken to complete all orders*

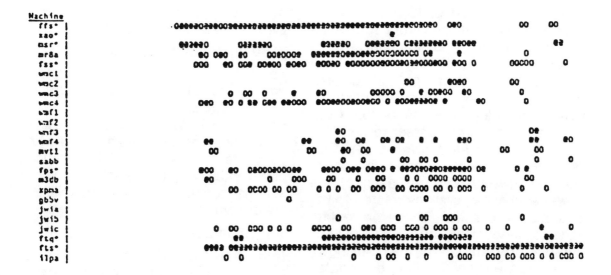

Figure 5.2: Version 7 gantt chart

fourteen. Moreover, a much lower average work-in-process time of 186.73 days was achieved, resulting in an overall makespan of 583.25 days. In this case, inadequate machine capacity in the 'final straightening area' (fts*) appeared to be the principal limitation affecting order tardiness. While these results are encouraging, further testing of ISIS continues.

6. Interactive scheduling

The discussion of the previous two sections centered on the automatic generation of job shop schedules via constraint-directed search. As mentioned at the outset, ISIS also provides the user with the 'hands on' capability to construct and alter schedules interactively. In this capacity, ISIS plays the role of an intelligent assistant, using its constant knowledge to maintain the consistency of the schedule under development and identify scheduling decisions that result in poorly satisfied constraints. Capabilities provided by the interactive scheduling subsystem include:

- *Lotting* — ISIS provides the user with an interactive lotting facility for searching and examining orders, and grouping them into lots.

- *Resource scheduling* — resources may be scheduled by reserving them for use in a particular operation at user specified time. Such resources are noted both with the resource and the reserver (lot or order).

- *Hierarchical scheduling* — the user may construct schedules at different levels of abstraction, and ISIS will automatically fill in the other levels. For example, the scheduler may schedule only the critical facilities, and ISIS will complete the schedule at the detailed lineup level.

- *Overlap flagging* — if user defined reservations for resources result in conflicting assignments, ISIS will inform the scheduler, and may automatically shift other reservations.

- *Constraint checking* — whenever a reservation for a resource is made, ISIS will check all relevant constraints, and inform the user as to their satisfaction. For example, if the reserved machine cannot be used for that sized product, the user will be informed at the time the reservation is made.

This section considers the strategy employed by ISIS to provide these capabilities.

As indicated above, ISIS allows the user to interactively construct schedules at various levels of abstraction. This is accomplished by exploiting a hierarchical model of the process routings associated with an order, and maintaining reservations at all levels of abstraction. Consider a decision by the user to create a new reservation for a given order. This reservation creates a need for corresponding reservations for each of the lower-level sub-operations related to the operation in question. These are established by determining the duration of each sub-operation and scaling the resulting intervals to the interval of time designated by the user. The reservations of temporally related operations residing at higher levels are also adjusted (and created if necessary) to reflect the presence of the newly imposed lower level reservations. A decision by the user to remove a reservation is propagated to other levels in a similar fashion.

The imposition of a new reservation, and the resulting propagation of effects, may introduce conflicts into the partially developed schedule. Specifically, conflicts may arise due to 1] a violation of the temporal constraints associated with previous and/or subsequent operations in the process routing (detectable at the level of the imposition), 2] contention for the same resource by different orders (detectable at the level where actual resources are involved), or 3] the scheduling of operations belonging to mutually exclusive process routings (detectable as the imposition is propagated upward). The resolution of such conflicts involves the invalidation of one of the offending reservations. Currently, all conflicts are resolved in favor of the more recently created reservation, although other strategies (e.g. an authority model) could be straightforwardly applied. The user is informed of the schedule changes that have been made. ISIS also checks all other constraints relevant to the scheduling decision imposed by the user, and signals the user as to their satisfaction or violation.

7. Summary of ISIS features

The ISIS system has been designed to provide complete facilities for practical use in job shop production management and control. Moreover, ISIS has been designed and implemented so that its functions are independent of the particular plant under consideration. This section summarizes the additional capabilities of the current version.

7.1. Model perusal

ISIS provides full interactive model perusal and editing from multiple users in parallel. The user may alter the model of the plant from any terminal. Perusal is provided in a number of forms including menus, a simple subset of English, graphic displays, and a logic programming-based question-answering system.

7.2. Reactive plant monitoring

ISIS provides the user with interfaces to update the status of all orders and resources. If the new status does not coincide with its schedule, then ISIS will reschedule only the affected resources. For example, if a machine breaks down, then all affected orders are rescheduled. Hence, ISIS can be used to provide real-time reactive scheduling of plants. It can also be extended to connect to an online data gathering system on the plant floor, providing real-time updating of plant status.

7.3. Generative process planning

One of ISIS's features is that its constraint representation allows it to perform a subset of generative process planning. Currently, ISIS has knowledge of a product's basic physical characteristics, and can choose machines based on them. These constraints can be extended to include geometric information.

7.4. Resource planning

Since ISIS schedules all specified resources, the user is informed of the resource requirements needed to satisfy the production. Constraints on the use of resources (e.g., machines, tools, personnel, etc.) may be specified and used to guide detailed scheduling. This enables departments such as advance planning to specify resource use constraints directly to ISIS.

7.5. Accessibility: flexible interfaces

The ISIS interface is menu/window-based. The user is presented with multiple windows of information on the terminal screen, plus a menu of commands to choose from. The menu system provides a network of displays ranging from order entry/update to interactive lotting to report generation. Reports may be printed directly on the screen or directed to an attached printer. A device independent color graphics display system is also available to ISIS. It is currently used to view a blueprint-like display of the plant, and to zoom in on work areas and machines. It can be used to display the status of the plant during operation. Finally, ISIS provides a simple natural language interface for use in perusing the plant model.

ISIS has been designed to be a multi-user system. Its model can be shared amongst multiple programs. Hence, the model may be perused and altered from multiple locations in the plant, allowing departments to get the information they need to perform their tasks, and to provide information directly to ISIS. ISIS is being extended to determine who the user is and restrict access and alteration capabilities depending on their function.

7.6. Simulation

ISIS is a component of the larger Intelligent Management System Project [10] underway at the CMU Robotics Institute. Hence, it can use other functions available in the project. For example, KBS, a knowledge-based simulator [15], can interpret the organization model directly to perform simulations. Since ISIS already has a model of the plant, KBS can use that model to perform simulations. All the user has to do is modify the model to reflect environment they wish to simulate.

8. Concluding remarks

The ability of ISIS to construct realistic job shop production schedules is due to a number of representational and search techniques for reasoning with constraints. These are summarized in Figure 8.1. In adopting these techniques, the ISIS scheduling system provides, for the first time, a general methodology for incorrating the wide variety of constraints present in the job shop scheduling domain for the automatic construction of a schedule. The robustness of the constraint representation employed makes possible the introduction of almost any constraint that is deemed appropriate by a user of the system. The attention paid to the relaxations, interactions, and relevance of constraints allows constraint knowledge to be effectively applied to control the combinatorics of the underlying search space. Constraint knowledge may be used to bound the solution space, generate and discriminate among alternative solutions according to the relative importance of various constraints, communicate information between various levels of search, and diagnose unsatisfactory solutions that are proposed. In addition, the constraint representation provides the basis for a flexible interactive scheduling facility.

Work is currently underway on the next iteration of ISIS where the emphasis is on giving constraints an even more active role in the reasoning process. Specifically, we envision a system architecture that conducts a more opportunistic form of search, focusing initially on the most critical (i.e. the most highly constrained) decisions that have to be made.

Representational Techniques:

- **Specification:** explicitly specify constraints as distinct schemata in the representation, attached as meta-information to the domain model.
- **Relaxation:** specify the full set of alternative values (or relaxations) for a given constraint.
- **Utility:** associate a particular utility with each alternative relaxation of a constraint to indicate the preferences that exist amongst them.
- **Context:** indicate the contextual applicability of a constraint implicitly by attaching it to portion of the domain model that it constraints, and explicitly by specifying the precise conditions under which it should apply.
- **Importance:** specify the relative importance of satisfying various constraints.
- **Interdependence:** relate constraints to one another according to the interdependencies that exist amongst them.

Search Techniques:

- **Definition:** derive the operators that define the search space from the constraints and their relaxations.
- **Hierarchy:** use the interdependencies among constraints to stratify the search into successive levels in which more and more constraints are considered. Independent constraints appear at the top, dependent constraints at lower levels.
- **Bounding:** select only a subset of the available search operators on the basis of the importance of their corresponding constraints and the utility of their relaxations.
- **Resolution:** dynamically resolve the set of constraints that are relevant to particular decisions (states).
- **Focus:** use a search state evaluation scheme that reflects the degree of satisfaction of the resolved constraints (i.e. a function of the utilities assigned) to focus attention during the search.
- **Diagnosis:** measure how well constraints are satisfied, and weight them according to their importance to assess the quality of the search results and detect poor solutions.
- **Repair:** exploit the interdependencies among constraints for guidance in repairing poor schedules.

Figure 8.1: Representational and search techniques for reasoning with constraints

9. Acknowledgements

This work could not have been completed without the contributions of the ISIS project members which include: Brad Allen, Ranjan Chak, Peng Si Ow, Gary Strohm and Doug Zimmerman. In addition, Ari Vepsalainen and Steve Miller contributed to the analysis of the scheduling problem at the turbine component plant. Tom Morton, Ari, Ram Rachamadugu, have contributed to the definition of constraint knowledge, and have evaluated critically our progress from a operations management perspective. Our expert scheduler, Bob Baugh, has contributed to the design of the interactive system interface, and has continually made us aware of the reality of the problem. Raj Reddy, Jose Isasi, Dwight Mize, and Bob Baugh have provided continued support during the ups and downs of this project.

10. References

[1] M.S. Fox, B.P. Allen and G.A. Strohm, 'Job Shop Scheduling: An Investigation in Constraint-Directed Reasoning,' *Proceedings of the 2nd National Conference on Artificial Intelligence*, American Association of Artificial Intelligence, August 1982, pp. 155–158.

[2] M.S. Fox, 'Constraint-Directed Search: A Case Study of Job Shop Scheduling,' PhD thesis, Carnegie-Mellon University, 1983.

[3] M.S. Fox, S.F. Smith, B.P. Allen, G.A. Strohm and F.C. Wimberly, 'ISIS: A Constraint-Directed Reasoning Approach to Job Shop Scheduling,' *Proceedings IEEE Conference on Trends and Applications 83*, Gaithersberg, Maryland, May 1983.

[4] L. Steels, 'Constraints as Consultants,' AI Memo 14, Schlumberger-Doll, December 1981.

[5] M. Stefik, 'Planning with Constraints (MOLGEN: Part 1),' *Artificial Intelligence*, **16**, 1981, pp. 111–140.

[6] G.J. Sussman and G.L. Steele, Jr. 'CONSTRAINTS — A Language for Expressing Almost-Hierarchical Descriptions,' *Artificial Intelligence*, **14**, 1980, pp. 1–40.

[7] D. Waltz, 'Understanding Line Drawings of Scenes with Shadows,' P.H. Winston (editor), *The Psychology of Computer Vision*. McGraw-Hill, New York, 1975.

[8] M.S. Fox, 'On Inheritance in Knowledge Representation,' *Proceedings of the Sixth International Joint Conference on Artificial Intelligence*. Tokyo, 1979.

[9] J.M. Wright, M.S. Fox and D. Adam, *SRL/1.5 User Manual*, Technical Report, Robotics Institute, Carnegie-Mellon University, 1984.

[10] M.S. Fox, *The Intelligent Management System: An Overview*, Technical Report CMU-RI-TR-81-4, Robotics Institute, Carnegie-Mellon University, August, 1981.

[11] S.F. Smith, *Exploiting Temporal Knowledge to Organize Constraints*, Technical Report CMU-RI-TR-83-12, Robotics Institute, Carnegie-Mellon University, 1983.

[12] C. Engleman, E. Scarl and C. Berg, 'Interactive Frame Instantiation,' *Proceedings of the 1st National Conference on Artificial Intelligence*, American Association of Artificial Intelligence, 1980, pp. 184–186.

[13] B. Lowerre, *The HARPY Speech Recognition System*, PhD thesis, Computer Science Department, Carnegie-Mellon University, 1976.

[14] B. Allen and J.M. Wright, 'Integrating Logic Programs and Schemata,' *Proceedings of the International Joint Conference on Artificial Intelligence*, Karlsruhe, Germany, Aug. 1983.

[15] Y.V. Reddy and M.S. Fox, *KBS: An Artificial Intelligence Approach to Flexible Simulation*, Technical Report CMU-RI-TR-82-1, Robotics Institute, Carnegie-Mellon University, 1982.

About the authors

Mark S. Fox

Mark Fox heads the Intelligent Systems Laboratory of the Robotics Institute at Carnegie-Mellon University and is an Assistant Professor of Management Science. His research interests span both computer and management science, including artificial intelligence, man–machine communication, databases, software system organisation, graphics, operations management, and organisation theory. He is the principal investigator of the Intelligent Management Systems project which performs research in the design and construction of AI-based systems to automate the management and control functions of factories. Dr. Fox received a B.Sc. in Computer Science from the University of Toronto in 1975, and his Ph.D. in Computer Science from Carnegie-Mellon University in 1983. He was twice awarded a National Research Council of Canada Post-Graduate Scholarship.

Stephen F. Smith

Stephen Smith is a Research Scientist in the Intelligent Systems Laboratory of the Robotics Institute at Carnegie-Mellon University. He received his B.S. degree (1975) in Mathematics from Westminster College and his M.S. (1977) and Ph.D. (1980) degrees in Computer Science from the University of Pittsburgh. Prior to joining the faculty of the Robotics Institute in 1982, he was an Assistant Professor of Computer Science at the University of Southern Maine. Dr. Smith's research interests include hierarchical and distributed problem solving, knowledge-based systems, machine learning, and AI applications to industrial problems. He has been involved with the ISIS project for the past two years. Dr. Smith is a member of the American Association of Artificial Intelligence, the ACM, and the IEEE Computer Society.

O-PLAN – CONTROL IN THE OPEN PLANNING ARCHITECTURE

Ken Currie & Austin Tate

Artificial Intelligence Applications Institute
University of Edinburgh
South Bridge
Edinburgh

ABSTRACT

This paper gives an overview of O-Plan - Open Planning Architecture. This is a prototype, computer based AI planning system. The design strategy aims to provide clear functional interfaces to the parts of the planner to allow for experimentation and integration of work underway in several aspects of knowledge based systems which together are an implementation of an opportunistic planner. The planner is part of an overall system for command, planning and control. As well as an overview of the O-Plan system, this paper concentrates on the control structure of the planner.

1. Introduction - the lead up to O-Plan.

The roots of O-Plan are to be found in earlier planning work on NONLIN by Tate [1] who investigated the process of constructing project networks. In turn that work was based on the early hierarchical planner NOAH [2] which spawned a new generation of non-linear planning systems. NONLIN identified the problem areas of domain representation and the capture of the "intent" of actions within plans.

The problem of domain representation led to the development of a high level language, called Task Formalism, for specifying the activities within a task domain and their more detailed representation as a set of subactivities and ordering constraints on them. A detailed plan is formed by chosing one suitable "expansion" of each high level (abstract) activity in the plan and including the relevant set of more detailed sub-activities. Any necessary ordering constraints are then imposed to ensure that the "effects" of some activities satisfy the necessary "conditions" before any activity can be used. The detailed descriptions of activities, called Schemas, describe how the planner should go about satisfying and maintaining each required condition within the schema by using "typing" of the conditions.

The main condition types are

supervised	satisfied by a sub-activity within the same overall activity.
unsupervised	satisfied outwith the overall activity by some outside agent (possibly another contractor working earlier or in parallel)
usewhen	satisfied by environmental information about the cases in which it is meaningful to use the activity.

The capture of the "intent" of the actions within the plan was achieved by a "Goal Structure" Table (GOST) [3] which records the condition(s) necessary for any action in the plan and the points in the plan where the effects to satisfy the condition have been asserted. GOST records the "scope" or "holding period" of these effects (possibly only one) which must extend at least as far as the condition. GOST therefore provides a mechanism for the detection of interactions between parallel activities.

The O-Plan planner builds on the concepts of NONLIN Task Formalism and GOST but within the framework of a totally new, more flexible architecture. This paper will give an overview of the O-Plan system, concentrating on the planner's control structure.

2. Objectives of the O-Plan Prototype.

O-Plan is intended to be part of a system for command, planning and control of tasks such as project management, job scheduling and vehicle control. Figure 1 shows how the O-Plan planner integrates into an overall system comprising

- a "workstation", which is the interface between the various types of user (human planner, domain specialists, etc) and the AI planner.

- the O-Plan AI planning system and resource allocation module.

- the plan execution and monitoring system.

The prototype O-Plan is based on the Task Formalism (TF) and GOST concepts introduced in NONLIN but improves on many features found in NONLIN and other planners.

The O-Plan planning process proceeds by gradual restriction of choices in the plan by the propagation of symbolic constraints (for example the restricting or binding of a variable in the plan) hence enabling some decisions to be made "later" in the planning process than in earlier systems. This allows the planner to find solutions to problems would have had many failure paths if choices of variable binding, for instance, were forced without reason. The implication of this is that there will be more information in the plan about why decisions were made.

O-Plan also copes with planning in temporal domains hence requiring management of time window information (earliest and latest start or finish times on activities), durations of activities and delays between successive activities in the plan. Allowing time to be expressed in a plan's domain clouds the definition of "beforeness" of activities in the partial order

Reprinted with the permission of Cambridge University Press

activity graph ("procedural net" in NOAH terms) so complicating the recording of Goal Structure and the answering of questions about the facts that hold at some point in a plan (in the question-answering module). The O-Plan temporal constraint propagation algorithms (Bell & Tate [4]) extend those of the DEVISER planner (Vere [5]).

Resource usage reasoning in O-Plan guarantees that a restricted class of resource constraints are satisfied. Several resource types have been identified (Bell [6]). Of these, two types are handled in O-Plan: "strictly consumable" and "single item re-useable" resources. Strictly consumable resources are those for which there is an initial stockpile which can only be depleted or untouched by any action in the plan and the management task is one of guaranteeing that the level of the stockpile never falls below zero. Re-usable resources can be reserved by an activity for a particular time period, during which the resource is not available to others, but after which the resource is returned to being available for use. Here the management task is one of ensuring that the use of a resource by competing, parallel activities do not exceed the amount of that resource at any instant. "Incremental" approaches to reasoning about these resource types are used in O-Plan. These allow up-to-date information about the validity of the resource constraints to be examined after any choice made by the AI planner. Other types of resource management are dealt with after the generation of the plan using algorithms from Operations Research.

3. How O-Plan will develop.

The present O-Plan prototype, or "early" O-Plan, provides a skeleton for further research and development. The following are active areas of development in the prototype:

(i)   User Interaction or Manual Control.

(ii) A rule based system for the control of the choices made by the planner (at its meta-level) to replace the present procedure which acts as the scheduler.

(iii) Interfacing to various sub-systems, specifically information sub-systems and special purpose sub-planners (for route finding, geometric manipulation, etc.)

(iv) The handling of scheduled and triggered events (for example, "the sun will rise at 6am", or "if A & B then C"). Events may be used in forwards or backwards search to contribute towards the triggering or achieving of an effect.

(v)   Clearly identifying the planner's use of its underlying database. This work centres on the "functions in context" data model (Tate [7])*.

* The "functions in context" data model provides a data store which holds entity/relationship data as statements with values which change in "context" and which can be inherited in various ways. The basic statements are of the form

4. Full O-Plan.

The "full" O-Plan design allows for dependency directed search and will at any stage retain only one solution (NONLIN and early O-Plan use a heuristic search strategy and keep many partial plan solutions spawned at each decision point). The action on plan failure in full O-Plan will be guided by decision dependency information, recorded at choice points earlier in the plan. The work is based on that of Hayes [8] and Daniels [9]. This will enable the failed, singly-retained solution to be "repaired" to remove the failed components. Then planning will re-start by re-making a choice at an appropriate previous decision point, allowing the planning process to continue hopefully to a solution. The planner will be restartable in the sense that it will be willing to receive back a partially executed plan for repair, and able to use the successful parts of the plan as the basis of its new starting point.

5. Main Areas of Research on the O-Plan Project.

The four main areas of research and development on the O-Plan project are obvious from Figure 1, namely:

(i)   AI Planner Design

(ii) Domain Knowledge Elicitation, including Task and Goal representation and User Interface.

(iii) Execution and Monitoring system and Replanning on Failure.

(iv) Realistic Trials

The work and ideas on these areas will now be presented in the following sections in sufficient detail to present a complete view.

6. Planner Design.

O-Plan is an abbreviation for "Open Planning Architecture" as the overall design is intended to provide a flexible base for AI planning work. The planner is being implemented as a co-operative venture, rather than the work of an individual, so the design reflects the use of formal software engineering techniques. Emphasis has been placed on independent modules with a well specified set of functional interfaces allowing for rapid prototyping of minimally operating modules in order to quickly provide a

$$f(arg1, arg2, ...) = \text{<value> in <context>}$$

The context mechanism provides efficient storage of a (rapidly) changing database by layering alterations made to earlier states of the database. These changes can be fully or partially ordered within a graph of layers, or contexts, of the database. The model also allows for the retrieval of partially specified items in the database at some point in the graph.

complete system. This modularity allows for experimentation within modules to achieve maximum efficiency, even to the extent of implementation of essential modules in hardware - at least one module has been designed with this in mind.

The design is data structure centred and at the heart of O-Plan there are a set of well defined data structures and some globally accessible data areas.

6.1. The Plan State.

The main data structure in the plan state is a graph of nodes reflecting the activities so far included in the plan, and a set of agendas which hold a list of pending tasks. Each pending task must be carried out by some method for the plan to be acceptable as a result. The current plan being developed and its associated information is called a "plan state". A building block of a plan state is the Pattern record as all statements in the database are of the form:

$$f(arg1, arg2, ...) - <value>$$

These are expressed in pattern form as for example in

$$(on\ a\ b) - true$$

Partial specification is possible within the pattern (except on the first, fixed word which is the function or relation) and the value hence the expression

$$(on\ ?x\ b) - ??$$

would be permissible and indicates that it will match any specification which matches the fixed words "on" and "b", the restriction on the variable "?x" and any value. Patterns occur in many different structures within O-Plan.

Early O-Plan employs three agenda lists which hold the following structures:

Agenda 0   As with NONLIN, the early prototype O-Plan saves partial plan states, along with the alternative choice(s), whenever a decision is taken in the planning process. These are kept on Agenda 0. Full O-Plan will record decision dependencies (e.g. why a variable was bound to a certain value to achieve a condition), to be used for the repair of the single partial plan state instead of using this alternatives agenda.

Agenda 1   This is the main task agenda, or posting area, for pending activities. These are operations which must be carried out for the plan to be valid. It may record failures to be repaired as well as normal steps to be taken to develop the plan to the level of detail required. Only task agenda records which refer to fully instantiated items (i.e. no variables) will be found on Agenda 1.

Agenda 2   The agenda for pending tasks which contain some non-fully bound variables in patterns. Only fully bound agenda 1 records are used in the planning process so the records on this agenda must become fully bound, by plan state variable instantiation, and then moved over to agenda 1 before being processed.

Other important structures in the plan state include:

- the detail of the activity nodes within the graph, recording temporal and resource information, activity type (normally "action" or "dummy") and pattern, and its successor and predecessor activities (to form the graph). Start and finish time windows, resource usage levels and other constraints are held as (minimum, maximum) pairs of numbers which represent numeric bounds on the (possibly symbolic) values of these entities.

- Variables, which can be specified within the Task Formalism schemas to permit a generic description of domain activities (e.g. (put ?x on top of ?y) is a description of a "put-on" action for a robot arm involving any two objects). When the activity is used within the plan then a choice of binding or restriction of the variable will be imposed and any further use of that variable will inherit this binding or restriction. Variables local to the TF schemas which do not get fully bound when the activity is used appear in the plan state as globally accessible variables awaiting further restriction and eventually binding. An agenda record is posted to ensure that a binding is eventually chosen - if it does not get fully instantiated. This plan state variable may be shared and hence restricted by many structures in the plan.

- The agenda records themselves which hold an identifier and type field, a pattern record, type specific information (e.g. that this is an "effect" (on a b) - true to be asserted at activity node 5 in the current plan state network) and a scheduling information field for the particular record. Figure 2 shows this structure.

With the exception of Agenda 0 (which is only present in early O-Plan) all the plan state structures, the values of items in the database and the plan state variables are "context layered". In early O-Plan these context layered plan states can be very deeply layered with many small changes between layers. In full O-Plan, the context layering will only be used for local hypothetical exploration of alternatives.

6.2. Globally Available Information.

The domain dependent information derived from the Task Formalism has the "schema" as its main structure. This is compiled into an internal data structure which holds information about the way in which the schema can be used (e.g. that it expands some action or achieves some effects), information on the requirements of the use of the schema and details the way in which it expands the activity network when used. Resource usage and activity time window information is also contained within a schema. Key "expand" or "achieve" patterns within the schema are used to index into a hash table for quick access to find relevant schemas. Schemas are also used to represent primitive actions, which cannot be further expanded out, and also to specify the initial conditions, or state of the world, in the application domain.

7. Agenda Lists and the Dynamics of O-Plan.

During the planning process the pending tasks are recorded on the agendas. These agenda records contain task specific information, including the task type and scheduling information (currently based on the agenda type, choice branching factor and various heuristic estimates). Associated with each agenda type is a "handler" which can act on an agenda record of the appropriate type and process that record. In doing so it may change the plan state and generate, modify and record new or existing agenda entries. The priority of triggering of these handlers on a particular agenda record is determined by the scheduling information of the agenda records on agenda 1 and the type associated with the agenda record.

The agenda records themselves are therefore the mechanism by which the system is driven in a "best-first" processing manner. The agenda priorities are put forward the "next-best" candidate which, at present, is picked up by a very simple controller which then invokes the appropriate handler for the agenda record type, with the type dependent information passed on as a parameter. Figure 3 shows the Controller Cycle of early O-Plan.

This approach has some similarities to Blackboard Architectures (e.g. see Hayes-Roth [10]) except that there is a difference in the dynamics of the problem solving process. Problem solving in O-Plan proceeds as a sequence of cycles, each of which is capable of generating new entries within the agendas. The handlers, or Knowledge Sources, are driven by the agenda records which hold the scheduling information determining the next best. The selected knowledge source then executes - possibly creating new, prioritised agenda records or modifying existing records. These events may even cause agenda priorities to change (e.g. by removing a record from an agenda, or by variable restriction or binding). This differs from full blackboard architectures in that they have greater flexibility on which knowledge sources are executable - changes to the triggering information being dynamically evaluated. However both systems support an opportunistic approach to problem solving.

The early O-Plan scheduling system is fairly rigid in its assignment of priorities to agenda records but full O-Plan will include a rule based system which will allow the scheduler to better reflect the understanding of the problem and how it relates to the applicability of the knowledge sources.

One interesting aspect of O-Plan's agenda record driven system is the ease with which the user can interrupt the process to take control. The cycle controller checks for user attention and adds a very high priority agenda record on to the agenda 1 list. This in turn drives the system in exactly the same way as any other record in that it calls a "user" handler or knowledge source to be executed. The user may then query the system, control the next few cycles or whatever. Other handlers can also request user assistance by a similar mechanism.

The cycle controller also has the capability of adding agenda records to the agenda list via a "diary" mechanism, which may do things such as "print a representation of the plan state every 10 cycles" or "review the satisfied conditions every minute of planning" or even modify some detail of an agenda record (e.g. up the priority or prune a tree of suggested arcs to be linked into the activity graph).

Knowledge sources have the power to "poison" any plan state if it is known that no solution can be found from the current plan state. In early O-Plan an agenda 0 record would then be used to go back to an earlier partial plan state and to choose an alternative to the decision made at that point. In full O-Plan a "repair" agenda record will be scheduled to use the assumptions recorded at decision points and to repair the plan state to allow the planning process to continue. If a plan state has been poisoned and there are no further agenda 0 records (or no relevant dependencies in full O-Plan) then there is no solution to be found within the specified domain and given constraints. A solution has been found when there are no further tasks outstanding on agenda 1 (and by implication agenda 2), however there may be further solutions to be found if there are still any agenda 0 alternatives left.

8. Knowledge within Plans.

An O-Plan solution for a planning task contains more information than simply the graph of activities with perhaps critical path information. From the Goal Structure Table (GOST) and the related Table of Multiple Effects (TOME) it is possible to extract information about why actions are inserted into the plans, specifically the conditions they contribute towards, and where effects are asserted which contribute to the satisfaction of conditions these actions require. Also it is possible to query the "context" or known state of the world, at any point in the plan. Hence it is possible to play through, or simulate, the operation of a plan - the potential here is enormous.

9. Domain Knowledge Elicitation.

The human planner or domain specialists interface to the AI planner through the TF Workstation [11]. This workstation communicates with the domain specialists or experts to elicit their knowledge about the application domain or with the human planner to build a description of the goal task or to show the resulting plan. The aim of the workstation is therefore to provide a natural, ergonomic interface for the creation of the structured Task Formalism and the presentation of plan results.

The current prototype TF Workstation provides a demonstration of the functions to be included in the user interface. It provides separate regions for structured text editing, using a TF-knowledgable editor, and for graphical editing of activity orderings within schemas. Control of operations within this graphics centred workstation is effected by mouse and pop-up menus. Figures 5a and 5b show typical sessions at the workstation's main window when editing a schema and viewing results respectively.

Consideration has been given to the imposition of a requirements analysis methodology onto the user interface to impose structure on the knowledge elicitation process. The use of Systems Designers' CORE methodology has been considered (on an M.Sc project [12]) as this has much in common with the structures used in the present Task Formalism. There is a clear overlap between knowledge elicitation for a planning domain and the specification of modules in a software engineering environment.

10. Plan Execution, Monitoring and Re-planning

Goal Structure is a high level representation of information about a plan which states the relationship between the individual actions in the plan and their purposes with respect to the goals or sub-goals they achieve. This information is used by the O-Plan planner to detect and correct conflicts when higher level plans are refined to greater levels of detail.

Goal Structure also represents information on which an execution monitor can operate effectively. The Goal Structure statements represent precisely the outcome of any operation which should be monitored. If lower level failures can be detected and corrected while preserving the stated Goal Structure, the fault need not be reported to a higher level. The implications of any propagated failure are computable and corrective action can be planned.

The techniques are equally applicable to the generation of plans and the monitoring of their execution for fully automated or fully manual situations as well as the more usual mixed environment. Intelligent sensors can be instructed as to what to monitor and by when to report. Hence we are suggesting an overall organisation within which individual modules for planning or control can operate. We have published a paper (Tate [13]) describing the proposed execution monitoring framework.

11. Applications of AI Planning.

O-Plan is being tested via the development of domain descriptions in the enhanced Task Formalism for various applications. The automatic generation of plans for representative tasks is being undertaken in these domains. The applications of interest to us at present include:

- small batch manufacturing and assembly systems

- logistics, command and control

- project management (such as in civil engineering and software production)

- spacecraft mission sequencing

Early O-Plan has generated simple plans (of between 30 and 60 activities) in house building and software production project management domains. The spacecraft mission sequencing example will use the published domain description given to the NASA Jet Propulsion Laboratory DEVISER planner (itself based on our own earlier NONLIN system). This will provide an early realistic trial and comparative data.

We are also engaged in an Alvey Community Club project (PLANIT) to show the benefits of manipulating pre-existing plans. This will provide detailed information on three domains:

- back axle assembly at Jaguar Cars

- a software production project at Price Waterhouse

- a job shop problem at Harwell Atomic Engergy Authority

The PLANIT project will also be of value in providing realistic data on which to try out the automatic production of plans in these domains (a development assumed by the Alvey Community Club project).

We are also concerned with the specification of suitable interfaces to an AI planning system from higher level management, design and aggregate (or capacity based rough-cut) scheduling software and to lower level detail planners, instruction generators, resource smoothing packages, intelligent sensors and robotic devices.

12. Conclusion.

This paper gave an overview of the O-Plan (Open Planning Architecture) project and the important concepts it builds on. These concepts are essential for domain and task description for input to the new planning system and for manipulating "knowledge-rich" information in the resulting plan.

The design approach, centred round clear functional interfaces to modules, was explained and an insight into the dynamics of the system, driven by the current plan state and its agenda lists, was given in enough detail to present a complete description of the system. O-Plan is currently operating at about the level of the earlier NONLIN planner although the potential which will be achieved in the near future will allow planning in more varied and realistic domains.

13. References

[1] Tate, A. (1977) Generating Project Networks, in IJCAI-77, Cambridge, MA, USA.

[2] Sacerdoti, E.D. (1977) "A Structure for Plans and Behaviour" Elsevier-North Holland.

[3] Tate, A. (1984) Goal Structure - Capturing the Intent of Plans, in ECAI-84, Pisa, Italy.

[4] Bell, C. and Tate, A. (1985) Using Temporal Constraints to Restrict Search in a Planner. Third Alvey IKBS Planning SIG Workshop, Sunningdale, UK. Also in AIAI-TR-5, Artificial Intelligence Applications Institute, University of Edinburgh.

[5] Vere, S. (1981) Planning in time: windows and durations for activities and goals. IEEE Trans. on Pattern Analysis and Machine Intelligence,

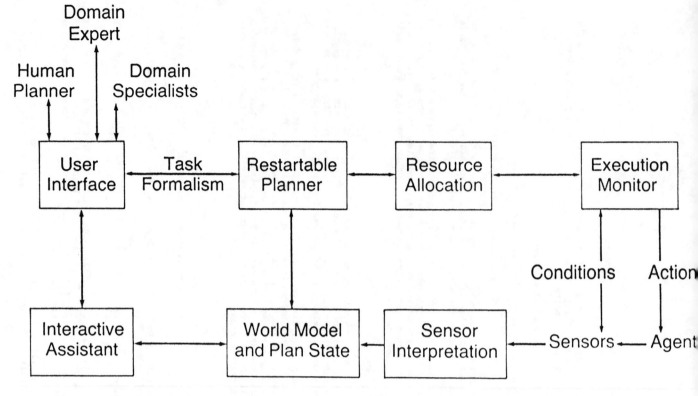

Vol. PAMI-5, No. 3, pp. 246-267, May 1983.

[6] Bell, C. (1985) Resource Management in Automated Planning, Fourth Alvey IKBS Planning SIG Workshop, Essex, UK. Also in AIAI-TR-7, Artificial Intelligence Applications Institute, University of Edinburgh.

[7] Tate, A. (1984) Functions in Context Data Base. Paper for the Second Alvey Workshop on Architectures for Large Knowledge Bases, Manchester University, July 1984. Also in AIAI-TR-1, Artificial Intelligence Applications Institute, University of Edinburgh.

[8] Hayes, P.J. (1975) A Representation for Robot Plans, in IJCAI-75, Tbilisi, USSR.

[9] Daniels, L. (1983) Planning and Operations Research, in Artificial Intelligence: Tools, Techniques and Applications (eds O'Shea and Eisenstadt).

[10] Hayes-Roth, B. (1983) The BlackBoard Architecture: a general framework for problem solving? Heuritic Programming Report HPP-83-30 Computer Science Dept. Stanford University

[11] Tate, A. and Currie, K. (1985) The O-Plan Task Formalism Workstation. Third Alvey IKBS Planning SIG Workshop, Sunningdale, UK. Also in AIAI-TR-6, Artificial Intelligence Applications Institute, University of Edinburgh.

[12] Wilson, A.C.M. (1984) Information for Planning, M.Sc Thesis, University of Edinburgh.

[13] Tate, A. (1984) Planning and Condition Monitoring in a FMS. Proceedings of the International Conference on Flexible Automation Systems. Institute of the Electrical Engineers, London, UK, July 1984. Also in AIAI-TR-2, Artificial Intelligence Applications Institute, University of Edinburgh.

O-Plan Control Loop

O-Plan Agenda Record

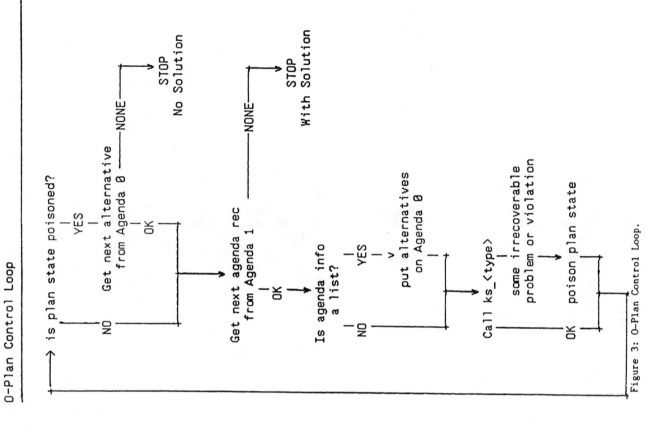

Figure 3: O-Plan Control Loop.

Figure 2: An Agenda Record.

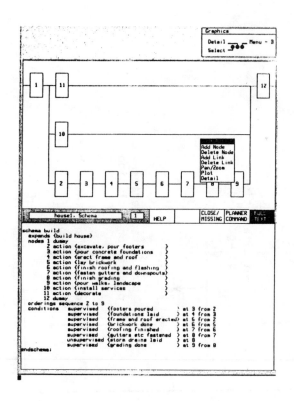

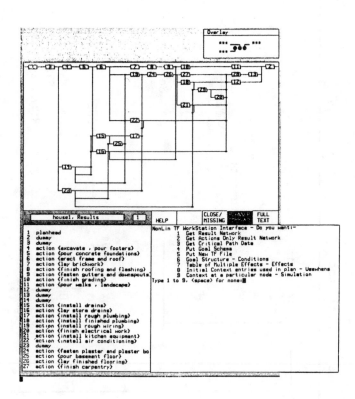

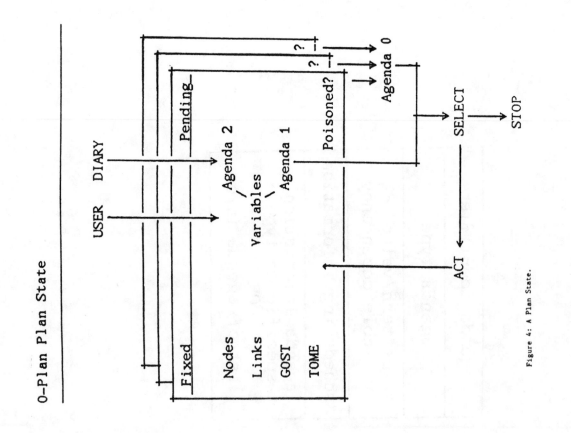

Figure 4: A Plan State.

Hierarchical planning involving deadlines, travel time, and resources

THOMAS DEAN[1]

Department of Computer Science, Brown University, Box 1910, Providence, RI 02912, U.S.A.

R. JAMES FIRBY

Department of Computer Science, Yale University, Box 2158, Yale Station, New Haven, CT 06520, U.S.A.

AND

DAVID MILLER

The Artificial Intelligence Group, Jet Propulsion Laboratory, California Institute of Technology, 4800 Oak Grove Drive, Pasadena, CA 91109, U.S.A.

Received July 30, 1987

Revision accepted September 19, 1988

This paper describes a planning architecture that supports a form of hierarchical planning well suited to applications involving deadlines, travel time, and resource considerations. The architecture is based upon a temporal database, a heuristic evaluator, and a decision procedure for refining partial plans. A partial plan consists of a set of tasks and constraints on their order, duration, and potential resource requirements. The temporal database records the partial plan that the planner is currently working on and computes certain consequences of that information to be used in proposing methods to further refine the plan. The heuristic evaluator examines the space of linearized extensions of a given partial plan in order to reject plans that fail to satisfy basic requirements (e.g., hard deadlines and resource limitations) and to estimate the utility of plans that meet these requirements. The information provided by the temporal database and the heuristic evaluator is combined using a decision procedure that determines how best to refine the current partial plan. Neither the temporal database nor the heuristic evaluator is complete and, without reasonably accurate information concerning the possible resource requirements of the tasks in a partial plan, there is a significant risk of missing solutions. A specification language that serves to encode expectations concerning the duration and resource requirements of tasks greatly reduces this risk, enabling useful evaluations of partial plans. Details of the specification language and examples illustrating how such expectations are exploited in decision making are provided.

Cet article décrit une architecture de planification qui soutient une forme de planification hiérarchique adaptée aux applications mettant en cause des limites, des temps de déplacement et des considérations au niveau des ressources. Cette architecture est fonction d'une base de données temporelle, d'un évaluateur heuristique et d'un processus décisionnel permettant de perfectionner des plans partiels. Un plan partiel consiste en une série de tâches ainsi que leurs contraintes au niveau de l'ordre, de la durée et des exigences possibles en matière de ressources. La base de données temporelle enregistre le plan partiel sur lequel le planificateur travaille et évalue certaines conséquences de ces données qui serviront à proposer des méthodes de perfectionnement du plan. L'évaluation heuristique examine l'espace des extensions linéarisées d'un plan partiel donné afin de rejeter les plans qui ne satisfont pas aux exigences de base (par ex. : dates limites serrées et limitations des ressources) et d'évaluer l'utilité des plans qui respectent ces exigences. Les renseignements fournis par la base de données temporelle et l'évaluation heuristique sont combinés à l'aide d'un processus décisionnel qui détermine la meilleure façon de perfectionner le plan partiel actuel. Ni la base de données temporelle, ni l'évaluateur heuristique ne sont complets. Sans des renseignements relativement précis concernant les exigences possibles au niveau des ressources des tâches d'un plan partiel, il y a un important risque que des solutions nous échappent. Un langage de spécification qui sert à encoder les attentes concernant les exigences au niveau de la durée et des ressources des tâches réduit grandement ce risque et permet des évaluations utiles de plans partiels. Des détails au sujet du langage de spécification et des exemples illustrant comment de telles attentes sont exploitées dans les processus décisionnel sont fournis.

[Traduit par la revue]

Comput. Intell. 4, 381–398 (1988)

1. Introduction

Planning is generally viewed as a process of incremental construction. At any point in the process, a planner will have before it a partially constructed plan that it is working to finish; the actions in the plan or the order in which they are to be executed may not be completely specified. For instance, while constructing a plan to manufacture a particular part, a planner may commit to using a specific manufacturing process without committing to a specific machine with which to carry out that process. Planning proceeds as a series of decisions concerning how to refine (or provide more detail to) the partially constructed plan. These decisions determine a search through a space in which each state is a partially constructed plan and each search operator serves to refine a partially constructed plan.

To direct the search, most planners employ some means of evaluating a partially constructed plan. Evaluation typically involves predicting the effects of actions already in the plan to determine whether or not they are likely to bring about some desired state of affairs. With appropriate knowledge, a planner can reason about actions and their effects at many different levels of detail and evaluate a partially constructed plan by predicting whether it brings about the desired state of affairs, given the current level of detail.

To support plan evaluation, the planner needs domain knowl-

---

[1]Much of the work described in this paper was carried out while all three of the authors were at Yale University. The order of names is alphabetical and has no other significance.

Printed in Canada / Imprimé au Canada

edge of two types: a database of rules that establish the cause-and-effect relations between actions and their results, and a database of rules that define the conditions for using certain methods for refining partially constructed plans. In addition to this static knowledge, a planner must maintain a database holding its partially constructed plan and the observed and predicted events corresponding to the context in which that plan is to be executed. The planner uses this temporal database and its rules for refining partially constructed plans to decide how best to add to the plan it is building.

In this paper, we build upon an approach to planning referred to as *hierarchical planning* (Sacerdoti 1977; Tate 1977; Vere 1983; Wilkins 1984). The main intuition that we borrow from hierarchical planning is that the search can often be directed so that decisions made early in planning are independent of decisions made later. To provide the necessary direction, the planning system described in these pages makes use of a powerful representation language that allows one to encode domain-specific information about the possible consequences of partially constructed plans. In addition, the system employs two programs that can make use of this information to predict further consequences. The first program, the temporal database manager, keeps track of consequences that are true of every completion of the currently partially constructed plan. The second program, the heuristic task scheduler, ensures that at all times there exists some completion of the current partially constructed plan that satisfies the planner's top level goals. The way these two programs are used in deciding what refinements to make to a partially constructed plan is central to this paper. Neither program is guaranteed to be complete; hence, there are situations in which the system will claim that there is no solution when there actually is one. However, if the system proposes a solution, then, barring inaccuracies in the system's knowledge, the solution is guaranteed correct.

The rest of this paper describes the FORBIN planner: a system for generating plans in domains involving mobile robots, deadlines, and limited resources. Throughout the paper we will use examples drawn from an automated factory domain. Most of the examples do not require detailed knowledge of the domain; Appendix A provides the details for those interested.

2. Planning as search in the FORBIN system

Each state in the FORBIN search space is a partially constructed plan. A partially constructed plan consists of a set of actions and a set of constraints on the expected duration and order of execution of those actions. An action is said to be *primitive* if breaking it down into simpler actions will reveal no additional useful information. Examples of primitive actions in the FORBIN domain are ''Pick up the widget'' and ''Push the lathe start button.''

A *task* is simply an action in the planner's current partially constructed plan. A task corresponding to a primitive action is said to be primitive; otherwise it is said to be *problematic*. Most planners deal with tasks that involve making certain facts true of the world. For example, if the desired fact is that block A is on block B (i.e., (ON A B)), then the associated task is (ACHIEVE (ON A B)). Carrying out such a task corresponds to executing primitive actions that bring about a state of the world in which the desired fact is true. Using this notion of task, planning is defined as the search for a sequence of primitive actions that will carry out all of the tasks that the planner has been assigned.

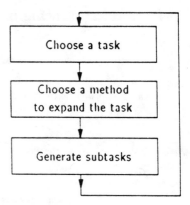

FIG. 1. Basic algorithm for task expansion.

In some approaches, each primitive action is associated with a unique search operator;[2] a partially constructed plan is a sequence of primitive actions, and applying an operator consists of appending the action associated with the operator to the end of the current partially constructed plan. In FORBIN, as in most hierarchical planners, the notion of a search operator is somewhat more complex. Transforming the current partially constructed plan may involve splicing in new tasks and imposing additional constraints on existing tasks. Planning proceeds by selecting a problematic task and attempting to replace or supplement its current specification with a set of other, hopefully less problematic, tasks. This process of transformation is referred to as *expansion*. For each nonprimitive action, the planner has a set of *methods* for carrying out these expansions.

Each method specifies a set of actions and constraints on their order and duration. In addition, each method is annotated with information that describes how good it is in a given set of circumstances. Applying a search operator in the FORBIN system consists of combining the actions and constraints in a particular method with those of the current partially constructed plan. Simplifying somewhat, the process of planning consists of choosing a problematic task that has yet to be expanded, choosing a method to expand that task, and transforming the current partially constructed plan using the chosen method. If there are no problematic tasks requiring expansion, then the plan is complete and the process stops. The basic cycle of activity is depicted in Fig. 1.

In FORBIN, the initial set of tasks describes a partially constructed plan, albeit a plan at a fairly high level of abstraction. Each task is associated with an interval of time during which it is to be carried out, and generally there are constraints on the order and conpletion time of the tasks. This partially constructed plan is represented in a *task network* (McDermott 1977). Figure 2a illustrates a simple task network corresponding to two initially supplied tasks. Expansion results in adding subtask and precedence links to the network. Figure 2b shows the result of expanding each of the two tasks in Fig. 2a. The task network encodes the basic decisions of the planner. As we will see, there is a great deal more that has to be represented to support hierarchical planning. In particular, the effects of the planner's proposed actions as well as the effects of events outside the planner's control all have to be taken into account in evaluating a partially constructed plan.

---

[2] In these approaches, operators and actions are in one-to-one correspondence, so the two terms are often used interchangeably.

(a)

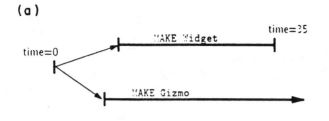

(b)

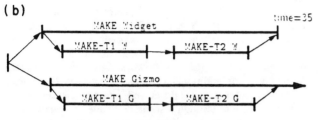

FIG. 2. Simple task networks.

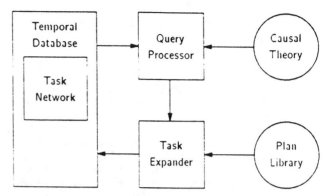

FIG. 3. Basic architecture for hierarchical planning.

Many hierarchical planners can be viewed as having the basic architecture of Fig. 3. Arrows indicate the flow of information between modules, circles represent static knowledge sources, and the box labeled "temporal database" indicates the dynamic component of the planner's knowledge. The task expander implements the algorithm sketched in Fig. 1, and the query processor assists in making choices by answering questions concerning the contents of the temporal database. Planners can be distinguished by the expressiveness of the languages used for representing plans and causal rules and by the techniques used for reasoning about such plans. The temporal database contains a set of cached deductions concerning the state of the partially constructed plan and (some of) the effects of the proposed actions. In the NASL planner (McDermott 1977), the temporal database and the task network are identical. In other planners, the temporal database may consist of a task network annotated with information concerning the truth of propositions corresponding to the effects of each task (e.g., the *table of multiple effects* of NOAH (Sacerdoti 1977)).

In general, the effects of one task are contingent upon the effects of preceding tasks. An *interaction* corresponds to a situation in which the effect of one task serves to undermine the intended effect of another task. The main difficulty with hierarchical planning is sorting out unexpected interactions involving the expansion method chosen for different tasks. The actions and the constraints on their order and duration within a single method will have been chosen so that they do not interfere with each other. However, when a plan is built for several tasks, subtasks from the different expansions may become interspersed and cause interactions that compromise the success of the plan under construction.

To notice and deal with such interactions, the planner must keep track of the expected state of the world resulting from each task in the plan it has built so far. By carefully choosing expansion methods and orderings that preserve the conditions required by actions already specified, interactions can often be avoided. The hard part is anticipating such interactions. One way to accomplish this is annotate methods with expectations concerning what conditions they will require. These expectations are then used to predict certain consequences of the current partially constructed plan and guide decision making so that any interactions that are encountered can easily be resolved. To make good decisions concerning which expansion method to use, the FORBIN planner must continually predict the expected future at each point in its plan. This process of prediction is referred to as *projection* and plays an integral role in decision making.

3. An overview of the planner and its algorithm

Broadly speaking, the FORBIN planning algorithm consists of two operations — expansion and projection — that are repeated until a completely refined plan is reached. The contribution of the FORBIN system is the way each operation is accomplished without becoming computationally intractable. As mentioned, the knowledge that the planner brings to each problem can be thought of as residing in two separate databases: one containing cause-and-effect relationships for use in projecting the expected results of the plan being constructed and one containing expansion methods for refining that plan to more detail. The plan under constructing is represented in a temporal database that keeps track of the tasks already in the plan, any events the planner does not control but knows will occur, and the expected effects of both the planned tasks and uncontrolled events. Each time that the planner refines one of the tasks in the plan, temporal projection is used to update the temporal database to include any new effects that can be derived from the new detail added to the plan.

To refine a partially constructed plan, the planner chooses a task to work on and consults the database of expansions to find available refinement methods. The temporal database is then consulted to determine which of those methods is appropriate under the circumstances expected at execution time. This consultation generally produces a small number of candidate methods suitable for the expansion. To choose between these candidates, a detailed projection is performed to determine which method is best. This projection step involves a search through the possible total orderings of the steps in the unfinished plan, and the only backtracking done by the FORBIN system is that required for this search. Once the best refinement method is found, it is integrated into the current plan and the temporal database is updated accordingly. Should FORBIN ever find itself with no appropriate refinement method for a particular task, it simply stops and signals failure. The FORBIN system does employ very sophisticated routines for tracking the reasons behind its expansion decisions, but currently there is no theory for recovering when those decisions turn out to be incorrect. As we will see, however, FORBIN goes to great lengths to make the right decisions the first time around.

Before we describe the FORBIN algorithm in more detail,

we will briefly consider some of the primary components of the reasoning system.

3.1. The causal theory

The causal theory describes the ways that each of the planner's actions will change the world. In particular, the theory contains two types of rules: those specifying the effects of executing tasks and those specifying the way effects interact with one another. Most task effects correspond to atomic propositions that are made true as a result of actions being executed or, more generally, events occurring. Other effects refer to quantities that change continuously over time: quantities the planner can add to, subtract from, or change with processes that continue without intervention once begun. For example, the action of starting an automatic milling machine has the simple effect of changing its state from off to on and the more complex effects of using up raw materials to make the part, causing wear on the cutting bit, and at some point in the future causing a finished part to exist where there was none before.

The causal theory must also concisely capture the interactions that occur between effects. Many of the results of a task come about indirectly and it is inappropriate to encode them in the task's effects. Turning on a light might cause a solar-powered sculpture to begin turning, but there should be no mention of solar-powered sculptures in the rules describing the effects of toggling the light switch. Rather, the connection between the switch and the sculpture should be encoded in a separate set of rules that refer to much more general physical principles.

3.2. The temporal database

The heart of the FORBIN system is its temporal datbase. The database maintains a picture of the expected future, given the plan so far, the causal theory, and any known external events. This representation of the future is used for two different purposes: (1) it gives the expected situation that each task in the plan will encounter (to use when choosing an expansion for the task) and (2) it prevents the plan under construction from becoming invalid by ensuring that task expansion preconditions do not get changed.

When planning begins, the temporal database contains the initial world state and the time and nature of any events under external control. As the plan is constructed, each new subtask the system commits to is added to the database along with its expected duration and starting time. The database then applies rules from the causal theory to determine the effects of that task and to propagate those effects into the future to compute the expected world state at all times.[3]

The choice of any particular action to add to the plan will usually depend on the situation expected when that action is to be executed. For example, the planner might decide that the best way to get a new widget by 2:00 p.m. is to make it on the lathe and add such a subtask to the database. During later planning, however, the planner might decide that to fill an important order, it would like to use the lathe to make gizmos all day. Simply adding this use of the lathe to the database would lead to an inconsistent future and to the planner mistakenly thinking it could make the widget and gizmos at the same time. To avoid such situations two precautions are taken. First, when a task is added to the database, facts assumed true when

---

[3]In general, projection need not terminate. FORBIN gets around this by imposing a lower limit on the duration of events and an upper limit on the interval over which projected events will be considered.

choosing the task are recorded along with the task. Second, before choosing a new task to use in the plan, the system checks the database to ensure that adding the task will not cause any previous assumptions to become invalid. Never adding a new task that violates a previous assumption avoids the creation of inconsistent futures.

This nice neat picture of the database as a complete description of the expected future is complicated by the fact that planned tasks may be only partially ordered. Projection of the sort required by FORBIN involving partially ordered events is *NP-hard* (Chapman 1987) even without the temporally varying quantities that FORBIN allows. To maintain computational tractability, an important heuristic is used: the temporal database only represents (or caches) those atomic assertions that can be derived from the task network, ignoring the possible consequences of additional ordering constraints (see Dean 1985). Order-dependent effects and quantity variations are taken into account through a separate detailed projection that explores a subset of all total task orders consistent with the partial order. This separate projection ensures the temporal database has at least one consistent ordering without having to constrain the task network to keep that ordering for the rest of the planning process.

3.3. The task expander

Refining a partially constructed plan proceeds by expanding a task into a set of simpler subtasks until only primitive actions requiring no further refinement remain. The routines responsible for performing the expansions are called the *task expander*. The database of refinement methods used by the task expander consists of "recipes" for expanding various task types into subtasks. Refinement in FORBIN proceeds hierarchically through several levels of methods culminating in expansions involving only primitive actions. Hierarchical refinement is used so that the temporal database always contains all planning goals, and hence the whole expected future, at some level of detail. Representing the entire future in the database provides a solid basis for each level of expansion and allows FORBIN to take account of important interactions early in planning.

3.4. The basic FORBIN algorithm

The basic planning algorithm is easy to understand in terms of the task expander, the temporal database, and the causal theory. The task expander selects a nonprimitive task from the database and looks up all appropriate refinement methods in the expansion library. It then asks the database which methods can be used in the context of the current task network (i.e., some methods will be based on assumptions that are not expected to be true, and some methods will have effects that invalidate previous assumptions). If no methods will work, then the task cannot be carried out in the current plan and FORBIN fails. If one or more methods will work, then the task expander scores them and chooses the "best." The best expansion is then added to the temporal database, and the database is updated in accordance with the causal theory. This cycle of choosing a task to work on, picking the best expansion based on the expected future, and then updating the temporal database continues until either some task cannot be expanded and failure occurs or all tasks have been reduced to primitive actions and the plan is complete. This basic cycle of activity is sketched in **Fig. 4**.

To support the selection of potential expansion methods, the temporal database handles a class of queries known as *abduc-*

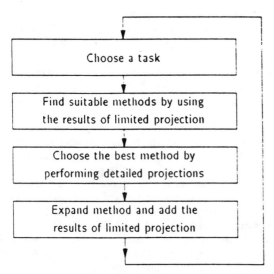

FIG. 4. FORBIN algorithm for task expansion.

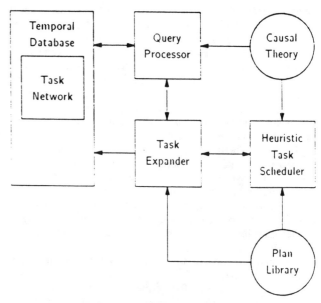

FIG. 5. FORBIN architecture.

tive queries. An abductive query is made to see whether the assumptions for a method are satisfied in the current temporal database. The answer returned from such a query includes a set of additional ordering constraints that may be added to the database to satisfy the assumptions. If a particular query can be satisfied in some totally ordered extension of the current partial order, then the temporal database is guaranteed to respond positively. However, because the temporal database only caches certain projection results and not all, it is possible that the database will respond positively even in cases where the query is not satisfied in any totally ordered extension.

To verify abductive queries, FORBIN employs an additional set of procedures for projecting the detailed consequences of the partially ordered task network. If a query is false in all totally ordered extensions of the current partial order, then these routines would detect this. The query routines of the temporal database act as an initial filter; the detailed projection routines are the final arbiter. The detailed projection routines are also used to score expansion methods by installing each expansion into the plan in a temporary database and then simulating the result considering various consistent total orders. Scoring is handled using domain-specific utility functions encoded with the various expansion methods. By actually looking at total orders, the simulation procedures are able to make very accurate predictions concerning the potential value of a given expansion. To avoid the possibility of doing an intractable amount of work in performing its evaluations, the simulation routines employ a strong heuristic component (for details see Miller 1985) which limits the number of total orders examined to only the few most promising ones. This method of evaluation is incomplete, since possible good total orderings may be missed and the corresponding methods rejected, but it is always correct. Within the limits of the causal theory, if a method is determined to work by the evaluation routines, it is correct.

Our initial hope was that the search done by the evaluation routines could be limited by passing them only the "relevant" parts of the current plan. Unfortunately, we never developed a theory of "relevance" and FORBIN was forced to apply the heuristic task scheduler, as the simulation routines were collectively called, to the entire set of tasks. It is our opinion that the knowledge necessary for restricting the application of the heu-

ristic task scheduler would be largely domain specific, as our attempts to derive a purely domain-independent theory met with little success.

3.5. *The basic FORBIN architecture*

Figure 5 shows the architecture of the FORBIN planner simplified to emphasize its interesting aspects. The temporal database manager is responsible for selectively caching deductions (limited projection) concerning the state of the partially constructed plan. The task expander implements the algorithm sketched in Fig. 4. The heuristic task scheduler handles the detailed predictions required for selecting among methods. In addition, FORBIN employs a *task queue manager* (not shown in Fig. 5) that keeps track of the tasks in the database that still need further refinement and decides on the best order to make those refinements.

An important consideration when designing the FORBIN planning system was that planning and execution might occur together. In particular, refinement should concentrate on those tasks to be executed earliest so that their constituent primitive actions can be "peeled off the front" of the plan and executed even while tasks later in the plan are unexpanded. Also, new tasks should be allowed to be introduced by the user at any time and should be incorporated into the growing and executing plan with as little disruption as possible. The task queue manager handles both of these duties in a uniform manner by giving priority for refinement to those tasks whose deadlines are approaching and by inserting user-added tasks into the queue just like subtasks spawned through expansion. The FORBIN goal of concurrent planning and execution has been only partially fulfilled so far, but the need for a system with the right properties has been a driving force behind its structure.

4. The FORBIN plan language: causal theory

The FORBIN system gives the calculation of expected states of the world a central role in plan construction. Each new task added to the plan is designed to have a particular effect on the world but, typically, it will have that effect only if the world is in an appropriate state to begin with. For example, putting down a cup will not leave it on the kitchen table unless we are, at an absolute minimum. in the kitchen. To ensure that planned actions achieve their intended effects, the task network must be arranged so that each task will begin execution in the correct world state. The FORBIN planner makes such arrangements in two ways: first. the initial choice of where to place a task is based on predicted futures from the existing task network, and second, constraints are added to the task network to guarantee that existing tasks will have their intended effects. Predicting the possible futures of a task network and confirming they are compatible with known constraints is called projection.

To make FORBIN projection successful. the task network representation must incorporate a realistic notion of time. When tasks have completion deadlines and quantities can vary continuously through time, the duration of every action in the plan is critical in predicting the future. Two tasks that start at the same time may generate very different results depending on which takes longer. Proper projection requires representing the duration of each task in the task network, the start time of every change to the world state, and how long each new state continues in time.

The accuracy of FORBIN projection also depends on the expressiveness of its *causal theory*. It must specify not only the effect each task has on the world, but also the way those effects evolve through time after the task is complete. In most previous planning systems, causal theories are composed of rules specifying a list of assertions to add or delete in order to model each action being executed. The world state at any one time is seen as a set of assertions like (ON *A B*) or (COLOR *X* RED). By applying the add and delete lists from each action in the plan in turn, the expected world state at all times can be determined. Projection rules employing simple add and delete lists are quite powerful even in complex worlds, but they are inadequate for representing actions that make relative changes to quantities or actions that begin processes which change continuously on their own. For example, the action (DEPOSIT $10) might have the effect of increasing one's bank account by $10. The resulting balance, however, must be calculated from the previous balance and may depend on a complex function of previous changes that includes interest and instant-teller charges. Similarly, the action (TURN-ON FAUCET) might start filling the sink with water, but no set of add and delete lists alone can predict what time it will be filled. FORBIN must represent both *static effects*, previously handled with add and delete lists, and *dynamic effects* which have results that change with time and context.

4.1. Specifying the causal theory

The FORBIN causal theory comes in two parts: the *domain physics* and the *task descriptors*. The domain physics contains the system's knowledge about every aspect of the world relevant to projection. For example, the FORBIN factory domain physics declares that there are such things as lathes, that they can be used to make only one thing at a time, that if one is turned off it will stay off unless acted upon explicitly, and so on. The domain physics mentions all fact types to be used, how these facts evolve through time once they become true, and how facts interact with one another if they become true at the same time.

A task descriptor encodes the way a task is expected to change the world when executed. Task descriptors are analogous to the add and delete lists of past planners with extensions to include statements about dynamic effects as well. For example, the description of a (RUN-LATHE . . .)[4] task might specify that a metal blank will be used up, a volume of shavings will be produced, and a new product will be brought into being.

In most previous planning systems. the domain physics, task descriptors, and expansion methods were bundled into the single notion of an operator (Fikes and Nilsson 1971; Sacerdoti 1977). An operator represented the expansion of a task and included an add/delete list describing how that task changed the world. However, FORBIN must separate task-expansion methods from task effects because the hierarchical elaboration strategy that FORBIN uses initially places each task into the task network in an unexpanded state. Projecting the expected futures of such a network requires knowledge of a task's effects before it is expanded. Since a task may have many different expansions, its task descriptor gives a summary of expected effects from all of its expansions. The domain physics describes how these effects change during the time *between* the end of one task and the start of the next.

4.2. Domain physics

There are two subsections to the domain physics: one to deal with the static-fact types and the other to deal with dynamic-fact types. Static facts are used to represent facets of the world that become true and remain unchanged until specifically acted upon, while dynamic facts are used to represent quantities that are influenced by actions and may change over time without any intervention. For example, the task descriptor for (MOVE-TO WIDGET IN-BOX) might specify that the static fact (LOCATION WIDGET IN-BOX) becomes true and the dynamic fact representing the weight of the box is increased: (BOX-WEIGHT +(WEIGHT-OF WIDGET)).

The distinction between static and dynamic facts is not logically required, since static effects are a subset of dynamic ones. However, the FORBIN system separates the two for pragmatic efficiency reasons that allow different processing for each type during projection. Assertions that result from projecting static facts alone are cached to make up the temporal database used in choosing candidate task expansions. In contrast, the detailed results from projecting dynamic facts are not cached in the task network. After they are used to choose between candidate expansions and ensure the choice is compatible with previous commitments, they are dropped so as not to overconstrain future choices.

4.2.1. Static facts

Static facts represent aspects of the world state that are made true and remain true until explicitly changed. They are modeled in the FORBIN system as predicate calculus assertions and defined with the form:

(DEFINE-FACT (⟨name⟩ ⟨var1⟩ ⟨var2⟩ . . .))

For example, many of the properties of a lathe are static in nature and might be defined as:[5]

---

[4]In the FORBIN plan language, all tasks, facts, and states are referred to in terms of *patterns*. A pattern is a list with the first element representing the task, fact, or quantity type. Remaining elements in the pattern are arguments that modify the type. Arguments will often appear as variables in the language but during planning all variables will be instantiated.

[5]Variables are specified by prefacing their name with a "?". This notation is drawn from the DUCK programming language (McDermott 1985) used to implement much of the FORBIN system.

```
(DEFINE-FACT (SETUP-LATHE ?lathe ?type))
(DEFINE-FACT (BIT ?lathe ?type))
(DEFINE-FACT (STATUS ?machine ?status))
```

All static features of the world referred to by task descriptors must be defined in this way. Static facts are exactly facts previously represented in add and delete lists.

Once a static fact has been defined, the projection machinery knows that whenever such a fact becomes true, it will remain true until specifically altered. The traditional way of altering a static fact is to delete it from the current state and add a new fact reflecting the change. However, the explicit deletion of a fact is subsumed in the FORBIN system by the clipping rule. Clipping rules declare that the beginning of one static fact causes the end of another. For example, asserting (STATUS LATHE-1 RUNNING) should cause the fact (STATUS LATHE-1 IDLE) to stop being true. There is no need to explicitly delete (STATUS LATHE-1 IDLE) as long as that rule is known. Clipping rules are specified with the form:

```
(DEFINE-CLIP ⟨fact 1⟩ ⟨fact 2⟩ ⟨condition fact⟩)
```

which states that whenever ⟨fact 1⟩ becomes true while the ⟨condition fact⟩ is true, it causes ⟨fact 2⟩ to end (and vice versa). For the example above one might use

```
(DEFINE-CLIP (STATUS ?machine ?status1)
             (STATUS ?machine ?status2)
             (NOT ( = ?status1 ?status2)))
```

Clipping rules allow task descriptors to assert only static facts they make true because facts they clip are taken care of automatically. Clipping rules are more general than delete lists because they work with facts generated by temporal forward chaining rules as well as those from task descriptors.

The FORBIN causal theory can represent more complex interactions between static facts than just clipping between static facts through the use of temporal forward chaining rules. The two most important rule types are DEFINE-OVERLAP and DEFINE-CAUSE which declare that whenever certain static facts overlap in time, new facts should be asserted.[6] With DEFINE-OVERLAP the new fact extends over the interval of time the initiating facts overlap, whereas a new fact spawned by DEFINE-CAUSE persists indefinitely (unless clipped). The basic temporal forward chaining rule syntax is

```
(DEFINE-[OVERLAP | CAUSE]
         (AND ⟨fact 1⟩ ⟨fact 2⟩ . . .) ⟨result fact⟩)
```

For example, to encode that the lathe and milling machine running together are very noisy, one might write

```
(DEFINE-OVERLAP (AND
        (STATUS LATHE RUNNING)
        (STATUS MILLING-MACHINE RUNNING))
                (NOISE-LEVEL HIGH))
```

while stating they will crack the window requires

```
(DEFINE-CAUSE (AND (STATUS LATHE RUNNING)
                   (STATUS MILLING-
                      MACHINE RUNNING))
              (HEALTH WINDOW CRACKED))
```

All three types of temporal inference (i.e., clipping, overlap, and cause) might best be thought of as if-then rules with different temporal scoping on the initiating and resulting facts.

A final static-fact type is the *pool*. A pool is a collection of objects that are essentially interchangeable and are referred to primarily by type rather than name. By referring to the pool, an object of the appropriate type can be identified. Pools are managed using an interconnected set of facts and clipping rules set up with a special syntax because of their frequent use. A pool is initialized with the form:

```
(DEFINE-POOL ⟨type⟩ (⟨member 1⟩ ⟨member 2⟩ . . .))
```

For example, a factory containing two identical lathes might represent them as a pool from which either can be selected for a particular job:

```
(DEFINE-POOL LATHE (LATHE-1 LATHE-2))
```

The task-expansion language contains forms for reserving an object from a pool and freeing it when finished. Pools are used extensively to manage discrete resources in the FORBIN example problems.

Static facts, clipping rules, and temporal forward chaining rules give the FORBIN planner a powerful model for many aspects of the world (see Dean (1985) for more background on reasoning about static facts). However, to handle task effects that vary with detailed context, dynamic facts must be used as well.

4.2.2. Dynamic facts

Dynamic facts represent those facets of the world that are best modeled as continuous quantities.[7] Static facts change value instantaneously and are always specified in terms of their new value. Dynamic facts, on the other hand, are often specified in terms of a change to their value (hence the new value depends on the old) and once changed, a dynamic fact may continue to change without further intervention. In the FORBIN plan language, dynamic facts are called *quantities*.

The schema for a quantity is shown below and consists of four parts: a name and three functions called MOVE, DELAY, and UPDATE.

```
(DEFINE-QUANTITY ⟨name⟩
   (MOVE   (lambda ( ⟨current-value⟩ ⟨change⟩
           ⟨time⟩) . . . ))
    DELAY  (lambda ( ⟨current-value⟩ ⟨change⟩
           ⟨time⟩) . . . ))
    UPDATE (lambda ( ⟨current-value⟩ ⟨change⟩
           ⟨time⟩) . . . ))
```

---

[6]The temporal database manager (T.D.M.) which manages the interaction of static facts actually supports several more types of temporal chaining rules. However, rules other than these two were used infrequently in our trials. For further discussion of temporal reasoning and the abilities of the TDM, see Dean (1985).

[7]The syntax given here for quantities is a simplified version of what is possible. A quantity can be generalized from a scalar quantity to an arbitrary LISP object and can carry a great deal of internal information around. The three quantity functions can then refer to this information in an arbitrary manner. For such examples, the patterns used to refer to the quantity in expansions and descriptors will have more arguments. See Miller (1985) for more background on the heuristic task scheduler used to reason about quantity representations.

(a) Example A

```
(DEFINE-QUANTITY PLASTIC-RESIN
    (MOVE   (lambda (old change time) (positive?
            (+ change old))))
    (DELAY  (lambda (old change time) 0))
    (UPDATE (lambda (old change time) (+ change old))))
```

(b) Example B

```
(DEFINE-QUANTITY POSITION
    (MOVE   (lambda (begin end time)
            (and  (member? begin *valid-locations*)
                  (member? end *valid-locations*)
                  (know-route-between? begin end))))
    (DELAY  (lambda (begin end time)
            (/ (distance-between begin end) *nominal-speed*)))
    (UPDATE (lambda (begin end time)
            (ACTION (move-primitive begin end))
            end)))
```

FIG. 6. Examples of quantity definitions.

Each of the functions takes three arguments: the current value of the quantity, the change desired in the value, and the current time. During projection, these functions are called by the system to find out whether, and then how, a quantity can be changed as required by a task. The current value and time are filled in by the system for the temporal interval of interest and the change is taken from the quantity change statement that appears in the task's descriptor. The MOVE function returns a boolean value saying whether the desired change is possible, and the DELAY function returns an estimation of the time it will take to carry out that change. The UPDATE function returns the new value of the quantity after the change has been made. For example, the quantity representing a robot's location might be called POSITION with a current value of AT-LATHE-CHUCK. If a task has the effect of changing the robot's location to AT-WORKBENCH, then the MOVE function applied to AT-LATHE-CHUCK, AT WORKBENCH and the current time would return whether or not the move is possible. The DELAY function would return how long the move will take, and the UPDATE function would return the new value of POSITION (i.e., AT-WORKBENCH).

The three quantity functions are written by the causal-theory builder to reflect the way different dynamic facts are used. In the robot position example above, task descriptors specify changes to POSITION as new, absolute robot locations. It is just as easy to write quantity functions that take changes specified as relative to the current value. For example, the robot might have a store of plastic resin that is often taken from and occasionally replenished. Such a quantity could be represented as shown in Fig. 6a. Notice that in the PLASTIC-RESIN quantity functions, the change is treated in a relative way. In the plan language such changes would be represented as (PLASTIC-RESIN +10) or (PLASTIC-RESIN −10).

An important feature of quantity definitions is that the UPDATE function may generate action requests of the form: (ACTION ⟨pattern⟩). An action-request pattern corresponds to a primitive task to be incorporated as part of the final plan that FORBIN builds. During the planning process itself, however, action requests are ignored and play no part in decisions that influence the plan. Action requests allow the task network to grow without regard to certain necessary tasks and yet have those tasks added into the network at the finish. The most common example of such actions are robot travel tasks. In the

```
(TASK-DESCRIPTOR ⟨id⟩
    (TASK ⟨pattern⟩)
    (EXPECTED-DURATION ⟨low⟩ ⟨high⟩)
    (GENERATED-FACTS ...) )
    (QUANTITY-CHANGES ...)
```

FIG. 7. The basic form of a task descriptor.

FORBIN factory, the robot must travel from work station to work station and the final plan must contain a primitive task for each change of locale. However, the start and end position of these travel tasks cannot be determined until all other parts of the plan have been elaborated and the planner knows where the robot needs to be for every task. Thus, travel tasks are generated using action requests from the position quantity, shown in Fig. 6b, once the final task network has been determined. This ability to add actions to the final plan as required is used extensively in FORBIN example problems to deal flexibly, but effectively, with travel time.

4.3. Task descriptors

Each type of task in the system has a task descriptor that specifies the way it changes facts in the world. The task descriptor also gives the expected duration for its task. FORBIN task descriptors can specify only the *expected* behavior of a task because there may be several different ways for the task to be expanded. For example, to make a widget it may be possible to use either the drill press or the milling machine. Each of these expansions will tie up a different machine and will alter different facets of the world. However, the (MAKE WIDGET) task must be incorporated into the task network, with its expected behavior, before an expansion is chosen. Thus, the task descriptor for the (MAKE WIDGET) task must make some compromise between the facts that might be changed by the drill press expansion and the facts that might be changed by the milling machine expansion.

The schema for a task descriptor is given in Fig. 7 and consists of four sections: the TASK section of the descriptor identifies the task type to which this descriptor applies, the EXPECTED-DURATION gives an estimation of how long the task will take, and the QUANTITY-CHANGES and GENERATED-FACTS sections together specify the effects that the task is expected to have on the world.

4.3.1. Task specifier

Whenever a task is added to the FORBIN task network, a task descriptor with matching specification is taken from the causal theory and used to describe the effects of that task to the projection machinery. Task descriptor specification may contain variables and hence it is possible for a task in the network to match more than one descriptor. For this reason, task descriptors are ordered (like prolog clauses) and the first one to match a task is chosen. Tasks in the task network will never have variables in their specifications and, after matching, all of the variables in a task descriptor will be instantiated. Some example task specifications are

```
(TASK (MAKE ?thing))
(TASK (SETUP-LATHE ?lathe WIDGET))
(TASK (SETUP-LATHE ?lathe ?type))
```

4.3.2. Expected duration

The expected duration of each task is crucial when temporal considerations are important to the success of a plan. Planning for deadlines requires knowledge of how long execution of all tasks in the plan is expected to take. The expected duration section of the task descriptor gives this information. A duration is specified as an estimated interval with a lower and upper bound. Some sample duration specifications are

(EXPECTED-DURATION 5.0 6.0)
(EXPECTED-DURATION (* 3 (SIZE-OF ?thing))
                   (* 10 (SIZE-OF ?thing)))

Once an expansion is chosen for a task, its expected duration is replaced with the composite durations of the subtasks in the expansion. Thus, as tasks are refined, so are the estimates of how long they will take.

4.3.3. Generated facts

The generated facts section of the task descriptor specifies those static effects that are expected to be made true by the task. The specification is a simple list of facts like a traditional add list. It is assumed during projection that each of these facts will be made true at some time during the execution of the task. No delete list is required because of the clipping rules specified in the domain physics. The following generated facts specification declares that executing the task will cause the lathe to be ready, the lathe bit to be of the correct type, and for the robot to be positioned at the lathe's chuck:

(GENERATED-FACTS
  (READY ?lathe ?type)
  (BIT ?lathe (BIT ?type))
  (LOCATION ROBOT (LOC-OF CHUCK ?lathe)))

4.3.4. Quantity changes

The final section of a task descriptor specifies a list of quantity changes or dynamic effects. Each change is augmented with an indication of when during the task the quantity will take on (or be changed by) the value specified. A quantity may be specified to change at the start, at the end, or sometime during the execution of the task. A quantity change has the form (⟨when⟩ ⟨pattern⟩), where ⟨when⟩ can be of START, END, or DURING. It is most enlightening to think of quantity changes as specifying "island states" or places in time when particular changes to dynamic facts will occur. For example, the following specification for the quantity changes of a (MOVE ?thing ?loc1 ?loc2) task will put the robot's position at ?loc1 to start and ?loc2 at the end:

(GENERATED-STATES
  (START (ROBOT-POSITION ?loc1))
  (END (ROBOT-POSITION ?loc2)))

As with the expected duration, after a task is expanded, its generated facts and quantity changes are replaced with those of its composite subtasks.

4.3.5. An example

To pull everything together, consider the complete task descriptor in Fig. 8. This descriptor specifies the causal information required for projection of the effects of a lathe setup task. It states that each setup task is expected to take from 5.0 to 6.0 time units and will result in the lathe being set up for the correct type of operation with the correct bit installed. Also, at the end of the task the robot will be positioned at the lathe's chuck. Whenever a task of this type is added to the task network, it will be annotated with all of this information for use in projection.

This task descriptor also illustrates an interesting point with

(TASK-DESCRIPTOR SETUP-T1
  (TASK (SETUP-LATHE ?lathe ?type))
  (EXPECTED-DURATION 5.0 6.0)
  (GENERATED-FACTS
    (SETUP-FOR ?lathe ?type)
    (BIT ?lathe (BIT ?type))
    (LOCATION ROBOT (LOC-OF CHUCK ?lathe)))
  (QUANTITY-CHANGES
    (END (POSITION (LOC-OF CHUCK ?lathe)))))

FIG. 8. The task descriptor for a lathe setup task.

respect to the different processing of facts and quantities. Notice that there is both a generated fact entry for the robot's LOCATION and a quantity change entry for the robot's POSITION; obviously these two entries represent the same facet of the world and will take on the same values. However, the LOCATION models the robot's location as a static fact that can be changed at will, while the POSITION quantity is continuous and requires action requests to change it. The results of projecting the two together are the same as projecting either one, but the POSITION quantity will have more temporal accuracy. The reason for using both is to let LOCATION facts be cached for later use in temporal queries while having the POSITION quantity to calculate detailed travel times and preserve overall plan consistency. Also, in the final plan, the POSITION quantity will add the action requests necessary to generate actual robot movement tasks. Thus, the two complement each other with the LOCATION used as a basis for future plan choices and the POSITION used to add more detail.

5. The FORBIN plan language: expansion library

The task-expansion library contains the methods that FORBIN has available for accomplishing its tasks. The system cannot build a plan for a task that does not have an expansion method in the library. Each entry in the library describes one way of carrying out an abstract task. When there is more than one way to carry out a task, there is more than one entry in the library. For example, it might be possible to build a new gizmo with either the lathe or the milling machine. Since each one requires a different set of bits and setup procedures, it would make sense to enter each one into the library as a separate expansion. Each expansion entry is known as a *method* for expanding its type of task.

This section of the paper describes the notation used to specify task-expansion methods.

5.1. The expansion method

A FORBIN task-expansion method presents one possible way to carry out a task. Each method consists of four sections as shown in Fig. 9. The TASK section of the method is used as an index and specifies the type of task that the method can be used to accomplish. The ASSUMPTIONS section describes characteristics that must be true of the world state before and during execution of this method to ensure correct performance of the desired task. The actual subtasks, and their order, are detailed in the SUBTASKS section of the method, and the UTILITY section gives a way of comparing this method with other methods that perform the same task. All other things being equal, the highest utility method with satisfied assumptions is the best one to choose.

The ⟨identifier⟩ of the plan descriptor is a unique symbol used to differentiate one expansion method from another. It plays no role in the FORBIN algorithm. The other elements are described in some detail below.

5.1.1. Task type

The (TASK ⟨pattern⟩) portion of the plan descriptor is used to identify what task this method is an expansion for. The ⟨pattern⟩ portion may contain parameters or constants depending on whether the method may be used as an expansion for several tasks or just one. The TASK field serves the identical function in expansion methods as it does in the task descriptors described in the previous section.

5.1.2. Utility

The (UTILITY ⟨number⟩) portion of the plan descriptor is used to give relative "goodness" ratings to the various methods of carrying out the task. When a task has more than one plan descriptor, the one with the highest utility is given some small degree of preference over the others by the heuristic task scheduler (HTS) when it is choosing the best plan to use.

The utility value can either be a constant or a lambda expression. Thus the utility for a particular expansion can vary depending on the exact task for which the expansion is to be used. For example, consider

(UTILITY (lambda () (cond ((= ?type widget) 4)
                          ((= ?type gizmo) 2)))))

The method containing this statement has a higher utility if it is operating on widgets than if it is being used for working on a gizmo.

5.1.3. Assumptions

The (ASSUMPTIONS ...) section in the plan descriptor details those things that must be true before the plan can be used as a method for completing the task. Each assumption is a predicate that must be true in the temporal database. All of the assumptions together make up a conjunctive query to the database. A valid assumption is any predicate that might be true in the temporal database, but for the most part, the only predicates necessary are

- (TT ⟨begin⟩ ⟨end⟩ ⟨effect⟩) stating that the formula ⟨effect⟩ must be true throughout the time interval ⟨begin⟩ to ⟨end⟩.
- (RESERVE ⟨begin⟩ ⟨end⟩ ⟨pool⟩ ⟨thing⟩ ⟨tag⟩) stating that the object ⟨thing⟩ from the ⟨pool⟩ must be available to be reserved by the task ⟨tag⟩ throughout the time interval ⟨begin⟩ to ⟨end⟩.

Throughout an expansion method, the special symbol *SELF* stands for the task that is being expanded. For example, the assumptions necessary for the GENERATE task in the FORBIN domain are

(ASSUMPTIONS
    (RESERVE (BEGIN *SELF*) (END *SELF*)
     LATHE ?LATHE (TAG *SELF*)))

The assumption states that this method will work only if a LATHE can be reserved for this task over the entire duration of the task. LATHE refers to a pool of lathes—several machines, any of which would be suitable for performing the GENERATE task. ?LATHE will be bound to a particular machine in the lathe pool. For a more detailed discussion of the RESERVE predicat, see Dean (1985).

(DEFINE-METHOD ⟨identifier⟩
    (TASK ⟨pattern⟩)
    (UTILITY ⟨number⟩)
    (ASSUMPTIONS ⟨assumption1⟩
                 ⟨assumption2⟩ ...)
    (SUBTASKS ((tag) ⟨pattern⟩
                 ⟨reason1⟩ FOR ⟨tag⟩
                 ⟨reason2⟩ FOR ⟨tag⟩ ...)
              ((tag) ⟨pattern⟩
                 ⟨reason1⟩ FOR ⟨tag⟩
                 ⟨reason2⟩ FOR ⟨tag⟩ ...)))

FIG. 9. The basic form of a task-expansion method.

The MOVE method of Appendix B requires the TT assumption:

ASSUMPTIONS
    (TT (BEGIN *SELF*) (BEGIN *SELF*)
        (LOCATION ?THING ?START)))

This assumption demands that the fact (LOCATION ?THING ?START) be true during the interval defined by the start of that MOVE expansion method. In other words, that fact must be true at the start of the move task if this method of doing the move is to be successful.

For most cases in which there are alternative methods for accomplishing a task, the assumptions will play an important role in choosing a particular method. The assumptions for a particular method constrain the time and the order in which that particular method may be used in the overall plan. The HTS, using the assumptions, picks the method that fits in "best" with the overall plan, as already developed. Thus, different assumptions will cause different methods to be picked—causing an overall different plan to be created.

5.1.4. Subtasks

The (SUBTASK ...) portion of the expansion method is used to define the piece of the task network into which the task should expand. This portion of the method includes some number of subtasks, each identified within the method by a ⟨tag⟩. Following the tag is some ⟨pattern⟩ which should match the TASK pattern of one or more expansion methods in the task library. After each pattern is a list of the ⟨reason⟩s for that subtask to be done. Reasons often will reference the tags, thereby defining some partial order over the subtasks.

There are three general types of reasons for a subtask:

- (ACHIEVE ⟨effect⟩): the purpose of the subtask is to create this effect. The effect will be entered into the temporal database.
- (CREATE ⟨pool⟩ ⟨object⟩): this subtask creates new object ⟨object⟩ that can be added to the group of objects specified by ⟨pool⟩.
- (CONSUME ⟨pool⟩ ⟨object⟩): the opposite of CREATE, this reason specifies an object to be taken out of a pool.

The reasons for a subtask are connected to other subtasks with the FOR operator. FOR indicates that the reason given is to satisfy a precondition for the execution of the named subtask (referenced by its tag). The subtasks and their reasons are then loaded into the temporal database where the projection machinery forms the appropriate partial order. Normally, all of the subtasks are constrained to fall within the temporal bounds of the task being expanded (i.e., *SELF*). However, the FOR

```
(SUBTASKS
   (T1 (REMOVE-BIT ?OTHER-BIT ?LATHE)
       (ACHIEVE (BIT ?LATHE NONE)) <FOR T2)
   (T2 (PUT ?BIT (LOC-OF CHUCK ?LATHE))
       (ACHIEVE (BIT ?LATHE ?BIT)))))
```

FIG. 10. The subtasks for the INSTALL-1 method.

```
(SUBTASKS
   (T1 (GET (BIT ?TYPE) (LOC-OF CHUCK ?LATHE))
       (ACHIEVE (HAVE *ME* ?BIT)) <FOR T2)
   (T2 (PUT (BIT ?TYPE) (LOC-OF BIT-RACK ?TYPE))
       FOR >)))
```

FIG. 11. The subtasks for the REMOVE-BIT method.

operator has three other forms: <FOR, FOR>, and <FOR>: which indicate that the indicated subtask may be positioned before, after, or on either side of the main task for which it is in service.[8] For example, the INSTALL-1 method has the two subtasks shown in Fig. 10. The first subtask takes the old bit out of the lathe chuck so that the lathe chuck will be empty. By using the <FOR, the fact that the lathe chuck is empty as a precondition for doing the second subtask is added into the temporal database. The < indicates that the first subtask may be accomplished any time prior to the second subtask, as long as the fact that the lathe chuck is empty remains true until the second subtask is started.

The REMOVE-BIT method has a slightly different subtask scheme (see Fig. 11). The first subtask must be performed before the second and during the scope of the REMOVE-BIT task (as shown by the vanilla FOR). The second subtask may be done any time after the first. The FOR > indicates it is not bound by the end of the REMOVE-BIT task.

5.2. An example method

Now it is time to put everything together and describe a full expansion method. Figure 12 shows the expansion methods for the MAKE, GENERATE, and MOVE tasks. From the preceeding discussion it should be fairly obvious how these methods work. What may not be obvious is why they were written this way rather than some other seemingly more simple way. The next section goes through an expansion in detail, keeping track of what is being added into the temporal database. The reasons for the detailed syntax should then become more apparent.

6. The FORBIN planning algorithm

Section 3 of this paper describes the FORBIN system as a planner that builds its task network using a combination of hierarchical expansion, which adds detail, and temporal projection, which ensures correctness. Section 4 describes the causal reasoning methods used to project the expected effects of a partially built task network and Sect. 5 describes the language used to write expansion strategies for specific task types that might appear in the network. This section of the paper gives a detailed description of the hierarchical search algorithm at the heart of the FORBIN planner.

---

[8]The FORs may have associated with them metric intervals that specify exactly how close or how far two subtasks may be separated in time. These intervals have been left out of this paper to help maintain clarity.

```
(DEFINE-METHOD MAKE
   (TASK (MAKE ?TYPE))
   (UTILITY 1.0)
   (ASSUMPTIONS nil)
   (SUBTASKS
      (T1 (GENERATE ?TYPE $NEW-THING)
          (CREATE ?TYPE $NEW-THING) FOR T2)
      (T2 (MOVE $NEW-THING (LOC-OF SHELF ?TYPE))
          (ACHIEVE (LOCATION $NEW-THING
          (LOC-OF SHELF ?TYPE)))))))
(DEFINE-METHOD GENERATE
   (TASK (GENERATE ?TYPE ?THING))
   (UTILITY 1.0)
   (ASSUMPTIONS
      (RESERVE (BEGIN *SELF*) (END *SELF*)
      LATHE ?LATHE (NAME *SELF*)))
   (SUBTASKS
      (T1 (SETUP-LATHE ?LATHE ?TYPE)
          (ACHIEVE (READY ?LATHE ?TYPE)) FOR T2)
      (T2 (RUN-LATHE ?LATHE ?TYPE)
          (CREATE ?TYPE ?THING)
          (ACHIEVE (LOCATION ?THING
          (LOC-OF HOPPER ?LATHE)))))))
(DEFINE-METHOD MOVE
   (TASK (MOVE ?THING ?FINISH))
   (UTILITY 1.0)
   (ASSUMPTIONS
      (TT (BEGIN *SELF*) (BEGIN *SELF)
      (LOCATION ?THING ?START)))
   (SUBTASKS
      (T1 (GET ?THING ?START)
          (ACHIEVE (HAVE *ME* ?THING)) FOR T2)
      (T2 (PUT ?THING ?FINISH)
          (ACHIEVE (LOCATION ?THING ?FINISH)))))))
```

FIG. 12. The methods for MAKE.

The FORBIN search algorithm is conceptually quite simple. At any point in the search there is a partially elaborated plan represented by the current task network. The object of the search is to expand each task in the network into more and more detail until only primitive tasks remain. The final plan produced by the system is the network of primitive tasks.

A naive backtracking implementation of this search algorithm is computationally much too expensive; therefore, the FORBIN system makes use of many heuristics to limit the number of partial task networks considered and the number of projected futures calculated. The detailed discussion below attempts to make these heuristics explicit and thus clarify which planning problems FORBIN can solve and which it cannot.

6.1. Introducing a new task into the task network

Throughout the remainder of this section we will illustrate the FORBIN algorithm on a simple example in the FORBIN domain. The causal theory and task-expansion methods are contained in appendices B and C. Initially FORBIN is given the task (or more precisely, tasks) of constructing two items in its factory: a gizmo and a widget. The system is given the further constraint that the widget must be completed (i.e., constructed and properly shelved) by time 35. An implicit constraint is that both projects be finished as quickly as is mechanically possible.

Figure 13 shows the initial task network (the state of the tem-

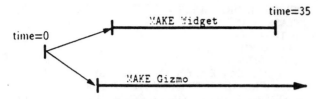

FIG. 13. The initial task network for constructing a widget and gizmo.

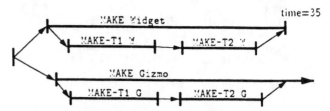

FIG. 14. The task network after one round of expansion.

poral database) after FORBIN has been given its task. The vertical line segments indicate the points in time actually dealt with by the planner. Time flows from left to right. The thin lines connect pieces of the network and represent ordering constraints, but not definite periods of time. The labeled horizontal segments indicate time to be spent doing whatever the label indicates; several activities may be going on in parallel. The network illustrated indicates that at some time after time zero the (MAKE WIDGET) task will be started; it will continue for a while, but will end by time 35. Meanwhile, some time after time zero (but not necessarily the same "some time" as in the previous sentence) the (MAKE GIZMO) task will be started. This task will also continue on for a while, but its end point is not presently constrained.

The network in Fig. 13 includes some information from the task descriptors for each task. In particular, the descriptors give the initial estimates of how long each task will take to execute.

Task-expansion choices are based on more than the task network shown in the diagram; they are also based on the temporal database derived from the task network and the task descriptors. There are many other things actually in the temporal database than are shown in the picture: the position of the robot, the bit currently in the lathe, what the robot is holding, and all other tasks known to the system, both past and future. However, for simplicity's sake, we will concentrate directly on the tasks at hand and show only the network itself.

5.2. Selecting a task to expand

Whenever FORBIN has unexpanded nonprimitive tasks in the task network, it attempts to expand them. Task expansions are done one at a time in an order based on several criteria:

- Since planning takes time, and some tasks have deadlines, tasks with approaching deadlines are given some priority in expansion.
- Tasks very high in the abstraction hierarchy should be expanded to sufficient detail that they may be placed in proper perspective in the task network.
- Heavily constrained tasks should be expanded so that none of their constraints are accidentally violated.

FORBIN will not retreat on an expansion decision, so the order that tasks are expanded may be critical to the plan that eventually evolves. Decisions about the way a task should be expanded (i.e., what method to use) are based on the facts in the task network and depend on the level of expansion for the tasks in the network. Since FORBIN does not retract expansion decisions, the algorithm may fail to find a successful plan where one exists. However, the search algorithm as a whole makes expansion decisions flexibly, by considering many alternatives before committing, so that the system is usually steered in an appropriate direction.

6.3. Queries and projections of possible expansions

Figure 14 shows the task network after both the widget and gizmo tasks have gone through one expansion. These expansions are easy to make because there is only one way to expand a MAKE task and it cannot interfere with other tasks in the network. Thus there are really no expansion decisions to worry about. FORBIN's decisions are not always this easy.

The MAKE plan is very high level. The only details that come out from its expansion are that two subtasks are required, the first generates the item, the second involves moving the item to its proper storage place. Both of these subtasks, as defined in the method, are constrained within the original bounds of their supertask. The unlabeled arrows between the subtasks indicate that the second subtask must follow the first by some amount of time that is only indirectly constrained by the starting constraint on the first subtask and the completion constraint on the second.

After another expansion cycle, the task network looks like that shown in Fig. 15. The expansion centered on the widget task because it is constrained by a deadline. The GENERATE subtask has been expanded and an assumption that the lathe is reserved was added to the temporal database. No conflicts with the assumption were detected, so the expansion was adopted. The left and right angle brackets linking items in the network (e.g., MAKE-T2 Widget and (MOVE WIDGET)) indicate the passing on of exact constraints (i.e., (MOVE WIDGET) has exactly the same constraints as the subtask from which it was expanded).

The choice of task to expand now switches to the gizmo task. The reason for this switch is that the (MAKE GIZMO) is now at too high an abstraction level with respect to the expanded (GENERATE WIDGET).

Exactly as with (MAKE WIDGET), the first subtask of (MAKE GIZMO) is expanded and a query is made using the temporal database machinery. This query asks when the assumption about lathe reservation that goes with the GENERATE method will be true. The query returns a disjunctive ordering constraint: the (GENERATE GIZMO) can occur either before or after the (GENERATE WIDGET) and have the lathe RESERVE come out true. Adopting this expansion and constraint leaves the task network with two distinct possible futures: one with the gizmo made on the lathe before the widget, and another with the widget produced first (shown in Fig. 16).

It should be noted that both of the orderings may not actually be feasible. The tasks have not really been expanded to sufficient detail to know for certain whether either will actually lead to a feasible plan, and the FORBIN algorithm, during each cycle, runs the task network through more detailed local projection where adverse interactions of dynamic effects may be spotted. As long as one feasible ordering for the task network can be found, however, it is left as is.

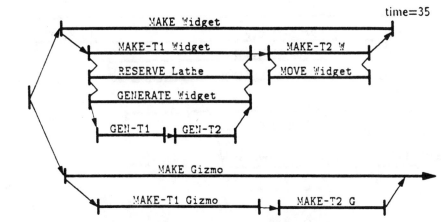

FIG. 15. The further expansion of the (MAKE WIDGET) task.

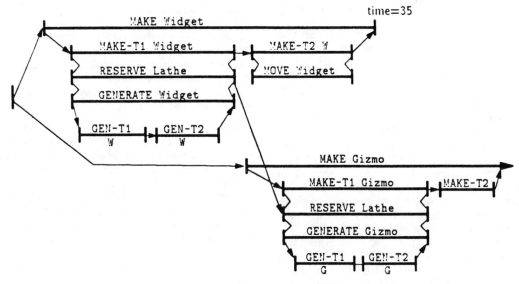

FIG. 16. The further expansion of the (MAKE GIZMO) task.

6.4. Comparing possible expansions

So far, in this discussion of the FORBIN algorithm, the relevant projection of the task network has been accomplished almost exclusively by the temporal database manager. This machinery has allowed the planner to identify possible trouble spots due to conflicts arising from separate tasks (e.g., the need for a lathe by both MAKE tasks) and it has automatically inserted disjunctive constraints to keep these potential conflicts from becoming actual plan bugs.

For some tasks FORBIN has several different methods for expansion. The first subtask of the GENERATE method is to set up the lathe. There is one method for expanding this task. It involves the FORBIN robot acquiring the correct lathe bit, and then installing that bit into the lathe. There are multiple methods for installing the bit. Which to use depends on whether there is a bit already in the lathe, and what type of bit is needed. Committing to a specific method for installing the bit into the lathe is committing the world to be in a particular state (or at least to having certain facts be true) at the time when that method is to be expanded. A partial order may not be sufficient to guarantee this, and further constraints may have to be added. The temporal database can determine what

constraints are necessary to keep a method's assumptions valid when those assumptions are queried, but it cannot decide which method and (or) constraint set is the "best." Thus, when FORBIN gets to the point of choosing between method and (or) constraint sets, all options are loaded into the heuristic task scheduler for more detailed projection.

The HTS efficiently explores the space of total orderings of the task network, propagating dynamic effects that occur in each ordering. As it explores these orderings, it may place any of the possible expansion methods into the schedule it is building, pursuing those with the greatest utility (and implicitly those with the shortest overall duration) first. When a feasible schedule is derived, the expansion method used is returned. This is the method that is inserted into the task network.

In the case of expanding the (INSTALL-BIT GIZMO LATHE) task, the assumptions can be met for either of two expansion methods. The assumptions for the INSTALL-1 method demand that the lathe already be set up, but for the wrong type of product. Thus this method includes steps for removing the old bit and inserting the new one. These assumptions are met in the task network if the INSTALL takes place after the lathe has been reserved for the GENERATE Gizmo

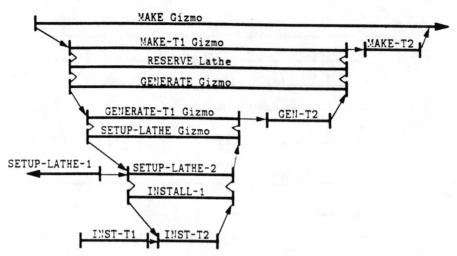

FIG. 17. Choosing the INSTALL-1 method.

task and after the lathe has been set up for the GENERATE Widget task (hence when the widget is made first).

The INSTALL-2 method also has its assumptions met. It demands that the lathe contains no bit. This condition exists in the task network at a time before either GENERATE task is done. Using this method causes a schedule to be created where the gizmo is produced first, but the HTS projects that this will cause a deadline violation for the (MAKE WIDGET) task (after all the travel tasks are added in by ACTION steps from the POSITION quantity) and the schedule is deemed non-viable. Thus, the HTS chooses the INSTALL-1 method for expanding the (INSTALL-BIT GIZMO LATHE) task.

Once this choice is made, the temporal database inserts the necessary constraints to maintain a temporally consistent task network. The resulting network is shown in Fig. 17.

It should be noted that the diagram also contains two subtasks linked to their supertasks via the <FOR operator. The first subtask in the (SETUP-LATHE LATHE GIZMO) method has such a link. That subtask involves having the robot acquire the proper lathe bit. This aquisition may be done at any time prior to the installation of the bit into the lathe. The first subtask in the INSTALL-1 method is similarly linked, but that task (which involves removing the old bit from the lathe) is constrained by having the lathe reserved.

6.5. Summary of FORBIN algorithm and solution

The FORBIN algorithm involves a cycle of operations that are performed on the task network. These are

1. Select a non primitive task descriptor from the network to expand. This selection is based on several heuristics involving the constraints on the tasks and the state of the network. Here the network acts as task queue.

2. From the library of expansion methods, extract all those whose pattern fields match the task being expanded.

3. Using the temporal database projection machinery, query the task network with the assumptions from each of the selected expansion methods. Eliminate those methods whose assumptions cannot be met. If all methods are eliminated then FORBIN has failed to successfully find a plan for that set of tasks.

4. Have the HTS try to create a viable schedule from the task network and its choice of expansion method. If the HTS is unable to find a viable schedule, FORBIN fails in planning for that set of tasks.

5. If the HTS finds a viable schedule, insert its choice of method into the task network.

6. Insert into the task network the task descriptors for each of the subtasks in the method just added.

7. Have the database machinery propagate effects through the network, and go to step 1.

This algorithm quickly fails on impossible tasks after exploring only a few candidate plans — a useful quality in a planner working in a highly exponential search space. When the algorithm is successful, a reasonably efficient plan will result. Efficiency stems from the flexibility of least-commitment planning tempered with the noticing of adverse dynamic effects early enough to plan around them. For the problem of widget and gizmo construction discussed above, FORBIN's solution is shown in Table 1.

7. Related work

The FORBIN planner borrows a great deal from existing systems. FORBIN builds on previous work in hierarchical planning (Sacerdoti 1977; Tate 1977; Wilkins 1984) by providing a specification language that allows one to encode expectations concerning deadlines, resources, and continuously changing quantities. The FORBIN specification language makes use of a temporal notation based loosely on McDermott's temporal logic (McDermott 1982). While FORBIN lacks even the full expressive power of propositional temporal logic, it is sufficiently expressive to encode many complex planning problems.

The FORBIN specification language is similar in many respects to the language used in the SIPE planner (Wilkins 1984). There are some problems that SIPE can handle and FORBIN cannot (e.g., certain restricted forms of quantification), but FORBIN excels in its treatment of metric time and continuously changing quantities.

FORBIN can also be viewed as a constraint-posting planner (Stefik 1981; Wilkins 1984; Chapman 1987) it attempts to avoid costly mistakes by making the constraints between tasks explicit. It is the manner in which FORBIN treats temporal constraints that sets it apart from other planners; FORBIN employs special routines (specifically, the heuristic scheduler and the temporal database query routines) that exploit the structure of time to efficiently detect possible inconsistencies and hence anticipate interactions involving resources and dead-

TABLE 1. FORBIN's solution to the example problem

Task	Place	Time		
		Travel	Task	Elapsed
(get (bit widget) hand1)	bit-rack	0	1	1
(put (bit widget) hand1)	lathe-chuck	3	1	5
(push (button widget) hand1)	lathe-control	1	1	7
(wait widget)	—	0	11	—
(get (bit gizmo) hand1)	bit-rack	3	1	11
(get (bit widget) hand2)	lathe-chuck	3	1	19[a]
(put (bit gizmo) hand 1	lathe-chuck	0	1	20
(push (button gizmo) hand1)	lathe-control	1	1	22
(wait gizmo)	—	0	14	—
(get widget hand1)	lathe-hopper	3	1	26
(put widget hand1)	(shelf widget)	5	1	32[b]
(get gizmo hand 1)	lathe-hopper	5	1	38[c]
(put (bit widget) hand2)	bit-rack	3	1	42
(put gizmo hand1)	(shelf gizmo)	3	1	46[d]

[a] End (wait widget) at 18.
[b] End (make widget).
[c] End (wait gizmo) at 36.
[d] End (make gizmo).

lines. Other planning systems have taken time into account (Allen and Koomen 1983; Cheeseman 1984), and some have even employed specification languages that allow metric constraints (Vere 1983; Hendrix 1973; Smith 1983), but FORBIN combines an expressive language for describing continuous processes with a sophisticated strategy for coping with the complexity that comes with the increased expressive power.

The FORBIN architecture was borne out of a realization that the combinatorics of temporal reasoning had to be dealt with directly. FORBIN attempts to solve a class of problems similar to that which the ISIS program (Fox and Smith 1985) and its various extensions were meant to handle. FORBIN attempts to capture much of the knowledge for reasoning about time and resources that is scattered throughout the ISIS knowledge base in a set of general-purpose routines and a strategy for using them.

8. Summary

Any useful approach to solving planning problems will involve some means of encoding knowledge concerning the domain of application. In addition to simply encoding this knowledge, there must be some means of drawing appropriate conclusions from this domain-specific knowledge and particular problem instances. In the case of reasoning about metric time and continuously changing quantities involving partially ordered events, computing all consequences that one might need to make the best choice is computationally prohibitive. The FORBIN architecture embodies one strategy for coping with the complexity of reasoning about time. Specifically, the FORBIN specification language allows one to encode descriptions of plans at several levels of detail, including information concerning expected resource use. This information is used during planning to eliminate plan expansions that cannot possibly lead to a solution, and rank those that can. This process of eliminating and ranking expansions is itself a potentially exponential process, and FORBIN employs a two-stage strategy for making these determinations. First, a set of candidates is generated using a temporal database query program that ignores interactions between partially ordered events. Second, this set of candidates is trimmed using a heuristic evaluation

program that eliminates candidates for which it cannot find an interaction-free total order. Using this two-stage evaluation strategy, if FORBIN terminates claiming success, then the solution it provides is correct. Moreover, FORBIN always terminates in time polynomial in the size of its knowledge base, and, supplied with reasonable expectations concerning the resource requirements of abstract actions, FORBIN will quite often terminate signalling success. The temporal database and heuristic evaluation routines exploit the structure of time and causation to realize high performance. FORBIN represents a practical and theoretically motivated concession to the complexity of real-world planning.

Acknowledgements

This paper was a long time in the writing and would not have been possible at all without the patience and support of Drew McDermott. The clarity of the paper, such as it is, also owes much to long discussions with Yoav Shoham and Steve Hanks. We would like to thank these three people and the many others whom we have harassed over the last two years.

This report describes work done by all three authors at Yale University supported in part by the Advanced Research and Projects Agency of the Department of Defense under Office of Naval Research contract N00014-83-K-0281. Subsequent discussion and writing was continued after two authors moved on and was further supported in part by DARPA Office of Naval Research contract N00014-85-K-0301 at Yale University, NSWC contract N60921-83-G-A165 at Virginia Polytechnic, and NSF grant IRI-8612644 at Brown University. In addition, Thomas Dean was supported at Brown University through an IBM Faculty Development Award and Jim Firby was supported at Yale University through a Canadian NSERC 1967 Science and Engineering Scholarship.

ALLEN, J., and KOOMEN, J. A. 1983. Planning using a temporal world model. Proceedings of the International Joint Conference on Artificial Intelligence, Karlsruhe, West Germany, pp. 741–747.

CHAPMAN, D. 1987. Planning for conjunctive goals. Artificial Intelligence, **32**: 333–377.

CHEESEMAN, P. 1984. A representation of time for automatic plan-

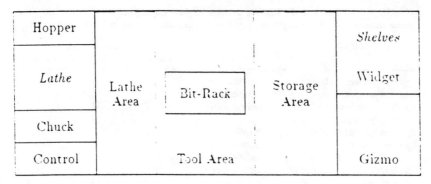

FIG. 18. Layout of the factory.

ning. Proceedings of the IEEE International Conference on Robotics.

DEAN. T. 1985. Temporal imagery: an approach to reasoning about time for planning and problem solving. Technical Report 433. Computer Science Department. Yale University. New Haven. CT.

FIKES. R. and NILSSON. N. J. 1971. STRIPS: a new approach to the application of theorem proving to problem solving. Artificial Intelligence. **2**: 189–208.

FOX. M. S.. and SMITH. S. 1985. ISIS: a knowledge-based system for factory scheduling. Expert Systems. **1**: 25–49.

HENDRIX. G. 1973. Modeling simultaneous actions and continuous processes. Artificial Intelligence. **4**: 145–180.

McDERMOTT. D. V. 1977. Flexibility and efficiency in a computer program for designing circuits. Technical Report 402. Artificial Intelligence Laboratory. Massachusetts Institute of Technology. Cambridge. MA.

———1982. A temporal logic for reasoning about processes and plans. Cognitive Science. **6**: 101–155.

———1985. The DUCK manual. Technical Report 399. Computer Science Department. Yale University. New Haven. CT.

MILLER. D. P. 1985. Planning by search through simulations. Technical Report 423. Computer Science Department. Yale University. New Haven. CT.

SACERDOTI. E. 1977. A structure for plans and behavior. American Elsevier Publishing Company. Inc.. New York. NY.

SMITH. S. F. 1983. Exploiting temporal knowledge to organize constraints. Technical Report CMU-RI-TR-83-12. Intelligent Systems Laboratory. Carnegie-Mellon University. Pittsburgh. PA.

STEFIK. M. J. 1981. Planning with constraints. Artificial Intelligence. **16**: 111–140.

TATE. A. 1977. Generating project networks. Proceedings of the International Joint Conference on Artificial Intelligence. Cambridge. MA.

VERE. S. 1983. Planning in time: windows and durations for activities and goals. IEEE Transactions on Pattern Analysis and Machine Intelligence. **5**: 246–267.

WILKINS. D. 1984. Domain independent planning: representation and plan generation. Artificial Intelligence. **22**: 269–302.

Appendix A. The FORBIN factory domain

The FORBIN planner is a general-purpose system. but for illustration we will present examples from a small automated factory domain. The factory consists of an automatic lathe. a storage area. and a robot operator that builds *widgets* and *gizmos* and places them in the storage area (see Fig. 18). Making either a widget or gizmo requires the robot to carry out the following steps:

1. Make sure the correct bit is in the lathe.
2. Start the lathe and let it run until finished (11 units of time for a gizmo and 14 units for a widget).

TABLE 2. Travel times in the factory

	Hopper	Chuck	Control	Rack	Widget	Gizmo
Hopper	0	2	3	3	5	6
Chuck	2	0	1	3	5	5
Control	3	1	0	3	6	5
Rack	3	3	3	0	3	3
Widget	5	5	6	3	0	2
Gizmo	6	5	5	3	2	0

3. Remove the finished item from the lathe hopper.
4. Place item on the correct shelf.

There are three primitive actions. get. put. and push, each taking one unit of time to complete and requiring the use of one of the robot's hands. The robot has two hands. each of which can carry one item or be used to operate a control. The robot can travel throughout the factory at a fixed velocity and the travel times between the various work stations are given in Table 2. A typical problem is to construct a number of widgets and gizmos where some of each must be done within specific deadlines.

This factory differs from typical job-shop factories like those handled by the ISIS program (Fox and Smith 1985) in two important respects. First. a complete "job" does not travel from work station to work station as a single entity (e.g.. not all of the widgets in an order need to be turned on the lathe before any can be moved to the storage shelves) and second. the travel time of the robot from one place in the factory to another can be a significant part of the overall factory production time.

This domain illustrates the importance of temporal representation and plan efficiency issues that have not been adequately handled by previous planning systems.

Appendix B. The FORBIN factory task expansion library

This appendix contains all of the task expansion methods referenced in Sect. 6 of the text. These methods are supplied for the sake of completeness. The world physics and task descriptors for this domain are supplied in Appendix C.

```
; -- (MAKE ?TYPE) --

(DEFINE-METHOD MAKE
  (TASK (MAKE ?TYPE))
  (UTILITY 1.0)
  (ASSUMPTIONS nil)
  (SUBTASKS
```

```
(T1 (GENERATE ?TYPE $NEW-THING)
    (CREATE ?TYPE SNEW-THING) FOR T2)
(T2 (MOVE SNEW-THING (LOC-OF SHELF ?TYPE))
    (ACHIEVE (LOCATION $NEW-THING
              (LOC-OF SHELF ?TYPE)))))))

(DEFINE-METHOD GENERATE
 (TASK (GENERATE ?TYPE ?THING))
 (UTILITY 1.0)
 (ASSUMPTIONS
   (RESERVE (BEGIN *SELF*) (END *SELF*)
     LATHE ?LATHE (NAME *SELF*)))
 (SUBTASKS
   (T1 (SETUP-LATHE ?LATHE ?TYPE)
       (ACHIEVE (READY ?LATHE ?TYPE)) FOR T2)
   (T2 (RUN-LATHE ?LATHE ?TYPE)
       (CREATE ?TYPE ?THING)
       (ACHIEVE (LOCATION ?THING
                 (LOC-OF HOPPER ?LATHE)))))))

; -- (SETUP-LATHE ?LATHE ?TYPE) --

(DEFINE-METHOD SETUP-LATHE
 (TASK (SETUP-LATHE ?LATHE ?TYPE))
 (UTILITY 1.0)
 (ASSUMPTIONS
   (TT (BEGIN *SELF*) (BEGIN *SELF*)
       (LOCATION (BIT-FOR ?TYPE) ?LOC1)))
 (SUBTASKS
   (T1 (GET (BIT-FOR ?TYPE) ?LOC1)
       (ACHIEVE (HAVE *ME* (BIT-FOR ?TYPE)))
       < FOR T2)
   (T2 (INSTALL-BIT (BIT-FOR ?TYPE) ?LATHE)
       (ACHIEVE (READY ?LATHE ?TYPE)))))

-- (RUN-LATHE ?LATHE ?TYPE) --

(DEFINE-METHOD RUN-LATHE
 (TASK (RUN-LATHE ?LATHE ?TYPE))
 (UTILITY 1.0)
 (ASSUMPTIONS nil)
 (SUBTASKS
   (T1 (PUSH BUTTON ?TYPE)
       (LOC-OF CONTROL ?LATHE)) FOR T2)
   (T2 (WAIT (TIME ?TYPE)))))

-- (INSTALL-BIT ?BIT ?LATHE) --

(DEFINE-METHOD INSTALL-1
 (TASK (INSTALL-BIT ?BIT ?LATHE))
 (UTILITY 2.0)
 (ASSUMPTIONS
   (TT (BEGIN *SELF*) (BEGIN *SELF*)
       (BIT ?LATHE ?OTHER-BIT))
   (NOT ?OTHER-BIT BIT)
   (NOT ?OTHER-BIT NONE))
 (SUBTASKS
   (T1 (REMOVE-BIT ?OTHER-BIT ?LATHE)
       (ACHIEVE (BIT ?LATHE NONE)) < FOR T2)
   (T2 (PUT ?BIT (LOC-OF CHUCK ?LATHE))
       (ACHIEVE (BIT ?LATHE ?BIT)))))

(DEFINE-METHOD INSTALL-2
 (TASK (INSTALL-BIT ?BIT ?LATHE))
 (UTILITY 1.0)
 (ASSUMPTIONS
```

```
   (TT (BEGIN *SELF*) (BEGIN *SELF*)
       (BIT ?LATHE NONE)))
 (SUBTASKS
   (T1 (PUT ?BIT (LOC-OF CHUCK ?LATHE))
       (ACHIEVE (BIT ?LATHE ?BIT)))))

-- (REMOVE-BIT ?BIT ?LATHE) --

(DEFINE-METHOD REMOVE-BIT
 (TASK (REMOVE-BIT (BIT-FOR ?TYPE) ?LATHE))
 (UTILITY 1.0)
 (ASSUMPTIONS nil)
 (SUBTASKS
   (T1 (GET (BIT-FOR ?TYPE)
       LOC-OF CHUCK ?LATHE))
       (ACHIEVE (HAVE *ME* ?BIT)) FOR T2)
   (T2 (PUT (BIT-FOR ?TYPE)
       (LOC-OF BIT-RACK ?TYPE))
       (ACHIEVE (LOCATION (BIT-FOR ?TYPE)
                 (LOC OF BIT-RACK ?TYPE))) FOR >)))

-- (MOVE ?THING ?FINISH) --

(DEFINE-METHOD MOVE
 (TASK (MOVE ?THING ?FINISH))
 (UTILITY 1.0)
 (ASSUMPTIONS
   (TT (BEGIN *SELF*) (BEGIN *SELF*)
       (LOCATION ?THING ?START)))
 (SUBTASKS
   (T1 (GET ?THING ?START)
       (ACHIEVE (HAVE *ME* ?THING)) FOR T2)
   (T2 (PUT ?THING ?FINISH)
       (ACHIEVE (LOCATION ?THING ?FINISH)))))
```

Appendix C. The FORBIN factory causal theory

This appendix contains the causal theory definitions necessary to complete the domain-specific knowledge FORBIN uses in the factory domain.

Fact declarations:

```
(DEFINE-FACT (BIT ?lathe ?bit))
(DEFINE-FACT (READY ?lathe ?type))
(DEFINE-FACT (LOCATION ?thing ?place))
(DEFINE-FACT (HAVE ?robot ?thing))
```

Clipping rules:

```
(DEFINE-CLIP (BIT ?lathe ?bit) (BIT ?lathe ?other)
            (NOT (= ?bit ?other)))
(DEFINE-CLIP (READY ?lather ?type1)
            (READY ?lathe ?type2)
            (NOT (= ?type1 ?type2)))
(DEFINE-CLIP (LOCATION ?thing ?place1)
            (LOCATION ?thing ?place2)
            (NOT (= ?place1 ?place2)))
(DEFINE CLIP (HAVE ?robot ?thing)
            (LOCATION ?thing ?place)
            (NOT (= ?robot ?place)))
```

; State declarations:

```
(DEFINE-QUANTITY POSITION
  (MOVE  (LAMBDA (ORIG DEST TIME) T))
  (DELAY (LAMBDA (ORIG DEST TIME)
```

```
                (LOOKUP-TRAVEL-TIME ORIG DEST)))
    (UPDATE(LAMBDA (ORIG DEST TIME)
                (ACTION (ROBOT-MOVE-TO DEST))
                DEST)))

; Pools of objects to be referenced:

(DEFINE-POOL LATHE   (LATHE-A LATHE-B))
(DEFINE-POOL WIDGET ())
(DEFINE-POOL GIZMO   ())

; Task Descriptors:

(TASK-DESCRIPTOR
  (TASK (MAKE ?TYPE))
  (ESTIMATED-DURATION 21.0 37.0)
  (QUANTITY-CHANGES
    ())
  (GENERATED-FACTS
    ())))

(TASK-DESCRIPTOR
  (TASK (GENERATE ?TYPE ?NAME))
  (ESTIMATED-DURATION 17.0 31.0)
  (QUANTITY-CHANGES
    ())
  (GENERATED-FACTS
    ())))

(TASK-DESCRIPTOR
  (TASK (SETUP-LATHE ?TYPE))
  (ESTIMATED-DURATION 5.0 6.0)
  (QUANTITY-CHANGES
    (END (POSITION (CHUCK ?LATHE))))
  (GENERATED-FACTS
    (READY ?LATHE ?TYPE)
    (BIT ?LATHE (BIT-FOR ?TYPE))
    (LOCATION *ME* (LOC-OF CHUCK ?LATHE))))

(TASK-DESCRIPTOR
  (TASK (INSTALL-BIT ?BIT ?LATHE))
  (ESTIMATED-DURATION 1.0 2.0)
  (QUANTITY-CHANGES
    ())
  (GENERATED-FACTS
    (BIT ?LATHE ?BIT)))

(TASK-DESCRIPTOR
  (TASK (REMOVE-BIT ?BIT ?LATHE))
  (ESTIMATED-DURATION 1.0 2.0)
  (QUANTITY-CHANGES
    ())
  (GENERATED-FACTS
    ())))

(TASK-DESCRIPTOR
  (TASK (RUN-LATHE ?LATHE ?TYPE))
  (ESTIMATED-DURATION 12.0 14.0)
  (QUANTITY-CHANGES
    (START (POSITION (CONTROL ?LATHE))))
  (GENERATED-FACTS
    ())))

(TASK-DESCRIPTOR
  (TASK (MOVE ?THING ?FINISH))
  (ESTIMATED-DURATION 7.0 8.0)
  (QUANTITY-CHANGES
    (START (POSITION (HOPPER ?LATHE)))
    (END (POSITION (SHELF ?TYPE))))
  (GENERATED-FACTS
    (LOCATION ?THING ?FINISH)
    (LOCATION *ME* ?FINISH)))
  -- PRIMITIVES --

(TASK-DESCRIPTOR
  (TASK-PRIMITIVE (GET ?THING ?PLACE))
  (ESTIMATED-DURATION 1.0 1.0)
  (QUANTITY-CHANGES
    (START (POSITION ?PLACE)))
  (GENERATED-FACTS
    (HAVE *ME* ?THING)
    (LOCATION *ME* ?PLACE)))

(TASK-DESCRIPTOR
  (TASK-PRIMITIVE (PUT ?THING ?PLACE))
  (ESTIMATED-DURATION 1.0 1.0)
  (QUANTITY-CHANGES
    (START (POSITION ?PLACE)))
  (GENERATED-FACTS
    (LOCATION ?THING ?PLACE)
    (LOCATION *ME* ?PLACE)))

(TASK-DESCRIPTOR
  (TASK-PRIMITIVE (PUSH ?BUTTON ?PLACE))
  (ESTIMATED-DURATION 1.0 1.0)
  (QUANTITY-CHANGES
    (START (POSITION ?PLACE)))
  (GENERATED-FACTS
    (LOCATION *ME* ?PLACE)))

(TASK-DESCRIPTOR
  (TASK-PRIMITIVE (WAIT ?TIME))
  (ESTIMATED-DURATION ?TIME ?TIME)
  (QUANTITY-CHANGES
    ())
  (GENERATED-FACTS
    ())))
```

Part III

Foundations of Planning

Chapter 6

Formal Models of Action

The papers in the chapter present general formal models of action and investigate how these models can be used to capture plan reasoning. These papers concern the representation of action within the larger context of general knowledge representation and do not generally specify practical methods for building planning systems. Rather, they attempt to stretch the limits of what situations can be represented and to show how complex knowledge about action can be.

The most influential formal model for planning is the situation calculus, as described in the first paper of this section, by McCarthy and Hayes (1969). This paper introduces the first temporal representation used in AI, accomplished by indexing each proposition by the situation in which it is true. It also presents a quite general model of "action as state change" which is formalized by the "result" function which maps an initial situation to a resulting situation. This paper also addresses many issues that are still beyond the capabilities of current planning systems, particularly in representing information about ability and the relationship between knowledge and action. This framework has influenced a majority of the formal work in planning since and is still the foundation for active research. For example, Pednault (1987, Chapter 10) builds from the situation calculus, as does McDermott (1982) in the second paper in this chapter.

McDermott develops a representation of action retaining the idea of situations, as developed in the situation calculus, but adds a rich temporal structure to them. In particular, he wishes to model continuous change by using a temporal model in which situations correspond to numbers on the real number line. In addition, he allows for indeterminacy by using a branching time model to represent the set of possible futures. Temporal intervals are constructed as sequences of all the situations between two other situations, and event types are then represented simply by the set of all the intervals over which the event occurs. Because of the explicit temporal model, McDermott has no problem stating that two actions or events may happen simultaneously and has no difficulty representing possible future states that may have to be considered in order to construct a reasonable plan. McDermott (1985) follows up on these ideas and further defines issues relevant to planning with such a representation.

The third paper in this chapter, Allen (1984), also introduces time to define the notion of action, but takes a different approach. Allen takes the notion of time intervals as primitive and builds a representation directly from intervals rather than from a notion of a situation. (A system for temporal inference using intervals was developed in Allen, 1983.) As does McDermott, Allen represents events as the set of intervals over which they occur and shows that simultaneous actions and future external events can be represented. Rather than use a branching time model, Allen uses a linear time model, which allows for only one future, and lack of knowledge about the future is used to simulate indeterminacy. Pelavin and Allen (1987) extend Allen's logic to include a branching time model and a notion of action executability that allows for rich interactions between simultaneous actions and external events.

The last paper in this chapter, Moore (1975), investigates a problem first addressed in the McCarthy and Hayes paper: namely, the relationship between action and knowledge. Moore combines the situations from the situation calculus with the possible worlds of Hintikka (1969) to represent knowledge and develops a representation that can capture a wide range of situations beyond the capabilities of the other approaches. In particular, he can reason about plans to acquire knowledge and then use this knowledge to perform action. For instance, to open a safe, one must know the combination. If one knows where to find the combination, a plan can be constructed to obtain the combination and then open the safe. Moore can prove that this plan can work even though the combination is not known.

There are many other papers that could be included in this chapter if there were the space. For instance, Georgeff (1987) and Schubert (in press) both extend the situation calculus in ways to deal with concurrent actions. Shoham (1987) analyzes McDermott's and Allen's temporal logics in depth and develops an alternative simpler formalism that identifies several important temporal characteristics that are not clearly identified in the earlier work. Bacchus, Tenenberg, and Koomen (1989) further simplify Shoham's logic without losing any generality. Morgenstern (1986) extends the work of Moore by further developing the relationship between action and knowledge.

Papers included herein but not referenced in the volume:

Allen, J. (1983). "Maintaining Knowledge about Temporal Intervals," *CACM* 26 (11).

Bacchus, F., Tenenberg, J., and Koomen, J. (1989). "A Non-reified Temporal Logic," in R. Brachman, H. Levesque, and R. Reiter (eds.), *Proc. of KR '89*, Morgan Kaufmann, San Mateo, CA.

Georgeff, M. (1987). "Actions, Processes, and Causality," in M. Georgeff and A. Lansky (eds.), *Reasoning about Actions and Plans*, Morgan Kaufmann, 1987, San Mateo, CA.

Hintikka, J. Semantics for Propositional Attitudes," in L. Linsky (ed.), *Reference and Modality*, 1971, pp. 145–167.

McDermott, D. (1985). "Reasoning about Plans," in J. Hobbs and R. C. Moore (eds.), *Formal Models of the Commonsense World*, Ablex, Englewood, NJ.

Morgenstern, L. (1986). "A First Order Theory of Planning, Knowledge and Action," in *Theoretical Aspects of Reasoning about Knowledge*, Morgan Kaufmann, San Mateo, CA.

Pelavin, R., and Allen, J. (1987). "A Model for Concurrent Actions Having Temporal Extent," *Proc. of the AAAI-87*.

Schubert, L. (in press) "Monotonic Solution of the Frame Problem in the Situation Calculus: An Efficient Method for Worlds with Fully Specified Actions," in H. Kyburg, R. Loui, and G. Carlson (eds.), *Knowledge Representation and Defeasible Reasoning*, Kluwer, Norwell, MA.

Shoham, Y. (1987). *Temporal Logics in AI, Artificial Intelligence*, 33.

SOME PHILOSOPHICAL PROBLEMS
FROM THE STANDPOINT OF ARTIFICIAL INTELLIGENCE

by John McCarthy, Stanford University

Patrick J. Hayes, Xerox PARC

Abstract

A computer program capable of acting intelligently in the world must have a general representation of the world in terms of which its inputs are interpreted. Designing such a program requires commitments about what knowledge is and how it is obtained. Thus, some of the major traditional problems of philosophy arise in artificial intelligence.

More specifically, we want a computer program that decides what to do by inferring in a formal language that a certain strategy will achieve its assigned goal. This requires formalizing concepts of causality, ability, and knowledge. Such formalisms are also considered in philosophical logic.

The first part of the paper begins with a philosophical point of view that seems to arise naturally once we take seriously the idea of actually making an intelligent machine. We go on to the notions of metaphysically and epistemologically adequate representations of the world and then to an explanation of *can, causes,* and *knows* in terms of a representation of the world by a system of interacting automata. A proposed resolution of the problem of freewill in a deterministic universe and of counterfactual conditional sentences is presented.

The second part is mainly concerned with formalisms within which it can be proved that a strategy will achieve a goal. Concepts of situation, fluent, future operator, action, strategy, result of a strategy and knowledge are formalized. A method is given of constructing a sentence of first order logic which will be true in all models of certain axioms if and only if a certain strategy will achieve a certain goal.

The formalism of this paper represents an advance over McCarthy (1963) and Green (1969) in that it permits proof of the correctness of strategies that contain loops and strategies that involve the acquisition of knowledge, and it is also somewhat more concise.

The third part discusses open problems in extending the formalism of Part 2.

The fourth part is a review of work in philosophical logic in relation to problems of artificial intelligence and a discussion of previous efforts to program 'general intelligence' from the point of view of this paper.

Machine Intelligence 4, pp. 463-502

1. PHILOSOPHICAL QUESTIONS

Why Artificial Intelligence Needs Philosophy

The idea of an intelligent machine is old, but serious work on the artificial intelligence problem or even serious understanding of what the problem is awaited the stored program computer. We may regard the subject of artificial intelligence as beginning with Turing's article *Computing Machinery and Intelligence* (Turing 1950) and with Shannon's (1950) discussion of how a machine might be programmed to play chess.

Since that time, progress in artificial intelligence has been mainly along the following lines. Programs have been written to solve a class of problems that give humans intellectual difficulty: examples are playing chess or checkers, proving mathematical theorems, transforming one symbolic expression into another by given rules, integrating expressions composed of elementary functions, determining chemical compounds consistent with mass-spectrographic and other data. In the course of designing these programs intellectual mechanisms of greater or lesser generality are identified sometimes by introspection, sometimes by mathematical analysis, and sometimes by experiments with human subjects. Testing the programs sometimes leads to better understanding of the intellectual mechanisms and the identification of new ones.

An alternative approach is to start with the intellectual mechanisms (for example, memory, decision-making by comparisons of scores made up of weighted sums of sub-criteria, learning, tree-search, extrapolation) and make up problems that exercise these mechanisms.

In our opinion the best of this work has led to increased understanding of intellectual mechanisms and this is essential for the development of artificial intelligence even though few investigators have tried to place their particular mechanism in the general context of artificial intelligence. Sometimes this is because the investigator identifies his particular problem with the field as a whole; he thinks he sees the woods when in fact he is looking at a tree. An old but not yet superseded discussion on intellectual mechanisms is in Minsky (1961); see also Newell's (1965) review of the state of artificial intelligence.

There have been several attempts to design intelligence with the same kind of flexibility as that of a human. This has meant different things to different investigators, but none has met with much success even in the sense of general intelligence used by the investigator in question. Since our criticism of this work will be that it does not face the philosophical problems discussed in this paper, we shall postpone discussing it until a concluding section. However, we are obliged at this point to present our notion of general intelligence.

It is not difficult to give sufficient conditions for general intelligence. Turing's idea that the machine should successfully pretend to a sophisticated observer to be a human being for half an hour will do. However, if we direct our efforts towards such a goal our attention is distracted by certain superficial aspects of human behaviour that have to be imitated. Turing excluded some of these by specifying that the human to be imitated is at the end of a teletype line, so that voice, appearance, smell, etc., do not have to be considered. Turing did allow himself to be distracted into discussing the imitation of human fallibility in arithmetic, laziness, and the ability to use the English language.

However, work on artificial intelligence, especially general intelligence, will be improved by a clearer idea of what intelligence is. One way is to give a purely behavioural or black-box definition. In this case we have to say that a machine is intelligent if it solves certain classes of problems requiring intelligence in humans, or survives in an intellectually demanding environment. This definition seems vague; perhaps it can be made somewhat more precise without departing from behavioural terms, but we shall not try to do so.

Instead, we shall use in our definition certain structures apparent to introspection, such as knowledge of facts. The risk is twofold: in the first place we might be mistaken in our introspective views of our own mental structure; we may only think we use facts. In the second place there might be entities which satisfy behaviourist criteria of intelligence but are not organized in this way. However, we regard the construction of intelligent machines as fact manipulators as being the best bet both for constructing artificial intelligence and understanding natural intelligence.

We shall, therefore, be interested in an intelligent entity that is equipped with a representation or model of the world. On the basis of this representation a certain class of internally posed questions can be answered, not always correctly. Such questions are

1. What will happen next in a certain aspect of the situation?
2. What will happen if I do a certain action?
3. What is 3 + 3?
4. What does he want?
5. Can I figure out how to do this or must I get information from someone else or something else?

The above are not a fully representative set of questions and we do not have such a set yet.

On this basis we shall say that an entity is intelligent if it has an adequate model of the world (including the intellectual world of mathematics, understanding of its own goals and other mental processes), if it is clever enough to answer a wide variety of questions on the basis of this model, if it can get additional information from the external world when required, and can perform such tasks in the external world as its goals demand and its physical abilities permit.

According to this definition intelligence has two parts, which we shall call the epistemological and the heuristic. The epistemological part is the representation of the world in such a form that the solution of problems follows from the facts expressed in the representation. The heuristic part is the mechanism that on the basis of the information solves the problem and decides what to do. Most of the work in artificial intelligence so far can be regarded as devoted to the heuristic part of the problem. This paper, however, is entirely devoted to the epistemological part.

Given this notion of intelligence the following kinds of problems arise in constructing the epistemological part of an artificial intelligence:

1. What kind of general representation of the world will allow the incorporation of specific observations and new scientific laws as they are discovered?

2. Besides the representation of the physical world what other kind of entities have to be provided for? For example, mathematical systems, goals, states of knowledge.

3. How are observations to be used to get knowledge about the world, and how are the other kinds of knowledge to be obtained? In particular what kinds of knowledge about the system's own state of mind are to be provided for?

4. In what kind of internal notation is the system's knowledge to be expressed?

These questions are identical with or at least correspond to some traditional questions of philosophy, especially in metaphysics, epistemology and philosophic logic. Therefore, it is important for the research worker in artificial intelligence to consider what the philosophers have had to say.

Since the philosophers have not really come to an agreement in 2500 years it might seem that artificial intelligence is in a rather hopeless state if it is to depend on getting concrete enough information out of philosophy to write computer programs. Fortunately, merely undertaking to embody the philosophy in a computer program involves making enough philosophical presuppositions to exclude most philosophy as irrelevant. Undertaking to construct a general intelligent computer program seems to entail the following presuppositions:

1. The physical world exists and already contains some intelligent machines called people.

2. Information about this world is obtainable through the senses and is expressible internally.

3. Our common-sense view of the world is approximately correct and so is our scientific view.

4. The right way to think about the general problems of metaphysics and epistemology is not to attempt to clear one's own mind of all knowledge and start with 'Cogito ergo sum' and build up from there. Instead, we propose to use all of our knowledge to construct a computer program that knows. The correctness of our philosophical system will be tested by numerous comparisons between the beliefs of the program and our own observations and knowledge. (This point of

view corresponds to the presently dominant attitude towards the foundations of mathematics. We study the structure of mathematical systems—from the outside as it were—using whatever metamathematical tools seem useful instead of assuming as little as possible and building up axiom by axiom and rule by rule within a system.)

5. We must undertake to construct a rather comprehensive philosophical system, contrary to the present tendency to study problems separately and not try to put the results together.

6. The criterion for definiteness of the system becomes much stronger. Unless, for example, a system of epistemology allows us, at least in principle, to construct a computer program to seek knowledge in accordance with it, it must be rejected as too vague.

7. The problem of 'free will' assumes an acute but concrete form. Namely, in common-sense reasoning, a person often decides what to do by evaluating the results of the different actions he can do. An intelligent program must use this same process, but using an exact formal sense of *can*, must be able to show that it has these alternatives without denying that it is a deterministic machine.

8. The first task is to define even a naive, common-sense view of the world precisely enough to program a computer to act accordingly. This is a very difficult task in itself.

We must mention that there is one possible way of getting an artificial intelligence without having to understand it or solve the related philosophical problems. This is to make a computer simulation of natural selection in which intelligence evolves by mutating computer programs in a suitably demanding environment. This method has had no substantial success so far, perhaps due to inadequate models of the world and of the evolutionary process, but it might succeed. It would seem to be a dangerous procedure, for a program that was intelligent in a way its designer did not understand might get out of control. In any case, the approach of trying to make an artificial intelligence through understanding what intelligence is, is more congenial to the present authors and seems likely to succeed sooner.

Reasoning programs and the Missouri program

The philosophical problems that have to be solved will be clearer in connection with a particular kind of proposed intelligent program, called a reasoning program or RP for short. RP interacts with the world through input and output devices some of which may be general sensory and motor organs (for example, television cameras, microphones, artificial arms) and others of which are communication devices (for example, teletypes or keyboard-display consoles). Internally, RP may represent information in a variety of ways. For example, pictures may be represented as dot arrays or a list of regions and edges with classifications and adjacency relations.

Scenes may be represented as lists of bodies with positions, shapes, and rates of motion. Situations may be represented by symbolic expressions with allowed rules of transformation. Utterances may be represented by digitized functions of time, by sequences of phonemes, and parsings of sentences.

However, one representation plays a dominant role and in simpler systems may be the only representation present. This is a representation by sets of sentences in a suitable formal logical language, for example ω-order logic with function symbols, description operator, conditional expressions, sets, etc. Whether we must include modal operators with their referential opacity is undecided. This representation dominates in the following sense:

1. All other data structures have linguistic descriptions that give the relations between the structures and what they tell about the world.

2. The subroutines have linguistic descriptions that tell what they do, either internally manipulating data, or externally manipulating the world.

3. The rules that express RP's beliefs about how the world behaves and that give the consequences of strategies are expressed linguistically.

4. RP's goals, as given by the experimenter, its devised subgoals, its opinion on its state of progress are all linguistically expressed.

5. We shall say that RP's information is adequate to solve a problem if it is a logical consequence of all these sentences that a certain strategy of action will solve it.

6. RP is a deduction program that tries to find strategies of action that it can prove will solve a problem; on finding one, it executes it.

7. Strategies may involve subgoals which are to be solved by RP, and part or all of a strategy may be purely intellectual, that is, may involve the search for a strategy, a proof, or some other intellectual object that satisfies some criteria.

Such a program was first discussed in McCarthy (1959) and was called the Advice Taker. In McCarthy (1963) a preliminary approach to the required formalism, now superseded by this paper, was presented. This paper is in part an answer to Y. Bar-Hillel's comment, when the original paper was presented at the 1958 Symposium on the Mechanization of Thought Processes, that the paper involved some philosophical presuppositions.

Constructing RP involves both the epistemological and the heuristic parts of the artificial intelligence problem: that is, the information in memory must be adequate to determine a strategy for achieving the goal (this strategy may involve the acquisition of further information) and RP must be clever enough to find the strategy and the proof of its correctness. Of course, these problems interact, but since this paper is focused on the epistemological part, we mention the Missouri program (MP) that involves only this part.

The Missouri program (its motto is, 'Show me') does not try to find strategies or proofs that the strategies achieve a goal. Instead, it allows the experimenter to present it proof steps and checks their correctness. Moreover, when it is 'convinced' that it ought to perform an action or execute a strategy it does so. We may regard this paper as being concerned with the construction of a Missouri program that can be persuaded to achieve goals.

Representations of the world

The first step in the design of RP or MP is to decide what structure the world is to be regarded as having, and how information about the world and its laws of change are to be represented in the machine. This decision turns out to depend on whether one is talking about the expression of general laws or specific facts. Thus, our understanding of gas dynamics depends on the representation of a gas as a very large number of particles moving in space; this representation plays an essential role in deriving the mechanical, thermal electrical and optical properties of gases. The state of the gas at a given instant is regarded as determined by the position, velocity and excitation states of each particle. However, we never actually determine the position, velocity or excitation of even a single molecule. Our practical knowledge of a particular sample of gas is expressed by parameters like the pressure, temperature and velocity fields or even more grossly by average pressures and temperatures. From our philosophical point of view this is entirely normal, and we are not inclined to deny existence to entities we cannot see, or to be so anthropocentric as to imagine that the world must be so constructed that we have direct or even indirect access to all of it.

From the artificial intelligence point of view we can then define three kinds of adequacy for representations of the world.

A representation is called metaphysically adequate if the world could have that form without contradicting the facts of the aspect of reality that interests us. Examples of metaphysically adequate representations for different aspects of reality are:

1. The representation of the world as a collection of particles interacting through forces between each pair of particles.

2. Representation of the world as a giant quantum-mechanical wave function.

3. Representation as a system of interacting discrete automata. We shall make use of this representation.

Metaphysically adequate representations are mainly useful for constructing general theories. Deriving observable consequences from the theory is a further step.

A representation is called epistemologically adequate for a person or machine if it can be used practically to express the facts that one actually has about the aspect of the world. Thus none of the above-mentioned representations are adequate to express facts like 'John is at home' or 'dogs chase cats' or 'John's telephone number is 321-7580'. Ordinary language is obviously adequate to express the facts that people communicate to each other in ordinary language. It is not, for instance, adequate to express what people know about how to recognize a particular face. The second part of this paper is concerned with an epistemologically adequate formal representation of common-sense facts of causality, ability and knowledge.

A representation is called heuristically adequate if the reasoning processes actually gone through in solving a problem are expressible in the language. We shall not treat this somewhat tentatively proposed concept further in this paper except to point out later that one particular representation seems epistemologically but not heuristically adequate.

In the remaining sections of the first part of the paper we shall use the representations of the world as a system of interacting automata to explicate notions of causality, ability and knowledge (including self-knowledge).

The automaton representation and the notion of 'can'

Let S be a system of interacting discrete finite automata such as that shown in Figure 1.

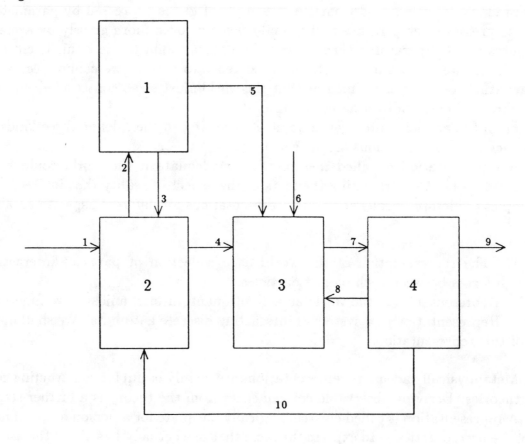

Figure 1

Each box represents a subautomaton and each line represents a signal. Time takes on integer values and the dynamic behaviour of the whole automaton is given by the equations:

$$(1)\ a_1(t + 1) = A_1(a_1(t),\ s_3(t))$$
$$a_2(t + 1) = A_2(a_2(t),\ s_1(t),\ s_2(t),\ s_{10}(t))$$
$$a_3(t + 1) = A_3(a_3(t),\ s_4(t),\ s_5(t),\ s_6(t),\ s_8(t))$$
$$a_4(t + 1) = A_4(a_4(t),\ s_7(t))$$

$$(2)\ s_2(t) = S_2(a_1(t))$$
$$s_3(t) = S_3(a_2(t))$$
$$s_4(t) = S_4(a_2(t))$$
$$s_5(t) = S_5(a_1(t))$$
$$s_7(t) = S_7(a_3(t))$$
$$s_8(t) = S_8(a_4(t))$$
$$s_9(t) = S_9(a_4(t))$$
$$s_{10}(t) = S_{10}(a_4(t))$$

The interpretation of these equations is that the state of any automaton at time $t + 1$ is determined by its state at time t and by the signals received at time t. The value of a particular signal at time t is determined by the state at time t of the automaton from which it comes. Signals without a source automaton represent inputs from the outside and signals without a destination represent outputs.

Finite automata are the simplest examples of systems that interact over time. They are completely deterministic; if we know the initial states of all the automata and if we know the inputs as a function of time, the behaviour of the system is completely determined by equations (1) and (2) for all future time.

The automaton representation consists in regarding the world as a system of interacting subautomata. For example, we might regard each person in the room as a subautomaton and the environment as consisting of one or more additional subautomata. As we shall see, this representation has many of the qualitative properties of interactions among things and persons. However, if we take the representation too seriously and attempt to represent particular situations by systems of interacting automata, we encounter the following difficulties:

1. The number of states required in the subautomata is very large, for example $2^{10^{10}}$, if we try to represent someone's knowledge. Automata this large have to be represented by computer programs, or in some other way that does not involve mentioning states individually.

2. Geometric information is hard to represent. Consider, for example, the location of a multi-jointed object such as a person or a matter of even more difficulty—the shape of a lump of clay.

3. The system of fixed interconnections is inadequate. Since a person may handle any object in the room, an adequate automaton representation would require signal lines connecting him with every object.

4. The most serious objection, however, is that (in our terminology) the automaton representation is epistemologically inadequate. Namely, we do not ever know a person well enough to list his internal states. The kind of information we do have about him needs to be expressed in some other way.

Nevertheless, we may use the automaton representation for concepts of *can, causes,* some kinds of counterfactual statements ('If I had struck this match yesterday it would have lit') and, with some elaboration of the representation, for a concept of *believes.*

Let us consider the notion of *can.* Let S be a system of subautomata without external inputs such as that of Figure 2. Let p be one of the subautomata, and suppose that there are m signal lines coming out of p. What p can do is defined in terms of a new system S_p, which is obtained from the system S by disconnecting the m signal lines coming from p and replacing them by m external input lines to the system. In Figure 2, subautomaton 1 has one output, and in the system S_1 (Figure 3) this is replaced by an external input. The new system S_p always has the same set of states as the system S. Now let π be a condition on the state such as, 'a_2 is even' or '$a_2 = a_3$'. (In the applications π may be a condition like 'The box is under the bananas'.)

We shall write

$$can(p, \pi, s)$$

which is read, 'The subautomaton p *can* bring about the condition π in the situation s' if there is a sequence of outputs from the automaton S_p that will eventually put S into a state a' that satisfies $\pi(a')$. In other words, in determining what p can achieve, we consider the effects of sequences of its actions, quite apart from the conditions that determine what it actually will do.

In Figure 2, let us consider the initial state a to be one in which all subautomata are initially in state *0*. Then the reader will easily verify the following propositions:

1. Subautomaton 2 *will* never be in state 1.
2. Subautomaton 1 *can* put subautomaton 2 in state 1.
3. Subautomaton 3 *cannot* put subautomaton 2 in state 1.

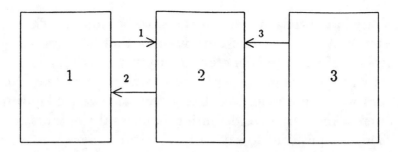

Figure 2. System S

$a_1(t + 1) = a_1(t) + s_2(t)$
$a_2(t + 1) = a_2(t) + s_1(t) + 2s_3(t)$
$a_3(t + 1) = $ **if** $a_3(t) = 0$ **then** 0 **else** $a_3(t) + 1$
$s_1(t) = $ **if** $a_1(t) = 0$ **then** 2 **else** 1
$s_2(t) = 1$
$s_3(t) = $ **if** $a_3(t) = 0$ **then** 0 **else** 1

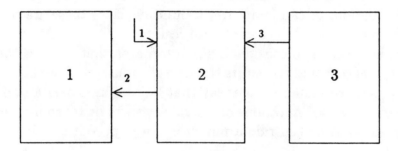

Figure 3. System S_1

We claim that this notion of *can* is, to a first approximation, the appropriate one for an automaton to use internally in deciding what to do by reasoning. We also claim that it corresponds in many cases to the common sense notion of *can* used in everyday speech.

In the first place, suppose we have an automaton that decides what to do by reasoning; for example, suppose it is a computer using an RP. Then its output is determined by the decisions it makes in the reasoning process. It does not know (has not computed) in advance what it will do, and, therefore, it is appropriate that it considers that it can do anything that can be achieved by some sequence of its outputs. Common-sense reasoning seems to operate in the same way.

The above rather simple notion of *can* requires some elaboration both to represent adequately the commonsense notion and for practical purposes in the reasoning program. First, suppose that the system of automata admits external inputs. There are two ways of defining *can* in this case. One way is to assert $can(p, \pi, s)$ if p can achieve π regardless of what signals appear on the external inputs. Thus, instead of requiring the existence of a sequence of outputs of p that achieves the goal we shall require the existence of a strategy where the output at any time is allowed to depend on the sequence of external inputs so far received by the system. Note that in this definition of *can* we are not requiring that p have any way of knowing what the external inputs were. An alternative definition requires the outputs to depend on the inputs of p. This is equivalent to saying that p can achieve a goal provided the goal would be achieved for arbitrary inputs by some automaton put in place of p. With either of these definitions *can* becomes a function of the place of the subautomaton in the system rather than of the subautomaton itself. We do not know which of these treatments is preferable, and so we shall call the first concept *cana* and the second *canb*.

The idea that what a person can do depends on his position rather than on his characteristics is somewhat counter-intuitive. This impression can be mitigated as follows: Imagine the person to be made up of several subautomata; the output of the outer subautomaton is the motion of the joints. If we break the connection to the world at that point we can answer questions like, 'Can he fit through a given hole?' We shall get some counter-intuitive answers, however, such as that he can run at top speed for an hour or can jump over a building, since these are sequences of motions of his joints that would achieve these results.

The next step, however, is to consider a subautomaton that receives the nerve impulses from the spinal cord and transmits them to the muscles. If we break at the input to this automaton, we shall no longer say that he can jump over a building or run long at top speed since the limitations of the muscles will be taken into account. We shall, however, say that he can ride a unicycle since appropriate nerve signals would achieve this result.

The notion of *can* corresponding to the intuitive notion in the largest number of cases might be obtained by hypothesizing an 'organ of will,' which makes decisions to do things and transmits these decisions to the main part of the brain that tries to carry them out and contains all the knowledge of particular facts. If we make the break at this point we shall be able to say that so-and-so cannot dial the President's secret and private telephone number because he does not know it, even though if the question were asked could he dial that particular number, the answer would be yes. However, even this break would not give the statement, 'I cannot go without saying goodbye, because this would hurt the child's feelings'.

On the basis of these examples, one might try to postulate a sequence of narrower and narrower notions of *can* terminating in a notion according to which a person can do only what he actually does. This notion would then be superfluous. Actually, one should not look for a single best notion of *can*; each of the above-mentioned notions is useful and is actually used in some circumstances. Sometimes, more than one notion is used in a single sentence, when two different levels of constraint are mentioned.

Besides its use in explicating the notion of *can*, the automaton representation of the world is very suited for defining notions of causality. For, we may say that subautomaton p caused the condition π in state s, if changing the output of p would prevent π. In fact the whole idea of a system of interacting automata is just a formalization of the commonsense notion of causality.

Moreover, the automaton representation can be used to explicate certain counterfactual conditional sentences. For example, we have the sentence, 'If I had struck this match yesterday at this time it would have lit.' In a suitable automaton representation, we have a certain state of the system yesterday at that time, and we imagine a break made where the nerves lead from my head or perhaps at the output of my 'decision box', and the appropriate signals to strike the match having been made. Then it is a definite and decidable question about the system S_p, whether the match lights or not, depending on whether it is wet, etc. This interpretation of this kind of counterfactual sentence seems to be what is needed for RP to learn from its mistakes, by accepting or generating sentences of the form, 'had I done thus-and-so I would have been successful, so I should alter my procedures in some way that would have produced the correct action in that case'.

In the foregoing we have taken the representation of the situation as a system of interacting subautomata for granted. However, a given overall situation might be represented as a system of interacting subautomata in a number of ways, and different representations might yield different results about what a given subautomaton can achieve, what would have happened if some subautomaton had acted differently, or what caused what. Indeed, in a different representation, the same or corresponding subautomata might not be identifiable. Therefore, these notions depend on the representation chosen.

For example, suppose a pair of Martians observe the situation in a room. One Martian analyzes it as a collection of interacting people as we do, but the second Martian groups all the heads together into one subautomaton and all the bodies into another. (A creature from momentum space would regard the Fourier components of the distribution of matter as the separate interacting subautomata.) How is the first Martian to convince the second that his representation is to be preferred? Roughly speaking, he would argue that the interaction between the heads and bodies of the same person is closer than the interaction between the different heads, and so more of an analysis has been achieved from 'the primordial muddle' with the conventional representation. He will be especially convincing when he points out that when the meeting is over the heads will stop interacting with each other, but will continue to interact with their respective bodies.

We can express this kind of argument formally in terms of automata as follows: Suppose we have an autonomous automaton A, that is an automaton without inputs, and let it have k states. Further, let m and n be two integers such that $m, n \geq k$. Now label k points of an m-by-n array with the states of A. This can be done in $\binom{mn}{k}!$ ways. For each of these ways we have a representation of the automaton A as a system of an m-state automaton B interacting with an n-state automaton C. Namely, corresponding to each row of the array we have a state of B and to each column a state of C. The signals are in 1–1 correspondence with the states themselves; thus each subautomaton has just as many values of its output as it has states. Now it may happen that two of these signals are equivalent in their effect on the other subautomaton, and we use this equivalence relation to form equivalence classes of signals. We may then regard the equivalence classes as the signals themselves. Suppose then that there are now r signals from B to C and s signals from C to B. We ask how small r and s can be taken in general compared to m and n. The answer may be obtained by counting the number of inequivalent automata with k states and comparing it with the number of systems of two automata with m and n states respectively and r and s signals going in the respective directions. The result is not worth working out in detail, but tells us that only a few of the k state automata admit such a decomposition with r and s small compared to m and n. Therefore, if an automaton happens to admit such a decomposition it is very unusual for it to admit a second such decomposition that is not equivalent to the first with respect to some renaming of states. Applying this argument to the real world, we may say that it is overwhelmingly probable that our customary decomposition of the world automaton into separate people and things has a unique, objective and usually preferred status. Therefore, the notions of *can*, of causality, and of counterfactual associated with this decomposition also have a preferred status.

In our opinion, this explains some of the difficulty philosophers have had in analyzing counterfactuals and causality. For example, the sentence, 'If I had struck this match yesterday, it would have lit' is meaningful only in terms of a rather complicated model of the world, which, however, has an objective preferred status. However, the preferred status of this model depends on its correspondence with a large number of facts. For this reason, it is probably not fruitful to treat an individual counterfactual conditional sentence in isolation.

It is also possible to treat notions of belief and knowledge in terms of the automaton representation. We have not worked this out very far, and the ideas presented here should be regarded as tentative. We would like to be able to give conditions under which we may say that a subautomaton p believes a certain proposition. We shall not try to do this directly but only relative to a predicate $B_p(s, w)$. Here s is the state of the automaton p and w is a proposition; $B_p(s, w)$ is true if p is to be regarded as believing w when in state s and is false otherwise. With respect to such a predicate B we may ask the following questions:

1. Are p's beliefs consistent? Are they correct?
2. Does p reason? That is, do new beliefs arise that are logical consequences of previous beliefs?

3. Does p observe? That is, do true propositions about automata connected to p cause p to believe them?

4. Does p behave rationally? That is, when p believes a sentence asserting that it should do something does p do it?

5. Does p communicate in language L? That is, regarding the content of a certain input or output signal line as in a text in language L, does this line transmit beliefs to or from p?

6. Is p self-conscious? That is, does it have a fair variety of correct beliefs about its own beliefs and the processes that change them?

It is only with respect to the predicate B_p that all these questions can be asked. However, if questions 1 thru 4 are answered affirmatively for some predicate B_p, this is certainly remarkable, and we would feel fully entitled to consider B_p a reasonable notion of belief.

In one important respect the situation with regard to belief or knowledge is the same as it was for counterfactual conditional statements: no way is provided to assign a meaning to a single statement of belief or knowledge, since for any single statement a suitable B_p can easily be constructed. Individual statements about belief or knowledge are made on the basis of a larger system which must be validated as a whole.

2. FORMALISM

In part 1 we showed how the concepts of ability and belief could be given formal definition in the metaphysically adequate automaton model and indicated the correspondence between these formal concepts and the corresponding commonsense concepts. We emphasized, however, that practical systems require epistemologically adequate systems in which those facts which are actually ascertainable can be expressed.

In this part we begin the construction of an epistemologically adequate system. Instead of giving formal definitions, however, we shall introduce the formal notions by informal natural-language descriptions and give examples of their use to describe situations and the possibilities for action they present. The formalism presented is intended to supersede that of McCarthy (1963).

Situations

A situation s is the complete state of the universe at an instant of time. We denote by *Sit* the set of all situations. Since the universe is too large for complete description, we shall never completely describe a situation; we shall only give facts about situations. These facts will be used to deduce further facts about that situation, about future situations and about situations that persons can bring about from that situation.

This requires that we consider not only situations that actually occur, but also hypothetical situations such as the situation that would arise if Mr. Smith sold his car to a certain person who has offered $250 for it. Since he is not going to sell the car for that price, the hypothetical situation is not completely defined; for example, it is not determined what Smith's mental state would be and therefore it is also undetermined how quickly he would return to his office, etc. Nevertheless, the representation of reality is adequate to determine some facts about this situation, enough at least to make him decide not to sell the car.

We shall further assume that the laws of motion determine, given a situation, all future situations.*

In order to give partial information about situations we introduce the notion of fluent.

Fluents

A *fluent* is a function whose domain is the space *Sit* of situational. If the range of the function is (*true*, *false*), then it is called a *propositional fluent*. If its range is *Sit*, then it is called a *situational fluent*.

Fluents are often the values of functions. Thus $raining(x)$ is a fluent such that $raining(x)(s)$ is true if and only if it is raining at the place x in the situation s. We can also write this assertion as $raining(x, s)$ making use of the well-known equivalence between a function of two variables and a function of the first variable whose value is a function of the second variable.

Suppose we wish to assert about a situation s that person p is in place x and that it is raining in place x. We may write this in several ways each of which has its uses:

1. $at(p, x)(s) \wedge raining\,(x)(s)$. This corresponds to the definition given.

2. $at(p, x, s) \wedge raining\,(x, s)$. This is more conventional mathematically and a bit shorter.

3. $[at(p, x) \wedge raining\,(x)](s)$. Here we are introducing a convention that operators applied to fluents give fluents whose values are computed by applying the logical operators to the values of the operand fluents, that is, if f and g are fluents then

$$(f \text{ op } g)(s) = f(s) \text{ op } g(s).$$

---

* This assumption is difficult to reconcile with quantum mechanics, and relativity tells us that any assignment of simultaneity to events in different places is arbitrary. However, we are proceeding on the basis that modern physics is irrelevant to common sense in deciding what to do, and in particular is irrelevant to solving the 'free will problem'.

4. $[\lambda s' . at(p, x, s') \wedge raining\,(x, s')](s)$. Here we have formed the composite fluent by λ-abstraction.

Here are some examples of fluents and expressions involving them:

1. $time(s)$. This is the time associated with the situation s. It is essential to consider time as dependent on the situation as we shall sometimes wish to consider several different situations having the same time value, for example, the results of alternative courses of actions.

2. $in(x, y, s)$. This asserts that x is in the location y in situation s. The fluent in may be taken as satisfying a kind of transitive law, namely:

$$\forall x . \forall y . \forall z . \forall s \; in(x, y, s) \wedge in(y, z, s) \supset in(x, z, s)$$

We can also write this law

$$\forall x . \forall y . \forall z . \forall . in(x, y) \wedge in(y, z) \supset in(x, z)$$

where we have adopted the convention that a quantifier without a variable is applied to an implicit situation variable which is the (suppressed) argument of a propositional fluent that follows. Suppressing situation arguments in this way corresponds to the natural language convention of writing sentences like, 'John was at home' or 'John is at home' leaving understood the situations to which these assertions apply.

3. $has(Monkey, Bananas, s)$. Here we introduce the convention that capitalized words denote proper names, for example, 'Monkey' is the name of a particular individual. That the individual is a monkey is not asserted, so that the expression $monkey(Monkey)$ may have to appear among the premisses of an argument. Needless to say, the reader has a right to feel that he has been given a hint that the individual Monkey will turn out to be a monkey. The above expression is to be taken as asserting that in the situation s the individual *Monkey* has the object *Bananas*. We shall, in the examples below, sometimes omit premisses such as $monkey(Monkey)$, but in a complete system they would have to appear.

Causality

We shall make assertions of causality by means of a fluent $F(\pi)$ where π is itself a propositional fluent. $F(\pi, s)$ asserts that the situation s will be followed (after an unspecified time) by a situation that satisfies the fluent π. We may use F to assert that if a person is out in the rain he will get wet, by writing:

$$\forall x . \forall p . \forall s . raining(x, s) \wedge at(p, x, s) \wedge outside(p, s) \supset F(\lambda s' . wet(p, s'), s)$$

Suppressing explicit mention of situations gives:

$$\forall x . \forall p . \forall\, raining(x) \wedge at(p, x) \wedge outside(p) \supset F(wet(p)).$$

In this case suppressing situations simplifies the statement.

F can also be used to express physical laws. Consider the law of falling bodies which is often written

$$h = h_0 + v_0 \times (t - t_0) - 0.5g \times (t - t_0)^2$$

together with some prose identifying the variables. Since we need a formal system for machine reasoning we cannot have any prose. Therefore, we write:

$$\forall b . \forall t . \forall s . falling(b, s) \wedge t \geq 0 \wedge height(b, s) + velocity(b, s) \times t - 0.5gt^2 > 0$$
$$\supset F(\lambda s' . time(s') = time(s) + t \wedge falling(b, s')$$
$$\wedge\, height(b, s') = height(b, s) + velocity(b, s) \times t - 0.5gt^2, s)$$

There has to be a convention (or declarations) so that it is determined that $height(b)$, $velocity(b)$ and $time$ are fluents, whereas t, v, t_1 and h denote ordinary real numbers.

$F(\pi, s)$ as introduced here corresponds to A. N. Prior's (1957, 1968) expression $F\pi$.

The use of situation variables is analogous to the use of time-instants in the calculi of world-states which Prior (1968) calls U-T calculi. Prior provides many interesting correspondences between his U-T calculi and various axiomatizations of the modal tense-logics (that is, using this F-operator: see part 4). However, the situation calculus is richer than any of the tense-logics Prior considers.

Besides F he introduces three other operators which we also find useful; we thus have:

1. $F(\pi, s)$. For some situation s' in the future of $s, \pi(s')$ holds.
2. $G(\pi, s)$. For all situations s' in the future of $s, \pi(s')$ holds.
3. $P(\pi, s)$. For some situations s' in the past of $s, \pi(s')$ holds.
4. $H(\pi, s)$. For all situations s' in the past of $s, \pi(s')$ holds.

It seems also useful to define a situational fluent $next(\pi)$ as the next situation s' in the future of s for which $\pi(s')$ holds. If there is no such situation, that is, if $\neg F(\pi, s)$, then $next(\pi, s)$ is considered undefined. For example, we may translate the sentence 'By the time John gets home, Henry will be home too' as

$$at(Henry, home(Henry), next(at(John, home(John)), s)).$$

Also the phrase 'when John gets home' translates into

$$time(next(at(John, home(John)), s)).$$

Though next (π, s) will never actually be computed since situations are too rich to be specified completely, the values of fluents applied to next (π, s) will be computed.

Actions

A fundamental role in our study of actions is played by the situational fluent

$$result(p, \sigma, s)$$

Here, p is a person, σ is an action or more generally a strategy, and s is a situation. The value of $result(p, \sigma, s)$ is the situation that results when p carries out σ, starting in the situation s. If the action or strategy does not terminate, $result(p, \sigma, s)$ is considered undefined.

With the aid of *result* we can express certain laws of ability. For example:

$$has(p, k, s) \wedge fits(k, sf) \wedge at(p, sf, s) \supset open(sf, result(p, opens(sf, k), s)).$$

This formula is to be regarded as an axiom schema asserting that if in a situation s a person p has a key k that fits the safe sf, then in the situation resulting from his performing the action $opens(sf, k)$, that is, opening the safe sf with the key k, the safe is open. The assertion $fits(k, sf)$ carries the information that k is a key and sf a safe. Later we shall be concerned with combination safes that require p to *know* the combination.

Strategies

Actions can be combined into strategies. The simplest combination is a finite sequence of actions. We shall combine actions as though they were ALGOL statements, that is, procedure calls. Thus, the sequence of actions, ('move the box under the bananas', 'climb onto the box', and 'reach for the bananas') may be written:

begin *move(Box, Under-Bananas); climb(Box); reach-for(Bananas)* **end;**

A strategy in general will be an ALGOL-like compound statement containing actions written in the form of procedure calling assignment statements, and conditional **go to**'s. We shall not include any declarations in the program since they can be included in the much larger collection of declarative sentences that determine the effect of the strategy.

Consider for example the strategy that consists of walking 17 blocks south, turning right and then walking till you come to Chestnut Street. This strategy may be written as follows:

```
begin
        face(South);
        n := 0;
    b : if n = 17 then go to a;
        walk-a-block; n := n + 1;
        go to b;
    a : turn-right;
    c : walk-a-block;
        if name-on-street-sign ≠ 'Chestnut Street' then go to  c
end;
```

In the above program the external actions are represented by procedure calls. Variables to which values are assigned have a purely internal significance (we may even call it mental significance) and so do the statement labels and the go to statements.

For the purpose of applying the mathematical theory of computation we shall write the program differently: namely, each occurrence of an action α is to be replaced by an assignment statement $s := result(p, \alpha, s)$. Thus the above program becomes

```
begin
        s := result(p, face(South), s);
        n := 0;
    b : if n = 17 then go to a;
        s := result(p, walk-a-block, s);
        n := n + 1;
        go to b;
    a : s := result(p, turn-right, s);
    c : s := result(p, walk-a-block, s);
        if name-on-street-sign ≠ 'Chestnut Street' then go to  c
end;
```

Suppose we wish to show that by carrying out this strategy John can go home provided he is initially at his office. Then according to the methods of Zohar Manna (1968a, 1968b), we may derive from this program together with the initial condition $at(John, office(John), s_0)$ and the final condition $at(John, home(John), s)$, a sentence W of first-order logic. Proving W will show that the procedure terminates in a finite number of steps and that when it terminates s will satisfy $at(John, home(John), s)$.

According to Manna's theory we must prove the following collection of sentences inconsistent for arbitrary interpretations of the predicates $q1$ and $q2$ and the particular interpretations of the other functions and predicates in the program:

$at(John, office(John)s_0)$,

$q1(O, result(John, face(South), s_0))$,

$\forall n . \forall s . q1(n, s) \supset$ **if** $n = 17$

         then $q2(result(John, walk\text{-}a\text{-}block, result(John, turn - right, s)))$

         else $q1(n + 1, result(John, walk\text{-}a\text{-}block, s))$,

$\forall s . q2(s) \supset$ **if** $name\text{-}on\text{-}street\text{-}sign(s) \neq$ '*Chestnut Street*'

         then $q2(result(John, walk\text{-}a\text{-}block, s))$

         else $\neg at(John, home(John), s)$

Therefore the formula that has to be proved may be written

$\exists s_0 \{ at(John, office(John), s_0) \wedge q1(O, result(John, face(South), s_0)) \}$

                 $\supset$

$\exists n . \exists s . \{ q1(n, s) \wedge$ **if** $n = 17$

         then $q2(result(John, walk\text{-}a\text{-}block, result(John, turn\text{-}right, s)))$

         else $\neg q1(n + 1, result(John, walk\text{-}a\text{-}block, s)) \}$

               $\vee$

$\exists s . \{ q2(s) \wedge$ **if** $name\text{-}on\text{-}street\text{-}sign(s) \neq$ '*Chestnut Street*'

         then $\neg q2(result(John, walk\text{-}a\text{-}block, s))$

         else $at(John, home(John), s) \}$

In order to prove this sentence we would have to use the following kinds of facts expressed as sentences or sentence schemas of first-order logic:

1. Facts of geography. The initial street stretches at least 17 blocks to the south, and intersects a street which in turn intersects Chestnut Street a number of blocks to the right; the location of John's home and office.

2. The fact that the fluent name-on-street-sign will have the value 'Chestnut Street' at that point.

3. Facts giving the effects of action α expressed as predicates about $result(p, \alpha, s)$ deducible from sentences about s.

4. An axiom schema of induction that allows us to deduce that the loop of walking 17 blocks will terminate.

5. A fact that says that Chestnut Street is a finite number of blocks to the right after going 17 blocks south. This fact has nothing to do with the possibility of walking. It may also have to be expressed as a sentence schema or even as a sentence of second-order logic.

When we consider making a computer carry out the strategy, we must distinguish the variable s from the other variables in the second form of the program. The other variables are stored in the memory of the computer and the assignments may be executed in the normal way. The variable s represents the state of the world and the computer makes an assignment to it by performing an action. Likewise the fluent name-on-street-sign requires an action, of observation.

Knowledge and Ability

In order to discuss the role of knowledge in one's ability to achieve goals let us return to the example of the safe. There we had

1. $has(p, k, s) \land fits(k, sf) \land at(p, sf, s) \supset open(sf, result(p, opens(sf, k), s))$,

which expressed sufficient conditions for the ability of a person to open a safe with a key. Now suppose we have a combination safe with a combination c. Then we may write:

2. $fits2(c, sf) \land at(p, sf, s) \supset open(sf, result(p, opens2(sf, c), s))$,

where we have used the predicate *fits2* and the action *opens2* to express the distinction between a key fitting a safe and a combination fitting it, and also the distinction between the acts of opening a safe with a key and a combination. In particular, $opens2(sf, c)$ is the act of manipulating the safe in accordance with the combination c. We have left out a sentence of the form $has2(p, c, s)$ for two reasons. In the first place, it is unnecessary: if you manipulate a safe in accordance with its combination it will open; there is no need to have anything. In the second place it is not clear what $has2(p, c, s)$ means. Suppose, for example, that the combination of a particular safe sf is the number 34125, then $fits(34125, sf)$ makes sense and so does the act $opens2(sf, 34125)$. (We assume that $open(sf, result(p, opens2(sf, 34111), s))$ would not be true.) But what could $has(p, 34125, s)$ mean? Thus, a direct parallel between the rules for opening a safe with a key and opening it with a combination seems impossible.

Nevertheless, we need some way of expressing the fact that one has to know the combination of a safe in order to open it. First we introduce the function $combination(sf)$ and rewrite 2 as

3. $at(p, sf, s) \land csafe(sf) \supset open(sf, result(p, opens2 \ sf, combination(sf), s)))$,

where $csafe(sf)$ asserts that sf is a combination safe and $combination (sf)$ denotes the combination of sf. (We could not write (sf) in the other case unless we wished to restrict ourselves to the case of safes with only one key.)

Next we introduce the notion of a feasible strategy for a person. The idea is that a strategy that would achieve a certain goal might not be feasible for a person because he lacks certain knowledge or abilities.

Our first approach is to regard the action $opens2(sf, combination\,(sf))$ as infeasible because p might not know the combination. Therefore. we introduce a new function $idea\text{-}of\text{-}combination(p, sf, s)$ which stands for person p's idea of the combination of sf in situation s. The action $opens2(sf, idea\text{-}of\text{-}combination(p, sf, s))$ is regarded as feasible for p, since p is assumed to know his idea of the combination if this is defined. However, we leave sentence 3 as it is so we cannot yet prove $open(sf, result(p, opens2(sf, idea\text{-}of\text{-}combination(p, sf, s)), s))$. The assertion that p knows the combination of sf can now be expressed as

5. $idea\text{-}of\text{-}combination(p, sf, s) = combination(sf)$

and with this, the possibility of opening the safe can be proved.

Another example of this approach is given by the following formalization of getting into conversation with someone by looking up his number in the telephone book and then dialing it.

The strategy for p in the first form is

> **begin**
>> $lookup(q, Phone\text{-}book)$;
>> $dial(idea\text{-}of\text{-}phone\text{-}number(sq, p))$
> **end**;

or in the second form

> **begin**
>> $s := result(p, lookup(q, Phone\text{-}book), s_0)$;
>> $s := result(p, dial(idea\text{-}of\text{-}phone\text{-}number(q, p. s)), s)$
> **end**;

The premises to write down appear to be

1. $has(p, Phone\text{-}book, s_0)$
2. $listed(q, Phone\text{-}book, s_0)$
3. $\forall s . \forall p . \forall q . has(p, Phone\text{-}book, s) \wedge listed(q, Phone\text{-}book, s)$
   $\supset phone\text{-}number(q) = idea\text{-}of\text{-}phone\text{-}number(p, q,$
   $\qquad\qquad\qquad\qquad result(p, lookup(q, Phone\text{-}book), s))$
4. $\forall s . \forall p . \forall q . \forall x . at(q, home(q), s) \wedge has(p, x, s) \wedge telephone(x)$
   $\supset in\text{-}conversation(p, q, result(p, dial(phone\text{-}number(q)). s))$
5. $at(q, home(q), s_0)$
6. $telephone(Telephone)$
7. $has(p, Telephone, s_0)$

Unfortunately, these premisses are not sufficient to allow one to conclude that

$$in\text{-}conversation(p, q, result(p, \textbf{ begin } lookup(q, Phone\text{-}book);$$
$$dial(idea\text{-}of\text{-}phone\text{-}number(q, p)) \textbf{ end}; s_0)).$$

The trouble is that one cannot show that the fluents $at(q, home(q))$ and $has(p, Tele\text{-}phone)$ still apply to the situation $result(p, lookup(q, Phone\text{-}book), s_0)$. To make it come out right we shall revise the third hypothesis to read:

$$\forall s . \forall p . \forall q . \forall x . \forall y .$$
$$at(q, y, s) \wedge has(p, x, s) \wedge has(p, Phone\text{-}book, s) \wedge listed(q, Phone\text{-}book)$$
$$\supset [\lambda r. at(q, y, r) \wedge has(p, x, r) \wedge phone\text{-}number(q)$$
$$= idea\text{-}of\text{-}phone\text{-}number(p, q, r)]$$
$$(result(p, lookup(q, Phone\text{-}book), s)).$$

This works, but the additional hypotheses about what remains unchanged when p looks up a telephone number are quite *ad hoc*. We shall treat this problem in a later section.

The present approach has a major technical advantage for which, however, we pay a high price. The advantage is that we preserve the ability to replace any expression by an equal one in any expression of our language. Thus if $phone\text{-}number(John)$ $= 3217580$, any true statement of our language that contains 3217580 or $phone\text{-}number(John)$ will remain true if we replace one by the other. This desirable property is termed referential transparency.

The price we pay for referential transparency is that we have to introduce $idea\text{-}of\text{-}phone\text{-}number(p, q, s)$ as a separate *ad hoc* entity and cannot use the more natural $idea\text{-}of(p, phone\text{-}number(q), s)$ where $idea\text{-}of(p, con, s)$ is some kind of operator applicable to the concept con. Namely, the sentence

$$idea\text{-}of(p, phone\text{-}number(q), s) = phone\text{-}number(q)$$

would be supposed to express that p knows q's phone-number, but $idea\text{-}of(p, 321\text{-}7580, s) = 3217580$ expresses only that p understands that number. Yet with transparency and the fact that $phone\text{-}number(q) = 3217580$ we could derive the former statement from the latter.

A further consequence of our approach is that feasibility of a strategy is a referentially opaque concept since a strategy containing $idea\text{-}of\text{-}phone\text{-}number(p, q, s)$ is regarded as feasible while one containing $phone\text{-}number(q)$ is not, even though these quantities may be equal in a particular case. Even so, our language is still referentially transparent since feasibility is a concept of the metalanguage.

A classical poser for the reader who wants to solve these difficulties to ponder is, 'George IV wondered whether the author of the Waverly novels was Walter Scott' and 'Walter Scott is the author of the Waverly novels', from which we do not wish to deduce, 'George IV wondered whether Walter Scott was Walter Scott'. This example and others are discussed in the first chapter of Church's *Introduction to Mathematical Logic* (1956).

In the long run it seems that we shall have to use a formalism with referential opacity and formulate precisely the necessary restrictions on replacement of equals by equals; the program must be able to reason about the feasibility of its strategies, and users of natural language handle referential opacity without disaster. In part 4 we give a brief account of the partly successful approach to problems of referential opacity in modal logic.

3. REMARKS AND OPEN PROBLEMS

The formalism presented in part 2 is, we think, an advance on previous attempts, but it is far from epistemological adequacy. In the following sections we discuss a number of problems that it raises. For some of them we have proposals that might lead to solutions.

The approximate character of $result(p, \sigma, s)$

Using the situational fluent $result(p, \sigma, s)$ in formulating the conditions under which strategies have given effects has two advantages over the $can(p, \pi, s)$ of part 1. It permits more compact and transparent sentences, and it lends itself to the application of the mathematical theory of computation to prove that certain strategies achieve certain goals.

However, we must recognize that it is only an approximation to say that an action, other than that which will actually occur, leads to a definite situation. Thus if someone is asked, 'How would you feel tonight if you challenged him to a duel tomorrow morning and he accepted?' he might well reply, 'I can't imagine the mental state in which I would do it; if the words inexplicably popped out of my mouth as though my voice were under someone else's control that would be one thing; if you gave me a long-lasting belligerence drug that would be another.'

From this we see that $result(p, \sigma, s)$ should not be regarded as being defined in the world itself, but only in certain representations of the world; albeit in representations that may have a preferred character as discussed in part 1.

We regard this as a blemish on the smoothness of interpretation of the formalism, which may also lead to difficulties in the formal development. Perhaps another device can be found which has the advantages of *result* without the disadvantages.

Possible Meanings of 'can' for a Computer Program

A computer program can readily be given much more powerful means of introspection than a person has, for we may make it inspect the whole of its memory including program and data to answer certain introspective questions, and it can even simulate (slowly) what it would do with given initial data. It is interesting to list various notions of $can(Program, \pi)$ for a program.

1. There is a sub-program σ and room for it in memory which would achieve π if it were in memory, and control were transferred to σ. No assertion is made that *Program* knows σ or even knows that σ exists.

2. σ exists as above and that σ will achieve π follows from information in memory according to a proof that *Program* is capable of checking.

3. *Program*'s standard problem-solving procedure will find σ if achieving π is ever accepted as a subgoal.

The Frame Problem

In the last section of part 2, in proving that one person could get into conversation with another, we were obliged to add the hypothesis that if a person has a telephone he still has it after looking up a number in the telephone book. If we had a number of actions to be performed in sequence we would have quite a number of conditions to write down that certain actions do not change the values of certain fluents. In fact with n actions and m fluents we might have to write down mn such conditions.

We see two ways out of this difficulty. The first is to introduce the notion of frame, like the state vector in McCarthy (1962). A number of fluents are declared as attached to the frame and the effect of an action is described by telling which fluents are changed, all others being presumed unchanged.

This can be formalized by making use of yet more ALGOL notation, perhaps in a somewhat generalized form. Consider a strategy in which p performs the action of going from x to y. In the first form of writing strategies we have $go(x, y)$ as a program step. In the second form we have $s := result(p, go(x, y), s)$. Now we may write

$$location(p) := tryfor(y, x)$$

and the fact that other variables are unchanged by this action follows from the general properties of assignment statements. Among the conditions for successful execution of the program will be sentences that enable us to show that when this statement is executed, $tryfor(y, x) = y$. If we were willing to consider that p could go anywhere we could write the assignment statement simply as

$$location(p) := y$$

The point of using *tryfor* here is that a program using this simpler assignment is, on the face of it, not possible to execute, since p may be unable to go to y. We may cover this case in the more complex assignment by agreeing that when p is barred from y, $tryfor(y, x) = x$.

In general, restrictions on what could appear on the right side of an assignment to a component of the situation would be included in the conditions for the feasibility of the strategy. Since components of the situation that change independently in some circumstances are dependent in others, it may be worthwhile to make use of the block structure of ALGOL. We shall not explore this approach further in this paper.

Another approach to the frame problem may follow from the methods of the next section; and in part 4 we mention a third approach which may be useful, although we have not investigated it at all fully.

Formal Literatures

In this section we introduce the notion of formal literature which is to be contrasted with the well-known notion of formal language. We shall mention some possible applications of this concept in constructing an epistemologically adequate system.

A formal literature is like a formal language with a history: we imagine that up to a certain time a certain sequence of sentences have been said. The literature then determines what sentences may be said next. The formal definition is as follows.

Let A be a set of potential sentences, for example, the set of all finite strings in some alphabet. Let $Seq(A)$ be the set of finite sequences of elements of A and let $L : Seq(A) \rightarrow \{\textbf{true}, \textbf{false}\}$ be such that if $s \in Seq(A)$ and $L(s)$, that is $L(s) = true$, and σ_1 is an initial segment of σ then $L(\sigma_1)$. The pair (A, L) is termed a *literature*. The interpretation is that a_n may be said after $a_1, \ldots, a_{n-1}$), provided $L((a_1, \ldots, a_n))$. We shall also write $\sigma \in L$ and refer to σ as a string of the literature L.

From a literature L and a string $\sigma \in L$ we introduce the derived literature L_σ. Namely, $\tau \in L_\sigma$ if and only if $\sigma * \tau \in L$, where $\sigma * \tau$ denotes the concatenation of σ and τ.

We shall say that the language L is universal for the class Φ of literatures if for every literature $M \in \Phi$ there is a string $\sigma(M) \in L$ such that $M = L_{\sigma(M)}$; that is, $\tau \in M$ if and only if $\sigma(M) * \tau \in L$.

We shall call a literature computable if its strings form a recursively enumerable set. It is easy to see that there is a computable literature $U(C)$ that is universal with respect to the set C of computable literatures. Namely, let e be a computable literature and let c be the representation of the Gödel number of the recursively enumerable set of e as a string of elements of A. Then, we say $c * \tau \in U_C$ if and only if $\tau \in e$.

It may be more convenient to describe natural languages as formal literatures than as formal languages: if we allow the definition of new terms and require that new terms be used in accordance with their definitions, then we have restrictions on sentences that depend on what sentences have previously been uttered. In a programming language, the restriction that an identifier not be used until it has been declared, and then only consistently with the declaration, is of this form.

Any natural language may be regarded as universal with respect to the set of natural languages in the approximate sense that we might define French in terms of English and then say 'From now on we shall speak only French'.

All the above is purely syntactic. The applications we envisage to artificial intelligence come from a certain kind of interpreted literature. We are not able to describe precisely the class of literatures that may prove useful, only to sketch a class of examples.

Suppose we have an interpreted language such as first-order logic perhaps including some modal operators. We introduce three additional operators: *consistent(Φ)*, *normally(Φ)*, and *probably(Φ)*. We start with a list of sentences as hypotheses. A new sentence may be added to a string σ of sentences according to the following rules:

1. Any consequence of sentences of σ may be added.
2. If a sentence Φ is consistent with σ, then *consistent(Φ)* may be added. Of course, this is a non-computable rule. It may be weakened to say that *consistent(Φ)* may be added provided Φ can be shown to be consistent with σ by some particular proof procedure.
3. *normally(Φ), consistent(Φ)* $\vdash$ *probably(Φ)*.
4. $\Phi \vdash$ *probably(Φ)* is a possible deduction.
5. If $\Phi_1, \Phi_2, \ldots, \Phi_n \vdash \Phi$ is a possible deduction then

$$probably(\Phi_1), \ldots, probably(\Phi_n) \vdash probably(\Phi)$$

is also a possible deduction.

The intended application to our formalism is as follows:

In part 2 we considered the example of one person telephoning another, and in this example we assumed that if p looks up q's phone-number in the book, he will know it, and if he dials the number he will come into conversation with q. It is not hard to think of possible exceptions to these statements such as:

1. The page with q's number may be torn out.
2. p may be blind.
3. Someone may have deliberately inked out q's number.
4. The telephone company may have made the entry incorrectly.
5. q may have got the telephone only recently.

6. The phone system may be out of order.

7. *q* may be incapacitated suddenly.

For each of these possibilities it is possible to add a term excluding the difficulty in question to the condition on the result of performing the action. But we can think of as many additional difficulties as we wish, so it is impractical to exclude each difficulty separately.

We hope to get out of this difficulty by writing such sentences as

$$\forall p \,.\, \forall q \,.\, \forall s \,.\, at(q, home(q), s)$$
$$\supset normally(in\text{-}conversation(p, q, result(p, dials(phone\text{-}number(q)), s))).$$

We would then be able to deduce

$$probably(in\text{-}conversation(p, q, result(p, dials(phone\text{-}number(q)), s_0)))$$

provided there were no statements like

$$kaput(Phone\text{-}system, s_0)$$

and

$$\forall s \,.\, kaput(Phone\text{-}system, s)$$
$$\supset \neg \, in\text{-}conversation(p, q, result(p, dials(phone\text{-}number(q)), s))$$

present in the system.

Many of the problems that give rise to the introduction of frames might be handled in a similar way.

The operators *normally*, *consistent* and *probably* are all modal and referentially opaque. We envisage systems in which $probably(\pi)$ and $probably(\neg \pi)$ and therefore $probably(\textbf{false})$ will arise. Such an event should give rise to a search for a contradiction.

We hereby warn the reader, if it is not already clear to him, that these ideas are very tentative and may prove useless, especially in their present form. However, the problem they are intended to deal with, namely the impossibility of naming every conceivable thing that may go wrong, is an important one for artificial intelligence, and some formalism has to be developed to deal with it.

Probabilities

On numerous occasions it has been suggested that the formalism take uncertainty into account by attaching probabilities to its sentences. We agree that the formalism will eventually have to allow statements about the probabilities of events, but attaching probabilities to all statements has the following objections:

1. It is not clear how to attach probabilities to statements containing quantifiers in a way that corresponds to the amount of conviction people have.

2. The information necessary to assign numerical probabilities is not ordinarily available. Therefore, a formalism that required numerical probabilities would be epistemologically inadequate.

Parallel Processing

Besides describing strategies by ALGOL-like programs we may also want to describe the laws of change of the situation by such programs. In doing so we must take into account the fact that many processes are going on simultaneously and that the single-activity-at-a-time ALGOL-like programs will have to be replaced by programs in which processes take place in parallel, in order to get an epistemologically adequate description. This suggests examining the so-called simulation languages; but a quick survey indicates that they are rather restricted in the kinds of processes they allow to take place in parallel and in the types of interaction allowed. Moreover, at present there is no developed formalism that allows proofs of the correctness of parallel programs.

4. DISCUSSION OF LITERATURE

The plan for achieving a generally intelligent program outlined in this paper will clearly be difficult to carry out. Therefore, it is natural to ask if some simpler scheme will work, and we shall devote this section to criticising some simpler schemes that have been proposed.

1. L. Fogel (1966) proposes to evolve intelligent automata by altering their state transition diagrams so that they perform better on tasks of greater and greater complexity. The experiments described by Fogel involve machines with less than *10* states being evolved to predict the next symbol of a quite simple sequence. We do not think this approach has much chance of achieving interesting results because it seems limited to automata with small numbers of states, say less than *100*, whereas computer programs regarded as automata have 2^{10^5} to 2^{10^7} states. This is a reflection of the fact that, while the representation of behaviours by finite automata is metaphysically adequate—in principle every behaviour of which a human or machine is capable can be so represented—this representation is not epistemologically adequate; that is, conditions we might wish to impose on a behaviour, or what

is learned from an experience, are not readily expresible as changes in the state diagram of an automaton.

2. A number of investigators (Galanter 1956, Pivar and Finkelstein 1964) have taken the view that intelligence may be regarded as the ability to predict the future of a sequence from observation of its past. Presumably, the idea is that the experience of a person can be regarded as a sequence of discrete events and that intelligent people can predict the future. Artificial intelligence is then studied by writing programs to predict sequences formed according to some simple class of laws (sometimes probabilistic laws). Again the model is metaphysically adequate but epistemologically inadequate.

In other words, what we know about the world is divided into knowledge about many aspects of it, taken separately and with rather weak interaction. A machine that worked with the undifferentiated encoding of experience into a sequence would first have to solve the encoding, a task more difficult than any the sequence extrapolators are prepared to undertake. Moreover, our knowledge is not usable to predict exact sequences of experience. Imagine a person who is correctly predicting the course of a football game he is watching; he is not predicting each visual sensation (the play of light and shadow, the exact movements of the players and the crowd). Instead his prediction is on the level of: team A is getting tired; they should start to fumble or have their passes intercepted.

3. Friedberg (1958,1959) has experimented with representing behaviour by a computer program and evolving a program by random mutations to perform a task. The epistemological inadequacy of the representation is expressed by the fact that desired changes in behaviour are often not representable by small changes in the machine language form of the program. In particular, the effect on a reasoning program of learning a new fact is not so representable.

4. Newell and Simon worked for a number of years with a program called the General Problem Solver (Newell *et. al.* 1959, Newell and Simon 1961). This program represents problems as the task of transforming one symbolic expression into another using a fixed set of transformation rules. They succeeded in putting a fair variety of problems into this form, but for a number of problems the representation was awkward enough so that GPS could only do small examples. The task of improving GPS was studied as a GPS task, but we believe it was finally abandoned. The name, General Problem Solver, suggests that its authors at one time believed that most problems could be put in its terms, but their more recent publications have indicated other points of view.

It is interesting to compare the point of view of the present paper with that expressed in Newell and Ernst (1965) from which we quote the second paragraph:

> We may consider a problem solver to be a process that takes a problem as input and provides (when successful) the solution as output. The problem consists of the problem statement, or what is immediately given, and auxiliary information, which is potentially relevant to the problem but

available only as the result of processing. The problem solver has available certain methods for attempting to solve the problem. For the problem solver to be able to work on a problem it must first transform the problem statement from its external form into the internal representation. Thus (roughly), the class of problems the problem solver can convert into its internal representation determines how broad or general it is, and its success in obtaining solutions to problems in internal form determines its power. Whether or not universal, such a decomposition fits well the structure of present problem solving programs.

In a very approximate way their division of the problem solver into the input program that converts problems into internal representation and the problem solver proper corresponds to our division into the epistemological and heuristic pats of the artificial intelligence problem. The difference is that we are more concerned with the suitability of the internal representation itself.

Newell (1965) poses the problem of how to get what we call heuristically adequate representations of problems, and Simon (1966) discusses the concept of 'can' in a way that should be compared with the present approach.

Modal Logic

It is difficult to give a concise definition of modal logic. It was originally invented by Lewis (1918) in an attempt to avoid the 'paradoxes' of implication (a false proposition implies any proposition). The idea was to distinguish two sorts of truth: *necessary* truth and mere *contingent* truth. A contingently true proposition is one which, though true, could be false. This is formalized by introducing the modal operator $\Box$ (read 'necessarily') which forms propositions from propositions. Then p's being a necessary truth is expressed by $\Box p$'s being true. More recently, modal logic has become a much-used tool for analyzing the logic of such various propositional operators as belief, knowledge and tense.

There are very many possible axiomatizations of the logic of $\Box$ none of which seem more intuitively plausible than many others. A full account of the main classical systems is given by Feys (1965), who also includes an excellent bibliography. We shall give here an axiomatization of a fairly simple modal logic, the system M of Feys – von Wright. One adds to any full axiomatization of propositional calculus the following:

> $Ax. 1 : \Box p \supset p.$
> $Ax. 2 : \Box(p \supset q) \supset (\Box p \supset \Box q).$
> Rule 1: from p and $p \supset q$, infer q.
> Rule 2: from p, infer $\Box p$.

(This axiomatization is due to Gödel.) There is also a dual modal operator ◇, defined as ¬□¬. Its intuitive meaning is 'possibly': ◇p is true when p is at least possible, although p may be in fact false (or true). The reader will be able to see the intuitive correspondence between ¬◇p—p is impossible, and □¬p—that is, p is necessarily false.

M is a fairly weak modal logic. One can strengthen it by adding axioms, for example, adding $Ax. 3 : \Box p \supset \Box\Box p$ yields the system called $S4$; adding $Ax. 4 :$ ◇$p \supset \Box$◇p yields $S5$; and other additions are possible. However, one can also weaken all the systems in various ways, for instance by changing $Ax. 1$ to $Ax. 1' : \Box p \supset$ ◇p. One easily sees that $Ax. 1$ implies $Ax. 1'$, but the converse is not true. The systems obtained in this way are known as the *deontic* versions of the systems. These modifications will be useful later when we come to consider tense-logics as modal logics.

One should note that the truth or falsity of □p is not decided by p's being true. Thus □ is not a truth-functional operator (unlike the usual logical connectives, for instance) and so there is no direct way of using truth-tables to analyze propositions containing modal operators. In fact the decision problem for modal propositional calculi has been quite nontrivial. It is just this property which makes modal calculi so useful, as belief, tense, etc., when interpreted as propositional operators, are all nontruthfunctional.

The proliferation of modal propositional calculi, with no clear means of comparison, we shall call the *first problem* of modal logic. Other difficulties arise when we consider modal predicate calculi, that is, when we attempt to introduce quantifiers. This was first done by Barcan-Marcus (1946).

Unfortunately, all the early attempts at modal predicate calculi had unintuitive theorems (see for instance Kripke 1963a), and, moreover, all of them met with difficulties connected with the failure of Leibniz' law of identity, which we shall try to outline. Leibniz' law is

$$L : \forall x . \forall y . x = y \supset (F(x) \equiv F(y))$$

where F is any open sentence. Now this law fails in modal contexts. For instance, consider this instance of L:

$$L_1 : \forall x . \forall y . x = y \supset (\Box(x = x) \equiv \Box(x = y))$$

By rule 2 of M (which is present in almost all modal logics), since $x = x$ is a theorem, so is □$(x = x)$. Thus L_1 yields

$$L_2 : \forall x . \forall y . x = y \supset \Box(x = y)$$

But, the argument goes, this is counterintuitive. For instance the morning star is in fact the same individual as the evening star (the planet Venus). However, they are not *necessarily* equal: one can easily imagine that they might be distinct. This famous example is known as the 'morning star paradox'.

This and related difficulties compel one to abandon Leibniz' law in modal predicate calculi, or else to modify the laws of quantification (so that it is impossible to obtain the undesirable instances of universal sentences such as L_2). This solves the purely formal problem, but leads to severe difficulties in interpreting these calculi, as Quine has urged in several papers (cf. Quine 1964).

The difficulty is this. A sentence $\Phi(a)$ is usually thought of as ascribing some property to a certain individual a. Now consider the morning star; clearly, the morning star is necessarily equal to the morning star. However, the evening star is not necessarily equal to the morning star. Thus, this one individual—the planet Venus—both has and does not have the property of being necessarily equal to the morning star. Even if we abandon proper names the difficulty does not disappear: for how are we to interpret a statement like $\exists x \,.\, \exists y(x = y \land \Phi(x) \land \neg \Phi(y))$?

Barcan-Marcus has urged an unconventional reading of the quantifiers to avoid this problem. The discussion between her and Quine in Barcan-Marcus (1963) is very illuminating. However, this raises some difficulties—see Belnap and Dunn (1968)—and the recent semantic theory of modal logic provides a more satisfactory method of interpreting modal sentences.

This theory was developed by several authors (Hintikka 1963, 1967a; Kanger 1957; Kripke 1963a, 1963b, 1965), but chiefly by Kripke. We shall try to give an outline of this theory, but if the reader finds it inadequate he should consult Kripke (1963a).

The idea is that modal calculi describe several *possible worlds* at once, instead of just one. Statements are not assigned a single truth-value, but rather a spectrum of truth-values, one in each possible world. Now, a statement is necessary when it is true in *all* possible worlds—more or less. Actually, in order to get different modal logics (and even then not all of them) one has to be a bit more subtle, and have a binary relation on the set of possible worlds—the alternativeness relation. Then a statement is necessary in a world when it is true in all alternatives to that world. Now it turns out that many common axioms of modal propositional logics correspond directly to conditions of alternativeness. Thus for instance in the system M above, *Ax. 1* corresponds to the reflexiveness of the alternativeness relation; *Ax. 3* ($\Box p \supset \Box\Box p$) corresponds to its transitivity. If we make the alternativeness relation into an equivalence relation, then this is just like not having one at all; and it corresponds to the axiom: $\Diamond p \supset \Box \Diamond p$.

This semantic theory already provides an answer to the first problem of modal logic: a rational method is available for classifying the multitude of propositional modal logics. More importantly, it also provides an intelligible interpretation for modal predicate calculi. One has to imagine each possible world as having a set of individuals and an assignment of individuals to names of the language. Then each statement takes on its truth value in a world s according to the particular set of individuals and assignment associated with s. Thus, a possible world is an interpretation of the calculus, in the usual sense.

Now, the failure of Leibniz' law is no longer puzzling, for in one world the morning star—for instance—may be equal to (the same individual as) the evening star, but in another the two may be distinct.

There are still difficulties, both formal—the quantification rules have to be modified to avoid unintuitive theorems (see Kripke, 1963a, for the details)—and interpretative: it is not obvious what it means to have the *same* individual existing in *different* worlds.

It is possible to gain the expressive power of modal logic without using modal operators by constructing an ordinary truth-functional logic which describes the multiple-world semantics of modal logic directly. To do this we give every predicate an extra argument (the world-variable; or in our terminology the situation-variable) and instead of writing '$\Box\, \Phi$', we write

$$\forall t\,.\,A(s,t) \supset \Phi(t),$$

where A is the alternativeness relation between situations. Of course we must provide appropriate axioms for A.

The resulting theory will be expressed in the notation of the situation calculus; the proposition Φ has become a propositional fluent $\lambda s\,.\,\Phi(s)$, and the 'possible worlds' of the modal semantics are precisely the situations. Notice, however, that the theory we get is weaker than what would have been obtained by adding modal operators directly to the situation calculus, for we can give no translation of assertions such as $\Box \pi(s)$, where s is a situation, which this enriched situation calculus would contain.

It is possible, in this way, to reconstruct within the situation calculus subtheories corresponding to the tense-logics of Prior and to the knowledge logics of Hintikka, as we shall explain below. However, there is a qualification here: so far we have only explained how to translate the propositional modal logics into the situation calculus. In order to translate quantified modal logic, with its difficulties of referential opacity, we must complicate the situation calculus to a degree which makes it rather clumsy. There is a special predicate on individuals and situation—*exists(i,s)*—which is regarded as true when i names an individual existing in the situation s. This is necessary because situations may contain different individuals. Then quantified assertions of the modal logic are translated according to the following scheme:

$$\forall x\,.\,\Phi(x) \rightarrow \forall x\,.\,exists(x,s) \supset \Phi(x,s)$$

where s is the introduced situation variable. We shall not go into the details of this extra translation in the examples below, but shall be content to define the translations of the propositional tense and knowledge logics into the situation calculus.

Logic of Knowledge

The logic of knowledge was first investigated as a modal logic by Hintikka in his book *Knowledge and belief* (1962). We shall only describe the knowledge calculus. He introduces the modal operator Ka (read 'a knows that'), and its dual Pa, defined as $\neg Ka\neg$. The semantics is obtained by the analogous reading of Ka as: 'it is true in all possible worlds compatible with a's knowledge that'. The propositional logic of Ka (similar to $\square$) turns out to be *S4*, that is $M + Ax.\,3$; but there are some complexities over quantification. (The last chapter of the book contains another excellent account of the overall problem of quantification in modal contexts.) This analysis of knowledge has been criticized in various ways (Chisholm 1963, Follesdal 1967) and Hintikka has replied in several important papers (1967b, 1967c, 1972). The last paper contains a review of the different senses of 'know' and the extent to which they have been adequately formalized. It appears that two senses have resisted capture. First, the idea of 'knowing how', which appears related to our 'can'; and secondly, the concept of knowing a person (place, etc.) when this means 'being acquainted with' as opposed to simply knowing *who* a person *is*.

In order to translate the (propositional) knowledge calculus into 'situation' language, we introduce a three-place predicate into the situation calculus termed 'shrug'. $Shrug(p, s_1, s_2)$, where p is a person and s_1 and s_2 are situations, is true when, if p is in fact in situation s_2, then for all he knows he might be in situation s_1. That is to say, s_1 is an *epistemic alternative* to s_2, as far as the individual p is concerned—this is Hintikka's term for his alternative worlds (he calls them model-sets).

Then we translate $K_p q$, where q is a proposition of Hintikka's calculus, as $\forall t . shrug(p, t, s) \supset q(t)$, where $\lambda s.q(s)$ is the fluent which translates q. Of course we have to supply axioms for *shrug*, and in fact so far as the pure knowledge-calculus is concerned, the only two necessary are

$$K1 : \forall s . \forall p . shrug(p, s, s)$$

and

$$K2 : \forall p . \forall s . \forall t . \forall r . (shrug(p, t, s) \wedge shrug(p, r, t)) \supset shrug(p, r, s)$$

that is, reflexivity and transitivity.

Others of course may be needed when we add tenses and other machinery to the situation calculus, in order to relate knowledge to them.

Tense Logics

This is one of the largest and most active areas of philosophic logic. Prior's book *Past, Present and Future* (1968) is an extremely thorough and lucid account of what has been done in the field. We have already mentioned the four propositional operators F, G, P, H which Prior discusses. He regards these as modal operators; then the alternativeness relation of the semantic theory is simply the time-ordering relation. Various axiomatizations are given, corresponding to deterministic and nondeterministic tenses, ending and nonending times, etc; and the problems of quantification turn up again here with renewed intensity. To attempt a summary of Prior's book is a hopeless task, and we simply urge the reader to consult it. More recently several papers have appeared (see, for instance, Bull 1968) which illustrate the technical sophistication tense-logic has reached, in that full completeness proofs for various axiom systems are now available.

As indicated above, the situation calculus contains a tense-logic (or rather several tense-logics), in that we can define Prior's four operators in our system and by suitable axioms reconstruct various axiomatizations of these four operators (in particular, all the axioms in Bull (1968) can be translated into the situation calculus).

Only one extra nonlogical predicate is necessary to do this: it is a binary predicate of situations called *cohistorical*, and is intuitively meant to assert of its arguments that one is in the other's future. This is necessary because we want to consider some pairs of situations as being not temporally related at all. We now define F (for instance) thus:

$$F(\pi, s) \equiv \exists t \,.\, cohistorical(t, s) \wedge time(t) > time(s) \wedge \pi(t).$$

The other operators are defined analogously.

Of course we have to supply axioms for 'cohistorical' and time: this is not difficult. For instance, consider one of Bull's axioms, say $Gp \supset GGp$, which is better (for us) expressed in the form $FFp \supset Fp$. Using the definition, this translates into:

$$(\exists t \,.\, cohistorical(t, s) \wedge time(t) > time(s)$$
$$\wedge \, \exists r \,.\, cohistorical(r, t) \wedge time(r) > time(t) \wedge \pi(r))$$
$$\supset (\exists r \,.\, cohistorical(r, s) \wedge time(r) > time(s) \wedge \pi(r))$$

which simplifies (using the transitivity of '>') to

$$\forall t \,.\, \forall r \,.\, (cohistorical(r, t) \wedge cohistorical(t, s)) \supset cohistorical(r, s)$$

that is, the transitivity of 'cohistorical'. This axiom is precisely analogous to the *S4* axiom $\Box p \supset \Box \Box p$, which corresponded to transitivity of the alternativeness relation in the modal semantics. Bull's other axioms translate into conditions on 'cohistorical' and time in a similar way; we shall not bother here with the rather tedious details.

Rather more interesting would be axioms relating 'shrug' to 'cohistorical' and time; unfortunately we have been unable to think of any intuitively plausible ones. Thus, if two situations are epistemic alternatives (that is, $shrug(p, s_1, s_2)$) then they may or may not have the same time value (since we want to allow that p may not know what the time is), and they may or may not be cohistorical.

Logics and Theories of Actions

The most fully developed theory in this area is von Wright's action logic described in his book *Norm and Action* (1963). Von Wright builds his logic on a rather unusual tense-logic of his own. The basis is a binary modal connective T, so that $p \, T \, q$, where p and q are propositions, means 'p, *then* q'. Thus the action, for instance, of opening the window is: *(the window is closed) T (the window is open)*. The formal development of the calculus was taken a long way in the book cited above, but some problems of interpretation remained as Castaneda points out in his review (1965). In a more recent paper von Wright (1967) has altered and extended his formalism so as to answer these and other criticisms, and also has provided a sort of semantic theory based on the notion of a life-tree.

We know of no other attempts at constructing a single theory of actions which have reached such a degree of development, but there are several discussions of difficulties and surveys which seem important. Rescher (1967) discusses several topics very neatly, and Davidson (1967) also makes some cogent points. Davidson's main thesis is that, in order to translate statements involving actions into the predicate calculus, it appears necessary to allow actions as values of bound variables, that is (by Quine's test) as real individuals. The situation calculus of course follows this advice in that we allow quantification over strategies, which have actions as a special case. Also important are Simon's papers (1965, 1967) on command-logics. Simon's main purpose is to show that a special logic of commands is unnecessary, ordinary logic serving as the only deductive machinery; but this need not detain us here. He makes several points, most notably perhaps that agents are most of the time not performing actions, and that in fact they only stir to action when forced to by some outside interference. He has the particularly interesting example of a serial processor operating in a parallel-demand environment, and the resulting need for interrupts. Action logics such as von Wright's and ours do not distinguish between action and inaction, and we are not aware of any action-logic which has reached a stage of sophistication adequate to meet Simon's implied criticism.

There is a large body of purely philosophical writings on action, time, determinism, etc., most of which is irrelevant for present purposes. However, we mention two which have recently appeared and which seem interesting: a paper by Chisholm (1967) and another paper by Evans (1967), summarizing the recent discussion on the distinctions between states, performances and activities.

Other Topics

There are two other areas where some analysis of actions has been necessary: command-logics and logics and theories of obligation. For the former the best reference is Rescher's book (1966) which has an excellent bibliography. Note also Simon's counterarguments to some of Rescher's theses (Simon 1965, 1967). Simon proposes that no special logic of commands is necessary, commands being analyzed in the form 'bring it about that p!' for some proposition p, or, more generally, in the form 'bring it about that $P(x)$ by changing x!', where x is a *command* variable, that is, under the agent's control. The translations between commands and statements take place only in the context of a 'complete model', which specifies environmental constraints and defines the command variables. Rescher argues that these schemas for commands are inadequate to handle the *conditional command* 'when p, do q', which becomes 'bring it about that $(p \supset q)$!': this, unlike the former, is satisfied by making p false.

There are many papers on the logic of obligation and permission. Von Wright's work is oriented in this direction; Castañeda has many papers on the subject and Anderson also has written extensively (his early influential report (1956) is especially worth reading). The review pages of the *Journal of Symbolic Logic* provide many other references. Until fairly recently these theories did not seem of very much relevance to logics of action, but in their new maturity they are beginning to be so.

Counterfactuals

There is, of course, a large literature on this ancient philosophical problem, almost none of which seems directly relevant to us. However, there is one recent theory, developed by Rescher (1964), which may be of use. Rescher's book is so clearly written that we shall not attempt a description of his theory here. The reader should be aware of Sosa's critical review (1967) which suggests some minor alterations.

The importance of this theory for us is that it suggests an alternative approach to the difficulty which we have referred to as the frame problem. In outline, this is as follows. One assumes, as a rule of procedure (or perhaps as a rule of inference), that when actions are performed, *all* propositional fluents which applied to the previous situation also apply to the new situation. This will often yield an inconsistent set of statements about the new situation; Rescher's theory provides a mechanism for restoring consistency in a rational way, and giving as a by-product those fluents which change in value as a result of performing the action. However, we have not investigated this in detail.

The Communication Process

We have not considered the problems of formally describing the process of communication in this paper, but it seems clear that they will have to be tackled eventually. Philosophical logicians have been spontaneously active here. The major work is Harrah's book (1963); Cresswell has written several papers on 'the logic of interrogatives', see for instance Cresswell (1965). Among other authors we may mention Åqvist (1965) and Belnap (1963); again the review pages of the *Journal of Symbolic Logic* will provide other references.

Acknowledgements

The research reported here was supported in part by the Advanced Research Projects Agency of the Office of the Secretary of Defense (SD-183), and in part by the Science Research Council (B/SR/2299).

References

Anderson, A.R. (1956). The formal analysis of normative systems. Reprinted in *The Logic of decision and action* (ed. Rescher, N.). Pittsburgh: University of Pittsburgh Press.

Åqvist, L. (1965). *A new approach to the logical theory of interrogatives, part I.* Uppsala: Uppsala Philosophical Association.

Barcan-Marcus, R.C. (1946). A functional calculus of the first order based on strict implication. *Journal of Symbolic Logic*, 11, 1-16.

Barcan-Marcus, R.C. (1963). Modalities and intensional languages. *Boston studies in the Philosophy of Science*. (ed. Wartofsky, W.). Dordrecht, Holland.

Belnap, N.D. (1963). *An analysis of questions.* Santa Monica.

Belnap, N.D. and Dunn, J.M. (1968). The substitution interpretation of the quantifiers. *Nous*, 2, 177-85.

Bull, R.A. (1968). An algebraic study of tense logics with linear time. *Journal of Symbolic Logic*, 33, 27-39.

Castañeda, H.N. (1965). The logic of change, action and norms. *Journal of Philosophy*, 62, 333-4.

Chisholm, R.M. (1963). The logic of knowing. *Journal of Philosophy*, 60, 773-95.

Chisholm, R.M. (1967). He could have done otherwise. *Journal of Philosophy*, 64, 409-17.

Church, A. (1956). *Introduction to Mathematical Logic.* Princeton: Princeton University Press.

Cresswell, M.J. (1965). The logic of interrogatives. *Formal systems and recursive functions.* (ed. Crossley, J.M. and Dummett, M.A.E.). Amsterdam: North-Holland.

Davidson, D. (1967). The logical form of action sentences. *The logic of decision and action.* (ed. Rescher, N.). Pittsburgh: University of Pittsburgh Press.

Evans, C.O. (1967). States, activities and performances. *Australian Journal of Philosophy,* 45, 293-308.

Feys, R. (1965). *Modal Logics.* (ed. Dopp, J.). Louvain: Coll. de Logique Math. serie B.

Fogel, L.J., Owens, A.J. and Walsh, M.J. (1966). *Artificial Intelligence through simulated evolution.* New York: John Wiley.

Follesdal, D. (1967). Knowledge, identity and existence. *Theoria,* 33, 1-27.

Friedberg, R.M. (1958). A learning machine, part I. *IBM J. Res. Dev.,* 2, 2-13.

Friedberg, R.M., Dunham, B., and North, J.H. (1959). A learning machine, part II. *IBM J. Res. Dev.,* 3, 282-7.

Galanter, E. and Gerstenhaber, M. (1956). On thought: the extrinsic theory. *Psychological Review,* 63, 218-27.

Green, C. (1969). Theorem-proving by resolution as a basis for question-answering systems. *Machine Intelligence 4,* pp. 183-205 (eds. Meltzer, B. and Michie, D.). Edinburgh: Edinburgh University Press.

Harrah, D. (1963). *Communication: a logical model.* Cambridge, Massachusetts: MIT Press.

Hintikka, J. (1962). *Knowledge and belief: an introduction to the logic of two notions.* New York: Cornell University Press.

Hintikka, J. (1963). The modes of modality. *Acta Philosophica Fennica,* 16, 65-82.

Hintikka, J. (1967a). A program and a set of concepts for philosophical logic. *The Monist,* 51, 69-72.

Hintikka, J. (1967b). Existence and identity in epistemic contexts. *Theoria,* 32, 138-47.

Hintikka, J. (1967c). Individuals, possible worlds and epistemic logic. *Nous,* 1, 33-62.

Hintikka, J. (1977). Different constructions in terms of the basic epistemological verbs. *Contemporary Philosophy in Scandinavia* (eds. Olsen, R.E. and Paul, A. M.), Baltimore: The John Hopkins Press, 105-122.

Kanger, S. (1957). A note on quantification and modalities. *Theoria,* 23, 133-4.

Kripke, S. (1963a). Semantical considerations on modal logic. *Acta Philosophica Fennica,* 16, 83-94.

Kripke, S. (1963b). Semantical analysis of modal logic I. *Zeitschrift fur math. Logik und Grundlagen der Mathematik,* 9, 67-96.

Kripke, S. (1965). Semantical analysis of modal logic II. *The theory of models* (eds. Addison, Henkin and Tarski). Amsterdam: North-Holland.

Lewis, C.I. (1918). *A survey of symbolic logic.* Berkeley: University of California Press.

Manna, Z. (1968a). *Termination of algorithms.* Ph.D. Thesis, Carnegie-Mellon University.

Manna, Z. (1968b). *Formalization of properties of programs* Stanford Artificial Intelligence Report: Project Memo AI-64.

McCarthy, J. (1959). Programs with common sense. *Mechanization of thought processes,* Vol. I. London: Her Majesty's Stationery Office. (Reprinted in this volume, pp. 000–000).

McCarthy, J. (1962). Towards a mathematical science of computation. *Proc. IFIP Congress* 62. Amsterdam: North-Holland Press.

McCarthy, J. (1963). *Situations, actions and causal laws.* Stanford Artificial Intelligence Project: Memo 2.

Minsky, M. (1961). Steps towards artificial intelligence. *Proceedings of the I.R.E.,* 49, 8-30.

Newell, A., Shaw, V.C. and Simon, H.A. (1959). Report on a general problem-solving program. *Proceedings ICIP.* Paris:UNESCO House.

Newell, A. and Simon, H.A. (1961). GPS - a program that simulates human problem-solving. *Proceedings of a conference in learning automata.* Munich: Oldenbourgh.

Newell, A. (1965). Limitations of the current stock of ideas about problem-solving. *Proceedings of a conference on Electronic Information Handling,* pp. 195-208 (eds. Kent, A. and Taulbee, O.). New York: Spartan.

Newell, A. and Ernst, C. (1965). The search for generality. *Proc. IFIP Congress* 65.

Pivar, M. and Finkelstein, M. (1964). *The Programming Language LISP: its operation and applications* (eds. Berkely, E.C. and Bobrow, D.G.). Cambridge, Massachusetts: MIT Press.

Prior, A.N. (1957). *Time and modality.* Oxford: Clarendon Press.

Prior, A.N. (1968). *Past, present and future.* Oxford: Clarendon Press.

Quine, W.V.O. (1964). Reference and modality. *From a logical point of view.* Cambridge, Massachusetts: Harvard University Press.

Rescher, N. (1964). *Hypothetical reasoning.* Amsterdam: North-Holland.

Rescher, N. (1966). *The logic of commands.* London: Routledge.

Rescher, N. (1967). Aspects of action. *The logic of decision and action* (ed. Rescher, N.). Pittsburgh: University of Pittsburgh Press.

Shannon, C. (1950). Programming a computer for playing chess. *Philosophical Magazine,* 41.

Simon, H.A. (1965). The logic of rational decision. *British Journal for the Philosophy of Science,* 16, 169-86.

Simon, H.A (1966). *On Reasoning about actions.* Carnegie Institute of Technology: Complex Information Processing Paper 87.

Simon, H.A. (1967). The logic of heuristic decision making. *The logic of decision and action* (ed. Rescher, N.). Pittsburgh: University of Pittsburgh Press.

Sosa, E. (1967). Hypothetical reasoning. *Journal of Philosophy,* 64, 293-305.

Turing, A.M. (1950). Computing machinery and intelligence. *Mind,* 59, 433-60.

von Wright, C.H. (1963). *Norm and action: a logical enquiry.* London: Routledge.

von Wright, C.H. (1967). The Logic of Action - a sketch. *The logic of decision and action* (ed. Rescher, N.). Pittsburgh:University of Pittsburgh Press.

A Temporal Logic for Reasoning About Processes and Plans*

DREW MCDERMOTT

Yale University
Department of Computer Science

Much previous work in artificial intelligence has neglected representing time in all its complexity. In particular, it has neglected continuous change and the indeterminacy of the future. To rectify this, I have developed a first-order temporal logic, in which it is possible to name and prove things about facts, events, plans, and world histories. In particular, the logic provides analyses of causality, continuous change in quantities, the persistence of facts (the frame problem), and the relationship between tasks and actions. It may be possible to implement a temporal-inference machine based on this logic, which keeps track of several "maps" of a time line, one per possible history.

1. INTRODUCTION

A common disclaimer by an AI author is that he has neglected temporal considerations to avoid complication. The implication is nearly made that adding a temporal dimension to the research (on engineering, medical diagnosis, etc.) would be a familiar but tedious exercise that would obscure the new material presented by the author. Actually, of course, no one has ever dealt with time correctly in an AI program, and there is reason to believe that doing it would change everything.

Because time has been neglected, medical diagnosis programs cannot talk about the course of a disease. Story understanding programs have trouble with past events. Problem solvers have had only the crudest models of the future, in spite of the obvious importance of future events.

*This research was supported by NSF grant MCS 8013710.

*Thanks to Ernie Davis for technical assistance and ideas; and to Chris Riesbeck and all the members of the Yale Learning Group, who came up with problems for a temporal notation in the field of economics; and to Tony Passera for work on the implementation. I had useful discussions with James Allen, Eugene Charniak, Patrick Hayes, and Robert Moore. The referee is responsible for some improvements in intelligibility. I am responsible for residual confusion and error.

Many researchers have compensated by modeling the course of external time with the program's own internal time, changing the world model to reflect changing reality. This leads to a confusion between correcting a mistaken belief and updating an outdated belief. Most AI data bases have some sort of operator for removing formulas. (e.g., ERASE in PLANNER, Hewitt, 1972) This operator has tended to be used for two quite different purposes: getting rid of tentative or hypothetical assertions that turned out not to be true, and noting that an assertion is *no longer* true. The confusion is natural, since some of the same consequences must follow in either case. For example, if "The car is drivable" follows from "There is gas in the car," then the former statement must be deleted when the latter is, whether you have discovered there to be no gas after all, or the gas has been used up.

But in many cases, the two behave quite differently, and efforts to make them the same have resulted in awkward, inextensible programs. For example, from "x is beating his wife," you are entitled to infer, "x is a bad man." But if x pauses to catch his breath, only the former statement must be deleted from the data base. Clearly, the proper inference is from "If x has beat his wife recently, he is a bad man," and "x is beating his wife," to "For the next year or so, x will have beaten his wife recently," and hence to "For the next year or so, x is a bad man." (We must allow for reform.) As far as I know, no AI program has been capable of such inferences.

An even worse flaw than the inability to model present change is the inability to model future possibility. To make this clear, I will sketch an example of where the standard approaches fail.

Say a problem solver is confronted with the classic situation of a heroine, called Nell, having been tied to the tracks while a train approaches. The problem solver, called Dudley, knows that

"If Nell is going to be mashed, I must remove her from the tracks."

(He probably knows a more general rule, but let that pass.) When Dudley deduces that he must do something, he looks for, and eventually executes, a plan for doing it. This will involve finding out where Nell is, and making a navigation plan to get to her location. Assume that he knows where she is, and she is not too far away; then the fact that the plan will be carried out is added to Dudley's world model. Dudley must have some kind of data-base-consistency maintainer (Doyle, 1979) to make sure that the plan is deleted if it is no longer necessary. Unfortunately, as soon as an apparently successful plan is added to the world model, the consistency maintainer will notice that "Nell is going to be mashed" is no longer true. But that removes any justification for the plan, so it goes, too. But that means "Nell is going to be mashed" is no longer contradictory, so it comes back in. And so forth. The data base manager might loop forever, or it might conclude erroneously that Nell is safe without any action by Dudley. The problem, however, lies deeper than the implementation level. The naive logic we used, a non-monotonic first-order situation calculus (McCarthy, 1968; McDermott, 1980a), is just inadequate: no implementation can do the right thing here, because the logic doesn't specify the right thing. We need to be able to express, "Nell is going to be mashed *unless* I save her," and *unless* is a non-trivial concept (Goodman, 1947; Lewis, 1973).

In this paper, I will begin an attempt to rectify these problems, by providing a robust temporal logic to serve as a framework for programs that must deal with time. This is in the spirit of Hayes's "naive physics" (Hayes, 1979a), and might be thought of as a "naive theory of time." I will sketch approaches within this framework to what I consider the three most important problems of temporal representation: causality, continuous change, and the logic of problem solving.

One difference between Hayes and me is that I have not been able to turn my eyes away from implementational details as resolutely as Hayes. Consequently, later in the paper I will discuss how these ideas might be embodied in a program. Of course, the use of logic does not constrain us to making the program look like a theorem prover.

So why do I plan to spend any time at all on logic? There are two reasons:

1. We want to be assured that our special-purpose modules are not prone to absurd interactions such as the one I just sketched. One way to guarantee this is to be sure that the modules' actions are sound with respect to an underlying logic. (It is relatively unimportant and in practice unattainable that the programs be logically complete.)

2. Recently it has become clear that a reasoning system must keep track of the justifications for its conclusions, in order to update the data base as assumptions change (Doyle, 1979). For example, a picture of the future based on the assumption that dinner will be done at 6:00 must be revised if there is a power failure at 5:30. It turns out that constructing and maintaining these justification records, called *data dependencies*, is not trivial. One useful guide is that the data dependencies be equivalent to proofs in the underlying logic.

Many cognitive scientists will not find these reasons reassuring enough. On the one hand, many of them will be intimidated by the use of logical notation. On the other, there is a widespread feeling that psychological experiments have proven that people cannot handle simple syllogisms (see, e.g., Johnson-Laird, 1980), and that, therefore, people cannot possibly operate on logical principles. Together, these considerations cause them to reject papers like this one out of hand.

Let me be a little more reassuring. There is no difference between logical notation and notations like those of Schank (1975) or Charniak (1981), except emphasis. The logical approach aims at expressing the implications used for *inference*, as well as providing an ontological framework (or set of primitives, or vocabulary) for expressing *facts*. But face it—we're all talking about computers performing formal operations on data structures representing beliefs. The only issue is which to nail down first, the organization of the information in memory, or the structure of the inferences.

The experimental results on human processing of syllogisms are much less relevant than they first appear. At best, they show that people have no natural syllogistic machinery accessible to consciousness. This says nothing about logics underlying various kinds of thinking. One might as well investigate frequency-domain analysis in the visual system by asking people to do Fourier transforms in their heads.

In any case, I hope that appreciation of the difficulties raised by time will cause you to stick with me.

2. ONTOLOGY

We shall be doing logic in the style of Robert Moore (1980). The logic of time appears at first glance to be like modal logic, with different instants playing the role of different possible worlds. An expression like "President of the US" seems to denote an intensional object, with a different denotation in different times (worlds). In fact, historically the exploration of this relationship has fueled temporal logic (Prior, 1967; Rescher, 1971).

Moore encountered a similar tradition in his study of knowledge. "Know" had typically been taken as a modal operator. This made it difficult to handle computationally (Moore, 1980). Moore's contribution was to work with a first-order, extensional language that described the *interpretation* of the original modal language. He retained the original modal language as a set of objects manipulated by the first-order semantic language.

We will carry this idea one step further and dispense with the object language altogether, although some of the terminology will hint at vestiges of it. We will talk about a temporal model using a first-order language. The resulting enterprise will look like a hybrid of Moore's work and that of Hayes (1979a).

There are two key ideas to capture in our logic: the "openness" of the future, and the continuity of time. The first idea is that more than one thing can happen starting at a given instant. We model this by having many possible futures. The second idea is that many things do not happen discontinuously. We model this by having a continuum of instances between any two instants. It will be clear eventually why these features are so important.

To capture these ideas, our language will talk of an infinite collection of *states* of the universe. A state is an instantaneous snapshot of the universe. States are partially ordered by a relation "= <." We write (= < s1 s2) to mean that s1 comes before or is identical to s2.

I use "Cambridge Polish" notation for logical formulas. Every term, atomic formula, and combination is of the form (p...), where p is a function, predicate, or connective. The rest of the formula after p will be the arguments or other subparts. If p is a quantifier ("forall" or "exists"), then the subparts are a list of variables and a formula:

(forall (-vars-) fmla)
(exists (-vars-) fmla)

For other connectives, the subparts are formulas, as in

(not fmla)
(if fmla1 fmla2)
(and fmla1 fmla2 ...)
(or fmla1 fmla2 ...)
(iff fmla1 fmla2)

If p is a binary transitive relation, (p w x y ... z) is an abbreviation for (and (p w x) (p x y) ... (p ... z)). I will generally use lower case for logical constants; upper case for sorts (which I will discuss shortly), for Skolem constants, and for domain-dependent predicates and functions; and italics for syntactic variables.

Axiom 1:   (iff (and (= < ?s1 ?s2) (= < ?s2 ?s1)) (= ?s1 ?s2))
           (iff (< ?s1 ?s2) (and (= < ?s1 ?s2) (not (= ?s1 ?s2))))

As usual, if (= < s1 s2) and s1 and s2 are distinct, we write (< s1 s2).

Axiom 2:   (Density)
(forall (s1 s2)
   (if (< s1 s2) (exists (s) (< s1 s s2))))

Axiom 3:   (Transitivity)
(forall (s1 s2 s3)
   (if (and (= < s1 s2) (= < s2 s3))
      (= < s1 s3)))

Notice that I assume a sorted logic. Variables beginning with s are states. All this means is that a formula (forall (x) p), where x is a sorted variable, is an abbreviation for

(forall (x) (if (is *sort* x) p),

where *sort* is x's sort, or "data type." Sorts will not appear very often, and will be capitalized when they do. They are not very important, and will only save a little typing. We can read (forall (s) ...) as "for all states ...," without having to mention explicitly the condition (is STATE s).

Unbound variables (prefixed with "?") are universally quantified with scope equal to the whole formula (after adding the sort conditions). Anonymous constants of a given sort (used in proofs), so-called "Skolem constants," will be written beginning with the appropriate upper-case letter, as in (= (d S1) D1). Any real number is a valid date: time is infinite and noncircular. Of course, no one in the universe can tell where zero is or what the scale is, so this is harmless. It does mean that two states will have comparable dates, even when they are not related by = <. I will use = < and < for ordinary numerical ordering as well as the partial ordering on states, since the use of sorts will disambiguate. I will not be rigorous about axiomatizing real numbers, but will just assume whatever properties I need as I go. Variables beginning with "r" or "t" are real numbers.

The two orderings are compatible:

Axiom 4:   (if (< s1 s2) (< (d s1) (d s2)))

States are arranged into chronicles. A *chronicle* is a complete possible history of the universe, a totally ordered set of states extending infinitely in time.

Axiom 5:   (Definition of Chronicle)
(iff (is CHRONICLE ?x)
   (and ;a set of states
      (forall (y) (if (elt y ?x) (is STATE y)))
      ;totally ordered
      (forall (s1 s2)
         (iff (and (elt s1 ?x) (elt s2 ?x))
            (or (< s1 s2) (> s1 s2) (= s1 s2))))
      ;infinite in time
      (forall (t)
         (exists (s)
            (and (elt s ?x) (= (d s) t))))))

(elt *a x*) means that *a* is an element of set *x*. We won't need any deep set theory, but I will feel free to introduce sets of elements previously introduced, including sets of sets of them. (If variables of some sort begin with a letter "l," then variables bound to sets of objects of that sort begin "ll." So "?ss" is a set of states.)

An immediate consequence of Axiom 5 is that a chronicle is "convex":

```
(if (is CHRONICLE ?x)
  (forall (s1 s2)
    (if (and (elt s1 ?x) (elt s2 ?x))
      (forall (s)
        (if (< s1 s s2)
          (elt s ?x))))))
```

Having defined (is CHRONICLE x), we can conceal most uses of it by declaring variables beginning "ch" to be of sort "CHRONICLE." A chronicle is a way events might go. There may be more than one of them, according to this logic. (See Figure 1.) Every state is in a chronicle. In fact,

Axiom 6:

```
(if ( = < ?s1 ?s2)
  (exists (ch) (and (elt ?s1 ch) (elt ?s2 ch)))))
```

whence, by convexity, every state between ?s1 and ?s2 is in ch.

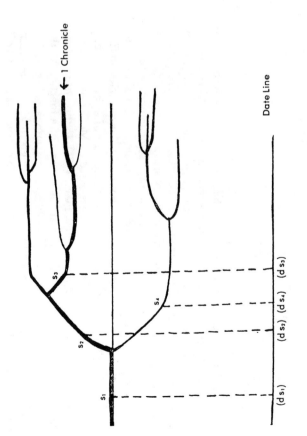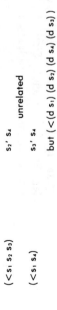

Figure 1. A Tree of Chronicles

Chronicles branch only into the future. (See Figure 1.)

Axiom 7:

```
(if (and ( = < ?s1 ?s) ( = < s2 ?s))
    (or ( = < ?s1 ?s2) ( = < ?s2 ?s1)))
```

The reason why this is so is that the future is really indeterminate. The past may be unknown, but there is only one past. By contrast, there may be more than one future from a given state. The reason for designing the logic this way is to provide for "free will," in the form of reasoning about actions that *select* one future instead of another. If there were only one future, the most we could do is *discover* it. Of course, both alternatives have unpleasant consequences: the one-future account implies that what we are going to do is unknown but fixed, while the many-futures account implies that the alternative futures to yesterday are as real as this one. For this reason, I do not include any reference to "yesterday," or even "now," in the logic, but simply talk about states in the abstract. The application to the state "now," and the fondness we feel for the "real" chronicle, are matters I defer until the section on implementation.[1]

States and chronicles are important only because they are the stage where facts and events are acted out. *Facts* change in truth value over time. By the usual mathematical inversion, we will take a fact to be a set of states, intuitively those in which it is true. For example, (ON A B) denotes the set of states in which A is on B. ON is a function from pairs of objects to sets of states, that is, facts; it is *not* a predicate.[2] This way of looking at facts is analogous to the logicians' trick of letting propositions denote sets of possible worlds (see e.g., Montague, 1974).

I will let variables beginning with "p" and "q" denote facts. The fact "always" is the set of all states. The fact "never" is the empty set.

We indicate that a fact is true in a state by (elt s p). As syntactic sugar, we usually write this as (T s p). ("T" suggests "true-in.") So, we have

Axiom 8:

```
(T ?s always)
(not (T ?s never))
```

We can think of facts as "propositions" in a Mooresque object language. In particular, we can combine them with connectives. For instance,

---

[1] I should point out that the logic I am developing is *not* intended as an analysis of the truth conditions of English or some other natural language. I doubt that this is at all a good way to think about natural language, and even if it is I see no reason why the internal representation should be constrained by the mere presence of words like "now" in natural language.

[2] It may be considered a predicate in an object language for which this temporal logic is a metalanguage; see below.

we can write (T s (& p q)), where the "&" is *not* part of our own logical notation; instead, it is simply syntactic sugar for set intersection; (& p q) is just the set of states that are elements of both p and q. Similarly, "∨" and "−" in this context denote union and complement (with respect to the set "always"). Then we have things like

```
(iff (T ?s ?p) (not (T ?s (− ?p))))
(iff (T ?s (& ?p ?q))
    (and (T ?s ?p) (T ?s ?q)))
```

as trivial set-theory results, after syntactic desugaring.

Events are more difficult to handle than facts. An event is something happening. In the past, the only kind of events handled by AI researchers and most philosophers is what might be called a *fact change*, such as a block being moved from one place to another (McCarthy, 1968; Rescher, 1971). The defining feature of an event on this theory are the changes in facts that the event brings about. This approach suppresses some important features of events. For instance, they take time. A fact change is just a list of two facts; how long it took is not describable. Further, it is meaningless in fact-change formalisms to ask what happens in the middle of a fact change.

Consider the usual emphasis in studies based on McCarthy's situation calculus (McCarthy, 1968; Moore, 1980; Fikes, 1971). In this system, an action like "moving x to y" is reasoned about in terms of a function MOVE that maps a block, a place, and an old situation into a new situation; (MOVE x y s) is the situation resulting from moving x to y in s. The axioms of the calculus talk entirely about the different facts true in s and (MOVE x y s). There is no mention of the infinite number of states occurring during the move.

Some of these problems can be eliminated by simply shifting emphasis, as I will show shortly. But a deeper problem is that many events are simply not fact changes. An example due to Davidson (1967) is "John ran around the track 3 times." The only fact change that occurs is that John is more tired. The amount of fatigue is not terribly different from the amount ensuing on running around 4 times. Besides, surely no one would argue that the *definition* of "run around the track 3 times" is "be here tired." Of course, John might have a memory of having done it, but even "be here tired with a memory of having run around 3 times" is still not a plausible definition, if for no other reason than that John might have lost count. Also, this definition is circular, since John's memory must make reference to the concept to be analyzed, and hence can only mean "I remember [bringing it about that I am tired and have a memory of [bringing it about that I am tired and have a memory of [....]]]"

If you still need to be convinced, consider the (large) class of actions that are done for their own sake, such as visiting Greece, eating a gourmet meal, or having sex. In all these cases, the fact changes are trivial, unappetizing, or only tangentially relevant. One could argue, I suppose, that these things are done only for the memory of having done them. It is true that doing them without remembering them would be a little pointless, but memory fades. Knowing you won't remember much of this trip, meal, or sexual activity 20 years from now is not much of a barrier to doing it now, and does not entail that doing it is logically impossible.

We need a fresh approach. One idea is that events be identified with a certain kind of fact, namely the fact that the event is taking place. Facts occupy time intervals, so we get the ability to talk about what happens during an event. This seems to be adequate for events that consist of some aimless thing happening for a while, such as a rooster crowing in the morning. The rooster-crowing event could just be defined to be the time during which the rooster is crowing. This event happens in a chronicle if any of its states are in that chronicle.

But most events do not fit this mold. Running around a track three times takes time, but cannot be identified with the states during which you are running on the track. The problem is that a given state may be part of a "3 times around" event in one chronicle, and a "2 times around" event in another. But the criterion would have the event happening in both.

We avoid this problem by identifying an event as a set of intervals, intuitively those intervals over which the event happens once, with no time "left over" on either side. An interval is a totally ordered, convex set of states. We can think of each interval as an event token, and the whole set as an event type. So "Fred running around a track 3 times" is the set of all intervals in which exactly that[3] happens.

Now we can indicate that an event happens between states s1 and s2 by writing (elt [s1, s2] e). As syntactic sugar for this, I will write (Occ s1 s2 e) Notice that I let variables beginning with "e" stand for events.

Can we always assume that an event occurs over a closed interval? Let us leave this question unanswered for the time being. In this paper, I will always used the Occ notation, and hence assume that they are closed, but it doesn't seem very important for most events whether they include two extra instants or not. Since we will want to allow for instantaneous events, at least some of them must be closed.[4] The notion of a fact being true over a period

---

[3] The phrase "exactly that" is intended to rule out "last Tuesday" as a token of this event if Fred ran around the track once on Tuesday (unless it took him 24 hr). But I do not mean to insist that an event happen over an interval only if it happens over no subinterval. When the event "Fred whistles" happens over an interval, it happens over an infinite number of subintervals. Incidentally, the idea of letting events be sets of intervals was stated by Montague (somewhat differently) in Montague (1960).

[4] Notice, by the way, that if we interpret event intervals consistently (as always closed, always half-open on the right, or whatever), then using them is equivalent to modifying McCarthy's situation calculus by letting actions be *relations* on situations (states) instead of functions.

of time is still valuable, even though it wouldn't carry the full load. This is written (subset [*s1*, *s2*] *p*), or, syntactically sugared, as (TT *s1 s2 p*).

Certain events and facts are closely related. For example, (sunion *S*), for any set *S* of sets, is the union of all its elements. The (sunion *e*) is a fact, true whenever *e* is "in progress," in the sense that in some possible chronicle *e* is in the process of occurring. I will use the syntactic sugaring (in-progress *e*) to mean the same thing as (sunion *e*), and (Tocc *s e*) to mean (T *s* (in-progress *e*)).

Given a fact, we can work our way back to events in more than one way. For instance, we can take the set of maximal intervals during which the fact is true, or the set of point intervals for all points where the fact is true.

Events can be related to each other in ways similar to those for facts. For instance, if *p* is a subset of *q*, then it is as if *p* implied *q*: at every state where *p* is true, so is *q*. For events, we write (subset *e1 e2*) as (one-way *e1 e2*): *e1* is one way *e2* can happen; every occurrence of *e1* is an occurrence of *e2*. For example, being squashed by a meteor is one way of being squashed.

We used boolean connectives like "&" to combine facts. These are not so useful with events. Instead, we need things like

```
(seq e1 e2 ... eN)
which stands for
{[s0, sN]: (exists (s1 ... sN-1)
             (and (Occ s0 s1 e1)
                  (Occ s1 s2 e2)
                  ...
                  (Occ sN-1 sN eN)) )}
```

Corresponding to "never," the fact that is never true, there is an event that never happens. This will also be the empty set, so we can call it "never," too, making this the only thing that is both an event and a proposition. There does not seem to be any useful notion of the event that always happens.

More such constructs will be introduced as we go.

Remember that this logic takes an Olympian view of states of the universe. "Now" is not distinguished, so there is no question about representing what has already happened versus what may happen. I will talk about this more in Section 6, below. I should point out, though, that representing tokens of past or expected events as ordered pairs of states, like (s34, s107), is not adequate. A given interval is a token of many different events, which happened to occur at that point. So event tokens must be represented as ordered pairs of events and intervals, or something equivalent.

I want to stress at this point that devising ontologies like this is not an empty philosophical enterprise. On the contrary, I am interested in purely utilitarian ends; I want a way of thinking about time that is useful to a robot. I am not interested in expressing all possible ways of thinking about time,

nor am I interested in calculating the truth values of English statements involving time. It may seem that logic and practicality have little to do with each other, that the problem for cognitive science is to build a computational model that reasons about time, and be done with it. Unfortunately, it is not so straightforward. Any program will be based on *some* ontology and assumptions about time. The wrong assumptions will mire us in a swamp of logical conundrums, which much be explicitly faced and conquered. The best way to do this is to make the logical machinery explicit (cf. McDermott, 1978a).

This is what I will be doing in the rest of this paper, examining three major problems that temporal reasoners will face: reasoning about causality and mechanism, reasoning about continuous change, and planning actions. There may be others, but these should suffice. They have been difficult in the past precisely because dangerous assumptions have been made about time, such as that there is a next moment, or that there is only one future. I will try to show that a program based on the logic I propose will have a better chance of avoiding these difficulties.

To illustrate how logical assumptions influence thought, I will try to prove a theorem about a mechanism, and show the power and weakness of what we have assumed so far. The theorem goes like this: Let DEV be a device with two states, DAY and NIGHT. DAY is always followed by NIGHT and NIGHT by DAY. DAY and NIGHT never overlap. Prove that if it is ever DAY or NIGHT, it will always be either DAY or NIGHT.

This may seem simple, but it is just the sort of inference that is beyond the capability of existing reasoning systems. Expressed in our notation, it is

```
DAY and NIGHT are mutually exclusive (except at boundaries):
(if (and (Occ ?s1 ?s2 DAY) (Occ ?s3 ?s4 NIGHT)
     (forall (s)
       (if (and (= < ?s1 s ?s2) (= < ?s3 s ?s4)
          (or (= s ?s2 ?s3)
              (= s ?s1 ?s4))) ) )

Each takes a nonzero amount of time:
(if (or (Occ ?s1 ?s2 DAY) (Occ ?s1 ?s2 DAY))
    (< ?s1 ?s2))

and each follows the other
(follows DAY NIGHT)
(follows NIGHT DAY)
where
(iff (follows ?e1 ?e2)
  (if (Occ ?s1 ?s2 ?e1)
    (forall (ch) (if (elt ?s2 ch)
      (exists (s3)
        (and (elt s3 ch)
             (Occ ?s2 s3 ?e2)))))))
```

That is, e2 follows e1 if every occurrence of e1 is followed immediately by an occurrence of e2 in every chronicle containing the occurrence of e1, i.e., in every way events might proceed.

Now to prove
(if (Occ S1 S2 DAY)
  (forall (s) (if (> s S2) (or (Tocc s DAY)
                               (Tocc s NIGHT)))))

This theorem may seem trivial, but in fact it does not follow from what we have assumed so far. If each succeeding DAY or NIGHT interval is half as long as the previous one, then an infinite number of them could go by in a finite amount of time, after which the state of DEV could be something else. However, this is something we wish to rule out. We do so with the axiom

Axiom 9:
(forall (s p)
  (and (exists (s0)
    (or (TTopen s0 s p))
        (TTopen s0 s (– p)))
  (forall (ch)
    (if (elt s ch)
      (exists (s1)
        (and (elt s1 ch)
          (or (TTopen s s1 p)
              (TTopen s s1 (– p)))))))))

where
  (iff (TTopen s1 s2 p)
    (and (< s1 s2)
      (forall (s)
        (if (< s1 s2) (T s p)))))

This axiom, due to Ernie Davis, assures us that, for every fact and an arbitrary state, there is an interval preceding the state during which the fact is always true or always false; and another one following the state, in every chronicle containing it. (See Figure 2.)

The presence of this axiom rules out any super powerful axiom of "comprehension,"[1] which would allow us to infer that any set of states was a fact, such as the set of states during which the temperature in Cleveland is a rational number. This is *not* a fact because, assuming the temperature is smoothly changing, it will change truth value infinitely often in any finite interval.

[1] An axiom or axiom schema of comprehension states that for every property, there is a set of objects satisfying it. Stating this formally in a way that avoids paradoxes is a major preoccupation of set theorists (Mendelson, 1964).

P violates Axiom 9 at s

Figure 2. How a Well-Behaved Fact Does Not Behave

So we will need special-purpose comprehension axioms for well-behaved facts. I will just assume these along the way as obvious. For example, if p and q are facts, (& p q) is also.[2] When I introduce a function like "in-progress," and announce that its values are from a given domain, like facts, I am implicitly declaring an axiom like

Axiom 10: (In-Progress Comprehension)
  (is FACT (in-progress ?e))

So you can take for granted that (in-progress e) satisfies Axiom 9. This axiom does away with any super powerful comprehension axiom for events, in case you were wondering.

You may now take it on faith that no further assumptions are required to prove that it will always be DAY or NIGHT, or you can bear with me through the following proof. (It is not as arbitrary as it seems; if anyone can find a simpler or clearer proof, I would like to hear about it.)

First, we need a few definitions. Letting sets of events be denoted by variables beginning with "ee," and integers be denoted by variables beginning with "n," we define

Axiom 11:
(iff (chain ?ee 0 ?s1 ?s2) (= ?s1 ?s2))
(iff (chain ?ee (+ ?n 1) ?s1 ?s3)
  (exists (e s2)
    (and (elt e ?ee)
      (Occ s2 ?s3 e)
      (chain ?ee ?n ?s1 ?s2))))

That is, there is an ee chain of length n from s1 to s2, if there is a sequence of abutting events from the set ee that reaches from s1 to s2.

[2] We could probably recast Axiom 9 as a biconditional and prove these axioms, but set-theoretic parsimony is not really important.

Now reachability is defined thus

Axiom 12:

```
(iff (reachable ?ee ?ch ?s1 ?s)
  (exists (n s2)
    (and (> = n 0)
      (elt s2 ?ch)
      (chain ?ee n ?s1 s2)
      (= < ?s1 ?s ?s2)) ))
```

We read this "?s is ?ee-reachable in ?ch from ?s1."
Some corollaries of these definitions (using Peano arithmetic) are:

```
(if (reachable ?ee ?ch ?s1 ?s)
  (forall (s')
    (if (< ?s1 s' ?s)
      (reachable ?ee ?ch ?s1 s')) ))

(if (reachable ?ee ?ch ?s1 ?s)
  (or (= ?s1 ?s)
    (exists (e s2 s3 n)
      (and (elt e ?ee)
        (elt s3 ?ch)
        (Occ s2 s3 e)
        (= < s2 ?s s3)) )))
```

These state that if ?s is ?ee-reachable from ?s1, then every state between ?s1 and ?s is reachable, and ?s occurs in the middle of some event in ?ee.

Now the proof goes as follows: Assume that S' is a state such that (> S' S2) and (not (Tocc S' DAY)) and (not (Tocc S' NIGHT)). Then by Axiom 6, there is a chronicle CH1 containing S' and S2. Clearly, (not (reachable {DAY, NIGHT} CH1 S2 S')). So, by the properties of real numbers and the first corollary above, there must be a state S, (< S2 S) and (= < S S'), such that every state between S2 and S is {DAY, NIGHT}—reachable in CH1 from S2, and every state from S on is not {DAY, NIGHT}—reachable in CH1 from S2. But, by Axiom 9, there must be an SD3 before S such that either DAY is in progress for all states between SD3 and S, or it is not in progress for all those states. Similarly, there must be an SN3 before S such that it's NIGHT or it isn't from SN3 to S. Since it can't be neither or both, let S3 be the one for which either it is DAY from S3 to S or NIGHT from S3 to S. Clearly, (< S2 S3) because both DAY and NIGHT occur at least once after S2. Every state from S3 to S is {DAY, NIGHT}—reachable, so, by the second corollary, one of DAY or NIGHT is occurring from S3 to S, and this occurrence ends in some state S4 in CH1. (See Figure 3.)

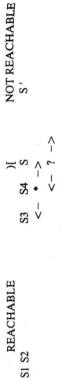

```
    REACHABLE                     NOT REACHABLE
S1 S2        S3 S4      )[ S              S'
             <- * ->
             <- ? ->
```

*either DAY or NIGHT in progress throughout this interval

S4 must come before S, or else S would be reachable, according to the definition, because S4 would end a chain from S2. But then starting at S4 NIGHT or DAY must occur, so DAY and NIGHT must coexist for more than an instant, which is impossible. So there is no such S, and all instants are reachable—QED.

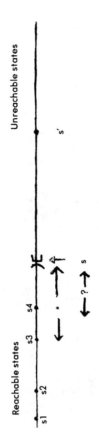

Reachable states   Unreachable states

*Either DAY or NIGHT is in progress throughout this interval

Figure 3. Proof of Eternal DAY or NIGHT

This may seem quite complicated. But it depended on only one new axiom, Axiom 9. Everything else came from definitions and arithmetic. Of course, this proof is much too complicated to expect a theorem prover to come up with it, but this was never my goal. My intent is similar to Hayes's: to express concepts in a form in which the intuitively plausible inferences are valid. If this is achieved, then we can start worrying about a practical inference program. In fact, I start worrying in Section 6, below. The only thing to point out here is that such a program has no hope of being complete.

I should also assure you that this paper is not crammed full of such long proofs of obvious results. The main purpose of showing you this was to let you get a feel for the generality of the ontological assumptions. They are so general that we have to tame them with Axioms like Axiom 9. But this is all the taming we will want to do.

Also, this result is not entirely academic. It is easily generalizable to a system with a finite number of mutually exclusive states which succeed each other the way DAY and NIGHT do. It gives us the ability to infer infinite loops in simple machines.

Now, as promised, I will examine three major problem areas from the point of view of this logic, before turning to implementation questions.

3. CAUSALITY

Causality is fundamental to a lot of problem solving. A problem solver brings things about by causing other things. What I mean by causality here is that one event (type) always follows another event (type). For example, if x is a loaded gun, pulling its trigger is followed by its firing.

Unfortunately, there must be more to it than that. For example, an exactly analogous case is, If a is approaching from the direction of the sun, the arrival of a's shadow is followed by the arrival of a. But we would not want to say that the arrival of a's shadow causes the arrival of a.

I assume that there is no way to get around this problem, and that there is no way to infer causality merely from correlation. So we will not try to define causality in terms of something more basic. Instead, we will assume whatever causal assertions we need, and infer events from them.

Events can cause two kinds of things: other events, and facts. The two cases are quite different, and the first is simpler.

When an event causes another, there is usually a delay. The scale of the date line attached to the chronicle tree is unknown in the logic, so we cannot use absolute time intervals. Instead, we assume that there are objects called *scales* which occupy some constant amount of time. If "hour" is such a scale, (* 5 hour) is a length of time equal to 5 times the size of hour (see McDermott 1980b for a fuller explanation). We will never be able to evaluate this, but we don't need to; we just need to be able to compare it to other things measured in hours or seconds. We can do the latter because we have as an axiom (= (3,600 second) hour). Note the elision of the * when it is clearly unnecessary.

With this out of the way, we introduce our basic predicate (ecause *p e1 e2 rf i*), which means that *e1* is always followed by *e2*, after a delay in the interval *i*, unless *p* becomes false before the delay is up. The delay is measured from a point *rf* through *e1*; if *rf*=0, this means from the start of *e1*; if *rf*=1, from the end.

Axiom 13:
```
(if (ecause ?p ?e1 ?e2 ?rf ?i)
    (if (Occ ?s1 ?s2 ?e1)
        (forall (ch)
            (if (elt ?s2 ch)
                (exists (s3)
                    (and (elt s3 ch)
                         (within-delay s3 ?rf ?i ?s1 ?s2)
                         (or (not (TT ?s2 s3 p))
                             (exists (s4)
                                 (and (elt s4 ch)
                                      (Occ s3 s4 ?e2)))))))))
```

where
$$\text{(iff (within-delay ?s ?rf ?i ?s1 ?s2)}$$
```
(elt { (d ?s) }
     { − (1 − ?rf)*(d ?s1) }
     { + ?rf*(d ?s2) } }
?i))
```

The (within-delay *s rf i s1 s2*) means that state *s* occurs after *s1* and *s2*, with delay *i*. An *rf* is a real number that says what point the delay is to be measured from. If it is 0, the delay is to be measured starting at *s1*; if 1, from *s2*; and so on for any number between 0 and 1. The *i* is a real interval, like <(3 min), (5 min)>, or [0, (5 hour)]. (An open side of an interval I denote by the usual angle bracket, as in <1, 3] or <1, 3>. A closed interval on the reals, while denoted with square brackets [..], is a completely different sort of thing from a state interval.)

As an example of ecause, we can express the idea that if a Republican is elected President, science will progress:

```
(ecause (POLPARTY ?x REPUBLICAN)
        (elected ?x)
        (INFLUX-MONEY-FOR-DESERVING-RESEARCHERS)
        1 [(1 year), (2 year)]))
```

In these examples, only the parts being illustrated are formalized in a reasonable way.

If the fuse on a powderkeg is lit, the keg will explode if the powder stays dry:

```
(ecause (& (DRY ?keg) (FUSE-OF ?fuse ?keg))
           (LIT ?fuse)
           (EXPLODE ?keg)
           1 [(30 sec), (2 min)]))
```

If a winch is rotated, an object gets hauled up:

```
(if (is WINCH ?x)
    (ecause (LOAD-OF ?x ?y)
            (ROTATE ?x)
            (RISE ?y)
            0
            [0, (2 sec)]))
```

Note that the object might not start rising for a second or two.

We also have the axiom:

Axiom 14:

```
(if (ecause ?p ?e1 ?e2 ?rf ?i)
  (forall (s3 s4)
    (if (Occ s3 s4 ?e2)
      (exists (pc ec s1 s2 rfc ic)
        (and (eecause pc ec ?e2 rfc ic)
          (Occ s1 s2 ec)
          (within-delay s3 rfc ic s1 s2))))))
```

That is, if an event is ever caused, then each of its occurrences is preceded by one of its causes (with the appropriate delay). This might be called the Principle of Paranoia. Its chief virtue is in enabling us to infer that an event must have occurred when it is known to be the only cause of another event that occurred.

The second kind of causality is the causation of a fact by an event. For example, if a boulder falls to the bottom of a mountain, it will *be* at the bottom of the mountain. This is important in problem solving, where the goal is often to bring about some fact by causing one or more events.

One approach might be to say that e causes p if, in all chronicles, p is true for some period of time after e. We could do this, but it would be useless. In this sense, shooting a bullet past someone would be a way of achieving that it was near him.

I must digress here to talk about the speed at which facts change. The real world doesn't change fast most of the time. Many facts remain true for long enough to be depended on. For example, that boulder will probably stay at the bottom of the mountain for years (or centuries). We normally use such facts with confidence, for example, when planning to build a house on the boulder.

On the other hand, we cannot infer with certainty that the boulder will be there. If we could, then there would be no way to plan confidently to remove it. Confidence in the plan would just land us in a contradiction between our belief that the boulder will be gone by next year, and our certainty that it will be there for many years.

This is a classic example of a *non-monotonic* reasoning pattern (McDermott, 1980a; McDermott, 1981a; and Reiter, 1980). The inference that the boulder will be there is good until you find out that someone is planning to move it. I have resisted introducing non-monotonicity into the logic so far, because it is not that well understood, and what is well understood about it is not all that encouraging. But we are going to need it here.

The problem here is closely related to the *frame problem*. That was the problem that arose in McCarthy's situation calculus (McCarthy, 1968)

of not being able to infer anything about a situation resulting from an action in a previous situation, without a large number of axioms of the form "p doesn't change in this transition." A typical axiom would say, "No block's color changes in the transition from s to (MOVE A B s)." The problem is even more acute for us, because almost anything could be happening in an interval. In McCarthy's calculus it was possible to pretend that a situation (MOVE A B S0) would persist until the next action, so that the situation after two actions could be denoted by something like (MOVE C A (MOVE A B S0)). Now the state of the world changes as the problem solver plans, so there is no term denoting the state of the world when the second action occurs. The frame problem becomes the problem of inferring what's true at the end of an arbitrary interval, given incomplete information about what happened during it.

Part of my expectation in developing a robust logic of time was that we could reason about facts "from the side," inferring that they were true for whole stretches of time. It's no loss that we can't work our way from one state to the "next" any more; that was always a bad idea. But now we find that in general you cannot infer that a fact is true for a period of time.

Let me distinguish this problem from another one that is often held to be solvable with non-monotonic notations. Every AI hacker knows that the example causality axioms I gave earlier are incomplete, and that there is no way to make them complete. For instance, the keg will not explode if the fuse is cut, or if all the oxygen is removed from the keg before the spark reaches it, or the keg is placed in an extremely strong box that can withstand the explosion, or .... But you see the point. It seems pointless to try to list all the ways the rule could fail.

This problem can be solved simply by letting our rules fail now and then. We can't hope to avoid errors, and it normally doesn't matter if a data base is "slightly" inconsistent. When it does matter, we can edit the rules to maintain consistency. So in a sense the theory is "approximately" true, and gets closer to the truth with every edit. Non-monotonic logic could play a role by letting rules "edit themselves" (McDermott, 1980a), but this hardly seems necessary.

The rule that a boulder stays put for years is not even approximately true in this sense. It would be approximately true only if it were used in a purely passive system. An astronomer observing an uninhabited planet might use the rule this way. He would simply live with errors caused by improbable occurrences like volcanic eruptions that moved boulders. But a problem solver knows full well *both* that it is counting on certain things to be true for a while, *and* that it could make them false any time it wanted to. (Other agents could also make them false, but we neglect this possibility.)

To capture these ideas in the logic, I introduce the notion of *persistence*. A fact p persists from s with a lifetime r, if in all chronicles it remains true until r has gone by or until it *ceases* to be true.

What this means is that a plan to remove the boulder five years from now cancels a persistence after that time, but leaves intact the inference that it will be there until then.

By the way, let me make a disclaimer. I try to appeal to non-monotonic deductions as seldom as possible. This is because the logics they are based on (McDermott, 1980a; McDermott, 1981a; Reiter, 1980; and McCarthy, 1980) are still rather unsatisfactory. For one thing, even some of the simple deductions in this paper may not be valid in any existing non-monotonic system. For example, the problem with existential quantifiers cited in (McDermott, 1981a) would probably block some of my proofs. (The system of (Reiter, 1980) avoids this problem, but has others.) For another thing, such logics do not distinguish between severities of contradictions; they use the same machinery for "rule edits" of the kind I described and for clipping off a persistent fact. In the usual terminology of such systems, this leads to unexpected "fixed points," or models, in which the wrong assumptions are retracted.

For the time being, we can view these not a problems with this paper, but as problems with non-monotonic logic. In attempting to represent things, it is helpful to be as formal as we can, but if the formal systems cannot keep up with the inferences we want to make, so much the worse for the formal systems. In the long run, I am confident that non-monotonic logics will be developed that capture the inferences we need. Probably the best way to see what inferences those are is to try to get along with the fewest possible non-monotonic inferences, but to feel free to use them when all else fails. If representation designers make it clear what they need, logicians will make it work.

Armed with the idea of persistence, we can make some progress on our original problem. First of all, it seems reasonable that most inferences of facts are actually about persistence of facts. For one thing, many facts have characteristic lifetimes. If x is a boulder, then (AT x *location*) has a lifetime measured in scores of years. If x is a cat, then (AT x *location*) has a lifetime measured in minutes (if the cat is sleeping) or seconds (if the cat is awake).

The senses actually tell you about persistences. I was driven to this by the following problem our logic appears to involve us in. At first blush, we might want an axiom to the effect that if a boulder is at a location loc in state S0, then (persist S0 (AT Boulder Loc) (50 year)). But then we can infer that the boulder will be there in 50 years, when another persistence will start, and so on. We can infer that the boulder will be there for any given time in the future. If this seems harmless, think about the cat instead.

The solution is to scrap such axioms. Instead, we normally start with a persistence and work our way to particular states, not vice versa. This requires that when we see a boulder, our eyes are telling our data base about a

Axiom 15: (Definition of Persist)

```
(iff (persist ?s ?p ?r)
  (and (T ?s ?p)
    (forall (s')
      (if (and (within-lifetime s' ?r ?s)
               (not (T s' ?p)))
          (Occbetween ?s s' (cease ?p)) )))
```

where

```
(iff (within-lifetime ?s2 ?r ?s1)
  (and (= < ?s1 ?s2)
    (< (- (d ?s2) (d ?s1)) ?r))

(iff (Occbetween ?s0 ?s3 ?e)
  (exists (s1 s2)
    (and (= < ?s0 s1 s2 ?s3)
      (Occ s1 s2 ?e)) ))
```

Ceasing does not mean merely that the fact goes from true to false. In fact, ceasing is so rare that it never happens unless we hear about it:

Axiom 16: (Fundamental Property of Ceasing)

```
(if (and (persist ?s ?p ?r)
         (within-lifetime ?s' ?r ?s)
         (M (nocease ?s ?p ?s')))
    (not (Occbetween ?s ?s' (cease ?p))))
```

M is a primitive sentence-forming operator, read "Consistent." Intuitively, if Q cannot be proven false, then (M Q) is true. The (nocease s p s') means that no occurrence of (cease p) occurs between s and s'. To conclude that p actually does not cease, we require only that it be consistent that it not cease; positive information is necessary to override this. The overriding occurs when other rules allow us to infer (not (nocease s p S1)) for some S1 within the lifetime of the persistence; then the M fails, we cannot infer the p does not cease. But if no such rule applies, then we can make the inference.

I hope that this application of non-monotonic logic will not mess everything up. I am depending on a property of the logic of (McDermott, 1981a), namely, that from Axiom 16 and an occurrence of a ceasing within the lifetime of a persistence, we can deduce (not (nocease s p s')). If a weaker logic is used, this should be made explicit in an axiom. However it is done, it is essential that (Occbetween s s' (cease p)) kill off a persistence after s', but leave the persistence "in force" for states between s and s'. Clearly, if (Occbetween s ?s' (cease p)), then (Occbetween s s'' (cease p)) for all states s'' between s' and the end of the persistence. Then we can infer (not (nocease s p s''))for all those states. We *cannot* infer such a thing for states *before* s'.

persistence, not about an instantaneous fact. Otherwise, as soon as we turned away, we would know nothing about the scene. Once you get used to this idea, it seems perfectly natural.

This brings us back to causation. Clearly, what events must cause directly is persistences, not the truth of facts. So our primitive predicate is (pcause p e q rf i rl), which means that event e is always followed by fact q, after a delay in the interval i, unless p becomes false before the delay is up. The delay is measured from a point rf through e; if rf=1, this means from the start of e; if rf=0, this means from the end. When q becomes true, it persists for lifetime rl. Formally,

Axiom 17:
```
(if (pcause ?p ?e ?q ?rf ?i ?r1)
    (if (Occ ?s1 ?s2 ?e)
        (forall (ch)
            (if (elt ?s2 ch)
                (exists (s3)
                    (and (elt s3 ch)
                        (within-delay s3 ?rf ?i ?s1 ?s2)
                        (or (not T s3 p))
                            (persist s3 ?q ?r1))) )))))
```

And we have examples like:

```
(pcause always)
    (KILL ?x)
    (DEAD ?x)
    1 [0, 0]
    FOREVER)
```

Another example is:

```
(if (is STOVE ?x)
    (pcause (− (BLACKOUT)
        (TURN-ON ?x)
        (HOT ?x)
        1 [(1 min), (2 min)]
        (24 hour)))
```

We pick "FOREVER" to be a very long time, equal to the largest number that can be stored on the machine the universe is being simulated on, or the length of time until the Last Judgement, depending on your religion.

Notice that the persistence time is picked as the time interval over which it is reasonable to infer that the state will remain in existence, assuming you have no intention of changing it. I pick 24 hours here because within that time, either one's spouse will find the burner and turn it off, or the house will burn down. Of course, normally you plan to turn it off sooner. If for some reason you wanted the burner to stay on longer (say you were cooking something that took a really long time), you would just need axioms about putting signs up, or other special tactics. These would say, "If you put a sign up telling someone not to alter a state they won't worry about if they see a sign, then the state will remain as long as the sign is up."[47]

Notice that not all instances of inferring facts "from the side" are direct instances of persistence. Part of the power of the notion comes from the fact that persistent facts have consequences. For example, if everyone in the American embassy is audible (while the embassy is bugged), and the fact that persistent facts have consequences. ... Henry is in the embassy for 15 minutes, then he is audible during that period. We don't have to come up with a general lifetime for audibility.

There is no Principle of Paranoia (Axiom 14) for pcause. This is because there are so many ways a fact can come about, including logical consequence, that it does not seem reasonable to look for a cause every time. Also, most true facts are "left-over" persistences. Most boulders in the world have been there longer than any lifetime you would use; the lifetime you can count on is much shorter than the times you observe. By the way, this should make it obvious that the logic does not imply that a persisting fact stops being true after its lifetime; we simply lose information after that point.

Since persistences, and not facts, are caused, and since there is usually no persistence that extends back to when a fact became true, there is really no cause for most facts, at least not in the technical senses I have been developing. Of course, many facts of interest are the result of observed or inferred events, and these will be caused. One interesting case is when an occurrence of (cease p) is inferred using Axiom 15. We can then infer that this ceasing was caused. In fact, we can call this the Special Principle of Paranoia:

Axiom 18:
```
(if (Occ ?s3 ?s4 (cease ?p))
    (exists (pc ec s1 s2 rfc ic)
        (and (ecause pc ec (cease ?p) rfc ic)
            (Occ s1 s2 ec)
            (within-delay ?s3 rfc ic s1 s2)) )))
```

[47] Several people (notably Ernie Davis, James Allen, and Ken Forbus) have suggested that the idea of lifetime should be dropped from persistences. Even though a burner rarely stays on for more than 24 hr, it would if left unattended, and my notation obscures this fact. My main reason for sticking with limited persistences is to take into account the fact that in many cases, we simply lose information about a system for moments too far from our last observation.

pcause and ecause work hand in hand. Consider the event (PUTON A B) that occurs within minutes after the beginnings of persistences of (CLEAR-TOP A) and (CLEARTOP B), with lifetimes of several hours. Suppose we have axioms like:

```
(pcause (& (CLEARTOP ?x) (CLEARTOP ?y))
         (PUTON ?x ?y)
         (ON ?x ?y)
         1 [0, 0]
         (10 hour))
```

and, of course,

```
(iff (T ?s (CLEARTOP ?X))
     (not (exists (y) (T ?s (ON y ?x)))))
```

We can deduce from the persistence of (CLEARTOP A) and of (CLEAR-TOP B) that (& (CLEARTOP A) (CLEARTOP B)) will be true for several hours. Hence it will be true during the PUTON. (We will need an axiom about how long PUTONs take.) Hence (ON A B) will persist from the end of the PUTON. Hence (CLEARTOP B), no longer true, must have ceased, and the rule that it doesn't cease is inapplicable. However, it still can be inferred not to have ceased up to the end of the PUTON, so there is no contradiction. I will say more on the subject of reasoning about plans later.

Before going on to other topics, I should pause to review previous work on representing causality. Curiously, Hayes (1979a) argues that there is no isolated body of knowledge about causality. Every branch of "naive physics" has its own way of accounting for things happening. He also says he has found no need for non-monotonicity. I envy him. I think the reason for his good fortune is the "passive" character of his theory. It says how to reason about physical systems; it takes a Buddhist attitude of resignation toward bad things. For example, Hayes's Theory of Liquids (Hayes, 1979b) can be used to infer that there will be a flood, in such a way that it is plain contradictory to suppose the flood can be prevented. (This is a bit unfair, since he would presumably make the move of changing the axioms, i.e., the physical setup, as a reflection of the action of the planner. I don't know if this would amount to letting non-monotonicity in by the back door or not.)

The most obvious competitor to the theory I have presented is that of Rieger, who developed a graphical notation for what he calls "Common-Sense Algorithms" (CSA) (Rieger, 1976; Rieger, 1975). This notation included devices for representing concepts like continuous causality, "gated one-shots," thresholds, and much more. There are several problems with this notation, all stemming from Rieger's refusal to state precisely what the links and nodes of his networks *mean*. Apparently, networks representing physical devices and plans are written exactly the same, or are freely mixed. There is a systematic ambiguity about whether a link drawn on a page indicates that *if* something is done, something else will follow; or *that the thing is actually done* and the consequence actually occurs. For example, does the "threshold" link indicate that if the threshold is passed something will happen, or that the threshold is *supposed* to be passed eventually? It seems as if you need to be able to say both. Apparently in the CSA notation you can only say the latter. It seems somehow perverse to make algorithms more basic than physics. In my system, algorithms come in later, in a different form (see Section 5).

Besides this major flaw, there are lots of little places where the CSA notation fails to be precise. For instance, time delays and lifetimes are not mentioned. How is it possible to reason about a plan involving several parallel actions if they are completely unsynchronized?

On the other hand, there is substantial overlap in what he and I have done. His gated causality, and my provision of a gating fact as the first argument to ecause and pcause, are both due to realization of a key fact about causality, that events' behaviors are modified greatly by background facts.

4. FLOW

A system cannot reason about time realistically unless it can reason about continuous change. This has been neglected by all but a handful of people (Hendrix, 1973; Rieger, 1975). The assumption that actions are instantaneous state changes has made it hard to reason about any other kind. If I am filling a bathtub, how do I describe what happens to the water level during (MOVE A B S0)?

I will use the term *fluent* for things that change continuously over time. (The term is due to McCarthy (1968), who used it in almost exactly the same sense.) Actually, the notion of fluent is more general than that. It is intended to do the work that is done by "intensional objects" in other systems. The President of the United States is a typical intensional object. Unlike most people, he has lived in the same house for over 150 years. His age sometimes decreases suddenly. These may seem like strange properties, but they are necessary (on some theories) to provide the correct truth value for sentences like "The President lives in the White House" (true), or "In 1955, the President was a movie actor" (false).

In my logic, such objects correspond to fluents. A fluent is a thing whose *value* changes with time. The value of a fluent in a given state s is written (V s v). I will use "v" for variables ranging over fluents. So, we can express two different readings for the last example sentence above:

(T 1955 (ACTOR (V 1955 President)))
(T 1955 (ACTOR (V 1981 President)))

In the first, "President" is taken to mean "President at the time of the fact." In the second, it is taken to mean "President at the time of the utterance (1981). The rules of English make the first reading more likely, under which the sentence comes out false.

Fluents are valuable, not for this sort of playing around, but because physical quantities may be thought of as fluents. For example, "the temperature in Cleveland" is a fluent, which takes on values in temperature space. The changes of the fluent can then be reasoned about. In particular, the fluent's being in a certain region is a fact which might be helpful in causal reasoning. All of the fluents I will look at from now on will have numbers as values. Such fluents I will loosely call "quantities." Most quantities are real-valued and vary continuously as well.

At this point a certain abuse of notation will make life simpler. Strictly speaking, (> *v1 v2*) is meaningless, because > relates numbers or states, not fluents. What we really need is a function (>* *v1 v2*), which takes two fluents and returns the fact which is true in all states *s* for which (V *s v1*) is greater than (V *s v2*). Similarly, (>! *v1 r*) might take a fluent and a real number, and return the fact which is true just when the quantity's value is greater than the number. Clearly, to do this rigorously would be tedious. Instead, I will just assume that all of the red tape can be cleared away, and use (> *alpha beta*) freely, where *alpha* and/or *beta* is a fluent, integer, real number, etc. If either *alpha* or *beta* is "polluted" by being a fluent, the result is a fact; if both are numbers, the result is either true or false. Similarly, (+ *alpha beta*) will produce a new fluent, unless both *alpha* and *beta* are numbers, when the result is a number. For safety's sake, I will not do this for anything but simple arithmetic predicates and functions.

By the way, notice that since facts like (> (− V1 V2) (* 5 V3)) are facts, they must obey Axiom 9. Ernie Davis has shown that this puts some fairly strong contraints on quantities. A quantity gives rise to a time function in every chronicle; given the time, the fluent delivers a unique value. Axiom 9 constrains this function not to jump around wildly, or ">" will chop it into pieces that disobey the axiom. For instance, we cannot have

$$(V\ s\ V0) = \sin \frac{1}{(d\ s) - t0}$$

in some chronicle, since then (> V0 0) will change truth value infinitely often around t0. One way to rule this out is to require that any such function be "finitely piecewise analytic," i.e., that, over any closed interval, the function consist of finitely many fragments that are analytic when extended to the complex plane. ("Analytic" means "infinitely continuously differen-

tiable.") This set of functions is closed under arithmetic operations and differentiation, and always produce well-behaved facts when compared. Restricting ourselves to this set allows for all the discontinuities that quantities exhibit in naive physics, and seems to capture the intuition that normal quantities jump a few times, but basically vary smoothly.

We won't look very hard at requirements like this. We simply let Axiom 9 take its course. But Davis's result is needed to justify the axiom, since otherwise there might not be interesting models satisfying it.

The fundamental event involving fluents is a "vtrans." A (vtrans *v r1 r2*) denotes the event consisting of all occasions when *v* changed from *r1* to *r2*.

Axiom 19:

```
(= (vtrans ?v ?r1 ?r2)
   {[s1, s2]: (and (= (V s1 ?v) ?r1)
                   (= (V s2 ?v) ?r2))})
```

For example, a winch's rotating corresponds to a vtrans of its phase angle. An increase in inflation is a vtrans of INFLATION from one value to another. A change of Presidents is a vtrans of "President of the US" from one statesman to another.

Knowing that a vtrans occurred tells you nothing about *how* it occurred, unless the quantity involved is *continuous*, when we have an intermediate-value axiom:

Axiom 20:

```
(if (continuous ?v)
  (if (Occ ?s1 ?s4 (vtrans ?v ?r1 ?r4))
    (forall (r2 r3)
      (exists (s2 s3)
        (and (= < ?s1 s2 s3 ?s4)
          (if (= < ?r1 r2 r3 ?r4)
            (and (Occ s2 s3 (vtrans ?v r2 r3))
              (forall (s)
                (if (= < s2 s s3)
                  (= < r2 (V s ?v) r3))))
          (if (> = ?r1 r2 r3 ?r4)
            (and (Occ s2 s3 (vtrans ?v r2 r3))
              (forall (s)
                (if (= < s2 s s3)
                  (> = r2 (V s ?v) r3)))))))))))
```

In English, if *v* changes continuously from *r1* to *r4*, and *r2* and *r3* lie between *r1* and *r4*, then there is a time interval in which *v* changes from *r2* to *r3* without going outside the bounds *r2* and *r3*. That is, it spends a certain period in every subinterval between *r1* and *r4*. (The conclusion of the axiom has two very similar conjuncts, one for the case when *v* is increasing, the other for when it is decreasing.)

Vtranses are normally inferred from "potranses." If (potrans *channel v r*) occurs, that means that "*v* was augmented through the given channel by an amount *r*." A potrans is a potential vtrans.

Potranses are intended to capture the way we reason about things like flows into tanks, and other more general changes. Often we know things like these:

I just poured five gallons of reagent into the vat.
I made 5 thousand dollars consulting today.
Decontrolling oil will tend to increase inflation by 5%.

In all these cases, we are given a fact which all by itself would translate directly into a vtrans: the vat's contents increased by five gallons, my net worth increased by $5,000, inflation increased by 5%. But, as we all know, life is not so simple. If you know about a leak in the vat, then the increase is actually 5 gallons MINUS pouring time * rate of leak. The IRS will make sure that my net worth doesn't go up by the amount I made. The Reagan administration hopes that other measures will offset the decontrol of oil.

I adopt a very abstract model of this kind of situation. Many quantities may be thought of as fed by various "channels." These may correspond to physical entities, such as pipes into tanks, but they are never identified with anything physical. They are there almost as a pure technical device to enable us to count potranses. We could not have a potrans of *r* into *v* be an event by itself, since then pouring five gallons into the same vat by two different pipes simultaneously would be just one occurrence of one event.

However, we do assume certain things about channels (which we denote by variables starting with the letter "h"). First, there is the fact (channel-into *h v*), for which we have the axioms:

Axiom 21:
```
(iff (exists (s)
     (and (= < ?s1 ?s2)
          (T s (channel-into ?h ?v))) )
     (exists (r)
          (Occ ?s1 ?s2 (potrans ?h ?v r))))
(if (and (Occ ?s1 ?s2 (potrans ?h ?v ?r1))
         (Occ ?s1 ?s2 (potrans ?h ?v ?r2)))
     (= ?r1 ?r2))
```

That is, that one unique amount "flows" through a given channel into a given quantity over any interval. No amount at all flows unless the channel actually "fed" the quantity at some time during the interval.

The fundamental fact about potranses and channels is then:

Axiom 22:
```
(if (real-valued ?v)
    (iff (Occ ?s1 ?s2 (vtrans ?v ?r1 ?r2))
         (= (- ?r2 ?r1)
            (sumpotrans ?s1 ?s2 ?v
               {h: (exists (s)
                   (and (= < ?s1 ?s2)
                        (T s (channel-into h ?v))) }))))
```

where
```
    (= (sumpotrans ?s1 ?s2 ?v {}) 0)
```

and
```
    (if (and (= (sumpotrans ?s1 ?s2 ?v ?hh) ?sum)
             (Occ ?s1 ?s2 (potrans ?h ?v ?r)))
        (= (sumpotrans ?s1 ?s2 ?v
               (union ?hh {?h}))
           (+ ? sum ?r)))
```

That is, the change in a real-valued fluent over an interval is the sum of the potential changes in it. (sumpotrans *s1 s2 v set-of-channels*) is the sum of all the potranses through the given channels into *v* from *s1* to *s2*.

Taken together, these two axioms enable us to count the contributions from all channels into a quantity over a given time interval.

Potranses are decomposable:

Axiom 23:
```
(iff (Occ ?s1 ?s2 (potrans ?h ?v ?r))
     (forall (s)
        (if (= < ?s1 ?s2)
            (exists (r1 r2)
               (and (Occ ?s1 s (potrans ?h ?v r1))
                    (Occ s ?s2 (potrans ?h ?v r2))
                    (= ?r (+ r1 r2)))))))
```

That is, the potrans through a channel over an interval is the sum of the potranses over each subinterval in a partition of it.

If a quantity is continuous, we can decompose potranses into it another way. If a certain amount "flows" into or out of a quantity, then for any smaller amount, the flow began with a sub-flow of this smaller amount. Formally:

Axiom 24: (An intermediate-value axiom)
(if (continuous ?v)
  (if (Occ ?s1 ?s2 (potrans ?h ?v ?r))
    (forall (r ')
      (if (or (= < 0 r ' ?r)
              (> = 0 r ' ?r))
        (exists (s)
          (and (= < ?s1 s ?s2)
               (Occ ?s1 s (potrans ?h ?v r '))
               (Occ s ?s2 (potrans ?h ?v
                          (− ?r r ')))))))))

Potranses are not instantaneous:

Axiom 25:
(if (T ?s (channel-into ?h ?v))
  (Occ ?s ?s (potrans ?h ?v 0)))

For example, let's say that we had:

(continuous (WATER-VOL TANK1))

(persist S0 (= {h: (channel-into h (WATER-VOL TANK1))}
               {(INFLOW TANK1), (OVERFLOW TANK1)})
          (6 weeks))

That is, only two channels into TANK1 exist. Notice how casually I sneak new constructs into the fact notation. The {x: p} is the set of all x such that p; this is, of course, a fluent. So (= {x: p} {A, B}) is a fact, with an obvious meaning.

The channels have certain special properties. Nothing ever flows in through the overflow, and there is no flow out of it while the level is below some capacity.

(if (Occ ?s1 ?s2
     (potrans (OVERFLOW TANK1) (WATER-VOL TANK1) ?x))
  (= < ?x 0))

(if (TT ?s1 ?s2 (< (WATER-VOL TANK1) (CAP TANK1)))
  (Occ ?s1 ?s2
     (potrans (OVERFLOW TANK1) (WATER-VOL TANK1) 0)))

Notice that the notation allows us to be ambiguous about whether (CAP TANK1) is a fluent or a number. If we decided on the former, we would have to talk about its persistence, so let's pretend it's the latter, and the capacity cannot vary with time. We assume that (> (CAP TANK1) 0). Nothing ever flows out through the inflow:

(if (Occ ?s1 ?s2
     (potrans (INFLOW TANK1) (WATER-VOL TANK1) ?x))
  (> = ?x 0))

The tank is built so that the capacity is never exceeded:

(= < (V ?s (WATER-VOL TANK1)) (CAP TANK1))

Now, let's say that for some S1 and S3 soon after S0, we have:

(= (V S1 (WATER-VOL TANK1)) 0)

(Occ S1 S3 (potrans (INFLOW TANK1) (WATER-VOL TANK1)
     (+ (CAP TANK1) (5 gal))))

Then we can infer that there is a state S2, such that:

(Occ S1 S2 (potrans (INFLOW TANK1) (WATER-VOL TANK1)
     (CAP TANK1)))

(Occ S2 S3 (potrans (INFLOW TANK1) (WATER-VOL TANK1)
     (5 gal)))

(Occ S2 S3 (potrans (OVERFLOW TANK1) (WATER-VOL TANK1)
     (−5 gal)))

Proof: By Axiom 24, there is a flow of (CAP TANK1) through (INFLOW TANK1), followed by a flow of (5 gal). But during this period, the flow through (OVERFLOW TANK1) must be zero, because it can't be positive, and if it were negative, then by Axiom 22 the volume would never get above (CAP TANK1) during this interval, so it would always be zero, a contradiction. Therefore, at the end of this period, the volume will be (CAP TANK1). This is state S2. Now 5 gal flow into the tank. At least 5 gal must flow out, or the tank capacity would be exceeded at S3. If more than 5 gal flowed out (i.e., less than −5 flowed in), then at the end the tank would be less than full. Then by Axiom 20 there must have been an interval between S2 and S3 during which the volume of water declined from (CAP TANK1) to the final value. But during this interval, either the flow into INFLOW would have had to be negative, or the flow into OUTFLOW would have had to be nonzero, both of which are impossible—QED.

5. PLANNING

With what I have talked about so far, we can reason about causal situations, but only as a spectator. In this section, I will talk about how a program might reason about its own actions. Part of my motivation in defining time the way I did was to support reasoning about interesting actions, like preventing events. The flexibility in my event ontology now carries over to the world of actions: An *action* is in this theory an entity, the doing-of which by an agent is an event. Formally, we just need a function (do *agent act*), which is used to name events consisting of an agent performing an action. In this paper, I will completely neglect multiple-agent situations, so the first argument to "do" will be dropped; it will simply map actions into events. Variables denoting actions will begin with "a."

In the first subsection below, I will see how far this takes us. Some actions, like preventing and allowing, just fall out of the ontology. Others, like protecting facts, are still problematical.

In the second subsection, I will explore the notion of "plan." A *plan* is a set of actions, often intended to carry out another action. In one form or another, this idea has been important to several AI researchers, from Sacerdoti (1977) to Schank (1977). I will show how the idea gets translated into my temporal-logic framework.

5.1. The Logic of Action

Many actions are quite straightforward, such as (PUTON x y), which is done whenever the problem solver, or "robot," actually puts x on y. These may correspond to primitive actions the hardware can execute. For each, there will be axioms giving their typical effects as persistences.

But many actions do not fit this mold, such as preventing, allowing, proving, observing, promising, maintaining, and avoiding.

Consider the action "Prevent e," where e is some event. To be concrete, let's have e be the event E1 = "Little Nell mashed by train TR1 in the 5 minutes after state S0." E1 will be prevented if it doesn't happen, assuming it was going to happen if not prevented. (You can't take credit for preventing an unlikely thing.)

This is the sort of thing that past problem solvers have neglected. In the present calculus, it is easy to do. First, we need a notion of event dependence.

Axiom 28:

```
(iff (not-occur-if ?e1 ?e2)
  (and (forall (ch)
        (if (hap ch ?e1) (not (hap ch ?e2))))
    (exists (ch) (hap ch ?e2) )
    (exists (ch) (not_hap ch ?e2)) ) ))
```

Other examples would be possible, but they would mainly illustrate reasoning about continuous functions. My main goal is the exploration of a logical framework, so I will leave this for somebody else.

Continuous quantities do not in general persist at the same value for very long. For example, the quantity of water in a reservoir will change with rain, evaporation and use. We could try to handle this by indicating that the persistence of time (= WATER-LEVEL k) is (say) one day. But this is almost never right. The level is not likely to stay exactly the same for more than an instant, but it is not likely to double in one day, either, no matter how hard it rains.

We need to introduce the "rate" predicate:

Axiom 26:

```
(if (> ?t 0)
  (iff (T ?s (rate ?v ?t ?i))
    (forall (s0 s1)
      (if (and (= < s0 ?s s1)
            (= (- (d s1) (d s0)) ?t))
```

$$\left(\text{elt} \quad \frac{?t}{(V\ s1\ ?v) - (V\ s0\ ?v)} \quad ?i\right)\ )))$$

(rate v t) means that the average rate of change of the quantity v over any interval of length t is within the given interval. The purpose of t is to smooth short-term fluctuations, and to allow us to talk of rates of change of non-continuous quantities. (t is not allowed to be 0, since then we would have to talk about derivatives, which are hard to define given multiple chronicles, and which don't seem to be necessary for "naive" reasoning about time.)

We also need to delimit rates of potransing:

Axiom 27:

```
(if (> ?t 0)
  (iff (T ?s (porate ?h ?v ?t ?i))
    (forall (s0 s1 r)
      (if (and (= < s0 ?s s1)
            (= (- (d s1) (d s0)) ?t)
            (Occ s0 s1 (potrans ?h ?v r)))
        (elt (?r / ?t)
          ?i)))))
```

Rather than infer persistences of values of numerical quantities, we can infer persistences of their rates of change. I will give an example of such an inference in the next section.

where

(iff (hap ?ch ?e)
(exists (s1 s2)
(and (subset [s1, s2] ?ch) (Occ s1 s2 ?e))))

For instance, (not-occur-if E1 E2), where E2 = "I move Little Nell in the 5 minutes after S0."

Now it is easy to define prevention:

Axiom 29:

(= (prevent ?e) (one-of {?a: (not-occur-if (do ?a) ?e)}))

So one may to prevent Little Nell from being mashed is to move her in the next 5 minutes.

In this axiom, I have used "event disjunction," written (one-of {e1 e2 ...}), although this is just syntactic sugar for "sunion." We extend the notation to actions, with the axiom

Axiom 30:

(= (do (one-of {?a1 ... ?aN}))
(one-of {(do ?a1) ... (do ?aN)}))

If there are no actions that E is negatively dependent on, then (do (prevent E)) is the empty set, "never." That is, (prevent E) never happens.

Axiom 31:

(= (do (one-of {})) never)

A finer analysis of impossibility appears below.

As an example, let us take another look at TANK1. Suppose that at S0,

(= (V S0 (WATER-VOL TANK1)) 0),

and (persist S0 (porate (INFLOW TANK1) (WATER-VOL TANK1))
(1 sec) [R1, R2])
T0)

where (> R2 R1 0) and (> T0 (/ (CAP TANK1) R1)).

A little more terminology: Let (anch s e) stand for `{[s, s2]: (Occ s s2 e)}`, the set of all occurrences of e starting in s. Let (culm p e) be

{[s1, s2]: (exists (s)
(and (= < s1 s s2)
(TT s1 s2 p)
(Occ s s2 e)))},

the set of all intervals in which p is true and then e happens. Let (holds p) be {[s, s]: (T s p)}, the set of all point intervals at which p is true.

What we want to find is an action to prevent

E0 = (anch S0
(culm (rate (INFLOW TANK1) WATER-VOL TANK1)
(1 sec) <0, infinity>)
(holds (= (WATER-VOL TANK1) (CAP TANK1)))))

That is, the overflow of the tank that will occur if the water is allowed to run.

We need the action (TURN-OFF (INFLOW TANK1)), defined by this axiom:

Axiom 32:

(pcause (channel-into ?h ?v)
(do (TURN-OFF ?h))
(porate ?h ?v (1 msec) [0, 0])
1 [0, 0]
(1 day))

This says that turning off ?h causes the flow through it to become zero. (The fourth argument, 1, says that the effect begins when the action is done; the fifth, [0, 0], says it happens immediately; and the sixth says it persists for one day. See Axiom 17.)

What we want to prove is that if E1 =

(do (within-time S0 (/ (CAP TANK1) R2)
(TURN-OFF (INFLOW TANK1))))

then

(not-occur-if E1 E0)

where

(= (do (within-time ?s ?t ?a))
{[s1, s2]: (and (Occ s1 s2 (do ?a)
(= < ?s s2)
(= < (- (d s2) (d ?s)) ?t))})

The (within-time s t act) is the action *act* done within t of state s.

The proof that turning off the tank in time will prevent the tank from filling requires three steps: (1) showing that E0 is possible; (2) showing that E0 might not happen; and (3) showing that E0 doesn't happen if E1 does.

The first requirement is met by a proof similar to that of Section 4.

But to make it go, we have to assume there is a chronicle in which the prob-

In English, (occur-if-not e1 e2) means that e2 will occur if e1 does not, and e2 may or may not occur.

We need a little bit more. First, the concept of "event negation," written "nev":

Axiom 35:
```
(iff (Occ ?s1 ?s2 (nev ?e))
     (and (T ?s1 (possible ?e))
          (T ?s2 (not possible ?e)))))
```

where

```
(iff (T ?s (possible ?e))
     (exists (s1 s2 ch)
        (and (elt ?s ch) (elt s2 ch)
             (Occ s1 s2 ?e)) ))
```

That is, the negation of an event occurs if that event becomes impossible. For instance, the negation of "Capitalism collapses by the year 1900" occurred in the last half of the nineteenth century.

Now we can define a related operator on actions, "forgo":

Axiom 36:
```
(iff (Occ ?s1 ?s2 (do (forgo ?a)))
     (Occ ?s1 ?s2 (nev (do ?a))))
```

Forgoing an action means doing something that makes doing the action impossible, which may mean just procrastinating until you have lost your chance. It is hard to forgo an action like "Whistling the Star-Spangled Banner" (except perhaps by having your lips removed), but easy to forgo an action like "Move Little Nell within 5 minutes after S0." If you don't move her within 5 minutes, you've forgone this action.

Now defining allow is straightforward:

Axiom 37:
```
(iff (Occur-if-not (do ?a) ?e)
     ( = (allow ?e) (forgo ?a)))
(if (not (exists (a) (occur-if-not (do ?a) ?e) ))
    ( = (do (allow ?e)) never))
```

Related to allowing and preventing are two other actions, forgoing preventing and forgoing allowing. To forgo preventing something is to make it impossible to prevent; this differs from allowing in that the thing might still fail to happen, whereas according to my definition an event that is allowed actually happens.

lem solver refrains from E1. It is tempting to devise an "Axiom of Free Will," which states that any action is avoidable; there is always a chronicle in which you don't do it. But there are counterexamples. If A1 = "snap your fingers within 1 minute of S0," and A2 = "keep from snapping your fingers for 1 minute after S0," then (one-of {A1, A2}) happens in every chronicle containing S0. There is no easy way to tell if an action is avoidable or not, so we must just provide axioms to tell in every case, which drive:

Axiom 33:
```
(iff (avoidable ?a ?s)
     (exists (ch)
        (and (elt ?s ch) (not (hap ch (do ?a))))))
```

In the present example, we have (avoidable (TURN-OFF (INFLOW TANK1)) S0). E1 is not exactly in this form, but we have the theorem

```
(if (avoidable ?a ?s)
    (avoidable (within-time ?s ?t ?a) ?s))
```

If you don't have to do ?a, you don't have to do it within some time. I won't spend any time on the theory of avoidable actions, since it is probably intricate and essentially trivial.

So there is a chronicle in which E1 does not occur. By Axiom 15 and Axiom 16, in this chronicle the water keeps running, so we can infer that the tank will reach capacity during the lifetime of the water's being on.

The third requirement is met by assuming that E1 happens in CH1, and showing that the fact required for "culm" will be cut off. This is pretty obvious.

The second requirement will follow from the third if we can show that the robot is able to turn off this channel. Clearly, we need an axiom to deduce this. For realism, it should be an axiom giving the exact circumstances under which a channel of this sort can be turned off. (You have to be near enough to the tap implementing the channel that you can reach it before (CAP TANK1) / R2.) But this is all tangential, so I won't give details.

To talk about allowing, I first introduce a notion complementary to not-occur-if:

Axiom 34:
```
(iff (occur-if-not ?e1 ?e2)
     (and (forall (ch)
        (if (not (hap ch ?e1)) (hap ch ?e2)) )
        (exists (ch) (hap ch ?e2) )
        (exists (ch) (not (hap ch ?e2)) )))
```

"primary" and "secondary" actions. A secondary action was one that was executed correctly when another action was executed in a particular way. For instance, in "Pick up this stick without moving any other stick," the subaction "Don't move any other stick" was a secondary modification of the primary action "Pick up this stick." Another word for a secondary action to which the system was committed was *policy*.

In the present calculus, the distinction does not get made this way. Secondary actions are no weirder than some intuitively primary actions. For instance, (avoid a), where a is an action, is simply an action which is done over any interval in which you don't do a. The key distinction now is between composing actions sequentially or in parallel. Before, I defined (seq e1 ... eN) to be an event consisting of all occurrences of e1, ... eN in order. We can define (seq a1 ... aN) in a similar way. For policies, we must define (par a1 ... aN):

Axiom 39:

$$(= (\text{par } ?e1 \ ... \ ?eN)$$
$$\{[s1, s2]: (\text{and } (\text{elt } [s1, s2] \ ?e1)$$
$$(\text{elt } [s1, s2] \ ?e2)$$
$$...$$
$$(\text{elt } [s1, s2] \ ?eN))\})$$

So to do A1 while avoiding doing A2, we do (par A1 (avoid A2)). (Here and from now on, I extend notations defined over events to actions in the obvious way without comment.)

Another secondary action is "protection." Sussman (1975). Intuitively, a fact is protected by a problem solver during an interval if it stays true during that interval. However, I think there is more to protection than this which I do not know how to formalize. There is a distinction between "restorable" and "unrestorable" protections. For instance, if you are protecting the fact, "The fuse (for some keg of dynamite) is not in contact with an open flame," then if the fact becomes false, you have failed. You might try to cut the fuse or run, but it is pointless to move the fuse away from the flame; the damage has been done. In most cases, though, it is worth it to reestablish the protected fact. If I am baby-sitting a child, I try to protect the fact that he is not out of my sight. I do not give up once he is invisible. So the act "Protect *p*," can often be successful, even if *p* lapsed a few times. I do not know how to formalize this. Perhaps you could put a time limit on how long the lapses are. So in the baby case, I have failed if he eludes me for more than 5 minutes, while in the dynamite case the maximum allowable lapse is zero. But this seems arbitrary. The only real criteria for success of actions like these are teleological. I am successful with the baby if he's around and in one piece when his parents arrive. I am successful with the dynamite if there's no explosion, and so forth.

Forgoing allowing an event is more complex. Let A be an action such that not doing it would entail that the event (E) occurs. To forgo allowing it is to forgo forgoing A. This means doing something that makes it impossible not to do A. This differs from preventing in that E might still occur.

Of course, there is a more mundane notion than either preventing or allowing, in which you actively work to make something happen. I will call this "bring-about." It is described by the axiom:

Axiom 38:

$$(= (\text{bring-about } ?e)$$
$$(\text{one-of } \{a: (\text{exists } (r \ i)$$
$$(\text{cause always } (\text{do } a) \ ?e \ r \ i))\}))$$

Bringing-about e is done by doing an action that (always) causes *e*.

James Allen (personal communication) has raised interesting objections to my analysis of allowing and preventing, which I will repeat here, since they are likely to seem weighty to many people:

> Since most things are possible, however improbably, ...every day I allow most of the events that happen in China. If someone was killed there, then since I did 'forgo' the action of boarding a plane, sneaking through customs, and throwing myself in front of the assailant's bullet, I allowed the killing. It gets even worse with prevent. There's probably no way I can ever prevent anything in this world. I have so little control over what happens that whatever I do, there is always some event (however improbable) that is possible and would nullify my efforts.

The first objection, that too many things get allowed, is no trouble for me; one does in fact allow an infinite number of things over any given day, without intending to allow most of them. (Note also that "I allow most of the events...in China," is ambiguous; one certainly does not allow the event consisting of the occurrence of all the events in China over a day.)

The second objection, that too few things get prevented, is more serious. Of course, there is a sense in which one could never *prove* that it is possible to prevent a given event, but this is just another case of excessive caution on the part of formal systems. A dose of non-monotonicity should cure it, one hopes. A deeper problem is that my analysis fails to take probabilities into account. We often plan to prevent something, *knowing* that the plan might not work because of improbable possibilities. But this point applies to all planning, not just prevention. In fact, it applies to a lot of reasoning. As far as I know, there is no theory combining formal logic with probability theory.

In McDermott (1978b), I discussed a classification scheme for actions, used in the NASL problem solver. An important distinction was between

In short, three notions of time were confused: the time of an action, the time of a task, and real-world time ("now"). Now that we have a good analysis of time, we can untangle these things.

The correct analysis of task and action seems to be this: A task is an action to which a problem solver is committed. The action must be well enough specified so that the time of commitment is not needed to know what it is the solver is committed to. Therefore, one may have a task like "Visit Greece," satisfiable any time, but usually the action must be more specified than that: "Put block A on block B within 5 minutes after ...."

A problem solver's being committed to an action is itself a fact. One may alternately have and not have the task of Visiting Greece. Entirely independently, one may actually visit Greece. There are several ways these might interact:

1. You might have the task and not have done the action yet: In this situation, a rational problem solver will devote resources to accomplishing the action, unless more urgent tasks intrude.

2. You might have the task and have already done the action: In this case, the task has succeeded, and nothing more need be done.

3. You might have done the action and not (now) have the task: This is quite common; an example would be insulting or cheering up someone yesterday without intending to now (or possibly then either).

4. You might have a task for an impossible action: This is quite common too. The action may have been possible when the task began; in this case, the task may be said to have *failed*. If it was never possible, it is wishful thinking. Philosophers have argued about whether it is ever rational to have such a task. I see no reason why not, in the case of task failure. It seems natural to say that I have a task of meeting that student at 2:30 yesterday as I promised, but I failed to do it.

The last two categories interact in an interesting way. Often when a task fails, there is some other action that was done *instead* of the intended one. For instance, you have a task of hitting the golf ball into the little hole, and you actually hit it into the big pond. Here is a combination of an action with no task and a task with no (possible) action. There should probably be a predicate relating the two: (did-instead act1 act2) would mean that act1 was a task and act2 was done instead (act1 never occurring). (In the example, act1 would be "Hit the ball into the hole on stroke 2 of hole 6 of the golf game played on Tuesday afternoon," and act2 would be "Hit the ball into the pond on stroke 2 of ....") Rather than examine this in detail, I will just point out an inadequacy in past representations of task networks. Prob-

I have already mentioned several ways of building new actions out of elementary actions, such as seq, par, forgo, and avoid. Another important class of action-building methods are the traditional programming constructs, like loops and conditionals. A complete study of how these composition methods fit together would start to resemble the study of programming-language semantics Milne (1976). I think we should avoid carrying this resemblance to an extreme. In particular, I think the ability to do simple reasoning about plans would go down the drain if variables and assignment were admitted into the plan language. In most loops that people execute, the outside world keeps all the state information. When a condition is no longer true, it will be false in the world, not in the robot's head.

5.2. The Logic of Problem Solving

So far in this section, I have analyzed actions, without ever introducing the concept of an action that "should be performed." A problem solver may be thought of as a program that takes an action that should be performed, a *task*, and performs it. Hence the notion is of some importance.

I tried once before, in McDermott (1977; and 1978b), to develop the logic of tasks. In that system, NASL, the fundamental predicate was (task *name act*) meaning, *name* denotes an action you should do, to wit, *act*. Unfortunately, the action of a task was usually underspecified. For instance, you might have the tasks:

```
(task T1 (PUTON A B))
(task T2 (PUTON B C))
(successor T1 T2)
```

This was where (PUTON B C) was an action that should be performed, but not at an arbitrary time; the "successor" formula constrained it to be after (PUTON A B).

The problem with this approach was that it distorted time relations, in three ways. First, the time dependence between the two actions was not part of their definition. This made it hard to say what "task" meant. If it meant "This action is to be done," then a task assertion didn't describe its action precisely, but only gave a generalization of it. (In the example, (PUTON B C) is a generalization of "Do (PUTON B C) after (PUTON A B).") Second, it wasn't made clear *when* something was a task. As with most previous AI representations, NASL lived only in the present; there was no way to talk about what had been a task or was going to be one. Third, to compensate for this, NASL changed the data base to reflect passing time. When something was no longer a task, it got erased. Unfortunately, when something had been assumed to be a task erroneously, it also got erased. There was no way to distinguish between these two (see Section 1).

lem solvers that maintain such networks (Sacerdoti, 1977; McDermott, 1978b) have failed to maintain a complementary *behavior network* that represents what actually happened (or is going to happen). If every task succeeds, the two networks would be isomorphic; where one had "Task a," the other would have "Did a." But if there was failure, there would be a link between the two networks, from "Task a," to "Did b." This would be more useful than simply recording that a task failed or succeeded, and would help the system in explaining its actions.

This is getting ahead of the story, into implementation and away from logic. We need to say more about logic first.

In both NOAH (Sacerdoti, 1977) and NASL (McDermott, 1978b), a key notion is that of one task being a *sub-task* of another. This means that the sub-task is part of the chosen plan for carrying out the super-task. Every task is either immediately executable or reducible to sub-tasks, which are executable or reducible, and so on.

A problem solver transforms a task into sub-tasks by *choosing* a plan for the task, and asserting that every element of the plan is a sub-task. This choice mechanism is probably not purely logical. That is, it seems that the solver probably doesn't *infer* a set of sub-tasks, but must actively choose them, whatever that means.[8]

The requirement that tasks be reduced to sub-tasks gives rise to a bug. In the current formalism, we can talk of reducing the action A1 to the action (seq B1 B2), but this reduces A to a single sub-task. Is there any sense in which B1 and B2 are sub-tasks of A? It makes sense for B1 to be thought of as a sub-task, but just any execution of B2 will cut no ice. We insist that B2 come after B1. To make B2 a sub-task would get us right back into the difficulty I raised at the beginning of this section, of tasks being underspecified.

The solution is to take as sub-tasks B1 and (just-after B1 B2), where just-after is defined as

Axiom 40:
(= (just-after ?a1 ?a2)
  {[s2, s3]: (and (Occ s2 s3 ?a2)
    (exists (s1) (Occ s1 s2 ?a1)))})

The set of actions {B1, (just-after B1 B2)} is such that A is executed in any chronicle in which they are executed; in other words, this set is a plan for A.

Of course, this is not really a solution to the problem, not until we provide rules for reducing tasks of the form (just-after a1 a2). But at least it suggests that what problem solvers do makes some logical sense. That is, in many cases, there is a well-defined plan for a task, each of whose elements must be done in order to carry out the task.

Another example is the classic plan for achieving a conjunction of facts. To analyze this, we need the action (achieve *prop until-prop*), which means "Bring it about that prop is true from the end of the achieve until the until-prop becomes true." This is clearly needed, for the reasons discussed in Section 3; if you were allowed to achieve things for a single instant, the achievement would usually be worthless. So we have:

Axiom 41:
(iff (Occ ?s1 ?s2 (do (achieve ?p ?q)))
  (and (T ?s2 ?p)
    (forall (s4)
      (if (and (< ?s2 s4) (not (T s4 ?p)))
        (exists (s3)
          (and (< ?s2 s3) (= (< s3 s4)
                (T s3 ?q))))))))

In English, doing (achieve ?p ?q) amounts to bringing it about that ?p, in such a way that if ?p ever becomes false thereafter, ?q must have become false first.

Historically, tasks of the form "achieve *p*" have been very important. Problem solvers like GPS (Ernst, 1969) concentrated on these (in the form of "difference reductions"), and this concentration has persisted. An especially interesting case is where *p* is a conjunction of facts (Sussman, 1975; Sacerdoti, 1977). The problem is, of course, that all the facts must be true at once, when the task is complete, and all too often the plan for one conjunct upsets another.

I will introduce the standard plan for achieving conjunctions after some useful definitions. First, we define "to-do" thus

Axiom 42:
(iff (to-do ?a1 ?a2)
  (one-way (do ?a2) (do ?a1)))

That is, *a2* is a way to do *a1* if (do *a2*) is one way that (do *a1*) can happen. Next, we let (plan *aa*) be the action corresponding to the plan consisting of all the actions *aa*.

Axiom 43:
(iff (Occ ?s1 ?s2 (do (plan ?aa)))
  (and (forall (a)

---

[8]"Perhaps I'm wrong on this. But if this relationship really is inferential, it must be an inference of the form: if p is the best plan for a, then every element of p is a sub-task of a. Unfortunately, it can happen that there are two equally good plans for a. Since we need to introduce a pure choice here, we may as well accept it in general. Amazingly little has been done on the logic of choices in AI. The work on medical diagnosis (e.g., Shortliffe, 1976), and work on choices by problem solvers (e.g., McDermott, 1978b; Doyle, 1980) are two examples.

```
        (if (elt a ?aa)
            (Occbetween ?s1 ?s2 a)) )
        (exists (a s)
          (and (elt a ?aa) (Occ ?s1 s a)) )
        (exists (a s)
          (and (elt a ?aa) (Occ s ?s2 a)) )))
```

That is, a plan is done in any minimal time span in which all of its elements are done. And finally,

```
Axiom 44:
  (iff (T ?s (finished ?a))
    (and (exists (s1 s2)
      (and (Occ s1 s2 (do ?a))
        (< s2 ?s)) )
      (forall (s1 s2)
        (if (= < ?s s2)
          (not (Occ s1 s2 (do ?a))) ))))
```

That is, an action is finished when its last execution is past.

The following theorem then states that one way to achieve a conjunction is to achieve each of its conjuncts, in such a way that each conjunct remains true until the other is achieved.

```
(if (and ( = ?a1 (achieve ?p1 (& ?q (finished ?a2))))
         ( = ?a2 (achieve ?p2 (& ?q (finished ?a1)))))
  (to-do (achieve (& ?p1 ?p2) ?q)
    (plan {?a1, ?a2})))
```

Proof: Assume that the task is to achieve P1 and P2 until Q, and let A1 and A2 be two actions that satisfy the antecedent. Assume that (do (plan {A1, A2})) occurs from S0 to S2. I will show that (do (achieve (& P1 P2) Q)) also occurs during that interval. According to Axiom 41, we must show that (T S2 (& P1 P2)), and that (& P1 P2) remains true until Q.

To show the first part, without loss of generality assume that A1 finishes before A2 (or no later). (See Figure 4.)

```
     ——A1 ->      (& P1 P2)        Q       (-P1)
SO       S1       S2               S3       S4
     ——— A2       ->
```

Then A2 is not finished until at least S2, so P1 must be true from S1 to S2. But P2 is true at S2, so (T S2 (& P1 P2)).

To show the second part, let S4 be an arbitrary state after S2 in which (& P1 P2) is false. Then either P1 or P2 is false there. Assume without loss of generality that it is P1. By Axiom 41, there must be a state S3 after S1 in which (& Q (finished A2)) is true, and hence Q is true. This must come after S2, since until then A2 is not finished—QED.

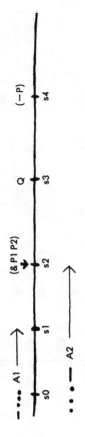

Figure 4. Conjunction Proof

There is one suspicious feature of this plan for conjunction achievement: there is no finite non-circular term for naming either sub-task. This rules out certain naive implementations of a problem solver based on this logic. A deeper problem is that there may be cases in which there are no actions satisfying the antecedent of my theorem, for instance if ?p1 and ?p2 contradict each other, or they require large amounts of a finite resource, or any of several other cases obtains. It is an open problem how one would go about proving the feasibility or unfeasibility of this plan.

The final problem to be examined in the light of this logic is the "plan decomposition" problem (pointed out by Eugene Charniak, personal communication). When you are writing a plan, say to paint something (Charniak, 1976), you have a choice whether to represent a step as "Dip brush in paint," or "Achieve (paint on brush)." The latter is the purpose of the former, but the former is the most common way of achieving this purpose, so common that it seems wrong not to make it part of the plan. But if the paint in the can is low, the usual step will not work. You will have to tilt the can and grope with the brush, or go buy more paint. On the other hand, it seems wasteful to make "Achieve (paint on brush)" the normal plan step, and rederive the normal sequence every time.

The solution seems to be to store two things: the usual plan, and a proof that it works. The proof in this case would have one fragment that said: "If you dip the brush in the paint, and there is paint deep enough to be dipped into, then you will get paint on the brush. If there is paint on the brush, then stroking the wall with it will get paint on the wall. . . ." The proof is not consulted until the plan fails, that is, until the "dip" step fails to bring about partial immersion of the brush. Then the proof would be consulted to see why this was done. The reason found would mention the bridging fact that "there is paint on the brush." The problem solver could then look for other ways to bring this about.

This sketch requires a lot of work to fill out, but I doubt that problem solvers will be robust and efficient until it is done. One big piece of work is to choose a format for these "proofs" that enables easy access to the relevant fragments. Presumably the proof would be broken into pieces festooned over the plan.

6. SKETCH OF AN IMPLEMENTATION

Up to now, I have avoided discussing data structures and algorithms. If Hayes (1979a) is right, I would be justified in avoiding them for a few more years. But I have not been able to keep from thinking about how these ideas would be expressed in a working program, and I think an occasional glimpse in that direction is necessary for even the most dedicated "AI logician." We are engaged in notational engineering, not philosophy.

An implementation must be able to do interesting, useful inferences. What is interesting and useful will vary from application to application. The one I am most interested in is problem solving. A problem solver must exploit the tree of possible chronicles, since it must reason about consequences of different courses of action. It must also be able to reason about the interactions between its actions and inanimate processes, and among its own actions. A typical interaction is the detection that a planned action will cause a persisting fact to cease.

Consider an example from (Sacerdoti, 1977). Say a problem solver has the tasks of painting the ladder and painting the ceiling. If it works on "paint the ceiling" first, it will notice that the ladder must be climbable, and that it is currently climbable. Therefore, it will persist in being climbable for years. The problem solver concludes that this state will last until the ceiling is painted, which will take a few hours. Now it turns to thinking about painting the ladder. It realizes that this will cause "ladder climbable" to cease, and remain untrue for a day (assuming paint dries this slowly). It then should see that it lacks sufficient information to decide if this is a problem, since it does not know whether it will paint the ladder before painting the ceiling. Since the situation is under its control, it imposes an order that didn't exist before, and decides to paint the ceiling first.

This is similar to Sacerdoti's algorithm, but with some important differences. First, the kind of retrieval that occurs is more generally applicable. If we found out someone was coming to repossess the ladder, exactly the same reasoning would go on, up to the point where we imposed extra order. A different response would be necessary if one of the events was outside our control. But the retrieval problem is the same.

Second, I do not model an action in terms of simple "addlists" and "deletelists," that is, lists of facts that change in truth value as a result of that action. Painting the ladder renders it unclimbable, but only for a while; we could always paint the ceiling tomorrow. In fact, there is no guarantee that we will catch the problem before we have already painted the ladder. Even if we do catch it, there may be some pressing reason why we should

paint the ladder first; for instance, we may want to paint the ladder blue, and the ceiling green, and the only way to get green may be to mix our blue with some yellow we have lying around.

In fact, there will in general be many factors on each side of an ordering decision, and I am skeptical that one can casually decide on the basis of one of them how the plan ought to go. Instead, it seems more reasonable to try simulating the plan both ways whenever there is an important uncertainty as to order or outcome (Wilensky, 1980).

For this to work, the implementation must recognize the existence of multiple chronicles. It might seem that we want to keep a description of every relevant chronicle, but, of course, there are an infinite number of chronicles, each with an infinite description; what we really want is a partial description of the typical element of an interesting set of chronicles. For instance, the set of all chronicles in which I fail to prevent Little Nell from being mashed by the oncoming train would be of (somewhat morbid) interest, as would the set of chronicles in which I succeed. A partial description is just a data structure that supports information retrieval, like the action-conflict detection I described before. Let us call this kind of data structure a "time line," without reading too much into the phrase. Every set of chronicles will be represented by a data structure called a *chronset*, which consists of a defining characteristic of the chronicles in the set, plus a time line for accessing the events and facts that occur in those chronicles.

Chronsets are hierarchically organized. When the problem solver detects an important uncertainty in a chronicle, it creates two (or more) new chronsets which represent the different outcomes. Almost everything true in the original chronset is true in the new ones; if I am on my way to visit Grandma when I hear Nell's cry for help, then the fact that I will see Grandma tonight is still true in both chronsets. Furthermore, the same chronset can be split more than one way. Before getting involved with Nell at all, I might have been speculating on whether nuclear war would occur by the year 2000, and what that would mean for civilization. The chronsets connected with this possibility have nothing to do with Nell.

Eventually, only one of a pair of alternative chronsets turns out to correspond to reality. This one becomes the new basis for further planning.

So, however time lines are implemented, they will have to be able to inherit properties from "superlines" belonging to higher chronsets. A flexible model of this kind of inheritance is the "data pool" model, developed in Sussman (1972) and McDermott (1981b). This allows a distributed data structure to be labeled so that different parts are "visible" in different data pools. Each data pool will correspond to a chronset. So, rather than have different time lines, we can have one big time line, with some parts invisible in some chronsets.

The next question is how time lines are implemented. The idea I am currently pursuing is that they are modeled "spatially," that is, using much

cle: We will call an event or fact being modeled in a time line in this way an *occurrence*.

With these restrictions, it makes sense to apply techniques for mapping time. The existence of chronsets merely forces there to be many competing maps.

Before I discuss time lines in more detail, let me issue a warning about the "real" chronicle and its relatives. I am convinced that no hint of this concept must appear in the logic, because it would lead to some serious paradoxes and a breakdown of the system. (I thank Ernie Davis for discussions leading to this conclusion.) For instance, how do you represent that something is inevitable? In the logic so far, you must say that it will happen in all chronicles. It seems tempting to explore the alternative way of putting this, that the thing will happen in the real chronicle. After all, what can it matter that something happens in an unreal chronicle? But then everything that actually happens was inevitable.

The only conclusion is that the logic we use makes some extreme assumptions about time, which our implementation resolutely ignored. If this bothers you because you think logic ought to encompass everything that goes on in a robot, then this should convince you that it can't. If this bothers you because you want to know who is right, the logic or the implementation, my guess is that the implementation is right, but so what? Neither alternative is very palatable, but neither can be neglected. A system that accepted the idea of many futures would have no grounds for any decision; but neither would a system that accepted the idea of one future. The trick is to resonate between them, betting that there is one real future that matters, relying on a logic that presupposes the opposite.

One other topic falls under the "Implementation" heading. A *data dependency* is a note of the support that an assertion has, expressed as a list of other assertions (Doyle, 1979). In the implementation I am describing, there will be two kinds of dependency: the support for the contention *that* an occurrence will take place in a chronset; and the support for the time *when* it occurs in that chronset. The former is relatively straightforward. A cause will be linked to the task. A bad occurrence will be linked to the task that prevents it. The only complication is that these links may have to cross chronset boundaries; for example, a task might be there because in another chronset, something bad will happen.

The second kind is more problematic. Times of occurrence are not asserted, but constrained. As constraints accumulate, they become more precisely known, just as in McDermott (1980b). How to erase such constraints is still an open problem in the spatial domain, and may also be a problem in the temporal domain.

Consider how this data-dependency system would solve the "Little Nell" problem I started with. Once the system (Dudley) has reasoned out the causal sequence involving the train and Nell, and sees that a bad event is

the same machinery as in a spatial reasoner like that of McDermott (1980b), Davis (1981), and McDermott (1981c).

In our spatial reasoner, every entity is modeled as a "frob"—a frame of reference attached to an object. The frobs are arranged in a graph. If the position of an object is known (fairly precisely) with respect to another object, its position with respect to that object's frame is stored explicitly; otherwise, it is computed when needed. Questions such as, How far is it from A to B? are answered by computation on the coordinates of A and B. Questions such as, What object is near A? are answered by searching through a *discrimination tree* of objects stored with respect to A (McDermott, 1981c, d).

Our working hypothesis is that events and facts can be modeled as frobs. The reason this approach may fail is that the frob graphs may just be too complicated; however, it is hard to think of a more promising approach. (But see Allen, 1981.)

In general, a frob's position and other features are "fuzzy," that is, known only to within an interval. Hence we call the aggregation of frobs a *fuzzy map*. The fuzziness is entirely due to uncertainty. The position of the object in the real world is assumed definite. (Objects are not quantum mechanical.) If an event is to be thought of as a frob, there must be a sense in which it is a definite object with uncertain attributes. Of course, this is not what an event is at all. Instead, it is an infinite collection of time intervals. The time during which I sang the Star Spangled Banner is a meaningless quantity, unless you mean the fuzzy interval of all dates from my first singing of it to my last. But this interval will never be reduced to a point by further information.

On the other hand, there does seem to be a notion of temporary uncertainty that gets resolved. I am not sure what time the plumber is coming tomorrow; after she had been here, I am sure. This notion is completely outside the realm of the logic I developed in Sections 1 through 5. Consider a problem solver at state S0, with a time line including tomorrow, and an event "Plumber comes." It is simply wrong to say that there is uncertainty in what time the plumber is going to come in the day following S0, because *there are lots of 24-hour periods following S0*, one per chronicle. Twenty-four hours later, there will be an infinite number of problem solvers, in an infinite number of incomparable states following S0, each with a slightly different idea of when the plumber came.

So for its own sanity, a problem solver is going to need the notion of the *real* chronicle, the one that is actually going to happen. Actually, for completeness, we will have every chronset contain a unique *realest* chronicle, which must be the real chronicle if the chronset contains it. The uncertainty surrounding the exact time of an event in a given chronset is then the uncertainty about the occurrence of the event in the realest chronicle in the set. And this only makes sense for events that happen at most once in a chroni-

going to happen, it looks for a plan to prevent it. Assuming it finds a candidate, it sets up an alternative chronset in which this plan is successfully executed. (See Figure 5.) It does an analysis of feasibility, and decides that this chronset probably corresponds to reality more closely than the one it started with. However, the data dependency supporting the assertion that "Move Nell" is a task specifies that the occurrence of "Nell is mashed" in the other, original chronset as the justification of the task. It is irrelevant that this chronset is not expected to be realized.

It *is* relevant that in the alternative chronset, she gets mashed. This assertion will be supported by a record of the causal argument (involving the persistence of being tied up, the train schedule, and so on) that led to Dudley's alarm in the first place. If this argument is upset, say by a new assertion that Dick Daring is planning to free Nell in two minutes (thus terminating a crucial persistence), then it is no longer true, even in the alternative chronicle, that Nell is in danger, and the assertion "I have the task of moving Nell" will disappear from Dudley's data base.

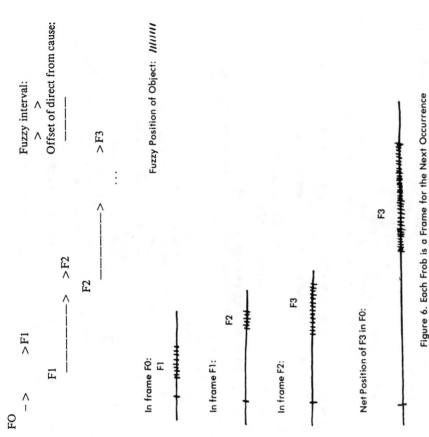

Figure 6. Each Frob is a Frame for the Next Occurrence

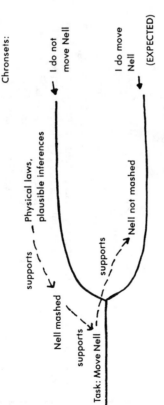

Figure 5. Tree of Chronsets for the Dudley-Nell Problem

As another illustration, let me sketch how this system would handle one straightforward kind of inference—system simulation. This kind of inference is the result of applying ecause and pcause rules to see how a system will behave. That is, starting in some state, we use these rules to predict future states, then start from there to predict more states, and so forth. Each application of a rule creates a new frob, corresponding to the caused effect. This frob will represent a persistence or event. It is also a frame of reference for further simulation; its effects will be frobs fuzzily located in its frame, and so on. Figure 6 shows how each occurrence is located more or less fuzzily, at some offset in the frame of its cause. Each effect then serves to answer queries, like "How soon after F1 will F3 occur?" This requires translating F3's fuzzy coordinates back into frame F0 for comparison. The more steps of translation, the fuzzier the coordinates get.

Just storing the coordinates does not suffice for answering questions such as "What's the first occurrence of...after F1?" This requires other sorts of indexing. (McDermott, 1981d)

This sketch is intended only to suggest what one might do. I feel that raw simulation of this sort is actually of little value, except for simple loop-free systems. If a loop is encountered, the unwary simulator will itself go into a loop. Instead, it should be on the lookout for "loopy" patterns, such as a quantity increasing twice, and try to step back and draw more interesting conclusions. I can only point at this problem here, and not hope to solve it.[9]

[9]I have implemented a preliminary version of a program for reasoning about simple mechanisms, including some with loops, and will report on it in a later paper.

7. CONCLUSIONS

I set out to develop a temporal logic which captured the openness and continuity of time. To this end, the basic ontology had to include states arranged into a branching set of continua, the "chronicle tree." Doing this enabled us to state facts about causes and effects, continuous change, and plans. In many cases, we could make useful deductions about the course of events. Here is a list of some of the situations considered:

- Causal sequences, including infinite loops
- Continuous change up to some threshold
- Actions taken to prevent the operation of causal systems
- Conflicts among actions done in the wrong order (cf. Sacerdoti, 1977)
- Changes in one's plans forced (or not forced) by changing circumstances

I look at some of these systems more formally than others, for which I emphasized implementational considerations.

I have found that logic and implementation fertilize each other. One often has a vague notion of what he wants a program to do, plus a pile of special cases that don't fit together too well. Sometimes one goes ahead and implements the special cases. I urge consideration of the alternative: temporarily to ignore hard-nosed programming issues, and try to achieve an elegant synthesis of the special cases in the logical domain. If you fail, it is likely that the logical bugs holding you up would have caused the program to exhibit bizarre behavior anyway. If you succeed, the results can often be transferred back to the programming domain. The ontology of the logic will be reflected in the data structures of the program (as chronicles gave rise to chronsets); the commonly encountered proofs will give rise to inference algorithms, and records of them become data dependencies, which help to make the program robust and less opaque. Of course, the program will fail to make inferences the logic allows (and hence, via non-monotonicity, jump to conclusions the logic forbids), but humans have these limitations too.

REFERENCES

Allen, J. *Maintaining knowledge about temporal intervals* (Technical Report TR86). University of Rochester, Department of Computer Science, 1981.

Charniak, E. *A framed PAINTING: the representation of a common sense knowledge fragment.* Working Paper 28, Fondazione Dalle Molle, 1976.

Charniak, E. A common representation for problem-solving and language-comprehension information. *Artificial Intelligence,* 1981 *16* (3), 225–255.

Davidson, D. In Rescher (Ed.), *The logical form of action sentences.* Pittsburgh, PA: Pittsburgh University Press, 1967.

Davis, E. *Organizing Spatial Knowledge* (Technical Report 193). Yale University, Computer Science Department, 1981.

Doyle, J. *A truth maintenance system* (Memo 521). MIT AI Laboratory, 1979.

Doyle, J. *A model for deliberation, action, and introspection* (TR 581). MIT AI Laboratory, 1980.

Ernst, G. W. & Newell, A. *GPS: A Case Study in Generality and Problem Solving.* New York: Academic Press, 1969.

Fikes, R. & Nilsson, N. J. STRIPS: A new approach to the application of theorem proving to problem solving. *Artificial Intelligence,* 1971 2, 189–208.

Goodman, N. The problem of counterfactual conditionals. *Journal of Philosophy,* 1947, *44,* 113–128.

Hayes, P. *The Naive Physics Manifesto.* Unpublished, 1979.

Hayes, P. *Ontology for Liquids.* Unpublished, 1979.

Hendrix, G. Modeling simultaneous actions and continuous processes. *Artificial Intelligence,* 1973, 4, 145–180.

Hewitt, C. *Description and theoretical analysis (using schemata) of PLANNER: a language for proving theorems and manipulating models in a robot* (Technical Report 258). MIT, AI Laboratory, 1972.

Johnson-Laird, P. N. Mental models in cognitive science. *Cognitive Science,* 1980, *4* (1), 71–115.

Lewis, D. K. *Counterfactuals.* Oxford: Basil Blackwell, 1973.

McCarthy, J. *Programs with common sense.* In Minsky (Ed.), 1968.

McCarthy, J. Circumscription: a non-monotonic inference rule. *Artificial Intelligence,* 1980, *13* (1, 2).

McDermott, D. V. *Flexibility and efficiency in a computer program for designing circuits* (Technical Report 402). MIT, AI Laboratory, 1977.

McDermott, D. V. Tarskian semantics or, no notation without denotation!. *Cognitive Science,* 1978, 2 (3). (a)

McDermott, D. V. Planning and acting. *Cognitive Science,* 1978, 2 (2), 71–109. (b)

McDermott, D. V. & Doyle, J. Non-monotonic logic I. *Artificial Intelligence,* 1980, *13* (1, 2). (a)

McDermott, Drew V. Spatial inferences with ground, metric formulas on simple objects (Technical Report 173). Yale University, Computer Science Department, 1980. (b)

McDermott, D. V. Non-monotonic logic II: non-monotonic modal theories. *Journal of ACM,* 1981. (Also Yale CS TR 174). (a)

McDermott, D. V. *Contexts and data dependencies: a synthesis.* Submitted to IEEE Transactions on Pattern Analysis and Machine Intelligence, 1981. (b)

McDermott, D. V. & Davis, E. Planning and executing routes through uncertain territory. Submitted to *Artificial Intelligence,* 1981. (c)

McDermott, D. V. *Finding objects with given spatial properties.* (Technical Report 195). Yale University, Computer Science Department, 1981. (d)

Mendelson, E. *Introduction to Mathematical Logic.* Van Nostrand, 1964.

Milne, R. & Strachey, C. *A Theory of Programming Language Semantics.* Halsted Press, 1976.

Minsky, M. (Ed.). *Semantic Information Processing.* Cambridge, MA: The MIT Press, 1968.

Montague, R. On the nature of certain philosophical entities. *The Monist,* 1960, *53,* 159–194. (Also in Montague, 1974.)

Montague, R. In R. Thomason, (Ed.), *Formal Philosophy.* New Haven, CT: Yale University Press, 1974.

Moore, R. *Reasoning about knowledge and action* (Technical Report 191). SRI AI Center, 1980.

Prior, A. *Past, Present, and Future*. Oxford University Press, 1967.

Reiter, R. A logic for default reasoning. *Artificial Intelligence*, 1980, *13* (1, 2).

Rescher, N. *The Logic of Decision and Action*. Pittsburgh, PA: Pittsburgh University Press, 1967.

Rescher, N. & Urquhart, A. *Temporal Logic*. New York: Springer-Verlag, 1971.

Rieger, C. The commonsense algorithm as a basis for computer models of human memory, inference, belief and contextual language comprehension. *Proc. Theoretical Issues in Nat. Lang. Processing Workshop*. Boston, MA, 1975.

Rieger, C. An organization of knowledge for problem solving and language comprehension. *Artificial Intelligence*, 1976, 1.

Sacerdoti, E. *A Structure for Plans and Behavior*. American Elsevier Publishing Company, Inc., 1977.

Schank, R. C. *Conceptual Information Processing*. American Elsevier Publishing Company, 1975.

Schank, R. C. & Abelson, R. P. *Scripts, Plans, Goals, and Understanding*. Hillsdale, NJ: Lawrence Erlbaum Associates, 1977.

Shortliffe, E. H. *Computer-Based Medical Consultations—MYCIN*. American Elsevier, 1976.

Sussman, G. J. & McDermott, D. V. From planning to conniving—a genetic approach. *Proc. FJCC 41*, 1171. IFIPS, 1972.

Sussman, G. J. *A Computer Model of Skill Acquisition*. American Elsevier Publishing Company, Inc., 1975.

Wilensky, R. *Metaplanning*. (Memo UCB/ERL M80/33). Berkeley Department of Computer Science, 1980.

Towards a General Theory of Action and Time

James F. Allen
Computer Science Department, University of Rochester, Rochester, NY 14627, U.S.A.

Recommended by Yorick Wilks

ABSTRACT

A formalism for reasoning about actions is proposed that is based on a temporal logic. It allows a much wider range of actions to be described than with previous approaches such as the situation calculus. This formalism is then used to characterize the different types of events, processes, actions, and properties that can be described in simple English sentences. In addressing this problem, we consider actions that involve non-activity as well as actions that can only be defined in terms of the beliefs and intentions of the actors. Finally, a framework for planning in a dynamic world with external events and multiple agents is suggested.

1. Introduction

The concept of action arises in at least two major subareas of artificial intelligence, namely, natural language processing and problem solving. For the most part, the formalisms that have been suggested in each subarea are independent of each other and difficult to compare, although there is recent work that attempts to merge work from both areas [1]. Even considering such work, however, there is presently no computational theory of action that is sufficiently powerful to capture the range of the meanings and distinctions expressible in English. The primary goal of this paper is to suggest a formalism that is considerably more expressive than current theories of action and to explore its use in defining the meanings of English sentences that describe actions and events.

A secondary, but important, requirement on the formalism is that it should be a useful representation for action reasoning (i.e., problem solving). Some effort will be made to describe how the representation could be used by a planning or plan recognition system. This is essential to the natural language research as well, because problem-solving techniques are being used more and more in our models of language comprehension (e.g., see [2]). While interest in this approach is growing, progress is inhibited by inadequate representations of actions and plans.

There are at least three major difficulties with nearly all existing models of action in AI. Such models cannot represent:

- actions that involve non-activity (e.g., "I stood on the corner for an hour");
- actions that are not easily decomposable into subactions (e.g., "I spent the day hiding from George");
- actions that occur simultaneously and many interact with each other.

The theory outlined below will allow all three of these situations to be represented. Each problem will be examined in detail below when discussing previous work.

1.1. Relevant work

Relevant work on this problem can be divided into three broad categories: representations for natural language systems, problem-solving systems, and work in linguistics and philosophy.

The most common formulation for actions in natural language systems is based on case grammar [3]. Each action is represented by a set of assertions about the semantic roles the noun phrases play with respect to the action denoted by the verb. Such a formalism is useful for interpreting the semantic structure of sentences, but doesn't address the issue of what an action is, or what inferences can be made from the fact that an action occurred. Typically there is only a simple temporal, or causal, ordering on the actions, which is not heavily used. Such representations only work in situations where actions are simply related to each other and no uncertainty exists.

Work in problem solving has used more sophisticated models of action and time. The most influential theory in this work has been the situation calculus [4]. The world is represented as a set of situations, each describing the world at a single instant in time. An action is a function from one situation to another, and can be described by a set of prerequisites on the initial situation and a set of effects that will hold in the final situation. While this model has been extremely useful in modeling physical actions by a single agent in an otherwise static world, it cannot easily be extended to account for simultaneous actions and events. For example, the action described by the sentence, "I walked to the store while juggling three balls," seems to be composed of the action of walking to the store and the action of juggling three balls. It is not clear how such a composite action would be defined if we view an action as a function from one instantaneous world description to another. Furthermore, since an action in the situation calculus is equated with change, actions that involve no activity, or restore the world to its original state (e.g., running around a track), cannot be modeled.

The most common implementation inspired by the situation calculus is the

Artificial Intelligence **23** (1984) 123–154
0004-3702/84/$3.00 © 1984, Elsevier Science Publishers B.V. (North-Holland)

state space model. The world is described by a data base containing what is presently true, and actions are simulated by adding and deleting facts from the data base. This model suffers from all the above criticisms of the situation calculus and in addition has no model of the past or the future.

None of these formulations can describe the following simple situation. In the blocks world, assume we have two actions, PUSHR, push to the right, and PUSHL, push to the left. Let us also assume that the effect of each of these actions is that the block moves one unit in the appropriate direction. But if two robots perform a PUSHR and a PUSHL simultaneously on the same block, the block doesn't move. Since we cannot express or reason about the simultaneity of actions in any of the above theories, we cannot express this situation. The best we can do will be to have the block oscillate as the robots push alternately.

McDermott [5] introduces a notion of event that is general enough to address the three problems above. To a first approximation, our two approaches are compatible; however, major differences exist. Some of these differences come about as a result of the difference in intended application, and some as a result of different underlying assumptions in our temporal logics. These issues will be discussed as they become relevant.

Work in linguistics and philosophy has provided many insights for this research, although the theories typically lack a computational viewpoint. The major influences on this paper come from Mourelatos [6], Jackendoff [7]. and Goldman [8].

Mourelatos presents a detailed analysis of the different classes of occurrences describable in English, and his terminology will be adopted here. The term *occurrence* is used to describe the class of all events, processes, actions. activities, and accomplishments. This effectively includes all forms of sentence meanings except for assertions of states such as "The building is red" or "I am ten years old". The class of occurrences is further subdivided by Mourelatos. and we will consider this subcategorization later as it becomes relevant.

Goldman presents a detailed theory of human action. At this stage, we need only examine the problem of action individuation, which is demonstrated by the question: if I pull the trigger of a gun, thereby shooting my friend. how many actions have I performed? One view is that only one action is performed. and that it exemplifies two action types [9], pulling the trigger and shooting my friend. Goldman's view is that two distinct—though intimately related—actions are performed. The latter view is adopted here as it provides for a simpler semantics. Thus a physical situation will typically be described as a set of distinct occurrences and actions. and actions may be distinct even if they have the same agent and occur at the same time.

1.2. The proposed theory

The world is described by a set of temporally qualified assertions outlining what is known about the past, present, and future. This includes descriptions of both static and dynamic aspects of the world. The static aspects are captured by *properties* (e.g., Cleo owning a car) that hold over stretches of time. The dynamic aspects are captured by *occurrences* (e.g., Cleo running a race) which describe change of forms of resistance to change over stretches of time. The distinction between properties and occurrences is usually obvious. but situations do arise where it is quite subtle. The most subtle cases arise from situations that can be described from either a static or dynamic perspective. For instance, adopting an example from Jackendoff [7]. we could describe the situation in which a light was on in a house all night by the static description, "the light was on all night", or by the dynamic description, "the light remained on all night". The only difference here appears to be that the latter suggests that it might have been otherwise. In most cases, however, the static/dynamic distinction will be straightforward.

It should be clear that a temporal logic is necessary to support this theory. Time plays a crucial role, and cannot be relegated to a secondary consideration as in most natural language systems or hidden in a search process as in most problem-solving systems. The temporal logic described below is based on temporal intervals, and denies the standard view of mapping time to points on the real number line.

Given a temporal logic, we address how *occurrences* can be defined. In particular, what do we know when we know an occurrence has occurred? In problem-solving systems, actions are described by prerequisites (i.e.. what must be true to enable the action), effects (what must be true after the action has occurred), and decomposition (how the action is performed, which is typically a sequence of subactions). While such knowledge is crucial for reasoning about what actions to perform in a given situation, it does not define what we know when we know an action has occurred. To clarify this, consider the simple action of turning on a light.

There are few physical activities that are a necessary part of performing the action of turning on a light. Depending on the context, vastly different patterns of behavior can be classified as the same action. For example, turning on a light usually involves flipping a light switch, but in some circumstances it may involve tightening the light bulb (in the basement) or hitting the wall (in an old house). Although we have knowledge about how the action can be performed, this does *not* define what the action is. The key defining characteristic of turning on the light seems to be that the agent is performing some activity which will cause the light, which was off when the action started, to become on when the action ends. An important side effect of this definition is that we could recognize an observed pattern of activity as "turning on the light" even if we had never seen or thought about that pattern previously.

Thus, we want a level of causal explanation that characterizes the consequences one can draw from a sentence describing an action. or, more generally, an occurrence. Such a description would not replace or subsume the prerequisite/effect/method characterization of actions, although there will be some overlap. For example, the effects of an action should be included, or be derivable from, the causal definition of the action. Some prerequisites would appear in the definition of an action, though others, dealing with an agent's abilities, might not be part of the action definition. Similarly, some parts of a method might be necessary in an action definition, but for the most part, method descriptions do not define what an action is. At a few places in the paper, we shall consider how problem-solving knowledge about actions can be integrated into the proposed framework.

1.3. An outline of the paper

Section 2 introduces an interval-based temporal logic and discusses properties than can hold over intervals. In Section 3, a logic for occurrences is introduced. Occurrences are subdivided into processes and events. Section 4 introduces the notion of action and makes the distinction between definitional knowledge of an action and generational knowledge which is needed for planning actions. Section 5 deals with intentional action and provides a semi-formal notion of plans and of an agent committing to a plan. The paper concludes with an analysis of the meaning of the verb 'to hide', using the formalism developed.

The following conventions will be used throughout. Predicates and constants will be in upper case, and variables will be in lower case. A full range of connectives and quantifiers will be used in their standard interpretation. I use:

& conjunction,
v disjunction,
~ negation,
⇒ implication,
⇔ equivalence,
∀ universal quantifier,
∃ existential quantifier,
∃! existence of a unique object.

Any variables that appear with no quantifier are assumed to be universal variables with global scope. I shall often resort to typing variables as in a many-sorted logic. In these cases, the type of the variable will be indicated by its name. Scoping of operators and quantifiers will be indicated by use of parentheses or by indentation of formulas. In general, quantifiers are assumed to be scoped as broadly as possible.

2. A Temporal Logic

Before we can characterize events and actions. we need to specify a temporal logic. The logic described here is based on temporal intervals rather than time points. This approach arises from the observation that the only times we can identify are times of occurrences and properties. For any such time, say the time I was opening the door, it appears to be possible to look more closely at the occurrence and decompose it; hence, times can be decomposed into subtimes. In other words, it seems that there is always a more detailed causal explanation if one cares, and is able, to look for it. A good analogy, then, is that times correspond to intervals on the real line. If we accept this, why not allow instantaneous time points as well? First, they do not appear to be necessary. Second, instantaneous time points will present difficulties with the semantics of our logic. If one allows time points, one must consider whether intervals are open or closed. For example, consider the time of running a race, R, and the time following after the race, AR. Let P be the proposition representing the fact that the race is on; P is true over R, and ~P is true over AR. We want AR and R to meet in some sense. Whether both ends of the intervals are open or closed, AR and R must either share a time point or allow time between them. Thus we have a choice between inconsistency or truth gaps, i.e., either there is a time when both P and ~P are true. or there is a time when neither P nor ~P is true. One solution to this problem is to stipulate by convention that intervals are open at the lower end and closed at the upper end, but then every interval has only a single endpoint. The artificiality of this solution reinforces the argument against allowing points. Events that appear to refer to a point in time (e.g., finishing a race) are considered to be implicitly referring to another event's beginning or ending. Thus time 'points' will be considered to be very small intervals. This will be made more precise below.

The logic is a typed first-order predicate calculus, in which the terms fall into many categories. The following three are needed at present:
- terms of type TIME-INTERVAL denoting time intervals:
- terms of type PROPERTY, denoting propositions that can hold or not hold during a particular time;
- terms corresponding to objects in the domain.

There are a small number of predicates. One of the most important is HOLDS, which asserts that a property holds (i.e., is true) during a time interval. Thus

$$\text{HOLDS}(p, t)$$

is true if and only if property p holds during t. As a subsequent axiom will state, this is intended to mean that p holds at every subinterval of t as well. Note that if we had introduced HOLDS as a modal operator we would not need to introduce properties into our ontology. We have not followed this route, however, since it seems more complicated in the later development of occurrences.

There is a basic set of mutually exclusive primitive relations that can hold between temporal intervals. Each of these is represented by a predicate in the logic. These relationships are summarized in Fig. 1.
- DURING($t1$, $t2$): time interval $t1$ is fully contained within $t2$:

Relation	Symbol	Symbol for inverse	Pictoral example
X before Y	<	>	XXX YYY
X equal Y	=	=	XXX / YYY
X meets Y	m	mi	XXXYYY
X overlaps Y	o	oi	XXX / YYY
X during Y	d	di	XXX / YYYYY
X starts Y	s	si	XXX / YYYYY
X finishes Y	f	fi	XXX / YYYY

FIG. 1. The thirteen possible relationships.

- STARTS($t1, t2$): time interval $t1$ shares the same beginning as $t2$, but ends before $t2$ ends;
- FINISHES($t1, t2$): time interval $t1$ shares the same end as $t2$, but begins after $t2$ begins;
- BEFORE($t1, t2$): time interval $t1$ is before interval $t2$, and they do not overlap in any way;
- OVERLAP($t1, t2$): interval $t1$ starts before $t2$, and they overlap;
- MEETS($t1, t2$): interval $t1$ is before interval $t2$, but there is no interval between them, i.e., $t1$ ends where $t2$ starts;
- EQUAL($t1, t2$): $t1$ and $t2$ are the same interval.

Given these predicates, there is a set of axioms that define their behavior. First, given any interval I, there exists an interval related to I by each of the above relationships. Thus, there exists an interval that is before I, that meets I, that is during I, etc. We have axioms asserting that each relationship is mutually exclusive of the others, and we have a large set of axioms describing the transitivity behavior. The full set of transitivity axioms, plus a description of an inference procedure using them, is given in [10]. Two examples of these are:

$$\text{BEFORE}(t1, t2) \,\&\, \text{BEFORE}(t2, t3) \Rightarrow \text{BEFORE}(t1, t3), \tag{T.1}$$

$$\text{MEETS}(t1, t2) \,\&\, \text{DURING}(t2, t3) \Rightarrow$$
$$(\text{OVERLAPS}(t1, t3) \vee \text{DURING}(t1, t3) \vee \text{MEETS}(t1, t3)). \tag{T.2}$$

It will be useful to define a predicate that summarizes the relationships in which one interval is wholly contained in another. We define IN as follows:

$$\text{IN}(t1, t2) \Leftrightarrow (\text{DURING}(t1, t2)$$
$$\vee \text{STARTS}(t1, t2) \vee \text{FINISHES}(t1, t2)). \tag{T.3}$$

Using this predicate, we can introduce the first crucial property of the HOLDS predicate: If a property p holds over an interval T, it holds over all subintervals of T, i.e.,

$$\text{HOLDS}(p, T) \Leftrightarrow (\forall t.\text{IN}(t, T) \Rightarrow \text{HOLDS}(p, t)). \tag{H.1}$$

For example, if I owned a car throughout 1982, then I owned a car throughout January of 1982, as well as February, etc.

In fact, it will turn out that we need a slightly stronger axiom in the later development. We shall introduce it here as a second axiom, even though (H.1) can be derived from this axiom plus the properties of the IN relation.

$$\text{HOLDS}(p, T) \Leftrightarrow$$
$$\forall t.\text{IN}(t, T) \Rightarrow (\exists s.\text{IN}(s, t) \wedge \text{HOLDS}(p, s)). \tag{H.2}$$

The proof that (H.1) can be derived from (H.2) is in Appendix A.

To allow properties to name complex logical expressions, there is a set of functions *and, or, not, all,* and *exists*, that correspond to the logical operators $\&, \vee, \sim, \wedge,$ and $\exists$ in the following manner. Conjunction moves through the HOLDS predicate freely:

$$\text{HOLDS}(and(p, q), t) \Leftrightarrow \text{HOLDS}(p, t) \,\&\, \text{HOLDS}(q, t). \tag{H.3}$$

Negation is defined by:

$$\text{HOLDS}(not(p), T) \Leftrightarrow (\forall t.\text{IN}(t, T) \Rightarrow \sim\text{HOLDS}(p, t)). \tag{H.4}$$

Contrast this with $\sim\text{HOLDS}(p, T)$, which by axiom (H.1) is equivalent to

$$\sim(\forall t.\text{IN}(t, T) \Rightarrow \text{HOLDS}(p, t)),$$

which, of course, is equivalent to

$$\exists t.\text{IN}(t, T) \,\&\, \sim\text{HOLDS}(p, t).$$

Thus, the latter asserts that there is at least one subinterval in which p doesn't hold, while the former asserts that p doesn't hold in all subintervals of T. Using the above definition, we can prove

$$\text{HOLDS}(not(p), T) \Rightarrow \sim\text{HOLDS}(p, T). \tag{H.5}$$

Also, using (H.4) and (H.2), we can derive

$$\text{HOLDS}(not(not(p)), T) \Leftrightarrow \text{HOLDS}(p, T) \tag{H.6}$$

as we would expect from intuition. Mirroring the normal definition of disjunction to define the function 'or', i.e.,

$$\text{HOLDS}(\text{or}(p, q), t) \equiv \text{HOLDS}(\text{not}(\text{and}(\text{not}(p),\text{not}(q))), t),$$

we can derive

$$\text{HOLDS}(\text{or}(p, q), T) \Leftrightarrow$$
$$\forall t.\text{IN}(t, T) \Rightarrow (\exists s.\text{IN}(s, t) \wedge (\text{HOLDS}(p, s) \vee \text{HOLDS}(q, s))). \qquad \text{(H.7)}$$

Many treatments of temporal logics introduce the notion of branching futures into the model. This is used to analyze the notion of possibility of some event (i.e., there is a branch in which it occurs), and necessity of some event (i.e., it occurs on all branches). The model has also been suggested as a computational framework for reasoning about future actions (e.g., [5, 11]).

There is no branching future in the model described here. This is because reasoning about the future is considered to be just one instance of hypothetical reasoning. Other examples include reasoning about the past (i.e., how could the world possibly have arrived at the present state), as well as reasoning independent of time and physical causality (such as mathematics). Since all these forms of reasoning are necessary, it seems arbitrary to put one subclass into the model of time. If there were a good reason to encode such reasoning in a branching time model, then the model should also include a branching past, for the types of mechanisms needed for reasoning about the past and future appear to be identical.

Thus there is a simple single time line (which would correspond to the actual past and actual future in a branching time model). Of course, the reasoner never can totally identify the actual past or future, and reasoning about what actually has occurred or will occur consists of constructing the most plausible hypotheses given what is known about the past, present, and future.

As a final comment, note that this does not mean that the reasoning agent is simply a passive observer of the world. By deciding to do actions, the agent changes his expectations about what the future will actually be. This will be discussed in further detail after we have introduced the notion of events and actions.

3. Defining Occurrences

In order to define the role that events and actions play in the logic, let us consider a possible logical form for sentences asserting that an event occurred and see how it fails. The suggestion is that we define a property for each event class such that the property HOLDS over an interval I just in the cases when an instance of the event class occurred over interval I. But this immediately presents problems, for axiom (H.1) would not hold for such properties. In

particular, an event such as turning on the light may occur over an interval T, but not occur over any subinterval of T. In other words, T could be the smallest interval over which "turning on the light" occurred. This cannot be captured by a property, for axiom (H.1) would imply the event occurred over subintervals of T as well.

We introduce a new type of object into our ontology, named an *occurrence*. By representing occurrences as objects in the logic, we are following Davidson's [9] suggestion for representing events. His major argument for this position is that it allows a clean formalism for modeling modifiers and qualifiers of events as predicates acting on the event objects.

Following many others, including Mourelatos [6], we will divide the class of occurrences into two subclasses, *processes* and *events*. Processes refer to some activity not involving a culmination or anticipated result, such as the process denoted by the sentence, "I am running". Events describe an activity that involves a product or outcome, such as the event denoted by the sentence "I walked to the store". A useful test for distinguishing between events and processes is that one can count the number of times an event occurs, but one cannot count the number of times a process is occurring.

Above, we saw that a property could HOLD over many different time intervals. For example, the property that "my wagon is red" might HOLD in the summer of 1981, but not in 1982, and yet again in 1983. We can view a property as defining a set of time intervals over which it holds. We treat occurrences similarly. For example, the occurrence "I walked from home to school" might OCCUR every weekday morning. We cannot specify a particular instance of an occurrence without specifying the unique time over which it occurred.

Properties, processes, and events may be distinguished by considering the characteristics of the set of temporal intervals that they hold or occur over. As we have already seen, the set of intervals over which a property holds is closed under the IN relation. In other words, if interval I is in the set, all intervals J such that $\text{IN}(J, I)$ are also in the set. In contrast, the set of intervals over which an event occurs contains no pair of intervals such that one is IN the other. In other words, an event occurs over the smallest time possible for it to occur. This is the same treatment of events as in McDermott [5]. Processes fall between events and properties. To see this, consider the process "I am walking" over interval I. Unlike events, this process may also be occurring over subintervals of I. Unlike properties, however, it is not the case that the process must be occurring over all subintervals of I. For example, if I am walking over interval I, then I am walking over the first half of I; however, there may be some subintervals of I where I paused for a brief rest.

Let us return to the more formal development of occurrences. We shall start with events, as they are the simplest. The predicate OCCUR takes an event and a time interval and is true only if the event happened over the time interval

t, and there is no subinterval of t over which the event happened. Thus for any event e, and times t and t', we have the axiom

$$OCCUR(e, t) \,\&\, IN(t', t) \Rightarrow \;\sim OCCUR(e, t'). \qquad (O.1)$$

Related classes of events can be described using functions. For example, consider the set of events consisting of an object changing location. We can define a function CHANGE-POS with three arguments: the object, the source location, and the goal location. Thus

$$CHANGE\text{-}POS(Ball, x, y)$$

generates the class of events that consists of a ball moving from x to y. This does not assert that a ball actually did move from x to y. That claim is made by asserting that the event occurred over some time interval. Thus to assert that BALL1 moved from POS1 to POS2 over time $T100$, we say

$$OCCUR(CHANGE\text{-}POS(BALL1, POS1, POS2), T100).$$

We can now define necessary conditions for the class of events involving a change of location:

$$OCCUR(CHANGE\text{-}POS(object, source. goal), t) \Rightarrow$$
$$\exists t1, t2.$$
$$MEETS(t1, t) \,\&\, MEETS(t, t2) \,\&$$
$$HOLDS(at(object, source), t1) \,\&\, HOLDS(at(object, goal), t2).$$

Notice that this definition is of the form

$$OCCUR(e, t) \Rightarrow P_t$$

where e is an event-defining function and P_t is a set of conditions involving t. If the P_t are necessary and sufficient conditions for an event's occurrence, we can define the event with an assertion of the form

$$OCCUR(e, t) \Leftrightarrow P_t \,\&\, \forall t'.IN(t', t) \supset \;\sim P_{t'}.$$

This more complicated form is necessary to ensure the validity of axiom (O.1), which insists that an event occurs only over the smallest interval in which it could have. For example, since the conditions above are sufficient to define a CHANGE-POS event, we could have the assertion

$$OCCUR(CHANGE\text{-}POS(object, source, goal), t) \Leftrightarrow$$
$$\exists t1, t2.$$
$$MEETS(t1, t) \,\&\, MEETS(t, t2) \,\&$$
$$HOLDS(at(object, source), t1) \,\&$$
$$HOLDS(at(object, goal), t2)) \,\&$$
$$(\forall t'.IN(t', t) \Rightarrow$$
$$\sim (\exists t3, t4.$$
$$MEETS(t3, t') \,\&\, MEETS(t', t4) \,\&$$
$$HOLDS(at(object, source), t3) \,\&$$
$$HOLDS(at. (object, goal), t4))).$$

For the sake of readability, we will summarize event definitions by only stating the P_t-conditions and noting whether they are only necessary or are necessary and sufficient. For example. the above example will be written as:

Necessary and Sufficient Conditions for
$OCCUR(CHANGE\text{-}POS(object, source, goal), t)$:
$$\exists t1, t2.$$
$$MEETS(t1, t) \,\&\, MEETS(t, t2) \,\&$$
$$HOLDS(at(object, source), t1) \,\&$$
$$HOLDS(at(object, goal), t2).$$

Axiom (O.1) allows us to count events and hence to construct events that are composites of other events. For example, the class of events of repeating an event twice can be defined by:

Necessary and Sufficient Conditions for
$OCCUR(TWICE(event), t)$:
$$\exists t1, t2.$$
$$IN(t1, t) \,\&\, IN(t2, t) \,\&\, t1 \neq t2 \,\&$$
$$OCCUR(event, t1) \,\&\, OCCUR(event, t2).$$

If we expand this definition out to its full form shown above, we can easily see that it captures repeating exactly twice rather than at least twice. An event that is a sequence of other events can be defined so that the times of each successive event MEET or are strictly AFTER each other. For example, a two-event sequence with MEET can be defined as follows:

Necessary and Sufficient Conditions for
$OCCUR(TWO\text{-}MEET\text{-}SEQUENCE(event1. event2), t)$:
$$\exists t1, t2.$$
$$STARTS(t1, t) \,\&\, FINISHES(t2, t) \,\&\, MEETS(t1. t2) \,\&$$
$$OCCURS(event1, t1) \,\&\, OCCURS(event2. t2).$$

Finally, a composite event that will be useful later is the simple composite of two events occurring simultaneously.

Necessary and Sufficient Conditions for OCCUR(COMPOSITE(event1, event2), t):

OCCUR(event1, t) & OCCUR(event2, t).

All of the event classes we have considered so far have been fully specified. For example, the CHANGE-POS event class specified both the starting position and ending position of the object. It is possible to deal with less specific events in the same framework as well. For instance, consider the class of events of moving to somewhere (without specifying where from). Thus we can define this new class as follows:

Necessary and Sufficient Conditions for OCCUR(MOVE-TO(obj, dest), T):

$\exists s.$OCCUR(CHANGE-POS(obj, s, dest), T).

It is here that we see that axiom (O.1) is crucial to allow us to count MOVE-TO events. For example, consider a simple world with three distinguished positions, A, B, and C, and a ball that moves from A to C via B during time T. Now there are three CHANGE-POS events that OCCUR over or within T. CHANGE-POS(Ball1, A, B), CHANGE-POS(Ball1, B, C), and CHANGE-POS(Ball1, A, C). So it would appear that we could have two MOVE-TO (Ball1, C) events that OCCUR over or within T corresponding to the latter two CHANGE-POS events above. If this were the case, we should report that the ball moved to C at least twice during T, an obviously ridiculous conclusion. Axiom (O.1), which is embedded in the definition of MOVE-TO above, guarantees that only the CHANGE-POS from A to C produces a MOVE-TO C event. Thus we have the desired conclusion that the ball moved to C only once during T.

The other major subclass of occurrences is the processes. Processes differ from events in that axiom (O.1) does not hold. If a process occurs over a time interval T, it appears to occur over at least a substantial number of subintervals. For example, if I am walking during interval T, I must be walking during the first half of interval T. I could have stopped walking for a brief period within T, however, and still have been walking during T. Thus we appear to need some notion of grain of interval size for a given process, where in any subinterval larger than the grain size, the process also occurred. This is too difficult to formalize adequately at present. Thus we will make a weaker claim for processes than we might. In particular, if a process is occurring over an interval T, it must also be occurring over at least one subinterval of T. To

formalize this, we introduce a new predicate, OCCURRING, for processes. We then have for all processes p, and time t:

$$\text{OCCURRING}(p, t) \Rightarrow$$
$$\exists t'.\text{IN}(t', t) \& \text{OCCURRING}(p, t'). \qquad (O.2)$$

Related classes of processes will be described using functions in a similar manner as with event classes. For certain classes of processes we can of course define stronger axioms than (O.2). For example, if we let FALLING(object) denote the class of processes involving the object falling, we could have an axiom that it is falling over all subintervals:

$$\text{OCCURRING}(\text{FALLING}(\text{object}), T) \Leftrightarrow$$
$$(\forall t.\text{IN}(t, T) \Rightarrow \text{OCCURRING}(\text{FALLING}(\text{object}), t)). \qquad (O.3)$$

Many event classes have closely associated process classes. For example, the event of an object falling from x to y necessarily involves the process of falling. In fact, we could define the falling event as a composite of the CHANGE-POS event introduced above and a falling process. Using a definition of COMPOSITE extended to include processes, we define:

FALL(object, source, goal) =
COMPOSITE(CHANGE-POS(object, source, goal),
FALLING(object)).

Using this definition, we can prove that

$$\text{OCCUR}(\text{FALL}(\text{object, source, goal}), t) \Leftrightarrow$$
$$\text{OCCUR}(\text{CHANGE-POS}(\text{object, source, goal}), t) \&$$
$$\text{OCCURRING}(\text{FALLING}(\text{object}), t).$$

Many events can be decomposed into a fairly 'neutral' event like CHANGE-POS and a process. This appears to formalize the intuition underlying many representations based on verb primitives (e.g., [12,7]).

The relation between processes and events becomes more complicated once one considers sentences that describe processes in terms of events. For example, the sentence "John is walking from home to the store" appears to describe a process because it is in the progressive tense, yet does it in terms closer to an event. This sentence may be true even if the event does not occur: John might change his mind on the way and return home. A suggested solution to this problem is that the above sentence really means that John is walking with the intention of going to the store. This does not solve the entire problem, however, for similar sentences can be constructed for inanimate objects, as in "The ball was falling to the ground".

The above solution might be adapted by using a notion of expected outcome to subsume the agent's intention. A solution along these lines, however, is beyond the capabilities of the present formalism. Without further comment, we shall allow such sentences to be expressed by allowing events to be arguments to the OCCURRING predicate. For example, let us assume the sentence "The ball fell onto the table over T" is represented as:

$$OCCUR(FALL(ball, s, table1), T).$$

Then the sentence "The ball was falling to the table over T" would be represented by:

$$OCCURRING(FALL(ball, s, table1), T).$$

Generalizing from this example, we can see that if an event occurred, then it was occurring. In other words, for any event e and time t,

$$OCCUR(e, t) \Rightarrow OCCURRING(e, t). \qquad (O.3)$$

The converse of this does not hold.

Defining necessary and sufficient conditions for many processes, especially those describing human activity, appears not to be possible. While there may be technical definitions of the differences between walking, strolling, and running, it is unlikely that they would be useful in language comprehension. Such terms appear to be primitive-like processes that may be recognized from the perceptual system. Of course, necessary conditions are likely to be found for these processes, and consequences, such as that they all involve moving, but at different rates, can be described if necessary.

Processes involving physical change, or motion (e.g., falling) may afford precise descriptions. What is necessary to describe these is a workable theory of naive physics (see [13]). Investigating these issues here will take us too far afield.

An important relationship that we shall need asserts that one event causes another. The nature of causality has been studied extensively in philosophy (e.g., [14]). Many of the issues considered there, however, will not affect this work. Let us introduce a predicate ECAUSE (event causation), where

$$ECAUSE(e1, t1, e2, t2)$$

is true only if event $e1$'s occurrence at time $t1$ caused event $e2$ to occur at time $t2$. The following facts about causality are important.

If an event occurred that caused another event, then the caused event also occurred.

$$OCCUR(e, t) \,\&\, ECAUSE(e, t, e', t') \Rightarrow OCCUR(e', t'). \qquad (O.4)$$

An event cannot cause events prior to its occurrence (though they may be simultaneous).

$$ECAUSE(e, t, e', t') \Rightarrow IN(t', t) \vee BEFORE(t, t') \vee MEETS(t, t') \vee OVERLAPS(t, t') \vee EQUALS(t, t'). \qquad (O.5)$$

Furthermore, the ECAUSE relation is transitive, anti-symmetric, and anti-reflexive.

None of the axioms above can be used to infer a new causal relation from a set of facts involving no causal relations. Thus all inferences about causality come from other already known causal relations, or must be induced from outside the logic. This seems consistent with common treatments in philosophy and artificial intelligence in which causality is irreducible (e.g., [15, 16, 12]).

4. Defining Actions

An important subclass of occurrences are those that involve animate agents performing actions. There are actions that are processes (e.g., "John is running"), and actions that are events (e.g., "John lost his hat"). An action is an occurrence caused in a 'certain' way by the agent. This relation is not simple causality between events, for an agent may be involved in an event without it being an action of that agent. For example, consider two distinct interpretations of the sentence. "Cleo broke the window". The first describes an action of Cleo. The second arises, say, if Cleo is thrown through the window at a wild party. In this case, Cleo is the instrument of the breaking of the window. Thus not all events that are caused by animate agents are actions by that agent.

To avoid this difficulty, we introduce a new form of causality termed agentive causality or ACAUSE. An agent ACAUSES an event only in those cases where the agent caused the event in an appropriate manner for the situation to be called an action of the agent's.

Classes of actions can be characterized by the function

$$ACAUSE(agent, occurrence)$$

which for any agent and occurrence produces the action of the agent causing the occurrence. As with all other occurrences, such actions may OCCUR or be OCCURRING over a set of time intervals. Particular instances of actions can only be specified by specifying the time of the action.

We can also classify actions in the same manner as all other occurrences by introducing a function for each related class of actions. For example, the class of actions consisting of an agent moving an object from one location to another can be generated by the function

MOVE-ACTION(agent, object, source-location, goal-location).

which can be defined as being equivalent to

ACAUSE(agent, CHANGE-POS(object, source-location, goal-location)).

It is hypothesized that every action can be characterized as an agent ACAUSEing an occurrence. For some actions, such as singing, an occurrence must be introduced that consists of the actual motions involved to produce the activity. Although such an occurrence might never occur independently of the action, introducing it preserves the simplicity of the model.

Again borrowing terminology from Mourelatos [6], we call the class of actions that consists of ACAUSEing an event to be *performances*, and those that consist of ACAUSEing a process to be *activities*.

We can capture much of the above discussion with the following axioms. If an agent ACAUSEs an occurrence over time t, then the occurrence was OCCURRING over t.

$$\text{OCCURRING(ACAUSE(agent, occurrence)}, t) \Rightarrow \text{OCCURRING(occurrence}, t). \qquad (A.1)$$

For every action there is a unique agent and a unique occurrence that the agent ACAUSEs which constitutes the action.

$$\forall \text{action } \exists! \text{ agent, occurrence}$$
$$\text{action} = \text{ACAUSE(agent, occurrence)}. \qquad (A.2)$$

For the subclass of performances, we have a stronger version of (A.1) with the OCCUR predicate.

$$\text{OCCUR(ACAUSE(agent, event)}, t) \Rightarrow \text{OCCUR(event}, t). \qquad (A.3)$$

The other important aspects of the ACAUSE relation remain to be considered in the section on intentional action. But first, let us reconsider the individuation of actions.

We have seen simple performances and activities as examples of actions. Using the constructors for composite events we can describe actions that

consist of a sequence of actions, or consist of actions being performed simultaneously. Note that a composite action composed of a performance and an activity (e.g., "walking to the store while juggling three balls") is itself a performance. This is easily seen from the observation that we can count the number of occurrences of such composite actions. The only composites that are activities are those that consist entirely of activities.

There are situations which might appear to be simple composite actions, yet, on closer examination, have considerably richer structure. The composite actions we have seen so far consist of actions that can be considered independently of each other; neither is necessary for the success of the other. Thus walking to the store while juggling three balls consists of walking to the store, which could have been done independently, and juggling three balls, which also could have been done independently. Many other composites have subactions that are related in a considerably stronger fashion. Consider the actions performed in the situation described as "Sam hid his coat by standing in front of it".

Taking the position outlined in the introduction, there are at least two distinct actions performed here; namely, "hiding the coat" and "standing in front of the coat". These actions, however, are not independent of each other. They are intimately related, as one was performed by means of performing the other, i.e., the coat was hidden by means of standing in front of it. Note that this is not simply a causal relationship: standing in front of the coat didn't cause John's hiding the coat, it actually constituted the hiding.

A wide range of similar examples exists in the speech act literature (e.g., [17]). For example, I may perform a promise by telling you that I will come to your party, provided I have the appropriate intentions. Again, the act of speaking did not simply cause the promise act, but, in conjunction with the appropriate intentions, it constituted the promise act.

Goldman [8] terms this relationship between actions as generation. An act A *generates* an act B iff:

(i) A and B are cotemporal (they occur at the same time);

(ii) A is not part of doing B (such as "playing a C note" is part of "playing a C triad" on a piano);

(iii) A occurs in a context C, where the occurrence of A and C jointly imply the occurrence of B.

Goldman distinguishes different types of generation, depending on the nature of the context C. I have not found this a useful division as most examples seem to be combinations of the different types. He identifies three major components of C:

- causal laws: A generates B because the occurrence of A causes the occurrence of B;
- conventional rules: for example, "signaling a left turn on your bike" is generated by "putting your arm out";

-simple (or definitional): A generates B simply by the fact that B is defined as doing A in a certain context; an example of this, namely hiding an object from someone, will be discussed in detail below.

To continue the formal development, let us introduce a predicate GENERATES that takes two actions and a time:

$$GENERATES(a1, a2, t).$$

This predicate is true only if action $a1$ generates action $a2$ during time t. GENERATES is transitive, anti-symmetric, and anti-reflexive with respect to its two action arguments.

For example, consider an agent JOHN playing a C triad on the piano. Other actions that JOHN performs simultaneously with this include playing a C note (a part of the first action) and waking up Sue (generated by the first action). We can express this in the formal notation using the following functions. Let:
- PLAY-C-TRIAD(agent, piano) be the action of the agent playing a C triad on the piano;
- PLAY-C(agent, piano) be the action of the agent playing a C note on the piano; and
- WAKE(agent, other) be the action of the agent waking up the other person.

Then the situation above is captured by

$$OCCUR(PLAY\text{-}C\text{-}TRIAD(JOHN, P), T1) \,\&$$
$$OCCUR(PLAY\text{-}C(JOHN, P), T1) \,\&$$
$$OCCUR(WAKE(JOHN, SUE), T1)$$

where
$$GENERATES(PLAY\text{-}C\text{-}TRIAD(JOHN, P),$$
$$WAKE(JOHN, SUE), T1)$$

and ∃-event

$$PLAY\text{-}C\text{-}TRIAD(JOHN, P) =$$
$$COMPOSITE(PLAY\text{-}C(JOHN, P), event).$$

The notion of generation is crucial for considering how an action was performed, or how to perform an action (i.e., planning). Investigating these issues will take us too far afield, but it is worth briefly considering how planning knowledge and definitional knowledge interact. We have seen two major classes of knowledge about actions. One, the definitional, outlines necessary (and sometimes sufficient) conditions for an action's occurrence. This is crucial for achieving a minimal understanding of what is implied by a sentence describing an action. The second, generational knowledge, outlines how actions can be performed, and is crucial for problem solving. But a sharp distinction in

the uses of this knowledge is artificial. Generational knowledge can be used in understanding to infer plausible ways in which an action might have been accomplished, whereas definitional knowledge can be used by a problem solver to identify what actions might be appropriate to solve a certain task that has not been encountered previously.

5. Intentional Action

Before developing the notion of intentional action, let us consider an example that motivates the remainder of the paper, namely, defining the action of hiding an object from someone. We shall not consider the sense of hiding that is equivalent to simply concealing from sight accidentally. The sense here is the sense that arises from an accusation such as "You hid that book from me!" As we shall see, this is an intentional action.

The definition of hiding an object should be independent of any method by which the action was performed, for, depending on the context, the actor could hide the object in many different ways. In other words, the action can be generated in different ways. For instance, the actor could:
- put the object behind a desk;
- stand between the object and the other agent while they are in the same room: or
- call a friend Y and get her or him to do one of the above.

Furthermore, the actor might hide the object by simply not doing something s/he intended to do. For example, assume Sam is planning to go to lunch with Carole after picking Carole up at her office. If, on the way out of his office, Sam decides not to take his coat because he doesn't want Carole to see it, then Sam has hidden the coat from Carole. Of course, it is crucial here that Sam believed that he normally would have taken the coat. Sam couldn't have hidden his coat by forgetting to bring it.

This example brings up a few key points that may not be noticed from the first three examples. First, Sam must have intended that Carole not see the coat. Without this intention (i.e., in the forgetting case), no such action occurs. Second, Sam must have believed that it was likely that Carole would see the coat in the future course of events. Third, Sam must have decided to act in such a way that he then believed that Carole would not see the coat in the future course of events. Finally, for the act to be successful, Sam must have acted in that way. In this case, the action Sam performed was "not bringing the coat", which would normally not be considered an action unless it was intentional.

I claim that these four conditions provide a reasonably accurate definition of what it means to hide something. They certainly cover the four examples presented above. It is also important to note that one does not have to be successful in order to have been hiding something. The definition depends on what the hider believes and intends at the time, not what actually occurs.

worlds where the only change is by the agent that constructs the plan. In more general settings, however, plans may involve actions by other agents as well as naturally occurring events. In addition, plans are not made starting from a blank world. There are many external events occurring, and the agent believes that certain other events may occur in the future. This even includes actions that the agent has already decided to do in the future. Thus a more general notion of planning is called for.

Let each *agent* maintain three partial descriptions of the world. Each description is a set of propositions asserting properties and occurrences over time intervals. The first description is called the *expected* world, the second the *planned* world, and the third the *desired* world. The expected world is what the agent believes will happen given that certain known future events will occur and assuming that the agent does nothing. It is a view of the world assuming all agents are as lazy as possible but remain in accordance with the known future events. The expected world obeys a generalized law of momentum. Things in the process of changing continue to change unless prevented, and everything else remains the same unless disturbed.

The desired world contains a description of the properties and occurrences that the agent desires. The planned world is the same as the expected world except that the agent may add or remove actions (by that agent). Thus it is a simulation of what the world would be like if the agent acted differently than what is expected. The goal, of course, is to make the planned world subsume the desired world and then act according to it. A possible algorithm for this would be a generalized GPS model of finding differences between the worlds and introducing actions to reduce the differences. There is not space here to consider the planning algorithm further, but for an initial attempt at building a planner, see [26].

A plan is a set of decisions about performing or not performing actions by the agent. Thus, at any time, there is a plan that specifies the mapping from the expected world to the planned world. A plan can be constructed without the agent intending to actually act in accordance with the plan. Such plans arise from a wide range of activities, from abstract problem solving to the recognition of plans of other agents. It will be important for us here to have a notion of an agent *committing* to a plan. An agent is committed to a plan over a certain time interval if that agent believes he or she will act in accordance with the plan. That is, the planned world becomes the expected world. This then becomes part of the agent's predictions about the future state of the world, and must be considered in any further planning activity done by the agent. For instance, in the hiding example, when Sam decided not to take the coat, he changed an action he had committed to do in order to hide his coat.

Most models of plans in the literature consider a subclass of the set of plans allowed here. In particular, they only allow planning into the immediate future, and with only a few exceptions (e.g., [27]), do not allow occurrences other than

However, the present definition is rather unsatisfactory, as many extremely difficult concepts, such as belief and intention, were thrown about casually. We shall investigate these issues in the next sections.

5.1. Belief and plans

There is much recent work on models of belief (e.g., [18, 19]). I will use a sentential model of belief based on the model of Haas [20], which is similar to that of Konolidge [21] and Kaplan [22]. In their work, belief is a predicate taking an agent and a description of a proposition as its arguments and is intended to mean that the agent believes that proposition. In computer models, it means that the agent has a data structure in its memory corresponding to the proposition. To develop this model requires a consistent method of introducing quotation into the predicate calculus so that the usual paradoxes are avoided. I will not develop this fully here as it is not necessary for this paper, but the interested reader should see [23, 20].

An important thing to notice, though, is that there must be two relevant time indices to each belief; namely, the time over which the belief is held, and the time over which the proposition is believed to hold. For example, I might believe *today* that it rained *last weekend*. This point will be crucial in modeling the action of hiding. To introduce some notation, let

"*A* believes (during T_b) that *p* holds (during T_p)"

be expressed as

   HOLDS(believes(*A*, "HOLDS(*p*, T_p)"), T_b).

and which we shall abbreviate using

   BELIEVES(*A*, *p*, T_p, T_b).

The quotation of formulas in this development must be viewed only as a notational convenience. A more elaborate system of quotation is required so that variables can be introduced into quoted expressions. In such cases, the variables range over names of terms. I will avoid these issues and simply allow variables within quotation marks. Once we have the capability of describing propositions in the logic, we can specify a wide range of beliefs using quantification over parts of formulas. Proof methods can be developed that allow the simulation of other agents' reasoning. For a rigorous treatment of these issues, see [20].

Plans are typically characterized in AI as a sequence or partial order of actions (e.g., [24, 25]). This characterization is adequate when modeling static actions by the planner. We can express plans which contain occurrences independent of the planner, including actions by other agents, as well as plans not to do some action.

Let us introduce a little notation for use later on. Let the predication

TO-DO(action, time, plan)

be true if the plan specified includes performing the action at the given time, and let

NOT-TO-DO(action, time, plan)

be true if the plan specified includes not performing the action at the given time. This is of course much stronger than asserting $\sim$TO-DO(action, time, plan), which simply asserts that the plan does not contain the indicated action.

The notion of a goal is not part of a plan directly. Rather, goals are part of the desired world and are the usual reason for committing to a plan. Let

IS-GOAL-OF(agent, goal, gtime, t)

be true if the agent's desired world at time t contains the specified goal holding during gtime. Finally, the predicate

COMMITTED(agent, plan, ctime)

is true if the agent is committed over ctime to act in accordance with the specified plan. Being committed to a plan means that the agent believes he or she will perform all actions (by the agent) in the plan.

One can think of a plan as a complex action, and it makes sense to talk of a plan occurring if all its decisions are carried out. This can be expressed by extending the OCCUR predicate to plans according to the following definition:

$$\text{OCCUR(plan, } t) \Leftrightarrow$$
$$\forall \text{action, } t_a.\text{TO-DO(action, } t_a, \text{plan}) \Rightarrow$$
$$\text{OCCUR(action, } t_a) \&$$
$$\forall \text{action, } t_a.\text{NOT-TO-DO(action, } t_a, \text{plan}) \Rightarrow$$
$$(\forall t.\text{IN}(t, t_a) \Rightarrow$$
$$\sim\text{OCCUR(action, } t_a)).$$

5.2. Intending

There are two senses of intention that are traditionally distinguished in the literature. The first has been termed *prior intention* (e.g. [28]) and arises in sentences such as

"Jim intends to run a mile today".

This intention is prior to the action, and can hold even if the action is never performed (i.e., Jim forgets or changes his mind). We shall model this form of intention simply by asserting that Jim has committed to a plan that has the action as a step. Thus

$$\text{INTEND(agent, ACAUSE(agent, occurrence), atime, itime)} \Leftrightarrow \quad (I.1)$$
$$(\exists \text{plan COMMITTED(agent, plan, time)} \&$$
$$\text{TO-DO(ACAUSE(agent, occurrence), atime, plan))}.$$

Note that Jim having this intention implies that he believes he will run the mile today. It does not imply that Jim wants to do the action, although in most cases this is a plausible inference. Also plausible is that Jim has some goal that results from this action being performed. The actual nature of this goal is uncertain. For instance, he may want to stay fit (and so he might change his mind and swim instead), or he may want to win a bet that he couldn't run a mile (and so swimming would not be a reasonable alternative). The example does not specify this information.

Many times an intention of an agent is so general that it is expressed in terms of a goal rather than an action. Examples are the actions of "achieving state x", "preventing event E", etc. To express these, we will simply use the IS-GOAL-OF predication introduced earlier.

The last sense of intention is that of intentional action, which arises in sentences such as

"Jack intentionally coughed".

This example is closely related to the notion of prior intention: it appears that Jack coughed as a result of a plan that he was committed to that involved him coughing. This is essentially the treatment suggested in Miller et al. [29].

But one must be careful with this definition. For instance, if one intentionally does an action A, does one intentionally do all the subparts of A? What about the actions one did to generate A, or the actions that A generates? For instance, if A was the action of Jack intentionally playing a C chord on the piano, did he also

(i) intentionally play a C note (a subpart of A);
(ii) intentionally move his finger (generating (i)); or
(iii) intentionally annoy his neighbors (generated by A).

One might say no to (i) and (ii), or allow subparts and not generation, or allow all as intentional. Each side has been proposed; which side we should take depends on what is counted to be in a plan. For instance. if a composite action is in a plan, are its subparts in the plan? If so, then (i) is always intentional. If an action is in a plan, the actions that it generates may or may not be in the plan, depending on the knowledge and goals of the actor. Thus, with (iii), it might go either way, depending on why Jack was playing the piano. This last case shows we cannot simply define how intentionality relates to generation. Some actions which are generated could not be denied, however. If Sam intentionally aims and fires a gun at Sue, knowing it is loaded, he intentionally shot her. This appears to be so because there is no other plausible plan that Sam could have had. Thus, if we assume Sam is a rational being, and does not act at random, we can assume his plan must have been to shoot Sue. Thus, we will only get into difficulty with the plan-based model of intentionality if we make hard and fast rules, such as that all subparts of an action must be in a plan, or all generated actions of an action must be in a plan. If the contents of a plan is left up to plausible reasoning about the motivation of an agent's behavior, the plan model appears to provide a reasonable definition of intentionality.

There are remaining problems with the plan model. however. Davis [30] gives an example of a person driving a car when a small child runs in front of it. He claims the person intentionally slams on the brakes yet has no time to form a plan to do so. This difficulty may arise from an inadequate model of plan-directed behavior. For the present, however, these examples will not cause us any problems. Searle [28] presents other difficulties that arise with this simple model, but again. the problems can be ignored at present, as the examples that present them are fairly bizarre.

On the basis of this discussion, and following Goldman [8]. we can say that an agent S intentionally performed an action A at time t iff

(i) S performed A at t:
(ii) A was part of a plan that S was committed to at time t: and
(iii) S performed A because of S's knowledge of (ii).

Introducing a new predicate, we can easily capture the first two conditions above, but it is not clear how to formalize condition (iii). For computational models in which an agent only acts because of an existing plan, however, this should not present any difficulties. Thus we can capture the first two conditions with:

$$\text{INTENTIONAL(ACAUSE(agent, occurrence), time)} \Rightarrow$$
$$\text{OCCURS(ACAUSE(agent, occurrence), time)} \,\&$$
$$\text{INTEND(agent. ACAUSE(agent, occurrence), time. time)} . \qquad (1.2)$$

Finally, let us return to questions about the nature of the ACAUSE relation. The examples in which we have used it have all been intentional actions, so the question arises as to whether it is possible to have an ACAUSE relation to an

unintentional action? For instance, if John broke the window unintentionally, did John perform an action? That, he certainly did, but the action he performed might not be breaking the window, it may have been hitting the baseball (which broke the window). If we claim that, even in this case, John performed the action of breaking the window, then we can make the example more complicated. What if John hit the baseball, which landed on the roof of a house, and a few minutes later rolled off and broke the window. Obviously, in this example, the delay and causal chain of events soon gets complicated enough that we would say John did not break the window. So where do actions stop and mere events caused by actions begin?

There seems no easy answer to this question, although a fruitful approach could be to consider the issue of responsibility. If an agent acts in a way that causes some effect which, while unintentional, should have been foreseen, we tend to term that as an action. We do not have the time to pursue this here, so make the simplifying assumption that all actions are intentional, i.e..

$$\text{OCCUR(ACAUSE(agent, occurrence), }t) \Rightarrow$$
$$\text{INTENTIONAL(agent, ACAUSE(agent, occurrence), }t) . \qquad (1.3)$$

In the unintentional case of "John broke the window", we analyze that as John did something intentionally that caused the window to break. This may seem to complicate the analysis of such sentences, but it can be handled in a relatively clean manner. The meaning of a sentence such as "John broke the window" could be

$$\exists e, t1, t2.\text{OCCUR(ACAUSE(John, }e), t1) \,\&$$
$$\text{OCCUR(BREAK-EVENT(Window), }t2) \,\&$$
$$((e = \text{BREAK-EVENT(Window)}) \vee$$
$$\text{ECAUSE}(e, t1, \text{BREAK-EVEN(Window), }t2)) .$$

The disjunction captures the ambiguity as to whether the breaking of the window was intentional or not. If $e = $ BREAK-EVENT(Window). then the event that John ACAUSEd was the breaking of the window. If e caused BREAK-EVENT(Window), then the event John ACAUSEd was something else which ECAUSEd the breaking of the window. Finally, if John intentionally broke the window by hitting the baseball, then he performed two actions (intentionally) which are related by the GENERATEs relation.

6. How to Hide Revisited

With these tools, we can attempt a more precise definition of hiding. We first define the function

$$\text{HIDE(agent. observer, object)}$$

to generate the class of hiding actions. Let us also introduce an event function

$$\text{SEE(agent, object),}$$

which generates events of an agent seeing an object, and a property SEEN (agent, object) defined by

$$\text{HOLDS(SEEN(agent, object), } t) \Leftrightarrow$$
$$\exists t1.\text{BEFORE}(t1, t) \ \&$$
$$\text{OCCUR(SEE(agent, object), } t1).$$

So the necessary and sufficient conditions for Sam to hide the coat from Carole over interval T_h are as follows. He must have initially believed (during T_b) that Carole would have seen the coat during T_h:

$$\exists t.\text{IN}(t, T_h) \ \& \ \text{STARTS}(T_b1, T_h) \ \&$$
$$\text{BELIEVES(Sam, SEEN(CAROLE, COAT), } t, T_b1). \qquad (1)$$

He must have had an intention (during T_h) that Carole not see the coat:

$$\text{IS-GOAL-OF(Sam, not(SEEN(CAROLE, COAT)), } T_h, T_h). \qquad (2)$$

Restating conditions (1) and (2) in terms of Sam's plan during T_b1, we see that in his expected world Carole will see the coat, while in the desired world, she will not.

The next conditions describe Sam as he formulates a new plan which achieves his goal of Carole not seeing the coat. To describe this we introduce two new event classes, first the event of an agent committing to a plan, and second the event of an agent changing his or her mind about something. Let

$$\text{COMMIT(agent, plan)}$$

denote the class of events defined by

Necessary and Sufficient Conditions for OCCUR(COMMIT(agent, plan), time):

$$\exists t1, t2.\text{MEETS}(t1, \text{time}) \ \&$$
$$\text{MEETS(time, } t2) \ \&$$
$$\sim\text{COMMITTED(agent, plan, } t1) \ \&$$
$$\text{COMMITTED(agent, plan, } t2).$$

Furthermore, let us define the event class

$$\text{CHANGE-MIND(agent, property, ptime)}$$

by

Necessary and Sufficient Conditions for OCCUR(CHANGE-MIND(agent, property, ptime), time):

$$\exists t1, t2.\text{MEETS}(t1, \text{time}) \ \&$$
$$\text{MEETS(time, } t2) \ \&$$
$$\text{BELIEVES(agent, property, ptime, } t1) \ \&$$
$$\text{BELIEVES(agent, not(property), ptime, } t2).$$

Using these events, we can state that Sam is adopting a plan with the goal that Carole not see the coat and that he believes it will work:

$$\exists \text{plan}, T_b2.\text{MEETS}(T_b1, T_b2) \ \&$$
$$\text{OCCUR(COMMIT(Sam, plan), } T_b2) \ \&$$
$$\text{ECAUSE(COMMIT(Sam, plan), } T_b2,$$
$$\text{CHANGE-MIND(Sam, SEEN(CAROLE, COAT), } T_h), T_b2). \qquad (3)$$

These three conditions capture Sam's intention to hide the coat, and if Sam acts in accordance with the plan hypothesized in condition (3), the hide action is performed.

We can put these conditions all together into one definition as follows:

Necessary and Sufficient Conditions for OCCUR(HIDE(agent, observer, object), T_h):

$$\exists t, T_b1, T_b2, \text{plan}.$$
$$\text{STARTS}(T_b1, T_h) \ \&$$
$$\text{MEETS}(T_b1, T_b2) \ \&$$
$$\text{IN}(t, T_h) \ \&$$
$$\text{BELIEVE(agent, SEEN(observer, object), } t, T_b1) \ \&$$
$$\text{IS-GOAL-OF(agent, not(SEEN(observer, object)), } T_h, T_h) \ \&$$
$$\text{OCCUR(COMMIT(Sam, plan), } T_b2) \ \&$$
$$\text{ECAUSE(COMMITS(Sam, plan), } T_b2,$$
$$\text{CHANGE-MIND(Sam, SEEN(CAROLE, COAT), } T_h), T_b2) \ \&$$
$$\text{OCCUR(plan, } T_h).$$

The conditions that the agent changed his mind can be derived from the above conditions and the definition of ECAUSE.

One can see that much of what it means to hide is captured by the above. In particular, the following can be extracted directly from the definition:
- if you hide something, you intended it not to be seen (and thus can be held responsible for the consequences of this);
- you cannot hide something if you believed it was not possible that it could be seen, or if it were certain that it would be seen anyway;

— one cannot hide something simply by changing one's mind about whether it will be seen.

In addition, there are many other possibilities related to the temporal order of events. For instance, you can't hide something by performing an action after the hiding is supposed to be done.

7. Conclusion

In the introduction, three problems in representing actions were discussed. These problems have been addressed throughout the paper, but sometimes only implicitly. Let us reconsider each problem. The first problem concerned actions that involve non-activity, such as standing still. These can be modeled with no difficulty. An action class can be defined so that the agent remains in one position over the time of the action's occurrence. Note that such a non-activity must be intentional if it is to qualify as an action in this framework. Otherwise, such non-activity can only be modeled as an event. A more complicated form of non-activity involves not doing an action that was previously expected. These actions can be defined in terms of the beliefs and intentions of the agent. In particular, the agent must have been intending to do the action and later changed his or her mind.

The second problem concerned actions that cannot be defined by decomposition into subactions. The example of "hiding a book from Sue" is a prime example from this class. Any particular instance of hiding a book can be decomposed into a particular set of subactions, but there is no decomposition, or set of decompositions, that defines the class of hiding actions. Rather, hiding can only be defined in terms of the agent's beliefs and intentions. The speech acts also fall into this class. Each occurrence of a speech act is partially decomposable into the act of uttering something, but otherwise depends crucially on the speaker's intentions.

The third problem concerned actions that occur simultaneously and possibly interact. Simultaneous actions can be described directly since the temporal aspects of a plan are separated from the causal aspects. This enables us to describe situations where actions may interact with each other. Building a system that can reason about such interactions while problem solving, however, remains a difficult problem.

This framework is currently being used to study general problem-solving behavior, as well as the problem-solving behavior that arises in task-oriented dialogues. A simple problem solver has been built using this framework and is described by Allen and Koomen [26]. The model is also being used both for plan recognition and plan generation in a system under development at Rochester that comprehends and participates in task-oriented dialogues. The action models are being used to describe a useful set of conversational actions which include the traditional notion of speech acts.

Appendix A. Proof that (H.2) Entails (H.1)

$$\text{HOLDS}(p, T) \Leftrightarrow$$
$$(\forall t.\text{IN}(t, T) \Rightarrow \exists s.\text{IN}(s, t) \wedge \text{HOLDS}(p, s)) . \tag{H.2}$$
$$\text{HOLDS}(p, T) \Leftrightarrow (\forall t.\text{IN}(t, T) \Rightarrow \text{HOLDS}(p, T)) . \tag{H.1}$$

We assume (H.2) as the definition, and prove (H.1) one direction at a time. The only assumptions we need about the IN relation is that it is transitive, and for every interval I, there exists an interval J such that $\text{IN}(J, I)$.

Proof of $\text{HOLDS}(p, T) \Rightarrow (\forall t.\text{IN}(t, T) \Rightarrow \text{HOLDS}(p, T))$:

(1)	$\text{HOLDS}(p, T)$	hypothesis;
(2)	$\forall t.\text{IN}(t, T) \Rightarrow (\exists s.\text{IN}(s, t)\ \&\ \text{HOLDS}(p, s))$	by defn.(H.2), (1):
(3)	$\text{IN}(T1, T)$	assumption;
(4)	$\text{IN}(T2, T1)$	assumption;
(5)	$\text{IN}(T2, T)$	transitivity of IN using (3), (4);
(6)	$\exists s.\text{IN}(s, T2)\ \&\ \text{HOLDS}(p, s)$	MP (2), (5);
(7)	$\forall t'.\text{IN}(t', T1) \Rightarrow$ $\quad(\exists s.\text{IN}(s, t')\ \&\ \text{HOLDS}(p, s))$	discharging assumption (4);
(8)	$\text{HOLDS}(p, T1)$	by defn.(H.2), (7);
(9)	$\forall t.\text{IN}(t, T) \Rightarrow \text{HOLDS}(p, T)$	discharging assumption (3) .

Proof of $(\forall t.\text{IN}(t, T) \Rightarrow \text{HOLDS}(p, t)) \Rightarrow \text{HOLDS}(p, T)$:

(1)	$\forall t.\text{IN}(t, T) \Rightarrow \text{HOLDS}(p, t)$	hypothesis;
(2)	$\text{IN}(T1, T)$	assumption;
(3)	$\text{HOLDS}(p, T1)$	MP (1), (2);
(4)	$\forall t.\text{IN}(t', T1) \supset$ $\quad\exists s'.\text{IN}(s', t')\ \&\ \text{HOLDS}(p, s')$	by defn.(H.2), (3);
(5)	$\exists s''.\text{IN}(s'', T1)$	axiom
(6)	$\text{IN}(T2, T1)$	existential elim., (5);
(7)	$\exists s'.\text{IN}(s', T2)\ \&\ \text{HOLDS}(p, s')$	MP (4), (6);
(8)	$\text{IN}(T3, T2)\ \&\ \text{HOLDS}(p, T3)$	existential elim., (7);
(9)	$\text{HOLDS}(p, T3)$	conj. elim., (8);
(10)	$\text{IN}(T3, T1)$	transitivity of IN, (6), (8);
(11)	$\text{IN}(T3, T1)\ \&\ \text{HOLDS}(p, T1)$	conj. intro.(9). (10);
(12)	$\exists s'.\text{IN}(s', T1)\ \&\ \text{HOLDS}(p, s')$	existential intro., (11);
(13)	$\exists s'.\text{IN}(s', T1)\ \&\ \text{HOLDS}(p, s')$	existential intro., [12];
(14)	$\forall t.\text{IN}(t, T) \supset \exists s'.\text{IN}(s', t)\ \&\ \text{HOLDS}(p, s')$	discharging assumption (2);
(15)	$\text{HOLDS}(p, T)$	by defn.(H.2), (14) .

ACKNOWLEDGMENT

The author wishes to thank Henry Kautz for his detailed criticism of the penultimate version of this paper that forced the clarification of several murky areas. I would also like to thank Jerry Feldman, Alan Frisch, Andy Haas, Margery Lucas, Dan Russell, and Stuart Goldkind for many enlightening comments and improvements on previous versions of this paper, and Drew McDermott and Pat Hayes for discussions on general issues in representing action and time.

REFERENCES

1. Charniak, E., A common representation for problem-solving and language-comprehension information, *Artificial Intelligence* **16** (1981) 225–255.
2. Allen, J.F. and Perrault, C.R., Analyzing intention in utterances, *Artificial Intelligence* **15** (1980) 143–178.
3. Fillmore, C.J., The case for case, in: Bach and Harms (Eds). *Universals in Linguistic Theory* (Holt, Rinehart and Winston, New York, 1968).
4. McCarthy, J. and Hayes, P.J., Some philosophical problems from the standpoint of artificial intelligence, in: B. Meltzer and D. Michie (Eds). *Machine Intelligence* **4** (Edinburgh University Press, Edinburgh, 1969).
5. McDermott, D., A temporal logic for reasoning about processes and plans. RR 196, Computer Science Dept., Yale Univ., New Haven, CT, 1981; also in *Cognitive Sci.* **6**(2) (1982).
6. Mourelatos, A.P.D., Events, processes, and states. *Linguistics and Philosophy* **2** (1978) 415–434.
7. Jackendoff, R., Toward an explanatory semantic representation, *Linguistic Inquiry* **7**(1) (1976) 89–150.
8. Goldman, A., *A Theory of Human Action* (Princeton University Press, Princeton, NJ, 1970).
9. Davidson, D., The logical form of action sentences, in: N. Rescher (Ed.), *The Logic of Decision and Action* (University Pittsburgh Press, Pittsburgh, PA, 1967).
10. Allen, J.F., Maintaining knowledge about temporal intervals, TR 86, Computer Science Dept., Univ. Rochester, January 1981; also in *Comm. ACM* **26** (1983) 832–843.
11. Mays, E., A modal temporal logic for reasoning about change, *Proc. 21st Meeting, Association for Computational Linguistics* (MIT, Cambridge, CA, 1983).
12. Schank, R.C., *Conceptual Information Processing* (North-Holland, New York, 1975).
13. Hayes, P.J., Naive physics I: Ontology for liquids. Working Paper 63, Institut pour les Etudes Semantiques et Cognitives, Geneva, 1978.
14. Sosa, E. (Ed.), *Causation and Conditionals* (Oxford University Press, Oxford, 1975).
15. Taylor, R., *Action and Purpose* (Prentice-Hall, Englewood Cliffs, NJ, 1966).
16. Norman, D.A. and Rumelhart, D.E., *Explorations in Cognition* (Freeman, San Francisco, CA, 1975).
17. Searle, J.R., *Speech Acts: An Essay in the Philosophy of Language* (Cambridge University Press, London, 1969).
18. Cohen, P.R., On knowing what to say: Planning speech acts, TR 118, Computer Science Dept., Univ. of Toronto, 1978.
19. Moore, R.C., Reasoning about knowledge and action, Ph.D. Thesis, MIT, Cambridge, MA, 1979.
20. Haas, A., Planning mental actions, TR 106 and Ph.D. Thesis, Computer Science Dept., Univ. of Rochester, Rochester, NY, 1982.
21. Konolidge, K., A first-order formalization of knowledge and action for a multiagent planning system, TN 232, AI Center, SRI International, Menlo Park, CA, 1980.
22. Kaplan, D., Quantifying in, *Synthese* **19** (1968) 178–214.
23. Perlis, D., Language, computation, and reality, TR 95 and Ph.D. Thesis, Computer Science Dept. Univ. of Rochester, Rochester, NY, 1981.
24. Fikes, R.E. and Nilsson, N.J., STRIPS: A new approach to the application of theorem proving to problem solving, *Artificial Intelligence* **2** (1971) 189–205.
25. Sacerdoti, E.D., The nonlinear nature of plans, *Proc. 4th IJCAI*, Tbilisi, USSR, 1975.
26. Allen, J.F. and Koomen, J.A., Planning using a temporal world model. *Proc. 8th IJCAI*, Karlsruhe, West Germany, 1983.
27. Vere, S., Planning in time: Windows and durations for activities and goals. Jet Propulsion Laboratory, California Institute of Technology, 1981.
28. Searle, J.R., The intentionality of intention and action, *Cognitive Sci.* **4**(1) (1980).
29. Miller, G.A., Galanter, E. and Pribram, K.H., *Plans and the Structure of Behavior* (Holt, Rinehart and Winston, New York, 1960).
30. Davis, L.K., *Theory of Action* (Prentice-Hall, Englewood Cliffs, NJ, 1979).

Received March 1982; revised version received October 1983

9   A Formal Theory of Knowledge and Action

Robert C. Moore

Artificial Intelligence Center
SRI International
Menlo Park, California

1 The Interplay of Knowledge and Action

Planning sequences of actions and reasoning about their effects is one of the most thoroughly studied areas within artificial intelligence (AI). Relatively little attention has been paid, however, to the important role that an agent's knowledge plays in planning and acting to achieve a goal. Virtually all AI planning systems are designed to operate with complete knowledge of all relevant aspects of the problem domain and problem situation. Often any statement that cannot be inferred to be true is assumed to be false. In the real world, however, planning and acting must frequently be performed without complete knowledge of the situation.

This imposes two additional burdens on an intelligent agent trying to act effectively. First, when the agent entertains a plan for achieving some goal, he must consider not only whether the physical prerequisites of the plan have been satisfied, but also whether he has all the information necessary to carry out the plan. Second, he must be able to reason about what he can do to obtain necessary information that he lacks. AI planning systems are usually based on the assumption that, if there is an action an agent is physically able to perform, and carrying out that action would result in the achievement of a goal P, then the agent can achieve P. With goals such as opening a safe, however, there are actions that any human agent of normal abilities is physically capable of performing that would result in achievement of the goal (in this case, dialing the combination of the safe), but it would be highly misleading to claim that an agent could open a safe simply by dialing the combination unless he actually *knew* that combination. On the other hand, if the agent had a piece of paper on which the combination of the safe was written, he could open the safe by reading what was on the piece of paper and then dialing the combination, even if he did not know it previously.

In this paper, we will describe a formal theory of knowledge and action that is based on a general understanding of the relationship between the two.[1] The question

---

[1] This paper presents the analysis of knowledge and action, and the representation of that analysis in first-order logic, that were developed in the author's doctoral thesis (Moore, 1980). The material in Sections 3.1 and 3.2, however, has been substantially revised.

"A Formal Theory of Knowledge and Action"
Reprinted with permission from Ablex Publishing Corporation.

of generality is somewhat problematical, since different actions obviously have different prerequisites and results that involve knowledge. What we will try to do is to set up a formalism in which very general conclusions can be drawn, once a certain minimum of information has been provided concerning the relation between specific actions and the knowledge of agents.

To see what this amounts to, consider the notion of a test. The essence of a test is that it is an action with a directly observable result that depends conditionally on an unobservable precondition. In the use of litmus paper to test the pH of a solution, the observable result is whether the paper has turned red or blue, and the unobservable precondition is whether the solution is acid or alkaline. What makes such a test useful for acquiring knowledge is that the agent can infer whether the solution is acid or alkaline on the basis of his knowledge of the behavior of litmus paper and the observed color of the paper. When one is performing a test, it is this inferred knowledge, rather than what is directly observed, that is of primary interest.

If we tried to formalize the results of such a test by making simple assertions about what the agent knows subsequent to the action, we would have to include the result that the agent knows whether the solution is acid or alkaline as a separate assertion from the result that he knows the color of the paper. If we did this, however, we would completely miss the point that knowledge of the pH of the solution is inferred from other knowledge, rather than being a direct observation. In effect, we would be *stipulating* what actions can be used as tests, rather than creating a formalism within which we can *infer* what actions can be used as tests.

If we want a formal theory of how an agent's state of knowledge is changed by his performing a test, we have to represent and be able to draw inferences from the agent's having several independent pieces of information. Obviously, we have to represent that, after the test is performed, the agent knows the observable result. Furthermore, we have to represent the fact that he knows that the test has been performed. If he just walks into the room and sees the litmus paper on the table, he will know what color it is, but, unless he knows its recent history, he will not have gained any knowledge about the acidity of the solution. We also need to represent the fact that the agent understands how the test works; that is, he knows how the observable result of the action depends on the unobservable precondition. Even if he sees the litmus paper put into the solution and then sees the paper change color, he still will not know whether the solution is acid or alkaline unless he knows how the color of the paper is related to the acidity of the solution. Finally, we must be able to infer that, if the agent knows (i) that the test took place, (ii) the observable result of the test, and (iii) how the observable result depends on the unobservable precondition, then he will know the unobservable precondition. Thus we must know enough about knowledge to tell us when an agent's knowing a certain collection of facts implies that he knows other facts as well.

From the preceding discussion, we can conclude that any formalism that enables us to draw inferences about tests at this level of detail must be able to represent the following types of assertions:

(1) After A performs ACT, he knows whether Q is true.

(2) After A performs ACT, he knows that he has just performed ACT.

(3) A knows that Q will be true after he performs ACT if and only if P is true now.

Moreover, in order to infer what information an agent will gain as a result of performing a test, the formalism must embody, or be able to represent, general principles sufficient to conclude the following:

(4) If 1, 2, and 3 are true, then, after performing ACT, A will know whether P was true before he performed ACT.

It is important to emphasize that any work on these problems that is to be of real value must seek to elicit general principles. For instance, it would be possible to represent (1), (2), and (3) in an arbitrary, ad hoc manner and to add an axiom that explicitly states (4), thereby ''capturing'' the notion of a test. Such an approach, however, would simply restate the superficial observations put forth in this discussion. Our goal in this paper is to describe a formalism in which specific facts like (4) follow from the most basic principles of reasoning about knowledge and action.

2 Formal Theories of Knowledge

2.1 A Modal Logic of Knowledge

Since formalisms for reasoning about action have been studied extensively in AI, while formalisms for reasoning about knowledge have not, we will first address the problems of reasoning about knowledge. In Section 3 we will see that the formalism that we are led to as a solution to these problems turns out to be well suited to developing an integrated theory of knowledge and action.

The first step in devising a formalism for reasoning about knowledge is to decide what general properties of knowledge we want that formalism to capture. The properties of knowledge in which we will be most interested are those that are relevant to planning and acting. One such property is that anything that is known by someone must be true. If P is false, we would not want to say that anyone knows P. It might be that someone believes P or that someone believes he knows P, but it simply could not be the case that anyone knows P. This is, of course, a major difference between knowledge and belief. If we say that someone believes P, we are not committed to saying that P is either true or false, but if we say that someone knows P, we are committed to the truth of P. The reason that this distinction is important for planning and acting is simply that, for an agent to achieve his goals, the beliefs on which he bases his actions must generally be true. After all, merely believing that performing a certain action will bring about a desired goal is not sufficient for being able to achieve the goal; the action must actually have the intended effect.

Another principle that turns out to be important for planning is that, if someone knows something, he knows that he knows it. This principle is often required for reasoning about plans consisting of several steps. Suppose an agent plans to use

ACT_1 to achieve his goal, but, in order to perform ACT_1 he needs to know whether P is true and whether Q is true. Suppose, further, that he already knows that P is true and that he can find out whether Q is true by performing ACT_2. The agent needs to be able to reason that, after performing ACT_2, he will know whether P is true and whether Q is true. He knows that he will know whether Q is true because he understands the effects of ACT_2, but how does he know that he will know whether P is true? Presumably it works something like this: he knows that P is true, so he knows that he knows that P is true. If he knows how ACT_2 affects P, he knows that he will know whether P is true after he performs ACT_2. The key step in this argument is an instance of the principle that, if someone knows something, he knows that he knows it.

It might seem that we would also want to have the principle that, if someone does not know something, he knows that he does not know it—but this turns out to be false. Suppose that A believes that P, but P is not true. Since P is false, A certainly does not know that P, but it is highly unlikely that he knows that he does not know, since he thinks that P is true.

Probably the most important fact about knowledge that we will want to capture is that agents can reason on the basis of their knowledge. All our examples depend on the assumption that, if an agent trying to solve a problem has all the relevant information, he will apply his knowledge to produce a solution. This creates a difficulty for us, however, since agents (at least human ones) are not, in fact, aware of all the logical consequences of their knowledge. The trouble is that we can never be sure which of the inferences an agent *could* draw, he actually *will*. The principle people normally use in reasoning about what other people know seems to be something like this: if *we* can infer that something is a consequence of what someone knows, then, lacking information to the contrary, we will assume that the other person can draw the same inference.

This suggests the adoption some sort of "default rule" (Reiter, 1980) for reasoning about what inferences agents actually draw, but, for the purposes of this study, we will make the simplifying assumption that agents actually do draw all logically valid inferences from their knowledge. We can regard this as the epistemological version of the "frictionless case" in classical physics. For a more general framework in which weaker assumptions about the deductive abilities of agents can be expressed, see the work of Konolige (Chapter 10, this volume).

Finally, we will need to include the fact that these basic properties of knowledge are themselves *common knowledge*. By this we mean that everyone knows them, and everyone knows that everyone knows them, and everyone knows that everyone knows that everyone knows them, ad infinitum. This type of principle is obviously needed when reasoning about what someone knows about what someone else knows, but it is also important in planning, because an agent must be able to reason about what he will know at various times in the future. In such a case, his "future self" is analogous to another agent.

In his pioneering work on the logic of knowledge and belief, Hintikka (1962) presents a formalism that captures all these properties. We will define a formal logic based on Hintikka's ideas, but modified somewhat to be more compatible with the additional ideas of this paper. So, what follows is similar to the logic developed by Hintikka in spirit, but not in detail.

The language we will use initially is that of propositional logic, augmented by an operator KNOW and terms denoting agents. The formula KNOW(A,P) is interpreted to mean that the agent denoted by the term A knows the proposition expressed by the formula P. So, if JOHN denotes John and LIKES(BILL,MARY) means that Bill likes Mary, KNOW(JOHN,LIKES(BILL,MARY)) means that John knows that Bill likes Mary. The axioms of the logic are inductively defined as all instances of the following schemata:

M1.   P, such that P is an axiom of ordinary propositional logic
M2.   KNOW(A,P) ⊃ P
M3.   KNOW(A,P) ⊃ KNOW(A,KNOW(A,P))
M4.   KNOW(A, (P ⊃ Q)) ⊃ (KNOW(A,P) ⊃ KNOW(A,Q))

closed under the principle that

M5.   If P is an axiom, then KNOW(A,P) is an axiom.

The closure of the axioms under the inference rule modus ponens (from (P ⊃ Q) and P, infer Q) defines the theorems of the system. This system is very similar to those studied in modal logic. In fact, if A is held fixed, the resulting system is isomorphic to the modal logic S4 (Hughes and Cresswell, 1968). We will refer to this system as the modal logic of knowledge.

These axioms formalize in a straightforward way the principles for reasoning about knowledge that we have discussed. M2 says that anything that is known is true. M3 says that, if someone knows something, he knows that he knows it. M4 says that, if someone knows a formula P and a formula of the form (P ⊃ Q), then he knows the corresponding formula Q. That is, everyone can (and does) apply modus ponens. M5 guarantees that the axioms are common knowledge. It first applies to M1–M4, which says that everyone knows the basic facts about knowledge: however, since it also applies to its own output, we get axioms stating that everyone knows that everyone knows, etc. Since M5 applies to the axioms of propositional logic (M1), we can infer that everyone knows the facts they represent. Furthermore, because modus ponens is the only inference rule needed in propositional logic, the presence of M4 will enable us to infer that an agent knows any propositional consequence of his knowledge.

2.2 A Possible-World Analysis of Knowledge

We could try to use the modal logic of knowledge directly in a computational system for reasoning about knowledge and action, but, as we have argued elsewhere (Moore, 1980), all the obvious ways of doing this encounter difficulties. (Konolige's recent work, this volume, suggests some new, more promising possibilities, but the details remain to be worked out.) There may well be solutions to these problems, but it turns out that they can be circumvented entirely by changing the language we use to describe what agents know. Instead of talking about the individual propositions that an agent knows, we will talk about what states of affairs are compatible with what he knows. In philosophy, these states of affairs are usually called "possible worlds," so we will adopt that term here as well.

This shift to describing knowledge in terms of possible worlds is based on a rich and elegant formal semantics for systems like our modal logic of knowledge, which was developed by Hintikka (1962, 1971) in his work on knowledge and belief. The advantages of this approach are that it can be formalized within ordinary first-order classical logic in a way that permits the use of standard automatic-deduction techniques in a reasonably efficient manner[2] and that, moreover, it generalizes nicely to an integrated theory for describing the effects of actions on the agent's knowledge.

Possible-world semantics was first developed for the logic of necessity and possibility. From an intuitive standpoint, a possible world may be thought of as a set of circumstances that might have been true in the actual world. Kripke (1963) introduced the idea that a world should be regarded as possible, not absolutely, but only relative to other worlds. That is, the world W_1 might be a possible alternative to W_2, but not to W_3. The relation of one world's being a possible alternative to another is called the *accessibility relation*. Kripke then proved that the differences among some of the most important axiom systems for modal logic corresponded exactly to certain restrictions on the accessibility relation of the possible-world models of those systems. These results are reviewed in Kripke (1971). Concurrently with these developments, Hintikka (1962) published the first of his writings on the logic of knowledge and belief, which included a model theory that resembled Kripke's possible-world semantics. Hintikka's original semantics was done in terms of sets of sentences, which he called *model sets,* rather than possible worlds. Later (Hintikka, 1971), however, he recast his semantics using Kripke's concepts, and it is that formulation we will use here.

Kripke's semantics for necessity and possibility can be converted into Hintikka's semantics for knowledge by changing the interpretation of the accessibility relation. To analyze statements of the form KNOW(A,P), we will introduce a relation K, such that $(K(A,W_1,W_2)$ means that the possible world W_2 is compatible or consistent with what A knows in the possible world W_1. In other words, for all that A knows in W_1, he might just as well be in W_2. It is the set of worlds $\{w_2 \mid K(A,W_1,w_2)\}$ that we will use to characterize what A knows in W_1. We will discuss A's knowledge in W_1 in terms of this set, the set of states of affairs that are consistent with his knowledge in W_1, rather than in terms of the set of propositions he knows. For the present, let us assume that the first argument position of K admits the same set of terms as the first argument position of KNOW. When we consider

---

[2] Chapters 6 and 7 of More (1980) present a procedural interpretation of the axioms for knowledge and action given in this paper that seems to produce reasonably efficient behavior in an automatic deduction system.

quantifiers and equality, we will have to modify this assumption, but it will do for now.

Introducing K is the key move in our analysis of statements about knowledge, so understanding what K means is particularly important. To illustrate, suppose that in the actual world—call it W_0—A knows that P, but does not know whether Q. If W_1 is a world where P is false, then W_1 is not compatible with what A knows in W_0; hence we would have $\neg K(A, W_0, W_1)$. Suppose that W_2 and W_3 are compatible with everything A knows, but that Q is true in W_2 and false in W_3. Since A does not know whether Q is true, for all he knows, he might be in either W_2 or W_3 instead of W_0. Hence, we would have both $K(A, W_0, W_2)$ and $K(A, W_0, W_3)$. This is depicted graphically in Figure 1.

Some of the properties of knowledge can be captured by putting constraints on the accessibility relation K. For instance, requiring that the actual world W_0 be compatible with what each knower knows in W_0, i.e., $\forall a_1(K(a_1, W_0, W_0))$, is equivalent to saying that anything that is known is true. That is, if the actual world is compatible with what everyone [actually] knows, then no one has any false knowledge. This corresponds to the modal axiom M2.

The definition of K implies that, if A knows that P in W_0, then P must be true in every world W_1 such that $K(A, W_0, W_1)$. To capture the fact that agents can reason with their knowledge, we will assume converse is also true. That is, we assume that, if P is true in every world W_1 such that $K(A, W_0, W_1)$, then A knows that P in

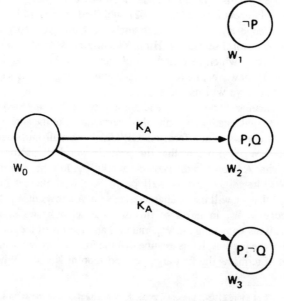

Figure 1. "A Knows That P"
"A Doesn't Know Whether Q"

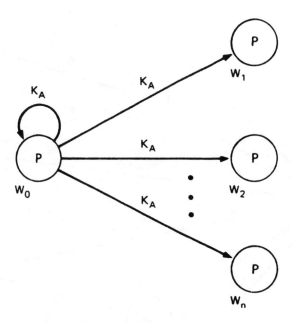

Figure 2. "P is True in Every World That is Compatible with What A Knows"

W_0. (See Figure 2.) This principle is the model-theoretic analogue of axiom M4 in the modal logic of knowledge. To see that this is so, suppose that A knows that P and that $(P \supset Q)$. Therefore, P and $(P \supset Q)$ are both true in every world that is compatible with what A knows. If this is the case, though, then Q must be true in every world that is compatible with what A knows. By our assumption, therefore, we conclude that A knows that Q.

Since this assumption, like M4, is equivalent to saying that an agent knows all the logical consequences of his knowledge, it should be interpreted only as a default rule. In a particular instance, the fact that P follows from A's knowledge would be a justification for concluding that A knows P. However, we should be prepared to retract the conclusion that A knows P in the face of stronger evidence to the contrary.

With this assumption, we can get the effect of M3—the axiom stating that, if someone knows something, he knows that he knows it—by requiring that, for any W_1 and W_2, if W_1 is compatible with what A knows in W_0 and W_2 is compatible with what A knows in W_1, then W_2 is compatible with what A knows in W_0. Formally expressed, this is

$$\forall a_1, w_1, w_2 (K(a_1, W_0, w_1) \supset (K(a_1, w_1, w_2) \supset K(a_1, W_0, w_2)))$$

By our previous assumption, the facts that A knows are those that are true in every world that is compatible with what A knows in the actual world. Furthermore, the facts that A knows that he knows are those that are true in every world that is

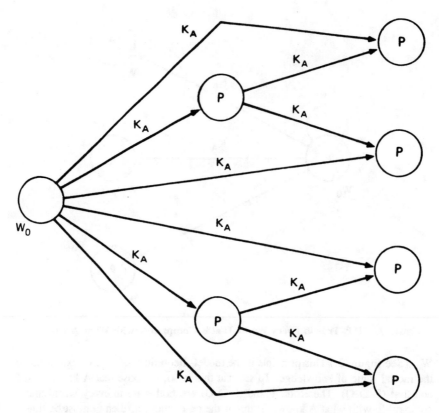

Figure 3. "If A Knows That P, Then He Knows That He Knows That P"

compatible with what he knows in every world that is compatible with what he knows in the actual world. By the constraint we have just proposed, however, all these worlds must also be compatible with what A knows in the actual world (see Figure 3), so, if A knows that P, he knows that he knows that P.

Finally, we can get the effect of M5, the principle that the basic fact about knowledge are themselves common knowledge, by generalizing these constraints so that they hold not only for the actual world, but for all possible worlds. This follows from the fact that, if these constraints hold for all worlds, they hold for all worlds that are compatible with what anyone knows in the actual world; they also hold for all worlds that are compatible with what anyone knows in all worlds that are compatible with what anyone knows in the actual world, etc. Therefore, everyone knows the facts about knowlege that are represented by the constraints, and everyone knows that everyone knows, etc. Note that this generalization has the effect that the constraint corresponding to M2 becomes the requirement that, for a given knower, K is reflexive, while the constraint corresponding to M3 becomes the requirement that, for a given knower, K is transitive.

Analyzing knowledge in terms of possible worlds gives us a very nice treatment

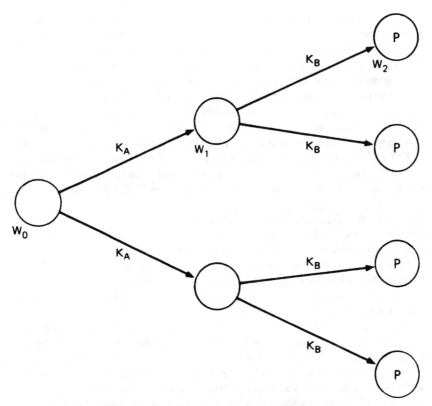

Figure 4. "A Knows That B Knows That P"

of knowledge about knowledge. Suppose A knows that B knows that P. Then, if the actual world is W_0, in any world W_1 such that $K(A,W_0,W_1)$, B knows that P. We now continue the analysis relative to W_1, so that, in any world W_2 such that $K(B,W_1,W_2)$, P is true. Putting both stages together, we obtain the analysis that, for any worlds W_1 and W_2 such that $K(A,W_0,W_1)$ and $K(B,W_1,W_2)$, P is true in W_2. (See Figure 4.)

Given these constraints and assumptions, whenever we want to assert or deduce something that would be expressed in the modal logic of knowledge by KNOW(A,P), we can instead assert or deduce that P is true in every world that is compatible with what A knows. We can express this in ordinary first-order logic, by treating possible worlds as individuals (in the logical sense), so that K is just an ordinary relation. We will therefore introduce an operator T such that T(W,P) means that the formula P is true in the possible world W. If we let W_0 denote the actual world, we can convert the assertion KNOW(A,P) into

$$\forall w_1(K(A,W_0,w_1) \supset T(w_1,P))$$

It may seem that we have not made any real progress, since, although we have gotten rid of one nonstandard operator, KNOW, we have introduced another one, T. However, T has an important property that KNOW does not. Namely, T "distributes" over ordinary logical operators. In other words, ⌐P is true in W just in case P is not true in W, (P ∨ Q) is true in W just in case P is true in W or Q is true in W, and so on. We might say that T is extensional, relative to a possible world. This means that we can transform any formula so that T is applied only to atomic formulas. We can then turn T into an ordinary first-order relation by treating all the nonintensional atomic formulas as *names* of atomic propositions, or we can get rid of T by replacing the atomic formulas with predicates on possible worlds. This is no loss to the expressive power of the language, since, where we would have previously asserted P, we now simply assert $T(W_0, P)$ or $P(W_0)$ instead.

2.3 Knowledge, Equality, and Quantification

The formalization of knowledge presented so far is purely propositional; a number of additional problems arise when we attempt to extend the theory to handle equality and quantification. For instance, as Frege (1949) pointed out, attibutions of knowledge and belief lead to violations of the principle of equality substitution. We are not entitled to infer KNOW(A,P(C)) from B = C and KNOW(A,P(B)) because A might not know that the identity holds.

The possible-world analysis of knowledge provides a very neat solution to this problem, once we realize that a term can denote different objects in different possible worlds. For instance, if B is the expression "the number of planets" and C is "nine," then, although B = C is true in the actual world, it would be false in a world in which there was a tenth planet. Thus, we will say that an equality statement such as B = C is true in a possible world W just in case the denotation of the term B in W is the same as the denotation of the term C in W. This is a special case of the more general rule that a formula of the form $P(A_1,...,A_n)$ is true in W just in case the tuple consisting of the denotations in W of the terms $A_1,...,A_n$ is in the extension in W of the relation expressed by P, provided that we fix the interpretation of = in all possible worlds to be the identity relation.

Given this interpretation, the inference of KNOW(A,P(C)) from B = C and KNOW(A,P(B)) will be blocked (as it should be). To infer KNOW(A,P(C)) from KNOW(A,P(B)) by identity substitution, we would have to know that B and C denote the same object in *every* world compatible with what A knows, but the truth of B = C guarantees only that they denote the same object in the actual world. On the other hand, if KNOW(A,P(B)) and KNOW(A,(B = C)) are both true, then in all worlds that are compatible with what A knows, the denotation of B is in the extension of P and is the same as the denotation of C; hence, the denotation of C is in the extension of P. From this we can infer that KNOW(A,P(C)) is true.

The introduction of quantifiers also causes problems. To modify a famous example from Quine (1971), consider the sentence "Ralph knows that someone is a spy." This sentence has at least two interpretations. One is that Ralph knows that there is at least one person who is a spy, although he may have no idea who that person is. The other interpretation is that there is a particular person whom Ralph knows to be a spy. As Quine says (1971, p. 102), "The difference is vast; indeed, if Ralph is like most of us, [the first] is true and [the second] is false." This ambiguity was explained by Russell (1949) as a difference of *scope*. The idea is that indefinite noun phrases such as "someone" can be analyzed in context by paraphrasing sentences of the form P("someone") as "There exists a person x such that P(x)," or, more formally, $\exists x(PERSON(x) \wedge P(x))$. Russell goes on to point out that, in sentences of the form "A knows that someone is a P," the rule for eliminating "someone" can be applied to either the whole sentence or only the subordinate clause, "someone is a P." Applying this observation to "Ralph knows that someone is a spy," gives us the following two formal representations:

$$KNOW(RALPH, \exists x(PERSON(x) \wedge SPY(x))) \tag{1}$$

$$\exists x(PERSON(x) \wedge KNOW(RALPH, SPY(x))) \tag{2}$$

The most natural English paraphrases of these formulas are "Ralph knows that there is a person who is a spy," and "There is a person who Ralph knows is a spy." These seem to correspond pretty well to the two interpretations of the original sentence. So, the ambiguity in the original sentence is mapped into an uncertainty as to the scope of the operator KNOW relative to the existential quantifier introduced by the indefinite description "someone."

Following a suggestion of Hintikka (1962), we can use a formula similar to (2) to express the fact that someone knows who or what something is. He points out that a sentence of the form "A knows who (or what) B is" intuitively seems to be equivalent to "there is someone (or something) that A knows to be B. But this can be represented formally as $\exists x(KNOW(A, (x = B)))$. To take a specific example, "John knows who the President is" can be paraphrased as "There is someone whom John knows to be the President," which can be represented by

$$\exists x(KNOW(JOHN, (x = PRESIDENT))) \tag{3}$$

In (1), KNOW may still be regarded as a purely propositional operator, although the proposition to which it is applied now has a quantifier in it. Put another way, KNOW still is used simply to express a relation between a knower and the proposition he knows. But (2) and (3) are not so simple. In these formulas there is a quantified variable that, although bound outside the scope of the operator KNOW, has an occurrence inside; this is sometimes called "quantifying in." Quantifying into knowledge and belief contexts is frequently held to pose serious problems of interpretation. Quine (1971), for instance, holds that it is unintelligible, because we have not specified what proposition is known unless we say what description is used to fix the value of the quantified variable.

The possible-world analysis, however, provides us with a very natural interpretation of quantifying in. We keep the standard interpretation that $\exists x(P(x))$ is true just in case there is some value for x that satisfies P. If P is $KNOW(A, Q(x))$, then a value for x satisfies P(x) just in case that value satisfies Q(x) in every world that is compatible with what A knows. So (2) is satisfied if there is a particular person who is a spy in every world that is compatible with what A knows. That is, in every such world the same person is a spy. On the other hand, (1) is satisfied if, in every world compatible with what A knows, there is some person who is a spy, but it does not have to be the same one in each case.

Note that the difference between (1) and (2) has been transformed from a difference in the relative scopes of an existential quantifier and the operator KNOW to a difference in the relative scopes of an existential and a universal quantifier (the "every" in "every possible world compatible with . . ."). Recall from ordinary first-order logic that $\exists x(\forall y(P(x,y)))$ entails $\forall y(\exists x(P(x,y)))$, but not vice versa. The possible-world analysis, then, implies that we should be able to infer "Ralph knows that there is a spy," from "There is someone Ralph knows to be a spy," as indeed we can.

When we look at how this analysis applies to our representation from "knowing who," we get a particularly satisfying picture. We said that A knows who B is means that there is someone whom A knows to be B. If we analyze this, we conclude that there is a particular individual who is B in every world that is compatible with what A knows. Suppose this were not the case, and that, in some of the worlds compatible with what A knows, one person is B, whereas in the other worlds, some other person is B. In other words, for all that A knows, either of these two people might be B. But this is exactly what we mean when we say that A does not know who B is! Basically, the possible-world view gives us the very natural picture that A knows who B is if A has narrowed the possibilities for B down to a single individual.

Another consequence of this analysis worth noting is that, if A knows who B is and A knows who C is, we can conclude that A knows whether B = C. If A knows who B is and who C is, then B has the the same denotation in all the worlds that are compatible with what A knows, and this is also true for C. Since, in all these worlds, B and C each have only one denotation, they either denote the same thing everywhere or denote different things everywhere. Thus, either B = C is true in every world compatible with what A knows or B ≠ C is. From this we can infer that either A knows that B and C are the same individual or that they are not.

We now have a coherent account of quantifying in that is not framed in terms of knowing particular propositions. Still, in some cases knowing a certain proposition counts as knowing something that would be expressed by quantifying in. For instance, the proposition that John knows that 321-1234 is Bill's telephone number might be represented as

KNOW(JOHN,(321-1234 = PHONE-NUM(BILL))),   (4)

which does not involve quantifying in. We would want to be able to infer from this, however, that John knows what Bill's telephone number is, which would be represented as

∃x(KNOW(JOHN,(x = PHONE-NUM(BILL)))).   (5)

It might seem that (5) can be derived from (4) simply by the logical principle of existential generalization, but that principle is not always valid in knowledge contexts. Suppose that (4) were not true, but that instead John simply knew that Mary and Bill had the same telephone number. We could represent this as

$$\text{KNOW(JOHN,(PHONE-NUM(MARY) = PHONE-NUM(BILL))).} \qquad (6)$$

It is clear that we would not want to infer from (6) that John knows what Bill's telephone number is—yet, if existential generalization were universally valid in knowledge contexts, this inference would go through.

It therefore seems that, in knowledge contexts, existential generalization can be applied to some referring expressions ("321-1234"), but not to others ("Mary's telephone number"). We will call the expressions to which existential generalization can be applied *standard identifiers,* since they seem to be the ones an agent would use to identify an object for another agent. That is, "321-1234" is the kind of answer that would *always* be appropriate for telling someone what John's telephone number is, whereas "Mary's telephone number," as a general rule, would not.[3]

In terms of possible worlds, standard identifiers have a very straightforward interpretation. Standard identifiers are simply terms that have the same denotation in every possible world. Following Kripke (1972), we will call terms that have the same denotation in every possible world *rigid designators.* The conclusion that standard identifiers are rigid designators seems inescapable. If a particular expression can always be used by an agent to identify its referent for any other agent, then there must not be any possible circumstances under which it could refer to something else. Otherwise, the first agent could not be sure that the second was in a position to rule out those other possibilities.

The validity of existential generalization for standard identifiers follows immediately from their identification with rigid designators. The possible-world analysis of KNOW(A,P(B)) is that, in every world compatible with what A knows, the denotation of B in that world is in the extension of P in that world. Existential generalization fails in general because we are unable to conclude that there is any particular individual that is in the extension of P in all the relevant worlds. If B is a rigid designator, however, the denotation of B is the same in every world. Consequently, it is the same in every world compatible with what A knows, and that denotation is an individual that is in the extension of P in all those worlds.

There are a few more observations to be made about standard identifiers and rigid designators. First, in describing standard identifiers we assumed that everyone

---

[3] "Mary's telephone number" *would* be an approriate way of telling someone what John's telephone number was if he already knew Mary's telephone number, but this knowledge would consist in knowing what expression of the type "321-1234" denoted Mary's telephone number. Therefore, even in this case, using "Mary's telephone number" to identify John's telephone number would just be an indirect way of getting to the standard indentifier.

knew what they referred to. Identifying them with rigid designators makes the stronger claim that what they refer to is common knowledge. That is, not only does everyone know what a particular standard identifier denotes, but everyone knows that everyone knows, etc. Second, although it is natural to think of any individual having a unique standard identifier, this is not required by our theory. What the theory does require is that, if there are two standard identifiers for the same individual, it should be common knowledge that they denote the same individual.

3 Formalizing the Possible-World Analysis of Knowledge

3.1 Object Language and Metalanguage

As we indicated above, the analysis of knowledge in terms of possible worlds can be formalized completely within first-order logic by admitting possible worlds into the domain of quantification and making the extension of every expression depend on the possible world in which it is evaluated. For example, the possible-world analysis of "A knows who B is" would be as follows: There is some individual x such that, in every world w_1 that is compatible with what the agent who is A in the actual world knows in the actual world, x is B in w_1. This means that in our formal theory we translate the formula of the modal logic of knowledge,

$$\exists x(KNOW(A,(x = B))),$$

into the first-order formula,

$$\exists x(\forall w_1(K(A(W_0),W_0,w_1) \supset (x = B(w_1)))).$$

One convenient way of stating the translation rules precisely is to axiomatize them in our first-order theory of knowledge. This can be done by introducing terms to denote formulas of the modal logic of knowledge (which we will henceforth call the *object language*) and axiomatizing a truth definition for those formulas in a first-order language that talks about possible worlds (the *metalanguage*). This has the advantage of letting us use either the modal language or the possible-world language—whichever is more convenient for a particular purpose—while rigorously defining the connection between the two.

The typical method of representing expressions of one formal language in another is to use string operations like concatenation or list operations like CONS in LISP, so that the conjunction of P and Q might be represented by something like CONS(P,CONS('∧,CONS(Q,NIL))), which could be abbreviated LIST(P,'∧,Q). This would be interpreted as a list whose elements are P followed by the conjunction symbol followed by Q. Thus, the metalanguage expression CONS(P,CONS('∧,CONS(Q,NIL))) would denote the object language expression (P ∧ Q). McCarthy (1962) has devised a much more elegant way to do the encoding, however. For purposes of semantic interpretation of the object language, which is what we want to do, the details of the syntax of that language are largely irrelevant. In particular, the only thing we need to know about the syntax of conjunctions is that there is *some* way of taking P and Q and producing the conjunction of P and Q. We can represent this by having a function AND such that AND(P,Q) denotes the conjunction of P and Q. To use McCarthy's term, AND(P,Q) is an *abstract syntax* for representing the conjunction of P and Q.

We will represent object language variables and constants by metalanguage constants; we will use metalanguage functions in an abstract syntax to represent object language predicates, functions, and sentence operators. For example, we will represent the object language formula KNOW(JOHN,$\exists$x(P(x))) by the metalanguage term KNOW(JOHN,EXIST(X,P(X))), where JOHN and X are metalanguage constants, and KNOW, EXIST, and P are metalanguage functions.

Since KNOW(JOHN,EXIST(X,P(X))) is a term, if we want to say that the object language formula it denotes is true, we have to do so explicitly by means of a metalanguage predicate TRUE:

$$\text{TRUE(KNOW(JOHN,EXIST(X,P(X)))).}$$

In the possible-world analysis of statements about knowledge, however, an object language formula is not absolutely true, but only relative to a possible world. Hence, TRUE expresses not absolute truth, but truth in the actual world, which we will denote by W_0. Thus, our first axiom is

L1. $\forall p_1(\text{TRUE}(p_1) \equiv T(W_0,p_1))$,

where $T(W,P)$ means that formula P is true in world W. To simplify the axioms, we will let the metalanguage be a many-sorted logic, with different sorts assigned to differents sets of variables. For instance, the variables w_1, w_2,... will range over possible worlds; x_1, x_2,... will range over individuals in the domain of the object language; and a_1, a_2,... will range over agents. Because we are axiomatizing the object language itself, we will need several sorts for different types of object language expressions. The variables p_1, p_2,... will range over object language formulas, and t_1,t_2,... will range over object language terms.

The recursive definition of T for the propositional part of the object language is as follows:

L2. $\forall w_1,p_1,p_2(T(w_1,\text{AND}(p_1,p_2)) \equiv (T(w_1,p_1) \land T(w_1,p_2)))$

L3. $\forall w_1,p_1,p_2(T(w_1,\text{OR}(p_1,p_2)) \equiv (T(w_1,p_1) \lor T(w_1,p_2)))$

L4. $\forall w_1,p_1,p_2(T(w_1,\text{IMP}(p_1,p_2)) \equiv (T(w_1,p_1) \supset T(w_1,p_2)))$

L5. $\forall w_1,p_1,p_2(T(w_1,\text{IFF}(p_1,p_2)) \equiv (T(w_1,p_1) \equiv T(w_1,p_2)))$

L6. $\forall w_1,p_1(T(w_1,\text{NOT}(p_1)) \equiv \sim T(w_1,p_1))$

Axioms L1–L6 merely translate the logical connectives from the object language to the metalanguage, using an ordinary Tarskian truth definition. For instance, according to L2, AND(P,Q) is true in a world if and only if P and Q are both true in the world. The other axioms state that all the truth-functional connectives are "transparent" to T in exactly the same way.

To represent quantified object language formulas in the metalanguage, we will introduce additional functions into the abstract syntax: EXIST and ALL. These functions will take two arguments—a term denoting an object language variable and a term denoting an object language formula. Axiomatizing the interpretation of quantified object language formulas presents some minor technical problems, however. We would like to say something like this: EXIST(X,P) is true in W if and only if there is some individual such that the open formula P is true of that individual in W. We do not have any way of saying that an open formula is true of an individual in a world, however; we just have the predicate T, which simply says that a formula is true in a world. One way of solving the problem would be to introduce a new predicate, or perhaps redefine T, to express the Tarskian notion of satisfaction rather than truth. This approach is semantically clean but syntactically clumsy, so we will instead follow the advice of Scott (1970, p. 151) and define the truth of a quantified statement in terms of substituting into the body of that statement a rigid designator for the value of the quantified variable.

In order to formalize this substitutional approach to the interpretation of object language quantifications, we need a rigid designator in the object language for every individual. Since our representation of the object language is in the form of an abstract syntax, we can simply stipulate that there is a function @ that maps any individual in the object language's domain of discourse into an object language rigid designator of that individual. The definition of T for quantified statements is then given by the following axiom schemata:

L7. $\forall w_1(T(w_1, \text{EXIST}(X,P)) \equiv \exists x_1(T(w_1, P[@(x_1)/X])))$

L8. $\forall w_1(T(w_1, \text{ALL}(X,P)) \equiv \forall x_1(T(w_1, P[@(x_1)/X])))$

In these schemata, P may be any object language formula, X may be any object language variable, and the notation $P[@(x_1)/X]$ designates the expression that results from substituting $@(x_1)$ for every free occurrence of X in P.

L7 says that an existentially quantified formula is true in a world W if and only if, for *some* individual, the result of substituting a rigid designator of that individual for the bound variable in the body of the formula is true in W. L8 says that a universally quantified formula is true in W if and only if, for *every* individual, the result of substituting a rigid designator of that individual for the bound variable in the body of the formula is true in W.

Except for the knowledge operator itself, the only part of the truth definition of the object language that remains to be given is the definition of T for atomic formulas. We remarked previously that a formula of the form $P(A_1, \ldots, A_n)$ is true in a world W just in case the tuple consisting of the denotations in W of the terms $A_1,...,A_n$ is in the extension in W of the relation P. To axiomatize this principle, we need two additions to the metalanguage. First, we need a function D that maps a possible world and an object language term into the denotation of that term in that world. Second, for each n-place object language predicate P, we need a corresponding $n+1$-place metalanguage predicate (which, by convention, we will write :P) that takes as its arguments the possible world in which the object language formula is to be evaluated and the denotations in that world of the arguments of the object language predicate. The interpretation of an object language atomic formula is then given by the axiom schema

L9. $\forall w_1, t_1,...,t_n$
$\quad (T(w_1, P(t_1,...,t_n)) \equiv :P(w_{f_1}, D(w_1, t_1),..., D(w_1, t_n)))$

To eliminate the function D, we need to introduce a metalanguage expression corresponding to each object language constant or function. In the general case, the new expression will be a function with an extra argument position for the possible world of evaluation. The axiom schemata for D are then

L10. $\forall w_1, x_1 (D(w_1, @(x_1)) = x_1)$

L11. $\forall w_1 (D(w_1, C) = :C(w_1))$

L12. $\forall w_1, t_1,...,t_n$
$\quad (D(w_1, F(t_1,...,t_n)) = :F(w_1, D(w_1, t_1),..., D(w_1, t_n))),$

where C is an object language constant and F is an object language function, and we use the ":" convention already introduced for their metalanguage counterparts.

Since $@(x_1)$ is a rigid designator of x_1, its value is x_1 in every possible world. In the general case, an object language constant will have a corresponding metalanguage function that picks out the denotation of the constant in a particular world. Similarly, an object language function will have a corresponding metalanguage function that maps a possible world and the denotations of the arguments of the object language function into the value of the object language function applied to those arguments in that world.

It will be convenient to treat specially those object language constants and functions that are (or can be used to construct) rigid designators. We could introduce additional axioms asserting that such expressions have the same value in every possible world, but we can accomplish the same end simply by making the corresponding metalanguage expressions independent of the possible world of evaluation. So, for object language constants that are rigid designators, we will have a variant of axiom L11:

L11a. $\forall w_1 (D(w_1, C) = :C)$ if C is a rigid designator.

We will similarly treat *rigid functions*—those that always map a particular tuple of arguments into the same value in all possible worlds:

L12a. $\forall w_1,t_1,\ldots,t_n(D(w_1,F(t_1,\ldots,t_n)) = :F(D(w_1,t_1),\ldots,D(w_1,t_n)))$
if F is a rigid function.

Finally, we introduce a special axiom for the equality predicate of the object language, fixing its interpretation in all possible worlds to be the identity relation:

L13. $\forall w_1,t_1,t_2(T(w_1,EQ(t_1,t_2)) \equiv (D(w_1,t_1) = D(w_1,t_2)))$

3.2 A First-Order Theory of Knowledge

The axioms given in the preceding section allow us to talk about a formula of first-order logic being true relative to a possible world rather than absolutely. This generalization would be pointless, however, if we never had occasion to mention any possible worlds other than the actual one. References to other possible worlds are introduced by our axioms for knowledge:

K1. $\forall w_1,t_1,p_1$
$(T(w_1,KNOW(t_1,p_1)) \equiv \forall w_2(K(D(w_1,t_1),w_1,w_2) \supset T(w_2,p_1)))$

K2. $\forall a_1,w_1(K(a_1,w_1,w_1))$

K3. $\forall a_1,w_1,w_2(K(a_1,w_1,w_2) \supset \forall w_3(K(a_1,w_2,w_3) \supset K(a_1,w_1,w_3)))$

K1 gives the possible-world analysis for object language formulas of the form KNOW(A,P). The interpretation is that KNOW(A,P) is true in world W_1 just in case P is true in every world that is compatible with what the agent denoted by A in W_1 knows in W_1. Since an object language term may denote different individuals in different possible worlds, we use $D(W_1,A)$ to identify the denotation of A in W_1. K represents the accessibility relation associated with KNOW, so $K(D(W_1,A),W_1,W_2)$ is how we represent the fact W_2 is compatible with what the agent denoted by A in W_1 knows in W_1.

As we pointed out before, the principle embodied in K1 is that an agent knows everything entailed by his knowledge. Since this is too strong a generalization, in a more thorough analysis we would regard the inference from the right side of K1 to the left side as being a default inference. K2 and K3 state constraints on the accessibility relation K that we use to capture other properties of knowledge. They require that, for a fixed agent :A, $K(:A,w_1,w_2)$ be reflexive and transitive. We have already shown this entails that anything that anyone knows must be true, and that if someone knows something he knows that he knows it. Finally, the fact that K1–K3 are asserted to hold for all possible worlds implies that everyone knows the principles they embody, and everyone knows that everyone knows, etc. In other words, these principles are common knowledge.

To illustrate how our theory operates, we will show how to derive a simple result in the logic of knowledge, that from the premises that A knows that P(B) and A knows that B = C, we can conclude that A knows that P(C). Our proofs will be in natural-deduction form. The axioms and preceding lines that justify each step will be given to the right of the step. Subordinate proofs will be indicated by indented sections, and ASS will mark the assumptions on which these subordinate proofs are based. DIS(N,M) will indicate the discharge of the assumption on line N with respect to the conclusion on line M. The general pattern of proofs in this system will be to assert the object language premises of the problem, transform them into their metalanguage equivalents, using axioms L1–L13 and K1, then derive the metalanguage version of the conclusion using first-order logic and axioms such as K2 and K3, and finally transform the conclusion back into the object language, again using L1–L13 and K1.

Given: TRUE(KNOW(A,P(B)))
            TRUE(KNOW(A,EQ(B,C)))

Prove: TRUE(KNOW(A,P(C)))

1.	TRUE(KNOW(A,P(B)))	Given
2.	$T(W_0,KNOW(A,P(B)))$	L1,1
3.	$K(D(W_0,A),W_0,w_1) \supset T(w_1,P(B))$	K1,2
4.	$K(:A(W_0),W_0,w_1) \supset T(w_1,P(B))$	L11,3
5.	TRUE(KNOW(A,EQ(B,C)))	Given
6.	$T(W_0,KNOW(A,EQ(B,C)))$	L1,5
7.	$K(D(W_0,A),W_0,w_1) \supset T(w_1,EQ(B.C))$	K1,6
8.	$K(:A(W_0),W_0,w_1) \supset T(w_1,EQ(B.C))$	L11,7
9.	$K(:A(W_0),W_0,w_1)$	ASS
10.	$T(w_1,P(B))$	4,9
11.	$:P(w_1,D(w_1,B))$	L9,10
12.	$:P(w_1,:B(w_1))$	L11,11
13.	$T(w_1,EQ(B,C))$	8,9
14.	$D(w_1,B) = D(w_1,C)$	L13,13
15.	$:B(w_1) = :C(w_1)$	L11,14
16.	$:P(w_1,:C(w_1))$	12,15
17.	$:P(w_1,D(w_1,C))$	L11,16
18.	$T(w_1,P(C))$	L9,17

19. $K(:A(W_0),W_0,w_1) \supset T(w_1,P(C))$ DIS(9,18)

20. $K(D(W_0,A),W_0,w_1) \supset T(w_1,P(C))$ L11,19

21. $T(W_0,KNOW(A,P(C)))$ K1,20

22. $TRUE(KNOW(A,P(C)))$ L1,21

A knows that $P(B)$ (Line 1), so $P(B)$ is true in every world compatible with what A knows (Line 4). Similarly, since A knows that $B = C$ (Line 5), $B = C$ is true in every world compatible with what A knows (Line 8). Let w_1 be one of these worlds (Line 9). $P(B)$ and $B = C$ must be true in w_1 (Lines 12 and 15), hence $P(C)$ must be true in w_1 (Line 16). Therefore, $P(C)$ is true in every world compatible with what A knows (Line 19), so A knows that $P(C)$ (Line 22). If $TRUE(EQ(B,C))$ had been given instead of $TRUE(KNOW(A,EQ(B,C)))$, we would have had $B = C$ true in W_0 instead of w_1. In that case, the substitution of C for B in $P(B)$ (Line 16) would not have been valid, and we could not have concluded that A knows that $P(C)$. This proof seems long because we have made each routine step a separate line. This is worth doing once to illustrate all the formal details, but in subsequent examples we will combine some of the routine steps to shorten the derivation.

4 A Possible-World Analysis of Action

In the preceding sections, we have presented a framework for describing what someone knows in terms of possible worlds. To characterize the relation of knowledge to action, we need a theory of action in these same terms. Fortunately, the standard way of looking at actions in AI gives us just that sort of theory. Most AI programs that reason about actions are based on a view of the world as a set of possible states of affairs, with each action determining a binary relation between states of affairs—one being the outcome of performing the action in the other. We can integrate our analysis of knowledge with this view of action by identifying the possible worlds used to describe knowledge with the possible states of affairs used to describe actions.

The identification of a possible world, as used in the analysis of knowledge, with the state of affairs at a particular time does not require any changes in the formalization already presented, but it does require a reinterpretation of what the axioms mean. If the variables w_1, w_2,... are reinterpreted as ranging over states of affairs, then "A knows that P" will be analyzed roughly as "P is true in every state of affairs that is compatible with what A knows in the actual state of affairs." It might seem that taking possible worlds to be states of affairs, and therefore not extended in time, might make it difficult to talk about what someone knows regarding the past or future. That is not the case, however. Knowledge about the past and future can be handled by modal tense operators, with corresponding accessibility relations between possible states-of-affairs/worlds. We could have a tense operator FUTURE such that FUTURE(P) means that P will be true at some time to come. If we let F be an accessibility relation such that $F(W_1,W_2)$ means that the state-of-affairs/world W_2 lies in the future of the state-of-affairs/world W_1, then we can define FUTURE(P) to be true in W_1 just in case there is some W_2 such that $F(W_1,W_2)$ holds and P is true in W_2.

This much is standard tense logic (e.g., Rescher & Urquhart, 1971). The interesting point is that statements about someone's knowledge of the future work out correctly, even though such knowledge is analyzed in terms of alternatives to a state of affairs, rather than alternatives to a possible world containing an entire course of events. The proposition that John knows that P will be true is represented simply by KNOW(JOHN,FUTURE(P)). The analysis of this is that FUTURE(P) is true in every state of affairs that is compatible with what John knows, from which it follows that, for each state of affairs that is compatible with what John knows, P is true in some future alternative to that state of affairs. An important point to note here is that two states of affairs can be "internally" similar (that is, they coincide in the truth-value assigned to any nonmodal statement), yet be distinct because they differ in the accessibility relations they bear to other possible states of affairs. Thus, although we treat a possible world as a state of affairs rather than a course of events, it is a state of affairs in the particular course of events defined by its relationships to other states of affairs.

For planning and reasoning about future actions, instead of a tense operator like FUTURE, which simply asserts what will be true, we need an operator that describes what would be true if a certain event occurred. Our approach will be to recast McCarthy's situation calculus (McCarthy, 1968; McCarthy & Hayes, 1969) so that it meshes with our possible-world characterization of knowledge. The situation calculus is a first-order language in which predicates that can vary in truth-value over time are given an extra argument to indicate what situations (i.e., states of affairs) they hold in, with a function RESULT that maps an agent, an action, and a situation into the situation that results from the agent's performance of the action in the first situation. Statements about the effects of actions are then expressed by formulas like P(RESULT(A,ACT,S)), which means that P is true in the situation that results from A's performing ACT in situation S.

To integrate these ideas into our logic of knowledge, we will reconstruct the situation calculus as a modal logic. In parallel to the operator KNOW for talking about knowledge, we introduce an object language operator RES for talking about the results of events. Situations will not be referred to explicitly in the object language, but they will reappear in the possible-world semantics for RES in the metalanguage. RES will be a two-place operator whose first argument is a term denoting an event, and whose second argument is a formula. RES(E,P) will mean that it is possible for the event denoted by E to occur and that, if it did, the formula P would then be true. The possible-world semantics for RES will be specified in terms of an accessibility relation R, parallel to K, such that $R(:E,W_1.W_2)$ means that W_2 is the situation/world that would result from the event :E happening in W_1.

We assume that, if it is impossible for :E to happen in W_1 (i.e., if the prerequisites of :E are not satisfied), then there is no W_2 such that $R(:E,W_1,W_2)$ holds. Otherwise we assume that there is exactly one W_2 such that $(:E,W_1,W_2)$ holds:[4]

R1. $\forall w_1,w_2,w_3,e_1((R(e_1,w_1,w_2) \wedge R(e_1,w_1,w_3)) \supset (w_2 = w_3))$

(Variables e_1, e_2,... range over events.) Given these assumptions, RES(E,P) will be true in a situation/world W_1 just in case there is some W_2 that is the situation/world that results from the event described by E happening in W_1, and in which P is true:

R2. $\forall w_1,t_1,p_1(T(w_1,RES(t_1,p_1)) \equiv \exists w_2(R(D(w_1,t_1),w_1,w_2) \wedge T(w_2,p_1)))$

The type of event we will normally be concerned with is the performance of an action by an agent. We will let DO(A,ACT) be a description of the event consisting of the agent denoted by A performing the action denoted by ACT.[5] (We will assume that the set of possible agents is the same as the set of possible knowers.) We will want DO(A,ACT) to be the standard way of referring to the event of A's carrying out the action ACT, so DO will be a rigid function. Hence, DO(A,ACT) will be a rigid designator of an event if A is a rigid designator of an agent and ACT a rigid designator of an action.

Many actions can be thought of as general procedures applied to particular objects. Such a general procedure will be represented by a function that maps the objects to which the procedure is applied into the action of applying the procedure to those objects. For instance, if DIAL represents the general procedure of dialing combinations of safes, SF a safe, and COMB(SF) the combination of SF, then DIAL(COMB(SF),SF) represents the action of dialing the combination COMB(SF) on the safe SF, and DO(A,DIAL(COMB(SF),SF)) represents the event of A's dialing the combination COMB(SF) on the safe SF.

This formalism gives us the ability to describe an agent's knowledge of the effects of carrying out an action. In the object language, we can express the claim that A_1 knows that P would result from A_2's doing ACT by saying that KNOW(A_1,RES(DO(A_2,ACT),P)) is true. The possible-world analysis of this statement is that, for every world compatible with what A_1 knows in the actual

---

[4] This amounts to an assumption that all events are deterministic, which might seem to be an unnecessary limitation. From a pragmatic standpoint, however, it doesn't matter whether we say that a given event is nondeterministic, or we say that it is deterministic but no one knows precisely what the outcome will be. If we treated events as being nondeterministic, we could say that an agent knows exactly what situation he is in, but, because :E is nondeterministic, he doesn't know what situation would result if :E occurs. It would be completely equivalent, however, to say that :E is deterministic, and that the agent *does not* know exactly what situation he is in because he doesn't know what the result of :E would be in that situation.

[5] It would be more precise to say that DO(A,ACT) names a *type* of event rather than an individual event, since an agent can perform the same action on different occasions. We would then say that RES and R apply to event types. We will let the present usage stand, however, since we have no need to distinguish event types from individual events in this paper.

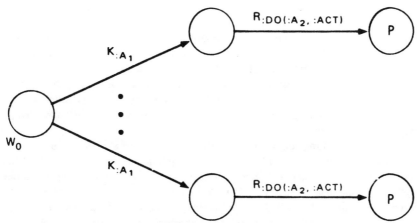

Figure 5. $\text{TRUE}(\text{KNOW}(A_1, \text{RES}(\text{DO}(A_2, \text{ACT}), P))) \equiv$
$$\forall w_1 (K(:A_1, W_0, w_1) \supset$$
$$\exists w_2 (R(:DO(:A_2 \text{ACT}), w_1, w_2) \wedge T(w_2, P)))$$

world, there is a world that is the result of A_2's doing ACT and in which P is true (see Figure 5). Formally, this is expressed by

$$\forall w_1 (K(:A_1, W_0, w_1) \supset \exists w_2 (R(:DO(:A_2, :ACT), w_1, w_2) \wedge T(w_2, P))),$$

if we assume that A_1, A_2, and ACT are rigid designators.

In addition to simple, one-step actions, we will want to talk about complex combinations of actions. We will therefore introduce expressions into the object language for action sequences, conditionals, and iteration. If P is a formula, and ACT_1 and ACT_2 are action descriptions, then $(\text{ACT}_1; \text{ACT}_2)$, $\text{IF}(P, \text{ACT}_1, \text{ACT}_2)$, and $\text{WHILE}(P, \text{ACT}_1)$ will also be action descriptions. Roughly speaking, $(\text{ACT}_1; \text{ACT}_2)$ describes the sequence of actions consisting of ACT_1 followed by ACT_2. $\text{IF}(P, \text{ACT}_1, \text{ACT}_2)$ describes the conditional action of doing ACT_1 if P is true, otherwise doing ACT_2. $\text{WHILE}(P, \text{ACT}_1)$ describes the iterative action of repeating ACT_1 as long as P is true.

Defining denotations for these complex action descriptions is somewhat problematical. The difficulty comes from the fact that, whenever we have an action described as a sequence of subactions, any expression used in specifying one of the subactions needs to be interpreted relative to the situation in which that subaction is carried out. For instance, if PUTON(X,Y) denotes the action of putting X on Y, STACK denotes a stack of blocks, TABLE denotes a table, and TOP picks out the top block of a stack, we would want the execution of

(PUTON(TOP(STACK),TABLE); PUTON(TOP(STACK),TABLE))

to result in what were initially the top two blocks of the stack being put on the table, rather than what was initially the top block being put on the table twice. The second occurrence of TOP(STACK) should be interpreted with respect to the situation in which the first block has already been removed. The problem is that, in general, what situation exists after one step of a sequence of actions has been excecuted depends on who the agent is. If John picks up a certain block, *he* will be holding the block; if, however. Mary performs the same action, *she* will be holding the block. If an action description refers to "the block Mary is holding," exactly which block it is may depend on which agent is carrying out the action, but this is not specified by the action description.

One way of getting around these difficulties conceptually would be to treat actions as functions from agents to events, but notational problems would remain nevertheless. We will therefore choose a different solution: treating complex actions as "virtual individuals" (Scott, 1970), or pseudoentities. That is, complex action descriptions will not be treated as referring expressions in themselves, but only as component parts of more complex referring expressions. In particular, if ACT is a complex action description (and A denotes an agent), we will treat the event description DO(A,ACT), but not ACT itself, as having a denotation. Complex action descriptions will be permitted to occur only as part of such event descriptions, and we will define the denotations of the event descriptions in a way that eliminates reference to complex actions. We will, however, continue to treat actions as real entities that can be quantified over, and simple action descriptions such as DIAL(COMB(SF),SF) will still be considered to denote actions.

The denotations of event descriptions formed from conditional and iterative action descriptions can be defined as follows in terms of the denotations of event descriptions formed from action sequence descriptions:

R3. $\forall w_1, t_1, t_2, t_3, p_1$
$((T(w_1, p_1) \supset (D(w_1, DO(t_1, IF(p_1, t_2, t_3))) = D(w_1, DO(t_1, t_2)))) \wedge$
$(\neg T(w_1, p_1) \supset (D(w_1, DO(t_1, IF(p_1, t_2, t_3))) = D(w_1, DO(t_1, t_3)))))$

R4. $\forall w_1, t_1, t_2, p_1$
$(D(w_1, DO(t_1, WHILE(p_1, t_2))) =$
$D(w_1, DO(t_1, IF(p_1, (t_2; WHILE(p_1, t_2)), NIL)))$

R3 says that performing the conditional action IF(P,ACT$_1$,ACT$_2$) results in the same event as carrying out ACT$_1$ in a situation where P is true or carrying out ACT$_2$ in a situation where P is false. R4 says that performing WHILE(P,ACT) always results in the same event as IF(P,(ACT; WHILE(P,ACT)),NIL), where NIL denotes the null action. In other words, doing WHILE(P,ACT) is equivalent to doing ACT followed by WHILE(P,ACT) if P is true, otherwise doing nothing—i.e., doing ACT as long as P remains true.

To define the denotation of events that consist of carrying out action sequences, we need some notation for talking about sequences of events. First, we will let ";" be a polymorphic operator in the object language, creating descriptions of event sequences in addition to action sequences. Speaking informally, if E$_1$ and E$_2$ are event descriptions, then (E$_1$; E$_2$) names the event sequence consisting of E$_1$ followed by E$_2$, just as (ACT$_1$; ACT$_2$) names the action sequence consisting of ACT$_1$

followed by ACT_2. In the metalanguage, event sequences will be indicated with angle brackets, so that $\langle :E_1, :E_2 \rangle$ will mean $:E_1$ followed by $:E_2$. The denotations of expressions involving action and event sequences are then defined by the following axioms:

R5. $\forall w_1, t_1, t_2, t_3$
$(D(w_1, DO(t_1, (t_2; t_3))) = D(w_1, (DO(t_1, t_2); DO(@(D(w_1, t_1)), t_3))))$

R6. $\forall w_1, w_2, t_1, t_2$
$(R(D(w_1, t_1), w_1, w_2) \supset (D(w_1, (t_1; t_2)) = \langle D(w_1, t_1), D(w_2, t_2) \rangle))$

R5 says that the event consisting of an agent A's performance of the action sequence ACT_1 followed by ACT_2 is simply the event sequence that consists of A's carrying out ACT_1 followed by his carrying out ACT_2. Note that, in the description of the second event, the agent is picked out by the expression $@(D(w_1, A))$, which guarantees that we get the same agent as in the first event, in case the original term picking out the agent changes its denotation after the first event has happened. R6 then defines the denotation of an event sequence description $(E_1; E_2)$ as the sequence comprising the denotation of E_1 in the original situation followed by the denotation of E_2 in the situation resulting from the occurrence of E_1. If there is no situation that results from the occurrence of E_1, we leave the denotation of $(E_1; E_2)$ undefined.

Finally, we need to define the accessibility relation R for event sequences and for events in which the null action is carried out.

R7. $\forall w_1, w_2, e_1, e_2$
$(R(\langle e_1, e_2 \rangle, w_1, w_2) \equiv \exists w_3 (R(e_1, w_1, w_3) \wedge (Re_2, w_3, w_2)))$

R8. $\forall w_1, a_1 (R(:DO(a_1, :NIL), w_1, w_1))$

R7 says that a situation W_2 is the result of the event sequence $\langle E_2, E_2 \rangle$ occurring in W_1 if and only if there is a situation W_3 such that W_3 is the result of E_1 occurring in W_1, and W_2 is the result of E_2 occurring in W_2.[6] We will regard NIL as a rigid designator in the object language for the null action, so :NIL will be its metalanguage counterpart. R8, therefore, says that in any situation the result of doing nothing is the same situation.

5 An Integrated Theory of Knowledge and Action

5.1 The Dependence of Action on Knowledge

As we pointed out in the introduction, knowledge and action interact in two principal ways: (a) knowledge is often required prior to taking action; (b) actions can

---

[6] R7 guarantees that the sequences $<<E_1, E_2>, E_3>$ and $<E_1, <E_2, E_3>>$ always define the same accessibility relation on situations; so, just as one would expect, we can regard sequence operators as being associative. Thus, when we have a sequence of more than two events or actions, we will not feel obliged to indicate a pairwise grouping.

change what is known. In regard to the first, we need to consider knowledge prerequisites as well as physical prerequisites for actions. Our main thesis is that the knowledge prerequisites for an action can be analyzed as a matter of knowing what action to take. Recall the example of trying to open a locked safe. Why is it that, for an agent to achieve this goal by using the plan "Dial the combination of the safe," he must know the combination? The reason is that an agent could know that dialing the combination of the safe would result in the safe's being open, but still not know what to do because he does not know what the combination of the safe is. A similar analysis applies to knowing a telephone number in order to call someone on the telephone or knowing a password in order to gain access to a computer system.

It is important to realize that even mundane actions that are not usually thought of as requiring any special knowledge are no different from the examples just cited. For instance, none of the AI problem-solving systems that have dealt with the blocks world have tried to take into account whether the robot possesses sufficient knowledge to be able to move block A to point B. Yet, if a command were phrased as "Move my favorite block back to its original position," the system could be just as much in the dark as with "Dial the combination of the safe." If the system does not know what actions satisfy the description, it will not be able to carry out the command. The only reason that the question of knowledge seems more pertinent in the case of dialing combinations and telephone numbers is that, in the contexts in which these actions naturally arise, there is usually no presumption that the agent knows what action fits the description. An important consequence of this view is that the specification of an action will normally not need to include anything about knowledge prerequisites. These will be supplied by a general theory of using actions to achieve goals. What we will need to specify are the conditions under which an agent knows what action is referred to by an action description.

In our possible-world semantics for knowledge, the usual way of knowing what entity is referred to by a description B is by having some description C that is a rigid designator, and by knowing that B = C. (Note, that if B itself is a rigid designator, it can be used for C.) In particular, knowing what action is referred to by an action description means having a rigid designator for the action described. But, if this is all the knowledge that is required for carrying out the action, then a rigid designator for an action must be an *executable description* of the action—in the same sense that a computer program is an executable description of a computation to an interpreter for the language in which the program is written.

Often the actions we want to talk about are mundane general procedures that we would be willing to assume everyone knows how to perform. Dialing a telephone number or the combination of a safe is a typical example. In many of these cases, if an agent knows the general procedure and what objects the procedure is to be applied to, then he knows everything that is relevant to the task. In such cases, the function that represents the general procedure will be a rigid function, so that, if the arguments of the function are rigid designators, the term consisting of the function applied to the arguments will be a rigid designator. Hence, knowing what objects the arguments denote will amount to knowing what action the term refers to. We will treat dialing the combination of a safe, or dialing a telephone number as being this type of procedure. That is, we assume that anyone who knows what combination he is to dial and what safe he is to dial it on thereby knows what action he is to perform.

There are other procedures we might also wish to assume that anyone could perform, but that cannot be represented as rigid functions. Suppose that, in the blocks world, we let PUTON(B,C) denote the action of putting B on C. Even though we would not want to question anyone's ability to perform PUTON in general, knowing what objects B and C are will not be sufficient to perform PUTON(B,C); knowing *where* they are is also necessary. We could have a special axiom stating that knowing what action PUTON(B,C) is requires knowing where B and C are, but this will be superfluous if we simply assume that everyone knows the definition of PUTON in terms of more primitive actions. If we define PUTON(X,Y) as something like

```
(MOVEHAND(LOCATION(X));
 GRASP;
 MOVEHAND(LOCATION(TOP(Y)));
 UNGRASP),
```

then we can treat MOVEHAND, GRASP, and UNGRASP as rigid functions, and we can see that executing PUTON requires knowing where the two objects are because their locations are mentioned in the definition. So, although PUTON itself is not a rigid function, we can avoid having a special axiom stating what the knowledge prerequisites of PUTON are by defining PUTON as a sequence of actions represented by rigid functions.

To formalize this theory, we will introduce a new object language operator CAN. CAN(A,ACT,P) will mean that A can achieve P by performing ACT, in the sense that A knows how to achieve P by performing ACT. We will not give a possible-world semantics for CAN directly; instead we will give a definition of CAN in terms of KNOW and RES, which we can use in reasoning about CAN to transform a problem into terms of possible worlds.

In the simplest case, an agent A can achieve P by performing ACT if he knows what action ACT is, and he knows that P would be true as a result of his performing ACT. In the object language, we can express this fact by

$$\forall a(\exists x(KNOW(a,((x = ACT) \land RES(DO(a,ACT),P)))) \supset$$
$$CAN(a,ACT,P)).$$

We cannot strengthen this assertion to a biconditional, however, because that would be too stringent a definition of CAN for complex actions. It would require the agent to know from the very beginning of his action exactly what he is going to do at every step. In carrying out a complex action, though, an agent may take some initial action that results in his acquiring knowledge about what to do later.

For an agent to be able to achieve a goal by performing a complex action, all that is really neccessary is that he know what to do first, and that he know that he will know what to do at each subsequent step. So, for any action descriptions ACT and ACT$_1$, the following formula also states a condition under which an agent can achieve P by performing ACT:

$$\forall a (\exists x (KNOW(a,((DO(a,(x;\ ACT_1)) = DO(a,ACT)) \wedge$$
$$RES(DO(a,x),CAN(a,ACT_1,P))))) \supset$$
$$CAN(a,ACT,P)).$$

This says that A can achieve P by doing ACT if there is an action X such that A knows that his execution of the sequence X followed by ACT$_1$ would be equivalent to his doing ACT, and that his doing X would result in his being able to achieve P by doing ACT$_1$.

Finally, with the following metalanguage axiom we can state that these are the only two conditions under which an agent can use a particular action to achieve a goal:

C1. $\forall w_1,t_1,t_2,t_3,p_1$
    $((t_2 = @(D(w_1,t_1))) \supset$
    $(T(w_1,CAN(t_1,t_3,p_1)) \equiv$
    $(T(w_1,EXIST(X,KNOW(t_1,AND(EQ(X,t_3),RES(DO(t_2,\ t_3),p_1)))))V$
    $\exists t_4(T(w_1,\ EXIST(X,KNOW(t_1,AND(EQ(DO(t_2,(X;\ t_4)),DO(t_2,t_3))),$
    $RES(DO(t_2,X),$
    $CAN(t_2,t_4,p_1)))))))))))$

Letting $t_1 = A$, $t_2 = A_1$, and $t_3 = ACT$, C1 says that, for any formula P, if A$_1$ is the standard identifier of the agent denoted by A, then A can achieve P by doing ACT if and only if one of the following conditions is met: (a) A knows what action ACT is and knows that P would be true as a result of A$_1$'s (i.e., his) doing ACT, or (b) there is an action description $t_4 = ACT_1$ such that, for some action X, A knows that A$_1$'s doing X followed by ACT$_1$ is the same event as his doing ACT and knows that A$_1$'s doing X would result his being able to achieve P by doing ACT$_1$.

As a simple illustration of these concepts, we will show how to derive the fact that an agent can open a safe, given the premise that he knows the combination. To do this, the only additional fact we need is that, if an agent does dial the correct combination of a safe, the safe will then be open:

D1. $\forall w_1,a_1,x_1$
    $(:SAFE(x_1) \supset$
    $\exists w_2(R(:DO(a_1,:DIAL(:COMB(w_1,x_1),x_1)),w_1,w_2) \wedge$
    $:OPEN(w_2,x_1)))$

D1 says that, for any possible world W$_1$, any agent :A, and any safe :SF, there is a world W$_2$ that is the result of :A's dialing the combination of :SF on :SF in W$_1$, and in which :SF is open. The important point about this axiom, is that the function :COMB (which picks out the combination to a safe) depends on what possible world it is evaluated in, while :DIAL (the function that maps a combination and a safe into the action of dialing the combination on the safe) does not. Thus we are implicitly assuming that, given a particular safe, there may be some doubt as to what its combination is, but, given a combination and a safe, there exists no possible doubt as to what action dialing the combination on the safe is. (We also simplify matters by omitting the possible world-argument to :SAFE, so as to avoid raising the question of knowing whether something is a safe.) Since this axiom is asserted to hold for all possible worlds, we are in effect assuming that it is common knowledge.

Now we show that, for any safe, if the agent A knows its combination, he can open the safe by dialing that combination: or, more precisely, for all X, if X is a safe and there is some Y, such that A knows that Y is the combination of X, then A can open X by dialing the combination of X on X:

Prove: TRUE(ALL(X,IMP(AND(SAFE(X),
  EXIST(Y,KNOW(A,EQ(Y,COMB(X))))))
  CAN(A,DIAL(COMB(X),X),OPEN(X))))

1. $T(W_0,$
  AND(SAFE($@(x_1)$),
  EXIST(Y,KNOW(A,EQ(Y,COMB($@(x_1)$)))))))   ASS

2. :SAFE(x_1)   1,L2,L9

3. $\forall w_1(K(:A(W_0),W_0,w_1) \supset$
  $(:C = :COMB(w_1,x_1)))$ 1,L2,L7,K1,L11,
  L13,L10,L12

4. $K(:A(W_0),W_0,w_1)$ ASS

5. $:C = COMB(w_1,x_1)$ 3,4

6. $:DIAL(:C,x_1) = :DIAL(:COMB(w_1,x_1),x_1)$ 5

7. $T(w_1,$
  EQ($@(:DIAL(:C,x_1))$,
  DIAL(COMB($@(x_1)$),$@(x_1)$))))   L10,L12,L12a,L13

8. $\exists w_2(R(:DO(:A(W_0),$
  $:DIAL(:COMB(w_1,x_1),x_1))$,
  $w_1,w_2) \wedge$
  $:OPEN(w_2,x_1)))$ 2,D1

9. $T(w_1,$
  RES(DO($@(D(W_0,A))$,
  DIAL(COMB($@(x_1)$),$@(x_1)$)),
  OPEN($@(x_1)$))))   L11,L10,L12a,L9,R2

10. $T(w_1,$
  AND(EQ($@(:DIAL(:C,x_1))$,
  DIAL(COMB($@(x_1)$),$@(x_1)$)),
  RES(DO($@(D(W_0,A))$,
  DIAL(COMB($@(x_1)$),$@(x_1)$)),
  OPEN($@(x_1)$)))))   7,9,L2

11. $K(:A(W_0),W_0,w_1) \supset$ DIS(4,10)
      $T(w_1,$
          $AND(EQ(@(:DIAL(:C,x_1)),$
                  $DIAL(COMB(@(x_1)),@(x_1))),$
              $RES(DO(@(D(W_0,A)),$
                      $DIAL(COMB(@(x_1)),@(x_1))),$
                  $OPEN(@(x_1)))))$

12. $T(W_0,$ 11,L11,K1
          $KNOW(A,$
                  $AND(EQ(@(:DIAL(:C,x_1)),$
                          $DIAL(COMB(@(x_1)),@(x_1))),$
                      $RES(DO(@(D(W_0,A)),$
                              $DIAL(COMB(@(x_1)),@(x_1))),$
                          $OPEN(@(x_1))))))$

13. $T(W_0,$ 12,L7
          $EXIST(X,$
                  $KNOW(A,$
                          $AND(EQ(X,$
                                  $DIAL(COMB(@(x_1)),$
                                      $@(x_1))),$
                              $RES(DO(@(D(W_0,A)),$
                                      $DIAL(COMB(@(x_1)),$
                                          $@(x_1))),$
                                  $OPEN(@(x_1)))))$

14. $T(W_0,$ 13,C1
          $CAN(A,$
              $DIAL(COMB(@(x_1)),@(x_1)),$
              $OPEN(@(x_1))))$

15. $T(W_0,$ DIS(1,14)
          $AND(SAFE(@(x_1),$
              $EXIST(Y,KNOW(A,EQ(Y,COMB(@(x_1))))))))) \supset$
          $T(W_0,$
          $CAN(A,DIAL(COMB(@(x_1)),@(x_1)),OPEN(@(x_1))))$

16. $TRUE(ALL(X,$ 15,L4,L8,L1
                  $IMP(AND(SAFE(X),$
                          $EXIST(Y,$
                              $KNOW(A,$
                                      $EQ(Y,COMB(X))))),$
                      $CAN(A,DIAL(COMB(X),X),OPEN(X))))$

Suppose that x_1 is a safe and there is some C that A knows to be the combination of x_1 (Lines 1–3). Suppose w_1 is a world that is compatible with what A knows in the actual world, W_0 (Line 4). Then C is the combination of x_1 in w_1 (Line 5), so dialing C on x_1 is the same action as dialing the combination of x_1 on x_1 in w_1 (Lines 6 and 7). By axiom D1, A's dialing the combination of x_1 on x_1 in w_1 will result in x_1's being open (Lines 8 and 9). Since w_1 was an arbitrarily chosen world compatible with what A knows in W_0, it follows that in W_0 A knows dialing C on x_1 to be the act of dialing the combination of x_1 on x_1 and that his dialing the combination of x_1 on x_1 will result in x_1's being open (Lines 10–12). Hence, A knows what action dialing the combination of x_1 on x_1 is, and that his dialing the combination of x_1 on x_1 will result in x_1's being open (Line 13). Therefore A can open x_1 by dialing the combination of x_1 on x_1, provided that x_1 is a safe and he knows the combination of x_1 (Lines 14 and 15). Finally, since x_1 was chosen arbitrarily, we conclude that A can open any safe by dialing the combination, provided he knows the combination (Line 16).

5.2 The Effects of Action on Knowledge

In describing the effects of an action on what an agent knows, we will distinguish actions that give the agent new information from those that do not. Actions that provide an agent with new information will be called *informative* actions. An action is informative if an agent would know more about the situation resulting from his performing the action after performing it than before performing it. In the blocks world, looking inside a box could be an informative action, but moving a block would probably not, because an agent would normally know no more after moving the block than he would before moving it. In the real world there are probably no actions that are never informative, because all physical processes are subject to variation and error. Nevertheless, it seems clear that we do and should treat many actions as noninformative from the standpoint of planning.

Even if an action is not informative in the sense we have just defined, performing the action will still alter the agent's state of knowledge. If the agent is aware of his action, he will know that it has been performed. As a result, the tense and modality of many of the things he knows will change. For example, if before performing the action he knows that P is true, then after performing the action he will know that P was true before he performed the action. Similarly, if before performing the action he knows that P would be true after performing the action, then afterwards he will know that P is true.

We can represent this very elegantly in terms of possible worlds. Suppose :A is an agent and $:E_1$ an event that consists in :A's performing some noninformative action. For any possible worlds W_1 and W_2 such that W_2 is the result of $:E_1$'s happening in W_1, the worlds that are compatible with what :A knows in W_2 are exactly the worlds that are the result of $:E_1$'s happening in some world that is compatible with what :A knows in W_1. In formal terms, this is

$$\forall w_1,w_2(R(:E,w_1,w_2) \supset \\ \forall w_3(K(:A,w_2,w_3) \equiv \exists w_4(K(:A,w_1,w_4) \wedge R(:E,w_4,w_3))))),$$

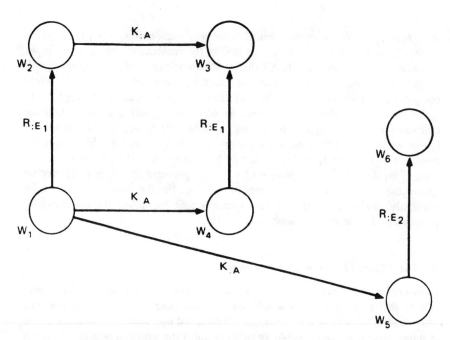

Figure 6. The Effect of a Noninformative Action on the Agent's Knowledge

which tells us exactly how what :A knows after $:E_1$ happens is related to what :A knows before $:E_1$ happens.

We can try to get some insight into this analysis by studying Figure 6. Sequences of possible situations connected by events can be thought of as possible courses of events. If W_1 is an actual situation in which $:E_1$ occurs, thereby producing W_2, then W_1 and W_2 comprise a subsequence of the actual course of events. Now we can ask what other courses of events are compatible with what :A knows in W_1 and in W_2. Suppose that W_4 and W_3 are connected by $:E_1$ in a course of events that is compatible with what :A knows in W_1. Since $:E_1$ is not informative for :A, the only sense in which his knowledge is increased by $:E_1$ is that he knows that $:E_1$ has occurred. Since $:E_1$ occurs at the corresponding place in the course of events that includes W_4 and W_3, this course of events will still be compatible with everything :A knows in W_2. However, the appropriate "tense shift" takes place. In W_1, W_4 is a possible alternative present for :A, and W_3 is a possible alternative future. In W_2, W_3 is a possible alternative present for :A, and W_4 is a possible alternative past.

Next consider a different course of events that includes W_5 and W_6 connected by a different event, $:E_2$. This course of events might be compatible with what :A knows in W_1 if he is not certain what he will do next, but, after $:E_1$ has happened and he knows that it has happened, this course of events is no longer compatible with what he knows. Thus, W_6 is not compatible with what :A knows in W_2. We can see, then, that even actions that provide the agent with no new information from the outside world still filter out for him those courses of events in which he would have performed actions other than those he actually did.

The idea of a filter on possible courses of events also provides a good picture of informative actions. With these actions, though, the filter is even stronger, since they not only filter out courses of events that differ from the actual course of events as to what event has just occurred, but they also filter out courses of events that are incompatible with the information furnished by the action. Suppose :E is an event that consists in :A's performing an informative action, such that the information gained by the agent is whether the formula P is true. For any possible worlds W_1 and W_2 such that W_2 is the result of :E's happening in W_1, the worlds that are compatible with what :A knows in W_2 are exactly those worlds that are the result of :E's happening in some world that is compatible with what :A knows in W_1, *and in which P has the same truth-value as in W_2*:

$$\forall w_1, w_2 (R(:E, w_1, w_2) \supset$$
$$\forall w_3 (K(:A, w_2, w_3) \equiv (\exists w_4 (K(:A, w_1, w_4) \wedge R(:E, w_4, w_3)) \wedge$$
$$(T(w_2, P) \equiv T(w_3, P)))))$$

It is this final condition that distinguishes informative actions from those that are not.

Figure 7 illustrates this analysis. Suppose W_1 and W_2 are connected by :E and are part of the actual course of events. Suppose, further, that P is true in W_2. Let W_4 and W_3 also be connected by :E, and let them be part of a course of events that is compatible with what :A knows in W_1. If P is true in W_3 and the only thing :A learns about the world from :E (other than that it has occurred) is whether P is true, this course of events will then still be compatible with what :A knows after :E has occurred. That is, W_3 will be compatible with what :A knows in W_2. Suppose, on the other hand, that W_5 and W_6 form part of a similar course of events, except that P is false in W_6. If :A does not know in W_1 whether P would be true after the occurrence of :E, this course of events will also be compatible with what he knows in W_1. After :E has occurred, however, he will know that P is true; consequently, this course of events will no longer be compatible with what he knows. That is, W_6 will not be compatible with what :A knows in W_2.

It is an advantage of this approach to describing how an action affects what an agent knows that not only do we specify what he learns from the action, but also what he does not learn. Our analysis gives us necessary, as well as sufficient, conditions for :A's knowing that P is true after event :E. In the case of an action that is not informative, we can infer that, unless :A knows before performing the action whether P would be true, he will not know afterwards either. In the case of an informative action such that what is learned is whether Q is true, he will not know whether P is true unless he does already—or knows of some dependence of P on Q.

Within the context of this possible-world analysis of the effects of action on knowledge, we can formalize the requirements for a test that we presented in Section I. Suppose that TEST is the action of testing the acidity of a particular

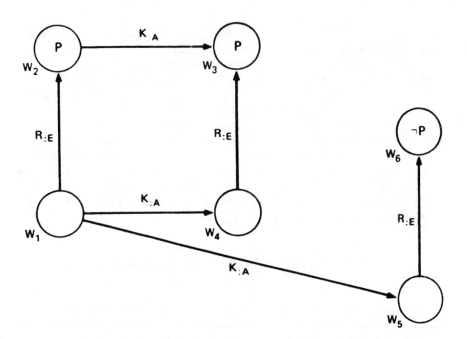

Figure 7. The Effect of an Informative Action on the Agent's Knowledge

solution with blue litmus paper, RED is a propositional constant (a predicate of zero arguments) whose truth depends on the color of the litmus paper, and ACID is a propositional constant whose truth depends on whether the solution is acidic. The relevent fact about TEST is that the paper will be red after an agent A performs the test if and only if the solution is acidic at the time the test is performed:

$$(ACID \supset RES(DO(A,TEST),RED)) \wedge$$
$$(\neg ACID \supset RES(DO(A,TEST), \neg RED))$$

In Section 1 we listed three conditions that ought to be sufficient for an agent to determine, by observing the outcome of a test, whether some unobservable precondition holds; in this case, for A to determine whether ACID is true by observing whether RED is true after TEST is performed:

(1) After A performs TEST, he knows whether RED is true.

(2) After A performs TEST, he knows that he has just performed TEST.

(3) A knows that RED will be true after TEST is performed just in case ACID was true before it was performed.

Conditions (1) and (2) will be satisfied if TEST is an informative action, such that the knowledge provided is whether RED is true in the resulting situation:

T1. $\forall w_1, w_2, a_1$
$(R(:DO(a_1,:TEST),w_1,w_2) \supset$
$\forall w_3(K(a_1,w_2,w_3) \equiv$
$(\exists w_4(K(a_1,w_1,w_4) \wedge R(:DO(a_1,:TEST),w_4,w_3)) \wedge$
$(:RED(w_2) \equiv :RED(w_3)))))$

If :RED and :TEST are the metalanguage analogues of RED and TEST, T1 says that for any possible worlds W_1 and W_2 such that W_2 is the result of an agent's performing TEST in W_1, the worlds that are compatible with what the agent knows in W_2 are exactly those that are the result of his performing TEST in some world that is compatible with what he knows in W_1, and in which RED has the same truth-value as in W_2. In other words, after performing TEST, the agent knows that he has done so and he knows whether RED is true in the resulting situation. As with our other axioms, the fact that it holds for all possible worlds makes it common knowledge.

Thus, A can use TEST to determine whether the solution is acid, provided that condition 1 is also satisfied. We can state this very succinctly if we make the further assumption that A knows that performing the test does not affect the acidity of the solution.[7] Given the axiom T1 for test, it is possible to show that

ACID $\supset$ RES(DO(A,TEST),KNOW(A,ACID)) and
$\neg$ ACID $\supset$ RES(DO(A,TEST),KNOW(A,$\neg$ ACID))

are true, provided that

KNOW(A,(ACID $\supset$ RES(DO(A,TEST),(ACID $\wedge$ RED)))) and
KNOW(A,($\neg$ ACID $\supset$ RES(DO(A,TEST),($\neg$ ACID $\wedge$ $\neg$ RED))))

are both true and A is a rigid designator. We will carry out the proof in one direction, showing that, if the solution is acidic, after the test has been conducted the agent will know that it is acidic.

Given: TRUE(KNOW(A,IMP(ACID,RES(DO(A,TEST),AND(ACID,RED)))))
TRUE(KNOW(A,IMP(NOT(ACID),
RES(DO(A,TEST),
AND(NOT(ACID),NOT(RED))))))
TRUE(ACID)

Prove: TRUE(RES(DO(A,TEST),KNOW(A,ACID)))

---

[7] We have to add this extra condition to be able to infer that the agent knows whether the solution *is* acidic, instead of merely that he knows whether it *was* acidic. The latter is a more general characteristic of tests, since it covers destructive as well as nondestructive tests. We have not, however, introduced any temporal operators into the object language that would allow us to make such a statement, although there would be no difficulty in stating the relevant conditions in the metalanguage. Indeed, this is precisely what is done by axioms such as T1.

1.	$\forall w_1(K(:A, W_0, w_1) \supset$	Given, L1, L4, R2,
	$\quad (:ACID(w_1) \supset$	L2, L9, L12, L11a
	$\quad\quad \exists w_2(R(:DO(:A, :TEST), w_1, w_2) \wedge$	
	$\quad\quad\quad :ACID(w_2) \wedge :RED(w_2))))$	
2.	$\forall w_1(K(:A, W_0, w_1) \supset$	Given, L1, L4, R2, L2,
	$\quad (\neg :ACID(w_1) \supset$	L6, L9, L12, L11a
	$\quad\quad \exists w_2(R(:DO(:A, :TEST), w_1, w_2) \wedge$	
	$\quad\quad\quad \neg :ACID(w_2) \wedge \neg :RED(w_2))))$	
3.	$:ACID(W_0)$	L1, L9
4.	$:ACID(W_0) \supset$	1, K2
	$\quad \exists w_2(R(:DO(:A, :TEST), W_0, w_2) \wedge$	
	$\quad\quad :ACID(w_2) \wedge :RED(w_2))$	
5.	$R(:DO(:A, :TEST), W_0, W_1)$	3, 4
6.	$:RED(W_1)$	3, 4
7.	$\forall w_2(K(:A, W_1, w_2) \equiv$	5, T1
	$\quad (\exists w_3(K(:A, W_0, w_3) \wedge$	
	$\quad\quad R(:DO(:A, :TEST), w_3, w_2)) \wedge$	
	$\quad (:RED(W_1) \equiv :RED(w_2))))$	
8.	$K(:A, W_1, w_2)$	ASS
9.	$K(:A, W_0, W_3)$	7, 8
10.	$R(:DO(:A, :TEST), W_3, w_2)$	7, 8
11.	$:RED(W_1) \equiv :RED(w_2)$	7, 8
12.	$:RED(w_2)$	6, 11
13.	$\neg :ACID(W_3) \supset$	2, 9
	$\quad \exists w_4(R(:DO(:A, :TEST), W_3, w_4) \wedge$	
	$\quad\quad \neg :ACID(w_4) \wedge \neg :RED(w_4))$	
14.	$\neg :ACID(W_3)$	ASS
15.	$R(:DO(:A, :TEST), W_3, W_4)$	13, 14
16.	$\neg :RED(W_4)$	13, 14
17.	$w_2 = W_4$	15, R1
18.	$\neg :RED(w_2)$	16, 17
19.	FALSE	12, 18
20.	$:ACID(W_3)$	DIS(14, 19)
21.	$:ACID(W_3) \supset$	1, 9
	$\quad \exists w_4(R(:DO(:A, :TEST), W_3, w_4) \wedge$	
	$\quad\quad :ACID(w_4) \wedge :RED(w_4))$	

22.	$R(:DO(:A,:TEST),W_3,W_4)$	20,21
23.	$:ACID(W_4)$	20,21
24.	$w_2 = W_4$	15,22
25.	$:ACID(w_2)$	23,24
26.	$K(:A,W_1,w_2) \supset :ACID(w_2)$	DIS(8,25)
27.	$R(:DO(:A,:TEST),W_0,W_1) \wedge$ $\forall w_2(K(:A,W_1,w_2) \supset :ACID(w_2))$	5,26
28.	$TRUE(RES(DO(A,TEST),KNOW(A,ACID)))$	27,L9,L11a,L12, K2,R2,L1

The possible-world structure for this proof is depicted in Figure 8. Lines 1 and 2 translate the premises into the metalanguage. Since A knows that, if the solution is acidic, performing the test will result in the litmus paper's being red, it must be true in the actual world (W_0) that, if the solution is acidic, performing the test will result in the litmus paper's being red (Line 3). Suppose that, in fact, the solution is acidic (Line 4). Then, if W_1 is the result of performing the test in W_0 (Line 5), the paper will be red in W_1 (Line 6). Furthermore, the worlds that are compatible with what A knows in W_1 are those that are the result of his performing the test in some world that is compatible with what he knows in W_1, and in which the paper is red if and only if it is red in W_1 (Line 7). Suppose that w_2 is a world that is compatible with what A knows in W_1 (Line 8). Then there is a W_3 that is compatible with what A knows in W_0 (Line 9), such that w_2 is the result of A's performing the test in W_3 (Line 10). The paper is red in w_2, if and only if it is red in W_1 (Line 11); therefore, it is red in w_2 (Line 12). Since A knows how the test works, if the solution were not acidic in W_3, it would not be acidic, and the paper would not be red, in w_2 (Line 13).

Now, suppose the solution were not acid in W_3 (Line 14). If W_4 is the result of A's performing the test in W_3 (Line 15), the paper would not be red in W_4 (Line 16). But w_2 is the result of A's performing the test in W_3 (Line 17), so the paper would not be red in w_2 (Line 18). We know this is false (Line 19), however, so the solution must be acidic in W_3 (Line 20). If the solution is acidic in W_3, it must also be acidic in the situation resulting from A's performing the test in W_3 (Lines 21–23), but this is w_2 (Line 24). Therefore, the solution is acidic in w_2 (Line 25). Hence, in W_1, A knows that the solution is acidic (Line 26), so in the situation resulting from A's performing the test in W_0, he knows that the solution is acidic (Line 27). In other words (Line 28), A's performing the test would result in his knowing that the solution is acidic.

By an exactly parallel argument, we could show that, if the solution were not acidic, A could also find that out by carrying out the test, so our analysis captures the sort of reasoning about tests that we described in Section 1, based on general principles that govern the interaction of knowledge and action.

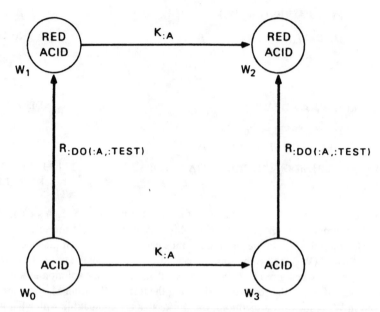

Figure 8. The Effect of a Test on the Agent's Knowledge

Acknowledgments

This research was supported in part by the Air Force Office of Scientific Research under Contract No. F49620-82-K-0031. It has also been made possible in part by a gift from the System Development Foundation as part of a coordinated research effort with the Center for the Study of Language and Information, Stanford University.

References

Frege, G. (1949). "On sense and nominatum," in *Readings in Philosophical Analysis*, H. Feigl & W. Sellars, Eds., pp. 85–102. New York: Appleton-Century-Crofts.

Hintikka, J. (1962). *Knowledge and Belief*. Ithica, NY: Cornell University Press.

Hintikka, J. (1971). "Semantics for propositional attitudes," in *Reference and Modality*, L. Linsky, Ed., pp. 145–167. London: Oxford University Press.

Hughes, G. E., & Cresswell, M. J. (1968). *An Introduction to Modal Logic*. London: Methuen.

Kripke, S. A. (1963). "Semantical analysis of modal logic," *Zeitschrift für Mathematische Logik und Grundlagen der Mathematik*, 9, pp. 67–96.

Kripke, S. A. (1971). "Semantical considerations on modal logic," in *Reference and Modality*, L. Linsky, Ed., pp. 63–72. London: Oxford University Press.

Kripke, S. A. (1972). "Naming and necessity," in *Semantics of Natural Language*, D. Davidson & G. Harmon, Eds., pp. 253–355. Dordrecht, Holland: Reidel.

McCarthy, J. (1962). "Towards a mathematical science of computation," in *Information Processing, Proceedings of IFIP Congress 62*, C. Popplewell, Ed., pp. 21–28. Amsterdam: North-Holland.

McCarthy, J. (1968). ''Programs with common sense,'' in *Semantic Information Processing*, M. Minsky, Ed., pp. 403–418. Cambridge: MIT Press.

McCarthy, J., & Hayes, P. J. (1969). ''Some philosophical problems from the standpoint of artificial intelligence,'' in *Machine Intelligence 4*, B. Meltzer & D. Michie, Eds., pp. 463–502. Edinburgh: Edinburgh University Press.

Moore, R. C. (1980). ''Reasoning about knowledge and action.'' Artificial Intelligence Center Technical Note 191. Menlo Park, CA: SRI International.

Quine, W. V. O. (1971). ''Quantifiers and propositional attitudes,'' in *Reference and Modality*, L. Linsky, Ed., pp. 101–111. London: Oxford University Press.

Reiter, R. (1980). ''A logic for default reasoning,'' *Artificial Intelligence*, 13, 81–113.

Rescher, N., & Urquhart, A. (1971). *Temporal Logic*. Vienna: Springer-Verlag.

Russell, B. (1949). ''On denoting,'' in *Readings in Philosophical Analysis*, H. Feigl & W. Sellars, Eds., pp. 103–115. New York: Appleton-Century-Crofts.

Scott, D. (1970) ''Advice on modal logic,'' in *Philosophical Problems in Logic: Some Recent Developments*, K. Lambert, Ed., pp. 143–173. Dordrecht, Holland: Reidel.

## Chapter 7

Formal Models of Planning Systems

Unlike the papers in the previous chapter, which dealt primarily with the general issue of representing action, the papers in this chapter formalize the techniques developed in actual planning systems. The first paper we present, Lifschitz (1987), formalizes the operation of STRIPS. This is a more complex task than it first might appear because the operations of STRIPS, namely, adding and deleting formulas to and from the database, cannot be captured directly as logical inference. In fact, designers of STRIPS systems must be very careful about what operations they allow in order to avoid deriving incorrect results. Lifschitz defines a semantics for these operations that allows the notion of soundness to be defined and yields a precise definition of the "good" uses of such systems.

The next paper presented, Rosenschein (1981), formalizes the operations of "regression" and "progression" found in many planning systems. Actions are formalized as state change, as in situation calculus, but within the dynamic logic framework as developed for the semantics of programming languages. The paper includes a formal definition of the planning problem and then defines what it means for a plan to solve a problem. The framework identifies the key techniques used by hierarchical and non-linear planning systems and clarifies several issues that were not clear in the systems that originated these techniques.

The next paper in this chapter, Chapman (1987), provides a precise definition of non-linear planning and defines the notions of soundness and completeness for such systems. The principal tool used in this development is the modal truth criterion, which defines what properties hold within a partial order of planning states. The definition of the modal truth criterion involves tracking the add and delete oper-

tions of the actions at each stage of the partial ordering. Using this framework, Chapman proves that plan verification can take polynomial time (rather than exponential time as one might expect). However, he shows this may involve enumerating the linear orderings consistent with the partial ordering, so non-linear planners offer no advantage over linear planners in the worst case. He also demonstrates that planning where the actions have conditional effects is an undecidable problem.

Allen and Koomen (1983), the next paper presented, develops a different approach to non-linear planning. Rather than maintaining a partial ordering of states, actions and their necessary consequences are represented in Allen's interval logic. Beside being able to explicitly represent simultaneous actions, they show that the resolve-conflicts critic, first developed by Sacerdoti (1975, Chapter 3) as an ad hoc procedure, could be formalized simply as a procedure for maintaining the consistency of the temporal database. A fuller description of this technique in a complete planning system can be found in Allen et al., 1990.

The last paper in this chapter, Korf (1987), analyzes planning as a search process. Korf classifies the different forms in which subgoals may interact and how these forms affect the techniques available for improving the heuristic search. With this framework in hand, he then gives some quantitative analysis about how using macro-operators and abstraction can affect the complexity of the search.

Papers referenced herein but not included in this volume:

Allen, J., Kautz, H., Pelavin, R., and Tenenberg, J. (1990). *Reasoning about Plans*, Morgan Kaufmann, Los Altos, CA.

ON THE SEMANTICS OF STRIPS

Vladimir Lifschitz
Computer Science Department
Stanford University
Stanford, CA 94305

Abstract

STRIPS is a problem solver which operates with world models represented by sets of formulas of first-order logic. A STRIPS system describes the effect of an action by a rule which defines how the current world model should be changed when the action is performed. The explanations of the meaning of these descriptions in the literature are very informal, and it is not obvious how to make them more precise. Moreover, it has been observed that minor and seemingly harmless modifications in standard examples of STRIPS systems cause STRIPS to produce incorrect results. In this paper we study the difficulties with interpreting STRIPS operator descriptions and define a semantics which draws a clear line between "good" and "bad" uses of the language of STRIPS.

1. Introduction

STRIPS (Fikes and Nilsson 1971) is a problem solver which operates with *world models*, represented by sets of formulas of first order-logic. A STRIPS system is defined by an *initial* world model, which describes the initial state of the world, and by a set of *operators*, which correspond to actions changing the current state. Using means-ends analysis, STRIPS attempts to find a sequence of operators transforming the initial world model into a model which satisfies a given *goal formula*.

The *description* of each operator consists of its *precondition* (the applicability condition, expressed by a first-order formula), its *add list* (the list of formulas that must be added to the current world model), and its *delete list* (the list of formulas that may no longer be true and therefore must be deleted). A resolution theorem prover is used for the verification of operator preconditions, for establishing the validity of the goal formula in the last world model, and also for directing the search.

The explanation of the meaning of operator descriptions in (Fikes and Nilsson 1971) is very brief and is almost completely reproduced in the parenthesized comments above. It is not immediately clear how to make this explanation more precise; more specifically, it turns out to be a non-trivial task to define under what conditions the delete list of an operator may be considered sufficiently complete. Moreover, some minor and seemingly harmless modifications in the main example of (Fikes and Nilsson 1971) cause STRIPS to produce incorrect results (see Sections 4 and 5 below). Alan Bundy observes that the AI literature "abounds with plausible looking formalisms, without a proper semantics. As soon as you depart from the toy examples illustrated in the paper, it becomes impossible to decide how to represent information in the formalism or whether the processes described are reasonable or what these processes are actually doing" (Bundy 1983). Is STRIPS a formalism of this sort?

In this paper we do the additional theoretical work needed to make sure that this is not the case. We study the difficulties with interpreting STRIPS operator descriptions and define a semantics which draws a clear line between "good" and "bad" uses of the language of STRIPS.

2. Operators and Plans

We start with an arbitrary first-order language L. A *world model* is any set of sentences of L. An *operator description* is a triple (P, D, A), where P is a sentence of L (the *precondition*), and D and A are sets of sentences of L (the *delete list* and the *add list*).

Consider an example from Section 3.2 of (Fikes and Nilsson 1971). In this example, the language contains some object constants and two predicate symbols, unary ATR and binary AT. Intuitively, the language is designed for describing the locations of a robot and of other objects. We think of the universe of the intended model as consisting of these objects and their possible locations. $ATR(x)$ means that the robot is at location x. $AT(x, y)$ means that the object x is at location y. Let now k, m, n be object constants of this language. The operator $push(k, m, n)$ for pushing object k from m to n is described by the triple:

Precondition: $ATR(m) \wedge AT(k, m)$.

Delete list: $\{ATR(m), AT(k, m)\}$.

Add list: $\{ATR(n), AT(k, n)\}$.

What we have defined here is a family of operator descriptions, one for each triple of constants k, m, n. The precondition shows that the corresponding action is possible whenever the robot and object k are both at location m. The delete list tells us that these two facts should be removed from the current world model when the operator $push(k, m, n)$ is applied. The add list requires that the information about the new location of the robot and of object k, represented by the formulas $ATR(n)$ and $AT(k, n)$, be added to the model.

A *STRIPS system* Σ consists of an *initial* world model M_0, a set Op of symbols called *operators*, and a family of operator descriptions $\{(P_\alpha, D_\alpha, A_\alpha)\}_{\alpha \in Op}$.

Section 4 of (Fikes and Nilsson 1971) introduces a STRIPS system which represents a world consisting of a corridor with several rooms and doorways, a robot and a few boxes and lightswitches. The language contains, in addition to ATR and AT, some other predicate symbols, for instance:

$TYPE(x, y)$: x is an object of type y,

$CONNECTS(x, y, z)$: door x connects room y with room z,

$NEXTTO(x, y)$: object x is next to object y,

INROOM(x,y): object x is in room y,

STATUS(x,y): the status of lightswitch x is y.

The initial world model in this example consists mostly of ground atoms, such as

$$TYPE(DOOR1, DOOR),$$
$$CONNECTS(DOOR1, ROOM1, ROOM5),$$
$$INROOM(ROBOT, ROOM1),$$
$$STATUS(LIGHTSWITCH1, OFF).$$

It contains also one universally quantified formula,

$$\forall xyz(CONNECTS(x,y,z) \supset CONNECTS(x,z,y)). \tag{1}$$

Among the operators we find:

*goto*1(m): robot goes to location m,

*goto*2(m): robot goes next to item m,

pushto(m,n): robot pushes object m next to object n,

gothrudoor(k,l,m): robot goes through door k from room l to room m,

turnonlight(m): robot turns on lightswitch m,

and a few others.

This system will be subsequently referred to as the "main example".

Given a STRIPS system Σ, we define a *plan* to be any finite sequence of its operators. Each plan $\overline{\alpha} = (\alpha_1, \ldots, \alpha_N)$ defines a sequence of world models $M_0, M_1, \ldots, M_N$, where M_0 is the initial world model and

$$M_i = (M_{i-1} \setminus D_{\alpha_i}) \cup A_{\alpha_i} \qquad (i = 1, \ldots, N). \tag{2}$$

We say that $\overline{\alpha}$ is *accepted* by the system if

$$M_{i-1} \vdash P_{\alpha_i} \qquad (i = 1, \ldots, N). \tag{3}$$

In this case we call M_N the *result* of executing $\overline{\alpha}$ and denote it by $R(\overline{\alpha})$.

In what terms do we want to describe the semantics of STRIPS?

We think of the world described by the language L as being, at any instant of time, in a certain *state*; we assume that one of the states, s_0, is selected as *initial*. We assume that it is defined for each state s which sentences of L are (known to be) *satisfied* in this state, and that the set of sentences satisfied in state s is closed under predicate logic. An *action* is a partial function f from states to states. If $f(s)$ is defined then we say that f is *applicable* in state s, and that $f(s)$ is the *result* of the action. We assume that an action f_α is associated with each operator α. A STRIPS system along with this additional information will be called an *interpreted* STRIPS system.

A world model M of an interpreted STRIPS system Σ is *satisfied* in a state s if every element of M is satisfied in s. For each plan $\overline{\alpha} = (\alpha_1, \ldots, \alpha_N)$ of Σ, we define $f_{\overline{\alpha}}$ to be the composite action $f_{\alpha_N} \cdots f_{\alpha_1}$.

3. Semantics: A First Attempt

Consider a fixed interpreted STRIPS system $\Sigma = (M_0, \{(P_\alpha, D_\alpha, A_\alpha)\}_{\alpha \in O_P})$. Our goal is to define under what conditions Σ can be considered *sound*. We start with the most straightforward formalization of the intuition behind operator descriptions.

Definition A. An operator description (P, D, A) is *sound* relative to an action f if, for every state s such that P is satisfied in s,

(i) f is applicable in state s,

(ii) every sentence which is satisfied in s and does not belong to D is satisfied in $f(s)$,

(iii) A is satisfied in $f(s)$.

Σ is *sound* if M_0 is satisfied in the initial state s_0, and each operator description $(P_\alpha, D_\alpha, A_\alpha)$ is sound relative to f_α.

Soundness Theorem. *If Σ is sound, and a plan $\overline{\alpha}$ is accepted by Σ, then the action $f_{\overline{\alpha}}$ is applicable in the initial state s_0, and the world model $R(\overline{\alpha})$ is satisfied in the state $f_{\overline{\alpha}}(s_0)$.*

Proof. Let $\overline{\alpha} = (\alpha_1, \ldots, \alpha_N)$ be a plan accepted by Σ. Let us prove that for every $i = 0, \ldots, N$ action $f_{\alpha_i} \ldots f_{\alpha_1}$ is applicable in s_0, and M_i defined by (2) is satisfied in state $f_{\alpha_i} \ldots f_{\alpha_1}(s_0)$. The proof is by induction on i. The basis is obvious. Assume that M_{i-1} is satisfied in $f_{\alpha_{i-1}} \ldots f_{\alpha_1}(s_0)$. By (3), it follows that P_{α_i} is satisfied in this state too. Since $(P_{\alpha_i}, D_{\alpha_i}, A_{\alpha_i})$ is sound relative to f_{α_i}, we can conclude that $f_{\alpha_i} f_{\alpha_{i-1}} \ldots f_{\alpha_1}(s_0)$ is defined, and that both $M_{i-1} \setminus D_{\alpha_i}$ and A_{α_i} are satisfied in this state. By (2), it follows then that M_i is satisfied in this state too.

There is a serious problem, however, with Definition A: it eliminates all usual STRIPS systems as "unsound". Consider, for instance, the description of $push(k, m, n)$ given in Section 2. The two atoms included in its delete list are obviously not the only sentences which may become false when the corresponding action is performed. Their conjunction is another such sentence, as well as their disjunction or, say, any sentence of the form $ATR(m) \wedge F$, where F is provable in predicate logic. To make the delete list complete in the sense of Definition A, we would have to include all such sentences in it. The delete list will become infinite and perhaps even non-recursive!

The designer of a STRIPS system cannot possibly include in a delete list all arbitrarily complex formulas that may become false after the corresponding action is performed. In our main example, the delete lists of all operator descriptions contain only atomic formulas. The same can be usually found in other examples of STRIPS systems. When describing an operator, we can try to make the delete list complete in the weaker sense that all *atoms* which may become false are included. More precisely, we may be able to guarantee condition (ii) for *atomic* sentences, but it is not realistic to expect that it will hold for all sentences in the language.

It would be a mistake, however, to restrict (ii) to atoms in Definition A and make no other changes, because that would make the assertion of the Soundness Theorem false. World models may include non-atomic sentences, and the weaker form of (ii) does not guarantee that such sentences are deleted when they become false. What is the right way to exploit this "atomic completeness" of delete lists?

One possible solution is to change the definition of a world model and require that it include atomic sentences only. In this case we should also allow only atomic formulas in add lists (otherwise $R(\overline{\alpha})$ will generally include non-atomic formulas and thus will not be a world model), and there will be no need to allow anything other than atoms in delete lists. (In this "atomic STRIPS", logical connectives and quantifiers would be still allowed in preconditions and in the goal formula).

This somewhat restrictive approach gives a satisfactory interpretation of many simple STRIPS systems. In fact, the description of STRIPS in (Nilsson 1980), for ease of exposition, allows only conjunctions of ground literals in world models, which is almost equally restrictive. But let us remember that our main example contains a non-atomic formula, (1). Why does that system appear to function correctly? This question is addressed in the next section.

4. Non-Atomic Formulas in World Models

Consider the description of the operator *turnonlight*($LIGHTSWITCH1$) in the main example. Its delete list is $\{STATUS(LIGHTSWITCH1, OFF)\}$. When the operator is applied, the atomic sentence $STATUS(LIGHTSWITCH1, OFF)$ (which is a part of the initial world model) will be deleted. Now let us change the example slightly and replace this atomic sentence in the initial world model by the stronger assumption that *all* lightswitches are originally turned off:

$$\forall x(TYPE(x, LIGHTSWITCH) \supset STATUS(x, OFF)). \qquad (4)$$

This formula will not be deleted when *turnonlight*($LIGHTSWITCH1$) is applied, which will cause STRIPS to malfunction.

Sentences (1) and (4) have the same logical complexity, and they are assumed to be both satisfied in the initial state of the world. What is wrong about including (4) in the initial world model? This example seems to confirm that "the frontier between "acceptable" and "ridiculous" (STRIPS-like) axiomatizations of the world is a very tenuous one" (Siklóssy and Roach 1975).

There is, however, an obvious difference between (1) and (4): the former is satisfied not only in the initial state, but in *every* state of the world. This difference is crucial. It is true that in the main example non-atomic formulas are never deleted from world models; but there can be no need to delete (1). This is why it is safe to include (1) in M_0.

A similar precaution should be taken with regard to including non-atomic formulas in add lists. We can extend the main example, for instance, by the operator *turnoffalllights*, with the add list consisting of one formula (4). If *turnonlight*(m)

is applied after this operator, we will have a difficulty similar to the one discussed above. A non-atomic formula may be included in an add list only if it is satisfied in every state of the world. (Of course, it can be included then in the initial world model as well.)

This discussion suggests the following modification of Definition A.

Definition B. An operator description (P, D, A) is *sound* relative to an action f if, for every state s such that P is satisfied in s,

 (i) f is applicable in state s,

 (ii) every atomic sentence which is satisfied in s and does not belong to D is satisfied in $f(s)$,

(iii) A is satisfied in $f(s)$,

(iv) every non-atomic sentence in A is satisfied in all states of the world.

Σ is *sound* if

 (v) M_0 is satisfied in the initial state s_0,

 (vi) every non-atomic sentence in M_0 is satisfied in all states of the world,

(vii) every operator description $(P_\alpha, D_\alpha, A_\alpha)$ is sound relative to f_α.

The Soundness Theorem remains valid for the new definition.

Proof. Let $\overline{\alpha} = (\alpha_1, \ldots, \alpha_N)$ be a plan accepted by Σ. Let us prove that for every $i = 0, \ldots, N$ action $f_{\alpha_i} \ldots f_{\alpha_1}$ is applicable in s_0, M_i is satisfied in state $f_{\alpha_i} \ldots f_{\alpha_1}(s_0)$, and every non-atomic formula in M_i is satisfied in all states. The proof is by induction on i. The basis is obvious. Assume that M_{i-1} is satisfied in $f_{\alpha_{i-1}} \ldots f_{\alpha_1}(s_0)$, and all non-atomic formulas in M_{i-1} are satisfied in all states. It follows from (3) that P_{α_i} is satisfied in state $f_{\alpha_{i-1}} \ldots f_{\alpha_1}(s_0)$. Since $(P_{\alpha_i}, D_{\alpha_i}, A_{\alpha_i})$ is sound relative to f_{α_i}, we can conclude that $f_{\alpha_i} f_{\alpha_{i-1}} \ldots f_{\alpha_1}(s_0)$ is defined, that every non-atomic formula in $M_{i-1} \setminus D_{\alpha_i}$ or in A_{α_i} is satisfied in this state, and that every atomic formula in any of these two sets is satisfied in all states. By (2), it follows then that M_i is satisfied in state $f_{\alpha_i} \ldots f_{\alpha_1}(s_0)$, and that every non-atomic formula in M_i is satisfied in all states.

5. The General Semantics of STRIPS

Our work has not come to an end yet. A careful examination of the main example reveals a small detail which shows that, in spite of all our efforts, that system is *not* sound in the sense of Definition B.

This peculiarity, pointed out in (Siklóssy and Roach 1975), is connected with the delete lists of some operators which change the position of the robot: $goto1(m)$, $goto2(m)$, $pushto(m, n)$ and $gothrudoor(k, l, m)$. As can be expected, the delete lists of these operators contain ground atoms which describe the robot's current position. They include all atoms of the form $ATROBOT(\$)$, where $\$$ is any object constant. They also include the atoms $NEXTTO(ROBOT, \$)$. However, they do *not* include $NEXTTO(\$, ROBOT)$.

This asymmetry is somewhat counterintuitive, because the authors apparently interpret $NEXTTO$ as a symmetric predicate. For instance, the delete list of $pushto(m, n)$ (the robot pushes object m next to object n) contains both $NEXTTO(\$, m)$ and $NEXTTO(m, \$)$, and its add list contains both $NEXTTO(m, n)$ and $NEXTTO(n, m)$. One may get the impression that the nonsymmetric treatment of $NEXTTO$ with $ROBOT$ as one of the arguments is an oversight.

However, this is not an oversight, but rather a trick carefully planned by the authors in the process of designing the main example. They make sure that assertions of the form $NEXTTO(\$, ROBOT)$ never become elements of world models in the process of operation of the system: there are no atoms of this form in M_0 or on the add lists of any operators. For example, the add list of $goto2(m)$ contains $NEXTTO(ROBOT, m)$, but not $NEXTTO(m, ROBOT)$, even though these atomic sentences both become true and, from the point of view of Definition B, nothing prevents us from adding both of them to the current world model.

The purpose of this is obvious: storing information on the objects next to the robot in both forms would have made the operator descriptions longer and would have led to computational inefficiency. In principle, it is possible to go even further in this direction and, for instance, store facts of the form $NEXTTO(BOXi, BOXj)$ only when $i < j$.

It is easy to accomodate the systems which use tricks of this kind by slightly generalizing Definition B. Let E be a set of sentences; the formulas from E will be called *essential*. Definition B corresponds to the case when E is the set of ground atoms.

Definition C. An operator description (P, D, A) is *sound* relative to an action f if, for every state s such that P is satisfied in s,
 (i) f is applicable in state s,
 (ii) every essential sentence which is satisfied in s and does not belong to D is satisfied in $f(s)$,
 (iii) A is satisfied in $f(s)$,
 (iv) every sentence in A which is not essential is satisfied in all states of the world.

Σ is *sound* if
 (v) M_0 is satisfied in the initial state s_0,
 (vi) every sentence in M_0 which is not essential is satisfied in all states of the world,
 (vii) every operator description $(P_\alpha, D_\alpha, A_\alpha)$ is sound relative to f_α.

It should be emphasized that Definition C defines the soundness of operator descriptions and STRIPS systems only with respect to a given class of sentences that are considered essential. The choice of this class E is an integral part of the design of a STRIPS system, along with its language, its initial model, and the set of its operators with their descriptions. When a STRIPS system is introduced, it is advisable to make the choice of E explicit; the description of the main example, for instance, will be more complete if we specify that a sentence is considered essential in this system if it is an atom and does not have the form $NEXTTO(\$, ROBOT)$. This information will help the user to avoid mistakes when the initial model is modified to reflect different assumptions about the initial state of the world, or when new operators are added to the system.

The treatment of $NEXTTO$ in the main example shows that it may be advantageous to make E a proper subset of the set of ground atoms. Sometimes it may be convenient to include some non-atomic formulas in E. For instance, we may wish to update negative information by means of adding and deleting negative literals; then E would be the set of ground literals, both positive and negative.

The proof of the Soundness Theorem given in the previous section can be easily generalized to soundness in the sense of Definition C.

Acknowledgements

This research was partially supported by DARPA under Contract N0039-82-C-0250. I would like to thank John McCarthy and Nils Nilsson for useful discussions, and Michael Gelfond for comments on an earlier draft of this paper.

References

A. Bundy, *The Computer Modelling of Mathematical Reasoning*, Academic Press, 1983.

R. E. Fikes and N. J. Nilsson, STRIPS: A new approach to the application of theorem proving to problem solving, *Artificial Intelligence* **2** (1971), 189-208.

N. J. Nilsson, *Principles of Artificial Intelligence*, Tioga Publishing Company, Palo Alto, Califormia, 1980.

L. Siklóssy and J. Roach, Model verification and improvement using DISPROVER, *Artificial Intelligence* **6** (1975), 41-52.

PLAN SYNTHESIS: A Logical Perspective

Stanley J. Rosenschein

Artificial Intelligence Center
SRI International

ABSTRACT

This paper explores some theoretical issues of robot system planning from the perspective of propositional dynamic logic. A generalized notion of "progression" and "regression" of conditions through actions is developed. This leads to a bidirectional single-level planning algorithm that is easily extended to hierarchical planning. Multiple pre-/postcondition pairs, complex (e.g., conjunctive, disjunctive) goals, goals of maintenance and prevention, and plans with tests are all handled in a natural way. The logical framwork is used to clarify gaps in existing "nonlinear" and "hierachical" planning strategies.

I INTRODUCTION

Although the connection between the artificial-intelligence (AI) planning problem and automated program syntheses is widely acknowledged, relatively little planning research has made explicit use of concepts from the logic of programs. Such logic, however, offers theoretical insight into various issues in AI planning, such as compound goals and levels of interaction (11, 12, 14, 4). Many of these issues arise in their purest form in domains describable in the propositional calculus (e.g. simple blocks worlds), as evidenced by the literature on the subject (13, 11, 15). Thus, for clarity and continuity, we choose the propositional setting to develop a unified, abstract treatment of these issues using propositional dynamic logic (PDL) as our primary logical tool (7, 5, 8, 9, 3).

PDL is a decidable modal propositional logic for reasoning about binary state relations induced by programs. In theory, the existence of such a logic provides an immediate "solution" to the propositional planning problem: One could systematically substitute all possible plans into a schema (the specification) that asserts the desired property of the plan. The resulting expressions could be tested for validity to filter out non-solutions. Unfortunately, this fact is of little practical consequence, as such a procedure is certain to be grossly inefficient. The approach developed here imposes additional structure by (1) considering a class of problems that require, in effect, only nonmodal reasoning, and by (2) using

suitable "progression" and "regression" operators to structure the search for a solution and allow early pruning of hopeless paths.

Surprisingly, even our restricted formulation covers a more general class of problems than are handled by most comparable AI planning methods. For instance, we allow goals to be arbitrary wffs, so that disjunctive goals (cited as an unsolved problem by Sacerdoti [12]) require no special treatment at all. The approach provides a theoretical basis for hierarchical plan generation that ties in directly with current ideas on hierarchical program development (see Section III C.) In addition, the use of program logic constitutes a formal basis for specifying and verifying the plan-generating system itself.

Although our work can be generalized along several dimensions (propositional axiom schemata, plans with loops, quantified pre-/postconditions, etc.), these are beyond the scope of the current paper, which focuses instead on the essential structure of the approach. At the same time, it should be noted that the use of axiom schemata seems to be a minimal requirement for practical application. This paper should be regarded as a foundational study aimed at deepening our understanding of planning; a separate paper will discuss problems of implementation [10].

II PRELIMINARIES

This section contains a brief presentation of the basic concepts of a loop-free fragment of propositional dynamic logic (PDL). The interested reader is referred to [7, 5, 3] for a more comprehensive treatment of dynamic logic. Although dynamic logic is ordinarily used to reason about <u>programs</u>, it is equally appropriate for reasoning about <u>plans</u> (in the AI sense); thus, in this paper the terms <u>program</u> and <u>plan</u> are used interchangeably.

A. Syntax

Let $\mathcal{P}$ and $\mathcal{Q}$ denote two symbol sets: <u>atomic propositions</u> and <u>atomic actions</u>, respectively. Define wffs $P_{\mathcal{P},\mathcal{Q}}$ and programs $A_{\mathcal{P},\mathcal{Q}}$ simultaneously (deleting subscripts for convenience):

1. $\mathcal{P} \subseteq P$

2. $\mathcal{Q} \subseteq A$

3. If $p, q \in P$, then $\neg p, p \vee q \in P$

4. If $p \in P$ and $\alpha \in A$, then $\langle \alpha \rangle p \in P$

The research described in this paper was supported by the Office of Naval Research under Contract Number N00014-80-C-0296.

Used by permission of the International Joint Conferences on Artificial Intelligence, Inc.

5. $\Lambda \in A$

6. If $p \in P$ and p is nonmodal (see below), then $p? \in A$

7. If $\alpha, \beta \in A$, then $\alpha;\beta$, $\alpha \cup \beta \in A$

A formula is <u>nonmodal</u> if it contains no subformula of the form $\langle \alpha \rangle p$. We abbreviate $\neg(\neg p \vee \neg q)$ as $p \wedge q$, $\neg p \vee q$ as $p \supset q$, $(p \supset q) \wedge (q \supset p)$ as $p \equiv q$, $\neg \langle \alpha \rangle \neg p$ as $[\alpha]p$, $p \vee \neg p$ as true, and $p \wedge \neg p$ as false. Parentheses are used conventionally as required.

B. Semantics

A structure S is a triple (W, π, m) where W is a nonempty set of "worlds," $\pi: \mathcal{P} \to 2^W$, and $m: \mathcal{Q} \to 2^{W \times W}$. That is, π assigns to each atomic proposition p the subset of W where p holds, and m assigns to each atomic action a the binary relation over W representing the next-state relation for a. Given a structure S, meanings can be assigned to arbitrary programs and formulas by extending m and π:

Meanings of Programs

1. $m(\Lambda) = \{(s,s) \mid s \in W\}$
   (identity relation over W)

2. $m(p?) = \{(s,s) \mid s \in \pi(p)\}$
   (identity relation restricted to worlds where p holds)

3. $m(\alpha;\beta) = m(\alpha) \circ m(\beta)$
   (composition of relations)

4. $m(\alpha \cup \beta) = m(\alpha) \cup m(\beta)$
   (union of relations considered as sets)

Meanings of Formulas

1. $\pi(\neg p) = W - \pi(p)$

2. $\pi(p \vee q) = \pi(p) \cup \pi(q)$

3. $\pi(\langle \alpha \rangle p) = \{ s \in W \mid \exists t \in W. (s,t) \in m(\alpha) \text{ and } t \in \pi(p)\}$

The last equation asserts that $\langle \alpha \rangle p$ is true in those worlds s from which another world t is reachable via α's next-state relation such that p holds in t. In general, our formulas will involve the dual of $\langle \alpha \rangle$, namely $[\alpha]$. $[\alpha]p$ can be read "after α, p." The formal meaning of $[\alpha]p$ is $\{ s \in W \mid \forall t \in W. (s,t) \in m(\alpha) \text{ implies } t \in \pi(p)\}$. In other words, $[\alpha]p$ holds in a world if p holds in all worlds accessible from that world via α. As expected, $\pi(\text{true}) = W$ and $\pi(\text{false}) = \emptyset$.

A formula p is <u>valid in a structure</u> $S = (W, \pi, m)$ (written $S \models p$) iff $\pi(p) = W$; p is <u>valid</u> (written $\models p$) iff it is valid in every structure.

C. Axiomatics

The following system captures the semantics given in the previous section:

Axioms

1. Axioms of the propositional calculus

2. $[\alpha](p \supset q) \supset ([\alpha]p \supset [\alpha]q)$

3. $[\Lambda]p \equiv p$

4. $[p?]q \equiv p \supset q$

5. $[\alpha;\beta]p \equiv [\alpha][\beta]p$

6. $[\alpha \cup \beta]p \equiv [\alpha]p \wedge [\beta]p$

Rules of Inference

1. From p, $p \supset q$ derive q   (modus ponens)

2. From p, derive $[\alpha]p$ (necessitation)

If a formula p follows from these axioms under the stated rules of inference, we say it is <u>provable</u> and write $\vdash p$; if p can be proved from a set of assumptions, Q, we write $Q \vdash p$.

D. A Restricted Class of Programs

PDL breaks the ordinary conditional statement into more primitive notions of "test" (?) and "nondeterministic choice" ($\cup$). Though we allow the primitive actions to be nondeterministic, we shall be interested only in deterministic combining forms. Thus, we limit the use of ? and $\cup$ to contexts of the form $(p?;\alpha) \cup (\neg p?;\beta)$ and require (for convenience only) that p be atomic. This corresponds to the ordinary conditional, so we abbreviate this program form to $p \to \alpha, \beta$ and call the class of programs obeying these syntactic restrictions <u>C-programs</u> (symbolically $\hat{A}_{\mathcal{P}, \mathcal{Q}}$). The requirement that p be atomic is not restrictive, since arbitrary Boolean combinations of tests can be expressed by appropriate use of (possibly nested) conditionals. For example, $\neg p \to \alpha, \beta$ is equivalent to $p \to \beta, \alpha$. $(p \wedge q) \to \alpha, \beta$ is equivalent to $(p \to (q \to \alpha, \beta), \beta)$, and so forth.

An important property of our combining forms is that they preserve termination; if the primitives always terminate, every C-program over those primitives will always terminate. (Loops are conspicuously absent.) In PDL, the fact that a program always terminates is expressed $\langle \alpha \rangle$true, since with true holding in every state, the only way for this formula not to hold is for there to be no states accessible via α--i.e., for α not to terminate.

III   A PLANNING METHOD

Having described a suitable language and logic, we are now in a position to discuss planning methods. Section A contains the formal definition of a (single-level) "planning problem" and the corresponding notion of a "solution." This leads directly (Section B) to a bidirectional (single-level) planning algorithm based on "progressing" and "regressing" conditions through actions. Section C describes how the hierarchical planning problem can be regarded as a succession of single-level problems in a way that makes the connection between the levels logically precise.

A. Definitions

A <u>planning problem</u> is a triple $(V, Q, R(u))$, where

$V = (\mathcal{P}, \mathcal{Q})$ is the <u>vocabulary</u> of the problem, consisting of the atomic propositions and the atomic actions.*

Q is a finite set of axioms, which we will refer to as <u>domain constraints</u>. Q is partitioned into two subsets: static constraints, which are nonmodal formulas, and dynamic constraints, which are always of the form $p \supset [a]q$, p and q being arbitrary nonmodal wffs and a an atomic action. We implicitly assume an axiom of the form $\langle a \rangle$**true** for every atomic action a; this expresses the fact that the action a always terminates, though Q may only partially specify in what state a terminates. We also assume that Q is consistent.

R(u) is a finite set of formulas called the <u>plan</u> <u>constraints</u>. Like the dynamic domain constraints, each of these is of the form $p \supset [u]q$ for nonmodal p and q. The symbol u is a distinguished atomic action not contained in $\mathcal{a}$.

A **solution** to a planning problem $(V,Q,R(u))$ is an expression α in the programming language A_V such that for every $r(\alpha)$ (obtained by substituting α for u in R), $Q \vdash r(\alpha)$. That is, it is provable from the domain constraints Q that α satisfies all the plan constraints.** (Because of the termination constraints on the atomic actions, α is guaranteed to terminate. Therefore, in the language of program logic, we are talking about "total correctness.")

B. <u>Finding Solutions</u>

Having defined "solutions," we turn our attention to methods for discovering them. A natural way of organizing the search for solutions is to follow the syntactic structure of the programming language.

Let us recall that a program is either Λ, an atomic action a, or a composite of the form $\alpha;\beta$ or $t \rightarrow \alpha,\beta$ where α and β are programs and t is an atomic proposition. It will simplify the algorithm to consider only programs in a normal form, which we now define.

1. Normal Form for Conditional Plans

A program is in normal form if it consists of a sequence* of zero or more atomic actions followed optionally by a conditional program, both branches of which are in normal form, followed in turn by 0 or more further atomic actions. More formally stated, a program is in normal form if it can be written as $A_1;\ldots;A_n$, $n \geq 0$, with at most one A_i not atomic, in which case A_i is of the form $t \rightarrow B_1, B_2$ where both B_j are themselves in normal form.** The null sequence is identified with Λ, and we take $\Lambda;\alpha = \alpha;\Lambda = \alpha$.

We have not precluded any essential solutions by insisting on this form, since every C-program can be put into normal form by transforming the longest (length > 1) sequence of steps whose first and last steps are conditionals into a single conditional as follows:

$(s \rightarrow A,B); \ldots ; (t \rightarrow C,D)$
$\quad ==> \quad (s \rightarrow A;\ldots;(t \rightarrow C,D), B;\ldots;(t \rightarrow C,D))$

and applying this transformation recursively to A, B, and the residual $\ldots;(t \rightarrow C,D)$.

2. An Algorithm

Let us suppose we are looking for a normal-form program α that satisfies one of the dynamic constraints $p \supset [\alpha]q$ in R. We consider the following cases corresponding to the possible forms of α:

1. $\alpha = \Lambda$. This is a solution if $Q \vdash p \supset q$.

2. $\alpha = a;\beta$ or $\alpha = \beta;a$ for some atomic action a. In the former case, α is a solution if $Q \vdash p/a \supset [\beta]q$, where p/a represents the strongest provable post-condition of p and a. Analogously, in the second case, α is a solution if $Q \vdash p \supset [\beta]a \backslash q$, where $a \backslash q$ is the weakest provable precondition of a and q. We call the former case "progression" and the latter "regression."

3. $\alpha = t \rightarrow \beta_1, \beta_2$. In this case, α is a solution if $Q \vdash p \wedge t \supset [\beta_1]q$ and $Q \vdash p \wedge \neg t \supset [\beta_2]q$.

We see that (1) defines success, (2) suggests forward and backward strategies for sequential steps, and (3) suggests a forward strategy for conditionals.

---

*For some applications it is desirable to constrain the programming language to use only a designated subset of the propositions as tests in conditionals. This requires a straightforward modification of our definition and will not be pursued here.

**Equivalently in semantic terms: Structures that satisfy the domain constraints also satisfy the α-instantiated plan constraints.

---

*Since ";" is associative, we write sequences $a;b;\ldots;c$ without indicating the order of association.

**Warren's method [17] for introducing conditionals produces plans of an even more restricted form: the conditional must be the <u>last</u> action in the sequence. That is, a plan, once split, may never rejoin. This is not an essential limitation, but it introduces a somewhat greater degree of redundancy than does our form. We note in passing that Warren's view of the conditional test as an action has much in common with PDL's p? action.

In addition, we observe that there are several obvious ways to limit the search. First, if $p \supset p/a$, the forward search need not consider action a. (A special case of this arises when $p/a = $ true.) Dually, if $a\backslash q \quad q$, the backward search need not consider a. (Here we have a special case when $a\backslash q = $ false.) These checks eliminate self-loops. We can eliminate cycling in the search space altogether if we are willing to pay the price of checking whether $p_i \supset p/a$ for any p_i in the leading chain of preconditions. Likewise we can check whether $a\backslash q \supset q_j$ for any q_j in the trailing chain of postconditions. It should also be noted that if $p \supset t$ or $p \supset \neg t$, the forward conditional search involving t need not be pursued. p/a can never be false, since this would imply failure of a to terminate, contradicting our assumptions about the domain constraints Q.

These observations lead directly to the following nondeterministic algorithm for computing solutions for the single constraint $p \supset [\alpha]q$: (Multiple constraints will be discussed later.)

BIGRESSION[*] ALGORITHM

Assume p, q are not false.

Solve(p,q) = Bigress(p,q,Λ,Λ).

Bigress(pre,post,leader,trailer):

IF $Q \vdash $ pre $\supset$ post THEN RETURN(leader;trailer).
CHOOSE:
  CHOOSE <a, pre/a> from LiveForward(pre):
    RETURN(Bigress(pre/a, post, leader;a, trailer))
  CHOOSE <a, a\post> from LiveBackward(post):
    RETURN(Bigress(pre, a\post, leader, a;trailer))
  CHOOSE t from NonTriv(pre):
    RETURN(leader;C;trailer)
      where C = (t $\rightarrow$ Bigress(pre $\wedge$ t, post,Λ,Λ),
                  Bigress(pre $\wedge \neg$ t, post,Λ,Λ))

LiveForward(p):
  IF $S \neq \emptyset$
    where S = { <a, p/a> | a $\in \mathcal{Q}$, $Q \not\vdash p \supset p/a$}
  THEN RETURN(S)
  ELSE FAIL().

LiveBackward(q):
  IF $S \neq \emptyset$
    where S = { <a, a\q> | a $\in \mathcal{Q}$, $Q \not\vdash a\backslash q \supset q$}
  THEN RETURN(S)
  ELSE FAIL().

NonTriv(p):
  IF $S \neq \emptyset$
    where S = { t | t $\in \mathcal{P}$, $Q \not\vdash p \supset t$, $Q \not\vdash p \supset \neg t$}
  THEN RETURN(S)
  ELSE FAIL().

The algorithm as presented finds solutions for a single plan constraint. However, the extension to the general case is straightforward: To ensure that all the plan constraints are satisfied, a

"Cartesian product" version of this algorithm must be run. A failure in any of the constraint components counts as failure and serves to prune that branch.

The bigression algorithm makes use of three additional auxiliary functions: "$Q \vdash$", "/", and "\". "$Q \vdash$" is a procedure that takes as input a nonmodal formula p and decides whether p is provable from Q. If the static axioms are rich enough,[*] this check can be done using only nonmodal reasoning, i.e., ordinary propositional decision methods. The functions "/" (progression) and "\" (regression) are the subject of the next section.

3. Progression and Regression

Ideally, we would like p/a to compute the strongest postcondition of condition p and action a. Similarly, we would like $a\backslash q$ to compute the weakest precondition. [1, 15] In PDL the weakest precondition of p and a can be expressed simply as [a]p, which is obviously the weakest formula implying "after a, p." The strongest postcondition can be expressed using a "converse" operator that we have not described. (See [5].)

However, given the restricted form of our dynamic axioms, there will be no propositional formula provably equivalent to either of these modal formulas. On the other hand, we can effectively compute the weakest precondition pre and strongest postcondition post for which it is **provable** from Q that pre implies "after a, q" and p implies "after a, post." It is these propositional formulae that we label p/a and $a\backslash q$.

The formula p/a is found by taking the conjunction of the set of formulas each of which is a disjunction of a set of q_i drawn from the "right-hand side" of the dynamic axioms of Q ($p_i \supset [a]q_i$) such that the disjunction of the corresponding p_i's is implied by p. Dually, $a\backslash q$ is found by taking the disjunction of the set of formulas, each of which is a conjunction of a set of p_i drawn from the "left-hand side" of the dynamic axioms of Q ($p_i \supset [a]q_i$) such that that conjunction of the corresponding q_i's implies q.

Let us consider the following sample axioms:
  A $\supset$ [a] (B $\vee$ C)
  G $\supset$ [a] $\neg$B
  (F $\wedge$ E) $\supset$ [a] D
In this case, $a\backslash(C \vee D) = (A \wedge G) \vee (F \wedge E)$. The reason for this is that (B $\vee$ C) conjoined with $\neg$B implies (C $\vee$ D), so the conjunction of the corresponding left-hand sides (A $\wedge$ G) is one disjunct of $a\backslash(C \vee D)$. Likewise, the formula D alone implies (C $\vee$ D), making the corresponding

---

---

[*]Specifically, the static axioms must generate all the nonmodal formulae generated by all of Q. In certain pathological cases, such as when Q contains a dynamic axiom of the form $p \supset [a]$false, Q would have to be extended to include extra static axioms, since $p \supset [a]$false and <a>true together imply $\neg$p--a nonmodal formula derivable only through modal reasoning.

left-hand side (F ∧ E) the second disjunct. These two cases exhaust the possibilities for getting (C ∨ D).

The reason the formulas p/a and a\q defined in this way are not exactly equivalent to the strongest postcondition and the weakest precondition lies in the nature of our atomic actions. Briefly stated, in the context of programming languages one typically begins with primitives whose semantics are fully characterized and focuses on characterizing the derived operations (sequencing, etc.) [1]. For example, the weakest precondition for the assignment primitive is given by the equation: wp("x:= E", P(x)) = P(E), which asserts that the weakest precondition for condition P and action "x gets E" is precisely P with E substituted for x.

In our case, however, the primitive actions are specified only by axioms stating one-way implications. Thus, unless we make assumptions of a "non-monotonic" nature, we would generally be able to consistently add axioms that "weaken" the precondition or "strengthen" the postcondition of an action. Since "provably weakest" is unattainable, we make do with "weakest provable." This does not affect the completeness of the search algorithm, since we are looking only for programs that <u>provably</u> satisfy the specifications.

C. Hierarchical Planning

The key observation to be made in extending the single-level algorithm to multilevel, hierarchical planning is that an atomic action at level k is a plan to be solved for at level k+1. This point of view is possible because of the way the planning problem was formalized. Specifically, an atomic action is described by a set of dynamic axioms in Q. Likewise, the desired program is described by a set of dynamic axioms in R. Since the same formal objects--namely, sets of dynamic axioms--are involved in both cases, it is natural to assume as primitive some action with given properties at level k and then to solve for a program having those properties at level k+1.

In formal terms, a hierarchical planning problem is a tree of single-level problems. If $\langle V_k = \langle \mathcal{P}_k, \mathcal{A}_k \rangle, Q_k, R_k(u_k) \rangle$ is the problem at nonleaf node k, then node k has one successor for each $a_{k,i}$ in $\mathcal{A}_k$, and that successor's problem has the form $\langle V_{k+1}, Q_{k+1}, Q'(a_{k,i}) \rangle$, where Q' denotes the subset of dynamic axioms of Q_k having the form $p \supset [a_{k,i}]q$. In other words, the domain constraints on the primitive "a" at level k become plan requirements at level k+1. A solution is a plan using the vocabulary of the leaf nodes that satisfies the requirements of the root node. That is, is a solution if it solves $\langle V_n, Q_n, R_1(u_1) \rangle$. The propositional vocabulary and the action vocabulary can change from level to level, provided that the domain axioms have enough inferential structure to make the transfer from level to level meaningful.

Obviously, for any node k, only the successor nodes corresponding to actions actually used in k's solution need be solved. Furthermore, finding a solution for each of these nodes guarantees that we have an overall solution.

As with other hierarchic planners, the main benefit of levels in our approach is heuristic: The selection of intermediate vocabularies and domain axioms constitutes a choice of "planning islands." Any algorithm that tries to solve a problem by solving the nodes in the hierarchy is, in essence, searching for a plan constrained to go through the states defined by the domain constraints of the intermediate actions. The main benefit of logic here is to define a reasonable relation between the levels, namely the relation: "correctly implements."

For a fixed determination of levels and a small number of actions it would be possible to precompute solutions to the subproblems, in which case, after solving the problem at the top level, the system would act more like a compiler than a problem solver. In dynamic situations in which the lower-level actions (in effect, the "tools" for solving the problem) are changing or when few actions are ever actually used, it seems more natural to solve subproblems as they arise.

IV DISCUSSION

A. Modeling Actions: The Legacy of STRIPS

Much of the research into the control of planning has been carried out in the STRIPS paradigm [2, 6]. In this approach, actions are regarded not as mappings from states to states, but rather as syntactic transformations of state descriptions to other state descriptions, where state descriptions are logical formulas. One consequence is the oft-cited advantage of not having to mention the various "frame conditions," i.e., the properties that are invariant under an action.* Unfortunately, the need for operators to be sensitive to the syntax of state descriptions led researchers to consider only very simple state descriptions (e.g. sets of atomic propositions) and very simple transformations (e.g., addlists and deletelists).

As an example of an action that is difficult to specify with a single addlist/deletelist pair, consider the action <u>toggle</u>, described by a pair of dynamic axioms:

On(light) ⊃ [toggle(switch)] ¬On(light)
¬On(light) ⊃ [toggle(switch)] On(light)

Since the consequents depend conditionally on the antecedents, it cannot be determined in isolation whether toggle adds or deletes the wff On(light). Nonetheless, a planning system given these axioms might reason that after two toggles, the light would surely have gone on at least once. Similar remarks hold for actions with disjunctive postconditions.

These possibilities notwithstanding, many

---

*However, these invariants need not be as large an obstacle to practical implementation as is commonly supposed (see [10]).

planning systems do make the assumption that the truth of a given atomic proposition in the state resulting from applying a sequence of operators is a determinate, calculable thing. Techniques that rely critically on these assumptions are sometimes difficult to adapt to less constraining assumptions. We offer two illustrations from NOAH [11].

B. Nonlinear Planning: Problems with Partial Orders and Shuffles

The basic idea behind nonlinear planning is the following. To solve a conjunctive goal G1 & G2, find a sequence S1 = a;b;...;c that achieves G1 and another sequence S2 = d;e;...;f that achieves G2. Represent the overall plan as a network of partially ordered actions with S1 and S2 as parallel branches. Now use the "resolve-conflicts critic" to detect interference between the plans and impose additional ordering constraints upon the actions to eliminate the interference. The network encodes the subset of the possible shuffles of S1 with S2 that are believed to achieve the overall goal G1 & G2.

For the resolve conflicts critic to filter interference correctly, it must know what is true at each node of the network. Unfortunately, for nodes that occur after joins, what is true depends critically on the ultimate linearization of the parallel branches. In the general case, the best that can be done is to represent the disjunction of the strongest postconditions of the alternative linearizations.* This requires considering the alternatives, of which there are $\binom{m+n}{m}$, where m and n represent the lengths of the action sequences in the two parallel branches. Since it is easy to imagine cases in which resolve-conflicts criticism would be an expensive operation, the belief that using a nonlinear strategy is computationally efficient seems to be grounded in the _empirical_ hypothesis that operators encountered in practice will permit easy detection of conflicts.

C. Hierarchical Planning: Problems with Heuristic Decompositions

The justification for partial orderings in NOAH is linked with a desire not to commit the system _prematurely_ to a particular linear order of actions which, though seemingly correct at one level, may expand into incorrect plans at lower levels. This possibility can arise, of course, only if the relation between levels ("Plan A achieves the same effect as Action a") is not exact. However, such inexactness undermines the original rationale for hierarchical planning-- namely, reducing complexity by means of factorization--since it destroys compositionality and requires that we check complex lower-level plans for "unexpected" _global_ interactions. Here too, an empirical hypothesis is presumably invoked, namely, that by some suitable metric the plan comes

"close" to implementing the abstract action. (It is not immediately obvious, though, what metric could be meaningful for the space in question.)

D. Some Benefits of Bigression

Some of the benefits of regression were first discussed by Waldinger [15] and appreciated by Warren [16]. These benefits accrue dually by including progression, which completes the logical symmetry and allows bidirectional search. As we have described them, the progression and regression operations handle arbitrary Boolean formulas, thus solving conjunctive and disjunctive goals as particular applications of a more general strategy. Goals of maintenance and prevention can be incorporated into the algorithm as well by expressing as (nonmodal) wffs the condition to be maintained (m) and the condition to be prevented (v). Since the planning algorithm actually develops a descriptive wff (d) for each state reachable during plan execution, it is straightforward to add a check to the procedures LiveForward, LiveBackward, and NonTriv eliminating paths through states where $Q \vdash d \supset \neg m \lor v$.* This simple approach will work in situations in which no dynamic replanning is anticipated; goals of maintenance and prevention involving execution monitoring, feedback, and replanning require more complex strategies. Further research should be directed at these problems as well as at efficiency issues, especially clarification of the role of heuristics and the compilation of deductive processes.

ACKNOWEDGEMENTS

I have profited considerably from discussions with Richard Waldinger, Vaughan Pratt, Kurt Konolige, Dave Wilkins, Jerry Hobbs, and Bob Moore.

------

*Actually, NOAH does not represent disjunctive postconditions--which may explain why disjunctive goals are considered problematical.

------

*For a more thoroughgoing treatment of reasoning about processes with intermediate states, see [9].

Planning for Conjunctive Goals*

David Chapman

Artificial Intelligence Laboratory, MIT, Cambridge, MA 02139, U.S.A.

Recommended by Robert Wilensky

ABSTRACT

The problem of achieving conjunctive goals has been central to domain-independent planning research; the nonlinear constraint-posting approach has been most successful. Previous planners of this type have been complicated, heuristic, and ill-defined. I have combined and distilled the state of the art into a simple, precise, implemented algorithm (TWEAK) which I have proved correct and complete. I analyze previous work on domain-independent conjunctive planning: in retrospect it becomes clear that all conjunctive planners, linear and nonlinear, work the same way. The efficiency and correctness of these planners depends on the traditional add/delete-list representation for actions, which drastically limits their usefulness. I present theorems that suggest that efficient general purpose planning with more expressive action representations is impossible, and suggest ways to avoid this problem.

1. Introduction

If you intend to use a domain-independent planner as a workhorse black-box part of something else, you care whether it works. Planners of the most promising ("nonlinear") sort have been complicated, heuristic, ill-defined AI programs, without clear conditions under which they work. This paper describes a nonlinear planner, TWEAK, that has few novel features, but is a simple, precise algorithm I have proved correct and complete.

*Revised version of a thesis submitted to the Department of Electrical Engineering and Computer Science on January 25, 1985 in partial fulfillment of the requirements for the degree of Master of Science.

This report describes research done in part at the Artificial Intelligence Laboratory of the Massachusetts Institute of Technology. Support for the laboratory's artificial intelligence research has been provided in part by the Advanced Research Projects Agency of the Department of Defense under Office of Naval Research contract N00014-80-C-0505, in part by National Science Foundation grants MCS-7912179 and MCS-8117633, and in part by the IBM Corporation.

The views and conclusions contained in this document are those of the author, and should not be interpreted as representing the policies, either expressed or implied, of the Department of Defense, of the National Science Foundation, or of the IBM Corporation.

Artificial Intelligence **32** (1987) 333–377
0004-3702/87/$3.50 © 1987, Elsevier Science Publishers B.V. (North-Holland)

I started work on planning because I wanted a planner to coroutine with a learner to make an integrated problem solver [5]. I'd heard that Earl Sacerdoti's NOAH was the state of the art in planning, and decided to copy it exactly, since I had no interest in the matter. Four readings of [50] and three misconceived implementations later, I had a planner that worked, but no idea why. To determine whether it would work as a reliable subroutine, I had to simplify the algorithm and representations and apply some mathematical rigor. To quote Sacerdoti:

[The basic operations of NOAH] were developed in an ad hoc fashion. No attempt has been made to justify the transformations that they perform, or to enable them to generate all transformations. However, it should be possible to define an algebra of plan transformations... a body of formal theory about the ways in which interacting subgoals can be dealt with. [50]

That is what I've done in this paper.

Rigor of formulation not only gives confidence in a program, it may be needed as a stable base for further research. AI comes in "neat" and "scruffy" styles. Nonlinear planning research to date has been scruffy: heuristic, ill-understood, unclear. As I discovered, scruffy research is hard to duplicate. That is not Sacerdoti's fault, or mine: most AI research is necessarily like that. When working at the frontiers of knowledge, you will make no progress if you wait to proceed until you understand clearly what you are doing. But it is also hard to know when progress has been made and where to go next before the scruffy work is neatened up. Neat and scruffy research on a particular domain should follow each other in cycles. Late in this neat paper, I will make some scruffy suggestions about how to go beyond the crucial limitation of the domain-independent planners that have been implemented to date.

1.1. Nonlinear conjunctive planning

The conjunctive planning problem has been a main focus of planning research for more than ten years. The problem is to achieve several goals simultaneously: to find a plan that makes a conjunctive formula true after it has been executed. To make a planner generally useful, it should be domain-independent. The difficulty in domain-independent conjunctive planning is in interactions between the means of achieving the individual goals. The following classic problem, known as the "Sussman anomaly," illustrates the difficulty. Suppose we have three blocks, a, b, and c; initially c is on a and a and b are on the table (situation (i) in Fig. 1). We want to have a stacked on b on c, or to achieve the conjunctive goal (and (on a b) (on b c)) (situation (ii)). Let's say you're only allowed to move one block at a time, so that the top of a block must be clear before it can be moved. If you try to put b on c first, when you go to put a on b

given in Section 2.1. Section 2.2 describes a nondeterministic procedure that transforms a plan so that it achieves a goal that it previously did not. The top-level control structure, described in Section 2.3, controls this nondeterminism. Because choosing how to make a plan achieve a goal is difficult, backtracking search is used to recover from wrong choices. Here I prove that TWEAK is complete: if a solution to a problem exists, TWEAK will find it.

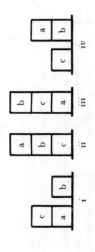

Fig. 1. The Sussman anomaly, with partial outcomes.

you fail, because c is on a and so prevents it from moving (situation (iii)). On the other hand, if you try first to put a on b (removing c to make a accessible), putting b on c is made impossible by a, which is in the way (situation (iv)).

I'll return to this problem later in the paper and show how nonlinear planning can solve it. The important idea, due to Sacerdoti, is that a plan (at least while it is being constructed) does not have to specify fully the order of execution of its steps. In other words, a plan is only a partial order on steps; this is what is meant by *nonlinear* planning.

1.2. Guide to this paper

The next section explains how and why TWEAK works. The section is divided into three subsections: the first explains what a plan is; the second shows how to improve incomplete plans; and the third describes the overall control structure of the planner.

Section 3 covers related and future work. I analyze previous planning research using the analytical tools developed in Section 2, showing that all domain-independent conjunctive planners work the same way. I suggest that the restrictions on representations of actions that these planners depend upon are their crucial limitation, and show that there are complexity-theoretic barriers to lifting these restrictions.

The last section presents brief conclusions.

2. TWEAK

TWEAK is a rigorous mathematical reconstruction of previous nonlinear planners. TWEAK is also an implemented, running program. This section describes the algorithm and proves it correct. TWEAK comes in three layers: a plan representation, a way to make a plan achieve a goal, and a top-level control structure. Each layer is described in more detail in one of the next three subsections of this section. The fourth subsection gives a detailed scenario of TWEAK solving the Sussman anomaly problem described in the last section.

The plan representation is the most complex layer. The basic operation provided by this representation determines whether a proposition will be true of the world after part of a plan has been executed. An efficient algorithm for this operation depends on a subtle theorem about incompletely defined plans,

2.1. The plan representation

In this section I define plans, problems, and what it means for a plan to solve a problem. I present a criterion which allows TWEAK to reason about what will be true in the world as a plan is executed. Inevitably most of this section is composed of dry and obvious definitions. Proofs are deferred to Appendix A.

TWEAK is a *constraint-posting* planner. Constraint posting is the process of defining an object, a plan in this case, by incrementally specifying partial descriptions (constraints) it must fit. Alternatively, constraint posting can be viewed as a search strategy in which, rather than generating and testing specific alternatives, chunks of the search space are progressively removed from consideration by constraints that rule them out, until finally every remaining alternative is satisfactory. The advantage of the constraint-posting approach is that properties of the object being searched for do not have to be chosen until a reasoned decision can be made. This reduction of arbitrary choice often reduces backtracking.

As TWEAK works on a problem, it has at all times an *incomplete plan,* which is a partial specification of a plan that may solve the problem. This incomplete plan could be completed in many different ways, depending on what constraints are added to it; thus it represents a class of complete plans. The incomplete plan supplies partial knowledge of the complete plan that will eventually be chosen; planning is finished when all the completions of the incomplete plan solve the given problem. I will say "necessarily p" if p is true of all completions of an incomplete plan, and "possibly p" if p is true of some completion. Adding a constraint to a plan can often rule out all the completions; the set of constraints is then *inconsistent,* and no longer defines a valid incomplete plan. At this point backtracking must be invoked. The number of completions of a plan is exponential in its size, so computing whether something is possible or necessary by searching completions would be very expensive. The heart of this section is a polynomial-time algorithm that computes possible and necessary properties of an incomplete plan.

TWEAK's plan representation is very simple. It is so restrictive that it cannot represent most domains; I will explain why in Section 3.2.1. A *complete plan* is a total order on a finite set of *steps.* The order represents time; the steps, actions. The plan is executed by performing the actions corresponding to the steps in the order given. A step has a finite set of *preconditions,* which are things that must be true about the world before the corresponding action can be performed. A step also has finitely many *postconditions*, which are things that the action guarantees will be true about the world after it has been performed. Pre- and postconditions are both expressed as *propositions*. Propositions have a *content*, which is a tuple of *elements*, and can be *negated* or not. Elements can be *variables* or *constants*; there are infinitely many of each. Functions, propositional operators and quantification are not allowed: all propositions are function-free atomic. (See Section 3.2.3 to understand why there must be infinitely many variables and constants and Section 3.2.1 for why propositions must be so simple.) Two propositions are negations of each other if one is negated and the other is not and they have the same content (strictly, necessarily codesignating content, a notion that I haven't introduced yet). I'll write propositions like this: (on a x) and this: ~ (on a x). These two propositions have the same content tuple, the three elements on, a, and x; the second is negated and the first is not.

Plans in TWEAK can be incomplete in two ways: the time order may be incompletely specified, using *temporal constraints*, and steps may be incompletely specified, using *codesignation constraints*. A temporal constraint is a requirement that one step be before another; thus a set of temporal constraints is simply a partial order on steps. A *completion* of a set of temporal constraints C is any total order O on the same set of steps such that sCt implies sOt. (Every ordering in the incomplete plan must also hold in the complete one.)

Codesignation is an equivalence relation on variables and constants. In a complete plan, each variable that appears in a pre- or postcondition must be constrained to codesignate with (effectively, be bound to) a specific constant. In execution, that constant will be substituted for the variable when the action is performed. Codesignation constraints enforce codesignation or noncodesignation of elements. Distinct constants may not codesignate. Two propositions codesignate if both are negated or both are not and if their contents are of the same length and if corresponding elements in the contents codesignate. For example, the propositions (on a x) and (on a y) codesignate iff x and y codesignate.

Recall the general definitions of necessary and possible; thereby, two propositions in an incomplete plan necessarily codesignate if they codesignate in all completions; in other words no matter what constraints are added. You can constrain two possibly codesignating propositions to necessarily codesignate by constraining all the corresponding elements of their contents to codesignate. This amounts to unification of the two propositions. You can constrain two possibly noncodesignating propositions to necessarily not codesignate by choosing some tuple index and constraining noncodesignation of the two elements at that index in the content tuples of the two propositions. For example, (on a x) and (on a y) can be made to necessarily codesignate by making x and y necessarily codesignate, and to necessarily not codesignate by making x and y necessarily not codesignate.

As steps are executed the state of the world changes. TWEAK represents states of the world with *situations*, which are sets of propositions. A plan has an *initial situation*, which is a set of propositions describing the world at the time that the plan is to be executed, and a *final situation*, which describes the state of the world after the whole plan has been executed. Associated with each step in a plan is its *input situation*, which is the set of propositions that are true in the world just before it is executed, and its *output situation*, which is the set of propositions that are true in the world just after it is executed. In a complete plan, the input situation of each step is the same as the output situation of the previous step. The final situation of a complete plan has the same set of propositions in it as the output situation of the last step. The time order extends to situations: the initial and final situations are before and after every other situation that is before the step; the output situation of a step is after the step and before any other situation that is after the step.

A proposition is *true in a situation* if it codesignates with a proposition that is a member of the situation. A step *asserts* a proposition in its output situation if the proposition codesignates with a postcondition of the step. A proposition is asserted in the initial situation if it true in that situation. A proposition is *denied* in a situation if its negation is asserted there. It's illegal for a proposition to be both asserted and denied in a situation.

A step can be executed only if all its preconditions are true in its input situation. In this case, the output situation is just the input situation minus any propositions denied by the step, plus any propositions asserted by the step. (The order matters. Also, this is not the same thing as the input situation plus the propositions asserted by the step: if p were true in the input situation and the step asserts $\sim p$, then the output situation must not contain both p and $\sim p$; input and output situations must be consistent sets of propositions, since they describe states of the world.) This model of execution does not allow for indirect or implied effects of actions or for uncertainty of execution; any changes in the world must be explicitly mentioned as postconditions. I will have more to say about this restriction in Section 3.2.1.

I use graphs, as in Figs. 2–4, to illustrate plans. Steps are boxes; the preconditions are put before or above the box and postconditions after or

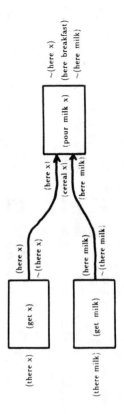

Fig. 2. An incomplete plan.

Modal Truth Criterion. *A proposition p is necessarily true in a situation s iff two conditions hold: there is a situation t equal or necessarily previous to s in which p is necessarily asserted; and for every step C possibly before s and every proposition q possibly codesignating with p which C denies, there is a step W necessarily between C and s which asserts r, a proposition such that r and p codesignate whenever p and q codesignate. The criterion for possible truth is exactly analogous, with all the modalities switched (read "necessary" for "possible" and vice versa).*

The necessary truth criterion is diagrammed in Fig. 6. Solid lines indicate necessarily time-relatedness and dashed lines possible time-relatedness; the dashed box, a disallowed step; the dotted box a step that would make the dashed step legal. I call situations *t* necessarily before *s* that necessarily assert *p establishers*; steps *C* defined as in the statement of the theorem *clobberers*, *white knights*. If a step *C* is before *t*, certainly it does not clobber *p*; but in such a case, the step of which *t* is the output situation acts itself as a white knight.

The part of the criterion about white knights is counter-intuitive, but it is needed, as illustrated by the previously illustrated odd plan. More complex codesignation implications can also occur: for example, the propositions (xy) and (yz) must codesignate if (xy) and (zx) do.

The truth criterion can usefully be thought of as a completeness/soundness theorem for a version of the situation calculus.

The criterion can be interpreted procedurally in the obvious way. It runs in time polynomial in the number of steps: the body of the criterion can be verified for each of the n^3 triples $\langle t, C, W \rangle$ with a fixed set of calls on the polynomial-time constraint-maintenance module. (The exponent in this polynomial can be reduced with dynamic programming; this is essentially what Tate's GOST does [68].) However, the modal truth criterion does exponentially much "work" by describing properties of the exponentially large set of completions of an incomplete plan. (Strictly, there may be infinitely many completions, since there are infinitely many constants the variables could codesignate with; but since all but finitely many constants are unconstrained and so equivalent, there are only exponentially many that are not isomorphic.) The remainder of TWEAK depends heavily on the criterion.

Now I will define problems and their solutions. A *problem* is an *initial situation* and a *final situation*, which are two sets of propositions. A *plan for a problem* is one such that every proposition in its initial situation is true in the initial situation of the problem. A *goal* is a proposition which must be achieved (true) in a certain situation. The goals of a plan for a problem are defined to be the propositions in the final situation of the problem, which must be true in the final situation of the plan, and the preconditions of steps in the plan, which must be true in the corresponding input situations. A complete plan for a problem *solves* the problem if all its goals are achieved. Thus, a complete plan

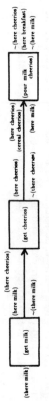

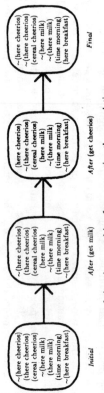

Fig. 3. One completion of the example plan.

Fig. 4. The sequence of situations resulting from executing the completion.

below. The steps may have labels inside, but these are only mnemonic. Arcs represent the partial time order. Ovals are situations.

During planning, incompleteness introduces uncertainty into the meaning of a plan. To use a blocks world example, if v is a variable, after asserting (on block v), there's no way to tell whether (on block c) is true or false, unless v necessarily codesignates with a particular constant. I will now sketch the derivation of a criterion that tells you when a proposition is necessarily true in a situation. Of course a proposition is necessarily true in a situation if it is necessarily asserted in it. Once a proposition has been asserted, it remains true until denied. Thus a proposition *p* is necessarily true in a situation if there is some previous situation in which it is necessarily true, and no possibly intervening step possibly denies it: for if there is a step that is even possibly in-between that even possibly denies *p*, there is a completion in which the step actually is in-between and actually denies *p*. (A step possibly denies *p* by denying a proposition *q* which possibly codesignates with *p*). Oddly, the converse of this criterion is not true; the incomplete plan in Fig. 5 illustrates an exception. If *p* and *q* are possibly codesignate, this plan has two classes of completions: ones in which *p* and *q* actually codesignate, so that *p* is asserted by step 3; and ones in which *p* and *q* do not codesignate, so that *p* is asserted by step 1, and is never denied. In either case, *p* is true in the final situation, even though no one step necessarily asserts *p* without an intervening step possibly denying it. The complete criterion, extended to cover such cases, is the following.

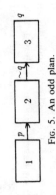

Fig. 5. An odd plan.

Fig. 6. The necessary truth criterion.

solves a problem if it can be executed in the initial situation of the problem and if the final situation of the problem is a correct partial description of the world after execution. The aim of TWEAK is to produce a plan that necessarily solves the problem it is given. This plan may be incomplete, in which case any of its completions can be chosen for execution.

2.2. Making a plan achieve a goal

TWEAK's contract is to produce a plan for a specific problem it is given. TWEAK has at all times an incomplete plan, initially null, which is an approximation to a plan that solves the problem. The top-level loop of the planner repeatedly chooses a goal and to tries to make the plan achieve it. This section describes TWEAK's procedure for making the plan achieve the goal.

The *goal-achievement procedure* is derived by interpreting the necessary truth criterion as a nondeterministic procedure. The criterion tells us all the ways a proposition could be necessarily true; the procedure chooses one of them and modifies the plan accordingly. To make a situation be before another or to make two propositions codesignate or not codesignate, the procedure just adds constraints. These constraints may be incompatible with existing constraints: for example, you can't constrain s before t if you have already constrained t before s. The constraint-maintenance mechanism signals failure in these cases, and the top-level control structure backtracks. Since the set of things possibly asserted in a situation cannot be changed, to make a proposition necessarily asserted there, the procedure constrains codesignation of the given existentially quantified situation nondeterministically: by choosing an existentially quantified situation nondeterministically: by choosing one of those asserted. There are two ways to instantiate an existentially quantified situation nondeterministically: by choosing an existing situation in the plan or by adding a new step to the plan and taking its output situation as the value of the existentially quantified variable. One of these two ways must be chosen nondeterministically. Logical operators in the statement of the criterion can also be interpreted procedurally: universal quantification over a set becomes iteration over that set; existential quantification a nondeterministic choice from a set; disjunction a simple nondeterministic choice; and conjunction, several things that must all be done.

Let $\approx$ and $\not\approx$ stand for codesignation and noncodesignation respectively; let $\square$ and $\diamond$ stand for "necessarily" and "possibly"; let $<$ represent the time order, and $\leq$ represent temporal precedence or equality. Then the necessary truth criterion in logical notation reads thusly:

$$\exists t\; t \leq s \wedge \square \text{ asserted-in}(p, t)\; \wedge$$
$$\forall C \;\square s \leq C \;\vee$$
$$\square q \;\forall \sim\!\text{denies}(C, q) \;\vee$$
$$\exists W\;\square C < W \;\wedge$$
$$\square W < s \;\wedge$$
$$\exists r \text{ asserts}(W, r) \wedge p \approx q \Rightarrow p \approx r$$

Figure 7 illustrates the structure of the nondeterministic procedure. This figure is a parse tree of the necessary truth criterion, modified according to the paragraph above on procedural interpretation. In the diagram, $\vee$ means to choose one of the alternate paths; $\wedge$ tells you to do all the paths; $\exists$ means "choose a"; $\forall$ tells you to apply the following path to every one. The leaf nodes are constraints that should be added to the plan. u ranges over the propositions necessarily true in t; q ranges over postconditions of C; r over postconditions of W. Choosing t and W may or may not require the introduction of a new step, as explained earlier.

A number of further comments are needed to fully specify the details of the procedure. Step addition involves choosing what step to add. Every step in a plan must represent an action that is possible to execute in the domain in which the problem is specified. To even possibly achieve a goal p by addition, the added step must assert a proposition possibly codesignating with p. The choice of steps, then, is among those that are allowed in the domain and that possibly assert the desired goal. The user must supply TWEAK with a set of template steps that TWEAK can use. These are formally identical to plan steps; they have preconditions and postconditions, which typically involve variables which may have codesignation constraints between them. Step templates are *instantiated* by copying the step, proposition, variable and codesignation constraint datastructures. Constants are not copied; if a step template refers to a specific object in the world, all instances should refer to the same one.

Making $p \approx q$ imply $p \approx r$ is tricky; this can not be expressed as a single codesignation constraint or even as a set of constraints. It is sometimes possible to constrain $p \approx q \Rightarrow p \approx r$ with a simpler constraint than either $p \not\approx q$ or $p \approx r$. (w x y) and (u y z) and (w z x) can be made to codesignate in case (w x y) and (w z x) do by constraining w ≈ u. In general, there may be several ways to ensure a codesignation implication using constraints between elements, and one of these must be chosen nondeterministically.

Alternative paths through the procedure are called *plan modification operations*, and are labeled in italics in the diagram. I'll refer to these individual operations later in the paper. The path that leads to constraining $s < C$ I call

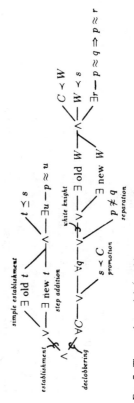

Fig. 7. The nondeterministic achievement procedure.

promotion. Demotion is a particular subcase of declobbering by white knight that is symmetric with promotion. Demotion is the case in which *t* is chosen to be the output situation of *W*, so that the clobberer is nullified by moving it before the establisher.

One additional way to achieve a goal is imaginable: to remove a clobbering step *C*. This would not help: every step is introduced to assert some goal proposition, and removing one makes negative progress. Moreover, the search control structure guarantees that the same plan without the clobbering step will be found eventually anyway, and it is never the case that the only way to achieve a goal is to remove a step. Apart from this, the achievement procedure encompasses *all* the ways to make an incomplete plan achieve a goal, because the modal truth criterion is sufficient as well as necessary. So in this respect TWEAK can not be improved upon.

The goal-achievement procedure has the useful property that so long as step addition is avoided, the new plan will continue to necessarily achieve any goals that it previously did. That's because the rest of the procedure operates only by adding constraints. When constraints are added, things that were previously possibly true become either necessarily true or necessarily false, but nothing that is necessarily true can change its truth value.

Step addition adds new preconditions to the plan that need to be achieved. and the added step may also deny, and so undo, previously achieved goals. This in unavoidable, and it can lead to infinite looping. Therefore, TWEAK prefers constraint posting to step addition.

2.3. The top-level control structure

TWEAK begins work on a problem with a first incomplete plan whose initial situation is the initial situation of the problem and which has no steps or constraints. It then enters a loop in which some goal not yet achieved is chosen and the procedure of the last section is applied, yielding a new plan. When all the plan's goals are achieved, the plan necessarily solves the problem. Choosing which goal to achieve and which choices to make in the achievement procedure is very difficult; certainly it is not always possible to choose right the first time. Therefore the top-level control structure of TWEAK is a search through the space of alternate paths through the goal-achievement procedure.

People have thought a lot about what sort of search to use; this work is reviewed in Section 3.4. Since none of the search strategies developed so far seem very good, I simply use dependency-directed breadth-first search in TWEAK. I shan't argue for breadth-first search; it's certainly too expensive for general use. However, the use of dependency-directed search deserves some justification.

Dependency-directed backtracking [15] is more efficient than chronological backtracking only if the search space is nearly decomposable into independent subparts, so that after a failure in one part, only the work done on that part needs to be undone; work on other parts can be saved. TWEAK does have this property when running in many domains. For example, in the blocks world, if the goal is to build two disjoint structures, the search space can be divided into the part concerned with building the one and the part concerned with building the other. Failure in building the one structure will not affect partial successes achieved thus far in building the other.

Because step addition can make the plan grow arbitrarily large, the search may never converge on a plan that necessarily solves the problem. In fact, there are three possible outcomes: success, in which a plan is found; failure, when the planner has exhaustively searched the space of sequences of plan modification operations. and every branch fails; and nontermination, when the plan grows larger and larger and more and more operations are applied to it, but it never converges to solve the problem.

Outcomes Lemma. *Each of the three outcomes is possible for some choice of domain and problem.*

This is a central theorem of this paper:

Correctness/Completeness Theorem. *If TWEAK, given a problem, terminates claiming a solution, the plan it produces does in fact solve the problem. If TWEAK returns signalling failure or does not halt, no solution exists.*

This theorem leaves little room for improvement. Perhaps loop-detection heuristics or techniques for proving no solution exists could make TWEAK fall into infinite loops less often. An obvious question is whether planning is in fact decidable: whether it is possible to make a complete planner that always halts.

First Undecidability Theorem. *Any Turing machine with its input can be encoded as a planning problem in the TWEAK representation. Therefore, planning is undecidable, and no upper bound can be put on the amount of time required to solve a problem.*

This theorem is weaker than it may appear, for two reasons. First, the proof uses an infinite (though recursive) initial state to model the connectivity of the Turing machine's tape. It may be that if problems are restricted to have finite initial states, planning is decidable. (This is not obviously true, though. A finite initial state does not imply a finite search space. There are infinitely many constants, and an action can in effect "gensym" one by referring to a variable in its postconditions that is not mentioned in its preconditions.) Section 3.2.1 shows in passing that planning is undecidable with even finite initial states if TWEAK's representation is extended a little. Second, what the proof shows is that the size of the shortest plan to solve a problem may be arbitrarily large, rather than that the process of planning itself is complex. In fact, no backtracking is required to solve the Turing machine-encoding problems.

2.4. Example

To give a feel for TWEAK doing its thing, I'll show how it solves the Sussman anomaly problem introduced in Section 1.1. Refer to Fig. 1 for the definition of the problem. Logically, only one action is available in this domain, puton. puton has three preconditions, (on x z), (clear x), and (clear y); and four postconditions, (on x y), ~(on x z), ~(clear y), and (clear z). z represents the block on which x lies before the puton takes place. There also must be noncodesignation constraints to the effect that x, y, and z are all distinct, and that x is not the table, which can't be moved. This isn't quite good enough: the table is always clear (always can have more put on it), and putting something on the table doesn't change that. We must constrain y not to codesignate with the table and use a different action, newtower, to put a block onto the table (and so start a new tower). newtower has preconditions (on x z) and (clear x) and postconditions (on x table), ~(on x z), and (clear z). Codesignation constraints ensure that x, z, and table are all distinct. See Fig. 8 for illustrations of the blocks world step templates.

I'll assume that the nondeterministic control structure always guesses right the first time. TWEAK begins with the two top-level goals (on a b) and (on b c). Each is achieved by adding a puton step; see Fig. 9. The variables instantiating x and y are constrained to codesignate with the goals. I have been somewhat sloppy and textually substituted constants for the variables that are bound to them. z_1 and z_2 are the instantiations of z.

Unachieved preconditions are starred. The on preconditions are achieved by being constrained to codesignate with propositions in the initial situation; see Fig. 10. The precondition (clear b) of the second step is unachieved because the first step is possibly before the second and denies the precondition. TWEAK

achieves (clear b) by promotion of (puton a b) (Fig. 11). Then the precondition (clear a) of (puton a b) is achieved by addition of a **newtower** step. This has a precondition (on x a) which is satisfied by being constrained to codesignate with (on c a), which is true in the initial situation. See Fig. 12. Finally TWEAK achieves (clear c) by promotion of (puton b c); see Fig. 13.

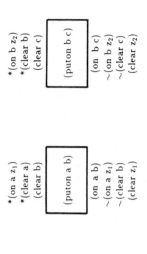

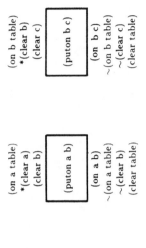

FIG. 9. A first incomplete plan for the Sussman anomaly.

FIG. 10. A second incomplete plan for the Sussman anomaly.

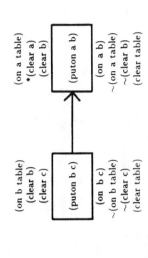

FIG. 11. A third incomplete plan for the Sussman anomaly.

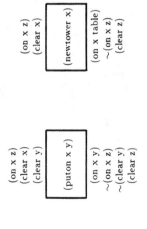

FIG. 8. The blocks world step templates.

one another, with particular emphasis on the history of the ideas embodied in TWEAK. The other three subsections are devoted to the history and future of the three levels of a conjunctive planner: representation, plan modification operations, and top-level search strategies. The most interesting suggestions for future research are in Section 3.2.1 on action representation; the most interesting analysis of past work is in Section 3.3 on plan modification operations.

3.1. Chronology

Two important "prehistorical" nonconjunctive planners introduced techniques that underlie all the conjunctive planning work. GPS [40], due to Allen Newell, J.C. Shaw, and Herbert Simon, introduced means-ends analysis, which is to say step addition or subgoaling: solving problems by applying an operator that would achieve some goal of the problem, and taking the preconditions of the operator as new goals. STRIPS [18], due to Richard Fikes and Nils Nilsson, contributed the action model—in which steps have postconditions that are the only things that get changed by the step—that is used by all domain-independent conjunctive planners.

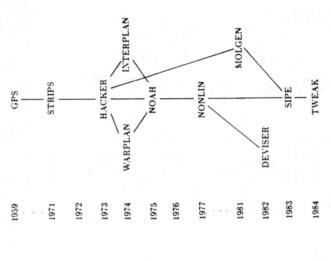

Fig. 14. Conjunctive planning: a family tree.

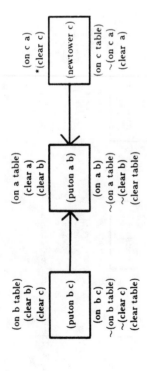

Fig. 12. A fourth incomplete plan for the Sussman anomaly.

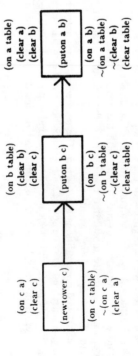

Fig. 13. A plan that solves the Sussman anomaly.

3. Past and Future Planning Research

The three main points of this section are that in retrospect all domain-independent conjunctive planners work the same way; that the action representation which they depend on is inadequate for the real-world planning; and that desirable extensions to this action representation make planning exponentially harder. It is much longer than such sections are in typical AI papers because domain-independent conjunctive planning is unusual as a subfield of AI in showing a clear line of researchers duplicating and building on each other's work. Science is supposed to be like that, but for the most part AI hasn't been.

I restrict attention to domain-independent conjunctive planning, ignoring planners and parts thereof that are domain-dependent or nonconjunctive. This may seem unfair at times. There are two previous survey articles on this topic, [51, 66]. The facts I consider are much the same as those covered by the other papers; my analyses of many points are different.

The first subsection in this section is a historical overview of domain-independent conjunctive planning, showing how different planners build on

Domain-independent conjunctive planning begins in 1973 with Gerald Jay Sussman's HACKER [60]. Sussman ended his thesis with the problem described in Section 1.1, due to Allen Brown but widely known as "the Sussman anomaly," which HACKER could not solve without resort to what Sussman called a "hack."

The urge to find a clean solution to the Sussman anomaly drove a series of rapid developments over the next four years. David Warren's WARPLAN [73] and Austin Tate's INTERPLAN [61–63], both of 1974, cleaned up Sussman's ad-hoc "hack": promotion, in fact. Richard Waldinger [72] further generalized promotion.

In 1975 came Earl Sacerdoti's NOAH [49,50], the first nonlinear planner. Besides his improvement in the representation of plans, Sacerdoti substantially expanded the set of plan modification operations. Tate (the same author of INTERPLAN) improved on NOAH in 1976. NONLIN [64,65] had a backtracking top-level control structure, so that it could find plans after NOAH would get stuck, and added to NOAH's set of plan modification operations.

After 1976, there was a great drought for many years. During this period, there was one important piece of work on nonconjunctive planning: Mark Stefik's MOLGEN [54] made constraints a central technique in planning for the first time. Conjunctive planning was not advanced until a new spurt of work beginning in 1982.

All the new conjunctive planners were NOAH-based. Several researchers [3, 36, 37, 70] extended NOAH by improving the representation of time, in quite different ways. (These improvements have not been incorporated in TWEAK.) David Wilkins' SIPE [77, 78] used MOLGEN-like constraints and incorporated a new technique for detecting clobbering.

3.2. Representation

A planner must represent events in time, actions the agent can take, and the world and the objects in it. Domain-independent planners all base their representations on those of STRIPS, and with the exception of the introduction of constraints, have not progressed much beyond that framework. Therefore, this section is more concerned with future than with past work.

The rest of this section is divided into four decreasingly interesting subsections. The first discusses action representation; the second, time; the third, codesignation constraints; and the fourth, miscellany.

3.2.1. Actions

TWEAK has an impoverished representation for actions; for example, it does not allow for indirect side-effects. Without these restrictions, the modal truth criterion would fail, and TWEAK would be no longer complete and perhaps not correct. These problems are largely a reflection of the state of the art and are

not specific to TWEAK. Linear planners can use more powerful action representations, but probably incur exponentially increased search. Previous nonlinear planners either have the same restricted action representation or are incorrect or incomplete or both.

The restrictions on action representation make TWEAK almost useless as a real-world planner. It is barely possible to formalize the cubical blocks world in this representation; HACKER's blocks world, with different-sized blocks, can not be represented. In the remainder of this section, I will explain the two major restrictions, the reason the truth criterion fails in each case, and some approaches to planning with richer action representations.

The action representation does not allow the effects of actions to depend on the situation in which they are applied. Consider a blocks world in which zero, one, or two blocks can be on any given block. (This example and its analysis are due to David McAllester, personal communication.) Every block still must be on zero or one other block. We need a function space that takes a block as an argument and returns an integer between zero and two inclusive that tells how much room is left on top of the block. A precondition of (puton a b) is that (space b) be greater than zero, and the corresponding postcondition is that (space b) be one less than before. TWEAK can not represent this puton; a representation with conditional postconditions or postconditions that are functionally dependent on the input situation could.

If TWEAK were extended to express this action, the modal truth criterion would fail. An example is provided by a plan with three unordered steps, (puton a d), (puton b d), and (puton c d), and with (space d) being two in the initial situation; see Fig. 15. A precondition of each step is that (space d) be at least one. Let us ask whether this precondition p is achieved in the input situation i of (puton a d). According to the modal truth criterion, it is achieved so long as there is a situation t (the initial situation will do) necessarily before i

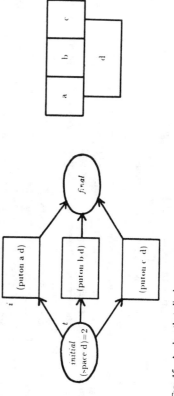

Fig. 15. A plan that displays synergy.

in which p is necessarily asserted (all true) and that there is not even possibly a step between t and i that denies p. Candidate clobbering steps are (puton b d) and (puton c d); they are possibly between t and i. Does one deny p? No. Because in the initial situation there is space for two, and each step only decrements space by one. Yet the two steps act synergistically to clobber p. This possibility is not accounted for in the modal truth criterion.

Another restriction is that all changes made by an action must be explicitly represented as postconditions; many actions can not be formalized in this representation. For example, if block b is on block a and we move a from room$_1$ to room$_2$, b will also move. This effect could be captured in an action representation in which deduction was allowed within situations, so that propositions logically following from postconditions would be considered true in the output situation of a step. Call the set of all propositions that follow from another set the deductive closure of the second set. The semantics of executing a step in a situation is to negate all the propositions in the deductive closure of the postconditions and remove that set from the input situation, add the postconditions to this result, and take the deductive closure of all that. It is again possible for two steps to act synergistically to assert or deny a proposition: if $q \wedge r \Rightarrow p$ and one step asserts q and the other r, together they assert p (equivalently deny $\sim p$). This is the reason that TWEAK requires all propositions to be atomic. Nonatomic propositions could be used, but would be simply treated as literals; the logical operators can't get their usual semantics without deduction.

There are two obvious ways of modifying the modal truth criterion to handle these problems of synergy. One is to consider all the completions of a plan. In a linear plan, the state of the world is completely known at all times, and no synergy is possible. Unfortunately, there are exponentially many linearizations of an incomplete plan, and so this approach, which amounts to reverting to linear planning, is not efficient. Another alternative is to consider sets of steps in trying to find establishers and clobberers. But again there are exponentially many subsets of a set of steps.

Among nonlinear planners, only SIPE allows derived effects or dependency of effects on the input situation of a step. SIPE's treatment of these features is incomplete and not generally correct. This is reasonable, as SIPE represents the state of the art in engineering, rather than a formal theory of planning.

Waldinger's planner allows for derived effects and for effects that depend on the input situation of a step. Because his planner is linear, the problems of synergy do not arise. To determine whether p holds in the output situation of a step S, he asks whether it or its negation is asserted there. If not, p is *regressed* over S. A regression, q, is computed from p and S such that q being true in the input situation of S guarantees that p is true in the output situation. Now the rule can be applied recursively to q and the output situation of the step preceding S.

There are two difficulties with Waldinger's approach. First, it depends on linearity; in a nonlinear plan there isn't a unique step preceding S to recurse to. (Pednault [41] is able to extend Waldinger's technique to a certain restricted form of nonlinearity.) In Section 3.2.2 I will suggest that linear planning is exponentially less efficient than nonlinear planning.

The second problem is that it is not obvious how to compute the regression of p given a step to pass it back over. Waldinger does not address this problem; his planner apparently was given specific techniques which worked only for particular action types. Rosenschein's planner [47] has a general procedure for computing regressions, which was further extended by Kautz [28, 29]. Because these systems incorporated complete deduction engines, they proved to be unworkably inefficient.

The regression formulation makes clearer how TWEAK depends on the simplicity of its action representation: the essential factor is that propositions are unchanged by regression. Extensions to the action representation that preserve this property would be safe. I haven't been able to find any such extensions, however.

The essential difficulty with extended action representation is the *frame problem* [27, 35, 42]. The frame problem is traditionally stated as that of discovering what propositions are left unchanged by an action; this is useful in practice in order to discover whether a proposition holds in a situation. Thus the frame problem can be viewed as that of finding an efficiently implementable truth criterion. The following theorem suggests that this may be impossible in general:

Intractability Theorem. *The problem of determining whether a proposition is necessarily true in a nonlinear plan whose action representation is sufficiently strong to represent conditional actions, dependency of effects on input situations, or derived side-effects is NP-hard.*

A somewhat related theorem is the following:

Second Undecidability Theorem. *Planning is undecidable even with a finite initial situation if the action representation is extended to represent actions whose effects are a function of their situation.*

What are we to make of these theorems? Naively, they suggest that writing planners for extended action representation is a quixotic enterprise. In the conclusion to this paper, I will make a radical suggestion in this regard. There are loosely three ways out, however. We might hope for the best, relax the correctness requirement on a planner, or relax the generality requirement. Hoping for the best amounts to arguing that for the particular cases that the precondition of a dependent operator can be achieved, if it is not already, by adding producers between t and s, by constraining consumers possibly between t and s to be before t or after s, or by constraining the amounts of consumption or production to be respectively small or large. In the HACKER blocks world. adding producers of space amounts to the "punting" strategy (see the discussion of "Strategy Conflict Brothers" in Section 3.3), and increasing the amount they increase space by suggests the "compacting" strategy.

Unfortunately, it turns out that planning with resources is NP-complete; it appears as "sequencing to minimize maximum cumulative cost" in [21]. However, the polynomial criterion and the achievement procedure will be extremely useful if additional domain constraints can be exploited to limit search.

3.2.2. Time

The representation of time is crucial to planning: a plan is really a representation of part of the future. The biggest advance in domain-independent conjunctive planning was probably the recognition that the time order can be partial, at least until execution. This observation first appears in print in [73, p.16], but the first implementation was in NOAH.

I believe that nonlinear planning is potentially exponentially more efficient than linear planning. In an extended action representation, linear planning avoids the potentially exponential amount of work required to compute the truth criterion; but the same exponential shows up in a different guise as the potentially exponentially greater amount of backtracking required to find the correct plan. That more search is required for linear planners is supported by intuition and empirical evidence, but has never been formally proved. It appears to be tricky, because it requires diagonalizing over the search strategy of the linear planner. Thinking about metalevel planning in attempting the proof might be good for this reason.

I have simplified the representation of plans from those used in NOAH and NONLIN. Those planners represent plans as directed acyclic graphs in which there are many different types of nodes, only a few of which represent anything much. My plans are simply partial orders on steps.

Much of the post-drought planning research in the last few years has focused on overlapping actions. All the old planners assume that actions are instantaneous and atomic; in the real world most actions take time, and several can happen at once. Steven Vere's DEVISER [70] treats actions as temporal intervals with numerical endpoints. James Allen and Johannes Koomen's planner [3] also treats actions as intervals, but is based on Allen's nonnumerical time logic. Drew McDermott [36] suggests using a time logic based on branching futures as a basis for planning. These approaches are combined in Miller et al.'s

come up in practice, extensions to current planning techniques will happen to be efficient. My intuition is that this is not the case, but the issue is an empirical one. Relaxing the correctness requirement would produce heuristic planners that sometimes produce plans that don't quite work. A number of current planning systems fit this category. In the remainder of this section, I'll discuss the third possibility, relaxing the generality requirement.

I have examined a number of specific domains, and found that for each of them it was easy to find an efficient truth criterion, but that these criteria were quite different. Perhaps then we should give up on domain-independent planning: the user of a planner must specify, together with the set of available actions, truth criteria to be used.

At the expense of some scruffiness, we can do better. In other work [7], I have been developing a theory of *intermediate techniques*, which are neither completely general, nor completely domain-specific. *Cognitive cliches*, formal structures occurring in many domains, have attached to them intermediate competence that is specific not to a domain, but to a cliche. Intermediate competence is applied by identifying instances of the associated cliche in the world. A cliche-based system has to know something about the domain it is running in, but is still domain-independent, since any cliche may show up in any domain. I envision a cliche-based constraint-posting planner for extended action representations which would have truth criteria specific to cliches that operators in the world might instantiate. A planner with truth criteria for a few dozen cliches might well cover most interesting domains.

For an example of planning with cliches, consider resources. An instance of the *resource cliche* consists of a state variable in the world which holds a quantity in some total order, together with at least one *consumer operator*, which decreases, relative to the order, the value of the state variable, and at least one *dependent operator*, which has as a precondition that the state variable have a value greater than some threshold. There may also be *producer operators* that increase the value of the state variable. (I'm using the term "resource" differently than Wilkins does.) Resources are found in many domains; puton in HACKER's blocks world is both a consumer and a dependent operator of space on any given block.

Associated with the resource cliche is a truth criterion. The value of the state variable in a situation s is no less than its value in situation t necessarily before s, minus the sum of the amounts of decrements due to consumers possibly between t and s, plus the sum of the amounts of increments due to producers necessarily between t and s. In fact, it is often possible to prove a higher lower bound than this; [43] describes a clever polynomial algorithm using network flow techniques that computes the exact least value the state variable could take on.

From this truth criterion we can derive three plan modification operations:

FORBIN [37]. In all these formulations, several actions can be executed in parallel. It would be interesting to analyze these planners in the same way I have analyzed TWEAK: particularly, to find a provable truth criterion that accounts for overlapping actions and to see what plan modification operations it engenders. This has been done for Allen's planner by Bruce Donald [14]. Allen's time logic can represent the constraint that two actions be disjoint in time without committing to which order they are to be performed in. This makes it possible to defer the choice of declobbering operation further than can be done in TWEAK. Promotion and demotion can be combined into a single constraint, which does not commit to which is to be used. This decrease in commitment may result in less search. Most generally, one could represent time propositionally, allowing general disjunctions between several possible constraints to be expressed. This would trade off commitment against the cost of deducing facts about a particular incomplete plan.

Plans are like programs in many ways; but programs have conditionals, iterations, and dataflows, which domain-independent planners have not for the most part been able to generate. A version of WARPLAN generated conditional plans [74], as did Rosenschein's planner [47]; see the discussion in Section 3.3. Jeffrey Van Baalen [69] describes a planner that uses numerical cost information to generate conditional plans. NOAH had a feature for representing simple iterations; however, this representation does not allow declobbering between steps inside the loop and steps outside, and so can not be called conjunctive. The Programmer's Apprentice [44, 45] uses a "plan calculus" historically derived in part from NOAH, which can represent conditionals, loops, and dataflow. Amy Lansky [31, 32] describes GEM, a plan representation derived from studies of concurrent programming systems, which can express a constraint such as "customers are served in the order in which they make requests" which is difficult in other representations. No program synthesizer has yet been written using the Programmer's Apprentice representation; a planner for GEM is now under construction.

3.2.3. Codesignation constraints

MOLGEN was the first planner to highlight the use of constraints; its author, Stefik, introduced the term "constraint posting." Constraints in MOLGEN are arbitrary predicates possibly on several variables. MOLGEN performs three operations on constraints: formulation, propagation, and establishment. Formulation is making new constraints, propagation creates new from old constraints, and establishment is binding variables to values. MOLGEN was the first planner to do propagation; unfortunately its propagation techniques are domain-dependent and not even described. Stefik describes a "build or buy decision" in achieving a goal involving a variable: either one can bind it to a constant already appearing in the plan ("buy"), or to a new constant

("build"). In this case it is often necessary to introduce new steps whose postconditions involve the constant, so as to guarantee properties of it. MOLGEN was first to introduce new steps to satisfy a constraint.

It is little recognized that HACKER used codesignation constraints. They were implemented as special type preconditions on variables. HACKER's clever techniques for achieving goals with variables make use of the CONNIVER [59] context mechanism and have not been duplicated since. However, only the "buy" option was considered, and it is not clear how general the implementation was.

SIPE's constraints are modeled on MOLGEN's. SIPE's truth criterion takes into account possible truths resulting from possibly codesignating propositions. Like TWEAK, SIPE propagates constraints only via a codesignation relation.

TWEAK uses only codesignation constraints, because preconditions already can represent predicates on variables, so that there is little loss in expressive power. If one looks at the way constraints are used in planning, almost all constraints correspond very naturally to preconditions of steps. There are some exceptions to this in MOLGEN, all of them constraints that have been created via propagation. Stefik's build or buy decision translates in the TWEAK framework into step addition versus simple achievement. Since preconditions are associated with times, predicates on variables are also; this solves problems MOLGEN had with time representation.

The difference in expressive power between MOLGEN or SIPE and TWEAK is that TWEAK cannot restrict the range of a variable to a finite set. There are two reasons I haven't put range restrictions into TWEAK: because constraint computations then become NP-complete (proof by reduction from graph coloring); and more seriously because the truth criterion fails if I allow them. The "pathological" plan in Fig. 16 illustrates the problem. Here the codesignation constraint and the range constraints together require that either x codesignate with a and y with b, or vice versa; either way $(p\ a\ b)$ holds in the final situation. Yet $(p\ a\ b)$ is not necessarily asserted by any particular step.

Variables are needed in the blocks world in which they originated for a "deep" reason. In [5] I describe a problem solver that uses a TWEAK-like planner as a subroutine. This problem solver views *puton* as both a POP and a PUSH. Towers can be seen as stacks; moving a block from one tower to another POPS the first and PUSHES the second. It is the PUSH aspect that is exploited in achieving on goals, and the POP aspect that is exploited in achieving clear goals. When *puton* is viewed as a POP, there is no explanation of what the second argument (the place to put the block moved) is for. So the problem solver uses

$(p\ y\ x)\qquad x\in\{a,b\}$
$y\in\{a,b\}$
$x\neq y$

$(p\ x\ y)$

Fig. 16. A pathological plan.

a variable to leave the second argument unspecified. Whatever value the second argument takes on, the puton acts as a POP.

3.2.4. Other problems for future research

A 1972 paper by Fikes, Hart, and Nilsson [19] lists a number of open research areas in planning. Most are still virtually untouched.

Representations of the world using nonassertional datastructures are simpler, more efficient, and better reflect its structure than the assertional databases used in current domain-independent planners. Many domain-specific planners use such representations effectively, and I see no inherent difficulty in using such simulation structures in linear domain-independent planning. In constraint-posting planning the state of the world is not completely defined at all times; this is easy to implement using assertional databases, in which it is easy to represent unknown truth values. It is much harder to represent partial knowledge with nonassertional datastructures. One approach to this problem is outlined in [48]. This or perhaps a hybrid technique, using both assertions and more direct representations, may lead to simpler, more powerful and efficient planners.

In most real-world domains actions can have any of several outcomes, depending on factors that the agent does not or cannot know, or even on genuinely random factors. Effectively, they are nondeterministic. There has been almost no work on planning in such domains. A related open problem is coping with events that are not planned for. These might be the actions of other agents or spontaneous physical happenings. DEVISER and Allen's planner can plan around "scheduled" unplanned events: these are specific events that will occur at known times. Many problem solvers have plan executives that, when unexpected events occur, call the planner to derive a new plan from the altered state of the world; [79], for example. In the real world, which has tigers in it, that isn't good enough; you have to prepare for contingencies during planning. Such plans need conditionals. Another area of current research is in planning for multiple agents or multiple effectors that have to be synchronized [19, 20, 46].

3.3. Making a plan achieve a goal

In this section, I treat first linear planners and then nonlinear planners. That isn't quite the chronological order, as some linear planners postdate NOAH. There are two interesting points to the section: one is the way the individual plan modification operations were developed by generalization, splitting, and merging. The other is to see that all conjunctive domain-independent planners work in substantially the same way, though they look very different, using apparently unrelated datastructures and algorithms. As time went by, features were added and alternative implementations were tried, but the fundamentals

are unchanged from HACKER down to TWEAK. This has not been generally realized, even by the people who wrote the planners. Forcing all the algorithms into the vocabulary of TWEAK modification operations makes them easy to compare. However, many of the early planning papers are very difficult to read, and some of what follows may be inaccurate in detail. Figure 17 summarizes the section, illustrating which parts of the achievement procedure were invented when.

The most important thing to understand about linear planners is that they work just the same way as nonlinear ones, except that the representation is awkward. The basic operation of all the linear planners is analogous to promotion. In a nonlinear planner this just adds temporal constraints; in a linear planner, a step must be picked up and moved to a different position in the plan.

There are two different versions of promotion that appear in linear planners. The first, *individual promotion*, moves the clobberer before the clobberee. (Alternatively, the clobberee could be moved backward before the clobberer; this is an uninterestingly different operation.) In a nonlinear planner, promotion automatically also puts everything before the clobberee before the clobberer and vice versa; individual promotion doesn't generally do so, with the result that a step can be separated from the steps that were to achieve its preconditions, so that they must be reachieved. *Block promotion* moves the clobberer, together with the steps that achieve its preconditions, and the steps that achieve their preconditions, transitively, as a block. This implies a *strong linearity assumption*: not only that the plan can be totally ordered, but also that if you have goals g and h and S achieves g and T achieves h then S is before T, then all the steps that achieve preconditions of S are before all the steps that achieve preconditions of T. In other words, the time order must respect the subgoaling hierarchy. Using only block promotion, it is impossible to solve optimally the Sussman anomaly problem. The optimal solution involves three steps: (puton c table), (puton b c), (puton a b). This plan violates the strong linearity assumption: the first step achieves the precondition (clear a) for the last

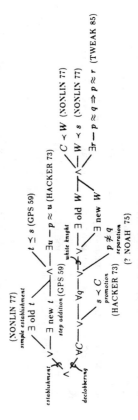

FIG. 17. A history of the plan modification operations.

step, but the middle step is not achieving a precondition of the last, but rather one of the top-level goals.

HACKER has, in effect, four plan modification operations. Step addition is used initially on each of the conjunct goals, and the resulting steps are arbitrarily linearly ordered. HACKER recognizes four bug types, each of which has a corresponding plan modification operation. "Prerequisite Missing" is a precondition that is not true anywhere before it is needed, and is patched with step addition. "Prerequisite Clobbers Brother Goal" is just clobbering, and block promotion is applied. "Prerequisite Conflict Brothers" is a "double cross": a pair of steps each of which clobbers the other. HACKER has a plan modification operation for this which does not appear in any other planner: a RESOLVE expert is called, which replaces the two steps with a single step that achieves all the goals the two steps together were intended to achieve. In practice, it seems that the only cases the RESOLVE expert could handle were pairs of steps that achieved the goals (spacefor a c) and (spacefor b c) (Sussman's blocks world allows more than one block on a given block). The expert would replace the two steps with a subplan that achieved (spacefor (both a b) c).

HACKER had many other nifty planning techniques that somehow got lost in the sands of time. For example, HACKER's addition operation is different from those of all subsequent planners. Addition in later planners uses one of the possibly several steps in later when one doesn't work. This leads to the fourth bug type, "Strategy Conflict Brothers," in which a step in one strategy (alternative achieving step) clobbers a precondition of another, later strategy. In this case, HACKER applies promotion. This "multiple addition" operation has many interesting properties. The principal use of it is in achieving (spacefor a b); the two strategies are "compacting" the blocks on top of b and "punting" blocks off of b that don't need to be there. Although either of these strategies may achieve an unachieved spacefor goal, neither is guaranteed to. Yet, if executed in the right order (punt then compact), they make space if it is possible to do so. This sort of synergy and partial goal fulfillment has never been duplicated.

Sussman called Allen Brown's problem "anomalous" because it could not be solved using block promotion. He presents a solution using individual promotion, but regards this as a "hack." Why? Sussman viewed HACKER as an automatic programming system, constructing programs, not plans. A conjunction (of the original goals or of the preconditions to a step) is achieved via a single subroutine. Promotion in HACKER was confined to permuting the order of lines of a subroutine; this amounts to block promotion, since subroutines encapsulate the subgoal hierarchy. In order to solve the Sussman anomaly, one must move program steps across subroutine boundaries, which HACKER wouldn't do.

It's a pity, though, that the view of planning as automatic programming got

lost in the shuffle. HACKER's performance in any given domain would improve as time went by, because the programs it wrote could be reused on new problems. Sussman describes techniques for generalization and subroutinization of programs so that less planning would need to be done later. Compilation can be viewed as constant-folding the source code into the interpreter; HACKER in effect constant-folded classes of problems into the planner. It would be interesting to build a problem solver that constant-folded into TWEAK, and incorporated what has been learned in the past ten years about generalization.

WARPLAN has two plan modification operations, step addition and an operation that combines addition with individual promotion. The latter operation ("regression") is to find a step that achieves the goal, then to search backward from the end for a place in the plan where the step can be put without being clobbered. WARPLAN was able to solve the anomalous problem because it doesn't make the strong linearity assumption; it represents plans as flat orders, without hierarchy.

Waldinger [72] generalizes Warren's technique by allowing the regression of a goal to be computed from the step it is being moved back over (as described in Section 3.2.1).

INTERPLAN has three plan modification operations: step addition and both versions of promotion (not combined with addition).

Rosenschein [47] describes a linear planner that uses both promotion and demotion. He also has an operation for introducing conditionals (if-then-else branches) into plans: it chooses an arbitrary proposition not provable or disprovable from the initial situation, and puts a branch on this proposition at the beginning of the plan. In unpublished work he has improved this technique so that the condition to branch on can be found deterministically.

With NOAH comes the great explosion in the set of plan modification operations. NOAH classifies clobberings into three classes: in the first, two steps each clobber the other (a "double cross"); in the second, the clobberer and the clobberee are unordered; and in the third, the clobberer is before the clobberee. The case (an "n-cross") in which a set of more than two steps clobber each other, arranged in a cycle, is neglected. I don't understand Sacerdoti's explanation of the plan modification operation to patch double crosses; it seems to be a version of step addition, possibly combined with separation. The other two cases are handled by promotion and demotion with the addition of a white knight step, respectively.

"Eliminate Redundant Preconditions" is a step removal operation. Step removal is useful because NOAH does not have a simple establishment operation. Thus, if two steps have the same precondition, they may both be achieved by addition, and then one of the two steps removed. "Use Existing Objects" binds variables to constants. Sacerdoti is very unclear on when it is applied and how the binding is chosen. NOAH has a simple but entirely adequate technique for achieving a disjunctive goal. Each of the disjuncts is planned for, until it is clear that one can be achieved; then an operation is applied that removes the plan fragments for the other disjuncts.

Sacerdoti presents two "task-specific" plan modification operations. "Tool Gathering" optimizes plans relative to a notion of the cost of performing correct plans: a correct plan may be made into a better, still correct one by some reorderings. "Limitations of an Apprentice" compensates for the inexpressibility in his action representation of many kinds of actions. The example he gives is very similar (a resource conflict, requiring a global view to do declobbering) to the blocks world example I analyze in Section 3.2.1. Unfortunately, the details of the operation are not given.

NONLIN was the first planner to use simple establishment. NONLIN also uses addition, promotion, and demotion.

SIPE introduced no new modification operations, but it does have a new technique for detecting clobbering. A particularly common sort of precondition is what Wilkins terms a *resource*: a binary variable that must be set to one value ("available") for an operation to be applicable, and which is set to a different value during the operation, then "released" or reset at the end. Two unordered steps that try to use the same resource clobber each other; SIPE then applies promotion. The techniques SIPE uses for resource clobbering detection are only heuristic; more work is needed to understand this maneuver.

Separation as a plan modification operation may appear first in TWEAK. I suspect that NOAH's double cross removal operation, which I don't understand, may combine step addition with separation; apart from this, there seems to be no precedent.

TWEAK is the first planner to use declobbering by white knight in the general case in which the white knight is distinct from the establishing situation t. This maneuver is actually pretty useless, because either the white knight will turn out to assert the goal, in which case we might as well have used separation as a situation as an establisher, or else it won't, in which case we'd have done as well to use its output to defeat the clobberer. The only possible advantage is slightly less commitment, and so possibly a little less backtracking. This plan modification, like all the others, falls out of interpreting the modal truth criterion as a nondeterministic procedure, and corresponds to the necessarily but odd clause about white knights. My implementation never actually uses it.

Because the modal truth criterion is sufficient as well as necessary, there are no more plan modification operations possible without extending the range of represented actions. Once that is done, new operations will be possible; again they can be derived from the truth criteria for the new representations. For example, the pathological plan illustrated in Section 3.2.3 suggests an operation of "establishment by separation": if the plan did not have the constraint $x \neq y$, adding this constraint would achieve p in the final situation. If the representation of time is extended to allow overlapping actions, a new operation ("simultaneous establishment") is possible. In this case, two actions must be performed simultaneously to achieve a result.

Kristian Hammond [22] describes WOK, a planner which although domain-specific and nonconjunctive has interesting things to say about goal interactions (the class of effects that includes clobbering). WOK achieves goals by introducing interactions of known sorts. This is the antithesis of the linear strategy: rather than assuming as a first approximation that goals don't interact, synergistic interactions are used as a basic tool for achieving goals. It is unclear how this approach can be applied to conjunctive planning, but it may be a useful line of future research. [76] also describes constructive use of goal interactions.

3.4. The top-level control structure

The top-level control structure of almost every domain-independent conjunctive planner is search. Search control is the aspect of domain-independent conjunctive planning that is understood least. Most of the domains to which domain-independent conjunctive planning has been applied have been forgiving: if more than one plan modification operation is applicable to a clobbering or unestablished goal, any of the possibilities will probably do. Thus, it hasn't been necessary to devote a lot of thought to which to choose. However, in real domains the choices probably are critical, and a lot of schemes have been proposed for making them. Since none of these has been adequately tested, little is known about which is best.

Almost every planner has a distinct control structure. I've loosely grouped them in eight classes, ordered roughly by the complexity of the backtracking algorithm. The classes are no backtracking, explicitly represented alternatives, dependency-directed modification, chronological backtracking, dependency-directed backtracking, heuristic search, metaplanning, and protection. Many of the planners I discuss actually fit into several of these classes.

The simplest control structure avoids backtracking altogether. Plan modification operations are applied in a fixed order according to fixed criteria until a correct plan is found or it is no longer possible to apply operations. This is not as bad as it sounds, because you can usually make a good guess as to which modification operation to apply: usually, one should prefer simple achievement to step addition, for example. HACKER uses this approach. NOAH comes very close; it backs up only from alternative choices of variable bindings. That NOAH solved several difficult problems shows that search strategy is unimportant in some domains.

A very simple solution to the problem of which modification operation to apply is to choose all applicable ones, splitting the plan into several explicitly represented copies. No planner fits altogether in this class as it is very inefficient in general. If some additional principle decides whether for a given choice to use this technique or to use search, the splitting technique may be useful. SIPE and a planning framework described by Barbara Hayes-Roth et al. [24] take this approach.

The simplest backtracking scheme is chronological: when a choice has to be made, one is chosen by some means and the others are saved away. If the plan cannot be extended to a solution by further modification, failure is signalled. The most recent choice point is backed up to, and an alternative for the choice is used. When no choices remain, the next most recent choice point is backed up to, and so on. WARPLAN, INTERPLAN, and SIPE use chronological backtracking.

Chronological backtracking can result in the exploration of more blind alleys than necessary. Dependency-directed backtracking backs up at failure not to the most recent choice point, but to one responsible for the failure. For a discussion of dependency-directed backtracking in general, see [15, 53]. The first planner to use dependency-direction was Hayes' 1975 route planner [23], which was not conjunctive. Hayes used backtracking to recover only from execution error, rather than from planning error (dead ends) as does TWEAK, although he explicitly considered the latter possibility. Thus his implemented control structure can be termed "dependency-directed modification" rather than backtracking. Hayes' conception of dependency-directed backtracking predates and seems to be independent of its discovery by Stallman and Sussman [53], to whom it is usually credited.

Daniel [11] added dependency-directed backtracking to NONLIN. The same year de Kleer et al. [12] described a dependency-directed linear planner. London's planner [33] represents plans and world states using a TMS, the utility underlying dependency-directed backtracking, but apparently does not use the TMS for backtracking.

Heuristic search uses some numerical estimate of "goodness" to decide which order to try choices in. INTERPLAN and NONLIN use heuristics to control their chronological search. Since making a wrong choice can result in searching a large dead-end subtree, it would be nice to eliminate wrong choices without having to explore their consequences. Kibler and Morris [30] present a control scheme based on negative search heuristics that prune obviously bad choices. However, these heuristics are domain-specific for the blocks world. Siklossy and Roach [52] use a similar strategy. Corkill [9] describes a NOAH-like planner in which control is distributed among several message-passing processors.

All the control structures discussed so far (with the possible exception of heuristic search) are "syntactic": they don't depend on the specifics of the plan being constructed, but blindly apply some simple algorithm for choosing among alternatives without considering what those alternatives are. Since control of planning is very hard, such methods may be inherently weak; perhaps we should apply the full power of a problem solver to choosing what to do next. This is the *metaplanning* approach. There is an increasing literature on this

[4, 10, 16, 55, 75, 76] most of which is very vague. I'll discuss just two meta-planning systems. Doyle's unimplemented SEAN uses (another copy of) the same planner to do metaplanning as to do planning about the domain. The metaplanner in turn is controlled by an identical metametaplanner and so on; Doyle discusses ways to implement this apparently infinite regress.

MOLGEN has only one level of metaplanning, and the metaplanner is quite unlike the domain-level planner. The domain-level planner creates plans for MOLGEN's domain, genetics experiment planning. It has operations that are analogous to the plan modification operations of TWEAK. These operations are selected by a metaplanner which chooses among plan modification operations. The metaplanner is very simple; it's perhaps exaggerated to call it a planner at all.

The idea of using a copy of TWEAK as a metaplanner is attractive: the plan modification operations can be thought of as having well-defined preconditions (that the constraints they impose not conflict with the existing ones, or that a suitable step exists to achieve a goal in the case of addition) and postconditions (the insertion of the new constraint or step). Unfortunately, TWEAK's action representation is too weak to represent the plan modification operations.

Protection is a technique introduced in HACKER; it guarantees that once a goal has been achieved, it stays achieved. Protection has not generally been seen as a search strategy, but is perhaps best viewed that way. Each time the goal achievement procedure is applied successfully, the achieved goal is stored in a protection list. This list consulted in future applications of the procedure; if the procedure would unachieve a protected goal as a side-effect of achieving a new goal, backtracking is invoked. Protection significantly decreases the size of the search space, but it is often overly strict and can result in excessive backtracking. Vere [71] describes "splicing," a technique which relaxes protection when it has caused a deadlock.

Planners can be classified along a dimension orthogonal to search strategy, that of technique used to recover from execution failures. This isn't part of planning proper, but many systems interleave planning with (simulated or actual) execution so that effectively a nonbacktracking planner performs search, failing during execution rather than planning, and then returning to the planner to obtain a new plan to recover. HACKER uses this approach. NOAH proper doesn't, but its planner is connected to an execution system that reinvokes the planner after execution failure, so that the system as a whole can be put in this class. HACKER makes use of CONNIVER techniques similar to dependency-direction in order to figure out which planning decision was responsible for the failure and to try another alternative in the choice.

Planning and AI language design have strongly influenced each other. Many of the planners that do search inherit their search discipline from the language they were written in, and many AI languages were designed to make writing the top-level control of planners easier. PLANNER [25, 26] was intended as a language for writing planners in; it was the first to supply backtracking automatically. HACKER and BUILD, a clever domain-specific blocks world planner [17], were written in and depend heavily on the abilities of CONNIVER [59]. CONNIVER was written in reaction to the difficulties with chronological backtracking in PLANNER. WARPLAN inherits its search from PROLOG. The planner of de Kleer et al. was the first program written in AMORD, and inherits its dependency-directed backtracking from AMORD's TMS [13]. TWEAK, too, inherits its dependency-directed backtracking from Dependency-Directed LISP, a language specifically designed for TWEAK. DDL looks like ordinary LISP but has an implicit dependency-directed backtracking control structure. It will be described in a forthcoming paper.

4. Conclusions

Perhaps the most important contribution of this paper is the introduction of the notion of a provably correct modal truth criterion and its use in the correctness/completeness proof. The first such correctness argument is given on [60, p. 100]; although it is very loose, my proof clearly descends from it. A series of five papers, [73, 72, 47, 29, 41], building on each other, rigorously prove correctness of linear planners. Those papers were motivated by many of the same considerations as this one: rigor requires simplicity, guarantees agreement about details, can unveil problems and suggest solutions. Thus these papers form the neat part of the scruffy-neat research cycle for linear planning. The neat part of the cycle for nonlinear planning begins with this paper.

Yet I wonder about the psychological reality of this sort of planning. It may be that the only solutions to the frame problem we can devise are heuristic. Anecdotal evidence suggests that humans solve problems by improvisation, doing something easy and debugging the result when it fails [58]. Sussman's HACKER worked that way; unfortunately the set of bugs that it could patch are ones that TWEAK never introduces, and so his specific debugging techniques are of no use. [1] describes the beginning of research on improvisation. [8] gives a theory of planning as a derivative activity, taking situated activity as the primary phenomenon. [2] (in preparation) describes in detail a theory of situated activity that does not involve planning.

Appendix A. Proofs

A.1. The modal truth criterion

I prove the criterion in three steps. First, I prove the *time's arrow lemma*, which says that only the steps executed before a situation are relevant to what is true in that situation. Time does not flow backward. I use the time's arrow lemma to prove a truth criterion for complete plans that is analogous to the modal truth criterion. I use that and a series of lemmas about consistent sets of constraints to prove the modal truth criterion. All these proofs except the last are by numerical induction. The proof of the modal truth criterion is more interesting; in it I construct specific completions of plans that satisfy various conditions.

Time's Arrow Lemma. *Let $\mathscr{P}$ and $\mathscr{Q}$ be complete plans whose initial situation and first n steps are identical. A proposition p is true in the initial situation or the input or output situation of one of the first n steps of $\mathscr{P}$ iff it is true in the corresponding situation in $\mathscr{Q}$.*

Proof. By induction on n. If $\mathscr{P}$ and $\mathscr{Q}$ have no steps, they have only one situation, which is both initial and final, and the same in both. Certainly p is true in this situation in $\mathscr{P}$ iff it is true in the corresponding situation in $\mathscr{Q}$. Suppose now that the lemma is true for plans whose initial situation and first $n-1$ steps are identical; I will show that it holds for plans whose initial situation and first n steps are identical. Let $\mathscr{P}$ and $\mathscr{Q}$ be such plans; they have the first $n-1$ steps identical, and by the induction hypotheses p is true in the initial situation and the input and output situations of the first $n-1$ situations of $\mathscr{P}$ iff p is true in the corresponding situation of $\mathscr{Q}$. The only remaining situation we need check is the output situation s of the nth step S. By definition, s is the input situation of S minus any propositions denied by S, plus any propositions asserted by S. If p is neither asserted nor denied by S, then it is true in s just in case it is true in the input situation of the analogous step of $\mathscr{Q}$. If p is asserted or denied by S, it is also asserted or denied by the analogous step in $\mathscr{Q}$ and so again is true in s iff it is true in the output situation of the nth step of $\mathscr{Q}$. By induction, then, the lemma holds for any n. □

Truth Criterion for Complete Plans. *In a complete plan, a proposition p is true in a situation s iff there exists a situation t previous or equal to s in which p is asserted and such that there is no step between t and s which denies p.*

Proof. It should be obvious that this criterion is correct. Informally, we start with the initial situation and at each step delete from the set of propositions representing the world what is denied by the step and add what is asserted by it. Everything else is preserved untouched.

A rigorous proof again uses induction on the length of plans. A plan with no steps has only an initial and a final situation, and the two contain the same set of propositions. A proposition is true in the initial situation iff it codesignates with something in the initial situation, in which case it is asserted there. A proposition is true in the final situation iff it is true in the initial situation. In both cases, there is no possibility of an intervening denying step.

Suppose now that the criterion is correct for complete plans of length $n-1$; I

Proof. There are enough constants because only finitely many of the infinite set can be mentioned in a plan. Since the gensymmed constants are not mentioned in the plan, they cannot have been constrained to not codesignate with any of the variables. Since the $\{v_i\}$ do not codesignate with any constants, there is no problem of distinct constants being constrained to codesignate. □

Noncodesignation Consistency Lemma. *If p is a proposition and $\{q_i\}$ is a finite set of propositions such that for all i possibly $q_i \neq p$, then possibly for all i $q_i \neq p$.*

Proof. Again by induction, on the size of $\{q_i\}$. p and q_i are constrained to not codesignate by constraining some pair of elements to not codesignate. I must show that doing so does not make p and some q_i necessarily codesignate. This is because the definition of the codesignation relation is such that a codesignation of elements cannot be made to follow by adding a noncodesignation. □

Modal Truth Criterion. *A proposition p is necessarily true in a situation s iff two conditions hold: there is a situation t equal or necessarily previous to s in which p is necessarily asserted; and for every step C possibly previous before s and every proposition q possibly codesignating with p which C denies, there is a step W necessarily between C and s which asserts r, a proposition such that r and p codesignate whenever p and q codesignate. The criterion for possible truth is exactly analogous, with all the modalities switched (read "necessary" for "possible" and vice versa).*

Proof. David McAllester helped debug and simplify this proof. I'll give the proof for necessary truth; possible truth follows by modal duality. Refer to Fig. 6 for a diagram of the necessary truth criterion.

The proof comes in three parts. The first two parts show the necessary truth of the proposition p implies the existence of an establisher and the absence of a clobberer. I do this by proving the contrapositive, that the absence of establisher or the presence of a clobberer ensures that p is not necessarily true. First I show that if there is no establisher, then p is not necessarily true. Then I show that if there is a clobberer, p is again not necessarily true. The third part of the proof shows the implication in the other direction: if there is an establisher and no clobberer, p is necessarily true. The basic proof technique is constructive: for each of these cases, I show how to construct a specific completion of the given incomplete plan in which the truth criterion for complete plans can be used to show that p is (or is not) true in s.

In the case where there is no establisher, to construct the completion falsifying p in s, first add constraints that put after s every step possibly after s. This can be done, by the temporal consistency lemma. The next step is to apply the codesignation consistency lemma and constrain every equivalence class of variables that is not already constrained to codesignate with some specific constant to codesignate with a distinct "gensymmed" constant. A completion

will show that it is correct for complete plans of length n. Let P be a plan of length n, f the final situation of P, S the last step in P, i the input situation of S, and 2 the plan of length $n - 1$ derived by removing S from P; see Fig. A.1. p is true in a situation in P other than f just in case p is true in the corresponding situation of 2, by the time's arrow lemma. Then by the induction hypothesis, the criterion holds for every proposition and every situation in P except perhaps f (which contains the same propositions as the output situation of S). f is by definition i minus things denied by S plus whatever is asserted by S. Thus p is true in f iff it is asserted by S or true in i and not denied by S. In the former case, p is asserted in f and no step can intervene, so the criterion holds. In the latter, by induction there is a situation t in which p is asserted and no step between t and i which denies p, and since S does not deny p, there is also no step between t and f that denies p. This same t is before f, so the criterion is satisfied. The converse is trivial: if the criterion holds, either p is asserted in f or it is true in i and not denied by S. □

I will next state and give only proof sketches for three technical lemmas needed in the proof of the modal truth criterion.

Temporal Consistency Lemma. *If s is a situation and $\{t_i\}$ is a finite set of situations such that each i. s is possibly before t_i, then possibly s is before all the t_i.*

Proof. By induction on the size of $\{t_i\}$. The main step is to see that constraining $s < t_j$ for some j leaves all the other $s < t_i$ possible. For $s < t_j$ to make $s < t_i$ impossible, it would have to make $t_i < s$ necessary. But, from the definition of the time order, from $s < t_j$ together with the previous constraints, there follow only constraints of the form $a < b$, where $a \leq s$ and $t_i \leqslant b$. □

Codesignation Consistency Lemma. *If $\{v_i\}$ is a finite set of variables none of which is constrained to codesignate with any constant, you can assign to each equivalence class (under the codesignation relation) a distinct "gensymmed" constant not previously appearing in the plan, and constrain codesignation of these constants with the variables in their respective classes.*

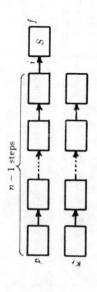

Fig. A.1. Constructions used in the proof of the criterion for complete plans.

in which p is not true in s is made by taking any completion of this modified plan. In the original incomplete plan there was no step that necessarily asserts p and that is necessarily before s; and any step that only possibly asserted p has been made not to assert it (but rather some other proposition involving gensymmed constants); and any step that necessarily asserts p but is only possibly before s has been put after s. So no situation before or equal to s asserts p, and by the truth criterion for complete plans p is not true in this completion.

The next case is that in which there is a clobberer C. To construct the falsifying completion first constrain C before s, which is possible because C is a clobberer. Then constrain every step still possibly after s to be actually after s, by application of the temporal consistency lemma, twice. Now constrain every step still possibly before C to be actually before C. This can be done, by application of the temporal consistency lemma, twice. Now constrain codesignation of q (the proposition possibly codesignating with p which C denies) and p, which can be done because C is a clobberer, and constrain noncodesignation with p of every postcondition of every step between C and s, which can be done by the noncodesignation consistency lemma and the observation that any such step, if it now necessarily asserted p, would be a white knight. Finally arbitrarily complete the result; see Fig. A.2. By the truth criterion for complete plans, in this completion p is false in s. C is a step that denies p, it is before s, and no step in-between asserts p.

The last case is that in which there is an establisher and no clobberer. In this case, I will show, p is necessarily true in s. Choose any completion; Fig. A.3 is illustrative. Since there is an establisher t, p is true in t. Consider the set of steps $\{C_i\}$ that possibly denied p in the incomplete plan. Each of these either does or does not actually deny p. The latter sort we can ignore; they do not endanger p's truth in s. Since remaining C_i are not clobberers, there is for each a corresponding white knight W_i asserting p (since the white knight asserts p whenever C_i denies it). There may in turn be a step after the white knight

denying p; but it must also have its own white knight. Since there are only finitely many steps in the plan. eventually p will be asserted by a white knight and not denied before s. Then by the truth criterion for complete plans, p is true in s. □

A.2. The outcomes lemma

Outcomes Lemma. *Each of the three possible outcomes of TWEAK's algorithm (success, failure, and looping) is possible for some choice of domain and problem.*

Proof. A trivial example of success is a problem with a single goal which is true in the initial situation. A trivial example of failure is provided by a problem that has at least one goal that is not true in the initial situation and which is not possibly asserted by any available step template. An example of nontermination is given by the problem whose initial state is $\sim g$ and $\sim h$ and whose goals are g and h in a domain in which there are two step templates, one with precondition $\sim h$ and postconditions g and $\sim h$ and the other with precondition $\sim g$ and postconditions h and $\sim g$. TWEAK loops on this problem, building plans that are longer and longer chains of steps that alternately assert g and h. □

A.3. The correctness/completeness theorem

Correctness/Completeness Theorem. *If TWEAK, given a problem, terminates claiming a solution, the plan it produces does in fact solve the problem. If TWEAK returns signalling failure or does not halt, no solution exists.*

Proof. This follows directly from the use of the necessary truth criterion in computing whether a plan solves the problem given and in constructing the goal achievement procedure. TWEAK's incomplete plan always has the same initial situation as the problem given. and the top-level loop continues until all the goals are achieved, at which point the plan must solve the problem. If a solution exists it must be a plan in some way achieves the problem's goals. Since TWEAK's search is breadth-first, and since the nondeterministic plan modification procedure generates only finitely many ways to produce a new plan from an old one, TWEAK eventually examines every way to satisfy a problem's goals. The plan must also have all preconditions achieved; but TWEAK also tries all ways to achieve preconditions. Thus, if a solution exists, TWEAK will find it. □

A.4. First undecidability theorem

First Undecidability Theorem. *Any Turing machine with its input can be encoded as a planning problem in the TWEAK representation. Therefore, plan-*

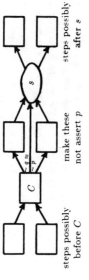

Fig. A.2. Falsifying p in a plan with a clobberer.

Fig. A.3. A completion of a plan satisfying the criterion.

ning is undecidable, and no upper bound can be put on the amount of time required to solve a problem.

Proof. The encoding is direct and straightforward. An infinite set of constants t, are used to represent the tape squares. The binary relation successor represents the connectivity of the tape. The functional binary relation contents represents the contents of the tape, and the set of constants a, represent the alphabet written on the tape. A predicate head holds of exactly one tape square, that under the head. A set of constants s, represent the finitely many states of the controller, and the predicate state holds of the current state only. For each arc from state s, to state s, in the controller's state graph there is an operator type. The operator has four preconditions: (state s,), (head t) where t is a variable representing the unknown square under the head, (contents t a), where a is the symbol the arc specifies to read, and (successor t u) if the arc says to move right, or (successor u t) if the arc says to move left. The operator has four postconditions: (state s,), ~ (state i), (head u), (contents t b), where b is the written symbol, and ~(contents t a).

The initial situation of the problem has (state i), where i is the initial state of the Turing machine controller, and (head t), where t is the initial tape square. The input to the machine is specified via the contents relation. There must be countably many successor propositions to encode the topology of the tape (and also countably many contents propositions to make all but finitely many squares blank). The final situation of the problem is just (state f), where f represents the halt state for the Turing machine.

It is easy to see that a valid plan for this problem amounts to a trace of the encoded Turing machine computation. Such a plan exists iff the Turing machine halts. Thus it is undecidable whether or not there exists a plan. □

A.5. The intractibility theorem

Intractibility Theorem. *The problem of determining whether a proposition is necessarily true in a nonlinear plan whose action representation is sufficiently strong to represent conditional actions, dependency of effects on input situations, or derived side-effects is NP-hard.*

Proof. This proof is based on an idea of Stan Rosenschein's. It is by direct reduction from PSAT, or rather from the equivalent problem of determining whether a Boolean formula is valid (true under every truth assignment).

Augment TWEAK's action representation by adding a new type of step, the conditional step. A conditional step is always applicable. but has two sets of postconditions, the if-true and the if-false postconditions. The if-true postconditions hold in the output situation if all the preconditions were satisfied in the input situation; otherwise the if-false postconditions hold.

Given a propositional formula p on atoms p_i, I construct a plan in this representation and a proposition such that the proposition is necessarily true in the final situation iff p is valid. The p_i are recycled as propositions in the plan, and all are made false in the initial situation. A set of steps S_i make the p_i true, so that a truth assignment on the p_i corresponds to a subset of $\{S_i\}$.

A set of conditional steps, $\{C_j\}$, check that p holds in every truth assignment. Let p be expressed as the disjunction of conjunctive clauses. There is a C_j for each clause; C_j has as its preconditions the conjunct p_i in the corresponding clause. The if-true postconditions assert a proposition called *satisfied*; the if-false postconditions are null. *satisfied* is false in the initial situation.

What remains is to guarantee that all the C_j evaluate their clauses relative to the same truth assignment. This is done by introducing a new "flag" proposition called *checking*, initially false, which is made true by a single step K and false by a single step U. K and U have no preconditions and the are ordered respectively before and after all the C_j. The S_i are made conditional, so that they assert *satisfied* if *checking* holds. Figure A.4 illustrates the plan I have constructed.

When does *satisfied* hold in the final situation? It holds whenever there are any S_i between K and U, by the mechanism of the last paragraph. If there are no S_i between K and U, the C_j evaluate their clauses in the truth assignment corresponding to the set of S_i before K. (The remaining S_i are after U and have no effect on *satisfied*.) Since every truth assignment is generated by some

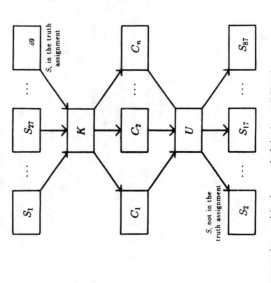

Fig. A.4. Construction used in the proof of the intractibility theorem.

completion of the plan, *satisfied* is necessarily true in the final situation just in case p is in fact valid.

This establishes the result for conditional actions. For the rest, it is easy to see that these conditionals can be simulated with dependency of effects on input situations or derived side effects. □

A.6. Second undecidability theorem

Second Undecidability Theorem. *Planning is undecidable even with a finite initial situation if the action representation is extended to represent actions whose effects are a function of their input situation.*

Proof. Papert and McNaughton [39] showed that any recursive function can be computed by a two-counter machine, i.e. a machine consisting of two positive-integer-valued registers and a finite state control which can test either register for equality to zero and can increment or decrement either register. I encode such a machine, with inputs, as a planning problem, the goal of which is to get the machine into the halt state. I use three unary predicates to represent the state of the machine, $counter_1$, $counter_2$, and state. States and integers are represented by constants. $counter_1$ and $counter_2$ hold of exactly one integer and represent the contents of the two counters; state holds of exactly one state of the finite state controller and represents the state the controller is in.

The initial situation of the problem has (state s) where s is the start state and $(counter_1 \ c_1)$ and $(counter_2 \ c_2)$ where c_1 and c_2 are the values the two-counter machine is started with. There is an operator for each arc in the finite state controller. The operator associated with the arc (s_1, s_2) has as a precondition (state s_1) and as postconditions (state s_2) and $\sim$(state s_1). The operators associated with increment and decrement arcs also have increment and decrements of $counter_1$ and $counter_2$ as appropriate. The branches are implemented in the finite state machine with nodes that have two arcs coming out of them, one labeled $c_i > 0$ and one labeled $c_i = 0$ (for i in $\{1, 2\}$). These correspond to operators that have those same tests as preconditions and no postconditions other than setting state.

Now any plan that solves this problem is a trace of the computation that would be executed by the two-counter machine. The planner has to do at least as much work as the simulated machine did. □

ACKNOWLEDGMENT

My intellectual debt to the great lineage of AI planning researchers is enormous and obvious. Part of the research described here was done during the summer of 1985 while visiting the SRI AI Center and supported by the Center of the Study of Language and Information. The opportunity provided me by Mike Georgeff and Stan Rosenschein to work with the largest concentration of planning researchers in the world was invaluable.

This paper incorporates suggestions from many readers. They made me reformulate TWEAK over and over again. Phil Agre, Steve Bagley, John Batali, Alan Bawden, Mike Brady, Randy Davis, Tom Dean, Gary Drescher, Margaret Fleck, Walter Hamscher, Leslie Kaelbling, Amy Lansky, Scott Layson, Tomas Lozano-Perez, David McAllester, Kent Pitman, Charles Rich, Stan Rosenschein, Dirk Ruiz, Mark Shirley, Yoav Shoham, Reid Simmons, Tom Trobaugh, Dan Weld, David Wilkins, and several anonymous but erudite reviewers contributed much.

Ken Forbus convinced me that my understanding of nonlinear planning would make a Master's thesis. Ed Giniger taught me biology and kept me sane trading stories about idiotic lab politics. My office mate David McAllester was a source of much mathematical wizardry and put up with my randomness. Jim Vanese and Naomi Leavitt got me through hard times.

My supervisor Chuck Rich supported me through six thesis topic changes and believed in me when I didn't. His ability to debug me when wedged was vital.

REFERENCES

1. Agre, P.E., Routines. MIT AI Memo 828, Cambridge, MA, 1985.
2. Agre, P.E. and Chapman, D., AI and everyday life: The concrete situated view of human activity, in preparation.
3. Allen, J.F. and Koomen, J.A., Planning using a temporal world model, in: *Proceedings IJCAI-83*, Karlsruhe, F.R.G. (1983) 741–747.
4. Batali, J., Computational introspection, MIT AI Memo 701, Cambridge, MA, 1983.
5. Chapman, D., Naive problem solving and naive mathematics, MIT AI Working Paper 249, Cambridge, MA, 1983.
6. Chapman, D., Planning for conjunctive goals, MIT AI TR 802, Cambridge, MA, 1985.
7. Chapman, D., Cognitive cliches, MIT AI Working Paper 286, Cambridge, MA, 1986.
8. Chapman, D. and Agre, P.E., Abstract reasoning as emergent from concrete activity, in: *Proceedings 1986 Workshop on Reasoning about Actions and Plans*, Timberline, OR, 1987.
9. Corkill, D.D. Hierarchical planning in a distributed environment, in: *Proceedings IJCAI-79*, Tokyo, Japan (1979) 168–175.
10. Davis, R., Meta-rules: Reasoning about control, *Artificial Intelligence* **15** (1980) 179–222.
11. Daniel, L., Planning: Modifying non-linear plans, Edinburgh AI Working Paper 24, Edinburgh University, 1977 (Cited in [67]).
12. de Kleer, J., Doyle, J., Steele Jr., G.L. and Sussman, G.J., Explicit control of reasoning, *ACM SIGPLAN Notices* **12** (8)/*ACM SIGART Newslet.* **64** (combined special issue), Proceedings of the Symposium on Artificial Intelligence and Programming Languages (1977) 116–125; also MIT AI Memo No. 427, Cambridge, MA, 1977.
13. de Kleer, J., Doyle, J., Rich, C., Steele Jr., G.L. and Sussman, G. J., AMORD, a deductive procedure system, MIT AI Memo 435, Cambridge, MA, 1978.
14. Donald, B.R., On planning: What is to be done?, Unpublished area exam, MIT, Cambridge, MA, 1986.
15. Doyle, J., Truth maintenance systems for problem solving, MIT AI TR 419, Cambridge, MA, 1978.
16. Doyle, J., A model for deliberation, action, and introspection, MIT AI TR 581, Cambridge, MA, 1980.
17. Fahlman, S.E., A planning system for robot construction tasks, *Artificial Intelligence* **5** (1974) 1–49.
18. Fikes, R.E. and Nilsson, N.J., STRIPS: A new approach to the application of theorem proving to problem solving, *Artificial Intelligence* **2** (1971) 198–208.
19. Fikes, R.E., Hart, P.E. and Nilsson, N.J., Some new directions in robot problem solving, in: B. Meltzer and D. Michie, (Eds.), *Machine Intelligence 7* (Edinburgh University Press, Edinburgh, 1972) Ch. 23.
20. Georgeff, M., A theory of action for multiagent planning, in: *Proceedings AAAI-84*, Austin, TX, (1984) 121–125.
21. Garey, M.R. and Johnson, D.S., *Computers and Intractability: A Guide to the Theory of NP-Completeness* (Freeman, New York, 1979).
22. Hammond, K.J., Planning and goal interaction: The use of past solutions in present situations, in: *Proceedings AAAI-83*, Washington, DC (1983) 148–151.
23. Hayes, P.J., A representation for robot plans, in: *Proceedings IJCAI-75*, Tbilisi, U.S.S.R. (1975).
24. Hayes-Roth, B., Hayes-Roth, F., Rosenschein, S. and Cammarata, S., Modeling planning as an incremental, opportunistic process, in: *Proceedings IJCAI-79*, Tokyo, Japan (1979) 375–383.
25. Hewitt, C., Procedural embedding of knowledge in PLANNER, in: *Proceedings IJCAI-71*, London, U.K. (1971) 167–182.

26. Hewitt, C., Description and theoretical analysis (using schemata) of PLANNER: A language for proving theorems and manipulating models in a robot, MIT AI TR 258, Cambridge, MA, 1972.

27. Janlert, L.-E., Modeling change—the frame problem, in: Z. Pylyshyn (Ed.), *The Frame Problem and Other Problems of Holism in Artificial Intelligence* (Ablex, Norwood, NJ, 1985).

28. Kautz, H., Planning within first-order dynamic logic, in: *Proceedings Fourth Biennial Conference of the Canadian Society for Computational Studies of Intelligence (CSCSI)*, Saskatoon, Sask., 1982.

29. Kautz, H., A first order dynamic logic for planning, Tech. Rept. CSRG-144, Department of Computer Science, University of Toronto, Ont. 1982.

30. Kibler, D. and Morris, P., Don't be stupid, in: *Proceedings IJCAI-81*, Vancouver, BC (1981).

31. Lansky, A.L., Behavioral specification and planning for multiagent domains, Tech. Note 360, SRI International, Menlo Park, CA, 1985.

32. Lansky, A.L., A representation of parallel activity based on events, structure, and causality, in: *Proceedings 1986 Workshop on Reasoning about Actions and Plans*, Timberline, OR, 1987.

33. London, P., A dependency-based modeling mechanism for problem solving, Computer Science Tech. Rept. 589, University of Maryland, College Park, MD, 1977.

34. London, P., Dependency networks as a representation for modeling in general problem solvers, Computer Science Tech. Rept. 698, University of Maryland, College Park, MD, 1978.

35. McCarthy, J. and Hayes, P.J., Some philosophical problems from the standpoint of artificial intelligence, in: B. Meltzer and D. Michie (Eds.). *Machine Intelligence 4* (Edinburgh University Press, Edinburgh, 1970) 463–502.

36. McDermott, D., Generalizing problem reduction: A logical analysis, in: *Proceedings IJCAI-83*, Karlsruhe, F.R.G. (9183).

37. Miller, D., Firby, R.J. and Dean, T., Deadlines. travel time, and robot problem solving, in: *Proceedings IJCAI-85*, Los Angeles, CA (1985).

38. Milne, A.A., *Winnie The Pooh* (Dell Publishing Company, New York, 1984) First copyright, 1926.

39. Minsky, M.L., *Computation: Finite and Infinite Machines* (Prentice-Hall, Englewood Cliffs, NJ, 1967).

40. Newell, A., Shaw, J.C. and Simon, H.A., Report on a general problem-solving program, in: *Proceedings International Conference on Information Processing* (UNESCO, Paris, 1960) 256–264. Reprinted in: *Computers and Automation* (1959).

41. Pednault, E.P.D., Preliminary report on a theory of plan synthesis, SRI AI Center Tech. Note 358, Menlo Park, CA, 1985.

42. Raphael, B., The frame problem in problem-solving systems, in: *Proceedings Advanced Study Institute on Artificial Intelligence and Heuristic Programming*, Menaggio, Italy, 1970.

43. Rhys, J., A selection problem of shared fixed costs and network flows, *Manage. Sci.* **17** (1970).

44. Rich, C., Inspection methods in programming, MIT AI TR 604, Cambridge MA., 1981.

45. Rich, C., A formal representation for plans in the programmer's apprentice, in: *Proceedings IJCAI-81*, Vancouver, BC (1981) 1044–1052.

46. Rosenschein, J.S., Synchronization of multi-agent plans, in: *Proceedings AAAI-82*, Pittsburgh, PA (1982) 115–119.

47. Rosenschein, S.J., Plan synthesis: A logical perspective, in: *Proceedings IJCAI-81*, Vancouver, BC (1981) 331–337.

48. Rosenschein, S.J., Formal theories of knowledge in AI and robotics, SRI AI Center Tech. Note 362, Menlo Park, CA, 1985.

49. Sacerdoti, E.D., The nonlinear nature of plans, in: *Advance Papers IJCAI-75*, Tbilisi, U.S.S.R. (1975) 206–214.

50. Sacerdoti, E.D., *A Structure for Plans and Behavior* (American Elsevier, New York, 1977). also SRI AI Tech. Note 109, Menlo Park, CA, 1975.

51. Sacerdoti, E.D., Problem solving tactics, in: *Proceedings IJCAI-79*, Tokyo, Japan (1979).

52. Siklossy, L., and Roach, J., Collaborative problem-solving between optimistic and pessimistic problem solvers, in: J.L. Rosenfeld (Ed.), *IFIP-74* (North-Holland, Amsterdam, 1974) 814–817.

53. Stallman, R.M. and Sussman, G.J., Forward reasoning and dependency-directed backtracking in a system for computer-aided circuit analysis. MIT AI Memo 380, Cambridge, MA, 1979.

54. Stefik, M.J., Planning with constraints, Ph.D. Thesis, Stanford University, Stanford, CA, 1980; also Stanford Heuristic Programming Project Memo 80-2 and Stanford Computer Science Department Memo 80-784.

55. Stefik, M., Planning and metaplanning (MOLGEN: Part 2), *Artificial Intelligence* **16** (1981) 141–169.

56. Shrobe, H.E., Dependency directed reasoning for complex program understanding, MIT AI TR 503, Cambridge MA, 1979.

57. Shrobe, H.E., Dependency directed reasoning in the analysis of programs which modify complex data structures, in: *Proceedings IJCAI-79*, Tokyo, Japan (1979) 829–835.

58. Suchman, L.A., Plans and situated actions: The problem of human-machine communication, Xerox Palo Alto Research Center, Palo Alto, CA, 1985.

59. Sussman, G.J. and McDermott, D.V., From PLANNER to CONNIVER—A genetic approach, in: *Proceedings Fall Joint Computer Conference* (1972) 1171–1179.

60. Sussman, G.J., *A Computational Model of Skill Acquisition* (American Elsevier, New York, 1975); also MIT AI TR 297, Cambridge, MA, 1973.

61. Tate, A., INTERPLAN: A plan generation system which can deal with interactions between goals, Machine Intelligence Research Unit Memorandum MIP-R-109, University of Edinburgh, Edinburgh, 1974.

62. Tate, A., Interacting goals and their use, in: *Advance Papers IJCAI-75*, Tbilisi, U.S.S.R. (1975).

63. Tate, A., Using goal structure to direct search in a problem solver, Ph.D. Thesis, University of Edinburgh, Edinburgh, 1975.

64. Tate, A., Project planning using a hierarchic nonlinear planner, Department of Artificial Intelligence Research Rep. No. 25, University of Edinburgh, Edinburgh, 1976.

65. Tate, A., Generating project networks, in: *Proceedings IJCAI-77*, Cambridge, MA (1975).

66. Tate, A., Planning in expert systems, Invited Paper Alvey IKBS Expert Systems Theme—First Workshop at Cosener's house, Abingdon, Oxford, 1984; also D.A.I. Research Paper 221, University of Edinburgh. Edinburgh, 1984.

67. Tate, A., Planning and condition monitoring in a FMS, in: *Proceedings International Conference on Flexible Manufacturing Systems*, London, 1984.

68. Tate, A., Goal structure—Capturing the intent of plans, in: T. O'Shea, (Ed.), *ECAI-84: Advances in Artificial Intelligence* (North-Holland, Amsterdam, 1984).

69. Van Baalen, J., Planning and exception handling, AI Laboratory, MIT, Cambridge, MA, 1985.

70. Vere, S.A., Planning in time: Windows and durations for activities and goals, *IEEE Trans. Pattern Anal. Mach. Intell.* **5** (3) (1983) 246–267.

71. Vere, S.A., Splicing plans to achieve misordered goals, in: *Proceedings IJCAI-85*, Cambridge, MA (1975) 1016–1021.

72. Waldinger, R., Achieving several goals simultaneously, SRI Artificial Intelligence Center Tech. Note 107, Menlo Park, CA, 1975.

73. Warren, D.H.D, WARPLAN: A system for generating plans, Department of Computational Logic Memo No. 76, University of Edinburgh, Edinburgh, 1974.

74. Warren, D.H.D, Generating conditional plans and programs, in: *Proceedings AISB Summer Conference*, University of Edinburgh, Edinburgh (1976) 344–354.

75. Wilensky, R., Meta-planning: Representing and using knowledge about planning in problem solving and natural language understanding, *Cognitive Sci.* **5** (1981) 197–233.

76. Wilensky, R., *Planning and Understanding: A Computational Approach to Human Reasoning* (Addison-Wesley, Reading, MA, 1983).

77. Wilkins, D.E., Representation in a domain-independent planner, in: *Proceedings IJCAI-83*, Karlsruhe, F.R.G. (1983).

78. Wilkins, D.E., Domain-independent planning: Representation and plan generation, *Artificial Intelligence* **22**(3) (1984) 269–301; also SRI International Tech. Note No. 266R, Menlo Park, CA, 1983.

79. Wilkins, D.E., Recovering from execution errors in SIPE, *Comput. Intell.* **1** (1985) 33–45.

Received November 1985; revised version received October 1986

Planning Using a Temporal World Model

James F. Allen and Johannes A. Koomen
Computer Science Department, University of Rochester
Rochester, NY 14627 U.S.A.

Abstract

Current problem-solving systems are constrained in their applicability by inadequate world models. We suggest a world model based on a temporal logic. This approach allows the problem solver to gather constraints on the ordering of actions without having to commit to an ordering when a conflict is detected. As such, it generalizes the work on nonlinear planning by Sacerdoti and Tate. In addition, it allows more general descriptions of actions that may occur simultaneously or overlap, and appears promising in supporting reasoning about external events and actions caused by other agents.

I. Introduction

Current problem-solving systems are constrained in their applicability by inadequate world models. In particular, in most systems, the model of time is such that actions must be considered to be instantaneous, and only one action can occur at a time. This is the case in state-space based systems such as those of Fikes and Nilsson [1971], as well as in other systems based on the situation calculus [McCarthy, 1968]. In addition, these systems can only consider domains in which changes are made only as a result of the planner's actions, and the goals that can be described are confined to a single time instant. Thus, one couldn't express a goal such as "Put block_A on B, and then later move A to C."

Recent work has extended these models in a few directions. Sacerdoti [1977], for example, allows for partial ordering of actions in his plans, but retains a simple world model. As a result, actions are still viewed as instantaneous, for two actions either occur simultaneously or one must be strictly before the other. No possibility is allowed that actions might overlap in any way. McDermott [1978] allows constraints on the solution of a problem of the form: "Don't violate goal X during the solution." Vere [1981] allows events not caused by the planner provided that there is a reasonable estimate of the date at which the event will occur.

The preparation of this paper was supported in part by the Defense Advanced Research Projects Agency under Grant N00014-82-K-0193, and in part by the National Science Foundation under Grants IST-8210564 and MCS-8209971. Many thanks to Rich Pelavin and Henry Kautz for comments on the initial drafts.

We propose a formalism that incorporates these extensions and relaxes most of the other restrictions discussed above. The world model consists of all the planner's knowledge of the past, present, and future, expressed in a temporal logic. In simulating the effects of an action, the state of the world is not updated temporally as in previous systems. Instead, the planner's knowledge, primarily the predictions about the future, are updated. To draw a loose analogy to state-space based planners, the states in this model are states of the planner's knowledge and are independent of the temporal aspects of the world.

Given this approach, a *plan* is a collection of assertions viewed as an abstract partial simulation of the future, including actions the planner intends to take as well as other predicted actions, events, and states. In a coherent plan, most--but not necessarily all--of these events and states are causally related. A *goal* is a partial description of the world desired. This description is not confined to a specific instant of time. It might consist of a sequence of states (e.g., get block A on B, then later get A on C), restrictions (e.g., never let ON(B,C) be true), or any other set of facts expressible in the temporal logic.

We will not suggest any new methods for problem solving here. Our current concern is simply to investigate the consequences of the more general world model. In fact, we consider it a major asset of this representation that it can be used with existing problem-solving methods (e.g., means-end analysis, decomposition, etc.). We will discuss some issues in this area later in the paper.

We will use a STRIPs-like action formalism (as in [Nilsson, 1980]), except that the preconditions and effects will be temporally qualified. The temporal representation used is that described in [Allen, 1981]. The basic unit is that of a temporal interval, and intervals can be related by any of seven primitive relations and their inverses. These are summarized in Figure 1.

Usually, the precise relationship between two intervals is not known. In such cases, we can express a disjunction of the primitive relations. For example, the fact that intervals A and B are disjoint can be expressed by asserting that A is *before*, *meets*, *is met by*, or *is after* B. This is generally summarized with the notation:

A (< m mi >) B.

Used by permission of the International Joint Conferences on Artificial Intelligence, Inc.

Relation	Symbol	Symbol for Inverse	Pictorial Example
X *before* Y	<	>	XXX YYY
X *equal* Y	=	=	XXX YYY
X *meets* Y	m	mi	XXXYYY
X *overlaps* Y	o	oi	XXX YYY
X *during* Y	d	di	XXX YYYYYY
X *starts* Y	s	si	XXX YYYYY
X *finishes* Y	f	fi	XXX YYYYY

Figure 1: The Thirteen Possible Relationships

Another complex relationship that will be useful later is the notion that one interval A wholly contains another interval B. We shall assert A *contains* B as an abbreviation for

A (di si fi) B.

A computationally effective inference procedure has been developed based on constraint propagation. There is not space to discuss it here, but see [Allen, 1981]. The inferences made by this system are simply those derivable from the transitivity behavior of the relations. A typical example of such an inference rule is:

If A *during* B and B *meets* C
then A is *before* C.

All of the examples following have been implemented and run in a prototype planning system.

II. A Simple Example

This problem consists simply of stacking three blocks into a tower. There is one type of action required: that of stacking two blocks. Nilsson [1980] formalizes STACK as follows:

STACK(x,y)
    Preconditions: CLEAR(x), CLEAR(y)
    Effects: ON(x,y)
    DeleteList: CLEAR(y)

The same action in our formalism is expressed as an axiom:

If STACK(x,y) occurs over time Sxy, then
    CLEAR(y) holds over time Cy,
        such that Sxy *finishes* Cy; and
    ON(x,y) holds over time Oxy,
        such that Sxy *meets* Oxy; and
    CLEAR(x) holds over time Cx,
        such that Sxy *during* Cx.

Note that the deletion information is implicit in the temporal annotation. The precondition CLEAR(y), for instance, is constrained to terminate at the end of the stacking action. This is not the only form of precondition expressible in our system. We might have preconditions that overlap the action, continue after the action, or even hold during a part of the action.

When the temporal intervals associated with an instance of an action are added to the temporal reasoner, other relationships are automatically derived. For instance, from the fact that Sxy *finishes* Cy and Sxy *meets* Oxy, the relation Cy *meets* Oxy will be inferred. In the examples below, we shall only mention such inferential behavior if it is crucial to the example.

The problem is to take three clear blocks, A, B, and C, on a table and construct a tower with A on B and B on C. The initial description of the problem consists simply of the initial state and the goal state. Introducing interval I for the time of the initial state, and G for the goal state, we can describe the situation as follows:

    I *before* G.
    CLEAR(A) holds over time Ca1, such that
        Ca1 *contains* I.
    CLEAR(B) holds over time Cb1, such that
        Cb1 *contains* I.
    CLEAR(C) holds over time Cc1, such that
        Cc1 *contains* I.
    ON(A,B) holds over time Oab, such that
        Oab *contains* G.
    ON(B,C) holds over time Obc, such that
        Obc *contains* G.

Planning is initiated on those assertions that have no causal explanation. For the purposes of this paper, this means that the assertion is not the effect of an action nor true at the initial time I. Thus we have two subgoals to achieve: ON(A,B) and ON(B,C). We use Sacerdoti's strategy for conjunctive subgoals [1977] and attempt to achieve each goal independently. The stack action is applicable for achieving goals of form ON(x,y). Thus we will introduce two stacking actions.

The action STACK(A,B) is added with its effect ON(A,B) set to hold over Oab. This results in the following new facts being added (facts irrelevant for the example are omitted):

    STACK(A,B) occurs over time Sab, such that
        Sab (> mi) I
    CLEAR(B) holds over Cb2, such that
        Sab *finishes* Cb2
    ON(A,B) holds over Oab, such that
        Sab *meets* Oab
    CLEAR(A) holds over Ca2, where
        Sab *during* Ca2.

Introducing the action STACK(B,C) over time Sbc for the goal ON(B,C) yields a similar set of constraints, namely

Sbc (> mi) I
Sbc *finishes* Cc2
Sbc *meets* Oab
Sbc *during* Cb3.

The problem solver, besides adding these action descriptions, also adds further constraints based on the structure of the domain. There are two constraints relevant here. The first is a general constraint imposed by the temporal representation, and the second is specific to the blocks world.

When we assert that a proposition P *holds over* a time interval T, T is assumed to be the largest possible interval over which the proposition holds. This means that two intervals associated with the same proposition cannot meet or overlap, otherwise they would be identical. This results in our first general constraint:

The Proposition Constraint: Two intervals associated with the same proposition are equal, or one is strictly before the other; in other words, if P holds over Tp1 and Tp2, then Tp1 (< > =) Tp2.

In our present example, there are three intervals associated with the proposition CLEAR(B). Using the above principle, we may add the facts:

Cb1 (< > =) Cb2
Cb2 (< > =) Cb3
Cb1 (< > =) Cb3

The temporal reasoner combines these constraints with those already derived from the action definitions and may derive stronger constraints. In particular, it derives:

(*) Cb1 (< =) Cb2

using the facts that Cb1 *contains* I and Sab (> mi) I to get Sab (d f > mi oi) Cb1, and then combining this with Sab *finishes* Cb2 to derive that Cb1 cannot be *after* or *met-by* Cb2. The details of how this is accomplished are not important here. Suffice it to say that (*) is simply a logical consequence of the facts added so far.

The other constraint arises from the observation that in the blocks domain a block cannot simultaneously be CLEAR and have another block on it. Thus we have:

Domain Constraint 1: If CLEAR(x) holds over Cx, and ON(y,x) holds over Oyx, then Cx and Oyx cannot overlap in any manner. In particular,

Cx (m mi > <) Oyx.

Using this rule, the problem solver adds a set of constraints between the times for all CLEAR and ON propositions. The one relevant for this example arises from the interaction of CLEAR(B) and ON(A,B):

Cb3 (m mi > <) Oab

which given the existing constraints becomes

(**) Cb3 (< m) Oab.

This was derived since ON(A,B) (over Oab) must hold in the goal state, whereas CLEAR(B) (over Cb3) must hold before the goal state.

Once (**) is derived, an ordering is imposed between the times of the two stacking actions. In particular, given (**) and the fact that Cb2 *meets* Oab, it is inferred that

Cb3 (< =) Cb2.

Since we also have from the action definitions that

Sbc *during* Cb3
Sab *finishes* Cb2

we have that Sbc must complete before Sab completes, i.e., Sbc (< o m s d) Sab. If we wish to add a constraint that only one stacking action can be done at a time, i.e., Sbc (< > m mi) Sab, we then have STACK(B,C) occurring before STACK(A,B), i.e., Sbc (< m) Sab.

In the NOAH system, such orderings between actions was accomplished using a special-purpose program called the *resolve conflicts* critic. This procedure, however, did not guarantee to make the correct ordering decision if the actions were simply required to be disjoint. Tate [1977] extended this approach by introducing backtracking to cover such cases. In both systems, a conflict had to be resolved by picking a specific ordering. Our system allows one to defer that choice as long as possible as it can simply note that the actions must be disjoint. Thus the same advantages for delaying the binding of variables by posting constraints in Stefik [1981] are achieved in the area of action ordering. In addition, it is satisfying to see this behavior arising simply as a logical consequence of the formalism without resorting to special-purpose techniques.

III. Planning Overlapping Actions

We can now outline the problem-solving system in more detail and then present an example that forces us to reason about overlapping actions. The planner uses hierarchical action descriptions mirroring the approach of Sacerdoti [1977]. In the example below, we shall see that when the two overlapping actions are decomposed, their subactions must interleave to produce a solution.

As mentioned in the introduction, we view planning as reasoning about a simulation of the world extending into the future. Goals are simply facts in the simulation that are required to hold but have no causal explanation. The problem solver continually repeats the process of finding causal gaps and eliminating them with new proposed actions. Some causal gaps, however, can be eliminated by making additional assumptions about the simulated world. For instance, assume that proposition P holds over times Tp1 and Tp2 such that Tp1 (< =) Tp2. Now, if P holding over Tp1 has a causal explanation but

P holding over Tp2 does not, we appear to have a causal gap. But we can eliminate this gap if we assume that in fact Tp1 = Tp2. If we can eliminate all causal gaps by collapsing such intervals, we have a completed plan at the current level of abstraction.

Given the above discussion, we can summarize our problem solver as follows:

Repeat the following two steps until done:

1) Examine the simulation description for causal gaps. If there are none, or they all can be eliminated by collapsing intervals, we are done. Otherwise, the facts without causal explanation become the new set of subgoals.

2) Solve each subgoal independently by introducing a new action. Add any constraints derived from the proposition constraint and the domain constraints.

This algorithm will produce a complete plan at one level of abstraction. The plan can then be refined by adding the decomposition of each action to the simulation and repeating the process described above.

The following example uses a blocks world in which the table is so small that it can only support one block. The robot has multiple arms and can hold multiple blocks at a time. The problem is to transform a stack with B on A and A on C into a stack with A on B and B on C.

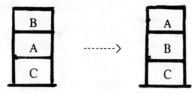

The main action supplied consists of moving a block x to another block t from a block f. This is defined as follows:

If MOVE(x,t,f) occurs over Mxtf, then
"Preconditions"
    CLEAR(x) holds over Cx1, such that Cx1 *meets* Mxtf,
    ON(x,f) holds over Oxf, such that Oxf *overlaps* Mxtf,
    CLEAR(t) holds over Ct, such that Ct (o s d) Mxtf,
"Effects"
    CLEAR(f) holds over Cf, such that Mxtf (o fi di) Cf,
    CLEAR(x) holds over Cx2, such that Mxtf *meets* Cx2,
    ON(x,t) holds over Oxt, such that Mxtf *overlaps* Oxt,

"Decomposition"
    PICKUP(x,f) occurs over PUxf, such that PUxf *starts* Mxtf,
    HOLDING(x) holds over Hx, such that PUxf *meets* Hx,
    PUTDOWN(x,t) occurs over PDxt, such that Hx *meets* PDxt and PDxt *finishes* Mxtf.

There are a few important things to note about this definition. CLEAR(x) must hold prior to the move action and after the move action, but does not hold while the action is occurring. The CLEAR(t) precondition specifies that t must be clear sometime during the move action, but need not necessarily hold at the start of the MOVE. In other words, this allows the possibility that block t will become clear as a result of some other event while the MOVE is in progress. This condition could be ignored at this level of abstraction, but including it eliminates the possibility of planning a move over a time where the block could not possibly be cleared. The generality of our representation allows us to specify such constraints without having to add the full detail of the decomposition, or alternatively, waiting until the decomposition is done to find the problem. Finally, the effect ON(x,t) begins to hold prior to the completion of the move. At that time, the blocks are stacked but the robot is still grasping the top block.

The actions of picking up a block and putting down a block are defined as follows:

If PICKUP(x,y) occurs over PUxy, then
    CLEAR(x) holds over Cx, such that Cx *meets* PUxy,
    ON(x,y) holds over Oxy, such that PUxy *finishes* Oxy,
    CLEAR(y) holds over Cy, such' that PUxy *meets* Cy,
    HOLDING(x) holds over Hx, such that PUxy *meets* Hx.

If PUTDOWN(x,y) occurs over PDxy, then
    HOLDING(x) holds over Hx, such that Hx *meets* PDxy,
    CLEAR(y) holds over Cy, such that Cy *meets* PDxy,
    ON(x,y) holds over Oxy, such that PDxy *starts* Oxy.

In addition to domain constraint 1 mentioned in the previous example, the following domain constraints are also valid in this blocks world:

A block cannot be held and be clear at the same time:

Domain Constraint 2: For any x, HOLDING(x) is disjoint from CLEAR(x), i.e., Hx (< > m mi) Cx;

A block cannot be held and have another block on it at the same time:

Domain Constraint 3: For any x,y, HOLDING(x) is disjoint from ON(y,x);

A block can only be on one block at a time:

Domain Constraint 4: For any x,y,z, ON(x,y) is disjoint from ON(x,z), assuming that y is not equal to z;

A block can only have one block on it at a time:

Domain Constraint 5: For any x,y,z, ON(x,y) is disjoint from ON(z,y), assuming that x is not equal to z.

We can now trace the planning procedure. The initial state is described by the facts ON(B,A), ON(A,C) and CLEAR(B) holding over the intervals Obc, Oac, and Cbl, respectively. Each of these intervals contains the initial time I. The final state is described by the fact ON(A,B) and ON(B,C) holding over Oab and Obc, both of which contain G.

In step 1 of the planning algorithm, two causal gaps are discovered, corresponding to the two facts ON(A,B) and ON(B,C). Solving each independently in step 2, two MOVE actions are introduced with their preconditions and effects, namely MOVE(A,B,z) over Mabz and MOVE(B,C,y) over Mbcy. The z and y are uninstantiated parameters in the actions to be considered as existentially quantified variables. Once all the domain constraints are added, the temporal reasoner infers that MOVE(B,C,y) must complete before MOVE(A,B,z) completes, i.e., Mbcy (< d m o s) Mabz. This is derived from the fact that ON(A,B), an effect of MOVE(A,B,z), conflicts with CLEAR(B), an effect of MOVE(B,C,y). Since ON(A,B) holds over the final time G, CLEAR(B) must hold before that.

Step 1 of the planning algorithm is repeated on this new world description. It is noticed that by collapsing Oba with Oby (thereby binding y to block A), and Oac with Oaz (binding z to block C), a plan is produced that is fully causally connected. When the new constraints that Oba *equals* Oby and Oac *equals* Oaz are added, the temporal reasoner concludes that MOVE(B,C,A) *overlaps* MOVE(A,B,C), i.e., Mbcy *overlaps* Mabz. Thus we can summarize the plan at this level of detail as shown in Figure 2, where time increases from left to right.

This plan can be further elaborated by expanding the overlapping MOVE actions using their decompositions and the definitions of the subactions PICKUP and PUT-DOWN. Once this is done, and the domain constraints have been asserted, the subactions will be constrained to be in the interleaved order shown in Figure 3.

```
|_ON(B,A)_|
|                    |
|        |__MOVE(B,C,A)_____|        |_CLEAR(B)_|
|                       |                         |        |_ON(A,B)_|
|             |_CLEAR(A)__|__MOVE(A,B,C)__|
```

Figure 2.

Most planners that exploit decomposition as a search technique have depended on the assumption that the actions to be decomposed are disjoint, and therefore their decompositions are independent of each other. Using the temporal world model, this restriction can be relaxed, as the above example demonstrates. We can exploit the efficiency of planning by decomposition without restricting the range of problems that can be solved with the technique.

IV. Current Areas of Research

A. Controlling Temporal Reasoning

The constraint propagation algorithm used in our temporal reasoning system is based on the transitivity of temporal relations. In any realistic application of this reaoning system, however, there will usually be a great many intervals with temporal relations defined between them, and the addition of a single assertion may have extensive effects throughout. Running the second example on our TIMELOGIC system, with 23 intervals defined, 37 task-specific and 52 domain constraints were explicitly asserted. These caused 856 additional constraints to be propagated, only a few of which are "interesting." Although the algorithm only runs while constraints are being further refined and hence activity tends to die down after a while, each newly introduced relation tends to be propagated through the entire system. Once a new interval X is asserted to lie after Y, then it follows immediately that, for every interval Z in the universe such that Y lies after Z, X also lies after Z.

It is clearly desirable to restrict this essentially exponential growth by somehow limiting the scope of constraint propagation. One way we are currently exploring is the use of a hierarchy of reference intervals [Allen, 1981]. We can group various intervals together by asserting their relations to a given reference interval. Then any constraint propagation occurs strictly within the group and its reference interval. Relations between intervals across groups can be deduced from the relation between their respective reference intervals.

```
|_____MOVE(B,C,A)_____|
|                                                     |
|_PICKUP(B,A)_|_____HOLDING(B)_____|_PUTON(B,C)_|
|             |                        |             |
|_clr A_|              |_clr C_|            |_clr B_|
|             |                        |             |
|_PICKUP(A,C)_|_____HOLDING(A)_____|_PUTON(A,B)_|
|                                                     |
|_____MOVE(A,B,C)_____|
```

A number of difficulties have arisen in the use of reference hierarchies, the principal one being the handling of explicitly asserted constraints between intervals with differing reference intervals. Simply asserting the relation does not result in any constraint propagation within either group because the original pair is not from a single group. For instance, in our second example, the interval for the MOVE operation could well serve as a reference interval for the PICKUP, HOLDING, and PUTON intervals. Clearly, any relation between PICKUP and HOLDING is not of interest outside this group. However, the domain constraints often introduce relations across reference groups. We are currently investigating various automatic ways of restructuring the reference hierarchy. Obviously, simply merging two reference groups when their members are found to interact quickly leads to a total flattening of the hierarchy in even as small a problem as our second example.

B. Temporal Durations

One ability that becomes feasible in this new framework concerns reasoning about temporal durations. Since actions take time in this model, we can consider how long they take and use this knowledge in plan construction. This is an important necessary step in designing planners that operate in more realistic domains. The temporal reasoner already can reason about durations. Relative information can be asserted (e.g., interval A takes two to three times as long as interval B), as well as ranges on precise scales (e.g., interval C takes 5 to 10 minutes). This system uses constraint propagation to derive the effects of new duration knowledge. Duration can also affect interval relationships. For example, if the system derives the fact that interval A takes less time than interval B, it adds the constraint that A cannot *contain* B. Similarly, the interval reasoner may constrain the duration reasoner.

Using this work, we hope to build a problem solver in a fairly complex domain, such as cooking or scheduling.

C. A General Model of Plan Reasoning

Because we only considered simple problems above, many details of this planning algorithm could be ignored. These need to be addressed to realize the full benefit of the approach. We shall outline two problems that are currently under consideration.

Problems arise when a complete causal explanation cannot be constructed simply by "collapsing" intervals together. In such cases, there may be alternate sets of assumptions, each producing a different set of causal gaps. In these cases, an arbitrary decision must be made by the planner. Once this decision is made, the assumptions motivating it can be removed restoring the world description to its most general case. We currently are examining different strategies for implementing this technique.

The other major problem area involves reasoning about future (or past) events (including actions by other agents). Currently, the existing formalism can express and reason about arbitrary future events, but cannot reason about interfering with them. Thus we can plan to interact with future events, but cannot change them. Reasoning about changing future events (such as preventing an event) requires an ability to change our predictions about the future.

Our approach to this problem is to develop a crude but workable model of hypothetical reasoning, and then use this general mechanism to reason about hypothetical futures. We prefer this approach over that of McDermott [1982], who introduces branching futures into his temporal logic. This is because a hypothetical reasoning ability is required for other purposes besides planning, and once such an ability is present, our simpler temporal model is sufficient. In addition, this framework will allow us to reason about other agents' plans from observing their actions (e.g., [Allen and Perrault, 1980]). Since time only branches into the future in McDermott's logic, it cannot support such reasoning about the past.

V. Summary

We have specified a world model for problem solving using an interval-based temporal logic. The formalism is notable for the following reasons:

-- It allows more general action descriptions than have previously been allowed. In particular, actions may take time, and their descriptions are not limited to simple precondition and effect descriptions and decomposition.

-- It allows more general goal descriptions, and more complicated worlds in which to achieve the goals. In particular, goals are not restricted to a single time, and future events may occur which will affect the planner's behavior.

-- The action ordering is more general than the nonlinear planners of Sacerdoti and Tate. In particular, actions may overlap, and when conflicts are detected, this method does not have to resort to arbitrary orderings as in Sacerdoti, or backtracking as in Tate, as required in certain situations.

REFERENCES

Allen, J.F., "An interval-based representation of temporal knowledge," *Proc.*, 7th IJCAI, Vancouver, B.C., August 1981.

Allen, J.F. and C.R. Perrault, "Analyzing intention in utterances," *Artificial Intelligence 15*, 143-178, 1980.

Fikes, R.E. and N.J. Nilsson, "STRIPS: A new approach to the application of theorem proving to problem solving," *Artificial Intelligence 2*, 189-205, 1971.

McCarthy, J., "Programs with common sense," in M. Minsky (ed). *Semantic Information Processing.* Cambridge, MA: The MIT Press, 1968.

McDermott, D., "Planning and acting," *Cognitive Science 2-2*, 1978.

McDermott, D., "A temporal logic for reasoning about processes and plans," *Cognitive Science 6*, 101-155, 1982.

Nilsson, N.J. *Principles of Artificial Intelligence.* Tioga Press, 1980.

Sacerdoti, E.D. *A Structure for Plans and Behavior.* New York: Elsevier North-Holland, Inc., 1977.

Stefik, M., "Planning with constraints (MOLGEN: Part 1)," *Artificial Intelligence 16*, 2, May 1981.

Tate, A., "Generating project networks," *Proc.*, 5th IJCAI, August 1977.

Vere, S., "Planning in time: Windows and durations for activities and goals," Jet Propulsion Laboratory, California Institute of Technology, November 1981.

Planning as Search: A Quantitative Approach

Richard E. Korf

*Computer Science Department, University of California,
Los Angeles, CA 90024, U.S.A.*

Recommended by Mark J. Stefik and David Wilkins

ABSTRACT

*We present the thesis that planning can be viewed as problem-solving search using subgoals,
macro-operators, and abstraction as knowledge sources. Our goal is to quantify problem-solving
performance using these sources of knowledge. New results include the identification of subgoal
distance as a fundamental measure of problem difficulty, a multiplicative time-space tradeoff for
macro-operators, and an analysis of abstraction which concludes that abstraction hierarchies can
reduce exponential problems to linear complexity.*

1. Introduction

As various subfields of artificial intelligence have matured, the state of
knowledge in those fields has been refined from qualitative statements to
quantitative results. For example, in the field of heuristic search, qualitative
wisdom of the form, "the more accurate a heuristic evaluation function is, the
more efficient search with that function becomes," has been replaced with
theorems such as, "if a heuristic function exhibits constant absolute error, then
best-first search using that function runs in linear time" [1]. There is now a
significant body of quantitative results concerning the performance of heuristic
search algorithms. The field of planning, however, remains at the stage of
qualitative wisdom, such as, "problem solving using a hierarchy of abstraction
spaces greatly improves search efficiency." This paper presents the first steps
toward a quantitative theory of planning. For example, one of the results is
that an abstraction hierarchy can reduce the time complexity of problem
solving from exponential to linear.

Ideally, the term planning applies to problem solving in a real-world
environment where the agent may not have complete information about the
world or cannot completely predict the effects of its actions. In that case, the
agent goes through several iterations of planning a solution, executing the plan,
and then replanning based on the perceived result of the solution.

Most of the literature on planning, however, deals with problem solving with
perfect information and prediction. What distinguishes planning from heuristic
search is that instead of using knowledge sources such as heuristic evaluation
functions, planning tends to make use of knowledge such as subgoals, macro-
operators, and abstraction spaces.

In this paper we view planning as search in the presence of subgoals,
macro-operators, and abstraction. We examine each of these knowledge
sources in turn, and present them in a unified framework. In each case, the
knowledge will be defined in terms of a *problem space*, and we will explain how
and to what extent the knowledge reduces search in that space.

The problem space model was formulated by Newell and Simon [7]. A
problem space consists of a set of *states*, and a set of *operators* that are
mappings from states to states. An operator is a partial mapping since it may
have preconditions which determine what states it can be applied to. A
problem, or *problem instance*, is composed of a problem space together with an
initial state and a set of *goal states*. The task is to find a *solution*, that is, a
sequence of operators that maps the initial state to one of the goal states. The
issues that we will be concerned with are the amount of time and space that are
required to find a solution, and the cost of the solution itself.

For example, consider the well-known Eight Puzzle (see Fig. 1). It consists
of a three by three square frame which holds eight movable square tiles, with
one space left over (the blank). The states of the Eight Puzzle are the different
possible permutations of the tiles in the frame. The allowable operators are to
move a tile which is horizontally or vertically adjacent to the blank into the
blank position. The object of the puzzle is to find a sequence of legal moves
that will map an initial arrangement of the tiles into the desired goal configuration. The cost of a solution to this problem is the number of moves required.

2. Brute-Force Search

Before examining how various knowledge sources reduce search effort, for
comparison we first consider the case where no knowledge is available, or
brute-force search. The complexity of brute-force search depends on two

FIG. 1. The Eight Puzzle.

Artificial Intelligence **33** (1987) 65–88

0004-3702/87/$3.50 © 1987, Elsevier Science Publishers B.V. (North-Holland)

exponential, the size of problems that it can solve effectively is severely limited. For example, on modern computers, brute-force techniques are sufficient to find optimal solutions to the Eight Puzzle, and heuristic search can find optimal solutions to its larger 4×4 relative, the Fifteen Puzzle, but finding optimal solutions to typical instances of the 5×5 Twenty-Four Puzzle is beyond the range of the best known heuristic techniques. Thus, more powerful sources of knowledge are needed, at the expense of sacrificing optimal solutions.

4. Subgoals

It is well known that the use of appropriate subgoals can greatly reduce the amount of search necessary to solve a problem. The reason is that decomposing an exponential problem into two or more simpler problems tends to divide the exponent, and hence drastically reduces the total problem-solving effort [9]. In this section we make this notion precise and quantitative. We first consider subgoals in general and then examine three special cases: independent subgoals, serializable subgoals, and non-serializable subgoals.

The simplest case of the use of a subgoal involves an initial state i, a single goal state g, and a single intermediate state s. Without additional knowledge, the best problem-solving algorithm is a brute-force search from i to s, followed by a brute-force search from s to g. If we define $d(x, y)$ to be the *distance* from state x to state y, or the length of the shortest sequence of operators that maps x to y, then the time complexity of our subgoal search is $O(b^{d(i,s)} + b^{d(s,g)})$ which is $O(b^{\max(d(i,s),d(s,g))})$. The length of the resulting solution is $d(i, s) + d(s, g)$. Thus, the subgoal will reduce search whenever $\max(d(i, s), d(s, g))$ is less than $d(i, g)$. The penalty for this search reduction, however, is that the optimal solution length $d(i, s) + d(s, g)$ will in general be longer than the optimal solution length $d(i, g)$. Note that the optimal subgoal lies exactly halfway along an optimal solution path from i to g, since this cuts the exponent of b in half yet still results in an optimal solution.

4.1. Subgoal distance

In general, a subgoal is not a single state but rather a property that is true of a number of states. For example. if we establish a subgoal for the Eight Puzzle of correctly positioning a particular tile, this subgoal is satisfied by any state in which that tile is in its goal position, regardless of the positions of the remaining tiles. Therefore. we formally define a subgoal to be a set of states. with the interpretation that a state is an element of a subgoal set if and only if it has the properties that satisfy the subgoal.

Correspondingly, we define the *subgoal distance* between subgoals S and T as

$$D(S, T) = \max_{s \in S} \min_{t \in T} d(s, t).$$

parameters of the problem, the branching factor and the depth. The *branching factor* (b) of a problem is the average number of new states that can be generated from a given state by the application of a single operator, and the *depth* (d) of a problem instance is the length of the shortest solution path from the initial state to a goal state.

The standard brute-force search algorithms are breadth-first and depth-first search. Breadth-first search uses $O(b^d)$ time to find an optimal solution of length d, but unfortunately also uses $O(b^d)$ space since all the states at a given level are stored before the next level is generated. Depth-first search uses only linear space since it stores just the current search path, but unfortunately requires an arbitrary depth cutoff in order to terminate. If that cutoff is less than the solution depth d, which is rarely known in advance, no solution is found, and if the cutoff is greater than d, then a great deal of extra computation will be performed and the first solution found may not be an optimal one.

These drawbacks are remedied by an algorithm called depth-first iterative-deepening (DFID). DFID performs a series of depth-first searches, starting with a depth cutoff of one, and incrementing the depth cutoff by one for each iteration until a solution is found. This algorithm finds a solution of length d in $O(b^d)$ time and $O(d)$ space. In fact, depth-first iterative-deepening is asymptotically optimal in terms of time and space, over all brute-force tree search algorithms that are guaranteed to find optimal solutions [2].

3. Heuristic Search

The source of knowledge that has been most extensively studied in the context of search problems is the heuristic evaluation function. In the case of single-agent problems, a heuristic evaluation function is an efficiently computable function that estimates the cost of reaching a goal from a given state. For example, a common heuristic function for the Eight Puzzle is Manhattan Distance: it is computed by determining for each tile the number of grid units between its current position and its goal position, and summing these values over all tiles. There are a number of search algorithms that utilize heuristic evaluation functions to reduce search, including hill-climbing, best-first search, A*, and iterative-deepening-A* (IDA*) [2, 10].

If the heuristic function never overestimates the actual cost of reaching the goal, a constraint satisfied by Manhattan Distance for the Eight Puzzle, then algorithms such as A* and IDA* will find an optimal path to the goal. In general, the effect of the heuristic in these algorithms is to reduce the time complexity of the search from $O(b^d)$ to $O(c^d)$, where c is the heuristic branching factor, which is less than the brute-force branching factor. This results in a significant savings and allows somewhat larger problems to be solved. On the other hand, since the complexity of heuristic search is still

The rationale for this definition is that min captures the idea that we consider a subgoal achieved when we reach the first state which satisfies it, and max allows us to do a worst-case analysis over all possible states in the first subgoal. Note that in general, $D(S, T)$ is not equal to $D(T, S)$, due to the asymmetry of the definition.

The usual relationship between successive subgoals in a problem-solving strategy is one of set inclusion. This is because latter subgoals in the sequence typically include the previous subgoals as well. For example, when we solve the Eight Puzzle one tile at a time, the first subgoal is the set of all states where the first tile is correctly positioned, the second subgoal contains all states in which the first two tiles are correct, etc.

Given a sequence of subgoals $S_0, S_1, \ldots, S_n$ where S_0 contains just the initial state and S_n is the goal set, the amount of time to find a solution in the worst case is

$$b^{D(S_0, S_1)} + b^{D(S_1, S_2)} + \cdots + b^{D(S_{n-1}, S_n)},$$

which is $O(b^{D_{\max}})$ where

$$D_{\max} \equiv \max_{0 \leq i \leq n-1} D(S_i, S_{i+1}),$$

or the maximum subgoal distance. Thus, the complexity of solving a problem using subgoals depends on the maximum gap between two successive subgoals.

This is analogous to the plight of a hiker trying to cross a stream on stepping stones. He doesn't care about the length of the stream (the size of the problem space), nor is he overly concerned with the width of the stream (the optimal solution length), nor the length of the actual path he must travel (the actual solution length). The parameter, however, that determines the difficulty of crossing the stream is the length of the largest jump between two successive stepping stones (the maximum subgoal distance).

The worst-case solution length using subgoals is the sum of the lengths of each segment of the solution, or

$$\sum_{i=0}^{n-1} D(S_i, S_{i+1}).$$

The *diameter* of a problem is the maximum distance between any two connected states in the problem space. This is equal to the worst-case optimal solution length, for an arbitrary pair of initial and goal states. Since the problem diameter is an obvious upper bound on all subgoal distances, if we have n subgoals then the worst-case solution length using subgoals is no more than n times the problem diameter.

Note that computing or even estimating subgoal distances is a hard problem. In principle, subgoal distances can be computed exactly by the formula which

defines them, but in practice the amount of computation which is required may be prohibitive. In general, efficiently providing even reliable estimates of subgoal distances is often very difficult. Note that heuristic evaluation functions, which estimate distance to a set of goal states, are the result of attempts to solve exactly this problem.

4.2. Subgoal distance as a predictor of solution lengths

The sum of the subgoal distances may be useful as a predictor of the number of moves that humans use to solve problems. In a series of experiments on human problem solving using the Eight Puzzle, Ericsson [11] found that the average number of moves required by ten human subjects to solve eight different problem instances was 38. If we choose the subgoals of positioning one tile at a time in numerical order, then the sum of the resulting subgoal distances (40 moves) is within five percent of the average human solution lengths in his experiments. While 80 data points from a single problem are insufficient to validate subgoal distance as a predictor of human problem-solving difficulty, the data is at least consistent with such a notion.

Given this general discussion of subgoals as a background, we now examine three special cases: independent subgoals, serializable subgoals, and non-serializable subgoals.

4.3. Independent subgoals

Consider the following somewhat contrived example: you are given two different physical copies of the Eight Puzzle with different initial configurations, and are asked to transform each of them to a different goal state. Ignoring for a moment the obvious decomposition of this problem into subgoals, if the branching factor of each problem is b, the branching factor of the combined problem is $2b$ since an operator from either puzzle can be applied at any point. Similarly, if d_1 and d_2 are the respective distances of each initial state from its corresponding goal state, the depth of the combined problem is $d_1 + d_2$ since this many operators must be applied to achieve the combined goal state. Thus, if we were to solve the combined problem directly without decomposing it into subgoals, its complexity would be $O((2b)^{d_1 \cdot d_2})$.

Obviously, a much better strategy for this problem would be to first solve one of the puzzles, ignoring the other, and then solve the remaining puzzle without disturbing the first. While the same number of moves $(d_1 + d_2)$ must be made in this case, the branching factor is reduced from $2b$ to b since we only consider operators on one puzzle at any given time. This reduces the time complexity from $O((2b)^{d_1 + d_2})$ to $O(b^{d_1} + b^{d_2})$ which is $O(b^{\max(d_1, d_2)})$. Note that this subgoal decomposition results in an optimal solution since the length of the optimal solution for the compound problem is the sum of the optimal solution lengths for the subproblems.

The above subgoals are an example of *independent subgoals*. A collection of subgoals are independent if each operator only changes the distance to a single subgoal. In other words, we can partition the complete operator set into subsets such that the operators in a given subset are only relevant to a single subgoal.

One of the important properties of independent subgoals, which is clear from the definition, is that an optimal global solution can be achieved by simply concatenating together optimal solutions to the individual subproblems in any order. Even more important is the fact that independent subgoals reduce the branching factor by allowing the problem solver to focus on only a subset of the operators at any given time. In general, independent subgoals tend to divide both the base and the exponent of the complexity function by the number of subgoals.

Before the reader dismisses independent subgoals as trivial and uninteresting, it is worth noting that most goals that we try to satisfy in everyday life are in fact independent or nearly independent. If we consider a typical mix of goals that must be accomplished in a day, from domestic chores through job-related tasks to recreational and social objectives, we find that for the most part different operators apply to different problems, thus justifying the sequential strategy that we usually apply in our daily routine. The only reason that we can cope with the multiplicity of these goals at all is their relative independence. The major exception to independence of everyday tasks is that we are often constrained by global resource limits such as time or money. These constraints, however, introduce dependence among subgoals only when we begin to approach the limits they impose.

There are at least two reasons why independent subgoals have not received much previous attention. One is that we do not normally consider independent subtasks as part of the same problem, and another is that we tend to focus our attention on the more interesting case of interacting subgoals, such as serializable subgoals.

4.4. Serializable subgoals

Even though two subgoals may not be independent, it may be possible to first solve one and then solve the other without ever violating the first. For example, if we solve the top row of the Eight Puzzle as a subgoal, then we can always solve the rest of the problem without disturbing the top row. We define a set of subgoals to be *serializable* if there exists an ordering among the subgoals such that the subgoals can always be solved sequentially without ever violating a previously solved subgoal in the order. In terms of our definition of a subgoal as a set of states, this means that for every state in a subgoal set, there exists a path into the next smaller subgoal set that lies entirely within the original subgoal set.

Note that serialization depends upon the actual order chosen. For example, if we were to first solve the bottom two rows of the Eight Puzzle, we would not in general be able to then solve the top row without disturbing the bottom two rows.

The idea of serializable subgoals comes from the General Problem Solver (GPS) of Newell and Simon [7]. Essentially, the serializable property of subgoals is equivalent to the existence of a triangular difference table for a problem. Solving a subgoal corresponds to removing a difference, and the ordering of the differences corresponds to the ordering of the subgoals that allows each to be solved without violating the previously solved ones.

Unlike independence, the serializability of a set of subgoals is usually not obvious. For example, the subgoal of first solving a $2 \times 2 \times 2$ corner subcube of the $3 \times 3 \times 3$ Rubik's Cube allows the remainder of the problem to be solved without disturbing this subcube, but this fact is surprising to most people who can solve the puzzle. In general, proving that a sequence of subgoals is serializable is as difficult as proving that a given problem is solvable from all initial states. For example, if we swap two tiles of the Eight Puzzle by temporarily removing them from the frame, then the original configuration of the tiles can no longer be reached by legal moves, but this result was not known until long after the puzzle became popular [3].

Furthermore, the value of serializable subgoals in reducing search is not immediately obvious. The reason is that protecting previously solved subgoals may increase the overall solution length since certain operators cannot be applied at certain points. For example, first solving the top row of the Eight Puzzle and then leaving it undisturbed while the remainder of the puzzle is solved in general requires more moves than solving the main goal directly. In fact, just solving the bottom two rows of the puzzle without disturbing the top row could require more moves on the average than solving the entire puzzle.

Why then do we preserve serializable subgoals? The reason is that it reduces the branching factor of the space. By protecting previously solved subgoals, the number of legal moves that remain is decreased because operators that violate the subgoals are ruled out. This effect usually more than compensates for the increase in solution length. For example, in Rubik's Cube, protecting a $2 \times 2 \times 2$ subcube and twisting only the remaining three faces increases the number of moves required to correctly position the last piece of the puzzle from twelve to fifteen moves in the worst case. This additional search depth, however, is more than compensated for by the fact that protecting the $2 \times 2 \times 2$ subcube cuts the branching factor in half.

4.5. Non-serializable subgoals

It is often the case that given a collection of subgoals, previously satisfied subgoals must be violated in order to make further progress towards the main goal, regardless of the solution order. Such a collection of subgoals will be called *non-serializable*. In terms of our subset model, non-serializability of a pair of subgoals means that for some state in the first subgoal set, all paths from that state into the second subgoal state temporarily pass outside of the first subgoal set, even when the second subgoal set is contained in the first.

A classic example of this phenomenon is Rubik's Cube: once part of the puzzle is solved, in general it must be messed up, at least temporarily, in order to make further progress. Non-serializable subgoals also occur in the Eight Puzzle: if the first two tiles in any row are correctly positioned, in general they must be moved in order to correctly position the third tile. Perhaps the simplest example of non-serializable subgoals comes from the blocks world and is commonly known as Sussman's anomaly [12] (see Fig. 2). Given a description of a stack of blocks as the conjunction of (ON A B) and (ON B C), regardless of the order in which we try to solve these subgoals, the first subgoal must be violated in order to solve the second. In this case, however, the non-serializability is not an inherent property of the problem, but an artifact of this particular goal description. If we describe the goal as the conjunction of (ON C Table), (ON B C), and (ON A B), then these three subgoals are serializable. This is in stark contrast with Rubik's Cube, where careful scrutiny by literally millions of people has failed to yield a sequence of serializable subgoals.

A fair bit of attention has been focused on the problem of non-serializable subgoals, mostly in the blocks world domain. Waldinger [15] provides a good survey of this research. The essential technique employed is to start with a plan for achieving the subgoals independently, and then modify that plan to deal with the subgoal interactions. This approach assumes that the subgoals are approximately independent. By contrast, we make no such assumption and instead use a full-fledged search to solve a sequence of subgoals where each subgoal includes all the previous subgoals as well.

Non-serializable subgoals do not decrease the branching factor since we must allow any operator to be applied at any point in the solution. Furthermore, passing through these subgoals will have the same effect of increasing solution lengths as do subgoals in general. Given these two facts, one might reasonably ask what the value of non-serializable subgoals is. There are two answers to this question, depending on whether the context is simple problem solving or machine learning. The first will be addressed below and the second will be deferred until Section 5.

In a pure problem-solving context where the goal is simply to solve a single instance of a problem, the value of non-serializable subgoals is that states which satisfy them are often closer to the goal state on the average than arbitrary states, even though the subgoal property cannot be preserved throughout the rest of the solution. The intuitive reason for this is that if our main goal is a conjunction of subgoals, we expect a state in which most of the subgoals are satisfied to be closer to the goal state than a state in which few subgoals are satisfied. Thus, satisfying even non-serializable subgoals usually constitutes progress toward the goal in terms of the number of remaining moves. For example, it turns out that a state of the $3 \times 3 \times 3$ Rubik's Cube in which almost all the components are correctly positioned is closer to the goal state on the average (12 moves) than an arbitrary state (≥ 18 moves), even though the correct pieces must be temporarily moved in order to make further progress. This is also the case with the subgoals of solving the Eight Puzzle one tile at a time, since the maximum subgoal distance is only fourteen moves [4] while the maximum distance from the goal state is 30 moves [5]. Note that these are simply empirical results derived from the work described in Section 5, and is not always the case, as we will see.

4.6. Block-serializable subgoals

Often a sequence of non-serializable subgoals can be made serializable simply by grouping together multiple subgoals into a single subgoal. Such a sequence of subgoals will be called *block-serializable subgoals*. As was mentioned above, the Eight Puzzle subgoals of positioning the tiles one at a time are not serializable since once the first two tiles in a row have been placed, in general they must be moved in order to place the third. We also pointed out, however, that once the entire top row is correctly positioned, the remainder of the puzzle can be solved without disturbing the top row. Thus, even though the individual subgoals are not serializable, they can be grouped together into blocks which are serializable. For example, for the goal state shown in Fig. 1, the blocks (1), (2, 3), (4, 5), and (6, 7, 8) form a sequence of serializable subgoals in the sense that once *all* the tiles in a block are correctly placed, they need not be disturbed to complete the remainder of the puzzle. Thus, we find that serializability is often a function of the granularity of the set of subgoals. The tradeoff is that increasing the grain size to achieve serializability also results in increased subgoal distances.

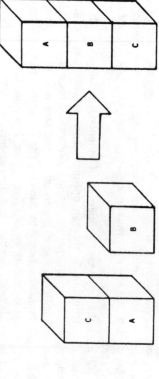

Fig. 2. Sussman's anomaly.

5. Macro-Operators

The reason that human problem solvers establish and solve these subgoals is that they know what sequence of operators to apply to solve the next subgoal from those states. A sequence of primitive operators is called a *macro-operator*. Progress toward the solution in this context is getting to a state from which the problem solver knows macro-operators that will achieve the next subgoal. Unfortunately, this explanation begs the question since it doesn't address where the macro-operators come from in the first place. In order to address that issue, we must broaden our perspective from pure problem solving to include learning behavior as well.

Strictly speaking, problem solving involves finding a solution to a particular problem instance. Learning, on the other hand, involves a collection of problem instances with some common structure. It may be a single problem instance that is to be solved repeatedly or a collection of related problem instances that are to be solved. In the former case, rote memorization of the solution is sufficient for learning. In the latter case, there must be some common structure to the collection of problem instances, such that the fixed cost of the learning plus the marginal cost of solving each problem instance using what was learned, is less than the total cost of solving each instance from scratch. In essence, the learning cost is amortized over all the problem instances to be solved.

In the case of a problem such as Rubik's Cube, the task of the human problem solver is not just to solve a particular instance of the problem, but rather to learn a general strategy for solving the problem from any given initial state. In fact, the problem is so difficult that an average problem instance cannot be solved without learning a general strategy. What people learn in order to solve this problem is a collection of macro-operators. Since an individual macro-operator can be used to solve more than one problem instance, the computational cost of learning a macro is amortized over all the problem instances for which it is useful.

5.1. Macros for non-serializable subgoals

In particular, the macros that are useful for non-serializable subgoals are those that leave previously satisfied subgoals intact. even though they may violate them temporarily. In other words. during the application of the macro, the previous subgoals may be disturbed. but by the end of the macro application, all previously satisfied subgoals will have been reestablished.

For example, consider the table of macro-operators for the Eight Puzzle in Table 1. corresponding to the goal state in Fig. 1. Each macro-operator is a sequence of primitive moves represented by the first letter of Left, Right, Up. or Down depending upon which direction a tile is moved. This table of macros can be used to solve the puzzle from any initial state with no search, as follows: First. locate the blank (or zero tile) in the initial state and note its position.

4.7. Pathological subgoals

We stated above that non-serializable subgoals often improve problem-solving efficiency by moving the problem solver closer to the goal, and gave Rubik's Cube and the Eight Puzzle as examples. This is not always the case, however. For some problems, solving subgoals does not decrease the distance to the main goal. For example, the obvious subgoals for solving Rubik's Cube are to position the individual components one at a time. Figure 3 shows a graph of the number of components, which are correctly positioned, versus the average distance to the goal state for the smaller 2 × 2 × 2 version of Rubik's Cube. Each data point shows the number of moves to the goal state via the shortest path, averaged over all states with the given number of components correctly positioned. One would expect the distance to the goal to decrease as more of the puzzle is solved.

What we find, however, is that as more components are positioned, the average distance to the goal remains constant. Even more surprisingly, the states in which the puzzle is almost completely solved are further from the goal than is the average state! Such a sequence of subgoals may be termed *pathological*. When people solve this puzzle, however, they pass through these states on their way to the solution. This raises the following question: by what measure do these subgoals represent progress towards the main goal?

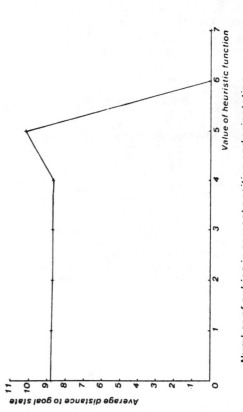

Number of cubies in correct position and orientation

Fig. 3. Average distance to goal state versus number of cubies in correct position and orientation for 2 × 2 × 2 Rubik's Cube.

(The label for any given position corresponds to the number of the tile that occupies that position in the goal state.) The position of the blank in the initial state is used as a row index into the zeroth column of the macro table to select a particular macro-operator. Applying that macro-operator will correctly move the blank to its goal position in the center of the frame. After that macro is applied, the resulting position of the one tile is used as a row index into the first column of the macro table to select the next macro-operator to be applied. The application of that macro will move the one tile to its correct position, and also return the blank tile to its goal position as well. Similarly, the resulting position of the two tile is used as a row index into the second column of the macro table to select a macro that will correctly position the two tile and also return the one and blank tiles to their goal positions. In general, at the *n*th stage of the algorithm, the position of the *n*th tile is used as a row index into the *n*th column of the macro table to select a macro that will correctly position the *n*th tile, and also restore the previous $n-1$ tiles to their goal positions.

Note that the effect of introducing these macro-operators is to serialize the subgoals of solving one tile at a time. While these subgoals are not serializable with respect to the primitive operator set, they are serializable with respect to this complex set of macro-operators. In general, the serializability of a set of subgoals depends upon the operator set to be applied to the problem.

The power of this approach lies in the fact that all 181,440 solvable initial states of the Eight Puzzle can be solved without any search using only the 35 macros shown. Such a table for the 4×10^{19} initial states of the $3 \times 3 \times 3$ Rubik's Cube requires only 238 macros. The reason is that each macro can usefully be applied to a large number of different states. This in turn is due to a structural property of these problems called *operator decomposability*.

If we represent the state of a problem by a vector of state variables, each one of which can take on a number of different values, then *total operator decomposability* requires that the effect of each operator on each state variable be a function only of that state variable. For example, in Rubik's Cube the state variables correspond to the individual movable components of the puzzle, and the values correspond to the different positions and orientations that the components can be in. Rubik's Cube is totally decomposable since the effect of any operator on the position and orientation of any component depends only on the position and orientation of that component and is independent of the other components of the puzzle. *Serial operator decomposability* is a more general form of operator decomposability, and requires only that there exist some ordering of the state variables for which the effect of each operator on each state variable depends only on that state variable and previous state variables in the ordering. For example, the Eight Puzzle is serially decomposable as long as the blank tile comes first in the ordering.

If a problem exhibits serial decomposability, which includes total decomposability as a special case, then a macro table similar to the one in Table 1

TABLE 1. Macro table for the Eight Puzzle

			Tiles				
	0	1	2	3	4	5	6
0							
1	UL						
2	U	RDLU					
3	UR	DLURRDLU	DLUR				
4	R	LDRURDLU	LDRU	RDLLURDRUL			
5	DR	ULDRURDLDRUL	LURDLDRU	LDRULURDDLUR	LURD		
6	D	URDLDRUL	ULDDRU	URDDLULDRRUL	ULDR	RDLLUURDLDRRUL	
7	DL	RULDDRUL	DRUULDRDLU	RULDRDLULDRRUL	URDLULDR	ULDRURDLLURD	URDL
8	L	DRUL	RULLDDRU	RDLULDRRUL	RULLDR	ULDRRULDLURD	RULD

(Positions — row labels 0–8)

exists for the problem. If n is the number of state variables and k is the number of different values that each state variable could be assigned, then in general the number of macros in the table is $O(nk)$ whereas the number of states in the problem space is $O(k^n)$. Note that in the case of the Eight Puzzle, the states are actually permutations of the tiles so the number of states is actually $O(k!)$. Since n and k are the problem size parameters, if we hold n fixed and allow k to grow, the number of macros grows linearly, the number of states grows polynomially, and hence the number of macros grows as the nth root of the number of states. Alternatively, if we hold k fixed and allow n to grow, the number of macros still grows linearly, but the number of states grows exponentially, and the number of macros grows only as the log of the number of states.

Thus, operator decomposability allows an exponential number of problem instances to be solved without any search, using only a linear amount of knowledge expressed as macro-operators. The amount of time required to learn the macros is $O(b^{D_{max}})$, where the subgoals are to map each state variable to its goal value. This is the same amount of time that would be required to solve a single instance of the problem using the same subgoals, with the difference being that in this case, the learning only has to be done once for all possible problem instances. The solution lengths resulting from this technique are simply the sum of the subgoal distances. A complete treatment of serially decomposable problems, including the formal definition of the property and the macro learning algorithm, can be found in [4].

5.2. Macros in arbitrary single-goal problem spaces

While macro-operators are particularly powerful for serially decomposable problems, they can be used to effectively reduce search in arbitrary problem spaces as well. We will first address the special case of problems with a single common goal state and then consider finding paths between arbitrary pairs of initial and goal states.

For example, consider the problem of navigating to your home along a network of roads. The states of this problem are different locations. If we adopt the definition of a primitive operator as one that does not admit intermediate states from which other operators can be applied, then the primitive operators in this space are sections of road between adjacent intersections. Clearly, we don't solve the problem of finding our way home from scratch every time we do it. Rather, with practice we learn enough so that the problem is normally solved with no search. Most of the knowledge in this task can be represented as macro-operators which indicate which sequence of roads to take to get home from various locations. Since different macros will share common paths, particularly as they get close to the goal, the entire set of macros can be viewed as a tree structure, rooted at the goal, where each branch has associated with it the direction to the goal.

Problem solving using this macro network consists of two steps: first search from the initial state to a state on the macro network, and then follow the macro network to the goal state. This reduces the search time at the expense of the space to store the macro network. In fact, we can quantify this space-time tradeoff.

Assume that the states in the macro network are uniformly distributed over the problem space so that the average distance from an arbitrary state to the closest state in the macro network is constant over the whole space. Actually, all that is required is that the distribution of the macro network match the distribution with which initial states are selected. Furthermore, we assume that a state on the macro network can be recognized in constant average time. This can be accomplished by hashing the states in the macro network. Finally, we assume that finding a path to the goal from any state in the macro network requires no search. This would be the case if every state in the network had associated with it the operator to apply to move toward the goal state.

Given these assumptions, let n be the total number of states in the space and let n/k be the number of states in the macro network, with k being the ratio of the size of the space to the size of the macro network. The probability that any given state is in the macro network is therefore $1/k$. Thus, starting from an arbitrary initial state, the expected number of states we would have to examine before finding one in the macro network is k. Since search time is proportional to the number of states explored and no search is required within the network itself, the total search time is $O(k)$ in the average case. The amount of space required to store the macro network is linear in the number of states in the network since only the operator which moves toward the goal need be stored with each state. Thus, the space required is $O(n/k)$. Note that the product of the space to store the network (n/k) and the time to search for a path from the initial state to the macro network (k) equals the number of states in the original space (n), independent of the size of the macro network. In other words, there is a multiplicative tradeoff between the size of the macro network and the amount of search required to solve problem instances in the resulting space.

5.3. Macros in arbitrary path-finding problems

The above analysis dealt only with the case of a single common goal state. We now relax that assumption and consider the use of macro networks to find paths between arbitrary pairs of initial and goal states. One solution to this problem is the following: First find a path from the initial state to the goal state of the macro network as above. Next, find a path from the actual goal state to the goal state of the network. Then, the first path followed by the inverse of the second path is a path from the initial state to the actual goal state, assuming that the operators are invertible.

A practical example of this approach is the system used by most overnight couriers. All packages are flown from their sources to a single common airport near the population center of the country, resorted, and then flown from this central hub to their destinations. This allows a quadratic number of source-destination pairs to be served by a linear number of flights.

The disadvantage of this approach is that the length of the path from initial state to goal state is proportional to the size of the problem space and not to the distance between the states. An overnight letter doesn't mind if it goes through Memphis to get from Los Angeles to San Francisco, but a passenger certainly would.

An alternative approach requires that the macro network be structured as a more highly connected graph rather than a tree. Problem solving then involves three steps: (1) finding a path from the initial state to a state on the macro network, (2) finding a path from the goal state to a state on the macro network, and finally (3) finding a path within the macro network between these two states on the macro network. In this case, the solution length depends on the distance between initial and goal states and on the density of the macro network, but is independent of the size of the problem space. The computational advantage of this approach over simply solving the problem directly in the original space is that much of the search will occur in the macro network, and since this network is sparser than the original space, this search will be more efficient. This idea is known as *abstraction*.

6. Abstraction

The value of abstraction is well known in artificial intelligence. The basic idea is that in order to efficiently solve a complex problem, a problem solver should at first ignore low-level details and concentrate on the essential features of the problem, filling in the details later. The idea readily generalizes to multiple hierarchical levels of abstraction, each focused on a different level of detail. Empirically, the technique has proven to be very effective in reducing the complexity of large problems.

Like many ideas in AI, the value of abstraction in human problem solving was pointed out by George Polya in *How to Solve It* [6]. The first explicit use of abstraction in an AI program was in the planning version of GPS [7]. The most thorough exploration of abstraction to date is Sacerdoti's work on the AB-STRIPS system [8].

This section presents a quantitative analysis of abstraction in problem solving. The essential reason that abstraction reduces complexity is that the total complexity is the sum of the complexities of the multiple searches, and not their product [9]. Our goal is to formalize and quantify this intuitive explanation. The questions we address are: how much search efficiency is gained by the use of abstraction, and what is the optimum level of detail for

each level of abstraction. To do so, we first formalize a model of abstraction. Next, we consider the special case of a single level of abstraction. Finally, we turn our attention to the general case of multiple abstraction levels. The analysis is done in the average case. The main result is that an abstraction hierarchy can reduce the amount of search to solve a problem from linear in the size of the problem space to logarithmic. A practical result of this analysis is that many levels of abstraction, with only small differences between them, reduce search the most.

6.1. A model of abstraction in problem solving

We model the states of an abstract space as a subset of the states in the original problem space (the base space). For example, in the road navigation problem, the states are street intersections and the operators are sections of road between intersections. In this domain, a suitable set of abstract states would be the set of major intersections, say at the centers of towns. An alternative model is for each state of the abstract space to correspond to a subset of the states in the base space. In the navigation example, a state of the abstract space would then correspond to a region in the base space. In many cases, however, operators only apply to particular states as opposed to sets of states. For example, while an interstate highway may serve an entire area, it can only be accessed from particular points in that area. In any case, the main difference between the subset and region models is that in the region model, no effort is required to get into the abstract space, since any state in a region is already a member of the region as a whole. This reduces the search complexity by a constant factor, and for this reason we adopt the more restricted subset model.

The operators of the abstract space map states in the abstract space to other states in the abstract space. In the case of GPS and Sacerdoti's work, the abstract operators were a subset of the primitive operator set that mapped abstract states to abstract states. In the transportation example, the operators of the abstract space would be direct means of transportation between major cities, such as interstate highways. Alternatively, the abstract operators may be macro-operators that go between abstract states. A necessary property of the macro-operators is that they be stored or otherwise known to the system and do not require search to find. In our example of road navigation, the abstract operators might be driving routes between major cities that are sequences of different roads marked by signs. Regardless of which type of abstract operators we choose, the assumption of known operators between abstract states is an important aspect of our model. An abstract space requires both a set of abstract states and a set of abstract operators between those states. If paths between the abstract states must be found by search among the operators of the base space, then abstraction by itself makes no improvement in search efficiency. For example, if we have to search for routes between nearby major cities, then the abstraction of major cities is of no use in route finding. Note

abstraction, if the base space is of size n, the optimum size for the abstract space is on the order of $\sqrt{n}$. This abstraction reduces total search time from $O(n)$ without any abstraction, to $O(\sqrt{n})$.

6.3. Multiple levels of abstraction

We now consider the general case of multiple hierarchical levels of abstraction. In order to solve a problem in a hierarchy of abstraction spaces, we first map the initial state to the nearest state in the first level of abstraction, then map this state to the nearest state in the second level of abstraction, etc., until the highest level of abstraction is reached. At the same time, this process is repeated starting from the goal state and working up through successive levels of abstraction until the paths from the initial and goal states meet at the highest abstraction level. The questions we want to answer are how much do multiple levels of abstraction reduce search, how many levels of abstraction should there be, and what should the ratios between their sizes be in order to minimize the search time to solve an average problem.

Again, let the number of states in the base space be n. Let k_1 be the ratio between the size of the base space and the size of the first level of abstraction, k_2 be the ratio of the sizes of the first and second levels of abstraction, etc. In order to make the formula for the search complexity at the top level the same as in the lower levels, let the highest level of abstraction consist of a single state. The task at the top level then is to find paths from both the initial and goal states to this single common state. With this slight simplification, the expected amount of time to find a solution to an average problem in this hierarchy of abstraction spaces is $2k_1 + 2k_2 + \cdots + 2k_m$, where m is the number of levels of abstraction, since two searches must be made at each level to find a state in the next higher level, one coming from the initial state and the other from the goal state. As in the case of a single abstraction, this is actually an upper bound on the expected time since it ignores the possibility that the actual goal state will be found before the highest level of abstraction is reached.

In order to minimize this expression, we must minimize the sum of the k_i. The constraint on the k_i is that their product must equal n, since they represent the ratios between the number of states at each level and n is the total number of states. Thus, the problem becomes one of factoring a number such that the sum of the factors is minimized, or in other words, finding a *minimum sum factorization*.

If the factors are constrained to be integers, then the prime factorization of n is a minimum sum factorization. However, in our case the k_i are ratios which need not be integral but rather can be arbitrary rational numbers. In that case, the minimum sum factorization of a number n consists of $\ln n$ factors, each of which is equal to e. To see this, first note that all the factors must be equal.

that we do not require an abstract operator between every pair of abstract states, but simply that the set of abstract states be connected by abstract operators.

For purposes of this analysis, we assume that the relative distribution of abstract states over the base space, while not necessarily uniform, is the same for all levels of abstraction. In our example, this corresponds to the observation that while there are more towns in the Eastern U.S. than in the West, the relative distribution of large cities is roughly the same as that of small cities. An average case analysis can be done independent of the actual distribution, as long as the distribution remains constant over different levels of abstraction.

6.2. Single level of abstraction

We begin our analysis with the special case of a single level of abstraction. As in the case of the macro network, let the number of states in the base space be n and the number of states in the abstract space be n/k, with k being the ratio of the size of the base space to the size of the abstract space. The issue we address is the expected amount of search required to find a solution to au average problem, using the abstraction. By average problem, we mean one where the initial and goal states are randomly selected from all states with equal probability.

We assume that the amount of time to search for a solution is proportional to the number of states visited in the search. The expected number of states visited is the sum of the expected numbers of states visited in the three phases of the search: getting into the abstract space, searching in the abstract space, and getting to the actual goal in the base space. Since we assume that the distribution of states in the abstract space is the same as in the base space, the probability that any randomly selected state is a member of the abstract space is $1/k$. Thus, the expected number of states that must be generated in a search before a state in the abstract space is encountered is k. This is both the expected number of states to be searched in going from the initial state to the abstract space and also in going from the abstract space to the goal state, since this latter search can be performed by searching from the goal state to the abstract space.

Since the total number of abstract states is n/k, to find a path between an arbitrary pair of abstract states, we would expect to have to examine $\frac{1}{2}n/k$ states on the average. Thus, the total expected number of states expanded is $t = 2k + \frac{1}{2}n/k$. Note that this is actually an upper bound on the expected number of states because it ignores the slight possibility that the goal state will be found before the abstract space is encountered when searching from the initial state.

What value of k minimizes this total search time? The minimum occurs at $k = \frac{1}{2}\sqrt{n}$, or $n/k = 2\sqrt{n}$, giving a value of $t = 2\sqrt{n}$. Thus, for a single level of

because two unequal factors could each be replaced by the square root of their product, which would reduce the sum without changing the product. This implies that there must be $\log_k n$ factors of k, and minimizing their sum. $k \log_k n$, yields $k = e$.

This implies that the optimum abstraction hierarchy for a problem space with n states consists of $\ln n$ levels of abstraction and that the ratio of the sizes of successive levels of abstraction is e. The average case time to find a solution given such an optimum abstraction hierarchy is proportional to $2k_1 + 2k_2 + \cdots + 2k_m$ or $2e \ln n$. Thus, the use of such an abstraction hierarchy can reduce the expected search time from O(n) to O(log n). This improvement makes combinatorial problems tractable. For example, if n is an exponential function of problem size, then log n is linear.

This same result was arrived at by Kleinrock and Kamoun [13] in the context of a closely related but somewhat different problem, that of hierarchical routing in large computer networks. In their problem, no search is performed, but each node stores a routing table which gives a destination node for each cluster at each level of abstraction. Their problem of minimizing the storage space for these routing tables turns out to be equivalent to minimizing, search time in our model.

In practice, there are a number of different factors that constrain the design of abstraction spaces, and hence an optimal abstraction hierarchy in the above sense will not be achievable in general. The point of the exercise is to illustrate the analysis of such a hierarchy and to see how much abstraction can reduce search complexity in the best case. The result does suggest, however, that in general a deep abstraction hierarchy, in terms of number of levels, will reduce search more than a shallow one.

The only quantitative empirical data in the literature on the use of abstraction in problem solving is Sacerdoti's comparison of STRIPS and ABSTRIPS on five different problems. For these problems, ABSTRIPS provided an approximately logarithmic speedup over STRIPS in time to find a solution. While five data points are too small a sample to validate the model, Sacerdoti's data is at least consistent with our theory.

6.4. Space requirements of abstraction

What about the space required to store abstract problem spaces? According to the model we used for the macro network, the amount of memory for an abstract space would be proportional to the number of abstract states. Thus. the optimal single level of abstraction would require $O(\sqrt{n})$ space and the optimal abstraction hierarchy would require $O(n)$ space, just for the first level.

In reality, however, the actual space requirements for abstraction are usually insignificant. In order to see this, it is necessary to distinguish two different kinds of problems: extensional and intensional. An extensional problem is one in which all the states of the problem space have an *extension* or exist in the world. For example. road navigation is an extensional problem. on the other hand, is characterized by a small set of rules which generate the entire problem space. The Eight Puzzle is an example of an intensional problem since all the states don't actually exist at once but rather are generated by the set of legal moves.

In an extensional problem the space requirement of an abstract problem space is negligible. This is because the space required is no more than linear in the number of states, and all the states already exist in the world. The small additional space is easily absorbed in the space required to represent the problem space. For example, in road navigation abstract states and abstract operators can be created simply by putting up road signs. Furthermore. the same abstractions can be used by any problem solver for any problem instance and hence the space cost is amortized over all problem solvers and all problem instances. Thus, while road signs indicating the direction to my house are not practical, more general road signs are cost-effective.

In the case of intensional problems, the additional space requirements are often avoided by creating abstract problems which are also intensional. For example, an abstract problem space for the Eight Puzzle can be created by ignoring the positions of some of the tiles. The states of the resulting abstract problem need not be represented explicitly, any more than those of the original problem, but rather implicitly by the legal moves. Similarly, in the case of ABSTRIPS, the abstract problems were created by ignoring certain details of the states. In general, when confronted with an intensional problem we design intensional abstractions.

Thus, in both extensional and intensional problems we find that in practice we incur no significant space overhead, albeit for different reasons in the two cases.

7. Conclusions and Further Work

We have presented the thesis that planning can be viewed as search using knowledge sources such as subgoals, macro-operators, and abstraction spaces, in addition to simple heuristic evaluation functions. Furthermore. we have taken the first steps in the quantitative analysis of problem solving performance using these sources of knowledge.

In the case of subgoals. we identified a measure called the subgoal distance as the parameter that. along with the branching factor. determines the time complexity of a search using subgoals. We then explored independent. serializable, and non-serializable subgoals in turn. We found that independent subgoals divide the branching factor of a problem, serializable subgoals reduce the branching factor by ruling out certain operators, and that solving non-serializable subgoals may reduce the distance to the main goal.

Even in those cases where the distance to the goal is not reduced, it may be worthwhile to solve non-serializable subgoals if the problem solver has available macro-operators which will achieve the goal from those subgoals. In the special case of serially decomposable problems, we found that exponentially increasing numbers of initial states can be solved by storing only logarithmically more macro-operators. In the more general case of single goal problems, a macro-network provides a multiplicative tradeoff between search time and storage space for macros. This can be extended to handle arbitrary initial and goal states by a central hub approach, but the penalty is that solution lengths are then proportional to the problem diameter rather than the distance between initial and goal states.

A more highly connected macro network for dealing with the general case of arbitrary pairs of initial and goal states amounts to an abstract problem space. We found that for a single level of abstraction, the optimal size for an abstract space is the square root of the size of the base space and that this reduces search from linear in the size of the space to the square root of the size of the space. In the case of multiple hierarchical levels of abstraction, we found that the optimal hierarchy has a logarithmic number of levels with a constant ratio between their sizes and that this hierarchy reduces search from linear in the number of states in the problem space to logarithmic. Since the number of states is often exponential in the problem size, this explains why abstraction hierarchies can reduce exponential complexity to linear complexity.

Further research along these lines is underway in several different directions. One is to extend the analyses to accurately predict solution lengths resulting from these different planning strategies. Another research direction is further exploration of independent subgoals that are subject to a common resource restriction. In addition, efforts are in progress to automate the learning of subgoals and abstraction spaces. Finally, we are exploring various hybrid strategies that combine two or more of these knowledge sources in a single algorithm. For example, the question of how heuristic techniques might be used to speed up individual subgoal searches is addressed in [14].

Our results represent the first steps toward a quantitative theory of planning. We hope that this paradigm will prove to be fruitful and that this body of work will eventually become as deep and rich as that dealing with problem solving with heuristic evaluation functions.

ACKNOWLEDGMENT

I would like to thank Herbert Simon and Judea Pearl for many helpful discussions concerning this research. In addition, Othar Hansson, Greg Korf, Andy Mayer, and Curt Powley read and made many constructive comments on the manuscript. This research was supported in part by NSF Grant IST 85-15302, an NSF Presidential Young Investigator Award, an IBM Faculty Development Award, and a grant from Delco Systems Operations, a division of Delco Electronics Corporation.

REFERENCES

1. Pohl, I., First results on the effect of error in heuristic search, in: B. Meltzer and D. Michie (Eds.), *Machine Intelligence* **5** (American Elsevier, New York, 1970) 219–236.
2. Korf, R.E., Depth-first iterative-deepening: An optimal admissible tree search, *Artificial Intelligence* **27** (1985) 97–109.
3. Johnson, W.A. and Storey, W.E., Notes on the 15 puzzle, *Am. J. Math.* **2** (1879) 397–404.
4. Korf, R.E., Macro-operators: A weak method for learning, *Artificial Intelligence* **26** (1985) 35–77.
5. Schofield, P.D.A., Complete solution of the eight puzzle, in: B. Meltzer and D. Michie (Eds.), *Machine Intelligence* **3** (American Elsevier, New York, 1967) 125–133.
6. Polya, G., *How to Solve It* (Princeton University Press, Princeton, NJ, 1945).
7. Newell, A. and Simon, H.A., *Human Problem Solving* (Prentice-Hall, Englewood Cliffs, NJ, 1972).
8. Sacerdoti, E.D., Planning in a hierarchy of abstraction spaces, *Artificial Intelligence* **5** (1974) 115–135.
9. Minsky, M., Steps toward artificial intelligence, in: E.A. Feigenbaum and J. Feldman (Eds.), *Computers and Thought* (McGraw-Hill, New York, 1963).
10. Pearl, J., *Heuristics* (Addison-Wesley, Reading, MA, 1984).
11. Ericsson, K.A., Approaches to descriptions and analysis of problem solving processes: The 8-puzzle, Ph.D. Thesis, University of Stockholm, 1976.
12. Sussman, G.J., *A Computer Model of Skill Acquisition* (American Elsevier, New York, 1975).
13. Kleinrock, L. and Kamoun, F., Hierarchical routing for large networks, *Comp. Networks* **1** (1977) 155–174.
14. Chakrabarti, P.P., Ghose, S. and DeSarkar, S.C., Heuristic search through islands, *Artificial Intelligence* **29** (1986) 339–347.
15. Waldinger, R., Achieving several goals simultaneously, in: N.J. Nilsson and B. Webber (Eds.), *Readings in Artificial Intelligence* (Tioga, Palo Alto, CA, 1981) 250–271.

Received December 1985; revised version received November 1986

Chapter 8

Time and the Frame Problem

The most important formal problem facing planning systems that use a rich representation of the world is the frame problem. This term has been used to refer to many different things, but it generally refers to reasoning about how the world changes as actions occur. Specifying the direct effects of actions is not so problematic—the frame problem arises from the need to specify what items in the world may or may not be indirectly affected by the action. The first paper in this chapter, Shoham and McDermott (1988), discusses the frame problem in general and shows that it is an inherent property of reasoning about change in the world, rather than a technical problem with any solution.

The next paper we present, Hayes (1973), is one of the first papers to specifically address the frame problem and contains a survey of several different techniques for dealing with the problem. While the paper is quite old by AI standards, most of the approaches discussed are still being pursued today.

The third paper in this chapter, Dean and McDermott (1987), describes the issues involved in building an explicit temporal representation that allows the efficient assertion and retrieval of temporally qualified facts. This paper also discusses in detail a technique that automatically "projects" the truth of properties into the future. Thus if a property P is asserted to be true at some time t, and nothing is known to contradict that P still holds at a later time t', then it is assumed that P still holds at time t'.

As mentioned above, attempts to formalize temporal projection have involved the use of non-monotonic logics to minimize change over time, or minimize causal effects. There has been a great amount of activity on this problem since the appearance of

Hanks and McDermott (1986), which described the Yale Shooting Problem, which they claimed could not be solved within existing frameworks. This paper raised considerable controversy, and many responses have been written since. For example, see Shoham (1988), Kautz (1986), Lifschitz (1986), and Haugh (1987). The next paper we present in this chapter, Hanks and McDermott (1987), includes a statement of the original problem and then contains a discussion of many of the responses the paper engendered.

Work on this problem continues and significant progress is being made. The final paper in this chapter, by Morgenstern and Stein (1988), is an excellent example of current work. In particular, while there have been many solutions to the problem that allow temporal projection into the future, Morgenstern and Stein cast the problem in a more general light, showing how the same techniques can be used for projecting backwards through time. Such a capability is essential for tasks such as generating explanations when something has gone wrong.

Papers referenced herein but not included in this volume:

Haugh, B. (1987) Simple causal minimization for temporal persistence and projection, Proc AAAI-87.

Hanks, S. and McDermott, D. (1986) Default Reasoning, Nonmonotonic logics, and the Frame Problem, Proc. AAAI-86.

Kautz, H. (1986) The logic of persistence, Proc AAAI-86.

Lifschitz, V. (1986) Pointwise Circumscription, Proc AAAI-86.

Shoham, Y. (1988) Reasoning about Change, MIT Press.

Problems in Formal Temporal Reasoning

Yoav Shoham

Department of Computer Science, Stanford University, Stanford, CA 94305, U.S.A.

Drew McDermott

Department of Computer Science, Yale University, New Haven, CT 06520, U.S.A.

Recommended by Patrick Hayes

ABSTRACT

Ever since its introduction by McCarthy and Hayes in 1969, the so-called frame problem *has been the object of much fascination and debate. Although it was defined in the narrow context of the* situation calculus, *a specific temporal formalism, it was clear from the start that it is in fact a manifestation of some fundamental problem in temporal reasoning.*

Our aim in this informal paper is to identify the general form of certain classes of problems that arise in formal temporal reasoning. We argue that problems such as the frame problem arise from the conflicting desires to reason both rigorously and efficiently about the future. This conflict does not depend on the particular underlying temporal formalism. In particular, we identify two formalism-independent problems, called the qualification problem *and the* extended prediction problem, *which subsume the frame problem. To illustrate the fact that these problems are indeed inherent to the prediction task and not to a particular formalism, we show that they arise in two distinct frameworks: classical mechanics, and Hayes' histories notation.*

Ever since its introduction by McCarthy and Hayes in 1969 [3], the so-called *frame problem* has been the object of much fascination and debate. Although it was defined in the narrow context of the *situation calculus*, a specific temporal formalism, it was clear from the start that it is in fact a manifestation of some fundamental problem in temporal reasoning. Despite its apparent universal nature, however, we know of no attempt within AI to define the problem in its most general form (but see [6] for discussion of what some philosophers take the problem to mean).

The general feeling has always been that we cannot define the frame problem, but we recognize it when we see it. We believe, however, that if we want to solve the frame problem then we will benefit from defining it first. We argue that the frame problem belongs to a class of problems that arise from the conflicting desires to reason both rigorously and efficiently about the future. This conflict does not depend on the particular underlying temporal formalism. In particular, we will identify two formalism-independent problems, called the *qualification problem* and the *extended prediction problem*, which subsume the frame problem.

Since the problems under discussion arise in the context of the prediction task, let us introduce them in that context. The first section describes a simple case of predicting the future, and brings up problems that arise if one tries to use either classical mechanics or the *histories* formalisms due to Hayes. The second section abstracts away from these two particular frameworks, and offers a general characterization of the problems.

1. A Specific Prediction Task

To see what problems are involved in predicting the future, let us consider a simple case of predicting the behavior of physical objects. Imagine an intelligent robot watching friends play a game of billiards. We join him when there are exactly two balls left on the pool table, and together with the robot we watch them roll towards a collision point as shown in Fig. 1.[1] We know exactly what is about to happen: the two balls will collide and bounce off appropriately, as shown in Fig. 2. The question is whether the robot can be expected to know

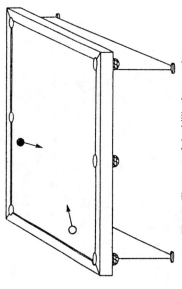

Fig. 1. First part of the billiards scenario.

---

[1] John McCarthy has prepared us for the wrath of some who might be offended by our terminology. It seems that in the following we have confused the vulgar game of billiards with the noble activity of shooting pool, or was it the other way around.

Artificial Intelligence **36** (1988) 49–61

0004-3702/88 $3.50 © 1988, Elsevier Science Publishers B.V. (North-Holland)

To summarize, then, the way Newtonian mechanics talk about temporal information is by having functions of time be their subject matter. These functions of time participate in sets of differential equations, in which all derivatives are taken with respect to time. We now come to the question of how one specifies the initial conditions in a physics problem, and what permits one to predict from this specification that, say, the two balls will collide. One would *like* to say that the initial conditions are the position and velocity of the balls at some time prior to the collision (in order to simplify the analysis, we can assume that the balls are elastic and that they are of equal mass and size). However, while this description is sufficient for humans, it is not, strictly speaking, complete, and therefore insufficient when subjected to formal inference techniques. The problem is that we have not stated that there are no *other* balls that affect the trajectory of the two particular balls. Even worse, it does not explicitly state that there are no holes in the table through which balls might drop, no strong winds that affect the trajectories of balls, and so on. What then constitutes a correct description of the scenario?

In [5], Montague offers a formal analysis of Newtonian mechanics. Actually, he talks of *particle mechanics* and *celestial mechanics*. Particle mechanics consist of Newton's three laws. Celestial mechanics is the specialization of it which specifies that the force between any two particles is given by the law of gravitation. Montague's interest lies in testing whether the formal theories have any of several formally defined properties such as that of being deterministic. For us what is interesting is the actual encoding of the theory of particle mechanics [5, pp. 311–318] (adding the gravitational axiom is a straightforward specialization of the theory that doesn't concern us immediately). Of that, much is devoted to axiomatizing the properties of the real numbers and of the integers [5, pp. 312–316]. These don't concern us here directly either since we assume those are well understood (in fact, even with Montague's axioms we are still left with "nonstandard" models of numbers, and he conditions subsequent theorems on assuming the standard model). What is important is Montague's encoding of Newton's laws, which relies on viewing the world as an *n-particle system*. In other words, the objects in the domain of discourse are exactly *n* particles, where *n* is some fixed integer. The initial conditions are exactly those envisioned by Laplace[2]: the mass, position and velocity of all the balls at some time prior to the collision. In general, one must have a finite number of quantities one is interested in, and the initial conditions are a complete listing of their values at some point. In our domain, this translates to fixing the number of balls, and giving their individual positions and velocities at some point as the initial conditions.

[2] The assertion due to Laplace is that the positions and momenta of all particles in the universe at one time completely determine their positions and momenta at all other times.

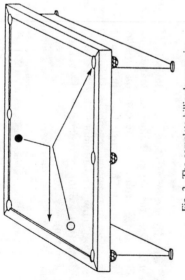

Fig. 2. The complete billiards scenario.

that too, and if so how. How does the robot represent what he sees on the pool table, and what physics does he employ to predict the outcome?

1.1. Classical mechanics

Let us first examine what happens if the robot uses classical, or Newtonian, mechanics. Newtonian mechanics keeps track of the values of *quantities*, which are functions of time. These quantities are represented by variables whose values range over some interval of the reals. Examples of quantities are force $f(t)$, acceleration $a(t)$ and mass $m(t)$. The latter is, of course, a constant function in classical mechanics. Typically, the time argument to the functions is omitted, so one writes simply f, a and m. The actual formulation of the physical laws comes in the form of *equations*, which are constraints on values the quantities may assume simultaneously. An example of an equation is $f = m \times a$, which is really shorthand for $\forall t\, f(t) = m(t) \times a(t)$. Two special quantities are spatial location $x(t), y(t), z(t)$ and time itself t, in both cases of which the laws of physics refer only to relative value. The way this is enforced is by using differentials. Time and space appear *only* as differentials, as in $vdt = dx$. By convention the formulations include only time derivatives, reflecting the intuition that what physics is about is keeping track of the values of quantities as they change in time. and so the last equation appears as $v = dx/dt$. or (since the only derivatives are time derivatives) simply as $v = x'$. One finds also equations in which time *seems* to appear as an undifferentiated quantity (as in $v = a \times t$), but in these cases the t really stands for "elapsed time", or interval duration, and the equations can be viewed simply as a particular solution of the original differential equations (in this case, $a = dv/dt$), given certain boundary conditions (in this case, $v_0 = 0$ and the fact that the acceleration is constant). The same applies to equations that seem to mention absolute spatial values.

There are some problems with this framework. First, all the initial conditions must refer to the exact same time point. That excludes questions of the form "If city A is 100 miles away from city B, train 1 leaves city A towards city B at 1:00 travelling at 20 mph, and train 2 leaves city B towards city A at 2:00 travelling at 15 mph, when will the two trains meet?," which are so common in textbooks. Second, it seems a little perverse to have to talk about scenarios with different numbers of balls as if they are unrelated. Is there no way to factor the number of balls out of the formulation? Furthermore, what if there are an infinite number of balls? In that case Montague's formulation does not apply, and for a good reason. as we shall see below when we discuss his encoding of the Newton's second law. Finally, even restricting ourselves to a single situation with a finite number of balls, what if there are very many of them? Do we really have to talk about millions of balls that are millions of miles away? In celestial mechanics these have an effect on the two balls under consideration (though a negligible one), but in the case of billiard balls they only do if they collide with one of the balls. While not a *logical* problem, it certainly poses a practical one.

We will return to these problems shortly, but for the moment let us proceed under the conditions that satisfy Montague's formulation. namely a finite number of balls whose initial conditions are given. In our example. suppose there are exactly five balls (including the two colliding balls), whose position. mass and velocity at some time instant prior to the collision are given. Our remaining task is to justify a modest version of Laplace's claim: given the description of all the balls at the initial time instant, one can deduce the collision and new trajectories of the two particular balls. To do that, we need to assign a precise meaning to the laws of physics. Consider Newton's second law. $f = m \times a$, whose intended meaning is that at any given instant in time. the net force on an object is equal to the product of its mass and acceleration (since we assume uniform mass, we can assume the law $f = a$ and the appropriate adjustment of units). The meaning of the phrase *net force* is the summation of all individual forces acting on the object, and this is where the assumption of a fixed finite number of balls is critical. If there are n balls, the number of individual forces on each ball is $n - 1$, one for each other ball. (Actually, Montague would say that there are n forces, thus allowing for "external" forces.) This assumption can only be made if we have fixed in advance the number of balls. Furthermore, it is easy to make sense of the notion of summation if there are a finite number of elements that are being summed. Montague's encoding in logic of the summation operator strongly relies on this finiteness. Things are less obvious if we allow infinite summation. and in fact it's not clear what it means for an infinite number of balls to collide. Of course, it makes perfect sense to speak of an infinite number of balls, only a finite number of which collide at any moment, but that too is outside the scope of Montague's formulation. Anyway. since we're making Montague-like as-

sumptions, all that remains for us is to specify the individual forces that the balls exert on one another. In Montague's case that force is the law of gravitation. In our case it is the law of conservation of momentum. Given the law of conservation of momentum, we can define the force between any two particles as follows:

(1) Two balls exert force on each other *only* if they touch.
(2) In this case the magnitude of this force is the appropriate function of their individual velocities, positions and directions at the time of the collision, and the law of conservation of momentum.

Given these assumptions, the laws of physics actually make the right prediction: they constrain the two balls to collide and bounce off appropriately. This "prediction," however, is purely model theoretic. No attention was paid to the problem of actually *computing* the point of collision. In fact, it is very unclear how to perform the computation, since all axioms refer to time *points*. Somehow we must identify the "interesting" points in time or space, and interpolate between them by integrating differentials over time. The problem seems a little circular, though, since the identity of the interesting points *depends* on the integration. For example, understanding where the two balls are heading logically precedes the identification of the collision: if we don't know that the two balls are rolling towards each other, there is no reason to expect something interesting at the actual collision point.

How do people solve such physics problems? The inevitable answer seems to be that they "visualize" the problem, identify a solution in some mysterious ("analog") way, and only then *validate* the solution through physics. Much of what goes on in the industry of so-called *qualitative physics* can be viewed as an attempt to lift that shroud of mystery and emulate the visualization process on a computer [1]. The solution offered in qualitative physics is related to another issue addressed by it and which was ignored here, the fact that precise numerical information (such as the precise distance between two billiard balls) is unnecessary and unavailable. In qualitative physics it is replaced by qualitative information (such as that whether the distance between the two balls is zero or nonzero, and whether it is increasing, constant or decreasing). A set of such qualitative values gives rise to a qualitative *state*, and, given one such state, one uses the "envisionment" procedure to determine the next state (or set of possible next states).

The details of qualitative physics are not crucial here; all that was needed was the principal idea behind the process of envisionment. The envisionment in the billiards domain is simple: it embodies the rule, which is a simple derivative of the physics, that a ball's velocity and travel direction is unchanged during an interval in which it collides with no other ball. But if in our domain the heuristic for identifying interesting points is simple, in richer domains it is more complex. When we throw a rock we know that the next interesting time point is when its parabolic trajectory is interrupted by our neighbor's window, and when we fix a flat tire we know that the next interesting point is when we next drive over a sharp object. In general it can be arbitrarily hard to identify interesting points from the physics.

To summarize the discussion of classical physics, we have said that if we start out with the complete description of the balls at some point in time, stipulate that those are the only balls that exist, assume that no other potentially influential events take place (no other objects touch the balls, there are no holes in the table, no ball is about to explode, etcetera), adopt a Montague-like description of Newton's kinematic equations, and formulate a dynamic rule about the force exerted between any two balls, then classical physics captures the future behavior of the balls. The most serious drawbacks associated with this approach are:

(1) The initial conditions must refer to a unique instant of time. Furthermore, we must give a *complete* description of the initial conditions, which unless abbreviated is too costly. So far we have no way of saying "this is all the information that is relevant to the problem."

(2) The physics specify which predictions are warranted by the initial conditions, but not how to make them. This information must be supplied from outside the physics.

(3) The rules of physics are constraints on the simultaneous values of quantities. This instantaneous flavor of the rules, which makes the formulation elegant and parsimonious, is not only the reason that prediction is hard but also the reason that physics rules seem so different from the knowledge that underlies human understanding of physical situations.

These shortcomings are actually manifestations of very general problems, ones that transcend the particular framework of classical physics. Before we explicate these general problems, though, let us first give a better feel for them by showing how they are manifested in a different setting, Pat Hayes' histories framework.

1.2. Histories

In [2] Pat Hayes suggested a new way of discussing physical scenarios: *histories*. A history is a contiguous chunk of spacetime with which we associate a *type*. Intuitively, the type corresponds to the period during which the behavior of the physical object is qualitatively the same. Hayes applied the theory to reasoning about the behavior of liquids. A piece of liquid can exhibit one of several behaviors: free falling, spreading on a surface, being contained in an upward-concave rigid object, entering a container, leaving it, and so on. Each of those is a history-type, and we can write axioms constraining the co-existence of several histories having various types. For example, no two histories may overlap in spacetime. Or, as another example, if there is an entering history

along the rim of a full container, then there must also be a leaving history (conservation of matter), and so on. The hope is that by creating a rich enough vocabulary of history-types and writing enough restrictions on them we will be able to capture the behavior of the physical objects.

Let us try to reason our billiards scenario in the histories framework. In our domain of billiards we may want to speak about various kinds of histories: rolling histories, falling histories, parabolic-flight histories, collision histories, strong-wind histories, and probably many others. Let us not worry too much about the precise taxonomy, since the problem will not be lack of expressiveness but rather difficulty of reasoning. For the sake of discussion let us assume two types of histories: ROLLING histories and COLLISION histories, where ROLLING histories describe the rolling of a billiard ball along a straight line. Thus we can represent the scenario involving the two balls by four ROLLING histories, two for each ball, as shown in Fig. 3: H11 denotes the history of the first ball until the collision and H12 denotes the history of the same ball after the collision, and similarly H21 and H22 denote the histories of the second ball before and after the collision, respectively. We could now write axioms describing the relation between H11, H12, H21 and H22. We won't do that; let us agree that such axioms could be written. The question we are interested in is, again, how to represent the initial conditions and from this representation deduce the rest of the scenario.

A natural representation of the initial conditions is by two histories, one for each ball. Those may be respective prefixes of H11 and H21, or the initial *slices* of those two histories. (A slice is the projection of a history onto a point in time. This option requires that we be able to speak about the *velocity* of a history.) Let us consider the first case, shown graphically in Fig. 4, in which the initial conditions are prefixes of H11 and H21, say H11' and H21' (the other case would behave similarly). We would need axiom(s) that guarantee that the two

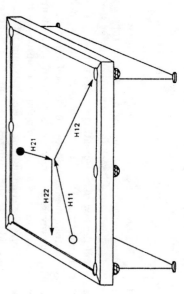

Fig. 3. Four ROLLING histories.

new history. We need to somehow capture the property of persisting "for as long as possible."

This brings us to another problem. One may say that since we have only one other history, it is trivial to determine when and where the first intersection between histories occurs. The problem with that is that we have not explicitly said that there are no other histories. For example, we have not explicitly ruled out the existence of a third ball deflecting one of the two original balls before the collision with the other original ball. It is tempting to say "ok, the *only* two histories are the ones I told you about, H11' and H21'." That, however, is simply false, since beside those two histories we have H11" and H21", the collision history, the two new ROLLING histories following the collision, and so on. Nor can we say "the only histories are the two given ones and those that follow from them," at least not until we define the notion of "following from."

These problems with using the histories framework are closely related to the problems with using classical mechanics, which were discussed in the previous subsection, and to the infamous frame problem. The general nature of the problems is discussed in the next section.

2. The problems of qualification and extended prediction, and their relation to the frame problem

The problems that arise in either classical mechanics or the histories framework are symptomatic of all systems for reasoning about change. The general problem is how to reason *efficiently* about what is true over extended periods of time, and it has to do with certain tradeoffs between risk-avoidance and economy in the process of prediction.

Any rules of change (or physics) must support inferences of the form "if *this* is true at this time then *that* is true at that time." Since we are interested primarily in predicting the future, a special case of this form will be of particular interest, the form "if this is true at this time then that is true at that *later* (or at least *no earlier*) time." The crux of the first problem is that the "if" part might get too large to be of practical use. For example, if we wish to be careful about our predictions, in order to infer that a ball rolling in a certain direction will continue doing so we must verify that there are no strong winds, that no one is about to pick up the ball, that the ball does not consist of condensed explosives that are about to go off in the next instant of time, and we can continue this list, getting arbitrarily ridiculous. Or, to use another example, when we pull the trigger of a loaded gun we would like to predict that a loud noise will follow, but strictly speaking there are a whole lot of other factors that need to be verified: that the gun has a firing pin, that the bullets are made out of lead and not marshmallows, that there is air to carry the sound, and so on.

balls continue rolling. In other words, we need to predict two new ROLLING histories. What should those two new histories look like? What should be their spatio-temporal extent? Surely neither can extend beyond the collision point. Should the two new histories end exactly at the collision point? If the answer is *no*, then clearly we are in trouble, since we can iterate this process indefinitely. We now have two new histories, say H11" and H21". From those we need to conclude yet two more histories, and so on (see Fig. 5). It follows that the two new ROLLING histories H11" and H21" must end exactly at the collision. What set of axioms could guarantee this property? Furthermore, suppose we managed to provide axioms that constrain the two new histories to end at the time of the collision. How could we effectively *compute* this time given the axioms?

The key property of each of the two new histories is that it will persist *until it meets another history in spacetime*, which in this case happens to be the other

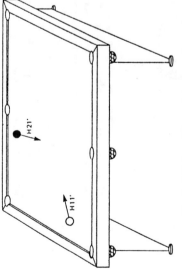

Fig. 4. Initial conditions of the scenario.

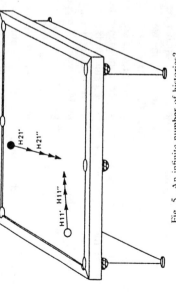

Fig. 5. An infinite number of histories?

The alternative is to be less conservative and base the predictions on only very partial information, hoping that those factors which have been ignored will not get in the way. This means that from time to time we must be prepared to make mistakes in our predictions (after all, the ball *might* turn out to be a miniature hand grenade whose fuse has just run out, and someone *might* have tampered with the gun), and be able to recover from them when we do. We will call this the *qualification problem*.[3] To summarize, it is the problem of making sound predictions about the future without taking into account everything about the past. Notice that the problem would disappear if we were willing to dramatically idealize the world: we could take it as a fact that noise always follows the firing of a loaded gun, and simply assume that guns always have firing pins, that there are never vacuum conditions, and so on. The premise, however, is that such an overidealization is a nonsolution, since the whole point is for our robots to be able to function in a realistically complex environment.

Severe as it is, the qualification problem is not the only problem that exists, and even if we solved it we would still be in trouble. Briefly, although we would be able to make individual inferences fairly easily, we might be forced to make very many of them. Since we are interested in the prediction task, let us explain the problem in the particular context of predicting the future.

The problem now has to do with the length of time intervals in the future to which the predictions refer (regardless of how much information about the past we require in order to make the predictions), or with the "then" part of the "if-then" inference mentioned earlier. Again, it involves a tradeoff between efficiency and reliability. The most conservative prediction refers to a very short interval of time, in fact an instantaneous one, but that makes it very hard to reason about more lengthy future periods. For example, if on the basis of observing a ball rolling we predict that it will roll just a little bit further, in order to predict that it will roll a long distance we must iterate this process many times (in fact, an infinite number of times). We will call this the *extended prediction* problem.[4]

We have seen the problem arise in classical physics: given (e.g.) the force f at time t, you can only deduce the velocity in the infinitesimal time period following t. In order to deduce the velocity after a finite amount of time you must perform integration over the appropriate interval, but you do not know which interval it is.

The disadvantages of the conservative prediction which refers to only a short time period suggest making predictions about more lengthy intervals. For example, when you hit a billiard ball you predict that it will roll in a straight line until hitting the edge of the table, and when you throw a ball into the air you predict that it will have a parabolic trajectory. The problem with these more ambitious predictions is again that they are defeasible, since, for example, a neighbor's window might prevent the ball from completing the parabola. Indeed, this is exactly the problem we encountered in the histories framework: we had no coherent criterion for determining the duration of the predicted ROLLING histories.

To summarize, the general extended prediction problem is that although we may be able to make predictions about short future intervals, we might have to make a whole lot of them before we can predict anything about a substantial part of the future. A special case of this is the *persistence* problem, which is predicting on the basis of the past that a fact will remain unchanged throughout a lengthy future interval (as opposed to the general problem of inferring arbitrary things about such an interval). For example, when we take the billiard ball out of the pocket and place it on a chosen spot on the table, we would like to predict that it will remain in that spot until we hit it.[5]

This problem was noticed a long time ago in the particular context of the *situation calculus*, the formalism introduced by John McCarthy and Pat Hayes in 1969 [3]. The situation calculus takes as basic the notion of *situations*, which are snapshots of the world at a given moment in time. The result of performing an *action* is the transition from one situation to another.[6]

For example, if the action PAINT(HOUSE17, RED) is taken in any situation s_1, the result is a situation s_2 in which the color of HOUSE17 is red. But now consider taking the action REARRANGE-FURNITURE in s_2, which results in a new situation s_3. What is the color of HOUSE17 in s_3? One would like to say that it is still red, since rearranging the furniture does not affect the color of the house, but unfortunately the formalism does not say that. We could add to the formalism the fact that after you rearrange the furniture the color of the house

---

[3] Naming history. In the past we have called it both the *intra-frame problem* and the *initiation problem*. Later we found these inappropriate, and since Matt Ginsberg pointed out the similarity between "our" problem and the problem John McCarthy called the *qualification problem*, it was decided to adopt the latter term. Although McCarthy's notion might have been broader than the one presented here, we think we are not misusing the terminology too badly.

[4] More naming history. In the past we called it the *inter-frame problem*. We then regretted that name and, borrowing from [4], renamed it the *persistence problem*. Finally, we realized that persistence was a special case of the general problem, that of predicting occurrences over extended periods of time, and hence the final (or, at least, current) name.

[5] A philosophical aside. In [4] it was noted that most facts in the world are persistent, and luckily so, because otherwise the world would appear very chaotic and unpredictable to us (or, to repeat the reinterpretation of the well-known phrase, the world would become a "blooming buzz"). Actually, an alternative view is possible, which relies on a cognitive version of the uncertainty principle. According to this view much of the world is indeed in a state of unfathomable flux, perhaps most of it, and we latch onto the (possibly scarce) time invariants simply because that is all we are capable of doing. The objects and properties of which we talk and think are exactly those out of which we can construct meaningful assertions that are not invalid by the time they are constructed.

[6] For those familiar with dynamic logic, this is precisely the view of the world in a dynamic logic with only deterministic atomic programs and only the composition operator.

remains unchanged, and this would be what McCarthy and Hayes call a *frame axiom*. The problem is that you'd need many such axioms: rearranging the furniture doesn't clean the floors, doesn't change the president of the United States, and the list can be continued infinitely.

(Notice that the problem becomes even worse if one allows concurrent actions, which the situation calculus did not. In this case the frame axioms are simply wrong: someone *might* paint your house while you are busy rearranging your furniture. So we must add an exception to the rule: rearranging furniture results in no change in the color of the house, unless in the meanwhile someone paints the house a different color. But even this isn't quite right, since although someone might paint your house, he might be using a paint that fades away immediately. Therefore we must state an exception to the exception, and so on.)

McCarthy and Hayes called this the *frame problem*. We have had mixed success persuading colleagues that the persistence problem and the frame problem coincide. Since the frame problem was never defined in more detail or generality than it was two paragraphs ago, it seems that the argument is somewhat futile. Certainly philosophers have read into the frame problem even more than the general extended prediction problem (see, e.g., [6]). At any rate, these terminological quibbles are not crucial. What is important is to agree on the problems.

3. Summary

We have defined two problems that arise when one tries to predict the future both reliably and efficiently, the *qualification problem* and the *extended prediction problem*. In contrast with the frame problem, these two problems do not depend on any particular underlying formalism. We have not offered a solution to either problem here; for that the reader is referred to [7].

REFERENCES

1. Bobrow, D.G. (Ed.). *Qualitative Reasoning about Physical Systems* (North-Holland. Amsterdam, 1984); also: *Artificial Intelligence* **24** (1984) Special volume.
2. Hayes, P.J., Naive physics 1—Ontology for liquids, in: *Formal Theories of the Commonsense World* (Ablex, Norwood, NJ, 1984).
3. McCarthy, J.M. and Hayes, P.J., Some philosophical problems from the standpoint of artificial intelligence, in: *Readings in Artificial Intelligence* (Tioga, Palo Alto, CA, 1981) 431–450.
4. McDermott, D.V., A temporal logic for reasoning about processes and plans, *Cognitive Sci.* **6** (1982) 101–155.
5. Montague, R., Deterministic theories, in: R.H. Thomason (Ed.), *Formal Philosophy: Selected Papers of Richard Montague* (Yale University Press, New Haven, CT, 1974).
6. Pylyshyn, Z.W. (Ed.), *The Robot's Dilemma* (Ablex, Norwood, NJ, 1986).
7. Shoham, Y., *Reasoning about Change* (MIT Press, Boston, MA, 1987).

Received May 1987; revised version received October 1987

PATRICK J. HAYES*

The Frame Problem and Related Problems in Artificial Intelligence

Summary

The frame problem arises in attempts to formalise problem–solving processes involving interactions with a complex world. It concerns the difficulty of keeping track of the consequences of the performance of an action in, or more generally of the making of some alteration to, a representation of the world. The paper contains a survey of the problem, showing how it arises in several contexts and relating it to some traditional problems in philosophical logic. In the second part of the paper several suggested partial solutions to the problem are outlined and compared. This comparison necessitates an analysis of what is meant by a representation of a robot's environment. Different notions of representation give rise to different proposed solutions. It is argued that a theory of causal relationships is a necessity for any general solution. The significance of this, and the problem in general, for natural (human and animal) problem solving is discussed, and several desiderata for efficient representational schemes are outlined.

Introduction

We consider some problems which arise in attempting a logical analysis of the structure of a robot's beliefs.

A *robot* is an intelligent system equipped with sensory capabilities, operating in an environment similar to the everyday world inhabited by human.robots.

* University of Edinburgh

By *belief* is meant any piece of information which is explicitly stored in the robot's memory. New beliefs are formed by (at least) two distinct processes: *thinking* and *observation*. The former involves operations which are purely internal to the belief system: the latter involves interacting with the *world*, that is, the external environment and, possibly, other aspects of the robot's own structure.

Beliefs will be represented by statements in a formal logical calculus, called the *belief calculus* L_b. The process of inferring new assertions from earlier ones by the *rules of inference* of the calculus will represent thinking (McCarthy, 1959, 1963; McCarthy and Hayes, 1969; Green, 1969; Hayes, 1971).

There are convincing reasons why L_b must *include* L_c – classical first-order logic. It has often been assumed that a moderately adequate belief logic can be obtained merely by adding *axioms* to L_c (a first-order theory); however I believe that it will certainly be necessary to add extra rules of inference to L_c, and extra syntactic richness to handle these extra rules.

One can show that, under very general conditions, logical calculi obey the *extension property*: If $S \vdash p$ and $S \subseteq S'$ then $S' \vdash p$. The importance of this is that if a belief p is added to a set S, then all thinking which was legal before, remains legal, so that the robot need not check it all out again.

Time and Change

For him to think about the real world, the robot's beliefs must handle *time*. This has two distinct but related aspects.

(a) There must be beliefs *about* time. For example, beliefs about causality.

(b) The robot lives *in* time: the world changes about him. His beliefs must accommodate in a rational way to this change.

Of these, the first has been very extensively investigated both in A.I. and philosophical logic, while the second has been largely ignored until very recently: it is more difficult. The first is solely concerned with thinking: the second involves observation.

The standard device for dealing with (a) is the introduction of *situation variables* (McCarthy, 1963; McCarthy and Hayes, 1969) or *possible* worlds (Hintikka, 1967; Kripke, 1963). Symbols prone to change their denotations with the passage of time are enriched with an extra argument place which is filled with a term (often a variable) denoting a *situation* which one can think of intuitively as a time instant; although other readings are possible. In order to make statements about the relationships between situations, and the effects of actions, we also introduce terms denoting *events*, and the function R (read: *result*) which takes events and situations into new situations. Intuitively, "$R(e,s)$" denotes the situation which results when the event e happens in the situation s. By "event" we mean a change in the world: "his switching on the light", "the explosion", "the death of Caesar". This is a minor technical simplification of the notation and terminology used in McCarthy and Hayes (1969) and Hayes (1971). Notice that all the machinery is defined within L_c. The situation calculus is a first-order theory.

Using situations, fairly useful axiomatisations can be obtained for a number of simple problems involving sequences of actions and events in fairly complicated worlds (Green, 1969; McCarthy and Hayes, 1969).

The Frame Problem

Given a certain description of a situation s – that is, a collection of statements of the form $\phi \llbracket s \rrbracket$, where the fancy brackets mean that *every* situation in ϕ is an occurrence of 's' – we want to be able to infer as much as possible about $R(e,s)$. Of course, what we can infer will depend upon the properties of e. Thus we require assertions of the form:

$$\phi_1[s] \ \& \ \psi(e) \supset \phi_2[R(e,s)] \tag{1}$$

Such an assertion will be called a *law of motion*. The frame problem can be briefly stated as the problem of finding adequate collections of laws of motion.

Notice how easily human thinking seems to be able to handle such inferences. Suppose I am describing to a child how to build towers of bricks. I say "You can put the brick on top of this one onto some other one, if that one has not got anything else on it." The child *knows* that the other blocks will stay put during the move. But if I write the

corresponding law of motion:

$$(\text{on}(b_1,b_2,s) \ \& \ \forall z.\ \neg\text{on}(z,b_3,s)) \supset \text{on}(b_1,b_3,R(\text{move}(b_2,b_3),s)) \tag{2}$$

then nothing follows concerning the other blocks. What assertions could we write down which would capture the knowledge that the child has about the world?

One does not want to be obliged to give a law of motion for *every* aspect of the new situation. For instance, one feels that it is prolix to have a law of motion to the effect that if a block is not *moved*, then it stays where it is. And yet such laws – instances of (1) in which $\phi_1 = \phi_2$ – are necessary in first-order axiomatisations. They are called *frame axioms*. Their only function is to allow the robot to infer that an event does *not* affect an assertion. Such inferences are necessary: but one feels that they should follow from more general considerations than a case-by-case listing of axioms, especially as the number of frame axioms increases rapidly with the complexity of the problem. Raphael (1971) describes the difficulty thoroughly.

This phenomenon is to be expected. Logically, s and $R(e,s)$ are simply different entities. There is no *a priori* justification for inferring any properties of $R(e,s)$ from those of s. If it were usually the case that events made widespread and drastic alterations to the world (explosions, the Second Coming, etc.), then we could hardly expect anything better than the use of frame axioms to describe in detail, for each event, exactly what changes it brings about. Our expectation of a more general solution is based on the fact that the world is, fortunately for robots, fairly stable. Most events – especially those which are likely to be considered in planning – make only small local changes in the world, and are not expected to touch off long chains of cause and effect.

Frame Rules

We introduce some formalism in order to unify the subsequent discussions. Any general solution to the frame problem will be a method for allowing us to transfer properties from a situation s to its successor $R(e,s)$; and we expect such a licence to be sensitive to the form of the assertion, to what is known about the event e, and possibly to other facts.

Consider the rule scheme FR:

$$\chi, \phi[s], \psi(e) \vdash \phi[R(e,s)] \qquad \text{(FR)}$$
$$\textit{provided } \aleph(e, \phi, \psi).$$

where $\aleph$ is some condition on e, ϕ and ψ, expressed of course in the metalanguage. We will call such a rule a *frame rule*. The hope is that frame rules can be used to give a general mechanism for replacing the frame axioms, and also admit an efficient implementation, avoiding the search and relevancy problems which plague systems using axioms (Green, 1969; Raphael, 1971).

One must, when considering a frame rule, be cautious that it does not allow contradictions to be generated. Any addition of an inference rule to L_c, especially if not accompanied by extra syntax, brings the risk of inconsistency, and will, in any case, have dramatic effects on the metatheory of the calculus. For instance, the deduction theorem fails. Thus a careful investigation of each case is needed. In some cases, a frame rule has a sufficiently simple $\aleph$ condition that it may be replaced by an *axiom scheme*, resulting in a more powerful logic in which the deduction theorem holds. This usually makes the metatheory easier and implementation more difficult.

Some Partial Solutions Using Frame Rules

The literature contains at least four suggestions for handling the problem which are describable by frame rules. In each case we need some extra syntactic machinery.

Frames

Following McCarthy and Hayes (1969), one assumes a finite number of monadic second-order predicates P_i. If $\vdash P_i(h)$ for a non-logical symbol h (predicate, function or individual constant) then we say that h is in the ith *block* of the frame. The frame rule is

$$P_{i_1}(h_1), ..., P_{i_n}(h_n), \phi[s], P_j(e) \vdash \phi[R(e,s)] \qquad \text{(3)}$$

where $h_1,...,h_n$ are all the non logical symbols which occur *crucially* in ϕ, and $i_k \neq j$, $1 \leq k \leq n$. Here *crucial* is some syntactic relation between h and ϕ; different relations give different logics, with a stronger or weaker frame rule.

Causal connection

We assume (Hayes 1971) that there is a 3-place predicate $\rightarrow(x,y,s)$ (read: x is connected to y in situation s) which has the intuitive meaning that if x is not connected to y, then any change to y does not affect x. It seems reasonable that $\rightarrow$ should be a partial ordering on its first two arguments (reflexive and transitive). The frame rule is:

$$\phi[s], \neg\rightarrow(h_1, e, s), ..., \neg\rightarrow(h_n, e, s) \vdash \phi[R(e,s)] \qquad \text{(4)}$$

where (i) ϕ is an atom or the negation of an atom; (ii) $h_1,...,h_n$ are all the terms which occur *crucially* in ϕ.

If we insisted only that $\neg\rightarrow(h_i,e,s)$ is not provable (rather than $\neg\rightarrow(h_i,e,s)$ *is* provable) then the rule is much stronger but no longer obeys the extension property. This is analogous to PLANNER's method below.

MICRO-PLANNER

The problem solving language MICRO-PLANNER (Sussman and Winograd, 1969) uses a subset of predicate calculus enriched with notations which control the system's search for proofs. We will ignore the latter aspect for the present and describe the underlying formalism. Its chief peculiarity is that it has no negation, and is therefore not troubled by the need for consistency.

Following MICRO-PLANNER we introduce the new unary propositional connective *therase*. Intuitively, *therase* ϕ will mean that ϕ is "erased". We also introduce the notion of a *transition*: an expression $\langle e: \phi_1,...,\phi_n \rangle$. This means intuitively "erase $\phi_1,...,\phi_n$ in passing from s to $R(e,s)$". The frame rule is:

$$\chi, \phi[s], \langle e: \phi_1,...,\phi_n \rangle \vdash \phi[R(e,s)] \qquad \text{(5)}$$

where (i) ϕ is an atom; (ii) ϕ contains no variables (other than s); (iii) χ, *therase* $\phi_1, ...,$ *therase* $\phi_n \nvdash$ *therase* $\phi[s]$. Notice the negated inference in (iii).

STRIPS

The problem-solving system STRIPS (Fikes and Nilsson, 1971) uses the full predicate calculus enriched with special notations ("operator descriptions") describing events, and ways of declaring certain predicates to be *primitive*. We can use transitions to describe this also. The frame rule is:

$$\phi[s], \langle e: \phi_1, \ldots, \phi_n \rangle \vdash \phi[R(e, s)] \tag{6}$$

where (i) ϕ is an atom or the negation of an atom; (ii) ϕ contains no variables (other than s); (iii) the predicate symbol in ϕ is *primitive*; (iv) $\phi[s]$ is not an instance of any ϕ_i, $1 \leqslant i \leqslant n$. Notice the similarity to (5). *Primitive* can be axiomatised by the use of a monadic second-order predicate, as in (1) above.

These four rules have widely divergent logical properties. Rule (3) is replaceable by an axiom scheme, and is thus rather elementary. It is also very easy to implement efficiently (theorem-proving cognoscenti may be worried by the higher-order expressions, but these are harmless since they contain no variables). Variations are possible, e.g., we might have disjointness axioms for the P_i and require $\neg P_j(h_k)$ rather than $P_{ik}(h_k)$: this would be closely similar to a special case of (4).

Retaining consistency in the presence of (3) requires in non-trivial problems that the P_i classification be rather coarse. (For instance, *no change in position ever affects the colour of things, so predicates of location could be classed apart from predicates of colour.) Thus frames, although useful, do not completely solve the problem.

Rule (4) is also replaceable by an axiom scheme, and the restriction to literals can be eliminated, with some resultant complication in the rule. Also, there is a corresponding model theory and a completeness result (Hayes, 1971), so that one can gain an intuition as to what (4) *means*. Retaining consistency with (4) requires some care in making logical definitions.

Rules (5) and (6) have a different character. Notice that (6) is almost a special case of (5): that in which *therase* $\phi \vdash therase\ \psi$ if ψ is not primitive or ψ is an instance of ϕ. The importance of this is that instantiation, and probably primitiveness also, are *decideable*, and conditions (iii) and (iv) in (6) are effectively determined solely by examining the transition, whereas condition (iii) in (5) is in general not decida-ble and in any case requires an examination of all of χ: in applications, the whole set of beliefs. MICRO-PLANNER uses its ability to control the theorem-proving process to partly compensate for both of these problems, but with a more expressive language they would become harder to handle. Notice also that (5) does not satisfy the extension property, while (6) does, provided we allow at most one transition to be unconditionally asserted for each event.

Maintaining "consistency" with (5) is a matter of the axiom-writer's art. There seem to be no general guidelines. Maintaining consistency with (6) seems to be largely a matter of judicious choice of *primitive* vocabulary. There is no articulated model theory underlying (5) or (6). They are regarded more as syntactic tools – analogous to evaluation rules for a high-level programming language – than as descriptive assertions.

A (Very) Simple Example: Toy Bricks

$$\neg above(x, x, s) \tag{A1}$$
$$x = Table \lor above(x, Table, s) \tag{A2}$$
$$above(x, y, s) \equiv .\,on(x, y, s) \lor \exists z.\,on(z, y, s) \,\&\, above(x, z, s) \tag{A3}$$
$$free(x, s) \equiv .\mathbf{A}\, y \sqsupset on(y, x, s) \tag{A4}$$

To enable activity to occur we will have events *move(x,y)*: the brick x is put on top of the brick y. Laws of motion we might consider include:

$$free(x, s) \,\&\, x \neq y. \supset on(x, y, R(move(x, y), s)) \tag{A5}$$
$$free(x, s) \,\&\, w \neq x \,\&\, on(w, z, s). \supset on(w, z, R(move(x, y), s)) \tag{A6}$$
$$free(x, s) \,\&\, w \neq x \,\&\, above(w, z, s). \supset above(w, z, R(move(x, y), s)) \tag{A7}$$

$$free(x, s) \,\&\, w \neq y \,\&\, free(w, s). \supset free(w, R(move(x, y), s)) \tag{A8}$$

Of these, (A6–A8) are frame axioms. (In fact, (A7) and (A8) are redundant, since they can, with some difficulty, be derived from (A6) and (A3), (A4) respectively.) (A5) assumes somewhat idealistically that there is always enough space on y to put a new brick.

Rule (3) cannot be used in any intuitively satisfactory way to replace A6–A8.

Rule (4) can be used. We need only to specify when bricks are connected to events:

$$\rightarrow (x, move(y, z), s) \equiv . \; x = y \lor above(x, y, s) \qquad (A9)$$

Using (A9) and (A3), (A4), it is not hard to show that

$$free(x, s) \; \& \; w \neq x \; \& \; on(w, z, s). \supset \lnot \rightarrow (w, move(x, y), s) \; \&$$
$$\lnot \rightarrow (z, move(x, y), s)$$

and thus, we can infer *on* {*w*, *z*, *R*[*move*(*x*, *y*), *s*]} by rule (7). (A7) and (A8) are similar but simpler. (One should remark also that (A4) is an example of an illegal definition, in the presence of (4), since it suppresses a variable which the rule needs to be aware of. It is easy to fix this up in various ways.)

Rule (5) can also be used, but we must ensure that *therase* does a sufficiently thorough job. Various approaches are possible. The following seems to be most in the spirit of **MICRO-PLANNER**. In its terms, *on* and *above* statements will be in the data-base, but *free* statements will not. The necessary axioms will be:

$$therase \; free(x, s) \qquad (A10)$$
$$therase \; on(x, y, s) \; \& \; above(y, z, s) \supset therase \; above \; (x, z, s) \qquad (A11)$$
$$free(x, s) \supset \langle move(x, y) \colon on(x, z, s) \rangle \qquad (A12)$$

To infer statements *free*[*x*, *R*(*e*, *s*)], we must first generate enough *on*[*x*, *y*, *R*(*e*, *s*)] statements by rule (5), and then use (A4), since by (A10), rule (5) never makes such an inference directly. (We could omit (A10) and replace (A12) by

$$free(x, y) \supset \langle move(x, y) \colon on(x, z, s), free(y, s) \rangle . \qquad (A13)$$

This would, in **MICRO-PLANNER** terms, be a decision to keep *free* assertions in the data base.

Notice that **MICRO-PLANNER** has no negation and hence no need to *therase* such assertions as $\lnot on(x, y, s)$. If it had negation we would replace (A12) by

$$free(x, y) \supset \langle move(x, y) \colon on(x, z, s), \lnot on(x, y, s) \rangle \qquad (A14)$$

and add

$$therase \; \lnot on(x, y, s) \; \& \; above(y, z, s) \supset therase \; \lnot above(x, z, s) \qquad (A15)$$

Notice the close relations between (A3), (A11) and (A15).

Rule (6) can be used similarly to (5), but we are no longer able to use axioms such as (A11) and (A15). The solution which seems closest in spirit to **STRIPS** is to declare that *on* is primitive but that *above* and *free* are not, and then simply use (A14). The "world model" (Fikes and Nilsson, 1971) would then consist of a collection of atoms *on* (*a,b*), or their negations, and the system would rederive *above* and *free* assertions when needed. This is very similar to MICRO-PLANNER's "data-base", and we could have used rule (5) in an exactly similar fashion.

Implementing Frame Rules

Some ingenuity with list structures enables one to store assertions in such a way that

(i) Given *s*, one can easily find all assertions φ[*s*].
(ii) Each symbol denoting a situation is stored only once.
(iii) The relationships between *s* and *R*(*e,s*), etc., are stored efficiently and are easily retrieved.
(iv) To apply a frame rule to *s*, one need only:
  (a) Create a new cell pointing to *s*.
  (b) Move two pointers.
  (c) Check each φ[*s*] for condition א: if it holds, move one pointer.

In the case of a rule like (5) or the variation to (4), where א is a negative condition (⊬), we need only examine those φ[*s*] for which the condition *fails*, resulting in greater savings.

Space does not permit a description of the method, but MICRO-PLANNER and STRIPS use related ideas. (The authors of these systems seem to confuse to some extent their particular implementations with the logical description of the frame rules, even to the extent of claiming that a logical description is impossible.)

Consistency and Counterfactuals

Frame rules can be efficiently implemented and, in their various ways, allow the replacement of frame axioms by more systematic ma-

and, more seriously, χ contains only assertions of the form $t_1 \neq t_2$ or of the form $P(t_1,...,t,...,t_n)$ and $P(t_1,...,u,...,t_n) \supset t = u$. Under these constraints, consistency is decidable and can even be computed quite efficiently. Moreover, MCSs are unique, so the second problem evaporates. However, it is not clear whether non-trivial problems can be reasonably stated in such a restricted vocabulary.

Conclusions

In the long run, I believe that a mixture of frame rules and consistency-based methods will be required for non-trivial problems, corresponding respectively to the "strategic" and "tactical" aspects of computing descriptions of new situations. In the short term we need to know more about the properties of both procedures.

One outstanding defect of present approaches is the lack of a clear model theory. Formal systems for handling the frame problem are beginning to proliferate, but a clear *semantic* theory is far from sight. Even to begin such a project would seem to require deep insight into our presystematic intuitions about the physical world.

Observations and the Qualification Problem

We have so far been entirely concerned with thinking. The situation calculus is a belief calculus for beliefs *about* time. Observations – interactions with the real world – introduce new problems. We must now consider the second aspect of time (b.p.).

Almost any general belief about the result of his own actions may be contradicted by the robot's observations. He may conclude that he can drive to the airport; only to find a flat tire. A human immediately says, "Ah, now I cannot go". Simply *adding* a new belief ("the tire is flat") renders an earlier conclusion false, though it was a valid conclusion from the earlier set of beliefs, *all of which are still present.* Thus we do *not* assume that the robot had concluded "*If* my tires are OK, *then* I can get to the airport" since there are no end of different things which might go wrong, and he cannot be expected to hedge his conclusions round with thousands of qualifications (McCarthy and Hayes, 1969).

chinery. But there is a constant danger, in constructing larger axiomatisations, of introducing inconsistency. An alternative approach avoids this by transferring properties ϕ from s to $R(e,s)$ *as long as it is consistent to do so*, rather than according to some fixed-in-advance rule.

Suppose we have a set χ of general laws which are to hold in every situation, and a description of – a set of assertions about – the situation s: $\{\phi_1[s],...,\phi_n[s]\}$. Using laws of motion we will directly infer certain properties $\psi_1,..., \psi_m$ of $R(e,s)$: the set of these constitutes a partial description $\phi_i[R(e,s)]$. To compute a more adequate one, we add assertions $\phi_i[R(e,s)]$ in some order, *checking at each stage for consistency with* χ; if a $\phi_i[R(e,s)]$ makes the set inconsistent, it is rejected. This continues until no more ϕ_i can be added. In this way we compute a maximal consistent subset (MCS) of the inconsistent set

$$\chi \cup \{\psi_1,...,\psi_m, \phi_1[R(e,s)],...,\phi_n[R(e,s)]\}.$$

There are two big problems: (1) Consistency is not a decidable or even semi-decidable property. Thus for practicality one has to accept a large restriction on the expressive power of the language. (2) There are in general many different MCSs of an inconsistent set, and so we must have ways of choosing an appropriate one. In terms of the procedure outlined above, we need a good ordering on the ϕ_i.

This procedure is closely similar to one described by Rescher (1964) to provide an analysis of counterfactual reasonings ("If I had struck this match yesterday, it would have lit", when in fact I didn't.). Rescher is aware of the first problem but gives no solution. His major contribution is to the second problem, which he solves by the use of *modal categories*: a hierarchical classification of assertions into grades of law-likeness. One never adds $\phi_i[R(e,s)]$ unless every ϕ_j with a lower classification has already been tested. This machinery is especially interesting as in (Simon and Rescher, 1966) it is linked to Simon's theory of causality (Simon, 1953). One puts ϕ_i in a lower category than ϕ_j just in case ϕ_i *causes* ϕ_j (or $\neg\phi_j$), more or less. Space does not permit a complete description of this interesting material which is fully covered in the references cited. In spite of its appeal, the first problem is still unsolved.

In unpublished work at Stanford, Jack Buchanan has independently worked out another version of the procedure. The first problem is handled by accepting a drastic restriction on the language. Every ϕ_i is an atom or the negation of an atom – c.f. frame rules (7), (8) and (9) –

Clearly this implies that the belief logic does not obey the extension property *for observations*: to expect otherwise would be to hope for omnipotence. However, we are little nearer any positive ideas for handling the inferences correctly.

John McCarthy recently pointed out to me that MICRO-PLANNER has a facility (called THNOT) which apparently solves the problem nicely. I will translate this into a slightly different notation.

We introduce a new unary propositional connective *proved*, which is supposed to mean "can be proved from the current collection of beliefs". Then we can write axioms like the following:

$$flat\,(tire) \supset kaput\,(car)$$

$$\neg proved\;kaput\,(car) \supset at\,\{robot,\,airport,\,R[drive(airport),\,s]\} \quad (A17)$$

from which $at(robot,\,airport,\,...)$ should be concluded *until* we add:

$$flat\,(tire) \quad (A18)$$

at which point the $\neg proved...$ becomes false. ($\neg proved$ is PLANNER's THNOT).

To make this work we could try the following rules of inference.

$$\phi \vdash proved\;\phi \quad (P1)$$

$$\chi \vdash \neg proved\;\phi \quad (P2)$$

where $\chi \nvdash \phi$.

(P2) fails the extension property, as expected. (It also has the difficulties of effectiveness which worry frame rule (5), but we will ignore these.)

Unfortunately, (P1) and (P2) are *inconsistent*. Suppose $\chi \nvdash \phi$, but that ϕ is consistent with χ. Then by (P2), $\neg proved\;\phi$. But if we now add ϕ (an observation: the flat tire), then by (P1) $proved\;\phi$: an overt contradiction. MICRO-PLANNER avoids this by denying (P1) and treating "ϕ and $\neg proved\;\phi$" as consistent. But this is a counsel of despair, since it clearly is not, according to the intuitive meanings.

The logical answer is to somehow make *proved* refer to the set χ of antecedents. The direct approach to this requires extremely cumbersome notation and a very strong logic which partly contains its own metatheory, thus coming close to Gödel inconsistency. Fortunately we do not need to *describe* sets χ of assertions, but only to *refer* to them, and this can be done with a very weak notation, similar to situation variables.

Assume that every belief is decorated with a constant symbol called the *index*: we will write it as a superscript. Indices denote the robot's internal belief states just as situation terms denote external situations. Observations are analogous to events. Assertions $proved\;\phi$ now have an extra index which identifies the state of belief at the time the inference was tested. The above rules of inference become:

$$\phi^s \vdash proved^s\;\phi^s \quad (P1')$$

$$\chi \vdash \neg proved^s\;\phi^s \quad (P2')$$

where $\chi \nvdash \phi^s$ and every member of χ has index s.

In applications we now insist that:
(i) in applying P2', χ contains *all* beliefs with index s;
(ii) whenever an *observation* is added to the beliefs, every index s is replaced by a new one s', *except* those on *proved* assertions.

This is just enough to avoid inconsistency; it clearly does not involve any Gödel-ish difficulties; and (ii) can be very efficiently implemented by frame-rule methods (see section Implementing Frame Rules). Indeed, more complex versions of (ii) which allow for direct contradiction between beliefs and observations can be similarly implemented.

The logic of these indices is trivial, but extensions have some interest. For instance, if we identify indices with situation terms, then expressions of the form $\phi[s]^s$ become legal, with the intuitive meaning "ϕ is true *now*".

Seen this way, the qualification problem is closely linked with the frame problem, and one expects progress in either area to help with the other.

Acknowledgements

This work was supported in part by the Advanced Research Projects Agency of the Office of the Secretary of Defense (SD−183), and in part by the Science Research Council.

I am also grateful for comment, criticism and contributions from Jack Buchanan, Richard Fikes, Malcolm Newey, Nils Nilsson, John

Rulifson, Richard Waldinger, Richard Weyrauch and from John McCarthy, to whom I am also grateful for the invitation to visit the Stanford Artificial Intelligence Project, where this paper was written. Most of all, I thank my wife, Jackie, for improving my English; controlling my verbosity, and typing innumerable drafts of the manuscript.

Temporal Data Base Management*

Thomas L. Dean

Department of Computer Science, Brown University, Providence, RI 02912, U.S.A.

Drew V. McDermott

Department of Computer Science, Yale University, New Haven, CT 06520, U.S.A.

Recommended by Mark Stefik

ABSTRACT

Reasoning about time typically involves drawing conclusions on the basis of incomplete information. Uncertainty arises in the form of ignorance, indeterminacy, and indecision. Despite the lack of complete information, a problem solver is continually forced to make predictions in order to pursue hypotheses and plan for the future. Such predictions are frequently contravened by subsequent evidence. This paper presents a computational approach to temporal reasoning that directly confronts these issues. The approach centers around techniques for managing a data base of assertions corresponding to the occurrence of events and the persistence of their effects over time. The resulting computational framework performs the temporal analog of (static) reason maintenance by keeping track of dependency information involving assumptions about the truth of facts spanning various intervals of time. The system described in this paper extends classical predicate-calculus data bases, such as those used by PROLOG, to deal with time in an efficient and natural manner.

1. Introduction

In most predicate-calculus data base systems (e.g., [4, 9, 16]), all (believed) assertions are considered timelessly true. Time, if it is dealt with at all, is handled by routines supplied by the application programmer. It seems unreasonable that a functionality as frequently invoked as reasoning about time has to be reimplemented by every researcher who finds it necessary to make use of that functionality. A significant amount of common-sense reasoning involves time in one aspect or another. Many of the facts we are accustomed to

deal with change over time, and hence many of the inferences we make depend crucially upon whether or not a fact or conjunction of facts is true at a point or throughout an interval. For a large number of applications, it makes sense to have the machinery for performing routine temporal inference built into the deductive engine underlying the data base.

The primary claim of this paper is that it is possible to implement a temporal data base that naturally and efficiently extends classical predicate-calculus data bases. The extension proposed here takes into account that temporal information is incomplete (e.g., our knowledge concerning the occurrence of events rarely admits to a total ordering), often metric (e.g., the duration or time of occurrence of certain events is known within metric bounds), and defeasible (i.e., temporal reasoning proceeds on the basis of assumptions concerning the persistence of certain facts; assumptions that may turn out to be unwarranted as new information is acquired and further inferences are made). In order to accomplish this extension, we replace the notion of an assertion in classical data bases with the *time token*, allowing us to refer to an *interval* of time during which a given fact or event *type* is alleged to be true. In addition, we extend the notion of (static) data dependency in predicate-calculus data bases [12] to deal with tokens spanning prespecified intervals.

The approach to temporal reasoning described in this paper is referred to as *temporal imagery* [7]. Temporal imagery was conceived as a process akin to visually scanning large amounts of data arranged in the form of a map. This analogy has limited usefulness, but it will serve as a starting point for our discussion.

The intuitive picture you should have of the process of temporal imagery is one of constructing maps, much like the maps used for plotting spatial information, and then scanning those maps to extract information and notice patterns. In many respects, time is a lot like space. The events in time are like the objects in a single-dimensional space. A temporal map can be described by a graph in which the nodes are instants of time associated with the beginning and ending of events, and the arcs connecting these nodes describe relations between pairs of instants. Certain pairs of instants are more important than others, as they indicate important events and spans of time over which facts are said to be true. Since the information stored in a temporal map corresponds to an agent's knowledge of the world, the instants are likely to be partially ordered. Reasoning about time in this framework consists of scanning this graph in order to determine how one event is related to another and what might be true during, before, or after an event. Since the instants are not totally ordered one can make hypotheses about what the consequences of certain additional ordering constraints might be and then proceed to explore some of those consequences. Moving from one instant in time to another should not require cranking a simulation backwards or forward; it is assumed that it is quite easy to jump about on this graph and simultaneously keep track of a number of situations occurring at different times.

*This work was supported by the Advanced Research Projects Agency of the Department of Defense and monitored by the Office of Naval Research under contract N00014-85-K-0301.

Artificial Intelligence **32** (1987) 1–55

0004-3702/87/$3.50 © 1987, Elsevier Science Publishers B.V. (North-Holland)

One of the important characteristics of this sort of graphical representation is that it can be updated incrementally. That is to say, as new events and facts are added only those parts of the graph that are affected need be changed. This is known as propagating the effects of a change. As this propagation proceeds it is important to be able to recognize when predictions formerly believed to be true are no longer so. This sort of graph scanning and updating is referred to as "reasoning about time from the side" [22]. It's as though all of what you know about the past, present, and future is laid out in front of you.

A program that supports temporal imagery should be capable of determining if a conjunction of facts is true at a time or could be made to be true with some additional constraints on the existing partial order. Using such a program, it should be straightforward to determine the consequences that follow from some proposed change. It should be possible to make conditional predictions (i.e., predictions that depend upon what is currently believed) and then easily notice when such conditions are no longer met. Described in this way the requisite programs sound less like a set of routines for scanning maps and more like a system for retrieving and maintaining information in a data base. Indeed another way of viewing our graphical representation is as an indexing scheme for assertions in a temporalized data base. In Section 3, we'll shift the discussion to explore this perspective, but first let's consider some more general aspects of temporal reasoning.

2. Shallow Temporal Reasoning

All reasoning requires some sort of exploration or search. It is difficult to keep track of all the possible repercussions implicit in the information stored in a person's head or a program's data base—the closure of one's knowledge so to speak. A temporal data base captures what is known about events and their effects occurring over time. The information in a temporal data base only partially specifies the way things could be; there may be a great number of possible completions. Exploration involves constructing some of those possibilities and then choosing the one (or ones) that appear to be most likely (or most appealing if we have a choice in the matter). In planning, exploration might involve determining if certain preconditions for a plan can be satisfied, given what is already known. In medical diagnosis, it might involve seeing if the known facts can be used to explain a symptom. In addition to extracting information from the data base concerning what is possible, it is necessary to confront the consequences of accepting certain possibilities. A diagnostician or planner will want to know what further commitments are required in order to accept an explanation or plan. For instance, if I'm to pick up a friend arriving on a 2:00 PM plane, I'll have to start for the airport right after my morning appointments; if I expect to meet my friend at the gate, I'll have to assume that the traffic on the turnpike will be light. Making commitments invariably leads to having to deal with certain *unforeseen* consequences: if I drive out to the

airport this afternoon, I'm going to miss the colloquium scheduled for 3:30. Noticing when the assumptions supporting a given prediction are undermined by new information is a critical part of coping with uncertain circumstances. If I'm driving along the turnpike and I hear that traffic on the bridge leading to the airport is backed up five miles due to an accident, I will want to be aware that I may be late to pick up my friend. My response might be to revise my strategy for finding my friend once I enter the airport terminal: I'll look in the baggage claim area before I go to the boarding gates. If I were meeting a child, I might feel compelled to stop at a pay phone and have someone at the airline meet the child at the gate.

A large part of temporal reasoning (and problem solving in general) consists of making predictions (guesses) on the basis of incomplete information, explicitly noting the assumptions under which those predictions are warranted, and then noticing when those assumptions are violated in the course of subsequent prediction and information gathering. This section introduces a general framework that supports this sort of reasoning. The framework is called *shallow temporal reasoning*. The reasoning is referred to as shallow because it is broken down into a number of steps, each of which is assumed to require only a small allowance of computational resources to carry out. Despite the relative simplicity of the individual steps, shallow temporal reasoning is not confined to making only simple inferences. Complex reasoning tasks are managed in this framework by performing the steps repeatedly in a cycle of inferences. Shallow temporal reasoning consists of the following steps:

(1) generate a set of candidate hypotheses,
(2) select one hypothesis from among the candidates,
(3) use the selected hypothesis as a basis for prediction,
(4) respond to unforeseen consequences noticed in the course of prediction.

These steps are quite similar to the expand/criticize cycle used in NOAH [27] and serve much the same purpose in general temporal reasoning. Hypotheses correspond to particular outcomes warranted by the currently available information about events, their effects, and their duration and time of occurrence. Committing to a given hypothesis may involve assumptions about the order in which various events occur, how long a fact will remain true, or which of several possible alternatives an agent is likely to choose. The selected hypothesis is used as the basis for making certain inferences or predictions, which are said to *depend upon* the selected hypothesis. These predictions can be divided into two broad categories: *projection* and *refinement*. Projection refers to positing the effects of an event (i.e., determining what new facts follow from the occurrence of an event). Refinement consists of providing a more detailed description of an event, usually by producing a sequence or partially ordered set of (sub)events. Noticing and responding to unforeseen consequences constitutes a form of *debugging*.

It should be noted that in reasoning about time there are a number of combinatorial problems lurking in the background. Job-shop scheduling, travel time optimization, and resource management are all generally assumed to be intractable. The techniques described in this paper are not aimed at "solving" such problems. Their "solution" will, in general, require the clever application of knowledge (usually knowledge specific to a given domain). Shallow temporal reasoning is meant to capture the reasoning of an adept: a problem solver that is good at dealing with the sort of problems that normally confront it. Such a problem solver rarely explores a significant portion of the full search space associated with the problem at hand. The problem solver is not perfect, however, and sometimes it must perform a bit of surgery on a flawed solution in order to deal with some unanticipated event or complicated interaction. The problem solver is knowledgeable enough to analyze the situation and propose a patch that will work in most cases. If after several patches there is no solution in sight, the problem solver should admit that it's in over its head.

3. Temporal Data Bases

A temporal imagery device supporting the sort of functionality outlined in the previous sections can be viewed as a special sort of data base management system. Such a system might consist of:

(1) A data base that captures what is known about events and their effects occurring over time. In particular, it is important to record information about the truth of propositions changing over time. The system should be able to handle the addition of new information and the removal of old information in an efficient manner using some criterion for internal consistency.

(2) A query language that enables application programs to construct and explore hypothetical situations. This language should support simple retrieval of the form: Is it possible that P is true at time T given what is currently known? It should also handle retrieval of the form: Find an interval satisfying some initial constraints such that the conjunction (and $P_1 ... P_n$) is true throughout the interval.

(3) A method for extending the information in the data base. On the basis of information extracted from the data base (antecedent conditions), the user should be able to engage in some sort of forward inference (prediction). The predictions added to the data base in this manner should depend upon the antecedent conditions in some meaningful way.

(4) A mechanism for monitoring the continued validity of conditional predictions. This mechanism would extend the functionality of reason maintenance systems [12] to temporal domains.

The data base is called a *time map* [22]. The routines for retrieval, maintaining internal consistency, and handling forward inference are combined in what is called a *time map management system* or TMM. We will devote the next two subsections to a more detailed introduction to time maps and the complications involved in temporal reason maintenance.

3.1. Time maps

A time map is a graph. Its vertices refer to *points* or *instants* of time corresponding to the beginning and ending of events. These points provide us with convenient frames of reference for reasoning about the temporal relationships between events. To relate one point to another, we introduce the notion of a *point-to-point constraint* or simply a *constraint*. Constraints are represented as directed edges linking two points. Each edge is labeled with an upper and lower bound on the distance separating the two points in time. There can be any number of constraints relating the same two points. If the constraints are consistent with one another, then the maximum of the lower bounds will always be less than or equal to the minimum of the upper bounds. You can relate any two points by finding a path from one point to the other, where a path from pt_0 to pt_n is just a sequence $pt_0 c_1 pt_1 ... c_n pt_n$ such that pt_0 through pt_n are points and c_i is a constraint relating pt_{i-1} to pt_i. Figure 1 shows three points related to one another by several constraints. For every constraint from a point pt_i to a point pt_j with lower bound *low* and upper bound *high* there is an implicit companion constraint (usually not shown in diagrams) from pt_j to pt_i with lower bound −*high* and upper bound −*low*. For each path connecting a pair of points, you can compute an estimate of the distance separating the two points by summing the upper (lower) bounds of the individual constraints in the path. There may be several such paths for any given pair of points. In Fig. 1, $pt_1 c_1 pt_2$, $pt_1 c_2 pt_3 c_3 pt_2$, and $pt_1 c_2 pt_3 c_4 pt_2$ are paths relating pt_1 and pt_2. Their respective bounds are $\langle 5,9 \rangle$, $\langle 6,8 \rangle$, and $\langle -1,11 \rangle$. Generally we're interested only in paths that give either the greatest lower bound or the least upper bound. In Fig. 1, $pt_1 c_2 pt_3 c_3 pt_2$ provides both the greatest lower bound 6 and the least upper bound 8 on the distance separating pt_1 and pt_2. A set of constraints is said to be consistent just in case for all pairs of points $\langle pt_0, pt_n \rangle$ and all paths $pt_0 c_1 pt_1 ... c_n pt_n$ where each c_i is in the set of constraints, the sum of the lower bounds of the c_i is less than or equal to the sum of upper bounds of the c_i. The set of constraints shown in Fig. 1 is consistent.

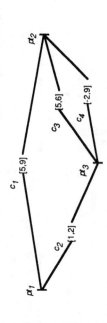

Fig. 1. Relating pairs of points with constraints.

An *interval* is just a pair of points. Each interval consists of a *begin* and an *end* point such that the beginning is constrained to precede or be coincident with the ending. Some intervals are more important than others, because they correspond to a particular occasion when a general type of occurrence happens. These intervals are referred to as *tokens* of that *type*. A type is denoted by a formula like (operational-status lathe17 in-service) or (malfunction assembly-unit34). An interval together with a type will often be referred to as a *time token* (or simply *token* in situations where it should cause no confusion).

Tokens corresponding to facts are referred to as *persistences*. If two tokens with contradictory types (e.g., (operational-status lathe17 in-service) and (operational-status lathe17 out-of-service)) are ordered such that one begins before the other and the earlier could persist longer than the beginning of the later, then the two are said to be *apparently contradictory*. The TMM resolves apparently contradictory tokens by forcing the end of the earlier to precede the beginning of the later. This is referred to as *clipping* the earlier occurring persistence.

Persistences are employed as part of a strategy for default reasoning about how facts change over time. It's convenient to be able to state that one effect of performing some action is that some fact will become true and persist for some period of time without having to be explicit about how long the fact will remain true. The default is simply that it will last just until something is known to make it false. The duration of an event, on the other hand, can generally be predicted to a reasonable degree of precision. The predicted duration of an event is one of its most important attributes. If it takes between 15 and 20 minutes to drive to the airport, then you will want to take that into account in planning to meet a plane. If you have three tasks to finish before leaving the office this evening, each of which take about half an hour, then you should consider this when setting up a dinner date. An important reason for choosing one plan over another is that it takes less time than any of its alternatives.

A classical data base assertion specifies a fact (type) that is timelessly true. Persistences, on the other hand, correspond to intervals during which a fact type is true. In general, there will be many persistences with the same type. Temporal data base queries generally refer to an interval or temporal index that defines the scope of the query. For example, the query (tt pt1 pt2 (and P Q)) is interpreted as "determine if both P and Q are true throughout (tt) the interval from pt1 to pt2." For this query to succeed, the data base management system must find a token of type P and a token of type Q such that each of their corresponding intervals span the interval pt1 to pt2. Since there are likely to be many tokens of a given type, it is important to store them in such a way that the above sort of query can be performed efficiently. Among other things, this involves keeping track of how long persistences can be assumed to endure.

Tokens as they are used in the time map are akin to intervals in James Allen's work [1]. The notion of persistence was developed by Drew McDermott in his temporal logic [22]. McDermott uses predications of the form

(persists some-fact from-some-instant for-some-length-of-time) to represent a guess about how long a fact, once made true, will endure. This guess can be amended to account for new information. Persistences are sometimes confused with histories in the sense that Hayes uses the term [15]. A Hayesian history describes a chunk of space/time in which a given proposition is true. While it is true that persistences have no spatial extent, that is not the critical difference. Histories form a record that is essentially complete. You can retract or modify a history, but you can't change its temporal extent by simply adding more information. In the approach described in this paper, persistences, like Hayes' histories and Allen's intervals, are first and foremost a device to be manipulated. Persistences, however, are first and foremost a device for default reasoning. They were designed so that their temporal extent can be easily modified in the face of new information. Persistences are used in the time map in order to efficiently update the temporal data base to reflect what events are believed to have occurred and the intervals of time over which certain facts are believed to be true.

The time map management system is not simply a simulator. You don't reason by stipulating a set of initial conditions and then simulating those events to generate a time line. As mentioned earlier, the time map is a means of viewing time "from the side." You reason with a time map by making modifications to the data base and then examining the repercussions of those modifications. The time map machinery sees to it that only important changes are brought to the attention of the calling program. As we'll see in the next subsection, the "important changes" are those that involve antecedent conditions used as a basis for making predictions. The TMM has to be able to detect when certain previously established antecedent conditions are no longer tenable and then alert the user that all predictions that depended upon these conditions are no longer supported.

3.2. Temporal reason maintenance

Resolving apparent contradictions is only one part of a strategy for handling shallow temporal reasoning. Most inconsistencies are neither so easily noticed nor so easily resolved. You can't go to a play in New York that starts at 8:00 PM and also attend a reception in Boston which begins at 7:30 PM on the same evening. The fact that these are not both possible depends upon the inference that attending both events requires traveling between their respective locations, a feat which is beyond most of us given the time constraints. Recognizing that some set of tasks or predictions are incompatible often requires a good bit of inference. That is to say the repercussions (projections and detailed descriptions) of a set of events must be explored in order to detect the source of their conflict. Since you can never tell in advance just where things might go wrong and what you may be forced to later retract, you have to keep track of why you believe things so that if the reasons for believing a fact go away, your belief in that fact and its consequences will evaporate as well. Hypothesis generation can be seen as the means for establishing the antecedent conditions supporting a given set of consequent predictions. Hypothesis generation is accomplished using the time map management system's query routines. Querying a changing data base is a tricky thing. It's not sufficient that the query mechanism return correct information; it must also keep track of the conditions under which that information continues to be warranted. If the antecedent conditions should fail, then the consequent predictions should be retracted or a new warrant established.

Systems that make the sort of conditional inferences described in the previous paragraph tend to be nonmonotonic (in the sense that Minsky used the term [25]) in that the addition of new information is likely to result in the removal of old. The term "nonmonotonic" is bandied about in today's literature as though systems exhibiting nonmonotonic behavior were something special, as though one could choose whether to introduce nonmonotonicity into a system for dealing with the real world. Actually, nonmonotonicity is inherent in just about every aspect of reasoning in nontrivial domains. Nonmonotonicity arises as a result of the need to commit to predictions about how the world might be, despite the fact that you are bound to guess wrong on occasion.

The time map machinery extends the functionality of reason maintenance systems like Doyle's [12] to handle temporalized assertions. A (temporal) antecedent condition is generally something of the form: P is believed to be true throughout an interval. In the time map this translates into: there exists a time token of type P such that the token begins before the beginning of the interval and can't be shown to end before the end of the interval. If such a condition obtains, we say that P is *protected* throughout the interval. Notice that this is nonmonotonic. While it may be true initially that it can't be shown that the token ends before the end of the interval, additional constraints may change this. Such conditions are monitored using nonmonotonic data dependencies called *protections* (after [30]). Protections and persistences can interact when one token is constrained by another (contradictory) token as a result of resolving an apparent contradiction. In order to deal with this and similar interactions, the TMM employs a temporal reason maintenance system that keeps track of what protections are warranted and hence what predictions are warranted and supported by protections are warranted.

The TMM takes care of constructing protections for antecedent conditions and installing justifications where necessary. The underlying machinations of the TMM are not visible to the user. The query language appears no more complex than the typical pseudo-predicate-calculus format used in PROLOG [4].

Using the time map to establish a set of antecedent conditions followed by the assertion of some set of consequent predictions illustrates a sort of controlled forward deduction which is typical in shallow temporal reasoning.

The deduction is controlled in that the calling program is responsible for asking the right questions and drawing appropriate conclusions in keeping with its current goals. This control enables the calling program to carefully direct search. The time map also handles a sort of general purpose temporal forward chaining rule that can be used to reason about the physics of a given situation. The advantage of such rules is that they don't require the application program to continually check to see that their antecedent conditions are met. It is assumed that whenever the antecedent conditions are met, it is appropriate to make the consequent inferences. Suppose that you are reasoning about some complex operations in a factory involving flammable liquids and machinery that might produce sparks or generate intense heat. You might want to be particularly sensitive to conditions in which the former is likely to be exposed to the latter. Monitoring such situations by continually querying the data base is clumsy and inefficient. Disallowing such situations altogether is overly restrictive. All you really want is to be alerted to such situations when they arise so that you can exercise caution or prepare for contingencies. The TMM allows one to implement a restricted (no loops) form of envisionment [10, 14] for reasoning about simple processes. The rules can be applied selectively by specifying the rule as a fact token with limited temporal extent. This sort of forward chaining, which we call *auto-projection*, can play an important role in reasoning about time and responding to complex situations. Auto-projection makes it particularly easy to reason about the effects of actions in planning. A plan need only specify the actions, the (partial) order in which they must occur, and the dependencies between the actions in terms of prerequisites. Side effects and actions with conditional effects are handled by the auto-projection facility.

4. Time Map Management

This section discusses how to use the time map management system for temporal reasoning tasks. The terminology presented in previous sections will be carried over into a notation for temporal queries and a set of procedures for constructing and modifying time maps. A pseudo-predicate-calculus notation is used for clarity and compatibility with an existing deductive retrieval system. The language presented here can be thought of as a variant of PROLOG [4], at least as far as the use of unification and backward chaining are concerned.

The techniques described in this paper extend traditional deductive retrieval systems and their associated predicate-calculus data bases to handle a wide class of temporal inference. The TMM is implemented as an extension (or temporalized version) of the deductive retrieval system DUCK [23] which follows in the tradition of MICRO-PLANNER [29], CONNIVER [20], and AMORD [9]. We will assume a general familiarity with deductive-retrieval and logic-programming issues such as unification and the use of forward and backward chaining. Readers who need more background are urged to consult [23] or any of a number of good introductory AI texts (e.g., [3, 26]). Aspects of DUCK that are nonstandard and critical to the discussion of the TMM will be introduced as required. We'll begin with some notational preliminaries.

4.1. Notation

A LISP-style notation will be used for predicate-calculus formulae. All formulae are of the form (q . . .), where q is a function, predicate, or connective, and the ". . ." corresponds to the arguments of a predicate or function or the subparts of a composite formed with a connective. Variables (notated ?name) are universally quantified unless otherwise stated. A substitution (or set of variable bindings) is notated as {($variablename_1$, $value_1$) . . . ($variablename_n$, $value_n$)} (e.g., unifying (foo ?x ?y) with (foo Fred Sally) results in the substitution {(x Fred)(y Sally)}). The connectives and and or have their standard interpretation. The negation-as-failure operator is thnot ((thnot P) succeeds just in case P fails). In places where one would normally use if, one of ← or → will be substituted, where the former indicates a standard backward chaining rule and the latter a forward chaining rule. A formula such as (← P (and Q_1 . . . Q_n)) (equivalently in PROLOG "P :- Q_1, . . . , Q_n") is interpreted as saying: to prove P, prove Q_1 through Q_n with appropriate substitutions made via unification. The formula (→ P Q) is interpreted as: if P is added to the data base, add Q as well. Variables appearing in formulae are declared to be a given type using the constructs define-predicate and define-function. Types will appear in upper case, all else in lower case. The initial types include: FIXNUM (either an integer or a special symbol like *pos-inf* and *neg-inf* (for plus or minus infinity)), PROP (a LISP representation of a predicate-calculus formula—if P is a PROP, then so is (not P)), and OBJ (all types are a subtype of OBJ). New types will be introduced as needed. Predicates are defined using a schema in which the arguments are replaced by a type. For instance (define-predicate (< FIXNUM FIXNUM)) declares < to be a predicate of arity 2, both of whose arguments are of type FIXNUM. Functions are defined similarly, except that the first element in the schema following the function name is the type which the function returns and the second element is a list of the types of the function arguments. So (define-function (+ FIXNUM (FIXNUM FIXNUM))) defines + to be a function of two FIXNUM arguments that returns a FIXNUM.

Lists are notated using the syntax !⟨*items-in-the-list-separated-by-spaces*⟩ (equivalent to the PROLOG [*items-in-the-list-separated-by-commas*]). The empty list is just !⟨ ⟩. There are also means of decomposing lists using unification. One can break a list consisting of one or more elements into its first element and the list consisting of the rest of the elements using !⟨?x !& ?y⟩, which is equivalent to [X|Y] in PROLOG.

4.2. Basic temporal notions

The principal items in our ontology of time are instants, constraints, and time tokens. Each of these correspond to a data type (respectively POINT, CONLINK, and TOKEN) in the TMM. An object of data type POINT designates an instant in time. That instant needn't be completely specified in any particular frame of reference. That is to say the system needn't be able to specify the precise position of a particular point on the time line laid down by a given clock. Every point is itself a frame of reference. You may know that exactly five minutes after starting the coffee maker this morning, you sat down at the kitchen table to read the paper. You may also recall that you started the coffee maker sometime after being disturbed from a sound sleep by a wrong number. The time between waking and sitting down at the table to read the paper is only approximately known. This is represented as an upper and lower bound on the distance separating two points in the time map. These bounds are computed by the underlying TMM machinery using heuristic search techniques to find paths connecting pairs of POINTs.

The following function is used to denote the distance between two points.

(define-function (distance FIXNUM (POINT POINT)))

We want to be able to add new constraints and determine what is known about the distance separating two points in the time map. The function distance allows us to refer to the distance separating two points in the time map. We now need a set of predicates so that we can retrieve and modify information about such distances. The time map is designed to efficiently compute the best bounds on the distance separating a pair of points in the time map. We'll refer to those bounds as the GLB (greatest lower bound) and LUB (least upper bound).

The predicate strict-elt (for "strictly an element of") is used to determine the best known (strictest) bounds on the value of terms denoting integers (FIXNUMs). In general, (strict-elt trm_1 trm_2 trm_3) means that trm_1 is bounded from below by trm_2 and from above by trm_3, and that there are no better bounds known. The predicate declaration is simply:

(define-predicate (strict-elt FIXNUM FIXNUM FIXNUM))

So, for instance, the query (strict-elt (distance pt1 pt2) ?low ?high) will return with ?low and ?high bound to the GLB and LUB respectively. As was mentioned in Section 4.1, a FIXNUM is either an integer or one of a small set of special symbols. In the TMM, there are four symbolic FIXNUMs. The symbols *pos-inf* and *neg-inf* denote numbers (respectively) larger and smaller than any other number. In addition, *pos-tiny* denotes a number greater than 0 but less than any positive number; *neg-tiny*, a number less than 0 but greater than any negative number. The only arithmetic operations used by the TMM involving symbolic FIXNUMs are addition and subtraction and these are quite straightforward. If pt1 and pt2 are unconstrained and ?low and ?high are unbound, (strict-elt (distance pt1 pt2) ?low ?high) will succeed with substitution {(low *neg-inf*) (high *pos-inf*)}.

Next we'll introduce a similar (though less restrictive) predicate called simply elt.

(define-predicate (elt FIXNUM FIXNUM FIXNUM))

The predication (elt trm_1 trm_2 trm_3) means that trm_1 is bounded from below by trm_2 and from above by trm_3. A query of the form (elt (distance pt1 pt2) 6 9) will succeed just in case there exists a path from pt1 to pt2 with lower bound greater than or equal to 6, and upper bound less than or equal to 9. Elt reports on whether or not a set of bounds is supported by the current set of constraints in the time map.

For the sake of convenience, we'll define a set of predicates, pt≤, pt<, pt>, pt≥, and pt=, which serve as shorthand for various uses of elt.

(define-predicate (pt< POINT POINT))
(←(pt< pt1 pt2)
   (elt (distance pt1 pt2) *pos-tiny* *pos-inf*))

(define-predicate (pt≤ POINT POINT))
(←(pt≤ pt1 pt2)
   (elt (distance pt1 pt2) 0 *pos-inf*))

The other definitions are quite similar.

So far we only know how to ask questions about the distance separating points in the time map. We need to be able to add information as well. You can add a new constraint to the time map by asserting something of the form (elt (distance pt1 pt2) low high) where low and high are FIXNUMs. This supplies an upper and lower bound (not necessarily the least upper or greatest lower) on the distance separating pt1 and pt2. It may also change the strict bounds (GLBs and LUBs) on distances separating other pairs of points in the time map, since the new constraint can be used to compute new paths between pairs of points besides those that it directly refers to.

Now that we can add constraints between points and determine information about the distance separating points, it would be nice to be able to create new points. What we're really interested in is the ability to create entities corresponding to events and facts. These entities will refer to time points, but it is the entities themselves that are of primary interest.

Objects of data type TOKEN are used to represent events and persistences. These are two obvious functions associated with TOKENs namely their beginning and end points.

(define-function (begin POINT (TOKEN)))
(define-function (end POINT (TOKEN)))

In addition, we define a predicate relating TOKENs and their (logical) types (PROPs).

(define-predicate (time-token PROP TOKEN))

Given a query of the form (time-token (malfunction lathe17) ?tok), the TMM would return a list of answers in which ?tok is bound to a TOKEN of type (malfunction lathe17). Asserting (time-token (malfunction lathe17) tok1) would add to the time map a new object tok1 of data type TOKEN with the (logical) type (malfunction lathe17).

The time map makes no internal distinction between TOKENs interpreted as events and those interpreted as facts. A distinction, however, is implied in the tokens and rules that the user adds to the data base. Certain fact types can be defined to contradict other fact types. Two tokens are said to be contradictory if their corresponding types are determined to be contradictory. Such tokens are treated as persistences by the TMM. Contradiction criteria are defined using the contradict predicate.

(define-predicate (contradict PROP PROP))

Example criteria are:

(contradicts (not ?p) ?p)

and

(←(contradicts (operational-status ?machine ?status1)
            (operational-status ?machine ?status2))
   (thnot (= ?status1 ?status2)))

As far as the time map is concerned, any token found to be in contradiction with another token is treated as a fact. The TMM performs no additional interpretation. It does, however, perform an important service involving contradictory tokens.

If one token is determined to be in contradiction with a second, and the first

tions in which it is reasonable to give a persistence a duration with an upper bound greater than 0. If you notice a light being on for some time and later are told that it was not on during the period you observed it, then you should be disturbed. It would be wrong for the TMM to resolve the inconsistency without notifying someone of a problem. In such a situation the TMM will describe the problem and then prompt the calling program to remove one or more constraints in order to resolve the contradiction. The important decisions are left up to the calling program.

4.3. Default reasoning about time

The information in a time map is generally incomplete. Event tokens are partially ordered, constraints on their occurrence are specified as fuzzy intervals, and the only information typically available concerning the duration of persistences is an upper bound. In order to make use of time maps, it is important to adopt a consistent strategy for interpreting the information they contain. The interpretation strategy built into the operation of the TMM is quite simple. Events occur as early as they can (the lower bound on the duration of an event token is most indicative of its start time), and fact tokens persist as long as possible (the duration of a persistence is best estimated by the upper bound on the distance separating its begin and end points). According to this strategy a fact P is true throughout an interval just in case there exists a fact token of type P that begins before, or is coincident with, the beginning of the interval, and it's consistent to believe that the token persists at least as long as the interval. In order to define a predicate that captures this, we first need to be able to reason about whether it's consistent to believe in certain relationships involving the distance separating points in the time map.

Earlier we defined a predicate elt and a function distance that were useful in reasoning about the duration of intervals separating points in the time map. A query of the form (elt (distance pt1 pt2) *low high*) allows us to determine whether or not a set of bounds (*low* and *high*) on the distance separating a pair of points are supported by the current set of constraints (i.e., the lower bound *low* is not greater than the GLB and the upper bound *high* is not less than the LUB). Now we want to consider an operator M such that a query of the form (M (elt (distance pt1 pt2) low high)) will succeed just in case the bounds on (distance pt1 pt2) are *consistent* with the current set of constraints.

Consider the following definition:

```
(←(M (elt (distance ?pt1 ?pt2) ?low ?high))
   (and (strict-elt (distance ?pt1 ?pt2) ?glb ?lub)
        (≤ ?low ?high)
        (≤ ?low ?lub)
        (≤ ?glb ?high)))
```

is constrained to begin before the second begins, then the first is constrained to end before the second (assuming such a constraint is consistent with the existing constraints). This is referred to as the *rule of persistence*, and while the rule is quite simple in form, it figures prominently in a number of important assumptions that are deeply woven into the fabric of time maps as used in the TMM.

The rule of persistence is used to modify the duration of fact tokens. If you assert that the light in the attic is on, then, lacking information to the contrary, you should be willing to believe it will stay on indefinitely. This willingness to believe that certain facts persist indefinitely, if unmolested, corresponds to there being no upper bound on the duration of the associated token (or perhaps an upper bound equal to the estimated life of the light bulb). It is also possible that subsequent information will lower that upper bound (e.g., someone fetches something from the attic and turns the light off). This readiness to reduce the duration of a fact in the face of evidence of its contradiction corresponds to the lower bound on the token's duration being zero (or at least very small). The rule of persistence is used to remove apparent but resolvable contradictions.

```
(←(apparent-contradiction ?tok1 ?tok2)
   (and (time-token ?p ?tok1)
        (time-token ?q ?tok2)
        (contradicts ?p ?q)
        (strict-elt (distance (begin ?tok1) (begin ?tok2)) ?blow ?bhigh)
        (≤0 ?blow)
        (strict-elt (distance (begin ?tok2) (end ?tok1)) ?elow ?ehigh)
        (≤0 ?ehigh)))
```

Two apparently contradictory tokens can be resolved if it is possible that the one beginning earlier can end before the later.

```
(←(resolvable-contradiction ?tok1 ?tok2)
   (and (apparent-contradiction ?tok1 ?tok2)
        (strict-elt (distance (begin ?tok2) (end ?tok1)) ?low ?high)
        (< ?low 0)))
```

Whenever the TMM discovers a resolvable contradiction, it removes it by adding a constraint to ensure that the earlier token ends before the later (the actual mechanism will be discussed in Section 5). Unfortunately, not all apparent contradictions are resolvable. There is no way to resolve apparently contradictory tokens with coincident beginning points. Also, there are situa-

Suppose that the GLB and LUB on the distance separating pt1 and pt2 are 4 and 8 respectively (i.e., (strict-elt (distance pt1 pt2) 4 8) succeeds). In this case the query (M (elt (distance pt1 pt2) 2 3)) should succeed, but (M (elt (distance pt1 pt2) 2 3)) should fail. This is obviously a nonmonotonic inference. The inference (M (elt (distance pt1 pt2) 3 5)) is valid as the example was given. However, if the constraint (elt (distance pt1 pt2) 7 *pos-inf*) is added, then the inference is no longer valid. Noticing when the status of such nonmonotonic inferences change (and what the consequences are) is an important part of temporal reason maintenance. In what follows, we'll assume that it is clear how the M operator behaves with regard to shorthand expressions for uses of elt involving point-to-point distances (e.g., pt≤ and pt>).

Now we can proceed to define a predicate tt (for "true throughout" an interval) that will help us reason about facts that change over time.

(define-predicate (tt POINT POINT PROP))

A query of the form (tt pt1 pt2 Q) is taken to mean, "Is it possible that Q is true throughout the interval from pt1 to pt2?" The definition is:

```
(<-(tt ?pt1 ?pt2 ?q)
  (and (time-token ?q ?tok)
       (pt≤ (begin ?tok) ?pt1)
       (M (pt≤ ?pt2 (end ?tok)))))
```

Understanding how the TMM handles queries involving the true throughout predicate is best done in the context of an example. The examples we'll be using in this paper are drawn from the machine shop domain [13] and deal with scheduling machines to perform various manufacturing tasks. In our first example, there are four machines lathe14, lathe17, lathe34, and lathe 9, each of which is available for use only over certain intervals (a machine is available for use at a particular time just in case its operational-status is in-service). The machines can also have various attachments installed over certain intervals. There is one event token corresponding to the task to complete (manufacture) a certain order (lot427). We're interested in determining which machines are available for assisting in the manufacturing process.

To illustrate the examples in this paper, it will help if we establish some conventions for depicting the contents of time maps. Time maps are rather hard to draw in just two dimensions. Each point in the time map represents a frame of reference. If the distance between all points is not known with precision, then, depending upon what point you choose as a reference, you will get a different picture of the contents of the time map. We will simplify the interpretation of time map diagrams by using examples in which most of the points are related to one another with precision. Tokens are diagrammatically

represented with a vertical bar indicating when the corresponding interval begins and either a second vertical bar providing some indication of when the interval ends or an arrow→indicating that the end of the interval is far enough in the future that it can't be drawn in the diagram. The delimiters for tokens are connected by a horizontal bar (e.g., ⊢→). Each time token is labeled with a symbol (e.g., task1) used to refer to the token and a formula denoting its type. Time tokens are laid out on the page so as to indicate their relative offset from a single reference point usually not explicitly stated. In cases where a token is not completely constrained with respect to the reference point, we use the notation |----| where the first two vertical bars indicate the earliest and latest the corresponding interval might begin and the distance separating the second and third vertical bars give some indication of the duration of the interval.

In our first example, the reference point *ref* corresponds to 12:00 noon, the base temporal unit is a minute, and the notation *hrs:min* is shorthand for ((*hrs* · 60) + *min*) minutes. The manufacturing task can't begin until after 10:30 AM (assume that some prerequisite operation won't be completed until that time) and must be finished by 1:00 PM. The task is estimated to take between an hour and an hour and fifteen minutes. The assertions below set up the situation shown in Fig. 2:

```
(time-token (operational-status lathe14 in-service) in-service1)
(time-token (operational-status lathe17 in-service) in-service2)
(time-token (operational-status lathe34 in-service) in-service3)
(time-token (operational-status lathe9 in-service) in-service4)
(time-token (installed milling-attachment lathe14) installed1)
(time-token (manufacture lot427) order721)
(elt (distance (begin in-service1) *ref*) 4:00 4:00)
(elt (distance (begin in-service2) *ref*) 1:00 1:00)
(elt (distance (begin in-service3) *ref*) 3:00 3:00)
(elt (distance (begin in-service3) (end in-service3)) 0 2:00)
(elt (distance (begin in-service4) *ref*) 2:30 2:30)
(elt (distance (begin in-service4) (end in-service4)) 0 3:00)
(elt (distance (begin installed1) *ref*) 3:30 3:30)
(elt (distance (begin order721) *ref*) 1:30 *pos-inf*)
(elt (distance (begin order721) (end order721)) 1:00 1:15)
(elt (distance *ref* (end order721)) *neg-inf* 1:00)
```

Now, consider the following query:

```
(and (time-token (manufacture lot427) ?tok)
     (tt (begin ?tok) (end ?tok)
         (operational-status ?machine in-service))
     (instance-of ?machine lathe))
```

continued validity of a query. In order to understand the complex interplay between backward and forward deduction in a changing data base it will be necessary to delve a bit deeper into the machinery of the underlying deductive retrieval system.

4.4. Deduction involving forward and backward chaining

A computation in a logic programming system like PROLOG can be described in terms of answering questions (or processing queries). In PROLOG, you ask a question by typing a goal (generally a form containing variables but no connectives) or a conjunction of goals to the PROLOG interpreter. An answer to a query consists of a substitution for the variables in the query. A given query may have no answers or it may have many, depending upon the facts and rules in the data base. DUCK also has an interpreter that you can invoke to process queries, but DUCK encourages a style of programming that blends logic-based computation (or deductive retrieval) and the applicative style of programming common to LISP. The LISP function fetch takes a single argument that evaluates to a goal or conjunction of goals. This function returns a list of answers that can be manipulated just like any other LISP data object, and we'll make use of this fact to control deduction in the TMM.

There are computations involving deductive retrieval systems in which the data base does not change over the course of the computation. But in many applications it is convenient or even necessary to modify the set of facts and rules as part of the computation. This might be done for efficiency or it might be done simply because new information becomes available while the program is running. PROLOG handles this by having operators (asserta and asertz) that can be used to add facts and rules to the data base during backward chaining. DUCK has an operator assert that serves the same basic function and a LISP function add that allows one to add facts and rules from LISP.

In both PROLOG and DUCK, exactly what is *asserted* or added to the data base will "depend" on the *current answer* or state of the computation. In PROLOG, this dependency can be stated totally in terms of the variable bindings (substitution) in force at the time the assertion is encountered in the computation. As an example let's assume that the data base consists of just the fact (brother-of Cain Abel). In the following query:

(and (brother-of ?x ?y) (assert (sibling ?x ?y)))

the assertion will occur in the context of the substitution {(x Cain)(y Abel)}, resulting in (sibling Cain Abel) being added to the data base. There is actually a more complicated implicit dependency in this; it would seem that the assertion (sibling Cain Abel) should somehow depend upon the assertion (brother-of Cain Abel). If the latter assertion is removed from the data base, then there seems to be no warrant for believing the former. In DUCK, this dependency is made

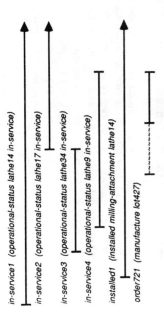

in-service1 (operational-status lathe14 in-service)

in-service2 (operational-status lathe17 in-service)

in-service3 (operational-status lathe34 in-service)

in-service4 (operational-status lathe9 in-service)

installed1 (installed milling-attachment lathe14)

order721 (manufacture lot427)

FIG. 2. Time map for demonstrating temporal backward chaining.

If we assume that each of lathe14, lathe17, lathe34, and lathe9 are probably instances of lathes, then this query should return with exactly two answers, one with substitution {(machine lathe14)(tok order721)}, and a second with substitution {(machine lathe9)(tok order721)}. The query will fail for {(machine lathe17)(tok order721)} (in-service2 doesn't begin early enough) and {(machine lathe34)(tok order721)} (in-service3 doesn't persist long enough).

For the slightly more complicated query:

```
(and (time-token (manufacture lot427) ?tok)
     (instance-of ?machine lathe)
     (tt (begin ?tok) (end ?tok)
     (and (operational-status ?machine in-service)
          (installed milling-attachment ?machine))))
```

there is only one answer (with substitution {(machine lathe14)(tok order721)}), since there is only one lathe that is both in service and has the necessary attachment throughout the required interval.

You might have noticed that the first query would have succeeded with lathe17 if we had made the additional assertion:

(elt (distance (begin in-service2) (begin order721)) 0 *pos-inf*)

Dean [7] describes a general method for exploring hypothetical situations that involves selectively accepting additional premises during backward chaining. These premises (referred to as *abductive premises*) allow a deduction to succeed in situations where otherwise it would not. This sort of abductive inference is critical in reasoning with partially ordered time maps.

The answers to questions returned by the TMM are not guaranteed to remain valid over the course of subsequent additions and deletions to the time map. Of course this is not an issue unless some further deduction depends upon the

explicit in what is called a *data dependency network*. Assertions that are no longer justified are labeled as such by what is referred to as a *reason maintenance system* (RMS).

4.4.1. Reason maintenance

A reason maintenance system is a program used for keeping track of the status of a set of items stored in a data base. Depending upon the particular RMS the *status* of a data base item may refer to the truth value of a proposition [18], whether a given proposition is believed or not [12], or the assumptions which, were they true, would entail a given proposition [11, 17]. The RMS manipulates a data structure referred to as a *data dependency network*. This network consists of nodes called *ddnodes* (for data dependency node): one node for each datum of interest to the user. Dean [7] describes an implementation of the TMM that employs an assumption-based RMS. In this paper, however, we will describe the TMM in terms of a system modeled after Doyle [12].

The ddnode and the item it refers to are generally spoken of interchangeably. The paradigmatic case is the ddnode associated with each assertion in the data base, but, in general, any explicit belief of the program must be associated with a ddnode, and any ddnode must have a *propositional content* that the program either believes or does not at any given time. Connecting all the program's beliefs in a data dependency network allows the RMS to enforce consistency among the beliefs. The connections between various items of data in the network are described in terms of *justifications*. A justification for a ddnode n_0 consists of a conjunction of other ddnodes in the following form: $\{\{n_1, \ldots, n_i\}\{n_{i+1}, \ldots, n_j\}\}$ where n_1 through n_i are referred to as *in-justifiers* and n_{i+1} through n_j are called *out-justifiers*. An assertion corresponding to a ddnode with the empty justification (i.e., $\{\{\}\{\}\}$) is said to be a *premise*; it's believed unconditionally. Justifications are used to capture conditions for belief and thus the node n_0 is said to depend upon belief in $n_1, \ldots, n_i$ and absence of belief in $n_{i+1}, \ldots, n_j$.

In addition to recording the reasons for believing something, it is also important to keep track of which things are currently believed. Deductions (such as forward and backward chaining) are generally performed using only items (rules and ground assertions) that are believed. Also it is often critical that the program using the reason maintenance system be notified of specific changes in the status of selected beliefs. Each ddnode has associated with it a *label* which is used to keep track of the status of the corresponding datum. In a Doyle-type RMS, the label for a ddnode is a Boolean value, one of IN or OUT. IN means that the corresponding datum is believed and OUT means that it's not believed. In the latter case the datum associated with the ddnode is essentially hidden from the deductive retrieval machinery; it is, from the user's point of view, not present in the data base. All premises are given the label IN. A ddnode with no justifications is said to be an *assumption* and is given the label

OUT. The labels for all other ddnodes have to be computed. The primary objective of a reason maintenance system is to find a *consistent* and *well-founded* assignment of states (IN or OUT) to all the ddnodes in the network which are neither premises nor assumptions. Intuitively a status assignment for a node is consistent if it follows from its justifications. In Doyle's system this requires that the label for a ddnode be IN iff at least one of its justifications is composed of in-justifiers with IN labels and out-justifiers with OUT labels. Intuitively a status assignment is well-founded if every IN ddnode can be shown to be grounded in premises. A ddnode with label IN is grounded (in premises) if it is a premise or it has at least one justification such that each in-justifier is either grounded or a premise and all the out-justifiers are labeled OUT.

When a justification is added or removed, the consequences of the change have to be propagated throughout the data dependency network. This involves recomputing the labels of some subset of the set of all ddnodes. The algorithm used in the Doyle RMS is described in [3] and won't be repeated here. Suffice it to say that this algorithm finds a consistent and well-founded assignment of statuses (IN or OUT) for all ddnodes in the network, and does so in an efficient manner. The algorithm for updating the dependency network also allows us to determine which ddnodes have changed status as a result of the most recent modification to the dependency network. The indexing machinery is responsible for seeing to it that all justifications for believing a given datum refer to a unique ddnode. One reason for uniquely identifying beliefs is to simplify responding to changes.

Each data dependency node serves as a location in which to store responses to specific changes in the status of that node. These responses, called *signal functions*, are executable objects that are "run" whenever the label for the ddnode changes in some predefined way. The ddnode gives you a handle on a given belief. If the dependency network is modified in any way, the RMS can easily determine the set of ddnodes that might possibly have changed status. It can then check to see which of those ddnodes have changed status and what the nature of those changes are by comparing the newly computed label with the previous one.

Data dependency systems of the sort we are discussing here are used for incrementally updating a set of beliefs upon the addition or removal of new beliefs or justifications, and then noticing and responding to specific changes in those beliefs. In order to make use of this functionality, we have to be clear about how the connections between beliefs (justifications) are set up and how you go about detecting and responding to changes in the status of these beliefs.

4.4.2. Setting up the justifications for belief

In addition to standard forms of forward and backward deduction, DUCK allows a third type of deduction which we'll refer to as *program-mediated* deduction. Forward and backward chaining always occur in some sort of "context," including a set of variable bindings. Program-mediated deduction involves the use of programs that directly manipulate this context, setting up data dependency justifications, modifying variable bindings, and controlling forward inference. Before explaining program-mediated deduction, we'll explain what these "contexts" are and how they are created and employed during backward and forward chaining.

In the TMM, the context of a deduction is an object of data type ANS (for "answer") that consists of a set of variable bindings and a set of ddnode/support-type pairs associated with the steps in the deduction thus far. For our purposes, a support-type is just one of the set $\{+, -\}$, where $+$ means that the deduction depends upon the ddnode being believed, and $-$ means that the deduction depends upon the ddnode not being believed. This set of ddnode/support-type pairs attempts to capture why or under what conditions the current answer should be believed to be true. The machinery responsible for forward and backward chaining sees to it that the *current answer* (the value of ans*, a global variable of data type ANS) is modified to reflect the current state of the deduction. When an assertion occurs, the system finds or creates the unique ddnode associated with that assertion. It then installs in that ddnode a new justification formed using the set of ddnodes in the current answer (in-justifiers consisting of ddnodes of support type $+$ and out-justifiers those of support type $-$). Assertions are allowed to occur during backward chaining. In backward chaining on the conjunctive goal (and $P_1 \ldots P_n$ (assert Q)), a system handling data dependencies should ensure that the ddnode corresponding to Q has a justification that depends upon on the ddnodes associated with deducing $P_1 \ldots P_n$. There is also the need to handle queries that make use of the "consistent" (nonmonotonic negation-as-failure) operator. So assuming that P cannot be deduced from the current contents of the data base, a query of the form (and (M (not P)) (assert Q)) should succeed, resulting in the ddnode associated with Q having a justification with an out-justifier corresponding to the ddnode associated with P. Forward chaining behaves similarly. If P is asserted and there is a rule ($\rightarrow$ PQ), then the ddnode associated with Q should have a justification which includes the ddnodes for P and ($\rightarrow$ PQ).

"Program-mediated deduction" refers to deduction done inside code using language constructs for forward and backward chaining (e.g., fetch and add). When an assertion is made, it is justified, intuitively, because the process has reached a certain point in the program, with the variables bound in a certain way. Often, it is possible to identify explicit reasons for the process to have reached this point, such that an assertion made at this point ought to depend upon those reasons. Suppose that the data base consists of:

```
ddnode:   corresponding datum:
n₁        (string-quartet Juilliard)
n₂        (list-of-members Juilliard !⟨Earl-Carlyss Robert-Mann
                                       Samuel-Rhodes Joel-Krosnick⟩)
```

```
n₃        (←(member ?x !⟨?y !& ?z⟩) (or (= ?x ?y) (member ?x ?z)))
```

And suppose that the following code is executed:

```
(cond ((fetch '(and (string-quartet ?q)
                    (list-of-members ?q ?l)
                    (member Robert-Mann ?l)))
       (add '(classical-musician Robert-Mann))))
```

The assertion (classical-musician Robert-Mann) is added to the data base *because* Robert Mann is known to be a member of the Juilliard string quartet. It should be made dependent upon the assertions (string-quartet Juilliard) and (list-of-members Juilliard !⟨Earl-Carlyss Robert-Mann Samuel-Rhodes Joel-Krosnick⟩) and the rule used by the deductive system to determine that one term is a member of a list of terms. Objects of data type ANS provide us with the means for keeping track of the reasons why a process has reached a certain point in a program. The following:

```
(fetch '(and (string-quartet ?q)
             (list-of-members ?q ?l)
             (member Robert-Mann ?l)))
```

would return:

```
((⟨(q Juilliard)
   (l !⟨Earl-Carlyss Robert-Mann Samuel-Rhodes Joel-Krosnick⟩)
   {(+ n₁) (+ n₂) (+ n₃)}⟩))
```

in the data base described above.

All deductions take place in the context of the current answer ans*. The answers returned by a "fetch" are said to *augment* the current answer. If we want an assertion to be dependent upon a particular "fetch," then we will have to bind ans* to be the value of some augmented answer returned by the "fetch." The *scope* of an answer refers to the time during which that answer is the value of ans*. For our example involving the Juilliard quartet, the dependencies would be handled correctly by the following:

```
(let (answers (fetch '(and (string-quartet ?q)
                           (list-of-members ?q ?l)
                           (member Robert-Mann ?l))))
  (cond (answers
         (bind ((ans* (car answers)))
               (add '(classical-musician Robert-Mann))))))
```

That is to say, the system will create a ddnode corresponding to (classical-musician Robert-Mann) with justification $\{\{n_1, n_2, n_3\}\{\}\}$.

The above code can be simplified using various LISP macros designed for that purpose. In a call of the form (for-first-answer (fetch *query*) *code*), if the list returned by the fetch is empty, the call returns with nil; if the list is not empty, then ans * is bound (locally) to the first augmented answer in the list and the code is executed returning whatever the code returns. In (for-each-answer (fetch *query*) *code*), the current answer is repeatedly bound to as many augmented answers as the fetch will allow, and the code is executed for each answer. The for-each-answer macro is generally used as follows:

```
(for-each-answer (fetch some-query)
        assorted-LISP-code
        (add some-assertion)
        more-assorted-LISP-code)
```

Each answer in the list returned by fetch is bound to ans * in turn, and add is called. Add makes the necessary substitutions and sets up the requisite dependencies. Suppose that the data base contains just (string-quartet Juilliard) and (string-quartet Guarneri) and the following code is executed:

```
(for-each-answer (fetch '(string-quartet ?q))
        (add '(repertoire ?q Mozart)))
```

Following execution, the data base will also contain (repertoire Juilliard Mozart) and (repertoire Guarneri Mozart), such that (repertoire Juilliard Mozart) depends upon (string-quartet Juilliard), and (repertoire Guarneri Mozart) depends upon (string-quartet Guarneri).

Notice that under certain conditions, the above code performs the same function as the forward chaining rule ($\rightarrow$ (string-quartet ?q) (repertoire ?q Mozart)). The main difference concerns timing. In the case of the for-each-answer version, if after executing the code you add (string-quartet Melos), then (repertoire Melos Mozart) will not be added to the data base. There are many cases in which this is exactly what you want. For example, suppose that the data base is consistent with several hypothetical situations, only one of which can actually occur. In such a case, the program will have to be careful to add only those assertions that follow from the hypothesis selected as best. As we'll see, this sort of carefully controlled deduction plays an important role in temporal reasoning. We will reserve the term *controlled forward inference* to refer to that class of deductions characterized by the pattern (for-each-answer (fetch *antecedent-conditions*) (add *consequent-predictions*)).

Whenever forward chaining occurs, either by using rules of the form ($\rightarrow$ **PQ**) or via other means of making assertions, the RMS is invoked to (re)compute the status of all possibly affected ddnodes. Now we can consider how to go about detecting and responding to changes in the status of ddnodes that occur during this process of updating.

4.4.3. *Detecting and responding to changes*

There are two main issues concerning the detection and response to changes in the status of ddnodes. The first concerns what sort of changes one has to be aware of. In a Doyle-type system, the sort of changes that can occur are rather simple. A ddnode label can toggle between IN and OUT and that's the extent of it. The second issue in responding to changes concerns the order in which responses are made. If there are several changes to be dealt with the order can be quite critical. Certain operations on the data base cannot be reliably or efficiently performed unless the data base satisfies some property. One way of getting the timing to work out involves the use of priority queues. Each priority level is associated with a set of executable objects (e.g., closures) such that when an object at one level is executed it can assume that all objects with higher priority have already been executed. The priority levels can be associated with data base properties, called *invariants* (see David McAllester's RUP system [19] for a discussion of the use of invariants in reason maintenance). In describing the implementation of the TMM (Section 5), we will introduce a number of invariants. In addition, the user is also given a range of priorities that are for his sole use. The time map invariants are of higher priority than any user invariants in order to discourage the user from making deductions on the basis of a partially updated time map.

Each signal function has associated with it a priority level and a condition which must be true in order to warrant the execution of the signal function. In the RMS update algorithm, once the status assignments have been recomputed, all ddnodes that have changed status have their signal functions checked. Any signal functions whose conditions are satisfied are placed in the priority queue at the appropriate level. When the update is completed all the objects in the queue are executed in such a way than an object can assume that all objects of higher priority have been executed. Just before execution the condition is checked once more to ensure that execution is still warranted.

DUCK provides utilities to enable the user to tell the system exactly what to do when an assertion toggles from IN to OUT or alternatively OUT to IN. The resulting programs are called *change-driven interrupts* and are implemented by attaching signal functions to the ddnodes corresponding to the assertions of interest. The simplest form of change-driven interrupt can be implemented using what are called *if-erased demons* [29]. The expression (if-erased *pattern* code) ensures that *code* is run whenever an assertion matching *pattern* becomes OUT.

4.5. Noticing assumption failures

The answers to the queries in the example of Section 4.3 are based on default assumptions concerning the persistence of fact tokens in the time map. It is often the case that steps in deductions involving the predicate tt are invalidated by subsequent additions and erasures from the time map. There are three ways in which this can happen corresponding to the three conjuncts in the definition of tt:

(1) (time-token ?q ?tok)
(2) (pt≤ (begin ?tok) ?pt1)
(3) (M (pt≤ ?pt2 (end ?tok)))

With regard to the first conjunct, the ddnode associated with the time token (bound to ?tok) used in making the deduction can become OUT. Relative to the second conjunct it is possible that certain constraints will become OUT so that it is no longer possible to conclude (pt≤ (begin ?tok) ?pt1). The third conjunct involves a nonmonotonic inference. By adding constraints it may become possible to conclude that (pt> ?pt2 (end ?tok)), thereby invalidating the conjunct (M (pt≤ ?pt2 (end ?tok))). Generally the only time you are interested in the continued validity of conclusions extracted from the time map is when you have used those conclusions as a basis for deriving further consequences. Whenever the TMM successfully processes a query involving tt, it augments the current answer (in particular the ddnode/support-type pairs) in such a way that assertions occurring in the context of that answer will be believed, just in case the above three conditions continue to hold. The details of how this is accomplished will be presented in Section 5.3; in this section we're only concerned with how we can put it to use.

The addition of new fact tokens and constraints on their occurrence can result in changes in the duration of existing time tokens. This change may serve to violate default assumptions concerning the persistence of fact tokens. We'll refer to such violations as *interactions*. An interaction occurs when a belief that was previously warranted is suddenly threatened by the addition of new information.

The rule of persistence has already been briefly described in Section 4.2. Its mandate is carried out automatically by the time map machinery. To reiterate: the rule of persistence detects when two tokens, T1 and T2, are ordered such that (begin T1) precedes (begin T2). Whenever the TMM finds a pair of tokens satisfying this criterion it determines if it is possible that (end T1) precedes (begin T2) (i.e., the least upper bound on the distance separating the

two points is greater than 0). If this last condition cannot be met then the data base is said to be inconsistent and some action must be taken to remove the inconsistency. If the condition is met, then the TMM adds the constraint (elt (distance (end T1) (begin T2)) *pos-tiny* *pos-inf*).[1] The operation of adding constraints via the rule of persistence is referred to as *persistence clipping*.

To illustrate, suppose we add the following to the time map shown in Fig. 3:

(time-token (malfunction lathe14) malfunction1)
(time-token (operational-status lathe14 out-of-service) out-of-service1)
(elt (distance *ref* (begin malfunction1) (end malfunction1)) 2 2)
(elt (distance *ref* (begin malfunction34)) 30 30)
(elt (distance (end malfunction1) (begin out-of-service1)) 0 0)

Figure 4 shows the result of having made the above assertions. Notice that the only thing that has changed, other than the addition of out-of-service1 and malfunction1, is the duration of in-service1; the persistence in-service1 has been clipped by the persistence out-of-service1 by the TMM in resolving the apparent contradiction between the two tokens.

Let's return to the time map of Fig. 3 and consider how we might go about choosing a plan for the task associated with order721 using controlled forward chaining. The following code fragment describes a simple method for plan choice:

```
(for-first-answer
  (fetch (and (time-token (manufacture lot427) ?tok)
              (instance-of ?machine lathe)
              (tt (begin ?tok) (end ?tok)
              (and (operational-status ?machine in-service)
                   (installed milling-attachment ?machine)))))
  (add '(and (time-token (setup lathe14 lot427) setup1)
             (time-token (batch-process lathe14 lot427) batch1)
             (elt (distance (begin setup1) (end setup1)) 20 20)
             (elt (distance (begin batch1) (end batch1)) 30 40)
             (pt≤ (begin ?tok) (begin setup1))
             (pt≤ (end batch1) (end ?tok))
             (pt≤ (end setup1) (begin batch1)))))
```

[1] Recall that *pos-tiny* denotes a number greater than zero but less than any positive number (except itself). This constraint in conjunction with the way we handle tt implies that persistences are closed on the left and open on the right. That is to say the fact associated with a persistence is believed at the beginning of the persistence interval and up to but not including the end of that interval.

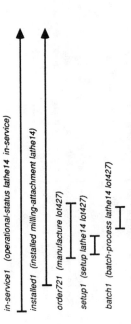

in-service1 (operational-status lathe14 in-service)

installed1 (installed milling-attachment lathe14)

order721 (manufacture lot427)

FIG. 3. Initial time map for demonstrating controlled forward inference.

You can think of the query as establishing the conditions for using a particular plan for performing the manufacturing task. The assertion describes the expansion of a simple plan (the refinement of order721). Figure 5 shows the result of executing the above code fragment in the time map of Fig. 3. Notice that the query establishing the conditions for the manufacturing plan would not have succeeded in the time map of Fig. 4, since in this time map lathe14 is not operational throughout order721. However, if, having already executed the above code fragment, we add the assertions involving the malfunction of lathe14, then we won't notice that the conditions for our plan are no longer met. So far we have said very little about what is done after a query succeeds with respect to the end points of persistences involved in satisfying a "true throughout" query. If an application program makes assertions on the basis of an answer returned by the TMM, then those assertions are dependent upon the state of the time map reflected in the query answer. We would like to ensure that the consequent assertions are believed just in case the antecedent conditions in the time map continue to hold. There are two ways that this might be accomplished. First, we could just add constraints that ensure the antecedent conditions. Second, we could keep track of the validity of the antecedent conditions and update the status of the consequent assertions accordingly. In the following, we will explore the advantages and disadvantages of both methods.

We would like to be able to keep track of the continued validity of conditional assertions. If believing in Q relies on believing in P being true

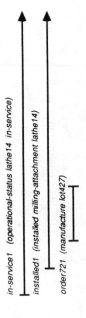

in-service1 (operational-status lathe14 in-service)

installed1 (installed milling-attachment lathe14)

malfunction1 (malfunction lathe14)

out-of-service1 (operational-status lathe14 out-of-service)

order721 (manufacture lot427)

FIG. 4. Time map demonstrating persistence clipping.

throughout an interval, then we want to be able to either guarantee the condition or be able to detect when it is no longer met. P is said to be *protected* throughout an interval pt1 to pt2 just in case there exists a persistence T1 with fact type P such that T1 begins before pt1 and T1 cannot be shown to end before pt2. A protection is *violated* if its corresponding fact is ever false during the interval.

One way we might guarantee a protection is by adding the constraint (pt≤ ?pt2 (end ?tok)) to ensure the continued validity of the nonmonotonic assumption (M (pt≤ ?pt2 (end ?tok))) in the definition of tt. If we were to get the TMM to do this whenever an assertion is made in the context of an answer containing a nonmonotonic temporal assumption, then the conditions for the plan to use lathe14 would be guaranteed. Using this method for handling protections, the TMM would not allow the addition of the assertions concerning the malfunction of lathe14 to the time map of Fig. 5; the assertions would be inconsistent with the (now firmly established) conditions for the plan to use lathe14 for the manufacturing task.

This technique of "stretching" persistences is one method of implementing protections. The only way that a protection violation can occur is by relaxing the constraints (i.e., removing one or more constraints). This means that the system is monotonic: adding new facts can never cause a protection violation. A protection in this scheme is equivalent to a pair of constraints: that a token with the required fact type begins before and ends after the interval over which the fact is being protected.

This persistence-stretching method has certain advantages. It is employed in the TMM as the method of choice for handling certain types of resource management [24]. It can also be used to implement a variant of Vere's DEVISER planner [31] that uses the point-and-token-based representation of time presented in this paper. One of its main advantages is that the constraints added in constructing protections act to enforce deadlines in a neat parsimonious way. The disadvantages, however, make it worth our while to consider alternatives. One disadvantage is flexibility. It is often convenient in debugging plans

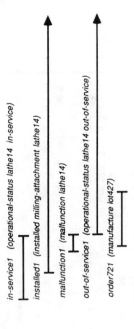

in-service1 (operational-status lathe14 in-service)

installed1 (installed milling-attachment lathe14)

order721 (manufacture lot427)

setup1 (setup lathe14 lot427)

batch1 (batch-process lathe14 lot427)

FIG. 5. Time map showing the results of controlled forward inference.

to determine the repercussions of modifying certain constraints in the time map. For instance, in building a house one might ask what problems would be encountered if the concrete basement floor was poured (installed) in the early stages of construction. Using the persistence-stretching method you would simply be informed (assuming that there are potential problems in pouring the concrete early) that such a modification cannot be made (i.e., it is inconsistent with the current data base). What you want, however, is a blow-by-blow account of what things might go wrong, so you can assess what might be done to make an early pouring feasible.

Ideally what we would like is a data base that, given some additional information, would do its best to accommodate the new data, reorganize itself to suit, and then spit out a list of beliefs that had to be modified in the revised data base in order to include the new information. Unfortunately this sort of magic data base in not likely to materialize. It is possible, however, to use data dependency methods in a highly controlled manner to get surprising flexibility out of a temporal data base.

By "highly controlled manner" we mean stipulate in advance what sort of behavior is expected of the system. The M operator serves as annotation to tell the deductive retrieval machinery what sort of default assumptions to incorporate into the current answer. The predication (MP) is said to indicate a default in that it effectively says believe P if you can, but be prepared to give it up (and anything that depends upon it as well) if you ever have reason to believe (not P). By using defaults what we are really doing is stating a priority on beliefs. Rules containing the M operator specify the conditions under which they can be overridden. Such rules are said to be nonmonotonic because the addition of new information can result in the falsification of old. In general the behavior of nonmonotonic systems is difficult to predict or analyze [21], but in cases where the defaults are few and of a simple form the behavior can be quite straightforward. In the TMM defaults are used to give precedence to the rule of persistence.

The dependencies set up in processing queries involving tt don't really serve to "protect" anything. They establish what might be more appropriately called "persistence assumptions." Nevertheless, because of the way in which these assumptions are used in planning systems (e.g., [24]). we will continue to refer to them as protections.

If we added the assertions concerning the malfunction of lathe14 to the time map of Fig. 4, the system would reconfigure the data base and note that something that was formerly believed is no longer so: the time tokens setup1 and batch1 are now OUT.

Simply labeling tokens as OUT obviously won't be sufficient for dealing with complex planning interactions. Some interactions are inconsequential; others are of minor interest, requiring at most a bit of bookkeeping; and still others are critical, demanding our immediate attention. Using the sort of change-

driven interrupts described in Section 4.4.3, a program can specify exactly what to do in the event that an assertion becomes OUT. Change-driven interrupts enable programs to detect and respond to specific changes in a complex set of beliefs.

4.6. Automatic projection and refinement

It is often convenient to be able to specify routine inferences that are to be performed whenever certain new facts are added to or removed from the data base. Standard forward chaining rules are an example of a technique for performing such inferences. Controlled forward inference of the sort characterized by the pattern (for-each-answer (fetch *antecedent-conditions*) (add *consequent-predictions*)) is unsuitable for certain applications due to timing problems. If, *after* executing (for-first-answer (fetch P) (add Q)), P is added to the data base where previously it was absent, then the planner will miss drawing the conclusion Q. One application in which such timing problems prove particularly irksome concerns reasoning about the effects of actions in planning.

A planner has to take into account the effects of actions proposed as steps in a plan for achieving a given task. However, the specification of a plan should not have to mention those effects of actions (performed as steps in the plan) that have no bearing on the plan achieving its stated objective. It's true that such side effects should be readily available as they are likely to figure prominently in integrating a set of steps into a larger plan. It's unreasonable to expect, however, that the plan specification for achieving an isolated task attempt to anticipate all possible interactions by providing a detailed account of the physics involved in carrying out the plan. The underlying physics should be represented elsewhere. A planner should expect that the deductive system responsible for managing its representation of actions, processes, and their effects occurring over time maintain the following invariant: the representation should reflect exactly those effects that are licensed by the rules describing the physics of the world. Relying on the deductive system to maintain a physically consistent view of the world frees the planner to concentrate on figuring out what to do when its actions fail to achieve their *intended* effects.

The TMM supports two basic types of temporal forward chaining. The first is a temporal analog of a (static) forward chaining rule extended to handle conjunctions as antecedents. A rule of the form ($\rightarrow$, (and $P_1, \ldots P_n$) Q) sees to it that whenever P_1 through P_n are simultaneously true, you can infer Q. That is, given any set of n tokens such that the first has type P_1, the second P_2 and so on up to P_n, then if the intersection of their corresponding intervals is nonempty, we can construct a new time token of type Q whose endpoints are coincident with the interval of intersection. The second type of temporal forward chaining is referred to as *auto-projection* and it is used to model the physics of a domain or project the consequences of holding certain beliefs. A rule of the form (project *antecedent-conditions trigger-event delay consequent-effect duration*) states that if an event of type *trigger-event* occurs, and the *antecedent-conditions* are true throughout the interval associated with the triggering event, then a token of type *consequent-effect* is added to the time map following the triggering event by an interval of time determined by *delay* and lasting for a length of time determined by *duration*. Delays and durations are normally supplied as bounds [*low, high*]. A single number n in either the *delay* or *duration* slot is taken to mean the interval [n, n]. In many cases, the delay and duration are omitted and the system supplies standard default bounds: [0,0] is the default delay and [0, *pos-inf*] is the default duration. The temporal reason maintenance system sees to it that exactly those tokens are IN as are licensed by the rules describing the physics of the domain and the conditions (premised tokens and constraints on their occurrence) specified by the calling program.

Temporal forward chaining rules can also be temporally "gated." That is to say you can temporally restrict the interval of time over which a rule is to apply. An assertion of the form ($\rightarrow_t$ (and $P_1 \ldots P_n$) Q) is timeless; it applies to any conjunction of appropriate tokens. An assertion of the form (time-token ($\rightarrow_t$ (and $P_1 \ldots P_n$) Q) tok) applies only within the interval (begin tok) to (end tok). To understand better how automatic projection rules can be used, we'll consider an example drawn from the factory domain. We begin by specifying rules that govern the behavior of processes involving machine tools and the equipment for moving items around in the factory. First of all we state that an object can't be in two distinct locations at the same time:

```
(← (contradicts (location ?object ?location1)
                (location ?object ?location2))
   (thnot (= ?location1 ?location2)))
```

Normally two syntactically different expressions describing locations are taken to describe distinctly different locations. but there are exceptions to this rule. If two machines are pipelined (i.e., the output of the first is fed into the input of the second), then the output bin of the first machine is considered identical to the input bin of the second:

```
(→t (and (pipelined ?machine1 ?machine2)
         (location ?object (output-bin ?machine1)))
    (location ?object (input-bin ?machine2)))
```

If the output of one machine is being piped into the input of a sorting machine and a batch job is carried out on the first machine, then 2 units following the batch job the sorter will be cycled for a period of exactly 4 units:

```
(project (and (pipelined ?machine1 ?machine2)
              (instance-of ?machine2 sorter))
         (batch-process ?machine1 ?production-lot)
         2 (cycle ?machine2) 4)
```

If an operational sorter is run with an item in its input bin, then following the run the item will be located in the staging area of its assigned pickup depot. The destination property of a production lot is not time-dependent.

```
(project (and (operational-status ?machine in-service)
              (instance-of ?machine sorter)
              (location ?production-lot (input-bin ?machine))
              (destination ?production-lot ?pickup-depot))
         (cycle ?machine)
         (location ?object (staging-area ?pickup-depot)))
```

If a batch job is performed on an operational machine, then following the job the resulting production lot will be located in the machine's output bin:

```
(project (operational-status ?machine in-service)
         (batch-process ?machine ?production-lot)
         (location ?production-lot (output-bin ?machine)))
```

Now suppose that we add a token of type (batch-process lathe14 lot427) to the time map shown in Fig. 6. The resulting time map is shown in Fig. 7 and is self-explanatory given the rules described above. The consequences of the batch process have been projected in accordance with the existing facts and the rules that determine the physics of such processes. The predictions shown in Fig. 7 are conditional upon certain facts that were assumed to be true of the time map in Fig. 6. We can upset those assumptions either by removing old facts or adding new ones. To demonstrate how the temporal reason maintenance machinery works, let's consider a simple projection rule that states whenever an operational machine malfunctions, it is no longer operational:

```
(project (operational-status ?machine in-service)
         (malfunction ?machine)
         (operational-status ?machine out-of-service))
```

If we add a time token of type (malfunction sorter43) to the time map of Fig. 7 and constrain this token to occur before the token batch1, then the TMM will predict that the sorter fails to perform its job and the output of the batch manufacturing process remains in the output bin of lathe14. Figure 8 depicts this outcome.

We'll conclude this section with an overview of the role of temporal imagery in planning. Let's consider the overall strategy suggested by the techniques presented thus far.

When you make a change to the data base (either the addition of new information or the removal of old), the TMM attempts to reorganize things to accommodate the change. Temporal forward chaining rules (e.g., auto-projection rules) assist in this reorganization by modeling some of the underlying physics of the domain (e.g., how objects move around under the influence of various processes). When this reorganization is complete, the repercussions that matter (those that the user has indicated using change-driven interrupts) are available for use as a summary of, or response to, the important developments in the data base (change-driven interrupts can be used in either capacity). It is the user's responsibility to decide what to do about these new developments. The system is only required to provide an accurate picture (time map) of the implications of what the user believes. A planner proceeds by providing more and more detail concerning how it intends to accomplish its current set of tasks. The "repercussions that matter" typically involve interactions between various steps in the plan proposed thus far. The time map represents how the proposed plan might turn out if it was executed as is. In planning, the TMM assists in choosing more detailed accounts of individual tasks, and in detecting interactions between tasks.

5. An Implementation of Temporal Reason Maintenance

In Section 3.2 the time map management system was advertised as performing *temporal* reason maintenance. The basic task of the TMM is the same as that for a conventional (static) reason maintenance system, namely, to keep track of the conditions for belief. In a temporalized data base, the conditions for belief are somewhat more complex than in the static case. A (temporal) condition for belief is generally something of the form: there exists a token asserting P that begins before a given interval and possibly persists throughout that interval. This sort of condition was referred to as a protection. Protections are, like Doyle's assumptions, nonmonotonic in that they can be undermined by the addition of new information. A protection can fail as a result of either adding or removing a constraint. In Section 4.5 we saw that constraints added by the TMM in resolving apparent contradictions can result in protection failures. From the user's perspective the task of a temporal data dependency system is to detect when an assertion is no longer justified and assist the user in responding in an appropriate manner. This section explains how the TMM detects and

in-service1 (operational-status lathe14 in-service)
pipelined1 (pipelined lathe14 sorter43)
in-service2 (operational-status sorter43 in-service)

FIG. 6. Initial time map for demonstrating automatic projection.

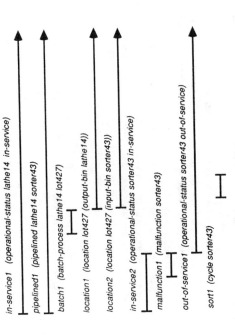

in-service1 (operational-status lathe14 in-service)
pipelined1 (pipelined lathe14 sorter43)
batch1 (batch-process lathe14 lot427)
location1 (location lot427 (output-bin lathe14))
location2 (location lot427 (input-bin sorter43))
in-service2 (operational-status sorter43 in-service)
malfunction1 (malfunction sorter43)
out-of-service1 (operational-status sorter43 out-of-service)
sort1 (cycle sorter43)

FIG. 8. Time map demonstrating temporal reason maintenance.

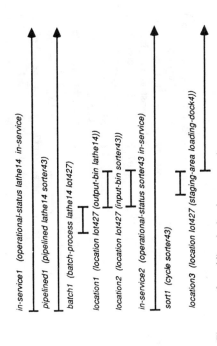

in-service1 (operational-status lathe14 in-service)
pipelined1 (pipelined lathe14 sorter43)
batch1 (batch-process lathe14 lot427)
location1 (location lot427 (output-bin lathe14))
location2 (location lot427 (input-bin sorter43))
in-service2 (operational-status sorter43 in-service)
sort1 (cycle sorter43)
location3 (location lot427 (staging-area loading-dock4))

FIG. 7. Time map after adding the batch process token.

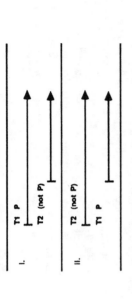

Apparent contradictions involving T1 and T2:

Data dependencies used for resolving apparent contradictions:

ddnode:	associated data type:	corresponding datum:
n_1	TOKEN	(time-token P T1)
n_2	TOKEN	(time-token (not P) T2)
n_3	TCONDIT	(pt< (begin T1) (begin T2))
n_4	TCONDIT	(pt< (begin T2) (begin T1))
n_5	CONLINK	(pt< (end T1) (begin T2))
n_6	CONLINK	(pt< (end T2) (begin T1))

n_5 has the justification $\{\{n_1, n_2, n_3\}\}$
n_6 has the justification $\{\{n_1, n_2, n_4\}\}$

Fig. 9. Dependency relations for managing persistence clipping.

resolves apparent contradictions and detects and responds to protection failures.

5.1. Apparent contradictions

Recall from Section 4.2 that two tokens are said to be apparently contradictory if they have contradictory types, one can be shown to begin before the other, and the two corresponding intervals possibly overlap. It is the responsibility of the system to resolve apparent contradictions by constraining the earlier token to end before the later one. The hard part, however, is noticing that resolution is required in the first place. Adding new tokens alone does not result in apparent contradictions. It is the addition of new constraints that the system has to be alert to. Every additional constraint results in new paths through the constraint network. Some of these new paths may enable the system to deduce new apparent contradictions.

The apparent contradiction criterion can be broken down into three tests: (1) do the two tokens contradict one another? (2) does one token precede the other? and (3) assuming that one token does precede the other, could the earlier token possibly overlap the later token? The result of the first test can be established once and for all at the time new tokens are created. This is because expressions corresponding to the types of time tokens contain no variables and contradiction criteria depend only upon properties of the terms appearing in these expressions that are timelessly true. The third test is not performed in the current implementation. If the two tokens could overlap, then adding the appropriate constraint will eliminate the possibility. If the two tokens can't overlap, then adding a constraint that ensures this fact shouldn't hurt. It is the second test that is used by the system to detect whether or not two contradictory tokens require resolution.

When a new token is asserted, the TMM finds all the tokens that contradict it (actually the TMM is a bit more selective than this [7]). For each pair of contradictory tokens T1 and T2 found in this way, the TMM creates a pair of what are called *clipping constraints*. For the tokens T1 and T2, the two clipping constraints would be (pt< (end T1) (begin T2)) and (pt< (end T2) (begin T1)). The purpose of the clipping constraints is to eliminate an apparent contradiction should one be detected. (When the end of one token is constrained to precede the beginning of a second (contradictory) token the second token is said to *clip* the first.) To make this work, the TMM adds a special justification to each clipping constraint in accordance with the second of the three tests described above. The easiest way to understand this is by looking carefully at the dependency structures and dependencies built by the TMM for the pair of contradictory token T1 and T2.

First, suppose that T1 and T2 have corresponding ddnodes n_1 and n_2. The system constructs two additional ddnodes n_3 and n_4 corresponding to the predications (pt< (begin T1) (begin T2)) and (pt< (begin T2) (begin T1)) respectively. These predications are referred to as *temporal conditions* and are associated with objects of data type TCONDIT. The system also constructs ddnodes n_5 and n_6 corresponding to the clipping constraints (pt< (end T1) (begin T2)) and (pt< (end T2) (begin T1)). The only justification for n_5 is $\{\{n_1, n_2, n_3\}\}$ and the only one for n_6 is $\{\{n_1, n_2, n_4\}\}$. Figure 9 shows the two situations leading to apparent contradictions involving T1 and T2 along with the data dependencies set up to resolve them.

The propositional content of a ddnode associated with a constraint will have the form (elt (distance pt1 pt2) *low high*). The justification for this ddnode is constructed from the current answer at the time the constraint is added to the data base. The propositional content of a ddnode associated with a temporal condition also has the form (elt (distance pt1 pt2) *low high*), but in this case the justification for the ddnode will be provided by the system. The system tries to make sure that each ddnode corresponding to a temporal condition (such as n_3 or n_4) is IN just in case there is path through the network of constraints (CONLINKs) whose bounds satisfy the condition corresponding to the propositional content of the ddnode. The TMM is said to manage the "virtual transitive closure" of a set of relations of which pt< is but one. We'll return to see how this is done after we see how the same sort of thing helps out in monitoring protections.

5.2. Protections

The notion of a protection is strongly connected with planning [30]. The idea of monitoring a protection came from trying to make sure that a prerequisite task served its purpose, where purpose was construed narrowly to mean making a fact true over an interval spanning the main task served by the prerequisite. In the time map we have stretched this notion to mean simply making sure that some proposition is believed to be true throughout an interval. The TMM supports three different types of protections. We will only consider *simple protections* here; see [7] for details on the other two.

All protections are implemented as ddnodes associated with an assertion of the form (passume P pt1 pt2) (passume stands for persistence assumption)

(define-predicate (passume PROP POINT POINT))

Every protection has one or more justifications, each of which refers to a specific time token. A simple protection has only one such justification. The justification is composed of three additional ddnodes: (1) n_1—a time token (call it T1) of type P, (2) n_2—the node associated with the temporal condition (pt≤ (begin T1) pt1), and (3) n_3—the node associated with the temporal condition (pt< (end T1) pt2). The data dependencies set up in a simple example of controlled forward chaining are shown in Fig. 10. The justification for the ddnode associated with (passume P pt1 pt2) is $\{\langle n_1, n_2\rangle\{n_3\}\}$ and corresponds to an instantiation of the *protection criterion*:

```
(← (passume ?p ?pt1 ?pt2)
   (and (time-token ?p ?tt)
        (pt≤ (begin ?tt) ?pt1)
        (M (pt≤ ?pt2 (end ?tt))))))
```

Noticing protection failures depends upon the ability of the system to keep track of the validity of temporal conditions such as (pt< pt1 pt2) and (pt≤ pt1 pt2). In the next section we'll see how to implement the "virtual transitive closure" of temporal conditions involving pairs of points.

5.3. Keeping track of temporal conditions

The objective of this subsection is to describe a method for maintaining the following invariant: each ddnode corresponding to a temporal condition (e.g., (pt< pt1 pt2) is IN just in case the constraints in the time map warrant it. We'll begin by being more precise about what is meant by "the constraints in the time map warranting a temporal condition."

The time map consists of POINTs linked by CONLINKs which bound the distance (in some units of time) separating pairs of points. CONLINKs, while they are created by TMM application programs, are not directly manipulated by such programs. We will use small caps and prefix notation to refer to system-defined functions and predicates in order to distinguish them from functions and predicates available to a TMM application program. A CONLINK is denoted $\langle pt_1, pt_2, low, high, dn\rangle$ where pt_1 and pt_2 are of type POINT, *low* and *high* are FIXNUMs, and *dn* is a data dependency node (an object of data type DDNODE). The only thing that we have to know about objects of data type DDNODE is that they have a label that is either IN or OUT (i.e., if *dn* is a DDNODE then LABEL(*dn*) ∈ {IN,OUT}). For each CONLINK $c = \langle pt_1, pt_2, low, high, dn\rangle$, we have LOW(*c*) = *low*, HIGH(*c*) = *high*, and DN(*c*) = *dn*. Recall that a path in the time map is a sequence of POINTs and directed edges corresponding to CONLINKs. For each *path* = $pt_0 c_1 pt_1 \ldots c_n pt_n$ we have BOUNDS(*path*) = $\langle low, high\rangle$ where $low = \Sigma_{i=1}^n$ LOW(c_i), and $high = \Sigma_{i=1}^n$ HIGH(c_i).

TCONDITs are denoted just as CONLINKs. Variables corresponding to TCONDITs and CONLINKs are prefixed *tc* and *c* respectively. The temporal condition $tc = \langle pt_{begin}, pt_{end}, tclow, tchigh, dn\rangle$ is warranted by the constraints in the time map just in case:

The following code fragment:

```
(for-first-answer (fetch '(tt pt1 pt2 P))
  (add '(and (time-token Q T2) (pt= pt2 (begin T2)))))
```

given the time map:

results in the augmented time map:

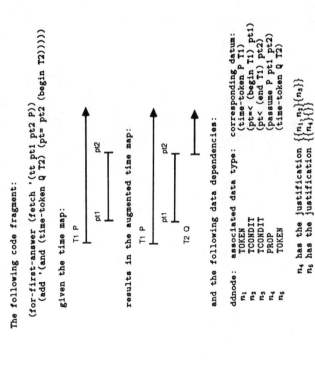

and the following data dependencies:

ddnode:	associated data type:	corresponding datum:
n_1	TOKEN	(time-token P T1)
n_2	TCONDIT	(pt< (begin T1) pt1)
n_3	TCONDIT	(pt< (end T1) pt2)
n_4	PROP	(passume P pt1 pt2)
n_5	TOKEN	(time-token Q T2)

n_4 has the justification $\{\{n_1, n_2\}\{n_3\}\}$
n_5 has the justification $\{\{n_4\}\{\}\}$

Fig. 10. Dependency relations for handling protections.

FIG. 11. Updating temporal conditions during constraint propagation.

For the TMM to work properly we need to be able to guarantee that the status (IN or OUT) of each ddnode corresponding to a TCONDIT accurately reflects the status of the constraints in the time map. This is done by attaching a signal function to each ddnode corresponding to a constraint such that whenever that ddnode becomes IN the consequences of that constraint are propagated throughout the time map. This signal function calls a function PROPAGATE defined as follows:[2]

$$\exists path = pt_{begin}c_1pt_1 \ldots c_npt_{end}:$$
$$(\text{BOUNDS}(path) = \langle plow, phigh \rangle) \wedge$$
$$(\mathbf{V}i: 1 \leqslant i \leqslant n: \text{LABEL}(\text{DN}(c_i)) = \text{IN}) \wedge$$
$$(tclow \leqslant plow) \wedge (phigh \leqslant tchigh)$$

PROPAGATE(c)
for each $path = pt_0c_1pt_1 \ldots c_npt_n$
if $(\exists j: 1 \leqslant j \leqslant n \wedge c = c_j) \wedge$
$\quad (\text{BOUNDS}(path) = \langle plow, phigh \rangle) \wedge$
$\quad (\mathbf{V}i: 1 \leqslant i \leqslant n: \text{LABEL}(\text{DN}(c_i)) = \text{IN}) \wedge$
then for each $tc = \langle pt_0, pt_n, tclow, tchigh, tcdn \rangle$
if $(tclow \leqslant plow) \wedge (phigh \leqslant tchigh)$
then INSTALL$(\{\{\text{DN}(c_i) | 1 \leqslant i \leqslant n\}\{\}\}, tcdn)$

Figure 11 shows a simple time map involving six points and the following five constraints:

$$c_1 = \langle pt_3, pt_5, 4, 5, dn_1 \rangle$$
$$c_2 = \langle pt_5, pt_1, 1, 2, dn_2 \rangle$$
$$c_3 = \langle pt_1, pt_2, 1, 1, dn_3 \rangle$$
$$c_4 = \langle pt_2, pt_4, 1, 2, dn_4 \rangle$$
$$c_5 = \langle pt_4, pt_6, 3, 4, dn_5 \rangle$$

Suppose that there is a temporal condition $tc_1 = \langle pt_3, pt_4, 0, \ast\text{pos-inf}\ast, dn_6 \rangle$ corresponding to the predication (pt $\leqslant$ pt3 pt4). Furthermore, dn_1, dn_2, dn_4, and dn_5 are IN, dn_6 is OUT, and the ddnode dn_3 corresponding to the constraint c_3 between pt_1 and pt_2 has just become IN. In this case PROPAGATE(c_3) will find the path $p = pt_3c_1pt_5c_2pt_1c_3pt_2c_4pt_4$ such that BOUNDS(p) = $\langle 7, 10 \rangle$ and execute INSTALL($\{\{dn_1, dn_2, dn_3, dn_4, dn_3\}\{\}\}$, dn_6) resulting in LABEL(dn_6) = IN.

The function PROPAGATE is implemented using heuristic graph searching techniques to find paths through the time map that might be used to update

temporal conditions. If the algorithm is allowed to enumerate all possible paths, this will guarantee that every temporal condition will be IN just in case it is warranted by the constraints in the time map. Of course this sort of exhaustive search can be prohibitively expensive. The complexity of the algorithm depends upon the number of constraints. Assuming a reasonable number of constraints, say n^2 where n is the total number of points, the algorithm will take time proportional to the cube of n. If n is large, as is expected in many applications, and constraints are frequently changed, then this sort of overhead cannot be absorbed. In most cases, however, you can get by with much less than exhaustive search. The easiest approach is to put an absolute limit on the search in terms of either CPU seconds or length of longest path considered. In most applications, the length of search paths required to update all critical temporal conditions is bounded by a small integer. For a given application this bound can be determined with a little experimentation. It might also be convenient in some instances to vary the bound to suit the type of problem being worked on or the time required for a solution. Adding a constraint (or having a constraint become IN) can be handled in constant time where the constant depends upon the sort of temporal connectivity expected for the application at hand. [7] considers techniques for caching distance estimates to improve performance in time maps having certain structural regularities.

5.4. The TRMS update algorithm

We can now describe the overall algorithm used by the temporal reason maintenance system (TRMS) in terms of a set of invariants to be maintained. The invariants are:[3]

(1) all TCONDITs are IN as the current set of constraints warrant,
(2) all apparent contradictions are resolved.

The temporal reason maintenance algorithm can be completely specified in terms of the dependency structures built by the TMM and the signal functions attached to various ddnodes. The important changes to the time map (those requiring significant reorganization and relabeling of ddnodes) result from

---

[2] INSTALL(*just*,*dn*) adds the justification *just* to the ddnode *dn* and updates the data dependency network accordingly.

[3] In the actual implementation of the TMM there are five invariants. Those not mentioned here are used for implementing special purpose protections, avoiding unnecessary calls to the static RMS, and caching distance estimates.

adding or removing constraints and erasing time tokens. When CONLINK ddnodes become IN, their signal functions propagate their corresponding point-to-point distance estimates. This propagation can result in the update of TCONDIT ddnodes which participate in the justifications for protections and clipping constraints. The former can directly affect the status of ddnodes corresponding to time tokens. Either update can result in a change in the status of ddnodes corresponding to constraints used to resolve apparent contradictions. If one of these ddnodes becomes IN then propagation occurs and the cycle repeats. In the next section we'll show that (under certain assumptions) this cycle of activity is guaranteed to terminate in a state that satisfies one interpretation of correctness for time maps.

5.5. Correctness of the temporal reason maintenance algorithm

The top level invariant maintained by the temporal reason maintenance system can be expressed as follows:

Each token, T1, can be shown to clip each contradictory token, T2, just in case T1 and T2 are IN and there exists a path through the time map consisting of CONLINKs with IN ddnodes such that the beginning of T2 can be shown to precede the beginning of T1.

Of course, tokens are typically justified by protections that are IN or OUT, depending upon the status of other tokens and the extent to which these (protecting) tokens are clipped. This gives rise to a circularity that could potentially cause problems. Figure 12 shows how changes instigated by an application program are translated into calls to the static RMS and execution of signal functions which, in turn, give rise to further calls to the static RMS. The circularity is plainly depicted in Fig. 12. The application program modifies the time map by adding new tokens and constraints in the course of controlled forward chaining. It is the addition of constraints which is of real interest. Modification to the status of a CONLINK ddnode can cause constraint propagation which, in turn, causes modification to the status of other CONLINK ddnodes. If one is not careful, this can go on indefinitely. Ensuring that it does not will require the cooperation of the user. In order to construct a proof of correctness, we will have to establish some conventions for using the TMM.

The situation that we're trying to avoid occurs when the action of clipping a persistence results in a chain of further actions that are ultimately responsible for undoing that clipping. For the temporal reason maintenance algorithm to terminate it must be the case that:

(1) clipping that results from resolving an apparent contradiction between two tokens cannot be the cause of a situation in which one of the two tokens becomes OUT;

(2) clipping that results from resolving an apparent contradiction between two tokens cannot be the cause of a situation in which one of the CONLINK ddnodes involved in establishing the apparent contradiction criterion (i.e., one of the CONLINKs in the path satisfying the TCONDIT used to determine that one token precedes a second) becomes OUT.

To ensure that the above conditions are met, we present a set of 5 specific rules[4] that guarantee correctness. The TMM will terminate correctly under considerably less restrictive sets of rules. The rules presented here were chosen because they make for a relatively short and simple proof of correctness.

Rule 1. Temporal data dependencies constructed in controlled forward chaining must conform to the following: All persistence tokens that depend upon protections are constrained to follow (by at least some infinitesimal amount) the intervals associated with their justifying protections.

What we really want to say here is that a time token of type P cannot depend upon (even indirectly) a time token of type R where P and R contradict one another and the token of type R is protected longer than the beginning of the token of type P. Simply put, a persistence cannot undermine its own reason for being.

[4] In [7] each rule is motivated with examples showing why violating the rule can get you into trouble, and why the rule will, in many cases, keep you from falling prey to certain conceptual misunderstandings.

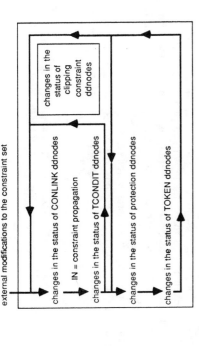

external modifications to the constraint set

changes in the status of CONLINK ddnodes

IN = constraint propagation

changes in the status of TCONDIT ddnodes

changes in the status of protection ddnodes

changes in the status of TOKEN ddnodes

changes in the status of clipping constraint ddnodes

Fig. 12. Flow of control in temporal reason maintenance.

5.6. Some preliminaries to a proof of correctness

Sections 5.1 and 5.2 introduced two important data dependency relations. The first concerned dependencies set up to clip persistences in keeping with the apparent contradiction criterion. In that case we had a special constraint called a clipping constraint whose ddnode was justified by a TCONDIT ddnode and the two ddnodes associated with the two contradictory tokens. The resulting data structures along with their associated ddnodes and justifications were shown in Fig. 9. The second type of dependency relation concerns protections and was illustrated in Fig. 10, again with its associated data structures. In each case, ddnodes corresponding to TCONDITs and TOKENs play the critical roles. Recall that a TCONDIT has justifications which take the form of some number of CONLINK ddnodes. These CONLINKs define a path through the time map that would satisfy the temporal condition given that all the ddnodes were IN. When a ddnode associated with a constraint becomes IN, this causes the propagation of the constraint. This, in turn, may result in certain TCONDITs being updated to reflect the change in temporal connectivity. When a constraint ddnode becomes OUT no propagation occurs, but TCONDIT ddnodes can become OUT as a result of justifications that depend upon the OUT constraint.

Rules 2 and 3 together guarantee that, after the constraint changed by the user (thus instigating the update) is propagated, the relative ordering of the beginning of the tokens in the time map will not change over the course of the rest of the update. This is because the only constraints that change (by Rule 3) are clipping constraints, and since they only constrain the end points of persistences (which are otherwise unconstrained by Rule 2) these constraints cannot change the relative order of the beginning of tokens.[5] So once the initial propagation occurs, the beginning of all tokens will remain in the same partial order throughout the rest of the update. When we say that one token is earlier than another, or refer to the set of all tokens which occur earlier than a given token, we are speaking only about the relative ordering of their beginning points.

Finally, before we get on with the proof, we introduce two properties of tokens. A token is said to be stable with respect to its status (abbreviated s/STATUS) just in case each earlier occurring token is both stable with respect to its status and stable with respect to the clipping that that token is licensed to perform (abbreviated s/CLIP). If a token is OUT, then it's not licensed to perform any clipping. In general, a token, T1, is licensed to clip any earlier contradictory, T2, just in case the ddnodes corresponding to T1 and T2 are IN, and there exists a path through the time map such that the beginning of T2 can be shown to precede the beginning of T1, and the ddnodes corresponding to

---

[5] We're assuming here that all apparent contradictions can be resolved. This is guaranteed given Rule 5 if the lower bound on all persistences is 0. If not and an apparent contradiction cannot be resolved the system will detect an inconsistency and prompt the user to resolve it.

Rule 2. Having initiated the TRMS update algorithm by changing the justification for a constraint or time token, the only additional constraints to change status are those added by the system in resolving apparent contradictions.

This rule is a bit harder to swallow than the previous one, simply because it forces a (partial) separation between temporal connectivity and inferential connectivity. From an aesthetic point of view, it would be nice if we could somehow integrate the two. Ideally, all constraints should be dependent upon the tokens whose points they constrain. If a token became OUT for one reason or another, then its associated constraints would evaporate as well, leaving the data base free of "phantom" constraints (i.e., constraints relating points belonging to tokens which are OUT). While this is desirable in certain circumstances, it can introduce circularities into the dependency graph that prevent termination. Rather than go into the details [7], we will simply forbid justifications for constraints that would cause one constraint to change status as a result of a change in the status of a second constraint. Note that this applies only to user-introduced constraints. Clipping constraints are guaranteed to be well behaved.

Rule 3. The only constraints that refer to the end points of a persistence are those added by the system in resolving apparent contradictions.

This rule essentially says that the end points of persistences must "float".

Rule 4. No new objects of data type TOKEN are added during TRMS update.

This rule just makes the proof simpler. The use of auto-projection rules obviously violates this mandate. In most situations auto-projection works fine, but if the user chooses to describe an oscillator with no termination condition then the TMM cannot guarantee termination.

Rule 5. No two time tokens asserting contradictory facts can be shown to have coincident beginning points.

This is just another criterion to ensure that the data base does not have any outright unresolvable contradictions.

The above five rules constitute basic assumptions about how the TMM is used sufficient to guarantee correctness. Before we present the proof of correctness we'll review some ideas presented in previous sections, point out some of the places where the 5 rules described above will come into play, and introduce some additional terminology that will be used in the proof.

the CONLINKs in the path establishing this ordering relation are also IN. Of course, this is just a restatement of the top level invariant which began Section 5.5. To prove correctness we want to show that the algorithm terminates in a state such that every token is both S/STATUS and S/CLIP. Intuitively (and simplifying somewhat), a ddnode is IN just in case all of the protections participating in its justification are IN. A protection is IN just in case the associated token is IN and it spans (persists throughout) the required interval. Every IN token clips all earlier occurring contradictory tokens.

5.7. Correctness

The proof will proceed by induction. The idea is to show that as the update progresses tokens become S/STATUS and S/CLIP on a regular basis, and, once they achieve this lofty position, they do not revert to an unstable state. The only thing that sustains the update is change in the status of tokens and, since there are a finite number of tokens and these are eventually all S/STATUS, the algorithm must terminate; and, since all the tokens are both S/STATUS and S/CLIP, it terminates correctly. Let m be the total number of tokens in the data base and assume that $m > 0$.

Basis step. When the initial propagation is finished, there is a nonempty set of tokens each of which have no earlier tokens in the partial order. These tokens are necessarily S/STATUS, since by Rule 1 they have no protections, as this would imply that there are earlier tokens. In addition, they must be S/CLIP since there are no earlier tokens and hence there are no earlier contradictory ones. The status of these tokens must have been given by fiat, and hence this status is correct and will not change during the remainder of the update.

Induction hypothesis. We assume that n tokens are both S/STATUS and S/CLIP where $0 < n < m$ and that further these tokens have the correct status and this status will not change during the remainder of the update.

Induction step. It's easy to see that there must exist some number (> 0) of tokens that are S/STATUS but not S/CLIP. By the induction hypothesis there are tokens which are not both S/STATUS and S/CLIP, so necessarily there are such tokens that are not earlier than any of the others and these must be S/STATUS by definition. Let's consider one such token, call it T1. First, we want to show that the status of T1 is correct and that it won't change. Since all earlier tokens have the correct status and have clipped just those tokens they are entitled to, the protection of T1 must be IN just in case their corresponding tokens are IN and span the required interval. If they are IN, then whether or not they span the required interval should be evident in the status of the protections' TCONDITs. The only tokens that could stop all the clipping from persisting long enough (by Rule 1) are those that are earlier than T1 and hence have done all the clipping they're entitled to. Propagation of constraints guarantees that the clipping constraints will be reflected in TCON-DITs which keep track of the status of protections. So T1 has the correct status and it can't change.

Now we have to show that T1 will clip all the tokens it's supposed to, and, once it has performed this clipping (and its associated constraint propagation), it won't do any more. All clipping constraints depend upon a pair of tokens and a TCONDIT which relates the beginnings of the two tokens. We can assume that the TCONDIT does not change status after the initial constraint propagation. So, the only thing that can initiate further constraint propagation is a change in the status of tokens. Since both T1 and any earlier tokens which it could clip will not change any further (by the induction hypothesis and the argument above), we can assume that the status of all clipping constraints that would result in T1 clipping an earlier token T1 are stable. Moreover, the signal functions associated with these clipping constraints will see to it that these constraints are reflected in the TCONDITs for protections justifying later tokens. This last may result in a change in the status of other later tokens, and hence cause further changes in clipping the next time the static RMS is called. However, T1 has done all the clipping it can do, and this will not change, since the status of T1 will not change. This shows that T1 is S/CLIP thus completing the induction argument.

In this way, we can see that the process will not stop as long as changes keep occurring in the status of tokens. However, since eventually all tokens are both S/STATUS and S/CLIP the process must terminate and terminate correctly.[6]

6. Problems and Possible Extensions

Time maps were originally developed for coping with large amounts of temporal information. The time maps in the applications explored so far have yet to exceed 300 time tokens. One ideal application of time maps would be to manage a large data base of facts dealing with the correspondence of a journal editor or publishing house. The time map would monitor publication deadlines, automatically generate nasty letters to laggard reviewers and writers, and notice when some reviewer was inadvertently swamped with more work than he or she could possibly handle. Such a data base for a large journal would easily involve thousands of time tokens and hundreds of auto-projection rules

---

[6] The changes in token status do not necessarily occur in the most efficient order. In the worst case, a single token could change status on the order of n times where n is the total number of tokens. In practice this would be hard to even purposely arrange, but less extreme situations occur frequently and can cause the RMS to do more work than is necessary. One way in which the RMS algorithm might be improved would be to sort the signal functions for clipping constraints so that they swept forward in time, never propagating a clipping constraint until both of the tokens associated with it were stable with respect to their status. It would take some experimentation to determine whether or not the sorting overhead would outweigh the cost of unnecessary token status toggling, but it would certainly pay off if anything like the worst case began to manifest itself regularly.

two methods whereby the user might be freed from adhering to such a criterion. First, it is possible that less restrictive criteria that still guarantee termination can be found. In fact, such criteria are more complicated and hence more difficult for the programmer to adhere to. The second method for relaxing the termination criterion would be to make it the system's responsibility to detect and recover from circular dependencies that would normally lead to the current algorithm failing to terminate. The latter might involve considerable processing overhead (we suspect that the general problem of detecting time map dependency circularities leading to nontermination is intractable). We hope that it will be easier to formulate a less restrictive criterion. Perhaps something akin to the *no-odd-loops* criterion for static data dependency systems [3] can be formulated for time maps.

There are occasions on which it would be convenient to handle apparent contradictions involving tokens whose schemata (types) contain variables or terms whose properties change over time. For instance, (color block37 c2) contradicts (color block37 c1) even though all we currently know about c1 and c2 is that (member c1 !(red green)) and (= c2 blue)). Noticing such contradictions might be handled using various nonmonotonic inference techniques, but keeping track of exactly which pairs of tokens are contradictory under the addition and deletion of facts is likely to be expensive. In planning, this sort of inference may play an important role in the process of managing the properties of partially instantiated parameters (or *script variables*) introduced in plan expansion [28]. For instance, suppose that the robot has decided to service either lathe7 or lathe34. One consequence of this is that the robot will be in either room41 or room17. From this the planner should be able to conclude that the robot will no longer be in room5. Furthermore, if the success of a particular plan depends upon the fact that the robot being in room5, then the planner should be made aware of the fact that this plan is endangered. Currently there is little work being done along these lines. The functionality as it has been described so far is disturbingly open ended.

In [6], a version of the TMM is described that is capable of reasoning about alternative choices and multiple outcomes for events. The ability to describe a robot's temporal knowledge in terms of a tree of predictions branching into the future is extremely useful in planning. The branching time implementation of the TMM (described in [7]) is essentially a temporalized assumption-based reason maintenance system [11]. Unfortunately, maintaining several time lines simultaneously can turn out to be relatively expensive. One problem is that with n binary choices there are $O(2^n)$ distinct time lines. Some of these can be eliminated as being impossible, but there are generally enough left to seriously degrade the system's performance. The main problem is that the constraint propagation routines used by the temporal reason maintenance machinery are currently not smart enough to keep the necessary computations within reason-

and change-driven interrupts. Without some additional strategies for partitioning large time maps and guiding search, the current implementation would be swamped by such applications. The techniques used in the TMM just begin to exploit the available structure for organizing time maps. Hierarchical organizations based on the calendar (days, weeks, months, years) suggest simple but highly effective techniques that could be used to partition time maps. Another problem involved in dealing with large time maps involves setting up data dependencies to detect apparent contradictions. Setting up such predictions for all possible pairs of contradictory tokens is prohibitive. Luckily, in most cases it's not necessary. Most information in a temporal data base is unlikely to ever change. If the galley proofs for a certain manuscript are sent to the copy center, then that fact is history. Every subsequent action that results in a change in the location of those proofs needn't worry about whether the action occurs before or after the proofs were sent to the copy center. It's highly unlikely that the data entry operator was mistaken about the time that the proofs were sent to the copy center. It would seem that the problem of selectively setting up data dependencies to detect and resolve apparent contradictions can be handled efficiently in many applications.

The current version of the TMM has difficulty reasoning about overlapping tokens of the same type. If you know that there's a light in the kitchen from 8:00 AM until midnight and a light in the living room from midnight until noon, then you know there is a light on in the house 24 hours a day. Currently the time map is not capable of making the general observation that if P is true throughout the interval from pt1 to pt2, P is true throughout the interval from pt3 to pt4, and pt3 is between pt1 and pt2, then P is true throughout the interval from pt1 to pt4. Getting the time map to handle this sort of inference appears to be one of the simpler extensions of the TMM. Dean [7] describes a solution to this problem, but it has yet to be implemented.

Another potentially useful extension involves nonmonotonic inferences of the form, if you have no reason to believe (not P) is true anywhere in the interval from pt1 to pt2, then you are licensed to believe P throughout this interval. Writing code to handle queries of the form (M (tt pt1 pt2 P)), and monitor the continued validity of the underlying default assumptions is not particularly difficult. The TMM supports such inferences using what are called anti-protections [7]. However, there are a number of efficiency considerations that have to be dealt with before this sort of inference can be relied upon not to bog down processing. In particular, anti-protections must keep track of *all* tokens of a particular type. There must be some method for concentrating on a restricted subset of the set of all tokens of a type. In this regard, the issues involved in handling anti-protections are much the same as those involved in setting up dependencies to detect and resolve apparent contradictions.

The proof of correctness for the temporal reason maintenance system provided a fairly restrictive criterion for guaranteeing termination. There are

able limits. The worst case we know is hard, but it seems that we should be able to build a version that works well in common planning situations.

7. Conclusions

This paper describes an extension of classical predicate-calculus data base techniques that naturally and efficiently handles a useful class of temporal reasoning chores. There are three issues to address in assessing the contribution of this extension:

(1) *Naturalness and expressive power of the notation.* How clear is the language for expressing temporally dependent facts, and what are the limitations on what can be said in this language?

(2) *Supported functionality.* What sort of operations on temporal data are handled by the augmented deductive engine?

(3) *Efficiency.* What sort of performance can be expected from the system in handling routine temporal reasoning chores of the sort that typically arise in artificial intelligence applications?

In the following three subsections we will speak of each of these in turn.

7.1. A notation for expressing temporal information

The basic ontological commitments (points, intervals, and constraints) are clearly necessary. In addition, the notion of time token provides a convenient means for speaking about particular periods of time during which an event occurs or a proposition becomes true and remains so for a time. We have chosen to take points as primitives and define intervals in terms of points, but that is essentially an implementation detail. Time tokens referring to intervals are the primary units of discourse in application programs using the TMM.

The language primitives introduced in Section 4.2 are again rather basic, though slightly more controversial. Some may question the emphasis on metric constraints, but we believe that the ability of the TMM to express and reason about duration and metric information is one of its strong points. There are those who claim that interval relations like precedes, overlaps. and meet [1, 2] deserve greater prominence in a theory of time. For the most part we would agree and hope that the fact that predicates like precedes. overlaps. and meet can be easily defined in terms of elt and the function distance with minimal computational overhead will appease these potential detractors. But while these interval relationships are important, reasoning about duration involving metric constraints is a critical prerequisite to a computational approach to reasoning about time. Purely qualitative information is easily handled using elt, distance, and the set { *neg-inf* , *neg-tiny* , 0, *pos-tiny* , *pos-inf* }. Incomplete information, in the form of partially ordered time tokens and "fuzzy" durations, is easily expressible in the notation for referring to upper and lower bounds on the time separating pairs of points. The TMM provides a suitable

foundation for reasoning about all sorts of temporal information, qualitative as well as quantitative. Suitable predicates can easily be defined to meet the individual programmer's representational requirements.

The class of useful queries possible using the predicates elt, time-token, and tt in conjunction with the M operator and the abductive techniques described in [5, 7] is quite extensive. The examples shown in Section 4 have demonstrated some of the TMM's range in this regard. There are also severe restrictions on what can be expressed using these language constructs. The most glaring deficiency concerns the expression of information about continuously changing quantities. Actually the notion of "continuous change" is a red herring. The time map cannot even deal effectively with discretely changing quantities like the number of lathes available for use on a production line. We have considered extensions to the time map for performing the requisite reasoning tasks, but the requirement that the extension deal with partial orders and provide a corresponding extension to the temporal reason maintenance algorithms has proved difficult to meet. The computational problems for the general case appear to be intractable. We believe that the techniques described in this paper can be extended to deal with certain aspects of reasoning about continuous change. The hard part will be isolating a useful functionality that can be efficiently supported.

7.2. Functional requirements for temporal data base management

The temporal information possessed by an agent in realistic situations is both incomplete and potentially defeasible. In order to contend with these factors, we introduced the notion of persistence (Section 3.1) and a strategy for interpreting the information stored in time maps (Section 4.3). This provided the basis for processing queries in partially ordered time maps involving default assumptions about the persistence of fact tokens. The notion of protection (Section 3.2) was extended to deal with defeasible antecedent conditions involving facts persisting over certain intervals, where these conditions are used as the basis for making various consequent predictions. These techniques for managing temporal deductions fit in quite nicely with methods for performing forward inference in static data base systems (e.g., [8]).

Since the information contained in a time map is typically incomplete, there has to be some method of exploring some of the possible completions. The query routines should make the application program aware of various possibilities that might provide a basis for supporting certain sought-after conclusions or consequences. The TMM facilitates this sort of reasoning by providing an abductive interpretation of the "true throughout" predicate. Using the abductive inference capability, the system can propose additional constraints (abductive premises) that restrict the current partially ordered time map in order to allow a deduction to precede that would fail otherwise. In addition, the use of abductive answers provides an application program with an inexpensive method for keeping around several hypothetical situations to facilitate the process of selecting the best such hypothesis.

In addition to techniques supporting what was termed controlled forward inference, the TMM also provides the necessary machinery for performing a temporal version of pattern directed inference. Section 4.6 described notation for expressing rules that support a simple form of temporal implication (rules of the form (→, *antecedent consequent*)), as well as a method for capturing certain causal effects of actions represented in the time map (automatic projection rules). These rules don't suffer from the timing complications inherent in controlled forward inference. They are especially useful in planning applications, as they free the planner to concentrate upon only those aspects of a planning situation that are of critical importance in achieving the desired coordination of a set of conjunctive tasks. Side effects of actions need only come to the attention of the planner when they are noticed to interfere with or somehow facilitate a plan currently under consideration.

7.3. Efficiently managing temporal data bases

The techniques described in this paper constitute a solution to the temporal data base update problem. There are two aspects to this problem. The first concerns determining whether or not a proposition is true at a point or throughout an interval. The second aspect concerns the reorganization of a temporal data base in response to various changes in its contents and the detection of important consequences that follow from those changes. The TMM addresses both of these aspects.

The organization of the time map makes it quite simple to determine whether or not a token of a given type spans a given point or interval. This determination can be made without taking into consideration all of the events and their associated effects that fall between the beginning of that token and the end of the period in question. The main techniques used in performing such operations involve the use of temporal conditions (used to monitor the validity of relationships between pairs of points) and clipping constraints (used in resolving apparent contradictions in order to restrict the duration of persistences). Simplifying somewhat, determining whether or not a fact P is true throughout an interval pt1 to pt2 requires finding the token of type P that most recently precedes pt1 and then determining whether or not the end of that token can possibly follow pt2. The most expensive part of this involves determining good estimates of the distance separating pairs of points in the time map, and this operation is optimized using the techniques of [7].

Incremental reorganization of the time map is an important consideration in efficiently maintaining the data base to support the above sort of queries. The techniques of temporal reason maintenance see to it that only those parts of

the data base affected by the most recent modifications have to be updated. The temporal reason maintenance algorithm effectively performs a sweep forward in time selectively updating only those aspects of the time map as are indicated by the dependencies recorded in time map protections. The methods described for propagating constraints, monitoring protections, and resolving apparent contradictions make this incremental reorganization possible. Temporal reason maintenance also plays an important role in noticing certain critical consequences that follow from modifications to the data base. Using special programs called change-driven interrupts, an application program can specify the type of consequences it is interested in being alerted to and exactly what response is to be made assuming that those consequences manifest themselves. The basic technique is quite common in AI languages [16, 20]. Its application to reasoning in time maps provides a natural generalization of the notion of a critic [27] that responds to the detection of interactions (or in the case of the TMM, protection failures).

It is ultimately up to those using the TMM to determine whether or not it represents an efficient and natural extension of classical predicate-calculus data base techniques. Without access to the program it will be difficult to assess its efficiency. Versions of the TMM have already been employed in planning applications [24], and there should be a distribution version within the coming year. As for the naturalness of the notation and the range of functionality supported, the examples of Section 4 should provide a basis for the reader to make his own judgements. Admittedly there is a great deal of research that has yet to be done. The hope is simply that the techniques presented here provide a reasonable start.

ACKNOWLEDGMENT

James Firby, Steve Hanks, Dave Miller, and Yoav Shoham influenced both the content and form of this paper. Gene Charniak, Chris Riesbeck, and Austin Tate read earlier drafts and provided constructive criticism.

REFERENCES

1. Allen, J., Maintaining knowledge about temporal intervals, *Commun. ACM* **26** (1983) 832–843.
2. Allen, J.F. and Hayes, P.J., A common-sense theory of time, in: *Proceedings IJCAI-85*, Los Angeles, CA, 1985.
3. Charniak, E., Riesbeck, C.K. and McDermott, D.V., *Artificial Intelligence Programming* (Erlbaum, Hillsdale, NJ, 1980).
4. Clocksin, W.F. and Mellish, C.S., *Programming in Prolog* (Springer, Berlin, 1984).
5. Dean, T., Planning and temporal reasoning under uncertainty, in: *Proceedings IEEE Workshop on Principles of Knowledge-Based Systems*, Denver, CO, 1984.
6. Dean, T., Temporal reasoning involving counterfactuals and disjunctions, in: *Proceedings IJCAI-85*, Los Angeles, CA, 1985.

7. Dean, T., Temporal imagery: An approach to reasoning about time for planning and problem solving, Tech. Rept. 433, Computer Science Department, Yale University, New Haven, CT, 1985.

8. de Kleer, J., Doyle, J., Steele, G.L. and Sussman, G.J., Explicit control of reasoning, *SIGPLAN Notices* **12**(8) (1977).

9. de Kleer, J., Doyle, J., Rich, C., Steele, G.L. and Sussman, G.J., AMORD: A deductive procedure system. Tech. Rept. AI TR-435. AI Laboratory, MIT, Cambridge, MA, 1978.

10. de Kleer, J. and Brown, J.S., Foundations of envisioning, in: *Proceedings AAAI-82*, Pittsburgh, PA, 1982.

11. de Kleer, J., An assumption-based TMS, *Artificial Intelligence* **28** (1986) 127–162.

12. Doyle, J., A truth maintenance system, *Artificial Intelligence* **12** (1979) 231–272.

13. Firby, R.J., Dean. T.L. and Miller, D.P., Efficient robot planning with deadlines and travel time, in: *Proceedings Sixth International Symposium on Robotics and Automation*, Santa Barbara, CA, 1985.

14. Forbus, K.D., Qualitative process theory, *Artifical Intelligence* **24** (1984) 85–168.

15. Hayes, P.J., The naive physics manifesto, in: D. Michie (Ed), *Expert Systems in the Microelectronic Age* (Edinburgh University Press, Edinburgh, 1979).

16. Hewitt, C., PLANNER: A language for proving theorems in robots, in: *Proceedings IJCAI-69*, Washington, DC. 1969.

17. Martins, J.P. and Shapiro. S.C., Reasoning in multiple belief spaces, in: *Proceedings IJCAI-83*, Karlsruhe, F.R.G., 1983.

18. McAllester, D.A., The use of equality in deduction and knowledge representation. Tech. Rept. 550, AI Laboratory, MIT, Cambridge, MA, 1980.

19. McAllester, D.A., Reasoning utility package user's manual, Tech. Rept. 667. AI Laboratory, MIT, Cambridge, MA, 1982.

20. McDermott, D.V. and Sussman, G.J., The Conniver reference manual, Tech. Rept. 259, AI Laboratory, MIT, Cambridge, MA, 1973.

21. McDermott, D.V. and Doyle, J., Non-monotonic logic I, *Artificial Intelligence* **13** (1980) 41–72.

22. McDermott, D.V., A temporal logic for reasoning about processes and plans, *Cognitive Sci.* **6** (1982) 101–155.

23. McDermott, D.V. The DUCK manual, Tech. Rept. 399, Computer Science Department, Yale University, New Haven, CT, 1985.

24. Miller, D.P., Firby, R.J. and Dean, T.L.. Deadlines, travel time, and robot problem solving, in: *Proceedings IJCAI-85*, Los Angeles, CA, 1985.

25. Minsky, M.. A framework for representing knowledge, in: J. Haugeland (Ed.). *Mind Design* (MIT Press, Cambridge, MA, 1981).

26. Nilsson, N.J., *Principles of Artificial Intelligence* (Tioga, Palo Alto, CA, 1980).

27. Sacerdoti, E., *A Structure for Plans and Behavior* (American Elsevier, New York, 1977).

28. Stefik, M.J., Planning with constraints (MOLGEN: Part 1), *Artificial Intelligence* **16** (1981) 111–139.

29. Sussman, G.J., Winograd, T. and Charniak. G., Micro-Planner reference manual. Tech. Rept. 203, AI Laboratory. MIT, Cambridge, MA. 1971.

30. Sussman, G.J., *A Computer Model of Skill Acquisition* (American Elsevier, New York, 1975).

31. Vere, S., Planning in time: Windows and durations for activities and goals. *IEEE Trans. Pattern Anal. Mach. Intell.* **5** (1983) 246–267.

Received January 1986; revised version received June 1986

Nonmonotonic Logic and Temporal Projection*

Steve Hanks and Drew McDermott**

Department of Computer Science, Yale University, New Haven, CT 06520, U.S.A.

Recommended by Daniel G. Bobrow

ABSTRACT

Nonmonotonic formal systems have been proposed as an extension to classical first-order logic that will capture the process of human "default reasoning" or "plausible inference" through their inference mechanisms, just as modus ponens provides a model for deductive reasoning. But although the technical properties of these logics have been studied in detail and many examples of human default reasoning have been identified, for the most part these logics have not actually been applied to practical problems to see whether they produce the expected results.

We provide axioms for a simple problem in temporal reasoning which has long been identified as a case of default reasoning, thus presumably amenable to representation in nonmonotonic logic. Upon examining the resulting nonmonotonic theories, however, we find that the inferences permitted by the logics are not those we had intended when we wrote the axioms, and in fact are much weaker. This problem is shown to be independent of the logic used; nor does it depend on any particular temporal representation. Upon analyzing the failure we find that the nonmonotonic logics we considered are inherently incapable of representing this kind of default reasoning.

The first part of the paper is an expanded version of one that appeared in the 1986 AAAI proceedings. The second part reports on several responses to our result that have appeared since the original paper was published.

1. Introduction

Logic as a representation language for AI theories has always held a particular appeal in the research community (or in some parts of it, anyway): its rigid syntax forces one to be precise about what one is saying, and its semantics provide an agreed-upon and well-understood way of assigning meaning to the symbols. But if logic is to be more than just a concise and convenient notation that helps us in the task of writing programs, we somehow have to validate the axioms we write: are the conclusions we can draw from our representation

(i.e., the inferences the logic allows) the same as the ones characteristic of the reasoning process we are trying to model? If so, we've gone a long way toward validating our theory. In fact several research efforts have been based around the idea that logic can describe both ontology and reasoning processes. Most notable among these are the "Naive Physics" program proposed by Hayes (e.g. in [9]) and the work done by McCarthy on circumscription (e.g. in [17]).

The limitation of classical logic as a representation for human reasoning is that its inference rule, modus ponens, is the analogue to human *deductive* reasoning, but for the most part everyday human reasoning seems to have significant nondeductive components. But while certain aspects of human reasoning (e.g. inductive generalization and abductive explanation) seem to be substantially different from deduction, a certain class of reasoning, dubbed "default reasoning," resembles deduction more closely. Thus it was thought that extensions to first-order logic might produce formal systems capable of representing the process of default reasoning.

While it is still not clear *exactly* what constitutes default reasoning, the phenomenon commonly manifests itself when we know what conclusions should be drawn about *typical* situations or objects, but we must jump to the conclusion that an observed situation or object *is* typical. For example, I may know that I typically meet with my advisor on Thursday afternoons, but I can't deduce that I will actually have a meeting *next* Thursday because I don't know whether next Thursday is typical. While certain facts may allow me to deduce that next Thursday is *not* typical (e.g. if I learn he will be out of town all next week), I will not generally be able to deduce that it *is* typical. What we want to do in cases like this is to jump to the conclusion that next Thursday is typical based on two pieces of information: first that most Thursdays *are* typical, and second that we have no reason to believe that this one is not. Another way to express the same notion is to say that I know that I have meetings on typical Thursdays, and that the only *atypical* Thursdays are the ones that I *know* (can deduce) are atypical. (Thus everything is typical that cannot be proved to be atypical.)

Research on nonmonotonic logics,[1] most notably by McCarthy (in [16, 17]), McDermott and Doyle (in [21]) and Reiter (in [24]) attacked the problem of extending first-order logic in a way that captured the intuitive meaning of statements of the form "lacking evidence to the contrary, infer α" or more

---

[1] So called because of the property that inferences allowed by the logic may be *disallowed* as axioms are added. For example I may jump to the conclusion that next Thursday is typical, thus deduce that I will have a meeting. If I later come to find out that it is *atypical*, I will have to *retract* that conclusion. In first-order logic the addition of new knowledge (axioms) to a theory can never diminish the deductions one can make from that theory, thus it is never necessary to retract conclusions.

[2] This sounds much more straightforward than it is: consider that the theorems of a logic are defined in terms of its inference rules, yet here we are trying to define an inference rule in terms of what is or is not a theorem.

*This is a revised version of the paper that won the AI Journal Best Paper Award at AAAI-86.

**This work was supported in part by ONR grant N00014-85-K0301.

axioms. Finally we point out the (unexpected) characteristics of the domain that the logics were unable to capture, and discuss proposed solutions to the problem.

The paper we originally published on this result, which first appeared as a Yale technical report [7], then in a shortened version in the AAAI-86 proceedings [8], generated a wide range of responses. In the second part of this paper we will discuss these replies and comment on the extent to which they actually address the issues we raised.

2. Nonmonotonic Inference

Since we are considering the question of what inferences can be drawn from a nonmonotonic theory, we should look briefly at how inference is defined in these logics. We will concentrate on Reiter's default logic and on circumscription, but the discussion and subsequent results hold for McDermott's nonmonotonic logic as well.

2.1. Inference in default logic

Reiter in [24] defines a *default theory* as two sets of rules. The first consists of sentences in first-order logic (and is usually referred to as *W*), and the second is a set of *default rules* (referred to as *D*). Default rules are supposed to indicate what conclusions to jump to, and are of the form

$$\frac{\alpha : M\beta}{\gamma},$$

where α, β, and γ are first-order sentences. The intended interpretation of this rule is "if you believe α, and it's consistent to believe β, then believe γ", or, to phrase the idea more like an inference rule, "from α and the *inability* to prove $\neg\beta$, infer γ." (But recall our note above about the futility of trying to define inference in terms of inference.)

In order to discuss default inference Reiter introduces the concept of an *extension*—a set of sentences that "extend" the sentences in *W* according to the dictates of the default rules. A default theory defines zero or more extensions, each of which has the following properties:

(1) any extension *E* contains *W*,

(2) *E* is closed under (monotonic) deduction, and

(3) *E* is faithful to the default rules.

By the last we mean that if there's a default rule in the theory of the form $(\alpha : M\beta)/\gamma$, and if $\alpha \in E$, and $(\neg\beta) \notin E$, then $\gamma \in E$. The extensions of a default theory are all the minimal sets *E* that satisfy these three properties. Extensions can be looked upon as internally consistent and coherent states of the world, and a reasoner should thus "pick" an extension from those

---

generally "infer β from the inability to infer α." But since that first flurry of research the area has developed in a strange way. On one hand the logics have been subjected to intense technical scrutiny (in the papers cited above, and also, for example, by Davis in [3]) and have been shown to produce counterintuitive results under certain circumstances. But these examples always have a certain contrived appearance to them. A favorite example is a theory containing a rule "infer α from the inability to infer α." Presumably there would be no *real* representation problem in which the inability of prove a formula should be a reason to believe that formula, so we wonder whether the anomalous technical results really should matter to us in representing the real world.

At the same time we see in the literature practical representation problems such as story understanding (Charniak [1]), social convention in conversation (Joshi, Webber, and Weischedel [17]), and temporal reasoning (McDermott [19] and McCarthy [10]), in which default rules would *seem* to be of use, but in these cases technical details of the formal systems are for the most part ignored. At best the researchers admit that they don't understand exactly what they're writing when they resort to the language of default logic (see [19], for example); at worst they just go ahead and use the syntax without further analysis.

The middle ground—whether the technical workings of the logics correctly bear out one's intentions in representing practical default-reasoning problems—is for the most part empty, though the work of Reiter, Etherington, and Criscuolo (in [4,5] and elsewhere) is a notable exception. Logicians have for the most part ignored practical problems to focus on technical details, and "practitioners" have used the default rules intuitively, with the hope (most often unstated) that the proof theory or semantics of the logics can eventually be shown to support those intuitions.

We explore that middle ground by presenting a problem in temporal reasoning that involves default inference, writing axioms in nonmonotonic logics intended to represent that reasoning process, then analyzing the resulting theory.

Reasoning about time is an interesting application for a couple of reasons. First of all, the problem of representing the tendency of facts to endure over time (the "frame problem" of McCarthy and Hayes [18] or the notion of "persistence" of McDermott [19]) has long been assumed to be one of those practical reasoning problems that nonmonotonic logics would solve. Second, one has strong intuitions about how the problem *should* be formalized in the logics, and even stronger intuitions about what inferences should then follow, so it will be clear whether the logics have succeeded or failed to represent the domain correctly.

In the first part of this paper we discuss briefly some technical aspects of nonmonotonic logics, then go on to pose formally the problem of temporal projection. We then analyze the inferences allowed by the resulting theory and show that they do *not* correspond to what we had intended when we wrote the

generated by the default theory and reason within it. Although an extension is by definition consistent, the union of two extensions may be inconsistent.

Finding a satisfying definition of default inference—what sentences can be said to follow from a default theory—is tricky. Reiter avoids the problem altogether, focusing on the task of defining extensions and exploring their properties. He ascribes to the view of reasoning that we noted in the paragraph above: that default reasoning is really a process of selecting *one* extension of a theory, then reasoning "within" this extension until new information forces a revision of one's beliefs and hence the selection of a new extension.

This view of default reasoning, while intuitively appealing, is infeasible from a practical standpoint: there is no way of "isolating" a single extension of a theory, thus no procedure for enumerating or testing theoremhood within an extension. So any definition of default reasoning based on discrimination among extensions is actually beyond the expressive power of default logic. Reiter does provide a proof procedure for asking whether a sentence is a member of *any* extension, but, as he points out, this is not a satisfying definition of inference since both a sentence and its negation may appear in different extensions.

Our view is that *some* notation of inference is necessary to judge the representational power of the logic. A logic that generates one intuitive extension and one unintuitive extension does not provide an adequate representation of the problem. since there is no way to distinguish between the two interpretations. For that reason we will define inference in the manner of McDermott's logic: a sentence δ can be inferred from a default theory just in case δ is in *every* extension of that theory. (This definition is also consistent with circumscriptive inference as described in the next section.)

While there is no general procedure for determining how many extensions a given theory has, as a practical matter it has been noted that theories with "conflicting" default rules tend to generate multiple extensions. For example, the following default theory

$$W = \{Q(N), R(N)\}.$$

$$D = \left\{ \frac{Q(x) : MP(x)}{P(x)}, \quad \frac{R(x) : M \neg P(x)}{\neg P(x)} \right\}$$

has two rules that would have us jump to contradictory conclusions. Applying one of the default rules means that the other cannot be applied. since its precondition is not met. This default theory has two extensions: $E_1 = \{Q(N), R(N). P(N)\}$ and $E_2 = \{Q(N), R(N), \neg P(N)\}$ that correspond to the two choices one has in applying the default rules. (One interpretation of this theory reads Q as "Quaker," R as "Republican," P as "Pacifist," and N as "Nixon.") Thus according to our definition of inference the above theory entails only the sentences in W, plus tautologies (for example $P(N) \vee \neg P(N)$).

We are not claiming that the admission of multiple extensions is a fault or deficiency of the logic—in this particular example it's hard to imagine how the logic could license any *other* conclusions. (It would be our responsibility to add additional rules to resolve the conflict, saying, for example, that one's Quaker tendencies always win out over one's Republican tendencies, or vice versa. McCarthy [17] and McDermott [20] both discuss techniques for restructuring the default rules to mediate their application.)

The point is that when a theory generates multiple extensions it's generally going to be the case that only weak conclusions can be drawn. Further, if one extension captures the *intended* interpretation but there are other different extensions, it will not be possible to make only the intended inferences.

2.2. Inference in circumscription

To describe inference in circumscribed theories we will have to be rather vague: there are several versions of the logic, defined in [14, 16, 17] and elsewhere, and we will not spend time discussing these differences.

We will speak generally of *predicate circumscription.* in which the intent is to minimize the extension of a predicate (say P) in a set of first-order axioms. Using terms like those we used in describing default logic, we might say that when we circumscribe axioms over P we intend that "the only individuals for which P holds are those individuals for which *P must hold*," or alternatively we might phrase it as "believe '*not P*' by default."

To circumscribe a set of axioms A over a predicate P one adds to A an axiom (the exact form of which is not important for our discussion) that says something like this: "any predicate P' that satisfies the axioms A, and is at least as strong as P, is *exactly* as strong as P." The intended effect is (roughly) that for any individual x,

if $A \not\vdash P(x)$,
then $\mathrm{Circum}(A, P) \vdash \neg P(x)$.

where Circum(A, P) refers to the axioms in A augmented by the circumscription axiom for P. This formulation is oversimplified: in addition to deciding what predicate(s) to circumscribe over, one must also decide on a set of predicates that are allowed to vary as parameters in the circumscription axiom. We will not discuss this complication further—in a previous paper [7] we do so at some length.

To talk about circumscriptive inference we should first note that since Circum(A, P) is a first-order theory we want to know what *deductively* follows, but we are interested in characterizing those deductions in terms of the original axioms in A. In brief, the results are these: if a formula φ is a theorem of Circum(A, P) then φ is true in all models of A *minimal in P.* (this property is called *soundness*), and if a formula φ is true in all models of A minimal in P then φ is a theorem of Circum(A, P) (this property is called *completeness*). Completeness does not hold for all circumscribed theories, but it does hold in certain special cases—see Minker and Perlis [22].

Minimal models, the model-theoretic analogue to default-logic extensions, are defined as follows: a model $\mathcal{M}$ is minimal in P just in case there is no model $\mathcal{M}'$ that agrees with $\mathcal{M}$ on all predicates *except* for P, but whose extension of P is a *subset* of $\mathcal{M}$'s extension of P.

As with default logic, there is no effective procedure for determining how many minimal models a theory has. And note that the converse of the soundness property says that if φ is *not* true in all models minimal in P it does *not* follow from Circum(A, P). So once again, if we have multiple minimal models we can deduce only those formulas true in all of them. Because of the obvious parallels between extensions and minimal models (and "NM fixed points" in McDermott's logic, which we will not discuss here), we will use the terms interchangeably when the exact logic or object doesn't matter.

3. The Temporal Projection Problem

The problem we want to represent is this: given an initial description of the world (some facts that are true), the occurrence of some events, and some notion of causality (that an event occurring can cause a fact to become true), what facts are true once all the events have occurred?

We obviously need some temporal representation to express these concepts, and we will use the *situation calculus* [18]. We will thus speak about *facts* holding true in *situations*. A fact syntactically has the form of a first-order sentence, and is intended to be an assertion about the world, such as SUNNY, LOADED(GUN-35), or $\forall x.$HAPPY(x). Situations are individuals denoting intervals of time over which facts hold or do not hold, but over which *no* fact changes its truth value. This latter property allows us to speak unambiguously about what facts are true or false in a situation. To say that a fact f is true in a situation s we assert $t(f, s)$, where t is a predicate and f and s are terms. In fact t and *ab*, which we will define below, are the *only* predicates in our logic.

Events are things that happen in the world, and the occurrence of an event may have the effect of changing the truth value of a fact. So we think of an event as a transition from one situation to another—from the situation in which it occurs to one in which its effects are reflected. The function *result* maps an event and a situation into another situation. So if S_0 is a situation and *result*(WAKEUP(JOHN), S_0) is also a situation denoting the one resulting from JOHN waking up in situation S_0. We might then want to state that JOHN is awake in this situation:

$$t(\text{AWAKE(JOHN)}, result(\text{WAKEUP(JOHN)}, S_0)),$$

or more generally we might state that

$$\forall p.s.\ t(\text{AWAKE}(p), result(\text{WAKEUP}(p), s)).$$

A problem arises when we try to express the notion that facts tend to *stay* true from situation to situation as irrelevant events occur. For example, is JOHN still awake in the state S_2, where

$$S_2 = result(\text{EAT-BREAKFAST(JOHN)}, result(\text{WAKEUP(JOHN)}, S_0))?$$

Intuitively we would like to assume so, because it's typically the case that eating breakfast does not cause one to fall asleep. But given the above axioms there is no way to deduce

$$t(\text{AWAKE(JOHN)}, S_2).$$

We could add an axiom to the effect that if one is awake in a situation then one is still awake in the situation resulting from his eating breakfast, but this seems somewhat arbitrary and will occasionally be false. And in any reasonable description of what one might do in the course of a morning there would have to be a staggering number of axioms expressing something like "if fact f is true in a situation s, and e is an event, then f is still true in the situation $result(e, s)$." McCarthy and Hayes (in [18]) called axioms of this kind "frame axioms," and identified the "frame problem" as the problem of having to explicitly state many such axioms. Deductive logic forces us into the position of assuming that an event occurrence may potentially change the truth value of all facts, thus if it does *not* change the value of a particular fact in a particular situation we must explicitly say so. We would like to assume just the opposite: that most events do *not* affect the truth of most facts under most circumstances.

Intuitively we want to solve the frame problem by assuming that in general an event happening in a situation is *irrelevant* to a fact's truth value in the resulting situation. Or, to make the notion a little more precise, we want to assume "by default" that

$$t(f, s) \supset t(f, result(e, s))$$

for all facts, situations, and events. But note the quotes: the point of this paper is that formalizing this assumption is not as straightforward as the phrase might lead one to believe.

McCarthy's proposed solution to the frame problem (described in [17]) involves extending the situation calculus a little, to make it what he calls a "simple abnormality theory." We state that all "normal" facts persist across occurrences of "normal" events:

where $ab(f, e, s)$ is taken to mean "fact f is abnormal with respect to event e occurring in state s," or, "there's something about event e occurring in state s that causes fact f to stop being true in $result(e, s)$." We would expect, for example, that it would be true that

$$\forall p, s. \; ab(AWAKE(p), GOTOSLEEP(p)), s)$$

and we would have to add a specific axiom to that effect.

Of course we still haven't solved the frame problem, since we haven't provided any way to deduce $\neg ab(f, e, s)$ for most facts, events, and situations. As an alternative to providing myriad frame axioms of this form. McCarthy proposes that we circumscribe over the predicate ab, thus "minimizing" the abnormal temporal individuals.[3] The question is whether this indeed represents what we intuitively mean by saying that we should "assume the persistence of facts by default," or "once true, facts tend to stay true over time."

As an illustration of what we *can* infer from a simple situation-calculus abnormality theory, consider the axioms of Fig. 1. For simplicity we have restricted the syntactic form of facts and events to be propositional symbols. so the axioms can be interpreted as referring to a single individual who at any point in time (situation) can be either ALIVE or DEAD and a gun that can be either LOADED or UNLOADED. At some known situation S_0 the person is alive (axiom (1)), and the gun becomes loaded any time a LOAD event happens (axiom (2)). Axiom (3) says that any time the person is shot with a loaded gun he becomes dead, and furthermore that being shot with a loaded gun is abnormal with respect to staying alive. Or to express our intent as we did above: there is something about a SHOOT event occurring in a situation in which the gun is loaded that causes the fact ALIVE to stop being true in the situation resulting from the shot. Axiom (4) is just the assertion we made above that "normal" facts persist across the occurrence of "normal" events.

Then we circumscribe axioms (1)–(4) over ab, varying t, and recall that what follow from the augmented axiom are those formulas true in all models

$$t(ALIVE, S_0) \tag{1}$$

$$\forall s. \; t(LOADED, result(LOAD, s)) \tag{2}$$

$$\forall s. \; t(LOADED, s) \supset ab(ALIVE. SHOOT, s) \wedge$$
$$t(DEAD. result(SHOOT. s)) \tag{3}$$

$$\forall f, e, s. t(f. s) \wedge \neg ab(f, e, s) \supset t(f, result(e. s)) \tag{4}$$

FIG. 1. Simple situation-calculus axioms.

[3] More precisely. the proposal should be to circumscribe over ab while allowing predicate t to vary. Again. we will ignore this point.

minimal in ab. We will refer to axioms (1)–(4) as A, and to the circumscribed axioms as $Circum(A, ab. t)$.

Now consider the problem of projecting what facts will be true in the following situations:

$$S_0 \, ,$$
$$S_1 = result(LOAD, S_0) \, ,$$
$$S_2 = result(WAIT, S_1) \, ,$$
$$S_3 = result(SHOOT, S_2)$$
$$= result(SHOOT, result(WAIT. result(LOAD, S_0))) \, .$$

In other words, our individual is initially known to be alive, then the gun is loaded, then he waits for a while, then he is shot with the gun. The projection problem is to determine what facts are true at the situations S_i. The event WAIT is supposed to signify a period of time when nothing of interest happens. Since according to the axioms no fact is abnormal with respect to the occurrence of event WAIT occurring, we intend that every fact true before the WAIT event occurs should also be true *after* it occurs.

One interpretation of the axioms (1)–(4) is shown in Fig. 2(a). This first picture represents facts true in all models of A (thus what we can deduce if we *don't* circumscribe). From axioms (1) and (2) we can make the following deductions:

$$t(ALIVE, S_0) \, , \qquad t(LOADED, S_1) \, ,$$

but we can deduce nothing about what is true in S_2 or in S_3. We also cannot

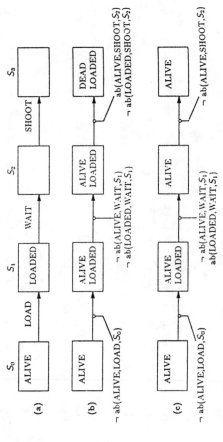

FIG. 2. Three models of axioms (1)–(4) of Fig. 1.

deduce any "abnormalities" or their negations. But this is pretty much as expected: the ALIVE fact did not persist because we could not deduce that it was "not *ab*" with respect to loading the gun, and the gun being loaded did not persist through the WAIT event because we could not deduce that it was "not *ab*" with respect to waiting.

Intuitively we would like to reason about "minimizing abnormalities" like this: we know ALIVE must be true in S_0, and nothing compels us to believe *ab*(ALIVE, LOAD, S_0), so we assume its negation. From this assumption and from axiom (4) we deduce *t*(ALIVE, S_1). Reasoning along the same lines, we can deduce *t*(LOADED, S_1) and we are free to make the assumptions ¬*ab*(ALIVE, WAIT, S_1) and ¬*ab*(LOADED, WAIT, S_1) so we do so and go on to deduce *t*(ALIVE, S_2) and *t*(LOADED, S_2). Again moving forward in time, we can deduce from axiom (3) that *ab*(ALIVE, SHOOT, S_2) so we cannot assume its negation, but we *can* assume ¬*ab*(LOADED, SHOOT, S_2). At this point we can deduce *t*(DEAD, S_3) and *t*(LOADED, S_3).

This line of reasoning leads us to the interpretation of Fig. 2(b). We can easily verify that this interpretation is indeed a model of *A* (that axioms (1) through (4) are satisfied). Furthermore, this model is minimal in *ab*: any submodel would have to have an empty extension for *ab*, which cannot be the case.[4]

The interesting question now is whether the model of Fig. 2(b)—our *intended* model of *A*—is the *only* minimal model, or, more to the point, whether *t*(DEAD, S_3) and *t*(LOADED, S_3) are true in *all* minimal models. Because if they're not true in all minimal models they don't follow from Circum(*A*, *ab*, *t*).

Consider the situation in Fig. 2(c). The picture describes a state of affairs in which the gun ceases to be loaded "as a result of" waiting. Then the individual *does not* die as a result of the shot, since the gun is not loaded. Of course this state of affairs directly contradicts our stated intention that since nothing is explicitly "*ab*" with respect to waiting everything should be "not *ab*" with respect to waiting. Does this interpretation describe a minimal model? First recall that there can be no models having a null extension for *ab*, so if this interpretation is a model at all it must be minimal in *ab*.

One can "build" this model in much the same way we constructed the model of Fig. 2(b), except this time instead of starting at S_0 and working forward in time, we will start at S_3 and work backward. In other words, we will start by noting that *t*(ALIVE, S_2) must be true, then consider what must have been true at S_2 and in earlier situations for that to have been the case.

The first abnormality decision to make is whether *ab*(ALIVE, SHOOT, S_2) is

---

[4] To see why this is true, consider that *t*(ALIVE, S_2) must be either true or false in any model of *A*. If it's true we can immediately deduce an abnormality from axiom (3). But if it's false then either *ab*(ALIVE, LOAD, S_0) or *ab*(ALIVE, WAIT, S_0) or *ab*(ALIVE, WAIT, S_2) would have to be true. In either case we must have at least one abnormality.

true. Since we haven't made a decision to the contrary, we will assume its negation. But then from the contrapositive of axiom (3), we can deduce ¬*t*(LOADED, S_2). But if that is the case, and since it must also be the case that *t*(LOADED, S_1) is true, we can deduce from axiom (4) that *ab*(LOADED, WAIT, S_1) is true. The rest of Fig. 2(c) follows directly, since we can assume that ALIVE is "not *ab*" with respect to LOAD and WAIT, thus deduce that ALIVE is true in both S_1 and S_2.

What, then, can be deduced from the (circumscribed) abnormality theory? It's fairly easy to verify that the two models we have presented are the only two models minimal in *ab*, so the theorems of Circum(*A*, *ab*, *t*) are those common to those two models. We can therefore deduce that ALIVE and LOADED are true in S_1, that ALIVE is true in S_2, but we can say nothing about what is true in S_3, except for statements like *t*(ALIVE, S_3) ∨ *t*(DEAD, S_3). What we can deduce from Circum(*A*, *ab*, *t*) is therefore considerably weaker than what we had intended.

4. How General Is This Problem?

The question now arises: how dependent is this result on the specific problem and formulation we just presented? Does the same problem arise if we use a different default logic or a different temporal formalism?

We can easily express the theory above in Reiter's logic: we use the same first-order axioms from Fig. 1 but instead of circumscribing over *ab* we represent "minimizing abnormal individuals" with a set of default rules of the form

$$D = \left\{ \frac{: M\neg ab(f, e, s)}{\neg ab(f, e, s)} \right\}$$

(where any individual may be substituted for *f*, *e*, and *s*). Recall that extensions are defined proof-theoretically instead of model-theoretically, so we must translate the minimal models shown in Figs. 2(b) and (c) into sets of sentences. The question becomes whether the following sets are default-logic extensions:

E_a			E_b	
(1a)	*t*(ALIVE, S_0)		*t*(ALIVE, S_0)	(1b)
(2a)	¬*ab*(ALIVE, LOAD, S_0),		¬*ab*(ALIVE, LOAD, S_0),	(2b)
(3a)	*t*(ALIVE, S_1),		*t*(ALIVE, S_1),	(3b)
(4a)	*t*(LOADED, S_1),		*t*(LOADED, S_1),	(4b)
(5a)	¬*ab*(ALIVE, WAIT, S_1),		¬*ab*(ALIVE, WAIT, S_1),	(5b)
(6a)	¬*ab*(LOADED, WAIT, S_1),		*ab*(LOADED, WAIT, S_1),	(6b)
(7a)	*t*(ALIVE, S_2),		*t*(ALIVE, S_2),	(7b)
(8a)	*t*(LOADED, S_2),		¬*t*(LOADED, S_2),	(8b)
(9a)	*ab*(ALIVE, SHOOT, S_2),		¬*ab*(ALIVE, SHOOT, S_2),	(9b)
(10a)	¬*ab*(LOADED, SHOOT, S_2),		¬*ab*(LOADED, SHOOT, S_2),	(10b)
(11a)	*t*(DEAD, S_3),		*t*(ALIVE, S_3).	(11b)
(12a)	*t*(LOADED, S_3).			

Of course these are partial descriptions of extensions. Each set must also contain A and all tautologies, and in E_a, for example, we must also include all sentences of the form $\neg ab(f, e, s)$ for all individuals (f, e, s) *except* (ALIVE, SHOOT, S_2).

To show that E_a and E_b are both extensions we can use a theorem from Reiter's paper [24, p. 89], which says that a set of sentences E is an extension just in case it is equal in the limit to the sequence of sets $E_0, E_1, \ldots$ formed as follows:

(1) $E_0 = \text{Th}(A)$.
(2) $D_i = \{\neg ab(f, e, s): ab(f, e, s) \notin E\}$,
(3) $E_{i+1} = \text{Th}(E_i \cup D_i)$,

where "Th" is deductive closure. Note that this is a way of verifying that a known set of sentences E, is an extension, not a way of building an extension. Since the set of default instances D_i is defined in terms of the proposed extension E, that set must be known ahead of time.

In practical terms, this definition suggests the following algorithm: Start with A. Add all sentences of the form $\neg ab(f, e, s)$ such that their negations do not appear in the proposed extension. Deduce all you can. Continue until you reach a point where no more deductions can be made and no more default instances can be added. The set is an extension if all the sentences in the set have been deduced (and no others).

To demonstrate on E_a, start with Th(A), which is the set $A \cup \{(1a), (4a)\}$. Add the defaults $D_0 = \{(2a), (5a), (6a), (10a)\}$. Now we can make the following deductions:

deduce (3a) from (1a) and (2a) and (4) ,
(7a) from (3a) and (5a) and (4) ,
(8a) from (4a) and (6a) and (4) ,
(9a) from (8a) and (3) ,
(11a) from (8a) and (3) ,
(12a) from (8a) and (10a) and (4) .

At this point there are no more default instances to be added, and no more deductions to be made, so $E_1 = E_2 = \cdots = E_a$. Furthermore, since all the sentences in E_a have been deduced, we can also conclude that E_a is an extension. (By rights we should also verify that E_a is minimal—that *only* sentences in E_a have been deduced. We will skip this part of the proof, since it would require a more precise definition of E_a than we supplied above. In an earlier paper [7], we prove the minimality of the two extensions, though using a different technique.)

Next we turn our attention to E_b. The sentence of interest is (6b), since intuitively it's not true, and we would hope that it wouldn't follow from *any* set of "$\neg ab$" assumptions. We can rearrange a couple of the axioms in A in order to clarify the example:

$$\forall s.\ \neg ab(\text{ALIVE, SHOOT}, s) \vee \neg t(\text{DEAD}, result(\text{SHOOT}, s)) \tag{3'}$$
$$\supset \neg t(\text{LOADED}, s),$$

$$\forall f, e, s.\ t(f, s) \wedge \neg t(f, result(e, s)) \supset ab(f, e, s). \tag{4'}$$

Again we start with Th(A), which includes (1b) and (4b). Add defaults $D_0 = \{(2b), (5b), (9b), (10b)\}$. And

deduce (3b) from (1b) and (2b) and (4) ,
(7b) from (3b) and (5b) and (4) ,
(8b) from (9b) and (3') ,
(6b) from (4b) and (8b) and (4') ,
(11b) from (7b) and (9b) and (4) .

Again there are no more default instances to add, and nothing more to deduce, and all the sentences in E_b follow from A and D_0, therefore E_b is also an extension.

So circumscription is not the culprit here—Reiter's proof-theoretic default logic has the same problem. We can also express the same problem in McDermott's nonmonotonic logic and show that the theory has the same two fixed points.

Nor is the situation calculus to blame: in a previous paper [7] we use a simplified version of McDermott's temporal logic and show that the same problem arises, again for all three default logics. In the next section we will show what characteristics of temporal projection lead to the multiple-extension problem, and why it appears that the three default logics are inherently unable to represent the domain correctly.

5. A Minimality Criterion for Temporal Reasoning

We noted above that default-logic theories often generate multiple extensions. But characteristic of all the usual examples, like the one we used in Section 2, is the fact that the default rules of these theories were mutually exclusive: the application of one rule rendered other rules inapplicable by blocking their preconditions.

Thus it comes as somewhat of a surprise that the temporal projection problem should exhibit several extensions. How can there be conflicting rules in the same way we saw above when our theory has only a single default rule? It turns out that conflict between rules arises in our domain in a different, more subtle, manner. To see how, recall how we built the first minimal model (that of Fig. 2(b)). The idea was that we assumed one "normality," then went on to make all possible deductions, then assumed another "normality," and so on. The picture looks something like this:

$$\neg ab(\text{LOADED, WAIT, } S_1) \Rightarrow t(\text{LOADED, } S_2)$$
$$\Rightarrow \cdots \Rightarrow ab(\text{ALIVE, SHOOT, } S_2),$$

where the conflict to notice is that as a result of assuming a "normality" we could deduce an *abnormality*. The same thing happened when we built the model in Fig. 2(c), except the picture looks like this instead (reading from right to left):

$$ab(\text{LOADED, WAIT, } S_1) \Leftarrow \cdots \Leftarrow \neg t(\text{LOADED, } S_2)$$
$$\Leftarrow ab(\text{ALIVE, SHOOT, } S_2).$$

The only difference between the two models is that in the first case we started at the (temporally) earliest situation and worked our way forward in time, and in the second case we started at the latest point and worked our way backward in time. Another way to express the idea is that in the first model we always picked the "earliest possible" (f, e, s) triple to assume "normal" and in the second model we always picked the latest.

So the class of models we want our logic to select is not the "minimal models" in the set-inclusion sense of circumscription, but the "chronologically minimal" models (a term due to Yoav Shoham): those in which normality assumptions are made in chronological order, from earliest to latest, or, equivalently, those in which abnormality occurs as late as possible.

Let us make clear what we are claiming here: that chronological minimality is the correct minimality criterion for the temporal projection problem we proposed above, and that neither predicate circumscription, nor Reiter's default logic, nor McDermott's nonmonotonic logic, can represent this criterion. Why they cannot do so is pretty clear: the concept of minimality in circumscription is intimately bound up with the notion of set inclusion, and chronological minimality cannot be expressed in those terms. As far as Reiter and McDermott's logics go, what we need is some way to mediate *application* of default rules in building extensions or fixed points, which is beyond the expressive power of (Reiter's) default rules or of NML sentences involving the M operator.

One thing we are *not* claiming (our critics notwithstanding) is that chronological minimality so defined is the only criterion one would ever need in representing problems in temporal reasoning. One can easily imagine the "temporal explanation" problem, for example, in which one is presented with a state of the world and causal rules and asked to speculate on what the world might have been like in the past so as to generate the given state. For this problem one might argue that "reverse chronological minimality"—working backward in time, making normality assumptions from latest to earliest—would be appropriate.

For reasoning about the real world the criterion will be more complicated than either of the criteria we proposed above. Is it more reasonable to assume the gun was loaded and our friend died, or that it was not loaded and he lived? That depends on a lot of different domain-dependent factors: how reliable is the gun, how much time elapsed between the WAIT and the SHOOT. One can easily build realistic scenarios where one might jump to either conclusion (or perhaps neither). The point is that if these formal systems cannot express the simple minimality criterion we presented above, they won't be able to express the more realistic, complex criteria either.

6. Criticisms and Proposed Solutions

A flurry of replies greeted our original paper. The responses can be grouped into five classes, making the following arguments:

(1) that there really is no problem at all,
(2) that other domain-independent formal systems can solve the problem,
(3) that the temporal axioms can be revised so the existing nonmonotonic logics will select the intuitive interpretation.
(4) that circumscription can be extended in expressive power so as to represent chronological minimality and similar criteria,
(5) that the right way to think about default reasoning is directly through the notion of "preferred models" rather than indirectly through devices like circumscription axioms or default rules.

6.1. Arguing that there is no problem

The first argument, put forth by Loui in [15] says basically that we don't want our formal systems to favor the chronologically minimal models, either because other temporal reasoning problems might involve other such criteria, or because the function of a logic is to constrain admissible models rather than to mirror reasoning in any way.

The first interpretation we have already responded to: granted that chronological minimality is not the only criterion one might want to express, it certainly is *one* such criterion. It seems to express what McDermott was getting at in his temporal logic [19], and what McCarthy has referred to as the "inertial property of facts" (e.g. in [17]). It is hard to imagine any criterion that might arise in temporal reasoning that does not in some way mention temporal ordering, yet we have showed that all of these logics fail to discriminate on the basis of concepts like "temporally earlier" or "temporally later."

A second interpretation of the "no problem" argument takes a stand on what role logic should play in the process of theory development in AI. It goes something like this: Axioms are supposed to describe constraints on the world, and do not need to support reasoning in any direct way. We fix a temporal ontology, but may want to reason about that ontology in a number of different ways: from past to future, from future to past, starting with the most strongly believed premise, etc. The axioms should reflect our ontological choices, but should be neutral about the ways in which we might reason using the resulting theories.

Now it is true that one can take this lofty view of the relation between logic and thought, but from that distance mundane phenomena like the frame problem simply become invisible. The whole point behind the development of nonmonotonic formal systems for reasoning about time has been to augment our logical machinery so that it reflects in a natural way the "inertia of the world." All of this effort is wasted if one is trying merely to express constraints on the physics of the world: we can solve the problem once and for all by saying "once a fact becomes true it stays true until the occurrence of some event causes it to become false." This is in effect our axiom (4) above. As we noted, this principle will allow us to conclude almost nothing, since we can generally not conclude that a terminating event has *not* occurred. But if trying to conclude such things is not our aim, then there indeed is no problem. Many researchers, however, would not be satisfied with using logic only as a notation for expressing ontological theories.

6.2. Arguing for an alternative minimality criterion

Loui, in [15, Section III.1.1], makes the argument that with a change in our axioms an alternative formal system actually favors the correct extension. The implication is that the minimization we really intended to do can be captured by another domain-independent criterion for preferring one model over another, though set inclusion did not work. He claims that the theory-comparison logic of Poole, as reported in [23], chooses the right interpretation of the axioms. We will explain Poole's system quickly, then move on to Loui's analysis.

To use Poole's logic we divide our axioms into three sets: a set of noncontingent facts, or laws (labelled F_n), a set of contingent, or problem-specific facts (labelled F_c), and a set of default rules (labelled Δ). F_p and F_c are just sets of first-order sentences. The former expresses truths about the world in general, and the latter describes one particular situation. Default rules look a lot like Reiter's default rules; our "persistence of facts" rule would appear as follows:

$$\langle f, e, s \rangle \; \text{ASSUME} \; t(f, s) \supset t(f, result(e, s)),$$

where f, e, and s are variables that can be instantiated in the rule, and ASSUME is just syntactic sugar.

From a triple (F_n, F_c, Δ) we can build *theories* of the form (F_n, F_c, D), where D is a set of instances of the default rules in Δ (formed by plugging in constants for all the variable names that appear to the left of ASSUME). Note that theories formed in this way are first-order theories, so we can speak of the sentences that follow deductively from them. We say a sentence φ is *explained* by a theory (F_n, F_c, D) if

$$F_n \cup F_c \cup D \models \varphi$$

and

$$F_n \cup F_c \cup D \text{ is consistent}.$$

When context makes the identity of F_n and F_c clear, we will refer to a theory just by its default instances D.
Applying this model to our original axioms we might get the following:

$F_n = \{\forall s. \; t(\text{LOADED}, result(\text{LOAD}, s)),$
$\qquad\quad \forall s. \; t(\text{LOADED}, s) \supset t(\text{DEAD}, result(\text{SHOOT}, s))\},$

$F_c = \{t(\text{ALIVE}, S_0)\},$

$\Delta = \{\langle f, e, s \rangle \; \text{ASSUME} \; t(f, s) \supset t(f, result(e, s))\}.$

Now we build two different theories by choosing two different sets of default instances. We'll call the theories D_a and D_b to identify them with the extensions we built in Section 4:

$D_a = \{t(\text{ALIVE}, S_0) \supset t(\text{ALIVE}, S_1),$
$\qquad\quad t(\text{ALIVE}, S_1) \supset t(\text{ALIVE}, S_2),$
$\qquad\quad t(\text{LOADED}, S_1) \supset t(\text{LOADED}, S_2),$
$\qquad\quad t(\text{LOADED}, S_2) \supset t(\text{LOADED}, S_3)\},$

$D_b = \{t(\text{ALIVE}, S_0) \supset t(\text{ALIVE}, S_1),$
$\qquad\quad t(\text{ALIVE}, S_1) \supset t(\text{ALIVE}, S_2),$
$\qquad\quad t(\text{ALIVE}, S_2) \supset t(\text{ALIVE}, S_3)\}.$

Theory D_a explains the sentence $t(\text{DEAD}, S_3)$ (we'll call this sentence g_a, following Poole's notation) and theory D_b explains $t(\text{ALIVE}, S_3)$ (which we'll call g_b). Poole's system addresses the question of which of these two theories we should prefer.

Poole's system would have us prefer the "most specific solution," where a solution is a theory plus a sentence it explains, e.g. $\langle D_a, g_a \rangle$. Specificity can loosely be thought of as "the extent to which the solution depends on contingent facts.'' Recall that contingent facts are the sentences in F_c. To illustrate using an example from Poole, assume we have a *noncontingent* fact of the form "all emus are birds," default rules of the form "birds fly" and "emus do not fly," and a *contingent* fact of the form "Edna is an emu.'' One can build a theory that explains "Edna can fly'' as well as a theory that explains "Edna cannot fly.'' According to Poole's specificity criterion the second theory is strictly more specific than the first because it depends on the contingent fact "Edna is an emu'' and the first theory depends on no contingent facts.

Specificity is defined formally as follows: given two solutions

$$S_1 = \langle D_1, g_1 \rangle \quad \text{and} \quad S_2 = \langle D_2, g_2 \rangle,$$

we say that S_1 is more specific than S_2 if the following holds for all sets of sentences F_p:

if $F_p \cup D_1 \cup F_n \models g_1$
and $F_p \cup D_2 \cup F_n \not\models g_1$,
then $F_p \cup D_2 \cup F_n \models g_2$.

Solution S_1 is *strictly more specific* than S_2 if S_1 is more specific than S_2 but S_2 is *not* more specific than S_1. So the analogue of circumscriptive minimal models are those solutions that are strictly more specific than all others. We will write "$S_1 \geq S_2$" to mean "S_1 is more specific than S_2," and "$S_1 > S_2$" to mean "S_1 is strictly more specific than S_2.''

Now returning to the "shooting" theories we built above, we ask which is most specific between

$$S_a = \langle T_a, g_a = t(\text{DEAD}, S_3) \rangle$$

and

$$S_b = \langle T_b, g_b = t(\text{ALIVE}, S_3) \rangle?$$

First let's establish whether $S_a \geq S_b$. To do so we must show that

if $F_p \cup D_a \cup F_n \models t(\text{DEAD}, S_3)$
and $F_p \cup D_b \cup F_n \not\models t(\text{DEAD}, S_3)$,
then $F_p \cup D_b \cup F_n \models t(\text{ALIVE}, S_3)$.

Crucial to determining specificity is figuring out for each solution what facts must be in F_p in order that the solution's conclusion follows. (This is the first condition in the specificity criterion above.) We will call this set the solution's "necessary F_p facts.'' Some of these facts will be uninteresting. Consider solution S_a, for example: certainly putting $t(\text{DEAD}, S_3)$ in F_p allows us to draw

that conclusion from $F_p \cup D_a \cup F_n$, but it also allows any *other* solution to draw that conclusion too, so the second condition in the specificity criterion will not be satisfied. When we speak about necessary F_p facts, then, we will generally only be concerned with the "interesting" ones: those that satisfy both conditions of the specificity criterion.

Turning our attention now to comparing S_a and S_b, we note that the set of necessary F_p facts for S_a is empty: g_a follows from $D_a \cup F_n$ alone. Any set F_p will satisfy the first antecedent. To get g_b from $D_b \cup F_n$, however, we *do* need additional information: either $t(\text{ALIVE}, S_3)$ or $t(\text{ALIVE}, S_2)$ or $t(\text{ALIVE}, S_1)$ or $t(\text{ALIVE}, S_0)$. So it's easy to find an F_p that does not satisfy the definition: $F_p = \emptyset$. Therefore S_a is *not* more specific than S_b.

Conversely, to show that $S_b \geq S_a$ we note that the consequent of the new specificity condition.

$$F_p \cup D_a \cup F_n \models t(\text{DEAD}, S_3),$$

is true for any choice of F_p, thus the conditional is always true and $S_b \geq S_a$; in fact $S_b > S_a$. The upshot: for our reformulation of the axioms in Poole's default logic, Poole's specificity criterion favors the *wrong* conclusion.

Loui claims that we can fix the problem by changing the axioms in two ways: by making the "shooting" law ($\forall s. t(\text{LOADED}, s) \supset t(\text{DEAD}, s)$) into a default rule, and by strengthening its antecedent. Thus he reformulates our axioms as follows (we are actually inferring his intentions here, since he never explicitly states his reformulation):

$F_n = \emptyset,$
$F_c = \{t(\text{ALIVE}, S_0), t(\text{LOADED}, S_1)\},$
$\Delta = \{(s) \quad \text{ASSUME } t(\text{LOADED}, s) \wedge t(\text{ALIVE}, s)$
$\qquad\qquad\qquad \supset t(\text{DEAD}, result(\text{SHOOT}, s)),$
$\qquad (f, e, s) \text{ ASSUME } t(f, s) \supset t(f, result(e, s))\}.$

Loui has actually made *three* changes here: in addition to changing the "shoot" laws into a default rule and adding $t(\text{ALIVE}, s)$ to its antecedent, he also chose to express the "loading a gun causes it to be loaded" law as a situation-specific fact. Expressing this axiom as a fact (in F_c) instead of as a law (in F_n) turns out to have an important effect on which theories are more specific than others, though Loui does not mention this in his paper. We will return to that poin later.

Now the two theories look like this:

$D_a = \{t(\text{ALIVE}, S_0) \supset t(\text{ALIVE}, S_1),$
$\qquad t(\text{ALIVE}, S_1) \supset t(\text{ALIVE}, S_2),$
$\qquad t(\text{LOADED}, S_1) \supset t(\text{LOADED}, S_2),$
$\qquad t(\text{LOADED}, S_2) \wedge t(\text{ALIVE}, S_2) \supset t(\text{DEAD}, S_3),$
$\qquad t(\text{LOADED}, S_2) \supset t(\text{LOADED}, S_3)\}.$

We can easily verify that S_a is now strictly more specific than S_b: in order to conclude $t(ALIVE, S_3)$ from D_a we need both $t(LOADED, S_2)$ and $t(ALIVE, S_2)$. To get the former we need in F_p either $t(LOADED, S_0)$ or $t(LOADED, S_1)$ or $t(LOADED, S_2)$. To get the latter we need in F_p either $t(ALIVE, S_0)$ or $t(ALIVE, S_1)$ or $t(ALIVE, S_2)$. On the other hand, to get $t(ALIVE, S_3)$ from D_b we need in F_p either $t(ALIVE, S_2)$ or $t(ALIVE, S_1)$ or $t(ALIVE. S_0)$, and one of those has to be in the F_p set for S_a. So the F_p set for S_a must be a superset of the F_p set for S_b, and therefore $S_a > S_b$.

How are we to know that $t(ALIVE, s)$ is the right conjunct to add to the "shoot" rule? Loui says only "[the added conjunct is] a genuine part of what is claimed to be known about the causal law in this domain." The reason Hanks and McDermott want to clip *alive*-ness instead of *loaded*-ness is that intuitively, they know that [$t(ALIVE, S_2)$] is one of the assertions that can be in the antecedent of (the defeasible version of) their rule." This hardly amounts to a policy for deciding which conjuncts to put in our causal rules. unless he is suggesting that we qualify *every* causal rule with *every* condition that does not interfere with the conclusion. That simple a scheme will not work.

Consider an extended version of our original example. We look a little further forward in time, and consider a situation S_4, which is *result*(LEAVE-HOUSE, S_3). We also add a causal rule that says if one is alive. and if it is raining, then one is wet as a result of LEAVE-HOUSE. We will defer to Loui here and couch this as a default rule. (It turns out to be irrelevant to the specificity analysis whether it is a default rule or a law: indeed, it turns out to be irrelevant whether the "shoot" rule is a default or a law.) We will also say that it is raining at S_0. Our logic now becomes:

$F_n = \emptyset,$
$F_c = \{t(ALIVE, S_0), t(LOADED, S_1), t(RAINING, S_0)\},$
$\Delta = \{(s) \qquad ASSUME\ t(LOADED, s) \supset t(DEAD,\ result(SHOOT, s)),$
$\quad (s) \qquad ASSUME\ t(ALIVE, s) \wedge t(RAINING, s)$
$\qquad\qquad\qquad \supset t(WET,\ result(LEAVE-HOUSE, s)) .$
$\quad (f, e, s)\ ASSUME\ t(f, s) \supset t(f, result(e. s))\} .$

(We will have to add qualifications to the default rules' antecedents.) The two solutions to compare are:

$D_a = \{t(ALIVE, S_0) \supset t(ALIVE, S_1) ,$
$\quad t(ALIVE, S_1) \supset t(ALIVE, S_2) .$
$\quad t(LOADED, S_1) \supset t(LOADED. S_2) .$
$\quad t(LOADED, S_2) \wedge t(ALIVE, S_2) \supset t(DEAD, S_3) .$
$\quad t(LOADED, S_2) \supset t(LOADED. S_3)\} .$

$D_b = \{t(ALIVE, S_0) \supset t(ALIVE, S_1) ,$
$\quad t(ALIVE, S_1) \supset t(ALIVE, S_2) ,$
$\quad t(ALIVE, S_2) \supset t(ALIVE, S_3) ,$
$\quad t(RAINING, S_0) \supset t(RAINING, S_1) ,$
$\quad t(RAINING, S_1) \supset t(RAINING, S_2) ,$
$\quad t(RAINING, S_2) \supset t(RAINING, S_3) ,$
$\quad t(ALIVE, S_3) \wedge t(RAINING, S_3) \supset t(WET, S_4)\} ,$

$S_a = \langle D_a, t(DEAD, S_3) \rangle ,$
$S_b = \langle D_b, t(WET, S_4) \rangle .$

What do we add to the antecedents of these rules? Do we add $t(ALIVE, s)$ to the "shoot" rule? Apparently so. Do we add $t(RAINING, s)$ to the "shoot" rule? We have to: S_b depends on a "raining" fact, so if S_a is to be more specific than S_b it must *also* depend on a "raining" fact. So now the "shoot" rule reads like this: if ALIVE and LOADED and RAINING then DEAD follows from SHOOT. Now what should we qualify the "get wet" rule with? We already qualify it with ALIVE and RAINING; should we qualify it with LOADED too? It would seem at least as reasonable as qualifying the "shooting" rule with RAINING. It doesn't matter whether we do so or not. Since the "get wet" rule is applied *temporally later than* the "shoot" rule, an F_p set of the form $\{t(ALIVE, S_3),$ $t(RAINING, S_3), t(LOADED, S_3)\}$ would, with D_b, entail (WET, S_4), but this F_p would not entail $t(DEAD, S_3)$.

Now we're beginning to see where the temporal aspect of the problem has been hidden: not in the axioms themselves, but in the choices one makes as to how one qualifies the default rules. The way one strengthens the causal rule antecedents depends on the temporal order in which they are to be applied. Now deciding on these qualifications itself becomes an exercise in temporal reasoning, and to *formalize* this process would presumably require formalizing the temporal-ordering criteria that have proved so difficult. Furthermore, what to add to the rule antecedents depends not just on the syntactic form of the rules themselves, but on the particular theory comparison being made. Compare two new theories and you have to rethink the form of the causal rules.

As far as we're concerned, there is no justification for qualifying the "shooting" rule with a "raining" precondition, except that it makes the theory comparison come out right. Is this sort of decision "a genuine part of what is claimed to be known about the causal law in this domain," as Loui claims? We think not. Domain knowledge to us means knowledge about being alive, about guns being loaded, about shooting, about raining, about getting wet—in short, exactly what we put into our original, unqualified axioms.

What's worse is that under some circumstances *no* reasonable specialization of the antecedents works right. Consider the following example, pictured in Fig. 3:

The necessary F_p fact for S_a is $t(Q, S_0)$, while S_b must have $t(R, S_2)$ and either $t(P, S_0)$ or $t(P, S_1)$ or $t(P, S_2)$. As is, neither solution is more specific than the other. To make S_a more specific we can strengthen the antecedent of the first causal rule, as Loui suggests. Following his example we will specialize the first causal rule so it reads "if P and Q are true at s then P is false at $result(E_1, s)$." That takes care of S_b's P precondition: now S_a needs either $t(P, S_0)$ or $t(P, S_1)$, and either of these will lead to a deduction of $t(P, S_2)$ from D_b. But can we specialize the rule further to take care of S_b's R precondition? Apparently not. If we further specialize the "shoot" rule to include R in the antecedent, not only does it not make S_a more specific than S_b, but S_a is no longer a valid solution: its conclusion, $\neg t(P, S_1)$, no longer follows from $F_n \cup F_c \cup D_a$. In fact the only specialization that *would* work would say explicitly that the causal rule being applicable *at situation* S_1 depends on R being true at *situation* S_2. To have the applicability of a causal rule depend on some *future* state of affairs is absurd.

We should make one last comment about Loui's reformulation of our problem. We mentioned above that he made a subtle, but crucial. decision in building his version of our shooting example. Whereas we expressed the "loaded gun" rule as as general law (thus in F_n) of the form "guns are loaded in all situations resulting from a loading event." Loui expresses this information in a much more specific form—by adding a *situation-specific fact* of the form "the gun is loaded in situation S_0." If this axiom is expressed as a law then the "shot therefore dead" theory no longer depends on a fact in F_p of the form "the gun is loaded," because that fact is already in F_n. The theory is therefore less specific than it was before. In fact even if one strengthens the antecedent of the "shoot" rule as Loui suggests, the "shot therefore dead" theory is still not strictly more specific than the "unloaded therefore alive" theory. Thus Loui's analysis depends on a representational decision that is arguably arbitrary, and certainly left unstated in his paper.

To summarize, we find Loui's proposed solution singularly unsatisfying. First of all it is extremely brittle, depending, as it does, on the assignment of axioms to the set of universal laws instead of the set of problem-specific facts. His solution is based on coding temporal information in the causal rules in a way that depends not on issues of causality, but on the specific theory comparison one is undertaking. Further. he provides no general method to do this coding, but it is clear that this method must include exactly the temporal minimality criterion we are trying to formalize. Finally, there are cases where no reasonable specialization of the causal rules does the projection right.

6.3. Arguing for a change in temporal ontology

The proposal here is to revise the axioms so that one of the standard nonmonotonic formal systems actually licenses the right conclusions. The

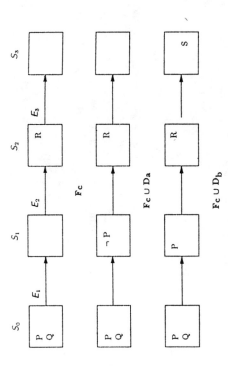

FIG. 3. Another simple projection example.

$F_n = \emptyset$.
$F_c = \{t(P, S_0), t(Q, S_0), t(R, S_2)\}$,
$\Delta = \{(s) \quad$ ASSUME $t(Q, s) \supset \neg t(P, result(E_1, s))$,
$\quad (s) \quad$ ASSUME $t(P, s) \land t(R, s) \supset t(S, result(E_3, s))$,
$\quad (f, e, s) \quad$ ASSUME $t(f, e, s) \supset t(f, e, result(e, s))\}$,

where the states are

S_0,
$S_1 = result(E_1, S_0)$,
$S_2 = result(E_2, S_1)$,
$S_3 = result(E_3, S_2)$.

There is a single chronologically minimal model—one in which the P fact is "clipped" at S_1 so that the second causal rule does not apply, and S is not true at S_3. A second interpretation has P persisting to S_2, thus S becomes true at S_3. The corresponding Loui solutions are:

$D_a = \{t(Q, S_0) \supset \neg t(P, S_1)\}$,
$D_b = \{t(P, S_0) \supset t(P, S_1)$,
$\quad t(P, S_1) \supset t(P, S_2)$,
$\quad t(P, S_2) \land t(R, S_2) \supset t(S, S_3)\}$,
$S_a = \langle D_a, \neg t(P, S_1) \rangle$,
$S_b = \langle D_b, t(S, S_3) \rangle$.

S_a describes the chronologically minimal model.

best-developed effort in this direction is that of Vladimir Lifschitz, in his paper "Formal Theories of Action" [12]. He revises the situation calculation so as to make certain notions of causality more specific. First of all, he assumes a predicate of the form

$$causes(action, fluent_1, fluent_2)$$

which means "if *action* is feasible, then whenever it is executed it causes $fluent_1$ to take on the value of $fluent_2$." A fluent is a function from situations to truth values, so it corresponds to what we called a *fact*. For example one might say

$$causes(SHOOT, ALIVE, FALSE),$$

where FALSE is a fluent that is true in no situations. Similarly TRUE is a fluent true in all situation. We enforce this by adding axioms of the form:

$$\forall s. \; t(TRUE, s) \quad \text{and} \quad \forall s. \; \neg t(FALSE, s).$$

The predicate *precond* determines whether an action is feasible—whether it will succeed in a given situation. Saying *precond(fluent, action)* means that *action* can succeed only if *fluent* is true in the situation in which *action* is attempted. An example would be *precond(LOADED, SHOOT)*.

An action is successful in a situation just in case all its preconditions in that situation are true:

$$\forall a, s. \; success(a, s) \Leftrightarrow \forall f. \; precond(f, a) \supset t(f, s) .$$

Another predicate, *affects*, can then be defined for actions, fluents, and situations, to mean "a successful action would affect the value of the fluent in the situation"

$$\forall a, f, s. \; affects(a, f, s)$$
$$\Leftrightarrow success(a, s) \wedge \exists v. \; causes(a, f, v) .$$

That is, an action affects the value of a fluent just in case the action is feasible and causes the fluent to take on some truth value.

With these definitions we can define how an action can change a fluent's value. These axioms simplify Lifschitz's treatment somewhat:

$$\forall a, s, f, v. \; success(a, s) \wedge causes(a, f, v)$$
$$\supset (t(f, result(a, s)) \Leftrightarrow t(v, s)))$$

$$\forall a, s, f. \; \neg affects(a, f, s) \supset (t(f, result(a, s)) \Leftrightarrow t(f, s)) .$$

Then for a given problem we list all the known *causes* and *preconditions*:

$$causes(LOAD, LOADED, TRUE),$$
$$causes(SHOOT, ALIVE, FALSE),$$
$$precond(LOADED, SHOOT),$$

and then we circumscribe on the predicates *causes* and *precond* (letting *t* vary as a parameter), which has the effect of making the explicit *causes* and *preconditions* the *only* *causes* and *preconditions*. So from the circumscribed axiom we get:

$$\forall a, f, v. \; (causes(a, f, v)$$
$$\Leftrightarrow (a = \text{LOAD} \wedge f = \text{LOADED} \wedge v = \text{TRUE}) \vee$$
$$(a = \text{SHOOT} \wedge f = \text{ALIVE} \wedge v = \text{FALSE})) .$$

$$\forall a, f. \; (precond(f, a) \Leftrightarrow f = \text{LOADED} \wedge a = \text{SHOOT}) .$$

(This is called *predicate completion*, as in Clark [2].)

From here conventional deduction yields the desired result: we can infer from the circumscribed axioms:

$$\neg t(\text{ALIVE}, result(\text{SHOOT}, result(\text{WAIT}, result(\text{LOAD}, S_0)))) .$$

Loui, in [15, Section III.1] makes a proposal like that of Lifschitz in spirit, though not in detail. He suggests adding a predicate *original-event*, which apparently refers to event instances that are imagined but not necessarily realized. So we say that a firing, a waiting, a dying, and an unloading are all *original-events*. Furthermore we say that the loading and the firing are both "real events," (*event-instances*, to use his notation) and that the dying is a real event only if the gun is loaded, and the gun becomes unloaded only if there's a "real event" unloading. The axioms provide no way to deduce that a "real" unloading occurred, so one never does, the gun remains loaded through the wait, and the individual dies.

We see two problems with proposals like these. The first is that if we adopt one of these solutions we have in effect allowed technical problems in the logic to put too much pressure on our knowledge representation. Part of the presumed appeal of expressing theories in logic is that the language should allow us to explore our intuitions about domains like naïve physics (as in [9]). What we should be thinking about at the logical level are issues like whether time is continuous or discrete, how many modalities there are, whether time is made out of points or intervals, etc. But if we follow the example of those who would have us change our ontology, we in effect have to phrase our axioms in one particular way (which seems only slightly different—and slightly more awkward—than the situation calculus) just to get around the inadequacies of the inference mechanism. Why is it that *causes* and *precond* are exactly the predicates we should have used to describe our problem? What was it about the domain (not about the technical details of the logic) that should have told us that? Will Lifschitz be around to bail us out when we come up against the next inferential bug?

The second objection we have to solutions like the one Lifschitz proposes is that at the point one takes heroic measures to patch the circumscription machinery, the machinery itself becomes epiphenomenal. We will present this argument in the next section.

6.4. Arguing for an enhanced circumscription

Two proposals, one by Lifschitz (in [13]) and one by Kautz (in [11]), propose a more robust (and hence more complex) circumscription axiom that expresses the chronological minimality criterion directly, and uses our original ontology. Since Lifschitz's proposal is more general, we will present it below.

Lifschitz's logic is called "pointwise circumscription"—the notion being that it may not be adequate to circumscribe "globally" over a set of predicates, that instead one may want to minimize predicates differently at different points. In our example we want to minimize abnormalities, so a point is actually a triple (f, e, s) where f is a fact type, e is an event type, and s is a situation.

We need to beef up our axioms a little bit. We want to minimize over temporally earlier situations first. so in all fairness we need to introduce the notion of temporally earlier into the logic. We will do so in a rather ad hoc manner, just by defining a new predicate $<$ and enumerating the situations over which it holds:

$$\forall s_1, s_2 \cdot \; s_1 < s_2 \Leftrightarrow (s_1 = S_0 \land s_2 = S_1) \lor$$
$$(s_1 = S_0 \land s_2 = S_2) \lor$$
$$(s_1 = S_0 \land s_2 = S_3) \lor$$
$$(s_1 = S_1 \land s_2 = S_2) \lor$$
$$(s_1 = S_1 \land s_2 = S_3) \lor$$
$$(s_1 = S_2 \land s_2 = S_3) \tag{5}$$

and we can then define an ordering relation over fact event situation triples:

$$\forall f, e, s, f', e', s' \cdot \; (f, e, s) <_P (f', e', s') \Leftrightarrow s < s'. \tag{6}$$

As we did with global circumscription, we minimize the ab predicate, allowing t to vary as a parameter. But the pointwise circumscription axiom allows us to minimize according to the temporal ordering defined by $<_P$. This is the axiom Lifschitz proposes:

$$\forall f, e, s, ab', t' \cdot$$
$$\neg(ab(f, e, s)) \tag{C1}$$
$$\land \forall f', e', s' \cdot \; (f', e', s') <_P (f, e, s)$$
$$\supset (ab'(f', e', s') \Leftrightarrow ab(f', e', s')) \tag{C2}$$
$$\land A(\lambda f', e', s' \cdot (ab(f', e', s') \land (f, e, s) \neq (f', e', s')) \cdot t')). \tag{C3}$$

(For any alternative choice of ab (ab') and of t (t') it cannot be the case that the original ab is true at (f, e, s) and that ab and ab' agree on all points temporally earlier than s and that ab' satisfies A at all points other than (f, e, s).)

Now the question springs to mind: how do we know whether this works? What follows from the circumscribed axiom, which we henceforth call Circum(A; $ab/<_P$, t) using Lifschitz's notation? The time-honored approach to analyzing circumscribed theories, which Kautz carries out in some detail, goes like this: first admit that you already know the right answer. In our case this answer takes the form of choices for ab' and t' that correspond to our preferred model. We'll call them ab_C and t_C and t to stand for the "correct" ab and t:

$$ab_C(f, e, s) \Leftrightarrow (f, e, s) \in \{(\text{ALIVE, SHOOT, } result(\text{SHOOT}, S_1)),$$
$$(\text{ALIVE, SHOOT, } S_2),$$
$$(\text{ALIVE, SHOOT, } S_3),$$
$$(\text{ALIVE, SHOOT, } result(\text{SHOOT}, S_3))\} \; .$$

$$t_C(f, x) \Leftrightarrow (f, e, s) \in \{(\text{ALIVE, } S_0),$$
$$(\text{ALIVE, } S_1), (\text{LOADED, } S_1),$$
$$(\text{ALIVE, } S_2), (\text{LOADED, } S_2),$$
$$(\text{DEAD, } S_3), (\text{LOADED, } S_3),$$
$$(\text{DEAD, } result(\text{SHOOT}, S_1)),$$
$$(\text{DEAD, } result(\text{SHOOT}, S_3))\} .$$

(You may notice that we refer to some situations we're not really interested in, e.g. $result(\text{SHOOT}, S_3)$. We include these just to satisfy the original axioms, which say, for example, that if a shot *did* occur in S_3, the ALIVE fact *would* be abnormal.)

One fact we're very much interested in is whether or not $ab(\text{LOADED, WAIT, } S_1)$ is true in the augmented axioms. We hope it is not. We will check. To do so we create an instance of the circumscription axiom, using our choices for ab_C, t_C, f, e, and s. That gives us:

$$\neg(ab(\text{LOADED, WAIT, } S_1) \tag{C1'}$$
$$\land \forall f', e', s' \cdot \; (f', e', s') <_P (\text{LOADED, WAIT, } S_1)$$
$$\supset (ab_C(f', e', s') \Leftrightarrow ab(f', e', s')) \tag{C2'}$$
$$\land A(\lambda f', e', s' \cdot (ab_C(f', e', s') \land (\text{LOADED, WAIT, } S_1) \neq (f', e', s')) \cdot t'))$$
$$\land (\text{LOADED, WAIT, } S_1) \neq (f', e', s') \tag{C3'}$$

which roughly means that if ab_C and ab agree on all points temporally prior to S_1, and if ab_C and t_C are strong enough to satisfy the original axioms A, then ab(LOADED, WAIT, S_1) is false—thus the gun is loaded and the individual dies.

What we have to do, then, is verify that the second two conjuncts, (C2') and (C3'), are true. Start with (C3'). We have to substitute t_C for t, and substitute

$$\lambda f', e', s'(ab_C(f', e', s') \wedge (\text{LOADED, WAIT, } S_1) \neq (f', e', s'))$$

for ab_C into the original axioms (1)–(4) (from Fig. 1). Axioms (1) and (2) involve only t, and become:

t_C(ALIVE, S_0),   (1')

$\forall s. \ t_C$(LOADED, $result$(LOAD, s)),   (2')

both of which can be verified by examining the enumeration of t_C above. Axioms (3) and (4) become:

$\forall s. \ t_C(\text{LOADED, } s)$
$\supset ab_C(\text{ALIVE, SHOOT, } s)$
$\wedge \ (\text{ALIVE, SHOOT, } s) \neq (\text{LOADED, WAIT. } S_1)$
$\wedge \ t_C(\text{DEAD, } result(\text{SHOOT, } s)),$ (3')

$\forall f, e, s. \ t_C(f, s) \wedge \neg(ab_C(f, e, s) \wedge (f, e, s) \neq (\text{LOADED, WAIT. } S_1))$
$\supset t_C(f, result(e, s))$ (4')

For instance (3') we note that the only values of s that satisfy the antecedent are S_1, S_2, and S_3, so the conjuncts must be satisfied for each of those situations:

(ALIVE. SHOOT, S_1) $\in ab_C$
and (ALIVE, SHOOT, S_1) $\neq$ (LOADED WAIT, S_1)
and (DEAD, $result$(SHOOT, S_1)) $\in t_C$;

(ALIVE. SHOOT, S_2) $\in ab_C$
and (ALIVE, SHOOT, S_2) $\neq$ (LOADED, WAIT, S_1)
and (DEAD, $result$(SHOOT, S_3)) $\in t_C$;

(ALIVE. SHOOT, S_3) $\in ab_C$
and (ALIVE, SHOOT, S_3) $\neq$ (LOADED, WAIT, S_1)
and (DEAD, $result$(SHOOT, S_3)) $\in t_C$.

Again we can verify each conjunct by examining the enumeration of ab_C and of t_C.

Finally, axiom instance (4') can be enumerated and checked in the same way, but we will omit this step.

Now we have verified conjunct (C3). and we must do the same for (C2):

$$\forall f', e', s'. \ (f', e', s') <_P (\text{LOADED, WAIT, } S_1)$$
$$\supset ab_C(f', e', s') \Leftrightarrow ab(f', e', s').$$

Note that the only abnormality points that satisfy the precondition are those involving situation S_0, so (C2) reduces to

$$\forall f, e. \ ab(f, e, S_0) \Leftrightarrow ab_C(f, e, S_0),$$

but since ab_C includes *no* abnormalities at situation S_0, (C2) further reduces to

$$\forall f, e. \ \neg ab(f, e, S_0),$$

so the original circumscription instance becomes

$$\neg ab(\text{LOADED, WAIT, } S_1) \vee \exists f, e. \ ab(f, e, S_0).$$

So we didn't get quite what we wanted, which was just the first disjunct. To eliminate the second disjunct we would next have to prove

$$\forall f, e. \ \neg ab(f, e, S_0).$$

The proof works the same way: we produce an instance of the circumscription axiom, substituting ab_C for ab, t_C for t, and S_0 for s, and go about eliminating all terms in the negation except for the first conjunct, leaving us with $\neg ab(f, e, S_0)$. We omit the proof, but note that it works out easily enough: verifying the third conjunct involves essentially the same analysis we did above, and since there are no points temporally earlier than S_0, the second conjunct is immediately true.

Thus pointwise circumscription (and Kautz's logic of persistence) can be shown to produce as theorems exactly those formulas true in all chronologically minimal models. But we must ask at this point what purpose the circumscription served in the first place? So far the only way to use circumscribed theories has been to perform analyses such as the one we performed above: you know what conclusion you want to get out of the theory, you use the conclusion to build an instance of the circumscription axiom, and you see if the desired result pops out.

It's the need to know the solution beforehand that is troublesome here. If we really can provide no general theory as to how to instantiate the circumscription axiom, in no sense have we provided a formal inferential theory. We're always going to have to know the right answer ahead of time in order to instantiate the axiom, and at that point the circumscription provides us with no new information. On the other hand, if we *can* find some way to generate appropriate axiom instances we can just view that process itself as an axiom schema and dispense with circumscription altogether.

There was some hope with earlier versions of circumscription that the axioms could actually be put into an automated theorem prover, and through that mechanism we might learn unexpected things about our theory (see, e.g., [17, Appendix A]). But pointwise circumscription in its full generality is not a first-order axiom, nor can the chronological minimality criterion be expressed by a first-order axiom, so barring some serious advances in theorem proving for higher-order logics, circumscription seems to be putting us in the position of using our insight into the problem to validate the formal system, rather than the other way around. We can never get more out of circumscription than we already know, and, if we don't do it just right, we may get a good deal less.

6.5. Arguing for model-theoretic minimality criteria

It is probably clear by now that what we're really interested in is the answer to two questions: (1) given a logical theory that admits more than one model, what are the preferred models of that theory (that is, what is the preference criterion) and (2) given a theory and a preference criterion, how do we find the theorems that are true in all "most preferred" models?

The last proposal for solving our representation problem, and the most promising, in our view, involves answering these questions directly: by describing preference relations on models and describing algorithms that generate the theorems true in the preferred models. This is the approach advocated by Shoham (in [25]), though it is also suggested in the writings of Kautz [11], Poole [23], and Goebel and Goodwin [6].

Shoham's theory of causal inference involves a logic for reasoning about time in which knowledge appears as a key modality. We can make statements like "$K(f, s)$," which is to be interpreted as "fact f is known in situation s." His preference criterion—chronological minimization extended to the notion of "facts being known," instead of "facts being true"—is called *chronologically maximal ignorance*. Just as above we advocated preferring those models in which abnormalities, or clippings, occurred as (temporally) late as possible, Shoham's criterion directs us to prefer those models in which knowledge is acquired (facts are known) as late as possible.

Frame axioms are then phrased like "if you know that the gun is loaded at t and you don't know that an unloading occurs between t and $t + 1$, then you know the gun is loaded at $t + 1$." The "shot therefore dead" model of our shooting axioms is preferred to the "unloading therefore alive" model because the latter model admits knowledge of an "unloading" event unknown in the former model, and the unloading event occurs temporally earlier than the "clipping aliveness" event that is known in the former model but unknown in the latter.

Minimizing knowledge (as opposed to clippings, or gun firings, or abnormalities, or something else) turns out to be an advantage because minimizing knowledge amounts to minimizing all propositions simultaneously. We can't do this by minimizing the *truth* of propositions because minimizing the points where P holds implies maximizing the points where $\neg P$ holds. On the other hand, we can simulteneously minimize the points where P is *known* to hold and the points where $\neg P$ is known to hold.

Having defined and justified this preference criterion, Shoham goes on to define theories, which he calls *causal theories*, that have the property that all maximally chronologically ignorant models agree on what is known. Further, he provides an algorithm that efficiently computes the set of atomic sentences known in all of these models.

So Shoham's solution, though it is very specific to the problem of temporal projection, indeed gives us what we were looking for in a logic: a way of expressing what models our theory of projection prefers, and a way of generating the sentences true in the preferred models.

7. Conclusion

Much of the controversy surrounding our first paper, [7], centered around a statement we made at the end:

[If it is indeed that case that] a significant part of defeasible reasoning can't be represented by default logics, and if in the cases where the logics fail we have no better way of describing the reasoning process than by a direct procedural characterization (like our program or its inductive definition), then logic as an AI representation language begins to look less and less attractive.

In retrospect that was an oversimplification—on the one hand, it almost certainly is the case that nonmonotonic inference (or default reasoning, or whatever you want to call it) is idiosyncratic and domain dependent, and that there is no reason to expect that a simple syntax for describing when "leaps of faith" should be made, or a simple minimality criterion such as set inclusion, should handle all the cases. On the other hand, this does not doom to ultimate failure all uses of logic in AI (or even in describing nonmonotonic reasoning).

There are a variety of ways to describe nonmonotonic reasoning within a logical framework. Many of them depend on classifying models more finely than classical logic allows. One's effort in describing nonmonotonic reasoning, then, should be directed toward describing the classification (i.e. developing a preference criterion) and finding out what is true in those preferred models, as Shoham eloquently argues in [25].

Circumscription—especially the new, more expressive versions—seems only obliquely concerned with these goals. The circumscription axiom does not allow a perspicuous statement of minimality criteria. Indeed, in many cases one *starts* with the notion of minimality and works backward to find a circumscription axiom that expresses it. And circumscription offers no help at all in generating the theorems true in preferred models. As we noted, the only way we know of to find that out is to show ahead of time what follows.

But while our conclusion about the role of logic in theory development was admittedly overstated, our second conclusion, about the acceptable uses of nonmonotonic logics, was not. One thing that our result, and even the responses, makes clear is that the relationship between these logics and human reasoning is not well understood. We can no longer engage in the logical "wishful thinking" that led us to claim that circumscription solves the frame problem [17], or that "'consistent' is to be understood in the normal way it is construed in nonmonotonic logic. [1]" From a technical standpoint, there *is* no "normal way" to understand the *M* operator. or the Reiter default rules, or a theory circumscribed over some predicate, apart from the proof or model theory of the chosen logic.

The term "consistent" has too often been used informally by researchers (e.g. in [10]) as if it had an intuitive and domain-independent meaning. We have shown that in at least one case a precise definition of the term is much more complex than intuition would have us believe, and that the definition is tightly bound up with the problem domain.

So researchers concerned with issues in nondeductive inference are not going to be able to rely on nonmonotonic logics to solve their problems for them, but perhaps in revealing the inadequacies of the formal systems we have also pointed out fruitful ways to attack these problems.

REFERENCES

1. Charniak, E. Motivation analysis, abductive unification, and non-monotonic equality, *Artificial Intelligence*, to appear.
2. Clark, L., Negation as failure, in: H. Gallaire and J. Minker (Eds.), *Logic and Databases* (Plenum Press, New York, 1978) 293–322.
3. Davis, M., The mathematics of non-monotonic reasoning. *Artificial Intelligence* 13 (1980) 73–80.
4. Etherington. D.W., Formalizing non-monotonic reasoning systems, Computer Science Tech. Rept. No. 83-1, University of British Columbia, Vancouver. BC, 1983.
5. Etherington. D.W. and Reiter, R... On inheritance hierarchies with exceptions, in: *Proceedings AAAI-83*, Washington, DC (1983) 104–108.
6. Goebel, R.G. and Goodwin, S., Applying theory formation to the planning problem, Research Rept. CS-87-02, Logic Programming and AI Group, Department of Computer Science, University of Waterloo. Waterloo. Ont. 1987.
7. Hanks, S. and McDermott, D. Temporal reasoning and default logics, Computer Science Research Rept. No. 430, Yale University, New Haven. CT. 1985.
8. Hanks, S. and McDermott, D. Default reasoning, nonmonotonic logics, and the frame problem, in: *Proceedings AAAI-86*, Philadelphia, PA (1986) 328–333.
9. Hayes, P.J., The second naïve physics manifesto, in: J.R. Hobbs and R.C. Moore (Eds.), *Formal Theories of the Commonsense World* (Ablex, Norwood. NJ, 1985) 1–36.
10. Joshi, A.. Webber, B. and Weischedel. R., Default reasoning in interaction, in: *Proceedings of the Non-Monotonic Reasoning Workshop* (1984) 141–150.
11. Kautz, H., The logic of persistence. in: *Proceedings IJCAI-85*, Los Angeles, CA (1985) 401–405.
12. Lifschitz, V., Formal theories of action, in: F. Brown (Ed.). *The Frame Problem in Artificial Intelligence: Proceedings of the 1987 Workshop* (Morgan Kaufman, Los Altos, CA, 1987).
13. Lifschitz, V.. Pointwise circumscription: Preliminary report. in: *Proceedings IJCAI-85*, Los Angeles, CA (1985) 406–410.
14. Lifschitz, V.. Some results on circumscription, in: *Proceedings of the Non-Monotonic Reasoning Workshop* (1984) 151–164.
15. Loui, R.P.. Response to Hanks and McDermott: Temporal evolution of beliefs and beliefs about temporal evolution, *Cognitive Sci.*, to appear.
16. McCarthy, J.. Circumscription—a form of non-monotonic reasoning. *Artificial Intelligence* 13 (1980) 27–39.
17. McCarthy, J.. Applications of circumscription to formalizing common sense knowledge, in: *Proceedings of the Non-Monotonic Reasoning Workshop* (1984) 295–324.
18. McCarthy, J. and Hayes, P.J.. Some philosophical problems from the standpoint of artificial intelligence, in: B. Meltzer and D. Michie (Eds.), *Machine Intelligence 4* (Edinburgh University Press, Edinburgh, 1969) 463–502.
19. McDermott, D.V., A temporal logic for reasoning about processes and plans, *Cognitive Sci.* 6 (1982) 101–155.
20. McDermott. D.V.. Nonmonotonic modal theories: Nonmonotonic modal logic II, *J. ACM* 29 (1) (1982) 33–57.
21. McDermott, D.V. and Doyle, J., Non-monotonic logic I, *Artificial Intelligence* 13 (1980) 41–72.
22. Perlis, D. and Minker, J., Completeness results for circumscription. Computer Science Tech. Rept. TR-1517, University of Maryland, College Park, MD, 1985.
23. Poole, D., On the comparison of theories: Preferring the most specific explanation, in: *Proceedings IJCAI-85*, Los Angeles, CA (1985) 144–147.
24. Reiter, R., A logic for default reasoning, *Artificial Intelligence* 13 (1980) 81–132.
25. Shoham, Y., Time and causation from the standpoint of artificial intelligence, Computer Science Research Rept. No. 507, Yale University, New Haven. CT. 1986.

Received April 1987

Why Things Go Wrong:
A Formal Theory of Causal Reasoning

Leora Morgenstern and **Lynn Andrea Stein**
Department of Computer Science
Brown University
Box 1910, Providence, RI 02912

Abstract

This paper presents a theory of generalized temporal reasoning. We focus on the related problems of

1. Temporal Projection—determining all the facts true in a chronicle, given a partial description of that chronicle, and

2. Explanation—figuring out what went wrong if an unexpected outcome occurs.

We present a non-monotonic temporal logic based on the notion that actions only happen if they are *motivated*. We demonstrate that this theory handles generalized temporal projection correctly, and in particular, solves the Yale Shooting Problem and a related class of problems. We then show how our model lends itself to a very natural characterization of the concept of an adequate explanation for an unexpected outcome.

1 Introduction

A theory of generalized temporal reasoning is a crucial part of any theory of commonsense reasoning. Agents who are capable of tasks ranging from planning to story understanding must be able to predict from their knowledge of the past what will happen in the future, to decide on what must have happened in the past, and to furnish a satisfactory explanation when a projection fails.

This paper present a theory that is capable of such reasoning. We focus on the related problems of

1. Temporal Projection—determining all of the facts that are true in some chronicle, given a partial description of that chronicle, and

2. Explanation—determining what went wrong if an unexpected outcome occurs.

Most AI researchers in the area of temporal reasoning have concentrated their efforts on parts of the temporal projection task: in particular, on the problem of forward temporal projection, or prediction ([McCarthy and Hayes, 1969], [McDermott, 1982], [Hayes, 1985], [Shoham, 1987]). Standard logics are unsuitable for the prediction task because of such difficulties as the frame problem. Straightforward applications of non-monotonic logic to temporal logics (suggested by [McDermott, 1982], [McCarthy, 1980]) are also inadequate, as [Hanks and McDermott, 1986] demonstrated through the Yale Shooting Problem.

Several solutions to the Yale Shooting Problem, using extensions of default logic, have been proposed ([Shoham,

1986] [Shoham, 1987], [Kautz, 1986], [Lifschitz, 1986] [Lifschitz, 1987], [Haugh, 1987]). All of these solutions, however, while adequate for the Yale Shooting Problem itself, handle either forward or backward projection incorrectly, and/or work only within a very limited temporal ontology. Thus, they cannot serve as the basis for a theory of generalized temporal reasoning.

In this paper, we present a solution to the problems of both forward and backward temporal projection, based upon the concept that actions happen only if they have to happen. We then show how our model lends itself to a very natural characterization of the concept of an adequate explanation for an unexpected outcome.

In the next section, we survey the solutions that have been proposed to the YSP, and explain why they cannot handle general temporal projection accurately. We then present our theory of default temporal reasoning and demonstrate that it can handle the Yale Shooting Problem as well as the problems that give other theories difficulty. Finally, we extend our theory of temporal projection to a theory of explanation.

2 Previous Approaches to the Prediction Problem

2.1 Default Reasoning and the Yale Shooting Problem

The frame problem—the problem of determining which facts about the world stay the same when actions are performed—is an immediate consequence of the attempt to subsume temporal reasoning within first order logic. McCarthy and Hayes first discovered this problem when they developed the situation calculus ([McCarthy and Hayes, 1969]); however, it is not restricted to the situation calculus and in fact arises in all reasonably expressive temporal ontologies ([McDermott, 1987]). In order to deal with the frame problem, McCarthy and Hayes suggested using frame axioms to specify the facts that don't change when certain actions are performed; critics (*e.g.* [McDermott, 1984]) have argued that such an approach is unsatisfactory given the difficulty of writing such axioms, the intractability of a theory containing so many axioms, and the fact that frame axioms are often false. This last point is especially relevant for temporal ontologies which allow for concurrent actions.

[McDermott, 1982] introduced the notion of a persistence: the time period during which a property typically persists. He argued that we reason about what is true in the world, not via frame axioms, but through our knowledge of the persistences of various properties. Such reasoning is inherently non-monotonic.

These considerations led [McDermott, 1982] to argue that temporal reasoning is best formalized within a non-monotonic logic. The discovery of the Yale Shooting Problem ([Hanks and McDermott, 1986]), however, demonstrated that this might not always yield desirable results.

The Yale Shooting Problem can briefly be described as follows: Assume that a gun is loaded at time 1, and the gun is fired (at Fred) at time 5. We know that if one loads a gun at time j, it is loaded at time j+1[1] that if a loaded gun is fired at a person at time j, the person is dead at time j+1, that if a gun is loaded at j, it will typically be loaded at time j+1 ("loaded" persists for as long as possible), and that if a person is alive at time j, he will typically be alive at time j+1 ("alive" persists for as long as possible).

We would like to predict that Fred is dead at time 6. Relative to standard non-monotonic logics ([McDermott and Doyle, 1980], [McCarthy, 1980], [Reiter, 1980]), however, the chronicle description supports (at least) two models: the expected one, in which one reasons by default that the gun is loaded at time 5, and in which Fred is dead at time 6, and the unexpected model in which one reasons by default that Fred is alive at time 6, and in which, therefore, the gun must be unloaded at time 5. Standard non-monotonic logic gives us no way of preferring the expected, intuitively correct model to the unexpected model.

Like the frame problem, the Yale Shooting Problem was first presented within the situation calculus framework, but is not restricted to that particular ontology ([McDermott, 1987]).

2.2 Proposed Solutions to the YSP and Their Limitations

In their original discussion of the Yale Shooting Problem, Hanks and McDermott argued that the second, unexpected model seems incorrect because we tend to reason forward in time and not backward. The second model seems to reflect what happens when we reason backward. Such reasoning, they argued, is unnatural: the problem with non-monotonic logic is that there is no way of preferring the forward reasoning models to the backward reasoning models.

2.2.1 Chronological Minimization

The first wave of solutions to the Yale Shooting Problem ([Shoham, 1986], [Kautz, 1986], [Lifschitz, 1986]) all independently set out to prove that such a preference could indeed be expressed in non-monotonic logic. We discuss Shoham's work here: criticisms of his theory apply equally to the others in the group.

Shoham defines the following preference relation on models: $\mathcal{M}_1$ is preferable to $\mathcal{M}_2$ if $\mathcal{M}_1$ and $\mathcal{M}_2$ agree up to some time point j, but at j, there is some fact known to be true in $\mathcal{M}_2$, which is not known to be true in $\mathcal{M}_1$. $\mathcal{M}_1$ is said to be chronologically more ignorant than $\mathcal{M}_2$. This preference defines a partial order; models which are minimal elements under this ordering are said to be chronologically maximally ignorant.

The expected model—in which Fred is dead—is preferable to the unexpected model—in which Fred is alive, since, in the unexpected model, it would be known that at some point before 5, something happened to unload the gun. In fact, in all chronologically maximally ignorant models for this set of axioms, the gun is loaded at time 5, and therefore, Fred is dead.

Solutions based upon forward reasoning strategies have two drawbacks. In the first place, agents perform both backward and forward reasoning. In fact, agents typically do backward reasoning when performing backward temporal projection. Consider, for example, a modification of the Yale Shooting Problem, where we are told that Fred is alive at time 6. We should know that the gun must somehow have become unloaded between times 2 and 5; however, we should not be able to say exactly when this happened. In contrast to this intuition, the systems of Shoham and Kautz would predict that the gun became unloaded between time 4 and time 5. This is because things stay the same for as long as possible.[2]

A second objection to the strategy of chronological minimization is that it does not seem to address the real concerns underlying the Yale Shooting Problem. We don't reason that Fred is dead at time 6 *because* we reason forward in time. We conclude that Fred is dead because we are told of an action that causes Fred's death, but are not told of any action that causes the gun to be unloaded.

2.2.2 Circumscribing Over Causes

[Lifschitz, 1987] and [Haugh, 1987] independently proposed solutions which were not based upon forward reasoning strategies. We present Lifschitz's; again criticisms of his theory apply to both. Lifschitz's solution is based on the intuition that "all changes in the values of fluents are caused by actions." Lifschitz introduces a predicate causes(act,f,v), where action act causes fluent f to take on value v, and a predicate precond(f,act). Success is defined in terms of precond, affects in terms of causes and success. He circumscribes over both the causes and precond predicates; circumscribing over causes solves the frame problem.[3] Things are only caused when there are axioms implying that they are caused. Necessary preconditions for an action are satisfied only when the axioms force this to be the case. Actions are successful exactly when all preconditions hold; actions affect the values of fluents if and only if some successful action causes the value to change. Assuming, now, the following axioms: causes(load,loaded,true), causes(shoot,loaded,false), causes(shoot,alive,false), precond(loaded,shoot), and a chronicle description stating that a load takes place at 1, a wait at 2,3, and 4, and a shoot at 5, we can predict that Fred is dead at time 6. There is no way that the wait action can cause the fluent loaded to take on the value false.

This solution doesn't force reasoning to go forward in time. Nevertheless, Lifschitz's solution is highly problematic. It works only within rigid formalisms like the situation calculus, and cannot be extended to—and in fact yields incorrect results in—a more flexible, realistic theory.

---

[1] It is implicitly assumed that actions take unit time.

[2] This point was noted by Kautz when he first presented his solution to the Yale Shooting Problem.

[3] Lifschitz introduces the precond predicate in order to solve the qualification problem, which we don't discuss here.

Moreover, a closer examination of the solution shows that it does not address one of the major intuitions underlying the Yale Shooting Problem.

It is crucial to realize that the causes predicate over which Lifschitz circumscribes ranges over action types as opposed to action instances. Circumscribing over causes thus entails that state changes will not happen spontaneously, but does not in general entail that as little will change as possible. Since the situation calculus framework itself entails that as little as possible happens, the solution will work as long as we stay within this rigid framework. Problems arise, however, in frameworks in which not all actions are known.

Consider what would happen in a world in which concurrent actions were allowed, and in which we were to add the rule causes(unload,loaded,false) to the theory. We could then have a model $\mathcal{M}_1$ where an unload occurs at time 2, the gun is thus unloaded, and Fred is alive at time 6. There would be no way to prefer the expected model where Fred dies to this model.[4] This cannot in fact happen in Lifschitz's formulation because in the situation calculus, concurrent actions aren't allowed. Since a wait action occurs at times 2, 3, and 4, nothing else can occur, and unload actions are ruled out.

Lifschitz's solution thus works only in frameworks where all the acts in a chronicle are known. In these cases, circumscribing the cause predicate gives us exactly what we want—it disables spontaneous state changes. The intuition underlying the Yale Shooting Problem, however, is that we can make reasonable temporal projections in worlds where concurrent actions are allowed, even if we aren't necessarily told of all the events that take place in a chronicle. The fact is that even if we are given a *partial* description, we will generally not posit additional actions unless there is a good reason to do so.

The temporal projection problem is thus a dual one: we must reason that actions don't cause fluents to take on values in unexpected ways, and we must reason that unexpected events don't in general happen. Lifschitz solved the first of these problems; in the next section, we turn our attention to the second.

3 Temporal Projection: A Theory of Motivated Actions

In this section, we develop a model of temporal projection which yields a satisfying solution to the Yale Shooting Problem, and which lends itself nicely to a theory of

explanation. Our model formalizes the intuition that we typically reason that events in a chronicle happen only when they "have to happen". We formalize the idea of a *motivated action*, an action that *must* occur in a particular model.

3.1 The Formal Theory

We begin by formally describing the concepts of a theory and a chronicle description. We work in a first order logic L, augmented by a simple temporal logic. Sentences are of the form True(j,f) where t is a time point, and f is a fluent—a term representing some property that changes with time. True(j,¬f) iff ¬True(j,f). Occurs(act) and loaded are examples of fluents. If φ = True(j,f), j is referred to as the *time point* of φ, time(φ). Time is isomorphic to the integers. Actions are assumed to take unit time.

A *theory*, T, and a *chronicle description*, CD, are sets of sentences of L. The union of a theory and a chronicle description is known as a *theory instantiation*, TI. Intuitively, a theory contains the general rules governing the behavior of (some aspects of) the world; a chronicle description describes some of the facts that are true in a particular chronicle. A theory includes *causal rules* and *persistence rules*. A causal rule is a sentence of the form $\alpha \wedge \beta \Longrightarrow \gamma$, where:

α is a non-empty set of sentences of the form True(j,Occurs(act))—the set of *triggering events* of the causal rule,

β is a conjunction of statements stating the preconditions of the action, and

γ describes the results of the action.

Note that γ can include sentences of the form True(j+1,Occurs(act)). We can thus express causal chains of action.

A persistence rule is of the form

$$\text{True(j,p)} \wedge \beta \Longrightarrow \text{True(j+1,p)}$$

where β includes a conjunction of statements of the form

$$\text{True(j,¬Occurs(act))}$$

These persistence rules bear a strong resemblance to frame axioms. In reality, however, they are simply instances of the principle of inertia: things do not change unless they have to.

We have hand coded the persistence rules for this simple case, although it is not necessary to do so. They can in fact be automatically generated from the theory's causal rules, relative to a closed world assumption on causal rules: that all the causal rules that are true are in the theory. This is indeed exactly what Lifschitz achieves by circumscribing over the causes predicate in his formulation. It is likely that such a strategy will be an integral part of any fully developed theory of temporal projection. Since the automatic generation of persistence rules is not the main thrust of this paper, we will not develop this here.

It is important to note that all of the rules in any theory T are monotonic. We achieve non-monotonicity solely by introducing a preference criterion on models: in particular, preferring models in which the fewest possible extraneous actions occur. Typically, we will not be given

---

[4]Haugh seems to address a related point in his paper. Haugh considers the case where we have an axiom stating that unload causes loaded to be false, and that the precondition for unload is that the performing agent knows how to perform the action (we recast into Lifschitz's formalism here for ease of comparison). Then, if it is known that an unload(attempt) Occurs, there will be no way of preferring models where loaded is true to models where loaded is false. Haugh says that this is to be expected; if we know of an unload attempt, we do not want to conclude that loaded is true. This argument is really beside the point. It is quite clear that if we are told of an unload (attempt), we will not conclude that Fred is dead. The point of the YSP is that, if you are not explicitly told of an unload, you will not seriously consider the possibility when making a prediction.

enough information in a particular chronicle description to determine whether or not the rules in the theory fire. However, because persistence rules explicitly refer to the non-occurrence of events, and because we prefer models in which events don't occur unless they have to, we will in general prefer models in which the persistence rules do fire. The facts triggered by persistence rules will often allow causal rules to fire as well.

3.2 Motivated Actions

Given a particular theory instantiation, we would like to be able to reason about the facts which ought to follow from the chronicle description under the theory. In particular, we would like to be able to determine whether a statement of the form True(j,p) is true in the chronicle. If j is later than the latest time point mentioned in *CD*, we call this reasoning *prediction*, or *forward projection*, otherwise, the reasoning is known as *backward projection*.

Given $TI = T \cup CD$, we are thus interested in determining the preferred models for TI. $\mathcal{M}(TI)$ denotes a model for TI: *i.e.*, $(\forall \varphi \in TI)[\mathcal{M}(TI) \models \varphi]$. We define a preference criterion for models in terms of *motivated* actions: those actions which "*have to happen.*" Our strategy will be to minimize those actions which are *not* motivated.

Definition: Given a theory instantiation $TI = T \cup CD$, we say that a statement φ is *motivated* in $\mathcal{M}(TI)$ if it is strongly motivated in $\mathcal{M}(TI)$ or weakly motivated in $\mathcal{M}(TI)$.

A statement φ is *strongly* motivated with respect to TI if φ is in all models of TI, *i.e.* if $(\forall \mathcal{M}(TI))[\mathcal{M}(TI) \models \varphi]$. If φ is strongly motivated with respect to TI, we say that it is motivated in $\mathcal{M}(TI)$, for all $\mathcal{M}(TI)$.

A statement φ is *weakly* motivated in $\mathcal{M}(TI)$ if there exists in TI a causal or persistence rule of the form $\alpha \wedge \beta \Longrightarrow \varphi$, α is (strongly or weakly) motivated in $\mathcal{M}(TI)$, and $\mathcal{M}(TI) \models \beta$.

Intuitively, φ is motivated in a model if it *has to be* in that model. Strong motivation gives us the facts we have in *CD* to begin with as well as their closure under T. Weak motivation gives us the facts that have to be in a *particular* model relative to T. Weakly motivated facts give us the non-monotonic part of our model—the conclusions that may later have to be retracted.

We now say that a model is preferred if it has as few unmotivated actions as possible. Formally, we define the preference relation on models as follows:

Definition: Let φ be of the form True(j,Occurs(act)). $\mathcal{M}_i(TI) \unlhd \mathcal{M}_j(TI)$ ($\mathcal{M}_i$ is *preferable* to $\mathcal{M}_j$) if $(\forall \varphi)[\mathcal{M}_i(TI) \models \varphi \wedge \mathcal{M}_j(TI) \not\models \varphi \Longrightarrow \varphi$ is motivated in $\mathcal{M}_i(TI)$.

That is, $\mathcal{M}_i(TI)$ is preferable to $\mathcal{M}_j(TI)$ if any action which occurs in $\mathcal{M}_i(TI)$ but does not occur in $\mathcal{M}_j(TI)$ is motivated in $\mathcal{M}_i(TI)$. Note that such actions can only be weakly motivated; if an action is strongly motivated, it is true in all models.

Definition:
If both $\mathcal{M}_i(TI) \unlhd \mathcal{M}_j(TI)$ and $\mathcal{M}_j(TI) \unlhd \mathcal{M}_i(TI)$, we say that $\mathcal{M}_i(TI)$ and $\mathcal{M}_j(TI)$ are *equipreferable* ($\mathcal{M}_i(TI) \bowtie \mathcal{M}_j(TI)$).

$\unlhd$ induces a partial ordering on acceptable models of TI. A model is *preferred* if it is a minimal element under $\unlhd$:

Definition: $\mathcal{M}(TI)$ is a *preferred model* for TI if $\mathcal{M}'(TI) \unlhd \mathcal{M}(TI) \Longrightarrow \mathcal{M}'(TI) \bowtie \mathcal{M}(TI)$.

Since not all models are comparable under $\unlhd$, there may be many preferred models. Let $\mathcal{M}^*(TI)$ be the union of all preferred models.

We define the following sets:

$\cap_{\mathcal{M}^*} = \{\varphi \mid (\forall \mathcal{M} \in \mathcal{M}^*(TI))[\mathcal{M} \models \varphi]\}$—the set of statements true in all preferred models of TI

$\cup_{\mathcal{M}^*} = \{\varphi \mid (\exists \mathcal{M} \in \mathcal{M}^*(TI))[\mathcal{M} \models \varphi]\}$—the set of statements true in at least one preferred model of TI

Consider, now, the relationship between any statement φ and TI. There are three cases:

Case I: φ is in $\cap_{\mathcal{M}^*(TI)}$. In this case, we say that TI *projects* φ.

Case II: φ is in $\cup_{\mathcal{M}^*(TI)}$. In this case, we say that φ is *consistent with* TI. However, TI does not project φ.

Case III: φ not in $\cup_{\mathcal{M}^*(TI)}$. In this case, we say that φ is *inconsistent with* TI. In fact, it is the case that TI projects $\neg\varphi$.

If TI projects φ, and time(φ) is later than the latest time point mentioned in TI, we say that TI *predicts* φ.

3.3 Prediction: The Yale Shooting Problem, Revisited

We now show that our theory can handle the Yale Shooting Problem. We represent the scenario with the following theory instantiation:
CD:

> True(1,alive)
>
> True(1,load)
>
> True(5,shoot)

T contains the causal rules for shoot, load, and unload, as well as the persistences for loaded and alive:

T: Causal Rules:

True(j,Occurs(load))	$\Longrightarrow$	True(j+1,loaded)
True(j,Occurs(shoot))	$\wedge$	True(j,loaded)
	$\Longrightarrow$	True(j+1,¬alive)
True(j,shoot)	$\Longrightarrow$	True(j+1,¬loaded)
True(j,unload)	$\Longrightarrow$	True(j+1,¬loaded)

Persistence Rules:

True(j,alive)	$\wedge$	(True(j,¬Occurs(shoot))
		$\vee$ True(j,¬loaded))
	$\Longrightarrow$	True(j+1,alive)
True(j,loaded)	$\wedge$	True(j,¬Occurs(shoot))
	$\wedge$	True(j,¬Occurs(unload))
	$\Longrightarrow$	True(j+1,loaded)

Let $\mathcal{M}_1$ be the expected model, where the gun is loaded at 5, and Fred is dead at 6; and let $\mathcal{M}_2$ be the unexpected model, where an unload takes place at some time between 2 and 5, and therefore Fred is alive at 6. Both $\mathcal{M}_1$ and $\mathcal{M}_2$ are models for *TI*. However, we will see that $\mathcal{M}_1$ is preferable to $\mathcal{M}_2$, since extra, unmotivated actions take place in $\mathcal{M}_2$.

We note that the facts True(1,alive), True(1,Occurs(load)), and True(5,Occurs(shoot)) are strongly motivated, since they are in *CD*. The fact True(2,loaded) is also strongly motivated; it is not in *CD*, but it must be true in all models of *TI*. In $\mathcal{M}_1$, the model in which the gun is still loaded at 5, True(6,¬alive) is weakly motivated. It is triggered by the shoot action, which is motivated, and the fact that the gun is loaded, which is true in $\mathcal{M}_1$. In $\mathcal{M}_2$, the occurrence of the unload action is unmotivated. It is not triggered by anything.

According to this definition, then, $\mathcal{M}_1$ is preferable to $\mathcal{M}_2$. There is no action which occurs in $\mathcal{M}_1$ that does not occur in $\mathcal{M}_2$. However, $\mathcal{M}_2$ is not preferable to $\mathcal{M}_1$: there is an action, unload, which occurs in $\mathcal{M}_2$, but not in $\mathcal{M}_1$, and this action is unmotivated.

In fact, it can be seen that in any preferred model of *TI*, the gun must be loaded at time 5, and therefore Fred must be dead at time 6. That is because in a model where the gun is unloaded at 5, a shoot or unload action must happen between times 2 and 5, and such an action would be unmotivated. Since the facts that loaded is true at time 5 and that Fred is dead at time 6 are in all preferred models of *TI*, *TI* projects these facts.

Note that preferring models in which the fewest possible unmotivated actions occur is not equivalent to preferring models in which the fewest possible actions occur. Consider, *e.g.*, a theory of message passing in which messages go through several checkpoints before completion. The message is passed as long as the control switch is open. An action is needed to close the switch. If we know that the message is started, we would like to predict that the switch remains open and the message completes. This is in fact what our preference criterion projects. However, since each stage of the message passing can be regarded as a separate action, a theory minimizing occurrences will predict that the switch is turned off, eliminating additional message passing segments.

3.4 Backward Projection

We now show that our theory handles backward projection properly. As an example, consider TI', where $TI' = TI \cup \{True(6,alive)\}$. That is, TI' is the theory instantiation resulting from adding the fact that Fred is alive at time 6 to the chronicle description of *TI*. Since we know that a shoot occurred at 5, we know that the gun cannot have been loaded at 5. However, we also know that the gun was loaded at 2. Therefore, the gun must have become unloaded between 2 and 5.[5] Our theory tells us nothing more than this. Consider the following acceptable models

----

[5]As we know, either an unload or a shoot will cause a gun to be unloaded. However, because we know that shooting will cause Fred to be dead, that dead persists forever, and that Fred is alive at 6, all acceptable models for TI' must have an unload.

for TI':

- $\mathcal{M}_1'$, where unload occurs at 2, the gun is unloaded at 3,4, and 5
- $\mathcal{M}_2'$, where unload occurs at 3, the gun is loaded at 3 and unloaded at 4 and 5
- $\mathcal{M}_3'$, where unload occurs at 4, the gun is loaded at 3 and 4, and unloaded at 5.

Intuitively, there does not seem to be a reason to prefer one of these models to the other. And in fact, our theory does not: $\mathcal{M}_1'$, $\mathcal{M}_2'$, and $\mathcal{M}_3'$ are equipreferable. Note, however, that both $\mathcal{M}_1'$ and $\mathcal{M}_3'$ are preferable to $\mathcal{M}_4'$, the model in which unload occurs at 2, load at 3, and unload at 4. $\mathcal{M}_4'$ is acceptable, but has superfluous actions. In fact, it can be shown that $\mathcal{M}_1'$, $\mathcal{M}_2'$, and $\mathcal{M}_3'$ are preferred models for TI'. All that TI' can predict, then, is the disjunction:

$$True(2,Occurs(unload)) \lor True(3,Occurs(unload))$$
$$\lor\ True(4,Occurs(unload))$$

which is exactly what we wish.

4 Explanation

A theory of temporal reasoning that can handle both forward and backward projection properly is clearly a prerequisite for any theory of explanation. Now that we have developed such a theory, we present a theory of explanation.

Intuitively, the need to explain something arises when we are initially given some partial chronicle description accompanied by some theory, we make some projections, and then we subsequently discover these projections to be false. When we find out the true story, we feel a need to explain "*what went wrong*"—that is, why the original projections did not in fact hold true.

Formally, we can describe the situation as follows: Consider a theory instantiation $TI_1 = T \cup CD_1$, with $\cap_{\mathcal{M}^*(TI_1)}$ equal to the set of facts projected by TI_1. Consider now a second theory instantiation $TI_2 = T \cup CD_2$, where $CD_2 \supset CD_1$. That is, TI_2 is TI_1 with a more fleshed out description of the chronicle. We say that there is a *need for explanation of TI_2 relative to* TI_1 if there exists some fact $\kappa \in CD_2$ such that TI_1 does not project κ, *i.e.* if $(\exists \kappa \in CD_2)[\kappa \notin \cap_{\mathcal{M}^*(TI_1)}]$. For any such κ, we say that κ *must be explained* relative to TI_1 and TI_2.

The need for explanation may be more or less pressing depending upon the particular situation. There are two cases to be distinguished:

Case I :

κ is not projected by TI_1, *i.e.* $\kappa \notin \cap_{\mathcal{M}^*(TI)}$. However κ is consistent with TI_1, *i.e.* $\kappa \in \cup_{\mathcal{M}^*(TI_1)}$. That is, κ is true in some of the preferred models of TI_1, it just is not true in all of the preferred models. For example, consider $TI_1 = T \cup CD_1$, where T is the theory described in the previous section, and $CD_1 = \{True(1,loaded), True(2,\neg loaded)\}$, and $TI_2 = T \cup CD_2$, where $CD_2 = CD_1 \cup \{True(1,Occur(unload))\}$.

The set of preferred models for TI_1 contains models in which the gun becomes unloaded via an unload action, and models in which the gun becomes unloaded via a shoot action. Neither action is in the intersection of the preferred models, so neither action is projected by TI_1. TI_1 will only project that one of the actions must have occurred; *i.e.* the disjunct True(1,Occurs(shoot)) $\vee$ True(1,Occur(unload)).

The extra information in CD_2 does not contradict anything we know; it simply gives us a way of pruning the set of preferred models. Intuitively, an explanation in such a case should thus characterize the models that are pruned.

Case II :

κ is not projected by TI_1. In fact, κ is not even consistent with TI_1, *i.e.* $\kappa \notin \cup_{\mathcal{M}^*(TI_1)}$. In this case, it is in fact the case that $\neg\kappa \in \cap_{\mathcal{M}^*(TI_1)}$, *i.e.*, TI_1 projects $\neg\kappa$.

Such a situation is in fact what we have in the Yale Shooting Scenario, if we find out, after predicting Fred's death, that he is indeed alive at time 6. This is the sort of situation that demonstrates the non-monotonicity of our logic, for TI_1 projects True(6,¬alive), while $TI_2 \supset TI_1$ projects True(6,alive). Here the need for explanation is crucial; we must be able to explain why our early projection went awry.

Intuitively, an informal explanation of what went wrong in this case must contain the facts that an unload occurred and that the gun was thus unloaded at time 5. That is, an adequate explanation is an account of the facts leading up to the discrepancy in the chronicle description.

We formalize these intuitions as follows: Given TI_1, TI_2, and a set of facts Q which are unprojected by TI_1, we define an adequate explanation for the set of facts Q relative to TI_1 and TI_2 as the set difference between the projections of TI_2 and the projections of TI_1:

Definition: Let $Q = \{\kappa \mid \kappa \in CD_2 \wedge \kappa \notin \cap_{\mathcal{M}^*(TI)}\}$

An adequate explanation for Q is given by $\cap_{\mathcal{M}^*(TI_2)} - \cap_{\mathcal{M}^*(TI_1)}$

As an example, let $TI_1 = T \cup CD_1$ be the description of the Yale Shooting Scenario (as in the previous section); let $TI_2 = T \cup CD_2$, where $CD_2 = CD_1 \cup \{\text{True}(6,\text{alive})\}$. The explanation of True(6,alive) relative to TI_1 and TI_2 would include the facts that an unload occurred either at time 2 or time 3 or time 4, and that the gun was unloaded at time 5—precisely the account which we demand of an explanation.

5   Conclusions and Future Work

We have developed a theory of default temporal reasoning which allows us to perform temporal projection correctly. Central to our theory is the concept that models with the fewest possible unmotivated actions are preferred.

We have demonstrated that this theory handles both forward and backward temporal projection accurately. We have given an intuitive account of the ways in which the need for explanation arises, and have shown how we can define explanation in a natural way in terms of our theory of projection.

We are currently extending the work described in this paper in two directions. We are examining several different characterizations of the explanation process, and determining the relationships between these characterizations within our model. In addition, we are investigating the properties of a theory which minimizes unmotivated state changes, as opposed to unmotivated actions. Preliminary

investigations suggest that such a theory would eliminate the need for both persistence rules and the principle of inertia.

Acknowledgements:

We'd like to thank Ernie Davis, Tom Dean, Vladimir Lifschitz, John McCarthy, and Yoav Shoham for ideas, advice, and many helpful discussions.

References

[Hanks and McDermott, 1986]
Steven Hanks and Drew McDermott, "Default Reasoning, Nonmonotonic Logics, and the Frame Problem", *Proc. AAAI*, 1986.

[Haugh, 1987] Brian Haugh "Simple Causal Minimizations for Temporal Persistence and Projection", *Proc. AAAI*, 1987.

[Hayes, 1985] Patrick Hayes, "Naive Physics I: Ontology for Liquids", in J. Hobbs and R. Moore, editors, *Formal Theories of the Commonsense World*, Ablex 1985.

[Kautz, 1986] Henry Kautz, "The Logic of Persistence", *Proc. AAAI*, 1986.

[Lifschitz, 1986] Vladimir Lifschitz, "Pointwise Circumscription: Preliminary Report", *Proc. of AAAI*, 1986.

[Lifschitz, 1987] Vladimir Lifschitz, "Formal Theories of Action: Preliminary Report", *Proc. of IJCAI*, 1987.

[McCarthy, 1980] John McCarthy, "Circumscription—A Form of Nonmonotonic Reasoning", *Artificial Intelligence*, Vol. 13, 1980.

[McCarthy and Hayes, 1969] John McCarthy and Patrick Hayes, "Some Philosophical Problems from the Standpoint of Artificial Intelligence", In Donald Michie and Bernard Meltzer, editors, *Machine Intelligence*, Vol. 4, 1969.

[McDermott and Doyle, 1980] Drew McDermott and Jon Doyle, "Non-Monotonic Logic I", *Artificial Intelligence*, Vol. 13, 1980.

[McDermott, 1982] Drew McDermott, "A Temporal Logic for Reasoning about Processes and Plans", *Cognitive Science*, Vol. 6, 1982.

[McDermott, 1984] Drew McDermott, "The Proper Ontology for Time", Unpublished paper, 1984.

[McDermott 1987] Drew McDermott, "AI, Logic, and the Frame Problem", *Proc. The Frame Problem in Artificial Intelligence*, 1987.

[Reiter, 1980] Ray Reiter, "A Logic for Default Reasoning", *Artificial Intelligence*, Vol. 13, 1980.

[Shoham, 1986] Yoav Shoham, "Chronological Ignorance: Time, Nonmonotonicity, Necessity, and Causal Theories", *Proc. AAAI*, 1986.

[Shoham, 1987] Yoav Shoham, "Reasoning about Change: Time and Causation from the Standpoint of Artificial Intelligence", Phd Thesis, Tech. Report 507, Yale Univ. 1987.

Part IV

New Directions in Planning Systems

Since the mid-1980's a new look has come over the planning literature. As planning systems emerged from AI laboratories, it was realized that many of the assumptions underlying the classical framework could not hold in many real-world applications. This lead to three new directions for planning systems: the identification of domains in which the classical approach could be used, the engineering of domain-specific heuristics that could be used to provide individual planning systems with the ability to handle the domains in which they had to function, and the use of new techniques to extend planners to function in domains for which they had not originally been designed.

Much of the work focusing on addressing the extension of planning systems has involved a new awareness of the roots of planning systems. This has caused many researchers to reexamine control, decision, and information theories, and to attempt to apply these approaches in the field of planning. While this is leading to an increasing ability to develop real-world planning systems, it is sometimes hard to read such papers and know where the control theory (etc.) ends and the planning begins. Thus, although such papers are now making a major impact on the field of planning, we believe it is too early to present such papers in this collection.

Instead, in this, the final part of this volume, we present papers (several of which have previously been available only as technical reports) that demonstrate three important directions in which the field of planning is growing. Unlike many of the papers appearing earlier in this volume, these are not articles that have stood the test of time or been regarded as "classics" in the planning literature. Rather, they are recent papers that we feel present a good discussion of issues currently being examined and approaches currently being explored. The topics we have chosen to present include:

Learning and Reuse: Describes the integration of machine learning and case-based reasoning into planning.

Extending the Classical Framework: Expands on the directions described in Part II of this volume.

Planning and Execution: Questions the separate generation and execution of plans.

Part IV

New Directions in Planning Systems

Chapter 9

Learning and Reuse

In Chapter 4, we presented a paper by Fikes, Hart, and Nilsson (1972) describing how the STRIPS system could learn to group sets of operators into single "macro-operators" which could then be used in new planning situations. This technique could not be directly applied, however, in the non-linear, hierarchical planning systems that grew to replace the STRIPS approach. Recent work in the field of machine learning has focused on the development of approaches that can use past experience to help modify behavior. Two of these in particular, explanation-based learning and case-based reasoning, are proving to be useful for planning systems.

In this chapter we present three papers chosen to indicate differing approaches to the issues of learning in planning. The first paper, by Minton (1985), describes the use of an explanation-based learning algorithm to expand on the idea developed in the early work of Fikes et al. In that system, new operators were derived by generalizing solutions to planning problems and replacing the constants found in specific plans with variables. Minton's system uses a similar approach, but applies an explanation-based learning (EBL) algorithm to provide more accurate generalizations. Other work in applying EBL to planning include the work of Segre, 1988, and Chien, 1989.

The second paper we present, Hammond (1986), describes a case-based approach to planning. In such a system an old plan is chosen and modified to run in a different situation. This work concentrates on guiding the search for the old plan and then using a mapping strategy to produce the new plan. The paper presented herein describes Hammond's CHEF system, which attempts to learn from failures arising in the domain of Chinese cooking. (Kolodner [1987] describes JULIA, an alternative case-based approach

to learning from failures in planning.) A comprehensive description of Hammond's work can be found in his 1989 book.

The work on CHEF (and JULIA) concentrated primarily on finding relevant plans. Another important issue is how the plans that are retrieved can be reused in the current situation. The last paper we present in this chapter, Alterman (1988), describes the PLEXUS system, which uses information about a new context to guide the reuse of an existing plan. This work also served as the motivation for another plan-reuse system that functioned in the classical planning framework, Kambhampati's (1989) PRIAR system. PRIAR is an extension to Tate's NONLIN program (1977, Chapter 5) which allows the planner to annotate plans being created with information about the dependency structure between operators. This information is then used to guide retrieval, reuse, and replanning.

Papers referenced herein but not included in this volume:

Chien, S. (1989). "Using and Refining Simplifications: Explanation-based Learning of Plans in Tractable Domains," *Proc. of the IJCAI-89.*

Hammond, K. (1989). "Case-based Planning," Academic Press, MA.

Kambhampati, S. (1989). "Flexible Reuse and Modification in Hierarchical Planning: A Validation Structure-Based Approach," Ph.D. Thesis, Dept. of Computer Science, University of Maryland. College Park.

Kolodner, J. (1987). "Case-based Problem Solving," 4th International Workshop on Machine Learning, Irvine, CA.

Segre, A. (1988). "Machine Learning of Robot Assembly Plans," Kluwer Academic Publishers, Norwell, MA.

Selectively Generalizing Plans for Problem-Solving

Steven Minton[1]

Computer Science Department, Carnegie-Mellon University
Pittsburgh, PA 15213, USA

Abstract

Problem solving programs that generalize and save plans in order to improve their subsequent performance inevitably face the danger of being overwhelmed by an ever-increasing number of stored plans. To cope with this problem, methods must be developed for selectively learning only the most valuable aspects of a new plan. This paper describes MORRIS, a heuristic problem solver that measures the utility of plan fragments to determine whether they are worth learning. MORRIS generalizes and saves plan fragments if they are frequently used, or if they are helpful in solving difficult subproblems. Experiments are described comparing the performance of MORRIS to a less selective learning system.

1 Introduction

Building problem-solving programs that improve their performance by generalizing and re-using past solutions is one of the goals of machine-learning research. It has been demonstrated that generalized solution sequences, or plans, can be produced by analyzing the constraints inherent in solution instances [3, 8]. This method of learning has been successfully employed in domains as diverse as game-playing [6] and mathematical problem-solving [7].

One drawback to learning plans is that the number of stored plans may increase quickly as the problem-solver gains experience. Furthermore, the applicability conditions of long plans tend to be highly specific. Searching through the space of stored plans to find one that is best-suited to the current problem may be as expensive as searching through the original search space. This leads to the following paradox: as the system gains experience it gradually becomes swamped by the knowledge it has acquired. In some cases performance can eventually degrade so dramatically that the system operates even more poorly than a non-learning system.

One of the earliest and best-known plan learning systems was the STRIPS problem solver [4, 3]. Having solved a problem, STRIPS produced a parameterized version of the solution, called a Macrop, by generalizing constants while maintaining the dependencies among the steps in the solution. The Macrop might subsequently be used – either in whole or in part – to aid in rapidly solving similar problems. This paper explores how the degradation problem manifests itself in STRIPS-like learning systems. Moreover, two methods are considered whereby a heuristic problem-solver may selectively save fragments of generalized solutions in order to stave off degradation.

2 STRIPS and MACROPS

The generic term "macro-operator" will be used hereafter to refer to a parameterized sequence of operator applications, eg.:

```
GOTO-OBJ(KEYS)
PICK-UP(KEYS)
GOTO-DOOR(drx)
UNLOCK(drx)
OPEN(drx)
GOTHRU-DOOR(drx, rmy)
```

Constants are denoted by capitalized strings, and variables by lower case strings. The macro-operator shown above describes a series of actions for getting the keys and unlocking, opening, and going through a door.[2]

A STRIPS problem-space consists of a world model, represented by a set of well-formed formulas (wffs) in the predicate calculus, and a set of operators. Each operator includes an add-list, a delete-list and a precondition wff. An operator is applicable if its precondition wff is satisfied. Applying an operator simply involves making the changes indicated in the add and delete lists.

STRIPS, like many other problem-solvers, searched through the space of operator sequences in order to solve a problem. Means-ends analysis [1] was used to guide the search. Once a sequence of operators that solved the problem was found, STRIPS produced a Macrop by replacing the problem-specific constants in the operator sequence with problem-independent parameters. Any subsequence of the Macrop could then be used as a composite operator during future planning.

Fikes et al. [3] described a series of 5 problems that STRIPS solved more rapidly when Macrops were learned after each trial. They claimed that "the search tree sizes [were] all smaller when Macrops were used and the Macrops allow longer plans to be formed without necessarily incurring an exponential increase in planning time".

---

[1]The author is supported by an AT&T Bell Laboratories Scholarship

[2]STRIPS's Macrops also included information helpful for monitoring execution of the operator sequence in the real world.

Used by permission of the International Joint Conferences on Artificial Intelligence, Inc.

There appear to be two distinct factors that can contribute to the effectiveness of macro-operators in problem-solving. First, since macro-operators represent sequences of operators, the preconditions and postconditions of the individual operators can be compiled into aggregate preconditions and postconditions for the macro-operator as a whole. Therefore it can be quicker to test whether a macro-operator is applicable than to test whether the corresponding sequence of operators is applicable.[3] . Even more importantly, the use of macro-operators can bias the order in which the search space (of operator sequences) is explored. If relevant Macro-operators tend to be considered before relevant operators, then previously successful paths will generally be explored before other paths. This experiential bias can be a significant source of heuristic power.

Unfortunately, a problem solver that uses macro-operators in this manner may find that as the number of macro-operators increases, the experiential bias gradually disappears. In the extreme case, if eventually every operator sequence that the problem-solver might conceivably consider in solving a problem becomes a macro-operator, then the ordering advantage will have been effectively negated.

In practice, however, only a subset of these sequences become macro-operators. For any given domain, the crucial issue is whether or not the use of macro-operators will effectively compress the search space associated with that domain. If a small set of macro-operators can be generated that "cover" the relevant problems in the domain, then search will be confined within this smaller space. For example, Korf's Macro Problem Solver [5] is powerful enough to generate a set of macros that completely eliminates search, unfortunately, his technique only works for domains that exhibit operator decomposability. With STRIPS, every unique subsequence of all previously acquired solutions is a potential macro-operator; the STRIPS technique for generating macro-operators does not have strong domain requirements, but neither does it guarantee that the search space will be adequately compressed. Indeed, it has been our experience that even in small domains, the STRIPS approach can quickly lead to an explosion of macro-operators. For example, in STRIPS even "useless" operator sequences, such as STACK(x, y) followed by UNSTACK(x, y), can become macro-operators due to STRIPS's methods of generating and editing solution sequences.

3 MORRIS: A Selective Learner

To avoid being swamped by too many macro-operators, a problem-solver can endeavor to retain only those macro-operators that are most useful. MORRIS ("the finicky learner") is a heuristic problem-solver in the STRIPS

tradition[4] that demonstrates the importance of selective learning. Currently MORRIS saves two types of macro-operators, s-macros and t-macros. S-macros, or "scripts", are frequently used operator sequences. T-macros, or "tricks", are operator sequences for solving difficult problems.

3.1 S-Macros

The strategy of retaining only the most frequently used macro-operators was suggested by Fikes et. al. [3], but never implemented in STRIPS. MORRIS accomplishes this by maintaining a record of the problems solved and their generalized solutions. Each time a new solution is acquired, it is compared to the previously acquired solutions in order to locate common subsequences. When two unifiable subsequences are found, the more general of the two subsequences is added to the list of s-macros.

A limit is maintained on the number of s-macros kept active by the system. Once this limit is exceeded, the s-macros that were least-used during their lifetimes are deleted from the active set. The net result of this process is a set of relatively short macro-operators, which is desirable, since the time cost of evaluating whether a macro-operator is applicable can grow exponentially with the number of preconditions it has[5].

3.2 T-Macros

T-macros are macro-operators that represent "non-obvious" solutions to difficult problems. The notion of non-obviousness is defined by MORRIS's heuristic evaluation function, called H_{diff}. H_{diff} is used to estimate the progress that an operator (or macro-operator) makes with respect to the current set of goals. At each node in the search tree, MORRIS collects the relevant set of operators (and macro-operators) for extending the current path and evaluates them with respect to H_{diff}. Since MORRIS employs a best-first search through the tree, operators that appear to make the most progress are considered before less promising operators.

In evaluating the progress made by an operator, H_{diff} takes into the account the number of goals that remain to be solved as well as the *criticality* of each of these goals. A criticality value is a difficulty estimate assigned to each literal (i.e. potential goal) in the domain [10]. Higher criticality goals are attacked before goals of lesser criticality. (Generally one literal is given a higher criticality value than another literal if achieving the first literal typically undoes the second literal.)

---

[3]Clever methods for storing macro-operators and ordering their preconditions may also effect the efficiency of the search, although less attention has been given to these issues

---

[4]Although patterned after STRIPS, MORRIS operates within a closed world, and therefore uses matching rather than theorem proving to test whether the preconditions of an operator are satisfied.

[5]There is generally a linear relationship between the average number of preconditions and the length of a macro.

Occasionally the values given by H_{diff} will be misleading; if the real solution path is estimated to be less promising than alternative paths, MORRIS may be led far astray in its search. For example, consider the situation depicted in Figure 1. Paths A and B appear to be productive, but eventually lead to dead ends. Path C, despite its unpromising rating at node N_0, actually leads to a solution. (The heuristic is of the hill-climbing variety; up indicates apparent progress towards the solution.) In such cases, the mistaken estimate may be uncovered only after many alternatives have been explored, since MORRIS uses a best-first search to traverse the search space.

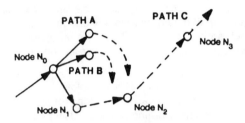

Figure 1: Misleading Path Ratings

The operator subsequence from node N_0 to node N_3 is *locally anomalous*. Its initial segment appears to make no progress, but the subsequence as a whole is rated as advantageous. Parameterizing and saving this 3-step operator sequence as a t-macro will enable MORRIS to avoid similar pitfalls in the future. If the goal at node N_0 is encountered again, MORRIS will evaluate its relevant operators as usual, but now the saved t-macro will be among them. Consequently, a more accurate heuristic estimate of this path will be generated. This strategy helps MORRIS avoid states which, in hill-climbing terms, are local maxima.

T-macros are also relevant to problems involving interacting goals. Many well-known problems fall into this class; for example, a robot planning problem might require the robot to move a box from a room and turn off the light to the room. If the robot first tries to turn off the light, it will not be able to move into the room to get the box. Because the two goals interact, ordering considerations are important.

If MORRIS finds that re-ordering goals succeeds in solving a problem that could not be solved otherwise, it must be the case that that some interaction between these goals occurred. The eventual solution to such a problem will always include a locally anomalous subsequence. This happens because re-ordering goals corresponds to attacking a lower criticality problem before a higher criticality problem (usually an unproductive undertaking), and consequently a low H_{diff} rating is generated at that point.

Once the solution is found, MORRIS identifies the goals involved in the re-ordering and constructs a t-macro in the normal fashion. T-macros of this type are particularly effective, since their use can be restricted to situations where the combination of these goals reoccurs.[6]

4 Experimental Results

In order to compare the effectiveness of MORRIS against a less-selective learner, a problem-solver called MAX was constructed that closely follows the STRIPS philosophy of saving all usable macro-operators. As does STRIPS, MAX generalizes the entire solution sequence whenever a problem is solved, and considers all composable subsequences to be potential macro-operators. MAX's procedures for saving, editing, and eliminating subsumed macro-operators are all modeled after those used by STRIPS with Macrops.

Once an operator (or macro-operator) is determined to be relevant to the current goal, both MAX and MORRIS use the same method to instantiate the operators. The bindings necessary to produce the relevant additions are first substituted into the operator's precondition list and then a partial-matching process is instituted to find potential instantiations. Since the time cost of the matching process is sensitive to the ordering of the preconditions, the matcher re-orders the preconditions to decrease the cost. Furthermore, during the matching operation, partial instantiations with many unsatisfied conditions may filtered out if the number of potential instantiations grows exceptionally high. Each instantiation produced by the matcher is then evaluated by H_{diff}.

MAX and MORRIS are identical programs with respect to their method of exploring the problem space. Since both programs employ a best-first search, misleading heuristic estimates can be costly. The only difference between them is in the types and numbers of macro-operators saved.

MAX and MORRIS were compared in a robot world consisting of 26 operators. This world is similar to the STRIPS experimental domain, but is richer in that many interacting problems can occur. There are 5 rooms, and operators for going to objects, going through doors, standing on, picking up, stacking, unstacking and putting down objects. Boxes can be pushed to various locations. Objects can be fixed and broken with various tools. Lights can be turned on and off, doors can be opened, closed, locked and unlocked. Food can be eaten. Sample problems include the following: "Go into room1 and lock the door to room1"; "Push boxA and boxB together and stand on BoxA"; "Take the keys from room1 to the room3".

The experimental results for a sampling of problems from a series of 25 are shown in Table 1. The table includes results for MORRIS, MAX, and a non-learning problem-solver that uses H_{diff} but does not save any macro-operators. (The non-learning program is a stripped down version of MORRIS). The timing data does not include the time taken to generalize macro-operators, only the time necessary to find a solution. Typically, the learning time is considerably less than the search time.

---

[6]Presently, MORRIS does not attempt to fully analyze why the interaction occurred. In order insure that application of the t-macro is restricted to circumstances under which the interaction occurs, a slightly weaker form of generalization is used whereby identical constants in the goals are replaced by single variables.

Problem Number	1	10	17	22	26
NON-LEARNING SYSTEM					
# Branches evaluated	24	63	704	558	930
# Nodes expanded	10	22	137	110	186
Solution length	4	10	16	16	*
CPU Seconds	1.5	3.9	78.1	62.4	100
MORRIS					
# Branches evaluated	24	47	55	123	95
# Nodes expanded	10	20	13	24	19
Solution length	4	10	11	16	16
CPU Seconds	1.5	3.6	8.0	17.0	14.1
MAX					
# Branches evaluated	24	201	128	781	1131
# Nodes expanded	10	20	10	26	17
Solution length	4	10	12	16	*
CPU Seconds	1.5	13.0	15.0	68.0	100

* No solution generated within 100 CPU seconds

Table 1: Experimental Results

Since small variations in the problems can cause large differences in performance for each of these systems, Table 1 is only partially indicative of their relative abilities. However, some points do stand out.

The benefits attributable to MORRIS's strategy of selectively saving macrops are revealed by the smaller number of branches - relevant operators and macro-operators - that were evaluated by MORRIS during each search as compared to MAX. Saving fewer macro-operators did not hurt MORRIS's overall performance. Consider, for example, that in solving problem 10 MAX and MORRIS followed the same path to the solution, but MAX evaluated more alternatives along the way. The problem with MAX is that it gradually loses the efficiency advantage provided by H_{diff}. Whenever H_{diff} indicates the correct branch, MAX will waste considerable time instantiating many macro-operators, in effect, performing look ahead. Whenever H_{diff} is wrong, MORRIS will be as well prepared as MAX assuming the appropriate t-macro has been saved.

Compared to the non-learning problem-solver, MORRIS generally performed better. Admittedly, the sequence of problems was arranged so that the smaller problems were presented first. In many cases, the t-macros learned while solving these earlier problems were necessary for solving later, more difficult problems. Once a wrong path was taken by the non-learning program, recovery was impossible to achieve if the number of alternatives was very high, as was typically the case in complex problems.

In the later stages of the experiment, the contrast between MAX and the non-learning program became evident: if the non-learning program could find a solution to a problem, it generally did so more quickly than MAX. Because MAX was busy performing look-ahead at each node (by evaluating all the relevant macro-operators), it it could not take full advantage of H_{diff} in pruning the search.

Overall, the results confirm our expectations. MORRIS's t-macros appeared to extend the heuristic advantage provided by H_{diff}, resulting in a significant improvement in problem-solving ability. S-macros were more frequently useful, but resulted in less significant gains. Occasionally the extra time necessary to test for the applicability of s-macros slowed MORRIS down enough so that the non-learning system performed more efficiently. In either case, the extra computational expense incurred by saving these macros was more than offset by their benefits. We have yet to perform extensive experiments comparing t-macros and s-macros.

5 Conclusions

The approach to learning embodied in MORRIS is rather unusual, since we have focused on the issue of "What to learn?" rather than "How to learn?". This issue can be crucial for a macro-operator learning system; if the acquisition of macro-operators is unbridled, the size of the search space defined by the set of macro-operators may grow rapidly, approaching the size of the original search space.

The two strategies MORRIS employs for evaluating the worth of a macro-operator have been found to be effective in controlling the learning process. Using these strategies, MORRIS maintains a balance between its reliance on knowledge, and its reliance on search.

In the future we hope to improve MORRIS by having it explicitly reason about the utility of control knowledge in order to direct its learning. We suspect that as machine-learning becomes better understood, the problem of deciding what is worth learning will assume greater importance.

6 Acknowledgements

The author thanks Jaime Carbonell for his many contributions to this research.

References

1. Ernst, G. and Newell, A.. *GPS: A Case Study in Generality and Problem Solving.* Academic Press, 1969.
2. Fikes, R. *Monitored execution of Robot Plans produced by STRIPS.* Proceedings IFIP Congress, 1971.
3. Fikes, R., Hart, P. and Nilsson, N. "Learning and Executing Generalized Robot Plans." *Artificial Intelligence* 3, 4 (1972).
4. Fikes, R. and Nilsson, N. "STRIPS: A new approach to the application of theorem proving to problem solving." *Artificial Intelligence* 2 (1971).
5. Korf, Richard E. *Operator Decomposability: A New Type of Problem Structure.* Proceedings AAAI-83, 1983.
6. Minton, S. *Constraint-Based Generalization.* AAAI Proceedings, 1984.
7. Mitchell, T., Utgoff, P. and Banerji, R. Learning by Experimentation: Acquiring and Refining Problem-Solving Heuristics. In *Machine Learning*, Carbonell, J., Michalski, R. and Mitchell, T., Ed.,Tioga Publishing Co., 1983.
8. O'Rorke, Paul. *Generalization for Explanation-based Schema Acquisition.* Proceedings AAAI, 1984.
9. Porter, B. and Kibler, D. *Learning Operator Transformations.* AAAI Proceedings, 1984.
10. Sacerdoti, E. "Planning in a Hierarchy of Abstraction Spaces." *Artificial Intelligence* 5 (1974).

CHEF: A Model of Case-based Planning.*

Kristian J. Hammond

Department of Computer Science
Yale University

ABSTRACT

Case-based planning is based on the idea that a machine planner should make use of its own past experience in developing new plans, relying on its memories instead of a base of rules. Memories of past successes are accessed and modified to create new plans. Memories of past failures are used to warn the planner of impending problems and memories of past repairs are called upon to tell the planner how to deal with them.

Successful plans are stored in memory, indexed by the goals they satisfy and the problems they avoid. Failures are also stored, indexed by the features in the world that predict them. By storing failures as well as successes, the planner is able to *anticipate and avoid* future plan failures.

These ideas of memory, learning and planning are implemented in the case-based planner CHEF, which creates new plans in the domain of Szechwan cooking.

I WHAT IS CASE-BASED PLANNING?

Case-based planning is planning from experience. A case-based planner differs sharply from planners that make use of libraries of goals and plans in that it relies on an episodic memory of past planning experiences. As a result, memory organization, indexing, plan modification, and learning are central issues in case-based planning. Because this sort of planner has to be able to reuse the plans that it builds, it must be able to understand and explain why the plans that it has built succeed or fail in order to properly store them for later use. This means that a cased-based planner not only needs to have a powerful memory organization, it must also have a strong model of the causality of the domain in which it operates.

The case-based approach to planning is to treat planning tasks as memory problems. Instead of building up new plans from scratch, A case-based planner recalls and modifies past plans. Instead of seeing plan failures as planning problems alone, it treats them as expectation failures that indicate a need to modify its understanding of the world. And instead of treating plans as disposable items that are used once and then forgotten, a case-based planner treats them as valuable commodities that can be stored and recalled for later use. In general, a case-based planner treats at the problem of building and maintaining plans as an interaction between its knowledge base and the world. Any problem that arises out of a disparity between what the planner knows and what is requires that it alter not only its plan but also the expectations that led to the creation of that plan.

II WHY CASE BASED?

The argument for case-based planning is straightforward: we want a planner that can learn complex plans rather than replan every time

*This report describes work done in the Department of Computer Science at Yale University. It was supported in part by ONR Grant #N00014-85-K-0108.

it has to achieve an already planned for set of goals. In the case of a single plan from the CHEF domain, a plan for stir fried chicken and peanuts for example, the plan itself has seventeen steps performed on a dozen ingredients. While such a plan can be built up from a set of rules or plan abstractions, it is more efficient to save the entire plan and recall it for reuse when the same situation reoccurs. Further, the case-based approach seems to much more closely reflect human planning behavior than do those approaches that suggest replanning for every new case.

Even going back to the earliest rule-based planners such as STRIPS [1], there has always been the desire to save completed plans in a way that makes them accessible to the planner in later situations. This was especially the case in those situations where a past plan included information about how to avoid problems that the planner's base of rules tended to lead into. But the planning algorithm used by most planners does not allow for anything but the most obvious reuse of existing plans. Most planners build plans for multiple goal situations out of the individual plans for each of the goals that the planner is handed and then deal with any interactions as they arise. Unfortunately, this algorithm has resulted in set of planners that recreate and then debug past mistakes rather than using the plans that they have developed before that avoid those mistakes altogether [2,4,5].

The approach taken in CHEF is to *anticipate and avoid* problems due to plan interaction. To do this, CHEF keeps track of what features in its domain are predictive of particular problems so it can predict when it has to plan for them. It also saves plans in memory, indexed by the goals that they satisfy and the problems that they avoid. So the prediction of a problem allows CHEF to find the plans in memory that avoid it. CHEF's basic algorithm is to find a past plan that satisfies as many of the most important goals as possible and then modify that plan to satisfy the other goals as well.

III CHEF'S OVERALL STRUCTURE

CHEF is a case-based planner that builds new plans out of its memory of old ones. CHEF's domain is Szechwan cooking and its task is to build new recipes on the basis of a user's requests. CHEF's input is a set of goals for different tastes, textures, ingredients and types of dishes and its output is a single recipe that satisfies all of its goals. Its output is a single plan, in the form of a recipe, that satisfies all of the users goals.

Before searching for a plan to modify, CHEF examines the goals in its input and tries to anticipate any problems that might arise while planning for them. If a failure is predicted, CHEF adds a goal to avoid the failure to its list of goals to satisfy and this new goal is also used to search for a plan. Because plans are indexed in memory by the problems they avoid, this prediction can be used to find a plan that solves the predicted problem. Much of CHEF's planning power lies in this ability to predict and thus avoid failures it has encountered before.

CHEF consists of six processes:

- **Problem anticipation:** The planner anticipates planning problems by noticing features in the current input that have previously participated in past planning problems.

- **Plan retrieval:** The planner searches for a plan that satisfies as many of its current goals as possible while avoiding the problems that it has predicted.

- **Plan modification:** The planner alters the plans it has found to satisfy any goals from the input that are not already achieved.

- **Plan repair:** When a plan fails, the planner fixes the faulty plan by building up a causal explanation of why the failure has occurred and using it to find the different strategies for repairing it.

- **Credit assignment:** Along with repairing a failed plan, the planner wants to repair the characterization of the world that allowed it to create the failed plan in the first place. It does this by using the causal explanation of why the failure occurred to identify the features in the input that led to the problem and then mark them as predictive of it.

- **Plan storage:** The planner places successful plans in memory, indexed by the goals that they satisfy and the problems that they avoid.

The flow of control through these processes is simple. Goals are handed to the problem anticipator, which tries to predict any problems that might occur as a result of planning for them. If a problem is predicted, a goal to avoid it is added to the set of goals to be planned for. Once this is done, the goals are handed to the plan retriever, which searches for a plan that satisfies as many of the planner's goals as possible, including any goals to avoid any predicted problems. In order to do this, the plan retriever makes use of a memory of plans indexed by the goals they satisfy and the problems they solve. Once a base line plan is found, the plan modifier alters the plan to satisfy any goals that it does not already deal with. The alteration of the plan is done using a set of modification rules that are indexed by the goal to be added and the type of plan being altered.

After the plan is built it is handed to a simulator, which runs the plan using a set of rules concerning the effects of each action in CHEF's domain under different circumstances. If the plan runs without fail, it is placed in memory, indexed by the goals that it satisfies. If there are failures, the plan is handed to the plan repair mechanism. This process builds a causal description of why a plan has failed and then uses that description to find the repair strategies that will alter the causal situation to fix the fault. After the plan has been repaired, it is placed in memory, indexed by the goals it satisfies and the problems it now avoids. Because a problem has to be anticipated before it can be planned for, however, the planner has to do more than just store plans by the fact they they solve particular problems. It also has to build up a knowledge base that can be used to infer problems on the basis of the features in the world that predict them. The planner must decide which features in the input are responsible for the problem and mark them as such. This credit assignment is done whenever a failure occurs and the features that are blamed for the failure are linked to the memory of the failure itself. These links are later used to predict failures so that plans can be found that avoid them.

These six processes make up the basic requirements for a case-based planner. Plan retrieval, modification and storage are essential to the basic planning loop that allows old plans to be modified in service of new goals. A plan repair process is need for those situations in which plans fail. A process that assigns blame to the features responsible for failures is required for the planner to be able to later anticipate problems. And problem anticipation is needed in order for the planner to avoid making mistakes that it has already encountered.

In the sections that follow, each of these modules will be discussed in turn. These sections will discuss two examples: one in which CHEF creates and then repairs a faulty plan for a stir fry dish including beef and broccoli and one in which CHEF uses the knowledge gained from the first example to create a plan for a stir fry dish including chicken and snow peas. Most of this paper will attend to the second example in which the knowledge learned by CHEF in dealing with the first example is actually used, so as to show the power of the processes of problem anticipation, plan retrieval and plan modification. In discussing the processes of failure repair, plan storage and credit assignment, however, the first example is discussed. This is because CHEF learns from the problems encountered in dealing with this example and these three modules make-up CHEF's repair and learning abilities.

IV PROBLEM ANTICIPATION

CHEF's initial input is a set of goals to include different tastes and ingredients in a type of dish. The first step that CHEF takes in dealing with them is to try to anticipate any problems that might arise in planning for them. CHEF wants to predict problems before they occur so it can find a plan in memory that already avoids them.

The planner anticipates problems on the basis of a memory of past failures that is linked to the features that participated in causing them. These links are used to pass markers from the features in an input to the memory of failures that those features predict. When the features that are related to a past problem are all present, the memory of the failure is activated and the planner is informed of the possibility of the failure reoccurring.

For example, one of the failures the planner has in memory relates to an attempt to make a stir-fry dish with beef and broccoli. In making the dish, the liquid produced when stir frying the beef ruined the texture of the broccoli while it was cooking. The failure is indexed in memory by the features of the goals that interacted to cause it: the goal to include meat, the goal to include a crisp vegetable and the goal to make a stir fry dish. When these features are present in an input the planner can predict that the failure will occur again. Once a problem is predicted, the planner can add a goal to avoid the problem to the set of goals that will be used to find a plan.

In planning for the goals to include SNOW PEAS and CHICKEN in a STIR FRY dish, the planner is is reminded of the past failure it encountered in building the beef and broccoli plan. This failure was due to the fact that CHEF tried to stir fry some beef and broccoli together in a past plan, allowing the liquid from the beef to make the broccoli soggy. The surface features of the goal to include meat and the goal to include a crisp vegetable are the same, so the planner predicts that it will make this mistake again if it does not attend to this problem.

```
Searching for plan that satisfies input goals -
  Include chicken in the dish.
  Include snow pea in the dish.
  Make a stir-fry dish.

Collecting and activating tests.

  Is the dish STYLE-STIR-FRY.
  Is the item a MEAT.
  Is the item a VEGETABLE.
  Is the TEXTURE of item CRISP.

Chicken + Snow Pea + Stir frying = Failure
"Meat sweats when it is stir-fried."
"Stir-frying in too much liquid makes
  crisp vegetables soggy."
Reminded of a failure in the
BEEF-AND-BROCCOLI plan.
Failure = 'The vegetable is now soggy'
```

Once a failure has been anticipated, CHEF builds a goal to avoid it and adds this goal to the set of goals which will be used to search for a plan. This set of goals is then handed to the plan retriever.

V PLAN RETRIEVAL

The function of the plan retriever is to find the best plan to use in satisfying a set of goals. It seeks what we call the "best match" in memory, the plan for a past situation that most closely resembles the current situation. In CHEF, this notion of "best match" is defined as finding a plan that satisfies or partially satisfies as many of the planner's most important goals as possible. Finding a raspberry soufflé recipe that can be turned into a strawberry soufflé or finding a beef stir fry dish that can be turned into one for pork. The plan retriever uses three kinds of knowledge in finding the best match for a set of goals: a plan memory that is indexed by the goals that the plans satisfy and the problems that they avoid, a similarity metric that allows it to notice partial matches between goals and a value hierarchy that allows it to judge the relative importance of the goals it is planning for.

When CHEF's retriever is searching for a past case on which to base its planning, it is searching for a plan that was built for a situation similar to the one it is currently in. The idea behind this search is that the solution to a past problem similar to the current one will be useful in solving the problem at hand. But this means that the vocabulary used to describe the similarity between the two situations has to capture the relevant aspects of the planning problems that the planner deal with. This vocabulary consists of two classes of objects: the goals in a situation, (which in the case of stored plans are satisfied by those plans) and the problems that have been anticipated (which in the case of the stored plans are avoided by them). CHEF gets its goals directly from the user in the form of a set of constraints that have to be satisfied. It gets information about the problems that it thinks it has to avoid while planning for those goals from its problem anticipator, which examines the goals and is reminded of problems that have resulted from interactions between similar goals in the past.

CHEF's domain is Szechwan cooking, so the goals that it plans for are all related to the taste, texture and style of the dish it is creating. The basic vocabulary that CHEF uses to describe the effects of its plans, and the effects that it wants a plan to accomplish include descriptions of the foods that it can include, (*e.g.*, Beef, chicken, snow peas and bean sprouts), the tastes that the user wants (*e.g.*, Hot, spicy, savory and fresh), the textures that the dish should include, (*e.g.*, Crunchy, chewy and firm) and the type of dish that the user is looking for, (*e.g.*, STIR-FRY, SOUFFLE, and PASTA). In searching for a past situation which might be useful, the plan retriever uses the goals that it is handed to index to possible plans. The plan it finds, then, will satisfy at least some of the goals it is looking for.

The problems that CHEF tries to avoid, by finding plans that work around past instances of them, also relate to the planner's goals. In searching for a plan, CHEF uses the predictions of any problems that it has anticipated to find plans that avoid those problems. Because plans are indexed by the problems that they solve, the planner is able to use these predictions to find the plans that will avoid the problems they describe. In searching for a base-line plan for the chicken and snow peas situation, CHEF searches for a plan that, among other things, avoids the predicted problem of soggy vegetables. Because the beef and broccoli plan is indexed by the fact that it solves the problem of soggy vegetables due to stir frying with meats, the plan retriever is able to find it on the basis of the prediction of this problem, even though the surface features of the two situations are dissimilar.

In searching for a plan that includes chicken and snow peas, the planner is also trying to find a plan that avoids the problem it has predicted of the vegetables getting soggy as a result of being cooked with the meat. The fact that it has predicted this problem allows it to find a plan in memory that avoids it, even though the plan deals with surface features that are not in the current input. The planner is able to find this plan even though a less appropriate plan with more surface features in common with the current situation, a recipe for chicken and green beans, is also in memory.

The planner's goals, including the goal to avoid the problem of the soggy vegetable are all used to drive down in a discrimination network that organizes past plans.

```
Driving down on: Make a stir-fry dish.
 Succeeded -
Driving down on:
  Avoid failure exemplified by the state
  'The broccoli is now soggy' in recipe BEEF-AND-BROCCOLI.
 Succeeded -
Driving down on: Include chicken in the dish.
 Failed - Trying more general goal.
  Driving down on: Include meat in the dish.
  Succeeded -
Driving down on: Include snow pea in the dish.
 Failed - Trying more general goal.
  Driving down on: Include vegetable in the dish.
  Succeeded -

Found recipe -> REC9 BEEF-AND-BROCCOLI
```

Here CHEF finds a past plan that avoids the problem due to goal interactions that has been predicted while still partially satisfying the other more surface level goals.

VI PLAN MODIFICATION

CHEF's memory of plans is augmented by the ability to modify plans for situations that only partially match the planner's present problems. CHEF's plan modifier, the module that handles these changes, makes use of a modification library that is indexed by the changes that have to be made and the plan that they have to be made in. The modification rules it has are not designed to be complete plans on their own, but are instead descriptions of the steps that have to be added and deleted from existing plans in order to make them satisfy new goals. Along with the modification rules are a set of *object critics* that look at a plan and, on the basis of the items or ingredients involved, correct difficulties that have been associated with those ingredients in the past.

The process used by CHEF's modifier is simple. For each goal that is not yet satisfied by the current plan, the modifier looks for the modification rule associated with the goal and the general plan type. If no modification rule exists for the particular goal, the modifier steps up in an abstraction hierarchy and finds the modification rule for the more general version of the goal. Once a rule is found, the steps it describes are added to the plan, merged with existing steps when possible.

If the goal in question is already partially satisfied by the plan, (this happens when the plan satisfies a goal that is similar to the current one), the planner does not have to go to its modification rules. It replaces the new item for the old item, removing any steps that were added by the old item's ingredient critics and adding any steps required by the new item's ingredient critics.

In altering the BEEF-AND-BROCCOLI plan to include chicken and snow peas, the planner has the information that both new ingredients are partial matches for existing ones and can be directly substituted for them. A critic under the concept CHICKEN then adds the step of boning the chicken before chopping.

```
Modifying new plan to satisfy:
    Include chicken in the dish.
Substituting chicken for beef in new plan.

Modifying new plan to satisfy:
    Include snow pea in the dish.
Substituting snow pea for broccoli in new plan.

Considering critic:
```

```
Before doing step: Chop the chicken
   do: Bone the chicken. - Critic applied.
```

VII PLAN REPAIR

Because CHEF cannot avoid making errors, it has to be able to repair faulty plans in response to failures. As it is, CHEF's plan repairer is one of the most complex parts of both the CHEF program and the case-based theory that it implements. It is complex because it makes the most use of the planner's specific knowledge about the physics of the CHEF domain and has to combine this knowledge with a more abstract understanding of how to react to planning problems in general.

Once it completes a plan, CHEF runs a simulation of it using a set of causal rules. This simulation is CHEF's equivalent of the real world. At the end of the simulation, it checks the final states that have been simulated against the goals of the plan it has run. If any goal is unsatisfied or if any state has resulted that CHEF wants to avoid in general, an announcement of the failure is handed to the the plan repairer.

CHEF deals with plan failure by building a causal explanation of why the failure has occurred. This explanation connects the surface features of the initial plan to the failure that has resulted. The planner's goals, the particular steps that it took and the changes that were made are all included in this explanation. This explanation is built by back chaining from the failure to the initial steps or states that caused it, using a set of causal rules the describe the results of actions in different circumstances.

The explanation of the failure is used to find a structure in memory that organizes a set of strategies for solving the problem described by the explanation. These structures, called Thematic Organization Packets or TOPs [3], are similar in function to the critics found in HACKER [4] and NOAH [2]. Each TOP is indexed by the description of a particular type of planning problem and each organizes a set of strategies for deal with that type of problem. These strategies take the form of general repair rules such as REORDER steps and RECOVER from side-effects. Each general strategy is filled in with the specifics of the particular problem to build a description of a change in the plan that would solve the current problem. This description is used as an index into a library of plan modifiers in the cooking domain. The modifications found are then tested against one another using rules concerning the efficacy of the different changes and the one that is most likely to succeed is chosen.

The idea behind these structures is simple. There is a great deal of planning information that is related to the *interactions* between plans and goals. This information cannot be tied to any individual goal or plan but is instead tied to problems that rise out of their combination. In planning, one important aspect of this information concerns how to deal with problems due to the interactions between plan steps. Planning TOPs provide a means to store this information. Each TOP corresponds to a planning problem due to the causal interaction between the steps and the states of a plan. When a problem arises, a causal analysis of it provides the information needed to identify the TOP that actually describes the problem in abstract terms. Under each TOP is a set of strategies designed to deal with the problem the TOP describes. By finding the TOP that relates to a problem, then, a planner actually finds the strategies that will help to fix that problems.

CHEF does not run into any failures while planning for the stir fry dish with chicken and snow peas. This is because it is able to avoid the problem of the liquid from the meat making the vegetables soggy by anticipating the failure and finding a plan the avoids it. It can only do this, however, because it has handled this problem already in that it built a similar plan that failed and was then repaired. This earlier plan is the same one that CHEF selected as the base-line plan for this situation, because it knows that this is a plan that it repaired in the past to avoid the same problem of liquid from the meat making the vegetables soggy that is now predicted as a problem in the current situation.

This past failure occurred when CHEF was planning for the goals of including beef and broccoli in a stir fry dish. CHEF originally built a simple plan in which the two main ingredients were stir fried together. Unfortunately, this plan results in the liquid produced by stir frying the beef making the vegetables soggy as they are cooking. This explanation of the failure in this example indexes to the TOP SIDE-EFFECT:DISABLED-CONDITION:CONCURRENT, a memory structure related to the interaction between concurrent plans in which a side effect of one violates a precondition of the other. This is because the side effect of liquid coming from the stir-frying of the beef is disabling a precondition attached to the broccoli stir-fry plan that the pan being used is dry.

The causal description of the failure is used to access this TOP out of the twenty that the program knows about. All of these TOPs are associated with causal configurations that lead to failures and store strategies for fixing the situations that they describe. For example, one TOP is DESIRED-EFFECT:DISABLED-CONDITION:SERIAL, a TOP that describes a situation in which the desired effect of a step interferes with the satisfaction conditions of a later step. The program was able to recognize that the current situation was a case of SIDE-EFFECT:DISABLED-CONDITION:CONCURRENT because it has determined that no goal is satisfied by the interfering condition (the liquid in the pan), that the condition disables a satisfaction requirement of a step (that the pan be dry) and that the two steps are one and the same (the stir fry step). Had the liquid in the pan satisfied a goal, the situation would have been recognized as a case of DESIRED-EFFECT:DISABLED-CONDITION:CONCURRENT because the violating condition would actually be a goal satisfying state.

```
Found TOP TOP1 -> SIDE-EFFECT:DISABLED-CONDITION:CONCURRENT
TOP -> SIDE-EFFECT:DISABLED-CONDITION:CONCURRENT has 3
    strategies associated with it:
   SPLIT-AND-REFORM
   ALTER-PLAN:SIDE-EFFECT
   ADJUNCT-PLAN
```

These three strategies reflect the different changes that can be made to repair the plan. They suggest:

- ALTER-PLAN:SIDE-EFFECT: Replace the step that causes the violating condition with one that does not have the same side-effect but achieves the same goal.

- SPLIT-AND-REFORM: Split the step into two separate steps and run them independently.

- ADJUNCT-PLAN:REMOVE: Add a new step to be run along with a step that causes a side-effect that removes the side-effect as it is created.

In this case, only SPLIT-AND-REFORM can be implemented for this particular problem so the change it suggests is made. As a result the single stir fry step in the original plan in which the beef and broccoli were stir fried together is changed into a series of steps in which they are stir fried apart and joined back together in the final step of the plan.

Once a plan is repaired it can be described as a plan that now avoids the problem that has just be fixed. When it is stored in memory, then, it is stored as a plan that avoids this problem so it can be found if a similar problem is predicted.

VIII PLAN STORAGE

Plan storage is done using the same vocabulary of goals satisfied and problems avoided that plan retrieval uses. Once a plan has been built and run, it is stored it in memory, indexed by the goals it satisfies and the problems it avoids. The plans are indexed by the goals that they satisfy so the planner can find them later on when it is asked to find a plan for a set of goals. They are also stored by the problems that they avoid so that CHEF, if it knows that a problem is going to result from some planning situation, can find a plan that avoids that problem.

The repaired BEEF-AND-BROCCOLI is indexed in memory under the goals that it satisfies as well as under the problems that it avoids. So it is indexed under the fact that is a plan for stir frying, for including beef and so on. It is also indexed by the fact that it avoids the problem of soggy vegetables that rises out the interaction between meat and crisp vegetables when stir fried. The fact that the plan is associated with the problem that it solves allows the plan retriever to later find the plan to use when confronted with the later task of finding a plan that avoids the problem of soggy vegetables that results when meats and crisp vegetables are stir fried together.

```
Indexing BEEF-AND-BROCCOLI under goals and problems:

If this plan is successful, the following should be true:
    The beef is now tender.
    The broccoli is now crisp.
    Include beef in the dish.
    Include broccoli in the dish.
    Make a stir-fry dish.


The plan avoids failure  exemplified by the
state 'The broccoli is now soggy' in
recipe BEEF-AND-BROCCOLI.
```

IX CREDIT ASSIGNMENT

CHEF's approach to failures is two fold. It repairs the plan to make it run and it repairs itself to make sure that it will not make the same mistake again. Part of assuring that the same mistake will not be repeated is storing the repaired plan so that it can be used again. But the fact that the original plan failed and had to be repaired in the first place indicates that CHEF's initial understanding of the planning situation was faulty in that it built a failure when it thought it was building a correct plan. When it encounters a failure, then, CHEF has to also find out why the failure occurred so that it can anticipate that failure when it encounters a similar situation in the future.

CHEF's makes use of the same causal explanation used to find its TOPs and repair strategies to figure out which features should be blamed for a failure. The purpose of this blame assignment is to track down the features in the current input that could be used to predict this failure in later inputs. This ability to predict planning failures before they occur allows the problem anticipator to warn the planner of a possible failure and allow it to search for a plan avoiding the predicted problem. The power of the problem anticipator, then, rests on the power of the process that figures out which features are to blame for a failure.

CHEF's steps through the explanation built by the plan repairer to the identify goals that interacted to cause the failure. After being pushed to the most general level of description that the current explanation can account for, these goals are turned into tests on the input. This allows the planner to later predict failures on the basis of surface features that are similar to the ones that participated in causing the current problem.

As a result of the beef and broccoli failure, a test on the texture of vegetables, is built and associated with the concept VEGETABLE because a goal for a crisp vegetable predicts this failure while goals for other vegetables do not. It is associated with VEGETABLE rather than BROCCOLI because the rule explaining the failure is valid for all crisp vegetables not just broccoli. Because any meat will put off the liquid like that which participated in the failure no test is needed and a link is built directly from the presence of the goal to the memory

of the failure.

```
Building demon: DEMON0 to anticipate interaction between rules:
"Meat sweats when it is stir-fried."
"Stir-frying in too much liquid makes crisp vegetables soggy."

Indexing marker passing demon under item: MEAT
by test: Is the item a MEAT.

Indexing marker passing demon under item: VEGETABLE
by test:
    Is the item a VEGETABLE.
and Is the TEXTURE of item CRISP.


Goal to be activated = Avoid failure exemplified
by the state 'The broccoli is now soggy' in
recipe BEEF-AND-BROCCOLI.
```

These links between surface features and memories of failures are used later to predict the same problem when it is handed the goals to makes a stir fry dish with chicken and snow peas. This prediction is then used to find the plan that avoids the problem.

X CHEF

The idea behind CHEF is to build a planner that learns from its own experiences. The approach taken in CHEF is to use a representation of those experiences in the planning process. To make this possible, CHEF requires what any case-based planner requires, a memory of past events and a means to retrieve and store new them, a method for modifying old plans to satisfy new goals, a way to repair plans that fail, and a way to turn those failures into knowledge of how to better plan.

By choosing plans on the basis of the problems that they solve as well as the goals they satisfy, CHEF is able to avoid any problem that it is able to predict. By also treating planning failures as understanding failures and repairing its knowledge base as well as its plans, CHEF is able to predict problems that it has encountered before. And by using an extensive causal analysis as a means of diagnosing problems, CHEF is able to apply a wide variety of repairs to a single failure.

REFERENCES

[1] Fikes, R., and Nilsson, N., *STRIPS: A new approach to the application of theorem proving to problem solving*, Artificial Intelligence, 2 (1971).

[2] Sacerdoti, E., *A structure for plans and behavior*, Technical Report 109, SRI Artificial Intelligence Center, 1975.

[3] Schank, R., *Dynamic memory: A theory of learning in computers and people*, Cambridge University Press, 1982.

[4] Sussman, G., *Artificial Intelligence Series*, Volume 1: *A computer model of skill acquisition*, American Elsevier, New York, 1975.

[5] Wilensky, R., *META-PLANNING*, Technical Report M80 33, UCB College of Engineering, August 1980.

An Adaptive Planner

Richard Alterman

Computer Science Division
University of California, Berkeley
Berkeley, California 94720

ABSTRACT

This paper is about an approach to the flexible utilization of old plans called **adaptive planning**. An adaptive planner can take advantage of the details associated with specific plans, while still maintaining the flexibility of a planner that works from general plans. Key elements in the theory of adaptive planning are its treatment of background knowledge and the introduction of a notion of planning by situation matching.

1. Introduction

A planner that has access to general plans (alternately abstract or high-level plans) is flexible because such plans will apply to a large number of situations. A problem for a planner working exclusively with general plans is that many of the details associated with more specific plans (e.g. sequencing information and causal relationships) must be recomputed. For a planner that works from more specific plans the situation is reversed: There is a wealth of detail, but there are problems with flexibility. I will refer to planners with the capacity to use a mix of old specific plans and general plans as **adaptive planners** [1-3]. Adaptive planners foreground specific plans, but gain flexibility, in situations where the old plan and the planner's current circumstances diverge, by having access to more general plans.

The adaptive planning techniques that will be described in this paper are sufficiently robust to handle a wide range of relationships between an old specific plan and the planner's current circumstances. For example, suppose a planner is about to ride the NYC subway for the first time, and attempts to treat an old plan for riding BART (Bay Area Rapid Transit) as an example to guide the current planning activity. Consider the steps involved in riding BART. At the BART station the planner buys a ticket from a machine. Next, the ticket is fed into a second machine which returns the ticket and then opens a gate to let the planner into the terminal. Next the planner rides the train. At the exit station the planner feeds the ticket to another machine that keeps the ticket and then opens a gate to allow the planner to leave the station. Compare that to the steps involved in riding the NYC subway: buy a token from a teller, put the token into a turnstile and then enter, ride the train, and exit by pushing thru the exit turnstile. There are a great number of differences between the BART Plan and the plan that the planner must eventually devise for riding the NYC Subway.

- In the BART case a ticket is bought from a machine, in the NYC subway case there is no ticket machine and instead a token is bought from a teller.

- In the BART case the ticket is returned after entering the station, in the NYC subway case the token is not returned after entry.

- In the BART case the ticket is needed to exit, in the NYC subway case the token is not needed to exit.

This paper will describe an adaptive planner called **PLEXUS** that can overcome these differences and in an effective manner use the BART Plan as a basis for constructing a plan for the NYC subway situation. Two versions of PLEXUS have already been constructed. This paper gives an overview of adaptive planning and PLEXUS. It includes a discussion of adaptive planning in relation to the literature, descriptions of four key elements of adaptive planning, and some details of PLEXUS' adaptation mechanism.

2. Adaptive Planning

There are four keystones to the adaptive planning position on the flexible utilization of old plans.

- An adaptive planner has access to the **background knowledge** associated with an old plan.

- In adaptive planning the exploitation of the background knowledge is accomplished by a process of **situation matching**.

- An adaptive planner foregrounds **specific plans**.

- Adaptive planners treat the failing steps of a plan as **representative of the category of action** which is to be accomplished.

Adaptive planning makes the background knowledge associated with an old specific plan explicit. Previous approaches to re-using old plans have dealt with an old plan in relative isolation and therefore the task of re-using an old plan has been considerably more complicated. By making the content and organization of the background knowledge explicit, it becomes possible to re-use an old plan in a wider variety of situations. Background knowledge includes general plans, categorization knowledge, and causal knowledge.

Exploitation of the background knowledge is accomplished by a process of **situation matching**. Adaptive planning uses the position of the old plan in a planning network

This research was sponsored in part by the Defense Advance Research Projects Agency (DOD), Arpa order No. 4031, Monitored by Naval Electronic System Command under Contract No. N00039-C-0235. This research was also supported by the National Science Foundation (ISI-8514890).

as a starting point for finding a match to the planner's current circumstances. The **interaction** of planning knowledge and the current situation determine a plan which fits the current context and realizes the goal. The interaction works in both directions. In the direction of planning knowledge to situation, the old plan serves as a basis for interpreting the actions of other agents and the various objects in the new situation. Moreover, it provides the planner with a course of action. In the direction of situation to planning knowledge, it is the situation which provides selection cues that aid the planner in determining an alternate course of action when complications arise.

Adaptive planning foregrounds **specific plans**. It has been previously argued by Carbonell [4] that the importance of being able to plan from more specific plans is that many times a more general plan is not available. But there are other reasons why the capacity to work from more specific examples is important. Many times a more specific plan is tailor-made for the current planning situation. Furthermore, the more specific plans make available to the planner previously computed causal and ordering relationships between steps. For a more general plan these can not be determined until that steps are instantiated. Consequently, even in the cases where the more specific plan must be re-fit, many times the cost of such changes are much less than the cost of dealing with the subgoal and subplan interactions inherent in a process that works by instantiating more general plans.

Adaptive planning treats the failing steps of the old plan as **representative of the category of action** which is to be accomplished. In the case of the BART-NYC planning problem, each of the failing steps is representative of the category of action the planner eventually wants to take. An adaptive planner uses the category knowledge, as represented by the failing step, to access more general versions of that step and also to determine its eventual course of action. For example, the first step of the BART Plan, 'buying a BART ticket', is representative of the planner's eventually course of action - adapting a plan to 'buy a theatre ticket'.

3. PLEXUS - An adaptive planner

For PLEXUS the background knowledge associated with an old plan is determined by the old plan's position in a knowledge network. The network includes **taxonomic, partonomic, causal,** and **role** knowledge; the network acts as a structural backbone for its contents. PLEXUS uses the taxonomic structure not only for the purposes of property inheritance, but also as a basis for reasoning about categories. The partonomic structure (i.e. step-substep hierarchy) is used to aid in determining the pieces of network which need to be refitted in a given situation. The causal knowledge serves several functions: The **purpose** relation identifies the abstraction which maintains the purpose of a step in a plan. The **precondition, outcome,** and **goal** relations act as appropriateness conditions. The **reason** relation provides dependency links between a step and its justification (c.f Stallman & Sussman, 1977) [5]. Roughly, in PLEXUS, **purpose** is synonymous with 'intent', **goal** with 'aim', and **reason** with 'justification'. The purpose of 'buying a BART ticket' is to 'gain access', the goal associated with it is to 'have a ticket', and the reason for doing it is that it makes it possible to 'enter the BART station' (see figure 1). Associated with roles are type constraints on the types of objects which can fill them. The **role** relations are used by PLEXUS for both cross indexing purposes and to control inferencing. For further arguments on the importance of

background knowledge see Alterman (1985), and for more details on the representation of the background knowledge see Alterman (1986) [3].

PLEXUS uses the old plan to interpret its course of action in its current circumstances. It considers the steps, one step at a time, in order. If a step is not an action it adapts substeps in a depth-first fashion before moving onto the next step in the plan. When a given step of the old plan has been adapted to the current circumstances, PLEXUS simulates a planner taking action on that step before moving onto the next step in the plan - thus, as did NASL (McDermott, 1978 [6]), PLEXUS interleaves **planning and acting**.

Associated with each step (substep) in a plan are **appropriatness conditions**. The appropriateness conditions are intended to be suggestive that a particular course of action is reasonable to pursue. Before a step is applied, PLEXUS treats the preconditions and goals of the old plan as appropriateness conditions. After a step has been applied, PLEXUS treats the expected outcomes as appropriateness conditions. Appropriateness conditions are checked by testing the type constraints associated with each of the roles attached to the appropriateness condition. The type constraints are interpreted in terms of the network.

A rough outline of the top-level decision procedure is shown below:
1) Are any of the before conditions associated with the old plan failing?
   a) Is this a case of step-out-of-order?
   b) Is this a case of failing precondition?
2) Has the current circumstances aroused a goal not accounted for by the current step?
   a) This is a case of differing goals.
3) Is the current step an action?
   a) If yes, perform the action.
   b) If no, proceed to adapt substeps.
4) Are any of the outcomes associated with the current step failing?
   a) This is a case of failing outcome?
5) Adapt next step.

If one of the before appropriatness conditions fails, or the current circumstances indicate a goal not accounted for by the old plan, one of three different types of **situation difference** is occurring: failing precondition, step-out-of-order, or differing goals. There is a fourth kind of situation difference, failing outcome, that occurs when one of the expected outcomes of a given step fails to occur. Associated with each of the types of situation difference are varying strategies that will be briefly described in the fifth section of this paper. PLEXUS does not always consider the steps in order, under certain circumstances it looks ahead to the latter steps of the plan and adjusts them in anticipation of certain changes - thus PLEXUS has an element of **opportunism** (Hayes-Roth & Hayes-Roth, 1979) [7].

The core of PLEXUS are the matching techniques it uses for finding an alternate version of a step once it determines that the step needs to be refit. To find an alternate matching action for a given situation, PLEXUS treats the failing step as **representative of the category** of action it needs to perform, and then it proceeds to exploit the background knowledge in two ways.

By a process of **abstraction** PLEXUS uses the background knowledge to determine a category of plans in common between the two situations.

By a process of **specialization** PLEXUS uses the background knowledge to determine an alternate course of **action** which is appropriate to the current circumstances.

PLEXUS accomplishes abstraction by moving up the categorization hierarchy until it finds a plan where all the before appropriatness conditions are met. PLEXUS accomplishes specialization by moving down the categorization hierarchy until it finds a plan that is sufficiently detailed to be actionable.

4. Core of the Matcher (Managing the Knowledge)

There are at least two important considerations concerning the control of access to knowledge. One consideration is that there is a danger of the planner becoming overwhelmed by the wealth of knowledge (c.f. **saturation,** Davis 1980 [8]) that is available. The problem is that there are potentially too many plans that the planner might have to consider, and consequently, the planner could get bogged down in evaluating each candidate plan. Somehow the planner needs to be able to selectively consider the various alternatives available to it.

Another consideration in the control of access to knowledge comes form the cognitive science literature and is referred to as the problem of **enumeration** (e.g. Kolodner, 1983 [9]). The problem of enumeration is that humans do not appear to be capable of listing all the instances of a category without some other kind of prompting. When asked to list the states of the union, human subjects do not accomplish this by simply listing all the members of the category of states. For the concerns of adaptive planning the problem of enumeration comes in a slightly different guise. Given an abstract plan it is not reasonable to assume that a human planner could enumerate all of the specializations of that abstract plan.

The first of these considerations dictates that PLEXUS be **selective** in its choice of planning knowledge to use. The second of these considerations acts as a sort of **termination condition:** sometimes the planner knows the right plan but circumstances are such that it cannot find it. As a result of these considerations, PLEXUS' abstraction and specialization processes must be constrained. While moving up the abstraction hierarchy PLEXUS maintains the function of the step in the overall plan. Movement down the abstraction hierarchy, towards more detailed plans, is controlled by the interaction between the planner's knowledge and the current circumstances.

4.1. Abstraction

The way to think about abstraction of a plan is that it removes details from that plan: if a particular plan fails to match the current situation, some of the details of that particular plan must be removed. Moving up the abstraction hierarchy removes the details that do not work in the current situation while maintaining much of what is in common to the two situations. Effectively, the movement of abstraction is discovering the generalization which holds between the old and new situations given that a difference has occurred.

A given plan step can have any number of abstractions associated with it. Choosing the wrong abstraction can lead to the wrong action. The planner can avoid this problem by applying the following general rule:

Ascend the abstraction hierarchy that maintains the purpose of the step in the plan that is being refitted.

By moving up the abstraction hierarchy that maintains the purpose of the step, PLEXUS attempts to maintain the function of the step in the overall plan and thereby mitigate the propagated effects of changes.

In general PLEXUS uses two techniques for moving up the abstraction hierarchy.

- If a plan is failing due to the existence of a particular feature of a plan, move to the point in the abstraction hierarchy from which that feature was inherited.

- Incremently perform abstraction on a failing plan

The first technique applies in situations where there is a specific feature in the old plan that does not exist in the current situation. The second technique of abstraction applies in situations where there is no identifiable feature which has to be removed. In such cases, PLEXUS incrementally moves up the abstraction hierarchy. In either case, for each abstraction it tries to find a specialization that will work in the current context. If it fails to find a specialization for a given abstraction, it moves to the next abstraction in the abstraction hierarchy.

4.2. Specialization

Via the process of specialization PLEXUS moves from a more abstract plan towards more specific examples. PLEXUS navigation thru the network is dependent on the planner's current circumstances. PLEXUS descends down the classification hierarchy one step at a time. PLEXUS tests the applicability of a specialization by checking the before appropriateness conditions; if one of these conditions fails the movement is rejected. At each point in the hierarchy PLEXUS is faced with one of five options:

1) Is the plan sufficiently detailed to act on?
2) Is there a feature suggested by the type of situation difference which cross indexes some subcategory of the current category of plan?
3) Is there an observable feature which cross indexes some subcategory of the current category of plan?
4) Is there an observable feature with an abstraction that cross indexes a subcategory of the current category?
5) Is there a salient subcategory?

PLEXUS stops descending the categorization hierarchy when it gets to a leaf node (option 1). If the node is not a leaf it continues to descend (options 2-5). Sometimes the type of situation difference suggests cues for subcategory selections (option 2). Sometimes 'observable features' act as cues for subcategory selection (options 3-4). These 'observable features' can either directly cross index some subcategory of plan (option 3), or have an abstraction which cross indexes a subcategory of plan (option 4). Certain subcategories are salient regardless of context and can always be selected (option 5).

Many of these techniques are employed in the following example: Suppose a planner wants to transfer between planes at the Kennedy Airport in NYC. The planner's normal plan for transferring between planes is to walk from the arrival to the departure gate. But when the planner arrives at Kennedy Airport the arrival and departure gates turn out to be in different terminals. Suppose the planner decides that the walk between terminals is too strenuous, and thus a new goal is aroused: preserve energy. The detection of this goal has no correspondent in the old plan and it is determined that the plan must be adjusted to account for this goal; this is a case of the **differing goals** type of situation difference. By a process of abstraction, PLEXUS moves up the categorization hierarchy from the plan to 'walk' to the more general plan of 'travelling'. Next PLEXUS must determine an alternate plan, within the category of 'travelling', from which to act. The newly aroused goal acts as a cue for selecting 'vehicular travel' as a potential subcategory of plan from which to act (option 2). Suppose the planner has never used a shuttle before at an airport, but it sees (observable feature) a sign concerning 'airport shuttles'. An abstraction of 'shuttle' acts as a cue for selecting 'mass transit travel' as a subcategory of 'vehicular travel' (option 4). Moreover, 'shuttle' is a cue for selecting 'shuttle travel' as a subcategory of 'mass transit travel' (option 3). 'Shuttle travel' is sufficiently detailed for PLEXUS to attempt to adapt (option 1). See Alterman (1986a) [3] for further details and a trace of PLEXUS handling this planning problem.

5. Four Types of Situation Difference

PLEXUS currently recognizes four kinds of situation difference: failing precondition, failing outcome, different goals, step-out-of-order.

A **failing precondition** situation difference occurs when one of the preconditions of a step (plan) fails. For failing preconditions PLEXUS moves up the abstraction hierarchy, according to the **purpose** of the step, to a point at which the failing condition has been abstracted out. In the event that PLEXUS cannot find a specialization of that category of plans, it continues to incrementally move up the abstraction hierarchy indicated by the **purpose** relation. For failing preconditions either of PLEXUS specialization techniques are appropriate.

A **failing outcome** situation difference occurs, if after applying a plan (step) PLEXUS discovers that one of the expected outcomes of that plan was not achieved. There are three courses of action available. The obvious course of action is to try the plan again. A second course of action, is to use the **reason** relation to determine the other steps of the plan which are effected by the failed outcome, and determine, via abstraction and specialization, if the planner can continue on its course action because there is an alternate interpretation of the latter step which does not require the failed outcome. If all else fails, the third option available to the planner is to find and perform an alternate version of the failing step. For failing outcomes, if the current plan step is being re-interpreted, abstraction occurs incrementally. If PLEXUS is trying to re-interpreted a step related to the current step by a **reason** relation, abstraction occurs using the failing outcome as a feature to abstract out of the plan. For the second and third cases PLEXUS uses both of the specialization techniques available to it.

A **differing goal** situation difference occurs if the planner's current circumstances arouse a new goal not accounted for by the old plan. For this kind of situation difference, abstraction occurs incrementally, and specialization requires that the new plan be indexed under both old and new goals.

A **step-out-of-order** situation difference occurs, when PLEXUS encounters a situation where it needs to apply a step out of order. There are two adjustments that are possible when a step-out-of-order situation difference occurs, PLEXUS can either delete the intermediate step(s), or re-order the steps of the old plan. If a step can be applied out of order, PLEXUS uses abstraction and specialization in an attempt to find an alternate version of the plan with the correct ordering of steps. Under such a situation, PLEXUS can use the new ordering constraint as an index for specialization purposes. In the event an alternate plan with a different ordering of steps can not be found, PLEXUS per-

forms the step-out-of-order, removes it from the sequence of steps, and proceeds with attempting to apply the failing step.

6. An example

The BART-NYC subway planning problem provides examples of three of the types of situation difference (see figure 1).

Adapting buy a BART ticket.
The first step of the BART plan fails in the NYC subway situation because there is no ticket machine. This is a case of **failing precondition**, and therefore PLEXUS abstracts out the failing condition, 'exist ticket machine', and specializes, using the salient subcategory, to 'buy theatre ticket', which it proceeds to adapt to the NYC subway situation. During the process of adapting this step 'ticket' gets bound to 'token'.

Adapting enter BART station.
The second step of the BART plan involves entering the station. The first substep of this step is to insert the token into the entrance machine, which the planner successfully accomplishes. The next step of 'BART enter' is that the ticket is returned by the machine. But in the NYC subway situation the ticket is not accessible, but it is possible to push thru the turnstile (the third step of 'BART enter'). Hence this is a case of **step out of order**. Having accomplished the last step of 'BART enter', PLEXUS must determine whether it should act on the intermediate step or instead delete it.

Re-interpreting BART exit.
In order to delete intermediate steps PLEXUS must treat the outcomes of each intermediate step as a case of a **failing outcome** and test to see if the latter steps in the plan effected by the failing outcome can be adapted. In this case there is only one intermediate step, 'ticket returned'. The *outcome* associated with this intermediate step is that the planner 'has the ticket' (or in this case 'token'). PLEXUS applies the second strategy associated with the situation difference type **failed outcome**: Find an alternate interpretation of the situation where that outcome is no longer necessary. PLEXUS uses the *reason* relation associated with 'ticket return' to determine which of the latter steps are effected by the failing outcome. In this case, the reason that the ticket is returned is so it can be used when exiting the station. PLEXUS must try to re-interpret 'BART-EXIT' in such a manner that it can exit without a ticket. This leads to a situation of **failed precondition** for the step 'BART-EXIT'. Via abstraction PLEXUS extracts that 'exiting an institution' is what is in common between the old plan and the new situation. PLEXUS 'observes' the exit turnstile and uses it as a cue for determining 'exit_building' as an alternate plan for 'exiting the station', where 'exit turnstile' plays the role of 'locking door'. Since it can find an alternate interpretation to 'exiting the station' that does not involve using a ticket, PLEXUS treats the **step-out-of-order situation** that occurs during execution of the plan 'BART enter' as a case of deletion. For a more detailed discussion of this problem and a trace see Alterman (1986) [3].

7. Discussion

Like the early general problem solving planners [10,11] adaptive planning is concerned with the problems of **generality** and **flexibility**. Unlike them it explores these issues in the context of increased amounts, and larger chunks of, knowledge. Where the early general problem solvers accomplished generality and flexibility by working with a small number of atomic operators, adaptive planning works with increased amounts of knowledge and achieves these twin goals by exploiting the **structure** of that knowledge. Like the work on MACROPS [12], adaptive planning is concerned with larger chunks of actions, but adaptive planning extends their utilization to planning problems like the BART-NYC subway problem. Adaptive planning is concerned with **tasks** [6] and **commonsense planning** [13] problems. It is **knowledge-based** in that its approach to refitting old plans is based on the accessibility of the structure and content of the **background knowledge** associated with an old plan. As in the case of other knowledge-based planning approaches [8,14,15], adaptive planning is concerned with **control of access to knowledge**; its approach is dependent on the interaction of the planner's knowledge with the planner's current circumstances. Like the work on analogical planning [4,16,17], adaptive planning attempts to re-use old specific plans, but its strategies take greater advantage of the available knowledge, exploit categorization knowledge, and its processing is novel in that it takes the form of **situation matching**. Where other researchers have emphasized the problem of initial retrieval of old plans [18-21], the work on adaptive planning balances that view by investigating issues concerning flexibility and usage. Although knowledge acquisition is not the focus of the current research, adaptive planning does provide a framework for dealing with these issues. It promises to promote **additivity** because its procedures are largely based on the structure of the knowledge and not its content. Moreover, as a by-product of abstraction **and specialization**, PLEXUS discovers the generalizations over the steps of the old plan and the steps of the new plan, and consequently it provides a framework for the planner to do automatic re-organization and generalization [22-25].

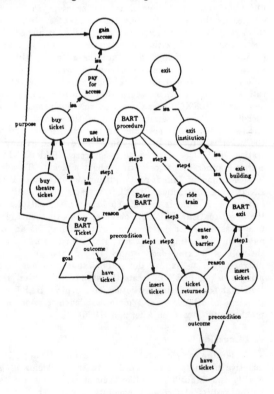

Figure 1: BART Plan with some background knowledge.

References

1. Alterman, R., Adaptive Planning: Refitting old plans to new situations, in *The seventh annual conference of the cognitive science society*, 1985.

2. Alterman, R., Adaptive Planning: Refitting old planning experiences to new situations, *Second Annual Workshop on Theoretical Issues in Conceptual Information Processing*, 1985.

3. Alterman, R., Adaptive Planning: A case of flexible knowing, Technical Report, University of California at Berkeley, 1986.

4. Carbonell, J. G., Derivational analogy and its role in problem solving, *AAAI-83*, 1983, 64-69.

5. Stallman, R. and Sussman, G., Forward reasoning and dependency-directed backtracking in a system for computer-aided circuit analysis, *Artificial Intelligence 9*, 2 , 135-196.

6. McDermott, D., Planning and Acting, *Cognitive Science 2* (1978), 71-109.

7. Hayes-Roth, B., A cognitive model of planning, *Cognitive Science 3* (1979), 275-310.

8. Davis, R., Meta-Rules: Reasoning about Control, *Artificial Intelligence 15* (1980), 179-222.

9. Kolodner, J. L., Reconstructive memory a computer model, *Cognitive Science 7* (1983), 281-328.

10. Ernst, G. and Newell, A., *GPS: A case study in generality in problem solving*, Academic Press, 1969.

11. Fikes, R. and Nilsson, N., STRIPS: a new approach to the application of theorem proving to problem solving, *Aritificial Intelligence 2* (1971), 189-208.

12. Fikes, R., Hart, P. and Nilsson, N., Learning and Executing Generalized Robot Plans, *Artificial Intelligence Journal 3* (1972), 251-288.

13. Wilensky, R., *Planning and Understanding*, Addison-Wesley Publishing Company, 1983.

14. Wilensky, R., Meta-Planning: Representing and using knowledge about planning in problem solving and natural language understanding, *Cognitive Science 5* (1981), 197-233.

15. Stefik, M., Planning and meta-planning, *Artificial Intelligence 12*, 2 (1981), 141-170.

16. Carbonell, J. G., A computation model of analogical problem solving, *IJCAI 7*, 1981.

17. Carbonell, J. G., Learning by analogy: formulating and generalizing plans from past experience, in *Machine learning, and artificial intelligence approach*, Mitchell, M. C. (editor), Tioga Press, Palo Alto, 1983.

18. Kolodner, J. L. and Simpson, R. L., Experience and problem solving: a framework, *Proceedings of the sixth annual conference of the cognitive science society*, 1984.

19. Kolodner, J. L., Simpson, R. L. and Sycara-Cyranski, K., A process model of cased-based reasoning in problem solving, *Proceedings of the ninth international joint conference on artificial intelligence*, 1985.

20. Hammond, K., Indexing and Causality: The organization of plans and strategies in memory., Yale Department of Computer Science Technical Report 351, 1985.

21. Hendler, J., Integrating Marker-Passing and Problem Solving, in *The sevent annual conference of the cognitive science society*, 1985.

22. DeJong, G., Acquiring Schemata through Understanding and Generalizing Plans, *IJCAI 8*, 1983.

23. Schank, R. C., *Dynamic Memory*, Cambridge University Press, Cambridge, 1982.

24. Kolodner, J. L., Maintaining organization in a dynamic long-term memory, *Cognitive Science 7* (1983), 243-280.

25. Lebowitz, M., Generalization from natural language text, *Cognitive Science 7* (1983), 1-40.

Chapter 10

Extending the Classical Framework

As new logics for formalizing temporal events have been developed (see Part III), attempts have been made to base planning systems on these logics. In addition, modeling the increasingly complex domains being attacked by planning systems has put new requirements on the representations that planners must use. In this chapter we present three papers that focus on extending the classical planning framework to handle conditional iteration, multi-agent coordination, and complex domain interactions. While this is in no way a comprehensive list of the ways that numerous researchers are extending the classical planning framework, we feel that these three papers are indicative of some potentially important directions.

One important type of reasoning, often overlooked in the planning literature, is the ability to reason about repeated or conditional actions. For example, a plan for driving in a nail might include a repeated hitting of the nail with a hammer until the head of the nail is flush with the surface. The first paper in this chapter, Drummond (1985), addresses this issue.

The second paper we present, Lanksy (1989), is a short description of the GEMPLAN system (a more detailed description can be found in Lansky, 1988).

This program works by utilizing heuristics that exploit the naturally occurring structures within a domain. The planner uses "locality," or domain structure, to provide a way of partitioning the planning search space into smaller, localized search spaces. This paper is an example of work that is motivated by the need to reduce the overall complexity of planning systems (the need for such a reduction is based largely on the results of Chapman, 1987, Chapter 7, and Korf, 1987, Chapter 7).

Another important direction in planning research is based on the new work in temporal logics. One example is the effort being made to extend temporal representations to handle simultaneously occurring events and event interactions—items that are critical for reasoning about the kinds of complex domains that planning systems are now being designed for. The use of these extended representations for planning is discussed by Pednault (1987), the last paper we present in this chapter.

Papers referenced herein but not included in this volume:

Lansky, A.L. (1988). "Localized Event-Based Reasoning for Multiagent Domains," *Computational Intelligence Journal*, Special Issue on Planning, 4(4).

REFINING AND EXTENDING THE PROCEDURAL NET

Mark E. Drummond

Department of Artificial Intelligence
University of Edinburgh
Hope Park Square
Edinburgh, Scotland, U.K.

Abstract

This paper presents a new definition for Plans. The objects defined are called Plan Nets, and are similar in spirit to Sacerdoti's Procedural Nets (1975). It is argued that Plan Nets are more descriptive than Procedural Nets, because they can easily describe iterative behaviour. The Plan Net definition is motivated by providing an operational semantics for the Procedural Net, and noticing that all Procedural Net state spaces are "loop free". This is seen to restrict the behaviours that can be described by the Procedural Net to those which do not include iteration. It is suggested that Plan Net state spaces can contain loops, and thus can describe iterative behaviour.

1. Paper Overview

In the next section we give Sacerdoti's definition of the Procedural Net. A simple method for deriving Procedural Net behaviours is also presented, and it is argued that the Procedural Net cannot describe iteration. Section 3 defines and discusses the Plan Net. Two sample Plan Nets are given. An operational semantics is _suggested_ for the Plan Net, and it is argued that Plan Nets can describe iteration. The Procedural Net and the Plan Net are compared in Section 4. Section 5 concludes.

2. The Procedural Net

A _Procedural_ _Net_ has been defined as "a network of actions at varying levels of detail, structured into a hierarchy of partially ordered time sequences." (Sacerdoti, 1975, p. 10). The basic objects in a Procedural Net are actions, and some ordering relations on the actions. Because of this, we refer to the Procedural Net as an "event space" representation. A net can be drawn as an action-on-node graph, with directed arcs between nodes. An arc running from one node α to another node β means that the action denoted by α must occur "before" the action denoted by β.

We can derive the possible behaviours of a given Procedural Net by analyzing the state space which it describes. A net's state space can be produced by playing a version of the "pebbling game" (Pippenger, 1980). While pebbling was not developed with this application in mind, it does capture our

intuition of what "before" means in a Procedural Net. In our version of this game, we place "pebbles" on the nodes of a Procedural Net as they are executed. The net starts out pebble-free, and finishes up pebble-laden — each node must be pebbled; that is, each action must be executed. Pebble placement is carried out according to the rule: A node may be pebbled if all of its immediate predecessors are pebbled.

The Procedural Net has been criticized recently (McDermott, 1983; Rosenschein, 1984). This paper addresses the Procedural Net's inability to describe "iterative" behaviour. Such behaviour is difficult to model in a natural way using a Procedural Net. Since the arcs of a net are taken to mean "before", one cannot simply direct an arc from an action "back into" the net.

It is obvious that all Procedural Net state-spaces will be loop-free, since the number of pebbles on a net must increase monotonically. There will never be an action which removes a pebble; thus never an action which can produce an earlier state. This is due to the strict "before" interpretation of the Procedural Net's arcs.

While Sacerdoti did include a mechanism for dealing with iteration, it hides the notion of "process" inside a special _replicate_ node. His treatment of iteration poses problems. Below, we suggest that by defining an alternative "event space" representation for plans, we _can_ describe iterative behaviour. This new definition follows the belief that iteration must be expressed in terms of the structure of a plan, so that a planner can _reason_ about the iteration.

3. The Plan Net

In this section, we define _Plan Nets,_ using some basic concepts from Net Theory (Brauer, 1979).

Definition 1. A _Plan Net_ is a 6-tuple $<P,T,R_a,R_b,R_c,R_e>$, where $P = \{p_1,p_2,...,p_N\}$, a finite set of places; $T = \{t_1,t_2,...,t_M\}$, a finite set of transitions; $N \geq 0$, $M \geq 0$; and $T \cap P = \phi$, the empty set. $R_a = \{(t_i,t_k) \mid \exists p_j \in P \ [(t_i,p_j) \in R_c \ \& \ (p_j,t_k) \in R_e]\}$, the Allow relation. $R_e \subseteq (P \times T)$, the Enable relation; $R_c \subseteq (T \times P)$, the Cause relation. $R_b \subseteq (T \times T)$, the Before relation; R_b must be a strict partial order on T.

IJCAI 1985 pp. 1010-1012
Used by permission of the International Joint Conferences on Artificial Intelligence, Inc.

Definition 2. Place p_i is an <u>input place</u> of transition t_j if and only if $(p_i,t_j) \in R_e$. Place p_i is an <u>output place</u> of transition t_j if and only if $(t_j,p_i) \in R_c$.

Definition 3. A <u>marking</u> of a Plan Net is a mapping μ: $P \to \{0, 1\}$.

Definition 4. A transition t_j is <u>enabled</u> if for each input place, p_i, $\mu(p_i) = 1$. A transition t_j may <u>fire</u> when enabled. Firing t_j in a marking μ produces a new marking μ' such that

1) If p_i is an input place of t_j
     then $\mu'(p_i) = 0$;
2) If p_i is an output place of t_j
     then $\mu'(p_i) = 1$;
3) If p_i is not an input place
     and not an output place of t_j
     then $\mu'(p_i) = \mu(p_i)$.

A place is thought of as a "condition", a static thing which does or does not hold. If a place p_i is marked ($\mu(p_i) = 1$) it is considered to be believed [by the planning system], and if it is unmarked ($\mu(p_i) = 0$), it is considered to be not believed [by the planning system].

Transitions are events, the Plan Net counterparts of a Procedural Net's actions. Events are dynamic entities; conditions are static. Events are things which "happen".

The Allow relation (R_a) is an abstraction of two simpler relations: Cause (R_c), and Enable (R_e). Events cause conditions, and conditions enable events. The input places of a transition describe those conditions which must be believed to hold in the world for the event the transition denotes to be enabled. The firing of a transition models the activation of its event. After firing, the output places of the transition describe the new conditions that are believed to hold.

Sample plans in this formalism are given in Figures 1 and 2. The plan of Figure 1 is designed to solve a canonical Blocks World problem. An initial marking is included. The plan of Figure 2 is one for (endlessly) hammering a nail. The plans look large, but this is due to redundant information being included in the formalism. When a plan is drawn as a graph it shrinks to more modest proportions (see Drummond, forthcoming).

4. Comparing the Nets

In this section we argue that the Plan Net representation is more powerful than the Procedural Net because of an explicit epistemological commitment to conditions and events. The Procedural Net makes no <u>clear</u> distinction between them. Using the Allow and Before relations as defined above, we can produce state spaces which contain cycles; that is, ones which correspond to iterative behaviour.

$C = \langle P,T,R_a,R_b,R_c,R_e \rangle$

$P = \{$ (on c a), (on c t3), (on a t1),
      (on b t2), (on b c), (on a b),
      (clear t3), (clear a), (clear t1),
      (clear b), (clear t2), (clear c)$\}$

$T = \{$ (move c a t3), (move a t1 b),
      (move b t2 c) $\}$

$R_c = \{$ ((move c a t3), (clear a)),
      ((move c a t3), (on c t3)),
      ((move c a t3), (clear c)),
      ((move b t2 c), (clear b)),
      ((move b t2 c), (on b c)),
      ((move b t2 c), (clear t2)),
      ((move a t1 b), (clear a)),
      ((move a t1 b), (clear t1)),
      ((move a t1 b), (on a b)) $\}$

$R_e = \{$ ((on c a), (move c a t3)),
      ((clear t3), (move c a t3)),
      ((clear c), (move c a t3)),
      ((clear a), (move a t1 b)),
      ((clear b), (move a t1 b)),
      ((on a t1), (move a t1 b)),
      ((clear c), (move b t2 c)),
      ((clear b), (move b t2 c)),
      ((on b t2), (move b t2 c)) $\}$

$R_a = \{$ ((move c a t3), (move b t2 c)),
      ((move b t2 c), (move a t1 b)),
      ((move c a t3), (move a t1 b)),
      ((move b t2 c), (move b t2 c)),
      ((move a t1 b), (move a t1 b)),
      ((move c a t3), (move c a t3)) $\}$

$R_b = \{$ ((move c a t3), (move b t2 c)),
      ((move b t2 c), (move a t1 b)) $\}$

$\mu(p) = 1$ if $p \in \{$(on c a), (clear t3),
        (clear c), (clear b),
        (on b t2), (on a t1)$\}$
$\mu(p) = 0$ otherwise.

Figure 1: A plan. (move X Y Z) means "Move block X from Y to Z".

NOAH (Sacerdoti, 1975), and its descendents, such as NONLIN (Tate, 1976), DEVISER (Vere, 1981), and SIPE (Wilkins, 1983) all use plans based on Sacerdoti's original Procedural Net. The following comments are expressed principally in terms of NOAH, but apply equally to these newer planners.

The Allow relation takes the form of a "before" link in a Procedural Net which has been introduced by pattern-directed operator invocation. Such a link might appear, for instance, between an action which must make block **A** clear, and an action which must stack **A** on **B**.

$C = <P,T,R_a,R_b,R_c,R_e>$

$P = \{Hammer\text{-}Up, Hammer\text{-}Down\}$

$T = \{Lift\text{-}Hammer\text{-}Up, Pound\text{-}Hammer\text{-}Down\}$

$R_a = \{(Pound\text{-}Hammer\text{-}Down, Lift\text{-}Hammer\text{-}Up),$
$\qquad (Lift\text{-}Hammer\text{-}Up, Pound\text{-}Hammer\text{-}Down)\}$

$R_e = \{(Hammer\text{-}Up, Pound\text{-}Hammer\text{-}Down),$
$\qquad (Hammer\text{-}Down, Lift\text{-}Hammer\text{-}Up)\}$

$R_c = \{(Pound\text{-}Hammer\text{-}Down, Hammer\text{-}Down),$
$\qquad (Lift\text{-}Hammer\text{-}Up, Hammer\text{-}Up)\}$

$R_b = \{\}$

Figure 2:   A plan for hammering a nail.

The Before relation appears in a Procedural Net as a "before" link introduced by the Resolve Conflicts critic. This critic analyzes operator preconditions and effects, and introduces "before" orderings because of unfavourable interactions.

In Section 2, it was shown that one can take a Procedural Net, and through repeated application of the pebbling rule, determine possible net behaviours. The situation is slightly more complex when we consider deriving a Plan Net's possible behaviours. To do this, we require an initial marking of the net, the net itself, and the firing rule as provided in Definition 4. Using the initial net marking, we repeatedly fire transitions until either no enabled transitions remain, or a marking is reached that has been seen previously. A tree or graph structure can be built in this manner, in which the nodes contain states (markings) of the Plan Net, and the arcs are transitions for moving from one state to another. In net Theory, this structure is often called a reachability tree (or graph), and is precisely the sort of behavioural account we generated for the Procedural Net by using the Pebbling rule. (See Peterson, 1980, for more on net reachability.) The important thing is that the state space constructed from a Plan Net need not be loop free. Using these nets, it is possible to model iterative behaviour in a natural way.

A planning system called Selah has been implemented which uses the Plan Net representation. Selah is currently able to solve "Blocks World" problems, and work is underway to extend its construction algorithms to allow it to create iterative plans.

5. Summary

This paper has defined the Plan Net using Sacerdoti's Procedural Net as a starting point. Through the introduction of a simple operational semantics, the Procedural Net was shown to be incapable of describing iterative behaviour. It was argued that the Plan Net can describe such behaviour. The implementation of a planner able to construct iterative plans is underway, and results from it will be reported.

Acknowledgements

Thanks are given to the Edinburgh University AI Planning Group, and to Dave Wilkins for providing useful comment on an earlier version of this paper. I am indebted to Karl Kempf and Barry Fox of the University of Missouri for introducing me to Pebbling. The supervision of Austin Tate has been invaluable.

References

Brauer, W. (ed.). 1979. Springer-Verlag LNCS series. Net theory and applications. Proceedings of the Advanced Course on General Net Theory of Processes and Systems, Hamburg.

Drummond, M. 1985. Ph.D. dissertation, University of Edinburgh. (To appear.)

McDermott, D. 1983. Generalizing problem reduction: a logical analysis. Proceedings of IJCAI-83. pp. 302-308.

Peterson, J.L. 1980. Petri Net theory and the modeling of systems. Prentice-Hall.

Pippenger, N. 1980. Pebbling. RC 8258 (#35937), IBM TJ Watson Research Center, Yorktown Heights, NY.

Rosenschein, S. 1984. Invited lecture at AAAI-84, In Austin, TX: "A perspective on planning".

Sacerdoti, E.D. 1975. A structure for plans and behaviour. SRI Technical Note #109.

Tate, A. 1976. Project planning using a hierarchic non-linear planner. University of Edinburgh, Department of Artificial Intelligence Research Report #25.

Vere, S.A. 1981. Planning in time: windows and durations for activities and goals. Jet Propulsion Laboratory, Information Systems Research section, research report.

Wilkins, D.E. 1983. Representation in a domain independent planner. Proceedings of IJCAI-83. pp. 733-740.

Localized Representation and Planning

Amy L. Lansky

Artificial Intelligence Center
SRI International
333 Ravenswood Avenue, Menlo Park. California 94025

Abstract

This paper describes how the inherent structural properties of a domain (*locality*) can be used to alleviate tractability problems faced by multiagent planners. The domain structuring mechanisms of the GEM concurrency model are presented, as are the frame or "locality" rules imposed by these structures. The GEMPLAN planner applies these rules to subdivide the planning search space into *localized search spaces*. A domain's structural semantics can also be used to guide reasoning about regional interactions and to cope with the problem of replanning in dynamic environments.

1 Introduction

By now it is well-recognized that the enormous search space requirements and algorithmic complexity of planning make it a formidable task [Chapman 1985]. Indeed, it has become popular to give up on the notion of domain-independent planning altogether; instead, "reactive planners" (which simply react using prescribed knowledge forms) [Georgeff and Lansky 1987] [Kaelbling 1987] have come into vogue. However, it is clear that people *do* plan, especially to coordinate their actions with those of others. For example, factories and organizations spend substantial effort to come up with schedules and other mechanisms to coordinate their activities. If a planning capability is needed at all, it is to generate coordinated multiagent plans – a task that is even more formidable than single-agent planning!

This paper describes how the use of *locality* (i.e., the inherent structural properties of a domain) can alleviate some of the tractability problems faced by multiagent planners. (Actually, the techniques described herein are equally applicable to single-agent planners.) The basis of my work is GEM, a concurrency model capable of describing the complex temporal and structural properties of multiagent domains, and GEMPLAN, a multiagent planner based on this model.

Previous papers [Lansky 1988] [Lansky 1987] [Lansky and Fogelsong 1987] have focused on the full complexity of the GEM model and GEMPLAN. In this paper, I shall focus solely on the use of locality to structure and guide domain reasoning. The underlying motivation is similar to that of hierarchical methods; considerable savings can be had by subdividing a problem into smaller subproblems. In the case of planning, the size of planning search spaces can be reduced, as well as the size of the plans to which expensive algorithms are applied. (An exponential algorithm is certainly cheaper when it is applied locally to a set of 10 actions rather than applied globally to a set of 100 actions!) I will show how GEM's use of locality is not only more general than the notion of hierarchy, but more semantically meaningful and powerful than the hierarchical operators found in such planners as NOAH [Sacerdoti 1977] and SIPE [Wilkins 1984]. While these traditional planners decompose actions into subactions, their use of hierarchy helps little in resolving plan interactions.

2 GEM Locality Structures

GEM models a domain as a *set of interrelated events clustered into regions of activity*.[1] Events may be related by three relations: a temporal order $\implies$, a causal or "enabling" relation $\leadsto$, and a simultaneity relation $\rightleftharpoons$ (modeling required simultaneity). GEM utilizes two kinds of regions: *elements* and *groups*.[2] Each element or group may be associated with explicit constraints on the event behaviors occurring within it. Thus, a domain is viewed as a myriad of interrelated events that are partitioned into regions and subject to regional constraints.

Elements are the most basic type of region. Every event must belong to exactly one element, and all events belonging to the same element must occur sequentially. Thus, elements are loci of sequential activity. Elements (and their constituent events) are then clustered into groups – regions whose boundaries impose barriers on

---

[0]This paper appeared in *The Proceedings of the 1989 Stanford Spring Symposium Workshop on Planning and Search*. Research was made possible in part by NSF Grant IRI-8715972.

[1]I shall use the terms "event," "action," and "event instance" synonymously.

[2]GEM stands for the Group Element Model.

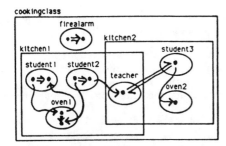

Figure 1: Cooking Class Domain

various forms of domain interaction. The motivation behind the selection of these particular kinds of regions was to mimic the structures found in the world and how people reason about them. For example, at some level, most physical objects in the world are subject to sequentiality constraints. Such regions may be suitably represented as elements. And the fact that humans are capable of dealing with the complexities of the world is evidence that they utilize some form of regional independence – e.g., the kind imposed by groups.

GEM's domain regions may be structured so that they overlap, are disjoint, or form hierarchies – i.e., they may take on *any* structural configuration that the domain describer wishes. The key idea is to partition a domain in such a way that domain properties are *localized*. That is, if a set of events is affected by a specific set of constraints, that set should be represented as a distinct region of activity. A domain's physical structure, its functional decomposition, the extent of causal effect, the processes that may occur — all of these factors may play a role in structuring a domain. Indeed, the regional structure of a domain may reflect many decompositions simultaneously – for instance, a physical decomposition may be overlapped with a functional decomposition.

As an illustration, Figure 1 depicts a cooking class. The domain is modeled as a group composed of a fire alarm element and two kitchen subgroups, both of which share a teacher element. Each kitchen also contains a set of student elements and an oven element. Typical constraints that might be used in this domain include rules regarding individual student behavior, limitations on the use of the oven in each kitchen, requirements for teacher and student cooperation on certain tasks, descriptions of appropriate reactions to teacher instructions, and constraints on the behavior of the fire alarm.

Syntactically, a GEM domain description is composed of a set of element and group declarations.[3] Each element declaration is associated with a set of event types, describing the kinds of events that may occur within it. A group declaration describes the elements and groups which comprise it. Both element and group declarations

---
[3] GEM also includes a facility for declaring and instantiating element and group types.

are then associated with first-order linear-temporal-logic constraints on event behaviors. These constraints are highly expressive, especially for describing the complex synchronization properties common to multiagent domains [Lansky 1988, Lansky 1987].

GEM constraints are *localized*, constraining the event behaviors occurring within the element or group with which they are associated. Thus, one of the primary reasons for structuring a domain into elements and groups is to localize the effect of constraints upon event behaviors – i.e., *constraint localization*. The second reason for GEM's locality structures is to impose additional *structural constraints* on events. As already stated, elements impose a sequentiality constraint on their constituent events, and groups limit event interrelationships that cross their boundaries.

3 Locality Rules

This section presents a more formal definition of constraint localization and GEM's structural constraints. Together, these locality properties can be used to infer the scope of effect of domain events and to determine potential interactions among events and constraints or other properties – i.e., they provide a way of addressing the frame problem [Georgeff 1987] [Hayes 1973]. While the use of domain structure to define frame axioms and to guide reasoning has been suggested in the AI literature, it has not been explored extensively until now.

Let us begin with a few definitions. We say that a constraint ψ belongs to a region x if it is explicitly associated with x in the domain description: constraint-belongs(ψ,x). We say that a region x structurally belongs to a group g if it is explicitly declared as a *direct* component of g within g's declaration: structure-belongs(x,g). For example, in the cooking class, we have structure-belongs(student1,kitchen1), but ¬ structure-belongs(student1,cookingclass).

Next, we introduce the use of *ports* – events declared to be "holes" in a group boundary. Both ports and group overlap are used to model potential interactions between groups. There are two kinds of ports: input and output. Input ports are used to allow causal flow *into* a group, and output ports, flow *out* of a group. Let us assume that domain specifications include the relations input-port(e,g) and outputport(e,g), and that inputport(e,g) ∨ outputport(e,g) ⊃ port(e,g). We can then define the relation event-belongs as follows:

event-belongs(e,x) ≡ (element(x) ∧ e∈x) ∨
group(x) ∧
[(∃ elem:ELEMENT)
    e∈elem ∧ structure-belongs(elem,x)] ∨
[(∃ g:GROUP) structure-belongs(g,x) ∧ port(e,g)]

If event e belongs to element x, we have event-belongs(e,x). For a group x, event-belongs(e,x) is true if e belongs to an element that structurally belongs to x or is a port of a subgroup of x. Intuitively, event-belongs(e,x) is true if e's containment within x is not blocked by a group boundary. For example, although an event bake belonging to oven1 also belongs to kitchen1 (event-belongs(bake,kitchen1)), that same event does not "belong" to the cooking class (¬ event-belongs(bake,cookingclass)). If, however, bake were designated a port of kitchen1, we would have event-belongs(bake,cookingclass).

We are now able to define formally the concept of constraint localization:

Constraint Localization:
constraint-influence(e,ψ) ≡
($\exists$ x) constraint-belongs(ψ,x) $\wedge$ event-belongs(e,x)

In other words, an event e can potentially be affected by or affect a constraint ψ if and only if e and ψ belong directly to the same group or element. For example, as currently structured, firealarm events are the only events that can influence constraints belonging to the cooking-class group. If, however, all Bake events were made ports of their Kitchen group, they too could potentially influence cookingclass constraints.

The reader has probably already noticed the similarity between the notion of constraint localization and scoping in programming languages. An event can interact with a constraint if it occurs within the constraint's region of definition or if it has been "made visible" by a subregion through a port. One can also see how constraint-influence can be viewed as a frame rule. Namely, if an event has no influence on a constraint or property, it can be assumed to be independent of it – the occurrence of the event will have no effect upon it.

Of course, events may also influence constraints by interacting with other events. For example, if e1 $\rightsquigarrow$ e2 and constraint-influence(e2,ψ), one might think of e1 as influencing ψ, at least indirectly. We now define *structural constraints*, which limit potential event interrelationships.

Element Structural Constraint:
e1$\in$elem $\wedge$ e2$\in$elem $\supset$ e1$\Longrightarrow$e2 $\vee$ e2$\Longrightarrow$e1

Group Structural Constraint:
e1$\rightsquigarrow$e2 $\vee$ e1$\rightleftharpoons$e2 $\supset$ access(e1,e2)

The first structural constraint describes the required sequential behavior of elements. The second constraint deals with the limitations imposed by group boundaries; an event e1 may cause or be necessarily simultaneous with an event e2 only if e1 has *access* to e2. Stated informally, an event e1 has access to another event e2 if and only if:

1. e1 has direct access to e2 (they both belong directly to the same group – i.e., they are siblings) or

2. e1 has indirect access to e2 because of the way groups are structured and associated with input and output ports. In particular, access can permeate group boundaries directionally through ports.

Because of space limitations, I cannot provide a full definition of access here (see [Lansky 1988]). Some examples from the cooking class domain, however, are illustrative. For instance, while a student2 event has access to a teacher event, and the teacher has access to student3, the two students do not have access to each other. As another example, suppose that *all* events in every kitchen are declared to be output ports. This would enable all student, teacher, and oven events to cause events at the fire alarm.

Note that the predicate access captures purely structural information about a domain. Thus, we have defined the behavioral notion of allowed effect strictly in terms of domain structure. GEM's structural constraints can also be used to strengthen the notion of event/constraint independence beyond that provided by constraint localization. Specifically, if there can be no possible chain of effect between e and any event that influences ψ, event e cannot influence ψ, either directly or indirectly. This is clearly a stronger form of independence than provided by most frame rules.

4 Localized Planning

This final section describes the localized planning architecture of the GEMPLAN multiagent planning system. Implemented in Prolog on a Sun workstation, GEMPLAN has already been used to generate multiagent solutions to blocks-world problems, the Tower of Hanoi, and a building construction domain. Current work on GEMPLAN is aimed toward handling larger scheduling and coordination applications.

Given the structure of a domain and its applicable constraints, GEMPLAN's task is to construct a world model or *plan* (i.e., a set of interrelated events) that is subdivided into regions ("subplans"), each of whose executions satisfies all applicable regional constraints and goal constraints. Thus, GEMPLAN's reasoning process may be viewed as one of constraint satisfaction. Given an initial world plan (possibly empty), the planner repeatedly chooses a constraint, checks to see whether the constraint is satisfied and, if it is not, either backtracks to an earlier decision point in the planning process or continues on, modifying the world plan so that the constraint is satisfied.

This constraint satisfaction process may be seen as the search of a set of trees, one for each region (see Figure 2). Each search tree focuses on building a regional plan that

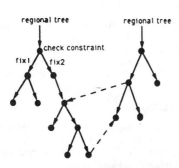

Figure 2: Localized Search Trees

satisifies all regional constraints. At each tree node is stored a representation of the currently constructed plan for that region. When a node is reached during planning search, a constraint is checked. To satisfy it, the search space branches for each of the possible ways of repairing or "fixing" the world plan. A *fix* typically involves the addition of new events and event interrelationships; in essence, it massages an ever-growing partial order. The placement of events within this partial order depends on the nature of the constraint and fix.

In principle, a GEM constraint can be *any* first-order temporal-logic formula. However, because of the intractability of satisfying arbitrary first-order temporal-logic constraints, GEMPLAN's approach is to use *predefined* fixes for common constraint forms. The system can currently satisfy event-prerequisite constraints, constraints based on regular-expression patterns of events, nonatomic-event expansion, and the achievement of state-based conditions and goals (using Chapman's *modal truth criterion* [Chapman 1985]). GEMPLAN also includes a facility for *accumulating* constraints on the values of unbound event-parameter variables, similar to the constraint accumulation facility in Wilkins' SIPE system [Wilkins 1984]. This allows some forms of least-commitment planning to be utilized. Future research plans include the addition of priority constraints as well as other forms of temporal constraints and constraint satisfaction mechanisms.

Of course, the order in which constraints and fixes are applied has an effect on the speed with which a correct plan is found and the actual composition of the plan — indeed, on whether or not any solution is found at all. GEMPLAN tries to provide for as much flexibility as possible in the control of planning search. The order in which constraint checks and fixes are tried (including moves between regional search trees) and decisions about when and where to backtrack or halt are all guided by user-modifiable *regional search tables*. Whenever backtracking occurs, the node left behind is retained. The search may thus utilize a mixture of depth- and breadth-oriented exploration, depending on the strategy deter-

mined by the table. If a user does not supply domain-specific search information, a default depth-first search strategy is used. The constraints and fixes within each region are chosen in the order in which they are supplied within the domain description. Once constraint checking in a specific region is complete, other regions that may be affected are rechecked.

It is interesting to note the differences between this approach to planning and more traditional methods. While most planners can handle only one or two forms of domain constraints (goal conditions and preconditions, nonatomic-event expansion), GEMPLAN can handle any form of constraint, as long as it is furnished a suitable plan-fixing method. Thus, planning "operators" that have been given distinctive status by traditional planners become unified as constraint satisfaction methods. Second, GEMPLAN's constraint satisfaction search is much more flexible than those found in most planners. Because constraints and fixes can be applied in *any* order (determined by the regional search tables), the planning process need not be rigidly broken up into distinct phases.

GEMPLAN is also unique in its use of locality to partition the construction of plans and the planning search into localized search spaces. These search spaces are tied to one another in accordance with the structure of a domain – group search spaces can affect accessible events belonging to their subregions. For example, because kitchen1 constraints apply to the students, oven, and teacher within it, the kitchen1 search space will have access to the subplans belonging to these subelements. GEMPLAN's internal representation for constructed plans is based on a scheme of data *inheritance*; each plan inherits a set of previously defined plan information, supplemented by a set of new events and relationships. This inheritance-based representation is compact and useful for consolidating local plan information to form more global plans. Each GEMPLAN group plan is composed of its subelements' plans (plus port events belonging to its subgroups) along with relations among these that are added by virtue of group constraints.

Of course, planning for one region may affect planning within another. Thus, the flow of reasoning among regional search spaces must be guided by a domain's potential interactions – i.e., those delineated by GEM's locality rules. When plan modifications are made, only those constraints that could possibly be affected need be rechecked. In practice, shifts between regional search spaces are enacted by virtue of search table information or the particular nature of a fix. For example, if a group fix needs to add an event to a subregion, search will be pursued within that subregion.

Given this regional planning architecture, planning complexity is directly related to the amount of regional interaction — which is as it should be. Planning for tightly coupled regions may involve considerable interaction among their regional search spaces, but planning for domains in which there is little regional interaction will be loosely coupled and could potentially be performed in parallel. In addition, GEMPLAN's constraint satisfaction algorithms are applied locally to relevant subplans rather than to a global plan, thereby mitigating their possibly expensive nature. In contrast, traditional hierarchical planners, which partition the *expansion* of subplans, do not cope with the potential interactions among those subplans in any disciplined manner. As a result, event interactions within a plan must be checked during a costly global interaction analysis.

The locality properties of GEM and GEMPLAN could also be used to deal with the problem of replanning in dynamic environments. GEMPLAN stores a link between each event and relation in a plan to the search tree node where it was added. This link can be used for plan explanation as well as plan repair. If a particular event goes awry during execution, GEMPLAN could use the link between the offending event and the node where it was created to guide planning search directly to a point where other strategies might be tried. By knowing which events have already taken place and which events are affected by which constraints (locality), GEMPLAN could determine which events are retractable and which portions of a plan must be repaired.

Similarly, suppose that the set of constraints to be solved suddenly changes. Using the links between events and relations in the old plan and the constraints that caused them to be inserted into that plan, GEMPLAN could determine which events should be removed from the older plan (i.e., those that have not yet occurred and correspond to constraints that were removed). Locality could then be used to distinguish those parts of the plan that will be affected from those that will not. Starting from a newly pared-down initial plan (that saves as much information as possible from the old plan), replanning could then proceed as an instantiation of a new planning problem with a new set of constraints to be solved.

Of course, the ultimate utility of locality is predicated on the assumption that a domain *can* be appropriately subdivided. This will depend on the skill of the domain expert in subdividing a domain description and on the nature of the domain itself. If a domain can be structured so that regional interactions are limited, planning will be cheaper. Tradeoffs must obviously be made between allowing possibly relevant, but costly, interactions and the ultimate tractability of domain reasoning. However, experiences thus far with GEM (as well as the fact that humans *are* able to plan in a complex world) is evidence that localizing principles can be effectively used.

Acknowledgments

David Fogelsong was an important contributor to the construction of GEMPLAN. Thanks also to Michael Georgeff and Martha Pollack for critical comments and advice. This research was made possible by the National Science Foundation, under Grants IST-8511167 and IRI-8715972.

References

[Chapman 1985] Chapman, D., 1985. "Planning for Conjunctive Goals," Masters Thesis, Technical Report MIT-AI-TR-802, MIT Laboratory for Artificial Intelligence, Cambridge, Massachusetts.

[Georgeff 1987] Georgeff, M.P., 1987. "Many Agents are Better Than One," in *The Frame Problem in Artificial Intelligence, Proceedings of the 1987 Workshop*, F. Brown (editor), Morgan Kaufmann Publishers, Los Altos, California.

[Georgeff and Lansky 1987] Georgeff, M.P. and A.L. Lansky, 1987. "Reactive Reasoning and Planning," in *Proceedings of the Sixth National Conference on Artificial Intelligence (AAAI-87)*, Seattle, Washington.

[Hayes 1973] Hayes, P.J., 1973. "The Frame Problem and Related Problems in Artificial Intelligence," in *Artificial Intelligence and Human Thinking*, A. Elithorn and D. Jones (editors), Jossey-Bass, Inc. and Elsevier Scientific Publishing Company, pp. 45-59.

[Kaelbling 1987] Kaelbling, L.P., "An Architecture for Intelligent Reactive Systems," in *Reasoning about Actions and Plans: Proceedings of the 1986 Workshop*, M. Georgeff and A. Lansky (editors), Morgan Kaufmann Publishers, Los Altos, California, 1987.

[Lansky 1988] Lansky, A.L., 1988. "Localized Event-Based Reasoning for Multiagent Domains," *Computational Intelligence Journal, Special Issue on Planning*, Volume 4, Number 4.

[Lansky 1987] Lansky, A.L., 1987. "A Representation of Parallel Activity Based on Events, Structure, and Causality," in *Reasoning About Actions and Plans, Proceedings of the 1986 Workshop at Timberline, Oregon*, M. Georgeff and A. Lansky (editors), Morgan Kaufmann Publishers, Los Altos, California, pp. 123-160.

[Lansky and Fogelsong 1987] Lansky, A.L. and D.S. Fogelsong, 1987. "Localized Representation and Planning Methods for Parallel Domains," in *Proceedings of the Sixth National Conference on Artificial Intelligence (AAAI-87)*, Seattle, Washington, pp. 240-245.

[Sacerdoti 1977] Sacerdoti, E.D., 1977. *A Structure for Plans and Behavior*, Elsevier North-Holland, Inc., New York. New York.

[Wilkins 1984] Wilkins, D.E., 1984. "Domain Independent Planning: Representation and Plan Generation," *Artificial Intelligence*, Volume 22, Number 3, pp. 269-301.

FORMULATING MULTIAGENT, DYNAMIC-WORLD PROBLEMS IN THE CLASSICAL PLANNING FRAMEWORK

Edwin P.D. Pednault*

Aritificial Intelligence Center

SRI International

333 Ravenswood Avenue

Menlo Park, CA 94025

ABSTRACT

This paper demonstrates how some multiagent, dynamic-world planning problems may be formulated as single-agent, static-world problems, thereby permitting them to be solved with techniques originally intended for the latter. This approach to formulating such problems requires that dynamic worlds be modeled in the same manner as their static couterparts, and that simultaneous actions be modeled as sequential actions. The former is accomplished by introducing time as a parameter in the description of dynamic worlds. To model simultaneous actions as sequential ones, the idea of a *boundary condition* is introduced. A boundary condition exists at a point in time and determines the future course of events, up to the next boundary condition. The effect of simultaneous actions is then modeled by modifying boundary conditions sequentially. To provide concrete examples, a new language is introduced for the purpose of describing actions and their effects. This language, called ADL, combines the the notational convenience of the STRIPS operator language with the semantics and expressive power of the situation calculus. ADL thus has the same facilities as the STRIPS language for coping with the frame problem, but it is a more expressive language in that it permits actions to be described whose effects change according to the circumstances underwhich they are performed. In addition, ADL overcomes the semantic pitfalls of the STRIPS language that are discussed by Lifschitz.

---

*Current address: AT&T Bell Laboratories, Crawfords Corner Road, Holmdel, New Jersey 07733.

1. INTRODUCTION

Until recently, virtually all work in automatic planning has been concerned with ways of representing and solving what might be called the *classical planning problems*. In this type of problem, the world is regarded as being in one of a potentially infinite number of states. Performing an action causes the world to pass from one state to the next. In the specification of a problem, we are given a set of goals, a set of allowable actions, and a description of the world's initial state. We are then asked to find a sequence of actions that will transform the world from any state satisfying the initial-state description to one that satisfies the goal description. This framework has typically been used to model real-world problems that involve a single agent (e.g., a robot) operating in an environment that changes only as the result of the agent's action, and otherwise remains static.

Much contemporary research, on the other hand, is concerned with broader classes of planning problems, particularly those that involve multiple agents operating in dynamic worlds; for example, two children playing on a seesaw. To model such problems, appropriate representations for simultaneous actions and continuous processes are required, along with mechanisms for solving problems by using such representations. Hendrix [15] was one of the first to address these representational issues, having developed a system for simulating the effects of simultaneous actions in a dynamic world. More recent contributions have been made by Allen [2], Georgeff [9–12], Lansky [16, 17], and McDermott [21, 23], each of whom has used a different approach to the problem of representing actions and processes: Allen advocates a logic of time intervals, Georgeff employs a modified state-based approach, Lansky uses an event-based logic, while McDermott prefers a logic that combines states with continuous time lines. Stuart [29, 30] has examined the problem of synchronizing plans executed by different agents to avoid undesirable interactions among plans. Cheeseman [4], Dean [6], Tate [5, 33], Vere [35, 36], and Vilain [37] have concentrated primarily on representing and reasoning about the time and duration of events.

At this stage in the game, the primary objective is to develop epistemologically adequate [20] formalisms for representing and reasoning about simultaneous actions and continuous processes. The next step is to construct planning techniques that utilize these formalisms. Some work has already been done in this direction, notably by Allen and Kooman [1], Cheeseman [4], Georgeff and Lansky [10], Lansky [16], and McDermott [22]. However, these techniques are still in their infancy. The purpose of this paper is to help further these efforts by showing how some multiagent, dynamic-world problems may be formulated and solved in the classical planning framework. It is hoped that, by looking at the classical planning framework in this new light, it may be possible to discern how solution techniques developed for the classical problems can be transferred to frameworks that are more suitable for solving multiagent, dynamic-world problems.

This paper focuses primarily on ways of formulating multiagent, dynamic-world problems as classical planning problems. As part of our exposition, a new language, called ADL, will be introduced for the purpose of describing actions and their effects. ADL differs from its predecessors in that it combines the notational convenience of the STRIPS operator language [7] with the semantics and expressive power of the situation calculus [20] and first-order dynamic logic [13]. From the point of view of syntax, descriptions in ADL resemble STRIPS operators with conditional add and delete lists. This syntax permits actions to be described whose effects are highly state-dependent. At the same time, it allows the frame problem [14] to be circumvented to the extent that one need only specify what changes are made when an action is performed, not what remains unaltered. However, the semantics of ADL is drastically different from that of STRIPS. Whereas STRIPS operators define transformations on state descriptions, ADL schemas define transformations on the states themselves. In this respect, the semantics of ADL is similar to that of the situation calculus and first-order dynamic logic. Furthermore, by adopting a different semantics, ADL avoids the pitfalls of the STRIPS language that are discussed by Lifschitz [18].

As we shall see, ADL is well suited to the multiagent, dynamic-world problems that are presented. Once a problem is formulated with ADL, it can be solved by means of the techniques described in my thesis [25] and in a earlier technical report [24]. An explicative review of these techniques, however, is beyond the scope of this paper.

2. DEFINING THE CLASSICAL PLANNING PROBLEMS

To make clear the issues involved in formulating multiagent, dynamic-world problems as classical planning problems, the latter will now be defined mathematically. This definition is set-theoretic in nature and is based on ideas borrowed from first-order dynamic logic [13].

As previously stated, the world is regarded, in classical planning problems, as being in any one of a potentially infinite number of states. The effect of an action is to cause the world to jump from one state to another. This permits an action to be characterized as a set of current-state/next-state pairs, summarizing the possible state transitions that could occur when the action is performed. Stated mathematically, an action is a set a of ordered pairs of the form $\langle s, t \rangle$, where s and t are states, s being the "current state" and t being the "next state."

In many situations, there is no uncertainty as to how the world will change when an action is performed. In such cases, performing an action will cause the world to jump from one state to a unique next state. Mathematically speaking, an action a has this property if and only if for every state s there is at most one state t such that $\langle s, t \rangle \in a$ (i.e., such that the ordered pair $\langle s, t \rangle$ appears in a). Hence, performing action a when the world is in state s will always cause the world to jump to state t.

In other situations, the effect of an action might be unpredictable. In such cases, there will be a collection of states that the world could jump to when the action is performed, but the exact state would not be known beforehand. In mathematical terms, the effect of performing action a in state s will be uncertain if and only if there is more than one state t such that $\langle s, t \rangle \in a$. For example, if performing action a in state s will cause the world to jump to one of the states $t_1, \ldots, t_n$, but it is not known beforehand which it will be, then this is modeled by having each of the ordered pairs $\langle s, t_1 \rangle, \ldots, \langle s, t_n \rangle$ appear in the set a.

Although some actions can be performed under any circumstances, most actions can occur only when the world is in one of a limited number of states. For example, to walk through a doorway, the door must be open. If the world is in a state in which the door is closed, the action of walking through the doorway becomes impossible. In our mathematical framework, an action a may be executed in a state s if and only if there is some state t such that $\langle s, t \rangle \in a$. The set of states in which a may take place is given by

$$\mathrm{dom}(a) = \{s \mid \langle s, t \rangle \in a \text{ for some state } t\}$$

The function dom is borrowed from set theory [27, 31], where $\mathrm{dom}(a)$ is called the *domain* of the set of ordered pairs a.

In the statement of a classical planning problem, we are given a set of allowable actions, a set of possible initial states, and a set of acceptable goal states. Told that the world is currently in one of the possible initial states, we are then asked to find a sequence of allowable actions that, when executed, will leave the world in one of the acceptable goal states. A classical planning problem can therefore be viewed as an encoding of this information:

Definition 2.1. A *classical planning problem* is a quadruple of the form $\langle \mathcal{W}, \mathcal{A}, \mathcal{I}, \mathcal{G} \rangle$, where

(1) $\mathcal{W}$ is the set of all possible states of the world

(2) $\mathcal{A}$ is the set of allowable actions

(3) $\mathcal{I}$ is the set of possible initial states

(4) $\mathcal{G}$ is the set of acceptable goal states.

A solution to a classical planning problem is a sequence of actions $a_1 a_2 \cdots a_n$ that will transform the world from any of the possible initial states into one of the acceptable goal states. To guarantee this result, a number of conditions must be satisfied. First, it must be possible to execute each of the actions in the given order. This requires that it be possible to first perform a_1 in any of the possible initial states, then a_2 in any state that could result from performing a_1, then a_3 in any state that could result from performing a_2, etc. If these conditions hold, the sequence is said to be *executable*. Finally, for the sequence to be a solution, the world must necessarily be in one of the goal states once all the actions have been carried out.

To express these conditions mathematically, the following notation is introduced.

(1) Let ϵ denote the empty sequence; that is, the sequence containing no actions. "Executing" ϵ therefore leaves the world undisturbed.

(2) If σ and γ are two sequences of actions, then $\sigma\gamma$ is the sequence obtained by appending γ to the end of σ. For example, if $\sigma = a_1 a_2$ and $\gamma = a_3 a_4 a_5$, then $\sigma\gamma = a_1 a_2 a_3 a_4 a_5$. Note that $\sigma\epsilon = \epsilon\sigma = \sigma$.

(3) If there exists a sequence γ such that $\sigma\gamma = \theta$, then σ is said to be a *prefix* of θ. For example, the prefixes of the sequence $a_1 a_2 a_3 a_4 a_5$ are ϵ, a_1, $a_1 a_2$, $a_1 a_2 a_3$, $a_1 a_2 a_3 a_4$, and $a_1 a_2 a_3 a_4 a_5$.

The concept of a prefix permits us to express the executability conditions for a sequence as follows: a sequence θ is executable if and only if, for every prefix σa of θ, where a is an action, a can be performed in every state that could result from the execution of σ. The set of states that could result when σ is executed is given by the function $\text{Result}(\sigma, I)$, which is defined recursively as follows:

$$\text{Result}(\epsilon, I) = I \tag{2.2a}$$

$$\text{Result}(\gamma a, I) = \{t \mid \langle s, t \rangle \in a \text{ for some } s \in \text{Result}(\gamma, I)\} \tag{2.2b}$$

Thus, if no actions task place, the set of possible resulting states is merely the set of possible initial states. If one or more actions are performed, the set of resulting states is obtained by considering every state transition that could possibly occur when the sequence is executed. Thus, an action a can be performed in every state that could result from the sequence σ if and only if $\text{Result}(\sigma, I) \subset \text{dom}(a)$ (i.e., every state in $\text{Result}(\sigma, I)$ also appears in $\text{dom}(a)$). This permits the following definitions to be formulated:

Definition 2.3. A sequence of actions θ is said to be *executable* with respect to a set of possible initial states I if and only if $\text{Result}(\sigma, I) \subset \text{dom}(a)$ for every prefix σa of θ such that a is an action.

Definition 2.4. A *solution* to a classical planning problem $\langle \mathcal{W}, \mathcal{A}, I, \mathcal{G} \rangle$ is a sequence of actions θ drawn from $\mathcal{A}$ such that θ is executable with respect to I and $\text{Result}(\theta, I) \subset \mathcal{G}$.

3. THE ONTOLOGY OF ACTIONS IN CLASSICAL PLANNING

When a formalism is proposed for describing some aspect of the real world, two questions naturally arise: in what sense does the formalism reflect reality, and to what degree? This section is intended to at least partially answer these questions with respect to the classical planning problems. Specifically, we shall consider how various kinds of real-world planning problems may be modeled as classical planning problems, particularly those problems involving dynamic environments and multiple agents. In each case, our primary emphasis will be on establishing a correspondence between actions in the real world and the formal notion of an action used in classical planning problems. Our goal, however, is not to understand the true nature of actions in the real world, but rather to determine how a particular mathematical construct may be used to model problems of interest.

Historically, the formal notion of an action developed in Section 2 was used to model problems that involve a single agent operating in an environment that remains essentially static, except while the agent is performing an action. To illustrate, imagine a robot in a closed room that contains a table on which a number of wooden blocks of equal size are stacked. The robot may be commanded (say, by radio) to move the blocks one at a time, either placing them elsewhere on the table or stacking them on top of other blocks. When issued a command, the robot will reach for the block to be moved, pick it up, position it over the desired location, and deposit it. Once the block has been deposited, the robot will stand motionless until the next command is received. Thus, except for those periods when the robot is carrying out a order, the robot and the blocks remain static (i.e., their respective positions remain fixed).

Imagine further that our goal is to have the robot arrange the blocks in a particular configuration. To determine an appropriate sequence of commands, all we need to know about each command are its net effects–that is, what the final respective positions of the robot and the blocks would be once the command has been carried out. The exact motion of the robot and the blocks during execution is unimportant. This leads us directly to the classical planning framework: First we can define a state to be a particular arrangement of the robot and blocks. Then we can catalogue the effects of a command by means of a set of current-state/next-state pairs specifying what the final disposition of the robot and blocks would be for each possible arrangement at the moment a command is invoked. This way of formalizing the problem ignores the details of the robot's motion while retaining all of the information relevant to planning a sequence of commands. It should be noted, however, that this formalization is possible only because the robot and the blocks remain stationary between the completion of one task and the start of the next.

In many real-world situations, though, the world is not static but is in continuous state of flux. For example, suppose that our robot is trying to land a spacecraft on the moon. At any point in time, the robot may change the vehicle's flight path by adjusting the attitude of the vehicle and/or its thrust. Unlike the blocks in the previous example, however, the vehicle is in continuous motion until it lands (safely, we hope) on the lunar surface.

Single-agent, dynamic-world problems, such as the one just described, can be formulated in the classical planning framework by assigning new interpretations to the mathematical notions of state and state transition. In the static case, the world does not change between the end of one action and the beginning of the next. This permits a state to represent everything that is true of the world at a given point in time between one action and the next. In a dynamic situation, however, this is not sufficient, since the world may be continually changing of its own accord from one moment to the next. Hence, what may be true at one point in time might not be true an instant later. How, then, is it possible to model actions in a dynamic environment as sets of current-state/next-state pairs? The key is to use states not for cataloguing what is true of the world at given instants in time, but rather for cataloguing what is true at each individual point in time, for all such points. To use McDermott's terminology [21, 23], a state according to this new interpretation is a *chronicle* of all that is true, was true, and will be true of the world, from the beginning of time through to the end of time.

Since we are interpreting states as chronicles, how should we interpret state transitions? The most sensible answer is to interpret a state transition as the initiation of an action or course of action at a particular point in time. Under this interpretation, when a state transition is made from one chronicle to the next, the past with respect to the new chronicle must be identical to the past with respect to the preceding chronicle. This reflects the commonsense intuition that the past is inaccessable and therefore cannot be changed. The future portion of the new chronicle, however, may be different. That portion must catalogue everything that would be true henceforth, *provided that no further actions are initiated*. In particular, it would record the events that take place as a result of executing the action whose initiation the state transition represents. If a new action is initiated, it must obviously follow all prior initiations. This corresponds to the commonsense intuition that time always moves forward, never backward.

This new way of interpreting states and state descriptions is illustrated in the figure below. States (i.e., chronicles) are shown as time lines, while state transitions are depicted as jumps from one time line to another that has the same past.

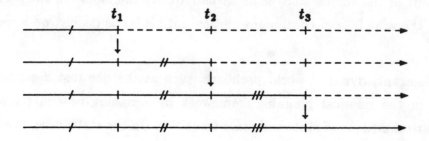

As an example, consider again the problem of landing a spacecraft on the moon, where the allowable actions are to adjust the attitude of the vehicle and the thrust. For a given adjustment, the future course of events will be dictated by the physics of the situation and will not change unless further adjustments are made. Each new adjustment places the spacecraft on a new trajectory, do that a new chronicle of events comes into force. Each new chronicle has the same past as the preceding one, since the previous history of the vehicle does not change; only the future is changed.

It is interesting to note that the ontology of time and action presented above is identical, within isomorphism, to the ontology put forth by McDermott [21, 23]. This isomorphism becomes evident from the fact that each of McDermott's forward-branching trees can be expanded into a set individual chronicles and a set of transitions from one chronicle to the next. Furthermore, a set of chronicles, together with a set of transitions between chronicles that share the same past, can be collapsed into a forward-branching tree. This isomorphism is significant, since it reinforces our earlier conjecture that it may be possible to transfer techniques for solving classical planning problems to frameworks that are better suited to the modeling of simultaneous actions and dynamic processes. A first step toward effecting this transfer is to establish such an isomorphism.

Thus far, we have considered problems involving a single agent acting in a world that may be static or dynamic. In some real-world situation, though, there may be several agents capable of performing tasks simultaneously. To maximize productivity, as many agents as possible should be working at any given time. Therefore, we would like to construct plans that coordinate the simultaneous execution of actions by these agents. In attempting to formulate such problems in the classical planning framework, though, we are faced with a major incongruity—i.e., that actions in the classical planning framework may be performed only sequentially whereas multiple agents tend to act simultaneously. In some situation, however, the effect of executing actions simultaneously is the same as doing them sequentially, regardless of the order of execution. This happens, for example, when the actions affect independent parts of the world and so do not interact. If such is the case, we can solve the problem by assuming that actions are to be carried out sequentially, and then transform the resulting sequential plan into a parallel plan for coordinating their simultaneous execution. This parallel plan could be in the form of a partial ordering of actions that specifies which actions may be performed simultaneously, which sequentially.

Such a partial order may be constructed in the following manner. First, to each action in the sequence we assign a unique symbol that identifies that action and its position in the sequence. Next, we construct a binary relation $\prec$ on these identifiers that will be used to define the partial order. The binary relation itself is defined as follows: We start by writting $x \prec y$ as shorthand for $\langle x, y \rangle \in \prec$. Then, for any pair of identifiers x and y, we define $x \prec y$ to be true if and only if the action corresponding to x precedes the action corresponding to y in the sequential plan and these two actions cannot be performed simultaneously. The desired partial order is then given by the *transitive closure* [27, 31] of $\prec$, which we write as $\prec^*$. Mathematically speaking, $\prec^*$ is the smallest binary relation such that

(1) If $x \prec y$ then $x \prec^* y$

(2) If $x \prec^* y$ and $y \prec^* z$ then $x \prec^* z$.

The relation $\prec^*$ specifies in the following way which actions may be performed simultaneously and which sequentially. If $x \prec^* y$, the action corresponding to x must be carried out before the action corresponding to y. On the other hand, if neither $x \prec^* y$ nor $y \prec^* x$, then the actions corresponding to x and y may be executed simultaneously.

It should be emphasized that the procedure just outlined works correctly if and only if the effect of performing actions simultaneously is the same as performing them sequentially. However, not all actions behave this way. Some actions have synergistic effects when performed simultaneously. As a result, their effects are different when performed simultaneously as compared with their sequential execution. For example, consider the effect when two agents lift opposite ends of a table upon which various objects have been placed. If the ends of the table are raised sequentially, the objects on the table might slide around and perhaps even fall off. On the other hand, if the ends are lifted simultaneously and with equal force, the objects on the table will remain more or less fixed. Chapman [3] gives a similar example involving the assembly of LEGO™ blocks. In his example, two agents are pressing down on opposite ends of a LEGO™ block that is resting on top of another LEGO™ block. If the agents apply equal force simultaneously, the first block will mate with the bottom block. On the other hand, if unequal force is applied or if equal force is applied sequentially, the first block will merely pivot and jam.

On the surface, it would appear that synergistic simultaneous actions cannot be dealt with in the classical planning framework, since the latter requires that actions be performed sequentially. Nevertheless, by choosing the appropriate representation, some synergistic simultaneous actions can be made to look like sequential actions, thereby permitting their formulation in the classical planning framework. In the table illustration given above and in Chapman's LEGO^{TM} example, this property can be achieved by modeling the forces that are acting upon on the objects. The overall motion of the objects is determined by the sum of the applied forces and the physical constraints. The primary effect of an action is to apply a force. Since the individual forces acting upon an object can be combined in any order to determine the net force, the actions of applying force can be considered sequentially. This allows the actions to be formulated as sets of current-state/next-state pairs, where each state is a chronicle of all that is true, was true, and will be true of the world, and where each state transition represents the effect of adding or subtracting a force vector at a particular instant. When a transition occurs, not only is the future portion of the chronicle modified, but a record is made noting the force that was added or deleted, along with the time at which this occurred. In this way, the net effect of simultaneously adding or subtracting forces can be determined through a sequence of state transitions.

This approach to determining the net effect of synergistic simultaneous actions can be generalized in the following way. The primary effect of an action is to establish a boundary condition at the point in time at which the action is initiated. The future course of events is then determined by these boundary conditions. In the table example and in Chapman's LEGO^{TM} example, the boundary conditions are the forces applied to the objects. When actions are performed simultaneously, they add to and modify one another's boundary conditions. The resulting boundary conditions then determine the net effect of the actions. Furthermore, the boundary conditions is are modified in a way that enables the actions and their contributions to the boundary conditions to be considered sequentially and in any order. In this way, synergistic simultaneous actions can be made to resemble sequential actions, thus permitting the problem to be formulated in the classical planning framework.

A concrete example of this technique is presented in Section 5. First, however, suitable languages need to be established for representing states and actions.

4. DESCRIBING STATES AND ACTIONS

When solving complex problems, it is often impossible to deal with states and state transitions explicitly, since the number of possible states of the world may be infinite—or at least so large as to make it impractical to enumerate them all. In such cases, states and actions must be dealt with implicitly by creating languages that can express facts about states and actions. The problem would then be specifed and solved by using these languages. Facts in the languages would relate not just to individual states/actions, but to groups thereof. This is necessary so that an infinite number of states and state transitions can be described by a finite number of facts. For example, the lunar landing problem of Section 3 involves uncountably many states; nevertheless, only a page or two of mathematical formulas will suffice to define the problem precisely. Languages for describing states and actions can also be useful when solving problems that involve only a small number of states, as it may be more convenient to present the problems in terms of facts about states and actions than in terms of the states and actions themselves.

The principal requirement of languages for describing states and actions is unambiguousness. Descriptions are intended to represent facts, which are by definition not subject to interpretation. Hence, there can be no ambiguity as to whether or not a given state or action satisfies a given description. Therefore, a description must either be true with respect to a state or an action, or it must be false. Additionally, a description need not be complete: certain details might be left out, either because they are not known or because they are thought to be unimportant. Moreover, if a description is incomplete, there will be a multiplicity of states or actions that satisfy it.

Provided the above conditions are met, literally any language could be used to express facts about states and/or actions. For the purposes of this paper, two particular lanuages will be used. In keeping with much of the previous work in automatic planning, formulas of first-order logic [27, 34] will be used to express facts about states. To describe actions, a new language called ADL will be introduced. ADL has an advantage over its predecessors in that it can be used to define actions whose effects change depending on the circumstances in which they are performed. This feature is necessary to illustrate how multiagent, dynamic-world problems may be formulated in the classical planning framework.

ADL relies on a nonstandard semantics for first-order logic derived from the semantics of first-order dynamic logic [13]. It is also similar to the semantics of first-order logic as presented by Manna and Waldinger [19]. Since a nonstandard semantics is being used, let us examine it in detail.

4.1 STATE DESCRIPTIONS AND FIRST-ORDER LOGIC

Since formulas shall be used to express facts about states, a given state will either satisfy a given formulas or it will not. To express this relationship symbolically, we shall write

$$s \models \varphi$$

to mean that state s satisfies the formula φ (or, equivalently, that φ is true when the world is in state s). Similarly,

$$s \not\models \varphi$$

means that state s does not satisfy the formula φ (or, equivalently, that φ is false when the world is in state s). One use of this notation is to define the set of initial states I and the set of goal states $\mathcal{G}$ for a planning problem in terms of state descriptions. Specifically, if Γ is a formula that describes the initial state of the world, and if G is a formula that describes the goals to be achieved, then

$$I = \{s \mid s \models \Gamma\}$$
$$\mathcal{G} = \{s \mid s \models G\}$$

The concept in first-order logic that most closely satisfies the above relationship between states and formulas is that of an *algebraic structure*. An algebraic structure M is a tuple of the form

$$M = \langle D; r_1, \ldots, r_n; f_1, \ldots, f_m; d_1, \ldots, d_k \rangle \, .$$

where

(1) D is a nonempty set of objects called the *domain* of the structure

(2) $r_1, \ldots, r_n$ are relations on D

(3) $f_1, \ldots, f_m$ are functions on D

(4) $d_1, \ldots, d_k$ are distinguished elements of D.

As in set theory [31], relation r_i holds among elements $x_1, \ldots, x_n$ of D if and only if $\langle x_1, \ldots, x_n \rangle \in r_i$, and $f_i(x_1, \ldots, x_n) = y$ if and only if $\langle x_1, \ldots, x_n, y \rangle \in f_i$ (note that, in set theory, a function is just a special kind of relation). Also, the functions that appear in an algebraic structure must be defined everywhere; that is, if f_i is a function of n variables, then, for every combination of n elements $x_1, \ldots, x_n$ of D, there must exist an element y of D such that $\langle x_1, \ldots, x_n, y \rangle \in f_i$. In this way, an algebraic structure completely specifies which relations and functions hold among the elements of D, and which do not. Borrowing the terminology of set theory, we shall call a function of n variables an *n*-ary function (i.e., *unary*, *binary*, *ternary*, etc.) and a relation among n elements an *n*-ary relation.

Algebraic structures are used to model a situation in the real world by choosing an appropriate set of objects for the domain of the structure, together with an appropriate collection of relations, functions, and distinguished elements for cataloguing the relevant information about the situation. For example, suppose we have a world that consists of a $TABLE$ and three blocks A, B, and C, where blocks A and B are resting on the $TABLE$ and block C is stacked on top of block A. This arrangement of blocks can be described by a single binary relation ON such that $\langle x, y \rangle \in ON$ if and only if x is on top of y. Thus, we can use the algebraic structure BLK given below to represent this state of affairs:

$$BLK = \langle D_{BLK}; ON_{BLK}; ; A, B, C, TABLE \rangle .$$

where

$$D_{BLK} = \{A, B, C, TABLE\}$$

and

$$ON_{BLK} = \{\langle C, A \rangle, \langle A, TABLE \rangle, \langle B, TABLE \rangle\} .$$

In this algebraic structure, A, B, C, and $TABLE$ have all been identified as distinguished elements. The double semicolon indicates that there are no functions in the structure.

Formulas of a first-order language are used to describe facts about algebraic structures. In a first-order language, each relation, function, and distinguished element of an algebraic structure has a corresponding symbol in the language: the symbols corresponding to relations are called relation symbols, for functions they are called function symbols, and for distinguished elements they are called constant symbols. These symbols are commonly referred to as the *nonlogical symbols* and are defined by the user of the logic. For example, we might use the symbol On to stand for the ON relation discussed above, and the symbols A, B, C, and $TABLE$ to stand for the distinguished elements $\mathcal{A}$, $\mathcal{B}$, $\mathcal{C}$, and $\mathcal{TABLE}$ respectively. For notational purposes, we shall write $M(Y)$ to mean the component of the algebraic structure M that corresponds to the nonlogical symbol Y. Thus, for the algebraic structure BLK defined above,

$$
\begin{aligned}
BLK(\text{On}) &= \{\langle \mathcal{C}, \mathcal{A} \rangle, \langle \mathcal{A}, \mathcal{TABLE} \rangle, \langle \mathcal{B}, \mathcal{TABLE} \rangle\} \\
BLK(A) &= \mathcal{A} \\
BLK(B) &= \mathcal{B} \\
BLK(C) &= \mathcal{C} \\
BLK(TABLE) &= \mathcal{TABLE}
\end{aligned}
\tag{4.1}
$$

We shall often refer to $M(Y)$ as the *interpretation* of symbol Y in structure M.

In addition to the nonlogical symbols supplied by the user, a first-order language has a second group of symbols, called the *logical symbols*, that are built in. They are used to connect nonlogical symbols together to produce formulas. This group consists of variable symbols (e.g., $x_1, x_2, \ldots$) that range over objects in the domain of an algebraic structure, the symbols $TRUE$ and $FALSE$, the equality symbol "$=$", the universal quantifier "$\forall$" (meaning *for all*), the existential quantifier "$\exists$" (meaning *there exists*), and the logical connectives "$\wedge$", "$\vee$", "$\neg$", "$\rightarrow$", and "$\leftrightarrow$" (corresponding in meaning, respectively, to *and, or, not, implies,* and *if and only if*).

To show how the logical symbols are used to construct formulas in a first-order language, we need to introduce the notion of a *term*. Terms are syntactic constructs that denote objects in the domain of an algebraic structure. For example, in Equation 4.1, the constant symbol A is a term that denotes the object $\mathcal{A}$ in the algebraic structure BLK. Terms are constructed from constant symbols, function symbols, and variables according to the following rules:

(1) Every constant symbol and every variable symbol is a term.

(2) If $t_1, \ldots, t_n$ are terms and F is an n-ary function symbol, then $F(t_1, \ldots, t_n)$ is a term.

(3) Nothing else is a term.

Using the notion of a term, the syntax for formulas of a first-order language is defined as follows:

(1) *TRUE* and *FALSE* are formulas.

(2) If t_1 and t_2 are terms, then $(t_1 = t_2)$ is a formula.

(3) If $t_1, \ldots, t_n$ are terms and R is an n-ary relation symbol, then $R(t_1, \ldots, t_n)$ is a formula.

(4) If φ and ψ are formulas, then $\neg\varphi$, $(\varphi \wedge \psi)$, $(\varphi \vee \psi)$, $(\varphi \rightarrow \psi)$, and $(\varphi \leftrightarrow \psi)$ are formulas.

(5) If φ is a formula and x is a variable, then $\forall x\, \varphi$ and $\exists x\, \varphi$ are formulas.

(6) Nothing else is a formula.

To make formulas more readable, parentheses will be omitted whenever possible as long as this omission does not render the reading of the formula ambiguous. Also, formulas of the form $\neg(t_1 = t_2)$ will be written as $t_1 \neq t_2$ and sequences of quantifiers of the same type will be simplified by grouping the variables involved under one quantifier. For example, the formula

$$\forall x_1 \forall x_2 \forall x_3 \left(\left(\left(\mathrm{On}(x_1, x_3) \wedge \mathrm{On}(x_2, x_3) \right) \wedge \neg(x_3 = \mathit{TABLE}) \right) \rightarrow (x_1 = x_2) \right)$$

may be written as

$$\forall x_1\, x_2\, x_3 \left(\left(\mathrm{On}(x_1, x_3) \wedge \mathrm{On}(x_2, x_3) \wedge x_3 \neq \mathit{TABLE} \right) \rightarrow x_1 = x_2 \right).$$

This particular formula is true if and only if all blocks are stacked so that at most one block is on top of another.

In the usual semantics of first-order logic, algebraic structures are used to assign truth-values to *closed formulas* (i.e., formulas in which all variables are associated with quantifiers). The formula given above is an example of a closed formula, since the variables x_1, x_2, and x_3 are all associated with the universal quantifier $\forall$. Given an algebraic structure, a closed formula will either be true or false with respect to the structure. The formula given above, for example, is true with respect to the algebraic structure BLK defined earlier. The relationship between algebraic structures and closed formulas is therefore identical to the relationship we desire between states and formulas. However, formulas that contain *free variables* (i.e., variables not associated with any quantifier) do not necessarily have unique truth values with respect to algebraic structures. For example, the formula $\neg On(x, A)$ would be true with respect to the algebraic structure BLK if x had the value A, B, or $TABLE$; however, if x had the value C, the formula would be false. What is usually done with free variables is to view them as being universally quantified. The formula $\neg On(x, A)$ would then be equivalent to the formula $\forall x \neg On(x, A)$.

When constructing plans, however, it is often convenient to use free variables as placeholders for terms yet to be chosen [1–6, 16, 25, 26, 28, 33, 35, 36, 38], or as parameters in a generalized plan [8]. Consequently, if the same free variable appears in more than one formula, we want that free variable to represent the same object in each of the formulas. This use, however, is inconsistent with the usual interpretation of free variables as being universally quantified. What is required is that free variables be assigned interpretations in a manner similar to constant symbols. This can be accomplished by defining states as follows:

Definition 4.2. A state is a pair of the form $\langle M, V \rangle$, where M is an algebraic structure and V is a function that maps variable symbols to elements of the domain of M.

The function V serves to assign interpretations to free variables. For notational convenience, we shall define $s(Y)$ to mean the interpretation of the symbol Y in state s; that is, if $s = \langle M, V \rangle$, then

$$s(Y) = \begin{cases} M(Y), & \text{if } Y \text{ is a relation, function, or constant symbol} \\ V(Y), & \text{if } Y \text{ is a variable symbol} \end{cases}$$

Also, we will refer to the domain of the algebraic structure of a state as the domain of the state.

Given a state s as defined above, and a formula φ, either φ will be true with respect to s or it will be false. To define this relation precisely, we first need to define a *denotation function* for terms. Terms refer to objects; hence, for a particular state, each term will denote a particular object in the domain of that state. Let $[\![\tau]\!]_s$ be the denotation of term τ in state s. Then $[\![\tau]\!]_s$ can be defined recursively as follows:

(1) $[\![C]\!]_s = s(C)$ for any constant symbol C

(2) $[\![x]\!]_s = s(x)$ for any variable x

(3) $[\![F(\tau_1,\ldots,\tau_n)]\!]_s = s(F)\,([\![\tau_1]\!]_s,\ldots,[\![\tau_n]\!]_s)\ ,$

where F is a function symbol, $\tau_1,\ldots,\tau_n$ are terms, and $s(F)\,([\![\tau_1]\!]_s,\ldots,[\![\tau_n]\!]_s)$ is the result of applying the function denoted by F in state s to the denotations of the terms $\tau_1,\ldots,\tau_n$ in s.

To define the truth value of a quantified formula, an additional bit of notation is required. We shall write $s[x \mapsto d]$ to mean the state obtained by changing the interpretation of variable x to d in state s. Thus, the interpretation of a symbol Y in $s[x \mapsto d]$ is given by

$$s[x \mapsto d](Y) = \begin{cases} s(Y) & \text{if } Y \text{ is not the variable } x \\ d & \text{if } Y \text{ is the variable } x \end{cases}$$

The above notation permits the satisfaction relation $s \models \varphi$ between a state s and a formula φ to be defined recursively as follows:

(1) $s \models TRUE$

(2) $s \not\models FALSE$

(3) $s \models (\tau_1 = \tau_2)$ if and only if $[\![\tau_1]\!]_s = [\![\tau_2]\!]_s$

(4) $s \models R(\tau_1,\ldots,\tau_n)$ if and only if $\langle [\![\tau_1]\!]_s,\ldots,[\![\tau_n]\!]_s \rangle \in s(R)$

(5) $s \models (\varphi \wedge \psi)$ if and only if $s \models \varphi$ and $s \models \psi$

(6) $s \models (\varphi \vee \psi)$ if and only if $s \models \varphi$ or $s \models \psi$, or both

(7) $s \models \neg\varphi$ if and only if $s \not\models \varphi$

(8) $s \models (\varphi \rightarrow \psi)$ if and only if $s \not\models \varphi$ or $s \models \psi$, or both

(9) $s \models (\varphi \leftrightarrow \psi)$ if and only if $s \models \varphi$ and $s \models \psi$, or $s \not\models \varphi$ and $s \not\models \psi$

(10) $s \models \forall x\,\varphi$ if and only if $s[x \mapsto d] \models \varphi$ for every element d in the domain of s

(11) $s \models \exists x\,\varphi$ if and only if $s[x \mapsto d] \models \varphi$ for some d in the domain of s.

4.2 ADL: A LANGUAGE FOR DESCRIBING ACTIONS

Let us now consider a language for describing actions. This language, called ADL for Action Description Language, has the interesting property that it is syntactically similar to the STRIPS operator language of Fikes and Nilsson [7], yet it has relatively the same expressive power as the situation calculus of McCarthy and Hayes [20]. In fact, any classical planning problem that can be formulated in the situation calculus can also be formulated with ADL, and vice versa (a formal proof of the equivalence appears elsewhere [25], but is beyond the scope of the current paper). As a result, ADL can be used to describe actions whose effects are highly dependent upon the state of the world in which the action is performed. However, the syntactic properties of ADL enable the frame problem of the situation calculus to be circumvented—at least to the extent that one has only to specify the changes that take place when an action is performed, not what remains the same. The latter is provided implicitly by the language. Consequently, ADL has an advantage over other languages in that it is powerful yet convenient to use. The version of ADL presented here is an extension of a similar language introduced in an earlier technical report [24].

ADL is intended to be a practical language for describing actions. To arrive at this language, certain constraints were imposed on the kinds of actions that could be described in ADL. The first constraint is that the set of states in which an action can be performed must be representable as a well-formed formula. In other words, for an action a to be describable in ADL, there must exist a formula π^a such that

$$\text{dom}(a) = \{s \mid s \models \pi^a\}.$$

This formula is called the *precondition* of the action. Note that this is a standard requirement incorporated into all planning systems to date.

The second constraint is that an action should not alter the domain of a state. That is, for any action a that can be described in ADL, and for any pair of states $\langle s, t \rangle \in a$, the domains of s and t must be identical. This requirement is of concern only when we wish to describe actions that create or destroy objects in the world. An example of such an action would be the GENSYM function in LISP, which creates new LISP atoms. Because actions are required to preserve the domain of a state, the effect of creating or destroying objects must be simulated by introducing a unary relation, say U, where $U(x)$ is true if and only if object x "actually" exists. Objects would then be "created" or "destroyed" by modifying the interpretation of U. Of course, this would require that the domain of a state include all objects that could possibly exist. Note that this is precisely the way in which GENSYM is implemented in a real computer: GENSYM does not create LISP atoms "out of thin air," but rather locates an area of unused memory and claims it for use as a new atom.

The third constraint is that an action must preserve the interpretations of free variables; that is, for any action a that can be described in ADL, and for any pair of states $\langle s, t \rangle \in a$, it must be the case that $s(x) = t(x)$ for every variable symbol x. The reason for this is that we shall want to use free variables as parameters in a plan. Consequently, a free variable that appears at more than one point in a plan should represent the same object at each of those points. Hence, we must require that actions preserve the interpretations of free variables.

The fourth constraint is that actions described in ADL be deterministic; that is, for any state $s \in \text{dom}(a)$, there is a unique state t such that $\langle s, t \rangle \in a$. The rationale for this constraint is that it allows an action to be decomposed into a collection of functions—one for each relation symbol, function symbol, and constant symbol. Each function in the collection is a mapping from states to interpretations of the corresponding symbol in the succedent states. Thus, if f_Y is the function corresponding to symbol Y for action a, and if $\langle s, t \rangle \in a$, then $t(Y) = f_Y(s)$.

To provide a way of specifying these functions, we shall introduce our fifth and final constraint, which is that each function be representable as a formula. That is, each function f_Y corresponding to a symbol Y is then defined by a formula φ_Y, such that

(1) For each n-ary relation symbol R, $R(x_1, \ldots, x_n)$ is true in the succedent state if and only if $\varphi_R(x_1, \ldots, x_n)$ was true previously (where $x_1, \ldots, x_n$ are the free variables of φ_R).

(2) For each n-ary function symbol F, $F(x_1, \ldots, x_n) = w$ is true in the succedent state if and only if $\varphi_F(x_1, \ldots, x_n, w)$ was true previously.

(3) For each constant symbol C, $C = w$ is true in the succedent state if and only if $\varphi_C(w)$ was true previously.

Stated mathematically, for every pair of states $\langle s, t \rangle \in a$, and for every n-ary relation symbol R, every n-ary function symbol F, and every constant symbol C, there must exist formulas $\varphi_R(x_1, \ldots, x_n)$, $\varphi_F(x_1, \ldots, x_n, w)$, and $\varphi_C(w)$, such that

(1) $t(R) = \{\langle d_1, \ldots, d_n \rangle \mid s[x_i \mapsto d_i] \models \varphi_R(x_1, \ldots, x_n)\}$

(2) $t(F) = \{\langle d_1, \ldots, d_n, e \rangle \mid s[x_i \mapsto d_i][w \mapsto e] \models \varphi_F(x_1, \ldots, x_n, w)\}$

(3) $t(C) = d$ such that $s[w \mapsto d] \models \varphi_C(w)$.

For example, suppose we have an action for placing block B on top of block C. After this action is applied, block B is situated atop block C and every block except B remains where it was. Therefore, $\mathrm{On}(x, y)$ is true following the action if and only if

$$(x = B \wedge y = C) \vee (x \neq B \wedge \mathrm{On}(x, y))$$

was true just prior to execution. In other words, if the action is performed in state s, the interpretation of On in the succedent state is the set of ordered pairs $\langle d, e \rangle$, such that

$$s[x \mapsto d][y \mapsto e] \models (x = B \wedge y = C) \vee (x \neq B \wedge \mathrm{On}(x, y)) .$$

If this action were performed with the blocks stacked as described in Section 4.1, where the interpretation of On was $\{\langle B, \mathcal{TABLE} \rangle, \langle C, \mathcal{A} \rangle, \langle \mathcal{A}, \mathcal{TABLE} \rangle\}$, then the resulting interpretation of On would be $\{\langle B, C \rangle, \langle C, \mathcal{A} \rangle, \langle \mathcal{A}, \mathcal{TABLE} \rangle\}$.

When solving a planning problem, it is important to know exactly what modifications an action induces in a state before the appropriate actions for achieving the intended goals can be selected. Therefore, we shall express the above-defined φ_R's, φ_F's and φ_C's in terms of other formulas that make the modifications explicit, and then deal exclusively with these other formulas. For relation symbols, this means expressing each φ_R associated with an action a in terms of two other formulas, α_R and δ_R, which, respectively, describe the additions to and the deletions from the interpretation of R. In other words, if action a is performed in state s, the interpretation of R in the succedent state is given by

$$t(R) = (s(R) - D_R) \cup A_R \,,$$

where $s(R)$ is the interpretation of R in state s, D_R the set of tuples to be deleted from $s(R)$, and A_R the set of tuples to be added to $s(R)$, and where A_R and D_R are given by

$$A_R = \{\langle d_1, \ldots, d_n \rangle \mid s[x_i \mapsto d_i] \models \alpha_R(x_1, \ldots, x_n)\}$$
$$D_R = \{\langle d_1, \ldots, d_n \rangle \mid s[x_i \mapsto d_i] \models \delta_R(x_1, \ldots, x_n)\} \ .$$

We shall further require that A_R and D_R be nonoverlapping (i.e., $A_R \cap D_R = \emptyset$), so that additions and deletions may be done in any order. Consequently,

$$(s(R) - D_R) \cup A_R = (s(R) \cup A_R) - D_R$$

This requires that, for every state $s \in \text{dom}(a)$,

$$s \models \neg\exists x_1 \cdots x_n \, (\alpha_R(x_1, \ldots, x_n) \wedge \delta_R(x_1, \ldots, x_n))$$

Given formulas α_R and δ_R, as defined above, formula φ_R is expressed by

$$\alpha_R(x_1, \ldots, x_n) \vee (\neg\delta_R(x_1, \ldots, x_n)) \wedge R(x_1, \ldots, x_n) \tag{4.3}$$

To paraphrase, $R(x_1, \ldots, x_n)$ is true after performing action a if and only if action a made it true, or it was true beforehand and action a did not make it false. Note that it is possible to find appropriate formulas α_R and δ_R for any given formula φ_R; for example, we can let $\alpha_R(x_1, \ldots, x_n)$ be the formula $\varphi_R(x_1, \ldots, x_n)$ and $\delta_R(x_1, \ldots, x_n)$ be $\neg\varphi_R(x_1, \ldots, x_n)$. For efficient problem solving, though, α_R and δ_R should be chosen to reflect the minimal modifications required in the interpretation of R. For example, for the block-stacking action described previously, a suitable $\alpha_{\text{On}}(x, y)$ would be $(x = B \wedge y = C)$ and a suitable $\delta_{\text{On}}(x, y)$ would be $(x = B \wedge y \neq C)$. Note that $\delta_{\text{On}}(x, y)$ cannot be $(x = B)$, since $\alpha_{\text{On}}(x, y)$ and $\delta_{\text{On}}(x, y)$ are constrained from being true simultaneously.

The formulas defining the interpretations of the function symbols in the succedent state can be restructured in much the same way as the formulas for relation symbols. In the case of functions, however, we can take advantage of the fact that a function must be defined everywhere, as required by the definition of an algebraic structure. Consequently, $F(x_1, \ldots, x_n) = w$ is true after an action has been performed if and only if the action changed the value of $F(x_1, \ldots, x_n)$ to w, or the action preserved the value of $F(x_1, \ldots, x_n)$ and $F(x_1, \ldots, x_n) = w$ was true previously. These modifications can be described by a single formula $\mu_F(x_1, \ldots, x_n, w)$ that is true if and only if the value of $F(x_1, \ldots, x_n)$ is to be changed to w when the action is applied. Since functions have unique values, μ_F

must have the property that, for any instantiation of $x_1, \ldots, x_n$, either there is a unique w for which $\mu_F(x_1, \ldots, x_n, w)$ is true or there are no w's for which $\mu_F(x_1, \ldots, x_n, w)$ is true. Given such a μ_F, the formula φ_F defining the interpretation of F in the succedent state is expressed by

$$\mu_F(x_1, \ldots, x_n, w) \vee (\neg \exists w \, [\mu_F(x_1, \ldots, x_n, w)] \wedge F(x_1, \ldots x_n) = w) \ . \tag{4.4a}$$

As with α_R and δ_R, an appropriate μ_F can be found given any formula φ_F; for example, we can let $\mu_F(x_1, \ldots, x_n, w)$ be $\varphi_F(x_1, \ldots, x_n, w)$. However, for efficient problem solving, μ_F should be chosen to reflect the minimal modifications required in the interpretation of F. As an example, suppose that we wish to model the assignment statement $U \leftarrow V$, where U and V are program variables. To do so, we could have a function Val that maps program variables to their values, plus an action that updates $\mathrm{Val}(U)$ to be the value of $\mathrm{Val}(V)$. An appropriate update condition $\mu_{\mathrm{Val}}(x, w)$ for this action would then be $(x = U \wedge w = \mathrm{Val}(V))$.

Constant symbols are handled in exactly the same way as function symbols, since the former may be thought of as functions without arguments. Therefore, φ_C is given by

$$\mu_C(w) \vee (\neg \exists w \, [\mu_C(w)] \wedge C = w) \tag{4.4b}$$

Note that Formula (4.4b) is simply a special case of Formula (4.4a) in which $n = 0$.

The syntax of ADL is designed to provide a convenient means of specifying the α, δ, μ, and π formulas that define an action. To illustrate the syntax of ADL, consider the following two actions described in ADL:

$\mathrm{Put}(p, q)$
    PRECOND: $p \neq q$, $p \neq TABLE$, $\forall z \, \neg \mathrm{On}(z, p)$,
                  $[q = TABLE \vee \forall z \, \neg \mathrm{On}(z, q)]$
        ADD: $\mathrm{On}(p, q)$
    DELETE: $\mathrm{On}(p, z)$ for all z such that $z \neq q$

$\mathrm{Assign}(u, v)$
    UPDATE: $\mathrm{Val}(u) \leftarrow \mathrm{Val}(v)$

The first action, Put(p, q), is a block-stacking action for placing a block p on top of an object q, where q may be either another block or the table. The second action, Assign(u, v), simulates a statement that might appear in a programming language for assigning to variable u the value of variable v.

As the examples illustrate, a description in ADL consists of a name, an optional parameter list, and four optional groups of clauses labeled PRECOND, ADD, DELETE, and UPDATE. The PRECOND group consists of a list of formulas that define the set of states in which an action may be performed. Every formula in the list must be true when the action is performed; hence, the precondition π for the action is the conjunction of these formulas. If the list is empty, π is taken to be the formula *TRUE*, meaning that the action may be performed in every state. Thus, the precondition of Assign(u, v) is the formula *TRUE*, whereas the precondition of Put(p, q) is the formula

$$p \neq q \wedge p \neq \textit{TABLE} \wedge \forall z \, \neg\text{On}(z, p) \wedge [q = \textit{TABLE} \vee \forall z \, \neg\text{On}(z, q)]$$

The α and δ formulas for an action are specified by the ADD and DELETE groups, respectively. Each group consists of a set of clauses of the following forms:

(1) $R(t_1, \ldots, t_n)$
(2) $R(t_1, \ldots, t_n)$ if ψ
(3) $R(t_1, \ldots, t_n)$ for all $z_1, \ldots, z_k$
(4) $R(t_1, \ldots, t_n)$ for all $z_1, \ldots, z_k$ such that ψ ,

where R is a relation symbol, $t_1, \ldots, t_n$ are terms, ψ is a formula, and $z_1, \ldots, z_k$ are variable symbols that appear in terms $t_1, \ldots, t_n$ but not in the parameter list. Each of the clauses in an ADD group corresponds to an *add condition*, $\hat{\alpha}_R$, for some relation symbol R. The formula α_R that defines the set of tuples to be added to the interpretation of R is obtained by taking the conjunction of each of the add conditions for R defined in the group. If no add conditions are specified for symbol R, α_R is taken to be the formula *FALSE*, meaning that no tuples are to be added to the interpretation of R. The semantics of the DELETE group is similar to the ADD group except that, in this case, each clause corresponds to a *delete condition*, $\hat{\delta}_R$, for some relation symbol R. The conjunction of the delete conditions for R defines the formula δ_R. If no delete conditions are specified for R, δ_R is taken to be the formula *FALSE*, meaning that no tuples are to be deleted from the interpretation of R. The add/delete conditions that correspond to each of the four types of clauses are listed in the table below:

Clause	$\hat{\alpha}_R(x_1,\ldots,x_n)/\hat{\delta}_R(x_1,\ldots,x_n)$
$R(t_1,\ldots,t_n)$	$(x_1 = t_1 \wedge \cdots \wedge x_n = t_n)$
$R(t_1,\ldots,t_n)$ if ψ	$(x_1 = t_1 \wedge \cdots \wedge x_n = t_n \wedge \psi)$
$R(t_1,\ldots,t_n)$ for all $z_1,\ldots,z_k$	$\exists z_1 \cdots z_n \, (x_1 = t_1 \wedge \cdots \wedge x_n = t_n)$
$R(t_1,\ldots,t_n)$ for all $z_1,\ldots,z_k$ such that ψ	$\exists z_1 \cdots z_n \, (x_1 = t_1 \wedge \cdots \wedge x_n = t_n \wedge \psi)$

Thus, $\alpha_{On}(x,y)$ for $\text{Put}(p,q)$ is given by

$$\alpha_{On}(x,y) \equiv (x = p \wedge y = q).$$

Similarily, $\delta_{On}(x,y)$ is given by

$$\delta_{On}(x,y) \equiv \exists z \, (x = p \wedge y = z \wedge z \neq q),$$

which simplifies to

$$\delta_{On}(x,y) \equiv (x = p \wedge y \neq q).$$

In the above equations, the symbol "$\equiv$" is used to denote equality between formulas. A separate symbol is used so as to avoid possible confusion with the logical symbol "$=$".

The UPDATE group is used to specify the μ-formulas that define the interpretations of the function symbols in the succedent state. The UPDATE group consists of a set of clauses of the following forms:

(1) $C \leftarrow t$

(2) $C \leftarrow t$ if ψ

(3) $C \leftarrow t$ for all $z_1,\ldots,z_k$

(4) $C \leftarrow t$ for all $z_1,\ldots,z_k$ such that ψ

(5) $F(t_1,\ldots,t_n) \leftarrow t$

(6) $F(t_1,\ldots,t_n) \leftarrow t$ if ψ

(7) $F(t_1,\ldots,t_n) \leftarrow t$ for all $z_1,\ldots,z_k$

(8) $F(t_1,\ldots,t_n) \leftarrow t$ for all $z_1,\ldots,z_k$ such that ψ ,

where C is a constant symbol, F is a function symbol, $t_1, \ldots, t_n, t$ are terms, ψ is a formula, and $z_1, \ldots, z_k$ are variable symbols that appear in terms $t_1, \ldots, t_n, t$ but not in the parameter list. Each clause in an UPDATE group corresponds to an *update condition*, $\hat{\mu}_F$, for some function symbol F, or to an update condition, $\hat{\mu}_C$, for some constant symbol C. The formula μ_F that defines the modifications in the interpretation of F is obtained by taking the conjunction of each of the update conditions $\hat{\mu}_F$ defined in the group. Likewise for the formula μ_C. If no update conditions are specified for a function/constant symbol F/C, μ_F/μ_C is taken to be the formula *FALSE*, meaning that no modifications are made in the interpretation of F/C. The update conditions that correspond to each of the eight types of clauses are listed below:

Clause	$\hat{\mu}_C(w)/\hat{\mu}_F(x_1, \ldots, x_n, w)$
$C \leftarrow t$	$(w = t)$
$C \leftarrow t$ if ψ	$(w = t \wedge \psi)$
$C \leftarrow t$ for all $z_1, \ldots, z_k$	$\exists z_1, \ldots, z_k \, (w = t)$
$C \leftarrow t$ for all $z_1, \ldots, z_k$ such that ψ	$\exists z_1, \ldots, z_k \, (w = t \wedge \psi)$
$F(t_1, \ldots, t_n) \leftarrow t$	$(x_1 = t_1 \wedge \cdots \wedge x_n = t_n \wedge w = t)$
$F(t_1, \ldots, t_n) \leftarrow t$ if ψ	$(x_1 = t_1 \wedge \cdots \wedge x_n = t_n \wedge w = t \wedge \psi)$
$F(t_1, \ldots, t_n) \leftarrow t$ for all $z_1, \ldots, z_k$	$\exists z_1 \cdots z_n \, (x_1 = t_1 \wedge \cdots \wedge x_n = t_n \wedge w = t)$
$F(t_1, \ldots, t_n) \leftarrow t$ for all $z_1, \ldots, z_k$ such that ψ	$\exists z_1 \cdots z_n \, (x_1 = t_1 \wedge \cdots \wedge x_n = t_n \\ \wedge w = t \wedge \psi)$

For example, for the Put(p, q) action defined earlier,

$$\mu_A(w) \equiv FALSE \qquad\qquad \mu_C(w) \equiv FALSE$$
$$\mu_B(w) \equiv FALSE \qquad\qquad \mu_{TABLE}(w) \equiv FALSE$$

and, for the Assign(u, v) action,

$$\mu_{\text{Val}}(x, w) \equiv (x = u \wedge w = \text{Val}(v)) \, .$$

As the forgoing discussion demonstrates, ADL has a well-defined semantics. Actions are defined by providing the appropriate add, delete, and update conditions for the appropriate symbols. As long as these formulas obey the constraints imposed earlier, the descriptions in ADL will define a unique set of current-state/next-state pairs. To summarize these constraints, $\alpha_R^a(x_1, \ldots, x_n)$ and $\delta_R^a(x_1, \ldots, x_n)$ must be mutually exclusive for every n-ary relation symbol R, and $\mu_F^a(x_1, \ldots, x_n, w)$ must define a partial function mapping $x_1, \ldots, x_n$ to w for every n-ary function symbol (constant symbol) F. Because actions are described directly in terms of their effects on the state of the world, and not in terms of the formulas they make true/false, ADL avoids the semantic pitfalls of the STRIPS operator language that are discussed by Lifschitz [18].

To reason about what formulas are made true/false by actions described in ADL, *regression operators* [38] are first constructed for these actions. A regression operator for an action described in ADL is a function mapping formulas to formulas that defines the necessary and sufficient conditions that must hold before an action is performed for some condition to be true afterward. Regression operators enable us to determine whether some formula φ holds at a point p in a plan by providing us with a formula ψ that would have to be true in the initial state for φ to be true at point p. The formula ψ can then be compared with the initial state to ascertain the truth of φ at point p. The construction of regression operators from ADL descriptions and their use in plan synthesis are described elsewhere [24, 25].

5. EXAMPLES

In this section, we shall present a number of examples illustrating how multiagent, dynamic-world problems can be formulated and solved as classical planning problems. Let us first consider a specific multiagent, static-world problem. Suppose we have a world consisting of four blocks, A, B, C and D, stacked on a table, A initially on top of B, C atop D, and both B and D resting on the table. Let us suppose further that our goal is to have A on top of D and C on top of B. However, instead of having only a single robot to control, we now have two robots, R_1 and R_2. They may be commanded to both pick up and deposit blocks. But these particular robots are unable to carry more than one block at a time. Their actions can be described in ADL as follows:

PickUp (rbt, blk)

> PRECOND: Robot(rbt), $blk \neq TABLE$, $\forall z \neg$Holding(rbt, z),
>
> $\forall z \neg$Holding(z, blk), $\forall z \neg$On(z, blk)
>
> ADD: Holding(rbt, blk)
>
> DELETE: On(blk, z) for all z

PutDown (rbt, obj)

> PRECOND: Robot(rbt), $obj = TABLE \vee \forall z \neg$On$(z, obj)$
>
> ADD: On(z, obj) for all z such that Holding(rbt, z)
>
> DELETE: Holding(rbt, z) for all z

Both actions require the parameter rbt to designate one of the robot, R_1 or R_2. The PickUp action corresponds to the command that causes robot rbt to pick up object blk. For the robot to do so, blk cannot be the table, the robot cannot be holding any other object, no other robot can be holding blk, and nothing can be on top of blk. After robot rbt performs this action, it will be holding block blk, and block blk will be removed from its prior resting place. The PutDown action corresponds to the command that causes robot rbt to put whatever it is holding on top of object obj. To do so, either obj must be the table or there must be nothing on top of obj. When this action is executed, all objects held by robot rbt are placed on top of obj, with rbt releasing its hold on these objects.

Using the planning technique described in an earlier paper [24], we can obtain the following plan for placing block A atop block D, and block C atop block B:

$$\text{PickUp}\,(R_1, A) \rightarrow \text{PickUp}\,(R_2, C) \rightarrow \text{PutDown}\,(R_1, D) \rightarrow \text{PutDown}\,(R_2, B)$$

To construct a parallel plan, we note that PickUp (R_1, A) and PickUp (R_2, C) can be performed simultaneously by the robots, as can PutDown (R_1, D) and PutDown (R_2, B). However, neither PickUp (R_1, A) nor PickUp (R_2, C) can be executed at the same time as PutDown (R_1, D) or PutDown (R_2, B). Thus, the parallel plan would be to allow PickUp (R_1, A) and PickUp (R_2, C) to be performed simultaneously, after which actions PutDown (R_1, D) and PutDown (R_2, B) could also be concurrent.

Let us now consider a single-agent, dynamic-world problem: specifically, the lunar-landing problem described in Section 3. In this example, the thrust and attitude of the vehicle are adjusted simultaneously by a single robot. We shall assume a two-dimensional version of the problem in which the controls can be set at any point in time to provide a desired acceleration at a desired angular orientation. Once set, the acceleration and orientation are maintained until the next adjustment. If we disregard the possibility of running out of fuel or crashing into the moon, the effect of setting the controls can be formulated in ADL as follows:

Adjust (a, θ, t')

> PRECOND: $t_0 \leq t'$, $min \leq a \leq max$
>
> UPDATE: $a_0 \leftarrow a$, $\theta_0 \leftarrow \theta$, $t_0 \leftarrow t'$
>
> $x(t) \leftarrow \frac{1}{2} a \sin \theta \, (t - t')^2 + v_x(t')(t - t') + x(t')$ fa t st $t \geq t'$
>
> $y(t) \leftarrow \frac{1}{2}(g - a \cos \theta)(t - t')^2 + v_y(t')(t - t') + x(t')$ fa t st $t \geq t'$
>
> $v_x(t) \leftarrow a \sin \theta \, (t - t') + v_x(t')$ fa t st $t \geq t'$
>
> $v_y(t) \leftarrow (g - a \cos \theta)(t - t') + v_y(t')$ fa t st $t \geq t'$

where a is the net acceleration, θ the angular orientation, and t' the time at which the controls are adjusted, and where "fa" is shorthand for "for all", and "st" shorthand for "such that". The constants a_0, θ_0, and t_0 denote the acceleration, orientation, and time of the most recent adjustment, respectively. The functions $x(t)$ and $y(t)$ define the x and y coordinates of the vehicle as functions of time, while $v_x(t)$ and $v_y(t)$ define the component velocities of the vehicle along the x and y axes. Since t_0 is the time of the most recent adjustment, Adjust (a, θ, t') has the precondition that t' be greater than or equal to t_0. Adjust (a, θ, t') also has the precondition that the net acceleration lie within certain bounds, reflecting the limitations of the vehicle's engine. When an adjustment is made, the future is thereby altered, placing the vehicle on a new trajectory. The history of the vehicle's travel, however, is preserved.

The goal of a lunar-landing problem is to land safely within a certain distance of some targeted point. To ensure a safe landing, the x and y velocities must be sufficiently small and the attitude of the vehicle must be sufficiently close to vertical. This goal can be expressed as follows:

$$\exists t\, [\; y(t) = 0 \wedge \; -d_x \leq x(t) \leq d_x \; \wedge \quad 0 \leq v_y(t) \leq d_{v_y}$$
$$\wedge -d_{v_x} \leq v_x(t) \leq d_{v_x} \wedge -d_\theta \leq \; \theta_0 \; \leq d_\theta \;]$$

In the initial state, t_0 would represent the time at which control of the vehicle is turned over to the planner, a_0 would represent the net acceleration at that time, and θ_0 would represent the angular orientation. The functions $x(t)$, $y(t)$, $v_x(t)$, and $v_y(t)$ would have to be defined accordingly, and would have to reflect the position and velocity of the craft at time t_0. In addition, the arithmetic and trigonometric functions would have to be defined. With the appropriate formulas selected for initial-state description, the problem could then be solved by using the techniques presented elsewhere [25].

To give an example of a multiagent, dynamic-world problem, let us again consider a lunar-landing situation, but this time with the thrust and attitude adjusted independently by different robots. Although this is not the most representative of multiagent problems, it does serve to illustrate how the concept of boundary conditions can be used to handle the problem of synergistic simultaneous actions. As discussed in Section 3, by applying this notion, synergistic simultaneous actions can be made to resemble sequential actions. In the case of the lunar-landing problem, we can use acceleration and angular orientation as boundary conditions. This permits us to define the actions for setting the thrust and attitude as follows:

Thrust(a, t')

PRECOND: $t_0 \leq t'$, $min \leq a \leq max$

UPDATE: $a_0 \leftarrow a$, $t_0 \leftarrow t'$

$x(t) \leftarrow \frac{1}{2}a\sin\theta_0\,(t - t')^2 + v_x(t')(t - t') + x(t')$ fa t st $t \geq t'$

$y(t) \leftarrow \frac{1}{2}(g - a\cos\theta_0)(t - t')^2 + v_y(t')(t - t') + x(t')$ fa t st $t \geq t'$

$v_x(t) \leftarrow a\sin\theta_0\,(t - t') + v_x(t')$ fa t st $t \geq t'$

$v_y(t) \leftarrow (g - a\cos\theta_0)(t - t') + v_y(t')$ fa t st $t \geq t'$

Angle(θ, t')

> PRECOND: $t_0 \leq t'$

> UPDATE: $\theta_0 \leftarrow \theta, \ t_0 \leftarrow t'$

$$x(t) \leftarrow \tfrac{1}{2}a_0 \sin\theta \ (t - t')^2 + v_x(t')(t - t') + x(t') \ \ \text{fa} \ t \ \text{st} \ t \geq t'$$

$$y(t) \leftarrow \tfrac{1}{2}(g - a_0 \cos\theta)(t - t')^2 + v_y(t')(t - t') + x(t') \ \text{fa} \ t \ \text{st} \ t \geq t'$$

$$v_x(t) \leftarrow a_0 \sin\theta \ (t - t') + v_x(t') \ \text{fa} \ t \ \text{st} \ t \geq t'$$

$$v_y(t) \leftarrow (g - a_0 \cos\theta)(t - t') + v_y(t') \ \text{fa} \ t \ \text{st} \ t \geq t'$$

Adjusting the thrust does not affect the attitude of the vehicle; hence, the effect of this action is to update the acceleration boundary condition and thus to adjust the vehicle's future trajectory in accordance with the new acceleration and the previous angular orientation. Similarly, adjusting the attitude does not affect the thrust; hence, the effect of this action is to update the angular-orientation boundary condition and to adjust the vehicle's future trajectory in accordance with the new angular orientation and the previous acceleration. By defining the above actions in this manner, we obtain the desired property that performing Thrust(a_1, t_1) followed by Angle(θ_1, t_1) has the same effect as performing Angle(θ_1, t_1) followed by Thrust(a_1, t_1). Furthermore, their combined effect is the same effect as Adjust(a_1, θ_1, t_1). Thus, by using acceleration and angular orientation as boundary conditions, we have effectively made synergistic simultaneous actions resemble sequential actions. A problem involving these actions can therefore be solved by first constructing a sequential plan and then transforming it into a parallel plan as described in Section 3.

Technically speaking, the position and velocity of the vehicle at the time an adjustment is made should also be considered as boundary conditions, since the future motion of the vehicle depends on them. However, it is the thrust and attitude that are being modified directly by the actions; the position and velocity at the time of adjustment are not modified, but instead serve as continuity constraints. This suggests that, when the concept of boundary conditions is applied, it is important to distinguish between those conditions that are modified by an action directly and those that play the role of continuity constraints.

6. SUMMARY

We have shown how some multiagent, dynamic-world problems may be formulated in the classical planning framework, thereby enabling them to be solved using classical planning techniques. The two main obstacles to formulating such problems this way is representing simultaneous actions and representing continuous processes. As was explained, continuous processes can be represented in the classical planning framework by interpreting (1) a state as a chronicle of all that is true, was true, and will be true of the world at every point in time, and (2) a state transition as the initiation of an action or course of action. It was also shown that the classical framework is adequate for handling some simultaneous actions in spite of the fact that actions in that must be performed sequentially. By representing a problem in the appropriate manner, some simultaneous actions can be made to look like sequential ones, permitting their formulation in the classical planning framework. A general approach to representing actions, based on the concept of boundary conditions, was introduced to accomplish this objective. Whether this approach can be applied in all cases is left to subsequent research. In any event, the fact that some simultaneous actions can be represented in the classical planning framework suggests the feasibility of transferring techniques for solving classical planning problems to other frameworks that are specifically designed for modeling simultaneous actions and dynamic processes.

As part of the presentation, ADL, a new language for describing actions and their effects, was introduced. Because it combines the best features of the STRIPS operator language [7] and the situation calculus [20], ADL offers the advantage of both expressive power and notational convenience. Furthermore, ADL avoids the semantic pitfalls of the STRIPS operator language that are discussed by Lifschitz [18]. This is done by describing the effects of actions directly in terms of state transformations, as opposed to transformations on descriptions of states.

Acknowledgments

The research reported herein was conducted at SRI International and was supported by the Office of Naval Research under Contract N00014–85–C–0251. The views and conclusions expressed in this document are those of the author and should not be interpreted as necessarily representing the official policies or endorsements, either expressed or implied, of the Office of Naval Research or the U.S. Government. The author wishes also to thank AT&T Bell Laboratories for providing the facilities to complete the final draft of this report.

References

[1] Allen, J.F. and J.A. Kooman, "Planning Using a Temporal World Model," *Proc. IJCAI-83*, Karlsruhe, West Germany, pp 741–747 (August 1983).

[2] Allen, J.F., "Towards a General Theory of Action and Time," *Artificial Intelligence*, Vol. 23, pp 123–154 (1984).

[3] Chapman, D., "Planning for Conjunctive Goals," Technical Report 802, Artificial Intelligence Laboratory, Massachusetts Institute of Technology, Cambridge, Massachusetts (November, 1985).

[4] Cheeseman, P., "A Representation of Time for Automatic Planning," *Proc. IEEE Int. Conf. on Robotics*, Atlanta, Georgia (March 1984).

[5] Currie, K. and A. Tate, "O-Plan: Control in the Open Planning Architecture," Report AIAI-TR-12, Artificial Intelligence Applications Institute, University of Edinburgh, Edinburgh, Scotland (1985).

[6] Dean, T., "Temporal Imagery: An Approach to Reasoning about Time for Planning and Problem Solving," Research Report 433, Computer Science Department, Yale University, New Haven, Connecticut (October 1985).

[7] Fikes, R.E. and N.J. Nilsson, "STRIPS: A New Approach to the Application of Theorem Proving to Problem Solving," *Artificial Intelligence*, Vol 2, pp 189–208 (1971).

[8] Fikes, R.E., Hart, P. and N.J. Nilsson, "Learning and Executing Generalized Robot Plans," *Artificial Intelligence*, Vol. 3, No. 4, pp 251–288 (1972).

[9] Georgeff, M.P., "A Theory of Action for Multiagent Planning," *Proc. AAAI-84*, Austin, Texas, pp 121–125 (August, 1984).

[10] Georgeff, M.P. and A.L. Lansky, "A System for Reasoning in Dynamic Domains: Fault Diagnosis on the Space Shuttle," Technical Note 375, Artificial Intelligence Center, SRI International, Menlo Park, California (January 1986).

[11] Georgeff, M.P., "Actions, Processes, and Causality," in M.P. Georgeff and A.L. Lansky (eds.), *Reasoning about Actions and Plans: Proceedings of the 1986 Workshop* (Morgan Kaufmann, Los Altos, California, 1987).

[12] Georgeff, M.P., "The Representation of Events in Multiagent Domains," *Proc. AAAI-86*, Philadelphia, Pennsylvania, pp 70–75 (August 1986).

[13] Harel, D., "First-Order Dynamic Logic," *Lecture Notes in Computer Science*, Vol. 68, G. Goos and J. Hartmanis eds. (Springer-Verlag, New York, New York, 1979).

[14] Hayes, P., "The Frame Problem and Related Problems in Artificial Intelligence," in *Artificial and Human Thinking*, A. Elithorn, and D. Jones eds., pp 45–59 (Jossey-Bass, 1973).

[15] Hendrix, G.G., "Modeling Simultaneous Actions and Continuous Processes," *Artificial Intelligence*, Vol. 4, pp 145–180 (1973).

[16] Lansky, A.L., "Behavioral Specification and Planning for Multiagent Domains," Technical Note 360, Artificial Intelligence Center, SRI International, Menlo Park, California (1985).

[17] Lansky, A.L., "A Representation of Parallel Activity Based on Events, Structure, and Causality," in M.P. Georgeff and A.L. Lansky (eds.), *Reasoning about Actions and Plans: Proceedings of the 1986 Workshop* (Morgan Kaufmann, Los Altos, California, 1987).

[18] Lifschitz, V., "On the Semantics of STRIPS," in M.P. Georgeff and A.L. Lansky (eds.), *Reasoning about Actions and Plans: Proceedings of the 1986 Workshop* (Morgan Kaufmann, Los Altos, California, 1987).

[19] Manna, Z., and R. Waldinger, *The Logical Basis for Computer Programming, Volume I: Deductive Reasoning* (Addison-Wesley, Reading, Massachusetts, 1985).

[20] McCarthy, J. and P. Hayes, "Some Philosophical Problems from the Standpoint of Artificial Intelligence," in *Machine Intelligence 4*, B. Meltzer and D. Michie eds., pp 463–502 (Edinburgh University Press, Edinburgh, Scotland, 1969).

[21] McDermott, D., "A Temporal Logic for Reasoning about Processes and Plans," *Cognitive Science*, Vol. 6, pp 101–155 (1982).

[22] McDermott, D., "Generalizing Problem Reduction: A Logical Analysis," *Proc. IJCAI-83*, Karlsruhe, West Germany, pp 302–308 (August 1983).

[23] McDermott, D., "Reasoning about Plans," in *Formal Theories of the Commonsense World*, Hobbs, J.R. and R.C. Moore eds., pp 269–317 (Ablex Publishing, Norwood, New Jersey, 1985).

[24] Pednault, E.P.D., "Preliminary Report on a Theory of Plan Synthesis," Technical Report 358, Artificial Intelligence Center, SRI International, Menlo Park, California (August 1985).

[25] Pednault, E.P.D., *Toward a Mathematical Theory of Plan Synthesis*, Ph.D. thesis, Department of Electrical Engineering, Stanford University, Stanford, California.

[26] Sacerdoti, E.D., "A Stricture for Plans and Behavior," Technical Note 109, Artificial Intelligence Center, SRI International, Menlo Park, California (August 1975).

[27] Shoenfield, J.R., *Mathematical Logic* (Addison-Wesley, Reading, Massachusetts, 1967).

[28] Stefik, M., "Planning With Constraints (MOLGEN: Part 1)," *Artificial Intelligence*, Vol. 16, No. 2, pp 111–140 (May 1981).

[29] Stuart, C, "An Implementation of a Multi-Agent Plan Synchronizer," *Proc. IJCAI-85*, University of California at Los Angeles, Los Angeles, California, pp 1031–1033 (August 1985).

[30] Stuart, C, "A New View of Parallel Activity for Conflict Resolution," in M.P. Georgeff and A.L. Lansky (eds.), *Reasoning about Actions and Plans: Proceedings of the 1986 Workshop* (Morgan Kaufmann, Los Altos, California, 1987).

[31] Suppes, P., *Axiomatic Set Theory* (Dover, New York, New York, 1972).

[32] Sussman, G.J., "A Computational Model of Skill Aquisition," Report AI TR-297, Artificial Intelligence Laboratory, Massachusetts Institute of Technology, Cambridge, Massachusetts (August 1973).

[33] Tate, A., "Goal Structure, Holding Periods and Clouds," in M.P. Georgeff and A.L. Lansky (eds.), *Reasoning about Actions and Plans: Proceedings of the 1986 Workshop* (Morgan Kaufmann, Los Altos, California, 1987).

[34] Van Dalen, D., *Logic and Structure* (Springer-Verlag, Berlin, Germany, 1980).

[35] Vere, S., "Planning in Time: Windows and Durations for Activities and Goals," *IEEE Trans. on Pattern Analysis and Machine Intelligence*, Vol 5., No. 3, pp 246–267 (May 1983).

[36] Vere, S., "Temporal Scope of Assertions and Window Cutoff," *Proc. IJCAI-85*, University of California at Los Angeles, Los Angeles, California, pp 1055–1059 (August 1985).

[37] Vilain, M.B., "A System for Reasoning about Time," *Proc. AAAI-82*, Pittsburgh, Pennsylvania, pp 197–201 (August 1982).

[38] Waldinger, R., "Achieving Several Goals Simultaneously," in, *Machine Intelligence 8*, E. Elcock and D. Michie eds., pp 94–136 (Ellis Horwood, Edinburgh, Scotland, 1977).

Chapter 11

Planning and Execution

Much recent work has dealt with designing mechanisms that can handle rapidly changing environments. Most of this work achieves responsiveness by giving up complex planning for shallow planning or by planning using tightly coupled sensing and action (Rosenschein, 1982; Chapman and Agre, 1987; Hendler and Sanborn, 1987). Some of this work, however, has dealt directly with the issues of how to map from planning to reaction. In this chapter we present four papers that indicate some of the directions in which such work is going.

The first two papers we present describe work by Kaelbling and Rosenschein (1988) in the design of the GAPPS system, a compiler that translates constraint expressions into directly executable circuits for use in robotic control systems. We then present a paper by Georgeff and Lansky (1987) which describes the use of a meta-reasoning system that can choose from a variety of execution-time options based on the goals being pursued by the system. The final paper, by Ambros-Ingerson and Steel (1987), proposes an approach to integrating planning and execution for changing domains using an agenda-driven control structure in which actions that are serially initiated can run concurrently, with information-acquiring actions (for monitoring the environment) included. Omitted for lack of space, but also of interest, is Firby (1989), who demonstrates the use of "reactive action packages" which essentially replace the operators in the system with procedures that include a reactive component. A mechanism for producing such reactions is described in Sanborn and Hendler, 1988.

There is another important dimension to this new work that we have had to omit due to lack of space. This work indicates that an important part of planning in dynamic domains involves making trade-offs—specifically, trading precision in decision making for time in responding to events. (This work is, essentially, the modern descendant of the work of Feldman and Sproull, 1977, Chapter 4.) In the last few years, a number of researchers have attempted to improve the responsiveness of planning systems operating in dynamic domains by directly reasoning about the utility of planning (Dean, 1987; Horvitz, 1988; Russell and Wefald, 1989). This work has involved an examination of reasoning about these trade-offs during plan generation (Kanazawa and Dean, 1989; Heckerman et al., 1989) and during execution (Boddy and Dean, 1989; Horvitz et al., 1989).

Papers referenced herein but not included in this volume:

Boddy, M., and Dean, T. (1989). "Solving Time-Dependent Planning Problems," *Proceedings of the IJCAI-89*, Detroit, MI.

Chapman, D., and Agre, P. (1987). "Abstract Reasoning as Emergent from Concrete Activity," in Georgeff, M., and Lansky, A. (eds.), *Reasoning about Actions and Plans*, Morgan Kaufmann, Los Altos, CA.

Dean, T. (1987). "Intractability and Time-Dependent Planning," in Georgeff, M., and Lansky, A. (eds.), *Reasoning about Actions and Plans*, Morgan Kaufmann, Los Altos, CA.

Firby, J. (1989). "Adaptive Execution in Complex Dynamic Worlds," Doctoral Dissertation, Department of Computer Science, Yale University, New Haven, CT.

Heckerman, D., Breese, J., and Horvitz, E. (1989). "The Compilation of Decision Models," *Proceedings of the 1989 Workshop on Uncertainty in Artificial Intelligence*, Windsor, Ontario, Canada.

Hendler, J., and Sanborn, J, (1987). "Planning and Reaction in Dynamic Domains," *Proceedings of the DARPA Workshop on Planning*, Austin, TX.

Horvitz, E. (1988). "Reasoning Under Varying and Uncertain Resource Constraints," *Proceedings of the AAAI-88*, St. Paul, MN.

Horvitz, E., Cooper, G., and Heckerman, D. (1989). "Reflection and Action Under Scarce Resources: Theoretical Principles and Empirical Study," *Proceedings of the IJCAI-89*, Detroit, MI.

Kanazawa, K., and Dean, T. (1989). "A Model for Projection and Action," *Proceedings of the IJCAI-89*, Detroit, MI.

Rosenschein, S. (1982). "Synchronization of Multi-agent Plans," *Proceedings of the AAAI-82*.

Russell, S., and Wefald, E. (1989). "Principles of Metareasoning," *Proceedings of the First International Conference on Principles of Knowledge Representation and Reasoning*, Morgan Kaufmann, Los Altos, CA.

Sanborn, J., and Hendler, J. (1988). Monitoring and Reacting: Planning in Dynamic Domains, *International Journal of AI and Engineering*, 3(2).

An Architecture for Intelligent Reactive Systems

Leslie Pack Kaelbling
Artificial Intelligence Center
SRI International

and

Center for the Study of Language and Information
Stanford University

Introduction

Any intelligent system that operates in a moderately complex or unpredictable environment must be *reactive*—that is, it must respond dynamically to changes in its environment. A robot that blindly follows a program or plan without verifying that its operations are having their intended effects is not reactive. For simple tasks in carefully engineered domains, non-reactive behavior is acceptable; for more intelligent agents in unconstrained domains, it is not.

This paper presents the outline of an architecture for intelligent reactive systems. Much of the discussion will relate to the problem of designing an autonomous mobile robot, but the ideas are independent of the particular system. The architecture is motivated by three main desiderata:

Modularity: The system should be built incrementally from small components that are easy to implement and understand.

Awareness: At no time should the system be unaware of what is happening; it should always be able to react to unexepected sensory data.

Robustness: The system should continue to behave plausibly in novel situations and when some of its sensors are inoperative or impaired.

Modularity

It is well-established principle of software engineering that the modular design of programs improves modifiability, understandability and reliability [4]. The ability

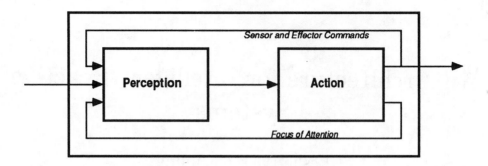

Figure 1: Top-Level Decomposition

to combine simple behaviors in different ways will facilitate experimentation in the design of a complex, reactive system.

Brooks [5] has proposed a *horizontal* decomposition of a robot's control system, in which the fundamental units of the program are task-accomplishing behaviors. Each behavior consists of both an action and a perception component and may, in a structured manner, depend on other behaviors in the system. This is in contrast with the standard approach, which he refers to as *vertical* decomposition—namely, a division into many subsystems, each of which is essential for even the most elementary behavior. Such a vertical decomposition might include the following components: perception, modeling, planning, execution, and effector control.

Horizontal decomposition is attractive because the system can be built and debugged incrementally, allowing the programmer to test simple behaviors, then build more complex ones on top of them. There are some difficulties involved in having perception distributed throughout multiple behavior components, however. The first is that special-purpose perception mechanisms tend to be weak. Raw sensory data is often noisy and open to a variety of interpretations; to make perception robust, it is necessary to exploit the redundancy of different sensor systems and integrate the information from many sources. The second difficulty stems from the fact that, as behaviors become more sophisticated, they tend to be dependent on conditions in the world, rather than on the particular properties of sensor readings. A general perception mechanism can synthesize information from different sensors into information about the world, which can then be used by many behaviors.

We propose a hybrid architecture with one major vertical division between the perception component and the action component. There is to be a horizontal decomposition within each of these components, but any of the action subcomponents may take advantage of any of the perception component's outputs. This component will be decomposed into layers of abstraction, with uninterpreted sensor readings available at the lowest level and sophisticated world models available at the highest level. The action component will consist of a set of behaviors, each of which may undergo some further structural decomposition.

Figure 1 contains a block diagram of this architecture. The system receives raw data from the sensors and emits commands to the sensors and effectors. The action component takes the output of the perception component as input and, as in the preceding case, generates commands to both the sensors and effectors. This differs from many other systems, in which control of the sensors is the responsibility of the perception component. In many situations the sensors are a scarce resource; consequently, decisions must be made about where to point the camera or which ultrasonic sensor to fire at a given time. What should be done in such cases depends critically on the action strategy that is being followed at the moment: Is the robot following a wall on the left? Is it trying to locate an object in front of it? Since the action component is deciding on the strategy of the effectors, it is in the best position to do so for the sensors as well. For the same reasons, if the perception component is limited in the amount of processing it can do, the action component generates an attention command to the perception component, indicating where its computing power should be directed. It might focus attention on a particular region of the visual field, or on a certain kind of object. The entire sensory data stream goes directly into the perception component, along with the both the attention command of the action component and the commands that were last sent to the effectors.

Awareness

For a robot to be truly aware of its environment, it must be designed in such a way that there is a constant bound on the interval between the time the sensors get a particular reading and the time the effectors can react to that information. Many robots simply "close their eyes" while a time-consuming system, such as a planner or vision system, is invoked; the penalty for such unawareness is that perceptual inputs are either lost or stacked up for later processing. During this period of dormancy, a truly dynamic world might change to such an extent that the results of the long calculation would no longer be useful. Worse than that, something might happen that requires immediate action on the part of the robot, but the robot would be oblivious to it.

Our approach to this problem is to have a number of processes that work at different rates. We define a tick to be the constant minimum-cycle time for the entire system. During each tick, the inputs are read, some computation is done, and the outputs are set. If a process cannot complete its computation during its portion of a cycle, either because its run time is inherently non-constant, or has a large constant, it emits a signal indicating that its outputs are not yet available, whereupon its state is saved for resumed execution during the next tick. The Rex language, which is discussed below, allows such a system to be easily constructed.

Robustness

Once again we propose a solution similar to that of Brooks [5]. His system is broken down into *levels of competence* in such a way that, if higher levels break down, the lower levels will still continue to work acceptably. This is especially important for Brooks, since his levels are intended to be built on separate physical devices that can fail independently. Our system, on the other hand, will be implemented on a single piece of hardware, so we will concern ourselves with robustness only in relation to failed sensors or to the possibility of general confusion because of new or unusual situations. We shall refer to these two types of robustness as *perceptual* and *behavioral*.

Perceptual robustness can be achieved by integrating all sensory information into a structure that represents the robot's knowledge or lack of knowledge about the world. If a particular sensor fails and its failure has been detected, the robot's information about the world will be weaker than it would have been if all of the sensors had been working correctly. We say that the information I, carried by an agent is weaker than information I' if and only if the set of possible worlds compatible with I is a superset of the set of possible worlds compatible with I'. Thus, with weaker information, the robot can make fewer discriminations among the states of the world, but it can still be the case that information integrated from the remaining sensors will suffice for reasonable but degraded operation. If a particular behavior depended entirely on a single sensor, there would be no room for graceful degradation; it would simply fail. The problem of detecting sensor failure is a difficult one that we shall not be examining here. Eventually, however, work in fault detection mechanisms will have to be integrated into such a system.

Behavioral robustness depends upon the ability to trigger a system's actions in direct accordance with the strength of available information. Consider a behaviorally robust robot with a high-level path-planning module that generates actions based on a strong model of the environment. If the robot's actual information is insufficient for the path planner to produce a plan—perhaps because the robot has just been switched on or has become lost or confused, that module will simply emit a signal indicating its inability to form a plan. In this case, some less sophisticated module that is capable of operating with weaker information will know what to do; its actions might be directed toward gaining sufficient information to enable the first module to work and avoiding coming to any harm in the process. Another example of behavioral robustness concerns the robot's behavior in case any of the necessary action-computing processes, such as planners or visual matching systems, cannot run in real time. The high-level planning module may not know what to do for several ticks until it has finished computing its plan; during this time, however, lower-level, less competent action modules should be in control, attempting to maintain the status quo and to keep the robot out of danger.

Building Real-time Systems

Rex

Rex is a language designed for the implementation of real-time embedded systems with analyzable information properties [12,8]. It is similar to a hardware description language in that the user declaratively specifies the behavior of a synchronous digital machine. Johnson [7], exploring the idea of using purely functional notation and recursion equations for circuit description, found that it was indeed viable and, moreover, in many ways preferable to standard techniques. He presents techniques for synthesizing digital designs manually from recursion equations. In Rex, the programmer can use both recursion and functional style, as well as having the specifications be translated automatically into hardware descriptions. There are, however, many complex recursion equations that are not automatically translatable into Rex. The declarative nature of Rex makes programs amenable to analysis of semantic and behavioral properties. From a Rex specification, the compiler generates a low-level structural description that can then be simulated by sequential code in C or Lisp.

The resulting machine description can be visualized as a large collection of variables of some data type, D, and code that updates them once per tick. The variables can be divided into *input*, *state*, and *output*. The input variables, conceptually connected directly to the sensors, contain current sensory values at the beginning of each tick. The state variables are updated during each tick as a combined function of the values of the input variables and the old values of the state variables. The output variables, conceptually connected to the effectors, are updated during each tick as a combined function of the inputs and the old values of the state variables. Rex can be thought of as specifying a function $F : D^{i+s} \to D^{s+o}$, where i, s, and o are the numbers of input, state, and output variables, respectively, that maps the values of the inputs and the old values of the state variables into new values of the state variables and outputs. For any machine specified in Rex, the function F is guaranteed to be calculable in constant time. This in turn guarantees that the minimum reaction time (minimum time required for the value of an input to affect the value of an output) also has a constant bound, thereby making all machines defined in Rex real-time.

Embedding Slow Processes in Fast Systems

As control systems become more sophisticated, they almost always involve planning of some sort. Chapman has shown that a general planning problem is undecidable and that many restricted planning problems are intractable [6]; we must therefore consider methods for embedding processes that do not operate in constant time in systems with a constant tick rate. The intractability of planning, as well as other time-consuming problems, usually stems from the need for graph search. There are two methods for implementing search procedures in real-time systems. The first is to exploit the power of parallel processing and devote a large amount of dedicated hardware to doing the search in constant time. The second method is to conserve hardware and to search by using a conventional algorithm, such as backtracking, but to guarantee that the searching process will be "swapped out" in such a way that other processes are assured a chance to react to inputs in real time.

Production systems are often used to perform search and inference in problem solving and planning systems. In many of these systems, the rules are fixed and cannot be changed during execution. If this is the case, an inference net [13] can be explicitly implemented in hardware, allowing all search and inference to take place in parallel in constant time that is proportional to the maximum depth of the net. For many problems, the inference net will require less space than would have been needed to encode a rule interpreter and the production rules implicitly embodied by the net.

In general, any computation can trade time for space. Thus, if sufficient computing hardware is not available to implement large searching processes in parallel, they may be serialized and run on general-purpose hardware. Von Neumann computer architecture is an extreme example of this; it allows huge programs to be run on a very small amount of hardware, trading time for space. We propose a middle ground for embedding processes like planners into real-time systems, using general-purpose searching hardware for the processes that involve search, and iterating the searching process over time, while the other processes continue to run in parallel with it.

Planning

There are two problems that arise when a planner is run in a dynamic environment. The first is that, if the planner takes control of the processor, the robot can no longer respond, even at a reflex level, to events in the environment. The second problem is that, during the process of planning, the environment may have changed to such an extent that the newly created plan is no longer executable in the current situation.

A solution to the first problem is for the planner to work incrementally, doing a few computation steps during each state transition, then storing its state until the next tick. Other parts of the system that react more quickly to changes in the environment will be running in parallel with the planner, and will therefore be able to act even if the planner has not finished its computation. This behavior is in contrast to that of a program that "calls" the planner and waits for it to finish executing before doing anything else. When the planner is finished, it issues the plan; until that time, it emits a signal that says it is not ready yet and has no answer. The specification of a planner that works incrementally and saves its state is written easily in Rex. A similar system might also be constructed using an

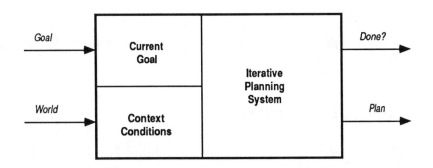

Figure 2: Schematic of an Embedded Planner

operating system with message passing and a round-robin scheduler. This would make it possible for other processes to respond to external events while the planner is working, although the informational analysis of the Rex version is much more tractable.

A planner is typically given a description of some initial state and a goal, and then activated. The planner constructs a plan that depends on the truth of some of the conditions in the initial state; we shall call these *context conditions*. The rest of the initial state is either irrelevant to the plan (for instance, the temperature is irrelevant to planning to go down the hall), or can be handled conditionally during plan execution (the robot might assume that it can navigate around local obstacles without planning). A planner embedded in a real-time system must be especially conscious of its context conditions; otherwise it cannot know whether the plan it is working on will be valid when it is done.

In Figure we present a schematic diagram of a planner that works flexibly in dynamic environments. Its inputs are a goal and the output of the world model; its outputs are a plan and a signal as to whether or not the plan is ready. When it is given a new goal, it remembers that goal and the current values of the context conditions in its local state. It begins planning with respect to those values of the goal and context conditions until the plan has been completed or until the goal or context conditions in the world differ from those that are stored in the planner.

If the goal or context conditions change before the completion of the plan, the planner stores their new values and begins planning again. This scheme has the property that the planner will notice at the earliest instant if its plan is no longer valid because of a change in goal or context conditions, and will therefore start working on a new one. The planner might be made more efficient if, when the goal or context is changed, it tried to salvage parts of the plan in progress. It is true that, if the context conditions or goal vary too rapidly, the planner will never succeed in generating a plan. This would happen only if the planner were not written with adequate generality for the environment in which it is embedded. One way to simplify the design of embedded planners, as well as to make the planning process more efficient, is to use many small planners that are domain-dependent, rather than one large, general, domain-independent planner. Much of the domain knowledge can be "procedurally represented" in a domain-dependent planner, eliminating the need for its run-time manipulation.

The Perception Component

As in the domain of actions, perception can be done at many levels of abstraction. Normally, the higher the level of abstraction, the more processing power is required to integrate new information. Thus, we will break the perception component of this architecture down into several levels of abstraction that can be made to work at different speeds, using the techniques that were applied to the planner in the preceding section. At the lowest level, we might simply store the most recent raw perceptual readings. Since this level requires no interpretation or integration, the data are immediately available to highly time-critical behavior components, such as obstacle-avoidance reflexes. More advanced behaviors will require information that is more robust and abstract. Eventually this will culminate in a representation that integrates data from all of the sensors into a coherent world model. The world model itself might exist at various levels of abstraction, from Cartesian locations of obstacles, to a topological map of interconnections of hallways, doors, and rooms.

It is important to note that these levels of perception may have no direct mapping to the levels of competence in the action component. The highest level of action competence will consist of behaviors at many different levels of abstraction; it thus relies on many or all of the layers of the perception component. It is likely however, that the lower action levels will not make use of the higher perception levels, thereby allowing each of the major components to be constructed incrementally.

For a system to be behaviorally robust, the representation of perceptual data must explicitly encode the robot's knowledge and lack of knowledge about the world. If we consider the propositional case, the robot can stand in three relations to a proposition φ: it can know that φ holds ($K(\varphi)$), it can know that φ doesn't hold ($K(\neg\varphi)$), or it can be unaware as to whether φ holds ($\neg K(\varphi) \wedge \neg K(\neg\varphi)$). If φ were the proposition "I'm about to run into the wall," we might have the following set of action rules:

$$
\begin{aligned}
K(\varphi) &\rightarrow stop \\
K(\neg\varphi) &\rightarrow go \\
\neg K(\varphi) \wedge \neg K(\neg\varphi) &\rightarrow stop \wedge look\_for\_wall
\end{aligned}
$$

These rules do something reasonable in each case of the robot's knowledge, or lack thereof, guaranteeing that it will not hit a wall but will go forward if it knows that such a collision is not imminent. It also tries to strengthen its information in case of uncertainty. For many applications, this approach may have to be extended to the probabilistic case, substituting $P(\varphi) > a \rightarrow \alpha$ for $K(\varphi) \rightarrow \alpha$, where a

is the necessary degree of belief in the proposition φ to make α an appropriate action. We would similarly substitute $P(\varphi) < b$ for $\neg K(\varphi)$ and $b \leq P(\varphi) \leq a$ for $\neg K(\varphi) \wedge \neg K(\neg\varphi)$.

Framework for Hierarchical Control

This section presents a scheme for the hierarchical decomposition of robot control in terms of compositions of behaviors. We define a *behavior* to be a procedure that maps a set of inputs, which in this case are the outputs of the perception module, into a set of outputs to the effectors of the system. Each behavior has the same input/output structure as the action module in Figure 1, with possibly some additional outputs that are intended to be used internally. To compose behaviors, we use procedures called *mediators*. A mediator's inputs are outputs of several *subbehaviors* and the perception module. Since it generates outputs of the same type as a behavior, the complex module consisting of the subbehaviors and a mediator is itself a behavior.

Mediating Behaviors

One scheme for mediation between subbehaviors, described by Kurt Konolige [9], is a "bidding" system in which each behavior outputs in the form of sensor effector commands not only what it wants to do, but also some measure of its "desire" to do it. The mediator decides what to do on the basis of some weighted average of the outputs of the subbehaviors and their respective degrees of urgency. There are two possible difficulties with such a scheme. One is that, when the behaviors are at a higher level than simple motor control, the mediation will have to be more than a simple average; for example, a robot performing the average of going to office A and office B probably won't get far. A logical response to this difficulty is that the two behaviors (the office A behavior and the office B behavior) would have to know something about each other, and so would only request actions that are compatible. But this seems to require mediation again, albeit internal to the behaviors, and it brings us to the second difficulty. One of the greatest advantages of a compositional methodology is that a particular component can be independently designed and tested, then used in more than one place in a system. In Konolige's approach there is something crucially context-dependent about each low-level behavior, since its urgency parameters will have to be tuned for each specific application, depending on what other behaviors it is being combined with.

One approach that appears to overcome these difficulties is to move all the intelligence governing behavior selection into the mediator function itself. In this scheme, the mediator would take the outputs of the subbehaviors, as well as the world model and other perceptual data, as inputs. Then, on the basis of these data, the mediator could output some weighted combination of the input behaviors or, alternatively, simply switch through the output of a particular behavior. If there are very different effectors, it might make sense to perform part of one behavior and part of another; for example, a walking and a talking behavior could be mediated by outputting the speech commands of the talker and the motor commands of the walker. Each behavior can be designed and debugged independently, then used without modification as a building block for other, more complex behaviors. Another advantage of this approach is that proofs of correctness of complex behaviors can be done compositionally. A proof involving a complex behavior need only involve the switching behavior of the mediator and those properties of the subbehaviors that can be proved independently.

Hierarchically Mediated Behaviors

We will approach the design of a robot's action component as a top-down decomposition of behaviors into lower-level behaviors and mediators. At the top level, adopting the scheme of Brooks, we have a number of behaviors that represent different levels of competence at executing the main task of the system. Each behaviors, unlike those of Brooks, computes its outputs independently of the outputs of the other modules. Included in the set of possible outputs of each behavior is `no-command`, a signal denoting that the behavior does not know what to do in the current situation. We have some intuitive idea of what competence is, and, given two modules, can make subjective judgements about which works "better." We hope to formalize the notion of what makes one action or strategy better than another with respect to some goal; since that has not yet been done, however, the balance of this discussion must be based on our intuitive understanding of "better." If the following four properties hold of a system whose top-level mediation function switches through the entire output of the most competent behavior that knows what to do, the system as a whole will always do the best thing of which it is capable, given the available information.

- The lowest level of competence never outputs `no-command`

- No level emits a command other than `no-command` unless it is a correct command

- Lower levels of competence require weaker information

- If any two levels both emit commands in the same tick, the output of the higher level is better

Thus, if the more competent levels fail or have insufficient information to act, the robot will be controlled by a less competent level that can work with weak information until the more competent components recover and resume control.

Within each of the levels of competence, decomposition is based on abstraction rather than competence. The highest-level behavior is constructed by mediating among medium-level behaviors. Those behaviors are constructed by mediating among low-level behaviors. The structure will typically be a graph rather than a tree, since many high-level behaviors will ultimately be constructed from a few low-level ones. In practice, it will also happen occasionally that the hierarchy will not be strict; that is, a certain behavior might be present at two different levels in the graph.

There has been other work exploring the use of a hierarchy of abstraction for reactive control. Albus [1,2,3] in the RCS (Real-time Control System), employs an abstraction hierarchy of "multivariant servos" for controlling factory automation systems. Although his approach is similar to ours, it does not allow the simultaneous combining of components of more than one behavior, even if they are potentially compatible. This is equivalent to having the mediating functions always switch through one entire behavior. Nils Nilsson has proposed using triangle tables as a robot programming language[11]. They were originally used in the SRI robot *Shakey* [10] for plan execution monitoring, but the formalism can be extended to hierarchical systems that are very much like the one described by Albus.

Example

This section presents an example that illustrates the methods of hierarchical decomposition discussed in the preceding section. After sketching the top-level decomposition of a complex behavior into levels of competence, it will show how the most competent module is broken down into levels of abstraction. A block diagram of this example is presented in Figure 3.

The task of this robot is to traverse a very long hall without crashing into anything. It is more important to avoid crashes than to get to the end of the hall. The robot's construction is such as to make it highly unlikely that it can roll straight down the hall without veering into the sides unless it corrects its course along the way. The robot has distance sensors pointing forward and to each side. We decompose this problem into three behaviors at different levels of competence, as follows:

Level 1 This behavior looks at accumulated raw sensor data. If any of the measurements in taken from the front of the robot too short, or a significant interval has elapsed since the last measurement was made by the front sensor, it stops; otherwise it moves forward.

Level 2 This behavior also looks at accumulated raw sensor data. As in the preceding behavior, it stops if the measurements are too short or too old. If it has stopped and cannot move forward, but the sensor data imply that it is safe to turn, the robot turns until the sensor data are no longer too short, then moves. If it is not save to turn, it emits `no-command`.

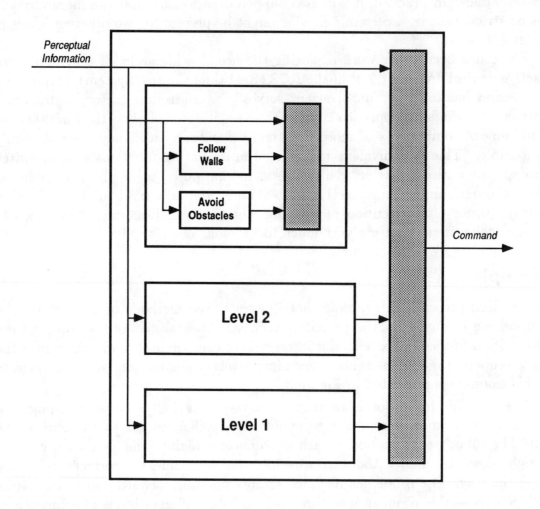

Figure 3: Example of Hierarchies of Competence and Abstraction. (The shaded boxes are mediators).

Level 3 This behavior looks at data that has been combined at a higher level of abstraction. It can tell whether there is a wall to the front or side, how far away it is, and how tight the bounds on its knowledge of its position are. If it knows that there is no wall too close to it,[1] and knows fairly tight bounds on the locations of the walls on either side, it moves in such a way as to go forward in the middle of the hall, staying parallel to the walls. If it does not know this, it emits `no-command`.

This set of behaviors satisfies the rules given above for a correct decomposition. The lowest level always either moves or stops. Each level acts only when it knows the particular action is safe — that is, when executing it will not cause the robot to crash into something. The lowest level requires only sensor readings, which, although weak, are available instantly. The second level requires information about whether it is safe to turn; this information, stronger than that needed by the first level, must be synthesized from the raw sensor readings. The highest level requires very strong wall-location data that must be derived from the aggregation of many sensor readings and knowledge about the world. If each level knows what to do, it is intuitively obvious that the highest-level behavior is "best." It is better to proceed along a hall by staying parallel to the walls than by zig-zagging from side to side (which is what the second behavior is likely to do), or just by going to one side of the hall and stopping when obstructed.

The highest level of competence can be divided into subbehaviors at different levels of abstraction, as shown in Figure 3. The first division is into a behavior that stays parallel to the walls on the sides and one that causes the robot to slow down linearly as a function of its distance to an obstacle in front of it. Each of these behaviors is composed of subbehaviors that cause the robot to move at certain velocities and request certain sensor measurements. Let us assume that each behavior consists of a motor command and sensor command (the robot can poll only one sensor at a time.)

Then, in pseudocode, the `follow-walls` behavior is

```
sensor-command := if left-info-weak then left-sensor
                  else if right-info-weak then right-sensor
                  else *no-op*
motor-command  := if K-location-of-left-wall and
                     K-location-of-right-wall then servo-to-midline
                  else *no-command*
```

This behavior requests a sensor measurement if it has weak information about one side or the other, and returns *no-op* if it has no immediate need for sensor information. If it knows the location of the left and right walls to a close enough tolerance, it performs the behavior that servos to the middle line of the hallway; otherwise, it emits *no-command*, indicating that it does not know what to do.

---

[1] A wall is too close to the robot if it will crash into the wall unless it begins its stopping action immediately.

The `no-crash` behavior is described by

```
sensor-command := if front-info-weak then front-sensor
                  else *no-op*
motor-command := if K-location-of-front-obstacle then linear-speed-limit
                  else *no-command*
```

This behavior requests a sensor measurement from the front sensor if it needs it and, if it knows the location of the nearest obstacle in front to sufficient tolerance, it performs the behavior that causes the robot slow down in proportion its distance from the obstacle. If it does not know that location, it emits *no-command*.

Now it remains only to combine these two behaviors. The mediator is

```
sensor-command := if no-crash-sensor-command = *no-op*
                  then follow-wall-sensor-command
                  else no-crash-sensor-command
motor-command  := if (follow-wall-motor-command = *no-command*) or
                  (no-crash-motor-command = *no-command*)
                  then *no-command*
                  else rescale (follow-wall-motor-command, no-crash-motor-command)
```

If the `no-crash` behavior does not request a sensor command, the mediator does what the `follow-wall` behavior wants to do; otherwise it does what the `no-crash` behavior wants to do. This gives priority to acquiring information that is relevant to the more important goal of avoiding obstacles. If either motor command is *no-command*, the motor command of the mediator will be the same. If both motor commands are defined, the wall-following motor command defines a set of differential velocities for maintaining the heading of the robot down the center of the hall and the crash-avoidance motor command defines a limit for safe speed, given the knowledge of the distance to obstacles in front of the robot. These values are input to the function `rescale` which performs a ratiometric scaling of the servo velocities. This is done so that neither velocity will exceed the speed limit, but their ratio will maintained.

Future Work

This methodology has been applied to simple tasks, such as the one described above, with a large degree of success. As well as expanding the implemented example, we will continue research on the formal specification of goals and the ranking of the "goodness" of behaviors with respect to particular sets of goals. The problem of perceptual organization also requires more attention, with the aim of devising algorithms that use predictions about the environment from old information to facilitate analysis of new information.

Acknowledgments

This work was supported in part by a gift from the Systems Development Foundation, in part by FMC Corporation under contract 147466 (SRI Project 7390), in part by the office of Naval Research under contract N00014-85-C-0251, and in part by General Motors Research Laboratories under contract 50-13 (SRI Project 8662). It was done in the context of programming the SRI Artificial Intelligence Center's mobile robot (Flakey) to perform hallway navigation tasks. Many of these ideas arose from discussions with Stan Rosenschein and debugging sessions with Stan Reifel and Sandy Wells.

References

[1] James S. Albus. *Brains, Behavior, and Robotics*. BYTE Books, Subsidiary of McGraw-Hill, Peterborough, New Hampshire, 1981.

[2] James S. Albus, Anthony J. Barbera, and Roger N. Nagel. Theory and practice of hierarchical control. In *Proceedings of the 23rd IEEE Computer Society International Conference*, 1981.

[3] Anthony J. Barbera, M. L. Fitzgerald, and James S. Albus. RCS: The NBS real-time control system. In *Proceedings of the Robots 8 Conference and Exposition*, Detroit, Michigan, 1984.

[4] Grady Booch. *Software Engineering with Ada*. The Benjamin/Cummings Publishing Company, Menlo Park, California, 1983.

[5] Rodney A. Brooks. A robust layered control system for a mobile robot. Technical Report AIM-864, MIT Artificial Intelligence Laboratory, Cambridge, Massachusetts, 1985.

[6] David Chapman. Planning for conjunctive goals. *Artificial Intelligence*, 32(3):333–378, 1987.

[7] Steven D. Johnson. *Synthesis of Digital Designs from Recursion Equations*. The MIT Press, Cambridge, Massachusetts, 1983.

[8] Leslie Pack Kaelbling and Nathan J. Wilson. Rex programmer's manual. Technical Report 381R, Artificial Intelligence Center, SRI International, Menlo Park, California, 1988.

[9] Kurt Konolige. Personal communication, 1986.

[10] Nils J. Nilsson. Shakey the robot. Technical Report 323, Artificial Intelligence Center, SRI International, Menlo Park, California, 1984.

[11] Nils J. Nilsson. Triangle tables: A proposal for a robot programming language. Technical Report 347, Artificial Intelligence Center, SRI International, Menlo Park, California, 1985.

[12] Stanley J. Rosenschein and Leslie Pack Kaelbling. The synthesis of digital machines with provable epistemic properties. In Joseph Halpern, editor, *Proceedings of the Conference on Theoretical Aspects of Reasoning About Knowledge*, pages 83–98. Morgan Kaufmann, 1986. An updated version appears as Technical Note 412, Artificial Intelligence Center, SRI International, Menlo Park, California.

[13] Patrick Henry Winston. *Artificial Intelligence*. Addison Wesley, Reading, Massachusetts, second edition, 1984.

REACTIVE REASONING AND PLANNING

Michael P. Georgeff
Amy L. Lansky

Artificial Intelligence Center, SRI International
333 Ravenswood Avenue, Menlo Park, California
Center for the Study of Language and Information, Stanford University

Abstract

In this paper, the reasoning and planning capabilities of an autonomous mobile robot are described. The reasoning system that controls the robot is designed to exhibit the kind of behavior expected of a rational agent, and is endowed with the psychological attitudes of belief, desire, and intention. Because these attitudes are explicitly represented, they can be manipulated and reasoned about, resulting in complex goal-directed and reflective behaviors. Unlike most planning systems, the plans or intentions formed by the robot need only be partly elaborated before it decides to act. This allows the robot to avoid overly strong expectations about the environment, overly constrained plans of action, and other forms of overcommitment common to previous planners. In addition, the robot is continuously reactive and has the ability to change its goals and intentions as situations warrant. The system has been tested with SRI's autonomous robot (Flakey) in a space station scenario involving navigation and the performance of emergency tasks.

1 Introduction

The ability to act appropriately in dynamic environments is critical for the survival of all living creatures. For lower life forms, it seems that sufficient capability is provided by stimulus-response and feedback mechanisms. Higher life forms, however, must be able to anticipate future events and situations, and form plans of action to achieve their goals. The design of reasoning and planning systems that are *embedded* in the world and must operate effectively under real-time constraints can thus be seen as fundamental to the development of intelligent autonomous machines.

In this paper, we describe a system for reasoning about and performing complex tasks in dynamic environments, and show how it can be applied to the control of an autonomous mobile robot. The system, called a *Procedural Reasoning System* (PRS), is endowed with the attitudes of belief, desire, and intention. At any given instant, the actions being considered by PRS depend not only on its current desires or goals, but also on its beliefs and previously formed intentions. PRS also has the ability to reason about its own internal state – that is, to reflect upon its own beliefs, desires, and intentions, modifying these as it chooses.

This research has been made possible by a gift from the System Development Foundation, the Office of Naval Research under Contract N00014-85-C-0251, by the National Aeronautics and Space Administration, Ames Research Center, under Contract NAS2-12521, and FMC under Contract FMC-147466.

This architecture allows PRS to reason about means and ends in much the same way as do traditional planners, but provides the reactivity that is essential for survival in highly dynamic and uncertain worlds.

For our the task domain. we envisaged a robot in a space station, fulfilling the role of an astronaut's assistant. When asked to get a wrench, for example, the robot determines where the wrench is kept, plans a route to that location, and goes there. If the wrench is not where expected, the robot may reason further about how to obtain information as to its whereabouts. It then either returns to the astronaut with the desired tool or explains why it could not be retrieved. In another scenario, the robot may be midway through the task of retrieving the wrench 'when it notices a malfunction light for one of the jets in the reactant control system of the space station. It reasons that handling this malfunction is a higher-priority task than retrieving the wrench and therefore sets about diagnosing the fault and correcting it. Having done this, it resumes its original task, finally telling the astronaut.

To accomplish these tasks, the robot must not only be able to create and execute plans, but must be willing to interrupt or abandon a plan when circumstances demand it. Moreover, because the robot's world is continuously changing and other agents and processes can issue demands at arbitrary times, performance of these tasks requires an architecture that is both highly reactive and goal-directed.

We have used PRS with the new SRI robot, Flakey, to exhibit much of the behavior described in the foregoing scenarios, including both the navigational and malfunction-handling tasks [8]. In this paper, we concentrate on the navigational task; the knowledge base used for jet malfunction handling is described elsewhere [6,7].

2 Previous Approaches

Most existing architectures for embedded planning systems consist of a plan constructor and a plan executor. As a rule, the plan constructor formulates an entire course of action before commencing execution of the plan [5,12,14]. The plan itself is typically composed of primitive actions – that is, actions that are directly performable by the system. The rationale for this approach, of course, is to ensure that the planned sequence of actions will actually achieve the prescribed goal. As the plan is executed, the system performs these primitive actions by calling various low-level routines. Execution is usually monitored to ensure that these routines will culminate in the desired effects;

Used by permission of the International Joint Conferences on Artificial Intelligence, Inc.

if they do not, the system can return control to the plan constructor so that it may modify the existing plan appropriately.

One problem with these schemes is that, in many domains, much of the information about how best to achieve a given goal is acquired during plan execution. For example, in planning to get from home to the airport, the particular sequence of actions to be performed depends on information acquired on the way – such as which turnoff to take, which lane to get into, when to slow down or speed up, and so on. To overcome this problem, at least in part, there has been some work on developing planning systems that interleave plan formation and execution [3,4]. Such systems are better suited to uncertain worlds than the kind of system described above, as decisions can be deferred until they *have* to be made. The reason for deferring decisions is that an agent can acquire *more* information as time passes; thus, the quality of its decisions can be expected only to improve. Of course, because of the need to coordinate some activities in advance and because of practical restrictions on the amount of decision-making that can be accommodated during task execution, there are limitations on the degree to which such decisions may be deferred.

Real-time constraints pose yet further problems for traditionally structured systems. First, the planning techniques typically used by these systems are very time-consuming, requiring exponential search through potentially enormous problem spaces. While this may be acceptable in some situations, it is not suited to domains where replanning is frequently necessary and where system viability depends on readiness to act.

In addition, most existing systems are overcommitted to the planning phase of their operations; no matter what the situation or how urgent the need for action, these systems *always* spend as much time as necessary to plan and reason about achieving a given goal before performing any external actions whatsoever. They lack the ability to decide when to stop planning or to reason about possible compromises between further planning and longer available execution time.

Traditional planning systems also rely excessively on constructing plans solely from knowledge about the primitive actions performable by the robot. However, many plans are not constructed from first principles, but have been acquired in a variety of other ways – for example, by being told, by learning, or through training. Furthermore, these plans may be very complex, involving a variety of control constructs (such as iteration and recursion) that are normally not part of the repertoire of conventional planning systems. Thus, although it is obviously desirable that an embedded system be capable of forming plans from first principles, it is also important that the system possess a wealth of precompiled *procedural knowledge* about how to function in the world [6].

The real-time constraints imposed by dynamic environments also require that a situated system be able to react quickly to environmental changes. This means that the system should be able to *notice* critical changes in the environment within an appropriately small interval of time. However, most embedded planning systems provide no mechanisms for reacting in a timely manner to new situations or goals during plan execution, let alone during plan formation.

Another disadvantage of most systems is that they commit themselves strongly to the plans they have adopted. While such systems may be reactive in the limited sense of being able to

replan so as to accomplish fixed goals, they are unable to change their focus completely and pursue new goals when the situation warrants. Indeed, the very survival of an autonomous system may depend on its ability to modify its goals and intentions according to the situation.

A number of systems developed for the control of robots do have a high degree of reactivity [1]. Even SHAKEY [10] utilized reactive procedures (ILAs) to realize the primitive actions of the high-level planner (STRIPS). This idea is pursued further in some recent work by Nilsson [11]. Another approach is advocated by Brooks [2], who proposes decomposition of the problem into *task-achieving* units whereby distinct behaviors of the robot are realized separately, each making use of the robot's sensors, effectors, and reasoning capabilities as needed. Kaelbling [9] proposes an interesting hybrid architecture based on similar ideas.

These kinds of architectures could lead to more viable and robust systems than the traditional robot-control systems. Yet most of this work has not addressed the issues of general problem-solving and commonsense reasoning; the research is instead almost exclusively devoted to problems of navigation and the execution of low-level actions. These techniques have yet to be extended or integrated with systems that can change goal priorities completely, modify, defer, or abandon its plans, and reason about what is best to do in light of the immediate situation.

In sum, existing planning systems incorporate many useful techniques for constructing plans of action in a great variety of domains. However, most approaches to embedding these planners in dynamic environments are not robust enough nor sufficiently reactive to be useful in many real-world applications. On the other hand, the more reactive systems developed in robotics are well suited to handling the low-level sensor and effector activities of a robot. Nevertheless, it is not yet clear how these techniques could be used for performing some of the higher-level reasoning desired of complex problem-solving systems. To reconcile these two extremes, it is necessary to develop reactive reasoning and planning systems that can utilize both kinds of capabilities whenever they are needed.

3 A Reactive Planning System

The system we used for controlling and carrying out the high-level reasoning of the robot is called a *Procedural Reasoning System* (PRS) [6,7]. The system consists of a *data base* containing current *beliefs* or facts about the world, a set of current *goals* or *desires* to be realized, a set of *procedures* (which, for historical reasons, are called *knowledge areas* or KAs) describing how certain sequences of actions and tests may be performed to achieve given goals or to react to particular situations, and an *interpreter* (or *inference mechanism*) for manipulating these components. At any moment, the system will also have a *process stack* (containing all currently active KAs) which can be viewed as the system's current *intentions* for achieving its goals or reacting to some observed situation. The basic structure of PRS is shown in Figure 1. A brief description of each component and its usage is given below.

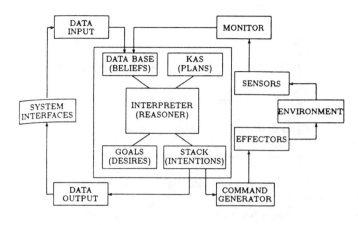

Figure 1: System Structure

3.1 The System Data Base

The contents of the PRS data base may be viewed as representing the current beliefs of the system. Some of these beliefs may be provided initially by the system user. Typically, these will include facts about static properties of the application domain — for example, the structure of some subsystem, or the physical laws that some mechanical components must obey. Other beliefs are derived by PRS itself as it executes its KAs. These will typically be current observations about the world or conclusions derived by the system from these observations.

The data base itself consists of a set of *state descriptions* describing what is believed to be true at the current instant of time. We use first-order predicate calculus for the state description language. Data base queries are handled using unification over the set of data base facts. State descriptions that describe *internal* system states are called *metalevel* expressions. The basic metalevel predicates and functions are predefined by the system. For example, the metalevel expression (goal g) is true if g is a current goal of the system.

3.2 Goals

Goals appear both on the system goal stack and in the representation of KAs. Unlike most AI planning systems, PRS goals represent desired *behaviors* of the system, rather than static world states that are to be [eventually] achieved. Hence goals are expressed as conditions on some interval of time (i.e., on some sequence of world states).

Goal behaviors may be described in two ways. One is to apply a *temporal predicate* to an n-tuple of terms. Each temporal predicate denotes an *action type* or a *set* of state sequences. That is, an expression like "(walk a b)" can be considered to denote the set of state sequences which embody walking actions from point a to b.

A behavior description can also be formed by applying a temporal operator to a state description. Three temporal operators are currently used. The expression (!p), where p is some state description (possibly involving logical connectives), is true

of a sequence of states if p is true of the last state in the sequence; that is, it denotes those behaviors that *achieve p*. Thus we might use the behavior description (!(walked a b)) rather than (walk a b). Similarly, (?p) is true if p is true of the first state in the sequence – that is, it can be considered to denote those behaviors that result from a successful *test* for p. Finally, (#p) is true if p is preserved (maintained invariant) throughout the sequence. Behavior descriptions can be combined using the logical operators ∧ and ∨. These denote, respectively, the intersection and union of the composite behaviors.

As with state descriptions, behavior descriptions are not restricted to describing the external environment, but can also be used to describe the internal behavior of the system. Such behavior specifications are called metalevel behavior specifications. One important metalevel behavior is described by an expression of the form (=> p). This specifies a behavior that places the state description p in the system data base. Another way of describing this behavior might be (!(*belief p*)).

3.3 Knowledge Areas

Knowledge about how to accomplish given goals or react to certain situations is represented in PRS by declarative procedure specifications called *Knowledge Areas* (KAs). Each KA consists of a *body*, which describes the steps of the procedure, and an *invocation condition* that specifies under what situations the KA is useful.

The body of a KA is represented as a graphic network and can be viewed as a plan or plan schema. However, it differs in a very important way from the plans produced by most AI planners: it does not consist of possible sequences of primitive actions, but rather of possible sequences of *subgoals* to be achieved. Thus, the bodies of KAs are much more like the high-level "operators" used in traditional planning systems [13]. They differ in that (1) the subgoals appearing in the body can be described by complex temporal expressions and (2) the allowed control constructs are richer and include conditionals, loops, and recursion.

The invocation part of a KA contains an arbitrarily complex logical expression describing under what conditions the KA is useful. Usually this consists of some conditions on current system goals (in which case, the KA is invoked in a goal-directed fashion) or current system beliefs (resulting in data-directed or *reactive* invocation), and may involve both. Together the invocation condition and body of a KA express a declarative fact about the effects of performing certain sequences of actions under certain conditions.

The set of KAs in a PRS application system not only consists of procedural knowledge about a specific domain, but also includes *metalevel* KAs — that is, information about the manipulation of the beliefs, desires, and intentions of PRS itself. For example, typical metalevel KAs encode various methods for choosing among multiple relevant KAs, determining how to achieve a conjunction of goals, and computing the amount of additional reasoning that can be undertaken, given the real-time constraints of the problem domain. Metalevel KAs may of course utilize knowledge specifically related to the problem domain. In addition to user-supplied KAs, each PRS application contains a set of system-defined default KAs. These are typically domain-independent metalevel KAs.

3.4   The System Interpreter

The PRS interpreter runs the entire system. From a conceptual standpoint, it operates in a relatively simple way. At any particular time, certain goals are active in the system and certain beliefs are held in the system data base. Given these extant goals and beliefs, a subset of KAs in the system will be relevant (i.e., applicable). One of these relevant KAs will then be chosen for execution by placing it on the process stack.

In the course of executing the chosen KA, new subgoals will be posted and new beliefs derived. When new goals are pushed onto the goal stack, the interpreter checks to see if any new KAs are relevant, chooses one, places it on the process stack, and begins executing it. Likewise, whenever a new belief is added to the data base, the interpreter will perform appropriate consistency maintenance procedures and possibly activate other relevant KAs. During this process, various metalevel KAs may also be called upon to make choices among alternative paths of execution, choose among multiple applicable KAs, decompose composite goals into achievable components, and make other decisions.

This results in an interleaving of plan selection, formation, and execution. In essence, the system forms a partial overall plan, determines a means of accomplishing the first subgoal of the plan, acts on this, further expands the near-term plan of action, executes further, and so on. At any time, the plans the system is intending to execute (i.e., the selected KAs) are both *partial* and *hierarchical* — that is, while certain general goals have been decided upon, the specific means for achieving these ends have been left open for future deliberation.

Unless some new fact or request activates some new KA, PRS will try to fulfill any intentions it has previously decided upon. But if some important new fact or request does become known, PRS will reassess its goals and intentions, and then perhaps choose to work on something else. Thus, not all options that are considered by PRS arise as a result of means-end reasoning. Changes in the environment may lead to changes in the system's beliefs, which in turn may result in the consideration of new plans that are not means to any already intended end. PRS is therefore able to *change its focus completely* and pursue new goals when the situation warrants it. PRS can even alter its intentions regarding its own reasoning processes – for example, it may decide that, given the current situation, it has no time for further reasoning and so must act immediately.

3.5   Multiple Asynchronous PRSs

In some applications, it is necessary to monitor and process many sources of information at the same time. Because of this, PRS was designed to allow several instantiations of the basic system to run in parallel. Each PRS instantiation has its own data base, goals, and KAs, and operates asynchronously relative to other PRS instantiations, communicating with them by sending messages. The messages are written into the data base of the receiving PRS, which must then decide what to do, if anything, with the new information. As a rule, this decision is made by a fact-invoked KA (in the receiving PRS), which responds upon receipt of the external message. In accordance with such factors as the reliability of the sender, the type of message, and the beliefs, goals, and current intentions of the receiver, it is deter-

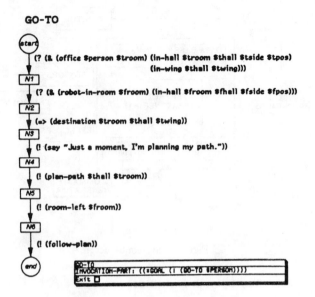

Figure 2: The Top-Level Strategy

mined what to do about the message – for example, to acquire a new belief, establish a new goal, or modify intentions.

4   The Domain Knowledge

The scenario described in the introduction includes problems of route planning, navigation to maintain the route, and such tasks as malfunction handling and requests for information. We shall concentrate herein on the tasks of route planning and navigation. However, it is important to realize that the knowledge representation provided by PRS is used for reasoning about all tasks performed by the system.

The way the robot (under the control of PRS) solves the tasks of the space station scenario is roughly as follows. To reach a particular destination, it knows that it must first plan a route and then navigate to the desired location (see the KA depicted in Figure 2). In planning the route, the robot uses knowledge of the station's topology to work out a path to the target location, as is typically done in navigational tasks for autonomous robots. The topological knowledge is not detailed, stating simply which rooms are in which corridors and how the latter are connected. The route plan formed by the robot is also high-level, typically having the following form: "Travel to the end of the corridor, turn right, then go to the third room on the left." The robot's knowledge of the problem domain's topology is stored in its data base, while its knowledge of how to plan a route is represented in various route-planning KAs. Throughout this predictive-planning stage, the robot remains continuously reactive. Thus, for example, should the robot notice indication of a jet failure on the space station, it may well decide to interrupt its route planning and attend instead to the task of remedying the jet problem.

Once a plan is formed by the route-planning KAs, that plan must be used to guide the activities of the robot. To achieve this, we defined a group of KAs that react to the presence of a plan (in the data base) by translating it into the appropriate sequence of subgoals. Each leg of the original route plan generates subgoals – such as turning a corner, travelling along the hallway, and updating the data base to indicate progress. The second group of navigational KAs reacts to these goals by actually doing the work of reading the sonars, interpreting the readings, counting doorways, aligning the robot in the hallway, and watching for obstacles up ahead.

ROOM-LEFT

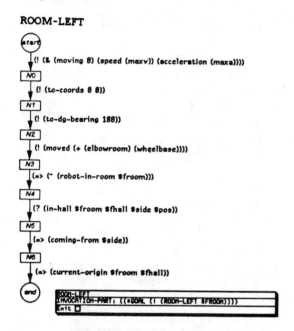

Figure 3: Route Navigation KA

FOLLOW-PLAN

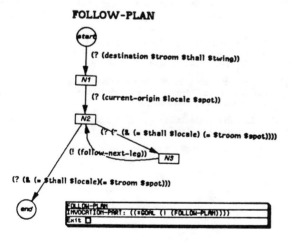

Figure 4: Plan Interpretation KA

For example, let us consider the KAs in Figures 3 and 4. After having used the KA in Figure 2 to plan a path, the robot acquires the goal (!(room-left $froom)), where the variable $froom is bound to some particular constant representing the room that the robot is trying to leave. The KA in Figure 3 will respond, causing the robot to perform the steps for leaving the given

room. The last step in this KA will insert a fact into the system data base of the form (current-origin $froom $fhall), where the variables are again bound to specific constants. Next, the KA in Figure 2 issues the command (!(follow-plan)). This activates the KA in Figure 4, which assures that each leg of the plan is followed until the goal destination is reached. Beliefs of the form (current-origin $locale $spot) are repeatedly updated to readjust the robot's bearings and knowledge about its whereabouts.

A third group of KAs reacts to contingencies encountered by the robot as it interprets and follows its path. These will include KAs that respond to the presence of an obstacle ahead or the fact that an emergency light has been seen. Such reactive KAs are invoked solely on the basis of certain facts' becoming known to the robot. Implicit in their invocation, however, is an underlying goal to "avoid obstacles" or "remain safe."

Yet other KAs perform the various other tasks required of the robot [7]. Metalevel KAs choose among different means of realizing any given goal and determine the respective priority of tasks when mutually inconsistent goals arise (such as diagnosing a jet failure and fetching a wrench). Each KA manifests a self-contained behavior, possibly including both sensory and effector components. Many of these KAs can be simultaneously active, performing their function whenever they may be applicable. Thus, while trying to follow a path down a hallway, an obstacle avoidance procedure may simultaneously cause the robot to veer from its original path. We elsewhere provide a more detailed description of the KAs used by the robot [8].

5 Discussion

The system as described here was implemented using the new SRI robot, Flakey, to accomplish much of the two scenarios described in the introduction. In particular, the robot managed to plan a path to the target room, maneuver its way out of the room in which it was stationed, and navigate to its destination via a variety of hallways, intersections, and corners. It maintained alignment in the hallways, avoided obstacles, and stopped whenever its path was completely blocked. If it noticed a jet malfunction on the space station (simulated by human interaction via the keyboard), it would interrupt whatever it was doing (route planning, navigating the hallways, etc.) and attend to diagnosing the problem. The diagnosis performed by the robot was quite complex and followed actual procedures used for NASA's space shuttle [7].

The features of PRS that, we believe, contributed most to this success were (1) its partial planning strategy, (2) its reactivity, (3) its use of procedural knowledge, and (4) its metalevel (reflective) capabilities. The partial hierarchical planning strategy and the reflective reasoning capabilities of PRS proved to be well suited to the robot application, yet still allowed the system to plan ahead when necessary. By finding and executing relevant procedures only when sufficient information was available, the system stood a better chance of achieving its goals under the stringent real-time constraints of the domain. For example, the method for determining the robot's course was dynamically influenced by the situation, such as whether the robot was between two hallway walls, adjacent to an open door, at a T-intersection, or passing an unknown obstacle.

Because PRS expands plans dynamically and incrementally, there were also frequent opportunities for it to react to new situations and changing goals. For example, when the system noticed a jet-fail alarm while it was attempting to fetch a wrench, it had the ability to reason about the priorities of these tasks and, if it so decided, to suspend the wrench-fetching task while it attended to the jet failure. Indeed, the system even continued to monitor the world while it was *planning* its route and could interrupt the planning whenever the situation demanded.

The wealth of procedural knowledge possessed by the system was also critical in allowing the robot to operate effectively in real-time and to perform a variety of very complex tasks. In particular, the powerful control constructs allowed in KAs (such as conditionals, loops, and recursion) proved highly advantageous. PRS also makes it possible to have a large number of diverse KAs available for achieving a goal. Each may vary in its ability to accomplish a goal, as well as in its applicability in particular situations. Thus, if there is insufficient information about a given situation to allow one KA to be used, another (perhaps one less reliable) might be available instead. Parallelism and reactivity also helped in providing robustness. For example, if one PRS instantiation were busy planning a route, other instantiations could remain active, monitoring environmental changes, keeping the robot in a stable configuration, and avoiding dangers. This has much in common with, and yields the same advantages as, the vertical robot architecture proposed by Brooks [2].

The metalevel reasoning capabilities of PRS were particularly important in managing the application of the various KAs in different situations. Such capabilities can be critical in deciding how best to meet the real-time constraints of a domain. However, the current system was really too simple to serve as an adequate test of the system's metalevel reasoning abilities; indeed, the system performed quite well with only a few [well-chosen] metalevel KAs.

Despite these encouraging results, the research is only in its initial stages and there are a number of limitations that still need to be addressed. First, there are many assumptions behind the procedures (KAs) used. For example, we have assumed that hallways are straight and corners rectangular and that all doors are open and unobstructed. A greater variety of KAs and increased parallelism would also have been preferable, allowing the robot to perform its tasks under more demanding conditions. For example, we could have included many additional low-level procedures for, say, avoiding dangers and exploring the surroundings. Finally, PRS does not reason about other subsystems (i.e., other PRS instantiations) in any but the simplest ways. However, the message-passing mechanisms we have employed should allow us to integrate more complex reasoning about interprocess communication.

Acknowledgments

Marcel Schoppers carried out the experiment described here. Pierre Bessiere, Joshua Singer, and Mabry Tyson helped in the development of PRS. Stan Reifel and Sandy Wells designed Flakey and its interfaces, and assisted with the implementation described herein. We have also benefited from our participation and interactions with members of CSLI's Rational Agency Group (RATAG), particularly Michael Bratman, Phil Cohen, Kurt Konolige, David Israel, and Martha Pollack. Leslie Pack Kaelbling, Stan Rosenschein, and Dave Wilkins also provided helpful advice and interesting comments.

References

[1] J. S. Albus. *Brains, Behavior, and Robotics*. McGraw-Hill, Peterborough, New Hampshire, 1981.

[2] R. A. Brooks. *A Robust Layered Control System for a Mobile Robot*. Technical Report 864, Artificial Intelligence Laboratory, Massachusetts Institute of Technology, Cambridge, Massachusetts, 1985.

[3] P.R. Davis and R.T. Chien. Using and reusing partial plans. In *Proceedings of the Fifth International Joint Conference on Artificial Intelligence*, page 494, Cambridge, Massachussets, 1977.

[4] E. H. Durfee and V. R. Lesser. Incremental planning to control a blackboard-based problem solver. In *Proceedings of the Fifth National Conference on Artificial Intelligence*, pages 58–64, Philadelphia, Pennsylvania, 1986.

[5] R. E. Fikes and N. J. Nilsson. STRIPS: a new approach to the application of theorem proving to problem solving. *Artificial Intelligence*, 2:189–208, 1971.

[6] M. P. Georgeff and A. L. Lansky. Procedural knowledge. *Proceedings of the IEEE Special Issue on Knowledge Representation*, 74:1383–1398, 1986.

[7] M. P. Georgeff and A. L. Lansky. *A System for Reasoning in Dynamic Domains: Fault Diagnosis on the Space Shuttle*. Technical Note 375, Artificial Intelligence Center, SRI International, Menlo Park, California, 1986.

[8] M. P. Georgeff, A. L. Lansky, and M. Schoppers. *Reasoning and Planning in Dynamic Domains: An Experiment with a Mobile Robot*. Technical Note 380, Artificial Intelligence Center, SRI International, Menlo Park, California, 1987.

[9] L. P. Kaelbling. An architecture for intelligent reactive systems. In *Reasoning about Actions and Plans: Proceedings of the 1986 Workshop*, Morgan Kaufmann, Los Altos, California, 1987.

[10] N. J. Nilsson. *Shakey the Robot*. Technical Note 323, Artificial Intelligence Center, SRI International, Menlo Park, California, 1984.

[11] N. J. Nilsson. *Triangle Tables: A Proposal for a Robot Programming Language*. Technical Note 347, Artificial Intelligence Center. SRI International, Menlo Park, California, 1985.

[12] S. Vere. Planning in time: windows and durations for activities and goals. *IEEE Transactions on Pattern Analysis and Machine Intelligence*, 5(3):246–267, 1983.

[13] D. E. Wilkins. Domain independent planning: representation and plan generation. *Artificial Intelligence*, 22:269–301, 1984.

[14] D. E. Wilkins. Recovering from execution errors in SIPE. *Computational Intelligence*, 1:33–45, 1985.

Integrating Planning, Execution and Monitoring*

José A. Ambros-Ingerson
Dept. of Info. and Computer Science
University of California
Irvine, CA 92717
jambros@ics.uci.edu

Sam Steel
Dept. of Computer Science
University of Essex
Colchester, CO4 3SQ
United Kingdom

Abstract

IPEM, for Integrated Planning, Execution and Monitoring, provides a simple, clear and well defined framework to integrate these processes. Representation integration is achieved by naturally incorporating execution and monitoring information into [Chapman, 1987] TWEAK's partial plan representation. Control integration is obtained by using a production system architecture where IF-THEN rules, referred to as flaws and fixes, specify partial plan transformations. Conflict resolution is done using a scheduler that embodies the current problem solving strategy.

Since execution and plan elaboration operations have been designed to be independently applicable, and execution of an action is a scheduling decision like any other, the framework effectively supports interleaving of planning and execution (IPE). This renders a local ability to replan after both unexpected events and execution failure.

The framework has served as the basis for an implemented hierarchical, nonlinear planning and execution system that has been tested on numerous examples, on various domains, and has shown to be reliable and robust.

1   Introduction

As early as 1974, [Sacerdoti, 1974] writes "[F]or a system that deals with complex problems in a real world, as opposed to a simulated one, it is undesirable to solve an entire problem with an epistemologically adequate plan. There are too many reasonably likely outcomes for each real-world operation." (133) Further on he suggests that this can be achieved in a hierarchy of abstraction spaces where "[T]he process of alternatively adding detailed steps to the plan and then actually executing some steps can continue until the goal is achieved." (134)

This problem solving strategy needs a framework that allows interleaving planning and execution, and furthermore, a control policy to indicate when to plan and when to execute.

*The research reported herein has been partly supported by an Overseas Research Student Award by the CVCP of the UK (ORS/85281); the Teamwork Project funded by the SERC of the UK (GR/C/44938); and Hewlett Packard México through a fellowship administered by UC-Mexus. This research has *not* been supported by a military agency. Any use of the results presented here for military purposes is contrary to the intentions of this research.

IPEM is an attempt to provide such framework, not only to support Interleaving of Planning and Execution (IPE) but also to support replanning in dynamic environments where unexpected events can occur, and where actions can fail to bring about their intended effects.

We should note that IPE is present in replanning, planning in dynamic environments, plan repair, etc. If a system is to execute its plans, IPE will be the norm and not the exception.

The present document presents an overview of the IPEM framework and system. For a detailed description please see [Ambros-Ingerson, 1987].

2   Related Work

IPEM relates to other work in the field along three important dimensions:

1. *The representation used for actions and plans.* This relates it to planning systems like STRIPS [Fikes and Nilsson, 1971], NOAH [Sacerdoti, 1974], NONLIN [Tate, 1977], and more recently, TWEAK [Chapman, 1987].

2. *The control mechanism used in the elaboration of the plan.* The great majority of systems use fixed control strategies. Alternatives explored have been MOLGEN [Stefik, 1981], Bartle's Cross-Level Planning [Bartle, 1986] and, in Blackboard Architectures, the use of a task scheduler as in HEARSAY-II [Lesser and Erman, 1977], which is the approach taken by IPEM and in Tate's O-Plan system [Currie and Tate, 1985].

3. *The execution monitoring and replanning capabilities.* Very few planning systems execute their plans (either controlling some robot or in a simulated environment) and consequently aren't faced with this problem. Of those that do the most relevant are PLANEX [Fikes, 1971] (the execution module for STRIPS), NASL [McDermott, 1978], ELMER-a taxi driver in a simulated city- [McCalla and Reid, 1982], Phil Hayes's work on replanning using dependency records [Hayes, 1975], and [Wilkins, 1985] addressing the issue of recovering from execution errors in SIPE. More recently attention has been devoted to reactive planning; e.g., the work of [Georgeff and Lansky, 1987] on procedural logic and [Schoppers, 1987] on universal plans.

3   IPEM: Framework and Implementation

The IPEM system was designed with the goal of supporting interleaving planning and execution. An integrative approach requires that both execution and planning decisions be based upon and recorded on a common representation. We use a partial plan representation similar to the one used in other systems (e.g., TWEAK), extended to include the current world description, the actions in the process of being executed, etc. We also maintain a decision list that records the history of the problem solving process (e.g., for backtracking).

A problem solving strategy that interleaves planning and execution should not be constrained by dependencies between planning and execution operations. Thus, all our transformations – the flaws and fixes that are used to elaborate and execute a plan – were designed to preserve the well-formedness and semantics of partial plans and can be applied independently of each other.

Our bias has been to design plan transformations that are clean, simple and composable, instead of powerful ones, that are often complex and ad-hoc. Complex powerful transformations are obtained by the application of a sequence of simple ones.

We use a production system architecture since it provides the flexibility in control that we need [Lesser and Erman, 1977]. IF-THEN rules map to flaws and fixes in our framework. A flaw is a property or condition in a partial plan that corresponds to the IF part of an IF-THEN rule; each fix – there is usually more than one – corresponds to the THEN part, and specifies a plan transformation to get rid of (i.e., fix) the flaw. Conflict resolution is done using a scheduler that embodies the current problem solving strategy along with weak and domain specific heuristics. Alternative options at a choice point are retained so that full backtracking is supported whenever possible.

IPEM has been implemented in C-Prolog at Essex (Sun3/50 and GEC-63) as the core of a multi-actor planning and execution system [Doran, 1987]. It allows the user to input unexpected events at any stage of execution and plan development. The examples presented here, and others that involve interactions in a multi-actor setting [Doran, 1986], run satisfactorily. The system is currently being used at Essex for research in plan delegation and organization emergence [Doran, 1988].

3.1 Assumptions

Our action representation is – by historical accident, since it was developed independently – almost identical to Chapman's TWEAK, so all his assumptions are our assumptions (e.g., STRIPS assumption).

We further assume a continuously updated Current World Description (CWD), in the form of a set of ground (i.e., variable free) propositions. We do not assume the description is complete but we do assume it contains no errors of commission. We don't make the closed world assumption. Note however, that:

- we do not assume a static world – the CWD can change while the plan is being elaborated, possibly making the current partial plan inapplicable;

- actions can fail to achieve its intended effects; partial success is exploited;

- actions are not assumed to achieve their effects immediately – in fact, different effects of the same action can have different delays without preventing the execution of those parts of the plan that can be safely executed, and;

- we don't assume the CWD holds all the information

needed to elaborate a complete, detailed plan at planning onset – so the problem may be unsolvable without interleaving planning and execution.

We say that an incomplete (partial) plan P *necessarily* satisfies property S if S holds in every possible completion (elaboration) of P. It *possibly* satisfies S if there is at least one completion that satisfies S. See [Chapman, 1987] for more details.

3.2 Plan Elaboration

The plan transformations used to elaborate the plan are very similar to those used in other systems (e.g., NONLIN, TWEAK). We will only give a brief description here.

A (well-formed) partial plan[1] consists of:

1. a partially ordered set of actions including two special ones, BEGIN (the minimum) and END (the maximum) – the postconditions (effects) of BEGIN are the propositions in the CWD and the goals to be achieved are the preconditions of END.

2. a set of (protection) ranges – each range connects a postcondition (supplier) with a precondition (consumer) indicating the (sub)goal dependency and requiring both propositions to necessarily codesignate (necessary codesignation is equivalent to unification). Note that the supplier has to be necessarily before the consumer.

The initial partial plan has of two actions, BEGIN and END, to which the following transformations are applied.

3.2.1 Unsupported Precondition; Reduce

An action A in the plan with a precondition with no range (i.e., it has no assigned producer) has an *unsupported precondition* flaw. The postcondition to be used as producer for the new range can be assigned in any of three ways:

1. by simple establishment on an action already in the plan which is necessarily before A (*reduction prior*), or

2. by simple establishment on an action B already in the plan which is possibly before A (*reduction parallel*). B is now constrained to be necessarily before A; or

3. on a new step (action) now added to the plan (*reduction new*).

3.2.2 Unresolved Conflict; Linearize

A plan with a range R that protects proposition p and an action A, possibly after the producer and possibly before the consumer of R that asserts the negation of q, where p and q necessarily codesignate, has an *unresolved conflict* flaw (clobbering). This is fixed by promotion (A is constrained to be necessarily after the consumer of R) or demotion (A is constrained to be necessarily before the producer of R). In both cases the plan is partially *linearized*.

3.2.3 Unexpanded Action; Expand

A plan with an action which is expandable (i.e., not primitive) has an *unexpanded action* flaw. Actions and their expansions up and down the hierarchy are linked

---

[1]See [Ambros-Ingerson, 1985] for a detailed definition of well-formed partial plan.

by their pattern – an *action based description* (e.g., 'dance *style*') – and codesignation of patterns constrain variable bindings in the same way as with ranges. Expansion consists of replacing such action (together with the ranges attached to it) with an appropriate expansion instance – a partial plan in itself (e.g., a sequence of foot moves that realize the dance).

This contrasts with the *state based description* expressed through pre and post-conditions that reduction uses (e.g., an action that takes 'foot@loc1' to 'foot@loc2').

3.2.4 Completeness and Correctness

A comparison between IPEM's and TWEAK's plan transformations shows that IPEM has no fixes equivalent to separation and white night while TWEAK has no action expansions. Can we claim IPEM complete and correct?

Correctness follows from the fact that both IPEM and TWEAK detect the same set of flaws. Provided expansion schemas are correct, their inclusion in the plan can't generate incorrect plans (although they can certainly introduce new flaws). In fact, action expansions can be defined in terms of a sequence of reductions and linearizations.

Although our clobbering (unresolved conflict) definition is narrower than TWEAK's (it requires necessary instead of possible codesignation), we can show that they only yield different results on plans that are complete except for unbound variables in the post-conditions of some action(s). There is more than one way to define the semantics of executing such an action. We return to this issue in Section 5.

Completeness follows from noticing that a white knight fix is equivalent to replacing a range with a far producer for one with a closer one. This transformation can be avoided by selecting the final producer correctly in the first place. The same argument holds for separation; it can be avoided by selecting bindings right in the first place. Note that the completeness claim has to be dropped if unexpected events or execution failure is allowed, since the notion is ill defined in this case.

What *can* be affected is the efficiency of plan generation. If used with the same search regime, IPEM will probably backtrack more often because it posts more stringent constraints than it needs to. Our selection of few fixes however, matches our bias for simplicity referred to previously.

3.3 Plan Monitoring and Execution

We extend the action representation to accommodate the necessities of execution and monitoring. We associate a procedure and a time-out with every primitive action as explained below.

3.3.1 Unsupported Range; Excise Range

A plan with a range R produced by BEGIN, protecting a proposition no longer in the CWD, has an *unsupported range* flaw. Note that ranges produced by BEGIN are precisely those propositions in the CWD that are currently relied upon (assumed) by the partial plan.

Excising R fixes this flaw but automatically creates an unsupported precondition on R's consumer. On the other hand, since the codesignation constraint is also removed (it is part of the range) new bindings might be permissible.

The effect of the REINSTANTIATE operator in SIPE [Wilkins, 1985] is analogous to the application of an ex-

cise range followed by a reduction prior on BEGIN. We return to this relationship in Section 4.

3.3.2 Unexecuted Action; Execute

A plan with an action ready for execution has an *unexecuted action* flaw. We consider an action A ready for execution if

- A is primitive and not END;
- all its preconditions have ranges produced by BEGIN, none of which is unsupported;
- it is immediately after an executed action (BEGIN is considered executed);
- it is not involved in an unresolved conflict flaw; and
- there is no "live" action B (i.e., not timed-out) before A that expects a post-condition that can clobber any of A's post-conditions.

Executing the action consists of :

- adding order constraints so that all parallel actions are made necessarily after A;
- calling the associated procedure (after substitution of the appropriate bindings) which in turn should instruct some effector to carry out a movement, a measurement, etc.;
- if active monitoring by a lower level system is desired, posting the action's postconditions as expected; and
- recording that the action has been executed.

Note that the action is kept in the plan (see time-out below).

Although this execution model does not allow simultaneous execution initiation, it does allow the execution initiation of actions before their predecessors have finished (timed-out). Thus, if the planner's cycle is fast with respect to execution completion times, actions executing in parallel can be present.

3.3.3 Timed Out Action; Excise Action

An executed action *times out* when no further effects are expected to come about as consequence of its execution. Note that time-out is not defined in terms of success or failure; every action must time-out, whether it achieved its intended effects or not.

Fixing this flaw entails removing the action – together with all the ranges for which some postcondition is a producer or some precondition a consumer – from the plan.

We previously pointed out that actions are kept in the plan when executed. It's important to note that this is consistent with the semantics of an action in a partial plan. In fact. since incorporating the expected effects into the postconditions of BEGIN would violate the semantics of the CWD. deleting the action from the partial plan would necessitate the creation of new structures to record the expected effects and their interaction with other parts of the plan. However, this is what planning is all about and is done for every action in the plan. So why duplicate this effort in another structure? An unexecuted action and an executed one that hasn't timed-out are both predicting a future state of affairs over which the same kind of planning reasoning applies.

3.3.4 Unextended Range; Extend Range

If, in a plan, we can remove a range R and replace it with a range R' where

- *R* and *R'* have the same consumer;
- the producer of *R'* is before the producer of *R*; and
- the new range *R'* does not create an unresolved conflict flaw (clobber);

we have an *unextended range* flaw. The fix is to replace *R* with *R'*, which can be seen as extending range *R* on the producer side to the location of the producer of *R'*; hence its name: *range extension*.

We distinguish the special case where the producer of the new range is BEGIN and the consumer is a post-condition of an executed action *A*. In this case the appearance of the proposition at BEGIN that makes the extension possible can be correlated with a (partially, at least) successful execution of *A*.

The general case where no execution has taken place can be considered to be a serendipitous occurrence, especially if the extension is to some postcondition of BEGIN. Range extensions have to be done with care in the general case (only) since there is a tradeoff between having long ranges, that are more likely to generate interactions, and short ones, that take no advantage of serendipitous occurrences to remove redundant actions.

3.3.5   Redundant Action; Excise Action

A plan with an action *A* not producing for any range (i.e., no range has *A* as producer) has a *redundant action* flaw. Excising the action – its fix – can result in further action redundancies since ranges are removed along with the action.

3.4   Control: The Scheduler

Conflict resolution for the application of a given fix at a given moment is done through a scheduler similar to the one used in HEARSAY-II [Lesser and Erman, 1977]. It maintains an agenda (priority queue) of tasks. Each task consists of a flaw, along with its possible fixes. Tasks and fixes for a flaw are ordered using weak and user supplied domain heuristics.

Although the search space is not a strict AND-OR graph, we use some of the heuristics that work well there. Since all flaws have to be fixed, we select the one that is "harder" to fix, and select the fix that introduces less constraints into the partial plan (e.g., in the case of reductions, the preference order we use is prior, parallel and new).

In our runs we have set to fix flaws in the following order: unsupported range, unextended range, timed-out action, unresolved conflict, unsupported precondition, unexpanded action, unexecuted action. Within a flaw class, the flaw which appears harder to fix (e.g., has only one fix) is preferred. If some flaw has no fixes, then backtracking is attempted when possible.

3.4.1   Backtracking

The system uses full chronological backtracking up to decision points that involve non-backtrackable fixes (e.g., excision of an unsupported range caused by an unexpected event, action execution, etc.). Beyond this point two general approaches can be taken, where the choice is domain and case dependent. Note however, that all replanning options will be attempted before backtracking is chosen.

The first is to ignore such decision points (they have only one fix anyway) and carry on up the tree to other choice points with open alternatives. Note however that completeness is compromised; e.g., it is possible that the very same option currently being backtracked over is now viable thanks to a just occurred unexpected event.

Alternatively, we can scrap the old plan and start afresh on a new plan with the same goals. Simplicity makes this approach more appealing.

4   Unexpected Events and Replanning

This section will illustrate IPEM's replanning adaptability to both a dynamic world and to execution failure. This example is very similar to the one presented by Wilkins [Wilkins, 1985] and fits the scenario proposed by Schoppers [Schoppers, 1987], where a mischievous baby makes the state of the world all but static.

The goal is to achieve $((a \text{ on } c) \wedge (u.x \text{ on } r.y))$ from the blocks configuration presented in Figure 1:i. The initial plan (move a from b to c) in parallel to (move u.2 from t.5 to r.1) is at the top left labeled 'i'.

Before execution of this plan can commence, our baby (moves d from t.3 to r.1). This causes the addition of $((\text{clear t.3}) \wedge (\text{d on r.1}) \wedge \neg(\text{d on t.3}) \wedge \neg(\text{clear r.1}))$ to the CWD creating an unsupported range flaw on (clear r.1). The range is excised, creating an unsupported precondition on (clear z), which is fixed by reduction prior on (clear r.2) (see ii). The overall effect is very similar to the REINSTANTIATE operator described by Wilkins [Wilkins, 1985].

At this point our baby interferes again, (moving a from b to u.2). This interferes with both actions in the plan. Two unsupported ranges result; for (clear u.2) and for (a on b). The ranges are excised, generating the corresponding unsupported preconditions for (clear u.2) and (a on y). The first one is fixed by reduction parallel to the effect (clear y) of the action moving block a (now necessarily before as a consequence of the constraint that for a given range, the producer is necessarily before the consumer). The second one is fixed with a reduction prior to (a on u.2) at BEGIN. The resulting plan is shown at 'iii': (move a from u.2 to c) followed by (move u.2 from t.5 to r.2).

There is an unexecuted action flaw on the first action, now fixed by execution. The effector starts by picking block a up. (clear u.2) is added to the CWD, generating an unextended range flaw, fixed by extension. Now the effector screws up and bumps into d and r.1 producing the state shown in 'iv'. Now the action times-out (say the manipulator sends a signal indicating it bumped into something and that it is no longer attempting to carry out the procedure) and must be excised. This generates an unsupported precondition at (a on c) of END. Note that execution of (move a from u.2 to c) was *partly* successful and that IPEM took notice; execution of (move u.2 from t.5 to r.2) could have proceeded if another manipulator were available even though the other action hadn't timed-out yet.

A number of other propositions are added to the CWD as a consequence of the bumping (e.g., (clear r.1), (d on c), ¬(a on u.2), etc.). The unsupported precondition for (a on c) is now fixed with two reduction new fixes and a number of reduction priors. The resulting plan is shown in 'iv'.

It is important to point out the adaptability displayed by IPEM under unexpected events and execution failure. This it shares with reactive planners (e.g., [Schoppers, 1987],

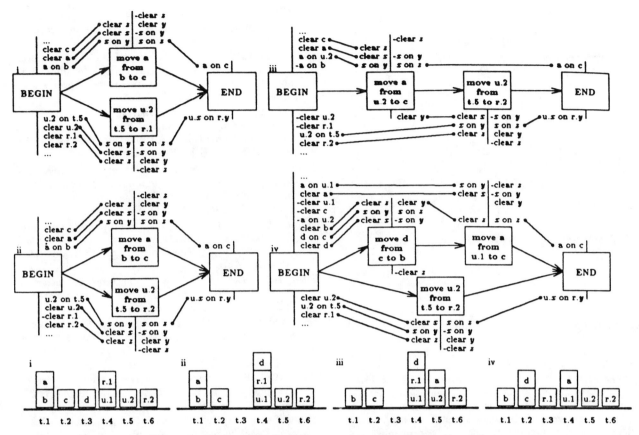

Figure 1: Replanning after unexpected events and execution failure.

[Firby, 1987]). On the other hand it retains the flexibility and power of a hierarchical nonlinear planner. It is capable of dealing with action interactions where reactive planners are incapable of doing so.

5   Interleaving Planning and Execution

We are having dinner with Sandy. When having dinner with somebody we want that somebody to *like* the food and we also *need* to have the food. We don't know what Sandy likes but it does make a difference since the choice determines the restaurant, the way to dress, whether to make a reservation, etc. Asking is a way of finding what a person likes.

This example illustrates a class of problems that can hardly be solved without interleaving planning and execution. A conditional plan is a poor option since it must plan for a potentially large number of alternatives, most of which won't be used. On the other hand, replanning after execution failure can be harmful to our relationship with Sandy.

To solve this problem using IPEM we need to make an extension to the action representation to cope with information acquiring actions (IAA's). TWEAK's semantics define an otherwise complete plan with an unbound variable on the postconditions of an action to be completed to *any* constant. This is unsatisfactory for an action which yields a particular – yet unknown – value when executed.

We introduce a new set of variables, *Ivar* to handle such actions. The variable in the postcondition intended to provide information in an IAA is defined as an Ivar. We allow Ivar's to codesignate with variables, but not with constants. The scheduler is slightly modified to put on hold those flaws whose fixes would bind an Ivar to a constant. This results in plan elaboration up to the point where all flaws are on hold with the exception of unexecuted actions, then chosen for execution by the scheduler.

For example, consider Figure 2. The top presents a plan to solve our dining example problem, where *thing* is an Ivar at ASK, our IAA action. At this point every expansion for GET *meal* in the action schema repertoire known to the system would bind *meal* to some constant. Since *meal* codesignates with *thing* its expansion is placed on hold. Note that this is the maximally elaborated plan that doesn't commit the binding of *meal*.

Unexecuted action at ASK is the only remaining flaw not on hold. ASK is executed and made necessarily before GET *meal* (see bottom of Figure 2). "Sandy likes fondue" is eventually added to the CWD creating an unextended range from DINE to BEGIN. The range is extended (the solid range added, the dotted one removed) so that *meal* now codesignates with a constant (fondue) and not with *thing*. Planning can proceed now that it has been established that the correct expansion for GET *meal* is GET fondue.

Note that an action has been executed before the plan was fully elaborated and the outcome of its execution was used to decide the expansion to use (i.e., for a planning

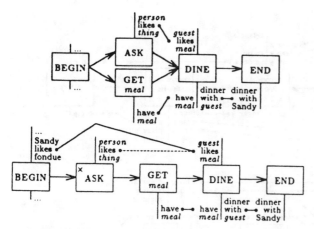

Figure 2: Interleaving Planning and Execution

decision).

Conclusions

IPEM successfully integrates the processes of planning, execution and monitoring. Control integration was obtained by using a production system architecture where the IF-THEN rules operate as transformations between partial plans. In IPEM's context IF-THEN rules are referred to as flaws and fixes. Representation integration was achieved by using a common partial plan representation extended to include monitoring and execution information.

The primary goal of providing a system to support interleaving of planning and execution in a principled and clear way has been attained.

Furthermore, the system exhibits a robust capacity to replan either after execution failure or after the occurrence of unexpected effects. One must caution however, that this capability is seriously limited by its locality.

A planning and execution system embodying the framework has been successfully implemented. It has been tested on numerous examples from various domains, including the ones in this document. It is currently being used at Essex in research concerning Multi-Actor systems [Doran, 1988].

Acknowledgements

Many thanks must go to Jim Doran for support, encouragement and valuable insights and suggestions. We also thank David Aha, Tony Lawson, Chris Trayner, Edward Tsang and Wayne Wobcke for useful comments in the course of this research.

References

[Ambros-Ingerson, 1985] J. A. Ambros-Ingerson. *Planning; a Theory, an Application and a Tool.* Master's thesis, University of Essex, Colchester CO4 3SQ, U. K., 1985.

[Ambros-Ingerson, 1987] J. A. Ambros-Ingerson. IPEM: Integrated planning, execution and monitoring. M. Phil. Dissertation, University of Essex, Colchester CO4 3SQ, U. K., 1987.

[Bartle, 1986] R. A. Bartle. *Three Ways to Cross-Level Plan.* Technical Report CSM-84, University of Essex, University of Essex, Colchester CO4 3SQ, U.K., 1986.

[Chapman, 1987] David Chapman. Planning for conjunctive goals. *Artificial Intelligence*, 32:333–377, 1987.

[Currie and Tate, 1985] K. Currie and A. Tate. *Control in the Open Planning Architecture.* Technical Report AIAI-TR-12, Artificial Intelligence Applications Institute, Edinburgh, U.K., 1985.

[Doran, 1986] Jim E. Doran. *Distributed Artificial Intelligence and the Modelling of Sociocultural Systems.* Technical Report CSM-87, University of Essex, Colchester CO4 3SQ, U.K., September 1986.

[Doran, 1987] Jim E. Doran. *A Computational Investigation of Three Models of Specialisation, Exchange and Social Complexity.* Technical Report, University of Essex, Colchester CO4 3SQ, U.K., August 1987.

[Doran, 1988] Jim E. Doran. The structure and emergence of hierarchical organisations. In *Alvey Workshop on Multiple Agent Systems*, Philips Research Labs, Redhill U.K., April 1988.

[Fikes, 1971] Richard E. Fikes. *Monitored Execution of Robot Plans Produced by STRIPS.* Technical Note 55, Stanford Research Institute, 1971.

[Fikes and Nilsson, 1971] R. E. Fikes and N. J. Nilsson. Strips: a new approach to the application of theorem proving to problem solving. *Artificial Intelligence*, 2:189–208, 1971.

[Firby, 1987] R. J. Firby. An investigation into reactive planning in complex domains. In *AAAI'87*, pages 202–206, 1987.

[Georgeff and Lansky, 1987] M. P. Georgeff and A. L. Lansky. Reactive reasoning and planning. In *AAAI'87*, pages 677–682, 1987.

[Hayes, 1975] P. J. Hayes. A representation for robot plans. In *IJCAI'75*, pages 181–188, 1975.

[Lesser and Erman, 1977] V. R. Lesser and L. D. Erman. A retrospective view of the Hearsay-II architecture. In *IJCAI'77*, pages 27–35, 1977.

[McCalla and Reid, 1982] G. I. McCalla and L. Reid. Plan creation, plan execution and knowledge acquisition in a dynamic microworld. *International Journal of Man Machine Studies*, 16:189–208, 1982.

[McDermott, 1978] Drew McDermott. Planning and acting. *Cognitive Science*, 2:71–109, 1978.

[Sacerdoti, 1974] Earl D. Sacerdoti. Planning in a hierarchy of abstraction spaces. *Artificial Intelligence*, 5:115–135, 1974.

[Schoppers, 1987] M. J. Schoppers. Universal plans for reactive robots in unpredictable environments. In *IJCAI'87*, pages 1039–1046, 1987.

[Stefik, 1981] M. Stefik. Planning and meta-planning (Molgen: part 1 and 2). *Artificial Intelligence*, 16:111–170, 1981.

[Tate, 1977] Austin Tate. Generating project networks. In *IJCAI'77*, pages 888–893, 1977.

[Wilkins, 1985] D. E. Wilkins. Recovering from execution errors in SIPE. *Computational Intelligence*, 1:33–45, 1985.

Author Affiliations

Credits

Index

AUTHOR AFFILIATIONS

James F. Allen
University of Rochester
Dept. of Computer Science
Hylan Building
Rochester, NY 14627

Richard Alterman
Brandeis University
Computer Science Dept.
415 South St.
Waltham, MA 02254

Jose Ambros-Ingerson
Dept. of Information
  and Computer Science
University of California, Irvine
Irvine, CA 92717

David Chapman
MIT
545 Technology Square
Cambridge, MA 02139

Ken Currie
Artificial Intelligence
  Applications Institute
University of Edinburgh
80 South Bridge
Edinburgh, EHI IHN

Thomas Dean
Department of
  Computer Science
Brown University Box 1910
Providence, RI 02912

Mark E. Drummond
Sterling Federal Systems
NASA Ames Research Center
Mail Stop 244-17
Moffett Field, CA 94035

Jerome Feldman
International Computer Science Institute
1947 Center Street Suite 600
Berkeley, CA 94704

Richard Fikes
Price Waterhouse
68 Willow Rd.
Menlo Park, CA 94025

R. James Firby
Department of Computer Science
Yale Unviversity, Box 2158
Yale Station
New Haven, CT 06520

Mark S. Fox
Carnegie-Mellon University
Pittsburgh, PA 15213

Michael P. Georgeff
The Australian AI Institute
1 Grattan Street
Carlton 3053
Victoria, Australia

Cordell C. Green
Kestrel Institute
1801 Page Mill Rd.
Palo Alto, CA 94304

Kristian Hammond
University of Chicago
Computer Science Dept.
1100 E. 58th Street
Chicago, Ill 60615

Steve Hanks
Dept. of Computer
  Science and Engineering
University of Washington FR-35
Seattle, WA 98195

Peter E. Hart
Stanford Research Institute
Menlo Park, CA 94025

Patrick Hayes
XEROX PARC
3333 Coyote Hill Rd.
Palo Alto, CA 94304

Philip J. Hayes
Carnegie Group, Inc.
650 Commerce St. AI Station
Pittsburgh, PA 15219

Barbara Hayes-Roth
Stanford University
701 Welch Rd.
Stanford, CA 94304

Frederick Hayes-Roth
Cimflex-Teknowledge
1850 Embarcadero Rd.
Palo Alto, CA 94304

James Hendler
Computer Science Department
University of Maryland
College Park, MD 20742

Leslie Pack Kaelbling
SRI International
333 Ravenswood Avenue
Menlo Park, CA   94025

Feliks Kluźniak
Dept. of Computer and Information Science
Linköping University
S-581 83 Linköping
Sweden

Johannes A. Koonen
Computer Science Department
University of Rochester
Rochester, NY   14627

Richard E. Korf
Computer Science Department
University of California
Los Angeles, CA 90024

Amy L. Lansky
Nasa Ames Research Center
MS 244-17
Moffett Field, CA   94035

Vladimir Lifschitz
Computer Science Department
Stanford University
Stanford, CA   94305

John McCarthy
Computer Science Dept.
Stanford University
Stanford, CA   94305-2140

Drew McDermott
Yale University
   Computer Science Dept.
P.O. Box 2158, Yale Station
New Haven, CT   06520

David P. Miller
Jet Propulsion Lab
California Institute of Technology
Pasadena, CA   91109

Steven Minton
NASA Ames Research Center
Mail Stop 244-17
Moffett Field, CA   94035

Robert Moore
SRI International AI Center
333 Ravenswood
Menlo Park, CA 94025

Leora Morgenstern
IBM T. J. Watson Research Center
P.O. Box 704
Yorktown Heights, NY 10598

Allen Newell
Carnegie-Mellon University
Computer Science Dept.
Pittsburgh, PA 15213

Nils J. Nilsson
Computer Science Department
Stanford University
Stanford, CA 94305

Edwin Pednault
AT&T Bell Laboratories
Crawfords Corner Rd.
Holmdel, NJ   07733

Stanley J. Rosenchein
Teleos Research
576 Middlefield Rd.
Palo Alto, CA   94301

Earl D. Sacerdoti
The Copernican Group
430 Cowper Street
Palo Alto, CA   94301

Yoav Shoham
Computer Science Dept.
Stanford University
Stanford, CA   94305

Herbert A. Simon
Dept. of Psychology
Carnegie-Mellon University
Pittsburgh, PA   15213-3875

Stephen F. Smith
The Robotics Institute
Carnegie-Mellon University
Pittsburgh, PA 15213

Sam Steel
Dept. of Computer Science
University of Essex
Colchester, CO4 3SQ
United Kingdom

Lynn Andrea Stein
Dept. of Computer Science
Brown University
Providence, RI   02912

Mark J. Stefik
XEROX PARC
3333 Coyote Hill Rd.
Palo Alto, CA 94304

Gerald Sussman
MIT AI Lab
545 Technology Square
Cambridge, MA   02139

S. Szpakowicz
Computer Science Dept.
University of the Witwatersrand
P.O. Wits
Johannesburg 2050
South Africa

Austin Tate
Artificial Intelligence
  Applications Institute
University of Edinburgh
80 South Bridge
Edinburgh EHI IHN

Steven Vere
Lockheed AI Center 90-06/259
3251 Hanover Street
Palo Alto, CA 94304-1187

Richard Waldinger
SRI International
AI Center
333 Ravenswood Ave.
Menlo Park, CA 94025

Robert Wilensky
Computer Science Dept.
571 Evans Hall
UC Berkeley
Berkeley, CA 94720

David Wilkins
SRI International AI Center
333 Ravenswood
Menlo Park, CA 94025

CREDITS

Allen, J. F., "Towards a General Theory of Action and Time". This article first appeared in Volume 23, 1984 of the journal *Artificial Intelligence* published by North-Holland Publishing Co., Amsterdam. Copyright North-Holland Publishing Co. It is reprinted here with the permission of the publisher and author.

Allen, J. F., and J. A. Koomen, "Planning Using a Temporal World Model", IJCAI 1983 Proceedings, pp. 741-747. Copyright 1983 IJCAI. Used by permission of the author and the International Joint Conferences on Artificial Intelligence, Inc.,: copies of this and other IJCAI Proceedings are available from Morgan Kaufmann Publishers, Inc., P. O. Box 50490, Palo Alto, Ca 94303, USA.

Alterman, R., "An Adaptive Planner", AAAI 1986 Proceedings, pp. 65-69, copyright 1986 by the American Association for Artificial Intelligence. Reprinted with the permission of the publisher and author.

Ambros-Ingerson, J. and S. Steel, "Integrating Planning, Execution, and Monitoring", AAAI 1988 Proceedings, pp. 83-88, copyright 1988 by the American Association for Artificial Intelligence. Reprinted with the permission of the publisher and author.

Chapman, D., "Planning for Conjunctive Goals". This article first appeared in Volume 32, 1987 of the journal *Artificial Intelligence* published by North-Holland Publishing Co., Amsterdam. Copyright North-Holland Publishing Co. It is reprinted here with the permission of the publisher and author.

Currie, K. and A. Tate, "O-Plan-Control in the Open Planning Architecture", *Expert Systems* 85, pp. 225-240. Copyright 1985, Cambridge University Press. Reprinted with the permission of Cambridge University Press and the author.

Dean, T., and D. McDermott, "Temporal Data Base Management". This article first appeared in Volume 32, 1987, of the journal *Artificial Intelligence* published by North-Holland Publishing Co., Amsterdam. Copyright North-Holland Publishing Co. It is reprinted here with the permission of the publisher and author.

Dean, T., J. Firby, and D. Miller, "Hierarchical Planning Involving Deadline, Travel Time and Resources", *Computational Intelligence* 4(4), 381:398, (c) 1988 NRC Research Journals. Reprinted with the permission of the publisher and the author.

Drummond, M., "Refining and Extending the Procedural Net", IJCAI 1985 Proceedings, pp. 1010-1012. Copyright 1985 IJCAI. Used by permission of the author and the International Joint Conferences on Artificial Intelligence, Inc.,: copies of this and other IJCAI Proceedings are available from Morgan Kaufmann Publishers, Inc., PO Box 50490, Palo Alto, Ca 94303, USA.

Feldman, J. A., and R. F. Sproull, "Decision Theory and AI II: The Hungry Monkey", *Cognitive Science* 1, 158:192. Copyright 1977 Ablex Publishing Corporation. Reprinted with the permission of the publisher and author.

Fikes, R. E., P. E. Hart, and N. Nilsson, "Learning and Executing Generalized Robot Plans". This article first appeared in Volume 3, no. 4, 1972 of the journal *Artificial Intelligence* published by North-Holland Publishing Co., Amsterdam. Copyright North-Holland Publishing Co. It is reprinted here with the permission of the publisher and author.

Fikes, Richard E., and Nils Nilsson, "STRIPS: A New Approach to the Application of Theorem Proving to Problem Solving". This article first appeared in Volume 5, no. 2, 1971 of the jounal *Artificial Intelligence* published by North-Holland Publishing Co., Amsterdam. Copyright North-Holland Publishing Co. Published here with the permission of the publisher and author.

Fox, M. S., and S. Smith, "ISIS—A Knowledge-Based System for Factory Scheduling", *Expert Systems* 1(1), 1984, pp. 25-49. Copyright 1984, Learned Information (Europe) Ltd. Reprinted with the permission of Learned Information (Europe) Ltd. and the author.

Georgeff, M., "Planning", Reproduced, with permission, from the *Annual Review of Computer Science*, Volume 2, copyright 1987 by Annual Reviews, Inc, and the author.

Georgeff, M., and A. Lansky, "Reactive Reasoning and Planning", AAAI 87 Proceedings, Copyright 1987 by the American Association for Artificial Intelligence. Reprinted with the permission of the publisher and author.

Green, C., "Applications of Theorem Proving to Problem Solving", IJCAI 1969 Proceedings, pp. 741-747. Copyright 1969 IJCAI. Used by permission of the author and the International Joint Conferences on Artificial Intelligence, Inc.,: copies of this and other IJCAI Proceedings are available from Morgan Kaufmann Publishers, Inc., PO Box 50490, Palo Alto, CA 94303, USA.

Hammond, K. J., "CHEF: A Model of Case-Based Planning", AAAI 1986 Proceedings, pp. 261-271, copyright 1986 by the American Association for Artificial Intelligence. Reprinted with the permission of the publisher and author.

Hanks, S., and D. McDermott, "Nonmonotonic Logic and Temporal Projection". This article first appeared in Volume 33, 1987, of the journal *Artificial Intelligence* published by North-Holland Publishing Co., Amsterdam. Copyright North-Holland Publishing Co. It is reprinted here with the permission of the publisher and author.

Hayes, P. J., "A Representation for Robot Plans", IJCAI 1975 Proceedings, pp. 181-188. Copyright 1975 IJCAI. Used by permission of the author and the International Joint Conferences on Artificial Intelligence, Inc.,: copies of this and other IJCAI Proceedings are available from Morgan Kaufmann Publishers, Inc., PO Box 50490, Palo Alto, CA 94303, USA.

Hayes, P., "The Frame Problem and Related Problems in Artificial Intelligence". In Elithorn and Jones (eds.) *Artificial and Human Thinking*. Copyright P. Hayes. Reprinted with the permission of the author.

Hayes-Roth, B. and Hayes-Roth, F., "A Cognitive Model of Planning", *Cognitive Science* 3(4) 275:310, copyright 1979 by Ablex Publishing Corporation. Reprinted with the permission of the publisher and author.

Hendler, J., "Integrating Marker-Passing and Problem Solving", Proceedings of the Cognitive Society Conference, copyright 1985, Cognitive Science Society Incorporated. Reprinted with the permission of the publisher and author.

Kaebling, L., "An Architecture for Intelligent Reactive Systems". In Georgeff and Lansky (eds.) *Reasoning About Actions and Plans*. Copyright L. Kaebling. Reprinted with the permission of the author.

Korf, R. E., "Planning as Search: a Quantitative Approach". This article first appeared in Volume 33, 1987 of the journal *Artificial Intelligence* published by North-Holland Publishing Co., Amsterdam. Copyright North-Holland Publishing Co. It is reprinted here with the permission of the publisher and author.

Kluźniak, F., and S. Szpakowicz, *Prolog for Programmers* (extract from). In the series, APIC Studies in Data Processing, no. 24. Copyright 1974 by Academic Press. Reprinted with permission of the publisher and authors.

Lansky, A., "Localized Representation and Planning". Copyright by A. Lansky. Reprinted with the permission of the author.

Lifschitz, V., "On the Semantics of STRIPS". In Georgeff and Lansky (eds.) *Reasoning About Actions and Plans*. Copyright V. Lifschitz. Reprinted with the permission of the author.

McCarthy, J., and P. J. Hayes, "Some Philosophical Problems From the Standpoint of Artificial Intelligence". Copyright 1969 by Edinburgh Press. This excerpt appeared in *Machine Intelligence 4* edited by B. Meltzer and D. Michie and is reprinted with the permission of Edinburgh University Press and the author.

McDermott, D., "A Temporal Logic for Reasoning About Processes and Plans", *Cognitive Science 6*, 101:155, copyright 1982 by Ablex Publishing Corporation. Reprinted with the permission of the publisher and author.

McDermott, D., "Planning and Acting", *Cognitive Science 2(2)*, 71:109, copyright 1978 by Ablex Publishing Corporation. Reprinted with the permission of the publisher and author.

Minton, S., "Selectively Generalizing Plans for Problem-Solving", IJCAI 1985 Proceedings, pp. 596-599. Copyright 1985 IJCAI. Used by permission of the author and the International Joint Conferences on Artificial Intelligence, Inc.,: copies of this and other IJCAI Proceedings are available from Morgan Kaufmann Publishers, Inc., PO Box 50490, Palo Alto, CA 94303, USA.

Moore, R., "A Formal Theory of Knowledge and Action". Reprinted from *Formal Theories of the Commonsense World*, edited by J. R. Hobbs and R. C. Moore. Copyright 1985 by Ablex Publishing Corporation. Reprinted with the permission of the publisher and author.

Morgenstern, L., and L. Stein, "Why Things Go Wrong: A Formal Theory of Causal Reasoning", AAAI Proceedings 1988. Copyright 1988 by the American Association for Artificial Intelligence. Reprinted with the permission of the publisher and author.

Newell, A., and H. A. Simon, "GPS, A Program That Simulates Human Thought", reprinted from *Lernende Automaten*, Munich, copyright 1961 by R. Oldenbourg KG. Reprinted with the permission of the publisher and the author.

Lernende Automaten
Bericht uber die Fachtagung der Nachrichtentechnischen Gesellschaft im VDE (NTG, Karlruhe 1961)
Besorgt von Heinz Billing, 1961
Beihefte zur Zeitschrift Elektronische Rechenanlagen, Band 3

Pednault, E., "Formulating Multi Agent Dynamic World Problems in the Classical Planning Framework". In Georgeff and Lansky (eds.) *Reasoning About Actions and Plans*. Copyright E. Pednault. Reprinted with the permission of the author.

Rosenchein, S., "Plan Synthesis: A Logical Perspective", IJCAI 1981 Proceedings, pp. 331-337. Copyright 1981 IJCAI. Used by permission of the author and the International Joint Conferences on Artificial Intelligence, Inc.,: copies of this and other IJCAI Proceedings are available from Morgan Kaufmann Publishers, Inc., PO Box 50490, Palo Alto, CA 94303, USA.

Sacerdoti, E., "Planning in a Hierarchy of Abstraction Spaces". This article first appeared in Volume 5, no. 2, 1975 of the journal *Artificial Intelligence* published by North-Holland Publishing Co., Amsterdam. Copyright North-Holland Publishing Co. It is reprinted here with the permission of the publisher and author.

Sacerdoti, E. "The Non-linear Nature of Plans", IJCAI 1975 Proceedings, pp. 206-214. Copyright 1975 IJCAI. Used by permission of the author and the International Joint Conferences on Artificial Intelligence, Inc.,: copies of this and other IJCAI Proceedings are available from Morgan Kaufmann Publishers, Inc., PO Box 50490, Palo Alto, CA 94303, USA.

Shoham, Y., and D. McDermott, "Problems in Formal Temporal Reasoning". This article first appeared in Volume 36, 1988 of the journal *Artificial Intelligence* published by North-Holland Publishing Co., Amsterdam. Copyright North-Holland Publishing Co. It is reprinted here with the permission of the publisher and author.

Stefik, M., "Planning with Constraints - MOLGEN: Part I". This article first appeared in Volume 16, no. 2, 1981 of the journal *Artificial Intelligence* published by North-Holland Publishing Co., Amsterdam. Copyright North-Holland Publishing Co. It is reprinted here with permission from the publisher and author.

Sussman, G. J., "The Virtuous Nature of Bugs", Originally presented at the first conference of the Society for the Study of AI and the Simulation of Behavior, held at Sussex University, Brighton, UK, in 1974. Copyright G. J. Sussman. Reprinted with the permission of the author.

Tate, A., "Generating Project Networks", IJCAI 1977 Proceedings, pp. 888-89. Copyright 1977 IJCAI. Used by permission of the author and the International Joint Conferences on Artificial Intelligence, Inc.,: copies of this and other IJCAI Proceedings are available from Morgan Kaufmann Publishers, Inc., PO Box 50490, Palo Alto, CA 94303, USA.

Waldinger, R., "Achieving Several Goals Simultaneously". Reproduced with permission from *Machine Intelligence 8*, published in 1977 by Ellis Horwood Limited, Chichester. Reproduced with permission from the author and publisher.

Wilensky, R., "A Model for Planning in Complex Situations", *Cognition and Brain Theory*, Vol. IV, no. 4, 1981. Published by Laurence Erlbaum Associates, Hillsdale, N.J. copyright 1981 by Laurence Erlbaum Associates. Reprinted with the permission of the publisher and author.

Wilkins, D. E., "Domain-independent Planning: Representation and Plan Generation". This article first appeared in Volume 22, no. 3, 1984 of the journal *Artificial Intelligence* published by North-Holland Publishing Co., Amsterdam. Copyright North-Holland Publishing Co. It is reprinted with the permission of the publisher and author.

Vere, S. A. "Planning in Time: Windows and Durations for Activities and Goals", Pattern Analysis and Machine Intelligence, 5(246:267). Copyright 1983 IEEE. Reprinted with the permission of the publisher and author.

Index

A

A* algorithm, 31, 211, 567
Abstraction, 248, 249–50, 566, 574
  levels, 34, 37
  model of, 574–75
  multiple levels of, 575–76
  single level of, 575
  space, 99–100
  space requirements, 576
Abstraction hierarchy, 137, 566, 723
  in FORBIN, 380
  in PLEXUS, 662
ABSTRIPS (Abstraction-Based
    STRIPS), 15, 34, 37, 57, 98–108,
    162, 165, 181, 182, 574, 576
  comparison with STRIPS, 105
Accessibility relation, 485–87
Action logics, 38–39
Action regression, 35
Actions, 6, 28, 411
  ADL for describing, 686–87,
    693–701
  defining, 471–73
  DEVISER, 298
  influential, 133–34
  intentional, 473–75
  logic of, 452–56
  models of, 5–6
  opportunistic model, 250
  possible-world analysis, 500–505
  primitive, 370
  representations of, 17–18
  simultaneous, 477
  STRIPS, 190
  synergistic simultaneous, 684–85
  theories of, 430
  TWEAK, 545–47
  WARPLAN, 140
Action theory, 225–43
Activities
  DEVISER, 298
  windows for, 301–3
Adaptive planners, 660–64
Add list, 7, 29, 37
ADL (Action Description Language),
    675, 677, 686, 693–701
Aircraft Carrier Mission Planning, 28
Aircraft operations, 334
Airplan, 39
ALGOL, 411, 418–19, 422
Allen, James F., 50, 464, 559
Allowable formulas, 8
Alpha-beta technique, 211
Alterman, Richard, 660
Ambros-Ingerson, José A., 735
AMORD, 553, 600
Analytical adequacy, 225

AND/OR graph search, 227, 228
Answer literal, 68
AP/1, 132
Applicable plan, 29
Application independence, 225
Archeological model, 133, 134–35
Assumption failures, 609–11
Asynchronous system, PRS, 732
ATLAST, 278
Atomic actions, 9
Atomic plans, 9
Attitudes, 23
Automatic programming, 67–87
AUTOPILOT, 298
Awareness, 713, 715

B

Backtracking, 157, 182, 275, 286, 333,
    551–53
  ABSTRIPS, 101–2
  AND/OR graph search, 227
  chronological, 552, 738
  dependency-directed, 227–28, 542
  depth-first, 32–33
  in GEMPLAN, 673
  in IPEM, 737
  versus marker-passer use, 284
  one-then-best, 32
  in real-time systems, 718
  relative efficiency of, 547
Backward projection in time, 645
Bayesian decision theory, 207
Bayesian model, 213, 218
Bayes' rule, 213, 221
Beam search, 32
  scheduling, 354
Behavior, 5
  mediating, 721–23
Behavioral robustness, 716, 720
Behaviorism, 66
Belief, 23, 588
  justifications for, 606–8
  and knowledge, 483–84
  models of, 474–76
  in STRIPS, 591
Belief calculus, 588
Benchmark, ISIS test, 354
Bigression, 534
  benefits of, 536
Blackboard Architectures, 364, 735
Blackboard model, 253–55, 259, 332
  opportunistic, 250–51
Block promotion, 549
Blocks world, 233–40, 669

  in ADL, 703
  dependency-directed backtracking
    in, 542
  microexample, DEVISER, 306–7
  performance of SIPE, 334
  and TWEAK, 545
BNF description, task formalism, 293
Branch-and-bound methods, 221
Branch and case analysis, 37
Branch and re-join, 37
Branching factor, 567
Branching time model, 53–54
BUG, 114
Bugs, 111–17
BUILD, 553

C

Cambridge Polish notation, 438
Carnegie-Mellon University, 336
Case-based planning, 655–64
Causality, 18–19, 409–10, 444–48, 471
Causal theory, 639
  explanation, 658
  FORBIN, 372, 374
  formal theory of reasoning, 641–46
  inference, 639
Chaining
  deduction and, 605–6
  temporal, TMM, 611–12
Changes, detecting and responding to,
    TMM, 609–10
Chapman, David, 537
CHEF, 41, 649, 655–64
Choice, 9
Chronicles, 5, 438–40, 643, 682, 683
  multiple, 459–61
Chronological backtracking, 552, 553,
    738
Chronologically maximal ignorance,
    639
Chronological minimality, 631, 642
Chronsets, 459, 460
Circumscription, 630, 631, 639, 640,
    642–43
  enhanced, 637–39
Classical planning problems, 676
  defined, 677–80
  ontology of actions in, 680–85
Clipping constraints, 613
Clobberers, 540
Codesignation
  consistency lemma, 554
  constraints, 548–49
Cognitive cliches, 547